INTRODUCTION TO INTERNATIONAL DEVELOPMENT

Approaches, Actors, Issues, and Practice

Paul A. Haslam

Jessica Schafer

Pierre Beaudet

THIRD EDITION

Oxford University Press is a department of the University of Oxford.
It furthers the University's objective of excellence in research, scholarship,
and education by publishing worldwide. Oxford is a registered trade mark of
Oxford University Press in the UK and in certain other countries.

Published in Canada by
Oxford University Press
8 Sampson Mews, Suite 204,
Don Mills, Ontario M3C 0H5 Canada

www.oupcanada.com

First Edition published in 2009
Second Edition published in 2013

Library and Archives Canada Cataloguing in Publication
Introduction to international development : approaches,
actors, issues, and practice / edited by Paul Haslam, Jessica
Schafer, and Pierre Beaudet. — Third edition.

Previous edition has subtitle: Approches, actors, and issues.
Includes bibliographical references and index.
ISBN 978-0-19-901890-1 (paperback)

1. Economic development—Textbooks. 2. Political development—
Textbooks. I. Beaudet, Pierre, editor II. Haslam, Paul Alexander, editor
III. Schafer, Jessica, editor

HD82.I58 2016   338.91   C2016-905036-X

Cover image: Cultura RM Exclusive/Philip Lee Harvy, Getty Images

Oxford University Press is committed to our environment.
Wherever possible, our books are printed on paper which comes from
responsible sources.

Printed and bound in the United States of America

2 3 4 — 20 19 18

CONTENTS

Each chapter includes, at the beginning, Learning Objectives, and, at the end, Summary, Questions for Critical Thought, Suggested Readings, and Bibliography.

PART III Issues in International Development 261

PART IV Practice in International Development 461

LIST OF BOXES

IMPORTANT CONCEPTS

CRITICAL ISSUES

CURRENT EVENTS

LIST OF FIGURES AND TABLES

FIGURES

TABLES

FROM THE PUBLISHER

Oxford University Press is delighted to present the third edition of *Introduction to International Development*, which continues to offer comprehensive coverage of theories and topics in international development studies in a manner that is sophisticated yet proven to engage students from various backgrounds at the first- and second-year level.

Whereas most international development textbooks are anchored in a single discipline such as political science or economics, *Introduction to International Development* draws on contributions from internationally acclaimed experts representing the spectrum of subject areas that contribute to field, including anthropology, economics, education, geography, history, international affairs, politics, population studies, sociology, urban planning, and women's studies.

Organized into four parts examining the theories, actors, issues, and practice of international development, the third edition features new chapter-length coverage of alternatives to development, gender and development, China and the emerging economies, and climate change. Part IV, on the practice of international development, is entirely new and boasts chapters devoted to measuring poverty, planning projects, humanitarian assistance, ethics, global poverty reduction, and social policy. This edition also incorporates a full-colour, student-friendly design and a strong ancillary suite encompassing an instructor's manual, a student study guide, a test bank, and links to audio podcasts and videos.

KEY FEATURES OF THE THIRD EDITION

The third edition of *Introduction to International Development* brings together an assortment of features designed to enhance the experience of both students and educators.

20 Development and Health

Ted Schrecker

LEARNING OBJECTIVES

- To achieve familiarity with key concepts such as social determinants of health and socio-economic gradients in health.
- To be able to assess arguments about the relative contribution of health care or health systems and social determinants of health to socio-economic gradients in health and population health status.
- To be able to identify and assess the potential effects on health of domestic social and economic policy and international development policy in areas that are superficially unrelated to health.
- To become familiar with major elements of the changing landscape of global health governance.
- To be able to assess the prospects for future improvements in population health outside the high-income countries in light of key developments in the international political economy.

Female patients waiting on hospital beds in the Comprehensive Community Based Rehabilitation in Tanzania (CCBRT) hospital. | Source: Photo by Thomas Trutschel/Photothek via Getty Images

Learning Objectives help students focus their reading on the central themes of each chapter.

- **Three types of themed boxes** highlight important concepts, critical issues, and relevant current events.

IMPORTANT CONCEPTS

BOX 22.7 | Freedom of Information, Open Data, and Open Government

Freedom of information laws give people the right to access information from the government. Such laws often keep citizens in the know about their government.

Related to this is the concept of **open data**. According to Open Data Handbook, this refers to data that can be freely used, reused, and redistributed by anyone—subject only, at most, to the requirement to attribute and share alike. The argument for open data is that the best use of data is left for people/stakeholders, not necessarily the original generator of that data.

Both concepts are connected to the conc participation in public affairs, and for ways to m able, and effective.

Important Concepts boxes highlight the many theoretical perspectives that contribute to international development studies, along with the discipline's most influential scholars, activists, and institutions.

CRITICAL ISSUES

BOX 5.2 | HeForShe Campaign

The HeForShe is a strategy designed to engage men and boys in efforts to promote gender equality. It was initiated in 2014 by UN Women as an alternative to targeting girls as recipients of development aid by shifting the focus to understanding social relationships that support and reproduce gender inequality. The campaign includes a goal of ensuring that more than one million men and boys take the HeForShe pledge: a pledge that acknowledges that gender equality is not only an issue for women and girls but is a human rights issue that requires everyone's participation. The pledge calls for action to end forms of violence and discrimination faced by women and girls. The popularity of the HeForShe campaign was augmented by the endorsement of the initiative by the British actress Emma Watson, now the UN Women goodwill ambassador (and known for her role as Hermione in the Harry Potter movies). Emma Watson's impassioned speech in September 2014 has been vie video on YouTube and has circulated widely on other so sure to this particular strategy of addressing gender ine

Critical Issues boxes present cases from around the world that students can analyze using their new theoretical toolkit. Topics include the HeForShe campaign, "mobile money," and South–South cooperation in St Vincent and the Grenadines.

BOX 15.3 | Fair Trade Coffee in an Unfair World? **CURRENT EVENTS**

Research conducted on fair trade groups in the South suggests that fair trade provides important social and economic benefits to certified producers, although with important qualifications (Hudson et al., 2013; Fridell, 2007; Jaffee, 2007). This can be seen in the case of the Union of Indigenous Communities of the Isthmus Region (UCIRI), one of the most successful fair trade coffee co-operatives in the world, located in Oaxaca, Mexico. Through their participation in fair trade, UCIRI members have attained higher incomes and significantly better access to social services through co-operative projects in health care, education, and training. UCIRI also has constructed its own economic infrastructure, such as coffee-processing and transportation facilities, and has provided its members with enhanced access to credit, technology, and marketing skills. Yet, despite the co-operative's success in combatting extreme misery, UCIRI members still report the persistence of general poverty (Fridell, 2007). Fair trade prices are inadequately low because they must remain somewhat competitive with conventional coffee bean prices. Moreover, UCIRI members remain highly vulnerable to global market and climate conditions beyond their control. A major coffee leaf rust infestation, intensified by the impacts of climate change, destroying coffee harvests throughout Mexico and Central America beginning in 2012, has brought UCIRI to the verge of collapse, with members reporting: "Everything we have fought for over the past 30 years we are losing to climate change and rust" (quoted in Byrne and Sharpe, 2014: 124). How effective can the fair trade network be at the local level against the tide of global forces beyond its control?

Current Events boxes take a critical look at the media's coverage of topics ranging from fair-trade coffee to climate change, with a particular focus on the details of interest to students of international development.

- **End-of-chapter aids to student learning** include summaries, review questions, and recommended print and online resources, all designed to enhance the reader's engagement with the chapter's central concepts.

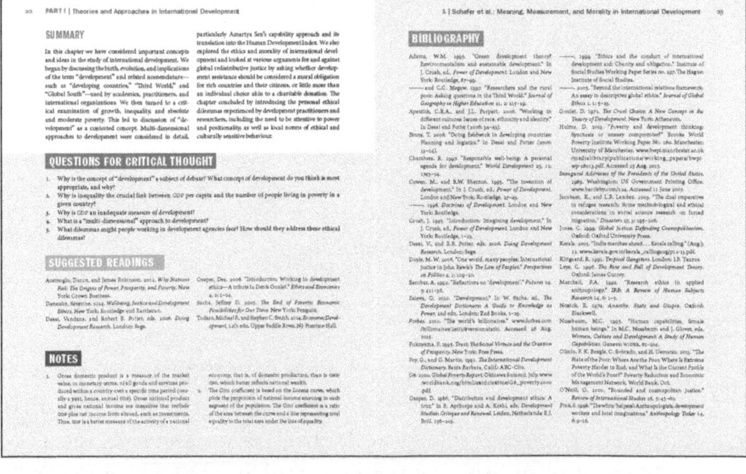
PART I | Theories and Approaches in International Development

SUMMARY

QUESTIONS FOR CRITICAL THOUGHT

SUGGESTED READINGS

NOTES

1 | Schafer et al.: Meaning, Measurement, and Morality in International Development

BIBLIOGRAPHY

- **Vivid photographs, maps, tables, and figures** help to introduce students to the on-the-ground reality of development work, as well as sites of importance and key statistical trends from around the globe.

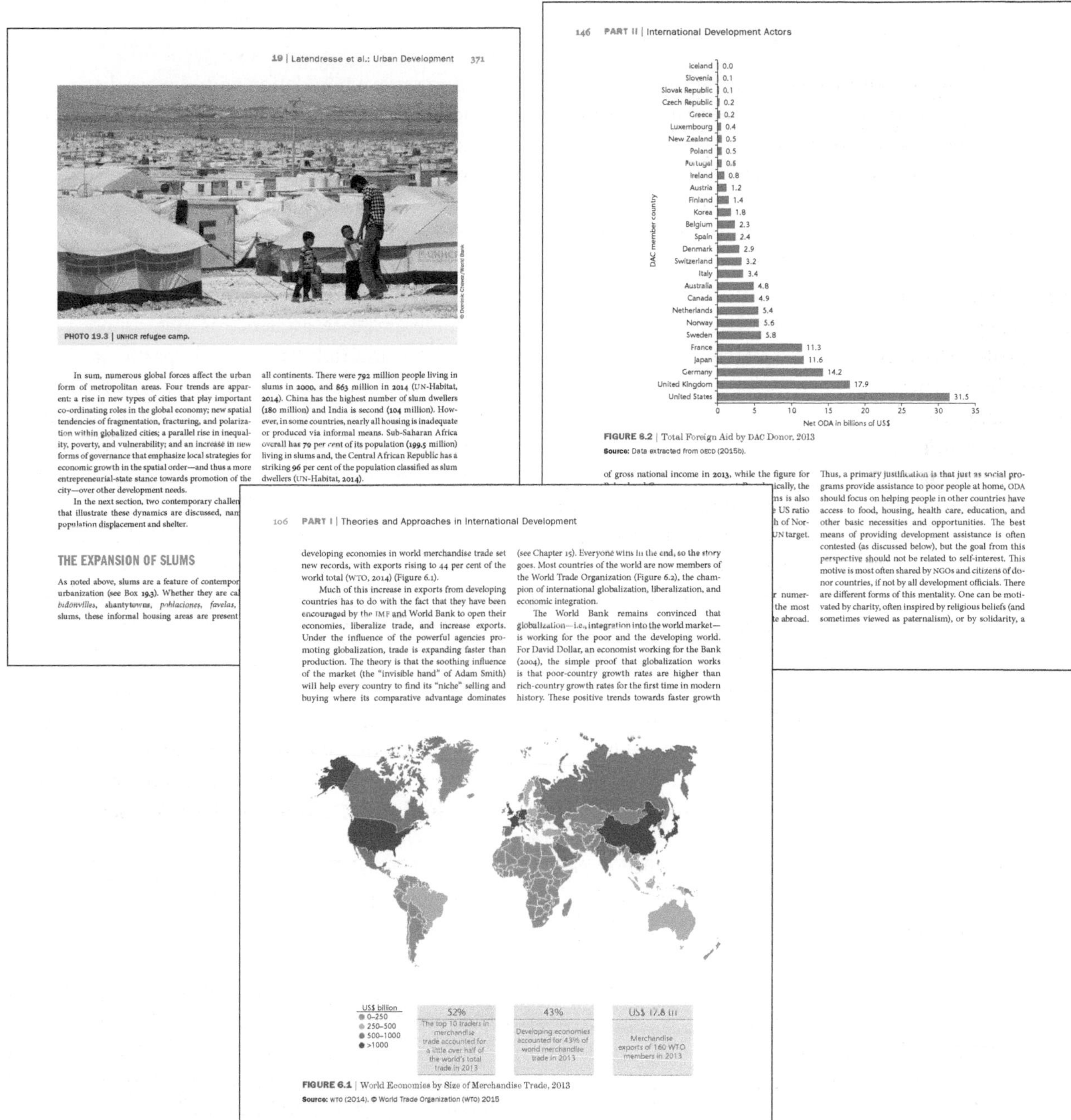

19 | Latendresse et al.: Urban Development 371

PHOTO 19.3 | UNHCR refugee camp.

In sum, numerous global forces affect the urban form of metropolitan areas. Four trends are apparent: a rise in new types of cities that play important co-ordinating roles in the global economy; new spatial tendencies of fragmentation, fracturing, and polarization within globalized cities; a parallel rise in inequality, poverty, and vulnerability; and an increase in new forms of governance that emphasize local strategies for economic growth in the spatial order—and thus a more entrepreneurial-state stance towards promotion of the city—over other development needs.

In the next section, two contemporary challen[ges] that illustrate these dynamics are discussed, nam[ely] population displacement and shelter.

THE EXPANSION OF SLUMS

As noted above, slums are a feature of contempor[ary] urbanization (see Box 19.3). Whether they are ca[lled] *bidonvilles*, shantytowns, *poblaciones*, *favelas*, slums, these informal housing areas are present

all continents. There were 792 million people living in slums in 2000, and 863 million in 2014 (UN-Habitat, 2014). China has the highest number of slum dwellers (180 million) and India is second (104 million). However, in some countries, nearly all housing is inadequate or produced via informal means. Sub-Saharan Africa overall has 70 per cent of its population (199.5 million) living in slums and, the Central African Republic has a striking 96 per cent of the population classified as slum dwellers (UN-Habitat, 2014).

146 PART II | International Development Actors

FIGURE 6.2 | Total Foreign Aid by DAC Donor, 2013

Source: Data extracted from OECD (2015b).

of gross national income in 2013, while the figure for ... ically, the ... ns is also ... US ratio ... h of Nor- ... UN target. ... numer- ... the most ... abroad.

Thus, a primary justification is that just as social programs provide assistance to poor people at home, ODA should focus on helping people in other countries have access to food, housing, health care, education, and other basic necessities and opportunities. The best means of providing development assistance is often contested (as discussed below), but the goal from this perspective should not be related to self-interest. This motive is most often shared by NGOs and citizens of donor countries, if not by all development officials. There are different forms of this mentality. One can be motivated by charity, often inspired by religious beliefs (and sometimes viewed as paternalism), or by solidarity, a

106 PART I | Theories and Approaches in International Development

developing economies in world merchandise trade set new records, with exports rising to 44 per cent of the world total (WTO, 2014) (Figure 6.1).

Much of this increase in exports from developing countries has to do with the fact that they have been encouraged by the IMF and World Bank to open their economies, liberalize trade, and increase exports. Under the influence of the powerful agencies promoting globalization, trade is expanding faster than production. The theory is that the soothing influence of the market (the "invisible hand" of Adam Smith) will help every country to find its "niche" selling and buying where its comparative advantage dominates (see Chapter 15). Everyone wins in the end, so the story goes. Most countries of the world are now members of the World Trade Organization (Figure 6.2), the champion of international globalization, liberalization, and economic integration.

The World Bank remains convinced that globalization—i.e., integration into the world market—is working for the poor and the developing world. For David Dollar, an economist working for the Bank (2004), the simple proof that globalization works is that poor-country growth rates are higher than rich-country growth rates for the first time in modern history. These positive trends towards faster growth

FIGURE 6.1 | World Economies by Size of Merchandise Trade, 2013

Source: WTO (2014). © World Trade Organization (WTO) 2015

- **Bolded key terms** throughout the text help students from different disciplines develop the working vocabulary needed to read and write about international development.
- A **glossary of key terms** at the back of the book serves as a convenient reference for readers and an indispensable review tool for students preparing for tests and exams.

A WORD FROM THE AUTHORS

This is the third, revised and updated edition of *Introduction to International Development: Approaches, Actors, Issues, and Practice*. The world of development has changed significantly since the launch of the first edition in 2008. To mention only a few of these changes, poverty rates have declined in most regions; a more active state has returned to manage development; China and emerging economies provide lessons that have yet to be fully understood; and climate change threatens some of the advances that have been made. This new edition addresses these changes head-on. Chapters from the earlier editions have been rewritten, and new chapters have been added to address these changes, including a new section on development practice.

Introduction to International Development sets out to respond to the particular needs of undergraduate international development programs. Given that many programs of study are multidisciplinary in nature, there is a clear need for a text that is explicitly multidisciplinary in its approach to the key issues. Multidisciplinarity has been at the heart of this project from the beginning; it has guided our selection of authors, who were drawn from disciplines as varied as political science, economics, sociology, anthropology, history, women's studies, and geography. Many of these authors also have been involved in working for and advising development agencies, are grounded by their solid experience of local realities, and represent the ideals of praxis to which our students aspire.

THE CHALLENGE OF MULTIDISCIPLINARITY

Introduction to international development courses are often highly popular electives in the first and second years of Bachelor of Arts programs. This means that textbooks in international development need to serve a population with diverse disciplinary experiences and without a common theoretical or conceptual background. Typically, students do not come just from the diverse fields of the social sciences but also from the faculties of "hard" or applied science and from other multidisciplinary programs with no common-core theoretical apparatus. The challenge of teaching development studies to such an undergraduate audience is not simply one of providing multiple views on particular issues or exposing students to the diversity of issues in development studies; it is also more fundamentally about grounding students with a common theoretical and conceptual intellectual toolkit applicable to the multidisciplinary nature of development problems. To our knowledge, no other textbook currently available has the explicit objective of grounding a multidisciplinary audience in a way that permits the sophisticated understanding of development issues.

In this respect, the core mission of this book is to build a conceptual toolkit for first- and second-year undergraduate students with no prior knowledge of development and with diverse disciplinary backgrounds. For this reason, the book is structured into four sections: Approaches; Actors; Issues; and Practice. The six chapters in Part I, Theories and Approaches in International Development, introduce the student to key concepts, historical contexts of development thinking and action, and theoretical approaches. A noteworthy feature of this section is the accessible account of postmodern and post-colonial approaches, which are rarely taught at this level but constitute the fundamental epistemology for much recent work in development. Part II, International Development Actors (Chapters 7–13), explains various key external and internal forces that shape developmental outcomes. Chapters 14–23, which comprise Part III, Issues in International Development, apply the toolkit learned in the first two sections to a wide variety of issue-areas. In Part IV, Practice in International Development,

Chapters 24–29 explore practical and policy issues in more detail, bringing together the student's knowledge of development approaches, actors, and issues. The book is designed to teach the student by establishing a series of layers that progressively deepen the student's knowledge of international development theory and practice.

At the end of a course, the student has not just accumulated knowledge about development issues but, much more fundamentally, has learned how to approach and study development.

FLEXIBILITY FOR TEACHING

In addition to the need to ground a multidisciplinary audience with a common theoretical toolkit, an introductory textbook also needs to be pedagogically flexible. Some programs minimize exposure to theory in favour of problem-solving and case studies, while others introduce students to development theory early on. To cover these diverse situations found across undergraduate development programs, the four distinct sections of this book (Approaches, Actors, Issues, and Practice) offer the instructor considerable flexibility. He or she may follow the logic of the book, which progressively builds towards a more sophisticated integration of concepts, actors, and issues, and their application to policy and practice, or may pick and choose, perhaps preferring to twin only approaches and actors, or actors and issues, or even to focus simply on issues and practice. Each chapter has been written to stand alone without requiring the assignment of previous chapters, although the collection is organized in such a way as to permit the instructor to draw connections between theory, actors, issues, and practice when the student moves sequentially from the first chapters to the last. At the same time, the range of chapters makes it possible for an instructor to pick and choose the elements of the text that correspond with his or her course design.

The chapters follow a common structure to facilitate the book's use in undergraduate teaching. Teaching tools are provided in each chapter, including learning objectives, questions for discussion, and sources for further reading. Text boxes draw on examples from a wide range of regional and historical experiences to illustrate the main text.

We hope that this new third edition of *Introduction to International Development* will play an important role in providing students from multidisciplinary backgrounds with the conceptual toolkit necessary to understand a wide range of development issue-areas and help to launch them into this challenging and rewarding discipline that combines values, reflection, and action.

Paul A. Haslam, Jessica Schafer, Pierre Beaudet
School of International Development
and Global Studies
University of Ottawa
September 2016

ACKNOWLEDGEMENTS

Over the last three editions, this textbook has been developed, edited, and improved by many people. The many authors who contributed chapters to this book are, of course, the foundation of its success. We'd also like to thank our editors at Oxford University Press: Kate Skene, who saw the potential of this book when it was only an idea in our heads; Dorothy Turnbull and Jennifer Charlton, who saw us through the first edition; Mary Wat and Richard Tallman, who produced the second edition; and Meg Farrell Patterson and Richard Tallman, who ably managed the third edition to its publication.

ACRONYMS

ACCCRN	Asia Cities Climate Change Resilience Network
ACP Group	African, Caribbean, and Pacific Group of States
AfDB	African Development Bank
AGTF	Africa Growing Together Fund
AIIB	Asia Infrastructure Investment Bank
ALBA	Bolivarian Alternative for the Americas
ANC	African National Congress
AOSIS	Alliance of Small Island States (UNFCCC)
APP	Asia-Pacific Partnership on Clean Development and Climate
APPO	Popular Assembly of the People of Oaxaca (Mexico)
ASEAN	Association of Southeast Asian Nations
AU	African Union
BCE	before the Christian era
BCR	benefit-cost ratio
BEE	Broad-Based Economic Empowerment (South Africa)
BHN	basic human needs
BIT	bilateral investment treaty
BKBBN	National Family Planning Coordinator Board (Indonesia)
BMGF	Bill & Melinda Gates Foundation
BRAC	Bangladesh Rural Advancement Committee
BRICS	Brazil, Russia, India, China, South Africa
BWIs	Bretton Woods institutions
CA	capabilities approach
CAFTA-DR	Central American Free Trade Agreement with the Dominican Republic
CAP	Consolidated Appeal Process (UN)
CBA	cost-benefit analysis
CBC	Bartolomé de Las Casas Centre
CBDR	common but differentiated responsibilities
CBDR+C	common but differentiated responsibility plus the capability principle
CCVI	Climate Change Vulnerability Index
CDM	Clean Development Mechanism
CE	Christian era
CEA	cost-effectiveness analysis
CEDAW	Convention on the Elimination of All Forms of Discrimination Against Women
CELAC	Comunidade de Estados Latino-Americanos e Caribe
CEO	chief executive officer
CEPCO	Oaxacan State Coffee Producers Network
CHS	Core Humanitarian Standards
CIA	Central Intelligence Agency (US)
CIDA	Canadian International Development Agency
CITES	Convention on International Trade in Endangered Species
CLs	compulsory licences
CNPC	China National Petroleum Company
COE	Council of Europe
COIN	US military doctrine for counter-insurgency
COP	Conference of Parties (UNFCCC)
CPAFFC	Chinese People's Association for Friendship with Foreign Countries
CPEs	complex political emergencies
CPHC	comprehensive primary health care
CRA	Contingent Reserve Arrangement
CRS	Catholic Relief Services
CSG	Child Support Grant (South Africa)
CSO	civil society organization
CSR	corporate social responsibility
DAC	Development Assistance Committee (OECD)
DAH	development assistance for health
DAWN	Development Alternatives with Women for a New Era
DDR	disarmament, demobilization, and reintegration
DDT	dichlorodiphenyltrichloroethane
DF	discount factor
DFID	Department for International Development (UK)
DG DEVCO	Directorate General for Development and Cooperation (European Commission)
DIRCO	Department of International Relations and Cooperation (South Africa)
DPA	Development Partnership Administration (India)

DPKO	Department of Peacekeeping Operations (UN)
DRC	Democratic Republic of the Congo
EC	European Commission
ECA	Economic Commission for Africa (UN)
ECHO	European Community Humanitarian Aid Department
ECLA/ECLAC	Economic Commission for Latin America and the Caribbean (UN)
ECOSOC	Economic and Social Council (UN)
EEAS	European External Action Service
EKC	Environmental Kuznets Curve
EMNC	emerging multinational corporation
EPZ	export processing zone
ESCAP	Economic and Social Commission for Asia and the Pacific (UN)
ESCWA	Economic and Social Commission for Western Asia (UN)
ESF	Emergency Social Fund (Bolivia)
EU	European Union
EZLN	Ejército Zapatista de Liberación Nacional
FAO	Food and Agriculture Organization (UN)
FDI	foreign direct investment
FGT	Foster-Greer-Thorbecke poverty measures
FOCAC	Forum on China–Africa Cooperation
FPI	foreign portfolio investment
FSR	farming systems research
FTAA	Free Trade Area of the Americas
G	shortfall from the poverty line
G7/8	Group of Seven/Eight
G20/G21	Group of 20/21
G24	Intergovernmental Group of Twenty-Four on International Monetary Affairs and Development
G77	Group of 77
GAD	gender and development
GATT	General Agreement on Tariffs and Trade
GAVI	Global Alliance for Vaccines and Immunization
GDI	Gender Development Index
GDP	gross domestic product
GHG	greenhouse gases
GLTN	Global Land Tool Network
GM	gender mainstreaming
GMP	Gates Malaria Partnership
GNH	Gross National Happiness Index
GNI	gross national income
GNP	gross national product
GTZ	German development agency
HCR	High Commission for Refugees
HDI	Human Development Index
HFCS	high-fructose corn syrup
HIPC	heavily indebted poor countries
HIV/AIDS	human immunodeficiency virus/acquired immune deficiency syndrome
HPI	Human Poverty Index
HYV	high-yielding varieties
IBRD	International Bank for Reconstruction and Development (World Bank)
IBSA	India, Brazil, and South Africa
ICA	International Coffee Agreement
ICRC	International Committee of the Red Cross
ICTs	information and communication technologies
IDA	International Development Association (World Bank)
IDGs	International Development Goals
IDL	international division of labour
IDM	Individual Deprivation Measure
IDP	internally displaced people
IDRC	International Development Research Centre
IEPL	International Extreme Poverty Line (World Bank)
IFAD	International Fund for Agricultural Development
IFI	international financial institution
IIA	international investment agreement
ILO	International Labour Organization (UN)
IMF	International Monetary Fund
INDCs	intended nationally determined contributions
INSTRAW	International Research and Training Institute for the Advancement of Women (UN)
IP	intellectual property
IPCC	Intergovernmental Panel on Climate Change
IRD	integrated rural development
IRR	internal rate of return
ISI	import substituting industrialization
ISP	Internet service provider
IT	information technology
ITT	International Telephone and Telegraph
LCD	low carbon development
LDCs	least developed countries
LEDS	low emission development strategies
LF	logical framework
LFA	logical framework approach
LGBT	lesbian, gay, bisexual, and transgender
LMICs	low- and middle-income countries
LPI	Living Planet Index
M&As	mergers and acquisitions

MCC	Millennium Challenge Corporation (US)
MDB	multilateral development bank
MDGs	Millennium Development Goals (UN)
MEF	Major Economies Forum on Energy and Climate Change
MERCOSUR	Common Market of the South
MGE	mainstreaming gender equality
MGNREGA	Mahatma Gandhi National Rural Employment Guarantee Act (India)
MNC	multinational corporation
MNE	multinational enterprise
MOF	Ministry of Finance (China)
MOFA	Ministry of Foreign Affairs (China)
MOFCOM	Ministry of Commerce (China)
MPI	Multidimensional Poverty Index
MSF	Médecins Sans Frontières
MSR	Maritime Silk Road (China)
MST	Landless Workers' Movement (Brazil)
MTEFs	Mid-Term Expenditure Frameworks
N	population size
NAFTA	North American Free Trade Agreement
NAM	Non-Aligned Movement
NAPs	National Action Plans
NASA	National Space Agency (US)
NATO	North Atlantic Treaty Organization
NDB	New Development Bank
NGO	non-governmental organization
NICs	newly industrialized countries
NIDL	new international division of labour
NIEO	New International Economic Order
NPV	net present value
OAS	Organisation of American States
OBOR	One Belt, One Road initiative (China)
OCHA	Office for the Coordination of Humanitarian Affairs (UN)
ODA	official development assistance
OECD	Organisation for Economic Co-operation and Development
OIF	Organisation internationale de la Francophonie
OLI	ownership, location-specific, and internalization
OPEC	Organization of Petroleum Exporting Countries
OPHI	Oxford Poverty and Human Development Initiative
OWG	Open Working Group on the SDGs
PA	participatory assessment
POPs	Stockholm Convention on Persistent Organic Pollutants
PPP	purchasing power parity
PPPs	public-private partnerships
PRA	participatory rural appraisal
PRI	Institutional Revolutionary Party (Mexico)
PRSs	national poverty reduction strategies
PRSPs	Poverty Reduction Strategy Papers
R&D	research and development
RBM	results-based management
RDA	Resources Development Administration (Pandora)
RRA	rapid rural appraisal
RTA	regional trading arrangement
RUF	Revolutionary United Front (Sierra Leone)
SADPA	South African Development Partnership Agency
SAPs	structural adjustment programs
SARS	severe acute respiratory syndrome
SDGs	Sustainable Development Goals
SDRs	special drawing rights
SE	social exclusion
SER	shadow exchange rate
SEWA	Self-Employed Women's Association (India)
SGBV	sexual and gender-based violence
SHE	Secretary of Hydrocarbons (Ecuador)
SIDA	Swedish International Development Cooperation Agency
SMART	specific, measurable, achievable, relevant, and time-bound
SME	small and medium-sized enterprise
SMS	short messaging systems
SOE	state-owned enterprise
SREB	Silk Road Economic Belt (China)
SRF	Silk Road Fund (China)
STABEX	export earnings stabilization system
SVG	St Vincent and the Grenadines
SWAPs	sector-wide approaches
SWR	shadow wage rate
TNC	transnational corporation
TPP	Trans-Pacific Partnership
TRIMs	trade-related investment measures
TRIPs	trade-related aspects of intellectual property rights
TRIPs-plus	stronger version of TRIPs
U5MR	under-five mortality rate
UCIRI	Union of Indigenous Communities of the Isthmus Region
UHC	universal health coverage
UK	United Kingdom
UN	United Nations
US	United States of America
UNASUR	Union of South American Nations
UNCBD	UN Convention on Biological Diversity
UNCCD	UN Convention to Combat Desertification

UNCDF	UN Capital Development Fund
UNCED	UN Conference on Environment and Development
UNCTAD	UN Conference on Trade and Development
UNCTC	UN Centre on Transnational Corporations
UNDP	UN Development Programme
UNECE	UN Economic Commission for Europe
UNEP	UN Environment Programme
UNESCO	UN Educational, Scientific and Cultural Organization
UNFCCC	UN Framework Convention on Climate Change
UNFP/UNFPA	UN Population Fund/UN Fund for Population Activities
UN-HABITAT	UN Human Settlements Programme
UNHCR	UN High Commissioner for Refugees
UNICEF	UN Children's Fund
UNIFEM	UN Development Fund for Women
UNOSSC	UN Office for South–South Cooperation
UNRISD	UN Research Institute for Social Development
UNRWA	UN Relief and Works Agency for Palestine Refugees in the Near East
UNV	UN Volunteers
USAID	United States Agency for International Development
USSR	Union of Soviet Socialist Republics
VAT	value-added tax
WAD	women and development
WBCSD	World Business Council of Sustainable Development
WCED	World Commission on Environment and Development (UN)
WFP	World Food Programme (UN)
WHA	World Health Assembly (WHO)
WHO	World Health Organization (UN)
WID	women in development
WIDER	World Institute for Development Economics Research
WMCCC	World Mayors Council on Climate Change
WMO	World Meteorological Organization
WSF	World Social Forum
WSIS	World Summit on the Information Society
WSSD	World Summit on Social Development
WTO	World Trade Organization
ZOPP/OOPP	objective-oriented project planning

CONTRIBUTORS

Erwin A. Alampay is associate professor in the National College of Public Administration and Governance (NCPAG) at the University of the Philippines.

Eric Allina is associate professor in the Department of History at the University of Ottawa.

Pierre Beaudet is Deputy Director and an associate professor at the School of International Development and Global Studies, University of Ottawa.

Stephen Brown is professor of political science at the University of Ottawa.

Lisa Bornstein is associate professor in the School of Urban Planning at McGill University.

Radhika Desai is professor in the Department of Political Studies at the University of Manitoba.

Gavin Fridell is a Canada Research Chair and associate professor of International Development Studies at Saint Mary's University.

Des Gasper is professor of States, Societies, and World Development at the International Institute of Social Studies at Erasmus University.

Jing Gu is Research Fellow and Director of the Centre for Rising Powers and Global Development, and Convenor of the Rising Powers in International Development Programme at the University of Sussex.

Arjan de Haan is program leader of the Employment and Growth Program at the International Development Research Centre, Ottawa.

Laura Hammond is reader and head of the Department of Development Studies at the School of Oriental and African Studies at the University of London.

Paul A. Haslam is an associate professor at the School of International Development and Global Studies, University of Ottawa.

Joseph Hanlon is visiting senior fellow at the London School of Economics and at the Open University (England).

Anil Hira is professor ofPolitical Science at Simon Fraser University.

David Hulme is professor in the School of Environment, Education, and Development at the University of Manchester.

Tim Jones is a senior policy and campaigns officer for the Jubilee Debt Campaign.

Cédric Jourde is associate professor in the School of Political Studies at the University of Ottawa.

Sophie King is a research fellow at UPRISE, a research centre within the School for the Built Environment at the University of Salford.

Anne Latendresse is professor in the Département de Géographie at the Université du Québec.

Nissim Mannathukkaren is associate professor in the Department of International Development Studies at Dalhousie University.

Marianne H. Marchand is Chair in International Relations in the Department of International Relations and Political Science at the Universidad de las Américas, Puebla.

Abu-Bakar Siddiq Massaquoi is doctoral researcher in the Department of Geography and Environmental Sciences at the University of Reading.

Chukwumerije Okereke is Reader in Environment and Development in the Department of Geography and Environmental Sciences at the University of Reading.

Jane Parpart is research professor in the Department of Conflict Resolution, Human Security, and Global Governance in the McCormack Graduate School at the University of Massachusetts.

David Potts is head of the Bradford Centre for International Development at the University of Bradford.

Joshua Ramisch is associate professor in the School of International Development and Global Studies at the University of Ottawa.

Jane Reid is a PhD student in the School of Urban Planning, McGill University

Keetie Roelen is a research fellow at the Institute of Development Studies and co-director of the Centre for Social Protection at the University of Sussex.

Jessica Schafer is Performance audit manager, Office of the Auditor General of British Columbia.

Ted Schrecker is professor of Global Health Policy in the School of Medicine, Pharmacy and Health at Durham University and a fellow at the Wolfson Research Institute.

David Sogge is an independent analyst based in Amsterdam and an associate of the Norwegian think-tank NOREF.

Astri Suhrke is senior researcher at the Chr. Michelsen Institute, Bergen, Norway.

Marcus Taylor is associate professor and graduate chair in the Department of Global Development Studies at Queen's University.

Rebecca Tiessen is associate professor in the School of International Development and Global Studies at the University of Ottawa.

Henry Veltmeyer is professor of Sociology and International Development Studies at Saint Mary's University.

Torunn Wimpelmann is post-doctoral researcher at the Chr. Michelsen Institute, Bergen, Norway.

Aram Ziai is professor in the Institute of Political Science at the University of Kassel.

PART I
Theories and Approaches in International Development

▲ **William Kamkwamba built a windmill out of a broken bicycle, a tractor fan blade, an old shock absorber, and blue gum trees to power his family's home in Malawi after borrowing books from a small community lending library. After hooking the windmill to a car battery for storage, William was able to power four light bulbs and charge neighbours' mobile phones.** | Source: Photo by Lucas Oleniuk/Toronto Star via Getty Images

1 Meaning, Measurement, and Morality in International Development

Jessica Schafer, Paul A. Haslam, and Pierre Beaudet

LEARNING OBJECTIVES

- To understand the commonality and diversity among developing countries.
- To differentiate among the meaning of various labels used to describe the developing world.
- To understand the relationship between national wealth, distribution of income, and poverty.
- To consider development as a multi-dimensional phenomenon and to identify the major scholars associated with this approach.
- To reflect upon the ethical dilemmas associated with foreign aid and development practice.

▲ **African schoolchildren playing with a globe in Vale Shingwedzi, Mozambique, where residents of areas within the newly created Great Limpopo Transfrontier Park have been resettled.** | Source: Photo by Ute Grabowsky/Photothek via Getty Images

WHAT IS THE DEVELOPING WORLD?

The 1968 photo of "Earthrise" taken by the Apollo 8 astronauts as they orbited the moon was the first image of our world as a whole, hanging in the blackness of space. For many, it made it possible to think of the common fate of humanity, without nations or borders, and regardless of wealth or poverty, making it an icon of the emerging **globalization**. Almost 45 years later, NASA released "Earth at Night," a composite image of the Earth taken by satellites, which showed the planet illuminated by millions of points of light originating from cities, towns, and villages. As David Hulme notes, these points of light can be used as indicators of urbanization, infrastructure, and development, and their absence, as a lack of development (Hulme, 2013: 17). In this regard, NASA's "Earth at Night" gives us an image of our world simultaneously unified and divided, rich and poor.

If you were to descend from the satellite-eye's view and traverse the many regions of the world, you would immediately notice the rich diversity of human experience and social organization. You would observe strikingly different landscapes; hear up to 7,300 different languages (SIL International, 2009); see the wide range of activities that people perform to earn a living; experience home life in many different forms, from nuclear families in suburbia to multi-generational households, families led by patriarchs with several wives, single-parent families, and groups of families in nomadic communities; and encounter a wide variety of political organizations from liberal democracies, to kingdoms, duchies, and principalities, Islamic and people's republics, and dictatorships.

At the same time, you could not fail to notice that certain areas—towns, cities, countries, and regions—exhibit signs of material wealth: sumptuously decorated

NASA

PHOTO 1.1 | NASA's "Earth at Night."

buildings; abundant consumer goods; energy-intensive activities; a highly developed infrastructure of roads, telecommunications, hospitals, and schools. By contrast, other regions and locales are devastatingly poor: human dwellings do not protect inhabitants from the elements; infrastructure is lacking for the movement of people, goods, and information; and the poorest have insufficient food and health care for survival. Many of these are the black areas in NASA's "Earth at Night."

Similarly, you would begin to realize that some human beings enjoy a wide range of opportunities and choices with respect to the way they live their lives, while others struggle to survive in conditions over which they exercise little control. And yet, you would see that there is no simple pattern to these opportunities. While there are richer and poorer countries, you would still see great wealth and great poverty existing side-by-side within both. And, even in these poor areas, few people are truly isolated from the global economy, as they are linked in to some degree by cheap consumer goods, cell phones, mass media, and migration flows.

The study of international development aims to explain both the diversity evident in the world in relation to human well-being and the common patterns that emerge when comparing people, social groups, nations, economic and political systems, and regions of the world. Some explanations are based on historical evidence, finding the causes of today's poverty in the actions (and injustices) of past societies (see Chapter 2). Other explanations for worldwide patterns of wealth and poverty focus on the results of economic "laws" and their functioning through individual rational action in impersonal market transactions. Still other theories of development hold that the economic logic of capitalism requires that some countries remain poor while others profit (see Chapter 3). And some theorists reject the concept of development altogether, heralding an era of "post-development" (see Chapter 4).

But before we get to the theories put forward to explain global development, poverty, wealth, and human well-being, we need to understand some concepts that are central to international development. The next section considers the words and labels that scholars, practitioners, and the popular media use in talking about development. Following that, we introduce different concepts of poverty and measurements of human development. The final two sections address global ethics and ethical issues for development researchers and practitioners.

IMPORTANT CONCEPTS

BOX 1.1 | President Truman's Point 4*

We must embark on a bold new program for making the benefits of our scientific advances and industrial progress available for the improvement and growth of underdeveloped areas. More than half of the people of the world are living in conditions approaching misery. Their food is inadequate, they are victims of disease. Their economic life is primitive and stagnant. Their poverty is a handicap and a threat both to them and more prosperous areas. For the first time in history, humanity possesses the knowledge and the skill to relieve the suffering of these people . . . our imponderable resources in technical knowledge are constantly growing and are inexhaustible. . . . The old imperialism—exploitation for foreign profit—has no place in our plans.

*This was the fourth foreign policy goal that President Truman outlined in his Inaugural Address and, therefore, has become known as his "Point 4."

Source: Inaugural Address, President Harry S. Truman, 20 January 1949, in *Inaugural Addresses of the Presidents of the United States* (1989), cited by Esteva (2010: 1).

LABELLING IN INTERNATIONAL DEVELOPMENT

The terms used to describe people, places, and processes within international development reflect the evolution of thinking about poverty, wealth, and the relationship among nations. Critical theorists have pointed out that labelling plays at least two important roles: labels make existing practices appear legitimate, and they also shape future policy-making (Sachs, 2010; Wood, 1985). Understanding the history of labelling within the field of international development therefore helps to track the progression of important concepts and approaches.

The modern concept of "development" is often traced back to US President Harry Truman's 1949 Inaugural Address (Box 1.1), when he spoke of "underdeveloped areas," a term still in common usage today. If we unpack the term "underdeveloped areas," the concept implies a universal measurement of development and that nations can be assessed against this standard. Those that meet the standards are considered "developed," while those that do not are considered "underdeveloped." In his speech, Truman suggested several criteria for measuring development: on the side of underdevelopment, he mentioned inadequate food, disease, primitive economic life, and poverty; on the side of development he placed scientific advancement and industrial progress, as well as skill and technical knowledge. The use of the word "imperialism" also suggests the areas to which Truman was referring: the large number of countries in Africa and Asia still at that time under political rule by European powers, and the countries of Asia and Latin America that had emerged from European colonial rule over the course of the previous 150 years.

Truman's use of the term "underdeveloped areas" implied a single, overarching scale on which to compare nations' success or progress in relation to each other. It also suggested the need for outside intervention by those who deemed themselves to have achieved progress or development success on behalf of those who have not yet done so or who do not possess the necessary conditions to do so. Indeed, this notion of "trusteeship" (acting for others) is considered by many to be a key element of the modern idea of "development," and has a long history that dates back at least as far as the colonial period (see Cowen and Shenton, 1996; Chapter 2).

In 1952, the French demographer Alfred Sauvy used the term "*tiers monde*" ("Third World") to refer to countries outside the two major power blocs of the West and the Soviet Union (Fry and Martin, 1991). His intent was to draw a parallel with the *tiers état* (Third Estate) in pre-revolutionary France, which referred to the bottom layer of the social pyramid, beneath the clergy and the nobility. The Third Estate had a very diverse membership, from peasants virtually enslaved under feudal lords to bourgeois merchants with great wealth, who had little in common apart from exclusion from the nobility and clergy. Similarly, the Third World to which Sauvy referred in the 1950s included countries with diverse economic, social, and political histories, which were following widely varied trajectories of development. Gradually, though, the term "Third World" took on connotations primarily related to poverty at the national level.

The deepening hostilities of the Cold War during the 1950s meant increasing political tensions and rivalries between the ideologically opposed First and Second Worlds (respectively, the nations of the North Atlantic Treaty Organization and those of the Warsaw Pact or Soviet bloc). The Non-Aligned Movement (NAM) brought some political unity to the group of countries outside the two superpower blocs following a conference in 1955 in Bandung, Indonesia, and the first official Non-Aligned Movement summit in 1961 in Belgrade, Yugoslavia. In this context, the term "Third World," like the NAM, suggested a political bloc that provided an alternative to the ideological power groupings (see Chapters 3 and 10). Although the First World and Second World designations became irrelevant with the fall of the Berlin Wall in 1989, and the Non-Aligned Movement declined in influence, the term "Third World" remains as a kind of catch-all category in international development circles. However, it is difficult to identify any enduring similarities among the countries that have been referred to under this category over the past 50-plus years, and numerous questions have been raised about its value.

Is it a sufficiently clear and useful term, given that there are no precise criteria to identify whether a given country falls within the category or not?

Does the label have negative connotations? Recent public discussions about which countries should be considered part of the Third World suggest that many people feel it is a pejorative, patronizing term and therefore prefer their own country not to be included within the category.

Is it ever possible for a country to move out of the Third World category, or is it a historically determined and static denotation? Some Eastern European countries with low scores on the Human Development Index (discussed below) are not commonly considered part of the Third World, whereas countries of South America may be automatically included even though some of them, such as Argentina and Chile, have achieved high human development scores.

Finally, many are unhappy with the way the term "Third World" seems to imply a world hierarchy and a single path to development success, just as the term "underdeveloped areas" did.

In the 1970s, a new term emerged as a result of economic transformation among a number of countries formerly considered part of the "developing world": the Newly Industrialized Countries (NICs). These countries included Hong Kong, South Korea, Singapore, and Taiwan. More recently, the term "emerging" has become more commonly used, and Thailand, India, Mexico, Brazil, China, South Africa, Turkey, and Malaysia have been included. The term "emerging markets" suggests they are perceived by the leaders of global capitalist enterprises as potential markets to target for profit but also that once they have embraced the rules of market economics, they may be admitted into the coveted circle of successful developed countries. In this regard, "emerging markets" and "emerging economies" imply an optimism for the future that is not captured by the terms "underdeveloped" or "Third World."

The most commonly used term for countries that have not yet reached the level of economic success necessary to be considered "developed" or "rich" is **"developing countries."** A country's **gross domestic product (GDP)** was the standard measure used in the past to classify countries as developed or developing, but this classification produced anomalies. GDP is a measure of the value of goods and services produced in a national economy and can be high as a result of natural resource wealth, even when other sectors of its economy and social well-being may not show signs of development such as industrialization, increased life expectancy, or higher levels of education. For example, Equatorial Guinea, an African country that saw its GDP shoot up in the mid-1990s with the discovery of oil reserves, could have been included in the "developed" category simply on the basis of per capita GDP. Yet other key indicators of human well-being in the country, such as life expectancy and literacy, remain very low. These problems with economic measurement are developed further in the next section.

The World Bank has established its own system of classification, partitioning countries into low-, middle-, and high-income groups as a basis for determining the loan programs for which a country is eligible to apply. It uses a measure of gross national income (GNI), calculated according to its own formula but basically similar to GDP or GNP (gross national product).[1] The wide range of national income levels across the globe is illustrated by Figure 1.1. The World Bank has further subdivided the categories to include lower-middle-income and upper-middle-income groups. There is also a second category of high-income countries: those belonging to the Organisation for Economic Co-operation and Development (OECD). In World Bank reports, the term "developing economies" is used to refer to low- and middle-income economies, but it officially recognizes that this terminology should not be taken to imply that these economies are making "progress" towards development or that those that do not fall into the two groups have already achieved "development." (See the World Bank website for more detail.)

The term **"Fourth World"** has come into usage more recently, although it is not yet common or central in the international development lexicon. It has been used in two quite distinct ways. One is to denote the poorest of the poor countries, often the "failed states" of recent parlance, which have experienced serious setbacks in human well-being and political governance, typically in connection with armed conflict, such as Somalia and Afghanistan (see Chapters 21 and 28). The other and earlier use of "Fourth World," derived

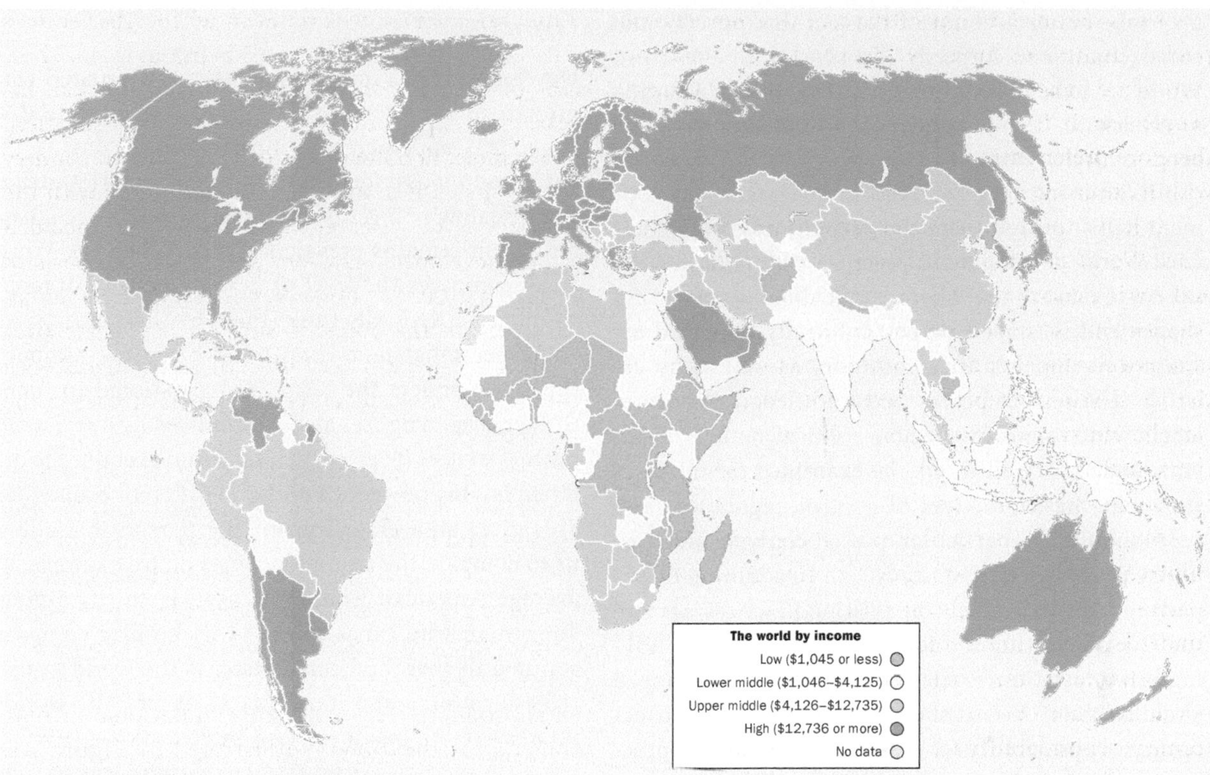

FIGURE 1.1 | Gross National Income Per Capita, 2014

Source: Based on World Bank estimates of 2014 GNI per capita.

from the work in the 1970s of the Canadian Aboriginal leader and writer George Manuel, is in reference to the internal colonization of Aboriginal peoples, whose status and citizenship rights vary considerably globally but who have frequently suffered dispossession and abrogation of political, economic, social, and cultural rights within countries where the dominant settler group has acted as a colonizer.

Discontent with "Third World" and "developing" or "underdeveloped," for many of the reasons mentioned, has prompted people to adopt alternative words to refer to the subjects of international development, such as "two-thirds world" and "majority world." These terms highlight the fact that the overwhelming majority of the world's population are the targets, subjects, or objects of development. The idea of strength in numbers underlies the hopefulness of these terms.

The label "South" seems to provide a neutral way of referring to countries because it emphasizes geographical location over other characteristics. Yet using "South" to refer to countries that qualify as the targets for development does imply characteristics beyond simply location in the southern hemisphere, since Australia and New Zealand, for example, are donor rather than recipient countries in international development, while some countries in the northern hemisphere receive aid and exhibit socio-economic characteristics similar to countries of the "South."

The term "Global South" has gained favour in the development community more recently and appears better able to incorporate the centrality of historical and contemporary patterns of wealth and power into a loosely geographically defined concept. The phrase may take better account of the fact that poverty and social conditions formerly identified with the Third World are to be found throughout the world (including in otherwise "rich" countries) and not simply in one geographical region.

Examining language and discourses of development helps to illuminate the deeper ideas and beliefs underlying development practice and policies. We need to be aware that how we talk about development shapes and is shaped by our culturally informed assumptions and historical position, as well as by existing relations of power and knowledge. Words or labels, which appear to be non-political, natural, or instinctively rational, should be examined for the ways they may mask practices of control, regulation, and reproduction of particular power configurations or policy processes (Crush, 1995: 15). In addition, by superimposing new labels on existing practices, we run the risk of creating the illusion of reform while leaving power relations underlying the labels unchanged (Adams, 1995). Yet, at the same time, we should recognize the possibility for creativity in discursive practice and search for ways in which language can be a force for transformation (Wood, 1985). We should not assume that concepts or practices of "development" are fully determined by those who believe themselves to be their architects. Instead, we need to recognize the agency exercised by those who have responded to, reacted to, and resisted being the objects of development (Crush, 1995: 8).

GROWTH, INEQUALITY, POVERTY, AND DEVELOPMENT

Although vast diversity exists in the standards of living between, among, and within developing countries—and even within the developed world—it remains difficult to define concisely what "development" is and how exactly to measure it. Different approaches to defining "development" reveal different aspects of the problem: the need to distinguish between levels of industrialization, the need to consider different segments of the population, the need to look specifically at poverty, and the need to consider development as an "ideal" or aspiration for betterment.

Growth

Development has most frequently been equated with growth of the economy over a prolonged period of time. This approach was most common during the 1950s and 1960s under the influence of theories such as Walt Rostow's *Stages of Economic Growth* (see Chapter 3), but remains prevalent today. When the World Bank compares the level of development of different countries, it typically ranks them by their average income per inhabitant—or **GDP per capita**—although the Bank prefers the term "gross national income." GDP per capita figures also are adjusted by **purchasing power parities** (PPPs), which take into account the different buying power of a dollar in different economies. This gives an average income per person that allows us to compare the annual incomes of, for example, an average American who earns $52,947 to the average Tanzanian who earns $1,654. This kind of comparison reveals that the United States is the world's ninth richest country and Tanzania is one of the world's poorest—159th out of 187 (see Table 1.2).

GDP per capita is an extremely useful way of comparing levels of development. It also gives us the most widely used measure of how countries are improving (or deteriorating) in their level of development. GDP growth rates (the percentage change in national income between any two years) are like the Academy Awards of the developing world, clearly indicating which economies have been performing (in terms of adding wealth) and which have not. The top-performing economies in the developing world may have growth rates exceeding 10 per cent per annum—such as China in the early 2000s—but others may post negative rates, as was the case for much of sub-Saharan Africa during the 1980s and early 1990s. However, growth rates in developing countries, where the economy might be based on a few exported products or resources, are very volatile and may be high one year and low the next. In contrast, developed countries generally have slower GDP growth rates, usually between 2 and 3.5 per cent, but these rates are more stable over time. One of the world's most prominent development economists, Jeffrey Sachs, has argued that the current gulf in wealth between the developed and developing countries is almost entirely caused by small differences in growth rates over the period since 1820. In 1820, he argues, the difference in GDP per capita between developed and developing countries was relatively small (only 4:1), but two centuries of differential growth rates have led to a twenty-fold gap (Sachs, 2005: 29–31).

Rapid growth in GDP is usually caused by rapid increases in productivity in agriculture, natural resource extraction, or industrialization. When GDP per capita reaches the level of a middle-income developing country, it usually means that a certain level of industrialization has been reached, including the production of manufactured goods such as textiles and consumer durables (refrigerators, cars) and of some intermediate goods such as steel and petrochemicals. It was generally assumed that growth of national wealth (as measured by GDP per capita) would "trickle down" to the poorest segments of society in such a way that most people would benefit. In other words, development, viewed through the prism of increasing GDP per capita, was about copying the industrialization experience of the West.

But it should not be forgotten that GDP per capita is a measure of the *average* income in a country. There are numerous problems with GDP per capita, including that it is an estimate that depends on the quality of information collected by government statistical agencies and that it fails to count the "value" of non-market subsistence activities, which may be quite important in less developed rural areas (for a trenchant critique, see Seers, 1979: 14–17). Although a good indicator of the degree of industrialization, GDP tells us relatively little about the extent of poverty—specifically, what proportion of the population is extremely poor—or whether growth is in fact "trickling down" to the poor. It is possible for countries to grow rapidly in GDP per capita but for only the richest segments of society to benefit. In this respect, development *cannot* be as simple as GDP growth, because growth does not necessarily reduce poverty.

Inequality

In order to know how many poor people there are in a given country and whether they are benefiting from the overall growth of the economy, we need to include another concept: the distribution of income. The **distribution of income** (also known as income inequality) is a measure of how the wealth of a country is distributed among its population: what share of that wealth is owned by the rich, and how much the poorest earn in comparison to the wealthiest. Indeed, income inequality is the direct link between GDP per capita and the number of people living in poverty.

Income inequality can be measured in two ways: a comparison of the income earned by different strata of the population and the Gini coefficient (see Chapter 26). Income inequality is often evaluated by dividing the population into five or ten equally populous strata, known respectively as "quintiles" or "deciles," and comparing the average incomes of these different strata to each other. A standard comparison is between the earnings of the wealthiest 20 per cent of the population and the poorest 40 per cent (the ninth and tenth deciles compared to the first to fourth deciles). However, the Gini coefficient is the most commonly used measure of income inequality. It is a number between 0 and 1, with relatively equal societies such as the Scandinavian countries scoring around 0.25 while very unequal societies like Brazil score around 0.6.[2]

Income inequality is important in part because it forces us to confront the injustice in most developing societies: that a privileged minority lead luxurious lives while the vast majority of their own countrymen and women struggle in abject poverty. But income inequality is also an important constraint on development. It means that growth often comes from the richer segment of the economy and is less likely to translate into poverty reduction by "trickling down" to the poor. Poverty is always eliminated more quickly when GDP growth is combined with improvements (greater equality) in the distribution of income.

Societies in developing countries tend to be much more unequal than societies in developed countries. Latin America, although an upper-middle-income area of the developing world, is also the region with the most unequal distribution of income. This means that the super-rich and the super-poor coexist in the same countries. Mexico, for example, has the second richest man on the list of the world's richest people, China has six people on the list, and India has five, while citizens of the developing world as a whole occupy 23 of the top 100 places (*Forbes*, 2015). Brazil, one of the most unequal countries in the world, has three billionaires on the Forbes list, European-trained elites, and a world-class aeronautics industry—but also *favelas* (Portuguese for "slums") surrounding its major modern and cosmopolitan cities such as São Paulo. The share of national income appropriated by the richest 20 per cent and that appropriated by the poorest 20 per cent hardly changed over the 1981–2001 period, despite significant growth that resulted in the doubling of per capita income (see Table 1.1). In 2001 the top quintile took home almost 62 per cent of the national income while the bottom quintile pocketed only 2.5 per cent. The degree of inequality between the top 10 per cent and the bottom 10 per cent is even more pronounced: 42 per cent and 1 per cent of the national income in 2013, respectively. Yet, there is also reason for hope. In the 2002–12 period (the latest date for which there are figures), the Brazilian government made a concerted attempt to channel resources to the poorest sectors of society, resulting in some improvement in the distribution of income.

The realization that income inequality makes the task of raising people out of poverty even more difficult has led to the current focus of international organizations and research on "growth with equity," which seeks to combine the goal of GDP growth with the goal of distributing the benefits of that growth to the poor. Growth remains important because it "grows the pie," but it is not enough in itself. Furthermore, some evidence suggests that countries that grow faster do not always improve the situation of the poorest (such as Brazil), while countries with low growth rates and GDP per capita may succeed relatively well in reducing the vulnerability of the poorest segments in society (such as Cuba or the Indian state of Kerala). This means that high GDP growth is not strictly necessary for poverty reduction, although it may make it easier. It is also worth underlining that the poorest and those who are least likely to benefit from the "trickle down" of growth are usually those who belong to disadvantaged ethnic, linguistic, and cultural groups. In Latin America, for example, this frequently means Indigenous peoples and people of African descent.

Although inequality undermines the opportunities for material advancement of the poor, it also has broader cultural effects on the rich. Dudley Seers writes, "The social barriers and inhibitions of an unequal society distort the personalities of those with high incomes no less than those who are poor" (1972: 23). When inequality becomes part of a national culture, it undermines the broad and diffuse social trust, what Robert Putnam, among others, has called **social capital** (Fukuyama, 1995; Putnam, 1993). Social capital refers to the extent to which individuals are willing to co-operate in the pursuit of shared goals and is usually thought to be essential to the development of a civic and democratic culture (see Chapters 12 and 16). Public opinion polling in highly unequal societies such as Latin America demonstrates that people are less trusting of strangers than is the case in the developed world. Gated communities and barred windows are commonplace. Furthermore, one may well ask if the traditional conservatism of elites in the developing world and their unwillingness to tolerate reformist groups or extend the rights of social citizenship to the poor comes from fear of loosening their grip on the masses, who know very well who benefits from the status quo and who does not.

Although inequality is a common feature of most developing countries, it is very difficult to explain why.

TABLE 1.1 | The Distribution of Income in Brazil by Quintiles, 1981–2012 (% share of national income)

Quintile	1981	1990	2001	2007	2012
1 (poorest)	2.89	2.36	2.45	3.02	4
2	6.01	5.27	5.84	6.85	8
3	10.59	9.72	10.79	11.78	12
4	18.84	18.19	18.94	19.62	19
5 (richest)	61.67	64.46	61.98	58.73	57
GNI/capita*	$1,850	$2,540	$3,310	$6,140	$12,390

*Atlas method, US$.

Source: World Bank 2014, World databank, at: databank.worldbank.org/ddp/home.do.

There are many possible reasons, some of which are discussed in more detail in subsequent chapters. At least three explanations seem plausible. First, the impact of colonial rule or neo-colonial economic relations may have forged or consolidated unequal social relations based on slavery, feudalism, and landownership patterns that continue to influence the present (see Chapters 2 and 3). Second, the characteristics of late industrialization—that is, the use of inappropriate capital-intensive technology—reduce the employment potential of GDP growth (see Chapters 7 and 22). Third, inadequate or non-existent social safety nets and regressive taxation systems prevent the redistribution of national income towards the poor and middle classes, as occurred in the developed economies after the Great Depression. The good news is that although income inequality makes development more difficult, it is not impossible to overcome. The recent expansion of targeted poverty reduction (see Chapters 24 and 25) and broad-based social programs (see Chapter 26) in much of the developing world has contributed to a significant reduction in the incidence of poverty and slight reductions in inequality.

Defining Poverty and Development

Income inequality leads us to the direct question of the proportion of poor people in a given country. (For a more detailed discussion of poverty and exclusion, see Chapters 24 and 25.) Poverty, however, is a difficult concept to define. It is usually defined as an extremely low level of income. For example, the World Bank distinguishes between absolute and moderate poverty in much of its work. **Absolute poverty** refers to being below the minimum level of income required for physical survival. The World Bank defines this level as US$1.25 per day measured in 2005 dollars at international purchasing power parity—that is, adjusted for the buying power of a US dollar in the local market. The definition of the absolute poverty line was revised in 2008 from the commonly cited US$1 a day level (in 1993 dollars). **Moderate poverty** is typically considered to be an income of US$2 per day, a level at which basic needs are barely met but survival is not actually threatened. According to these new measures, the World Bank reported that 1.2 billion people were below the absolute poverty line in 2013, more than had been estimated previously but approximately 700 million less than in 1980 (Olinto et al., 2013).

In the 1960s, however, American sociologists such as Talcott Parsons and Kenneth Clark, addressing poverty and in particular the status of African Americans in US society, began to develop the concepts of **relative poverty** and social exclusion. Relative poverty refers to a kind of poverty that does not threaten daily survival but in which an individual may not have the income necessary to fully participate in his or her society (Thomas, 2000: 13, citing Townsend). One may well imagine how an individual without computer access and knowledge would be seriously hampered in terms of his or her ability to access important information and even do basic tasks such as looking for employment. The poverty we refer to in developed countries is almost exclusively, even for the very poorest, an issue of relative rather than absolute or even moderate poverty. A related concept is "social exclusion" or social citizenship, which is discussed in greater detail in Chapter 26.

Nonetheless, the concept of relative poverty reveals that poverty is not just about income levels; it also has social, political, psychological, and moral elements—and this is true in both the developing *and* the developed world. In other words, although GDP per capita is a good indicator of poverty as income deprivation, it does not tell the whole story. Consequently, alleviating poverty or *doing development* also must be much more complicated than simply spurring economic growth or even reducing poverty. Three thinkers in particular have been fundamental in redefining how poverty, and therefore development, should be understood.

The idea that development involved much more than economic growth or an increase in income per capita began to gain ground in the late 1960s, promoted by development theorists and practitioners such as Dudley Seers and Denis Goulet. The arguments of these scholars have led to an understanding of poverty and development as *multi-dimensional*. Seers rephrased the question of how to develop by asking, "What are the necessary conditions for a universally acceptable aim, the realization of the potential of human personality?" (Seers, 1979: 10). He concluded that six conditions were necessary: adequate income to cover the needs of basic survival; employment (including any non-paid social role that contributes to self-respect and development of the personality); improvement in the distribution of income; an education, particularly literacy; political participation; and national autonomy (belonging to a politically and economically independent nation). Denis Goulet, writing at about the same time, asserted that development should promote "life-sustenance" (the basic requirements for survival—food, clothing, health, and shelter), self-esteem (or dignity and identity of the individual), and freedom (an expanded range of choice and freedom from "servitudes") (Goulet, 1971: 87–97; Seers, 1979: 10–13; Todaro, 1989).

It is evident that those closely involved in development were beginning to see growth as an inadequate measure of development and even entertained the possibility that rising incomes, although they improved the ability of individuals to meet basic physical needs, might not contribute to "development" in its more sophisticated and multi-dimensional aspects. These ideas were further developed in the work of Nobel Prize–winning economist Amartya Sen, who argues that development should not be seen simply as rising income levels but rather as an increase in individuals' substantive freedoms. His approach is often called "development as freedom," after the title of his popular 1999 book, or the **capability approach**. As Sen puts it, the real value of wealth and income is that "they are admirable general-purpose means for having more freedom to lead the kind of lives we have reason to value" (Sen, 1999: 14). In this respect, Sen sees poverty primarily as kinds of "unfreedom," or deprivation of freedoms, that limit the ability of individuals to improve their lives. Such unfreedoms may include a lack of access to health and welfare services, gender or ethnic **discrimination**, and limits on basic political, civic, and economic rights. According to Sen, lack of freedom can be the result of either processes (denial of rights normally considered "procedural," like political, civic, and human rights) or the opportunities that people do not have (inability to feed themselves, receive

Paul Haslam

PHOTO 1.2 | Inequality: hillside slums and the beachfront, Rio de Janeiro.

an education, access health services, avoid premature morbidity) (Sen, 1999: 14–17). It is worth underlining that these deprivations are absolute, not relative, as *all* people need a certain level of capabilities in order to function as fully human (live a good human life). Some of Sen's followers, such as Martha Nussbaum, have produced lists of these minimum but universal requirements (Nussbaum, 1995: 84–5).

The key to Sen's argument, therefore, is the way in which the expansion of people's capabilities—that is, their ability to lay claim to or access various resources (such as civil and political rights and government services)—can improve their ability to make choices that they value. At the same time, an increased ability to make choices feeds back to build their "capabilities." One can imagine, for example, how the right to vote and participate in politics could lead to governmental decisions that increase local educational opportunities, which in turn could expand the choices of those who participated in the political process by voting. Sen writes, "Greater freedom enhances the ability of people to help themselves and also to influence the world, and these matters are central to the process of development" (Sen, 1999: 18). Sen makes it clear, therefore, that level of income does not relate directly to "development" and that poverty is better seen as the deprivation of basic capabilities or freedoms.

Sen points to a number of compelling examples to illustrate his argument, including the fact that, using data from 1993, African Americans (on average) had a lower probability of reaching old age than citizens of China, Sri Lanka, or Costa Rica, despite having much higher incomes. Furthermore, male African Americans from Harlem were even worse off than the average, being less likely to reach the age of 40 than men in Bangladesh (Sen, 1999: 21–3). In this example, Sen shows that African-American men suffered from restrictions on their "capabilities" despite having incomes much higher than people in the other countries cited. It is important to underline that, for Sen, although freedom (including free markets) has intrinsic value and does not have to be justified in terms of outcomes, a significant part of the expansion of capabilities (ability to access freedoms) comes through access to government services. Therefore, Sen sees the ability to access education, health care, and unemployment insurance as central elements that expand people's capabilities. The inverse of this observation is that sometimes low income does not reflect the opportunities people have. This should be intrinsically clear to students in a university or college setting, where their income (measured by summer earnings or part-time jobs) would put them below the national poverty line. In no way does this income level reflect the real capabilities and freedoms commanded by students or the opportunities before them.

Sen's work has been instrumental (together with that of Seers and Goulet) in opening the door to more multi-dimensional measures of development that go beyond the ubiquitous GDP per capita. In defence of GDP per capita, it is easily measured, and levels of absolute and moderate poverty can be clearly established according to certain income cut-off points. Even one of its most ardent detractors, Dudley Seers, referred to GDP per capita as a "very convenient indicator" (Seers, 1979: 9). However, is it possible to measure a multi-dimensional concept like Sen's "development as freedom"? Some authors have criticized such an approach as being impossible to quantify (Rist, 1997: 10). Nonetheless, efforts have been made to construct measures that better capture the multi-dimensional aspects of development. The best known is the Human Development Index, or HDI, of the United Nations Development Programme (UNDP), constructed with input from Amartya Sen (Table 1.2).

The annual *Human Development Report*, which ranks the countries of the world by their HDI score, is the UNDP's flagship publication and was developed in 1990 as an alternative and more multi-dimensional measure of development than GDP per capita. Many people see it as an intellectual and philosophical challenge to the World Bank's annual publication, the *World Development Report*, which continues to use GNI per capita as a measure of development. The Human Development Index is a composite measure of three equally weighted factors: a long and healthy life, knowledge, and standard of living. A long and healthy life is measured by life expectancy at birth; knowledge is a composite of the adult literacy rate and the combined gross enrolment ratio for primary, secondary, and post-secondary schools; and standard of living is measured by GDP per capita. In this respect, the index recognizes that income levels are important but that other factors also are significant in human development. One may view the education and longevity measures as proxies that

TABLE 1.2 | Countries Ranked by HDI and GNI Per Capita, 2014

HDI Ranking 2014	Country (according to World Bank category)	HDI Score	GNI Per Capita (PPP US$)	GNI Per Capita Ranking
Very high human development				
1	Norway	0.944	64,992	6 ↑
8	United States	0.915	52,947	11 ↑
9	Canada	0.913	42,155	20 ↑
9	New Zealand	0.913	32,689	32 ↑
11	Singapore	0.912	76,628	4 ↓
14	United Kingdom	0.907	39,267	23 ↑
20	Japan	0.891	36,927	27 ↑
39	Saudi Arabia	0.837	52,821	12 ↓
42	Chile	0.832	21,290	53 ↑
High human development				
50	Russian Federation	0.798	22,352	49 ↓
72	Turkey	0.761	18,677	60 ↓
73	Sri Lanka	0.757	9,779	102 ↑
75	Brazil	0.755	15,175	74 ↓
90	China	0.727	12,547	83 ↓
Medium human development				
106	Botswana	0.698	16,646	65 ↓
110	Indonesia	0.684	9,778	101 ↓
115	Philippines	0.668	7,915	108 ↓
129	Tajikistan	0.624	2,517	156 ↑
130	India	0.609	5,497	126 ↓
142	Bangladesh	0.570	3,191	147 ↑
Low human development				
150	Swaziland	0.531	5,542	125 ↓
151	Tanzania	0.521	2,411	159 ↑
152	Nigeria	0.514	5,341	128 ↓
154	Madagascar	0.510	1,328	178 ↑
181	Sierra Leone	0.413	1,780	165 ↓
185	Chad	0.392	2,085	163 ↓
188	Niger	0.348	908	183 ↓

↑ Indicates country whose HDI ranking is higher than its GDP per capita ranking.

↓ Indicates country whose HDI ranking is lower than its GDP per capita ranking.

Source: UNDP, *Human Development Report 2015,* at: http://hdr.undp.org/en/statistics.

take account of the various government services that Seers, Goulet, and Sen see as crucial to expanding the range of individual choice. Indeed, the first *Human Development Report* (1990) was explicit about this link, noting that "Human development is a process of enlarging people's choices" (UNDP, 1990: 10).

For the UNDP, countries with a HDI score of 0.8 or more are considered highly developed, while those with a score of 0.5 or less are considered to have low development. In the 2015 *Human Development Report*, classifications are given for 188 countries in the following categories: very high human development (49), high human development (55), medium human development (38), and low human development (43), with HDI values ranging on a scale between 0 and 1. The HDI shows that many countries rank much higher in "human development" than average per capita income would predict. Even Norway, holding the number-one spot on the HDI (five spots higher than its GNI ranking), does not do as well in converting GNI per capita to human development as New Zealand, which is ninth in the HDI but thirty-secondth in GNI. New Zealand has almost half the per capita income of Norway but a very similar HDI outcome. Results can be even more divergent in developing countries: at almost the same GNI per capita of just over $9,000, we find both high-HDI Sri Lanka (#73) and medium-HDI Indonesia (#110). This shows that some countries do much better than others in converting income level into human development.

Perhaps most importantly, the HDI has embedded the idea of poverty and development as a multi-dimensional phenomenon in the modern approach to development. The UNDP has also developed a number of other multi-dimensional measures inspired by the HDI, in order to focus on other aspects of poverty, exclusion, and development. For example, the Inequality-adjusted Human Development Index combines the HDI with a measure of inequality; the Multidimensional Poverty Index (MPI) assesses how multiple "deprivations" affect people's quality of life; the Gender Inequality Index (GII) assesses the discrimination faced by women and girls; and the Gender Development Index (GDI) uses the same approach as the HDI, but tuned to the gap between male and female outcomes. Even the Millennium Development Goals (MDGs), the comprehensive framework developed to focus the activities of all bilateral and multilateral aid agencies between 2002 and 2015, and their successor, the Sustainable Development Goals (SDGs), can be viewed as operationalizing a multi-dimensional approach to development.

Recently, the multi-dimensional approach to understanding development has been twinned with a human-rights-based approach. The idea of development as a human right has been debated within the UN system since the early 1970s, but it was not until it was linked with Sen's capability approach that the human rights approach entered the mainstream (Uvin, 2010: 164–8). Proponents immediately saw the similarities between actions needed to increase people's capabilities on multiple dimensions and the various human rights treaties that governments had signed committing to improve access to food, education, health care, adequate housing, security, justice, and civil and political rights. Identifying development as a human right was supposed to put political pressure on governments to fulfill their existing obligations to improve the capabilities of their populations. In other words, activists wanted to use international law as a kind of "stick" to push recalcitrant countries forward. It was also hoped that international law would provide an opening for citizens to claim their rights from their own governments (Uvin, 2010: 170–4). The human-rights-based approach to development was officially launched with the publication of a framework linking development and human rights by the UN High Commission for Human Rights in 2006 (UNHCHR, 2006). Since that time, human rights considerations have become an increasingly important part of the debate over how to advance development goals.

GLOBAL ETHICS AND INTERNATIONAL DEVELOPMENT

Wherever you live, you are reading this book because you have an interest in international development and, by extension, in the global distribution of wealth and power, well-being, and poverty. It may seem obvious, therefore, that the negative consequences of poverty for human health and well-being are on the whole a bad thing, both within your own country and in other countries throughout the world. You probably also believe that it follows logically from this that we should take

CRITICAL ISSUES

BOX 1.2 | What Is Development?

"Development" is a contested term. There are debates surrounding the meaning of development, contestation over the best approach to achieve development, and even questions about whether it is worth pursuing at all (see Chapters 3 and 4). Today's dominant usage of "development," in which it is understood as virtually synonymous with economic growth and modernity, emerged in the post–World War II period. However, ideas about human progress that undergird this vision of development are rooted in the European Enlightenment.

With the rise of industrial capitalism in the eighteenth century, many philosophers began to see history as linear, as having an ultimate destination, a "progression to the better," as German philosopher Georg Hegel saw it (Leys, 1996: 4). At the same time, capitalism's transformation of society gave rise to new social ills, such as dispossession, unemployment, and poverty, and many saw the need for an antidote to these problems. Ideas of economic progress and social transformation were taken up and expressed through the European colonial enterprise, in complex ways and diverse forms. In particular, it has been suggested that the idea of development was based on the Eurocentric idea of "trusteeship"—those who were already "developed" could act on behalf of those individuals and societies that were yet to realize their potential (Cowen and Shenton, 1995).

Some thinkers, such as Arturo Escobar (1992), argue that the colonial roots of the concept and practice of development call into question the validity of the contemporary development enterprise. They emphasize the destructive and disciplinary power of development in its interventions in and transformations of non-Western societies (see Chapter 4). Development can be seen to have changed societies for the worse, rather than improving people's lives, as development discourse would have us believe (Watts, 1995: 45). Gilbert Rist (1997, 2007) refers to development as a "toxic word" because it necessarily entails the destruction of both the environment and social bonds in the process of transforming natural and human resources into economic commodities. In fact, Rist sees "development" as a discourse that legitimates the global expansion of capitalism while simultaneously obfuscating its negative effects on people.

However, development is not a homogeneous project. Development, "for all its power to speak and to control the terms of speaking, has never been impervious to challenge and resistance, nor, in response, to reformulation and change" (Crush, 1995: 8). Just as a body of scholarship has uncovered the interactions and mutual shaping that took place during the colonial encounter between (multiple) colonizers and (multiple) colonized peoples (see Chapter 2), research is also emerging that explores the ways people who are the "objects" of development policy subvert and in turn transform the people, ideas, projects, agencies, and societies that are held up as the paradigm of the developed world (Scott, 1990).

action to avoid, mitigate, or reverse poverty wherever possible—and not just within our own country.

However, while few people would argue that poverty is not a bad thing, the further belief that we should take action to address poverty is not universally shared. In addition, even among those who do accept that action should be taken to address global poverty, there are intense intellectual and political debates over how we can justify action on global poverty and what actions are justified. Several influential approaches to global poverty have had an impact on these debates within the field of international development and on policy action. We provide a brief overview of these approaches in this section, and then we explore dilemmas that you, as a student of international development, might face when assessing your options for action or when taking part in international development policy-making or practice.

Central to the international development arena is a simple question: Do our moral duties extend beyond our families, neighbours, and fellow citizens?

Over the course of the twentieth century, most Western societies developed systems of social support to ensure that no citizen would be left to die or suffer severe deprivation as a result of poverty. These systems became known as "welfare states."

However, while the welfare state in various forms became ubiquitous among European and North American nations, a global institution equivalent to national welfare state agencies has not emerged to take responsibility for guaranteeing security and meeting the basic needs of all people through similar forms of wealth redistribution and universal public service provisions. Nonetheless, many people believe that the principles of basic human rights and security should apply to all humans, regardless of where they happen to live in the world. Thus, we have moved from a time when most discussions about justice were concerned primarily with distribution within states to a time when many are considering arguments surrounding distributive justice globally, or what has become known as **global ethics**.

Cosmopolitan Arguments for Global Redistribution

Those who argue that principles of justice imply a moral obligation to address the needs of the poor not only within national boundaries but beyond these borders largely fall within the philosophical category referred to as **cosmopolitanism**. According to cosmopolitanism, justice is owed to all people regardless of where they happen to live or where they happen to have been born, and regardless of their race or gender, class or citizenship (O'Neill, 2000: 45). National boundaries are therefore of little or no moral importance in considerations of justice.

Within cosmopolitan thinking, Charles Jones (1999) identifies three main types of justification for global redistributive justice: a *consequentialist ethic* (as exemplified in the works of Peter Singer); a *contractarian ethic* (as in the works of Charles Beitz and Thomas Pogge); and a *rights-based ethic* (Jones's own position and that of Henry Shue). These three views are outlined in Box 1.3.

Peter Singer's argument is that if we can take action to prevent people from dying of starvation without compromising anything else of equal moral value, an impartial view of justice would clearly say that we are morally bound to take that action. Box 1.4 presents an example that he offers readers to persuade them of the moral correctness of this consequentialist position.

If Singer's position is correct, we can draw the conclusion that we should be giving away all of the "surplus" income we have as long as it does not cause us to give up something of *greater* moral value than the lives of people facing starvation anywhere in the world. One might characterize this as the "Mother Teresa" approach (Doyle, 2006) or radical sacrifice (Gasper, 1986: 141), since it seems to require that we give up

IMPORTANT CONCEPTS

BOX 1.3 | How to Judge Right and Wrong: Three Philosophical Approaches to Morality

Consequentialist philosophy assesses whether an action is morally just on the basis of the goodness or value of the outcomes it produces.

Contractarian philosophy holds that moral norms are justified according to the idea of a contract or mutual agreement (as in the political philosophy of Thomas Hobbes, John Locke, and, most recently, John Rawls).

Rights-based philosophy justifies moral claims on the basis of fundamental entitlements to act or be treated in specific ways. Justifications for rights-based morality are complex, but they include the idea that we have rights because we have interests or because of our status.

IMPORTANT CONCEPTS

BOX 1.4 | The Drowning Child Analogy

Peter Singer (2002) suggests that the following situation illustrates why justice requires us to act to prevent needless and extreme suffering regardless of national boundaries. Imagine you are walking to work and see a small child fall into a pond. She is in danger of drowning. You could easily walk into the pond and save her without endangering your own safety, but you would get your clothing and shoes muddy. You would have to go home and change, causing you to be late for work, and your shoes might be ruined. Our moral intuition tells us that you should clearly put aside those minor inconveniences in order to save the child's life—and that if you ignored her and continued on your way, you would have done something seriously morally wrong. Furthermore, it should make no moral difference whether this little girl is your own child, your neighbour's child, or someone you don't know at all. But, Singer argues, are we not in the same position, morally speaking, when we choose to spend money on frivolous or luxurious items that are no more important than the muddy shoes in the example, rather than use that money to prevent someone from dying of starvation (for example, through donation to humanitarian agencies that have proven competence in delivering aid to the starving and needy)? And, he argues, this is clearly true even if that starvation is occurring in another part of the world that we may never visit. Is that thousand-dollar bottle of champagne, that gold-encrusted tuna steak, that Tiffany diamond ring really more important, morally speaking, than a human life (or many of them)?

everything we have until we are in a similar position of poverty and have nothing left to give that would prevent another person from dying of starvation.

Thomas Pogge (2002, 2005) argues for the moral duty to address world poverty using different justifications. He suggests that one of the main reasons we have a moral duty to alleviate global poverty is because we are causally responsible for the current situation as a result of the colonial destruction of local economies and societies. Similar premises underlie the argument by Walter Rodney (1972), an influential Guyanese writer, that international development and assistance are simply a way to give back what had been taken from the Global South.

Another argument Pogge provides takes a contractarian approach (see Box 1.3). He holds that an economic order should be considered morally unjust if it causes massive and severe human rights deficits that could be avoided under a different and practically possible institutional arrangement. He argues that this is clearly the case with the current global economic order, which preserves the advantages of the wealthy and allows serious and avoidable deprivation among the poor, despite there being a "feasible institutional alternative under which such severe and extensive poverty would not persist" (Pogge, 2005: 4). Thus, according to Pogge, our obligation to address world poverty is based at least in part on our duty *not to harm* others.

Rights-based approaches to global justice and the problem of poverty take the idea of human rights as implying duties for individuals, states, and other institutions to protect and aid those whose basic needs are not being met through contemporary global market economies (see Chapter 24).

Charles Jones argues that the right to subsistence (principally food, shelter, and a level of health required for basic human functioning) is based on the recognition that these are universally shared human needs and, therefore, are morally important. They are the most basic interests we have, because "without food, shelter, and a reasonable level of health maintenance, human lives are simply not possible" (Jones, 1999: 58).

Not all states, however, are currently in a position to ensure the right to subsistence for all of their citizens, because some lack sufficient resources. This means that states with more than they need to ensure the fulfillment of the right to subsistence should redistribute wealth and resources to states unable either to provide subsistence rights to their citizens or to protect those rights (Jones, 1999: 70). Hence, a rights-based approach to justice also can provide moral justification for global redistribution of wealth in order to protect and aid all peoples in achieving the right to subsistence.

Arguments against Global Redistributive Justice

The two main ethical positions opposed to cosmopolitan approaches to redistributive global justice are communitarianism and libertarianism. **Communitarianism** takes issue with the cosmopolitan assumption that national borders have no moral importance. Instead, communitarians believe that political and social community is morally relevant. Thus, some communitarians hold that we are justified in giving (moral) preference to the needs of our fellow citizens, because membership in the nation creates special bonds, a kind of extended version of kinship.

Libertarian philosophy is best exemplified in the work of Robert Nozick, *Anarchy, State and Utopia* (1974). It has been influential among a number of development theorists (for example, Deepak Lal and Peter Bauer) in the formulation of what is now known as **neoliberalism** (see Gasper, 1986; see also Chapter 3). Nozick argues that individual rights to freedom and non-interference are the central moral good, and he places particular value on the right of individuals to acquire and retain private property. Therefore, libertarians oppose any form of obligatory redistribution of wealth, whether within one country or among countries.

Another aspect of Nozick's argument on justice is that the simple existence of (even extreme) inequality of wealth and poverty does not indicate injustice (Gasper, 1986: 143). As long as the wealth was obtained by legitimate means, the situation should be deemed just. Individuals should be free to give donations to poorer people if they choose to, but there is no moral obligation to do so, and there should be no corresponding demand on the part of a state or other body.

If we look at statements by actors and institutions operating in international development, many suggest a widespread belief in universal human rights and transnational duties to protect and assist people regardless of where they live in the world. Common values and human rights were an important justification for the adoption of the Millennium Development Goals in 2002 and the Sustainable Development Goals in 2015 (UN General Assembly, 2005). The G8 has posited that "fighting poverty is both a moral imperative and a necessity for a stable world" (G8, 2000). The UN High Commissioner for Human Rights has promoted a "right to development" (UNHCHR, 2006). "Rights talk" is fashionable, and it would be virtually unthinkable for a political leader to deny the principle underlying universal human rights—*that all human life is of equal worth*. And yet, much of the actual practice of Western aid allocation seems to imply a far less consistent view of the moral obligation to address global poverty, with aid often seen as non-obligatory charitable donations, serving the national interest, or rewarding allies (see Chapter 8). As you read this book, you should reflect on the moral principles that remain highly relevant to international development, and ask yourself what might be needed to bring our beliefs about justice in line with our actions in the global sphere (see Chapter 29).

ETHICAL BEHAVIOUR AND THE DEVELOPMENT PRACTITIONER

Development ethics also addresses the issue of how each of us should behave as development practitioners and researchers working in the developing world. As Des Gasper (1999: 6) puts it, those who work on the front line "need ethical frames by which they can better understand their situation, structure their choices, avoid debilitating degrees of doubt and guilt, and move forward." Gasper's contribution in Chapter 29 provides more detailed tools to assist in analysis and reflection about our ethical responsibilities as researchers, development practitioners, and students participating in internships and exchanges. Here, we introduce some key ideas that you should keep in mind as you are thinking about your role in the future of international development.

Although there are differences between the ethical responsibilities of researchers and those of practitioners, important commonalities between them are required for work in developing countries. Researchers tend to be principally concerned with the issues of informed consent and respect for the privacy and confidentiality of those who participate in their studies, the implications of relationships of reciprocity with key local informants (what researchers owe them, if anything), and the benefits of the research for the community (including how to share the findings with them) (Marchall, 1992: 1–3). An overriding injunction at all times is to "do no harm"—to ensure that the vulnerable are not put at risk as a result of their participation in the research or project (Adams and Megaw, 1997; Jacobsen and Landau, 2003: 193). These ethical responsibilities are salient for practitioners as well, although informed consent usually translates to ensuring that participation is willing and voluntary in the development project at hand.

Above all, being ethical as a development worker or researcher suggests a kind of permanent, ongoing self-critique and evaluation of one's actions and their effects, taking care to identify, privilege, and respect the rights of others over one's more narrow professional objectives (Adams and Megaw, 1997). In other words, development ethics subordinates the goals (what we want to do) to the means of development (how we do it).

We are always aware when we do not have the power in a relationship, but well-meaning people—such as the typical development worker or student—are not always aware when they do!

This situation is captured by the idea of **positionality**, which suggests that researchers or development

PHOTO 1.3 | A man with polio makes sandals in a UNDP-funded employment project in Makeni, Sierra Leone.

IMPORTANT CONCEPTS

BOX 1.5 | Ethics of Participatory Rural Appraisal

Robert Chambers's injunctions for participatory rural appraisal may be viewed as good ethical guidelines for the development practitioner: "ask them; be nice to people; don't rush; embrace error; facilitate; hand over the stick; have fun; relax; they can do it (i.e., have confidence that people are capable)" (Chambers, 1997: 1748).

practitioners must be aware of and reflect upon the social and power relationships in which they are embedded, particularly their position relative to the local people with whom they interact (Binns, 2006: 19). However, the development practitioner's positionality is not always easy to assess; as the representatives of donor agencies, they are often seen by locals as having power and authority. Choices made by researchers and practitioners—such as the social and political background of principal assistants and translators, the non-governmental organizations (NGOs) they work with, and the political "gatekeepers" who help them—all contribute to how local people interpret who they are and whose interests they represent. Resources distributed by practitioners create "relationships of 'help', 'trust', and 'friendship'" as they intersect with "people's strategies for earning money" (Pink, 1998: 9–10); at the same time, this distribution of resources also can create conflict among locals who struggle to capture benefits (Pouligny, 2001). Taking positionality seriously, therefore, means that the development practitioner needs to reflect on the implications of his or her power position on others.

Lifestyle, dress, and behaviour abroad are important to local perceptions. In general, development workers are expected to live modestly with the people they are supposed to assist. Professionalism and advanced technical capacity should go hand in hand with high moral and ethical standards based on transparency and democratic accountability. Most development experts see hiring and buying locally as an ethical obligation to spread the wealth. Likewise, participating in local cultural events, observing local standards of dress and modesty, and learning the local language are essential elements in building a healthy relationship with local partners (Apentiik and Parpart, 2006: 39–40; Binns, 2006: 20). Nonetheless, some development practitioners earn the derisory moniker "**development tourists**" as they jet in and out of poor countries dispensing advice with little understanding of local conditions (Adams and Megaw, 1997, citing Chambers, 1997). There are too many examples of development mission staff lecturing politicians from the Global South "like schoolboys" in a (deliberate?) attempt to leave them powerless (Klitgaard, 1991, cited in Gasper, 1999: 24).

Today, anyone who wishes to be involved in international development cannot but experience a great sense of modesty as compared to the kind of intellectual arrogance that was prevalent in the past. Modesty can mean many things, including a sense that the "Western" way is *not* the only way, that the achievements of richer countries are not necessarily replicable or even desirable in poor countries, that Western science and techniques are not always value-neutral, and that there are other narratives to explain reality and to change it in a pro-people way. Development agencies and practitioners should not assume they can solve local problems from the outside when solutions exist at the local level, which is frequently the case. Above all, development workers need to do more listening and less talking. This growing self-critical attitude among contemporary researchers and practitioners in what we may term the *post-naive* era of development represents a welcome break from the simplistic interpretations of the past.

In lieu of conclusion, we may ask future development practitioners and researchers to reflect upon the words of Mahatma Ghandi: "Recall the face of the poorest and the weakest man whom you may have seen, and ask yourself if the step you contemplate is going to be of any use to him. Will he gain anything by it? Will it restore him to a control over his own life and destiny? In other words, will it lead to *Swaraj* [self-rule] for the hungry and spiritually starving millions?" (Kerala, 2003: 12).

SUMMARY

In this chapter we have considered important concepts and ideas in the study of international development. We began by discussing the birth, evolution, and implications of the term "development" and related nomenclature—such as "developing countries," "Third World," and "Global South"—used by academics, practitioners, and international organizations. We then turned to a critical examination of growth, inequality, and absolute and moderate poverty. This led to discussion of "development" as a contested concept. Multi-dimensional approaches to development were considered in detail, particularly Amartya Sen's capability approach and its translation into the Human Development Index. We also explored the ethics and morality of international development and looked at various arguments for and against global redistributive justice by asking whether development assistance should be considered a moral obligation for rich countries and their citizens, or little more than an individual choice akin to a charitable donation. The chapter concluded by introducing the personal ethical dilemmas experienced by development practitioners and researchers, including the need to be attentive to power and positionality, as well as local norms of ethical and culturally sensitive behaviour.

QUESTIONS FOR CRITICAL THOUGHT

1. Why is the concept of "development" a subject of debate? What concept of development do you think is most appropriate, and why?
2. Why is inequality the crucial link between GDP per capita and the number of people living in poverty in a given country?
3. Why is GDP an inadequate measure of development?
4. What is a "multi-dimensional" approach to development?
5. What dilemmas might people working in development agencies face? How should they address these ethical dilemmas?

SUGGESTED READINGS

Acemoglu, Daron, and James Robinson. 2012. *Why Nations Fail: The Origins of Power, Prosperity, and Poverty*. New York: Crown Business.

Deneulin, Séverine. 2014. *Wellbeing, Justice and Development Ethics*. New York: Routledge and Earthscan.

Desai, Vandana, and Robert B. Potter, eds. 2006. *Doing Development Research*. London: Sage.

Gasper, Des. 2006. "Introduction: Working in development ethics—A tribute to Denis Goulet." *Ethics and Economics* 4, 2: 1–24.

Sachs, Jeffrey D. 2005. *The End of Poverty: Economic Possibilities for Our Time*. New York: Penguin.

Todaro, Michael P., and Stephen C. Smith. 2014. *Economic Development*, 12th edn. Upper Saddle River, NJ: Prentice-Hall.

NOTES

1. Gross domestic product is a measure of the market value, in monetary terms, of all goods and services produced within a country over a specific time period (usually a year, hence, annual GDP). Gross national product and gross national income are measures that include GDP plus net income from abroad, such as investments. Thus, GDP is a better measure of the activity of a national economy, that is, of domestic production, than is GNP/GNI, which better reflects national wealth.
2. The Gini coefficient is based on the Lorenz curve, which plots the proportion of national income accruing to each segment of the population. The Gini coefficient is a ratio of the area between the curve and a line representing total equality to the total area under the line of equality.

BIBLIOGRAPHY

Adams, W.M. 1995. "Green development theory? Environmentalism and sustainable development." In J. Crush, ed., *Power of Development*. London and New York: Routledge, 87–99.

——— and C.C. Megaw. 1997. "Researchers and the rural poor: Asking questions in the Third World." *Journal of Geography in Higher Education* 21, 2: 215–29.

Apentiik, C.R.A., and J.L. Parpart. 2006. "Working in different cultures: Issues of race, ethnicity and identity." In Desai and Potter (2006: 34–43).

Binns, T. 2006. "Doing fieldwork in developing countries: Planning and logistics." In Desai and Potter (2006: 13–24).

Chambers, R. 1997. "Responsible well-being: A personal agenda for development." *World Development* 25, 11: 1743–54.

Cowen, M., and R.W. Shenton. 1995. "The invention of development." In J. Crush, ed., *Power of Development*. London and New York: Routledge, 27–43.

———. 1996. *Doctrines of Development*. London and New York: Routledge.

Crush, J. 1995. "Introduction: Imagining development." In J. Crush, ed., *Power of Development*. London and New York: Routledge, 1–23.

Desai, V., and R.B. Potter, eds. 2006. *Doing Development Research*. London: Sage.

Doyle, M. W. 2006. "One world, many peoples: International justice in John Rawls's *The Law of Peoples*." *Perspectives on Politics* 4, 1: 109–20.

Escobar, A. 1992. "Reflections on 'development'." *Futures* 24, 5: 411–36.

Esteva, G. 2010. "Development." In W. Sachs, ed., *The Development Dictionary: A Guide to Knowledge as Power*, 2nd edn. London: Zed Books, 1–23.

Forbes. 2010. "The world's billionaires." www.forbes.com/billionaires/list/3/#version:static. Accessed 26 Aug. 2015.

Fukuyama, F. 1995. *Trust: The Social Virtues and the Creation of Prosperity*. New York: Free Press.

Fry, G., and G. Martin. 1991. *The International Development Dictionary*. Santa Barbara, Calif.: ABC-Clio.

G8. 2000. *Global Poverty Report*. Okinawa Summit, July. www.worldbank.org/html/extdr/cxtme/G8_poverty2000.pdf.

Gasper, D. 1986. "Distribution and development ethics: A tour." In R. Apthorpe and A. Krahl, eds, *Development Studies: Critique and Renewal*. Leiden, Netherlands: E.J. Brill, 136–203.

———. 1999. "Ethics and the conduct of international development aid: Charity and obligation." Institute of Social Studies Working Paper Series no. 297. The Hague: Institute of Social Studies.

———. 2005. "Beyond the international relations framework: An essay in descriptive global ethics." *Journal of Global Ethics* 1, 1: 5–23.

Goulet, D. 1971. *The Cruel Choice: A New Concept in the Theory of Development*. New York: Atheneum.

Hulme, D. 2013. "Poverty and development thinking: Synthesis or uneasy compromise?" Brooks World Poverty Institute Working Paper No. 180. Manchester: University of Manchester. www.bwpi.manchester.ac.uk/medialibrary/publications/working_papers/bwpi-wp-18013.pdf. Accessed 25 Aug. 2015.

Inaugural Addresses of the Presidents of the United States. 1989. Washington: US Government Printing Office. www.bartleby.com/124. Accessed 11 June 2007.

Jacobsen, K., and L.B. Landau. 2003. "The dual imperative in refugee research: Some methodological and ethical considerations in social science research on forced migration." *Disasters* 27, 3: 195–206.

Jones, C. 1999. *Global Justice: Defending Cosmopolitanism*. Oxford: Oxford University Press.

Kerala. 2003. "India marches ahead . . . Kerala calling." (Aug.): 12. www.kerala.gov.in/kerala_callingaug/p12-13.pdf.

Klitgaard, R. 1991. *Tropical Gangsters*. London: I.B. Taurus.

Leys, C. 1996. *The Rise and Fall of Development Theory*. Oxford: James Currey.

Marchall, P.A. 1992. "Research ethics in applied anthropology." *IRB: A Review of Human Subjects Research* 14, 6: 1–5.

Nozick, R. 1974. *Anarchy, State and Utopia*. Oxford: Blackwell.

Nussbaum, M.C. 1995. "Human capabilities, female human beings." In M.C. Nussbaum and J. Glover, eds, *Women, Culture and Development: A Study of Human Capabilities*. Geneva: WIDER, 61–104.

Olinto, P. K. Beegle, C. Sobrado, and H. Uematsu. 2013. "The State of the Poor: Where Are the Poor, Where Is Extreme Poverty Harder to End, and What Is the Current Profile of the World's Poor?" Poverty Reduction and Economic Management Network, World Bank, Oct.

O'Neill, O. 2000. "Bounded and cosmopolitan justice." *Review of International Studies* 26, 5: 45–60.

Pink, S. 1998. "The white 'helpers': Anthropologists, development workers and local imaginations." *Anthropology Today* 14, 6: 9–16.

Pogge, T. 2002. *World Poverty and Human Rights: Cosmopolitan Responsibilities and Reforms*. Cambridge: Polity Press.

———. 2005. "World poverty and human rights." *Ethics and International Affairs* 19, 1: 1–7.

Pouligny, B. 2001. "L'humanitaire non gouvernemental face à la guerre: Évolutions et enjeux." Centre d'études et de recherches internationales (CERI) Working Paper, 25 fév., Université de Sciences Po, Paris. www.ceri-sciences-po.org/cherlist/pouligny/huma.pdf.

Putnam, R.D. 1993. *Making Democracy Work*. Princeton, NJ: Princeton University Press.

Rist, G. 1997. *The History of Development: From Western Origins to Global Faith*. London: Zed Books.

———. 2007. "Development as a buzzword." *Development in Practice* 17, 4 and 5: 485–91.

Rodney, W. 1972. *How Europe Underdeveloped Africa*. London: Bogle-L'Ouverture.

Sachs, J.D. 2005. *The End of Poverty: Economic Possibilities for Our Time*. New York: Penguin.

Sachs, W. 2010. *The Development Dictionary*, 2nd edn. London: Zed Books.

Scott, J.C. 1990. *Dominations and the Arts of Resistance*. New Haven: Yale University Press.

Seers, D. 1972. "What are we trying to measure?" *Journal of Development Studies* 8, 3: 21–36.

———. 1979. "The meaning of development, with a postscript." In D. Lehmann, ed., *Development Theory: Four Critical Studies*. London: Frank Cass, 9–30.

Sen, A. 1999. *Development as Freedom*. New York: Anchor Books.

SIL International. 2009. "Ethnologue: Languages of the world." www.ethnologue.com/. Accessed 13 Aug. 2010.

Singer, P. 2002. *One World: The Ethics of Globalization*. New Haven: Yale University Press.

Thomas, A. 2000. "Poverty and the 'end of development'." In T. Allen and A. Thomas, eds, *Poverty and Development into the 21st Century*. Oxford: Oxford University Press and The Open University, 3–22.

Todaro, M.P. 1989. *Economic Development in the Third World*, 4th edn. New York: Longman.

United Nations Development Programme (UNDP). 1990. *Human Development Report 1990: Concept and Measurement of Human Development*. Geneva: United Nations. hdr.undp.org/reports/global/1990/en.

United Nations General Assembly. 2005. "Resolution adopted at the outcome of the World Summit." http://daccessdds.un.org/doc/UNDOC/GEN/N05/487/60/PDF/N0548760.pdf?OpenElement.

United Nations High Commission for Human Rights. 2006. *Principles and Guidelines for a Human Rights Approach to Poverty Reduction Strategies*. HR/PUB/06/12. Geneva: United Nations.

Uvin, P. 2010. "From the right to development to the rights-based approach: How 'human rights' entered development." In A. Cornwall and D. Eade, eds, *Deconstructing Development Discourse: Buzzwords and Fuzzwords*. Bourton on Dunsmore, UK: Practical Action Publishing, 163–74.

Watts, M. 1995. "'A New Deal in emotions': Theory and practice and the crisis of development." In J. Crush, ed., *Power of Development*. London and New York: Routledge, 44–62.

Wood, G.D. 1985. "The politics of development policy labelling." In G.D. Wood, ed., *Labelling in Development Policy: Essays in Honour of Bernard Schaffer*. London: Sage; The Hague: Institute of Social Studies, 5–31.

2 Imperialism and the Colonial Experience

Eric Allina

LEARNING OBJECTIVES

- To understand the causes for imperial expansion.
- To learn about the strategies indigenous rulers followed in their engagement with European empires.
- To differentiate between the colonial experience in various regions in the developing world.
- To appreciate the important consequences of colonial rule for indigenous societies.

▲ **Day of the Dead banners hanging in front of Parroquia De San Miguel Archangel Church Tower in San Miguel de Allende, Mexico.** | Source: Rob Tilley/Getty Images

"He was a sugar planter or something. Wasn't that it, Manuel?"
"Yes madam. He was sugar. He was sugar, wine, sugar brandy, coal, sardines, water, everything. . . . He took the water from the people and sold it back again."
"You mean he developed the country."

H.E. Bates, *Summer in Salandar*

From "First and Third World," to "centre and periphery," to "developed and developing," we have now arrived at "Global North and South" to describe the world's uneven distribution of political and financial capital. Each of these paired terms has a history, and as much as the compass-oriented labels now in vogue strive to elide that history, they cannot, if only because some parts of the "South" lie an inconvenient distance north of the equator, just as some parts of the "North" are inexplicably located south of the equator. What each pair unsuccessfully attempts to euphemize is a separation of the world along a gradient, a separation whose modern history began with the creation of European empires in what is now known as the "South." There are, of course, exceptions to prove this rule, perhaps none more outstanding than the United States, a world superpower for much of the twentieth century, a state composed of former British, French, Dutch, Russian, and Spanish colonies.

We might trace the history of interaction between this Global North and South back to the fifteenth-century explorations, led by the Portuguese and the Spanish, that gave rise to European expansion into the Americas and Asia. Yet the "age of exploration," as it has sometimes been called, is something of a misnomer: by the time Portuguese sailor Vasco da Gama's sea voyage in 1497–9 turned Europe's contact with Asia into one of regular (if not rapid) exchange, people, goods, and ideas had been travelling along the great Central Asian highway known as the "silk road" for centuries. Europeans besides Marco Polo had made the trip east, and Chinese and other inhabitants of Asia had gone west. This very long history of interaction was one reason that da Gama knew of his destination in advance: the world he entered was known to those who lived in it, if not to him (Newitt, 2005: 2–3). Such earlier interactions notwithstanding, most exchange between Europe and Asia had taken place through intermediaries, with merchants and traders all along the southern and eastern portions of the Mediterranean Sea marketing Asian and African products to European consumers. Previously, only the rare traveller moved from one sphere into the other, but such movement now became more routine.

EUROPEAN EXPANSION AND CONQUEST

Southern Europe's interactions with largely Muslim traders were an important factor in Portuguese and Spanish decisions to embark on the seafaring explorations that led to Europe's more direct contact with a wider world. The kingdoms of Portugal and Spain had only been established following the centuries-long military reconquest of the Iberian Peninsula (completed in 1492), territory the Christian rulers had seized from its Muslim occupants. This foundational conflict was one impulse that led the Spanish and Portuguese to confront their North African neighbours. Accordingly, in 1415 Portuguese forces invaded Ceuta, a city whose wealth made it known to the Portuguese as the "flower of all other cities of Africa" (Diffie and Winius, 1977: 53). The assault was successful, and following their conquest and occupation of the city, the Portuguese learned more about the sources of its great wealth, such as its access to a gold trade that came from points south of the Sahara northwards into the Mediterranean world. The motives for expansion were thus at once political-religious, born of a competitive tension with Muslim neighbours, and economic, owing to ambitious Europeans' desire for more direct access to goods—not only gold but spices and textiles as well, much sought after in Europe's growing towns and cities, now beginning to recover from the ravages of the Black Death.

The desire for more direct trade with African and Asian societies, eliminating Muslim middlemen, was fulfilled in the vast seaborne expansion during the sixteenth century. Spain and Portugal established their previously unplanned presence in the Americas and created footholds in Africa and Asia. They were soon joined by the French, the English, and the Dutch, leading to several centuries of expansion, occupation, and competition among the European empire-builders for control over these far-flung sources of wealth, power, and glory. Over the next three centuries, the Spanish, French, Portuguese, and British

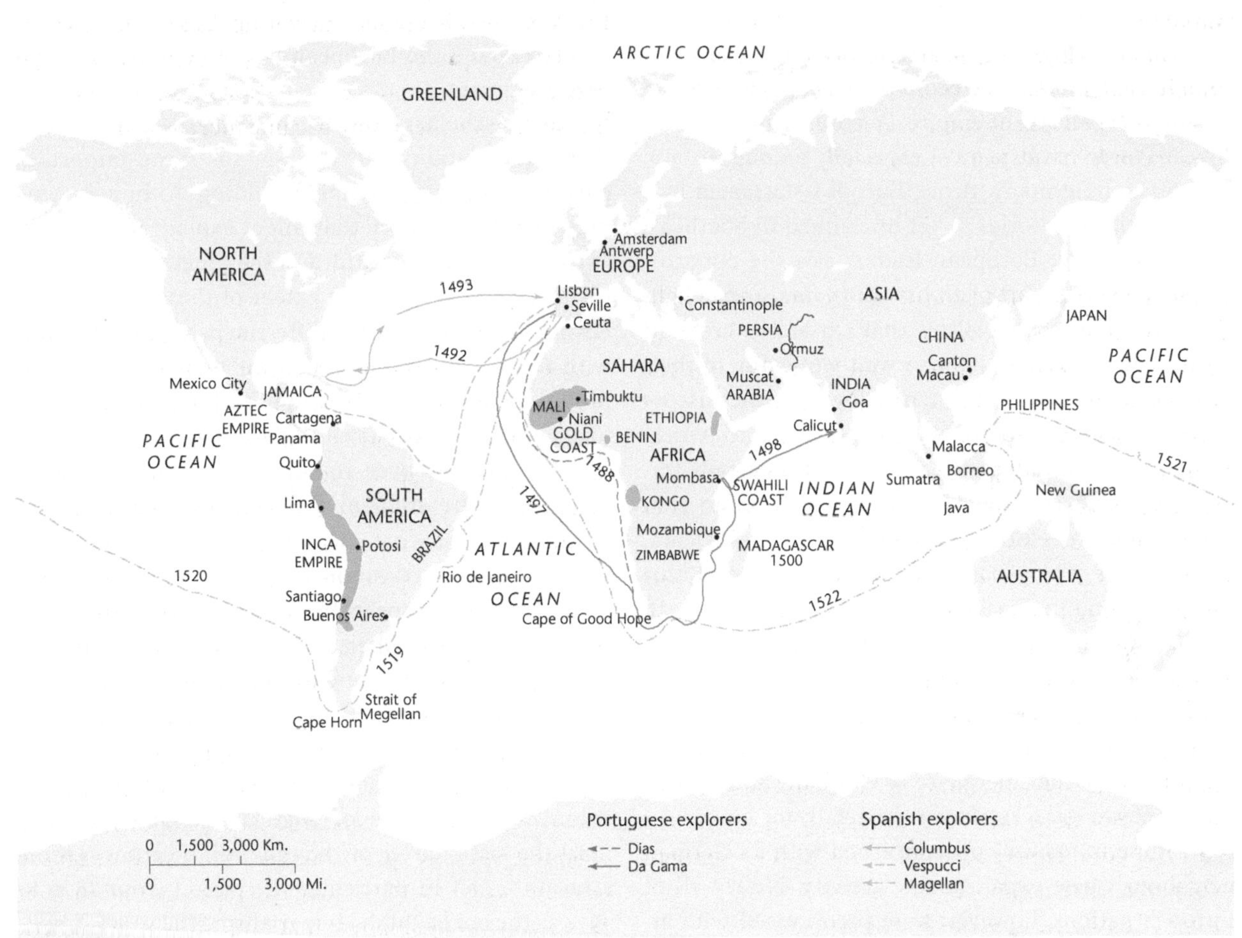

FIGURE 2.1 | European Exploration, 1420–1542

Source: Richard W. Bulliet et al., *The Earth and Its Peoples: A Global History*, 3rd edn (Boston: Houghton Mifflin, 2005), 427.

founded—and mostly lost—vast colonial possessions in the Americas, while their holdings in Africa and Asia only grew.

If there is consensus on the motives for Europe's initial phase of expansion, the same cannot be said for the final burst of conquest and occupation towards the end of the nineteenth century. Following an interpretation offered by English scholar John Hobson and also strongly associated with Vladimir Lenin (the Russian revolutionary and theorist who helped end the rule of Russia's Romanov dynasty and launch the October Revolution in 1917, bringing forth the Soviet Union), many scholars believe that economic motives linked to the **Industrial Revolution** launched the classic "high" **imperialism** of this period (Hobson, 1902; Lenin, 1920 [1916]). According to this view, the expansion of European empires was undertaken as part of a search for new markets: economic returns within Europe were dwindling, and industrial capitalism had to search abroad for new investment opportunities and consumers. Renewed expansion and the creation of new colonies were thus necessary, because most of Europe still practised protectionist trade policies. This economic explanation offers an appealing logic, and the emphasis on the role of capitalism dovetails neatly with the eventual exploitation, most especially of African labour, that followed during the era of "high" imperialism. The Hobson–Lenin thesis nonetheless has its critics, among them economic historians who point to the limited investment made in the new overseas colonies, as well as other scholars who find the model places too much importance on impersonal economic structures in general and ignores any role Asians and Africans may have played in particular.

Another approach also focuses on Europe but combines political and economic factors to explain the rapid expansion of empire. According to this view, "Great Power" rivalry, most especially among Britain, France, and Germany, drove Europe's statesmen in a rush to seize territories as yet unclaimed in Southeast Asia and Africa. European leaders saw the opportunity to expand as part of a zero-sum game, and in light of the tensions and rivalries that existed in crowded Europe, none were content to wait while any of their neighbours moved ahead, especially after the discovery of diamonds (1867) and gold (1886) in South Africa. Although a desire to secure access to strategically important industrial inputs, such as rubber, or to gain control over areas long believed to possess great riches, such as parts of tropical Africa, was not irrelevant, this understanding emphasizes the imperial powers' race to keep pace with their neighbours.

Associated with the Great Power explanation is the belief in the important role played by nationalist sentiment, which flourished at the end of the nineteenth century. Thus, the emergence of Germany and Italy as unified states was a key factor, especially for France, an older imperial power now concerned with its German neighbour's new expansionary activity. Nearly all of Europe's nations, however, were preoccupied with attaining the degree of prestige and sense of greatness they believed was their due. This explanation is often deployed to account for the outsized role played by Belgium and Portugal, two small and relatively minor European powers whose involvement in the "scramble for Africa" had no clear connection to political or economic interests, yet both countries ended up with vast African colonies.[1]

What none of these explanations include, however, is much room for the actions of what some historians call the "men on the spot," a term most common in studies of the British Empire though just as useful elsewhere. These men—for they were all men—often made decisions to expand European activity and territorial claims even when such moves (and the means by which they were achieved) went beyond or even ran counter to official metropolitan policy. Reacting to local crises or opportunities amid a wider atmosphere of tension and transformation, their improvisations may have had little immediate connection to industrial capitalism or domestic nationalism, but the effect was to expand the European field of action and build bigger empires.

Most scholars now accept the idea that each of these explanations can account for some important part of the history of empire-building. Although some may long for a theory that might explain all imperial expansion in the final third of the nineteenth century, the staggeringly far-flung extent of these endeavours, encompassing such very different parts of the world with accordingly different political and economic conditions, defies any such attempt short of writing a "total history" (Sanderson, 1974; Kennedy, 1977).

The debates over the causes of imperialism or **colonialism** are unfortunately matched by lack of consensus over just what either of the two terms may be said to mean. In common usage, "imperialism" refers to the era of European expansion that began in the sixteenth century, when first the Portuguese and the Spanish and then the English, French, and Dutch created empires of trade in the Americas and Asia and, to a lesser extent, Africa. African territory did not, for the most part, come under imperial control or witness **colonization** (outside of Algeria and South Africa) until the last quarter of the nineteenth century; some scholars target in particular the period from 1870 to 1914 as the era of "high" imperialism. The word "imperialism" itself first came into use in the late nineteenth century, when it referred to the operation of Britain's empire: a political system by which colonies are ruled from a central seat of power in the pursuit of largely if not entirely economic goals (Williams, 1983: 159). This meaning of "imperialism" neatly describes some of the earlier European empires (such as the Spanish, English, or French territories of the Caribbean and the Americas) as well as those that covered Africa and good parts of South and Southeast Asia from the last quarter of the nineteenth century through the mid-twentieth century.

Another meaning of "imperialism," however, casts it not as a political system but as an economic one in which a state pursues "external investment and penetration of markets and sources of raw materials" (Williams, 1983: 159–60). This idea of imperialism is closely associated with the concept of **neo-colonialism**, by which the economies of formally independent countries remain subject to the control of others, often their former colonial rulers. Such a system, of course, may continue past the formal end of colonial rule, with the former imperial power continuing to exert strong control over a nominally independent ex-colony. In some uses, prior colonization is not considered necessary, such as might be the case when imperialism is applied to the involvement of the United States in the Middle East since the mid-twentieth century or of China's increasing influence in sub-Saharan Africa—via the action of state-run enterprises but also the largely spontaneous initiative of individual Chinese immigrants looking to benefit from Africa's new growth (French, 2014)—since the turn of the twenty-first century.

Colonization, in the sense of settling and occupying a specified territory, can refer to other contexts as well. Some scholars of early African history, for example, consider the expansion of African societies into unpopulated or sparsely populated areas as a process of colonization. Similarly, most evidence suggests that the earliest human societies in Madagascar were established by colonists who travelled to the island from Southeast Asia. However, neither of these instances of distant settlement took place as part of an imperial expansion or resulted in ongoing political or economic links between the society of origin and the society of settlement. The foundation of a colony may simply indicate the displacement and resettling of a population; colonialism implies the rule of some people over others (Cooper, 2006: 28).

The relationship of imperialism and colonial rule with development has drawn great interest from scholars, politicians, and policy-makers alike, and many have sought to explain how European imperial expansion led to or prevented development in those areas of the world now considered to be developing countries. Few would question that colonial rule had an impact on economic development in colonized territories, but there is no consensus on just what kind of development European imperialism (and colonialism) brought about in Africa, the Americas, and Asia.

RIVAL EMPIRES OF TRADE

Ventures to the east brought Europeans into a crowded arena that joined together several regions, each one washed by the Indian Ocean. Local and regional trading networks had long linked South Asia to peninsular and insular Southeast Asia and to the Arabian and Red Sea regions and the coast of East Africa to the west. After the Portuguese arrival in South Asia in 1498, Europe soon established a permanent presence with Lisbon's conquest of Goa, an urban trading centre on present-day India's western coast, in 1510. The English, Dutch, and French quickly joined the expansion into Indian Ocean waters, all hoping to dislodge the Portuguese from the position of dominance they had seized as European pioneers. The Dutch and English soon created **chartered companies**—the Dutch and English East India companies—in an effort to enlist private investment in the service of empire. The English East India Company, established in 1600, was followed 70 years later in British North America with the formation of the Hudson's Bay Company, which had effective control over all the lands draining into Hudson Bay. The French organized similar companies, in North America and the Far East, in an effort to compete, while the Portuguese Crown retained more direct control over its eastern empire. The recruitment of private capital by the English and Dutch proved a shrewd decision, for it broadened the financial base for expansionary activity and provided a sturdier platform that better withstood the cut and thrust of imperial rivalries.

Out of this seaborne scrum, the rivals began to carve out areas of influence: the Dutch soon assumed a dominant position in the spice trade out of the Southeast Asian islands (present-day Indonesia and Malaysia, though in other areas, such as present-day Taiwan, they had to contend with the power of China's Ming dynasty, giving way to what some have called a "co-colonization" of the island under Dutch and Chinese efforts), leading the English East India Company to concentrate on the South Asian subcontinent. The French competed with the British on South Asia's east coast, while the Portuguese clung to their base on the west coast. The various European powers sought openings overseen by the Mughal emperors, the recently risen rulers of the South Asian subcontinent. The Mughals welcomed the outsiders' rivalry because the emperor could capitalize on the competition among them to demand better terms of trade, reversing the trend that had prevailed during the first decades of Portuguese monopoly, when the newcomers had been able to impose trade terms less favourable to them.

Image courtesy of the Melville J. Herskovits Library of African Studies Winterton Collection, Northwestern University

PHOTO 2.1 | Troops from German East Africa (present-day Tanzania), before 1919.

The "new" world that Europeans entered in the Americas differed greatly from the one they encountered in Asia. In Central and South America, European arrival and the labour practices imposed on conquered Amerindian societies produced a staggering population collapse, making any continuation of existing political systems a near impossibility. European sailors and explorers carried smallpox to the Americas; the indigenous peoples of the Americas had no prior exposure and virtually no resistance to the virus. The disease laid waste to the previously populous societies of Meso-America. Alongside this unintended biological assault, the Spanish, in their eagerness to acquire as much silver and gold bullion as possible from their rapidly growing empire, enslaved indigenous people by the thousands and worked them to death mining gold and silver. In some places, such as the island of Hispaniola (present-day Haiti and Dominican Republic), the death toll resulted in near extinction: the indigenous Taino people numbered at least one million (and perhaps as many as five million) in 1492 but by 1550 had disappeared. In present-day Mexico, the Aztec state collapsed as the population plummeted from perhaps 25 million in 1518 to just over a million in 1605 (Watts, 1999: 84–90). No political institution could survive this degree of social destruction, and that fact ensured that any political system that might be created in New World empires would be cut from whole cloth.

Imperial expansion, especially in Spain's New World possessions, brought an unimagined wealth to the Iberian *conquistadores*. The captured Inca ruler Atahualpa, for example, offered his Spanish captors a ransom of 6,000 kilograms of gold and 12,000 of silver. (The Spanish eagerly took the ransom but instead of granting Atahualpa his freedom only gave him a choice between being burned at the stake and being baptized, then strangled, as a believer in Christ. He chose baptism and strangulation.) The prospect of such immense wealth, together with the decimation of Amerindian societies, resulted in greater immigration to the Americas than to other imperial possessions. Spanish colonists sought their fortunes in gold and silver mining and wielded great power, staffing the viceroyalties of Peru and New Spain, as the Spanish territories were called. The large numbers and eventual strength of this colonial elite led to broad tensions with the Spanish Crown, which recognized the potential threat they posed to ongoing imperial control.

Meanwhile, along with gold diggers, the Portuguese introduced the cultivation and export of sugar, which they had pioneered on the Atlantic islands of Madeira and the Azores. Sugar production—and an important product thereof, rum—flourished in Brazil and especially on the Caribbean islands, and sugar became a major item in the so-called triangular trade with Europe and Africa. From the later 1600s, export of African slaves to the Americas grew enormously, largely to supply labour for sugar (and later cotton and tobacco) production. The elimination of the Amerindian population was a major factor in Europeans' decision to purchase millions of African slaves and export them to the Americas, although the ability of European merchants to purchase slaves in Africa in exchange for relatively low-cost manufactured goods was also important. Towards the end of the seventeenth century, this forced African migration far outstripped European settlement, and colonial masters depended mightily on their black slaves, who built the foundations of the New World colonies and ensured their economic growth for centuries to come.

In contrast to Meso-America, South America, and the Caribbean, South Asian polities remained robust in early and ongoing interactions with agents of European empire, both in defence of local sovereignty and in pursuit of economic interest. To a certain extent, agents of European empire were compelled to accept terms dictated by the Mughal emperor: as much as the Europeans held sway at sea—for the Mughals had no navy or merchant fleet—Indian rulers accepted no challenge to their dominance on land, strictly limiting the outsiders' rights even to self-defence. Unlike the situation in the Americas, Europeans arrived in Asia with no significant advantage in military technology, and local armies were more than their match. Such was all the more the case in East Asia, especially in present-day Taiwan, where four decades of Dutch rule ended in 1662 when the Dutch East India Company fought forces from mainland China, losing a war in which both sides used prolonged sieges, effective espionage, and breathtaking brutality (Andrade, 2010, offers a marvellous "global microhistory"). Technology alone, however, was not the critical factor of difference between the Americas and Asia. As noted above, the decimation by disease of indigenous populations in the Americas made European conquest relatively simple. Even more important, many Amerindian groups—especially those that had not formed hierarchical city-states, had a communitarian ethos and culture, which led at first to their sharing with and helping the European newcomers, and their often non-sedentary lifestyle and community organization led the Europeans to believe the Amerindians were "uncivilized." Such a Eurocentric assumption was not possible in South Asia.

The greater the number of European firms angling for access to Indian markets, the stronger the Indian negotiating position. The question of competition would come to be of great strategic importance in future years: as Mughal power began to fade around the turn of the eighteenth century, the British and French sought to expand their influence with the regionally based successor states that emerged. Through the first several decades of the eighteenth century, European trading companies found that by allying with and even fighting on behalf of the rulers of Indian states, they could secure valuable concessions, such as duty-free export rights, that could boost their profits significantly.

Through the middle of the eighteenth century, France and Britain vied for dominance in South Asia as in Europe and the Americas. Britain topped her rival in Asia, especially after the English East India Company gained control of Bengal province in 1765. Exploiting rivalries within Bengal's political and commercial elites, the Company defeated the Mughal armies, and although Bengal remained part of the Mughal empire on paper, the Company emerged as the real power in eastern India. The province was one of India's most economically productive, and the Company now held the rights to Bengal's revenue as well as free rein to trade there. As much as it was a significant political evolution, this development also marked an important turning point in the economic history of imperial activity. Previously, the Company had financed its purchase of Indian exports with gold bullion, but with rights to locally raised tax revenues, its operations were now locally financed. Thanks to its military adventures, the Company now exercised an economic dominance as well and could rely on its ability to raise local revenue to fund its military actions, a practice known as "military fiscalism."

From this point forward, the English East India Company became a virtual juggernaut; although it ruled only a part of India directly, it wielded great influence over a much wider area through alliances with the princely rulers of individual states. With control

IMPORTANT CONCEPTS

BOX 2.1 | An "Oriental Despot": British Company Rule in South Asia

Queen Elizabeth I's government created the English East India Company in 1600, granting it extensive powers and a measure of autonomy from the state, rights conveyed by a document known as a charter. At the same time, the English state devolved the burden of raising capital and the inevitable risk of the distant undertaking to private investors. With a monopoly on British trade with Asia and the right to arm its trading fleet, the Company possessed the economic and coercive force that would make it the most powerful actor in European imperial history.

For most of its first two centuries, the Company jockeyed for position with rival Dutch and French companies. It also vied to create a more secure relationship with Indian rulers who controlled the Company's access to the subcontinent's producers and to consumers. Outlasting its European competitors, whose position weakened in part because of a changing domestic political landscape, the Company, powered by England's early industrialization, was alone in a position to challenge India's princely rulers in the last quarter of the eighteenth century.

Having spent nearly two centuries as a naval or at most a coastal power, the Company expanded throughout South Asia in the late eighteenth century and the first half of the nineteenth century. Despite its new dominance, it continued to recognize the Mughal emperor as a symbol of Indian authority and in individual states left princes on their thrones as figureheads. Doing so meant that the public, visible face of authority—embodied in the "magnificence of princely courts [and] the gifting and patronage activities they sustained"—would remain Indian. Behind the throne, the Company's resident officers controlled military forces, negotiated relations with other rulers, and oversaw revenue collection, often seizing vast fortunes for their personal enrichment (Metcalf and Metcalf, 2006: 75). These "men on the spot" had tremendous latitude to make decisions independent of Company policy, which sometimes lagged behind their improvisations.

This indirect rule preserved a veneer of indigenous authority over the reality of Company power and was in keeping with British beliefs that essential cultural differences between South Asian people and Europeans made European-style representative government impossible. The Company (and later the British government, once the British Crown took charge of India following a rebellion in 1857) insisted on governance that represented a rule of law: a commitment to law, rather than the personal rule of a prince or emperor, believed to characterize "Oriental despotism," was part of the way that the Company justified its writ. Yet in refusing any role for South Asian representation in government and in establishing a legal code that privileged colonizers' rights and interests and those of the wealthy local elite, the English East India Company (and eventually the British colonial state) was the "Oriental despot" until the end of colonial rule in 1947.

over Bengal's vast revenues, the Company expanded its military forces, creating a professional army that made it among the most powerful of any in the region. Having squeezed out its European rivals (French influence receded rapidly through the last third of the eighteenth century, and the Dutch East India Company was dissolved in 1795), the Company held a commanding position in its relations with Indian elites—political, financial, and commercial—who saw in the Company a powerful partner that could secure their own interests. For some whose loyalties were locally rooted, the benefits that might come from alliance with the Company were far more important than the consequences of such partnerships for people in other parts of the subcontinent or for the overall balance of power. Absent any broadly shared identity, ambitious individuals in South Asia had no reason to resist the Company's influence if they might profit from its presence.

In tandem with the English East India Company's growing control over territory in South Asia came a more active role in economic life as well. No longer confined to importing and exporting goods, the Company used its influence to begin reshaping the regional economy. Of signal importance was the extensive rail network constructed in the middle of the nineteenth century. Linking the vast hinterland to port cities (and the ports to one another), the railway greatly reduced transport times and costs, transforming the economy. In the process, however, it also laid down in iron rails the features of an underdeveloped economy: an infrastructure suitable for the export of high-bulk, low-value products. It was a missed opportunity to develop closer ties among the subcontinent's different regions and to integrate potentially complementary economic sectors. Instead, the export-oriented network served the Company's interests, and with financing from British investors, the system generated profits that left the country instead of producing revenue that might have been invested locally.

"HIGH" IMPERIALISM IN AFRICA

If South Asia's encounter with European imperialism was a case of conquest in slow motion, with the better part of three centuries elapsing between Vasco da Gama's arrival and the English East India Company's emergence as a territorial power, the creation of European colonies in Africa occurred at a breakneck pace by comparison. The last two decades of the nineteenth century saw Europeans burst forth from scattered coastal enclaves, some of which they had held for centuries, to seize the entire continent, except for Ethiopia. In this era of "high" imperialism, Africa occupied centre stage, with Belgium, England, France, Germany, Portugal, Italy, and Spain all establishing African colonies, albeit the last two limited to comparatively small territories.

However, Europe's imperial powers felt such ambivalence about the colonial endeavour in Africa that nearly all sought to find a way to draw non-state actors into the process, mostly by granting charters to private companies that undertook many of the initial steps (and sometimes more). Perhaps the most famous of these companies was Cecil Rhodes's British South Africa Company (founded in 1889), a vehicle for his continent-sized ambition, which the diamond baron used to seize present-day Zambia and Zimbabwe. But the British also used companies in Kenya (the Imperial British East Africa Company) and Nigeria (the Royal Niger Company), as the Germans did in Tanganyika (the German East Africa Company).

Similarly, the French rented out a wide swath of Central Africa to concessionary companies, and the Belgian government was so uninterested in creating an African empire that King Leopold II on his own pursued a vast private fief in the present-day Democratic Republic of the Congo, parts of which he leased out to private companies in return for a percentage of the profits. (Only in the face of international protest over the abuses committed there was the Belgian state persuaded to take over the territory from Leopold.)

Most of these companies held their state-like powers for only a decade or so before being replaced by formal colonial administrations early in the twentieth century, but they carried out the strategically vital, expensive, and bloody tasks of conquest and construction of basic infrastructure. Rhodes's company lasted longer than most, ceding its powers only in 1923, although it was outlived by two companies Portugal had created in Mozambique in the 1890s, one of which endured until 1929 and the other until 1942.

The first generations of scholarship on the history of colonialism in Africa focused a good deal of attention on perceived differences between British, French, and Portuguese approaches to colonial rule. German rule, being comparatively short-lived,[2] tended to be ignored in these analyses, as was the Italian and Spanish colonial presence, while Belgian rule was similarly overlooked. The focus on metropolitan differences, largely confined to the realm of formal policy, made much of an apparent difference between British **indirect rule** versus French direct rule. The Portuguese, on the other hand, were judged to have followed a third path, an especially hands-on and, according to some, more violent version of direct rule. Yet conquest across the board was prosecuted with violence, and all colonial rule was backstopped by violence or its threat; the variation in actual practice on the ground owed more to time and place than to the national origin of the colonizer. As one historian noted, indirect rule was associated with Britain "not so much because the British applied more indirect rule but because they talked about it more than others" (Kiwanuka, 1970: 300).

The focus on the European origins of colonial policies misses the important ways in which policies imagined in London or Lisbon were transformed by the challenge of putting them into practice and by the opportunistic nature of many colonial administrators, who seized whatever openings were available in striving to meet their goals. Britain's policy of indirect rule for its African colonies was, in important respects, a product of failure more than anything else: an inability to break the power of local African rulers in northern Nigeria led the British administrator responsible for the region to declare instead his intention to keep them in place so that he might rule indirectly through them. If there was any genius to the policy, it was in public relations—in making virtue out of failure and proclaiming the result to be official policy (Cooper et al., 2000: 124–5).

Indirect rule in colonial Africa followed closely on the early model the British had established in South Asia. It was perhaps even more in this later case a

PHOTO 2.2 | Cecil Rhodes (centre) in the Matopo Hills, Zimbabwe.

CRITICAL ISSUES

BOX 2.2 | The "Scramble for Africa"

The late nineteenth-century European conquest of Africa is often referred to as the "**scramble for Africa**," a phrase that suggests both speed and disorder. On the eve of Africa's partition, European powers had only a handful of colonies on the continent despite having visited and traded with coastal African societies for more than 400 years. When German Chancellor Otto von Bismarck convened the Berlin Conference in late 1884 (with not a single African representative in attendance), the European powers agreed on ground rules for their land grab. Henceforth, a claim to African territory would be commonly recognized if the claimant had established "effective occupation" of the area. The effect was to accelerate the process, with the scramblers rushing to put "boots on the ground." In the resulting flurry of activity, seven European states divided the continent into 40 colonies, leaving only Ethiopia unclaimed or unoccupied, while resistant African leaders clung to a fragile and dwindling independence.

The political and economic topography of late nineteenth-century Africa at the time of partition was markedly uneven. Large African empires with powerful centralized rulers, some controlling long-distance trade in ivory and slaves, existed in most regions of the continent, while smaller independent polities ruled by local authorities were also common. In some areas, notably coastal West and East Africa and their littorals, regional economic networks had grown ever stronger since the abolition of the slave trade earlier in the century, and through these networks, local producers (mostly producers of vegetable products sought by European industry but also elephant hunters who supplied ivory for growing middle-class consumption overseas) were tied to international commercial networks. With their links to overseas finance, these areas became even more "extroverted" in their orientation, while other parts of the continent were characterized by locally oriented self-sustaining economies.

In many instances, the European powers inserted themselves into areas fraught with tension, at times born of friction between expanding states and at others resulting from competition over trade. Amid such tensions, African leaders were eager to sign treaties with Europeans, hoping to gain an edge over their neighbours or enemies. In view of these existing divisions, the European powers employed less of a strategy of "divide and rule," but they were deft in their manipulation of local rivalries. African rulers soon found that after a rival had been subdued or defeated, their erstwhile allies turned on them, now demanding their submission. Standing alone against encroaching European forces, sometimes reinforced by African troops drawn from among those already conquered, remaining African leaders faced a choice between signing treaties that presumed their submission or fighting to remain sovereign. Armed with the Maxim (machine) gun, fortified against malaria with quinine, and more manoeuvrable than ever before with easily assembled (and disassembled) steam-powered flat-bottomed riverboats, the scramblers' forces encountered few opponents who could withstand their attack.

decision based on practicality. By keeping local rulers in place (or creating them where indigenous authorities proved difficult to identify or co-opt), colonizers saved themselves the difficulty of establishing new forms of authority or the expense of employing large numbers of European administrators. European colonizers found quick profits in only a few parts of the continent, such as South Africa's gold and diamond strikes or the Congo Free State's short-lived rubber boom, and despite an enduring myth that African colonies would turn out to be another El Dorado, the colonizing powers were reluctant to invest much or incur ongoing costs in Africa. In much the same fashion that the English East India Company had done in South Asia, colonial administrators sought to identify and codify the "customary" law that they believed governed African societies; their aim was to rule Africans indirectly through their own laws, enforced by their own leaders, who answered to colonial administrators. If they could incorporate local African rulers at the lower rungs of colonial administration, they could achieve at low cost a dominance that they believed would be viewed legitimately by the African population at large: "hegemony on a shoestring" (Berry, 1992).

Colonial rule did not affect all colonized people in the same manner. Depending on their position in society, especially their exposure to specific economic or political practices, certain groups of individuals might lose (or gain) material or social capital. The clearest cases of such differential impact occurred with indirect rule, under which many local elites benefited: some helped to collect new tax levies and received a portion for their role, while others, with the tacit support of the colonial state, imposed new burdens on their subjects. But more broadly, the great political and economic changes associated with colonial rule created winners and losers, and some people gained influence over others in the process. The overall effect was to strengthen existing cleavages or to create new ones in indigenous societies, with resulting social tensions. Particularly towards the end of the colonial era (the 1930s and 1940s in Asia and the 1950s in Africa), political constituencies manoeuvred for position as independence approached, and these cleavages—along lines of religion, language, ethnicity, race, and class—became sources of heightened tension and outright conflict, at times very violently so.

PHOTO 2.3 | The sultan of Zanzibar, c. 1890s, with British naval officers and colonial officials. Zanzibar, an archipelago off the coast of East Africa, gained its independence in 1963 and joined with Tanganyika in 1964 to become Tanzania.

COMMON THEMES IN THE COLONIAL EXPERIENCE

The colonial rule established under imperial systems of government lasted long enough—two centuries or more in South Asia and parts of the Americas, less lengthy in Africa, where some scholars emphasize the brevity of the colonial era by pegging it at "only" eight decades—to transform indigenous societies in a fundamental manner. The breadth of change wrought in political and economic life was such that it is difficult to address overall in a cohesive fashion.[3] Rather than attempting an encyclopedic coverage, this section focuses on three broad themes that reflect common elements of the colonial experience: European faith in essential cultural differences and in the superiority of European peoples, often used to justify exploitative economic policies and violently abusive governance practices; metropolitan states' ambivalence regarding the overseas commitments of empire; and a movement, in the twilight years of colonial rule, towards the promotion of economic development in colonial territories.

Late-nineteenth-century imperial boosters rallied others, including sometimes reluctant government ministers, to their cause with claims regarding the inferiority of peoples and cultures outside of Europe. The idea of subject peoples as different and inferior was nothing new to the "high" imperial era—as a characteristic of imperialism it goes back to Roman times, if not earlier. Indeed, some scholars argue any system of imperial rule depends on the creation or maintenance of differences (cultural or otherwise), because as an empire incorporates new lands and peoples, a hierarchy of difference becomes necessary to order and legitimize the subordination of some people to others (Burbank and Cooper, 2010).

Influenced by so-called social Darwinist ideas, which had little to do with the evolutionary theory Darwin offered in *On the Origin of Species* in 1859, those advocating renewed imperial expansion applied the idea of evolution not to individual species but instead to human societies. They believed that European peoples represented a more evolved type of human being and human society, while other, darker-skinned people and societies were supposedly examples of still-surviving earlier forms. These beliefs powerfully shaped attitudes towards empire in two ways. First, with Asian or African cultures seen as inferior and even "primitive," their subordination and even destruction were easily justified in the name of progress. Following on this, because indigenous African or Asian societies were regarded as backward, their transformation, by force if necessary, was judged to be a moral duty of Europeans as the bearers of a higher civilization.

These secular beliefs were prosecuted with a zeal not unlike the longer-standing and persistent spiritual impulse to spread Christianity and "save" souls from what was believed to be their unhappy heathen fate. The belief in indigenous inferiority was so tightly held that, in its refusal to entertain the possibility that it was not correct, despite plenty of proof to the contrary, it resembled faith. Thomas Macaulay, a senior British official who served in India from the 1830s, exemplified this stance, infamously expressed in his claim that "the entire native literature of India and Arabia" was not worth "a single shelf of a good European library." The claim stands as a hallmark of European chauvinism, all the more remarkable in light of Macaulay's lack of knowledge of any Indian language. He instead was a proponent of anglicization for Britain's Indian subjects, supporting English-language education to create a "class who may be interpreters between us and the millions we govern; a class of persons Indian in blood and colour but English in tastes, in opinions, in morals, and in intellect" (Metcalf and Metcalf, 2006: 81; Bose and Jalal, 2004: 67).

Imperial expansion did not always occur quickly or decisively, for metropolitan governments were sometimes unsure of the benefits of expansion and leery of taking on new commitments, particularly overseas. Yet once imperial powers committed themselves to acts of colonial conquest—sometimes because they feared they might be outmanoeuvred by a European rival—they prosecuted these wars with maximum force. In the imperial era of the late nineteenth century, particularly in Africa, this meant marshalling the resources of a modern industrial state against opponents nearly always outmatched in military terms. There were exceptions. One of the most successful cases of indigenous resistance was that of Samori Touré, the ruler of a large state in West Africa, who fought French forces tenaciously for the better part of two decades before succumbing to conquest in 1898. (Ethiopia's successful stand against the Italians, dealing their forces a devastating blow in 1896, is the single case of a European empire defeated in Africa.) Still, even after imperial powers established control over the territories they sought, they remained ambivalent about investing the resources that would have brought the reality of colonial rule into line, even partly, with the rhetoric of the civilizing mission.

Those who examine colonial attitudes and policies towards indigenous peoples sometimes point to stated differences among French, Portuguese, and British approaches, such as the French intention to assimilate Africans and make them "black Frenchmen" as opposed to the British commitment to creating "civilized Africans." Although formal differences existed among these approaches, all were based on a faith in the superiority of European culture and in the benefit it could bring to African societies. In addition, for most of the period of colonial rule, these policies affected very few people: French "assimilation," for example, required attainment of literacy in French, an achievement beyond most people's means, given colonial neglect of African education. Instead, the underlying belief in cultural hierarchy and racial difference was used to justify a wide range of practices whereby indigenous people were forced—sometimes through great violence—to serve Europeans' objectives and needs.

Part of the progress that European powers claimed to be bringing to their colonial territories was a transformation of economic life to the "modern" level of European economies. What this meant in practice was an overwhelming orientation of African economies towards production of raw materials for export. Mineral extraction—especially of copper, gold, tin, and diamonds—was enormously important in many parts of western, central, and southern Africa, but so were agricultural commodities. Africans produced sugar, cocoa, cotton, peanut oil, and other tropical products to supply European markets, setting the stage for longer-term economic dependencies and vulnerabilities.

The "high" imperial era looked somewhat different in Latin America. The Spanish colonies and Brazil had won their independence early in the nineteenth century, as local elites had chafed under and eventually challenged imperial rule successfully. Formal independence did not bring equal status between colonizer and ex-colony, however. For example, Britain and the United States—a new member of the imperial ranks—sought to control trade rather than territory. The British financed a vast expansion of South American rail lines, aiming to seal their access to the continent's large consumer markets for the sale of industrially produced machine goods and textiles and to speed export of agricultural products. Argentina, for example, was able to export great quantities of wool, wheat, and beef, generating important revenue for those who controlled these industries. Such a concentration of primary commodity production, however, along with the neglect of investment in domestic industry, produced structural imbalances and laid a foundation for future weakness (see Chapter 3).

Only comparatively late in the history of colonialism—the early to mid-twentieth century for the most part—did colonizers begin to institute policies that brought significant investment intended to benefit indigenous populations. The field of development, as a professionalized and self-conscious effort to transform economies outside of the industrialized West, dates from this time and still bears some remnants of its origin in the colonial era. In Africa, the end of the 1930s brought what historians used to call the "second colonial occupation" but is now seen as the emergence of the development era. The shift came amid realization on the part of colonial governments that their past practices had not yielded the expected results. Coercive labour practices—by which hundreds of thousands of Africans were forced to engage in heavy manual labour without pay, a "modern slavery" that often undermined their ability to support themselves and their families—and heavy-handed unequal treatment did not result in the "civilized" Africans colonial boosters had promised but rather in an embittered and impoverished population.

World War II, a war in which Africans fought alongside Europeans for the right of European and Asian nations to **self-determination** and freedom from foreign rule, forced a re-examination of the colonial endeavour. Africans increasingly exhibited a new militancy. They refused to remain confined to the narrow grooves cut by the traditional society imagined by colonial rulers, but rather made demands and articulated rights by drawing on metropolitan principles—not only those of self-determination but also of labour rights.

Part of the colonial response to such actions on the part of colonial subjects was a new approach, at least by Britain and France, to social and economic policy in the colonies. The British passed the Colonial Development and Welfare Act in 1940, and the French established the Investment Fund for Social and Economic Development in 1946. Both expanded the scale of colonial development activities in the post-war period, partly by increasing the flow of funds from the metropole, primarily through loans. Beyond the greater scale of assistance, however, they also changed the nature of colonial efforts to promote economic and social change. The plan for a "modern future set against a primitive present" was part of an attempt to prolong empire amid growing anti-colonial mobilization; economic development would be the "antidote to disorder" (Cooper, 1997: 65, 67). Coming at the time it did, the shift did not have a great impact on Britain's or France's closing years of colonial rule in South Asia or Southeast Asia, but it powerfully shaped Africa for the future.

Alongside the growth in scale came an associated increase in the personnel involved: local administrators (who may have improvised on their own initiative, perhaps on the basis of observations of and interactions with the Africans whose lives they administered) were now replaced with a nascent bureaucracy charged with studying, planning, and executing projects conceived to meet priorities set by ministries based in Europe. Colonial intervention in agriculture, forestry, water supply, and livestock was not new, but there was now an emphasis on "harnessing scientific and technical expertise" to such efforts (van Beusekom and Hodgson, 2000: 31). It was a new approach to an older ideal—delivering modernity to "natives" who were believed to be incapable of achieving such progress on their own. With the assistance of European experts, indigenous societies and cultures would thus evolve to the norm established by the West. Rather than continuing the mission, spiritual and otherwise, to "civilize" indigenous societies in accordance with European norms, colonial rule in its final two decades shifted to the "development" of those societies. In the effort to modernize African economies, the new form of colonial rule took aim not merely at farming techniques or livestock grazing practices but also at the social relations that organized those economic activities. As such, colonial development focused on indigenous social life as much as on economic life, as being in need of modernization.

In the same way that an earlier generation of colonial policy-makers had aimed to foster cultural transformation and "evolution" in indigenous societies, in keeping with a belief that the European model presented a natural path to progress, colonial planners now demonstrated faith that an economic makeover would set African societies on a similarly inevitable path. The increasingly advanced degree of political mobilization in post-war African colonies made colonial administrations wary of overly forceful implementation and occasionally responsive to African opposition to some projects. The turn towards development of indigenous societies came at a time when the inevitability of Indian independence was becoming clear, but in Africa, colonial rulers saw development plans in part as a way to return the mercurial genie of nationalist sentiment back into its bottle (Cooper, 1997). Still, the timing was crucial for the future, because the new development approach was bequeathed to a generation of African leaders who were mostly products of colonial education and had absorbed the associated idea of African "backwardness." Science and technology, held to have originated in the industrialized West, were the metric by which economic practices were to be evaluated. Although most post-colonial African leaders embraced African cultural practices, they were also enamoured of scientific knowledge as distinct from local knowledge and were thus skeptical of the practical experience of anyone who lacked a formal education.

The full turn towards development took place in a world divided by the Cold War, with the West—including all the colonial powers—arrayed against the Soviet bloc and its mission of "exporting revolution." Many leaders of nationalist independence movements in Africa and Asia sought and received aid, both military and financial, from the Soviet bloc. As anti-colonial mobilization intensified, the colonial powers reassessed their commitment to political control in their colonies. They questioned the financial benefits and feared the political costs, perceiving that continued denial of self-determination, and the greater oppression it would entail, might drive anti-colonial movements and newly independent states into the arms of the Soviet Union. Fiercely fought

CRITICAL ISSUES

BOX 2.3 | Development Project as White Elephant: The Office du Niger

The Office du Niger, a sprawling agricultural project planned for the French Soudan (present-day Mali), exemplified the ambition and oversight of colonial development planning. Conceived in the 1920s, the project signalled its outsized aims in the area targeted for development: 18,500 square kilometres, some of which fell within the Niger River's inland delta but much of which lay considerably outside of it. The plan called for the construction of several dams to irrigate vast tracts of land to be planted with cotton and rice. Planners did not speak of making the desert bloom, but their aim was to develop what they saw as underused land on the edge of the Sahara Desert. Yet because much of the area was arid and the population density accordingly low, many of the one million farmers imagined for the project would have to be resettled from elsewhere in French West Africa.

The plan had shortcomings sufficient to doom it from the start, chief among them poor "expert" knowledge and a yawning gap between the projected objectives and the interests and desires of the Africans expected to participate. Of all the planning shortcomings, perhaps the most astonishing was that the irrigation network—the project's very backbone—provided inadequate or ill-timed water flows in some areas, making successful cultivation nearly impossible. Other problems abounded: some planned villages lacked wells, forcing settlers to collect water from irrigation ditches, while other wells were dry or contaminated (van Beusekom, 2002: 89, 94).

A rejection of African farmers' considerable knowledge and experience was of a piece with the hierarchical nature of the endeavour. Volunteers for resettlement on the project were few; in 1938, one colonial official estimated that 90 per cent of those settled in the villages had been forcibly recruited (Beusekom, 2002). The forced labour recruitment prevalent in the French colonies was quite useful for this purpose, and to secure settlers for the project the Office tapped into the lines of authority that extended down through district-level administrators to local African authorities. Amid the wider political setting of coercion under colonial rule, it is hardly surprising that most Africans had little interest in the project, where they could expect an especially high degree of surveillance and control.

As with other colonial projects, the plan imagined not only a transformation of African agriculture but also a re-engineering of African social and economic life, changing the way Africans farmed, the structure of their families, and the values that underlay the organization of work and community. In the end, the project fell far short of its goals, whether defined by the area cultivated, the number of settlers, the processes of cultivation, or the crops planted. To the extent that the African settlers on the scheme succeeded in creating a livelihood for themselves, it was owing to their insistence on choosing their own crops, cultivated according to unapproved methods and frequently outside the areas designated for planting. Many others fled the settlement scheme instead, and those who remained, forging their own path, found the freedom to do so after 1946, when France abolished forced labour in its colonies.

anti-colonial wars in Vietnam, Algeria, Cameroon, and Kenya—to name only a few—proved the limits to continued colonial rule. Economic links replaced colonial ministries as the means of influence, and delivering development to colonized peoples was seen as a way to present capitalism and the West in a good light. Looking forward into a post-colonial era, past colonial rulers and a new ally, the United States, sought to maintain the loyalty of former colonies as client states in the Cold War.

SUMMARY

The idea of development, as it is understood in the twenty-first century, has a history of not even a hundred years, yet political, economic, and cultural interactions between today's industrialized and developing regions go back half a millennium and more. In examining the long history of European expansion and conquest into what is now known as the developing world, this chapter puts those interactions and the ideas that underlay them in a longer time frame. The deeper historical context sets the stage for many of the themes and problems examined in subsequent chapters dealing with contemporary issues in development. Although the initial steps of expansion, often unplanned, were taken by traders, chartered companies, fortune-seekers, and "men on the spot," the Industrial Revolution marked the arrival of "high" imperialism, as the English, French, German, and Portuguese states raced to carve out rival empires that circled the globe. Europeans encountered diverse and different societies. In the Americas, the populous empires of the Aztecs and Incas as well as many other indigenous peoples suffered demographic collapse as a result of diseases, especially smallpox, brought by the Europeans. While Africa remained largely unsettled until the "scramble for Africa" after 1884, it provided the slaves that powered the plantation economies of the Americas. Throughout the colonial period, imperial powers remained ambivalent about the endeavour and sought to use private chartered companies for expansion, as well as to govern on the cheap through indirect rule. Despite important differences across countries, the colonial experience has played an important role in structuring developing societies in the post-colonial world. Indeed, the first concerns for "development" emerged as the colonial powers responded to national struggles for self-determination after World War II. Political and economic inequalities between individual countries (and within them) and world regions, often with origins in the imperial era, continue to figure in relations between the Global North and South. Finally, many of the questions and themes in development—including, but not only, the importance of gender, culture, and indigeneity; accounting for sustainability and environmental impact; the effect of politics, such as socialism and capitalism and the state in general—have clear antecedents in the "pre-history" of development during the colonial era.

QUESTIONS FOR CRITICAL THOUGHT

1. What continuities might be identified between economic conditions created under colonial rule and those that prevail today in former colonies?
2. How did colonial policies help to contribute, even if indirectly or unintentionally, to the end of colonial rule?
3. How might present-day conflicts in former colonies be seen as a legacy of specific colonial policies?
4. What colonial-era ideas about indigenous peoples in Africa, Asia, or Latin America are still present in contemporary understandings of the "Global South"?

SUGGESTED READINGS

Allina, Eric. 2012. *Slavery by Any Other Name: African Life under Company Rule in Colonial Mozambique.* Charlottesville: University of Virginia Press.

Andrade, Tonio. 2010. "A Chinese farmer, two African boys, and a warlord: Toward a global microhistory." *Journal of World History* 21, 4: 573–91.

Bose, Sugata, and Ayesha Jalal. 2004. *Modern South Asia: History, Culture, Political Economy*, 2nd edn. New York: Routledge.

Calhoun, Craig, Frederick Cooper, and Keven W. Moore, eds. 2006. *Lessons of Empire: Imperial Histories and American Power.* New York: New Press.

Coatsworth, John H., and Alan M. Taylor, eds. 1998. *Latin America and the World Economy since 1800.* Cambridge, Mass.: Harvard University Press.

French, Howard W. 2014. *China's Second Continent: How a Million Migrants Are Building a New Empire in Africa.* New York: Alfred A. Knopf.

Hochschild, Adam. 1998. *King Leopold's Ghost: A Story of Greed, Terror, and Heroism in Colonial Africa.* New York: Houghton Mifflin.

Thornton, John. 1998. *Africa and Africans in the Making of the Atlantic World, 1400–1800*, 2nd edn. Cambridge: Cambridge University Press.

NOTES

1. For broad syntheses of the debates about the motivations for the European colonial enterprise, see Sanderson (1974) and Kennedy (1977).
2. Following World War I, Britain and France divided most of Germany's colonies, with Belgium taking Rwanda and Burundi; southwest Africa was something of an exception, being entrusted to South African rule under a League of Nations mandate.
3. Central Asia is one area of colonial rule outside the context of colonization by Western European powers and is largely absent from comparative scholarship, with the exception of Beissinger and Young (2002). It came under Russian imperial rule in the eighteenth century, and the Soviet Union later asserted control. Empire and colonial rule thus may flourish in the absence of a capitalist economic system; many of the economic and political outcomes considered characteristic of post-colonial societies are evident in post-Soviet Central Asia.

BIBLIOGRAPHY

Beissinger, M. and C. Young. 2002. *Beyond State Crisis: Postcolonial Africa and Post-Soviet Eurasia in Comparative Perspective.* Washington and Baltimore: Woodrow Wilson Center Press and Johns Hopkins University Press.

Berry, S. 1992. "Hegemony on a shoestring: Indirect rule and access to agricultural land." *Africa* 62, 3: 327–55.

Bose, S. and A. Jalal. 2004. *Modern South Asia: History, Culture, Political Economy*, 2nd edn. New York: Routledge.

Burbank, J. and F. Cooper. 2010. *Empires in World History: Power and the Politics of Difference.* Princeton, NJ: Princeton University Press.

Cooper, F. 1997. "Modernizing bureaucrats, backward Africans, and the development concept." In F. Cooper and R. Packard, eds, *International Development and the Social Sciences: Essays on the History and Politics of Knowledge.* Berkeley: University of California Press, 64–92.

——. 2006. "A parting of the ways: Colonial Africa and South Africa, 1946–48." *African Studies* 65, 1: 27–44.

——, T.C. Holt, and R. J. Scott. 2000. *Beyond Slavery: Explorations in Race, Labor, and Citizenship in Postemancipation Societies.* Chapel Hill: University of North Carolina Press.

Diffie, B.W., and G.D. Winius. 1977. *Foundations of the Portuguese Empire, 1415–1580.* Minneapolis: University of Minnesota Press.

Hobson, J. A. 1902. *Imperialism: A Study.* London: J. Nisbet.

Kennedy, P. M. 1977. "The theory and practice of imperialism." *Historical Journal* 20, 3: 761–9.

Kiwanuka, M. S. 1970. "Colonial policies and administrations in Africa: The myth of the contrasts." *African Historical Studies* 3, 2: 295–315.

Lenin, V.I. 1920 [1916]. *Imperialism: The Highest Stage of Capitalism: A Popular Outline.* Moscow: Foreign Languages Publishing House.

Metcalf, B.D., and T.R. Metcalf. 2006. *A Concise History of Modern India*, 2nd edn. Cambridge: Cambridge University Press.

Newitt, M. 2005. *A History of Portuguese Overseas Expansion, 1400–1668.* New York: Routledge.

Sanderson, G.N. 1974. "The European partition of Africa: Coincidence or conjecture?" *Journal of Imperial and Commonwealth History* 3, 1: 1–54.

van Beusekom, M.M. 2002. *Negotiating Development: African Farmers and Colonial Experts at the Office du Niger, 1920–1960.* Portsmouth, NH: Heinemann.

—— and D.L. Hodgson. 2000. "Lessons learned: Development experiences in the late colonial period." *Journal of African History* 41, 1: 29–33.

Watts, S. 1999. *Epidemics and History: Disease, Power, and Imperialism.* New Haven: Yale University Press.

Williams, R. 1983. *Keywords: A Vocabulary of Culture and Society*, rev. edn. New York: Oxford University Press.

3 Theories of Development

Radhika Desai

LEARNING OBJECTIVES

- To understand development as an aspiration since the beginnings of capitalism and the centrality of the nation-state and industrialization in it.
- To learn how development as a project emerged from post-war political tensions.
- To identify the main theoretical approaches to development in their historical context.
- To understand the implications of the BRICS, other emerging economies, and multipolarity for the prospects for development in the twenty-first century.

▲ **To mark the 130th anniversary of the death of Karl Marx in May 2013, his hometown, Trier, Germany, hosted an installation of 500 figures of the author and theorist created by Ottmar Hoerl.** | Source: THOMAS WIECK/AFP/Getty Images

The economic and financial crises of the early twenty-first century opened a new phase in the history of capitalist development. Three changes marked it. First, neoliberalism, the free-market dogma responsible for the development crisis of recent decades, was discredited. Second, growth in the rich countries slowed to a near halt while some developing countries, the "emerging economies," continued their rapid growth, narrowing even faster the enormous gap that separated their incomes and welfare from rich countries. Closing that gap had been the goal of the post-war development project and, for decades, substantial progress had eluded all but a few rather small countries, such as South Korea and Taiwan. So the faster growth, particularly in China and India, which between them account for a third of humanity, constitutes a momentous development though it leaves out too many countries and too many people even in the rapidly developing countries. Finally, less spectacular but equally important, has been the turn, primarily in Latin America during the 2000s, to progressive policies that flout the tenets of neoliberalism and put popular welfare at the centre of the political agenda. This shift has signalled at least a start in confronting the region's legendary social and economic inequality.

After decades of pessimism under neoliberalism, development theory now has the altogether more hopeful task of assimilating the development experiences of today's fast-growing economies and centre-left governments for other poor countries and people. This involves rethinking development in a longer-term historical perspective, not as something that began after World War II and concerned only the poor countries but as an aspiration that arose with the first stirrings of capitalism and industrialism and involves today's rich and poor countries alike. Finally, the rising productivity of widening circles of humanity raises critical ecological questions that require development theory to (re)consider the definition of the good life. This will once again merge development theory with the wider body of modern social and political thought from which it originated.

It generally is agreed that the division of countries into rich and poor began with the rise of capitalism, and the colonialism and imperialism that went with it, more than five centuries ago. More importantly, with the onset of industrialism, the gap widened more or less continuously, and one writer estimates that average incomes in the rich countries were a stunning 23 times higher than those in the rest of the world in 2000 (Freeman, 2004: 47). The "development" project emerged at the end of World War II to abolish this divide when it was a fraction of what it is today but was already politically unacceptable. Its persistent widening was the clearest indicator of the failure of the development project.

Development suffered its worst setbacks in the recent decades. Beginning in the 1980s, neoliberalism rolled back earlier gains. "Globalization" and "empire" sidelined it. International showmanship disguised the actually very modest Millennium Development Goals as radical initiatives. "Post-development" currents rejected development outright as a worthy aspiration. Worse, the new reckoning of national incomes in "purchasing power parities" (PPPs) rather than in US dollars suggested that the problem was an optical, or rather statistical, illusion (see Chapter 1 for an explanation of PPPs). PPP measures systematically placed the incomes of poor countries with low wages higher (since their citizens could theoretically afford to buy more goods and services produced by their equally low-income fellow citizens). Such development by statistical redefinition added insult to the injury of low incomes by congratulating a people for those low incomes when raising them was precisely the goal of development.

However, as the rapid development of the emerging economies and the popular upsurges that have produced centre-left governments in so many Latin American countries make clear, the aspiration to development cannot be reversed, sidelined, diminished, rejected, or denied. Development may have emerged as a project only after World War II, and a body of theory dubbed development theory may have emerged only then to comprehend development's problems and prospects, but development as an aspiration has deep roots in history. It is effectively the most enduring national and social urge of modern times.

In this chapter we begin by recalling the historical experience that gave rise to the development aspiration and the ideas that articulated it. This helps put the development of today's rich countries in the same frame as that of today's fast developers and those yet to come. Then, we examine the origins of the development project after World War II and the record of development in the following decades. With this essential background, we can consider the succession of theories that attempted to explain and shape the course of development. Our conclusion assesses their theoretical and analytical gains and dwells on the new tasks that development theory must now undertake.

DEVELOPMENT *AVANT LA LETTRE*

Development is linked to the idea of universal progress. It began to become widely accepted with the Industrial Revolution, which, more than 200 years ago, hurled people in the northwest corner of Europe into "change" and "improvement" faster than ever before and portended similar changes for other peoples. Before that, economic and social improvement had been slow, easily reversed, and often at the expense of others. The Industrial Revolution promised *absolute* and *rapid* increases in wealth in which, theoretically at least, all individuals, groups, and societies could partake.

However, things proved more complicated. The Industrial Revolution took place amid a new social organization of production—**capitalism**. It organized production in private units whose owners had the *capital* to buy the means and materials of production and the *labour* of workers who had no other means of making a living but to sell their *labour power*, their capacity to work, on the *market*. The market was the main mechanism for matching workers, producers, and consumers. Capital and markets had hitherto been either absent or constrained by social custom and political regulation. Under capitalism, they came to govern more and more of the social product, and custom and regulation changed to serve rather than constrain them as new capitalist states became committed to creating and maintaining this type of productive order.

Production and human productive capacity, no longer bridled by any social or political estimate of need, expanded massively and societies that had been agricultural for millennia were transformed into industrial ones. As Karl Marx and Friedrich Engels memorably put it, the new industrial capitalists "created more massive and more colossal productive forces than . . . all preceding generations together" by systematically applying science to production and improving technology, remarking that earlier centuries had no idea that "such productive forces slumbered in the lap of social labour" (Marx and Engels, 1967 [1848]: 84–5).

Increased production did not, however, correspondingly increase demand since workers were not paid the full value of their product. So capitalism required, and created, a constantly expanding world market, bringing all societies into it. It was not created, as is popularly believed, through commerce alone: conquest was employed equally if not more often. No wonder the world's first industrial capitalist country—Britain—acquired a colossal colonial empire in the nineteenth century, despite its proclaimed commitment to "free trade." Both imperial control and world market dynamics augmented the economic advantage of the industrial and colonizing nations and compounded the disadvantage of the colonized (see Chapter 2). Capitalism's geographical spread was uneven, creating agglomerations of wealth in some societies and pools of poverty and misery in others.

Industrial capitalist society's promise of generalized prosperity was broken in at least two other ways. First, because workers were paid only a fraction of the value of what they produced, incomes were unjustly and unequally distributed. Second, market co-ordination of privately organized production often broke down and crises, such as the Great Depression of the 1930s and today's Great Recession, interrupted and occasionally reversed increases in production. Karl Marx's famous critique of capitalism (*Capital*, the first volume of which was published in 1867) encompassed all of these problems. Never before in human experience had societies been governed by such unjust, impersonal, and uncontrolled institutions.

Ideas of "progress," what we now call "development," emerged out of the tension between the tantalizing possibilities for general human welfare that **industrial capitalism** offered and their failure to materialize for a majority of the people in the world under capitalism. Modern social thought is largely a series of attempts to comprehend and master the deeply contradictory dynamic of capitalism for human societies. Except for short-sighted and vulgar celebrations and condemnations, all accounts of industrial capitalist society, whether "economic" or "philosophical," reflect capitalism's double-sidedness. Marx's critique of capitalism's injustice and anarchy was balanced by an appreciation of its prodigious productivity. Adam

Smith's *An Inquiry into the Nature and Causes of the Wealth of Nations* (1937 [1776]) may have celebrated the Industrial Revolution but Smith was no advocate of unbridled free markets. Rather, Smith was a thinker who believed that markets needed to be controlled by the moral sentiments and relations that constituted society's necessarily human basis (Göçmen, 2007). As the onward march of capitalism tended to replace those sentiments and relationships with the dreaded "cash nexus," a mere four decades after the publication of Smith's *Wealth of Nations*, thinkers such as the great German philosopher Georg Wilhelm Friedrich Hegel saw the state as indispensable for correcting and opposing corrosive market forces.

State regulation is not necessarily socialist. The frequency of "market failure" in capitalism more or less guarantees that economic or market regulation will be supplemented by state or political regulation. Karl Polanyi's idea of a "double movement" captures this aptly. Market failure was endemic to capitalism, he argued, because it treated land, labour, and capital (i.e., social and productive organization) as commodities even though they were not produced for sale. Therefore, markets alone cannot regulate an economy and "no economy has existed that, even in principle, was controlled [purely] by markets" (Polanyi, 1944: 44). The nineteenth-century spread of market society provoked a countervailing movement: "While on the one hand markets spread all over the face of the globe and the amount of goods involved grew to unbelievable proportions, on the other hand a network of measures and policies was integrated into powerful institutions designed to check the action of the market relative to labour, land and money." It was "a deep-seated movement" through which "[s]ociety protected itself against the perils inherent in a self-regulating market system." This "double movement" was "the one comprehensive feature of the history of the age" (Polanyi, 1944: 76).

While Polanyi thought of the "double movement" operating within societies, the emergence of nations and the problem of national development can be seen as part of the operation of a similar sort of double movement at a geopolitical level. Although nations often are seen as cultural entities, they are products of the "machinery of world political economy" (Nairn, 1981: 335–6), specifically, of its uneven and combined development (Trotsky, 1934: 26). Capitalist development occurred unevenly, concentrated in some parts of the world and economically subjugated, through colonization or other means, other parts of the world. Colonized or less powerful peoples experienced capitalism not as development but as lack, deprivation, imposition, domination, and exploitation. They "learned quickly enough that Progress in the abstract meant domination in the concrete, by powers which they could not help apprehending as foreign or alien." Development elsewhere threatened to wash over them like a "'tidal wave' . . . of outside interference and control" (Nairn, 1981: 338).

In response, colonized and less powerful peoples sought to create nations as barriers against such tidal waves to avoid being "drowned" by them. Such national assertion worked against economic and imperial pressures to undertake combined development—hot-housed, state-led development of production. Though these efforts were not universally successful, this process eventually resulted in the nation-state system. As Benno Teschke (2003: 265) has noted:

> the expansion of capitalism was not an *economic* process in which the transnationalising forces of the market or civil society surreptitiously penetrated pre-capitalist states, driven by the logic of cheap commodities that eventually perfected a universal world market. It was a *political* and, *a fortiori, geopolitical* process in which pre-capitalist state classes had to design counterstrategies of reproduction to defend their position in an international environment which put them at an economic *and* coercive disadvantage.

Some countries, pre-eminently the United States, Germany, and Japan, not only defended themselves against economic and political subjugation to the world's first industrialized country, Britain, but also challenged its supremacy. Armed with the ideas of thinkers who exposed the ruling free trade ideology as merely the dogma and ruling ideology of British supremacy, they promoted the *national* development of their countries through political means. For thinkers such as Alexander Hamilton and Henry Carey in the United States and Friedrich List in Germany, free trade concentrated and reinforced the economic advantage of some countries as much as conquest did, creating an international division of labour in which some countries produced higher-value manufactured goods and others lower-value agricultural, primary, or (today also) cheap, low-tech, manufactured products. It could be challenged only by non-market, political means.

Contrary to ideologies of free trade and its modern-day equivalents, neoliberalism and globalization, national development has always been, and remains, a matter of state management of trade and production to enable the economy to produce higher-value goods, while managing a transition in agriculture to make it more productive and capable of fulfilling the greater demands of industrial society. This understanding exposes the conventional economic idea of "comparative advantage," in which the productive specialization of each nation—essentially, industrial powers producing industrial goods and colonies or weaker countries producing raw materials and agricultural goods—was to be accepted without question, as little more than a justification for the unequal international division of labour. Since it was created both by commerce and by conquest, political means are indispensable for breaking out of inherited specialization in low-value goods and to begin producing higher-value goods as the road to prosperity.

This is exactly what is going on in the BRICS (Brazil, Russia, India, China, and South Africa) and emerging economies, China in particular, but with one critical difference. In the late nineteenth century, Britain's industrial challengers, rejecting the breezy free-market ideas that demand and supply would balance each other out—an idea that only served to disguise the critical role of colonies as suppliers and markets (Desai, 2010)—and that "comparative advantage" would ensure the common prosperity through free trade, aimed to ensure the supply of industrial raw materials and the markets for their products in part by creating and expanding formal empires. Imperial competition intensified in the closing decades of the nineteenth century and culminated in World War I. By contrast, the "developing" countries of the second half of the twentieth century had been formal or informal colonies that could not acquire colonies of any significance to facilitate their industrial development.

This difference keeps the question of development and imperialism intertwined. The way out of *potential* subjugation for the so-called "late industrializers," such as Germany, the US, and Japan, lay in an intellectual and practical critique of "free trade" and was aided by extensive colonies. The way out of *actual* subjugation for the developing countries of the post-war period and the emerging and BRICS economies of today requires, in addition, undoing the effects of imperialism and doing so without colonization. That effort was and remains much more difficult.

THE MOMENT OF DEVELOPMENT

The development project that began in earnest after World War II marked a historic turnaround. After centuries during which colonizers justified colonialism with racist rationales such as the **white man's burden** and his "civilizing mission," colonial and imperial exploitation, **oppression**, and plunder were at last recognized for what they were. As decolonization began, the development project aimed to reverse these realities and aid the poor countries' "catching up" to the rich world's levels of income and material welfare.

This historical moment was long in the making and the result of the interaction of a range of actors—the US government, the Soviet Union, and (not least) national governments of newly independent but poor nations, with different and sometimes even opposed motivations—emerging from the "30-year crisis" of 1914–45, spanning two world wars and a Great Depression (Mayer, 1981). It was the crucible of a new world order. Three massive changes produced and defined the "moment of development" as the Thirty Years' Crisis ended. First, the US temporarily emerged as the world's most powerful capitalist nation. Though it had become the largest single economy by1913, it came to account for fully half of world production by 1945, thanks to the destruction two world wars had caused in Europe and elsewhere. Without much of a formal empire of its own, the US began to sponsor decolonization, reconstruction, and development to cut its capitalist rivals down to size and to take up the capitalist world's leadership.

A second change made development urgent for the US-led capitalist world: the Soviet Union, formed after a Communist revolution in the midst of World War I, had experienced remarkably successful industrialization based on state planning and direction while the capitalist world languished in the Great Depression. This industrialization proved critical in the Allied victory in World War II, and Soviet power and prestige balanced US power in the Cold War that followed as the Communist world, which now also included the Communist regimes in Eastern Europe and China, not only truncated the size of the capitalist world but also became an alternative pole of attraction for newly independent countries, forcing the US into "altruistic" grooves to keep or wrest poor countries from the attractions of communism. Third, after World War I, many national liberation movements, supported by the revolutionary Soviet government, had demanded decolonization. Only after World War II, however, did the US consistently support it to undermine its capitalist rivals and compete against the Soviet bloc for the support of nationalist movements and governments.

Together these developments placed the "catch-up" of former colonies to the levels of prosperity of rich countries on the world agenda. This was the development project—in a critical sense the ransom that the capitalist world had to pay to keep poor countries from communism. They were the stakes in the Cold War, which turned hot in such cases as Korea, Cuba, and Vietnam.

Development has come to mean many things—rising levels of education, political participation and democracy, urbanization, technology, health and welfare—but higher incomes and greater material welfare were critical, and industrialization and state direction were seen as essential to achieving them. And they remain equally essential today even though populist, neoliberal, and postmodern discourses of the late twentieth century insist otherwise and portray states as inherently oppressive and industrialization as unnecessary, indeed positively harmful, for poor countries (for a critique, see Kitching, 1982). The poor countries were predominantly agricultural and the rich countries predominantly industrial. Industry provided the critical advantage in productivity. Thus, development involved industrializing predominantly agricultural economies, as had already happened in rich societies, and the state was its agent.

Intellectually, development was the product of the *confrontation* between capitalism and communism as much as of their *interaction*. The experience of the Great Depression in capitalist countries, the contemporaneous success of state-directed industrialization of a predominantly agrarian economy in the USSR, and the unavoidable necessity of comprehensive planning during war, which proved so popular for its egalitarian effects, had taught

> the politicians, officials and even many of the businessmen of the post-war West . . . that a return to laissez-faire and the unreconstructed free market were out of the question. Certain policy objectives—full employment, the containment of communism, the modernization of lagging or declining or ruined economies—had absolute priority and justified the strongest government presence. Even regimes dedicated to economic and political liberalism now could, and had to, run their economies in ways which would once have been rejected as "socialist." (Hobsbawm, 1994: 272–3)

This new consensus held that the ills of capitalism could be remedied by planning, state ownership, and a large state role in making capitalist economies more productive as well as more egalitarian through welfare and redistributive measures. The economist John Maynard Keynes, who witnessed the collapse of economic activity during the Great Depression, recommended that at such times the government could step up its activity to compensate and loosen money supply to restart private economic activity. **Keynesian policies**, which intruded less on the private capitalist economy than Soviet-style planning, formed the basis of post-war macroeconomic management in the rich countries and of early ideas of "development," though Keynes's ideas were actually far more radical than these policies implied (Desai, 2009). With the free market abolished in the Communist countries and restricted and regulated in the advanced capitalist and developing economies, a "golden age" of capitalism ensued, demonstrating that the "economy of private enterprise ('free enterprise' was the preferred name) needed to be saved from itself to survive" (Hobsbawm, 1994: 273) and, ironically, saved by the instruments of its enemy, socialism and communism.

The international counterpart of these domestic policy instruments was the governance of trade and finance through a set of rules, pre-eminently capital controls, and institutions—the so-called Bretton Woods institutions, of which the International Monetary Fund (IMF), the World Bank, and the General Agreement on Tariffs and Trade (GATT) were the most important (see Chapters 9 and 15). During the 1950s and 1960s, at least, these controls and institutions worked to enable national economic management for growth and development.

> Capital was not allowed to cross frontiers without government approval, which permitted governments to determine domestic interest rates, fix the exchange rate of the national currency, and tax and spend as they saw fit to secure national economic objectives. National economic planning was seen as a natural extension of this thinking, as were domestic and international arrangements to stabilize commodity prices. It is not a great oversimplification to say that "development theory" was originally just a theory about the best way for colonial, and then ex-colonial, states to accelerate national economic growth in this international environment. The goal of development was growth; the agent of development was the state and the means of development were these macroeconomic policy instruments. (Leys, 1996: 6–7)

Of the numerous terms and euphemisms that have emerged over the decades to refer to the poor countries of the world and what they shared despite their diversity of cultural and material endowments—developing, underdeveloped, post-colonial, less developed, backward, Southern, and so on—the term "Third World" best captures the tensions of the development project's formative historical moment (see also Chapter 1). First, these countries sought to balance the capitalist First World and the Communist Second World in international politics, particularly through the Non-Aligned Movement (NAM) formed at the Bandung conference of 1955 to assert independence from Cold War blocs and put issues of importance to development on the world agenda. Second, most nationalist leaderships and governments needed to balance politically weak capitalist forces against the strength of socialist and communist forces and popular hopes aroused by national liberation movements. In India, Egypt, and Indonesia, for example (Ahmad, 1992: especially 297–304), the "Third World" was understood as a "third way" between capitalism and communism. Although "development" meant the development of capitalism, planning and state direction were to make it a reformed capitalism: more productive and egalitarian than the liberal capitalism that had come to grief in the inter-war period. Indeed, so low had capitalism's reputation sunk in the Thirty Years' Crisis that the capitalist world was on the defensive and avoided using the term "capitalism," preferring to deploy "development" and "free world" in its ideological war with Communism.

DISPUTING DEVELOPMENT

With conducive national and international institutions and policies in place, a two-decade-long "golden age" of growth of unprecedented tempo and duration ensued. Third World economies were swept along, though critical problems remained. The continuing dependence of many Third World economies on commodity exports was the most important. Despite their attempts to industrialize, and despite some significant successes, too much of the growth of Third World economies in the 1950s and 1960s originated in high demand for primary products by the First World, perpetuating rather than breaking colonial economic relationships. Both First and Third World dominant classes had vested interests in the continuation of these relationships and were able to keep them in place: clearly, decolonization and development marked breaks from the past but often of an ambiguous sort.

Even with these shortcomings, in retrospect this "golden age" was development's best. Neither world growth nor Third World growth has reached such long-term rates since then. Beginning in this relatively optimistic period, and continuing over the next decades as prospects for development dimmed, a succession of development theories, outlined in Table 3.1, held sway, with stimulating debates punctuating each transition.

TABLE 3.1 | Theories of Development

Theory/ Theme	Emergence/ Dominance	Thinkers	Discipline/ Tradition	The Problem	The Solution
Development economics	1950s	Lewis, Rosenstein-Rodan	Keynesian economics	Low-level equilibrium	Injection of capital and management of disequilibria to put economy on a growth path to high-level equilibrium
Modernization theory	Late 1950s	Rostow, Shils, Pye, Almond, Huntington	Weberian/ Parsonian sociology	Traditional society	Modernization through diffusion of modern values and institutions
Dependency theory	1960s	Cardoso, Frank, Wallerstein, Amin	Prebisch-Singer thesis, Economic Commission for Latin America approach, Marxism	Dependency within a world capitalist system	Delinking, fully or partially, or socialism
Marxism	1970s	Brenner, Warren	Marxist theory of modes of production	Articulation of modes of production	Not prescriptive but development of capitalist relations of production/ socialism
Neoliberalism	1970s–present	Bauer, Balassa, Kreuger, Lal	Neo-classical, marginalist economics, Austrian economics	State intervention	Free markets
Developmental states	1970s–present	Amsden, Haggard, Chang, Reinert	Listian national "neo-mercantilist" political economy	Free markets	State management of the economy to increase productivity, equality, and technological upgrading

Development Economics

Development economics was the first theory of development and it was simply the contemporary form of posing the perennial questions of economics.

> For centuries economics was—at its very core—an art, a practice and a science devoted to "economic development," albeit under a variety of labels: from an idealistic promotion of "public happiness" to the nationalistic creation of wealth and greatness of nations and rulers, and the winning of wars. (Jomo and Reinert, 2005: vii)

Development economics was predominantly **Keynesian** and saw capitalist crises such as the Great Depression as products of cyclical deficits of demand, which made capitalists reluctant to invest in productive plant and eager to keep their capital "liquid." The state could remedy this through fiscal and monetary macroeconomic policies to increase state spending and expand credit at the beginning to buoy up investment and consumption and "smooth out" the highs and lows, restoring equilibrium at high levels of employment of labour and capital. The state was also seen to provide health care, education, and social safety nets, such as instituting unemployment insurance and public pensions, and to own and operate key industries.

Keynesians sought to accelerate growth in developing countries by injecting capital and pursuing macroeconomic policies adapted to developing economies. Assumptions that applied to developed economies, such as decreasing returns to scale, labour scarcity, and "perfect competition," did not apply to developing ones: labour was far from fully employed while capital and technology were very scarce. Equilibrium was also undesirable: discontinuities and disequilibria were necessary to achieve a quantum leap to a higher growth path in "stagnant" economies in low-level equilibrium. As W.A. Lewis saw it, for example, largely agrarian labour-surplus economies had to be put on an industrial growth path such that employment in industry made labour scarce enough for wages to rise (Ros, 2005: 89–91). The great initial effort needed to put an economy onto a self-sustaining growth path invited comparison with an airplane taking off: "Launching a country into self-sustaining growth is a little like getting an airplane off the ground. There is a critical ground-speed which must be passed before the craft can become airborne" (Rosenstein-Rodan, 1961, quoted in Ros, 2005: 81).

While Keynesianism legitimized national economic management, its tools were macroeconomic and aimed to adjust or massage national economies. They paled in comparison with the policies of **Listian industrialization** employed in the rise of the first set of nations (the US, Germany, and Japan) to challenge the then-existing world division of labour, let alone the means employed in Soviet industrialization. In retrospect, whether they could overturn the even wider gap in incomes and productivity that now lay between the First World and the Third was doubtful. At the time, however, the mood was optimistic and the effectiveness of Development Economics was not initially called into question.

Modernization Theory

Sure enough, by the late 1950s it was clear that, while most developing countries grew, none was launched on a path to self-sustaining industrial growth. **Modernization theory** now emerged to pin responsibility on social and political factors largely outside the purview of development economics and to supplement economics with sociology and political science in theorizing the preconditions for, and obstacles to, development, which it conceived as the "modernization" of "traditional" societies.

Walt Rostow's *Stages of Economic Growth*, in which economics was central without being the exclusive focus, marked the transition between development economics and modernization theory. Relying on the growth experience of the developed countries and combining it with an appreciation of key social and political factors that facilitated growth, Rostow discerned five broad states through which "traditional" societies passed to become modern "high mass consumption" societies—"traditional," "preconditions for take-off," "take-off," "drive to maturity" and "modern." Traditional agricultural societies had "pre-Newtonian" attitudes towards nature and thus suffered low levels of technology and growth. The preconditions for take-off were fulfilled by key economic changes, including trade expansion and increases in investment, but the creation of a national state was critical. While these changes had occurred more or less autonomously in England and Western Europe, in most countries they were the result of external pressures that undermined the structures of "traditional societies." Take-off would occur when total investment in the economy reached 10 per cent of GDP and both industrial and agricultural productivity outstripped population growth. The drive to maturity featured further instalments of growth and modernization of the economy with the production of a more diverse range of goods, including technologically sophisticated ones, and greater integration into the world economy. High mass consumption society was the end state where average incomes were high and consumption expanded beyond basic needs. Societies could then institute welfare states and also spend more on the military as they sought to project their power internationally.

Rostow's account bore all the marks of modernization theory: consciousness of the stakes in the Cold War (he subtitled his work *A Non-Communist Manifesto*); an assumption that the First World was the model and end state for the Third; optimism about the prospects for growth in the Third World; and an assumption that the First World would be instrumental in promoting it. His observation that the danger of Communism was greatest when the preconditions for take-off were being met because conflicts were most likely during that period also anticipated modernization theory's authoritarian turn under Samuel Huntington.

Unlike Rostow's economic history, the principal modernization theorists employed sociology and political science, relying particularly on Talcott Parsons's *The Structure of Social Action* (1937), a breezy adaptation of Max Weber's complex and rather gloomy sociology of modernity. "Modernity, Parsons believed, implicitly but fundamentally, formed a *coherent, unitary, uniform and worthwhile* whole, and had to be apprehended by a social science that shared these qualities" (Gilman, 2003: 75). Though not concerned with the Third World, the overall question that framed Parsons's study—"what made the West different?"—eminently suited Cold War modernization theory. His "pattern variables" (see Table 3.2) distinguished modern from traditional societies by opposing them and modernization theory merely added that development occurred when modern characteristics—values and institutions, in addition to capital and technology—from the formerly imperial "modern" were "diffused" to the ex-colonial "traditional" countries until they matched the former as closely as possible. For modernization

PHOTO 3.1 | Oil refinery and storage tanks on the outskirts of Kisumu town on the road to Maseno in western Kenya, East Africa.

TABLE 3.2 | Parsons's Pattern Variables or Roles in Traditional Society and Modern Society

Traditional Society	Modern Society
Affectivity	**Affective neutrality**
Predominance of roles that give affective or emotional gratification	Predominance of roles whose performance is affectively neutral
Ascription	**Achievement**
Predominance of roles according to non-achievable status or attributes (sex, age, family position, etc.) indifferent to quality of performance	Predominance of roles in which achievement is the basis of status
Diffusion	**Specificity**
Predominance of roles in which a number of functions may be combined: e.g., family memberships and work on a farm	Predominance of roles specific to particular functions, as in a bureaucracy
Particularism	**Universalism**
Predominance of roles in which expectations are particular to the status of the performer	Predominance of roles in which performance is measured irrespective of the status of the performer
Collectivity orientation	**Self-orientation**
Predominance of roles oriented towards the collective, such as society or kinship group	Predominance of roles in which private self-interest is the prime motivation

theory the obstacles to "modernization" lay in local and inherited "tradition."

This narrative of modernization simply assumed away the history of imperialism. The "traditional" society was in a state before capitalist development, which would now be brought to them through capital injection and/or "diffusion" of modern values and institutions that required increasingly close contact—economic, social, political, and cultural—with formerly imperial countries. While a liberal wing of modernization theory assumed that modernization was inevitable and imminent and would lead to democratic orders, there was also a darker side to the theory.

Modernization scholars identified closely with the world aims and activities of the US but, to their disappointment, most of them never became influential in making US or World Bank development policy. Instead they inhabited the well-funded US government sponsored "area studies" departments that sought to know parts of the world that Washington was interested in or had become involved in. A couple of modernization theorists did become influential in US foreign policy. Walt Rostow served as head of the policy planning staff under John F. Kennedy and as national security adviser under Lyndon Johnson. He was widely known as the chief architect of the Vietnam War.

> Rostowians saw the world locked in a communist–capitalist struggle whose outcome would be decided in the developing areas. South Vietnam was the linchpin in this struggle. Under Walt W. Rostow's guidance, the Doctrine became the primary tenet of American policy toward the developing areas in the 1960s and the principal rationale for US intervention and conduct in Vietnam. . . . The international order depended on whether the developing areas could be "modernized"—a process Rostow equated with Western-style economic development. (Grinter, 1975, quoted in Gilman, 2003: 249)

Samuel Huntington never attained high office but did exert a chilling influence on US policy in Vietnam. Having given up on democracy in the Third World, preferring "order" instead because "the most important political distinction among countries concerns not their form of government, but their degree of government," he advocated "urbanization" in Vietnam, including by bombing and defoliating, to undercut rural support for the enemy. As one of his colleagues remarked, "Sam simply lost the ability to distinguish between urbanization and genocide" (Ahmad, 1992, quoted in Gilman, 2003: 233).

Huntington's trajectory revealed the deeply anti-democratic currents in post-war US intellectual life: modernization theory's core understanding of development as a transition from traditional to modern society itself contained the seeds of its later anti-democratic turn. When optimism about, and then patience with, populations allegedly under this transition wore out, breezy optimism about democracy could easily turn into an authoritarian concern for order (Gilman, 2003: 45–63; see also Cammack, 1997; O'Brien, 1971; the key text is Huntington, 1969).

Modernization theory was less the basis of policy in the developing countries and more the basis of the US government's involvement in them. As such, its validity was protected from policy challenge. It remains the dominant paradigm governing the understanding of the Third World in the US to this day. By the end of the 1960s, however, the "golden age" of capitalist growth had ended. As it came to an end, the comfortable assumptions of modernization theory soon were challenged.

Dependency Theory

Dependency theory remains to this day the most significant challenge to mainstream understandings of development. The *dependentistas* reinstated the history of imperialism in the understanding of development, or lack thereof, and sought to theorize post-war *informal* imperialism through concepts like "neo-colonialism." Not surprisingly, perhaps, dependency theory originated in Latin America, the one region of the Third World where, although the vast majority of nation-states had been independent for more than a century, underdevelopment remained a problem and where some countries, such as Argentina, had had levels of income and welfare to rival the rich countries at the end of World War II but fell rapidly behind in the following decades.

Dependency theory turned the central assumptions of modernization theory on their heads. Whereas modernization theory studied countries, dependency theory studied the whole capitalist "world system." Whereas modernization theory assumed that the problem of development was an original state of *non*-development, dependency theory argued that a single and integrated historical process of world capitalist development developed some countries and *under*developed others. Whereas modernization theory assumed that development would help "traditional" societies "catch up" with "modern" ones, the stronger forms of dependency theory insisted that development was impossible under capitalism: socialism was the only solution. Whereas modernization theory saw the elites of "traditional" societies diffusing modern values, ideas, practices, and institutions to the rest, dependency theory saw them collaborating with imperialism to produce underdevelopment. Rather than conceiving the world economy as divided between "traditional" and "modern" societies, dependency theorists saw it as divided between an advanced industrial "core" and a largely agricultural "periphery."

The varied strands of dependency can be traced to two principal sources. The first was the UN's Economic Commission for Latin America (ECLA) under Raúl Prebisch in the 1950s. He challenged conventional development economics in two ways. First, Prebisch contested conventional development economics, which assumed that trade between the centre and the periphery would generate development. Rather, he argued, it would exacerbate inequalities between them. He pointed to the experience of the two world wars and the intervening Great Depression when trade between Latin America and the core countries was disrupted and Latin American countries diversified and industrialized. These gains were being lost in the post-war resumption of close trading relations with core countries. Second, reflecting on the experience of the peripheral countries during the "golden age" he, in parallel with Hans Singer, took issue with conventional trade theory. It supposed that trade between industrial and agricultural countries would eventually favour the latter because they would benefit from advances in technology in industrial countries, reducing the prices of industrial goods faster than the prices of agricultural goods. The Prebisch-Singer thesis argued that instead of permitting the prices of industrial goods to fall in tandem with technological progress, advanced industrial countries kept the benefits of technical progress by keeping prices high while prices of primary products tended to decline as more producers and countries entered the market.

The second major source of dependency theory was the work of Paul Baran. Baran sought to understand how imperialism worked in the second half of the twentieth century—when the Third World was composed of formally independent nation-states, not colonies. The classical theories of imperialism proposed by Marxist intellectuals and leaders, including Lenin, in the early twentieth century understood imperialism and imperialist competition of the time as endemic in, and necessary to, capitalism: both would be ended only by socialism. Baran furthered this analysis, arguing that capitalism was a hierarchical international system based on a transfer of surplus from underdeveloped to developed countries—a process in which multinational corporations played an increasingly important role, blocking industrial development and producing stagnation and underdevelopment in the poor countries.

Dependency theory had many strands: politically, many dependency theorists spoke as representatives of their own national bourgeoisie, "chafing at its subordination to the interests of foreign companies and the influence of the US state in domestic politics" (Leys, 1996: 12) or they sided with the working class and other radical currents. Theoretically, Gabriel Palma (1981) classified dependency approaches in terms of how much each theorist thought development possible. Some currents merely pointed to the difficulties of development. A second current, which included Palma himself, F.H. Cardoso (who would become president of Brazil), and Enzo Faletto, focused on "concrete situations of dependency" and on how external obstacles were complemented by domestic class configurations to impede development. They also believed that some capitalist development—"dependent development"—was possible within these parameters. Peter Evans (1979), for instance, analyzed how a "triple alliance" of state capital, domestic capital, and foreign capital had determined the actual pattern of industrialization in Brazil. Finally, there were those—pre-eminently Andre Gunder Frank—who argued that no real development was possible without socialism and a delinking from the structures of world capitalism.

To Palma's classification we must add the theories of Samir Amin, a major theorist of dependency from Africa; he differed from dependency theorists' claim that underdevelopment was a capitalist condition, seeing it instead as the result of a combination of capitalist and pre-capitalist structures in peripheral societies. He did, however, think that selective delinking from the world economy could be combined with a broadly based and internally generated process of capitalist accumulation and development.

No discussion of dependency theory is complete without mention of the related "world system" approach. It relied on the French *Annales* school of historians, in particular Fernand Braudel, whose detailed history of world capitalism drew on Marxism but also differed from it by defining capitalism in terms of markets, not the relations of production. For Immanuel Wallerstein, the most prominent representative of the world system approach, the *capitalist* world economy resulted from the centuries-long expansion of a world market centred on Europe from the fifteenth century. Though it contained various political and economic forms, it was and remained a worldwide capitalist economy with a unified character. No unit within it could be analyzed separately. This structure generated "unequal development and therefore differential rewards . . . there was the differential of the core of the European world economy versus its peripheral areas, within the European core between states, within states, between regions and strata" (Wallerstein, 1974: 86). This capitalist world economy was divided into a core, a periphery, and a semi-periphery, and though at times the position of individual countries changed, the overall structure was unchanging.

Dependency turned out to be a mere mirror image of modernization theory: the one inevitabilist, the other impossibilist. Most *dependentistas* dismissed the possibility of autonomous national development in the context of the powerful and varied structures and practices of imperialism that persisted despite the nominal independence of Third World countries. While this was one-sided, dependency scholarship deepened our understanding of the specific mechanisms of imperialist subjection and exploitation, which Marxists tended to ignore because they focused on how workers, rather than on how nations, were exploited. Dependency scholars generated a wealth of writing on the operation of "unequal trade" (Emmanuel, 1969); multinational capital (Hymer, 1972); and debt, aid, and the official development organizations (e.g., George, 1988; George and Sabelli, 1994; Hayter and Watson, 1985; Payer, 1991), all of which illuminated how imperialism and dependency characterized world capitalism.

Marxism

Marxists had long understood capitalism as a contradictory and unjust, crisis-prone and exploitative form of society that had nevertheless vastly improved human social productive capacity. Although they claimed to be Marxists, dependency and world system theorists focused on the negative effects of capitalism through the exploitation and subordination of countries. It was, however, the success of capitalism in spurring human social productive capacity that gave rise to the ideas of development and progress in the first place. A brief review of the Marxist critique of dependency makes some of the implications of dependency's one-sidedness clear.

Dependency and world system scholars maintained that the inclusion of new areas or countries into the world market was sufficient to deem them capitalist and if the results were different, even opposite, from those in the core lands of capitalist accumulation, well, that was imperialism and dependency for you! Their Marxist critics begged to differ: capitalism was a matter of the social relations of production (and not only exchange) and world market inclusion did not always lead to the development of capitalism: Latin American *latifundia* (large agricultural estates) and Eastern Europe's "second serfdom," not to mention the still-numerous peasantries of the world, all constituted forms of world market incorporation that did not lead to the development of capitalist relations

Paul Haslam

PHOTO 3.2 | The revolution in Cuba was central to the development of dependency theory.

of production. While the "articulation of modes of production" approach of these Marxists was theoretically rich (see, e.g., Laclau, 1977; Brenner, 1978; Banaji, 1977), and while the debates between Marxists and *dependentistas* enriched our understanding of the range of different types of world market inclusion and their specific effects—for instance, such inclusion on terms of merchant capital tended not to develop capitalism but only to reinforce pre-capitalist forms of exploitation—they also revealed that the Marxist idea of capitalist exploitation had been reduced to the extraction of surplus value from wage workers alone. It had little purchase on understanding how underdevelopment was created and how nations could subordinate and exploit other nations.

Marxists kept open the possibility of an end to underdevelopment through the development of capitalist relations of production, and some criticized them for underestimating the problems of the Third World (Lipietz, 1982). And in doing so, they did question the "impossibilism" of dependency approaches, pointing to counter-indications, particularly the "miraculous" rise of the East Asian Newly Industrializing Countries (NICs) and the more widespread phenomenon of industrialization in a great number of Third World countries that was becoming clear in the 1970s (Warren, 1973, 1980).

Neoliberalism

The 1970s marked a watershed in the story of development. Growth in the world economy slowed as the post-war recovery of Western Europe and Japan, which had been the main motor of "golden age" growth, was completed and new problems emerged, including slowing productivity growth, worker militancy, and oil price increases. Slow growth in the First World meant that primary exports, on which Third World countries with little or no industrialization had remained dependent, slowed perceptibly. Moreover, post-war international economic governance, which had proved relatively benign for developing countries, unravelled and the restructuring of the main Bretton Woods institutions by the 1980s made them positively hostile to development, while changes in the international monetary system vastly increased the invidious power of these institutions (see Chapter 9).

The US had imposed the dollar on the world at Bretton Woods but providing dollar liquidity by running current account deficits had never worked and never could work, thanks to the "Triffin Dilemma" pointed out by the Belgian economist Robert Triffin (Desai, 2009). The dollar was falling in value and, by 1971, its gold backing had been removed. Convertible currencies now floated against each other, creating great financial uncertainty while the expansions of international financial flows and inflation of asset bubbles that now became systematically necessary for the dollar to serve as world money (Desai, 2013) added vastly to it. The Third World became caught up in the earliest of these, the vast increase in international bank lending in the 1970s, in a way that would prove fateful for them.

In reaction to the falling dollar, the Organization of Petroleum Exporting Countries (OPEC) dramatically raised oil prices from approximately $2 per barrel to $39 in the 1970s. This had a devastating impact on all oil-importing countries and was particularly punishing for many in the Third World. However, the financial results of these oil price increases had the unexpected result of facilitating faster industrialization in many Third World countries. As some relatively successful industrializers broke ranks to forge ahead while most others began sinking into a mire of economic stagnation or decline (political instability and social disintegration that would worsen in coming decades), the already disparate Third World began to diverge even more.

Successful Third World industrialization in the 1970s occurred at a unique conjuncture. International interest rates, never very high in the post-war period thanks to the "repression of finance" during the "golden age," dipped even lower as First World growth slowed and demand for capital slackened. Indeed, given high inflation, real interest rates—the difference between the nominal interest rates and the rate of inflation—occasionally even turned negative. At this time the vastly inflated OPEC revenues from oil sales were deposited in US banks and they became eager, even desperate, to lend money (see also Chapter 14). The 1970s witnessed a boom in private bank lending to sovereign Third World governments through open variable-rate loans. They financed the substantial spurt in industrialization and seemed to promise practically free capital and potentially high industrial growth for Third World countries with the state capacity and political will to foster it. If this promise had been realized, the shift in the centre of gravity in the world economy that the BRICS and other emerging economies caused in the early twenty-first century would have happened decades earlier.

However, the US turn towards "monetarism" ended this hopeful prospect. Monetarism prescribed raising interest rates to end inflation. Whether it ended inflation remained moot, but it certainly caused a sharp recession and delivered a harsh financial shock to Third World borrowers who had accepted huge loans when interest rates were low and even negative and now faced sky-high principal and interest payments. In 1982, the Third World "debt crisis" broke out as Mexico, Brazil, and Argentina defaulted on their debt. Although not originally designed to do so, the IMF and the World Bank stepped in to manage the resulting financial crises in a way that helped First World bankers evade their responsibility (creditors' responsibility) for profligate lending and passed the whole burden of adjustment to the borrowers, mainly Third World governments. Acting more like instruments of US and Western power than the multilateral institutions they were supposed to be, the IMF and the World Bank rescheduled debts to avert repudiation and imposed **structural adjustment programs** (SAPs), which were stricter, more market-friendly versions of the "conditionalities" that the IMF was empowered to impose on countries in balance-of-payments difficulties (see also Chapter 9). These programs severely restricted consumption and investment in favour of production of largely primary goods for export to repay debts.

SAPs marked the single most important change in the theory and practice of development. The neoliberalism they embodied contested the original goals and methods of development—to which, as we have seen, state intervention to control and direct market outcomes and promote industrialization had been central—in favour of dogmatically market-friendly policies. While in the rich countries neoliberalism resulted in unprecedented rates of unemployment, poverty, inequality, and deindustrialization, ending the "golden age" of high growth and the Keynesian welfare state, its effects on the Third World were far worse, leading to two "lost decades" of development featuring low or even negative growth in already poor countries.

Neoliberalism and structural adjustment were anti-statist rhetorically and to a certain degree practically, but in reality they entailed comprehensive state intervention to re-engineer whole economies in favour of private capital—foreign capital more than domestic capital, financial capital more than productive capital.

Although a number of debt reschedulings followed the outbreak of the debt crisis and small parts of the debt were forgiven, little was done to alleviate the debt burden that had expanded so vastly with the interest rate increases. For the next two decades, countries under SAPs—a majority of Third World countries—were forced to expand exports of mostly primary commodities and low-value-added industrial products to pay back the debt. Consequently, the market for these commodities was glutted, lowering prices and making it harder for these countries to earn the foreign exchange needed to repay inflated debts. Meanwhile, First World consumers benefited as many tropical products, from higher-value teas and coffees to cotton, fresh fruits and vegetables, and even seafood, entered mass consumption in the 1980s for the first time. And contrary to all notions of development, neoliberalism also engineered a massive transfer of capital *from* the Third World to the First, as the now inflated repayments were not matched by new loans. The resulting crisis of development is often blamed on poor government policies in the Third World. However, with state spending restricted and interventionism ruled out, no attempt to break out of the production of low-value-added products—in effect, no development—could even be contemplated.

Neoliberalism's anti-state and pro-market dogma ended "development" as originally conceived, with the nation-state as its chief agent and industrialization its central component. In the 1990s, the dominance of neoliberalism was reinforced by the discourse of "globalization," which argued that nation-states were now irrelevant. Then, as the twenty-first century opened with 9/11 and the US's "war on terrorism," a new set of discourses on "empire" and "imperialism" portrayed a number of Third World states as "rogue states," and "failed states," to be dealt with, if necessary, by violence often dressed up as "humanitarian intervention" and protection of "democracy." Amid all this, prospects for development, industrialization, and "catching up" to

First World levels of prosperity receded farther into the distance for most of the Third World.

In retrospect, the story of development, in its original sense, seemed more or less to have ended in the 1970s:

> By the early 1970s the vision of "catching up" (culminating in Rostow's 1960 version, in a "high mass-consumption" society, which implicitly included equity and democracy) had already given way to more modest ambitions: "redistribution with growth"—i.e., some reduction in inequality but financed out of growth so that the better off in the developing countries might be less unwilling to agree to it—in a word, fewer illusions about democracy. And by the end of the 1970s, redistribution had given way to just trying to meet the "basic needs" of the poor who, it seemed, would always be with us after all; the goal of equity had disappeared. Then came structural adjustment; to get growth, underdeveloped societies were to adjust themselves to the Procrustean bed allocated to them by the market, and for this purpose even basic needs must be sacrificed. (Leys, 1996: 26)

Neoliberalism was favoured also by Third World elites disinclined to honour their obligations to their own working and peasant classes implied by developmentalism. Its policies involved cuts in state spending on welfare and subsidies, currency devaluation, deregulation of the economy and privatization, and restriction of the rights of labour. Indeed, governments, rather than being agents of development, were obstacles to it—profligate, corrupt, inefficient, and parasitic. Government intervention interfered with the market's way of "getting prices right" and balancing economic activity. Neoliberals also argued against the emphasis on industrialization, insisting that markets assured that each country would specialize in the economic activity—and it could be agriculture—in which it had a "comparative advantage." If governments sought to overturn the verdict of the market and to industrialize, they would only cause declines in welfare.

Neoliberalism appeared convincing insofar as many governments in the Third World had never represented the interests of all the citizenry, only of its propertied. A great many development failures could indeed be placed at their door. Critics of neoliberalism faced the uphill task of arguing that while that was true, not only were governments capable of better in the right circumstances, only they could promote development against the obstacles posed by the political and economic power of the First World. Only in following decades, when a new generation became acquainted with the costs exacted by the oversimplifications of neoliberalism and free-market thinking, would thinking about alternatives rekindle.

But the contradictions of neoliberalism could not be wished away. By the end of the 1980s, neoliberalism's first decade, the high priests in its temples—the World Bank and the IMF—were already qualifying neoliberal doctrine by admitting at least a limited role for the state, and by the 1990s they were no longer able to argue that free markets and free trade were desirable. Now neoliberalism was replaced by "globalization," which argued that free trade and markets were inevitable and, in the 2000s, by discourse that there was no alternative to subjection to US "empire" (see Chapter 6).

Amid all this, development discourse petered out in a range of only apparently similar discourses—of "post-development" or of NGOs—or in esoteric reflections on the condition of various parts of the Third World. All of these discourses differ from development discourse in one critical respect: they posit no project and address no agent (see Chapter 4).

However, in the first decade of the twenty-first century, two developments were already in train to alter the landscape of development radically by the end of the decade. A small number of countries, pre-eminently China but also India, Brazil, and others, grew spectacularly. Post-Communist Russia stabilized under Vladimir Putin after a decade of neoliberal "shock therapy" (in reality, all shock and no therapy) under Boris Yeltsin. Double-digit growth rates in China were, in particular, the result of the central role of the Communist party-state in fostering development, and it was clearly possible precisely because that apparatus retained its policy autonomy from the power of the rich countries (see Chapter 13). Elsewhere, also, growth was the result of policies that were not neoliberal or were "insufficiently" neoliberal, which the more powerful states such as India or Russia or Brazil, able to stand up to US, World Bank, and IMF pressure, were able to follow. The demonstration effect on the rest of the Third World can hardly be understated. Second, and only slightly less important, many countries in Latin America, which had suffered some of the worst of the IMF/World Bank's bitter neoliberal medicine, began electing left-of-centre governments. These countries, where not just the poor but vast swaths of the middle classes had been adversely affected by neoliberalism, explicitly rejected it. By prioritizing the repayment of loans from the IMF and the World Bank over loans to private creditors, they regained the policy autonomy they had lost since the early 1980s and began to pursue progressive economic policies, not only to strengthen their economies but also to reorient them to serve the interests of the poor and hitherto marginalized. Development theory in the twenty-first century will be centrally about assimilating these experiences and drawing their lessons for the rest of the poor countries of the world.

Developmental States

As it seeks to do this, development theory will be greatly aided by a current within it that arose as a critique of neoliberalism but was marginalized by the latter's political power (Wade, 1996). While neoliberalism attempted to claim the development success of the Newly Industrializing Countries (NICs) for neoliberalism, new scholarship reaching back to nineteenth-century anti-free trade economists (such as Hamilton, List, and Carey, mentioned above) emphasized the role of government in these industrial success stories. The resulting literature on developmental states—states that consciously fostered more or less successful capitalist development, often benefiting sectors broader than the capitalist classes alone—was part of a veritable "Other Canon" (Reinert, 2007a, 2007b) of economic or development theory going back several centuries. Marginalized with the emergence of the free-market bias of economics in the nineteenth century, this "other canon" converged with the Marxist emphasis on the social relations of production, the political character of the states to which they give rise, the range of policy options available to such states, and the circumstances in which the more progressive options could be expected to be exercised (Bagchi, 2004, 2005). It also confirmed dependency theory, arguing that autonomy from the structures and practices of imperialism was crucial for development (Chang, 2002, 2010).

CONCLUSION: WHITHER DEVELOPMENT?

As the twenty-first century advances, the prospects for development theory look very different from what they were at its beginning. The Great Recession has discredited neoliberal faith in free markets and, insofar as it still lingers in the shape of "austerity" in the First World, it only accelerates the shift in the world economy's centre of gravity away from the stagnant rich countries and towards the fast-growing emerging economies. While their growth is hardly without problems, the obstacles to this growth, like its motors, were clearly more internal than external.

The gap in per capita incomes and material well-being between the rich and poor countries, even the most dynamic among them, remains large, but may not be endemic. Incomes are contingent on wage levels, and they in turn depend on the self-organization of labour. Industrialization in developing countries "has more often than not led to the emergence of strong, new labour movements . . . rather than an unambiguous 'race to the bottom' and the subsequent expansion of capital intensive, mass-production industries created new and militant working classes with significant disruptive power" (Arrighi, 2003: 36–7).

While "development" has proved disappointing in relation to the high hopes that launched it, the end of colonialism and the generalization of the nation-states system at least slowed income divergence among countries. In his important survey of world income inequality, Branko Milanovic concludes that population-weighted international inequality in per capita incomes in the pre- and post-1950 periods exhibited very different trends:

> The first was characterised by (i) strong divergence between countries, (ii) relative decline of populous countries, (iii) increasing

> inequality among world citizens, and (iv) decreasing within-country inequality. In the second period, after 1950, (i) the divergence among countries continued though at a slower pace, (ii) populous and poor countries started to catch up with the rich world, (iii) inequality among world citizens moved slightly up, and (iv) the overlap [between the poor of rich countries and the rich of poor countries], and perhaps within-country inequalities, increased again. In other words, the features (i) and (iii) continued, but at a slower pace, while the features (ii) and (iv) reversed. In effect, it is the reversal of feature (ii)—namely, the end of India's and China's falling behind the rich world—that causes the increase in the overlap component, as some part of poor countries' populations now "mingle" with people from rich countries. (Milanovic, 2005: 144)

This is the record of the whole period from 1950 to 2000, including the "lost decades" under neoliberalism. With growth slowing in the rich countries and accelerating in the emerging economies, and with the prospect that, learning the lessons of their development, even more poor countries will join their ranks, the *possibility* of faster progress on this front cannot be discounted. The record of populous India is revealing. The *most* significant break in India's twentieth-century growth record came following independence in 1947: India's economic growth rate in the first half of the twentieth century under colonialism has been estimated at between 0.8 and 1 per cent per annum, whereas in the second half, when India became independent, it was 4.2 per cent per annum (Nayyar, 2006: 1452–3).

Decolonization was central to the story of India's growth in the twentieth century. Surplus extracted from colonies such as India, indeed pre-eminently India, had contributed to the initial accumulation that

Paul Haslam

PHOTO 3.3 | Working on infrastructure for development: bridge construction in northeast Brazil.

led to the Industrial Revolution in Britain, and a century later, when Britain's industrial supremacy began to decline, this surplus had helped it to balance its payments against new rising manufacturing powers (see Arrighi, 2005; Patnaik, 2001, 2006). In India, the loss of surpluses, and the whole panoply of the practices of colonialism, had meant stagnation.

Even without their own colonies to exploit, the industrial capitalist development of the former colonial countries of the South was substantial prior to the twenty-first century, though admittedly the development of South Korea and Taiwan, the most successful up to that time, was due in substantial part to the compulsions of the Cold War that forced the US to grant these two states on the "front line" against Communism levels of aid, policy freedom, and access to US markets denied all other ex-colonial countries. Moreover, at worst, national independence—and the national economic management that went with it—has been a barrier to worsening inequality. With the ascendancy of neoliberalism broken, the merits of the dependency, Marxist, and "developmental state" theoretical currents in understanding and rectifying underdevelopment can now be tested.

SUMMARY

The post-war development project emerged amid the Cold War and decolonization but this project must be understood in the longer historical perspective of the rise of modern capitalism. Aspirations to development—universal human progress—were rooted in and denied by capitalist industrialization. Production increased dramatically, but it rested on injustice and anarchy. Colonialism, under which colonizers produced high-value goods and colonies produced low-value goods, was its geopolitical face. With decolonization, which began in the late 1940s, newly independent countries attempted to address these international and domestic inequalities under the rubric of the development project.

A succession of development theories articulated this endeavour. Early development theories emerged from the United States as it sought to increase its influence in the hitherto European-dominated global order and to counter Communism, while later theories, reflecting the experience of the developing world and the difficulties of development there, criticized them. However, for them all, industrialization was the main goal and, given the deep crises—two world wars and the Great Depression—that capitalism had just suffered, the nation-state, rather than the market, was to be the main agent of achieving it. In the 1950s, Keynesianism focused on state corrections for market crises; by the late 1950s, modernization theory focused on the alleged social defects of developing countries that prevented development; then, in the 1970s, dependency theory pointed to the maldistribution of economic power in world capitalism. It was only in the 1980s that neoliberalism radically rejected state intervention and promoted free markets uncritically, while contemporaneous post-development theories rejected the idea of development altogether. However, theorists of the developmental state continued and expanded on the centrality of the state in promoting industrial development. The emerging economics and geopolitics of the twenty-first century corroborate them, and point to the strengths of the dependency theorists of several decades earlier.

QUESTIONS FOR CRITICAL THOUGHT

1. How has the Great Recession of the twenty-first century changed the prospects for development?
2. Why is it important to think about development as something that began not after World War II but centuries earlier?
3. What is neoliberalism? How has it affected development?
4. What are the enduring contributions of dependency theory? What were its chief problems?
5. Do you think developmental states are the key to development's future? If we are moving towards a post-state future, who or what will be the agent of development?

SUGGESTED READINGS

Larrain, Jorge. 1989. *Theories of Development: Capitalism, Colonialism and Dependency.* London: Polity Press.

Leys, Colin. 1996. *The Rise and Fall of Development Theory.* Nairobi: EAEP; Bloomington: Indiana University Press.

Polanyi, Karl. 2004 [1944]. *The Great Transformation: The Political and Economic Origins of Our Time.* New York: Beacon Press.

Reinert, Erik S. 2007. *How Rich Countries Got Rich and Why Poor Countries Stay Poor.* London: Constable.

BIBLIOGRAPHY

Ahmad, A. 1992. "Three worlds theory." In A. Ahmad, *In Theory: Classes, Nations, Literatures.* London: Verso.

Arrighi, G. 2003. "The social and political economy of global turbulence." *New Left Review* 2, 20: 5–71.

———. 2005. "Hegemony unravelling" (1 and 2). *New Left Review* 2, 32: 23–80 and 2, 33: 83–116.

Bagchi, A.K. 2004. *The Developmental State in History and in the Twentieth Century.* New Delhi: Regency.

———. 2005. *Perilous Passage: Mankind and the Global Ascendancy of Capital.* Lanham, Md: Rowman & Littlefield.

Banaji, J. 1977. "Modes of production in a materialist conception of history." *Capital and Class* 3: 1–44.

Brenner, R. 1978. "The origins of capitalist development: A critique of neo-Smithian Marxism." *New Left Review* 1, 104 (Mar.–Apr.): 25–92.

Cammack, P. 1997. *Capitalism and Democracy in the Third World. The Doctrine for Political Development.* London: Leicester University Press.

Chang, H.-J. 2002. *Kicking Away the Ladder: Development Strategy in Historical Perspective.* London: Anthem Press.

———. 2010. *23 Things They Don't Tell You About Capitalism.* London: Allen Lane.

Desai, R. 2009. "Keynes redux: World money after the 2008 crisis." In W. Anthony and J. Guard, eds, *Bailouts and Bankruptcies.* Halifax: Fernwood Press.

———. 2010. "The consumption demand problem in Marx and in the current crisis." *Research in Political Economy* 26: 101–43.

———. 2013. *Geopolitical Economy: After US Hegemony, Globalization and Empire.* The Future of World Capitalism Series. London: Pluto.

Evans, P. 1979. *Dependent Development: The Alliance of Multinational, State and Local Capital in Brazil.* Princeton, NJ: Princeton University Press.

Freeman, A. 2004. "The inequality of nations." In A. Freeman and B. Kagarlitzky, eds, *The Politics of Empire.* London: Pluto.

George, S. 1988. *A Fate Worse Than Debt.* New York: Grove Press.

——— and Fabrizio Sabelli. 1994. *Faith and Credit.* Boulder, Colo.: Westview Press.

Gilman, N. 2003. *Mandarins of the Future: Modernization Theory in Cold War America.* Baltimore: Johns Hopkins University Press.

Göçmen, D. 2007. *The Adam Smith Problem: Reconciling Human Nature and Society in The Theory of Moral Sentiments and The Wealth of Nations.* London: Tauris Academic Studies.

Grinter, L. 1975. "How they lost: Doctrines, strategies and outcomes of the Vietnam War." *Asian Survey* 15: 12.

Hayter, T., and C. Watson. 1985. *Aid: Rhetoric and Reality.* Harmondsworth, UK: Penguin.

Hobsbawm, E. 1994. *Age of Extremes: The Short Twentieth Century, 1914–1991.* London: Viking.

Huntington, S. 1969. *Political Order in Changing Societies.* New Haven: Yale University Press.

Hymer, S. 1972. "The multinational corporation and the law of uneven development." In J. Bhagwati, ed., *Economics and the World Order from the 1970s to the 1990s.* New York: Collier-Macmillan.

Jomo, K.S., and E. Reinert, eds. 2005. *The Origins of Development Economics.* London: Zed Books.

Kitching, G. 1982. *Development and Underdevelopment in Historical Perspective: Populism, Nationalism and Industrialization.* London: Methuen.

Laclau, E. 1977. "Feudalism and capitalism in Latin America." In E. Laclau, *Politics and Ideology in Marxist Theory.* London: NLB.

Leys, C. 1996. *The Rise and Fall of Development Theory.* Oxford: James Currey.

Lipietz, A. 1982. "Marx or Rostow?" *New Left Review* 1, 132: 48–58.

Marx, K., and F. Engels. 1967 [1848]. *The Communist Manifesto.* London: Penguin.

Mayer, A. 1981. *The Persistence of the Old Regime: Europe to the Great War.* New York: Pantheon Books.

Nairn, T. 1981. "The modern Janus." In T. Nairn, *The Break-up of Britain*. London: Verso.

Nayyar, D. 2006. "Economic growth in independent India: Lumbering elephant or running tiger?" *Economic and Political Weekly* (15 Apr.): 1452–3.

O'Brien, C. 1971. "Modernization, order and the erosion of a democratic ideal." *Journal of Development Studies* 7: 141–60.

Palma, G. 1981. "Dependency and development: A critical overview." In D. Seers, ed., *Dependency Theory: A Critical Reassessment*. London: Frances Pinter.

Parsons, T. 1937. *The Structure of Social Action*. New York: McGraw-Hill.

Patnaik, P. 2001. "Imperialism and the diffusion of development: Text of the Ansari Memorial Lecture." 15 Mar. www.macroscan.org/anl/mar01/anl150301Imperialism_Diffusion_Development_1.htm.

Patnaik, U. 2006. "The free lunch: Transfers from the tropical colonies and their role in capital formation in Britain during the Industrial Revolution." In K.S. Jomo, ed., *Globalization under Hegemony: The Changing World Economy*. New Delhi: Oxford University Press.

Payer, C. 1991. *Lent and Lost: Foreign Credit and Third World Development*. London: Zed Books.

Polanyi, K. 1944. *The Great Transformation: The Political and Economic Origins of Our Time*. Boston: Beacon Press by arrangement with Rinehart and Co.

Reinert, E.S. 2007a. *How Rich Countries Got Rich and Why Poor Countries Stay Poor*. London: Constable.

———. 2007b. "The other canon." In E.S. Reinert, ed., *Globalization, Economic Development and Inequality: An Alternative Perspective*, paperback edn. Cheltenham, UK: Edward Elgar.

Ros, J. 2005. "The pioneers of development economics and modern growth theory." In K.S. Jomo and E. Reinert, eds, *Development Economics: How Schools of Economic Thought Have Addressed Development*. London: Zed Books.

Rosenstein-Rodan, P.N. 1961. *Notes on the Theory of the Big Push in H.S. Ellis and Henry C. Wallach, Economic Development for Latin America*. New York: St Martin's Press.

Smith, A. 1937 [1776]. *Wealth of Nations*. New York: Modern Library.

Teschke, B. 2003. *The Myth of 1648*. London: Verso.

Trotsky, L. 1934. *The History of the Russian Revolution*. London: Gollancz.

Wade, R.H. 1996. "Japan, the World Bank, and the art of paradigm maintenance: The East Asian miracle in political perspective." *New Left Review* 1, 217 (May–June): 3–36.

Wallerstein, I. 1974. *The Modern World System*. New York: Academic Press.

Warren, B. 1973. "Imperialism and capitalist industrialization." *New Left Review* 1, 81: 3–44.

———. 1980. *Imperialism: Pioneer of Capitalism*. London: New Left Books.

4 Post-Development and Alternatives to Development

Aram Ziai

LEARNING OBJECTIVES

- To understand why post-development differs from earlier critiques of development policy.
- To understand the concept of development discourse.
- To understand the main argument of post-development.
- To get to know examples of "alternatives to development."
- To distinguish between anti-development and post-development.
- To evaluate the criticisms raised towards post-development.

▲ **Roy Sesana, lead applicant and leader of the First People of the Kalahari celebrates, 13 December 2006, his victory and the right for his people to go back to the Central Kalahari game reserve after the final hearing and judgement of their case against the Botswana government at the High Court in Lobatse, Botswana.** | Source: GIANLUIGI GUERCIA/AFP/Getty Images

During the last two decades, a novel and controversial approach in development theory has been discussed that also has been increasingly accepted in the academic debate: the post-development school. Whereas earlier criticisms, such as the dependency school, had criticized development theory and policy usually with a view to devising a better theory and policy of development (e.g., Hayter, 1971), the post-development school explicitly refused to do so, engaging in destructive instead of constructive criticism. In its first landmark publication, Gustavo Esteva called development an "unburied corpse . . . from which every kind of pest has started to spread" (Esteva, 1992: 6). And Wolfgang Sachs (1992: 1), in the introduction to the volume, proclaimed that "[t]he idea of development stands like a ruin in the intellectual landscape" and that "the time is ripe to write its obituary." Post-development thus can be seen as a fundamental critique, one intended to lay to rest "development" and that called for "alternatives to development" instead of "**alternative development**" (Escobar, 1995: 215). In this chapter, we explore what the authors meant by that criticism and why they opposed the concept and practice of development so vehemently. First, we will deal with the historical origins of the approach before engaging a number of its central arguments and the alternatives it proposes. At the end of this chapter, we discuss some criticisms that have been raised in opposition to post-development and reflect on the importance of this school of thought.

THE ORIGINS OF POST-DEVELOPMENT

While the first post-development publications emerged in the 1980s (Esteva, 1985; Escobar, 1985; Rahnema, 1985; Rist and Sabelli, 1986; Latouche, 1986), the approach has been influenced by three other bodies of work: the writings of Ivan Illich, of Michel Foucault, and of anti-colonial writers like Mohandas Gandhi and Frantz Fanon. In order to better understand and contextualize the approach, a look at their arguments is useful. All of them unsettle the notion that "development" is a good thing and that the "less developed societies" should become "developed."

During the 1960s and 1970s, Ivan Illich (1970, 1997), an Austrian theologian, criticized the institutions of Western industrial modernity because they would teach people to be dependent: dependent on doctors for healing, dependent on the school for education, dependent on the church for faith and spirituality. Concerning development aid in Latin America, he argued that an understanding of progress as the spread of these institutions was counterproductive, because it produced needs that could not be fulfilled for the majority of the population (e.g., for Coca Cola, for advanced surgery, and for high school education) while neglecting goods and services more suited to their situation (e.g., vehicles that can handle rough terrain and can easily be repaired, clean water, healing assistants, communal storage, and public transport). In terms of technology, not only goods produced as commodities were problematic (i.e., those produced to be sold on the market for profit—a view common among socialists) but all goods that would come either with the price of dependency on experts or that could be provided only for a privileged minority. Development policy thus would result in damaging institutions over which people themselves have control, subjecting them increasingly to institutions that threatened their autonomy and produced poverty in the sense of unfulfilled needs and dependence. Illich outlined a politics of "conviviality," based on tools and institutions that enhance people's autonomy and self-help capacity without having these drawbacks (e.g., bicycles, phones, mail), as well as on restraint in energy consumption.

The writings of French philosopher and historian Michel Foucault were hardly concerned with issues of the Global South. In his most popular writings he deals with questions of knowledge and power, and with the construction of what counts as normal and true. He contends that what is accepted as true—even in the sciences—is dependent on the historical, social, and political contexts, on a "regime of truth" of this society and epoch. In this way he cautions us not to believe that what is currently seen as true and acceptable is irrespective of history and place: it may easily be seen as mad and monstrous in the next century—or in a different discourse. The concept of **discourse**, understood here as a system of representation linked to relations of power with consequences on behaviour, is explained well by post-colonial theorist Stuart Hall in Box 4.1. It is used by a number of post-development writers.

A third body of work influencing post-development is that of anti-colonial writers like Mohandas Gandhi

IMPORTANT CONCEPTS

BOX 4.1 | Stuart Hall on Discourse

A discourse is a group of statements which provide a language for talking about—i.e., a way of representing—a particular kind of knowledge about a topic. When statements about a topic are made within a particular discourse, the discourse makes it possible to construct the topic within a certain way. It also limits the other ways in which the topic can be constructed. . . . A discourse can be produced by many individuals in different institutional settings (like families, prisons, hospitals, and asylums). Its integrity or "coherence" does not depend on whether it issues from one place or from a single speaker or "subject." Nevertheless, every discourse constructs positions from which alone it makes sense. Anyone deploying a discourse must position themselves as if they were the subject of the discourse. For example, we may not ourselves believe in the natural superiority of the West. But if we use the discourse of "the West and the Rest" we will necessarily find ourselves speaking from a position that holds that the West is a superior civilization. . . . Foucault argues that statements about the social, political, or moral world are rarely ever simply true or false; and "the facts" do not enable us to decide definitively about their truth or falsehood, partly because "facts" can be construed in different ways. The very language we use to describe the so-called facts interferes in this process of finally deciding what is true and what is false. For example, Palestinians fighting to regain land on the West Bank from Israel may be described either as "freedom fighters" or as "terrorists." It is a fact that they are fighting: but what does the fighting mean? The facts alone cannot decide. And the very language we use—"freedom fighters/terrorists"—is part of the difficulty. Moreover, certain descriptions . . . can be made "true" because people act on them believing that they are true, and so their actions have real consequences. Whether the Palestinians are terrorists or not, if we think they are, and act on that "knowledge," they in effect become terrorists because we treat them as such. The language (discourse) has real effects in practice: the description becomes "true."

Source: Hall (1992: 201–3).

Photo by Clinton A. Hutton, PhD

PHOTO 4.1 | Stuart Hall.

and Frantz Fanon. Mohandas ("Mahatma") Gandhi, the icon of the non-violent Indian struggle for independence, perceived centralization, also political centralization through states, as inherently violent and advocated decentralized village republics (*swaraj*). For some post-development writers, Gandhi has been a source of inspiration not only because of this concept, but also because of his ideal of a "simple life." The latter is manifest in the quote that "Earth provides enough to satisfy every man's needs but not for every man's greed" (Gandhi, 1997: 306). He was generally critical of technological progress and concentration of wealth, yet not in principle but—like Illich—because only a fraction of humankind had access to them under the current system.

Frantz Fanon, a psychologist and physician from Martinique, also was engaged in anti-colonial struggle, but in contrast to Gandhi he was no advocate of non-violence—certainly not after he witnessed the horrors of the war waged by French colonizers in Algeria against the independence movement. However, he was wary about the new elites emerging out of the anti-colonial movements and warned that merely to take over the states from the colonizers would reproduce many problems. In the conclusion of his book *The Wretched of the Earth*, he thus called on Africans not to imitate Europe and not to be "obsessed with the desire to catch up with Europe" as the former colonies that became the United States had been, leading that country to become a "monster." He suggested following neither the ideal of productivism nor that of a return to nature, but proposed to the Third World "starting a new history of Man," not oblivious to Europe's crimes or its achievements (Fanon, 1961: 251ff.).

These influences led the post-development authors to strike a new chord in the critique of development theory and policy. They were not opposed to the dependency critique of the capitalist world system as articulated, for example, by Walter Rodney (2009), but for them it was not enough to criticize capitalism. The reason was that many of the features they criticized—the desire to catch up with Europe, the unquestioned pursuit of industrialization and growth, the rule of experts—could be found in the socialist countries as well, and even in the newly independent countries. Another novelty was the focus on knowledge and discourse in the post-development school. They decried not only the exploitation of the "underdeveloped" countries but also the very definition that they are "underdeveloped" and in need of "development," as if the "developed" countries could provide a universal model to be followed.

POST-DEVELOPMENT: CORE ARGUMENTS

Post-development is not a homogeneous school of thought and there are no membership passes, but some arguments can be encountered in the writings of a number of different authors in a similar manner. In the words of Escobar, post-development is characterized by the "rejection of the entire paradigm" of development, an "interest in local culture and knowledge; a critical stance towards established scientific discourses; and the defense and promotion of localized, pluralistic grassroots movements" (Escobar, 1995: 215). Beyond the authors already cited (Esteva, Escobar, Sachs, Rist, Latouche, and Rahnema), writers like Vandana Shiva (Mies and Shiva, 1993), Ashis Nandy (1988), and Claude Alvares (1992) are often associated with post-development, as is James Ferguson—although he probably would not subscribe to all arguments of the other post-development writers. In contrast, the volumes edited by Apffel-Marglin and Marglin (1990, 1996) and the work of anthropologist Helena Norberg-Hodge (2009) and of subsistence feminists Maria Mies, Veronika Bennholdt-Thomsen, and Claudia von Werlhof (Bennholdt-Thomsen and Mies, 1999) are rarely mentioned in this context, although there are striking parallels to post-development to be found among this group. In this section, we will get to know some of the central arguments of post-development.

The Invention of Development

Probably the most important intellectual move of post-development is to conceive of "development" as a discourse, a certain way of representing the world that can be historically situated and is closely related to relations of power. The historical context in which this discourse emerged was the imminent decolonization of large parts of Asia and Africa after World War II and at the beginning of the Cold War. Post-development writers claim that when US President Harry Truman, in his inaugural address on 20 January 1949 (see Box 1.1), announced a "program of development" for the "underdeveloped areas," he inaugurated the "development age" and promoted "a new way of conceiving international relations" (Rist, 2014: 71ff.). This "new way" replaced the hierarchies between colonizers and colonized with the seeming equality of trading partners in a global economy, one group of which (the "underdeveloped") lagged behind and were in need of assistance to catch up, which the "developed" generously granted.

Yet, the promise of prosperity given by Truman had not only (if at all) humanitarian purpose but also geopolitical motives: its thrust was to keep the countries in Africa and Asia, which were already in the process of becoming independent or were likely to become so during the next decade or two, from joining the growing Communist camp. This, the containment of world Communism, was the prime imperative of US foreign policy during the Cold War, and this is why Truman saw the poverty of these "underdeveloped areas" as a "threat, both to them and the more prosperous countries." Unlike the view of a world divided between exploiters and exploited, the new era's discourse of "development" allowed the US and the European colonial powers "to maintain their presence in the ex-colonies, in order to continue to exploit their natural resources, as well as to use them as markets for their expanding economies or as bases for their geopolitical ambitions" (Rahnema, 1997a: ix).

Esteva emphasizes another aspect of this new discourse when he writes that through this new discourse, a "new perception of one's own self, and of the other" was created: "two billion people became underdeveloped" (Esteva, 1992: 6ff.). By this, he does not mean that they were materially impoverished by Truman giving his speech, but that they were perceived—and

PHOTO 4.2 | Tuareg man making a camel saddle, Agadez, Niger.

increasingly perceived themselves—as poor in comparison to the industrial capitalist societies, not merely as having a different model of society: they were judged and found lacking according to the allegedly universal standards of the West.

> [T]hey ceased being what they were, in all their diversity, and were transmogrified into an inverted mirror of others' reality: a mirror that belittles them and sends them off to the end of the queue, a mirror that defines their identity, which is really that of a heterogeneous and diverse majority, simply in the terms of a homogenizing and narrow minority. (Esteva, 1992: 7)

That is, Tuareg nomads of the Sahara, Zapotec farmers in Oaxaca, and Adivasi hunter-gatherers are perceived first and foremost as underdeveloped—"not seen as living diverse and non-comparable ways of human existence, but as somehow lacking in terms of what has been achieved by the advanced countries" (Sachs, 1992: 3). Therefore, "development," catching up with the "developed," was seen—by Truman and development experts from the North, but also by national elites—as a goal that was necessary and desirable, even ineluctable, for these countries. A significant point (which leads us to the next argument) was that this diagnosis was based on comparative statistical measurements of gross national product and per capita income, which "proved" that living conditions in Third World countries were far below US standards—but of course this narrow economic perspective neglected many aspects of life (see Box 4.2).

In this perspective, the lack of money to buy goods and the lack of modern conveniences are conflated with a lack of basic necessities of life and identified with poverty, in the sense of an undignified condition that deserves compassion and helping. Wolfgang Sachs tells the story where in 1985 he was shown around the quarter of Tepito in Mexico City and his remark that the people were still terribly poor was countered with the stiff remark: "We are not poor, we are Tepitans!" (Sachs, 1990: 8). Apparently, the Tepitans were not willing to be degraded by the supposedly rich Westerner; they wanted to be seen for what they were, on their own terms. That people can learn to perceive themselves as poor is illustrated by another story, told by Helena Norberg-Hodge. When she first arrived in the village of Ladakh in Tibet, her inquiry about where the poor people lived produced perplexity among the Ladakhi she talked to: there were no poor people in the village. But this confident attitude changed through contact with tourists, development experts, and the media. Some years later, the same Ladakhi told a Western tourist: "If only you could do something for us, we are so poor" (Norberg-Hodge, 1997: 35).

Opposing Economics and Economization

In the eyes of post-development writers like Esteva, the development era reformulated the quest for a good life as the pursuit of material wealth and ever-growing production; economic growth was seen as the answer to the problems identified as underdevelopment. As economies of subsistence were not recognized as productive (although they supplied all means of sustenance for indigenous communities), the economist's view did not see a difference between poverty defined as lack of cash income to buy goods through the market (frugality) and poverty defined as inability to satisfy basic needs of food and shelter (destitution or deprivation). According to post-development, the former is not necessarily problematic, and the latter occurs only after people have been deprived of access to land and forest through the enclosure of the commons that accompanied the spread of capitalism since the colonial era, forcing people into wage labour (Rahnema, 1992, 1997; Shiva, 1989)—a mode of production associated by some indigenous peoples with a pact with the devil (Taussig, 2010). For Vandana Shiva, "development" was a process of capital accumulation that continued a process of colonization based on the exploitation of women's "non-productive" labour, a "new project of Western patriarchy" (1989: 1).

Esteva (1992) argues that this process entailed establishing economic value on the one hand (goods and services were now traded as commodities on the market), but devaluing all those resources, skills, and activities that were not or could not be sold on the market. By conveying the message that a lack of consumer goods prevents a dignified and happy life, advertising, Western media, and tourists succeeded in creating

IMPORTANT CONCEPTS

BOX 4.2 | A Critique of GDP

Gross national product and gross domestic product measure the value of all the goods and services sold on formal markets in one state during one year, the difference being that GDP counts what is produced by foreigners in the country while GNP does not but incorporates the values "produced" by citizens abroad. The increase in GNP/GDP is what is regarded as economic growth. Per capita income is calculated by dividing GDP by the number of residents. Critics point out that production leading to environmental pollution (e.g., an oil spill) or other destructive results (e.g., guns and bombs) boost GDP twice: through the production of negative goods and services and through goods and services that try to negate the damage caused by this production. Abstaining from destructive production does not boost the GDP, thus, destruction of nature appears as wealth creation. Goods lasting for decades contribute to the GDP, but goods breaking down quickly, needing fixing or replacement, do so much more. Other criticisms include that the informal sector and unpaid labour (especially by women) are not being measured and that distribution is entirely ignored. To this day, the World Bank continues to measure "development" through GDP. An alternative is the gross national happiness index (GNH), which combines indicators from nine domains: psychological well-being, time use, community vitality, cultural diversity, ecological resilience, living standard, health, education, and good governance. It was coined by the King of Bhutan, Jigme Singye Wangchuck, in 1972 and has attracted some criticisms in terms of methodology as well as because of the oppression of minorities in Bhutan (see Ekins and Max-Neef, 1992; grossnationalhappiness.com; happyplanetindex.org).

needs that could only be satisfied by commodities, enticing people to abandon their subsistence lifestyle, adopt wage labour, and trust the promise of "development" that one day all could live like the people in the West did (see also Norberg-Hodge, 2009). Esteva links this to the "law of scarcity" in economics textbooks, according to which "man's wants are great, not to say infinite, whereas his means are limited though improvable" (1992: 19). He denies the universal validity of this claim: voluntary frugality, sufficiency, and the rejection of the desire to have more cannot be processed within the prejudices of economists (see also Sachs, 1999: 16–19), which confuses "well-being" with "the quantity of gadgets" (Latouche, 1997: 139). Thus, Escobar sees economics not as a science but as a "cultural discourse," belonging to a certain historical period and producing certain truths that are far from universal (1995: 58ff.) but based on the assumption of rational, profit-maximizing individuals, which emerged during capitalist modernity. (For a description of this discourse, see Escobar, 1995: ch. 3.) The economist Serge Latouche agrees and maintains that the concept of this individual (the *homo economicus* who constantly pursues his/her interest) cannot account for the host of actions based on love, friendship, and solidarity, and that the "currently dominating accounting categories [see Box 4.2] represent a radical form of cultural imperialism" (Latouche, 1993: 110, 203).

Development as an Amoeba

Representatives of development theory and policy, when faced with this critique, usually admit that early modernization theories may be guilty of the economism described above, but that the debate has progressed a great deal since then. Post-development also takes note of these changes but interprets them differently. Esteva (1992: 12–17) records the history of redefinitions of development beyond the central idea of economic growth, from basic needs to endogenous development, from sustainable to human development, but maintains that despite this "conceptual inflation" the concept was

Dan Sears, UNC News Services

PHOTO 4.3 | Arturo Escobar.

still operationalized (not exclusively, but centrally) through GDP. Sachs points out that because of all these new definitions, "development became a shapeless amoeba-like word" (1999: 7). It can mean just about anything and take almost any form: the building of dams, the introduction of high-yielding varieties in agriculture, primary schooling for girls, biodiversity conversation, population control, structural adjustment—all of these projects (and many more) went under the label of development. "Development thus has no content but it does possess a function: it allows any intervention to be sanctified in the name of a higher evolutionary goal" (Sachs, 1999: 7).

Therefore, Escobar (1995: 42) argues: "although the discourse has gone through a series of structural changes, the architecture of the discursive formation laid down in 1945–55 has remained unchanged, allowing the discourse to adapt to new conditions." Beyond the two features described above, there is a third one described by Sachs (1999: 7) as follows: "Development always entails looking at other worlds in terms of what they lack, and obstructs the wealth of indigenous alternatives." Even the more progressive representatives of development discourse maintain that there are "developed" and "less developed" societies, that the former are to be found in the North and the latter in the South, and that the search for a solution to the latter's problems benefits from the knowledge of the former. One could say that the subject position of this discourse is that of a clinical gaze identifying deficits in the Other, attributing knowledge about the cure to the Self while ignoring the Other's knowledge. In this gaze, the North does not become the object of development interventions. So, according to post-development, the constant features of development are:

- the imperative of economic growth;
- the legitimation of intervention into societies defined as "less developed";
- based on the **Eurocentric** gaze of the "developed Self" and its attribution of problems and problem-solving knowledge;
- based on a universal scale according to which societies can be compared.

The Anti-Politics Machine

Another feature of development discourse has been claimed by James Ferguson (and also by Arturo Escobar), namely, that it depoliticizes questions of inequality. To understand this claim, we have to briefly recapitulate some of the findings of Ferguson's work on an integrated rural development project in Lesotho (Ferguson, 1994). In his study, Ferguson documents and analyzes the failure of this project to reduce poverty in the district of Thaba-Tseka through measures designed to raise agricultural productivity. One major reason for this failure was that the target group was misperceived by the development organization as cattle farmers, while they were primarily migrant labourers in South African mines (who also owned cattle). The misperception is explained by Ferguson through a bias in development discourse deriving from the institutional necessities of development organizations: in order to be able to offer meaningful solutions for the problem of poverty in "developing" countries, they construct the problem in such a way that it can be

CRITICAL ISSUES

BOX 4.3 | Ferguson on the Structural Limitations of Development Discourse

An academic analysis is of no use to a "development" agency unless it provides a place for the agency to plug itself in, unless it provides a charter for the sort of intervention that the agency is set up to do. An analysis which suggests that the causes of poverty in Lesotho are political and structural (not technical and geographical), that the national government is part of the problem (not a neutral instrument for its solution), and that meaningful change can only come through revolutionary social transformation in South Africa has no place in "development" discourse simply because "development" agencies are not in the business of promoting political realignments or supporting revolutionary struggles. . . . For an analysis to meet the needs of "development" institutions, it must do what academic discourse inevitably fails to do; it must make Lesotho out to be an enormously promising candidate for the only sort of intervention a "development" agency is capable of launching: the apolitical, technical "development" intervention. (Ferguson, 1994: 68ff.)

solved through development projects, i.e., technocratic, apolitical interventions (see Box 4.3).

The unwillingness of development experts to abandon this discourse becomes visible in the following anecdote narrated by Ferguson: "After the failure of the Thaba-Tseka project, one of the experts asked what his country could do to 'help these people'. 'When I suggested that his government might contemplate sanctions against apartheid, he replied, with predictable irritation, 'No, no! I mean development!' The only advice in question here is advice about how to 'do development' better" (Ferguson, 1994: 284). However, while development organizations thus try to avoid politics, they are caught up in it all the time—if only because they are co-operating with some groups in the country (usually the government) and organizing a transfer of resources. In the Thaba-Tseka project, the transfer of resources and the recruitment for jobs took place through Village Development Committees, which were in fact front organizations of the ruling National Party. The suggestion to refuse co-operation with these committees was countered with the statement that the development organization could not afford to get involved with politics. Sabotage of the project was attributed by ruling party representatives to "enemies of development," which led an observer to comment that politics was nicknamed "development" nowadays (Ferguson, 1994: 244–7).

So, on the one hand, development discourse, according to Ferguson, tends to ignore the political dimension of problems, i.e., the conflicts and struggles between different social and economic groups in a country, because "development" is assumed to benefit the whole country and is a technical problem. "By uncompromisingly reducing poverty to a technical problem, and by promising technical solutions to the sufferings of the powerless and oppressed people, the hegemonic problematic of 'development' is the principal means through which the question of poverty is de-politicized in the world today" (Ferguson, 1994: 256). On the other hand, the apparatus of "development" interferes in these conflicts and struggles, expanding bureaucratic state power (or, one has to add, the reach of multinational corporations) and thus performing political operations without designating them as such. This is why Ferguson concludes that this apparatus effectively functions as an "anti-politics machine" (Ferguson, 1994: 256).

Two decades after Ferguson's research, Tanya Murray Li (2007) conducted a similarly rich and detailed study of an integrated development project in Central Sulawesi, Indonesia, and arrived at very similar conclusions. Li illustrates that in neglecting political-economic causes of poverty and reframing social and environmental problems "in terms amenable to a technical solution" (2007: 126), the project was bound to fail. Just like in Lesotho, she found that "findings suggesting that 'the government' is not dedicated to the public good cannot be processed by the development machine" (134). Enhancing Ferguson's view, which hardly took into account the neoliberal counter-revolution in development theory and policy that occurred since the 1980s, Li finds that "[c]apitalist enterprise and the search for profit appeared in the [development organization's] narratives only as a solution to poverty, not as a cause" (267). She identifies three "crucial limitations" still prevalent in contemporary development interventions (even those emphasizing participation and empowerment): the assumptions that "the state apparatus . . . can be made to operate . . . in the public interest"; the ignorance towards the power relation implicit in the self-positioning as experts "with the power to diagnose and correct a deficit . . . in someone else"; and the continuous exclusion of "structural sources of inequality" (275). **Depoliticization** of poverty and blindness towards relations of power can thus be added as another feature of development discourse in the perspective of post-development.

The End of Development

The name of post-development derives from two different claims: beyond the normative claim that we should overcome the discourse and practices of "development" there is the empirical claim that the era of "development" is ending. Sachs (1992: 2–4) gives the following reasons for this diagnosis:

1. The assumption of the superiority of industrialized countries has been "shattered by the ecological predicament," by the recognition that their productivity is based on patterns of resource consumption and environmental destruction that are not sustainable and can only be upheld if they remain the privilege of a minority. Therefore, such "productivity" would be an aberration rather than a model, and the pursuit of economic growth is "leading towards an abyss."
2. After the end of the Cold War, the geopolitical constellation that gave rise to the concept of development and the practice of aid no longer exists and the project therefore is "bound to lose ideological steam and to remain without political fuel": the promise of universal material well-being and "industrial paradise" will be given up.
3. The whole project appeared as a "blunder of planetary proportions" because the gap between rich and poor countries had been growing ever wider during the era of "development," on the one hand. And on the other hand, while the traditional ways of subsistence and making a living have been smashed by colonialism and industrial capitalism, the new ways are not viable for a large part of the population in the South.
4. More and more people realize that "development's hidden agenda was nothing else than the Westernization of the world," leading to a loss of cultural diversity and a global monoculture.

The last two points are significant because the post-development authors claim they are not acting as a theoretical avant-garde, but are merely describing processes that take place in grassroots movements and local communities.

In a new edition of his book, Sachs (2010) has reflected on these hypotheses in the light of global change since the first edition. He states that for a number of people in the Global South, the promise of "development" has indeed come true, leading to the formation of a global middle class strongly defending it (2010: vii), but that the underside of this economic growth has been displacement and dispossession of the poor, increased polarization, and increased pollution (ix). Writing at a time where the threat of climate change is obvious, Sachs argues that delinking the desire for equity from economic growth (and linking it to new notions of well-being) and achieving a transition from economies based on fossil-fuel resources (and towards economies based on renewable resources) are the cornerstones of the post-development age (xii).

ALTERNATIVES TO DEVELOPMENT

Esteva claims that because of the exclusion produced by the project of "development," ordinary men and women would recover "their own definition of needs" as well as "autonomous ways of living" (1992: 21). They would be creating alternatives to "development." According to the post-development school, "alternative development" is not enough, because it reproduces the idea that the majority of the world's population is "underdeveloped" and needs to live like the West does. In other words, it merely seeks alternative ways to the same goal: "development," understood as a way of life similar to that of the modern industrial societies. In contrast to that, post-development identifies "alternatives to development" in grassroots movements and communities reclaiming their lives in different spheres: reclaiming politics vis-à-vis the state, reclaiming the economy vis-à-vis capitalism, and reclaiming knowledge vis-à-vis science. In all these spheres, Western models were universalized during the eras of colonialism and "development," but those excluded by these models have turned to alternatives, according to post-development authors.

Various social movements have been referred to by post-development authors, such as the Chipko movement of Indian women struggling against the destruction of forest ecosystems (Shiva, 1989) and the Process of Black Communities in Colombia defending their way of life, their territory, and their identity against capitalist corporations and socialist guerrillas alike (Escobar, 2008). Yet the social movement cited most often as an alternative to development is probably that of the Mexican Zapatistas, which will be described in the next subsection.

However, a closer look reveals that in many other countries we find concepts that reject the self-description of modern industrial capitalism as superior, assert non-Western cultural identities, and articulate different values and world views, concepts, therefore, that are closely connected to post-development (Dinerstein and Deneulin, 2012). The concept of ***buen vivir***, rooted in Andean indigenous cosmology, has become famous during the last decade, in particular after it was adopted by the governments of Ecuador and Bolivia (see Box 4.4). In many African societies, the philosophy of Ubuntu, which stresses the interconnectedness of human beings, can also be seen as one of these concepts. It derives from the Xhosa phrase "*Ubuntu ungamntungabanyeabantu*," which means "A person is a person through other persons" (Murithi, 2006: 28). In Iran, the concept of Gharbzadegi ("Occidentosis") was popular during the 1970s, promoted by intellectuals like Ale-e Ahmad and Ali Shariati (Mahmoodi and Zeiny Jelodar, 2011), and has become something like an implicit state doctrine after the Islamic Revolution in 1979. It reminds us that post-development concepts can also be abused—or simply used—by conservative forces.

Post-Development in Mexico

On 1 January 1994, a rag-tag army of mostly indigenous soldiers calling itself the Zapatista Army of National Liberation (Ejército Zapatista de Liberación Nacional, EZLN) occupied seven towns in the southeastern Mexican state of Chiapas and declared themselves to be insurgent and at war with the Mexican government. Demanding democracy, freedom, and justice, they claimed that violence was their last resort after a long history of discrimination and exclusion. After public pressure arising from sympathy with the insurgents and their demands had halted the ensuing military response by the government, the EZLN entered into negotiations that finally resulted in the San Andrés Accords (not adhered to by the government) and in an uneasy truce constantly threatened by low-intensity warfare. Yet the Zapatista insurgents have successfully upheld their autonomy from the Mexican government since then. During this period, they have captured the attention of a left-leaning public not only with their eloquent and poetic communiqués, but through their slogans manifesting a more modest and less self-assured revolutionary spirit ("A world of many worlds"; "questioning, we proceed"; "all for all, nothing for us"; "we don't need to conquer the world. It is enough to remake it"; "we walk at the pace of the slowest") they have been an inspiration for many groups active in the global protest movement since the 1990s (Muñoz Ramírez, 2003; Kerkeling, 2006; Esteva, 2013).

However, what renders them interesting for this chapter is that the principles guiding their autonomous municipalities resonate clearly with some of post-development's characteristics. Esteva (2013) claims they have successfully "reclaimed their commons" and are living "according to their own ways" "outside the logic" of capitalism and the state, and have managed to improve their living conditions "without receiving or accepting funds from the national government." How does that look on the ground? Do the Zapatistas really reclaim politics, the economy, and knowledge, as post-development proponents envision? Based on Esteva and Prakash (1998), Muñoz Ramírez (2003), Kerkeling (2006), Esteva (2013), and Gilgenbach and Moser (2013), the following can be said.

The political system of the around 200,000 Zapatistas living in about 1,000 communities (which form

IMPORTANT CONCEPTS

BOX 4.4 | *Buen Vivir*

There is no single concept of *buen vivir*, but many similar ideas expressed by different indigenous communities gained prominence under this label in the early 2000s. Most notable among these are "*sumakkawsay*," the Kichwa expression for "fullness of life" in a community, in Ecuador, and "*sumaqamaña*," a related Aymara concept, in Bolivia. Leaving aside particularities, *buen vivir* denotes a good life, which can only take place in community with other persons and nature. The indigenous cosmology, which includes a spiritual dimension and sees nature not as dead matter, but as "mother earth" (*pachamama*) and a subject of rights, is of central importance. According to Eduardo Gudynas (2011: 445), the concept promotes the "dissolution of the Society–Nature dualism."

Concerning the paradigm of development, Gudynas (2011: 445) sees *buen vivir* as "a replacement of the very idea of development." Acosta (2009: 219) stresses that it does not include the ideas of social evolution and an "underdevelopment" that has to be overcome, and Walsh (2010: 17) points out that "the very idea of development itself is a concept and word that does not exist in the cosmovisions, conceptual categories, and languages of indigenous communities." Further, the relationship to nature of *buen vivir* is entirely incompatible with the idea that nature has to be conquered and governed (Bacon's "*natura parendi vincitur*"), which is at the root of Western science and in turn constitutes the foundation of development thinking (Bajaj, 1988).

The growing influence of indigenous movements in Ecuador and Bolivia has led to the incorporation of *buen vivir* into the constitutions of these two states in 2008 and 2009, respectively, as well as to the explicit recognition of the rights of nature (Ecuador) and the plurinationality of the state (Bolivia). However, there are heated controversies regarding the extent to which the concept is actually followed in everyday politics in both countries, especially visible in the Yasuní–ITT case. The Yasuní Ishpingo Tambococha Tiputini Initiative, launched by the Ecuadorian government in collaboration with the UN Development Program, had the objective of abstaining from the extraction of oil in the Yasuní biosphere reserve in exchange for compensation payments by the international community. After the international community of states was not willing to finance the initiative at a sufficient level, the Ecuadorian government announced its plans to drill for oil in 2013, provoking accusations that it used the concept of *buen vivir* as window dressing for its extractivist policies (Guardiola and García-Quero, 2014).

over 100 municipalities, which in turn form five caracoles) is based on grassroots democracy, equal participation in decision-making of all members, and the principle of subsidiarity, i.e., the villages decide autonomously on most issues. Elected representatives have an imperative mandate and can be stripped of office at any time, and they are supposed to "govern through obeying" (the people) (see Photo 4.4). Political offices are for the most part unremunerated (merely, the person's fields are tilled by other villagers) and rotating. The most important political bodies beyond the community councils are the councils of delegates from the municipalities ("*Juntas de buengobierno*"—councils of good government). Despite a women's law and attempts to outlaw discrimination of women, their participation in the political system is perceived as insufficient. A tax law decrees that 10 per cent of any financial support that communities receive through development projects has to be given to another one without such support. There is no police force, alcohol and drugs are banned, and norm violation is sanctioned with warnings, advice, and support, and later, also, with community work. Domestic violence has been largely eliminated.

A large part of the Zapatista economy is based on collective forms of ownership and production. Work on the land has provided livelihoods for many thousands of poor (mostly indigenous) peasants. But next to subsistence production (guaranteeing some degree of autonomy), there is also production for the world market, e.g., fair trade coffee. In the production for the market, volatile prices, middlemen, and pressure on prices through competition are enumerated as problems, but monetary income is seen as precious by many. Self-organized production structures can also contribute to processes of empowerment, as is the case with artisanal women's co-operatives. On the other hand, no state subsidies are accepted in order to maintain independence from the "bad government."

In the field of knowledge, there have been attempts to recover practices of traditional medicine based on a holistic model. Midwives and herbal women (and a few men), the *promotores de herbolaría*, are passing on to the next generation the knowledge that was suppressed during the eras of colonialism and development. Yet "ordinary" physicians also are part of the health system, and their methods and instruments prove to be very useful, according to the midwives and health promoters, especially regarding surgery. So, just like in the other areas, there is a hybrid of traditional and modern practices.

Hajor/Wikimedia

PHOTO 4.4 | Top sign: "You are in Zapatista rebel territory. Here the people command and the government obeys." Bottom sign: "North Zone. Council of Good Government. Trafficking in weapons, planting and use of drugs, alcoholic beverages, and illegal sales of wood are strictly prohibited. No to the destruction of nature."

Post-Development in Germany?

If we take seriously post-development's demand to avoid the Eurocentric gaze, which sees problems in the South and problem-solving knowledge in the North, we should also look for "alternatives to development" in Europe and North America. The example of debates and practices in Germany based on the rejection of the current model of society can show us that maybe it is imprecise to talk about the Western model of society when we talk about a capitalist economy, state-based polity, and positivist universal science, because there is some degree of dissatisfaction with it in the West. It is more precise to talk about the hegemonic model. This model is rejected in some theoretical debates as well as in some practices that exhibit clear parallels to post-development.

Concerning the theoretical debates, there have been those inspired by Ivan Illich in the 1970s, but especially the subsistence feminism of Bennholdt-Thomsen, Mies, and Werlhof has to be mentioned here (Bennholdt-Thomsen and Mies, 1999). This standpoint envisions opting out of global capitalism and patriarchy by "returning to the soil" and living closer to nature. Leftists inspired by but dissatisfied with this approach because it evaded the system instead of confronting it—and because they found some modern technologies very useful (or were too lazy to engage in subsistence agriculture)—came up with a new concept entitled "Undeveloping the North." It entails an end to the oligarchic lifestyle based on the appropriation of cheap labour and resources from the South (what

Brand [2013] calls the "imperial way of living"), the prevention of military intervention, the downscaling of technology insofar as it is based on exploitative forms of production, and the appropriation of spaces needed for survival and regional autonomy (Spehr, 1996: 209–37). More recently, the debate about **degrowth** has become prominent (e.g., Paech, 2012), yet the concept comes in radical, liberal, and conservative variants.

Regarding alternatives to the current political system, there still is a small anarchist community in Germany. But even beyond that, the political culture in the radical left is strongly influenced by ideas of local autonomy and direct democracy. Decision-making in political groups and camps is often based on consensus in order to minimize domination, even in the name of the majority. Acts of civil disobedience in the context of protest against nuclear transports, coal mining, or infrastructure projects like the Stuttgart train station renewal are a recurring feature. In the latter case, participation extended far beyond the radical left groups.

In the area of the economy, an estimated 2,000 people still are living in communes, and a far higher and increasing number of people engage in community-supported agriculture, local exchange and trading systems, give-away shops, and similar initiatives (Habermann, 2013).

In the area of knowledge, it seems difficult at first to find people in Germany rejecting the system of science, but if we add up all those interested in (among others) esotericism, mysticism, new age spirituality, spiritual healing, hypnosis, acupuncture, Ayurvedic and other alternative medicine, the figure may become more impressive.

DEBATING POST-DEVELOPMENT

Since its rise to prominence during the 1990s, the post-development school has been widely and controversially discussed. In this last section, some of the criticisms raised against it will be discussed, as well as responses by post-development authors and the distinction between anti- and post-development. In the end, two different readings and positions towards the approach are sketched.

"The Last Refuge of the Noble Savage": Criticisms of Post-Development

A frequent critique is that post-development romanticizes the grassroots movements and local communities in the South in two respects: On the one hand, it neglects relations of domination and exploitation within these movements and communities, in particular but not exclusively of women. On the other hand, it assumes that the people in these communities were not interested in accumulation and Westernization—projecting the romantic image of the "noble savage" onto them (Kiely, 1999: 44).

Another critique claims that while post-development overlooks the negative features of traditional subsistence societies, it ignores the huge achievements of modernity and "development." Corbridge (1998: 144ff.) argues that the progress achieved in terms of significant improvement in life expectancy, for example, is based precisely on what post-development criticizes: the diffusion of Western models of society across the globe, including science and the growth of productivity. Therefore, to simply declare the "failure" of the "development project" was entirely inappropriate.

According to Nederveen Pieterse (1998: 363), there are methodological deficits at the base of these points: instead of looking at differences and discontinuities, post-development authors constructed a monolithic development discourse impervious to more nuanced constellations. One of these constellations is described by Cooper (1997: 84) as follows:

> Much as one can read the universalism of development discourse as a form of European particularism imposed abroad, it could also be read . . . as a rejection of the fundamental premises of colonial rule, a firm assertion of people of all races to participate in global politics and lay claim to a globally defined standard of living.

Meera Nanda (1999: 11) adds another point: the high value attributed to tradition and cultural identity leads to cultural relativism, i.e., to the belief that cultures exist separately and no culture can be judged from the outside. This would allow elites in the South to glorify the defence of their traditional privileges against modern claims and practices (e.g., human rights) as an act of anti-imperialism, sidelining political and economic conflicts within the country by pointing at alleged cultural conflicts and blaming the West.

In the literature, it has been remarked that the criticisms are valid for some post-development texts, but not for others. Consequently, we actually have to differentiate between approaches. Some scholars have advocated the rejection of modernity and the return to subsistence agriculture, and regard cultural difference as central and cultures as static (designated as anti-development approaches by Hoogvelt [2001] and as neo-populist post-development by Ziai [2004]). The perspective of others' approaches (genuine or skeptical post-development, respectively) is summed up as follows: "The idea, then, in spite of 'development,' is to organize and invent new ways of life—between modernization, with its sufferings but also some advantages, and a tradition from which people may derive inspiration while knowing it can never be revived" (Rist, 1997: 244). Table 4.1 outlines these important differences.

"Slaying the Development Monster": Responses to the Criticisms

Although post-development authors like Rist (2012: 273), Sachs (2009: vi), and Escobar (2012: vii) concede that their proclamation about the end of the era of "development" was premature, they reaffirm the necessity of performing a "decolonization of the imagination" (Sachs, 2010: ix).

Responding to the criticism that post-development had presented "development" as monolithic while in fact it was heterogeneous and contested, Escobar concedes that the critics were right. But, he continues, they "fail to acknowledge . . . that their own project of analyzing the contestation of development on the ground was in great part made possible by the deconstruction of development discourse" (Escobar, 2000: 12). Post-development's project had been to "slay the development monster," i.e., to break the consensus about "development" being necessary, self-evident, positive, and unquestionable and thus pave the way for more nuanced analyses. Romanticization, however, was an accusation used against any and all visions of societies that transcend the current model (Escobar, 2000: 13).

Sachs (2010: viii) also engages with the idea of contestation and admits:

> we had not really appreciated the extent to which the development idea has been charged with hopes for redress and self-affirmation. It certainly was an invention of the West, as we showed at length, but not just an imposition on the rest. On the contrary, as the desire for recognition and equity is framed in terms of the civilizational model of the powerful nations, the South has emerged as the staunchest defender of development.

This resonates with Cooper's criticism, mentioned above, concerning the discourse of "development" that could also (!) be read as a discourse of rights.

Another interesting response comes from Rist, who engages with the criticism of cultural relativism

TABLE 4.1 | Anti-Development and Post-Development

Anti-Development	Post-Development
Rejection of Western modernity	Some elements of modernity can be useful; hybridization of modernity and tradition
Return to subsistence agriculture	Different (also Western) lifestyles possible; no universal blueprint
Valorization of cultural traditions	Cultural traditions not necessarily superior to the West
Culture as static	Culture as dynamic; constructivist view of culture

Sources: Hoogvelt (2001); Ziai (2004).

and supporting groups who disrespect human rights. He argues:

> It may well be true that certain movements which oppose "development" have scant regard for certain articles in the Declaration of Human Rights; or that they force boys to look after goats instead of going to school; or that, as in the case of our grandmothers in Europe, they do not allow women to go out of the house "bareheaded." Nevertheless, if respect for the values linked to modernity is the only criterion for judging the social order, what should be said of our own society, which amid general indifference is increasing the numbers of those excluded in the name of economic growth? And what of the wars that cause countless victims, especially civilians, in the name of democracy and human rights? (Rist, 2012: 276)

The argument can be interpreted, of course, as countering the accusation of abusive practices in one group with a reference to abusive practices in some other group—not an entirely convincing argument. However, it could also be interpreted not as indifference towards abusive practices, but as a refusal to attribute these practices to the non-Western Other while exempting the Western Self, a stance that allows us to affirm our "civilizational superiority."

CONCLUSION: TWO POSITIONS

Post-development has been criticized vehemently by representatives of development theory and policy. This may have to do with the implication of post-development that the whole discipline is Eurocentric and blind to the relations of power inherent in its categorizations.

Today, even the most ardent academic critics of post-development, such as Corbridge or Nederveen Pieterse, have implicitly adopted post-development arguments concerning the Eurocentrism of development discourse and the relations of power constituting it (Ziai, 2015). But even if one subscribes to the arguments about the invention of "development," the "amoeba," or the "anti-politics machine," one can still easily reject the call for "alternatives to development" and side with Corbridge that the achievements of the project of "development" must not be underestimated—nothing less than the number of dying children is at hand, and few would doubt that modern medicine can provide significant advances in this issue. Opposing this view, post-development authors (e.g., Rahnema, 1992) have pointed towards the difference between frugality and destitution: in subsistence communities not sabotaged by the expansion of global capitalism there is (or rather was) a lack of money but all basic needs are provided for. And DuBois (1991) has argued that even in successful development projects, which result in improvements in health or productivity of the target population, relations of power are involved that create social group hierarchies and establish the superiority of one and the inferiority of the other culture. Apffel-Marglin (1990) has vividly described the violence of the vaccination squads in India in their crusade against smallpox and the fervour with which the (Indian!) modernizers tried to replace the old, "superstitious" medical practices with new "scientific" and only slightly more effective ones. Yet, is the preservation of culture worth human lives? One could easily consider relations of power the lesser evil. On the other hand, can the destruction of subsistence and dignity be compensated for by a more modern health system that allows us to live a little bit longer? Is the quantity of life always more important than the quality? These are ethical—and maybe even political—questions to which no universally valid answer can be given. And to give the answer in someone else's stead is to lay claim to a powerful form of knowledge. Here lies the contribution of post-development: it has lucidly pointed not only to the Eurocentrism but especially to the relations of power involved in development discourse and practice, as well as to the resistance and alternatives of those no longer willing to be classified and governed in the name of "development." It suggests that we look at global inequality using different concepts.

SUMMARY

This chapter has presented the post-development approach to development theory and policy. It is characterized as a fundamental critique that questions the very categories and objectives of the discipline. After outlining the origins of the school in Illich and Foucault, the chapter has dealt with post-development's central arguments: the invention of "development," how the concept evolved into an "amoeba" and functions like an "anti-politics machine," what is problematic about conventional economics, and why the era of "development" is ending. We also encountered some of the "alternatives to development" in the North as well as in the South and learned that there are numerous, different post-development concepts to be found in various contexts. Finally, we engaged the criticism that has been raised against post-development (among other issues, concerning the romanticization of subsistence communities and cultural relativism), as well as the response given by post-development authors. Summarizing, post-development does not provide an explanation of global inequality like other development theories, but it has revealed the Eurocentrism and relations of power implicit in the concept of "development."

QUESTIONS FOR CRITICAL THOUGHT

1. Do you find the post-development arguments convincing? Which ones?
2. Do you agree that the era of "development" is ending? Or that it should be?
3. According to Ferguson, how does the "anti-politics machine" work?
4. What would be the consequence of a post-development position for practical politics?
5. What do you think of the criticisms raised against post-development?
6. Which of the two positions outlined in the conclusion would you take? Or is there a third one?
7. Which other concepts could be used to describe and analyze situations of global socio-economic inequality?

SUGGESTED READINGS

Escobar, Arturo. 1995. *Encountering Development: The Making and Unmaking of the Third World*, 2nd edn. Princeton, NJ: Princeton University Press.

Ferguson, James. 1994. *The Anti-Politics Machine: "Development," Depoliticization and Bureaucratic Power in Lesotho*. Minneapolis: University of Minnesota Press.

Nandy, Ashis, ed. 1988. *Science, Hegemony and Violence: A Requiem for Modernity*. Tokyo: Oxford University Press.

Rahnema, Majid, with Victoria Bawtree, eds. 1997. *The Post-Development Reader*. London: Zed Books.

Rist, Gilbert. 2012. *The History of Development. From Western Origins to Global Faith*, 4th edn. London: Zed Books.

Sachs, Wolfgang, ed. 2010: *The Development Dictionary: A Guide to Knowledge as Power*, 2nd edn. London: Zed Books.

Ziai, Aram, ed. 2007. *Exploring Post-Development: Theory and Practice, Problems and Perspectives*. London: Routledge.

BIBLIOGRAPHY

Acosta, A. 2009. "Das 'Buen Vivir.' Die Schaffungeiner Utopie." *Juridikum* 4: 219–23.

Alvares, C. 1992. *Science, Development and Violence: The Revolt against Modernity*. Delhi: Oxford University Press.

Apffel-Marglin, F. 1990. "Smallpox in two systems of knowledge." In Apffel-Marglin and Marglin (1990: 102–44).

—— and S. Marglin, eds. 1990. *Dominating Knowledge: Development, Culture and Resistance*. Oxford: Clarendon.

——— and ———, eds. 1996. *Decolonizing Knowledge. From Development to Dialogue.* Oxford: Clarendon.

Bajaj, J.K. 1988. "Francis Bacon, the first philosopher of modern science: A non-Western view." In Nandy (1988: 24–67).

Bennholdt-Thomsen, V., and M. Mies. 1999. *The Subsistence Perspective: Beyond the Globalised Economy.* London: Zed Books.

Brand, U. 2013. "Green economy and green capitalism: Some theoretical considerations." Paper for the 8th Pan-European Conference on International Relations. Warsaw, 18–21 Sept. www.eisa-net.org/be-bruga/eisa/files/events/warsaw2013/SGIR_TA41-1_BRAND.pdf . Accessed 18 July 2015.

Cooper, F. 1997. "Modernising bureaucrats, backward Africans, and the development concept." In F. Cooper and R. Packard, eds, *International Development and the Social Sciences: Essays on the History and Politics of Knowledge.* Berkeley: University of California Press, 64–92.

Corbridge, S. 1998. "'Beneath the pavement only soil': The poverty of post-development." *Journal of Development Studies* 34, 6: 138–48.

Dinerstein, A.C., and S. Deneulin. 2012: "Hope movements: Naming mobilization in a post-development world." *Development and Change* 43, 2: 585–602.

DuBois, M. 1991. "The governance of the Third World: A Foucauldian perspective on power relations in development." *Alternatives* 16, 1: 1–30.

Ekins, P., and M. Max-Neef. 1992. *Real-Life Economics: Understanding Wealth Creation.* London: Routledge.

Escobar, A. 1985. "Discourse and power in development: Michel Foucault and the relevance of his work to the Third World." *Alternatives* 10: 377–400.

———. 1995. *Encountering Development: The Making and Unmaking of the Third World*, 2nd edn. Princeton, NJ: Princeton University Press.

———. 2008. *Territories of Difference: Place, Movements, Life, Redes.* Durham, NC: Duke University Press.

Esteva, G. 1985. "Development: Metaphor, myth, threat." *Development: Seeds of Change* 3: 78–9.

———. 1992. "Development." In Sachs (1992: 6–25).

———. 2013. "New forms of revolution (part 1): The Lacandona Commune."http://upsidedownworld.org/main/mexico-archives-79/4620-new-forms-of-revolution-part-1-the-lacandona-commune. Accessed 15 July 2015.

——— and M.S. Prakash. 1998. *Grassroots Post-Modernism: Remaking the Soil of Cultures.* London: Zed Books.

Fanon, F. 1963 (1961). *The Wretched of the Earth.* New York: Grove Press.

Ferguson, J. 1994 (1990). *The Anti-Politics Machine: "Development," Depoliticization, and Bureaucratic Power in Lesotho.* Minneapolis: University of Minnesota Press.

Gandhi, M. 1997. "The quest for simplicity: My idea of swaraj." In Rahnema with Bawtree (1997: 306–7).

Gilgenbach, D., and B. Moser. 2013. "Lieber autonom als entwickelt? Zapatistische Autonomie als empirische Stütze des Post-Development?" *Journal für Entwicklungspolitik* 28, 4: 8–29.

Guardiola, J., and F. García-Quero. 2014. "Nature and buen vivir in Ecuador: The battle between conservation and extraction." *Alternautas* 1: 100–5.

Gudynas, E. 2011. "Buen vivir: Today's tomorrow." *Development* 54, 4: 441–7.

Habermann, F. 2013. "Von post-development, postwachstum & peer ecommony: Alternative lebensweisen als 'Abwicklung des Nordens.'" *Journal für Entwicklungspolitik* 28, 4: 69–87.

Hall, S. 1992. "The West and the rest." In B. Gieben and S. Hall, eds, *Formations of Modernity.* London: Polity Press, 276–320.

Hayter, T. 1971. *Aid as Imperialism.* Harmondsworth: Penguin.

Hoogvelt, A. 2001. *Globalization and the Postcolonial World: The New Political Economy of Development*, 2nd edn. Baltimore: Johns Hopkins University Press.

Illich, I. 1973. *Tools for Conviviality.* New York: Harper & Row.

———. 1997. "Development as planned poverty." In Rahnema with Bawtree (1997).

Kerkeling, L. 2006. *La Lucha Sigue! Der Kampfgehtweiter*, 2nd edn. Münster: Unrast.

Kiely, R. 1999. "The last refuge of the noble savage? A critical assessment of post-development theory." *European Journal of Development Research* 11, 1: 30–55.

Latouche, S. 1986. *Faut-il réfuser le développement? Essai sur l'anti-économique du tiers monde.* Paris: Presses Universitaires de France.

———. 1993. *In the Wake of the Affluent Society: Explorations in Post-Development.* London: Zed Books.

———. 1997. "Standard of living." In Sachs (1992: 250–63).

Li, T.M. 2007. *The Will to Improve: Governmentality, Development, and the Practice of Politics.* Durham, NC: Duke University Press.

Mahmoodi, K., and E. Zeiny Jelodar. 2011. "Orientalized from within: Modernity and modern anti-imperial Iranian intellectuals. Gharbzadegi and the roots of material wretchedness." Asian Culture and History 3, 2: 19–28.

Mies, M., and V. Shiva. 1993. *Ecofeminism.* London: Zed Books.

Muñoz Ramírez, G. 2003. *EZLN: 20+10. Il fuego y la palabra.* México D.F.: Revista Rebeldía.

Murithi, T. 2006. "Practical peacemaking: Wisdom from Africa: Reflections on Ubuntu." *Journal of Pan African Studies* 1, 4: 25–35.

Nanda, M. 1999. "Who needs post-development? Discourses of difference, green revolution and agrarian populism in India." *Journal of Developing Societies* 15, 1: 5–31.

Nandy, A., ed. 1988. *Science, Hegemony and Violence: A Requiem for Modernity.* Tokyo: Oxford University Press.

Nederveen Pieterse, J. 1998. "My paradigm or yours? Alternative development, post-development, reflexive development." *Development and Change* 29: 343–73.

Norberg-Hodge, H. 1997. "The pressure to modernize and globalize." In Jerry Mander and Edward Glodsmith, eds, *The Case against the Global Economy and for a Turn toward the Local.* San Francisco: Sierra Club Books, 33–46.

———. 2009 (1991). *Ancient Futures. Learning from Ladakh.* Thousand Oaks, Calif.: Sierra Club.

Paech, N. 2012. *Befreiung vom Überfluss: Auf dem Weg in die Postwachstumsökonomie.* Stuttgart: Oekom.

Rahnema, M. 1985. "NGOs—Sifting the wheat from the chaff." *Development: Seeds of Change* 3: 68–71.

———. 1992. "Poverty." In Sachs (1992: 158–76).

———. 1997. "Introduction." In Rahnema with Bawtree (1997: ix–xix).

———with Victoria Bawtree, eds. 1997. *The Post-Development Reader.* London: Zed Books.

Rist, G. 2014 (1997). *The History of Development: From Western Origins to Global Faith.* London: Zed Books.

———. 2012. *The History of Development: From Western Origins to Global Faith,* 4th edn. London: Zed Books.

——— and F. Sabelli, eds. 1986. *Il était une fois le développement.* Lausanne: Editions d'en bas.

Rodney, W. 2009 (1972). *How Europe Underdeveloped Africa.* Abuja, Nigeria: Panaf Publishing.

Sachs, W. 1990. "The archaeology of the development idea." *Interculture* 23, 4: 1–37.

———, ed. 1992. *The Development Dictionary: A Guide to Knowledge as Power.* London: Zed Books.

———. 1999. *Planet Dialectics. Explorations in Environment and Development.* London: Zed Books.

———, ed. 2010. *The Development Dictionary. A Guide to Knowledge as Power,* 2nd edn. London: Zed Books.

Shiva, V. 1989. *Staying Alive: Women, Ecology and Survival in India.* London: Zed Books.

Spehr, C. 1996. *Die Ökofalle. Nachhaltigkeit und Krise.* Wien: Promedia.

Taussig, M. 2010 (1980). *The Devil and Commodity Fetishism in South America.* Chapel Hill: University of North Carolina Press.

Walsh, C. 2010. "Development as buen vivir: Institutional arrangements and (de)colonial entanglements." *Development* 53, 1: 15–21.

Ziai, A. 2004. "The ambivalence of post-development: Between reactionary populism and radical development." *Third World Quarterly* 25, 6: 1045–61.

———. 2015. "Post-development: Premature burials and haunting ghosts." *Development and Change* 46, 4: 833–54.

5 Gender and Development: Theoretical Contributions, International Commitments, and Global Campaigns

Rebecca Tiessen, Jane Parpart, and Marianne H. Marchand

LEARNING OBJECTIVES

- To understand the linkages between gender and development approaches and their applications in development policy and practice.
- To understand the historical and feminist theoretical foundations of gender and development.
- To learn about the range of strategies addressing women's rights, girls' rights, and gender equality, including United Nations' commitments and popular campaigns.
- To underscore past and contemporary challenges to addressing gender and development.

▲ **Members of the Gulabi Gang and villagers walk together as they seek ways to improve the condition of an agricultural field. The Gulabi Gang, or "the pink gang" in direct translation from Hindi, is a group of women who came together as a response to domestic abuse and other violence against women. Its main purpose is to help promote better living conditions for women around India. Since its formation in 2010, the Gulabi Gang is reported to have recruited more than 20,000 members and have saved thousands of women's lives across the country.** | Source: Photo by Jonas Gratzer/LightRocket via Getty Images

INTRODUCTION

Feminist theory, gender analytical frameworks, international commitments, and global campaigns are intertwined and shape each other. It is not possible to understand United Nations' (UN) commitments to women, girls, and gender equality without understanding how they have been influenced by feminist theory and gender and development thinking over time. Commitments to gender equality can be traced back many decades. For example, in 1970 Ester Boserup argued for the inclusion of women and women's needs in development, particularly their economic contributions to development (Boserup, 1970). More than four decades have passed since the First World Conference on Women, held in Mexico in 1975, adopted a global plan of action for implementing the objectives of the International Women's Year. At the start of the new millennium, the international community signed Security Council Resolution 1325 designed to promote women, peace, and security, and countries signed on to the Millennium Development Goals (MDGs)—with two goals dedicated to gender equality and women's empowerment and to reproductive health for women. As the global community reorients international programs from the MDGs to the Sustainable Development Goals (SDGs), this moment offers an important space for reflecting on past challenges and successes, as well as future opportunities for the promotion of gender equality.

Many high-profile strategies and global campaigns have been employed to raise awareness about gender inequality and women's rights. With the help of feminist insights and gender and development analytical frameworks, we have a better understanding of the complexity of gender relations, the persistence of masculinities that perpetuate gender inequality, and how structural processes and cultural practices shape and reinforce unequal social relationships and organizational practices. We have also achieved important milestones in the promotion of human rights (particularly for women and girls) and gender equality. Nonetheless, persistent challenges to achieving gender equality continue to raise notable concerns for women's and girls' empowerment, and for marginalized groups. Strategies to promote gender equality in international development have frequently slipped back into charitable models of development that **essentialize** women and girls. For example, women are portrayed almost exclusively as mothers or victims with little agency, or they are stripped to essentialist stereotypes of femininity. Women and girls are frequently presented as the primary recipients of donor programs that often serve other purposes, such as using the protection and/or education of girls as a means to justify military spending when engaging in war. A focus on women and girls has also overshadowed other important gender equality concerns, including the oppression of marginalized communities and transgender individuals, and the role of masculinities in shaping societal relations that benefit some groups at the expense of others.

While feminist scholarship on development often presents a continuum of development thinking beginning with the women in development (WID) approach, moving on to deeper analyses of gender inequality and masculinities, the programs and policies that have emerged over time do not follow a neat historical and linear trajectory. Rather, strategies to promote gender equality continue to represent a range of charitable and transformative approaches. Charitable development strategies target women and girls with specific activities without due consideration of—and strategies for addressing—the root causes of gender inequality. While addressing gender inequality in international development is a human rights imperative, as well as central to development projects' success and efforts to improve the quality of life for all, achieving gender equality requires involvement of diverse actors and stakeholders informed by critical and theoretical insights. The chapter outlines some of the important advances in feminist thinking about gender and development, and documents how these analytical frameworks have shaped international commitments and global campaigns on gender equality while also identifying some of the ongoing challenges to moving beyond simplistic strategies that primarily target women and girls.

THEORETICAL CONTRIBUTIONS AND FEMINIST INSIGHTS

Early Analytical Frameworks: The Welfare Approach, Women in Development, and Women and Development

This section provides a brief discussion of early contributions to feminist literature in development studies, particularly the welfare approach, women in development (WID), and women and development (WAD). The welfare approach was highly influenced by prevailing theories of modernization and economic growth. Development issues were constructed as "problems" to be solved with policies and programs geared to addressing "overpopulation," rurality, and lack of modernization (Moser, 1993). As such, the family planning approach involved treating women as the "focus of social control of fertility." Indonesia, for example, introduced a strong national family planning program that dates back to the 1950s with the introduction of contraceptives. By 1970, President Suharto had introduced the National Family Planning Coordinator Board (BKBBN) to control population growth in the country. Family planning fieldworkers visited individual households and Village Contraceptive Distribution Centres were set up around the country. This comprehensive national policy provided most rural and remote communities with contraceptives; however, the contraceptive choices were limited, and the delivery of services was shaped by authoritarian state structures and coercion (Hartmann, 1995). Targeting women for population control and essentializing them in relation to biological functions as mothers continues to dominate some contemporary approaches to addressing maternal and newborn health, treating women as "walking wombs" (Tiessen, 2015). Box 5.1 provides a summary of maternal and reproductive health strategies from a gender perspective (see also Chapter 20).

PHOTO 5.1 | **A poster praising the value of family planning in the city of Panaji, Goa, India.**

CRITICAL ISSUES

BOX 5.1 | Maternal and Reproductive Health Strategies

A number of maternal and reproductive health strategies have been promoted globally since the 1950s. In 2000, the international community agreed to a set of strategies to improve maternal health, including targets specified under MDG #5 to reduce maternal mortality and increase access to reproductive health services. Access to effective contraception is linked to maternal deaths. The World Health Organization (WHO) argues that meeting family planning needs through safe and effective contraception will reduce maternal deaths by almost one-third (WHO, 2015). Yet women around the world continue to face high maternal death rates. For example, 8,000 women die every day from preventable causes related to pregnancy and childbirth and 99 per cent of those deaths occur in developing countries, particularly in sub-Saharan Africa. Between 1990 and 2013, maternal mortality dropped by 50 per cent (WHO, 2014); however, high death rates continue to be a development issue. As we move into the next phase of global development commitments (the SDGs), the focus on sexual and reproductive health and rights will remain on the post-2015 development agenda under the broader health goal: "Ensure healthy lives and promote well-being for all at all ages." This goal includes a number of strategies, including the reduction of maternal mortality by 2030 to fewer than 70 per 100,000 live births. One of the ongoing and most significant challenges in the international efforts to address maternal mortality and reproductive health programs is the failure to address the gender dynamics and social relations that prevent women from seeking out the support and services they need to prevent or space pregnancies and/or to have healthy pregnancies. A WID approach to maternal health and other strategies that target women and girls essentialize women as "walking wombs," reducing women to the biological functions of giving birth. Gender and development approaches, alternatively, have highlighted the need for recognizing the social relations that shape women's decision-making power and access to reproductive services and resources.

By the early 1970s, some aid programs began to recognize the importance of involving women in development projects. In addition to family planning, the WID framework began to address sexual violence, discrimination, inequality in access to resources, and women's limited participation in positions of power or influence. The WID approach challenged the assumption that women would automatically gain from modernization/development policies and projects (Boserup, 1970). It called for specific attention to women as development actors, drawing on liberal feminist demands for improving women's positions in social, economic, and political realms. Encouraged by the 1975 United Nations World Conference on Women, women's issues began to take a more prominent place in development agencies. Some development agencies set up WID offices, hired personnel, and developed programs that addressed women's development issues. WID experts called for more accurate measures of women's access to education, training, property and credit, political power, and economic livelihoods. Development programs addressing these issues were established and operationalized, and high hopes were held out for improving women's positions in societies around the world (Moser, 1993).

Yet, while WID policies and projects improved some women's lives, inequality between women and men remained stubbornly high. Some WID personnel, influenced by **radical feminist** thinking and **socialist feminist** concerns with gender inequality in the workplace, began to consider new ways of fostering women's development. Drawing on the radical feminist argument that women can never achieve equality in a male-dominated world, some development experts argued for women-only projects that would protect women from patriarchal power structures and sexist cultural practices. Socialist feminists also raised questions about the difficulties facing women in a world shaped by Western patriarchal structures. These feminist critiques inspired the women and development

(WAD) approach, which focused on women's knowledge, work, goals, and responsibilities and called for women-only projects that would enhance women's powers and sideline patriarchal forces. They called for recognition of women's special role in the development process. While an important corrective to the uncritical assumption that gender power relations could be easily changed by development projects, WAD remained a minority approach to development. Yet its concern with women's cultures, economic exploitation, and the need for alternatives to capitalist development in some cases led local grassroots organizations to develop women-only projects that were intended to keep women sheltered from the worst effects of capitalist development. These concerns would resurface in some of the theorizing emerging from the Global South considered below (Parpart, Connelly, and Barriteau, 2000).

Gender and Development

The limitations of both WID and WAD inspired a growing concern with gendered practices, relations, and hierarchies and their impact on gender equality. Influenced by socialist feminist thought, gender and development (GAD) emerged in the 1980s as an approach that brought a gendered perspective to the social, economic, and political realities of development. It coincided with, but did not equate to, the Development Alternatives with Women for a New Era (DAWN) network, led by feminists from the Global South. DAWN launched critiques of mainstream development, especially its neoliberal approach to women's issues and development goals and its ties to colonial legacies (Sen and Grown, 1987). Drawing on these critiques, GAD's goals have been twofold: to demonstrate that unequal gender relations hinder development and female participation in economic and political arenas, and to show the need to transform structures of power in order to facilitate more equal partnerships between the genders. In this fashion, both women and men, it is believed, can be empowered as decision-makers and beneficiaries of development (Rathgeber, 1990).

The shift from women to gender was driven by the limited success of two decades of development programs aimed at improving women's economic, political, and social positions. Acknowledgement of this failure coincided with critiques from the Global South. Drawing on critical political economy to explain the Global North's continuing domination over the Global South, feminist scholars and activists from the South, with a few northern allies, condemned liberal women-centred development programs for their uncritical acceptance of modernity and their failure to analyze women's lacklustre position in economic, political, and social institutions. They called for greater attention to the complexities of women in the Global South (Sen and Grown, 1987).

These critiques, particularly the call for greater attention to the complex realities of poverty, race, ethnicity, and class facing women (and men) living in the Global South, inspired a gradual shift to gender and development, with its focus on the power relations shaping the lives of poor women and men in the Global South (and North). The concept of gender emphasized the socially constructed attitudes and practices associated with women, femininities, and men and masculinities, and especially their impact on the gender relations and hierarchies that shape gendered access to power and influence in particular societies. For example, the Japanese International Cooperation Agency (JICA) discovered that the attitudes of men and women towards women's responsibilities in the economy, politics, and community life defined the gender division of labour and reinforced gender hierarchies that limited women's possibilities for advancement in economic and political institutions. Development projects that ignored these assumptions were bound to fail.

The initial focus of GAD projects aimed to transfer resources and support to women in the Global South to enable them "to put their own agendas and priorities into action and challenge the current top-down, male-biased model of global development" (Sweetman, 2013: 3). The central focus remained on women's position and the way gendered assumptions have shaped the possibilities for women's advancement. Programs for men generally focused on their role in this process rather than on the deeper issues facing men and boys, particularly masculine norms associated with manly "success" and the difficulties of achieving these goals in an increasingly global, neoliberal world (Connell, 2005; Cornwall et al., 2011). While raising important issues about gender inequality, the GAD approach has largely operated within established development goals seeking to improve women's positions in a neoliberal world (Chant, 2012).

Scholars and activists from the Global South began to question the Western bias in most gender and development policies and programs. They argued that Western development "experts" measured gender progress with Western lenses (Mohanty, 1988) and called for attention to the lived experiences of women (and men) in the Global South, particularly the impact of race, ethnicity, class, colonization, and culture on women's and men's lives and relations. The focus on difference highlighted the importance of placing gender within specific cultural and historical context, as well as socio-economic and historical contexts. In particular, Mohanty's intervention set the tone for post-colonial feminist scholarship to contribute to and intervene in debates about gender and development. Its concerns about representation, homogenizing, **othering**, and silencing of so-called "Third World" women influenced further theorizing about gender and development (Marchand and Parpart, 1995).

However, not everyone has accepted the term "post-colonial" (see Chapter 4). Some Latin American scholars, for example, argue that many present-day societies in the Global South are still embedded in a colonial context and culture. Indeed, Walter Mignolo (1998), Arturo Escobar (1998), and Enrique Dussel (1992) argue that the construction of Latin America as a region is a Western creation that prevents local scholars from understanding and analyzing its social, economic, political, and cultural complexities through the use of homegrown theories and concepts. They call for a decolonial perspective that aims to decolonize our (colonial) knowledge and knowing about Latin America and the Global South in general. Decolonial feminists from the region have joined these efforts by focusing on the continuing power of colonial knowledge about Latin American women, which has been internalized by feminists in the region. They argue that dominant or hegemonic feminist knowledges need to be decolonized and opened up to other knowledges and ways of knowing produced through the everyday practices of local women, particularly Indigenous and Afro-descended women. This endeavour they call "ecology of knowledges," and its aim is to deconstruct hierarchies between different knowledges and forms of knowing (Red de Feminismos Decoloniales, 2014).

The question implicitly as well as explicitly raised by post-colonial and decolonial feminists is whether it is possible to create alliances among women from different parts of the Global North and South. Such alliances, based on the idea that women worldwide have something in common, have been referred to as Global Sisterhood. The critiques of women from the Global South, in particular DAWN and other post-colonial and decolonial feminists, reveal serious problems with the idea of a Global Sisterhood as it often reinforces the dominant position of Western feminisms. Instead, feminists from the Global South have looked for alternative ways of creating alliances that would recognize and respect differences and adopt more democratic agenda-setting and prioritizing of issues related to gender and development (Mohanty, 2003). One such response has been **transnational feminism**. Challenging the idea of Global Sisterhood and insisting on intersectional and transversal theorizing of women's differences, transnational post-colonial feminist scholarship also emphasizes the importance of incorporating political economy into analyses of gender and development (Mendoza, 2002). At the same time, transnational feminism has been challenged for primarily being a product of feminist academics from the Global South situated at (academic) institutions in the Global North (Mendoza, 2002).

In sum, post-colonial and decolonial scholarship continues to develop and expand, with consequences for the analysis of gender relations and hierarchies. As transnational feminism suggests, political economy is increasingly seen as a central feature of these new approaches (Sisson Runyan and Marchand, 2011). Feminists from around the world are also raising questions about sexuality and family forms, challenging the development industry's tendency to assume a heterosexual (and often nuclear family) model, based on Western practices and assumptions (Bergeron, 2011; Lind, 2011). Thus, while incorporation of critical feminist work from the Global South is uneven, GAD continues to evolve in response to feminist scholarship from many different perspectives and contexts.

Empowerment

Empowerment was initially regarded as a key tool for challenging and transforming unequal political, economic, and social structures. It was seen as a weapon for the weak—best wielded through participatory, grassroots community-based non-governmental organizations (NGOs). However, in the mid-1990s mainstream development agencies began to adopt the term, and subsequently the language of participation, partnership, and empowerment increasingly entered mainstream development discourse (World Bank, 1995; Elson and Keklik, 2002). While the wording remained the same, meanings varied. Mainstream institutions and their practitioners for the most part envisioned empowerment as a means for enhancing efficiency and productivity within the status quo rather than as a mechanism for social transformation (Parpart, Rai, and Staudt, 2002).

Empowerment first surfaced in gender and development debates when Sen and Grown argued that women needed "to develop a collective vision, a set of strategies and new methods for mobilizing political will and empowering women (and men) to transform society" (Sen and Grown, 1987: 87). Caroline Moser and others picked up this thread in the 1990s. Moser concluded that women needed to gain self-reliance and internal strength in order "to determine choices in life and to influence the direction of change, through the ability to gain control over crucial material and non-material resources" (1993: 74). Scholar/activists from the Global South joined the discussion, noting that the concept of "empowerment" had begun to lose its transformative edge. They called for a more precise understanding of power and empowerment, arguing that empowerment must challenge "existing power relations and [with an aim] of gaining greater control over the sources of power" (Batliwala, 1994: 130). Placing empowerment at the centre of efforts to achieve gender equality required self-understanding that enabled the transformative potential of *power within*—a power rooted in the ability to recognize and challenge gender inequality in the home and the community (Kabeer, 1994: 224–9). These critiques focused on collective, grassroots participatory action—the *power to* work *with* others "to control resources, determine agendas and to make decisions" (Kabeer, 1994: 229); the transformative nature of empowerment arguing that it is personal, relational and collective, and involves moving from insight into action (Rowlands 1997: 14–15); and emphasizing empowerment's ability to move beyond enhancing choice to extending the limits of the possible (Mosedale, 2005: 252).

At the same time, mainstream development institutions increasingly adopted the language of empowerment, especially for women. The Beijing Declaration, produced at the 1995 Fourth UN Women's Conference, stated unequivocally that women's empowerment is "fundamental for the achievement of equality, development and peace" (United Nations, 1995: para. 13). Official development institutions adopted the language of empowerment, gender equality, and gender mainstreaming as central to achieving gender equality and improving women's lives around the world, particularly in the MDGs and other development policies (Parpart, 2014).

Despite the widespread adoption of the term, and the tendency to assume empowerment was a feasible, reachable, and measureable goal, some criticisms began to emerge. Kabeer critiqued empowerment projects for assuming that they could "somehow predict the nature and direction that change is going to assume" (1999: 462). Parpart, Rai, and Staudt (2002) warned that the empowerment approach has often ignored the entrenched opposition to empowering marginal groups around the world. Cornwall and colleagues have brought a critical edge to the term, exploring its potential while fully aware of its limitations (Cornwall et al., 2011). Empowerment thus continues to be seen as a critical concept for achieving gender equality, but one that requires greater attention to the impact of cultural differences, economic and political power, colonial histories, and gendered practices and relations. This is a welcome expansion of the term and key to addressing gender empowerment in an increasingly complex, global, and still very patriarchal world.

Gender Mainstreaming

Gender mainstreaming (GM), with its promise of gender equality, empowerment, and transformation, has become a central pillar of development discourse, policy, and practice, supported by mainstream as well as more alternative development institutions. In the 1990s it emerged as a key mechanism for achieving gender equality and women's empowerment. GM was defined by the United Nations as the integration of gender into the design, implementation, monitoring and evaluation of the policies and programs in all political, economic and societal spheres (UNESCO, 1997). The optimistic, policy-oriented, "can-do" language of GM entered the development lexicon, becoming a central pillar of development agencies. The *Platform for Action* produced by the 1995 UN Conference on Women in Beijing adopted gender mainstreaming as the central mechanism for ensuring gender equality. GM soon became a necessary tool for every development agency concerned with women and gender and the improvement in gender equality (Parpart, 2014).

An impressive list of analytical tools such as checklists, gender impact assessments, awareness-raising, training manuals, expert meetings, and data collection reinforced the assumption that gender mainstreaming could be both achieved and measured. Gender mainstreaming began to be seen as beyond politics and economics—something that had to be planned for and executed. The possibility that intractable resistances to GM might derail these plans has been largely ignored.

Yet the achievements of gender mainstreaming policies and projects have often been disappointing. There have been some success stories—law reform, increases in the number of women in parliaments, participation in peace processes, and building organizational skills—yet these have been exceptions rather than the norm (Rao and Kelleher, 2005). While the Beijing Declaration called for the development of gender expertise within political institutions to ensure that GM would be implemented at all levels, the practice has been quite the opposite. Under pressure to rationalize (and downsize) bureaucracies, and thus reduce government spending, so-called national machineries, created to pursue gender equality policies, have been dismantled. Many critical development experts argue that despite an increasingly sophisticated stock of analytical tools and gender experts, gender mainstreaming's transformative potential remains in question (Parpart, 2014; Tiessen and Tuckey, 2015).

To understand the limitations of gender mainstreaming, we need to explore resistances that undermine its practice. Widespread skepticism about GM's effectiveness within development agencies, government offices, and other institutions has limited the potential for change of gender mainstreaming. Indeed, the African Development Bank discovered uneven support for GM from leadership in mainstream development agencies in most of 30 major GM projects. Efforts to mainstream women into politics have often failed to assess potential resistances, particularly masculinist cultures opposed to women's participation in political and economic institutions (Parpart, 2014). The recent shift to a focus on women and girls and the celebration of "girl power" by development agencies have also ignored the impact of gender relations and structural inequality on their potential to effect change. This approach also ignores the fact that some women (and girls) benefit from associating with powerful men and consequently support gender hierarchies that privilege masculine power and authority.

Given the limits of gender mainstreaming, some development scholars and practitioners have suggested that GM should give up its transformative agenda, scale back expectations to limited and doable reforms, and leave transformative goals to politics (Standing, 2007). Others are more optimistic, arguing that transformative policies will require new ideas, language, and practice, collaboration with NGOs involved in transformational work, and greater attention to the policies that have improved gender equality as well as lessons learned from those that do not. This approach holds out the possibility for meaningful change and realistic approaches to gender mainstreaming.

Men and Masculinities

Women remained the central development issue for gender experts throughout the 1970s and 1980s. Men and **masculinities** were rarely addressed, except as potential or actual impediments to women's and girls' progress. The 1980 World Conference on Women in Copenhagen called for the inclusion of men into development work supporting women's equality and empowerment, but for the next 15 years the role of men in promoting (or inhibiting) women's rights received little attention. Gender inequality persisted. Patriarchal privilege reinforced women's subordinate positions in economic and political institutions, and men continued to be seen largely as impediments to women's empowerment rather than part of the solution to gender inequality (Sweetman, 2013; White, 1997).

In the 1990s, men and masculinities were increasingly identified as development issues. Early projects focused on the role of men in the spread of HIV/AIDS, violence against women, and opposition to women's empowerment. Men were also encouraged to co-operate with gender mainstreaming efforts, although the focus remained on women. Since the turn of the century, increasing attention has been paid to the developmental problems of men and boys, particularly their underperformance in schools, their high levels of youth unemployment, their involvement in crime, and their role in the spread of HIV/AIDS. Programs for men have generally focused on their role in the struggle for gender equality (such as the HeForShe campaign summarized in Box 5.2) rather than on the deeper issues facing men and boys, particularly masculine norms associated with manly "success" and the difficulties of achieving these goals in an increasingly global, neoliberal world (Cornwall et al., 2011).

There has been some talk about a crisis of masculinity, of the need to change toxic masculine practices and to create sensitized men who will be allies in the struggle for gender equality. Less has been said about the material and social consequences of patriarchal privilege and its significance for men and women around the world.

As a result, the few projects focusing on men as key players in the creation of a more gender-equal world have often been criticized by men who saw these projects as inhibiting their advancement in a world where increasing numbers of men have been having difficulty meeting the ideals of masculine privilege and dominance. The subsequent insecurity has fuelled a backlash against projects seen as threatening masculine privilege. This hostility has intensified in the twenty-first century, which has witnessed an expansion of educational and employment opportunities for women along with a global economic crisis that has undermined many traditionally male-dominated sources of employment such as construction, manufacturing, and investment. Young men in particular have found it difficult to live up to expected roles as breadwinners. Many (along with some women) have turned to illegal activities to survive, including the drug trade and smuggling of persons and goods. Others have preferred to migrate and risk their lives on a dangerous journey to a new destination in an attempt to support their families. While migrations have become increasingly feminized, involving more women who are also migrating independently, women's lives have been affected in multiple ways by migrating male family members. They are now responsible for keeping the household going while also becoming increasingly dependent on remittances. Consequently, new attention has been drawn to the gendered migration–development nexus (Marchand, 2008). Armed conflicts have drawn young men (and some women) into battle, inuring them to violence and highlighting militarized masculine values. Resentment against more "successful" males and females has fuelled violence against vulnerable women and children (and some men) in marginalized households and communities.

The recognition that many males are facing development challenges has inspired an interest in policies and programs that pay attention to the many men

CRITICAL ISSUES

BOX 5.2 | HeForShe Campaign

The HeForShe is a strategy designed to engage men and boys in efforts to promote gender equality. It was initiated in 2014 by UN Women as an alternative to targeting girls as recipients of development aid by shifting the focus to understanding social relationships that support and reproduce gender inequality. The campaign includes a goal of ensuring that more than one million men and boys take the HeForShe pledge: a pledge that acknowledges that gender equality is not only an issue for women and girls but is a human rights issue that requires everyone's participation. The pledge calls for action to end forms of violence and discrimination faced by women and girls. The popularity of the HeForShe campaign was augmented by the endorsement of the initiative by the British actress Emma Watson, now the UN Women goodwill ambassador (and known for her role as Hermione in the Harry Potter movies). Emma Watson's impassioned speech in September 2014 has been viewed by nearly a million people on the official UN video on YouTube and has circulated widely on other social media sites, thus providing significant exposure to this particular strategy of addressing gender inequality.

frustrated with their inability to live up to masculine gender norms, particularly the expectation that they should protect and control women, children, and subordinate males. Organizations such as the UN Commission on the Status of Women and the United Nations Population Fund (UNFP) have designed programs to encourage the adoption of more progressive gender norms built around ideals of non-violence and "a sense of male pride and dignity based on progressive, gender based ideals" (Sweetman, 2013: 5). The programs aim to foster progressive gender relations that support transgender rights, women's rights, and gender equality in ways that benefit all individuals and the social worlds in which they live. The focus of many of these programs has been on addressing male roles, masculinities, and gender-based violence.

MASCULINITIES, GENDER-BASED VIOLENCE, AND (IN)SECURITY

Gender-based violence has become increasingly visible in the twenty-first century. Policy-makers, academics, and development practitioners have begun to focus on the destructive patterns that encourage and legitimate gender-based violence. Projects have been created to challenge such masculine attitudes and behaviours, and have urged men to change their behaviour and take personal responsibility for confronting these practices (Barker and Ricardo, 2006). In 2008, UN Security Council Resolution 1820 officially recognized rape as a weapon of war, building on earlier UN resolutions to promote women, peace, and security (see Box 5.3).

CRITICAL ISSUES

BOX 5.3 | Resolution 1325

The adoption of Security Council Resolution 1325 on women, peace, and security (SCR1325) on 31 October 2000 was a monumental achievement because it recognized sexual and gender-based violence (SGBV) as a human rights issue and introduced gender perspectives to the peace and security work of the United Nations. Specifically, Resolution 1325 acknowledges that armed conflict has a unique impact on women and girls and that specific gender strategies are required to address the needs of women and girls during conflicts and in the post-conflict stages. The recommendations arising from Resolution 1325 include the prevention of SGBV; a gender perspective in peace negotiations, disarmament, demobilization, and reintegration (DDR) strategies, peacekeeping operations, and reporting; and increased participation of women in international institutions and training, and as UN humanitarian personnel and military observers. To facilitate these recommendations, many UN member states have adopted National Action Plans (NAPs) documenting the country's commitments, policies, and strategies to address gender equality in armed conflict as well as, more broadly, the related issues of women, peace, and security (Tiessen and Tuckey, 2014). NGOs have played an important role in many countries in ensuring that the NAPs are prepared, reviewed, and updated and include reporting of successes and challenges. Since 2000, the successes internationally include greater attention to—and reporting on—gender issues in conflict and women's post-conflict participation in peace-building, including consultations with women's organizations. However, those committed to gender equality face many ongoing challenges, including the limited participation of women in peace negotiations and inadequate efforts to mainstream gender into DDR and peacekeeping operations. Most significantly, there remain high rates of SGBV and continued impunity for those who commit these crimes. Ongoing issues include continued reports of sexual abuse and exploitation by peacekeeping forces, women's limited participation in post-conflict decision-making, and continuing violence targeted at women. Furthermore, financial resources earmarked for women's protection and the promotion of gender equality are limited.

Civil societies began tracking the incidence of rape and other forms of sexual violence against women and girls, and the International Criminal Court now considers rape as a punishable war crime. Such efforts are imperative to the promotion of gender equality. Yet, other forms of gender-based violence—such as male-on-male rape, violence directed at LGBT (lesbian, gay, bisexual, and transgender) communities, and femicide (the murder of women because they are women, a sexual and gender-based hate crime particularly prevalent in Mexico and Guatemala)—have been met with fewer commitments.

Despite a tendency to revert to a focus on women and girls, development practitioners and researchers concerned with men and masculinity have sought to understand and address the beliefs and practices among men and boys (and some females) that legitimate male privilege and oppose efforts to produce a more gender-equitable world. Challenging these toxic beliefs and practices and encouraging new, more gender-sensitive ways of thinking and behaving have become important strategies for encouraging support for gender equality and reducing gender-based violence, HIV/AIDS, and gender disparities in education and employment.

At the same time, efforts to challenge and alter masculine attitudes and behaviour opposed to gender equality take place in a world where gendered assumptions still largely define which sexed bodies, performances, sexuality, and positionalities are seen as deserving the material and social rewards offered in particular societies. Trying to change long-held assumptions about what kinds of men (and a few women) should wield power is extremely difficult as those who benefit from such systems are rarely willing to step aside for a more equitable system. Convincing the powerful to give up their privileges is never easy, and it is even more difficult if many men (and some women) who benefit more indirectly from masculinist privilege still believe even their minimal power and authority will be threatened if gendered structures of power are altered. The World Bank, despite its *World Development Report 2012* supporting gender equality, has remained focused on women. Indeed, women and girls are increasingly seen as the "solution" to achieving that goal (Chant, 2012).

Yet, the twenty-first century has produced conditions that are beginning to shift perceptions about gender relations, men, and masculinity/ies, particularly their role in causing or challenging gender-based violence. Some development agencies now see gender-based violence not only as a threat to women's empowerment, but also as a systemic reaction of men grappling with their own struggles with (dis)empowerment on shifting economic and political sands. As most of the world continues to suffer from growing inequality, high levels of unemployment especially among young men and competition from increasingly skilled women entering the workforce are giving rise to new social tensions that sometimes have dangerous outcomes (Catala et al., 2012). Recognizing the psychological implications of these social changes for many men is essential for understanding and responding to gender-based violence and promoting more equitable gender relations.

Some NGOs and development agencies have begun to recognize the role socialization plays in shaping and responding to traditional patriarchal masculine ideals and expectations. Small, local workshops where men are able to openly discuss and negotiate their masculinity with other men have provided an alternative vision of how men might explore their understanding and acting out of masculinity, as practised in the CBC's (Centro Bartolomé de las Casas) Masculinities Program initiative in El Salvador (Bird et al., 2007). In 2000 UNICEF produced a series of educational films on masculinities designed to help young men explore the role of masculinity and how it relates to gender-based violence in South Asia. A UNFP project worked with boys between 10 and 15 years old to reflect on machismo culture and its impact on sexual violence. These are just a few examples of the many development projects confronting gender-based violence by addressing the role of masculinity as it impacts and shapes men on an individual psychological level. They are signs of progress. The current economic and political crises provide an opening, but also a challenge—witness both the resurgence of patriarchal power and resistances to it in the post-Arab Spring Middle East (see http://harassmap.org/en/). The need for broad social change has never been greater, but it will require collaboration and commitment to creating a more gender-equitable and fairer world. Such commitments will arise, in large part, from international efforts to ensure gender equality remains a priority in development programming. In the section that follows, we examine some of the international commitments and global campaigns to promote gender equality.

INTERNATIONAL COMMITMENTS AND GLOBAL CAMPAIGNS

Feminist scholarship has increasingly documented the gendered nature of rape and sexual violence as weapons of war (see Baaz and Stern, 2013) and the role that masculinities play in perpetuating gender-based violence (see Parpart, 2010). Getting to the point where sexual violence was recognized by the UN as a human rights violation has been a long road. However, the foundation for a more comprehensive understanding of human rights and women's/gender rights as they pertain to security can be found in earlier commitments, including the 1979 Convention on the Elimination of All Forms of Discrimination Against Women (CEDAW) and the 1993 UN Declaration on the Elimination of Violence against Women. The latter document highlighted a range of important issues facing women and called for "the universal application to women of the rights and principles with regard to equality, security, liberty, integrity and dignity of all human beings." In this document, the relationship between gender inequality and women's achievements in development and peace was highlighted, and nations and governments were called on to ensure the "effective implementation" of the 1979 Convention (UN General Assembly, 1993).

The CEDAW, adopted by the UN General Assembly in 1979, continues to serve as an important international bill of rights for women. The most important contributions of the Convention include its documentation of what constitutes discrimination against women and how to address these forms of discrimination through national actions. The Convention called on states to undertake a series of measures to end discrimination against women through legal means, such as abolition of discriminatory laws, and more generally to protect women from discrimination. It has served as a foundation for the promotion of women's rights for nearly four decades.

International commitments and UN resolutions are also the basis for global campaigns. The campaign to stop rape and gender violence in conflict, for example, grew out of UN Resolution 1325 and includes 25 partners from the NGO sector, particularly the Peace Laureates of the Nobel Women's Initiative. It calls for improved leadership at all levels to prevent and stop rape and gender violence; an increase in resources to prevent and protect survivors and their families, including the end to stigma associated with survivors; and justice for victims, including an end to impunity and prosecution of perpetrators. The website for this organization lists a number of "take action" events to promote awareness of sexual and gender-based violence around the world and initiatives to pressure governments into making this issue a priority.

The Beijing Conference represents another important international commitment to the promotion of gender equality. The Fourth World Conference on Women organized by the United Nations—the Beijing Conference—was attended by 17,000 participants plus 30,000 activists. An important outcome from Beijing is the highly celebrated *Platform for Action*, which outlined 12 strategic objectives and actions pertaining to gender issues ranging from poverty to political participation. Earlier UN conferences on women (Mexico City in 1975, Copenhagen in 1980, and Nairobi in 1985) also paved the way for the promotion of a global agenda for gender equality. The documents arising from the Beijing Conference—the *Beijing Declaration* and the *Platform for Action*—were adopted unanimously by 189 countries, and numerous programs and campaigns were spearheaded based on the recommendations and strategies outlined in these documents. In particular, a focus on the girl child spawned a series of global campaigns from corporations and NGOs. Two of those strategies are addressed in greater detail in Boxes 5.4 and 5.5: Nike's Girl Effect and Plan International's Because I am a Girl campaigns.

The *Platform for Action* remains a defining framework today, and since the Beijing Conference, additional international meetings (occurring in five-year intervals) have influenced efforts to promote gender equality.

CRITICAL ISSUES

BOX 5.4 | Nike and the "Girl Effect"

The "Girl Effect," a slogan coined by Nike in 2008, was used to promote the importance of play in childhood for girls but also girls' role and involvement in development. The marketing around the Girl Effect included a number of athletic women sporting pink Nike shoes as the symbol of Nike's commitment to promoting women's and girls' rights. A series of videos were also prepared by the Nike Foundation to raise awareness about issues affecting girls, but without a clear connection to the Nike brand. This Nike Foundation initiative on the Girl Effect, in collaboration with international agencies such as the United Nations Foundation, advocates for girls to be included in social programming as part of a strategy for ending poverty. The focus on targeting girls for development projects was met with some criticism from development experts as the campaign essentialized girls by stereotyping specific roles and activities for girls, and ignored the social relations that cause gender inequality in the first place, thereby putting the expectations on girls to stimulate gender equity-based development.

Nonetheless, the Girl Effect was a rather effective marketing campaign as part of Nike's corporate social responsibility (CSR) strategy. Simplified messages of "giving girls a chance" and other charitable acts were promoted as means to change communities and end poverty. Over the years, Nike has evolved its work on the Girl Effect by adding Accelerator, noting that girls are the "most powerful force for change on the planet" for entrepreneurship (http://www.girleffect.org/). It is important to track the role of private companies and foundations because their marketing power has had a major influence on the nature of the messages that are disseminated (see Chapter 11). The Girl Effect highlights a particular message that, on the surface, can be effective in raising awareness about girls' rights and opportunities. However, this approach is limited by its nature which offers targeted programs for girls rather than community-based solutions that address the masculinities and deep-seated inequalities that cause gender inequality.

An important set of commitments taking shape at the time this chapter was written is the post-2015 Sustainable Development Goals and development agenda. Among the 17 goals proposed in the SDGs, a commitment to "Achieve Gender Equality and Empower all Women and Girls" remains a core priority (Goal #5). The SDGs build on a long series of international commitments (some of which have been emphasized in this chapter). Building on the MDGs (in particular MDG #3 and its commitment to eliminate gender disparity in primary and secondary education), the SDGs aim to make advancements in ending poverty and promoting equality and sustainability in a 15-year period. However, numerous challenges remain. For example, many countries continue to limit access to education for girls. Pakistan is such an example, yet the importance of promoting girls' education has gained prominence through the efforts of Malala Yousafzai (see Box 5.6) and through the Malala Fund to empower girls through equal access to quality secondary education.

In addition to the lack of educational opportunities for women and girls, several other limitations of gender equality policies and commitments are worth noting. For example, countries may not track measures of gender equality; policies may not translate into practice; organizations may not have funds at their disposal to put gender equality commitments into practice; and individuals may resist efforts to promote gender equality.

TAKING STOCK: ACHIEVEMENTS, POSSIBILITIES, AND ONGOING GAPS IN GENDER AND DEVELOPMENT

The contemporary and historical commitments addressed above offer an important context for examining international actions, national strategies, and individual, private, or NGO campaigns to address

CRITICAL ISSUES

BOX 5.5 | Plan International and the "Because I am a Girl" Campaign

Among its core priorities, Plan International focuses on the girl child and improved access to education for girls, including quality secondary education and increased funding for these educational programs; an end to child marriage; an end to gender-based violence in and around schools; and greater participation for girls and boys in decision-making and programming. The slogan adopted for the Plan International campaign is "Because I am a Girl." This campaign involved extensive marketing employing banners, billboards, posters, and other advertising strategies that could be found in diverse locations from bus station walls to websites. The goal of the Because I am a Girl campaign is to directly improve the quality of life for at least four million girls by ensuring better access to school, enhanced skills, improved livelihoods, and greater protection. Through gender programming, Plan International also advocated for reaching 40 million girls and boys in indirect ways and 400 million girls through changes in policy (Plan International, 2015).

Plan International continues to work to promote improved education and to end early and forced child marriage. The awareness that Plan and other organizations have brought to the pressing problem of early and forced marriages culminated in a resolution to end early and forced marriage adopted by the United Nations in 2014. The resolution recognizes that early marriage has longer-term development impacts, such as threats to women's health, to their educational and economic opportunities, and to their overall social status. Furthermore, this resolution understands the practice of early and forced marriage as a symptom of deeply rooted gender inequalities and practices that discriminate against girls. Child marriage affects both boys and girls; however, the majority of children who face early marriage are female and the age gap between girls and men can be substantial. UNICEF estimates that, globally, one in six adolescent girls (aged 15 to 19) is currently married or in union. South Asia has the highest proportion of married adolescents (29 per cent), followed by West and Central Africa (25 per cent) and Eastern and Southern Africa (20 per cent) (UNICEF, 2015). Efforts to promote the negative impacts of early and forced marriage have led to important changes in practice in some countries. For example, in July 2015, a Malawian village chief annulled 300 child marriages and sent the girls back to school. A female senior chief, Inkosi Kachindamoto, used recent legislation passed in Malawi that sets the legal age of marriage at 18 to annul marriages that affected 175 girls and 155 boys (*This is Africa*, 2015). This is an important first step in a country where half of the women have entered into child marriages (marriage before 18 years of age). Ending early and forced marriage requires changes in laws across the world; improved understanding of the many negative impacts on children; and a commitment from men, women, boys, and girls to put an end to this practice.

gender inequality on a range of issues. Feminist theoretical and conceptual insights have challenged development actors and policy-makers to incorporate strategic commitments to ending gender inequality by moving beyond the targeting of women and girls for development initiatives and towards a deeper analysis of the masculinities, structural constraints, and social relations that perpetuate inequalities. The future of gender and development includes a number of commitments that will shape the next phase of global activities in the promotion of gender equality. One such initiative will be the commitments to gender equality within the Sustainable Development Goals (SDGs) between 2015 and 2030, as noted above. In addition, the United Nations Development Programme's *Gender Equality Strategy 2014–2017: The Future We Want: Rights and Empowerment* puts gender equality and the empowerment of women at the centre of

CRITICAL ISSUES

BOX 5.6 | Malala Yousafzai

Individuals can play an important role in shaping how we understand gender inequality. Malala Yousafzai, for example, has demonstrated the impact that one young woman can have on promoting a particular cause, in this case the promotion of girls' education. Malala is a Pakistani activist and a Nobel Prize laureate. Her name spread across the world when she was shot by a Taliban gunman at the age of 15 while travelling on a school bus to complete her exams in northwest Pakistan. After a lengthy and remarkable recovery, Malala continues to champion girls' education around the world. The United Nations dubbed 12 July 2013 Malala Day—Malala's sixteenth birthday—in honour of her speech to the UN where she noted that "Malala day is not my day. Today is the day of every woman, every boy and every girl who have raised their voice for their rights" (*The Independent*, 2013). The Malala Fund was inspired by Malala's dedication to girls' education and empowerment. As a co-founder of the Malala Fund, Malala Yousafzai advocates for girls' right to a minimum of 12 years of quality education.

PHOTO 5.2 | Malala Yousafzai speaks at a press conference during the United Nations Sustainable Development Summit in September 2015.

international development commitments. The starting point for this UNDP initiative is recognizing that gender equality is central to human rights and to progress in international development.

The commitments and theoretical insights identified in this chapter provide an overview of some of the diverse ways that international commitments to the promotion of gender equality have taken shape over the past several decades and how they have been influenced by feminist scholarship. Much has been achieved in terms of promoting improved understanding of the nature and extent of gender inequality. However, many strategies remain focused on simplified, targeted solutions aimed at improving maternal health, educating girls, or providing opportunities for girls' and women's involvement in sports, political decision-making, and/or economic opportunities. These are important strategies that must, however, be accompanied by broader commitments to understanding the root causes of gender inequality and how inequalities are shaped and sustained through power imbalances and social relations. Key concepts such as empowerment are important to this analysis, but so too are critical reflections on the basic causes of pervasive inequalities that disproportionately affect women and girls in many contexts, and more importantly, on the institutions, norms, and processes that facilitate inequality and perpetuate practices favouring particular kinds of masculinities. In order to make sense of the underlying factors that perpetuate gender inequality, we must continue to revisit the feminist insights addressed above as a guide for tackling gender inequality in development practice.

SUMMARY

In this chapter we have provided a range of examples of feminist insights, gender and development analytical frameworks, international commitments, and global campaigns. More importantly, we have demonstrated how ways of understanding gender and development over time have influenced development programs and international strategies. Gender inequality remains an important issue in international development and successful international development projects must include gender issues as central to the planning and implementation of development outcomes. Much like other challenges in international development, comprehensive and complicated approaches are necessary to ensuring development success. These strategies must involve the beneficiaries of development in all stages, but they also must consider the important historical, structural, and normative challenges to development.

QUESTIONS FOR CRITICAL THOUGHT

1. What do you consider to be some of the most effective campaigns to promote girls' and/or women's rights? Why were they effective? Did they promote targeted interventions specific to women and girls and/or address gender inequality?
2. What have been the most influential United Nations commitments to addressing gender inequality and what are the priorities identified in these commitments?
3. Why are masculinities important to the study of gender and development?
4. How has feminist theory contributed to improved commitments to gender equality?

SUGGESTED READINGS

Cornwall, A., J. Edstrom, and A. Grieg, eds. 2011. *Men and Development*. London: Zed Books.

Kabeer, N. 1994. *Reversed Realities: Gender, Hierarchies in Development Thought*. London and New York: Verso.

Marchand, M.H., and J. Parpart, eds. 1995. *Feminism, Postmodernism and Development*. London and New York: Routledge.

—— and A. Sisson Runyan. 2011. *Gender and Global Restructuring: Sightings, Sites and Resistances*, 2nd edn. London and New York: Routledge.

Momsen, J. 2004. *Gender and Development*, 2nd edn. London and New York: Routledge.

Parpart, J., P. Connelly, and E. Barriteau. 2000. *Theoretical Perspectives on Gender and Development*. Ottawa: International Research Centre.

Tiessen, R. 2007. *Everywhere/Nowhere: Gender Mainstreaming in Development Agencies*. Bloomfield, Conn.: Kumarian Press.

Tinker, I. 1990. *Persistent Inequalities: Women and World Development*. Oxford and New York: Oxford University Press.

Vişvanathan, N., L. Duggan, N. Wiegersma, and L. Nisonoff, eds. 2011. *The Women, Gender and Development Reader*. London: Zed Books.

BIBLIOGRAPHY

Baaz, M.E., and M. Stern. 2013. *Sexual Violence as a Weapon of War? Perceptions, Prescriptions, Problems in the Congo and Beyond*. London: Zed Books.

Barker, G., and C. Ricardo. 2006. "A key to HIV prevention: Understanding what drives young men in Africa." *Global AIDS Link* 100 (Nov./Dec.).

Batliwala, S. 1994. "The meaning of women's empowerment: New concepts from action." In G. Sen et al. eds, *Population Policies Reconsidered: Health, Empowerment and Rights*. Cambridge, Mass.: Harvard University Press, Harvard Series on Population and International Health, 127–38.

Bergeron, S. 2011. "Governing gender in neoliberal restructuring: Economics, performativity and social reproduction." In Marchand and Sisson Runyan (2011).

Bird, S.R., et al. 2007. "Constructing an alternative masculine identity: The experience of the Centro Barlolome de las Casas and Oxfam American in El Salvador." *Gender and Development* 15, 1: 112–21.

Boserup, E. 1970. *Women's Role in Economic Development*. London: George Allen and Unwin.

Catala, V., S. Colom, L. Santamaria, and A. Casajust. 2012 "Male hegemony in decline? Reflections on the Spanish case." *Men and Masculinities* 15, 4: 406–23.

Chant, S. 2012. "The disappearing of 'smart economics'? The World Development Report 2012 on gender equality: Some concerns about the preparatory process and the prospects for paradigm change." *Global Social Policy* 12, 2: 198–218.

Connell, R.W. 1995. *Masculinities*. London: Polity.

Cornwall, A., J. Edstrom, and A. Grieg, eds. 2011. *Men and Development*. London: Zed Books.

Dussel, E. 1992. *1492: El Encubrimiento del Otro. Hacia el Origen del Mito de la Modernidad*. Madrid: Nueva Utopía.

ECOSOC. 1997. *Mainstreaming the Gender Perspective into All Policies and Programmes in the United Nations System*. New York: United Nations.

Elson, D., and H. Keklik. 2002. *Progress on the World's Women 2002: Gender Equality and the Millennium Development Goals*. New York: United Nations Development Fund for Women.

Escobar, A. 1998. *La Invención del Tercer Mundo: Construcción y Deconstrucción del Desarrollo*. Bogotá: Editorial Norma.

Hartmann, B. 1995. *Reproductive Rights and Wrongs: The Global Politics of Population Control*. New York: Harper and Row.

Kabeer, N. 1994. *Reversed Realities: Gender Hierarchies in Development Thought*. London and New York: Verso.

———. 1999. "Resources, agency, achievements: Reflections on the measurement of women's empowerment." *Development and Change* 30, 3: 435–64.

Lind, A. 2011. "Querying globalization: Sexual subjectivities, development and the governance of intimacy." In Marchand and Sisson Runyan (2011).

Marchand, M.H. 2008. "Labor migration in a North-American context: The violence of development and the migration/insecurities nexus" *Third World Quarterly* 29, 7: 1375–88.

——— and A. Sisson Runyan, eds. 2011. *Gender and Global Restructuring: Sightings, Sites and Resistances*, 2nd edn. London and New York: Routledge.

Mendoza, B. 2002. "Transnational feminisms in question." *Feminist Theory* 3, 3: 313–32.

Mignolo, W.D. 2007. *La Idea de América Latina. La Herida Colonial y la Opción Decolonial*. Barcelona: Gedisa.

Mohanty, C.T. 1988. "Under Western eyes: Feminist scholarship and colonial discourses." *Feminist Review* 30: 61–88.

———. 2003. "'Under Western eyes' revisited: Feminist solidarity through anticapitalist struggles." *Signs* 28, 2: 499–535.

Mosedale, S. 2005. "Assessing women's empowerment: Towards a conceptual framework." *Journal of International Development* 17: 243–57.

Moser, C. 1993. *Gender Planning and Development: Theory, Practice and Training*. London: Routledge.

Parpart, J. 2010. "Masculinity, gender and the 'new wars'." *Nordic Journal for Masculinity Studies* 5, 2: 85–99.

———. 2014. "Exploring the transformative potential of gender mainstreaming in international development institutions." *Journal of International Development* 26: 382–95.

———. 2015. "Men, masculinities and development." In A. Coles, L. Gray, and J. Momsen, eds, *The Routledge Handbook of Gender and Development*. London: Routledge, 14–23.

———, S. Rai, and K. Staudt. 2002. *Rethinking Empowerment*. London: Routledge.

Plan International. 2015. "Because I am a Girl." http://plan-international.org/girls/. Accessed 23 July 2015.

Rao, A., and D. Keller. 2004. "Is there life after gender mainstreaming?" *Gender and Development* 13, 2: 57–69.

Rathgeber, E. 1990. "WID, WAD, GAD: Trends in research and practice." *Journal of Developing Areas* 24, 4: 489–502.

Red de Feminismos Descoloniales. 2014. "Descolonizando nuestros feminismos, abriendo la mirada." In Yuderkys Espinosa Miñoso, Diana Gómez Correal, and Karina Ochoa Muñoz, eds, *Tejiendo de Otro Modo: Feminismo, Epistemología y Apuestas Descoloniales en Abya Yala. Popayán*, Colombia: Universidad del Cauca.

Rowlands, J. 1997. *Questioning Empowerment*. Oxford: Oxfam Publications.

Sen, G., and C. Grown. 1987. *Development Crises and Alternative Visions: Third World Women's Perspectives*. London: Earthscan.

Sisson Runyan, A. and M.H. Marchand. 2011. "Conclusion." In Marchand and Sisson Runyan (2011).

Standing, H. 2007. "Gender, myth and fable: The perils of mainstreaming in sectoral bureaucracies." In A. Cornwall, E. Harrison, and A. Whitehead, eds, *Feminisms in Development*. London: Zed Books, 101–11.

Sweetman, C. 2013. "Introduction: Working with men on gender equality." *Gender and Development* 21, 1: 1–13.

The Independent. 2013. "The full text: Malala Yousafzai delivers defiant riposte to Taliban militants with speech to the UN General Assembly." 12 July. www.independent.co.uk/news/world/asia/the-full-text-malala-yousafzai-delivers-defiant-riposte-to-taliban-militants-with-speech-to-the-un-general-assembly-8706606.html. Accessed 23 July 2015.

This is Africa. 2015. "Malawian chief annuls 300 child marriages, sends kids to school." 2 July. http://thisisafrica.me/malawian-chief-annuls-300-child-marriage-send-kids-to-school/. Accessed 23 July 2015.

Tiessen, R. 2015. "Walking wombs: Making sense of the Muskoka Initiative and the emphasis on motherhood in Canadian foreign policy." *Global Justice—The Journal* 8: 1–22.

——— and S. Tuckey. 2014. "Loose promises and vague reporting: Analyzing Canada's National Action Plan and reports on women, peace, and security." In *Worth the Wait? Reflections on Canada's National Action Plan & Reports on Women, Peace & Security*. WPSN. https://wpsncanada.files.wordpress.com/2012/05/worth-the-wait-report.pdf. Accessed 24 July 2015.

——— and ———. 2015. "Losing gender along the way: The failure to mainstream gender in Canada's commitments to international security and development." In R. Warner, ed., *Unsettled Balance: Ethics, Security and Canada's International Relations*.Vancouver: University of British Columbia Press, 183–207.

UNICEF. 2015. "Child marriage is a violation of human rights, but is all too common." http://data.unicef.org/child-protection/child-marriage#sthash.sSGWFNwh.dpuf and http://data.unicef.org/child-protection/child-marriage. Accessed 31 July 2015.

United Nations. 1995. *The United Nations and the Advancement of Women, 1945–1995*. New York: United Nations Department of Public Information

———. 2014. *The Millennium Development Goals Report 2014*. New York: United Nations.

United Nations Development Programme (UNDP). 2015. *Annexes to the UNDP Gender Equality Strategy 2014–2017: The Future We Want: Rights and Empowerment, Annex 2: Key Global and Regional Commitments to Gender.* www.undp.org/content/dam/undp/library/gender/Annex%202%20Global%20and%20Regional%20Commitments%20to%20Gender%20Equality.pdf. Accessed 23 July 2015.

United Nations General Assembly. 1993. "Declaration on the Elimination of Violence against Women." 20 Dec. www.un.org/documents/ga/res/48/a48r104.htm. Accessed 19 Feb. 2016.

United Nations Population Fund. 2014. "International Conference on Population and Development Programme in Action." www.unfpa.org/publications/international-conference-population-and-development-programme-action#sthash.euhnzXcK.dpuf. Accessed 23 July 2015.

UN Women. 2015. "The girl child." *The Beijing Platform for Action Turns 20*. http://beijing20.unwomen.org/en/in-focus/girl-child. Accessed 23 July 2015.

White, S. 1997. "Men, masculinities and the politics of development." In S. Sweetman, ed., *Men and Masculinity*. Oxford: Oxfam, 14–22.

World Bank. 1995. *World Bank Participation Source Book*. Washington: World Bank Environment Department Papers.

World Health Organization (WHO). 2014. "Maternal mortality." Fact Sheet No. 348, updated May 2014. www.who.int/mediacentre/factsheets/fs348/en/. Accessed 14 Aug. 2015.

———. 2015. "MDG 5: Improve maternal mortality." Reviewed May 2015. www.who.int/topics/millennium_development_goals/maternal_health/en/. Accessed 14 Aug. 2015.

6 Globalization and Development

Pierre Beaudet

LEARNING OBJECTIVES

- To acquire a critical understanding of globalization in relation to development theories.
- To understand how globalization changes developing countries.
- To examine the impact that alternate globalization approaches have on development theories and practices.

▲ **A woman in Jiangsu province works on stuffed monkeys destined to be Valentine's Day gifts in North America. The most densely populated province in China, Jiangsu also has the highest GDP and is home to many of the world's leading exporters of electronics, chemicals, and textiles.** | Source: STR/AFP/Getty Images

INTRODUCTION

Over the past decade, the concept of globalization has invaded public space as well as the social sciences, including development studies. In many ways, the internationalization of the world economy has changed the way societies and states are structured and governed, simultaneously with the **contraction of time and space**, as explained by geographer David Harvey (2005). Scholars, practitioners, and experts debate the scope, depth, and impact of globalization's reach into economics, politics, culture, the environment, and so on. There is an abundance of excellent analysis on this "hot" topic (see the suggested readings at the end of this chapter).

Changing Paradigms?

This chapter focuses on the impact of globalization on development and developing countries. It aims to trigger new debates and reflections, especially for those who are working on and studying development. The development "community," indeed, faces many questions:

- Is globalization really transforming the architecture of the world we live in?
- How can we understand the contradictory patterns of economic growth, as evidenced by growing social gaps in many parts of the world?
- How are China and other "emerging" developing countries becoming economic leaders? Is this phenomenon changing the reality of what used to be called the "developing world"?
- Is the pattern of globalization forcing development scholars and practitioners to revise their perspectives and theories?

These questions are both theoretical and practical. On the one hand, they relate to the way concepts are constructed in development studies. On the other, they are translated into actions, programs, and projects by many governmental and non-governmental development agents.

GLOBALIZATION AND DEVELOPING COUNTRIES

In the early 1990s, when the concept of globalization became widely used, many scholars and policy-makers working on development were taken aback. One of those was Fernando Henrique Cardoso, one of the founders of the famous dependency school that had such great influence on thinking in development studies in the 1970s (see Chapter 3). He changed his earlier analysis, giving this globalization-and-development debate a rather provocative spin. After becoming the president of Brazil in 1994, Cardoso (2007) argued that past development theories were dead and buried and that everything he had said about development was wrong! At that time, he proposed that development required full integration into the world system, which implied, in turn, accepting the terms of current macroeconomic policies as they were defined a decade before in the Washington Consensus (Box 6.1). Under Cardoso's presidency, the social and economic priorities of Brazil were refocused to adjust to the needs and requirements of international markets. Yet a few decades previously, Cardoso and many of his colleagues in development studies had been arguing that the only path to development was to "delink" from international capitalism.

While Brazil and other developing countries were changing paths, most of the nations of the world sought to further integrate into the capitalist system. These broad policies were promoted by the G8, an informal association of the richest countries in the world (Canada, France, Germany, Italy, Japan, Russia, the United Kingdom, and the United States).

Success Stories?

For former President Cardoso and other heads of state of the developing world, there was simply no alternative in the early stage of globalization. His argument was fairly simple: the world had changed. Capitalism had triumphed worldwide with the end of the Cold War. Developing countries had to conform, and if they did not, they would be left out. During that period, the World Bank (2004), in particular, produced an enormous volume of analysis, arguing that developing countries could and should prosper and progress through fully "globalizing" and integrating into the world economy (and not going against it).

The Bank specifically documented what it presented as the "East Asian miracle" (see Chapter 7), where the combination of shared Confucian cultural

IMPORTANT CONCEPTS

BOX 6.1 | The Washington Consensus

The Washington Consensus was put on the agenda in 1989 by the economist and former World Bank official John Williamson. The term has been associated with neoliberal policies first adopted by the United States and Britain in the early 1980s and later promoted by the World Bank and the IMF in developing countries. The "consensus" recommended the liberalization of capital flows and trade (through free trade agreements), the privatization of the public sector, and the abolition of market-restricting regulations. It became a central component of structural adjustment programs imposed by the Bank and the IMF on countries that required loans.

heritage, strong government guidance, and export-led economies produced high economic growth and prosperity. The idea was that East Asia was *the* model whereby developing countries that opened their borders would find competitive niches and attract foreign capital, thereby triggering economic growth, as indeed happened in countries like China, South Korea, and smaller "tigers" and "dragons"[1] that emerged as big players in the global economy. Not only did these countries experience rapid economic growth (Asian Development Bank, 2013), but in addition, poverty declined rapidly, from 78 per cent in 1981 to 8 per cent in 2011. In China, 753 million people moved above the benchmark for extreme poverty ($1.25 per day) (World Bank, 2015).

Parallel to these achievements, China's economy continues to grow, while North America and Western Europe are struggling to come out of the financial and economic slump of 2008, the most severe since 1929. Indeed, China has become the workshop of the world, exporting a vast surplus of industrialized goods and, increasingly, high-tech products. Between 1990 and 2012, China's share of total world exports rose from 1.8 per cent to 10.4 per cent. China is on track to become the world's biggest exporter, overtaking Germany (World Trade Organization, 2012). (Also see Chapter 13.)

Time and Space Contracting

Put simply, globalization translates into new sets of relations and activities, mostly in the economic arena, that are taking place irrespective of the geographical location of participants. Globalization underpins a transformation in the organization of human affairs by linking together and expanding human activity across regions and continents (Held and McGrew, 2003). Territory as a geographic reality no longer constitutes the whole of the "social space" in which human activity occurs (see Box 6.2). Because of these major changes, social geographer David Harvey (2005) believes that modern capitalism has integrated the world much more profoundly than ever before. Time and space are no longer insurmountable, as they were in the past, because with modern communication and transportation, everything moves everywhere, including goods, services, and people. Therefore, the geographic divide between the North and the South appears to have become blurred (WTO, 2009). This is not to say that the gap has disappeared. Rather, globalization is generating a new pattern whereby poverty and wealth are redistributed through a reconstituted structure of exclusion. For Harvey (1990: 147), current patterns of development under globalization lead to "shifts in the patterning of uneven development, both between sectors and between geographical regions."

Trade and Growth

No one could deny that enormous changes have taken place in the past two decades in developing countries and at a broader level as well. World trade, in particular,

Photo by Yassine Gaidi/Anadolu Agency/Getty Images

PHOTO 6.1 | People from the World Social Forum gather to denounce terror in Tunis, Tunisia, on 24 March 2015. In Tunisia a corrupt dictatorship was overthrown during the "Arab Spring."

CRITICAL ISSUES

BOX 6.2 | A Global Age?

Globalization is a transplanetary process or set of processes involving . . . growing multi-directional flows of people, objects, places and information, as well as the structures they encounter and create that are barriers to, or expedite, those flows. Although globalization and transnationalism are often used synonymously, the latter is a more limited process which refers largely to interconnections across two, or more, national borders. The sheer magnitude, diversity and complexity of the process of globalization today lead to the conceptualization of the current era as the "global age."

Source: Ritzer (2010: 28).

has reached an unprecedented level. In 2013, exports and imports of goods and services exceeded $23 trillion, an increase of over 2 per cent from the previous year (WTO, 2014). At the same time, exports from developing countries are growing much faster in comparison with the rest of the world. In 2013, the share of developing economies in world merchandise trade set new records, with exports rising to 44 per cent of the world total (WTO, 2014) (Figure 6.1).

Much of this increase in exports from developing countries has to do with the fact that they have been encouraged by the IMF and World Bank to open their economies, liberalize trade, and increase exports. Under the influence of the powerful agencies promoting globalization, trade is expanding faster than production. The theory is that the soothing influence of the market (the "invisible hand" of Adam Smith) will help every country to find its "niche" selling and buying where its comparative advantage dominates (see Chapter 15). Everyone wins in the end, so the story goes. Most countries of the world are now members of the World Trade Organization (Figure 6.2), the champion of international globalization, liberalization, and economic integration.

The World Bank remains convinced that globalization—i.e., integration into the world market—is working for the poor and the developing world. For David Dollar, an economist working for the Bank (2004), the simple proof that globalization works is that poor-country growth rates are higher than rich-country growth rates for the first time in modern history. These positive trends towards faster growth

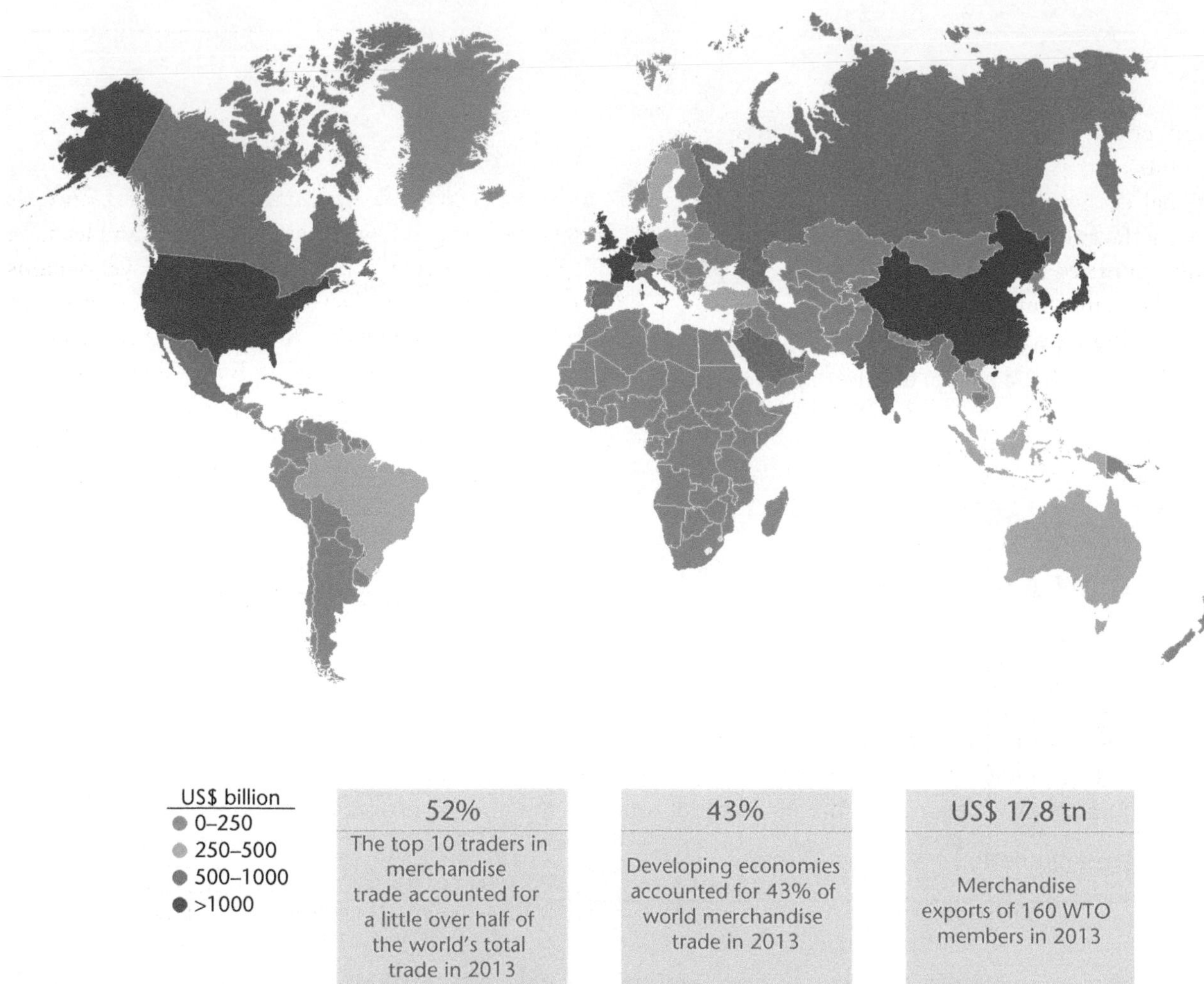

FIGURE 6.1 | World Economies by Size of Merchandise Trade, 2013

Source: WTO (2014).

CRITICAL ISSUES

BOX 6.3 | Are Things Getting Better?

According to the World Bank (2015), the number of the poorest of the poor (income of $1.25 per day or less) has declined from 43 per cent of the world's population (1990) to 17 per cent in 2011, leaving over a billion people at risk. The improvement is not as impressive for the "moderately" poor: there are still 2.2 billion people living on an average of $2 per day, as compared to 2.5 billion in 1981. China alone accounts for a large proportion of the people who escaped extreme poverty (more than 750 million). Poverty levels remain stubbornly—and unacceptably—high in sub-Saharan Africa, where there has been little growth, and in South Asia, despite more rapid and sustained growth. Eighty per cent of the extremely poor lived in South Asia (399 million) and sub-Saharan Africa (415 million). Experience has shown that economic growth alone is not sufficient to greatly reduce poverty in its many dimensions. Indeed, the mixed record of poverty reduction calls into question the efficacy of conventional approaches involving economic liberalization and privatization.

and poverty reduction are strongest in developing countries that have integrated most rapidly into the global economy. The World Bank is also encouraged by the fact that the growth of exports from developing countries is mostly in manufactured products. At the same time, **foreign direct investment (FDI)** in developing countries accounted for 52 per cent of all FDI (Figure 6.3). However, the flows are asymmetrical. Four countries (China, India, Brazil, and South Africa) have received most of the FDI flows to developing countries.

Who Is Benefiting?

In fact, when we look at the details, the picture is more complex. Sub-Saharan Africa, for example, has a high ratio of exports to GDP (30 per cent), yet remains poor because its products are cheap. By contrast, rich and powerful countries concentrate their productive capacities and exports on high-value goods and services. Also, only 12 developing countries are really participating in this expansion of trade. For the United Nations Conference on Trade and Development

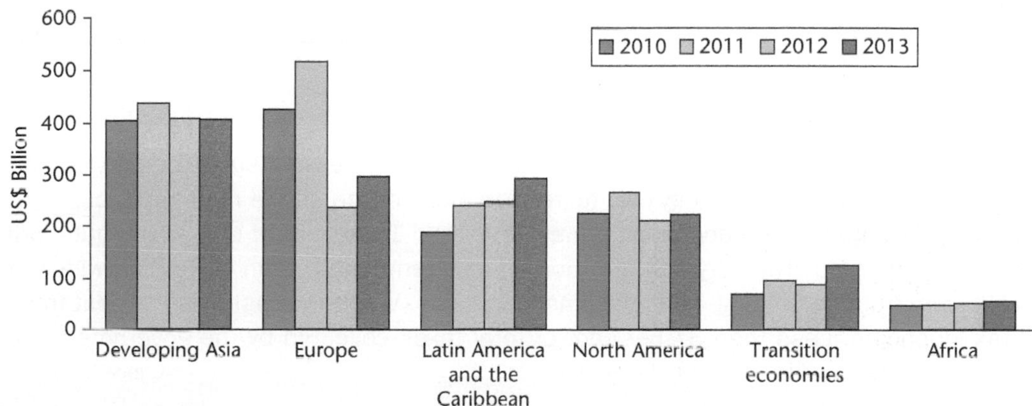

FIGURE 6.2 | FDI Inflows, by Region, 2010–13

Source: UNCTAD (2014). From *Global Investment Trends Monitor*, No. 15, 28 January 2014 © 2014. Reprinted with the permission of the United Nations.

(UNCTAD, 2014), the growth of exports in many poor countries does *not* necessarily lead to poverty reduction. The United Nations Food and Agriculture Organization estimates that about 805 million people were suffering from chronic undernourishment in 2012–14, out of which 791 million live in developing countries (FAO, 2015).

According to Oxfam International, the contrasting experiences of Latin America and East Asia illustrate that globalization-induced growth and poverty can coexist. Even when the market expands, "poor people are often excluded from opportunities by a lack of productive assets, weak infrastructure, poor education and ill-health" (Oxfam International, 2000). Since the 1950s, the income gap between rich countries and poor countries has widened considerably.

Amartya Sen (2002), a well-known economist originally from India who is critical of the World Bank and IMF policies, believes that the main issue is not globalization itself but inequitable sharing of its benefits. According to the World Commission on the Social Dimension of Globalization (2004) set up by the International Labour Organization, "Wealth is being created, but too many countries and people are not sharing in its benefits." The bottom half of the world's population owns the same as the richest 85 individuals in the world. All in all, the richest 1 per cent account for 48 per cent of world income (Oxfam International, 2014a).

Sub-Saharan Africa on the Margins

Even the most ardent promoters of globalization will admit that Africa is facing a tough challenge (see Box 6.5). Exclusion from the benefits of globalization of the poorest countries, defined by the UN as the "least developed countries" (LDCs), remains a dreadful reality. Currently, many African countries appear to be trapped in a vicious circle of interlocking handicaps, including poverty, illiteracy, civil strife, environmental pressures, poor governance, and inflexible economies largely dependent on a single commodity.

This bleak picture, however, needs to be nuanced. In the last decade, African social global indicators have been improving, in great part because of the good economic performance of a small group of countries. In countries rich in oil and other natural resources, such as Angola and Nigeria, high growth rates have been registered. Some countries have even been able to improve access to basic social services, making progress towards achievement of the Millennium Development Goals (UN Department of Economic and Social Affairs, 2010).

More critical views, however, suggest that economic growth has not led to major social improvements and, moreover, remains fragile, linked principally to the scramble for African natural resources by developed-country investors from the US, the European Union, and China. In addition, Africa's recent surge in growth was driven by commodity exports that did not induce much structural change. Instead, they merely reinforced

CRITICAL ISSUES

BOX 6.4 | Billionaires in India

According to Oxfam, there are currently 61 billionaires in India (there were six in the previous decade) in a country of 1.2 billion. Collectively, they own more than $250 billion. In the meantime, public resources for basic services like health and education remain less than 1 per cent of GDP, which puts India at the bottom of Asian standards. The very rich are thought to often benefit from corruption widely prevalent in sectors like construction, mining, and telecommunications. Wealthy people also benefit from low taxation and tax loopholes. Less than 37 per cent of total taxes collected by the government come from direct taxes on income, profits, and capital gains.

Source: Oxfam (2014b).

CRITICAL ISSUES

BOX 6.5 | Poverty in Sub-Saharan Africa

- Seventy-five per cent of the world's poorest countries are located in Africa. In 2010, 415 million people were living in extreme poverty across the continent (48.5 per cent of the total African population).
- Approximately 589 million Africans live without electricity. Because of lack of clean water and proper sanitation, 50 per cent of Africans catch water-related illnesses. Approximately 900,000 Africans die every year of malaria, out of which 80 per cent are children.
- Fewer than 20 per cent of African women have access to education. One in 16 women living in sub-Saharan Africa will die during childbirth or pregnancy (compared with one in 4,000 women in North America).

Source: Borgen Project (2014).

Africa's narrow export base. Moreover, since 2013, these commodities have lost much of their previous value while external markets have been squeezed because of the slump in Europe and Asia (IMF, 2014). In the meantime, Africa accounts for less than 1 per cent of the world's GDP. To add to the catastrophe, external debt has exploded—from $89 billion (1980) to $149 billion (2010). In 2014, while aid and investment flows into Africa represented $134 billion, financial outflows from Africa were almost $192 billion (Jubilee Debt Campaign, 2014), thus creating a net deficit of nearly $60 billion for the African economy.

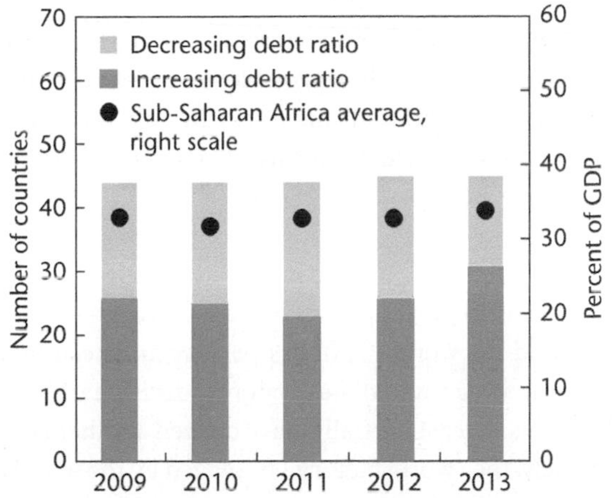

FIGURE 6.3 | Debt Ratio for Sub-Saharan Africa

Source: IMF (2014), p. 11.

China: Exception or Trend?

If African countries are generally in decline, other countries, most notably China, seem to be profiting from globalization. Indeed, China has now surpassed Japan to become the second biggest economy in the world. Most of the FDI to the Global South is absorbed by China, creating hundreds of thousands of jobs, chiefly in coastal areas (Sung, 2005). Vast masses of rural people have moved to the cities, where they have relatively better access to food, health care, and education. The rate of extreme poverty at the national level declined from 84 per cent in 1981 to 7 per cent in 2012 (Phelps and Crabtree, 2013). According to mainstream institutions such as the World Bank, most of that success can be attributed to the integration of China into the world economy (China joined the WTO in 2001).

But not everyone agrees. Some analysts argue that changes in China (such as land reform and nationalization of productive assets) after the 1948 revolution, but before globalization, have had a more lasting impact on economic and social progress than recent changes related to globalization. Other China experts focus on the flip side of the miracle in terms of class polarization,

CRITICAL ISSUES

BOX 6.6 | Is Globalization Reducing or Increasing Poverty and Inequality?

Vandana Shiva (2000a), a well-known ecologist and advocate of peoples' movements in India, puts globalization on trial using the example of peasants in India:

> Globalization is leading to a concentration of the seed industry, the increased use of pesticides, and, finally, increased debt. Capital-intensive, corporate-controlled agriculture is being spread into regions where peasants are poor but, until now, have been self-sufficient in food. In the regions where industrial agriculture has been introduced through globalization, higher costs are making it virtually impossible for small farmers to survive. The globalization of non-sustainable industrial agriculture is evaporating the incomes of Third World farmers through a combination of devaluation of currencies, increase in costs of production and a collapse in commodity prices.

For Robert I. Lerman (2002), on the other hand, globalization is benefiting the poor:

> It has helped the poor countries that adopted sound policies and contributed to income convergence among the countries participating in the global system. In principle, allowing trade, investment and migration should reduce global poverty. Less clearly, it should also shrink the gap between rich and poor. As firms move from high to low-wage areas, the demand for workers should grow in low-wage areas and decrease in high-wage areas, again lowering inequality.

environmental degradation, and deteriorating governance. According to Wen and Li (2006), China's growth is not sustainable. It is triggering an immense energy crisis coupled with declining food and water resources. They predict that the current trend, if not reoriented, could create an uncontrollable public health crisis as well as ecological disasters (see Chapter 17).

What Is New?

Given this global panorama, we arrive at a simple question: what is new about globalization? Are we not seeing the same thing, under new conditions perhaps, that has been restructuring the world since the expansion of Western capitalism? Is it not the same pattern observed by Karl Marx and Friedrich Engels over 160 years ago?

> The bourgeoisie has, through its exploitation of the world market, given a cosmopolitan character to production and consumption in every country. Instead of the old local and national seclusion and self-sufficiency, we have intercourse in every direction, the universal interdependence of nations. National one-sidedness and narrow-mindedness become less and less possible, and from the numerous national and local literatures, there arises a world literature. (Marx and Engels, 1967 [1848])

What does appear to be new is the speed and intensity of interconnections among entities across the world. Around the world, 24 hours per day, financial markets are imposing immediate economic decisions. New technologies, at least partially, have created another reality—namely, the "world factory," managed by the world firm, under a world label, where everything from production to marketing and design is integrated across continents and communities. For Luis Hebron and John F. Stack (2009), for example, globalization is powerful because it brings together politics, economics, law, social structures, media, and information technologies.

Who Makes the Decisions?

Globalization has a profound impact on politics. The nation-state, at the centre of the political architecture of the modern world, is losing parts of its sovereignty as economic actors such as large **multinational corporations** and financial institutions make transactions freely across borders (see Chapters 9 and 11). Kenichi Ohmae, in a provocative book, *The End of the Nation State*, explains: "the workings of genuinely global capital markets dwarf their ability to control exchange rates or protect their currency." Consequently, "nation states have become inescapably vulnerable to the discipline imposed by economic choices made elsewhere by people and institutions over which they have no practical control" (Ohmae, 1995: 12).

For many experts, political structures inherited from the nation-state are becoming obsolete. Fundamental policies governing macroeconomics are discussed and determined by agencies far removed from the public arena (Lenhard, 2010). While the powerful have influence, most developing countries are left out of the process. For example, the IMF and the World Bank are directed by a small group of countries because these institutions, unlike the United Nations, are governed by powerful states that have larger voting shares because of their greater financial contributions to institutional functioning, contrary to the UN system where all member states, in principle at least, have an equal footing (see Chapters 9 and 10).

The governments of smaller or weaker states are therefore losing their influence in the international arena—but also at their own national level. At worst, this process ends up in a breakdown, as we have seen in several sub-Saharan countries (as well as in Southeast Europe and elsewhere). This disjuncture between the economic/private and the political/public spaces is creating a vacuum. It remains to be seen, for example, whether the United Nations will be able to recover from its current semi-marginalization, considering that the rich and powerful may not want it to do so.

The United Nations is frequently bypassed by multilateral and bilateral structures and economic and trade accords, such as the North American Free Trade Agreement (NAFTA), that make decisions over a wide range of matters, including the maintenance of peace. Most countries have now joined the WTO and are negotiating their place on the ladder within this institution that imposes new rules for international trade. The G8, and now the more inclusive G20, an enlarged grouping of the most powerful countries, is there to "set the agenda," i.e., to define broader policies, norms, and targets that will be later adopted by or forced upon other national governments.

ANOTHER GLOBALIZATION?

Clearly, globalization appears set to remain at the centre of hot debates. The Global South is "re-" and "de"-composing itself into a myriad of contradictory processes.

CRITICAL ISSUES

BOX 6.7 | Governance

Joseph Stiglitz, former Chief Economist of the World Bank, wrote:

> Unfortunately, we have no world government, accountable to the people of every country, to oversee the globalization process. Instead, we have a system that might be called *global governance without global government*, one in which a few institutions—the World Bank, the IMF, the WTO—and a few players—the finance, commerce, and trade ministries, closely linked to certain financial and commercial interests—dominate the scene, but in which many of those affected by their decisions are left almost voiceless.

Source: Stiglitz (2002: 21–2).

The New Face of Imperialism?

Some analysts believe that globalization is basically just "another face" of imperialism, allowing the powerful, mostly in the Global North, to extend their reach and widen the net of international capitalism (Watts, 2011). The core, not to say the bulk, of key economic, commercial, and financial transactions remains concentrated in the "triad," the traditional centre of power composed of Western Europe, Japan, and North America. Although representing less than 15 per cent of the world's population, the triad accounts for most of the economic output, even if the emergence of new economic powers is eroding this supremacy.

For Samir Amin, a radical economist from Egypt, "their domination is exercised directly on all the huge companies producing goods and services, like the financial institutions (banks and others) that stem from their power" (Amin, 2009). Amin and other critics contend that even most of the "success stories" of East Asia (except for China) represent a set of "arrangements" with the triad, delocalizing some of the labour-intensive activities to countries that remain dependent, peripheral, and under the dominating influence of the rich countries. This situation is compounded by the fact that, in many respects, the East Asian "tigers" still depend on the Global North in key sectors such as finance and high technology.

"Global South"?

Walden Bello, a political economist from the Philippines, reminds us that the income gap continues to grow between "rich" and "poor" countries even if, within these countries, similar patterns are at play between social groups (Bello, 2013). According to a UN report on inequality (2014), 55 per cent of the global income is concentrated in countries accounting for 16 per cent of the population.

Bello (2005) summarizes the process as the reconfiguration of a Global South, which is no longer just a simple geographic definition but a reflection of new relations unfolding throughout the world. Bello describes a "restructured" worldwide capitalism where the traditional South (the Third World) is now split between "emergent" countries with growing segments of their populations enriching themselves and countries and people who are being left further behind; at the same time, in the traditional North (North America, Western Europe, Japan), the mix of economic decline and political/cultural fractures is producing growing pockets of poverty to an extent not known in the last 80 years.

Other scholars explain that this deterritorialization is by no means confined to the delocalization of economic activities (for example, industrial plants moving from Europe, Canada, or the United States to China or Mexico). It also implies the adoption of common policies on major issues governing the economy and society. Every country has to accept the rules established by the WTO and the IMF in order to maintain their "macroeconomic stability," as it is usually worded. This implies cutting down on social expenditures such as education and health care and providing more incentives to investors and financial institutions.

Pursuing that line of thinking, Amin (2004) suggests that globalization is setting the stage for a new offensive from the United States to protect its imperial interests. The empire relies on unlimited military might and the overwhelming influence of transnational corporations (TNCs), compelling other countries to submit.

Obviously, enthusiasm for globalization has been challenged by many, such as the Indian scientist and ecologist Vandana Shiva:

> Globalization is not a natural, evolutionary or inevitable phenomenon [but rather] a political process that has been forced on the weak by the powerful. . . . "Global" in the dominant discourse is the political space in which the dominant seeks control, freeing itself from local, regional, and global sources of accountability arising from the imperatives of ecological sustainability and social justice. (Shiva, 2000b: 92)

Within this context, a growing body of research and policy argues that current globalization needs to be "fixed" or eventually replaced.

Beyond the Triad

Globalization remains a process led by a few countries, mostly in North America and the European Union (with Japan). It has been noted, however, that a small number of countries in the Global South are now important economic actors (see Chapter 13). According to the World Bank, three of these countries (China, Brazil, and India) are now among the top 10 economies in the world.

Until recently, China was very quiet if not invisible in international forums. But China's role is changing, as one can see in the United Nations concerning controversial matters implicating Syria, Iran, and North Korea. In some of the past proceedings of the WTO (the "Doha round"), China sided with countries such as Brazil and India to oppose agreements that excessively favoured northern countries on issues such as agricultural protectionism and liberalization of trade and services. Like previous southern-led initiatives such as the Group of 77 and platforms such as UNCTAD, where the call for a "new economic order" was launched in the 1970s, these efforts are not intended as much to oppose globalization as to rebalance its impact. In addition to seeking to open northern markets and protect southern assets, these countries also are critical of the liberalization of the financial sector. Despite many demands from the US and the international financial institutions, China thus far has refused to alter its exchange control system, which keeps the Chinese currency outside speculative manoeuvres of large (mostly Western) financial institutions.

Apart from defending their assets and policies, countries of the Global South are trying to reinvent what used to be called "South–South solidarity." In this context, for example, a regional grouping such as the Association of Southeast Asian Nations (ASEAN) is trying to create a regional economic bloc bringing together 10 countries including China. In parallel, China is promoting a regional security association called the Shanghai Cooperation Organization (SCO) (see Box 6.8). The idea is to bring together China, Russia, Kazakhstan, Kyrgyzstan, Tajikistan, and Uzbekistan, and eventually India, Iran, Pakistan, and Mongolia, in a program of regional integration and security that would *not* be controlled by the northern powers. In reality, the SCO is very far from being anything but a discussion platform. But it might represent the beginning of an important process.

In terms of substance, China and the other "BRICS" countries (Brazil, Russia, India, China, South Africa) want to renegotiate, not destroy, international economic integration and trade. BRICS is an informal intergovernmental network where "emerging" countries discuss how to improve their status in the world system. These countries feel entitled to more influence in global governance because they have 25 per cent of the world's land coverage, have 40 per cent of the world's population, and hold a combined GDP of US$15.435 trillion. The BRICS want to reform organizations such as the WTO so that southern interests are better integrated into the mainstream. The economic liberalization of these still underdeveloped economies, as the BRICS see it, needs to be done gradually, protecting vulnerable and strategic sectors while improving access to northern markets. China, India, Brazil, and other emerging countries also want to further regionalize economic links, not necessarily against global integration but as a platform to gain strength and access to the global market on an equal footing. Through growing South–South linkages, the idea is to diversify (or reduce dependency on northern markets and investments) and enlarge the economy. China is involved in financial initiatives to enhance these linkages through the Asian Infrastructure Investment Bank, the Asian Bond Fund Initiative, and, in 2014, with the participation of Brazil, India, Russia, and South Africa, the founding of the New Development Bank (NDB) (formerly the BRICS Bank), with a starting fund of $50 billion. It is too early to say if the NDB will be able to compete with traditional institutions such as the World Bank. In the meantime, the United States has not been in favour of the creation of the NDB. It is also working to promote its own regional scheme under the Trans-Pacific Partnership (TPP), which would link up several Asian countries (but not China) with the United States, Canada, Mexico, Chile, Peru, New Zealand, and Australia. It is widely seen as another manifestation of the US–China competition that is bound to become more extensive in the decades ahead.

Will China and the BRICS face the challenge? Since 2010, China's economy has entered into a period of "slow growth" (in relative terms). Brazil, Argentina, and Algeria as well as other "emerging" countries have been battered by the declines in the prices of commodities on which their growth was based (mineral and agricultural resources). South–South relations are on a bumpy road since China has the capacity to flood its southern trade partners with industrial goods, which prevents these countries from industrializing and confines them to primary-sector activities.

CRITICAL ISSUES

BOX 6.8 | Shanghai Cooperation Organization

Created in 2001, the Shanghai Cooperation Organization aims to form a comprehensive network of co-operation among member states on several issues, such as military security, economic development, trade, and cultural exchange, with the implicit goal of curbing Washington's influence in Central Asia. Both Russia and China want to have the dominant influence over the rich energy resources of this region and also to link up with Middle Eastern countries concerned with Washington's policy of "regime change" in the region.

"Rebels" with a Cause

Some countries, mostly in South America, want to go even further within their region, demanding a reversal of the policies of trade liberalization and privatization and openly challenging the Washington Consensus. There are, of course, big differences between economic giants like Brazil, Argentina, and Mexico, and, on the other hand, small and poor countries like Ecuador and Bolivia. The idea of coming together in the tradition of Simón Bolívar (1783–1830), the leader of South American independence, in the "*Patria grande*" (one big country) is alive, but it clashes with contradicting economic, political, and social realities.

Nevertheless, in the last two decades, South American countries have made serious efforts to make their strength and capacities converge. One of the most important projects is MERCOSUR, a trade alliance between five states with a collective GDP of $2.9 trillion, which means that this South American bloc is the fourth largest in the world after the European Union, NAFTA, and ASEAN. Parallel to MERCOSUR are other initiatives such as the Bolivarian Alternative for the Americas (ALBA) launched initially by Venezuela, with the goal of focusing on social development, equality, and access for the poorest of the population. Practically, Venezuela, Cuba, Bolivia, Ecuador, and other nations are engaged in several programs to support one another in such areas as health, education, oil, and the media. It remains to be seen whether these projects will last, given the vulnerabilities of the main actors.

MOVEMENT FROM BELOW

Beyond the recent phenomenon of states challenging neoliberal globalization, of course, is the ascendancy of a **global civil society** expressing itself through numerous demands, demonstrations, movements, and networks (see Chapter 12). And beyond the image of anti-globalization protests and riots, a "movement of movements" seems to be in the process of becoming a significant factor in world politics. Radical authors such as Michael Hardt and Antonio Negri (2000) and Naomi Klein (2015) think that new alternative "alter-globalist" movements and demands could eventually turn globalization upside down. Thus, just as the empire appears to be expanding, an alternative political organization of global flows and exchanges is growing alongside it.

From Chiapas via Seattle to Bangkok and Tunis

In 1994 in southern Mexico, indigenous communities represented by a group known as the Zapatista National Liberation Army, otherwise known as simply the Zapatistas, appeared on the world stage, apparently out of the blue, to express their rejection of NAFTA and the neoliberal globalization policies attached to that process, which, according to them, was threatening the livelihood of the large peasant and indigenous populations of that region. The movement captured the imagination of media around the world, partly because of

CRITICAL ISSUES

BOX 6.9 | Latin America at a Crossroads

Created in 1985, MERCOSUR is a regional trade bloc comprising Brazil, Argentina, Uruguay, Venezuela, and Paraguay. Chile, Colombia, Ecuador, Bolivia, Peru, and Suriname are associate members. The combined population of the five member states (not counting the population of associate members) is over 275 million people. Although focusing on trade issues, MERCOSUR is seen by its member states as the beginning of a more comprehensive regional union that would take the path followed by the European Union. The discussion is continuing currently under a larger forum, the Union of South American Nations (UNASUR), launched in Brasilia in 2008, which intends to look at issues such as economic integration, defence, and migration. UNASUR still has a long way to go before it looks like the European Union. This process of South American integration has risen in parallel with the decline of American domination in South America. South American trade relations with China and the European Union have surpassed those with the US. In the meantime, South America actually killed a North–South integration scheme (Free Trade Area of the Americas or FTAA) proposed by US President Bill Clinton back in 1994. The United States and Canada saw the proposed FTAA as an extension of NAFTA southward.

the symbolism attached to Emiliano Zapata (a leader of the Mexican revolution in the early twentieth century) and also, more substantially, because the revolt was led by farmers and indigenous people who had traditionally been left out of the political arena, even by anti-systemic movements. In rather unique poetic language, Zapatistas demanded the end of neoliberal policies (see Marcos, 2001). They became widely known through their audacious use of modern communications at a time when use of the Internet was still embryonic for social movements and radical projects. Moreover, the Zapatistas were capable of creating and deploying new codes and modes of social interaction and communication, different from the traditional leftist approaches. They clearly asserted, for example, that their rebellion was not about "taking" power, but about "changing" it. It might have been just a brilliant formula, but it has indeed changed the paradigm for many social movements.

In Seattle in 1999, that cry was taken up by a wide coalition of US and international NGOs and social movements that was later defined as an alliance of "teamsters" (trade unions) and "turtles" (environmentalists). The occasion was the ministerial meeting of the recently formed World Trade Organization. A large "movement of movements" became visible after Seattle, with its adherents demonstrating in the streets of many cities in different parts of the world. Later the anti-globalization movement spread out in Europe, Asia, and Africa.

Then, in 2008, the world seemed to enter a new phase. The crash of large financial institutions on Wall Street and across the planet led to social and economic dislocation of a scale not seen since the Great Depression of 1929. As millions of people lost their jobs and sometimes their houses while others had to face scarcity and uncertainty, a widespread sentiment came about that the status quo was untenable. A few years later, several popular uprisings have erupted across the world. The "Arab Spring" in 2011 pushed out long-established dictatorships in Tunisia and Egypt. It was triggered by the self-immolation in December 2010 of a young unemployed street vendor, Mohamed Bouazizi, in protest of his condition. Thousands of Tunisians took to the streets and, unarmed, confronted security forces—leading ultimately to the collapse of the regime.

The Arab Spring was followed by protests against economic austerity in Southern Europe, notably in Spain and Greece. The occupation of public places, the takeover of closed-down factories, and the massive use of social media to spread the word and to systematically expose the negative impacts of neoliberal policies, massive corruption, and elite complicity across state boundaries have continued for several years.

In the United States and Canada, the "Occupy Wall Street" movement reached over 70 cities in North America, led by a new generation of educated youth, dispirited by the lack of suitable job opportunities. The third country of North America that we sometimes forget, Mexico, was also shaken by protests and mobilizations against state and gang violence and corruption.

Many anti-or alter-globalization movements are not caught up in the idea of replacing a "system" with another, but in articulating a new perspective that proposes to break down the structures of domination

CRITICAL ISSUES

BOX 6.10 | Occupy!

In October 2011, a group of mostly young people decided to occupy an area right in the middle of the famous financial district of Wall Street in New York City. Zuccoti Park became for a few weeks the epicentre of a series of demonstrations, cultural events, and workshops in which many hundreds of people protested against the corporate influence over the political system and political institutions and against the privileges enjoyed by the "1 per cent," that is, the very rich people in the United States. Being located in New York City, the protest attracted world attention and went on until May 2012, when 50,000 people demonstrated in the streets. One of the causes of that protest was the growing inequality in the US, where those with higher incomes have gained a much larger share of the national revenue over the last decades. Among the important features of the movement were its decentralized nature, the apparent absence of hierarchy, and the fact that nobody appeared to be in charge other than the people themselves functioning through daily general assembly. The Occupy movement impressed onlookers as a flash mob of serious intent, and public opinion was struck, as were some of the political actors, including Barack Obama. The US President said that the movement was expressing "the frustrations the American people feel, that we had the biggest financial crisis since the Great Depression, huge collateral damage all throughout the country . . . and yet you're still seeing some of the same folks who acted irresponsibly trying to fight efforts to crack down on the abusive practices that got us into this in the first place" (Memoli, 2011). Similar protests were held in Toronto, and in Los Angeles, Chicago, Seattle, San Francisco, Boston, Houston, and many other American cities. The Occupy process later appeared in several other Canadian cities, and in Europe, Asia, and South America.

After a while, the camps were dismantled and Occupy disappeared from the limelight. However, similar processes of engagement continued in 2012 in North African and Arab countries during the Arab Spring of 2011 and in the following years, and protests crossed the Mediterranean when thousands of people took the streets in Spain and Greece. These citizen actions criticize governments for their inaction in front of important social problems such as youth unemployment, massive corruption and diversion of public funds, and recurrent violation of human rights. Although different from one another, these social movements expressed the aspirations of a large segment of the new generations for whom the traditional channels to express dissent and demand changes, such as political parties and trade unions, are becoming irrelevant.

It is still too early to evaluate the impact of Occupy except to say that the idea of citizen mobilization is getting more and more credibility in the world as economic hardship and political deadlocks appear, to many people, as obstacles that cannot be confronted by working within state and international institutions as these are currently structured (Rowe and Carroll, 2014).

Alternatives/Dominic Morissette and Catherine Pappas

PHOTO 6.2 | Massive street demonstration in Caracas, Venezuela.

and exclusion that marginalize the poor. This push has been exemplified in South America, where progressive governments came into power after the first wave of anti-globalization protests in Venezuela, then Brazil, Argentina, Ecuador, Bolivia, Uruguay, etc. After more than a decade in power, people's movements are still struggling, facing unfulfilled promises and manipulative rules preventing popular movements from effectively participating in the process of power.

CAN THE WORLD CHANGE?

The demand for "another" globalization is captured by important national and international movements and social forces. Since 2001, many movements and initiatives have started a new international dialogue to build what they call a "counter-hegemonic project." One of the manifestations of that collective search is the World Social Forum (WSF), which had its roots in Latin American activism and held its first annual conference in Brazil in 2001 as a counter to the World Economic Forum held annually in Davos, Switzerland. The WSF has become a truly world process led by civil society groups, not only to protest the neoliberal institutions of globalization but to define alternatives to the current system. Currently, more than 500,000 small and large social movements in the world participate in the WSF process, decentralized into many local, national, and thematic forums and widely using the most advanced information technologies to stage ongoing and complex debates. In 2013 and 2015, after many years in

CRITICAL ISSUES

BOX 6.11 | Pope Francis: Solidarity Is the Key

In October 2014, an unusual gathering of popular movements came to the Vatican for discussions with Pope Francis. Since his inauguration in 2013, Francis has demarcated himself from previous papal administrations by his open support for social justice and his critique of social exploitation and environmental neglect. Here is an extract from his presentation to the gathering of social movement activists:

> The poor not only suffer injustice but they also struggle against it! They are not content with empty promises, excuses or alibis. . . . You feel that the poor will no longer wait; they want to be protagonists; they organize themselves, study, work, claim and, above all, practice that very special solidarity that exists among those who suffer, among the poor, whom our civilization seems to have forgotten, or at least really like to forget. . . . Solidarity is a word that means much more than some acts of sporadic generosity. It is to think and to act in terms of community, of the priority of the life of all over the appropriation of goods by a few. It is also to fight against the structural causes of poverty, inequality, lack of work, land and housing, the denial of social and labor rights. It is to confront the destructive effects of the empire of money: forced displacements, painful emigrations, the traffic of persons, drugs, war, violence and all those realities that many of you suffer and that we are all called to transform. . . . The scandal of poverty cannot be addressed promoting strategies of containment that only tranquilize and convert the poor into domesticated and inoffensive beings. . . . Climate change, the loss of bio-diversity, deforestation are already showing their devastating effects in the great cataclysms we witness, and you are the ones who suffer most, the humble, those who live near coasts in precarious dwellings or who are so vulnerable economically that, in face of a natural disaster, lose everything. . . . The Popular Movements express the urgent need to revitalize our democracies, so often kidnapped by innumerable factors. It is impossible to imagine a future for society without the active participation of the great majorities and that protagonism exceeds the logical proceedings of formal democracy. . . .

Source: Pope's address to popular movements, Vatican City, 29 Oct. 2014, http://www.zenit.org/en/articles/pope-s-address-to-popular-movements.

South America, the WSF moved to Tunis, the "capital" of the Arab Spring, where it was attended by 65,000 delegates. Social movements there agreed on a program of social action:

> We have forged a common history and a common stream of work which has led to some progress, with the hope to achieve a decisive victory against the ruling system and to create alternatives for a socially just development that respects nature. People all over the world are suffering the effects of the aggravation of a profound crisis of capitalism, in which private transnational corporations, banks, media conglomerates and international financial institutions are trying to increase their profits by applying interventionist and neocolonial policies with the complicity of neoliberal governments. . . . We denounce the false discourse of human rights defense and fight against fundamentalism, which is often used to justify military occupations. We defend the right to people's sovereignty and self-determination. (Declaration of the Assembly of Social Movements, World Social Forum, 2015)

FACING THE BIGGEST CHALLENGE

Critics of the current model of globalization insist on the non-sustainability of the process. "Hyper-growth" and the unrestricted exploitation of the planet's resources are seen as challenges that social movements need to face and surmount. The International Forum on Globalization (2002), an independent think-tank based in Washington with a mandate to nourish social movements with alternative perspectives, argues that the economy should be geared to "meet human genuine needs in the present without compromising the ability of future generations to meet theirs, and without diminishing the natural diversity of life on Earth."

Since the Earth Summit in Rio de Janeiro in 1992, the world has been warned that the hyper-exploitation of resources was creating an unprecedented problem for humanity. However, after more than 20 years of talks and negotiations, the problem remains as our planet is threatened by a number of factors, including the tremendous growth in emissions from fossil-fuel combustion. Based on scientific evidence, there is a real possibility that the climate will alter significantly in the next 25–50 years so that many life forms and human settlements, particularly in the Global South, will be at risk (see Chapter 17). Despite various attempts to reach a consensus, the United States and a number of other governments seem unable to identify affirmative policies to face the climate challenge, for example, firm targets to limit emissions and legal recourse to enforce an agreement. As a result, it is up to the diverse spectrum of social movements and NGOs to take on the issue.

LOOKING AHEAD

For more than 70 years, the development debate has been dominated by the issue of economic growth. As the US and the Soviet Union were competing to win allies, a limited number of states, mostly in Asia, were able to use these processes to their benefit. But the reality is that for many southern countries the development project has not yet tackled the main issues of poverty and exclusion, although opinions differ about the variety of causes that led to that result. As this debate continues, macro and meta changes are taking place. In many countries an astonishing number of social movements have mobilized broad sectors of society. They are

CRITICAL ISSUES

BOX 6.12 | Climate Change: Time Is Running Out

Canadian author and social activist Naomi Klein is one among many who have sounded the call for immediate action to stem the impending disaster of global climate change:

> Climate change is not a problem that can be solved simply by changing what we buy—a hybrid instead of an SUV, some carbon offsets when we get on a plane. At its core, it is a crisis born of overconsumption by the comparatively wealthy, which means the world's most manic consumers are going to have to consume less. . . . Our changing climate is like the landscape out the window [of a racing bullet train]: from our racy vantage point, it can appear static, but it is moving, its slow progress measured in receding ice sheets, swelling waters and incremental temperature rises. If left unchecked, climate change will most certainly speed up enough to capture our fractured attention—island nations wiped off the map, and city-drowning superstorms, tend to do that. But by then, it may be too late for our actions to make a difference, because the era of tipping points will likely have begun.

Source: Klein (2014).

doing so (at least partially) by reinventing the language of protest while seeking more inclusionary politics. While political issues of power remain important, social movements increasingly do not focus exclusively on the state.

The strengths of this vast alter-globalist movement are obviously impressive—such as the capacity to create immediate coalitions to resist policies and propose alternatives, sometimes to the extent of changing the political leadership. At the same time, the weaknesses of these movements are apparent as mirror images of their assets—i.e., their dispersion, their fragmentation, their inability to propose coherent and long-term programs because such proposals could jeopardize the narrow limits of the alliances on which the movements are built. In the last while, many popular movements were unable to stop the descent into violent conflicts manipulated by unscrupulous elites who skilfully played on ethnic, linguistic, religious differences, as we see in many countries in Asia and Africa. States have broken down not for the benefit of democratic aspirations and movements, but to abandon wide areas to the rule of the gun. Yet "alter" experiments continue, even in war-torn countries and regions where people literally fight for peace. Many of these networks are "glocal," meshing local issues with global perspectives.

The old saying "think globally, act locally" no longer applies, because alter-globalists are indeed acting globally. A striking example of this phenomenon concerns the devastating HIV/AIDS epidemic. It was first addressed by gay communities in northern California, later afflicted poor communities (mostly women) in sub-Saharan Africa with terrible consequences, and then was confronted by large-scale coalitions in such places as South Africa. That led to the creation of an extraordinary "rainbow coalition" of movements intervening at the very heart of international processes: in the UN, with powerful agencies like the World Bank, as well as directly with large pharmaceutical corporations. The pressure built up, until the rich countries were forced to concede that the countries most affected by the epidemic could have access to generic medication, bypassing the usual system of patents and protection for the giant pharmaceutical companies. It was by no means a 100 per cent victory, but the struggle allowed poor people access to some treatment. Today, the struggle continues. These efforts from below in combatting AIDS are mirrored in various other global movements that have risen from the grassroots. Now, governments and agencies are being challenged by well-organized and structured movements operating across borders, able to share information and elaborate strategies across the planet (Gibson, 2006).

SUMMARY

In this chapter, readers have learned that globalization means that new sets of relations and activities, mostly in the economic arena, are taking place irrespective of the geographical location of participants. In the meanwhile, even if the North–South gap remains and even if the rich countries of North America and Western Europe remain powerful, a few countries like China have become economic powerhouses. Out of these changes emerges a new geopolitical and geo-economic architecture. In parallel, globalization also ends up at the societal level, where citizens interacting worldwide come up with important demands on social development and human rights.

These changes have a huge impact over what traditionally has been considered as "development," in particular, the struggle against poverty. Poverty and economic exclusion are no longer confined to the developing countries, which explains, therefore, a new expression: the "Global South." It means that the "South," i.e., regions affected by underdevelopment and poverty, is not only a geographic term but a reality crossing borders.

This new globalization, therefore, needs to be integrated into the understanding and analysis of contemporary development issues. From the reform of the United Nations to the struggle for global health or the rehabilitation of decaying environments, new actors, new methodologies, and new approaches are acquiring a growing importance. The world we live in, along with it all its development challenges, will never be the same.

QUESTIONS FOR CRITICAL THOUGHT

1. How is globalization changing the meaning of "development"?
2. Why might some countries be characterized as "winning" in the globalization process? What explains that others appear to be losing?
3. What is "alter-globalization"? What are the strengths and weaknesses of the various alternatives to neoliberal globalization?

SUGGESTED READINGS

Globalizations, journal edited by Barry Gills, Newcastle University, UK, and published by Routledge.

Klein, Naomi. 2015. *This Changes Everything: Capitalism vs. the Climate*. New York: Simon & Schuster.

Pleyers, Geoffrey. 2010. *Alter-Globalization: Becoming Actors in a Global Age*. Cambridge: Polity Press.

Ritzer, George. 2010. *Globalization: A Basic Text*. Chichester, UK: Wiley-Blackwell.

NOTE

1. "Tigers" were countries like Taiwan, Indonesia, and Thailand that had succeeded in diversifying their economies and augmenting their exports. They were preceded by "dragons" (Hong Kong, Singapore, etc.), which had done the same at a smaller scale. Later, "dragons" came to include other "emerging" Asian economies like Malaysia and Vietnam.

BIBLIOGRAPHY

Amin, S. 2004. *Obsolescent Capitalism: Contemporary Politics and Global Disorder*. London: Zed Books.

———. 2009. "The battlefields chosen by contemporary imperialism: Conditions for an effective response from the South." Paper presented at World Forum for Alternatives conference "The World Crisis and Beyond," organized by the Rosa Luxembourg Foundation, Brussels, 28 Oct. www.forumdesalternative.org/docs/bruselas/ Programme.pdf.

———. 2013. "China 2013." *Monthly Review* 64, 10 (Mar.). http://monthlyreview.org/2013/03/01/china-2013/.

Asian Development Bank. 2013. *Asian Development Outlook*.

Bello, W. 2005. *Dilemmas of Domination: The Unmaking of the American Empire*. New York: Metropolitan Books, Henry Holt and Co.

———. 2013. *Capitalism's Last Stand? Deglobalization in the Age of Austerity*. London: Zed Books.

Borgen Project. 2014. "Top 10 poverty in Africa facts." http://borgenproject.org/10-quick-facts-about-poverty-in-africa/.

Cardoso, F.H. 2007. *The Accidental President of Brazil: A Memoir*. Washington: Perseus.

Food and Agriculture Organization, United Nations (FAO). 2015. *World Hunger and Poverty Facts and Statistics*. www.worldhunger.org/articles/Learn/world%20hunger%20facts%202002.htm.

Gibson, N., ed. 2006. *Challenging Hegemony: Social Movements and the Quest for a New Humanism in Post-Apartheid South Africa*. Trenton, NJ: Africa World Press.

Hardt, M., and A. Negri. 2000. *Empire*. Cambridge, Mass.: Harvard University Press.

Harvey, D. 1990. *The Condition of Postmodernity: An Enquiry into the Origins of Cultural Change*. Oxford: Blackwell.

———. 2005. *A Brief History of Neoliberalism*. Oxford: Oxford University Press.

Hebron, L., and J.F. Stack. 2009. *Globalization: Debunking the Myths*. Upper Saddle River, NJ: Pearson Prentice-Hall.

Held, D., and A. McGrew. 2003. *The Global Transformations Reader*. 2nd edn. London: Polity Press.

International Forum on Globalization. 2002. *Alternatives to Economic Globalization: A Better World Is Possible*. www.ifg.org/pdf/cancun/alter-SumChaRe.pdf.

International Monetary Fund (IMF). 2014. *Sub-Saharan Africa: Fostering Durable and Inclusive Growth*. Washington: IMF.

Jubilee Debt Campaign. 2014. "The true story of Africa's billion dollar losses." 15 July. http://jubileedebt.org.uk/reports-briefings/honest-accounts-true-story-africas-billion-dollar-losses.

Klein, N. 2014. "The change within: The obstacles we face are not just external." *The Nation*, 22 Apr. www.naomiklein.org/articles/2014/04/change-within-obstacles-we-face-are-not-just-external.

———. 2015. *This Changes Everything: Capitalism vs. the Climate*. New York: Simon & Schuster.

Lenhard, J. 2010. *Is Globalization Causing the Decline of the Nation-State?* Munich: Grin Verlag.

Lerman, R.I. 2002. "Globalization and the fight against poverty." www.urban.org/publications/410612.html.

Marcos, Subcommandante. 2001. *Our World Is Our Weapon*. New York: Seven Stories Press.

Marx, K., and F. Engels. 1967 [1848]. *The Communist Manifesto*. London: Penguin.

Memoli, M. A. 2011. "Obama news conference: Obama: Occupy Wall Street protests show Americans' frustration." *Los Angeles Times*, 13 July. Accessed 7 Oct. 2011.

Ohmae, K. 1995. *The End of the Nation State: The Rise of Regional Economies*. New York: Free Press.

Oxfam International. 2000. *Growth with Equity Is Good for the Poor*. Oxfam Policy Papers, 6-2000. team. http://univparis1.fr/teamperso/DEA/Cursus/L3/Memoire/Growth_Inequality%20OXFAM.pdf.

———. 2014a. "Rigged rules mean economic growth increasingly 'winner takes all' for rich elites all over world." www.oxfam.org/en/pressroom/pressreleases/2014-01-20/rigged-rules-mean-economic-growth-increasingly-winner-takes-all

———. 2014b. *Working for the Few: Political Capture and Economic Inequality*. www.oxfam.org/sites/www.oxfam.org/files/bp-working-for-few-political-capture-economic-inequality-200114-en.pdf.

Phelps, G., and S. Crabtree. 2013. "More than one in five worldwide living in extreme poverty." Gallup, 23 Dec. www.gallup.com/poll/166565/one-five-worldwide-living-extreme-poverty.aspx.

Ritzer, G. 2010. *Globalization: A Basic Text*. London: Wiley-Blackwell.

Rowe, J., and M. Carroll. 2014. "Reform or radicalism: Left social movements from the Battle of Seattle to Occupy Wall Street." *New Political Science* (Mar.).

Shiva, V. 2000a. "Globalization and poverty." *Resurgence* no. 202 (Sept.–Oct.).

———. 2000b. "War against nature and the people of the South." In Sarah Anderson, ed., *Views from the South: The Effects of Globalization and the WTO on Third World Countries*. Oakland, Calif.: Food First Books, 91–125.

Stiglitz, J.E. 2002. *Globalization and Its Discontents*. New York: W.W. Norton.

Sung, Y.-W. 2005. *The Emergence of Greater China: The Economic Integration of Mainland China, Taiwan and Hong Kong*. New York: Palgrave Macmillan.

United Nations. 2013. "Growing gulf between rich and poor 'reproach to the promise of the United Nations Charter,' Secretary-General tells General Assembly during thematic debate." Press release, 8 July. www.un.org/press/en/2013/ga11391.doc.htm.

United Nations Conference on Trade and Development (UNCTAD). 2014. *Trade and Development Report*. http://unctad.org/en/PublicationsLibrary/tdr2014_en.pdf.

United Nations Department of Economic and Social Affairs. 2010. *Rethinking Poverty: Report on the World Social Situation 2010*. New York: UN. www.un.org/esa/socdev/rwss/docs/2010/fullreport.pdf.

Wall Street Journal. 2013. "Poverty decline in China." 18 Apr. http://blogs.wsj.com/chinarealtime/2013/04/18/heres-how-much-poverty-has-declined-in-china/.

Washington Post. 2014. "What the new bank of BRICS is all about." 17 July.

Watts, C.P. 2011. "Is globalization another name for US imperialism?" *Politics Review Online* 20, 3 (Feb.). www.academia.edu/2001346/Is_globalization_another_name_for_US_imperialism.

Wen, D., and M. Li. 2006. "China: Hyperdevelopment and environmental crisis, in coming to terms with nature." In *Socialist Register 2007*. London: Merlin Press.

World Bank. 2004. *Global Development Prospects: Realizing the Development Promise of the Doha Agenda*. Washington: World Bank.

———. 2015. "Overview and strategy." www.worldbank.org/en/topic/poverty/overview.

World Social Forum. 2015. "Declaration of the Assembly of Social Movements—World Social Forum 2015." http://cadtm.org/Declaration-of-the-Assembly-of,11452.

World Trade Organization (WTO). 2012. *World Trade Prospects 2012*. www.wto.org/english/news_e/pres12_e/pr658_e.htm.

———. 2014. *International Trade Statistics*. www.wto.org/english/res_e/statis_e/its2014_e/its14_toc_e.htm.

PART II

International Development Actors

▲ Activists from the New Trade Union Initiative (NTUI)—a national platform of non-partisan left-democratic trade unions of formal and informal sector workers in agriculture, forest, construction, manufacturing and services—stage a sit-in in New Delhi to protest against the arrest of the Union leader Binayak Sen. | Source: RAVEENDRAN/AFP/Getty Images

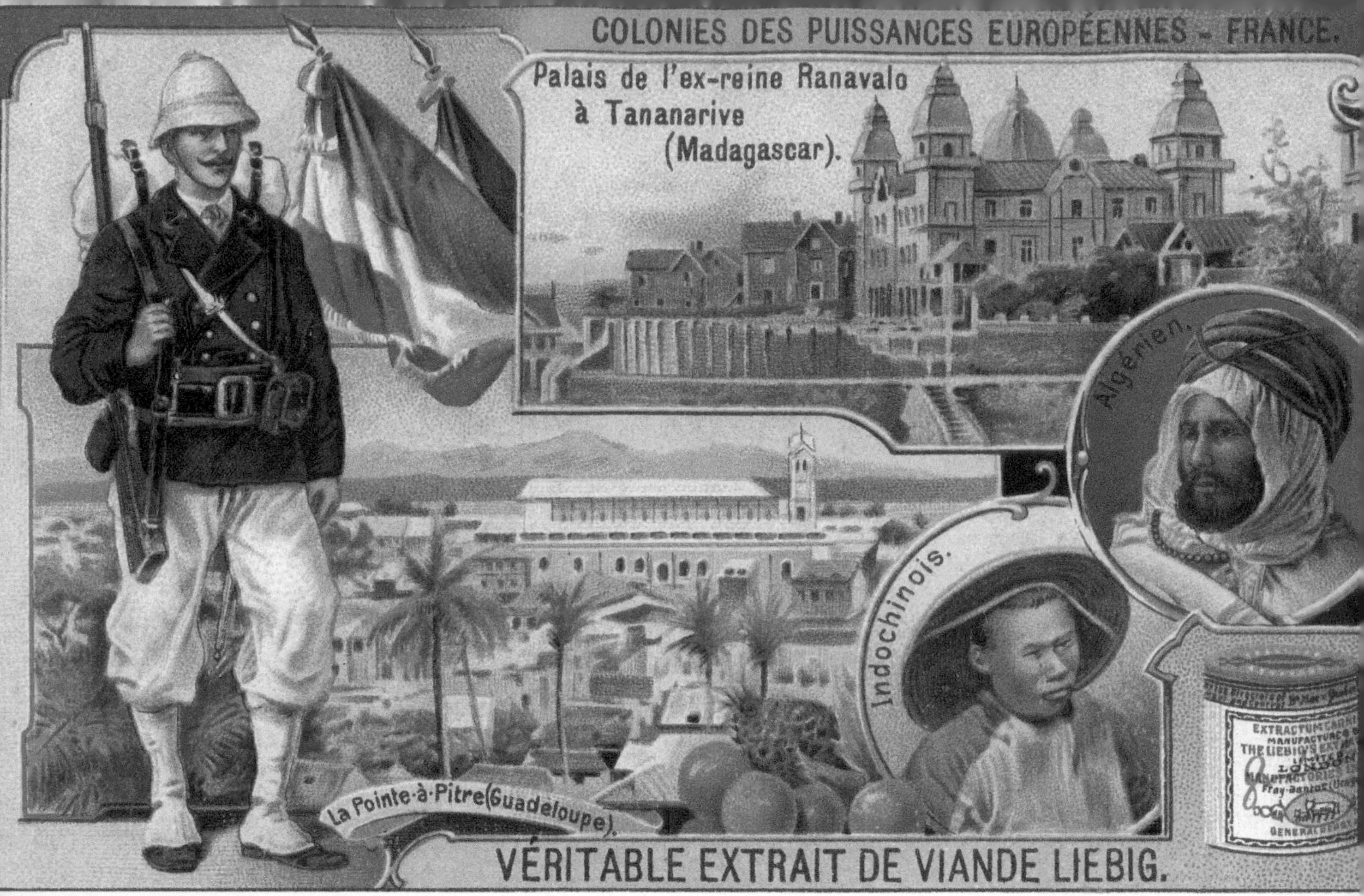

7 State of the State: Does the State Have a Role in Development?

Anil Hira

LEARNING OBJECTIVES

- To gain familiarity with the historical context of debates about the role of states in development.
- To understand the differences between northern and southern states and why simple policy prescriptions do not seem to gain traction in the South.
- To be able to explain the differences between the market-led and state-led views of development and related debates.
- To appreciate both the opportunities and constraints upon state leadership and responsiveness.
- To understand the basic concepts and issues behind good governance.

▲ **A historic poster depicting the colonies of the European powers: France, with illustrations of a French soldier, the palace of former queen Ranavalo at Tananrive, Magagascar, along with certain exports and drawings of the colonized.** | Source: © Lebrecht Music and Arts Photo Library/Alamy Stock Photo

WHAT IS THE STATE? THE LEGACY OF COLONIALISM

Before we get to the role of the state, we first should define it. The most prominent approaches—international relations and Weberian theory—rely on simple criteria to define the **state**: it is an entity with monopoly over the means of force within a designated territory that it controls, enjoying legitimate support for that monopoly from the majority of the population residing in the territory and recognition of its control by other states, and is empowered by the population with making public decisions.

While this definition may seem straightforward, it is problematic in a developing-country context and has been accused of **Eurocentrism**—that is, being based on European experience by those who consider this experience to be normative. The most obvious problem is that states in the European context, such as the United Kingdom, developed a historical identity over thousands of years, along with slow political centralization, that in part reflect natural geographic communities (Poggi, 1978). For example, the UK's physical separation from the European continent has and continues to have consequences for its view of itself as a force independent of Europe, demonstrated by its policies towards European integration. Even relatively new states such as Germany and Italy, formed in the 1870s, share a common language and cultural and religious identity as well as historical experiences, including civil wars and wars fought as a **nation**.

In the developing world, there was generally no such historical evolution. Rather, states were carved out through European conquest and division, and national identities and states were forged over short periods in response to European imperialism. In some cases, nations such as Brazil had no centralized entity that would resemble a modern state at the time of conquest. In others, genocide through direct means and population loss caused by disease imported from Europe, as happened in many parts of the Americas, wiped out large portions of the indigenous population, opening the way for the transplantation of completely new populations, including slaves from Africa. In Africa, the Middle East, and parts of Asia, colonial states were created with the express purpose of mixing different populations together, a divide-and-conquer strategy that allowed colonial masters to impose a relatively privileged minority's control over a large, resistant native population in spite of the relatively low numbers of colonizers in relation to local populations. In several colonies, the imposition of a new colonial elite made up of a different group from another area was added to local divide-and-conquer strategies, such as administrators from South Asia imported as bureaucrats and military officers in South Africa. In others (as in Japan's control over Korea or the British favouring the Sunnis over the Sh'ia in Iraq), the colonial masters simply created or chose a local minority to be their surrogates. Colonial powers planted further seeds for ethnic strife in the way borders were drawn, often across ethnic or religious lines, creating permanently divided states. The privileged locals chosen for administration formed the core of the emerging states, through power structures that often continued after independence. Thus, a relatively small external power could control a vast empire through its local allies, who then had a vested interest in the continuation of the system, whether through direct control or other ties (see Chapter 2).

While "artificial" in the sense of not representing the natural evolution of historical and cultural identity forces over prolonged periods, the states set up by colonizers nonetheless enjoy the other aspects of statehood: control of the means of force (e.g., the army and police) and the ability to make public decisions. What they seem to lack in many cases is a strong sense of **legitimacy** in terms of support among the population. This does not diminish their central role in development, but it does begin to shed light on the myriad additional difficulties that developing states face above and beyond those of Western states.

Even in states without a system of direct colonial control, the colonial economic system created incentives for compliance. Colonial economies were set up under a system called mercantilism to serve the interests of the colonizing or "mother" country. They provided raw materials or slaves to the colonizing country, receiving the home country's finished goods in return. They generally were banned from selling directly to other countries, including colonies within the same system, thus ensuring a profit for the home country acting as a middleman. The system also stifled or shut down existing industries; in India, a budding textile

IMPORTANT CONCEPTS

BOX 7.1 | The Nature of Authority in the State

What is the source of legitimate authority within a state? There are a number of competing theories about how a government can come to power with the acceptance of the vast majority of its citizens. While empires formed early, such as China, were based on family dynasties, the situation was much more complex than solving the problem of political succession by family lineage. Even in China, a strong set of values based on the teachings of Confucius insisted that leadership should have a meritocratic basis and that it had a paternalistic duty to govern its citizens well. Similarly, military governments that have taken over states in the South have always given reasons as to why their actions were necessary. Thus, even in non-Western empires and military dictatorships that we sometimes deem despotic, there is a sense of the need for a government to gain popular support and acceptance (legitimacy). While not dismissing the fact that many governments also use repression, no state in history relied solely on repression.

Much of political philosophy is concerned, therefore, with the terms and means by which a state gains legitimacy. Idealized notions based on the writings of John Locke suggest a legitimate state is one in which people come together voluntarily to create a compact for mutual defence and collective action; this is why political scientists often have focused on constitutions as the reflection of political will. Others, such as Thomas Hobbes, felt that passion guides men as much as reason and that a central authority, one with a monopoly on the means of coercion but with the agreement of the population, was the only way to create peace. With the Enlightenment in eighteenth-century Europe, which emphasized reason over tradition, a more group-oriented view of the state started to develop. For example, Jean-Jacques Rousseau suggested that the state had to reflect the collective will of the people; thus the freely agreeing individuals of Locke's perspective could be superseded by what was best for the nation as a whole. This created the idea that a state might sometimes make decisions that were unpopular in the short run but that, nonetheless, were for the general good. It also supported popular revolutions in the American colonies and in France. As the twentieth century progressed, more cynical views of the state's sources of legitimacy appeared. One set of Marxist critiques sees the state as reflecting only the interests of the powerful. These arguments reverberate today with questions about the undue influence of corporations on political decision-making. Political theorists continue to work on these ideas, with much activity going into how vibrant participatory democracies can be created, ones in which citizens participate in decision-making well beyond an occasional vote.

industry collapsed under British pressure. For colonial elites, many of whom had nobility status and/or had been given large mineral and land rights from the colonizing or metropolitan country during colonization, their well-being depended on the system's continuation.

As colonies grew, local administrations relied almost exclusively on taxes on exports of their products, so the colonial state was very much tied into the commodity trade of the mercantilist system. This also was true in countries not directly colonized, such as China, where control by European imperial powers over trade and investment, extending at one point to dividing up control over various ports, led to a strongly dependent relationship between local Chinese administrations and European states. In many cases, outside investors controlled large and key strategic assets of the state, such as the British building and owning Argentina's railway. This system of economic control extended even after many colonies achieved independence in the post–World War II period. Thus, even though the

Paul Haslam

PHOTO 7.1 | Brazil has invested in oil exploration and exploitation via its state-owned enterprise Petrobras, as indicated by these oil rigs off Rio de Janeiro.

formal mercantilist system broke down long ago, economies continue to exhibit many of the patterns of the colonial era. Those patterns include the frequent intrusion of the military into state affairs and widespread corruption in the state. This also can be seen in good part as a colonial legacy, as the military and administration were the instruments of colonial power, reflecting the combination of force and co-optation used to control populations and extract resources.

Some analysts see this neo-colonial system as having both pressures and opportunities for state leadership. During the Cold War, for instance, the rivalry between the United States and the Soviet Union allowed some smaller states, such as Cuba, to play off the two superpowers and thereby receive large amounts of aid, in this case from the Soviets. Mainstream economists point to the rapid expansion of the world economy during the 1960s and large US expenditures and imports as an environment that allowed for the development of the East Asian economies of Japan, South Korea, and Taiwan, the (temporary) "miracle" economies of Brazil and Mexico, and rapid growth in states such as Kenya. On the other side of the debate, critics suggest that there is now far less leeway for states to break away from neo-colonialism. The continuing reliance of many countries on commodity exports and on external technology, investment (highlighted by the debt crisis throughout the developing world in the 1980s—see Chapter 14), and imports, and the "brain drain" of the best and brightest to the West all are signs of the persistent difficulty that developing states face in engendering economic development. A further difficulty is the link between military rule in much of the developing world over extended periods and the influence of outside powers, such as US support of a variety of dictators and strongmen during the Cold War.

DEFINING THE STATE'S ROLE IN DEVELOPMENT

With this historical background, we can now turn to the task of analyzing the role of the state in fostering development. At the most general level, the debate revolves around whether a state should be an active leader or a responsive follower. Part of the answer to this question depends on whether you see the nature of the state as **compradorial** or Weberian. The term "compradorial" was coined by radical (Marxist-influenced) development analysts to describe the ties of the developing state to external interests, whether foreign governments, investors, or military, and to the local resource-owning and internationally oriented capitalist class. Thus, this line of thinking sees the post-colonial state as continuing to be colonial in nature, run by an elite "bought out" by and/or in alliance with foreign interests. By contrast, a **Weberian** view emphasizes the rational-purposeful nationalism of a modern state, regardless of its origin. Thus, in this view, even though India, for example, was created by colonial fiat, that does not prevent it from developing a government that is purposeful, rational, and legitimate.

State Capacity and Autonomy

Political economists such as Grindle (1996) have long pointed out that developing states struggle in several areas. The term **state capacity** is often used to suggest that developing states may not be as capable of weighing technical decisions as their counterparts in the North. Their personnel may not be as well-trained; they may not have as up-to-date equipment; and their budgets are likely

Anil Hira

PHOTO 7.2 | Paraguay has developed an ethanol industry in an effort to reduce dependency on oil imports.

to be considerably smaller. The term **state autonomy** is often used in this context to mean the degree of "insulation" that a state enjoys from social and external forces. The governments of states overrun with political pressures are more likely to make politically rather than merit-based decisions. In short, they may make decisions that favour a small group and themselves rather than the nation as a whole. For example, many developing-country civil services appear to lack meritocratic hiring and promotion practices. States that are insulated may be better able to resist pressures to escalate spending as a means of gaining political support. On the other hand, insulation can mean greater opportunity either for enlightened leadership or for corrupt and incompetent administration. Scholars such as Evans (1995) point out that the situation is much more complex in practice. Evans uses the term **embedded autonomy** to refer to states that develop strong network ties with foreign and domestic elites yet manage to retain some degree of autonomy for the pursuit of national interest. Miguel Angel Centeno's study of Latin America (2002) adds other important insights into why state autonomy is so often lacking in the developing world. He suggests that Latin American states lack a strong sense of nationalism, using as examples the lack of shared national cultural symbols.

CENTRAL DEBATES ABOUT THE ROLE OF THE STATE IN ECONOMIC DEVELOPMENT

The Push for Early Industrialization

Considering the role of the state in terms of economic development opens up a more detailed level of analysis. Over the course of the twentieth century, Keynesians argued for a significant state role in managing the economy while free-market theorists (neoliberals) proposed that the state's role should be minimal (see Chapter 3).

Scholars such as Sir Arthur Lewis (1955) posited that as previous colonies' agricultural sectors were modernized, the natural labour surplus of agricultural workers would be free to move to cities. In fact, continuing urbanization remains a central feature of almost every economy. However, Lewis also expected that the labour surplus would lower wages to the point where the natural comparative advantage of abundant labour would begin to attract industries, creating a positive cycle of growth and employment and thus no need for state leadership. In the aftermath of World War II, when many of the independent states of Africa and Asia were created, the lack of evidence for "natural" industrialization à la Lewis led to the adoption of Keynesian-oriented policies, favoured for obvious reasons by states (because it required their leadership) and by organizations such as the International Monetary Fund (IMF), the World Bank, and the regional development banks (which later would change their advice to promote the free-market approach; see Chapter 9).

In the early 1960s, the push for industrialization became one of the central goals of developing states in order to "modernize." Industrialization would help to diversify exports, reduce the commodity and other dependency aspects of post-colonial economies, and help to create a middle-class domestic market of highly skilled workers. However, a second axis of debate about the role of the state then became central: how was industrialization to be accomplished? At one extreme, many saw the Soviet Union at the time as a paradigm of efficient and rapid industrialization, accomplishing large and rapid increases in basic industrial production (such as steel) as a result of successful five-year plans. Countries as diverse as India, Ghana, Cuba, and Egypt began to emulate the state planning model by the late 1950s and early 1960s. The Soviet model, and later the Chinese model, was also attractive in terms of socialism—an example of state leadership in creating a more equitable nation that would correct the inequities rooted in colonialism and exacerbated by capitalism's privileging of elite classes. Skepticism, however, gradually emerged regarding the ability of the model to create viable industries or improved equity. The standard of living in Soviet bloc countries appeared to be well below that of the West, and the gap was increasing over time. Large amounts of steel did not translate into the same price for or quality of middle-class consumer goods such as automobiles. With regard to equity, the image of socialism as a benign policy for the betterment of people everywhere took a hit with the Soviet repression of rebellions in the areas it controlled, such as East Germany, Hungary, and Czechoslovakia, and Chinese repression of internal dissent. There was also

IMPORTANT CONCEPTS

BOX 7.2 | The Debate between Keynesians and Free Marketeers

While many of the pioneering works of economics are based on markets and free trade, such as the work of Adam Smith and David Ricardo, the belief in markets was severely shaken by the worldwide Depression marked at the outset by the 1929 New York stock market crash. The crash led to a ratcheting up of tariff walls, and as unemployment rates soared throughout North America and Europe, the beginnings of the welfare state were constructed. John Maynard Keynes (1936) gained the attention of the Franklin Roosevelt administration in the US and of various European governments by creating a new set of theories about why the market might fail, including the possibility of a liquidity trap of low interest rates and high unemployment (Hall, 1989). Keynesianism also reflected massive popular and social uprisings and demands (Polanyi, 1944). In such cases, the state should step in to "prime the pump" by spending to reactivate the economy. The state's role in addressing "market failures" then extended to many of the aspects of life we take for granted in the West: subsidized education and health care, unemployment insurance and pensions, and public aid for those who are not able to work. Around the same time, scholars such as the Austrian economist Friedrich Von Hayek (1944) suggested that states, not markets, were more likely to fail. This view resonated during the Cold War, with fears of totalitarianism spreading from the Soviet Union and also following the diagnosis that the increase in tariffs had choked off international trade, leading to the Great Depression. As we discuss below, Milton Friedman, a University of Chicago economist, became the new champion of markets and helped to "win" this battle of ideas in the political arena by the 1980s. Of course, with the most recent financial crisis, which began in the US in 2008, the neoliberal free-market solution to all that ails economies once again has been found wanting—for the simple reason that markets are not simply neutral, self-operative entities; rather, they reflect all the positive and negative aspects of human individual and collective behaviour.

Source: PBS, *"The Commanding Heights,"* at: www.pbs.org/wgbh/commandingheights/.

growing awareness that the Communist states were creating their own coddled elites within the state party and the bureaucracy. It is now well documented that the cost of militarization and global conflict by proxy imposed a heavy burden on the state socialist economies, particularly the Soviet Union.

Industrialization in other areas began to occupy a middle ground between market and state. In Latin America, a school of thought called "structuralism" began to emerge (Hira, 1998). Structuralist thinkers, led by Raúl Prebisch (1950), suggested that the state was needed, at least initially, to destroy the "bottlenecks" that prevented a market-based industrialized economy from developing naturally as expected. Prebisch, who later became the head of UNCTAD (United Nations Conference on Trade and Development), was highly influential throughout the world. One of his basic ideas, the Prebisch-Singer hypothesis, suggested that commodity prices were more volatile and earned less, over time, than industrial goods—because manufactured goods became more sophisticated (while coffee remained coffee). Therefore, developing economies needed industry to be able to reach the same standard of living as northern economies; the policies adopted became known as "import substituting industrialization" (ISI).

Prebisch's ideas about bottlenecks refer to the foundations of any economy: its productive, financial, and labour systems. In terms of productive systems, for example, too many developing states rely on outside technology and know-how. They need to develop their own technology to avoid being left behind and having to pay for it and adapt it to local conditions.

As Gerschenkron (1962) pointed out, protectionism was part of the industrialization experience for northern states. Most developing states have poorly functioning financial systems. Because local populations do not trust their banking systems, for which regulatory oversight is generally poor (such as a lack of government-backed deposit insurance), those who can do so place their money in foreign accounts, while others have little formal means of saving or borrowing. In terms of labour systems, the poor educational systems in developing countries mean that only a small number of people are well-trained and, lacking opportunities at home, they tend to emigrate. Thus, large-scale access to higher education is needed to create viable middle-class-based economies that can function as a domestic market for goods. Prebisch also suggested integrating southern economies to achieve more efficient industries that can sell to each other until they can compete with well-established Western industries.

While Prebisch's ideas have been highly influential, they still leave a great deal of ambiguity in terms of how the industrialization process could best be pushed forward: where, precisely, does the state's role lie in the spectrum of possibilities between state planning and laissez-faire markets as a means of eliminating bottlenecks? On this foggy ground, a secondary level of debate has emerged.

Many of the World Bank projects in the early 1960s centred on large infrastructure projects, such as airports and hydroelectric dams, which were expected to create the foundation for a modern economy. At this time, argument ensued over whether a "big push" or a targeted industrialization strategy would work best. Scholars such as Rosenstein-Rodan (1961) argued that a "big push" of capital investment across a variety of industries would be needed to sustain industrialization. This idea was reinforced to some extent by Albert O. Hirschman's idea of "linkages." Hirschman (1971) noted that some industries, such as the automotive industry, rely on a series of other industries for production of its final product—mining and smelting to provide the steel; rubber and tire manufacturers; and a variety of other producers for inputs. It also relies on a retail network to sell the product. However, for a developing country to pursue all industrial and infrastructure avenues simultaneously might not only be impossible in terms of its financial means but also might overwhelm the technical and managerial capacity of the state. As an alternative, the state could start by targeting specific industries and then extend the effort to other industries. Japan, for example, initiated advanced industrialization with electronics, with now well-known brands such as Sony and Toshiba leading the way under state guidance. Later, the Japanese began pushing into the more sophisticated and challenging auto industry.

By the early 1970s, economists and policy-makers had become disillusioned about the state's role in development. In 1973, when the Organization of Petroleum Exporting Countries (OPEC) ramped up the price of petroleum, the world economy went into a tailspin of low growth and high inflation ("stagflation"), which Keynesian theory seemed inadequate to explain. In the short term, the situation created a large increase in liquidity in the form of petrodollars lent by newly wealthy oil sheiks to other developing countries via New York and London banks, which then used the free-floating dollar as the common currency. In the long run, this rash of increased borrowing for state projects created an extremely high level of indebtedness that continues to haunt the developing world today (see Chapter 14). Determination to end inflation led the US Federal Reserve to raise interest rates precipitously in 1982. Along with a drop in oil prices, this action ended the period of easy borrowing and created a major debt crisis for developing states that had borrowed on adjustable interest rate terms in dollar denominations. With limited international borrowing and no mechanism of default (declaring bankruptcy), developing nations began to embrace or were forced into a new set of neoliberal policies, signalling the end of the era of state leadership for industrialization.

The Rise of and Justification for Neoliberalism

A number of factors lay behind the international wave of conservatism that swept the world in the 1980s. Stagflation was one factor, but on the political side, the sense of loss of power in the US and Europe also played a role. For example, the US under President Jimmy Carter had suffered a prolonged humiliation when its embassy was stormed and hostages were taken during the 1979 revolution in Iran, followed by a rescue attempt that failed miserably. These events resonated deeply with the earlier defeat in Vietnam and other historic "losses" on the part of US allies in China, Nicaragua, and Iran itself. Conservatives pushed for a return to the "good old days" of power and security in the North. The market-based economics they promoted was appealing to many southern economists and policy-makers because it seemed to offer a solution to the new constraints on spending created by the debt crisis.

Challenges to neoliberalism sprang up almost immediately. While poverty diminished in some areas, income inequality, by most measures, has increased in most of the world (and between the North and South) outside of the "miracle" economies of East Asia. And are the gains sustainable in terms of the environment? Moreover, efforts to create textbook free-market models à la Chile (allegedly)—for example, in Ghana and Jamaica—led to short-term monetary stability but to long-term stagnation and worsening equity (see Box 7.3).

The most serious challenge to neoliberalism comes from a wave of literature that sought to explain the precipitous rise of East Asian states and their achievements in both growth and equity. Authors such as Chalmers Johnson (1982) led the charge that the state—not markets—was responsible for these achievements. Johnson coined the term "developmentalist" state to suggest that a state could target particular sectors for successful promotion, which would lead to improvements in equity through job creation. This concept raised the question as to why such efforts had apparently failed in the rest of the developing world. The answer is complicated, but Johnson and others suggest that the ability of the state to "govern" the market, or to guide the domestic private sector through incentives,

CRITICAL ISSUES

BOX 7.3 | "The Chilean Miracle"

In 1973, General Augusto Pinochet led a coup that took over Chile. By 1975, he had adopted economic policies that followed his largely University of Chicago–trained economic advisory team, nicknamed "the Chicago Boys." Chile's monetary stability, despite a crisis in 1982 and relatively high growth rates, acted as a demonstration of the ability of markets, rather than of states, to lead to economic development. In the case of Chile, the state reduced legislation and regulation regarding labour unions and strikes, which the economists claimed made the Chilean labour market more flexible and adaptable (though these moves clearly also served political purposes). These legislative and regulatory changes were made possible by extreme repression of dissidents after 1973, which left thousands dead or in exile. The Chilean government also reduced many import barriers that had been set up under the ISI system to protect domestic producers, and unified and then, at least initially, floated the exchange rate. While maintaining some requirements for how long capital should stay in the country, the state also invited in foreign capital and investment. Chile went through a second wave of reforms in the 1980s, featuring the privatization of many state-owned companies (though not the copper company), including the state energy companies, to foreign interests, which would have been unthinkable in the 1960s, when anti-imperialist sentiments surged. Another major reform, also previously unthinkable, was to privatize the social security system, allowing individuals to choose their own pension funds, overseen by government regulation. Similar market-friendly reforms were carried out in education and health. Though Chile is now a democracy, the same neoliberal policies have continued. Increased social spending has reduced absolute poverty, and there has been a successful transition of government from left-wing to right-wing parties (with both moving to the centre). Yet the success of new exports, such as fish, wood, wine, and fruit, based on state policies, has not reduced income inequalities or a strong dependence on copper exports. Therefore, the Chilean case remains controversial, both in its accomplishments and in its "lessons" for other developing states (Hira, 1998).

distinguishes the path followed in East Asia from that of other states (Wade, 1990). For example, the developmentalist state provides subsidies and/or protection only if certain performance targets are achieved, and it requires competition among domestic companies in a bid for state help.

Arguably, the relative dominance of the East Asian state enables it to provide greater leadership to the private sector than is possible in other regions with less dominant states (Hira, 2007). Moreover, other authors (Haggard, 1990; Gereffi and Wyman, 1990) who have compared East Asian and Latin American industrialization conclude that East Asia's export orientation represents another key difference. Export orientation means that domestic producers have to produce goods and services that can compete in world markets. Export earnings offer a new source of revenue that the state can then funnel into new investments, including new industries, and thereby reduce pressure to borrow from abroad, as well as decrease exchange rate and interest rate volatility. However, mainstream economic institutions have not taken such challenges to market supremacy lying down (see Box 7.4). In 1993, the World Bank produced a rejoinder entitled *The East Asian Miracle*, suggesting that markets and macroeconomic balance were primarily responsible for growth, although it grudgingly conceded some role for the efficient Asian institutions that allowed markets to function well (World Bank, 1993).

From Neoliberalism to Governance

Mainstream economists, the vast majority of whom continue to support neoliberal policies because they are in line with mainstream economic theories, have begun to consider institutions an important variable for economic growth as they seek to explain the disappointing results of market reforms (Stiglitz, 2002). Economists such as Anne O. Krueger (2000), who went on to become head of the IMF, suggest that a second generation of neoliberal reforms is needed for markets to function well. The state must become an efficient market regulator, ensuring adequate contract enforcement and market-based information (such as price information); it must be capable of taxing and restricting spending; and it must be free of corruption in its decision-making. Thus, for mainstream economists, what went "wrong" with neoliberal reforms was not the need to pare back the state and allow markets to make decisions, but simply an underestimation of the importance of state regulation for the minimization of transactions costs. Transactions costs involve running a

CRITICAL ISSUES

BOX 7.4 | Good Governance and Good Institutions

The early work of economist Douglass North (1981) as well as James M. Buchanan and Gordon Tullock (1962) of the Virginia School presaged a slow but steady shift of economists, from the 1990s onwards, to begin to acknowledge that non-market factors, particularly institutions, could play a major role in the healthy functioning of markets, implying a subtle but important shift away from neoliberal perspectives. These perspectives focus on impediments to market functioning—such as lack of information and uncertainty and inadequately enforced contracts or property rights. A somewhat more activist approach in development economics is starting to gel around the work of celebrated Harvard economist Dani Rodrik. Rodrik (2006) suggests an even more active state approach might be needed, acknowledging its role in East Asian development. Rodrik does not endorse any clear prescription, stating that diagnostics for each situation must be conducted. His general approach is to suggest a market-conforming role for the state, such as investing in education or an industrial policy that helps to build upon existing export industries or ones where a clear comparative advantage exists. A weakness of these good governance approaches is that they do little to distinguish what makes for a "good" versus "bad" institution, other than the results, or how one goes about creating "good" institutions.

market, such as transporting goods from buyers to sellers, and the costs of a lack of clear information, which creates uncertainty and risk, and the lack of standards (an example would be appliances that run on different voltages). So, the second generation of reforms, particularly developing sound judiciaries to enforce property rights and contracts and to eliminate corruption, is really the key to spurring development in the South. According to this view, while the state regulates to reduce transactions costs, it cannot replace the market as the primary economic decision-maker.

The World Bank has picked up on this theme, using the term **governance** to refer to its new-found concern with how well states function in managing markets. It is interesting to note that this new tack still allows economists to avoid overtly political analyses (see Chapter 9). Governance thus came into the debate to encompass a variety of attempts to reform the state since the 1990s. Like globalization, it has been used in different ways and contexts to mean different things. In the most general sense, the idea of governance developed in response to the crisis of the state caused by neoliberal market-friendly policies. Shackled with debt and forced to retrench, the state lost its role as the leader in economic development. Even in welfare programs and utilities, privatization, subcontracting, or **public–private partnerships** are viewed as superior to the post-World War II Keynesian state, which was disparaged for the economic crises of the 1970s and 1980s. On the other hand, the general lack of economic growth and worsening income distribution between the North and many parts of the South led some to re-examine state capacity for development.

Jean-Marc Fleury, IDRC

PHOTO 7.3 | Worker preparing small ornamental fig trees for export, Las Palmas, Canary Islands.

Rent-Seeking and State Capture: The Battle against Corruption

The idea that the state was the problem with—not the solution to—economic development resonated with many people who had seen colonial states transformed into patronage-heavy and highly inefficient public projects and enterprises. Scholars such as Krueger (1974) coined the term "rent-seeking" to describe how states, even in the North, could become "captured" by special interest groups in the private sector, leading to policies that benefited a privileged minority. The charge of state corruption had broad appeal in the South and led initially to the success of neoliberal populists such as Carlos Salinas in Mexico, Alberto Fujimori in Peru, Fernando Collor de Melo in Brazil, Carlos Andres Pérez in Venezuela, and Carlos Menem in Argentina. The fact that all these leaders were later pushed out on corruption charges helped to sour the popular appeal of neoliberalism but did not eliminate the central problem of state capture. State capture now often includes the idea that powerful private interests, such as, but not limited to, foreign corporations, can undermine the ability of the state to pursue national policies in the collective interest and thereby undercut the democratic process.

The focus on good governance for mainstream development agencies has meant a battle against corruption. Various scoring indices have been developed for an annual rating of the level of corruption of a country, such as those of Transparency International, the World Bank, and the World Economic Forum. The data for these exercises are largely gathered from surveys of international business executives. While valuable, indices based on such a limited and understandably biased perspective only tell a part of the story, that is, how "friendly" a particular country is to the interests of international business, such as full profit repatriation, which might not be in national interests.

The focus on good governance does not just stop at how conducive to business the social and political environment is in a particular country. Most development agencies have adopted some form of "results-based management" and, at least rhetorically, a recognition of the need to consult stakeholders. The Millennium Development Goals, adopted in 2000 by a wide range of multilateral and bilateral aid agencies, were designed to create some clear, measurable targets for donor assistance levels, with results to be achieved (such as the wiping out of certain diseases) over certain periods of time, and the requirement for good governance by recipients. The goals were to be achieved in 2015, and while progress was made in some areas, such as levels of aid and trade, in other areas, such as access to medicines, the results are both more ambiguous and limited. While poverty has been reduced in the world, that reduction has been concentrated in certain countries, particularly China. Moreover, it is difficult to say whether achievements, such as Bangladesh's policy efforts to reduce infant mortality, are a result of the goals or independent of them. In 2016, the UN introduced the Sustainable Development Goals (SDGs) to replace them. The SDGs expand the number of goals to 17, to include many related to the environment. Goal 16 is specifically focused on "peace, justice and strong institutions," reflecting the governance agenda. The goals, such as wiping out extreme poverty, are to be achieved by 2030.

What may be normal in regard to governance in one place, such as allowing a friend speedier service, may be viewed as corruption in another. For example, Robinson (2009), reflecting findings by others, relates how a serious overhaul of the civil service in Uganda, including raising salaries and creating anti-corruption agencies and independent revenue authorities, had initially promising results but ultimately ebbed into failure. More ironically still, strong evidence indicates that donor agencies and NGOs themselves suffer from a lack of accountability and transparency (Berkman, 2008; Cremer, 2008).

Thus, it is important to distinguish **clientelism** from corruption. Clientelism is favouritism for particular groups that may be perfectly legal (unlike corruption) but inimical to social interests. Continual scandals in the North, from the fraudulent accounting that led to the collapse of US companies Enron and World.com in 2001–2 to investment misinformation by Goldman Sachs and others in 2009, have brought a new wave of interest in corporate ethics. Moreover, a review of corruption indices over time, such as that of Transparency International, shows little movement from high to low corruption, and offers no real explanation for why corruption occurs. All of this indicates that much deeper (possibly cultural and political) roots are at play in the fight against corruption and clientelism, and that it is a universal, not an exclusively southern, problem that deserves a lot more attention.

GOVERNANCE AS A PROCESS OF DEMOCRATIZATION

For non-economists, "governance" has come to mean a wide variety of other things related to a supposed crisis of the state throughout the world. The crisis of the state in the North refers to the lack of interest and electoral participation among large segments of the population, as well as a supposedly growing cynicism about the increasing reach of the state over the course of the twentieth century. In the South, the crisis stems from the fragility of democracy, as well as from dissatisfaction with the ability of democracies to address long-standing structural inequalities. Therefore, the original economic definition of "governance" that focused on good regulation of markets is now matched with an emphasis on finding additional means of enhancing the participation of citizens, called "civil society," as individuals and groups in collective decision-making through state co-ordination (see Chapter 12).

For most economists and in practice, this evolution has meant state co-ordination with the private sector. Studies have suggested that greater civic and political engagement ("social capital") leads to higher economic growth and development (e.g., Putnam, 1993). Certainly, southern democracies have a host of deficiencies, ranging from common voter fraud to extremely weak opposition parties and judiciaries. These shortcomings have been viewed as both reflecting and exacerbating the often polarized nature of their polities. This line of thought led to a different use of "governance" to mean co-ordination of collective decision-making among stakeholders, and had profound effects on development policy-making and practice, which now actively solicits outside parties (the stakeholders, generally limited to certain acceptable points of view) to take part in the decision-making process, including civil society or the general public. Such an approach is different from allowing only well-organized and well-funded lobby groups into the decision-making process. Thus, the state becomes as much a facilitator as a leader. In theory, all those affected have a say in collective decision-making, and the process is as important as the decision itself. For example, experimentation with participatory budgeting in certain municipalities in Brazil is seen as a new model for how to govern. The emphasis on client-based and results-based management is essential to what is called the "new public management" approach.

In practice, such noble efforts are quite difficult to consummate. This new kind of open state requires a new level and set of skills in terms of state capacity that go well beyond simply posting information on a website. Even on the local level, where participation is easier, studies show that those with more means tend to participate more. Similarly, gender, ethnicity, literacy, and free time could affect rates of participation. Then there is the question of how to deal with highly technical issues, such as how to best set the central bank interest rate. Moreover, the general public could be wrong—for example, in underestimating the long-term costs of climate change. This version of governance aims (or claims) to enable equitable representation of the different segments of the population, as well as to weigh collective interest in decision-making. Yet strong critiques suggest that governance of this sort is impossible, given the structural inequalities rife in the South.

On the other hand, others hold hope that a more open system will increase transparency and accountability to previously unheard constituents. This sea change of thought is behind the new forms of democratic populism, such as the attempts by Venezuela and Bolivia to create new constitutions and more representative constituent assemblies in the past decade. For an external agency, taking local participation seriously potentially changes the whole way that development operates, from defining a mission to delivering resources to evaluating the "success" or "failure" of a project, and the same could be said of any public service in general (Hira and Parfitt, 2004).

Globalization and the Role of the State

Concern about representative accountable states that are engaged with equity as well as growth has increased in a globalizing world. By globalization, authors such as Manuel Castells (1996) refer to increasing economic and social transactions and ease of communication across states. The explosive power of the Internet demonstrates the way that states may be losing some aspects of their control—in this case, the ability to control information and the means of communication within a state territory (see Chapters 6 and 22).

In addition, the movement towards policies that encourage foreign investment has been paralleled by the increasing dominance of large global companies such as Microsoft and DaimlerChrysler. Some argue that these companies have no real national identity, provide few benefits to their home country, and drive hard bargains with the developing states that want to attract their activities (see Chapter 11). They are increasingly challenged by upstarts from the BRICS countries whose state backing allows them to make different types of bargains, such as infrastructure building, in exchange for investment (see Chapter 13).

There is even greater fluidity in financial transactions. Much of the world's financial transactions now take place "offshore" in small tax havens, such as the Cayman Islands, where terrorists, drug traffickers, and corporations share banks. While most financial activity continues to occur in New York and London, the offshore centres serve as important routes to tax evasion. In 2016, the "Panama Papers" brought the staggering volume of unaccounted for financial transactions into broad daylight. The papers, consisting of 11.5 million documents, were leaked information from Panama-based attorneys acting on behalf of clients all over the world to set up tax havens and launder money. Prominent leaders, including the Prime Ministers of the UK and Iceland, were associated with the Papers; the latter was forced to resign. The Papers also revealed

CRITICAL ISSUES

BOX 7.5 | Does the 2008 Financial Crisis Mark a Shift Away from Neoliberalism?

The 2008 worldwide financial crisis further polarized both sides of the debate about states and markets. The financial crisis was traced by many back to the deregulation of financial markets from the 1980s as an extension of neoliberal macroeconomic reforms. The end result was the delinking of banking assets and investment decisions from collateral as new financial instruments were created. Many of these instruments included highly complex packages of mortgage debts, bets on financial futures, and "dark pools" of trading among banks that were beyond regulation. Alan Greenspan, the celebrated Federal Reserve Chairman, had an unshakeable faith that markets would sort out the most efficient solutions. This perspective was encapsulated in the "rational expectations" school of economics that suggested that markets were efficient not only in the present but also in smoothing out future volatility of markets through arbitrage. Surprisingly, the use of highly mathematical quantitative models upon which investment decisions were made ignored long-term cycles in market valuations that occasionally led to major "corrections" unanticipated on the downside by the models. On top of all this, the freeing of the financial sector from regulation was accompanied by the linking of investment and capital across Europe and the US, increasing the likelihood of contagion, or spreading of panic, if one centre went down. The lack of transparency and an overall move to deregulation arguably resulted in the worst financial situation for the West since the Great Depression (Hira, 2013).

States were left with no choice but massive bailouts of their financial sectors, ironically begun by neoliberal believers such as Hank Paulson, US Treasury Secretary. Even Greenspan admitted that he may have misjudged human nature and its propensity for "irrational exuberance." On top of these developments, two other challenges have shaken what once seemed an unassailable neoliberal consensus. First, the rise of China as a global powerhouse through state backing/control of key industries extends the aforementioned challenge from the East Asian model. Second, the increasingly pressing challenge of climate change and the inability of markets to reduce emissions raise questions about whether the market equilibrium is an acceptable one. Even some mainstream economists such as Nicholas Stern of the London School of Economics and Politics have weighed in on the side of major government intervention to avoid considerably higher, potentially disastrous, economic costs of climate change down the road. At the same time, the lack of employment recovery amid a return to financial solvency of companies has led some to question whether capital and labour are even more delinked in a globalized economy. All of this led to a mini-revival of Keynesian calls for further stimulus of Western economies to revive demand, and a broader questioning of neoliberalism. Even such stalwart institutions as the IMF and World Bank have begun to moderate their ideology towards markets, for example, by admitting that capital controls may sometimes make sense and by holding a conference on the potential for industrial policy, respectively.

For the developing world, there is a willingness to experiment, but the constraints pushing them towards market models, through dependency on global financial flows and trade ties, are still very strong. Still, there are a number of interesting experiments beyond China, such as Bolivia's market-based socialism and Rwanda's attempt to become the information technology hub of Africa. These still fall far short of an alternative model, however.

massive corruption in the developing world as well as conduits for capital flight, a far cry from expectations during the neoliberal period for the benefits of financial reform.

During the 1980s, part of the neoliberal reforms involved setting up stock exchanges in much of the developing world. The expectation was that these emerging markets would be able to attract increasing amounts

CRITICAL ISSUES

BOX 7.6 | Global Chains of Production

In 2005, *New York Times* journalist Thomas L. Friedman released a blockbuster book entitled *The World Is Flat*. Friedman suggests that global chains of production create a "level playing field" through which developing countries will start to participate fully in the world economy. Friedman points to the recent experience of Chinese and Indian companies springing up to compete in world markets, and uses as an example the production of a computer: programming may be done in one place, while the manufacture of components, the assembly, and the testing are done in several other locations. This modularization of production is what some scholars signalled as global commodity chain production. Friedman sees the rapid development of global production chains as largely beneficial, leading to greater participation and reduced poverty as well as reducing prices for consumers. Expansion of this participation means larger world markets, so employment does not have to decline in the West. Some scholars (Gereffi and Korzeniewicz, 1994) note that the nature of the product and what parts of the production chain countries are able to capture will determine the earnings they receive. For example, we pay some $4 for a fancy coffee at Starbucks, but coffee farmers in developing states receive a tiny fraction of that amount. This discrepancy has led to the fair trade movement (see Chapter 15).

of capital for their cash-starved growing businesses; markets, not the state, would provide leadership, taking on the risks and the analysis required to develop new businesses. However, the experience with emerging financial markets has been largely disappointing (Lavelle, 2004). Questions also have been raised about the international trade agreements that multiplied during the neoliberal period (see Chapter 15). For example, NAFTA, signed by Canada, the US, and Mexico in 1994, was supposed to lead to an age of prosperity for Mexico because its comparative advantage—cheap labour—would be soaked up in US production chains. However, the effects of NAFTA on Mexico have been highly controversial. Critics suggest that only a limited number of low-paying jobs have been created and that many sectors, such as sugar cane production, have been adversely affected. They also note that with China's emergence, many of the labour-intensive industries have left Mexico and relocated in a lower-wage environment. Moreover, products such as computers are manufactured in a modular fashion, with components that can be sourced and assembled in many different locations. All of this has led some to suggest that the state has weakened in the face of globalization (Strange, 1996). Some critics even suggest that the state is dying, not only in the developing world but also in the developed world, and point to diminishing social welfare protection in many states as evidence.

Yet other analysts, such as Linda Weiss (1998), argue that such ideas are "greatly exaggerated" and that the state is more important than ever. The state still determines the rules for foreign investment and trade within its own territory. The state is still the dominant actor that chooses whether to trade and fixes the terms for signing international trade and investment agreements. The state still can improve the nation's ability to compete in global markets through strategic investment in infrastructure and its own people. We can observe that, as in the story of blind men describing different parts of an elephant, both perspectives are correct. Globalization has weakened labour protections and power across the North as labour-intensive manufacturing has been replaced by cheaper imports of manufactured goods from overseas, where labour regulations and enforcement are less stringent. This does not mean that developing states that capture new production are in control, because production can move from one country to another fairly quickly in response to global business supply decisions. For example, textile production has moved from Taiwan and South Korea to China and Central America. At the same time, several analysts argue that strategic state intervention, not markets, explains the ability of states such as China and India to attract new global industries and services (Hira and Hira, 2005). Certainly, the state still may choose to create forms of insulation from and adjustment to global forces—Malaysia, for example, imposed controls over the movement of capital from outside the country for many years. Thus, the role of the state remains at the forefront in the development debate.

SUMMARY

The state as an instrument of the public will is at the centre of most development debates and action. The state is the arena where political, social, and economic debates and conflict are played out in terms of which public policies are adopted and implemented. The state is highly controversial, with some seeing it as an instrument for preserving the concentration of benefits, while others believe it is the sole instrument capable of leading a nation forward for the collective interest. This chapter has explored the role of the state in economic development through historical, discursive, and empirical analysis. The state in post-colonial societies has different origins, constraints, pressures, and possibilities for leadership from its Western counterparts. Late entry into the industrialization and technological development processes and domestic institutional weaknesses create serious challenges for finding stable and inclusive economic development paths. Contemporary issues such as globalization and the call for better governance are central to this discussion. A number of case studies exemplify questions regarding whether the state can and has been a positive force for economic development in the South.

QUESTIONS FOR CRITICAL THOUGHT

1. Is the traditional international relations theory view of a state adequate to understand the types of states we find in the developing world? Do states vary by region?
2. Select a developing state and identify the major issues it faces by examining current news reports. Then examine something about its history (a basic online encyclopedia will do). To what extent are its current problems tied to its colonial origins?
3. What are the advantages and disadvantages of market-based as opposed to state leadership? Consider efficiency and equity outcomes, economic stability, and employment.
4. If you were a state planner, what arguments could you see for and against a big push versus a targeted strategy for development? What kinds of blockages can you see in a typical developing economy, and to what extent are they related?
5. Is there a disadvantage to producing commodities instead of manufactured goods? Why or why not?
6. Why is the issue of corruption so polarized, with some claiming it is at the heart of poor development performance in the South and others suggesting it is just a way for external agents to ensure their investments in the South are safe? How would you judge the merits and weaknesses of each explanation, and what is your perspective?

SUGGESTED READINGS

Chang, Ha-Joon. 2002. *Kicking Away the Ladder: Development Strategy in Historical Perspective*. NY: Anthem.

Evans, Peter. 1995. *Embedded Autonomy: States and Industrial Transformation*. Princeton, NJ: Princeton University Press.

Gerschenkron, Alexander. 1962. *Economic Backwardness in Historical Perspective*. Cambridge, Mass.: Belknap Press of Harvard University Press.

Hira, Anil. 2007. *An East Asian Model for Latin American Success: The New Path*. Burlington, Vt: Ashgate.

North, Douglass C. 1990. *Institutions, Institutional Change, and Economic Performance*. New York: Cambridge University Press.

Wade, Robert. 1990. *Governing the Market: Economic Theory and the Role of Government in East Asian Industrialization*. Princeton, NJ: Princeton University Press.

BIBLIOGRAPHY

Berkman, S. 2008. *The World Bank and the Gods of Lending.* Sterling, Va: Kumarian Press.

Castells, M. 1996. *The Information Age: Economy, Society and Culture*, vol. 1: *The Rise of the Network Society.* Cambridge, Mass.: Blackwell.

Centeno, M.A. 2002. *Blood and Debt: War and the Nation-State in Latin America.* University Park: Pennsylvania State University Press.

Cremer, G. 2008. *Corruption and Development Aid: Confronting the Challenges.* Boulder, Colo.: Lynne Rienner.

Evans, P. 1995. *Embedded Autonomy: States and Industrial Transformation.* Princeton, NJ: Princeton University Press.

Friedman, T.L. 2005. *The World Is Flat: A Brief History of the Twenty-First Century.* New York: Farrar, Strauss and Giroux.

Gereffi, G., and M. Korzeniewicz, eds. 1994. *Commodity Chains and Global Capitalism.* Westport, Conn.: Greenwood.

——— and Donald L. Wyman. 1990. *Manufacturing Miracles: Paths of Industrialization in Latin America and East Asia.* Princeton, NJ: Princeton University Press.

Gerschenkron, A. 1962. *Economic Backwardness in Historical Perspective.* Cambridge, Mass.: Belknap Press of Harvard University Press.

Grindle, M.S. 1996. *Challenging the State: Crisis and Innovation in Latin America and Africa.* Cambridge: Cambridge University Press.

Haggard, S. 1990. *Pathways from the Periphery: The Politics of Growth in the Newly Industrializing Countries.* Ithaca, NY: Cornell University Press.

Hall, P. 1989. *The Political Power of Economic Ideas: Keynesianism across Nations.* Princeton, NJ: Princeton University Press.

Hira, A. 1998. *Ideas and Economic Policy in Latin America: Regional, National and Organizational Case Studies.* Westport, Conn.: Greenwood.

———. 2007. *An East Asia Model for Latin America: The New Path.* Burlington, Vt: Ashgate.

———. 2013. "Irrational exuberance: An evolutionary perspective on the underlying causes of the financial crisis." *Intereconomics: Review of European Economic Policy* 48, 2 (Mar./Apr.): 116–23.

——— and Trevor Parfitt. 2004. *Development Projects for a New Millennium.* Westport, Conn.: Greenwood.

Hira, R., and A. Hira. 2005. *Outsourcing America.* New York: Amacom.

Hirschman, A.O. 1971. *A Bias for Hope: Essays on Development and Latin America.* New Haven: Yale University Press.

Johnson, C. 1982. *MITI and the Japanese Miracle: The Growth of Industrial Policy, 1925–75.* Stanford, Calif.: Stanford University Press.

Keynes, J.M. 1936. *The General Theory of Employment, Interest, and Money.* New York: Harcourt Brace.

Krueger, A.O. 1974. "The political economy of the rent-seeking society." *American Economic Review* 64: 291–303.

———, ed. 2000. *Economic Policy Reform: The Second Stage.* Chicago: University of Chicago Press.

Lavelle, K.C. 2004. *The Politics of Equity Finance in Emerging Markets.* New York: Oxford University Press.

Lewis, W.A. 1955. "Economic development with unlimited supplies of labour." *The Manchester School* 22 (May): 139–92.

Poggi, G. 1978. *The Development of the Modern State: A Sociological Introduction.* Stanford, Calif.: Stanford University Press.

Polanyi, K. 1944. *The Great Transformation: The Political and Economic Origins of Our Time.* Boston: Beacon Press by arrangement with Rinehart and Co.

Prebisch, R. 1950. *The Economic Development of Latin America and Its Principal Problems.* New York: United Nations.

Putnam, R.D., with R. Leonardi and R.Y. Nanetti. 1993. *Making Democracy Work: Civic Traditions in Modern Italy.* Princeton, NJ: Princeton University Press.

Robinson, M. 2009. "The political economy of governance reforms in Uganda." In Mark Robinson, ed., *The Politics of Successful Governance Reforms.* New York: Routledge, 50–72.

Rosenstein-Rodan, P.N. 1961. "Notes on the theory of the big push." In H.S. Ellis and Henry C. Wallach, eds, *Economic Development for Latin America.* New York: St Martin's Press, 57–67.

Stiglitz, J. 2002. *Globalization and Its Discontents.* New York: W.W. Norton.

Strange, S. 1996. *The Retreat of the State: The Diffusion of Power in the World Economy.* Cambridge: Cambridge University Press.

Von Hayek, F. 1944. *The Road to Serfdom.* London: Routledge.

Wade, R. 1990. *Governing the Market: Economic Theory and the Role of Government in East Asian Industrialization.* Princeton, NJ: Princeton University Press.

Weiss, L. 1998. *The Myth of the Powerless State: Governing the Economy in the Global Era.* Cambridge: Polity Press.

World Bank. 1993. *The East Asian Miracle: Economic Growth and Public Policy.* New York: Cambridge University Press.

8 National Development Agencies and Bilateral Aid

Stephen Brown

LEARNING OBJECTIVES

- To understand the main terms and concepts applicable to bilateral foreign aid.
- To learn about the different reasons why donors provide assistance and how their priorities can vary.
- To appreciate current trends in and debates surrounding foreign aid.

▲ **Despite the importance of the agriculture sector in Ethiopia, access to credit is limited. USAID uses its Development Credit Authority to share risk with local banks, thus opening financing for underserved but credit-worthy borrowers. Abebaw Gesesse, the owner of a poultry farm in Mojo, Ethiopia, received a $132,000 loan from Dashen Bank thanks to a USAID guarantee. Today Abe produces over five million eggs a year and enough chicken meat to feed 108,000 people.** | Source: Morgana Wingard/USAID

This chapter provides an overview of the main actors, modalities, and resource flows involved in the aid that countries in the North provide to **recipients** in the South. It begins by explaining some key terms in what is known as **bilateral aid**. It then examines global aid flows, highlighting the differences among donors and analyzing the issue of their underlying motives. Finally, it explores which regions and countries receive the most aid, before turning to an overview of current trends and controversies in foreign aid.

CLARIFYING THE TERMINOLOGY

The providers of development assistance are usually referred to as **donors**, although "lenders" may be a more appropriate term in cases where the aid is in the form of loans. Most donors provide the majority of their aid—an average of 65–70 per cent—directly to developing countries (known as **bilateral** or government-to-government aid) and channel the remainder of their funds through multilateral organizations such as the World Bank or UN agencies, for example, UNICEF (**multilateral** aid). This chapter limits its discussion to bilateral aid and donors. Multilateral institutions and development assistance are discussed in Chapters 9, 10 and 28.

The expression "foreign aid" is often used interchangeably with the more technical term **official development assistance** (ODA), as we do in this chapter. The two, however, are not quite synonymous. While foreign aid can include a wide range of assistance, what can technically be counted as ODA is more restricted. According to its official definition, ODA refers to "flows of official financing administered with the promotion of the economic development and welfare of developing countries as the main objective, and which are concessional in character with a grant element of at least 25 per cent" (OECD, 2003). This means that to qualify as ODA, funding must be provided by governments and its main purpose must be improving economic or social well-being in developing countries (see Box 8.1). Thus, donations from individuals, foundations, or private corporations, whether directly to developing countries or through the intermediary of **non-governmental organizations** (NGOs), do not count as ODA, nor do military assistance and export credits meant primarily to promote the sale of goods from the donor country. Aid to countries not classified as developing, such as Russia, does not qualify as ODA and is usually referred to as "official assistance." ODA financing can be provided in the form of a grant (a non-reimbursable donation) or a loan (to be repaid), but to be counted as ODA the terms of the loan would have to be significantly better than what is available on the commercial market (with a lower interest rate, an extended period of repayment, and/or a "grace period" before the first repayment falls due). For this reason, private investment and commercial loans are excluded as well. However, ODA does include administrative costs, such as the costs of maintaining aid agency offices and the salaries of staff both at home and abroad.

There is some controversy over what should be included as ODA. For instance, donor governments have agreed to count as ODA the expenses incurred during the first year of resettling refugees in their countries. In this case, it is not clear that this fulfills the requirement that the main objective be "economic development and welfare of developing countries"; moreover, the period of one year is rather arbitrary. Some accounting measures are also contentious. For example, when debt is cancelled, the full outstanding amount is counted for the year in which the loan was forgiven, even if the scheduled repayment would not have been completed for decades. This allows donors to boost their ODA for a given year without actually spending any additional funds, which produces a temporary "blip" that distorts true aid trends. Furthermore, when development assistance is closely integrated with military and diplomatic initiatives—in Iraq and Afghanistan, for instance—it can be hard to determine exactly what constitutes ODA and what does not. A few countries are trying to revise the guidelines to include the cost of peacekeeping operations as ODA, even if the funds are spent on the donor country's troops. (Currently, this only counts as ODA if the donor country is funding the participation of personnel from a developing country.) Critics object to the expansion of the definition of ODA, arguing that it leads to the militarization or securitization of aid and can prioritize the interests of donor countries rather than those of the recipients.

IMPORTANT CONCEPTS

BOX 8.1 | The Many Uses of Foreign Aid

Foreign aid can be spent in numerous sectors and ways, including:

- To provide training and build local capacity.
- To promote social services, including education and health care.
- To promote the building of infrastructure, such as roads, bridges, dams, railways, and airports.
- To support policy reform, for instance, drawing up new legislation and regulations to protect the environment, fight corruption, or liberalize trade.
- To promote agriculture, including the adoption of new crop techniques.
- To promote industry, such as processing food or natural resources.
- To purchase technology.
- To provide humanitarian assistance, notably emergency housing, food, or health care, especially in cases of war or natural disaster.

OVERVIEW OF AID DONORS

Most industrialized countries that provide foreign aid belong to a donors' club known as the Development Assistance Committee (DAC) of the Organisation for Economic Co-operation and Development (OECD), headquartered in Paris. DAC members regularly provide the OECD with a breakdown of their aid figures, and the OECD in turn compiles the information, making it publicly available. Not all donors, however, are members of the DAC. Some OECD members have foreign aid programs but do not belong to the DAC, such as Hungary, Israel, and Turkey. Several Arab states, including oil-producing Kuwait, Saudi Arabia, and the United Arab Emirates, also provide assistance, as do some developing countries themselves, such as Cuba, Taiwan, and Venezuela, but none of these is a member of the OECD (see Table 8.1). China in recent years has gained much attention for its foreign aid, especially to Africa. However, most of it is in the form of loans or investments that do not generally qualify as ODA. Moreover, it does not disclose full information on its aid, nor do other important providers of development assistance, such as Brazil, India, and South Africa. This chapter concentrates on the ODA provided by the 28 member nations of the DAC, which constitutes some 85–90 per cent of global ODA.

In 2013, DAC donors contributed US$134 billion in ODA. Of this, over $93 billion was in bilateral assistance and $41 billion in contributions to multilateral institutions. Of these amounts, $8 billion was spent on humanitarian aid and another $5 billion was spent on settling refugees in donor countries. Total ODA was half the total amount of private flows to developing countries (including direct and portfolio investment), which totalled $263 billion for that year. Additionally, NGOs contributed about $31 billion (OECD, 2014: Tables 2 and 13).

The total volume of foreign aid has followed various trends over the decades. As Figure 8.1 illustrates (using constant 2013 dollars to facilitate comparison), total aid increased slowly in the 1960s and then much more rapidly in the 1970s. In fact, total aid flows more than doubled between 1970 and 1980, even when adjusted for inflation. Donors cut their aid in the early and mid-1990s, a period of "aid fatigue." Between 1991 and 1997, total aid dropped by one-fifth. Contributions rose again quite dramatically after 2000, reaching an

TABLE 8.1 | ODA and "ODA-Like Flows" from Non-DAC Providers, 2013

Donors	US$ Millions	ODA/Gross National Income (%)
OECD Non-DAC		
Estonia	31	0.13
Hungary	128	0.10
Israel	202	0.07
Turkey	3,308	0.42
Other providers		
Bulgaria	50	0.10
Chile*	44	Not available
China*	3,009	Not available
Croatia	45	0.08
Colombia*	95	Not available
Cyprus	20	0.10
India*	1,257	Not available
Indonesia*	12	Not available
Kuwait	186	Not available
Latvia	24	0.08
Liechtenstein	28	Not available
Lithuania	50	0.11
Malta	18	0.20
Romania	134	0.07
Russia	714	0.03
Saudi Arabia	5,683	Not available
South Africa*	183	Not available
Taiwan	272	0.05
Thailand	46	0.01
United Arab Emirates	5,402	1.34

Notes: Countries whose names are followed by an asterisk do not report their ODA figures to the OECD. The figures are estimates of concessional finance for development ("ODA-like flows"). Data were not available for 2013 for Brazil, Mexico, and Qatar.

Source: OECD (2014: Tables 33 and 33a).

all-time high to date in 2013, the latest year for which figures are available, about 56 per cent higher than 10 years earlier, in 2003. The trend-breaking amounts for 2005 and 2006 were inflated by exceptionally high debt relief, which as explained above provides a one-time boost reflected in accounting but not in actual spending on development activities. Box 8.2 describes these aid cycles in greater detail.

The most generous donor by far in dollar terms was the United States, whose ODA totalled over $31 billion in 2013 (see Figure 8.2). The next four largest donors were the United Kingdom, Germany, Japan, and France, each of which contributed between $11 billion and $18 billion, roughly one-third to half of the disbursements of the US. At the other end of the scale, smaller countries, such as Slovakia, Slovenia, and Iceland, each contributed less than $90 million in that year. Of the non-DAC donors that report their ODA figures to the DAC, the largest in 2013 was Saudi Arabia, which contributed $6 billion, making it the world's sixth-largest donor, followed by the United Arab Emirates ($5 billion) and Turkey ($3 billion), all of which provided more ODA than what each of the 17 smallest DAC donors contributed. China's concessional finance for development is estimated to total $3 billion in 2013, similar in size to Turkey's ODA (see Table 8.1).

Although absolute figures in US dollars immediately reveal who the most—and least—significant players are in the area of foreign aid, they tell us little about how generous the countries actually are when measured against their capacity to provide assistance. Relative generosity is normally calculated by dividing ODA by gross national income (GNI), gross national product (GNP), or gross domestic product (GDP), each of which provides almost identical figures.

In 1970, the UN General Assembly passed a resolution whereby donors would provide at least 0.7 per cent of their GNP in ODA by 1975 (see Box 8.3). DAC donors as a whole failed miserably to reach that target. In 2013, 38 years after the deadline, they collectively provided 0.30 per cent, less than half the amount to which they had committed. Nonetheless, this was significantly higher than the 0.21 per cent provided in 1997–8 (OECD, 2014: Table 4).

Individual donors' relative generosity actually varies greatly from the average. In 2013, as illustrated in Figure 8.3, five countries met or exceeded the UN target of 0.7 per cent: Norway (1.07 per cent), Sweden (1.01 per cent), Luxembourg (1.00 per cent), Denmark (0.85 per cent), and the United Kingdom (0.70 per cent). At the bottom of the scale, Slovakia contributed 0.09 per cent

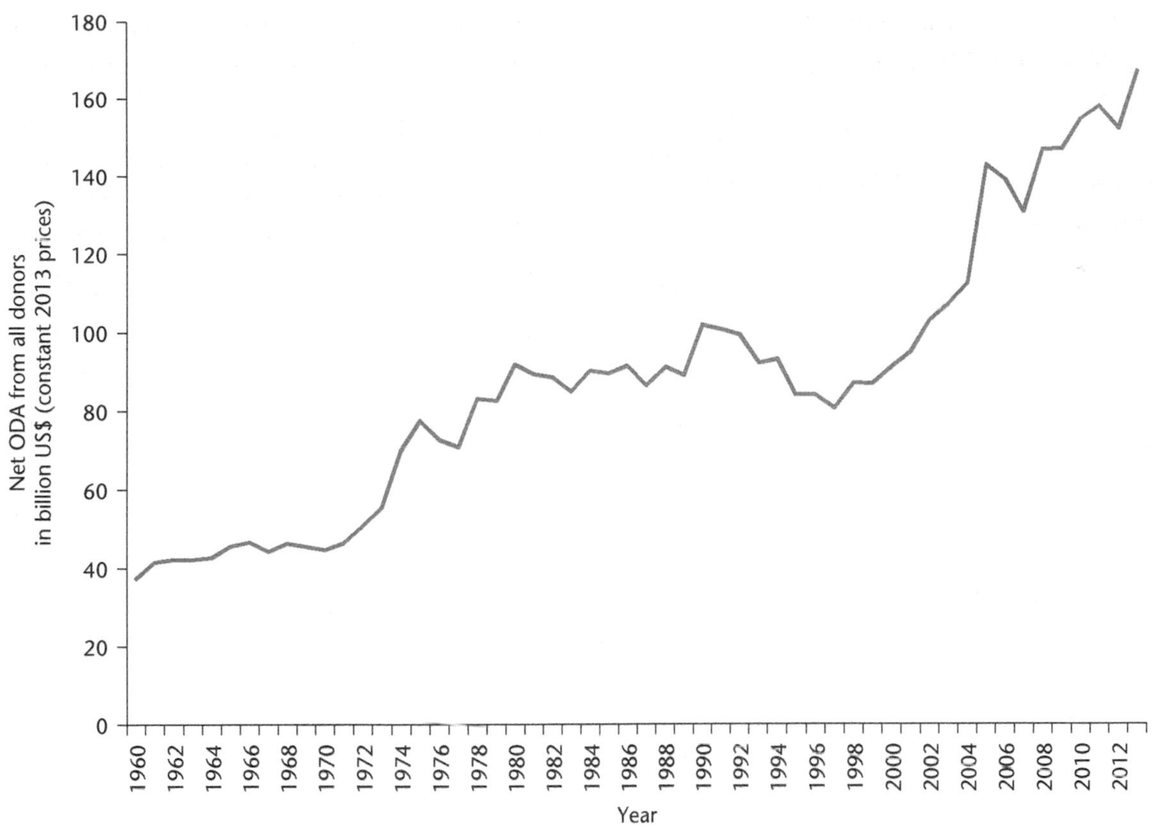

FIGURE 8.1 | Total Aid Flows, 1960–2013

Source: Data extracted from OECD (2015b).

CRITICAL ISSUES

BOX 8.2 | Foreign Aid Cycles

The 1970s were a period of great optimism regarding the use of foreign aid to promote development. Donors agreed at the United Nations in 1970 to steadily increase their ODA to reach a minimum of 0.7 per cent of their gross national product within five years. Although they failed to meet the target, as discussed above and in Box 8.3, donors did provide far more aid than ever before. In the 1980s, a period of slower growth in donor countries and severe economic crises in most recipient countries, new aid was often made conditional on major changes in economic policy. This slowed the growth of aid somewhat. In the 1990s, after the end of the Cold War and the collapse of the Soviet Union as a rival patron for many developing countries, Western donors cut their own foreign aid budgets, justifying the cuts mainly by invoking a need to trim their budget deficits. At the same time, donors were growing increasingly disenchanted with what they considered a lack of concrete results and unacceptably high levels of corruption in recipient countries. In 2000, the pendulum began to swing back the other way. A new consensus emerged on the urgent need to fight poverty, especially in Africa, leading to an agreement on the Millennium Development Goals (MDGs, discussed below and in Chapter 24) to be reached by 2015. Total aid increased at a rate not seen since the 1970s.

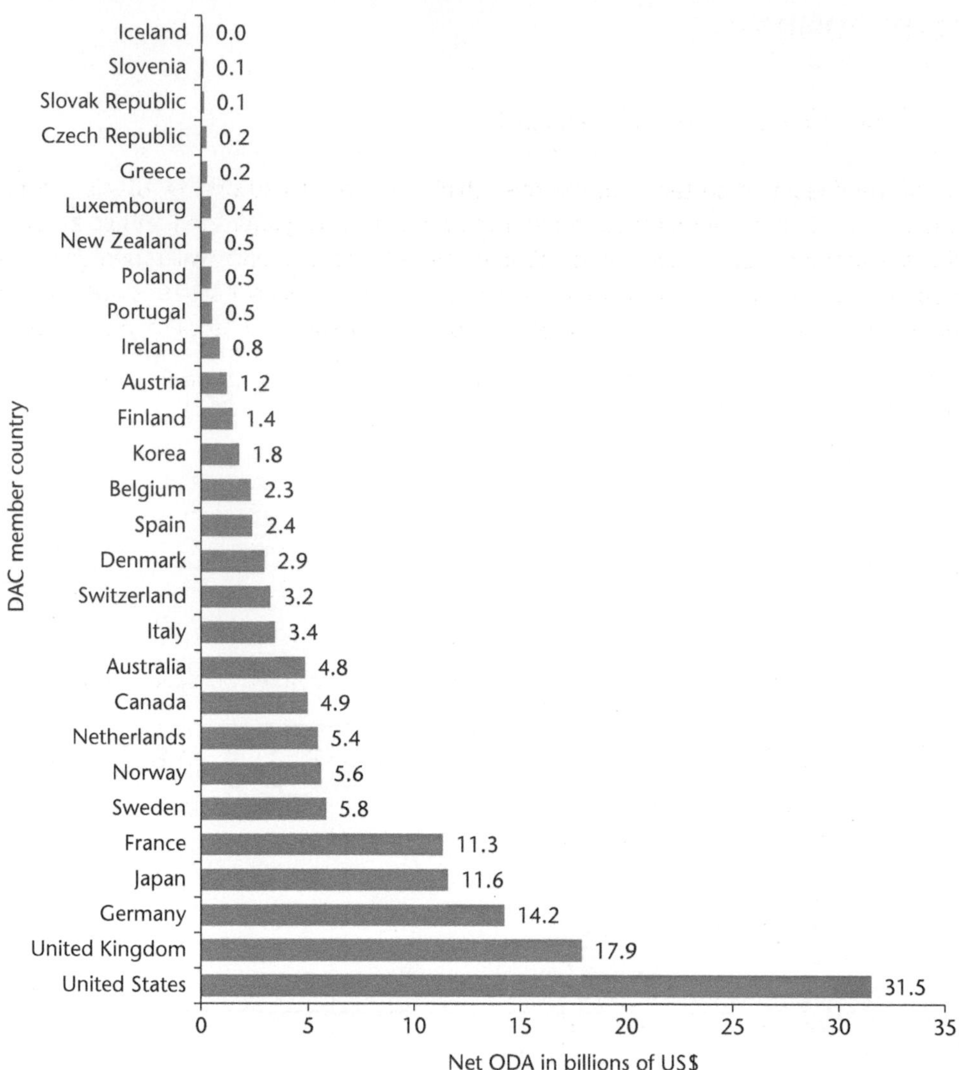

FIGURE 8.2 | Total Foreign Aid by DAC Donor, 2013

Source: Data extracted from OECD (2015b).

of gross national income in 2013, while the figure for Poland and Greece was 0.10 per cent. Paradoxically, the world's most generous donor in absolute terms is also one of the least generous in relative terms: the US ratio was only 0.18 per cent for that year, one-sixth of Norway's contribution and barely a quarter of the UN target.

DONOR MOTIVES

Donors provide development assistance for numerous reasons. One of them—and for many, the most important—is simply to help the less fortunate abroad. Thus, a primary justification is that just as social programs provide assistance to poor people at home, ODA should focus on helping people in other countries have access to food, housing, health care, education, and other basic necessities and opportunities. The best means of providing development assistance is often contested (as discussed below), but the goal from this perspective should not be related to self-interest. This motive is most often shared by NGOs and citizens of donor countries, if not by all development officials. There are different forms of this mentality. One can be motivated by charity, often inspired by religious beliefs (and sometimes viewed as paternalism), or by solidarity, a

IMPORTANT CONCEPTS

BOX 8.3 | The 0.7 Per Cent Aid Target

In recognition of the special importance of the role which can be fulfilled only by official development assistance, a major part of financial resource transfers to the developing countries should be provided in the form of official development assistance. Each economically advanced country will progressively increase its official development assistance to the developing countries and will exert its best efforts to reach a minimum net amount of 0.7 per cent of its gross national product at market prices by the middle of the Decade.

Source: International Development Strategy for the Second United Nations Development Decade, UN General Assembly Resolution 2626 (XXV), 24 Oct. 1970, para. 43.

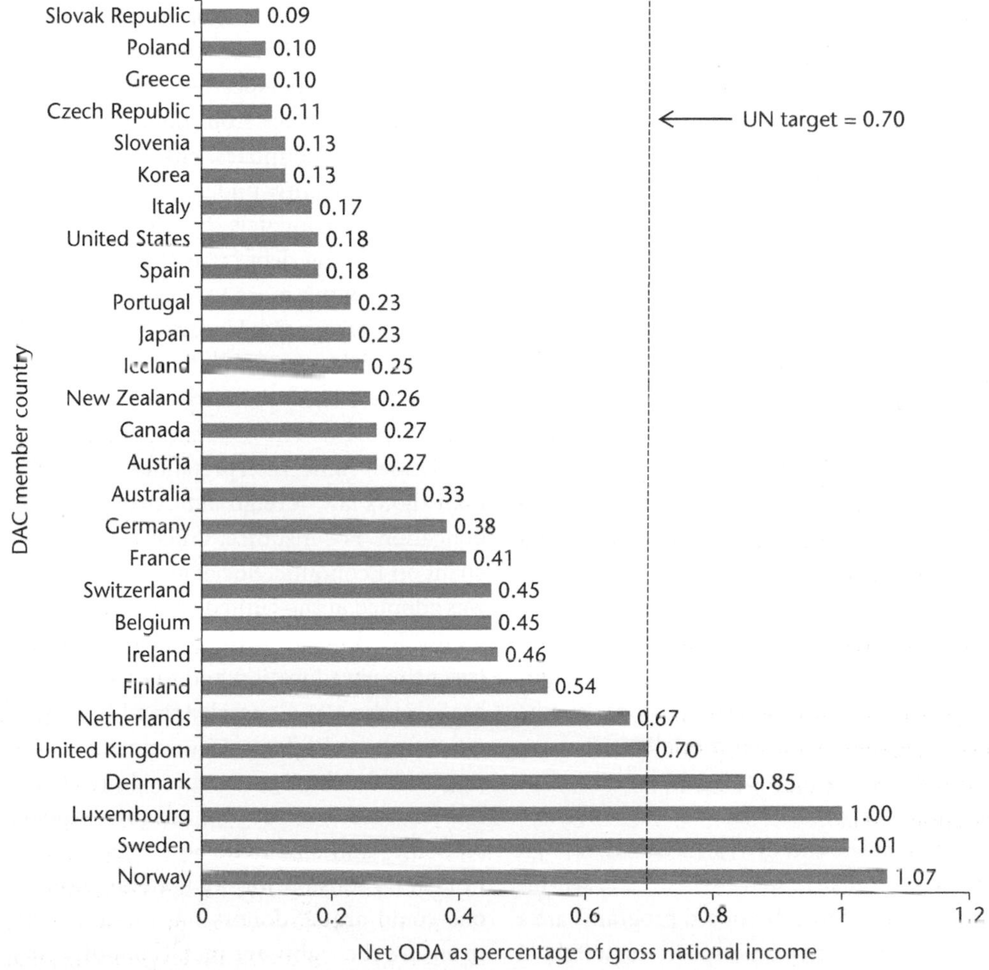

FIGURE 8.3 | Relative Generosity of DAC Donors, 2013

Source: Data extracted from OECD (2015b).

more left-wing concept that frames actors in the recipient country as equal partners. The latter is criticized by some as being naively idealistic and wilfully ignorant of the need for a donor to pursue its own national interest.

A more self-interested motive, however, is widely shared, especially among government officials not directly involved in aid delivery, including those working in national defence, foreign affairs, and international trade. From their perspective, aid is primarily a means to pursue other foreign policy objectives, including diplomatic, commercial, and security interests. Under this logic, aid should be used to promote diplomatic initiatives, including assisting "friendly" countries, pursuing security objectives (for instance, rewarding countries that take part in the "war on terror" or winning hearts and minds in a country where the donor country's troops are deployed), or facilitating trade relations, including the sale of donor nation goods and services in the recipient country. Aid programs also can serve to raise the donor's profile internationally, providing it with prestige among its peers as a country that makes an important contribution on the global level. The basic principle from this perspective is that foreign aid can be used to help people abroad, but that the selection of recipients and aid modalities should prioritize instances where it maximizes the direct and indirect benefits to the donor country.

Increasingly, donors are adopting a "whole-of-government approach" that integrates foreign aid more closely with other foreign policy objectives. This mentality is often criticized for using aid as a fig leaf, hiding the pursuit of naked self-interest behind claims that it is designed to help others. Simultaneously, donor countries are placing greater emphasis on supporting the private sector, often involving greater collaboration with their own multinational corporations. Depending on one's perspective, these partnerships can be described as innovative financing modalities to meet twenty-first century challenges or as corporate subsidies disguised as poverty reduction.

Since its origin at the end of World War II, foreign aid has simultaneously manifested altruistic and self-interested characteristics. Most donor aid programs are a compromise between these two perspectives, weighted differently from donor to donor. On the one hand, much foreign aid has been blatantly used as an instrument of foreign policy, most clearly during the Cold War, when foreign aid from the West often was explicitly targeted to prevent the expansion of Communism. Currently, ODA is more often linked to political and economic liberalization, including strengthening democracy, **good governance**, and the private sector in recipient countries (see Chapters 7 and 9). **Tied aid** (discussed in Box 8.4) is a clear manifestation of the principle that the donor's economy should benefit from the aid it provides, although most donors are phasing out the practice. On the other hand, many billions of dollars have been spent with no clear benefit to the donor. Emergency-related humanitarian assistance best embodies the principle of selflessness.

There are other justifications for the provision of foreign aid, although they are not as widely held. Some, especially in developing countries, view ODA as a form of compensation for past or present injustices, whether colonial exploitation or an unjust international system. From this perspective, northern countries have enriched themselves from their unequal relationships with southern countries, either under colonialism in the past or currently under a global trading system that still disproportionately benefits wealthier countries, with an ongoing debt crisis that has many developing countries paying more to service their debt than they receive in foreign aid. Under this logic, if the net transfer of wealth is from South to North, donors have a duty to increase their ODA to at least balance out the flow of resources.

Under some interpretations of international human rights law, foreign aid can also be considered an obligation. For instance, under the International Covenant on Economic, Social and Cultural Rights, which was adopted at the United Nations in 1966 and became legally binding in 1976, everyone has the right to a free primary education and to earn a livelihood. More broadly, the UN General Assembly adopted a Declaration on the Right to Development in 1986. In cases in which developing countries do not have the necessary resources to provide adequate opportunities for schooling and employment, for instance, they cannot be held responsible for not upholding those rights and, one could argue, donors must assume the obligation to ensure the rights are met. From this perspective, no distinction can be made among recipients based on donor interests—these rights are universal. Some would claim, however, that many developing countries have

CRITICAL ISSUES

BOX 8.4 | Tied Aid

Some ODA is conditional on the purchase of goods and services from the donor country, even if they are not the cheapest or the best value for money, a practice known as "tied aid." Tying aid increases costs by an average of 15 to 30 per cent, although in some instances the figure can be much higher (Jepma, 1991: 15). Sometimes the additional costs can be incurred for a decade or more. For instance, Canadian aid to Mongolia's agricultural sector might require that equipment such as tractors be purchased from Canadian companies. Not only might those tractors cost more and be no better than, say, Japanese or Chinese ones, but Mongolia would have to buy Canadian replacement parts for as long as the tractors were in use.

Aid that can be spent regardless of the country of origin of the goods and services is referred to as "untied." Donors have committed themselves to progressively untying aid, although they have not specified a deadline for eliminating the practice altogether (OECD, 2015a). Some countries, such as Sweden and the United Kingdom, have abolished tied aid altogether. Others, however, continue to tie a sizable proportion of their ODA, including Greece (90 per cent in 2013), Portugal (70 per cent), the Czech Republic (60 per cent), Austria (56 per cent), South Korea (45 per cent), Slovakia (37 per cent), and the United States (27 per cent) (OECD, 2014: Table 23).

the means to meet these basic rights but fail to do so because of waste, corruption, or emphasis on other priorities. In such cases, they believe, governments should be held accountable for their own failings, and donors should not be obligated to assume their responsibilities.

CHARACTERISTICS OF DONORS

Individual donor countries often choose to focus on a particular region on the basis of geography, security interests, or former colonial ties. For instance, in 2012–13, Australia, Japan, South Korea, and New Zealand gave between 54 and 81 per cent of their ODA to Asia and Oceania, their "neighbourhood." Ten donors—Belgium, Canada, Denmark, Finland, Iceland, Ireland, the Netherlands, Portugal, Sweden, and the United Kingdom—gave more than half of theirs to sub-Saharan Africa. No country concentrated the majority of its aid on the Middle East and North Africa or on Latin America and the Caribbean. The United States prioritized both Africa and Asia/Oceania (OECD, 2014: Table 28).

Some countries transfer a much larger proportion of their aid to multilateral institutions than they disburse directly to developing countries (see Chapter 10). By doing so, they reduce their administrative costs but also some of their control over where and how their funds are spent. Figures from 2013 range from Greece and Slovakia, which respectively provided 82 and 81 per cent of their aid through multilateral channels, to the United States and Iceland, which respectively disbursed only 15 and 16 per cent multilaterally (OECD, 2014: Table 13).

Donors also have varying institutional arrangements, priorities, and preferred aid modalities. The United States, for instance, the world's largest aid donor, has two main governmental aid agencies. The first, the United States Agency for International Development (USAID), since its creation in 1961 has been the principal government body for providing development assistance. A second government agency, the Millennium Challenge Corporation (MCC), was launched in 2004 with a narrower focus than that of USAID. The MCC aims to foster economic growth in a smaller number of countries that meet specific criteria regarding free markets, democracy, and good governance.

The US government openly acknowledges the simultaneously selfless and selfish motives of its ODA.

PHOTO 8.1 | USAID youth development project, San Salvador.

For example, the USAID website states that "U.S. foreign assistance has always had the twofold purpose of furthering America's interests while improving lives in the developing world. USAID carries out U.S. foreign policy by promoting broad-scale human progress at the same time it expands stable, free societies, creates markets and trade partners for the United States, and fosters good will abroad" (USAID, 2015). The links between US security interests and development assistance are not difficult to trace. In 2012–13, the top recipient of American ODA by far was Afghanistan, which alone received 7.1 per cent of total US assistance to all developing countries. Its other largest recipients were Kenya, Ethiopia, and Tanzania (OECD, 2014: Table 32).

From its founding in 1968 to its abolition in 2013, the Canadian International Development Agency (CIDA) was responsible for disbursing most of Canada's ODA. Absorbed into the Department of Foreign Affairs, Trade and Development (renamed Global Affairs Canada in 2015), Canada's aid program operates in more than 100 countries. Its top five recipients in 2012–13 were Tanzania, Haiti, Ethiopia, Mozambique, and Afghanistan (OECD, 2014: Table 32). More information on CIDA and its abolition can be found in Box 8.5.

France generally emphasizes aid to sub-Saharan and North Africa, where most of its former colonies are located. The top recipients of French aid in 2012–13 were Côte d'Ivoire, Morocco, Brazil, and Myanmar (OECD, 2014). Most of France's aid is managed by the French Development Agency, which provides assistance to more than 70 countries (Agence française de développement, 2015).

Sweden, one of the world's most generous aid donors in relation to the size of its economy, channels its aid mainly through the Swedish International Development Cooperation Agency (SIDA), which works under the authority of the Ministry of Foreign Affairs. It provides aid to more than 120 countries. In 2012–13,

CRITICAL ISSUES

BOX 8.5 | The Canadian International Development Agency

From its creation in 1968 to its abolition in 2013, the Canadian International Development Agency spent over $100 billion in foreign aid. As Canada's lead provider of ODA, CIDA had long been the subject of controversy. For decades, it has been widely criticized from a variety of perspectives.

Some criticisms are rather unfair, notably some unrealistic expectations placed on CIDA. For instance, when a Canadian Senate committee reviewed the agency's work in sub-Saharan Africa, it referred to "40 years of failure" (Canada, 2007). The authors of the report failed to understand that foreign aid is often not designed to deliver immediate results that can be attributed to the donor country. Increasingly, donors no longer provide aid to small-scale projects that they can identify as theirs, for example, six health clinics that Canadian aid made possible. Instead, they increasingly transfer funds to recipient governments in support for sector-wide programs, such as improving health care across the country. Especially if Canada pools its aid with other donors' assistance, it may be impossible to identify Canada-specific outputs, but that does not make CIDA's assistance any less worthwhile.

Better founded criticisms are directed against CIDA's activities that detract from its mission to "[l]ead Canada's international effort to help people living in poverty" (CIDA, 2009). Commercial, diplomatic, or security motives often influence the choice and amounts of assistance, such as, in recent years, Canada's massive injection of foreign aid to Afghanistan. Between 2001 and 2012, CIDA spent over Cdn$2 billion in Afghanistan, constituting Canada's largest aid program ever. In 2007, that one nation received 11 per cent of Canada's total bilateral assistance (DFATD, 2015: 18, 36). A large part of that assistance was meant to shore up Canadian military operations against the Taliban. Though many believe that ODA can be used to improve security in places like Afghanistan, others argue that foreign aid risks being squandered in an environment that lacks security. For example, aid can finance the building of schools, but the money will be wasted if it is unsafe for students and teachers to travel to and from school every day.

Canada—like most other donor countries—is seeking to make its aid more effective. Among other initiatives, it has been focusing its efforts on 20 to 25 "countries of concentration" and three to five priority themes. Though working in fewer countries and sectors has the potential to improve aid effectiveness, the selection process itself becomes politicized and every new government, if not every new minister, changes the list of countries and themes. The resulting volatility and inability to undertake long-term planning, a hallmark of development, actually make aid less effective (Brown, 2015).

The Canadian government justified CIDA's amalgamation into the newly created Department of Foreign Affairs, Trade and Development in 2013 in large part based on a desire to improve effectiveness. Integration, at least in theory, would allow for greater coherence between aid policies and those in other sectors, such as diplomacy and trade. Moving aid agencies under the authority of foreign ministries is, in fact, an important trend among donor countries. For instance, most Nordic countries have adopted that model. Soon after Canada abolished its stand alone aid agency, Australia followed suit. Though cohabitation in one ministry can promote policy coherence, critics fear that in Canada—as has been the case elsewhere—aid policies will be subservient to diplomatic and commercial self-interest, rather than trade and diplomacy increasing the degree of consideration they accord to the interests of developing countries.

its top five recipients were Mozambique, Tanzania, Afghanistan, Democratic Republic of the Congo, and Kenya. African countries made up seven out of the 10 largest recipients (OECD, 2014).

Most British aid is administered by the Department for International Development (DFID). Unlike its counterparts in most other countries, DFID is a full government department and is headed by a minister who sits at the cabinet table. Like France, the UK focuses its ODA mainly on its former colonies. Its top recipients in 2012–13 were Ethiopia, India, Pakistan, Afghanistan, Nigeria, and Bangladesh (OECD, 2014).

Although one can easily compare budgets and relative generosity, it is difficult to rank the overall performance of bilateral aid agencies. Some donors might be strong in one area, such as support to community development, but weak in another, for instance, being overly bureaucratic. Nonetheless, a few systematic comparisons of the main bilateral donors have been made. For example, the Center for Global Development, a US-based think-tank, annually assesses and ranks 27 donor countries' commitment to development in a number of areas, including the quantity and quality of their foreign aid. The aid component of the index considers each country's relative generosity and adds points for policies such as providing aid to the poorest recipients and allowing tax deductions for private donations. Points are deducted for tying aid, for providing aid to corrupt countries, and for splitting aid into a large number of small projects. Table 8.2 summarizes the results for 2014, with Denmark, Ireland, Sweden, and the United Kingdom ranked highest and Greece, Slovakia, Poland, and South Korea at the bottom of the list. This ranking is provided as just one example of a comparison of donors' aid policies. Other criteria and calculations, of course, could produce quite different results. The UK's Department for International Development is widely considered one of the top development agencies. Box 8.6 explains why.

TABLE 8.2 | Commitment to Development Index, Aid Component, 2014

Rank	Country	Score
1	Denmark	6.7
2	Ireland	6.6
3	Sweden	6.6
4	United Kingdom	5.9
5	Norway	5.9
6	Netherlands	5.7
7	Luxembourg	5.6
8	Finland	5.5
9	Canada	5.4
10	New Zealand	5.2
11	France	5.1
12	Portugal	5.0
13	Japan	5.0
14	Germany	4.9
15	Australia	4.8
16	Switzerland	4.6
17	Austria	4.6
18	Belgium	4.4
19	Spain	4.3
20	United States	4.3
21	Czech Republic	4.2
22	Italy	4.2
23	Hungary	4.2
24	Greece	4.1
25	Slovakia	4.1
26	Poland	4.1
27	South Korea	4.0

Note: Average score is 5.0.

Source: Center for Global Development (2015).

AID RECIPIENTS

The OECD's Development Assistance Committee maintains a list of countries and territories that qualify as recipients of ODA. The main goal is to be able to compile comparable statistics. Donors can still provide assistance to countries not on the list; they cannot, however, count it as ODA. The DAC periodically revises the list. For example, since 1989, following the collapse of the Soviet bloc, it has added a number of poorer European countries, including Albania, as well as a number of new countries, including Belarus, Moldova, Ukraine, and the former Soviet republics in Central Asia. The Palestinian Administered Areas/West Bank and Gaza Strip have been eligible for ODA since 1994

IMPORTANT CONCEPTS

BOX 8.6 | What Makes a Good Development Agency? Lessons from the United Kingdom

Since it was created in 1997, the UK's Department for International Development has gained the reputation of being one of the world's best bilateral development agencies. According to one study (Barder, 2007: 300–13), DFID's success can be attributed to a combination of factors, including:

- DFID has focused its aid policy on achieving outcomes, basing it on concrete evidence rather than ideological preferences.
- DFID has built strong in-house technical expertise but also consults widely with outside experts.
- DFID resists short-term pressures, including promoting British commercial interests, and focuses on long-term strategies centred primarily on poverty reduction in low-income countries.
- DFID is responsible for all British foreign aid, rather than its being split among various government departments.
- DFID has been represented at cabinet by ministers with strong leadership skills and important political profiles.
- DFID has enjoyed key support from the Prime Minister and the Chancellor of the Exchequer (finance minister).

(it was previously counted under ODA to Israel), while Kosovo and newly independent South Sudan were included on the list in 2009 and 2011, respectively.

Countries sometimes are removed from the list when they "graduate" to a higher income level. In the 1990s, these countries included Portugal, Greece, Singapore, Israel, some Caribbean nations, and a few oil-producing countries. Between 2000 and 2014, Bahrain, Oman, and Saudi Arabia, several countries in the Caribbean, and numerous Eastern and Central European countries were deemed no longer eligible for ODA, notably Russia and countries that had recently joined the European Union or were negotiating accession.

Overall, sub-Saharan Africa receives more foreign aid than any other region. In 2012–13, it received 37 per cent of DAC countries' ODA. As can be seen in Table 8.3, the second largest recipient region was South and Central Asia, receiving 23 per cent of total ODA, followed by "Other Asia and Oceania" (16 per cent) and the Middle East and North Africa (12 per cent). At the bottom of the list were Latin America and the Caribbean (9 per cent) and Europe (3 per cent).

Many of the increases in ODA since 2000 have been in the form of debt relief or in aid to Afghanistan and Iraq rather than increased spending in other developing countries. Most of the remaining aid went to Africa, whose proportion of aid has increased quite steadily from a low of about 20 per cent in 1999 to over 40 per cent a decade later.

The top recipients of foreign aid often vary from year to year, depending more on international politics

TABLE 8.3 | Proportion of Total ODA by Region, DAC Members, 2012–13

Region	Share (%)
Sub-Saharan Africa	37.0
South and Central Asia	22.7
Other Asia and Oceania	15.7
Middle East and North Africa	12.4
Latin America and Caribbean	8.9
Europe	3.3

Source: OECD (2014: Table 28).

TABLE 8.4 | Largest ODA Recipients, 2013

Country	Billion US$
Egypt	5.5
Afghanistan	5.3
Vietnam	4.1
Myanmar	3.9
Ethiopia	3.8
Syria	3.6
Tanzania	3.4
Kenya	3.2
Turkey	2.8
Bangladesh	2.6

Source: Data extracted from OECD (2015b).

TABLE 8.5 | Ten Most ODA-Dependent Countries, 2013

Country	ODA/GNI (%)
Tuvalu	48.3
Micronesia, Fed. States	41.7
Marshall Islands	41.4
Malawi	31.5
Liberia	30.5
Solomon Islands	30.0
Afghanistan	25.7
Kiribati	25.5
Burundi	20.1
West Bank and Gaza	19.1

Source: World Bank (2015).

than on anything else. For instance, as indicated in Table 8.4, Egypt was the top recipient in 2013, obtaining $5.5 billion, closely followed by Afghanistan, which received $5.3 billion. Aid to the former is closely related to the complex changes in the country in the wake of the 2010–12 Arab Spring. Afghanistan experienced a surge in foreign aid that followed the US-led invasion in 2001, and this increased aid has gone hand in hand with Western security interests and the presence of foreign troops. Aid to the sixth-largest recipient of ODA, Syria, does not necessarily go to the Syrian government: Vast amounts are spent on humanitarian aid (see Chapter 28). It is interesting to note that the ninth-largest recipient, Turkey, which obtained $2.8 billion in aid in 2013, is also an important non-DAC donor, providing $3.3 billion in ODA in the same year. This example illustrates how the categories of donors and receivers are becoming less distinct; a growing number of countries are both.

Because of great variations in the size of their economies, the top recipients of aid are not necessarily the most dependent on aid. The 10 most aid-dependent countries in 2013 can be found in Table 8.5. At the top of the list are three island nations in the Pacific Ocean. With the exception of Afghanistan, the top 10 are small countries, mainly in sub-Saharan Africa or the Pacific region. In these countries, donors potentially have tremendous leverage to influence domestic policy. Such aid dependence, however, is relatively rare.

Different countries receive aid from different donors and for widely varying purposes. In other words, the structure and purposes of ODA can vary tremendously. Bangladesh, for instance, has for many decades been a top recipient of foreign aid. Its chief bilateral donors in 2011–12 were the United Kingdom (the former colonial ruler) and Japan (a fellow Asian country), followed distantly by the United States and Australia (OECD, 2015c). A densely and highly populated country, Bangladesh is characterized by widespread poverty and is particularly prone to natural disasters that include cyclones and flooding. It is also known as the home of the Grameen Bank, one of the world's most successful and innovative micro-finance initiatives.

During the 1970s and 1980s, the Soviet Union and many social democratic Western European donors provided a high level of assistance to Mozambique. The former was motivated mainly by geostrategic interests related to a Cold War struggle for dominance in the developing world, the latter by solidarity with a socialist country in Africa on the front line of the fight against apartheid in South Africa. The Mozambican civil war, however, prevented this aid from translating into economic development. Since the end of the civil war in 1992 and the country's renouncement of socialism, a wide range of donors have disbursed huge amounts of aid to Mozambique, and the country has achieved a consistently high rate of growth, admittedly from a

IMPORTANT CONCEPTS

BOX 8.7 | Results-Based Management

Donors currently favour an approach known as results-based management (RBM). Although its goal of improving aid effectiveness is widely lauded, its requirement for measurable and verifiable results introduces distortions and biases in development assistance that, some believe, could outweigh its benefits. Not all goals can be easily or accurately quantified—for example, the rule of law, good governance, or independence of the judiciary. Setting indicators means that efforts will be deployed to improve those possibly arbitrarily chosen figures rather than meeting less tangible or undefined development objectives that could be of equal or greater utility, especially in the long term. See Chapter 27 for more on RBM.

low starting point. In 2011–12, the country's top bilateral aid donor was by far the United States (formerly its ideological opponent), followed by the UK, Portugal (its former colonizer), Canada, Sweden, and Denmark, many of which were continuing historical ties (OECD, 2015c).

Haiti, the poorest country in the western hemisphere, has long been plagued with social and political instability, notably since the Duvalier dictatorship was overthrown in the mid-1980s. Since then, the country has experienced a succession of democratic elections, military coups, and instances of violent unrest. It was widely hoped that the 2006 elections would mark the beginning of a new era of reconstruction and development. However, in 2010, a devastating earthquake killed hundreds of thousands of people and destroyed much of the infrastructure, seriously setting back Haiti's development process. In 2011–12, the top donors by far were the United States and Canada, both of which are in the same "neighbourhood" as Haiti and have large Haitian populations, followed by France, the former colonial ruler, and Spain (OECD, 2015c).

CURRENT TRENDS AND CONTROVERSIES

Some current trends in foreign aid are relatively uncontroversial. For instance, almost all donors are taking measures to greatly reduce or eliminate tied aid. Likewise, bilateral donors, for the most part, have phased out loans, preferring to provide grants. In 2012–13, only 5.1 per cent of DAC countries' ODA commitments were in the form of loans, while 100 per cent of the aid from many countries, such as Canada, the Netherlands, the United Kingdom, and the United States, was in the form of grants (OECD, 2014: Table 20). Multilateral institutions, however, continue to provide a high proportion of loans, which have led to an extremely high rate of indebtedness in many countries (see Chapter 14).

A long-standing debate in foreign aid is whether the focus of assistance should be primarily on fighting poverty or on promoting economic growth. For a long time, especially in the 1950s and 1960s, the argument was made that economic growth would eventually "trickle down" to help the poor—that "a rising tide lifts all boats." Faced with a lack of evidence to support that assumption, the pendulum swung the other way in the 1970s, and donors put a higher priority on meeting the more immediate basic needs of the poor. By the late 1980s, donors had turned to macroeconomic reform as a prerequisite for growth, encouraging—some would say forcing—recipient countries to implement programs that actually weakened the social safety net for the poor. A decade later, it became increasingly harder to argue credibly that poverty was being reduced at an adequate rate.

A new consensus emerged on the centrality of more immediate action to alleviate poverty, culminating in the United Nations Millennium Declaration in 2000.

The accompanying Millennium Development Goals set eight targets to be met by 2015, requiring urgent action to improve the lives of billions of people in all regions of the developing world (see Chapter 24). Although the MDGs signalled that the pendulum had swung back to placing priority on fighting poverty in the short run, many other donor policies and activities still favour an emphasis on longer-term economic growth. For instance, debt relief and assistance from international financial institutions and many bilateral agencies, notably the US's Millennium Challenge Corporation, depend on the presence of a broadly defined "enabling environment" deemed amenable to economic growth. These conditions are often in addition to, rather than instead of, the components of 1980s-style structural adjustment programs (see Chapter 9). Donors are thus supporting policies that place a greater priority on poverty reduction while simultaneously implementing others that tend to reduce government spending on the poor.

A related issue involves which countries aid should be focused on. As mentioned above, many donors are making sub-Saharan Africa a priority because of its higher rate of poverty. But even within a given region, which countries are more "deserving" of aid? Should resources go to the poorest countries, since they need it the most? Or should donors focus on well-governed countries, where they believe it will be used more effectively? Those who are pessimistic about aid's impact tend to favour the latter choice, which usually implies concentrating on middle-income countries, arguing that aid in poorly governed countries is all too often wasted. Critics respond that well-governed, wealthier countries are more able to attract investment or borrow money on financial markets and therefore do not need ODA as much. Low-income countries require aid, they argue, precisely so that they can improve governance and reach a stage at which they no longer need aid. Cutting them off, critics warn, would lead to "aid orphans" and great suffering, possibly even political or economic collapse, which could in turn threaten regional and international stability (and perhaps require costlier interventions later). Thus, those who believe that aid contributes to social or human development—a goal in and of itself, even if it does not quickly translate into economic growth—favour a greater emphasis on the poorest countries.

Similarly, there is no consensus on what specific recipient-country entity should be given ODA funds. Most disbursements are made directly to governments, but many worry that this only feeds bloated bureaucracies and leads to graft, especially in non-democracies. Left-leaning proponents of foreign aid are more likely to advocate providing funds to northern or southern NGOs, which they consider more likely to involve communities and meet people's actual needs. Critics respond that using voluntary organizations to deliver services actually undermines the state and deprives it

CRITICAL ISSUES

BOX 8.8 | How Effective Is Foreign Aid?

The contribution of ODA to development success stories is hotly debated. In instances where rapid economic growth and poverty reduction have occurred, notably in East Asia, there is no consensus on what role, if any, foreign aid played. In fact, some scholars of foreign aid have long argued that aid cannot help bring about development. Some claim that it distorts economies and is actually detrimental to long-term economic growth. Books by former World Bank staff members William Easterly, *The White Man's Burden: Why the West's Efforts to Aid the Rest Have Done So Much Ill and So Little Good* (2006), and Dambisa Moyo, *Dead Aid: Why Aid Is Not Working and How There Is Another Way for Africa* (2009), epitomize the belief, shared by many, that most aid is at best wasted and at worst counterproductive. By way of contrast, celebrity economist Jeffrey Sachs's optimistic book *The End of Poverty: Economic Possibilities for Our Time* (2005) argues that aid can be extremely effective and that, in particular, a "big push" of well-designed development assistance would help billions of people escape the "poverty trap."

of resources necessary to ensure national standards and coverage. From a more right-leaning perspective, it is better for funds to be channelled through and to promote the growth of the private sector, which is considered the key to long-term development—a perspective that gained prominence in most donor countries in the 2010s. This approach, however, is criticized as inadequate, because a business's primary motive is to make a profit, not to meet people's needs.

In the 2000s, donors recognized the importance of co-ordinating their aid, channelling funds through joint programs and working more closely with recipient governments. The Paris Declaration on Aid Effectiveness (2005) and subsequent Accra Agenda for Action (2008) epitomize this trend, attributing to recipient countries the lead role in the design and implementation of their national development strategy, to be supported by donors in an integrated and transparent manner. Advantages include the elimination of duplication—or even contradictory programs—and of the onerous requirement of reporting separately to donors.

Uniting around one single development strategy, however, also carries some risks. It could be described as "putting all the aid eggs in one basket," when past experience has shown that development plans do not always produce the desired results. Moreover, it places a tremendous amount of power in the planning and administrative capabilities of the recipient government, ignoring problems of lack of capacity or corruption. It also assumes that the government has consulted its population, represents it, or has its best interest at heart, which is not necessarily the case. Paradoxically, when donors act together, they are in a position of great power over the recipient country, which can hardly reject their opinions or pick and choose the advice it wishes to follow. After the aid funds have been transferred to the recipient government, however, donors generally lose control over how it is spent. Still, provisions for transparency may compensate for that, allowing donors to suspend further contributions if the funds are not used according to agreement or do not produce the expected results.

The prospect of aid harmonization weakened in the 2010s, with the rise of "non-traditional" or "emerging" donors, such as Brazil, China, India, and South Africa, among others. As their domestic economies gather strength, they increasingly seek a greater place in global political, economic, and commercial affairs. They have positioned themselves apart from the "traditional" DAC donors and, in fact, prefer to be called providers of development co-operation, rather than aid donors. The main label used to describe their development activities is "South–South Co-operation," which is much more encompassing than ODA. It includes not only aid-like assistance but often trade- and investment-related activities as well. These countries signed onto the Paris Declaration as recipients but do not want to be guided by its provisions when they act as aid providers. They usually prefer to frame their co-operation as "mutual benefit," rather than as altruism, and have retained many practices that generally are considered less effective in other contexts, such as tied aid (explained above) or sometimes, especially in the case of China, turnkey projects (for instance, building infrastructure with their own labour and handing it over once it is completed, without any local capacity-building). (See Chapter 13.)

S. Kalscheur/USAID

PHOTO 8.2 | USAID project on irrigation of urban agriculture, Ethiopia.

CRITICAL ISSUES

BOX 8.9 | Chinese Development Co-operation

Unlike most aid providers, China does not have a bilateral aid agency or a lead unit in its foreign ministry. The Ministry of Commerce manages foreign aid grants and zero-interest loans, while loans that charge interest at concessional rates fall under the responsibility of the state-run Export-Import Bank. In her comparison of Chinese and DAC aid, Deborah Bräutigam (2011) explains how Chinese development assistance places greater emphasis on building infrastructure and economic growth than do Western donors, who often prioritize social spending, such as primary education and poverty reduction. However, only a small fraction of China's financial support to developing countries meets the definition of ODA. Instead, the majority of funds consist of Chinese export and investment promotion and non-concessional loans. Bräutigam examined two prominent cases of Chinese development co-operation—a $10 billion loan to the Angolan government between 2003 and 2010 for reconstruction after the country's civil war and a $2 billion line of credit with the Nigerian government in 2006–9 to rebuild its railways—and found that neither should be counted as ODA, despite being described frequently as foreign aid. This does not mean that these forms of financing cannot promote development, but such spending should not be included in tallies of ODA—and used in comparisons with other countries' aid levels.

Some Western observers express great concern about the size of Chinese aid in particular and the way in which it serves as an alternative to Western ODA, which usually comes with conditions. Conditionality-free Chinese aid thus can help developing countries escape some of those pressures, such as for good governance. Usually, such fears are overstated. It is true that China supports some unsavoury dictatorships, but so do Western countries—just not necessarily the same ones. Also, there is a convergence of interests: commercial enterprises from all donor countries, whether "traditional" or "emerging," have a long-term interest in stability and the rule of law in the recipient country. Moreover, there is a tendency to report any form of co-operation from southern donors as aid, which generates misleading comparisons. Because southern donors usually mix in what would be considered ODA in the OECD context with commercial and investment activities and they do not make publicly available all the data, it is very difficult to compare their aid or development co-operation figures with those of DAC countries. As can be seen in Table 8.1 and Figure 8.2 above, estimated Chinese foreign aid was actually smaller than Italy's and Switzerland's in 2013, suggesting that its influence is usually exaggerated.

SUMMARY

This chapter has provided an overview of the main actors, modalities, and resource flows involved in the bilateral aid that countries in the North provide to recipients in the South. The chapter showed, for instance, how the size of a donor's aid program can differ greatly from its relative generosity. The United States, though by far the largest donor by volume, provides a much smaller proportion of its national income in foreign aid than do donors such as Norway and Sweden, which have considerably smaller economies.

Key terms were explained, including the different forms of aid, such as tied aid, as well as various types of aid donors. Aid can be provided by governments, international organizations, non-governmental organizations, private foundations, and individuals. To count as foreign aid, or "official development assistance," it must have as its main goal the promotion of well-being in developing countries. The chapter also explored the different reasons donors provide assistance: sometimes out of humanitarian concern, but often relating to their self-interests, including commercial, diplomatic, or security interests.

The chapter subsequently examined global trends in the provision of bilateral aid, including a comparison of important donors that illustrated how their motives, geographical focus, and priorities can vary. Some focus on their own security interests, while others concentrate their aid in former colonies, their "neighbourhood," or the world's poorest countries, mainly in sub-Saharan Africa. The chapter also considered which regions (above all, sub-Saharan Africa) and countries receive the most aid (Egypt and Afghanistan in 2013), as well as which ones are most dependent on it (mostly very small countries, often islands in the Pacific Ocean). Current trends and controversies in foreign aid were discussed. For instance: Should aid seek to create economic growth or should it target more directly poverty reduction? What kinds of countries should receive the most aid? Finally, the chapter summarized bilateral donors' most recent consensus on how to make aid more effective and highlighted some issues related to the rise in importance of non-traditional donors, suggesting that the latter might not have the negative influence that some fear. In sum, this chapter has introduced the reader to the main characteristics and debates regarding bilateral aid and the national agencies that contribute vast sums—almost $100 billion a year—to international development.

QUESTIONS FOR CRITICAL THOUGHT

1. Why should wealthier countries give aid to poorer ones? How much should they give and for what purposes?
2. What kinds of conditions, if any, should donor countries attach to their aid?
3. How should donors decide on which countries to concentrate their assistance?
4. Should donors provide their assistance directly to the recipient country's government, to northern or southern civil society organizations, or to the private sector in the donor or recipient country?
5. What are the responsibilities of recipient countries, if any, in using foreign aid?

SUGGESTED READING

Collier, Paul. 2007. *The Bottom Billion: Why the Poorest Countries Are Failing and What Can Be Done about It.* Oxford and New York: Oxford University Press.

Lancaster, Carol. 2007. *Foreign Aid: Diplomacy, Development, Domestic Politics.* Chicago: University of Chicago Press.

Mawdsley, Emma. 2012. *From Recipients to Donors: The Emerging Powers and the Changing Development Landscape.* London: Zed Books.

Riddell, Roger. 2007. *Does Foreign Aid Really Work?* New York: Oxford University Press.

Sumner, Andy, and Richard Mallett. 2012. *The Future of Foreign Aid: Development Cooperation and the New Geography of Global Poverty.* Basingstoke, UK: Palgrave Macmillan.

BIBLIOGRAPHY

Agence Française de Développement. 2015. "Who are we?" www.afd.fr/lang/en/home/AFD/presentation-afd. Accessed 21 June 2015.

Barder, O. 2007. "Reforming development assistance: Lessons from the UK experience." In Lael Brainard, ed., *Security by Other Means: Foreign Assistance, Global Poverty, and American Leadership.* Washington: Brookings Institution Press, 277–320.

Bräutigam, D. 2011. "Aid 'with Chinese characteristics': Chinese foreign aid and development finance meet the OECD-DAC aid regime." *Journal of International Development* 23, 5: 752–64.

Brown, S. 2015. "Aid effectiveness and the framing of new Canadian aid initiatives." In D. Bratt and C.J. Kukucha, eds, *Readings in Canadian Foreign Policy: Classic Debates and New Ideas*, 3rd edn. Don Mills, ON: Oxford University Press, 467–81.

Canada. 2007. *Overcoming 40 Years of Failure: A New Road Map for Sub-Saharan Africa*. Ottawa: Senate of Canada, Standing Senate Committee on Foreign Affairs and International Trade.

Center for Global Development. 2015. *The Commitment to Development Index*. www.cgdev.org/initiative/commitment-development-index/index. Accessed 20 June 2015.

DFATD. 2015. *Synthesis Report—Summative Evaluation of Canada's Afghanistan Development Program. Fiscal Year 2004–2005 to 2012–2013*. Gatineau, QC: Foreign Affairs, Trade and Development Canada.

Jepma, C. J. 1991. *The Tying of Aid*. Paris: OECD.

Organisation for Economic Co-operation and Development (OECD). 2003. "Official Development Assistance (ODA)." In *Glossary of Statistical Terms*. http://stats.oecd.org/glossary/detail.asp?ID=6043. Accessed 21 June 2015.

———. 2014. "Statistics on resource flows to developing countries." www.oecd.org/dac/stats/statisticsonresourceflowstodevelopingcountries.htm. Accessed 21 June 2015.

———. 2015a. *Paris Declaration and Accra Agenda for Action*. www.oecd.org/dac/effectiveness/parisdeclarationandaccraagendaforaction.htm. Accessed 21 June 2015.

———. 2015b. *Query Wizard for International Development Statistics*. http://stats.oecd.org/qwids/. Accessed 20 June 2015.

———. 2015c. "Recipient aid charts." www.oecd.org/dac/stats/recipientcharts.htm. Accessed 21 June 2015.

Sachs, J. 2005. *The End of Poverty: Economic Possibilities for Our Time*. New York: Penguin.

United States Agency for International Development (USAID). 2015. "Who we are." www.usaid.gov/who-we-are. Accessed 21 June 2015.

World Bank. 2015. "6.11 World Development Indicators: Aid dependency." http://wdi.worldbank.org/table/6.11. Accessed 20 June 2015

9 The International Financial Institutions

Marcus Taylor

LEARNING OBJECTIVES

- To understand why the IMF and the World Bank were created and how their operations changed over the subsequent decades.
- To comprehend their role in the process of structural adjustment and the ongoing controversy it created.
- To learn how the IMF has reacted to the current economic crisis, including the debates over granting developing countries more power within the institution.

▲ **People are seen in front of a banner during the 2016 International Monetary Fund, World Bank Spring Meetings at IMF headquarters.** | Source: MANDEL NGAN/AFP/Staff

INTRODUCTION

Few actors in international development have fuelled controversy to the same degree as the International Monetary Fund (IMF) and the World Bank. Notwithstanding their official objectives of ensuring global economic stability and promoting poverty reduction, these international financial institutions have attracted criticism from a wide range of social movements and political groups. Opponents from the left of the political spectrum have claimed that their policies serve to entrench global poverty and exacerbate inequalities. As a consequence, the annual meetings of the institutions are routinely confronted with protests. Conversely, conservative voices have often claimed that the expanding role of multinational corporations and global financial markets has undercut the purpose of both institutions. Editorials in the *Wall Street Journal*, for example, have argued that the institutions are increasingly irrelevant in today's globalized world and should be downsized or disbanded (*Wall Street Journal*, 2013).

To help to understand these debates, this chapter examines how and why the IMF and World Bank were established and how their roles have evolved. We begin with their creation at the Bretton Woods Conference of 1944 and examine how they assumed a growing influence on developing countries in the subsequent decades. By the 1980s, the IMF and World Bank began to use their considerable financial power to promote a controversial set of policies known as "structural adjustment." While the IMF and World Bank argued that structural adjustment was necessary to promote strong and stable economic growth, critics countered that these reforms exacerbated poverty and inequality. In examining this debate, we look at the ways in which the international financial institutions (IFIs) have reformed their practices in response to such criticism. Notably, current policies promoted by the World Bank focus not just on economic reforms but on a wider set of changes that incorporate such diverse features as "good governance" and "empowering the poor." We outline each of these in turn and ask whether they mark a change in direction from structural adjustment or are merely an appendage to the latter. Finally, we turn to the controversy surrounding the IMF over its interventions in the East Asian financial crisis in the late 1990s before reflecting on the impact of the current global economic crisis on the IMF and its governance structures, with special reference to the rise of China as a global power.

THE ORIGINS OF THE IMF AND WORLD BANK

The IMF and World Bank were created as part of the Bretton Woods Conference held in New Hampshire in July 1944. With World War II drawing to a close, the United States met with 44 allied countries to establish a new international economic system that would set formal rules to co-ordinate economic relations between countries. This goal stemmed from events in the 1930s, when unrestrained economic conflicts between European powers contributed to the outbreak of war. Owing to its overwhelming economic and military power, the US was able to ensure that its blueprint proposal set the basis for conference discussions despite the lack of a clear consensus. American delegates were explicit about the type of international order they envisioned. Given the superiority of the American industrial base, the US sought a system in which international trade could proceed relatively unhindered. This goal, the US delegates claimed, would not only help America to meet its goal of economic expansion but would also fuel global prosperity and mutual development. Ultimately, the US delegation successfully translated its vision of a global economic order into the final agreement that constituted what became known as the **Bretton Woods system**.

Monetary instability was blamed for the disintegration of international trade in the preceding era, therefore, the Bretton Woods system was founded on the establishment of fixed exchange rates between national currencies. Each country would peg its currency at an agreed amount of US dollars, which in turn had a fixed worth in gold. Only small variations to these exchange rates were permitted. The idea was that fixed currencies would provide stable monetary conditions necessary for an expansion of world trade.

Once the articles of agreement were ratified by member countries at the end of 1945, the International Monetary Fund was set up to oversee the workings of the system. Each member country paid into the IMF a quota of its own currency, as well as some gold or dollar holdings based on the size of its economy. When facing economic problems, countries would be permitted to draw temporarily on the reserves of the IMF to pay off international debts. Usage of these funds was intended to provide a country with sufficient time to stabilize its economy without resorting to measures such as currency devaluation that could destabilize the system. Notably, at this point, the IMF functioned as an important yet modest instrument to maintain international currency stability. This initial role gave no hint of the Fund's later emergence as a powerful agent within international development.

Along with the establishment of the IMF came the creation of the International Bank for Reconstruction and Development (IBRD), which later became known as the World Bank. The original role of the IBRD was to make loans at preferential rates of interest to European countries devastated by war. This function greatly diminished when the US's own Marshall Plan began to provide credit directly to European nations in 1947. Fortunately for the fledgling IBRD, a new and growing set of clients emerged through the ongoing process of decolonization. US President Harry Truman is widely considered to have formalized the project of international development in 1949 when he suggested that the collapse of European empires was creating an "underdeveloped world" that was in desperate need of a "program of development." By serving as a bank to provide development finance directly to these new countries, the IBRD found a key role in this project.

International Monetary Fund/Wikipedia

PHOTO 9.1 | John Maynard Keynes (right) and Harry Dexter White at the Bretton Woods Conference, 1944.

The new and soon-to-be post-colonial countries were commonly considered to be on a natural progression through a sequence of structural transformations leading from traditional agrarian societies to modern industrial ones (see Chapter 3). Development economists,

IMPORTANT CONCEPTS

BOX 9.1 | The US Aims for Bretton Woods

The purpose of the conference is . . . wholly within the American tradition, and completely outside political consideration. The United States wants, after this war, full utilization of its industries, its factories and its farms; full and steady employment for its citizens, particularly its ex-servicemen; and full prosperity and peace. It can have them only in a world with a vigorous trade. But it can have such trade only if currencies are stable, if money keeps its value, and if people can buy and sell with the certainty that the money they receive on the due date will have the value contracted for.

Source: US Department of State press release, cited in Peet (2003: 47).

IMPORTANT CONCEPTS

BOX 9.2 | IMF: Initial Function

Originally, the purpose of the IMF was quite limited: to provide financial resources to allow countries to solve balance-of-payments crises without devaluing their currencies. This would help to maintain the system of stable exchange rates established at Bretton Woods that facilitated stable international trade.

however, suggested that the rate of this development was limited by the stock of capital a country could draw upon for productive investment. In the post-colonial period, capital was scarce for most developing-world countries and many private international banks would not lend to these countries because they were viewed as a considerable risk. In this context the IBRD offered a solution by acting as an intermediary between private international banks and governments. Backed by the financial and political support of the leading Western countries, the IBRD was able to get loans from private international banks at low interest rates. In turn, the IBRD could then lend this money to governments in the developing world to finance development projects with only a small markup on the interest rate.

Initially, the Bank tended to fund very specific types of projects. In the first two decades of its existence, more than 60 per cent of its loans funded projects to build physical infrastructure such as highways, airports, electricity grids, and hydroelectric dams. To receive such funding, applications from developing countries needed to meet the criteria established by the Bank to ensure that the project was technically sound and would generate sufficient revenue to repay the loan. These criteria tended to exclude many of the poorer nations because they could not guarantee a significant rate of return.

To address this issue, the International Development Association (IDA) was formed in 1960 as a new organization within the World Bank. Like the IBRD, IDA loans funded large-scale infrastructure projects. However, these loans were provided at a virtually interest-free status over long periods of repayment. This allowed the IDA to fund a range of projects that did not qualify under the conditions. A clear separation of purpose was therefore created between the IBRD, which provided subsidized credit to middle-income countries, and the IDA, which provided zero-interest loans to poorer developing countries.

GOVERNANCE STRUCTURES

Before tracing the evolution of the IMF and the World Bank, it is useful to examine their governance structures and the exercise of power within them. Unlike the

IMPORTANT CONCEPTS

BOX 9.3 | World Bank: Initial Function

The original intent of the World Bank was to provide financing for post-war reconstruction and development projects. From 1950 on, however, the Bank focused on providing loans to developing-world countries at lower rates of interest than those of private international banks. These loans were directed mainly towards building infrastructure for development.

United Nations General Assembly, where each country has one vote, voting rights in the IMF and World Bank are weighted according to quota subscriptions that reflect the size of a country's economy. This ensures that advanced industrial countries have consistently held the majority of the voting power. At present, they hold approximately 57 per cent of voting rights, whereas the poorest 165 countries together have only 29 per cent. The US currently holds close to 17 per cent alone, providing it with a unilateral veto over constitutional amendments.

Voting power translates into direct representation at board meetings. While the IMF and World Bank are run on a day-to-day basis by an internal management structure, each has a Board of Executive Directors that oversees these actions, including approving loans and guarantees, setting the administrative budget, vetting country assistance strategies, and making borrowing and financial decisions. There are 24 seats on the Board, and the representatives are chosen through vote shares. As a consequence, the 46 sub-Saharan African countries together have only two representatives on each of the executive boards, while the five richest countries each have one, as do China, Saudi Arabia, and Russia. By convention, the US and the European Union also enjoy a unilateral power to choose presidents: the US appoints the president of the World Bank, and Europe designates the president of the IMF. This caused controversy in 2005 when the US government of George W. Bush insisted on placing Paul Wolfowitz at the head of the World Bank despite significant opposition from the developing world, European countries, and within the Bank itself.

Clearly, these power relations affect the conduct of IFIs. Although authors differ on the degree of power they ascribe to the US, there are numerous historical examples of American influence over decision-making. For example, in the Cold War period of the 1960s and 1970s, US governments used their influence to ensure that a disproportionate amount of financing was channelled to strategic US allies and, following the Cuban revolution of 1959, to governments seen as bulkheads against Communist revolutions (Caufield, 1996).

More recently, the record of US influence has been one of mixed success. For example, the US was successful in pressuring the World Bank's president to have controversial chief economist Joseph Stiglitz removed from his position at the Bank in 1999. However, it subsequently failed to significantly change the content of the Bank's *World Development Report 2000/2001* despite its opposition to the anti-poverty strategy it advanced (Wade, 2001). In a more constructive way, the

IMPORTANT CONCEPTS

BOX 9.4 | IMF Quotas and World Bank Subscriptions

On joining the IMF, each country must pay a subscription quota based loosely on the size of its economy and measured in SDRs (Special Drawing Rights), the IMF's unit of account. A member's quota determines both its financial commitment to the IMF and its voting power within the institution. These quotas also determine how much a country can borrow from the IMF in times of crisis. Technically, a country can borrow 100 per cent of its quota annually, to a limit of 300 per cent cumulatively. In special circumstances, however, these limits can be waived. Quota sizes are reviewed every five years, and the current levels can be viewed on the IMF's website (www.imf.org).

World Bank "subscriptions" also define voting rights. Upon joining the IBRD, member governments must "subscribe" to a portion of the Bank's capital stock by pledging to purchase a specified number of shares according to their financial capacity. Members are required to purchase only a small portion of their subscription ("paid-in capital"), while the remaining portion ("callable capital") remains outstanding. Given that the IBRD raises the vast majority of its capital through bond issues, it has never had to request "callable capital" from its members.

US Congress, under pressure from non-governmental organizations such as the Sierra Club, lobbied the US Treasury in 1989 to instruct the US director to vote against all Bank projects that did not have an environmental impact assessment available 120 days before the Board of Governors' vote. Two years later, this practice became incorporated into standard Bank policy. The relationship between the US and the IFIs is therefore quite complex and there is often considerable tension generated as the latter seek to juggle appeasing American interests with maintaining their multilateral credentials.

THE TURBULENT 1970s

During the first two decades of their existence, the activities of the IMF and World Bank were relatively modest and did not provoke the controversy that currently surrounds them. The decade of the 1970s, however, was a period of instability and crisis in the global economy that prompted transformation in both **Bretton Woods institutions**. Most notably, the 1971 decision of the United States to withdraw its support for the Bretton Woods system, when it ceased to back US dollars with gold reserves, undermined the official role of the IMF to maintain currency stability. In adapting to the new circumstances, the IMF did two things. First, it shed the aims of the collapsing Bretton Woods system to recast itself as an international lender of last resort. Countries that needed short-term injections of money to pay international debts could turn to the IMF without needing to maintain the value of their exchange rate. Indeed, the IMF now frequently recommended that countries devalue their currencies to strengthen their exporting sectors, which was the opposite of its original purpose.

Simultaneously, the IMF also began to expand the number of conditions attached to its loans and increase its surveillance of the policies pursued by borrowing countries. This trend would become increasingly important in the years that followed. By accepting financing from the IMF, countries were now forced to accept an IMF-sanctioned reform program. As we shall see below, in the 1970s and beyond, increasing numbers of developing-world countries found it necessary to borrow money from the IMF and this entrenched the power of the institution within the developing world. Through what were known as "stand-by arrangements," the standard IMF package involved austerity measures aimed at reducing government spending and lowering consumption within the economy so as to decrease imports and increase funds available for repaying international debts. In many countries, the financial solvency of the state was restored through cutting subsidies on basic consumption goods and reducing expenditures on social services (Körner, 1986). These programs, however, were widely criticized for their adverse effects on the poorer segments of society.

For the World Bank, the 1970s were also a period of notable transformation. Under the presidency of Robert McNamara (1968–81) the institution dramatically expanded its operations. McNamara viewed the Bank as an underutilized instrument in a fight against global poverty and Communism. On assuming office in 1968, McNamara challenged his staff to find ways to increase lending, including making loans to countries hitherto untouched by the World Bank. Lending activity swelled from $2 billion in 1970 to over $11 billion in 1980. At the same time, the Bank's lending profile shifted away from large-scale infrastructure projects to target a wider range of development objectives (see Box 9.5). McNamara emphasized the need for the Bank to fund direct anti-poverty efforts through social programs and projects aimed at modernizing the agricultural sector. Simultaneously, by focusing on health and education programs, McNamara's approach became known as the "basic needs" approach (see Chapter 24). Lending for infrastructure fell to about 30 per cent of total Bank funding, whereas loans for anti-poverty projects (including an emphasis on helping small-scale farmers increase productivity) rose to almost 30 per cent.

Two important changes stem from McNamara's tenure as head of the World Bank. First, like the IMF, the Bank became considerably more active and powerful on a global level. No longer was it content to lend cautiously to a limited number of developing-world countries. Rather, it was prepared to actively propagate projects in the developing world as part of a broader mission to spread its vision of development. Second, in emphasizing the need to focus on social objectives, the Bank opened up a debate about its own purpose and that of development finance in general. While McNamara's approach was well received by some members of the

IMPORTANT CONCEPTS

BOX 9.5 | Robert McNamara's Call for a "Basic Needs" Approach

Nations need to give greater priority to establishing growth targets in terms of essential human needs: in terms of nutrition, housing, health, literacy and employment—even if it be at the cost of some reduction in the pace of advance in certain narrow and highly privileged sectors whose benefits accrue to the few.

Source: Speech of the World Bank President to the annual meeting, Washington, Fall 1972.

international development community, there was a powerful conservative reaction that suggested the Bank should focus simply on promoting economic growth.

THE DEBT CRISIS, STRUCTURAL ADJUSTMENT, AND CONDITIONALITY

As the decade of the 1970s drew to a close, many developing-world countries were faced with the dual burden of high oil prices and falling prices for their key exports. To overcome budget deficits, they began to borrow heavily from private international banks that were keen to make lucrative high-interest loans to the developing world. In the glut of borrowing, countries across the developing world became heavily indebted to European and North American banks. In Latin America, for example, the total external debt (private and public) leapt from $100,000 million in 1976 to $336,230 million in 1983 (see Chapter 14). When, in 1982, the US made a unilateral decision to raise interest rates, numerous countries across Latin America and Africa faced daunting levels of debt. Mexico was the first to threaten default when it announced on 12 August 1982 that it could not meet payments on an outstanding $80 billion of loans. By October 1983, some 30 countries owing a total of $239 billion had or were attempting to reschedule debt payments. Given the magnitude of the loans facing default, a number of major US and international banks feared collapse and this raised the spectre of a financial crash engulfing the entire Western financial system.

In response, the IMF and World Bank began to pipeline billions of dollars to debt-stricken countries as a means for them to continue making payments on their old debt. In becoming the funnel for emergency loans to the South, the IMF and World Bank proposed dramatic reforms for developing countries to implement. The basic premise of their operations was that the policies pursued by most developing countries over the preceding decades were profoundly misguided. For the IMF and World Bank, these policies promoting state-led industrialization had created inefficient economies, drained national resources, and encouraged overinflated bureaucracies that distorted markets while breeding corruption.

To overcome the debt crisis, they argued, it was not enough merely to stabilize the economies of the developing world through standard austerity programs. Rather, a more profound process of transformation was necessary alongside austerity: one that would open countries to foreign trade and reorient them towards export production. To achieve these objectives, borrowing governments were mandated to rapidly cut back trade restrictions, end support to domestic industries, and remove subsidies to key consumer goods. The idea behind such liberalization was that market forces could then play a greater role in distributing resources across the economy, leading to improved efficiency and wealth creation. At the same time, foreign investment would flow into export-oriented sectors of the economy that would create new economic dynamism and earn the country valuable foreign earnings. This project became known as "structural adjustment" and the first explicit structural adjustment loan of US$200 million was granted to Turkey in March 1980, with many others following during the debt crisis.

Both the IMF and World Bank knew that structural adjustment would cause severe economic and social dislocation in the short to medium term. The theory held that this short-term pain was necessary for long-term gain. To ensure that countries undertook these difficult measures, World Bank and IMF loans came with binding conditions and the release of further portions of credit was made dependent on the successful implementation of prior requirements as decided by the IMF and the Bank. With both institutions seeking to impose mutually reinforcing cross-conditionality restrictions on lending, the two became embroiled in a far closer association than at any previous time. This rapprochement gave rise to the notion of the **Washington Consensus** as both IFIs wielded their considerable influence in order to propagate a common, US-supported development doctrine on a global scale.

The immediate phase of adjustment, usually managed by the IMF, consisted of severe austerity measures to restore macroeconomic balances. Through a "shock therapy" program of rapid liberalization of prices, currency devaluation, and fiscal cutbacks, a deflationary period could be engineered within which the government would balance its budget and inefficient industries would collapse. In the medium term, structural adjustment involved the rapid liberalization of trade, deregulation of markets, the privatization of state-owned industries, and the introduction of the private sector into social service provision such as health care. This was intended to allow market forces to play a greater role in distributing resources across different sectors of the economy and to encourage new and dynamic export-oriented industries to form.

While the emphasis of structural adjustment was on fostering long-term economic growth, these reforms were also intended to ensure rapid debt repayment and thereby re-establish the integrity of the international credit system. Unsurprisingly, the IMF and World Bank were widely perceived by post-colonial states and their populations as assuming the role of debt collectors for private banks. At no point did the institutions question the morality of the burden of debt crisis being placed on the post-colonial world rather than being shared with the international banks that had lent money irresponsibly (see Chapter 14). As an answer to the debt crisis, therefore, structural adjustment appealed greatly to the Western shareholders of the IMF and World Bank. New loans consolidated the financial systems of the North while structural adjustment opened avenues for investment in the South and refocused the industries in the South towards primary and secondary exports that lowered commodity costs in the West. The question remained, however, whether structural adjustment would also provide a route towards long-term economic stability and growth within the developing world as its proponents claimed.

BEYOND STRUCTURAL ADJUSTMENT?

In the 1990s, the IMF and World Bank came under growing pressure because structural adjustment was widely critiqued as being unable to deliver on its primary promises of stable growth and poverty reduction. The severe austerity programs put in place following the debt crisis often achieved their goals of reducing inflation, lowering government deficits, and ameliorating balance-of-payments problems. However, the broader reforms of liberalization, privatization, and deregulation did not appear to be producing a period of rapid and sustained economic growth. On the contrary, many countries in Latin America and Africa faced enduring stagnation, while the social costs of adjustment were often placed on the poorest segments of society (SAPRIN, 2004). Although the IMF and World Bank challenged negative interpretations of structural adjustment—often placing blame on countries' unwillingness to follow their prescriptions sufficiently—they nonetheless began to re-evaluate their primary goals and their policy prescriptions. Three factors in particular were important in forcing this rethink.

1. The "East Asian Miracle"

The countries of South Korea, Taiwan, Hong Kong, and Singapore did not follow the structural adjustment model. While they embraced export-oriented growth, they achieved it through sustained involvement of the state in protecting and subsidizing selected industrial sectors to compete on international markets. The successes of the East Asian countries were encapsulated in the notion of an "East Asian miracle," which seemed to contrast greatly with the experiences of countries in Latin America and Africa that had followed the orthodox structural adjustment model (see Chapter 7).

2. Stagnation in Sub-Saharan Africa

Owing to high levels of debt during the 1980s, the IMF and World Bank wielded considerable influence over many countries in sub-Saharan Africa. As a result, these countries often undertook profound structural adjustment programs. The results, however, were greatly disappointing. With only a few exceptions, the region was characterized by moribund economies and worsening social indicators during much of the 1980s and 1990s. Critics also claimed that the increase in armed conflict in the region and the escalating HIV/AIDS crisis were strongly related to the impact of structural adjustment on state capacity.

3. The Mexican Peso Crisis

In the late 1980s and early 1990s, Mexico was heralded as a success story that many advocates of structural adjustment used to justify its validity. The structural adjustment program pursued by Mexico in the 1980s had initially imposed considerable economic and social dislocation. However, with inflation tamed and market liberalization encouraging a stream of US investment into export-oriented industries in the early 1990s, Mexico appeared to be booming. Proponents suggested that rapid economic growth would remedy low wages and high poverty levels. In the latter part of 1994, however, the flows of investment turned into capital flight as investors became afraid that the Mexican boom was built on unstable foundations. Mexico was thrown into a deep recession, with wages falling further and unemployment increasing. The economic turmoil was resolved only when the US sponsored a massive IMF bailout package and the Mexican government took over the debts of private banks.

In view of the Mexican peso crisis, the East Asian successes, and the failures of structural adjustment in sub-Saharan Africa, the IFIs faced growing criticism. In response, both institutions—but especially the World Bank—have sought to reinvent themselves by making changes to their policy prescriptions and the ways in which they engage client countries. An ongoing question is whether these changes have been superficial—aimed primarily at improving public image—or reflect substantive changes in the way that the IFIs conceptualize development issues and orient their policy. This remains a matter of significant debate.

CRITICAL ISSUES

BOX 9.6 | The Bank Reflects on Structural Adjustment

In 2001, the World Bank published a report containing what it had learned from engaging with civil society over the successes and failures of structural adjustment:

- Adjustment should come "from within," based on local analysis, local knowledge, local perceptions of political "room for manoeuvre."
- In some cases, a step-by-step approach to adjustment is appropriate to allow complex reforms to be closely linked with the development of institutions.
- It is important to provide adequate safety nets to help mitigate potentially adverse effects of adjustment on the poor.
- Special attention should be paid to safeguarding social expenditures and maintaining access to health care and education.

Source: World Bank (2001).

THE WORLD BANK, GOOD GOVERNANCE, AND INSTITUTION-BUILDING

To explain the poor record of structural adjustment, the Bank introduced the concept of "good governance." Insisting that structural adjustment remained the only correct long-term solution to the problems of developing-world countries, the Bank argued that positive outcomes were often lost because poorly run state institutions were not enabling markets to work efficiently. In short, market liberalization was not failing the developing world but, rather, "bad governance" was failing the markets. In response, the World Bank has strongly promoted the goal of "good governance" as a remedy to development problems. The aim of good governance is to craft a political architecture that supports market economies through transparency, rule of law, and accountable decision-making. In the World Bank's view, corrupt government officials often make decisions favouring specific interests in return for monetary reward, and this skews the playing field and reduces the efficiency of the market. For good governance to prevail, the Bank argued, it was necessary to find mechanisms that would enforce transparency and accountability. The former would ensure that citizens could see how decisions were made and therefore could compel state officials to make decisions that benefited the common good, not special interests. Simultaneously, if the rule of law is not applied freely and fairly, the legal basis for a market system can falter. As Adam Smith argued some 200 years earlier, market actors must be certain that their private property is secure and their contracts will be upheld. If the law is not applied equally, a lack of confidence in the rules of the game will restrain market activity and frustrate development. As a consequence, good governance also must include judicial independence from both governmental influence and private actors, and requires an accountable police force to implement the rule of law with an even hand.

The notion of good governance offered a useful concept by which the Bank could explain the failures of structural adjustment and justify further reforms in developing countries. For market-oriented development strategies to be effective, the political systems that surround them must be made accountable, transparent, responsive, efficient, and inclusive. Critics, however, have delivered sharp responses. While few doubt that limiting corruption is an important goal in and of itself, they suggest that good governance has not been a necessary factor in the development of many countries, including those in the West where corruption was often rife during their early development. In a more contemporary setting, China—which has seen the most rapid expansion of any developing economy in recent decades—would fail on many counts of good governance owing to a systematic lack of transparency and accountability across government. By blaming the political environment for the failure of structural adjustment, the good governance doctrine denies that there may be weaknesses in the structural adjustment strategy itself. Moreover, given that the World Bank and IMF governing boards are Western-dominated and operate in secrecy, it seemed hypocritical to demand transparency and accountability from client countries when the institutions themselves have a democratic deficit.

The response from the World Bank to such critiques has been to broaden the scope of the debate by highlighting a wider spectrum of social and political institutions that are conducive to successful reform. Not only must accountability and transparency be present in all political and legal processes, but the state must play a proactive role in fashioning other social institutions to help markets work efficiently and fairly. Drawing on new theoretical trends in economics, such as the "new institutional economics" represented by such authors as Douglass North (see Harriss et al., 1995; Chapters 3 and 7), the World Bank now places greater emphasis on the institutional context in which development occurs. Along with good governance, governments are expected to enforce a clear, fair, and consistent set of rules by which all market actors must operate.

In emphasizing the role of institutions in development, the Bank is arguing that states need to facilitate and regulate the conditions for free economic exchange and to correct potential market failures caused by unequally distributed information among market agents. These situations are viewed to be particularly common in the developing world and require the state to proactively establish strong institutions that channel information about market conditions, goods, and opportunities to participants. This shift represented a partial re-evaluation of the role of the state in development. In contrast to the idea of a minimalist state promoted in early structural adjustment, the World Bank now envisaged a more expansive state that would undertake such tasks as preventing the establishment of monopolies that would strangle competition and ensuring the efficient operation of labour markets by constructing institutions that would maintain a suitably flexible labour force.

Consequently, in the early 2000s, the Bank introduced what it called a "comprehensive agenda" for development that encompassed not just economic policies but also the institutional, human, and physical dimensions of development strategy. These areas range from good governance and the rule of law through to social safety nets, education, health, rural and urban strategies, and environmental and cultural dimensions (Wolfensohn, 1999). Together, they form an ambitious policy agenda covering a holistic range of issues that broadens the scope of policy and institutional reform well beyond the original confines of structural adjustment. Critics, however, suggest that this expansion has drawn the World Bank into policy areas that far exceed its expertise. Others suggest that solidifying structural adjustment in this manner is unlikely to have a profound developmental effect. Instead, they advocate a move away from the market-centric model to one that acknowledges the central importance of the role played by the state in development, as evidenced by the experiences of countries as diverse as the United States, Norway, Japan, and South Korea (Chang and Grabel, 2004).

THE IMF AND THE ASIAN CRISIS

While the World Bank in the 1990s was expanding its range of policy advice, the IMF maintained a more consistent focus on macroeconomic policy. During the 1990s, the IMF further emphasized the need for developing countries to open themselves to foreign investment. By removing restrictions on the entry of foreign capital, the IMF suggested, developing countries could tap into a large source of finance for development. In particular, during the 1990s, the IMF argued that it was necessary for developing countries to attract **foreign portfolio investment** (FPI) by opening up their stock markets to foreign investors. This process is called "capital account liberalization," and the IMF suggests that it complements other forms of liberalization and enhances the ability of developing countries to attract capital. Using these arguments, the IMF attempted, unsuccessfully, to have the goal of furthering capital account liberalization written into its constitution.

The IMF's stance on capital account liberalization quickly came under pressure following the 1994 Mexican peso crisis, when investors panicked and rapidly withdrew their portfolio investment from the country, causing intense economic dislocation and social upheaval. Critics suggested that FPI is short-term, speculative, and prone to creating financial bubbles. Worse was to follow in 1997, when speculation on global financial markets against the Thai currency caused another crisis of confidence among investors, who quickly withdrew portfolio investments from across East Asia. Despite having been termed "miracle economies" because of periods of relatively sustained and stable growth, countries ranging from South Korea to Indonesia faced a massive crisis. The crisis did not stop in Asia: both Russia and Brazil faced capital flight and economic turmoil in 1998. The countries that were relatively least affected, however, were those that had either refrained from capital account liberalization or had quickly reestablished controls on the movement of capital out of the country (Soederberg, 2004).

In response to the Asian crisis, the IMF claimed the problems were homegrown and placed the blame on "crony capitalism." According to the IMF, the close relationships between East Asian governments and local businesses had made it impossible for foreign investors to judge the true conditions of the markets. This contributed to an overestimation of the strength of East Asian markets, leading to overinvestment and eventually financial panic once true market conditions were revealed. Good governance—i.e., openness, accountability, and transparency within East Asian governments—was prescribed as the solution, along with a series of new international institutions known collectively as the "new international financial architecture." These institutions were intended to promote financial transparency and co-ordinate actions among key nations at an international level.

PHOTO 9.2 | A Rainforest Action Network banner in Seattle at the time of the 1999 "Battle of Seattle" protests at the World Trade Organization meetings.

Critics, however, lambasted the IMF's position. They pointed out that the Fund had praised the East Asian countries just prior to the crash of 1997. The IMF, they claimed, had been cavalier in its approach to capital account liberalization, ignoring the potential risks by encouraging countries to liberalize rapidly without effective regulatory structures. This created the risk of rapid financial meltdown in countries with otherwise sound economies. Moreover, the immediate response of the IMF to the crisis was to make bailout loans conditional on reform measures similar to structural adjustment programs. The former World Bank chief economist Joseph Stiglitz was among those who argued that this IMF intervention was entirely inappropriate for the East Asian countries and greatly exacerbated the severity of the crisis. Besides denting the image of the IMF, another consequence of the Asian debacle has been the buildup of large foreign reserve stockpiles by East Asian countries in order to avoid having to turn to the IMF in the future.

INTO THE NEW MILLENNIUM: POVERTY REDUCTION AND COUNTRY OWNERSHIP

Stung by criticism over the Asian financial crises and facing large protests at their annual meetings, the IFIs entered the new millennium under mounting pressure. Their response has been to re-emphasize their role as global poverty alleviators and to restructure the form of their relationships with client countries. The emphasis placed on poverty reduction reflected the need for the IMF and World Bank to seek legitimacy for their programs. As one unhappy World Bank researcher put

AP Photo/Shakil Adil

PHOTO 9.3 | The IMF and World Bank are burned in effigy, Pakistan, 2011.

it, "The poverty issue is so red-hot that IMF and World Bank staff began to feel that every action inside these organizations, from reviewing public expenditure to vacuuming the office carpet, should be justified by its effect on poverty reduction" (Easterly, 2001).

First and foremost, structural adjustment lending has been remodelled under the new motif of Poverty Reduction Strategy Papers (PRSPs). According to the IMF, these lending agreements have replaced the older "structural adjustment facility" as the primary means of funding low-income countries to promote broad-based growth and reduce poverty. They formalize a clear division of labour between the IMF and World Bank, a relationship that former World Bank president James Wolfensohn referred to as "breathing in and breathing out" (Wolfensohn, 1999). While the IMF concentrates on a familiar range of macroeconomic policies and objectives, the World Bank is now responsible for overseeing the "social and structural" policies of participating countries.

The first innovation in the PRSP model was the introduction of "ownership." According to Wolfensohn (1999), ownership meant that "[c]ountries must be in the driving seat and set the course. They must determine the goals and the phasing, timing and sequencing of programs." By applying the concept of ownership, the World Bank argued that policies are no longer fashioned in a top-down manner by the IFIs but must find their initiative in the country itself. Reforms must be designed by the borrowing government and require the support of all affected social groups. When designing policies, therefore, governments must use participatory methods to ensure that all stakeholders—government, civil society, the private sector, and the international development community—are able to voice their opinions on what should be included within the PRSP.

CRITICAL ISSUES

BOX 9.7 | IFIs Embracing Anti-Poverty

The ultimate systemic threat today is poverty.

Michel Camdessus, IMF managing director, OECD forum speech, 15 May 2001.

Our dream is a world free of poverty.

World Bank mission statement (www.worldbank.org).

Although seemingly the opposite of conditionality, the notion of "ownership" has nonetheless caused controversy. The concept is taken from management theory, where it was developed to strengthen the commitment of employees to company projects. In that sense, the practices associated with "ownership" occur within power relationships between international finance providers and national governments. Ownership aims at improving the viability and efficiency of program design by allowing national governments to take the lead in establishing reforms that respect local conditions. However, since both IMF and World Bank boards must approve all PRSPs before funding is granted, it is highly improbable that the reforms will be allowed to diverge far from Bank and Fund orthodoxy. On the contrary, given the wide propagation of what the World Bank considers "best development practice," national governments are expected to internalize these lessons if they are to receive funding. Thus, ownership can also be viewed as a modification and extension of conditionality. Indeed, some critics have suggested that the ownership concept resembles the situation of a taxicab. The developing country is in the driver's seat, yet it goes nowhere until the World Bank gets in, announces where to go, and pays the fare (Pincus and Winters, 2002).

Beyond the notion of "country ownership," the World Bank widely championed a new approach to poverty reduction in the 2000s. Poverty, it suggested, not only represents a lack of income but also is manifested in the conditions of "voicelessness" and "vulnerability." Poor people suffer from an inability to influence political processes (voicelessness) and, because of a lack of assets, are unable to adapt to sudden shocks, such as the illness or unemployment of a primary wage earner (vulnerability). The Bank saw these three dimensions of poverty interacting and reinforcing each other. Despite this welcome new emphasis, the approach remains explicitly focused on promoting what it terms "market opportunities." The other aspects of poverty reduction are valued insofar as they aid the functioning of markets. The persistence of poverty within countries undergoing PRSPs, therefore, is explained by institutional and social barriers that prevent poor people from participating in markets. In the words of the World Bank (2000: 61), "Societies have to help poor people overcome the obstacles that prevent them from freely and fairly participating in markets." The possibility that markets themselves might create or reproduce voicelessness and vulnerability is downplayed in this approach.

How, then, does the Bank envisage fighting poverty and its related component of vulnerability? To combat vulnerability, the World Bank has lauded the concept of "social capital" as a "missing link" in development theory. Social capital is a concept used to identify the networks and linkages an individual or a household can use to gain access to resources. A household with high levels of social capital has greater support networks through family, friends, and the local community. These linkages facilitate access to extra assets and information—for example, loaned money to help pay medical bills or news about potential job opportunities. For the World Bank, the theory of social capital helps to explain the social dimensions of why some individuals and groups are more successful in gaining the assets to participate effectively in markets and also are less vulnerable to market fluctuations and other unforeseen events, such as ill health. As a consequence, the institution now funds programs designed to build up the social capital of the poor (see Chapter 12).

At the same time, to combat voicelessness, the Bank suggests that it needs to "empower the poor." It presents **empowerment** as a process through which the poor are mobilized to assist in generating reforms that reduce constraints on their economic activities and upward mobility. Corruption, such as officials demanding bribes in return for letting people sell their goods, is seen as blocking market access. Similarly, unaccountable officials frustrate the growth of market activity by failing to provide poor people with the physical (roads, electricity) or social (health, education) infrastructure necessary for market activities. The solution, according to the Bank, is to empower poor people by giving them voice: first, by promoting democracy and the rule of law; second, by promoting education; and third, through technical assistance to civil society groups in forming "pro-poor coalitions" that can enforce good governance.

The change in approaching poverty since the days of structural adjustment is marked. A World Bank that talks of "empowering the poor" would have been unthinkable prior to the new millennium. That said, the idea of empowerment promoted by the World Bank is relatively limited. Forms of empowerment that are not directly market-facilitating—such as the creation of trade unions or movements aimed at the redistribution of wealth within society—are given short shrift within the World Bank's framework, despite the important role they played in poverty alleviation in some Western countries. Most importantly for the critics, the Bank refuses to acknowledge that participation in markets, in some cases, can be a source of disempowerment. For example, jobs in the global textile industry are often characterized by extremely low wages, no job security, and repressive working conditions.

A NEW CRISIS OR A NEW BEGINNING?

More than six decades have passed since the creation of the IMF and the World Bank. Despite the constant evolution of their roles, they have not been able to shake controversy and debate. Immediately prior to the world economic crisis of 2008, their continued relevance was under scrutiny. With ever-larger flows of private investment circulating within the global economy, analysts questioned why the Bank still made loans to middle-income countries such as China and India, which have seen no shortage of private investment over the past decade. It was suggested that the World Bank should be scaled back. No longer should it lend to the BRICS and other middle-income countries, but rather should provide aid simply to the poorest countries. Similarly, given the wide criticism of the IMF for mishandling the East Asian crisis, many countries in that region built up considerable reserves to avoid having to draw on the IMF's resources (see Box 9.8). By 2007, Turkey was the only major borrower from the IMF. Without the revenues flowing from these countries, the institution even had trouble covering its own running costs.

CRITICAL ISSUES

BOX 9.8 | Argentina Pays Back the IMF

In 2005, just four years after suffering a crippling financial crisis, Argentinean President Néstor Kirchner announced that the country would immediately pay back the entirety of its remaining $9.8 billion debt to the IMF. Kirchner used the occasion to make pointed barbs at the institution, accusing it of fostering financial instability through its liberalization policies and then refusing to aid Argentina in its negotiations with creditors. Kirchner applauded the financial support of the Venezuelan government, which had bought $1 billion of Argentinean bonds, and encouraged other South American countries to affirm their sovereignty by severing links with the IMF. Whether such autonomy could withstand another major financial crisis, however, remains to be seen.

This context of gathering irrelevance dissipated, however, as many countries were faced with considerable economic distress following the worldwide financial crisis of 2008. Despite its origins in the West, a number of factors conspired to hurt developing economies, including the collapse of important commodity prices, diminishing demand for exports, declining investment flows, the reneging on aid promises by Western countries, and a considerable drop in remittances from migrant workers based abroad. Moreover, unlike Western countries that used large-scale deficit financing to attempt to prop up consumption and alleviate unemployment, many southern countries do not possess such means. They faced profound economic contraction with unsettling implications for wages and employment, as well as growing pressures on financing for social programs and other public-sector expenditures. These factors, moreover, act in combination with the elevated prices of food commodities that, despite falling from their 2008 peaks, still remain well above the levels established during the preceding decade. Indeed, this food crisis alone was judged to have thrust a further 100 million people into poverty during 2008.

Under these circumstances, the IMF and World Bank sought to promote a renewed relevance as global lenders. Once again, global economic crisis provided an opportunity for both institutions to reinvent and reassert their roles. To address the urgent financing needs of countries facing financial stress, the G20 boosted the Fund's concessional lending capacity to a level that, by 2014, was 10 times higher than before the crisis. Two new aspects were promoted as important to this resurgence. First, the IMF promised a less doctrinaire approach that could be more flexible in dealing with the crisis than in the 1980s and 1990s. Second, long promised changes to internal voting structures and the boards of governors were argued to make the institutions more reflective of a world in which former clients such as China appeared to be significant players in promoting a global economic recovery.

With regard to those issues, the jury is still out. At the start of the crisis, the IMF trumpeted a reduction in the strictness of its policy requirements as compared to the original structural adjustment programs. This new flexibility, however, appeared to apply unevenly. While major countries in the West were encouraged to spend their way out of recession with deficit-financed public spending and bailouts for banks, countries in the South that borrowed from the IMF were given constraining targets for budget deficits and monetary policy. This unequal approach was widely remarked to be a continuation of colonial double standards, although the IMF argued it simply reflected different fiscal capacities across countries. Regardless of the reasons, for countries in the South, the shift within the IMF represented a slightly more flexible approach rather than a substantive change of direction. Indeed, while some critics had hoped that the 2008 crisis might elicit a broader policy switch from export-oriented private-sector growth to a broader public-financed development strategy, this was not forthcoming. In a review of IMF lending to 13 low-income countries, one frustrated NGO document declared: "The traditional biases of the IMF continue to support macroeconomic frameworks where private interests supersede public interests and the role of the state, where the financial sector takes priority over the productive sector, and where foreign investors and corporate interests override those of domestic actors" (Third World Network, 2010).

The second focus of change centred on the governance of the institutions themselves. As addressed above, voting rights and seats on the boards of governors for both institutions are heavily weighted in favour of the Western countries. This seemed to negate the important shifts in relative economic power ongoing with the growth of China, India, and other key developing countries. Negotiations are currently ongoing to give greater presence to developing countries in terms of voting rights and seats on the board of the IMF. This process, however, is fraught with conflict because various European countries—which stand to be the prime losers in the process—have blocked numerous proposals for change. In January of 2015, the IMF Executive Board released a statement lamenting the lack of progress on reforms proposed five years previously. With the US supporting change, a compromise will likely emerge that will give more voice to the BRICS countries that today play a greater role in the global economy. That said, the present proposal seeks to redistribute just 5 per cent of voting rights, so any changes will be incremental and unlikely to alter fundamentally the operating structure of the IFIs. For a number of civil society groups seeking to overhaul simultaneously the policies and operating structures of the IFIs in a way that promotes a greater

CRITICAL ISSUES

BOX 9.9 | The World Bank and Climate Change

The World Bank has a notably ambiguous stance on global climate change. This reflects a key contradiction within contemporary development policy. Most of the established goals of development involve expanding consumption and the infrastructures that underscore the production and transportation of goods within a globalized economy: all of which remains a carbon-intensive process. As a result, the Bank finds itself pulled in two directions at the same time. On the one hand, it emphasizes the need for strong mitigation efforts—i.e., the reduction of greenhouse gas emissions. To this end, the Bank has championed the reduction of all subsidies in fossil fuels and invests some money in clean-energy projects. On the other hand, the Bank continues to directly fund projects that lead to considerable emissions increases. Notably, over the past decade the Bank has been a major lender for fossil-fuel-based energy projects in the name of development, including coal-fired power stations. By its own accounts, the Bank provided $1.3 billion in direct funding to fossil-fuel-related projects in 2013–14. If indirect funding to fossil-fuel projects was considered, that total could more than double, representing a significant subsidy.

Alongside mitigation goals, the World Bank also began to integrate climate change adaptation into its operations in the mid-2000s. The idea of adaptation is to build the ability of households, communities, and countries to better deal with the threats posed by climatic change while taking advantage of new opportunities. As a result, all current and future development projects funded by the Bank are projected to address climate change adaptation as integral parts of their design and operation. The aim of this "climate risk management" is to make existing development investments more resilient to climate variability and extreme weather events while simultaneously improving the impact of development efforts in the present. Critics, however, have questioned whether the concept of adaptation is a way of safeguarding existing development strategies and therein avoiding a more profound shift in the very idea of development to reflect pressing sustainability issues (see Taylor, 2015).

degree of influence for countries of the Global South, the reforms currently proposed are an opportunity lost rather than a success to be celebrated.

More dramatically, China has responded to the continued Western influence over the IFIs by announcing the creation of its own development bank that would directly rival the World Bank in Asia (see Chapter 13). Using its substantial holdings of foreign exchange, China has repeatedly sought to use development funding as a means to open markets and exercise leverage across the post-colonial world and in sub-Saharan Africa and Central Asia in particular. This initiative is closely connected to a desire to gain influence over key producers of raw materials and food. Proposed in 2013 and formally launched in October 2014, the Asian Infrastructure Investment Bank represents a bold attempt by China to assume a dominant role as a development funder in Asia. While the United States has implacably opposed the new bank—purportedly for a lack of clear governance protocols and environmental safeguards—other countries, including Britain, Germany, France, and Australia, have nonetheless subscribed to become joint members. This shift in support represents a major coup for the Chinese state, which now leads a development initiative that has a starting working capital of $50 billion, projected to rise to $100 billion. Notably, the explicit purpose of the Chinese initiative is to fund infrastructure, which was the founding goal of the World Bank 60 years previously, prior to the dramatic escalation of its role. For some observers—including Nobel Prize–winning economist Joseph Stiglitz—the Chinese state was conspicuously showing the World Bank where its priorities should lie in the twenty-first century.

SUMMARY

From this chapter you will have gained a detailed understanding of the history and policies of the International Monetary Fund and the World Bank. In many respects, these two institutions have been the official face of international development and have exercised a strong influence over both the idea of what development should look like as well as how it should be implemented. The chapter captured not only the profound impact on international development that both institutions have had over the past 60 years through their lending and policy prescription, but also how and why they have been repeatedly enmeshed in controversy. In particular, we examined the role of both institutions in promoting structural adjustment programs (SAPs) in the 1980s and 1990s, showing why these policies created considerable protest in affected countries. The chapter then charted how the institutions responded to criticisms during the 2000s, with specific reference to anti-poverty strategies in the new millennium. The question was raised as to whether these new policy approaches represented a substantive change or merely a shift in style. Finally, the chapter addressed how the institutions have reacted in the face of the global economic crisis emerging in 2008 and looked at recent reforms intended to increase the voice of developing countries within both institutions. While the 2008 crisis appeared as an opportunity for both institutions to reassert influence on a global scale, the continued growth of middle-income countries and—particularly—of China poses challenging questions for the future of the IMF and World Bank over the decade ahead.

QUESTIONS FOR CRITICAL THOUGHT

1. The IMF and World Bank remain powerful actors within international development. Is the power these institutions exercise over developing countries a positive force for ensuring equitable and sustainable development?
2. Structural adjustment was widely critiqued for its narrow focus on economic liberalization. Have the reforms that the World Bank introduced to its policy prescription during the 2000s suitably addressed such assessments?
3. The 2008 global economic crisis gave the IMF and World Bank a new sense of purpose within a changing world marked by the growth of China and other middle-income countries. To what extent is this new relevance simply a temporary reprieve?

SUGGESTED READING

James, Harold. 1996. *International Monetary Cooperation since Bretton Woods*. Washington: IMF; New York: Oxford University Press.

Lewis, John, Richard Webb, and Devesh Kapur. 1997. *The World Bank: Its First Half Century*, 2 vols. Washington: Brookings Institution Press.

Moore, David, ed. 2007. *The World Bank: Development, Poverty, Hegemony*. Scottsville, South Africa: University of KwaZulu-Natal Press.

Pincus, James, and Jeffrey Winters, eds. 2002. *Reinventing the World Bank*. Ithaca, NY: Cornell University Press.

Stiglitz, Joseph. 2002. *Globalization and Its Discontents*. New York: W.W. Norton.

World Bank. Various years. *World Development Report*. Washington: World Bank. econ.worldbank.org/wdr.

BIBLIOGRAPHY

Caufield, C. 1996. *Masters of Illusion: The World Bank and the Poverty of Nations*. New York: Henry Holt.

Chang, H.-J., and I. Grabel. 2004. *Reclaiming Development: An Alternative Economic Policy Manual*. London: Zed Books.

Easterly, W. 2001. *The Effect of International Monetary Fund and World Bank Programs on Poverty*. Washington: World Bank.

Harriss, J., J. Hunter, and C.M. Lewis, eds. 1995. *The New Institutional Economics and Third World Development*. London: Routledge.

Körner, P. 1986. *The IMF and the Debt Crisis: A Guide to the Third World's Dilemma*. London: Zed Books.

Peet, R. 2003. *Unholy Trinity: The IMF, World Bank, and WTO*. London: Zed Books.

Pincus, J., and J. Winters. 2002. "Reinventing the World Bank." In J. Pincus and J. Winters, eds, *Reinventing the World Bank*. Ithaca, NY: Cornell University Press, 1–25.

Soederberg, S. 2004. *The Politics of the New International Financial Architecture: Reimposing Neoliberal Domination in the Global South*. London: Zed Books.

Structural Adjustment Participatory Review International Network (SAPRIN). 2004. *Structural Adjustment: The SAPRIN Report: The Policy Roots of Economic Crisis, Poverty, and Inequality*. London: Zed Books.

Taylor, M. 2015. *The Political Ecology of Climate Change Adaptation: Livelihoods, Agrarian Change and the Conflicts of Development*. London: Routledge.

Third World Network. 2010. *Third World Resurgence* 237 (May): 26–8.

Wade, R. 2001. "Showdown at the World Bank." *New Left Review* 7: 124–37.

Wall Street Journal. 2013. "Doing in business at the World Bank: An annual survey on free enterprise is under attack." *Wall Street Journal*, 7 May. www.wsj.com/articles/SB10001424127887323372504578468802587910308. Accessed 11 August 2015.

Wolfensohn, J. 1999. *A Proposal for a Comprehensive Development Framework*. Washington: World Bank.

World Bank. 1989. *Sub-Saharan Africa: From Crisis to Sustainable Growth*. Washington: World Bank.

——. 2000. *World Development Report 2000–2001: Attacking Poverty*. Oxford: Oxford University Press.

——. 2001. *Adjustment from Within: Lessons from the Structural Adjustment Participatory Review Initiative*. www.worldbank.org/research/sapri/index.htm.

10 The United Nations and Multilateral Actors in Development

David Sogge

LEARNING OBJECTIVES

- To learn about key development and humanitarian institutions operating within the UN system and outside it.
- To understand how these organizations have advanced or retreated, as affected by internal challenges and geopolitical pressures.
- To assess the organizations' respective significance in various developmental spheres.

▲ **The UN Refugee Agency (UNHCR) resumed voluntary repatriation of tens of thousands of Ivorian refugees from Liberia, after a pause of more than a year because land borders were closed to prevent the spread of a deadly Ebola outbreak.** | Source: UN Photo/Abdul Fatai Adegboye

From killer viruses to tax evasion to the trade in weapons, major problems continue to show no respect for national boundaries. Needs to co-operate transnationally are more urgent than ever. To cope with such challenges, governments have committed themselves to international legal conventions, mutual defence pacts, international agencies, and economic blocs. Today there are more than 5,000 intergovernmental organizations (uia.org/igosearch) and more than 560 major agreements (treaties.un.org). These embody **multilateralism**, a term referring to formal arrangements among three or more states, commonly for peaceful purposes over extended periods. Multilateralism has developed over more than a century. Yet it has also met setbacks and spawned contradictions. In the name of the poor and powerless it has sometimes helped serve the rich and powerful. Questions continue to arise about multilateralism's scope, efficacy, and fairness in tackling problems.

Development has long been a multilateral pursuit. Rich countries have rallied under the banner of foreign aid, where multilateralism means singing from the same policy song sheets and contributing to the same collection boxes. Multilateral aid constitutes about 30 per cent of all net aid from Western governments. Yet that funding share understates its influence. Multilateral institutions design and transmit policy formulas about how non-Western countries should be run. Some observers claim that multilateral approaches are better than bilateral ones. Their virtues are said to include lower overhead costs, greater sectoral expertise, stronger capacities for long-term engagement, and lower risks that the self-interest of donor nations would dominate. Those are some assertions, but not everyone is convinced. This chapter begins with an overview of some of the main multilateral actors in development and some claims and counter-claims made about them.

Multilateral engagements can help governments improve their standing, influence, security, or economic advantage. So-called middle powers such as Australia, Canada, and the Netherlands often prefer working multilaterally because results can be better, at less cost and risk, than going it alone. They can allow governments to take lower profiles and in effect to subordinate themselves to others; political leaders can thereby sidestep sovereign responsibilities and pass the buck. Big powers such as the United States often pursue multilateralism "à la carte," co-operating only when it suits them and often acting on their own. This unilateralism has today become more common, as shown in one-to-one trade pacts and the use of bilateral funds under the banner of multilateral action. Nevertheless, governments face incentives to work together in the face of large issues—climate change, Internet access, organized crime—that transcend borders. States are increasingly bound by treaties, consultation systems, and agencies controlled jointly. Matters of international trade and investment are commonly framed and enforced under international "hard law" (see Chapter 11 on the private sector and Chapter 15 on free trade). Such arrangements allow powerful players in global capitalism to gain advantages. By contrast, global institutions with mandates regarding social development, human rights, and justice have far weaker suasion (see Normand and Zaidi, 2008), as their powers depend largely on normative guidelines or "soft law."

This chapter discusses multilateral organizations clustered according to the source of their oversight, as follows:

1. the United Nations system;
2. Western industrialized governments;
3. governments of non-Western countries.

The focus is on their functions and evolution according to shifting ideological currents and power balances. That perspective highlights distinctions between international organizations (the products) and international organization (the process) as a means of understanding their roles and significance.

THE UNITED NATIONS SYSTEM

The **United Nations** was conceived in the closing months of World War II. The triumphant great powers—Britain, the Soviet Union, and the United States—negotiated and eventually agreed on a design for a new body, the United Nations Organization, to replace its weak predecessor, the League of Nations (1919–46). The UN's design made it open to all countries but attuned to the strategic preferences of the great powers, especially the United States, the only state with the overwhelming military, diplomatic, and financial means to bring about such a global project at that time. Yet while the US may have wished to call all the shots, it could not act alone. To shape the post-war order according to its interests, it needed other nations' consent and active co-operation. It therefore agreed that France and China, together with Britain and the Soviet Union (Russia after 1991), would be permanent members of the UN Security Council, the world's pre-eminent forum on urgent issues of conflict and insecurity.

The UN was created under the banner of peace and security, but it rapidly took on mandates to promote development. During its first phase, up to the late 1950s, it helped launch many global initiatives in the name of economic and social well-being. It was the "mother church" of developmental optimism. At the same time, the UN served as a geostrategic instrument for a few powerful countries. It provided legitimacy and military power in support of US foreign policy, such as for the war in Korea in the early 1950s and during the upheaval in the Congo in the early 1960s. As chief source of funds, supplier of staff, and host of the UN headquarters in New York City, the US had decisive influence over the organization. However, the UN has not always behaved as an obedient servant to American overlords; indeed, it has often been a platform for non-Western countries to regroup and to resist Western pressures.

A second and more tumultuous phase began after 1960, by which time UN membership had risen to 99 nations, up from 51 at its founding in 1945. The one-state-one-vote balance in the General Assembly began to tilt towards the non-Western world. New issues emerged on the UN's agenda and expanded the scope of UN agency work. Colonial rule had largely ended, but post-colonial transitions did not always follow the scripts written by the Western "First World" or the "Second World" of the Communist bloc. New states often took independent positions as members of a "Third World" to chart their own ways forward.

In the 1990s, a third and far more troubled phase began for the UN, ushered in by the collapse of the Soviet Union and the expansion of an especially predatory and unaccountable kind of capitalism. Western nations supported the deployment of UN "blue helmet" troops to conflict zones where Western powers had not already intervened, such as in the former Yugoslavia, Haiti, and the Democratic Republic of the Congo. Yet where they initiated wars, those big powers bypassed the United Nations. In Afghanistan, Iraq, Libya, and Syria, "coalitions of the willing" under US leadership have disregarded some fundamental international rules, including UN safeguards against the use of armed force.

For many non-Western countries, Western powers have first defined the problems and then prescribed the solutions according to their preferred policy formulas (see Chapters 3, 9, and 15) through the International Monetary Fund (IMF), the World Bank, the World Trade Organization (WTO), and the G20 group of finance chieftains. However, those Western-backed bodies have regularly met dissent by non-Western nations, often in UN forums. In response, Western powers have lowered the priority and narrowed the roles they assign to the UN. Nevertheless, expressions of universal intent such as the UN's Millennium Development Goals and agreements such as the treaty banning landmines continue to emerge and to affect policy internationally. While trade and investment matters have driven both bilateral and multilateral deal-making, elites usually prefer multilateral co-operation on issues of the environment, public health, and humanitarian need. However, when challenged to respond to inequity and disrespect of rights or to create and maintain "global public goods," the founding norms of UN multilateralism face strong headwinds.

Origin and Oversight of UN Agencies

The twentieth century saw the birth of many international organizations, many of them with humanitarian and developmental mandates. Among the best known are UN agencies. The United Nations Children's Fund (UNICEF), for example, became a household word thanks to its appealing roles towards children and those caring for them.

These agencies arose amid certain assumptions. One was a widespread optimism about the power of expertise to solve problems. In the 1940s and 1950s, terms such as "modernization," "planning," and "population control" were commonplace. International agencies portrayed development as an essentially technical issue beyond politics. Its guides were to be professionals such as engineers, medical specialists, crop scientists, and economists. Such experts and managers could be trusted to define the problems properly and then get

epa european pressphoto agency b.v./Alamy Stock Photo

PHOTO 10.1 | UN Troops leaving Syria on 15 September 2014.

on with the job of solving them. Development agencies thus grew according to a logic of **technical functionalism**, in which each profession's know-how would be applied through sector-specific organizations managed from the top down. The approach embodied and indeed legitimated multilateralism as a pathway to universal development. Matters of national sovereignty or class interests were seen as harmful distractions. Framed in these ways, "development" became a conflict-free project insulated from left/right ideologies and from open debate. The technicians-in-white-coats image of multilateral action camouflaged its politics.

Later, donors began adjusting their approach. UN agencies came to focus more on each country's particular circumstances and plans rather than assuming that problems and solutions were the same in all new "modernizing" countries—an assumption justifying one-size-fits-all multilateral approaches to development.

According to the first article of its Charter, the UN is intended "to achieve international co-operation in solving international problems of an economic, social, cultural, or humanitarian character, and in promoting and encouraging respect for human rights and for fundamental freedoms for all." The Charter mandated the creation of the Economic and Social Council (ECOSOC), which is today composed of representatives of 54 states elected for three-year terms by the General Assembly. In formal terms, ECOSOC could be seen as the world's supreme forum for development policy; however, not long after its creation it was shown to have little authority, even over the specialized UN agencies formally answerable to it.

The UN categorizes its organizations mainly according to their lines of accountability. One category comprises *specialized agencies*. These are distinct bodies, established by **intergovernmental** treaties. They have their own charters and governance; they appoint their own chief executives. States may join or withdraw as they wish. Each specialized agency has an agreement linking it to the UN, although that seldom implies subordination. In formal terms, the World Bank and the IMF are specialized UN agencies, but in practice they operate in complete independence of the UN.

The second category is that of UN *organs*, also termed *programs* or *funds*. These are direct arms of the UN itself and are thus answerable ultimately to the General Assembly.

A third category comprises UN agencies, such as for peacekeeping and humanitarian action, that operate under the direct supervision of the Secretary-General's office. Major UN bodies with mandates for development and humanitarian tasks are depicted in Figure 10.1.

Overall contributions to the UN in 2011 were close to US$40 billion (equivalent to British Columbia's provincial government budget in that year). The ways by which it gets and spends money have departed significantly from its founding multilateral norms. Initially, UN bodies were funded chiefly by mandatory contributions from governments to a general budget, based on each country's capacity to pay.[1] That was multilateralism then. Today, UN agencies compete with each other to get most of their funding bilaterally from governments, who give on a voluntary basis, often with restrictions. If one "follows the money" supporting the United Nations, bilateralism has triumphed over multilateralism (see Jenks, 2014).

THE AGENCIES

The UN family tree has grown many branches over several generations. Its agencies, programs, funds, commissions, and other institutions number several dozen. This section discusses only the most prominent ones, grouped by sector.

Food, Agriculture, and Rural Development

Established in 1945, the Food and Agriculture Organization (FAO) is a UN specialized agency. Headquartered in Rome, where an earlier world body, the International Institute of Agriculture, had been based, the FAO's chief mandate is to provide governments with information and policy advice on food, agriculture, and rural development. It also runs development projects and provides emergency assistance in response to droughts and insect plagues. Together with crop research institutes financed by the Rockefeller and Ford foundations, it promoted controversial "green revolution" technologies designed for farmers and agri-businesses with sufficient land, skills, and financial assets (see Chapter 18).

Despite its reputation as a source of technical know-how, the FAO continues to meet criticism. It has been cited for its friendly stances towards global agri-businesses, such as its Private Sector Mechanism, an association involving many dozens of corporations and agri-business networks. Financial constraints have helped drive those relationships, and have also led it to frame some activities as emergencies (for which fundraising is easier) and to decentralize its management (which lowers staff costs).

Also based in Rome is the World Food Programme (WFP), a UN organ set up in 1961 by the FAO and tasked initially with channelling Western food surpluses into humanitarian relief efforts and labour-intensive public works projects. As both the WFP and the FAO respond to emergencies and seek support from the same donors, rivalry between them has grown.

Following the 1974 World Food Conference, a group of non-Western governments led by the Organization of Petroleum Exporting Countries (OPEC) established the International Fund for Agricultural Development (IFAD). A specialized UN agency, IFAD operates from Rome headquarters as a small international bank for member governments, channelling most of its loans through other UN bodies to support rural development projects. In the early 1990s a decline in OPEC funding left IFAD dependent on Western donor governments, with whom relations have been rocky.

Health, Children, and Women

In 1948, ECOSOC created the World Health Organization (WHO), a UN specialized agency based in Geneva. Having defined health as something more than the absence of disease or infirmity, WHO is supposed to promote general physical, mental, and social well-being. It is supposed to be on the front lines in combatting endemic diseases and epidemics. It further aims to

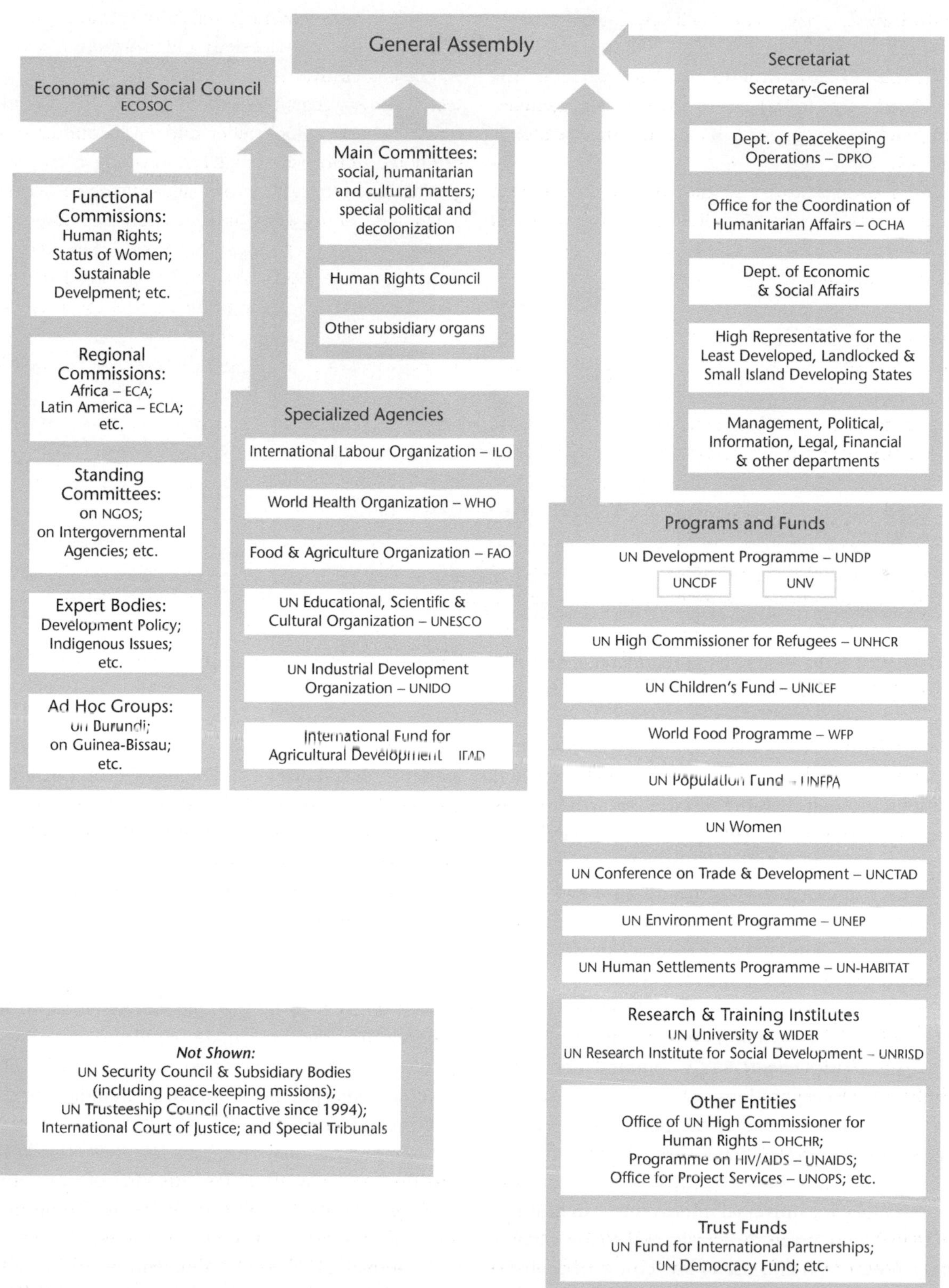

FIGURE 10.1 | Major UN Entities with Development and Humanitarian Functions

WFP/Colin Kampschoer

PHOTO 10.2 | The World Food Programme meets nutrition needs with a shipment destined for Pyongyang, the capital of the Democratic People's Republic of Korea.

promote health services and training, better nutrition, occupational health, and unharmful environmental conditions. Among its functions are research and the setting of standards for health practices and biological and pharmaceutical products. It has taken progressive stances by emphasizing basic health care and drawing attention to the causes of ill health and premature death, including smoking and road accidents. But its inept responses to crises (outbreaks of cholera in Haiti, and of Ebola in West Africa, etc.) and its failure to promote health services as a human right have left it open to criticism. Critics cite WHO's accommodation of big pharmaceutical corporations, whose interests seldom focus on health problems of the poor. "Big Pharma" promotes its corporate image through its donations and business "partnerships" with WHO. Yet corporations' relevance for universal improvement in health is open to question, given their resistance to low-income nations' production and use of low-cost generic drugs (see Chapter 20). Meanwhile, WHO is no longer the only player in global health. Competition comes from "philanthrocapitalist"organizations such as the Bill and Melinda Gates Foundation and from the World Bank (see Chapter 9), which also offers health policy advice. Despite these challenges, and Western pressures to restrict it to merely technical matters, WHO is often seen as among the more effective UN bodies. However, its effects in promoting change are harder to detect than those in promoting business-as-usual.

Set up in 1946 by the General Assembly to help feed, clothe, and vaccinate children in post-war Europe, the New York-based UN Children's Fund (UNICEF) today pursues a worldwide mandate for child survival and development, chiefly through community-based and national programs for preventive health, nutrition, and education. For this kind of work, it was awarded the 1965 Nobel Peace Prize. It also promotes legislation for child protection consistent with the 1990 International Child Rights Convention. In the 1980s, UNICEF stood out among aid agencies for its dissent against orthodox macroeconomic austerity policies imposed by the IMF, the World Bank, and most other official donors. It has sometimes joined activist NGOs in challenging corporations; it denounced, for example, the sale of infant formula foods sold by global corporations in low-income countries. However, UNICEF selectively pursues donations from corporations, and recruits showbiz and sport celebrities in its highly successful public relations efforts. UNICEF's data and analyses, much of them produced at its Innocenti Research Centre in Florence, Italy, focus on poverty, inequality, and powerlessness.

In 1946, ECOSOC established a Population Commission in response to fears of a "population explosion" in non-Western lands. In 1967, with monies from the United States, the General Assembly set up the UN Fund for Population Activities (UNFPA). Its mandate was to disseminate information and promote policies for better access to family planning knowledge and services. In Cairo in 1994, the UN convened its third decennial world gathering on Population and Development. At this conference, governments reached a unified view of linkages among population, development, and women's rights. Reinforced by this political consensus, and in the teeth of conservative religious and political opposition, the UNFPA has managed to advance thinking and action on reproductive rights and reproductive health, which have largely displaced the discourses of family planning and population control.

Helping to drive these achievements was a global movement for women's rights and gender equity. It helped to create and steer UN commissions, conferences, agencies, and research-and-training bodies. In 1946 the UN launched its Commission on the Status of Women. Along with other organizations, that body promoted legal statements such as the Convention on Political Rights of Women in 1952, followed by others on working life, human trafficking, marriage, and property. UN conferences related to women have shaped thinking and built global networks. The World Conference of the International Women's Year, held in Mexico in 1975, was unprecedented in scope and importance. Among its results was the establishment of the UN Development Fund for Women (UNIFEM) within the UN Development Programme. Extending the impact of these bodies are **knowledge-based institutes**. Among these was the International Research and Training Institute for the Advancement of Women (INSTRAW). Its work involved the promotion of women's rights as human rights. In July 2010, UNIFEM, INSTRAW, and two other UN bodies merged to form UN Women, the United Nations Entity for Gender Equality and the Empowerment of Women. Among its tasks are support to the UN Commission on the Status of Women, guidance to states seeking to implement policies and standards consistent with UN conventions, and pressures to hold the UN system accountable for its own commitments on gender equality (see also Chapter 5). Governments are expected to draw on these global policy commitments when framing national legislation, legal systems, and budgets. While no doubt adding to forward motion, however, the success of UN efforts ultimately remain dependent on pressures from emancipatory movements at all levels.

Education, Science, Culture, and Media

Established in 1946, the United Nations Educational, Scientific and Cultural Organization (UNESCO) is a specialized agency headquartered in Paris. UNESCO's mandate is both intellectual (promotion of education, culture, and media, exchange of knowledge, etc.) and normative (promotion of freedom of expression, of cultural rights, etc.). Those purposes are not easily reconciled, especially among the world's governments, who are UNESCO's "owners." The advance of economic orthodoxies and the interests backing them have put its normative mandate under stress. For example, its pursuit of rights to education has been frustrated. In 1990, at an intergovernmental conference held in Jomtien, Thailand, UNESCO achieved adoption of the "Education for All" declaration, holding that basic education should be a public good. Yet that resolution has encountered ideological opposition. Some business interests and governments, for example, have worked to turn knowledge and education into commodities. They frame them as products to be bought and sold in "marketplaces" rather than as public entitlements available to everyone regardless of ability to pay. As with many other UN agencies, UNESCO has had to seek financial and non-financial "partnerships" with businesses and other private-sector actors. Weak management has sometimes limited UNESCO's effectiveness. But external challenges—pressures to pursue "market-based" approaches and to sidestep demands for universal rights and freedoms—have been more detrimental. Meanwhile, the World Bank has become a competing source of expertise and influence over education policy in low-income countries.

Environment and Shelter

Following citizen initiatives in Europe and North America, the 1972 United Nations Conference on the Human Environment, held in Stockholm, Sweden, helped put global environmental issues on public and political agendas worldwide. It led the UN General Assembly in 1972 to create the United Nations Environment Programme (UNEP). Headquartered in Nairobi, Kenya, it has regional and specialized offices around the world. Its chief tasks are to monitor and assess global and regional environmental conditions, to facilitate negotiations of global agreements and supervise their enforcement, to raise awareness, and to manage specific projects on issues such as climate change and biodiversity. Some UNEP initiatives include anti-poverty dimensions, such as combatting the pollution of urban water supplies (see Chapter 17). UNEP is especially valued for the knowledge and norms it brings to the discussion of public policies.

The United Nations Human Settlements Programme (UN-HABITAT), also based in Nairobi, focuses on basic development and poverty issues. Founded in 1978, it was an outcome of the first Conference on Human Settlements, known as Habitat I, convened by the UN in 1976 in Vancouver, Canada. In 1996 a second conference, Habitat II, in Istanbul, Turkey, drew up a broad agenda for governments and others to tackle the fast-growing problems of cities in low-income countries. That agenda contrasts with market-led approaches. It holds that adequate shelter is a right, not merely a commodity available only to those who can afford to pay. Working with member governments and specialized NGOs, UN-HABITAT pursues its normative mandate through research and dialogue on policies, laws, and planning methods about housing, land use, water and sanitation, security, and urban governance (see Chapter 19).

Employment and Working Life

The International Labour Organization (ILO) emerged in 1919 after many decades of labour organizing and the advance of social democratic parties in industrialized countries. Today, as a UN specialized agency headquartered in Geneva, it is unique among official organizations in that representatives of civil society—organized labour and employers' organizations—participate in its governance. Historically, the ILO's main tasks have been normative: to define and promote standards for working and social conditions, chiefly through intergovernmental conventions. Most governments have ratified ILO conventions on "Fundamental Principles and Rights at Work," including the freedom of workers to associate together, as well as other agreements and guidelines to protect working people. Adherence to those rules, however, is not universal. The United States refuses to ratify conventions on freedom of association, on the right to organize and collective bargaining, on equal remuneration, and on discrimination in employment and occupation. They may enjoy overwhelming world support, but without US backing those covenants lack strong promotion and enforcement.

The ILO has promoted responses to globalization through studies, conferences, and thematic campaigns on "decent work" and social protection. It is the only UN body to have regularly paid attention to job creation and decent work. Its efforts to influence policies of the World Bank and IMF have met success only very recently, when those bodies began to accept that employment was an important goal. Originally focused on formal sectors, the ILO today addresses both the formal and informal labour markets. In training and technical assistance projects, such as labour-intensive public works, the ILO has contributed to practical measures. But in a world where workers are increasingly expendable and unprotected, the ILO's original normative purposes are under severe pressures (see Standing, 2008).

Trade, Investment, and Corporate Accountability

In 1964, at the initiative of non-Western governments wishing to end their disadvantages in the world economic system, the first UN Conference on Trade and Development (UNCTAD) was held. It was rapidly institutionalized, gaining a secretariat in Geneva. In its first three decades, UNCTAD tried to forge new trade policies, to serve as a forum for trade negotiations, and to influence UN development thinking. Concepts of dependency and Keynesian social democracy guided its campaign for a fairer world trade system (see Chapters 3 and 15). Non-Western countries were highly influential in UNCTAD, chiefly through the Group of 77 (discussed later in this chapter). Despite internal differences, those countries agreed that no single development path was best. UNCTAD was a global vehicle for them to gain occasional trade concessions, such as a 1970 agreement on a "generalized system of preferences."

Rich countries disliked UNCTAD because it often failed to follow Western prescriptions and posed disadvantages for multinational corporations. Western countries sought to downsize it and to promote the General Agreement on Tariffs and Trade (GATT), which evolved into the more highly structured WTO in 1995. The WTO (see Chapter 15) operates outside UN auspices and takes positions "diametrically opposed" to those of the UN (Wilkinson, 2014). In 1992, the rich countries decisively marginalized UNCTAD as a forum for negotiating trade rules. From that moment on its focus shifted; each government was expected to retool its economy along neoliberal lines. This meant privatizing public assets, lowering taxes on external trade and investment, and radically reducing business taxes and state control over flows of capital. Along these lines, the main obligation was to orient national economies in an outward direction; development of domestic markets could wait. UNCTAD's role shifted from helping non-Western countries negotiate better deals with the global economic system to promoting their integration into that system. Today, however, UNCTAD has regained some autonomy. It promotes alternatives to mainstream trade thinking through its conferences, research, and analysis, including the compilation of statistics on trade and investment. UNCTAD staff also provide technical assistance to governments on their trade and investment policies (see Chapter 15).

Humanitarian and Peacekeeping Action

From its earliest years, the United Nations has faced humanitarian emergencies. In 1948, the flight and expulsion of many hundreds of thousands from Palestine led the UN to set up its Relief and Works Agency for Palestine Refugees in the Near East (UNRWA). Nearly 70 years later, that UN program is still vital and effective despite pressures from within Israel and the United States. In 1950, the General Assembly created the office of the High Commissioner for Refugees (UNHCR) to co-ordinate action and raise money to help refugees. In the early Cold War years, its priority was on people seeking asylum from Communist Eastern Europe. In 1967, the UN broadened the UNHCR's mandate to include future as well as past refugee flows and to cover the entire world, thus effectively shifting its geographical focus from Western to non-Western settings.

Complex political emergencies, many of them arising from interventions by great powers, have produced much human suffering. In response, the UN has set up a number of multilateral agencies. Foremost among

BOX 10.1 | Transnational Corporations: The UN Changes Course

CURRENT EVENTS

In 1973, ECOSOC set up the UN Commission on Transnational Corporations and a research program managed by a New York–based Centre on Transnational Corporations (UNCTC). That centre acted as a watchdog; it commissioned studies, held workshops, and prepared a draft code of conduct for transnational corporations—a code that Western business interests contested and UN members never ratified. In 1994, following concerted pressure by business lobbies, the UN abolished the UNCTC and placed its residual responsibilities under UNCTAD's Investment, Enterprise and Development Commission, whose role is not that of a watchdog but mainly that of a *promoter* of global corporations (see Chapter 11).

them is the Office for the Coordination of Humanitarian Affairs (OCHA), headquartered in New York. Its director has the status of a UN undersecretary-general. OCHA's main tasks are to assess needs, raise money from governments, develop humanitarian policy, and co-ordinate field operations involving UN agencies, Red Cross organizations, and NGOs. It supports specialized organizations, including a news network, IRIN, set up in 1995 in recognition of the power of media to mobilize political and financial backing for humanitarian action.

The UN has frequently coupled humanitarian work with its peacekeeping missions. Between 1948 and 2015, it carried out 71 missions, 58 of them after 1988. The UN Department of Peacekeeping Operations (DPKO), headquartered in New York, is tasked with planning and directing UN efforts to bring stability and security to selected conflict-affected places. As of 2015, some 91,000 soldiers, 13,500 police personnel, and close to 16,800 civilian staff were on active duty under UN auspices in 16 countries; only the United States places more military personnel abroad. Yet, in 2014–15, UN peacekeeping accounted for less than half of 1 per cent of total military spending across the globe.

The UN "blue helmets" are recruited mainly from non-Western countries; as of 2015 the five leading sources were Bangladesh, Ethiopia, India, Pakistan, and Rwanda. Some UN missions, such as in Côte d'Ivoire and post-war Mozambique, clearly contributed to peace; others, such as in Angola, Congo, and Rwanda, largely failed to do so. That mixed record has led to criticisms that UN interventions in the name of peace often neglect the socio-political causes of conflict, and furthermore that they can put durable solutions out of

Khalil Mazraawi/AFP/Getty Images

PHOTO 10.3 | A Sudanese refugee from Darfur walks past tents during an open-ended sit-in outside the United Nations High Commissioner for Refugees (UNHCR) in the Jordanian capital Amman, demanding better treatment and acceleration of their relocation.

reach because strategies follow narrow "militarized" or "securitized" lines, even if carried out in the name of human security (see Chapter 21).

UN agencies have developed ties with non-governmental organizations, both international and domestic, often in "partnerships" to manage projects and deliver humanitarian aid. For example, the UN refugee agency UNHCR, headquartered in Geneva, has contracts with more than 800 NGOs and has referred to NGOs as "our right arm." In most cases the relationship is contractual rather than genuinely collaborative.

Steering Action, Influencing Thinking

In 1965, the General Assembly established the United Nations Development Programme (UNDP) under ECOSOC. Unlike other UN bodies, the UNDP has no specific mandate or formal charter. Yet it has high standing in the UN system; its chief executive officer, the Administrator, ranks third after the Secretary-General and Deputy Secretary-General. Set up originally to co-ordinate aid efforts, the UNDP has assumed strategic positions high on aid chains as a promoter of policy. Today, it describes itself as a network and advocacy organization for development. According to its *Strategic Plan* for 2015, the UNDP prioritized three "big ideas" for development action: "sustainability, democratic governance, and crisis response and prevention," with "special emphasis on the eradication of extreme poverty and reduction of inequalities and social exclusion."

Headquartered in New York, the UNDP operates in 177 countries and territories, giving it more extensive field presence than the World Bank. Because it is answerable to the UN General Assembly and to recipient governments, it should be among the most accountable and responsive development agencies. However, the UNDP's dependence on annual voluntary contributions from rich donor countries sets limits to what it can do for recipients.

Under UNDP co-ordination, UN agencies face pressures to perform well and to pursue results-based management (see Box 8.7). All agencies are supposed to follow a prescribed planning cycle, starting with a country-level assessment and leading to a UN Development Assistance Framework and a UN country program and action plan. Such systems of management may be technically competent and formulated through consultative processes, but their relevance is limited by aid system assumptions that poverty and governance problems are mainly domestic matters to be resolved by authorities within a given national territory. However, in a globalized world, important drivers of development problems are not confined to national territories. Indeed, many of them arise from *global* flows of money, information, people, weapons, and other commodities (see Chapter 6). For example, illicit capital flight takes much more money out of Africa than the aid system puts into it; yet illicit flows would be far smaller if tax havens under Western jurisdiction did not exist. Hence, major weaknesses of this new UN approach stem from failures to tackle harmful global flows and to curb the strong incentives that accompany them.

Several agencies operate under the UNDP. The UN Capital Development Fund (UNCDF) uses a model in which citizens co-determine the use of aid in local development. The UN Volunteers (UNV) program annually supports about 7,700 persons working in development or rehabilitation projects, most of them linked with UN agencies. The UN Office for South–South Co-operation (UNOSSC) began in 1974 at the initiative of non-Western governments and today operates an online Global South–South Development Academy, organizes an annual South–South Development Expo, and runs a South–South Global Assets and Technology Exchange.

Some of the UN system's most important work promotes *ideas*, *knowledge*, and *norms*. Together with the ILO, UNICEF, and UNCTAD, the UNDP has enabled alternative views to be voiced in policy debates in which organizations based in Washington, DC, are accustomed to having the last word. From its first issue in 1990 onward, the UNDP's *Human Development Report* has put forward social democratic viewpoints. It thus competes with, and sometimes dissents from, the World Bank's *World Development Report*, which despite policy flip-flops (switching from negative to positive stances towards the state, for example), follows an orthodox line. Policy research from the UNDP's International Policy Centre for Inclusive Growth, based in Brazil, provides counterpoints to centres of development orthodoxy.

Other units of the United Nations system also engage in policy research, thus helping to draw attention to issues and shape understanding of problems.

Founded in 1963, the Geneva-based UN Research Institute for Social Development (UNRISD) generates multi-disciplinary research on governance, market forces, social policy, and alternative models such as the "Social and Solidarity Economy." The United Nations University, established in 1973 and headquartered in Tokyo, comprises a worldwide network of research centres and programs in post-graduate education. One of these, the World Institute for Development Economics Research (WIDER), founded in 1984 and based in Helsinki, Finland, promotes research on poverty, inequality, and growth.

In its first decade, the UN set up economic commissions in most world regions. They are the UN Economic Commission for Europe (UNECE), based in Geneva; the Economic Commission for Latin America and the Caribbean (ECLAC), in Santiago, Chile; the Economic and Social Commission for Asia and the Pacific (ESCAP), in Bangkok, Thailand; the Economic Commission for Africa (ECA), in Addis Ababa, Ethiopia; and the Economic and Social Commission for Western Asia (ESCWA), in Beirut, Lebanon. These bodies gather statistics, monitor economic trends, help set standards, and develop trade arrangements. In some cases, such as the Commission for Europe, they promote expanded roles for private enterprise and the much-criticized "public–private partnership" approach (see Chapter 11). By contrast, since the 1950s ECLAC has promoted progressive policy alternatives, especially about world trade and investment.

TRENDS AND PROSPECTS FOR UN AGENCIES

The foregoing snapshots of UN agencies focus on the past. What of the future? The UN was established to allow for vigorous debate. In that spirit, the UN has allowed voices to be heard about domination and denial of rights. In the 1960s and 1970s in particular, non-Western governments tried using the UN as a forum where alternative ideas about development could compete and where issues of fairness and unequal power could gain a place on world agendas. However, many of those efforts have been deflected or blocked outright. From Washington to Frankfurt, powerful interests have insisted that "there is no alternative" to neoliberal orthodoxy. Increasingly harnessed to one school of thought, the UN has seen its fundamental mandates—promotion of new developmental norms and of dialogue—set aside. Nevertheless, for a few development questions, the UN continues to serve as a vehicle for **emancipatory** answers. It has helped to advance the status of women and widen access to reproductive health and reproductive rights (see Chapter 5). It has helped move problems of slums and environmental degradation higher on world agendas (see Chapters 17 and 19). Why have these initiatives met success? A major reason is the active presence of forceful social movements, such as for women's emancipation, for rights of minority peoples, and for environmental sanity.

UN agencies, like many others in the aid and development sector, struggle with internal deficiencies. Many of them suffer from technocratic ways of defining problems and solutions, non-transparency, high overhead costs, poor engagement with citizens' organizations, and unproductive working cultures that depress staff morale. In development operations, UN agencies, on average, are less effective than other multilateral players (Picciotto, 2014). Limits to effectiveness can stem from fragmentation driven by technical functionalism—agrarian issues for the FAO, children's issues for UNICEF, and so on. The lifeworlds of people targeted for interventions are not easily put into separate boxes. Yet aid agencies are seldom able to work flexibly amid this complexity and to respond "downward" to those in need. Rather, as new themes and funding possibilities arise, agencies respond by adding yet more objectives and tasks. The result is "mission creep." When a sense of crisis builds, such as at the height of the HIV/AIDS pandemic, new monies appear and agencies launch new programs. Duplication can be rife: at least 20 UN agencies work on issues of water supply. To promote coherence amid these overlapping agendas, UN agency heads committed themselves in 2005 to a "One UN" approach, with a single framework guiding all UN efforts in each country. It was supposed to streamline aid delivery and allow the UN to satisfy both states that receive aid and those using the UN to give aid. However, seven years later an independent evaluation found no convincing evidence that the "delivering as one" approach had made any real difference (United Nations, 2012).

But can management reform resolve deeper sources of dysfunction? Ultimately, the effectiveness of UN agencies depends on who holds the purse strings, who sets the agenda, and who makes the rules. Even when the UN's voting system favours lower-income countries because of their greater numbers, the power of money is decisive. Top-level UN jobs are held in disproportionate numbers by Americans or citizens of other big powers, and UN votes are often influenced by big donors' offers of aid or threats to withhold it. Agencies must increasingly compete with each other to gain funding from bilateral donors, usually according to those donors' personal and commercial interests. In short, the United Nations will go on suffering deficits in governance unless it can neutralize or sidestep the power of rich nations and the interests they promote.

There are further challenges. The influence of large corporations threatens the integrity and competence of the United Nations. That influence—the "privatization of multilateral institutions" (Bøås and McNeill, 2003: 142)—has led to a weakening of the UN's orientation to public service. This accelerated with the UN's "Global Compact," a public relations initiative launched in 1999 at the World Economic Forum, a gathering of business and political elites held annually in Davos, Switzerland. On that occasion, the UN Secretary-General appealed to corporations to engage more closely with the UN; by so doing they could improve their public image—something most of them badly need. In exchange, they had to endorse guidelines on corporate behaviour. That stipulation was easy to accept, since the guidelines are not legally binding, nor are they seriously monitored in any case. Concretely, the UN offered global companies so-called "partnerships" with UN bodies: McDonald's and Microsoft have teamed up with UNESCO, Novartis with WHO, Citigroup and Chevron-Texaco with the UNDP, and so forth. The Global Compact has sponsored conferences and publications with titles such as *Fighting Poverty: A Business Opportunity.* Many UN organizations added new departments to manage this strategy, such as the UNDP Division for Business Partnerships.

Collaborations between UN agencies and big business today number in the hundreds. Many corporations have thereby gained public goodwill (they have been **bluewashed**) through their association with UN agencies. In their turn, some UN agencies have gained a few more resources, while also adding to their overhead costs. Yet there has been embarrassment for the UN. Some big firms signed up to the Global Compact turned out to have violated OECD Guidelines for Multinational Enterprises (see Chapter 11). The UN's own Inspection Unit evaluated the Global Compact's first decade and found that direction was poor, regulation was weak, and means to verify results were lacking. According to the evaluators, in promoting better behaviour by corporations, the Global Compact had been largely toothless. Even more serious is evidence that close ties with corporations have weakened UN capacities to think and act critically on global issues (Utting and Zammit, 2009).

As a result, many voices (see Browne, 2014) today call on the UN to escape the shadow of these interests, reduce cumbersome and often ineffective tasks of co-ordination, and refocus its development efforts at strategic political levels, chiefly in setting emancipatory norms and in gaining compliance with those norms.

MULTILATERAL ORGANIZATIONS ANCHORED IN WESTERN GOVERNMENTS

Some multilateral arrangements are clubs open only to rich countries. The following organizations reflect the military or geostrategic interests of rich countries vis-à-vis non-Western states and regions.

Development Policy

Established in 1961 to succeed a European steering committee for Marshall Plan reconstruction aid from the US, the Organisation for Economic Co-operation and Development (OECD) is today a club of 34 governments of upper-income countries, including former aid recipients such as South Korea, Chile, and Poland. Guided mainly by orthodox economic precepts, it promotes consensus on aid and socio-economic development. The OECD's influence works through its vast linkages with governments and private-sector actors. It carries out "peer reviews" among official agencies and runs sophisticated communication strategies to make its findings virtually gospel among political classes. Rivalled only by the World Bank as an official think-tank, the OECD produces large streams of analytical reports, data, technical standards, and policy proposals. Some of those policies are generated through open, public processes, but many—notably about corporate investment and taxation—are prepared behind closed doors. For governments and opinion-makers, the OECD is a vital source of concepts, knowledge, and discourse. It has actively promoted macroeconomic orthodoxies, such as the Washington Consensus (see Chapter 9). More recently and positively, however, some units of the OECD have begun putting forward research findings and policy proposals on issues such as inequality, tax avoidance, quality-of-life indicators, and environmental threats.

European Organizations

The European Commission (EC), headquartered in Brussels, is the executive branch of the European Union (EU), which today consists of 27 Western and Eastern European countries. Only Norway, Switzerland, and most nations of the former Yugoslavia are not members of the EU. The EC is today one of the world's largest single sources of multilateral aid, accounting for about one-third of all multilateral aid spending and for about 10 to 12 per cent of total world official aid. Aid from the EC and from European bilateral donors together accounts for about two-thirds of total net aid from OECD countries.

The EC manages its relations with low-income countries through several ministries or Directorates General. In 2010 it created a "super-ministry" for foreign affairs, the **European External Action Service** (EEAS). Among sub-ministries is the Directorate General for Development and Cooperation (DG DEVCO), which designs and manages EU development and aid policies, with special attention to Europe's ex-colonies, formally referred to as the ACP (Africa-Caribbean-Pacific) countries. Working closely with it is the EC's Humanitarian Aid and Civil Protection Department (ECHO). As an interlocking set of bureaucracies, the EC is plagued by poor management, infighting over bureaucratic turf, above-average overhead costs, slow delivery, lack of transparency, an overload of objectives, and spending biases towards better-off countries in its near abroad—that is, North Africa and Southeast Europe. The coherence of its strategies is often in question. What Europe gives in aid is far surpassed by what it takes by way of trade deals, natural resource extraction (uranium and fish from West Africa, for example), and especially capital flowing to offshore financial centres under European jurisdictions. This redistribution from poor to rich underscores criticism that multilateralism helps to conceal old predatory relationships and to prettify them as neutral, market-based "partnerships."

Less well-known is a separate official European body, the Council of Europe (COE). In 1949, governments of 10 Western European countries signed a treaty creating it, with a mandate to promote human rights, democracy, and the rule of law throughout Europe. Its founding strategic purpose was socio-political cohesion and thus stability at a time when political and trade union movements were seeking greater social justice. Headquartered in Strasbourg, France, the COE now has 47 members, including lower-income countries, such as Armenia and Macedonia, formerly in the Soviet sphere of influence. Canada, Japan, and the US are among those with COE observer status.

In its human rights conventions, the COE sets standards for domestic legislation to combat discrimination and social exclusion. Under COE auspices, the European Court of Human Rights was set up in 1959 to enforce obligations established in 1950 under the European Convention for the Protection of Human Rights and Fundamental Freedoms—the first international legal instrument safeguarding human rights on a broad basis. The COE's committees, conferences, and research units regularly draw attention to gaps between formal adherence to and actual compliance with human rights norms. This includes socio-economic rights, notably those affirmed in the 1961 European Social Charter, an important but often neglected multilateral treaty ratified by more than 40 states.

The COE's Development Bank, founded in 1956 and based in Paris, is Europe's oldest multilateral financial institution and the only one with a mandate to promote social solidarity. Its loans go to public-sector bodies in support of social integration (housing, rehabilitation of poverty-hit zones), environmental protection, and human services in health and education. The COE is mandated to follow basic societal purposes rather than conventional "development" objectives. Perhaps for that reason it is often overlooked among multilateral organizations. Yet its mandate predates by four decades the normative themes of human rights, social cohesion, and democracy that are the talk of today's multilateral development organizations.

"Sphere of Influence" Organizations

Since recognizing the formal sovereignty of states in Africa, Asia, and Latin America, Western powers have sought to maintain ties with their former colonies or dependencies. To this end, they set up organizations with active secretariats mandated to promote policy dialogue, cultural ties, and even development efforts. The major Western **sphere of influence** bodies include the Organization of American States, la Francophonie, and the Commonwealth.

The Organization of American States (OAS) originated from US efforts in the 1880s to advance its commercial interests in Latin America. When the Cold War began, amid fears of left-leaning social movements, the US began to link its security and intelligence-gathering policies with its aid efforts. In 1948, twenty Latin American governments and the US signed the charter of the OAS; in later decades, 13 Caribbean countries and Canada also joined. Cuba was expelled in 1962. Headquartered in Washington, DC, the OAS works to influence political and business elites on issues of development, women's status, drug trafficking, and human rights. It convenes special committees and intergovernmental conferences. The US enlisted the OAS in efforts to create the Free Trade Area of the Americas, a larger version of its highly contested North American Free Trade Agreement (NAFTA) with Canada and Mexico, but after 2003 that US-driven initiative became a dead letter. Meanwhile, multilateral arrangements driven by Latin American governments, some of which are noted later in this chapter, are moving ahead.

The Organisation internationale de la Francophonie (OIF) comprises 57 member states in which French culture and the French language play at least some role in national identity. Canada is a member, and Quebec has the status of "participating government." Founded in 1970 as the Agence de coopération culturelle et technique, la Francophonie is headquartered in Paris, with regional offices in Gabon, Togo, and Vietnam. Promotion of the French language and encouragement of cultural diversity are its chief purposes. As with comparable bodies, it also supports activities to foster respect for human rights and democracy and to improve education, media, information technology, the environment, and the economy—in particular, the integration of member nations into the world economy. France's decline as an imperial power and weaknesses and divisions among members of the club have cumulatively weakened the OIF, despite some efforts by Canada to shore it up.

The Commonwealth of Nations, known before 1950 as the British Commonwealth, consists of 53 countries, all but two of them (Mozambique and Rwanda) ex-colonies of Great Britain. A number of Middle Eastern and Arab-aligned countries such as Sudan, though eligible, have declined to join. With a secretariat in London since 1965, the Commonwealth organizes gatherings of public officials and business people for diverse political, cultural, and commercial purposes. Its Commonwealth Foundation facilitates interchange among professional associations and non-governmental organizations. In 1997, the Commonwealth Business Council was set up to promote trade, investment, corporate social responsibility, and public–private partnerships.

MULTILATERAL ORGANIZATIONS ANCHORED IN NON-WESTERN GOVERNMENTS

In the twentieth century, the triumph of nationalist parties and insurgent armies over the colonial powers created optimism about collective action in non-Western countries. It also gave rise to a number of multilateral arrangements, including regional political alliances (e.g., the League of Arab States, 1945) and trade groups (e.g., the East African Community, from 1967 to 1977, then revived in 1999). Created on crests of enthusiasm, many of these groupings later became dormant or died altogether, the victims of internal difficulties or external pressures. Today, however, some of them are steering global politics towards complex yet possibly more equitable balances of power.

Lobbying Blocs

A 1955 conference in Bandung, Indonesia, was the first multilateral forum in which non-Western leaders voiced their collective demands for an end to colonialism. They also denounced their countries' adverse integration into the world economic system. Six years later, the same group, reinforced by newly independent African countries, set up the Non-Aligned Movement (NAM), an association without a charter but oriented by UN principles. Today it comprises 120 member states and 17 observer countries; its Co-Coordinating Bureau is based at the UN in New York. Founded to counter the Cold War, the NAM seeks to uphold "the right of independent judgement, the struggle against imperialism and neo-colonialism, and the use of moderation in relations with all big powers."

Wishing to form a coherent front in trade talks with rich countries, non-Western countries attending the UNCTAD in 1964 created the Group of 77 or G77 (see Toye, 2014). Today enlarged to 131 members, including China, the G77 operates as an informal caucus. Its representatives gather annually at the UN General Assembly meeting and sometimes at UNCTAD assemblies. In 1974 the G77 proposed a New International Economic Order (NIEO). Led by Iran, Venezuela, Mexico, and Algeria (countries whose treasuries were then filling up with petro-dollars on the strength of higher oil prices), the G77 wanted three things: faster economic growth, greater integration into the world trading system, and more foreign aid. These were hardly radical claims; indeed, they posed little threat to the global status quo. Yet Western powers rejected them and began sidelining UNCTAD. Since then, the attentions of key G77 members India, China, and Brazil have shifted to activities with Russia under the auspices of the BRICS (see below). Yet the G77 has gained new means to propose alternatives in the creation of two Geneva-based think-tanks: the South Centre, which accounts to some 51 non-Western governments, and the non-governmental International Centre for Trade and Sustainable Development.

Under G77 auspices, a smaller grouping, the Intergovernmental Group of Twenty-Four on International Monetary Affairs and Development (G24), emerged in 1971 to co-ordinate and sharpen views towards the IMF and World Bank. With a liaison office in Washington, DC, the G24 pursues policy dialogue and publishes hard-hitting research often critical of elite orthodoxies.

While some of the older non-Western blocs have suffered marginalization and decline, new linkages have emerged. Among them is a grouping of major economies of a non-Western bloc: Brazil, Russia, India, China, and South Africa—collectively known as BRICS (see Chapter 6). That semi-formal association exemplifies intentions by non-core governments to go their own way, sidestepping tutelage by institutions based in Washington, DC.

Regional Blocs

Governments across the world have sought to improve prospects, especially of their larger businesses, through economic pacts, or *regional trading arrangements* (RTAs). Sometimes called developmental regionalism, this strategy has advanced as an alternative to standard arrangements promoting economic openness towards the rich countries of the North—strategies that have exposed many to predatory globalization.

Among Asian nations, there is a veritable "noodle bowl" of RTAs. The oldest of these is the Association of Southeast Asian Nations (ASEAN), founded in 1967 by the leaders of Indonesia, Malaysia, the Philippines, Singapore, and Thailand. Initially fearful of Communist advances in Asia, ASEAN has since admitted Vietnam along with Brunei, Burma, Cambodia, and Laos. The year 2016 saw the proclamation of an overarching ASEAN Community, built on the original RTA economic pillar and newer pillars for collective security and socio-cultural relations. Meanwhile, bigger powers are pushing their own brands of multilateralism in Asia, such as the Regional Comprehensive Economic Partnership led by China and the Trans-Pacific Partnership led by the US and Japan.

In Latin America, a major RTA is the Mercado Común del Sur (MERCOSUR), or Southern Common Market, founded in 1991 by Brazil, Argentina, Uruguay, and Paraguay and joined in 2006 by Venezuela. Since 2004, a more ambitious initiative has developed—a Unión de Naciones Suramericanas (UNASUR), or Union of South American Nations, a merger of MERCOSUR with its older counterpart, the Comunidad Andina, or Andean Community, composed of Bolivia, Colombia, Ecuador, and Peru. Modelled on the European Union, UNASUR has helped lower barriers to trade and travel and has ambitions to issue a common South American currency. It has approved the idea of a common Latin American citizenship (including a single passport) and of a South American parliament, for which a building is now under construction in Cochabamba, Bolivia. In late 2011, regional leaders formally established a supranational bloc, Comunidade de Estados

Latino-Americanos e Caribe (CELAC) or Community of Latin American and Caribbean States, composed of 33 sovereign states. In essence, CELAC serves as an alternative to the OAS, whose legitimacy (as a US-dominated body) is in decline in Latin America.

Africa is home to a number of RTAs, many of them dormant. Large differences in economic capabilities and uneasy political relationships among governments, as well as the reinforcement of bilateral deal-making with richer countries, have set limits to integration in Africa.

Have regional blocs promoted equitable development? Results thus far have been modest at best. New trade arrangements may have boosted output, but that growth has usually been uneven and often inequitable, as stronger economies tend to reap larger shares of benefits. Nevertheless, multilateralism informed by principles of mutual advantage, especially within dynamic regions such as Latin America, provides impulses for more equitable development and political power.

ONE WORLD, MANY REGIONS

This chapter has noted the rise, and in some cases the decline, of three kinds of multilateral organizations. A factor found in the histories of many of them is the role of a hegemonic power, the United States. Together with several other "Anglo-Saxon" states, the US has influenced development agendas, determining which issues are to be managed multilaterally and how. Using their political, diplomatic, and especially economic power, Western states have successfully enlisted multilateral bodies in spreading standard policy formulas about how non-Western places should develop and be governed. Whereas terms such as "equity," "non-alignment," and "self-determination" once inspired multilateralism, today we hear private business terms such as "global competitiveness" and "public–private partnerships." Using the latter vocabulary, many multilateral bodies today propagate a new "common sense," thereby frustrating the emergence of more equitable and democratic norms of development. As a result, a number of UN and other multilateral institutions have lost legitimacy, especially for those outside zones of privilege and especially in non-Western regions of the world.

Nonetheless, transnational initiatives are emerging on other planes. Social and political movements are sharing ideas and demonstrating new solidarities. In the progressive camp of civil society some of this bottom-up multilateralism has created political leverage for responsive and equitable development, as demonstrated in the cases of women's rights, weapons control, and environmental sanity. In what measure this kind of public action will continue promoting emancipatory outcomes—or violent backlash born of humiliation and anger—is central to the unfolding dramas of change across the globe today.

BOX 10.2 | Multilateralism: Which Way Forward?

CURRENT EVENTS

Political analyst Jens Martens holds that multilateralism has reached a fork in the road. It could continue serving powerful interests, or it could reanimate founding norms and accountability rules that take needs and rights of the less advantaged fully into account.

> International politics is at a crossroads. On the one hand, the path towards an elite multilateralism, which shifts decisions on global policy increasingly into exclusive clubs and political circles while excluding democratic control and participation; on the other, the path to a multilateralism of solidarity, which emphasizes and strengthens the responsibility of democratically legitimate public institutions and complements this through a comprehensive involvement of civil society organizations and the well-regulated interaction with the private sector. In the spirit of the UN Charter, one can only hope that over time, this model of a multilateralism of solidarity will prevail over the elite club model of global politics. (Martens, 2007: 6)

SUMMARY

This chapter has aimed to widen understanding of multilateral organizations, particularly of the ideas and material measures that have guided and hindered these organizations' pursuit of developmental and humanitarian mandates. It has presented facts and analyses about their operations and lines of accountability within systems of geopolitics, especially the United Nations, after 1945. Those lines of accountability and funding routinely converge on Western powers, led by the United States. Some multilateral challenges to those powers have arisen from successful states in East Asia and Latin America, as well as from non-state actors elsewhere. Further, we have seen how corporations exert influence over multilateral bodies, especially those of the UN. Inasmuch as many of the ideas and policies outlined here are routinely debated, designed, set in motion, or frustrated by multilateral organizations, this chapter may allow deeper understanding of developmental issues discussed elsewhere in this book.

QUESTIONS FOR CRITICAL THOUGHT

1. Given the grossly unequal distributions of power and wealth, how can multilateral initiatives produce more equitable development outcomes?
2. Why would some countries prefer to engage in multilateral arrangements "à la carte" rather than to accept comprehensive international agreements?
3. How might multilateral arrangements among countries of a specific region, or among countries sharing cultural affinities, lead to positive development outcomes?
4. World politics today are said to face a choice between elite multilateralism and a multilateralism of solidarity (see Box 10.2). What forces have created this choice? Which kind of multilateralism would you bet on in the long run, and why?
5. Given the emergence of new powers in the Global South, to what extent will traditional North–South fractures continue to dominate multilateral processes?

SUGGESTED READINGS

Adams, Barbara, and Jens Martens. 2015. *Fit for Whose Purpose? Private Funding and Corporate Influence in the United Nations*. Bonn and New York: Global Policy Forum. www.globalpolicy.org/images/pdfs/images/pdfs/Fit_for_whose_purpose_online.pdf.

Bøås, Morten, and Desmond McNeill. 2003. *Multilateral Institutions: A Critical Introduction*. London: Pluto Press.

Cox, Robert W., ed. 1997. *The New Realism: Perspectives on Multilateralism and World Order*. Tokyo: United Nations University Press

Gowan, Peter. 2003. "US: UN." *New Left Review* 24: 5–28.

Jenks, Bruce, and Bruce Jones. 2013. *United Nations Development at a Crossroads*. New York: Center on International Cooperation, New York University. http://cic.nyu.edu/content/united-nations-development-crossroads.

McKeon, Nora. 2009. *The United Nations and Civil Society: Legitimating Global Governance—Whose Voice?* London: Zed Books

Malone, David, and Rohinton P. Medhora. 2014. *Development: Advancement through International Organizations*. Waterloo, Ont.: Centre for International Governance Innovation. www.cigionline.org/sites/default/files/cigi_paper_31.pdf.

Mazower, Mark. 2009. *No Enchanted Palace: The End of Empire and the Ideological Origins of the United Nations*. Princeton, NJ: Princeton University Press.

NOTE

1. Each UN member state's minimum contribution is 0.001 per cent of the UN's budget, an amount paid by 53 countries. Currently, the US pays about 22 per cent of the UN's budget. If assessments were based purely on each country's share of the world's gross domestic product, the US would pay about 30 per cent and some poor countries less than the 0.001 per cent minimum (CRS, 2013: 37).

BIBLIOGRAPHY

Browne, S. 2014. "A changing world: Is the UN development system ready?" *Third World Quarterly* 35, 10: 1845–59.

Congressional Research Service (CRS). 2013. *United Nations System Funding: Congressional Issues*. Washington: CRS.

Jenks, B. 2014. "Financing the UN development system and the future of multilateralism." *Third World Quarterly* 35, 10: 1809–28.

Martens, J. 2007. *Multistakeholder Partnerships—Future Models of Multilateralism?* Dialogue on Globalization, Occasional Paper 29. Berlin: Friedrich Ebert Stiftung.

Normand, R., and S. Zaidi. 2008. *Human Rights at the UN: The Political History of Universal Justice*. Bloomington: Indiana University Press.

Picciotto, R. 2014. *The UN Has Lost the Aid-Effectiveness Race: What Is To Be Done?* Briefing 14. Future United Nations Development System (FUNDS). New York: CUNY.

Standing, G. 2008. "The ILO: An agency for globalization?" *Development and Change* 39, 3: 355–84.

Toye, J. 2014. "Assessing the G77: 50 years after UNCTAD and 40 years after the NIEO." *Third World Quarterly* 35, 10: 1759–74.

United Nations. 2012. *Independent Evaluation of Delivering as One, Summary Report*. UN document A/66/859, June. www.un.org/en/ga/deliveringasone/.

Utting, P., and A. Zammit. 2009. "United Nations–business partnerships: Good intentions and contradictory agendas." *Journal of Business Ethics* 90: 39–56.

Wilkinson, R. 2014. *The WTO, the UN, and the Future of Global Development: What Matters and Why*. Briefing 15. Future United Nations Development System (FUNDS). New York: CUNY.

11 Private Enterprise and Development

Paul A. Haslam

LEARNING OBJECTIVES

- To understand the importance of the private sector in development and poverty alleviation.
- To identify the roles of small-scale entrepreneurship and large firms in development.
- To differentiate between different kinds of strategies employed by multinational corporations and their effects.
- To distinguish between the direct effect of the private sector on development and its indirect effect as mediated by government regulation and in collaboration with other actors via partnerships.

▲ **Olga Martinez at her outdoor workshop where she re-upholsters seats for vans and buses on Avenida La Castellana, south of Guatemala City. Work in the informal sector occupies an important place in Latin American economies.** | Source: ORLANDO SIERRA/AFP/Getty Images

The private sector is one of the most contentious, maligned, and misunderstood actors in international development. Important private-sector actors, particularly multinationals, are often associated, in the popular imagination, with various acts of malfeasance, including low wages and exploitation in sweatshops, environmental catastrophes, human rights abuses, unethical practices, and corruption. And yet, the domestic private sector and foreign multinationals operating in developing countries are responsible for much more investment and many more jobs than foreign aid programs—and good jobs are ultimately what development is about. At the same time, we can point to major multinationals, some of the same ones you might associate with some of the negative consequences listed above, that have also acted constructively to support local communities and economic development.

Increasingly, governments and development agencies are looking at ways to leverage private-sector investment to contribute to more and better economic development. And companies are beginning to realize that being a responsible corporate citizen in developing countries can be good for both profits and communities. The picture, then, is complex. Although the role of companies in development often generates heated debate between those who view them as scoundrels and those who view them as heroes, this chapter aims to steer between these polarized positions to present a balanced picture of the contribution the private sector can make to development, and how this role is affected by corporate strategy, the relations between firms and governments, and partnerships.

ENTREPRENEURSHIP AND SMALL-SCALE ENTERPRISE

In common parlance, when we refer to the "private sector," we generally include all privately owned organizations, the purpose of which is to make a profit for their owners or shareholders. In other words, we would include in this definition the smallest entrepreneur who sells coffee and fried food out of a shopping cart, a plumber, a web designer who works from home, a small shop owner, a medium-sized manufacturing company with 20 employees, and a multinational corporation that operates in 80 countries and makes billions of dollars in profits every year. Some privately funded organizations, such as corporate charities or philanthropic organizations built on private fortunes, occupy an ambiguous position: insofar as they are independent of corporate influence and pursue a social purpose, we generally consider them civil society organizations, although they may retain the "can-do" and entrepreneurial culture of their founders.

It is important to remember that the private sector is the engine of capitalist economies, even where there is an important role for the public sector. Businesses make investments and hire people to make and sell goods and services at a freely determined price on the market (without significant government interference). When they do well, growth, jobs, and usually development are the result. When businesses do less well, or fail, growth declines, jobs are lost, poverty increases, and individuals need the support of governments, communities, and family members to survive. In this respect, creating an environment in which the private sector can flourish and grow is essential to good development.

Joseph Schumpeter (1883–1950) was the first to theorize about **entrepreneurship** and its role in capitalist economic development. For Schumpeter, the function of the entrepreneur was to innovate: he or she had a kind of special ability to see new ways to put economic factors together to cause economic growth, such as new products, new productive processes, or accessing new markets. As an approach to explaining what pushes capitalism forward, his argument was agent-focused, rather than relying on abstract categories like "accumulation of capital" or "investment." Someone *does something* with capital. In this regard, Schumpeter links the leadership of special individuals, innovation, and economic growth and development (Thomas, 1987: 174). However, it fell to later theorists to address what conditions facilitated the emergence of entrepreneurs.

The distinction between small entrepreneurs and larger firms is fundamental. In many developing economies smaller firms are more likely to be locally owned, while large firms are more likely to be foreign. Formally registered small and medium-sized enterprises (SMEs) face many problems in developing countries and generally fail to develop into larger enterprises, but they do have some access to financing. In the **informal economy**, we find the micro-enterprises and independent entrepreneurs operating businesses that aren't legally registered, can't get bank financing, don't pay taxes, and don't follow labour or health and safety regulations. The informal economy is of principal interest for this discussion because in developing countries, most entrepreneurial activity (in terms of employment) takes place in this sector, and it is often a survival strategy for the very poor that is precarious and with little potential for growth.

Recent thinking on how entrepreneurship is held back in developing countries has focused on the problem of **informality**. Hernán de Soto, in his classic text *The Mystery of Capital*, argues that poor entrepreneurs are unable to convert the assets they control into capital because of an inadequate property rights regime. Those working in the informal sector in developing countries often don't have clear legal title to the assets they effectively control (such as a house built on unoccupied land in a slum), and without legal title they don't have the collateral to get a formal loan. From de Soto's perspective, property rights allow people to imagine the diverse ways that capital can be employed, while creating the right incentives for individual productivity (providing collateral, individual accountability by association with a credit history, and protection from theft). In this regard, the absence of enforceable property rights is a kind of "missing link" that condemns entrepreneurs to small-scale, unproductive, and precarious investments (de Soto, 2000).

This line of thinking was taken up by a high-level UN Commission on the Private Sector and Development (2004), which proposed a set of reforms to make business work for the poor. The Commission agreed with de Soto (who was a member) that widespread informality and weak property rights were the root causes holding micro-enterprise back in developing countries. However, they also noted that the excessively bureaucratic and costly process required to register a

IMPORTANT CONCEPTS

BOX 11.1 | Micro-Finance: Building Entrepreneurship?

One of the most widely used tools to promote entrepreneurship in developing countries is **micro-finance**: the granting of small nominal loans to would-be entrepreneurs. Micro-finance came to worldwide attention through the work of Muhammad Yunus, who established the Grameen Bank in Bangladesh and won the Nobel Peace Prize for his work in 2006. Yunus established a system in which small loans would be granted to individual women organized within a larger group under the principle of collective responsibility (if one failed to repay, they would all lose access to the loans). Repayment of the loan was a gateway to more loans, and failure to pay resulted in exclusion from the system. The system also involved compulsory savings by participants and intensive surveillance by caseworkers. This model of micro-finance used collective responsibility to substitute for a lack of collateral or property rights. It also promoted the empowerment of women in patriarchal societies by giving them access to loans and promoting solidarity and friendships with other women (Yunus, 2003).

Micro-finance is not without its problems. On the one hand, it can create indebtedness that is difficult for the poor to escape if their businesses are unsuccessful. As micro-finance has been scaled up to reach millions, there is also some evidence that normal financial criteria (such as having collateral) have become more important, meaning that micro-loans are not reaching the extremely poor. Perhaps most important is the gender critique (see Chapter 5), which points out that women are ideal clients for microcredit (more likely to repay) because they are disadvantaged by social norms (unable to move, dependent on their husbands, and with limited property rights or alternatives). In this regard, the microcredit system exploits the vulnerability of women while claiming to empower them. Studies have also shown that many women lose control over the use of their loans to male relatives, while remaining responsible for repayment (Goetz and Sen Gupta, 1996).

business made informality a logical choice for many entrepreneurs. For example, in Peru it takes an entrepreneur an estimated 278 days to formally register and open a business (de Soto, 2000). In this regard, the Commission insisted that three pillars were necessary to develop the entrepreneurial sector: a level playing field with fair rules and enforcement (to permit businesses to establish themselves easily); access to credit; and support for the development of skills and knowledge (human capital). This meant that the state had to work actively to create an enabling environment for entrepreneurship, including formalizing the economy. The authors of the report also recommended that multinational corporations work with governments to play an active role in coaching smaller companies through partnerships and developing skills.

WHAT IS A MULTINATIONAL CORPORATION?

While it is generally agreed that the promotion of small enterprise and local SMEs is good for development, the role of multinational corporations (MNCs) is much more contentious. Various terms are used to describe multinational corporations and their activities, including transnational corporations (TNCs), **multinational enterprises** (MNEs), and foreign direct investment (FDI). Overall, these terms can be and are used interchangeably. Differences between them stem principally from disciplinary and institutional divides and practices: MNC is the most widely used term, employed by political scientists, sociologists, and the media; TNC is the preferred terminology of the United Nations system; and MNE is used in international business studies. FDI is a catch-all phrase, often preferred by economists, which refers to investment that is made across borders. The word "direct" in "foreign direct investment" indicates that the investment has a physical presence or corporate form (such as a branch plant) and differentiates this mode of investment from indirect investment, also known as "foreign portfolio investment" or colloquially as "hot capital" flows, which include the purchase of foreign debt, loans, and stock market investments. Foreign direct investment is much more stable than portfolio investment, since it involves an investment in physical and productive assets such as buildings, technology, and labour, which are more costly to abandon.

John Dunning, the pre-eminent authority on the multinational corporation, defines it as an "enterprise that engages in foreign direct investment (FDI) and owns or controls value-adding activities in more than one country" (1993: 3). According to Dunning, the two key features of the MNC that distinguish it from other enterprises are that it co-ordinates value-adding activities across national borders (that is, it creates some kind of product based on bringing together productive assets from different places in the world, including capital, labour, technology, management expertise, and know-how); and it internalizes the cross-border transfer of inputs used in the production process (in other words, these transfers take place within the firm and do not occur on the open market) (Dunning, 1993: 4). In this respect, the MNC is a "hierarchy," meaning it has an organizational structure based on command and control, and is distinct from a market, in which the price mechanism, not management, co-ordinates relationships.

Although the two principles identified by Dunning apply to all multinationals, the reality of the universe of over 82,000 MNCs and 800,000 foreign affiliates is that their size and the degree to which they are internationalized vary greatly (Dunning, 1993: 3; UNCTAD, 2006: 10; UNCTAD, 2009: 223). Furthermore, the top 100 of these corporations are highly concentrated, controlling a significant proportion of total foreign assets, sales, and employment of all multinationals. Their proportion of sales and assets has increased significantly over recent years, illustrating that the world's largest multinational corporations are growing relative to the rest of the pack. Furthermore, the world's 100 largest MNCs are also disproportionately from the developed countries: 89 come from the US, Japan, and Europe, and only eight are from developing countries (UNCTAD, 2013). Although multinationals from developing countries remain much smaller, they are rapidly growing and becoming increasingly transnationalized (see Box 11.5).

Contrary to popular belief, MNCs from rich countries historically have invested more in other rich countries than in developing countries. However, in 2014, FDI to developing and transition countries reached a historically high proportion, amounting to 55 per cent of total flows. FDI to Asia drove these figures: that region received 68 per cent of the flows to developing and transition economies, while Africa received less than 8 per cent (UNCTAD, 2015a: 2–3). However, foreign direct investment constitutes the single most important source of new money for developing countries, with the possible exception of remittances from migrant workers, about which there are few reliable figures. If we compare the net inflows of different sources of capital to developing countries, FDI inflows to developing and transition economies accounted for US$681 billion in 2014, as compared to approximately $135 billion in official development assistance (ODA) (UNCTAD, 2015a: 3). These figures are in marked contrast to the beginning of the 1990s, when ODA, at just over $50 billion of net inflows, was twice as large as FDI, and commercial loans and portfolio flows were at a similar level to direct investment (UNCTAD, 2006: 5). In the least developed countries, total ODA (from bilateral and multilateral sources) exceeds the value of FDI ($47 billion to $23 billion in 2013), but both have doubled in value over the last decade (UNCTAD, 2015a: 78). Overall, foreign direct investment and the activities of multinational corporations have become relatively more important to many developing countries than other sources of capital over the past two decades.

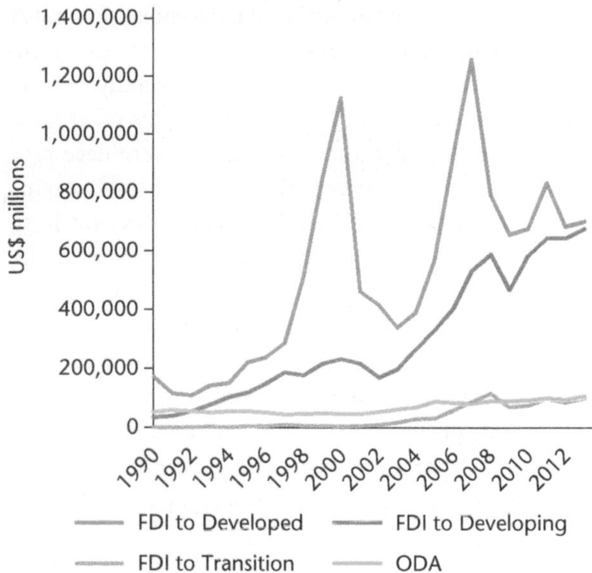

FIGURE 11.1 | FDI and ODA Flows to Developed and Developing Economies, 1990–2013

Sources: UNCTAD (2015b); World Bank (2015).

However, it must be stressed that most of the FDI inflows to the developing world are concentrated in a handful of the more dynamic and industrialized developing countries. Six countries—China, Hong Kong (considered separately from China in FDI figures), Singapore, Brazil, India, and Mexico—attracted over 60 per cent of all inflows to the developing world in 2014 and have consistently done so for a decade (UNCTAD, 2015a: 4). Furthermore, FDI figures do not always indicate new productive investments, known as "greenfield" investments, and thus should be viewed with caution. Mergers and acquisitions (M&As), in which a foreign company buys out a local company, involve only a transfer of funds, not an investment in building new facilities or in employing more people. In 2005, cross-border M&As made up 78 per cent of world FDI inflows; in 2014 they made up 36 per cent (UNCTAD, 2006: 9; UNCTAD, 2015a: 11). Foreign investment figures may also erroneously include domestic investment that has been routed through organizations and countries located abroad (known as "round-tripping") in order to benefit from preferential incentives and protection offered by some governments to foreign investors (UNCTAD, 2006: 12). Thus, the geographic concentration and the mode of entry of massive inflows of money indicated by global figures can be somewhat misleading as to their developmental impact. Such caveats about the available figures and their meaning point to the difficulty of evaluating the effect of FDI on host economies.

WHAT MOTIVATES MULTINATIONALS TO GO ABROAD?

Why firms internationalize by establishing branch plants or subsidiaries abroad, instead of by trade, is one of the most important questions in the study of multinational corporations. A second and related question is what effect this internationalization has on the politics, economy, and society of the host country. As in most areas of the social sciences, the answers to these questions vary according to the theoretical and ideological frameworks used to analyze them. At the risk of some

TABLE 11.1 | Largest Multinational Corporations by Assets, Including from Developing Countries, 2012 (US$ millions)

Rank	Corporation	Home Country	Industry	Foreign Assets	Total Assets	Foreign Assets as % of Total
1	General Electric	USA	electrical and electronic	338,157	685,328	49
2	CITIC Group	China	diversified	71,512	514,847	14
3	Volkswagen Group	Germany	motor vehicles	158,046	409,257	39
4	Toyota Motor Corporation	Japan	motor vehicles	233,193	376,841	62
5	Royal Dutch Shell	UK	petroleum	307,938	360,325	85
6	Exxon Mobile Corporation	USA	petroleum	214,349	333,795	64
7	EDF SA	France	utilities	103,015	330,582	31
8	BP plc	UK	petroleum	270,247	300,193	90
13	Vodafone Group	UK	telecom	199,003	217,031	92
24	Petronas Petroleum	Malaysia	petroleum	38,907	150,435	26
28	Statoil ASA	Norway	petroleum	71,127	140,511	51
30	Nestlé SA	Switzerland	food, beverages	132,686	138,212	96
34	Vale SA	Brazil	mining	45,721	131,478	35
35	BHP Billiton Group	Australia	mining	62,284	129,273	48
50	Hutchison Whampoa	Hong Kong	diversified	85,721	103,715	83
60	Vattenfall AB	Sweden	electricity, gas, and water	54,165	81,269	67
68	Hon Hai Precision Industries	Taiwan	electrical and electronics	65,471	70,448	93
70	América Móvil SAB de CV	Mexico	telecom	32,694	67,590	48
81	VimpelCom Ltd	Russia	telecom	33,381	55,360	60
82	AstraZeneca PLO	UK	pharmaceuticals	41,218	53,534	77
83	China Ocean Shipping (Group) Company (COSCO)	China	transport	40,435	52,230	77
86	Teva Pharma-ceutical Industries	Israel	pharmaceuticals	37,394	50,609	74
89	Barrick Gold Corporation	Canada	mining	45,335	47,282	96
97	Koninklijke Phillips Electronics	Netherlands	electrical and electronics	35,937	38,434	94
99	Cemex S.A.B. de Mexico	Mexico	mining	30,730	36,808	83

Source: UNCTAD (2013). Reprinted with the permission of the United Nations.

simplification, we can point to three main approaches to understanding the internationalization of the multinational corporation: a critical approach inspired by Marxism; the mercantile or nationalist approach; and the liberal or international business approach. Each approach reveals different facets of the MNC and its activities.

Dependency and Critical Approaches

Generally speaking, authors in the Marxist-inspired or critical tradition have tended to view multinational corporations as representatives of the global capitalist system and therefore as having a negative impact on the developing countries in which they invest. The dominant current in this approach has been dependency theory, although to be fair, dependency exhibits a wide range of attitudes towards foreign capital, some of which are quite ambivalent as to its beneficial or destructive effects (see Chapter 3). Much recent writing by activist scholars critical of the exploitation of workers and the environment by multinational corporations, although no longer embedded in Marxism, continues to be inspired by the vision if not by the letter of this perspective and its critique of global capitalism (see Klein, 2015; Korten, 2015).

The pioneers of dependency theory attributed an important role to multinational corporations in the maintenance of underdevelopment in the periphery. The structuralist critique in its original formulation by Raúl Prebisch was a trade-based explanation of underdevelopment (see Chapter 3). Later variations, drawing more explicitly on Marxism, focused on the role of multinational corporations in organizing this trading relationship and their impact on the productive structure of developing countries. Paul Baran argued that multinational corporations, through the **international division of labour** (IDL), in which high-value manufacturing remained in the core countries and commodity and resource extraction was conducted in developing countries, maintained and deepened the underdevelopment of the periphery. Profits made in the periphery were sent back to the head offices in the core countries of the North. Subsequent versions of this idea, known as the **new international division of labour** (NIDL), argued that manufacturing MNCs sought out Third World locations for their low-cost labour while maintaining high-value-added manufacturing in the developed countries with similar exploitative effects. Baran also pointed to the political alliances formed between multinational corporations and local elites uninterested in the social welfare of the poor in their countries. He described this alliance as a "political and social coalition of wealthy compradores, powerful monopolists [MNCs] and large landowners dedicated to the defense of the existing social order" (as cited in Evans, 1979: 20).

In this respect, multinational corporations change how countries (or rather, elites in those countries) perceive their interests. When multinational corporations control the major industries and a national bourgeoisie is absent, weak, or co-opted by MNCs, autonomous local development is impossible. That is, the logic of industrialization follows the needs of external agents, not internal ones (Amin, 1990: 11). This may lead to business choices that are dysfunctional for local development. For example, it is argued that foreign export-oriented multinationals are not interested in expanding local markets or in the buying power of local consumers (beyond sales to elites), use capital-intensive productive processes that create few jobs, have few links with local firms, and bring with them a cultural demonstration effect that encourages conspicuous consumption by elites.

More sophisticated dependency analyses pointed out that a specific kind of development and industrialization can occur under the aegis of multinational corporations in the larger Third World economies—what Cardoso and Faletto called "associated dependent development." Peter Evans (1979) made this argument most forcefully by pointing to the "triple alliance" among the Brazilian state, multinational corporations, and locally owned firms. He argued that the state can act as an autonomous class actor or state bourgeoisie by creating its own state-owned firms and promoting joint ventures involving the state, multinational corporations, and local firms. In this way, the state pushes industrialization forward by benefiting from the technology, management skills, and capital contributed by foreign firms. Evans argued, however, that this industrialization has its limits, since it is oriented towards production for upper-class consumption needs. It is therefore inevitably elitist and excludes the popular masses (Evans, 1979: 38).

The Mercantile Approach and the National Interest

Another common approach to the multinational corporation is to see it as a representative of the political and economic interests of its home country. This approach has been particularly important in the study of US-based multinationals by both advocates of US hegemony and its detractors. But it is also seen elsewhere in the nationalist literature of all countries (particularly in Japan and South Korea), which advocates the formation of large domestic firms or national champions capable of internationalizing and competing at the world level. Robert Gilpin argued that the era of multinationals corresponds with the era of American hegemony. The US actively promoted the expansion of its firms, particularly oil companies, for a number of reasons: to establish a safe supply of natural resources (a strategy currently being copied by India and China); to supply cheap petroleum to fund its political–military Western alliance during the Cold War; to create a worldwide liberal and business-friendly culture; and to improve its balance of payments and fund its military spending by means of repatriated profits (Gilpin, 1975).

Beyond these general goals, evidence suggests that US administrations during the Cold War used their connections with certain multinational corporations to pursue specific foreign policy objectives in the developing world, including US attempts to undermine or overthrow "unfriendly" governments. Two cases in particular reinforced this opinion, the CIA-sponsored *coup d'état* in Guatemala (1954), which was often portrayed as defending the interests of the United Fruit Co., and the contacts between the CIA and International Telephone and Telegraph (ITT) in Chile in the period 1968 to 1970, which preceded the overthrow of socialist President Salvadore Allende (see Sagafi-Nejad, 2008: 41–7). In the contemporary period, this perspective remains relevant. Close ties between large multinationals and their home countries continue to exist, and many governments seek to support the activities of their firms internationally. Most countries continue to build "national champions," subsidize them through various means, and defend their companies at the World Trade Organization—well illustrated in the aircraft industry, where Airbus, Boeing, Bombardier, and Embraer have become the national champions, respectively, of the EU, the United States, Canada, and Brazil. Multinationals in extractive industries continue to play an important role in guaranteeing supplies of needed raw materials for resource-poor countries, as illustrated by the internationalization of Brazil's Petrobrás, Malaysia's Petronas, and China's China National Petroleum Company.

International Business Perspective

Whereas the mercantile and dependency approaches tend to view multinationals as homogeneous actors that are structurally determined by the global distribution of power and wealth, the international business perspective views them as differentiated actors with diverse strategies. From this perspective, the dominant explanation for the characteristics and internationalization of multinational corporations is the "eclectic" or **OLI paradigm** developed by John H. Dunning. This approach turns around two questions: (1) Is there a common nature or feature of the multinational that distinguishes it from other kinds of firms? (2) What explains the myriad forms of internationalization chosen by multinationals (subsidiary, joint-venture, equity participation, licensing)? One question gets at the multinational as institution and the other as actor.

According to the OLI paradigm, the multinational corporation is distinguished by ownership (O), location-specific (L), and internalization (I) advantages. *Ownership advantages* are those elements unique to the firm in question and generally not available to other firms, such as patents, processes, organizational abilities, marketing and management, and access to capital, resources, and markets. *Location-specific advantages* are those factors in a country where the investment takes place that work with the firm's other advantages and may include political (stability, political access and coverage, investment regime and protection), social (cultural, linguistic, ethnic commonalities), and economic (market size, market access, resources, workforce) factors. When location-specific assets abroad add something truly important to the firm's activities, then it will internationalize (become multinational) instead of simply trading with that country (Dunning, 2000: 164).

Internalization advantages are the advantages of co-ordinating production within the hierarchical governance structure of the firm instead of buying and selling the parts needed to produce any given product through arm's-length market relationships. Indeed, one of the key reasons why multinationals invest in production across borders is because international markets are overwhelmed by a vast number of market imperfections (known as transaction costs). By organizing production inside the multinational, selling and buying from itself through administratively determined **transfer prices**, it benefits from lower transaction costs and is able to fully exploit ownership advantages without losing control of them on the open market. Open market relationships are much more likely to allow competitors to copy key ownership advantages like product design, technology, and industrial processes and are thus avoided (Dunning, 1993: 76–9; Eden, 1991: 204–7). Although the multinational corporation is often represented as the paragon of free markets, in fact the very existence of the multinational proves that "free" markets are imperfect and inefficient!

However, as globalization has intensified, many transportation, communication, and organizational costs (i.e., important transaction costs) have declined, and companies have become more experienced with international production. As a result, companies are now more likely to take on a networked structure where many key relationships are governed by the market (like subcontracting to suppliers outside the corporate structure), and only the most important core competencies remain internalized, such as design, research, technology, and software development. Thus, although modern multinationals rely on outsourcing more than their predecessors, functions that are essential to

IMPORTANT CONCEPTS

BOX 11.2 | Global Value Chains and the New International Division of Labour

In the 1970s, multinationals started to move some of their manufacturing processes to the developing world. The production process, co-ordinated by MNCs, became increasingly globalized and hierarchical—low-skill and labour-intensive processes were located in low-wage developing countries, while high-skill, high-wage activities remained at home in the North. This phenomenon, known as the new international division of labour, was characterized by the fragmentation of the production process across borders (Ietto-Gilles, 2005: 206). **Global value chain** theory emerged in the early 1990s to better understand this globally fragmented process in which different companies in different countries provided distinct inputs into the production of a single product. It described the interconnections between companies involved as suppliers and contractors to a lead firm—usually a multinational corporation—that are necessary to bring a product to market. It also established a clear hierarchy of activities within the chain, with a multinational co-ordinating, or governing, the multitude of relationships between separate companies (Gereffi and Sturgeon, 2005).

One of the most interesting contemporary questions about value chains is whether local firms in developing countries that supply particular parts within the value chain of an MNC can learn from the lead company over time and upgrade their technological and management capabilities, become more competitive, and move up the value chain into higher-value-added activities. When companies move up the value chain, it is expected that they will contribute more to the development of their national economies by increasing employment, developing the skills of their workforce, and exporting. The evidence, thus far, on **upgrading** is mixed. The ability of a firm to upgrade (move up the chain) depends to some extent on its prior capabilities and its pattern of learning, as well as the governance structure used by the multinational co-ordinating the chain. A governance structure that is more open, more akin to a market or a network, rather than a hierarchy, is usually more conducive to upgrading (Gereffi et al., 2005; Giuliani et al., 2005).

their competitiveness remain tightly guarded secrets internalized within the corporate structure (Buckley, 2014: 232).

The other very important contribution of international business studies is the recognition that multinational corporations can have four very different strategies when they go abroad to seek location-specific assets:

- *Resource-seeking strategy:* MNCs require specific resources that are only available abroad. Typically, these resources may include natural resources or agricultural goods, desirable services that can only be accessed locally, and specific managerial or technical skills.
- *Efficiency-seeking (or cost-reducing) strategy:* MNCs plan to make their global operations more efficient through exploiting differences in the availability and cost of labour, capital, and resources. The location of light manufacturing and assembly plants in low-wage countries is an example of this strategy.
- *Market-seeking strategy:* MNCs establish a subsidiary to serve the consumer demand of a local market directly instead of by trade. FDI is chosen over trade because it is required by law to enter the new markets, permits the product to be adapted to local conditions, is less expensive, or is a strategic response to competing firms. Direct investment in small market-seeking factories was a common response to import substituting industrialization (ISI) policies, which tended to restrict trade through high tariff barriers.
- *Strategic asset-seeking strategy:* MNCs buy up assets of other corporations as part of a global strategy to improve their competitiveness. Such a strategy may generate benefits such as "opening up new markets, creating R&D synergies or production economies, buying market power, lowering transaction costs, spreading administrative overheads, advancing strategic flexibility, and enabling risks to be better spread" (Dunning, 1993: 57–61).

Although it is important to consider the role of government policy, as we do in the next section of the chapter, it is generally thought that corporate strategies do affect development outcomes. Resource-seeking MNCs are thought to have the least beneficial effect, because they often operate as **enclaves** with few links to the rest of the economy. Efficiency-seeking MNCs that look for low-cost labour can increase employment, but the wages, working conditions, and benefits are relatively poor. Market-seeking MNCs depend on skilled workers, pay higher wages, and can contribute to a healthy domestic economy. The most beneficial MNC strategy for development is strategic asset-seeking, as it offers the potential for research and development activities, highly skilled jobs, and substantial growth.

RELATIONSHIP BETWEEN STATES AND MULTINATIONALS

The strategies of multinationals alone do not determine their effect on development. A crucial part of the impact of MNCs on development is how governments mediate this relationship. The historical record is full of small states that have succeeded in getting important concessions from big firms—as well as big firms that appear to have had their way with small states. The **obsolescing bargaining model** offers a dynamic and flexible approach to state–firm relations in that it allows for the reality that both firm and state strength (and ability to get what they want) vary by country, firm, sector of activity, and the historical conjuncture (Vernon, 1971). The obsolescing bargaining approach assumes that each actor—state and firm—wants to capture a greater share of the benefits of the foreign investment. That is, the firm wants more profits and the government wants to increase the developmental spillovers of the investment. Thus, multinationals and governments can bargain over a wide range of issues.

The outcome of this bargaining is affected by their relative bargaining power (the resources each controls that are desired by the other party and not available elsewhere), strategy (how the investment fits into the firm's and the country's economic strategy), and constraints (the existence of alternatives and pressure from domestic and international actors). The model generally assumes that firms hold the upper hand when they first invest, because governments try to out-compete other potential locations by offering attractive conditions. Once the investment is sunk, however, and the company cannot easily leave, the bargaining power begins to shift towards the government. At this point,

CRITICAL ISSUES

BOX 11.3 | Women and Export Processing Zones

Export processing zones (EPZs) are specially designated manufacturing-for-export areas in developing countries that attract efficiency-seeking FDI through offering a regulatory regime favourable to multinational corporations. Typically, EPZs allow duty-free imports and exports, have lower corporate taxation rates, may be exempt from minimum-wage legislation, and do not permit unionization of the labour force. Figures for 2007 from the International Labour Organization suggest that the EPZ labour force is 66 million worldwide (40 million in China alone), some 70 to 90 per cent of whom are women (Wick, 2010, citing Milberg and Amengual, 2008). In this respect, female labour is the backbone of the light manufacturing export industries based in developing countries (particularly in electronics, garments, and footwear).

There is a significant and unresolved debate about whether the employment of women under these conditions is liberating or exploitative. EPZ jobs involve low wages, long hours, and frequently poor working conditions. A spate of suicides by workers in Chinese plants drew media attention to these problems in 2010. On the one hand, entry into the wage labour force may allow women to escape the restrictive moral code of traditional households and cultures, form friendship and political networks, increase their power relative to men because of their contribution to household income, and provide a nest egg that increases their individual opportunities for advancement and education later on. On the other hand, light manufacturing firms may also reinforce gender stereotypes by selecting employees based on racialized or gendered characteristics, such as the "nimble fingers" that facilitate detail work, docility, youth, and marital status (Elson and Pearson, 1981). Young women also are considered "secondary wage earners" and therefore are paid less than men. Furthermore, the literature has recorded cases of factories using gender to control women: male floor managers; a paternalistic discourse to convince families that their daughters are being well looked after (and controlled); allocating "less-skilled" jobs (like sewing) to women while other "skilled" jobs (cutting) go to men; and beauty contests to reinforce traditional female norms. Evaluating whether EPZs liberate or exploit women is therefore a difficult question to resolve (see Wick, 2010).

the government may change the rules of the game and try to extract more benefits from the firm. The classic example of the obsolescing bargain can be found in the mining industry, which is a nationalist lightning rod for those who decry multinational investment as exploiting the national patrimony belonging to all citizens (Moran, 1974; Kobrin, 1987).

During the 1990s, analysts increasingly questioned the relevance of the obsolescing bargaining model. On the one hand, firms proved they could protect themselves using political risk insurance and prominent financiers like the World Bank, or the protection of bilateral investment treaties (see Box 11.4) (Moran, 1998). It also appeared that states, under the influence of neoliberal ideology, were giving a lot away to attract multinational corporations and doing very little to bargain with them once they were established (Haslam, 2007). Gone were the battles over ownership and performance requirements typical of the 1960s and 1970s. Some suggested that the obsolescing bargaining model had itself obsolesced as the overall mood in the 1990s became a co-operative one and governments and foreign corporations sought to complement each other in order to improve their ability to compete in world markets (Ramamurti, 2001; Stopford and Strange, 1991). Others argued that bargaining was counterproductive anyway, and policies to encourage firms to integrate backwards with local suppliers had failed.

Theodore Moran argued that the greatest spillovers in the local economy occur when the MNC is

Jessica Liu/iStockphoto

PHOTO 11.1 | Workers in a garment factory, Southeast Asia.

robas/iStockphoto

PHOTO 11.2 | Open-pit mine in the Atacama Desert, Chile.

the most free to take the productive decisions that make sense in terms of the company's global strategy. Companies not regulated by government are more likely to be larger (up to 10 times larger than import-substituting plants), to use more advanced technology, to develop and coach local suppliers to improve their product and production processes, and to use professional management techniques (Moran, 2005). Moran's thesis is contentious and may be most relevant to high-tech products like automobiles. Certainly, in the early years of the twenty-first century, the pendulum seems to be swinging towards more state regulation of MNCs, especially in the resource sector. In Latin America, since the early 2000s, left-of-centre governments have successfully put pressure on mining and petroleum producers to contribute more to development (Haslam and Heidrich, 2016). Indeed, the question "to bargain or not to bargain" may itself be too simplistic. Most of the literature on the successful developmental states of Southeast Asia points to the need for a close and supportive working relationship between foreign and domestic firms and governments (see Chapter 7).

INTERNATIONAL REGULATION OF MNCs

The state–firm relationship is no longer determined simply by the willingness of states to pursue either a co-operative or a bargaining strategy. Increasingly, international agreements limit the range of policy choices open to governments in their relationships with multinational corporations. In the 1960s and 1970s, developing countries organized themselves in the United Nations General Assembly and the Group of 77 (G77) to demand changes to the world trade regime that would be "fairer" for developing countries (see Chapters 10 and 15). These demands, inspired by nationalist and mercantile ideas, included controls on the activities of multinational corporations. The major projects of this period that reflected these concerns were the Charter of Economic Rights and Duties of States (1974) and the Draft Code of Conduct on Transnational Corporations. The draft code negotiations dragged out into the mid-1980s before being abandoned (UNCTAD, 2004: 9–11; Sagafi-Nejad and Dunning, 2008: 89–123). Their importance, however, was found in the counteroffensive it provoked from the rich countries to protect the rights of foreign investors in the developing world.

This counteroffensive took place on several fronts: (1) a campaign was launched to sign bilateral investment protection agreements with developing countries; (2) investment issues were included in the GATT negotiations; and (3) corporate social responsibility was promoted as a way to improve corporate behaviour in lieu of state regulation. The first two offensives sought to build a body of international law based on the principle of protection for foreign direct investors.

The first efforts in this direction involved the negotiation of **bilateral investment treaties** (or BITs) between developed and developing countries. Such agreements typically enunciated principles of treatment that foreign investors were entitled to receive from host governments, such as most-favoured-nation and national treatment (the same treatment as that accorded to the firms of any third country or locally owned firms), just and equitable treatment, full protection and security (from expropriation), and the right to sue host governments in international tribunals for breach of obligations. The first BIT was signed between Germany and Pakistan in 1959, but the web of agreements had expanded to approximately 3,271 worldwide by 2014 (UNCTAD, 2015a: xii). Few developing countries are not caught in this web, and many signed such agreements in the hope that demonstrating the "right" attitude towards foreign investors would encourage increased FDI inflows. Thus far, the evidence that international investment agreements contribute to increased investment flows is mixed.

At the global and regional levels, rules to protect foreign investors were included in trade agreements. The Uruguay Round (concluded in 1994) of GATT negotiations added agreements protecting the rights of foreign investors, the most notable of which are the TRIPs (Trade-Related Aspects of Intellectual Property Rights) agreement requiring respect for intellectual property and the TRIMs (Trade-Related Investment Measures) agreement forbidding the use of certain performance requirements (policies that imposed developmental obligations on MNCs). Since that time, a

CRITICAL ISSUES

BOX 11.4 | Investor–State Dispute Settlement

A major question related to international investment agreements (IIAs), such as bilateral investment treaties (BITs), is whether they restrict the **policy space** or the policy options open to governments in their dealings with multinational corporations (Gallagher, 2005: 10–12; Sánchez-Ancochea and Shadlen, 2008: 11–14; Van Harten, 2008). Most IIAs include investor–state dispute settlement provisions. These provisions permit a foreign corporation (but not a domestically owned firm) that believes its rights under an investment agreement have been violated to take the host government to "court" in binding international arbitration. Frequently, multinational corporations will claim they have not received "fair and equitable treatment" or that a particular governmental measure has affected their profitability to the extent that it may be considered "tantamount to expropriation." Known arbitration cases have skyrocketed from a total of 14 in April 1998 to 608 by the end of 2014, with some resulting in major damage awards, such as the US$834 million award against Slovakia in 2004 (UNCTAD, 2010: 1; UNCTAD, 2015a: xii). Argentina alone has faced over 40 known cases, most of which were related to its financial crisis and currency devaluation of 2002. This may represent the tip of the iceberg, since several of the arbitration venues open to investors conduct the proceedings in secret. Environmental and social activists have been particularly concerned that such investment protection could limit the ability of governments to make policy in the public interest if the interests of multinational corporations were damaged in the process, or that a **regulatory chill** could result in which a government never implements good public policy for fear of being sued by affected foreign investors. For example, most developing countries have private health-care delivery, but it might be too expensive to move to a universal public system if doing so damages the profits of multinational corporations and causes them to sue.

number of regional free trade agreements, such as the North American Free Trade Agreement, have included investment disciplines. The Doha Development Round (2001–present) also had investment on the agenda, although it was dropped in 2005 because of opposition from developing countries concerned about its effect on their policy space. As a result of this legalization of the rights of foreign investors, multinational corporations now enjoy more protection from governments and civil society groups than at any other time in history.

CORPORATE SOCIAL RESPONSIBILITY

The third element of this counteroffensive is the promotion of corporate social responsibility (CSR) as a way of forestalling or deflecting calls for government regulation of the activities of MNCs. Corporate social responsibility, broadly speaking, is the idea that corporations have a responsibility beyond their shareholders to a broader set of "stakeholders." Such stakeholders include any group that is affected by the activities of the firm, including employees, local communities, groups sharing the same resources (such as water), indigenous communities, and people involved in nearby economic activities (such as farming). CSR is a *voluntary* commitment of firms to improve the quality of their relationship with stakeholders. It is presented both as a moral argument that companies should behave ethically and as good business because it reduces operational risk, improves worker commitment, increases efficiency, and promotes profitability. The contrast between rights and obligations should be immediately apparent: on the one hand, corporate rights have been enhanced through international law and binding dispute settlement (Box 11.4); on the other, corporate responsibilities remain purely voluntary.

The immediate response of the OECD club of rich countries to the Draft Code of Conduct on Transnational Corporations was the *Guidelines for Multinational Enterprises* (1976). To this day, these guidelines constitute the most significant corporate social responsibility effort by developed countries, requiring each OECD country to establish an institution, the National Contact Point, to promote the guidelines and mediate disputes involving investors from that country. Another prominent international code is the Global Compact, an initiative of former UN Secretary-General Kofi Annan. Each set of codes advocates different principles, implies obligations for different actors, and involves different standards of verification and compliance. The Global Compact, for example, requires companies to voluntarily adhere to a set of 10 principles on human rights, labour standards, environmental stewardship, and anti-corruption. However, there is no independent audit or verification of company efforts, unlike codes that require "triple bottom-line accounting" (quantification of economic, social, and environmental impacts).

Most multinationals have developed their own codes of conduct, as well as adhering to global codes promoted by international organizations. Yet there is a debate as to whether CSR is appropriate for the developing world. Much of the thought on CSR was created in developed countries where a strong legal and social framework already forces high standards of responsible behaviour by corporations. In the Third World, where this framework is often either absent or not enforced, the appropriateness of putting the accent on voluntary efforts may well be questioned. Furthermore, there is little systematic evidence on the consequences of corporate social responsibility for development in poor areas. The argument for its value has mostly progressed through advocacy and case studies of good citizenship. Nonetheless, most world surveys of MNCs show an increasing uptake of CSR norms and practices by firms operating in the developing world. In this respect, the contribution of CSR to development may improve with time.

PARTNERSHIPS FOR DEVELOPMENT

Up to this point we have been discussing the largely accidental developmental effects that occur from self-interested behaviour by companies, sometimes mediated by the intervention of governments. Increasingly, however, private actors are purposefully playing the role of development agents. One of the most important vehicles for these actions has been **partnerships** with governments and civil society organizations. As of yet, there is no consensus definition for the term "partnership" and it is used in many ways by different authors. Nonetheless, a broad definition of the term is currently in vogue that sees it as synonymous with "cross-sectoral alliances," meaning co-operation that bridges the governmental, corporate, and civil society sectors (Jamali and Keshishian, 2008: 279). The classic definition from Waddock (1991) argues that different actors get together to "cooperatively attempt to solve a problem or issue of mutual concern that is in some way identified with a public policy agenda item" (cited in Kolk, 2013). Utting and Zammit (2006) add that within such alliances, actors have "a common purpose, pool core competencies, and share risks, responsibilities, resources, costs and benefits." Therefore, the key features of a partnership are as follows: (1) collaboration between business and other social actors; (2) a social or public purpose (such as responding to a policy or development problem); and (3) it should, ideally, be beneficial for all the partners.

There were four main reasons for this move towards partnerships. First, as many development agencies and civil society organizations saw their budgets stretched (or reduced) as needs grew, it was thought that the private sector could help fill the gap by mobilizing resources. Second, it was thought that the efficiency and specialized skills of private companies could create synergies with development agencies to do development *better*—sometimes known as "creating shared value." Third, many large companies began to see doing development as integral to their own activities, corporate image, and profitability. And, fourth, for ideological reasons, some development agencies and governments were willing to spend money to promote partnerships with the private sector. Of course, these changes occurred after neoliberalism, which was favourable to private enterprise, had become well entrenched.

CRITICAL ISSUES

BOX 11.5 | The Changing Face of FDI: The Third World Multinational

In recent years, some developing countries have established homegrown multinationals—**emerging multinational corporations** (EMNCs)—that invest in other developing countries and in the OECD countries. This change may prompt us to re-imagine some of the more simplistic approaches to the relationship between multinationals and developing countries. At the very least, it makes it harder to represent multinationals as simply the North exploiting the South.

Since some multinationals now call developing countries their "home," the issue of the impact of FDI on development is an issue of its impact not just on host countries but also on home countries. FDI from developing countries offers a number of potential benefits for the home country, such as increased profitability and competitiveness, access to foreign financing (in developed-country markets), technology transfer (especially if internationalization occurs through merger and acquisition of developed-country firms), integration into global production and distribution networks, secure supplies of natural resources, and spillovers for local firms. Indeed, it appears that Third World multinationals are expanding in a different way than American multinationals did in the 1950s. They are expanding more quickly, their ownership advantages are weak, they are used to unstable environments, they expand simultaneously in developed and developing countries, and frequently they use mergers and acquisitions as vehicles (Guillén and García-Canal, 2009: 26–30). Indeed, perhaps the most important and unique characteristics of Third World multinationals is that they seek to absorb First World technology and managerial practices through expansion, unlike First World MNCs, which seek to protect their ownership advantages from competitors (UNCTAD, 2006: 169–83; Hennart, 2012). Case studies suggest that EMNCs from India and China have been able to use expansion or participation in Western MNCs' global value chains (see Box 11.2) as a way of improving their global competitiveness and capabilities—in other words, to "absorb, adapt and build on technologies imported from abroad" (Kumar, 2007: 7). In both cases, the government has helped support the innovation capabilities of local MNCs by forcing foreign firms to establish relationships with local EMNCs (often in the geographic proximity of science parks) as the price of entry to the Chinese or Indian market (Altenberg et al., 2007). In addition to the impact on their home countries, Third World EMNCs also may be beneficial for other developing countries, as they frequently internationalize to poorer countries in their immediate regional environment. As a result, investment from developing countries is particularly important to nearby economies that are relatively unattractive to First World MNCs. In this way, South Africa is a source of more than 50 per cent of investment inflows in neighbouring southern Africa (UNCTAD, 2006: 120).

The relatively recent emergence of South–South FDI flows means that it is hard to judge whether this new phenomenon will have different developmental effects from those of North–South flows. Some possible benefits have been noted above. On the other hand, FDI from larger economies like China and India has shown little interest in the direct or indirect human rights violations (such as in Sudan) that might accompany their investments, and little permeability to pressure from domestic and transnational NGOs and civil society groups. This may represent a setback for activists who have successfully pushed Western MNCs to act more seriously regarding their responsibilities of corporate citizenship.

CRITICAL ISSUES

BOX 11.6 | Private Foundations and Development

Private foundations have emerged as important actors in international development. Strictly speaking, such civil society foundations are legally and financially independent from the companies that founded them, yet many retain an entrepreneurial culture that promotes innovative problem-solving and technological solutions. One of the most influential is the Bill & Melinda Gates Foundation, which has net assets of US$42.9 billion, spends annually up to US$3.9 billion (2014), and has disbursed a total of US$33.5 billion (www.gatesfoundation.org). The Foundation is well-known for its innovative, out-of-the-box thinking and its encouragement of partnerships. For example, the Gates Malaria Partnership (GMP) supported a program led by the London School of Hygiene and Tropical Medicine to research existing malaria tools, develop new tools, and build the capacity to do malaria research in Africa. The program developed a collaborative approach with African institutions, founding a Ph.D. program for African scholars, supporting two research laboratories in Africa, and establishing malaria training and advocacy centres (Greenwood et al., 2006). Table 11.2 compares the development spending of some notable private foundations and selected countries and international institutions.

The partnership ideal is best expressed in the concept of **shared value** developed by Harvard Business School professors Michael E. Porter and Mark R. Kramer, who argue that businesses should focus on how they can combine enhancing competitiveness with addressing the "needs and challenges" of society (Porter and Kramer, 2011: 64). The argument is a response to fears that business has lost respect and legitimacy in the public eye. The authors distinguish their idea from philanthropic activities, seeing these as only redistributing wealth. Instead, they argue that companies should creatively rethink products and markets with the purpose of addressing social problems, and redefine their relationship with suppliers and clusters to work constructively with small local firms in order to improve their performance and skills and to develop the communities in which they are located (Porter and Kramer, 2011: 68–73). In other words, investing in working with partners is not just a charitable act, but is good for the competitiveness and profitability of all. An example of such a partnership is found in the cultivation of fair trade coffee suppliers by Starbucks. Concerned that it would be the target of a sustained activist campaign, the company developed a partnership with

TABLE 11.2 | Development Spending in Billions of US$, Selected Foundations, Countries, and International Organizations, 2014

Private Foundations		Countries/International Organizations	
Bill & Melinda Gates Foundation	3.9	Australia	4.50
Open Society Foundation	0.82	Canada	4.42
Ford Foundation	0.56	New Zealand	0.49
W.K. Kellogg Foundation	0.34	United Kingdom	18.08
John & Catherine McArthur Foundation	0.23	UNDP	4.24*
Rockefeller Foundation	0.14***	WHO	5.31**

*UNDP provisional (April 2014); **WHO total funding 2014–15; ***2011 figures.

the Ford Foundation, Oxfam America, and the Oaxacan State Coffee Producers Network (CEPCO) in order to source fair trade coffee. This partnership allowed Starbucks to help raise the quality of CEPCO's coffee, improve the skills of small farmers, and encourage the dissemination of knowledge to other co-operatives, all while fulfilling the American company's commercial objectives (Argenti, 2004).

But the practice of partnership is more contentious than the idea itself. On the one hand, partnerships, especially those known as **public–private partnerships (PPPs)**, can be very similar to privatizations, in which a company is contracted and partially subsidized to provide a public service, such as building roads, electrification, or providing water (van der Wel, 2004). More problematically, the conditions for a truly successful and equitable partnership are rarely realized. When corporations provide resources to civil society organizations to perform some kind of social service, it can be a unidirectional relationship, where the firm controls the money, objectives, and ideas (Jamali and Keshishian, 2009: 278). NGOs often enter partnerships as subordinates or philanthropic subcontractors chasing the next paycheque, and can be pulled away from their core mission. At the same time, NGOs may be leery about their engagement with companies, fearing that the partnership might harm their legitimacy and reputation (Kolk, 2013). A substantive partnership requires a good fit between the strategic objectives of the different partners, as well as significant resources, a high level of ongoing collaboration, and frequent and high-level management interaction (Jamali and Keshishian, 2009: 281). In this regard, partnerships are not a panacea for development problems, but have to be carefully constructed and implemented, drawing on the core competencies of every partner, to work properly (Kolk, 2013).

CONCLUSION

There is general agreement that the promotion of entrepreneurship is good for developing countries (if very difficult to attain). But it is difficult to evaluate whether multinationals are good or bad for poor and developing countries, for two principal reasons discussed in this chapter. First, FDI is extremely heterogeneous (different MNC strategies and different firms have different effects on host countries), and second, the policy regime and bargaining outcomes vary greatly among states. In other words, some MNCs are better for development than others, and some states are simply better at getting the most out of multinationals. In this regard, it is essential to evaluate the effects of individual investments both for their economic contribution to capital inflows, exports, government revenue, and spillovers in the wider economy (Sumner, 2005: 277–81; UNCTAD, 1999: 279–83) and for their political, cultural, and social impact.

Above all, the chapter has sought to demonstrate that the private sector is not a monolithic, homogeneous actor whose effects are structurally determined and easily characterized as good or bad. Instead, private enterprises are diverse and complicated actors applying a wide range of strategies. Their developmental effects depend on the particular nature of their engagement with governments, international organizations, and civil society actors. Multinationals, which are often the focus of criticism, are neither entirely responsible for the successes of development nor can they simply be blamed for its failures. UNCTAD (1999: 149) has explained that multinational corporations "do not substitute for domestic effort: they can only provide access to tangible and intangible assets and catalyse domestic investment and capabilities. In a world of intensifying competition and accelerating technological change, this complementary and catalytic role can be very valuable."

SUMMARY

This chapter introduced one of the most important and yet most misunderstood and under-analyzed actors in international development—private enterprise. After reading the chapter, the student should be able to differentiate between small and large firms, and the different roles they play in development. Entrepreneurs, especially those in the informal sector, face important challenges related to a lack of property rights and government support, which can hamper economic development. Multinationals also should be regarded as differentiated actors that apply a wide range of strategies with diverse effects on development.

However, the chapter also underlined the need to consider the role of the state as a mediator. How well the state regulates and bargains with firms has a significant effect on whether they have a good or bad effect on development. Some states are better at getting more from multinationals than others. However, the student should note that international investment agreements sometimes reduce the policy space available to governments. In recent years, multinationals have begun to act directly as development agents, through corporate social responsibility programs that engage communities and by forming partnerships with government agencies and civil society organizations to address development problems. In brief, the effects of private enterprise on development depend on the size of the company, the strategy it employs, mediation by the state, and the way the company engages other actors such as civil society. Companies, by themselves, are not entirely responsible for the successes or the failures of development.

QUESTIONS FOR CRITICAL THOUGHT

1. How important is it to encourage small-scale entrepreneurship in developing countries?
2. If some multinationals do not adequately contribute to development, is it their fault or the fault of host governments that fail to regulate them?
3. Can corporate social responsibility contribute to good developmental outcomes? Why or why not? What are its limits?
4. Why would the emergence of Third World multinationals change how we evaluate MNCs' effects on developing countries?
5. Can MNCs successfully act as "aid agents" through partnerships with governments and civil society organizations?

SUGGESTED READINGS

Dunning, John H., and Sarianna M. Lundan. 2008. *Multinational Enterprises and the Global Economy.* Cheltenham, UK: Edward Elgar.

Eade, Deborah, and John Sayer, eds. 2006. *Development and the Private Sector: Consuming Interests.* Bloomfield, Conn.: Kumarian Press.

Gallagher, Kevin, and Daniel Chudnovsky, eds. 2010. *Rethinking Foreign Investment for Sustainable Development: Lessons from Latin America.* New York: Anthem Press.

Sagafi-Nejad, Tagi, and John H. Dunning. 2008. *The UN and Transnational Corporations: From Code of Conduct to Global Compact.* Bloomington: Indiana University Press.

United Nations Conference on Trade and Development (UNCTAD). Various years. *World Investment Report.* Geneva: UNCTAD.

BIBLIOGRAPHY

Altenberg, T., H. Schmitz, and A. Stamm. 2007. "Breakthrough? China's and India's transition from production to innovation." *World Development* 36, 2: 325–44.

Amin, S. 1990. *Delinking: Towards a Polycentric World.* London: Zed Books.

Argenti, P.A. 2004. "Collaborating with activists: How Starbucks works with NGOs." *California Management Review* 47, 1: 91–116.

Buckley, P.J. 2012. "Forty years of internalisation theory and the multinational enterprise." *Multinational Business Review* 22, 3: 227–45.

Commission on the Private Sector & Development. 2004. *Unleashing Entrepreneurship: Making Business Work for the Poor.* Geneva: United Nations.

de Soto, H. 2000. *The Mystery of Capital: Why Capitalism Triumphs in the West and Fails Everywhere Else.* New York: Basic Books.

Dunning, J.H. 1993. *Multinational Enterprises and the Global Economy.* Reading, Mass.: Addison-Wesley.

———. 2000. "The eclectic paradigm as an envelope for economic and business theories of MNE activity." *International Business Review* 9: 163–90.

Eden, L. 1991. "Bringing the firm back in: Multinationals in international political economy." *Millennium: Journal of International Studies* 20, 2: 197–224.

Elson, D., and R. Pearson. 1981. "'Nimble fingers make cheap workers': An analysis of women's employment in Third World export manufacturing." *Feminist Review* 7 (Spring): 87–107.

Evans, P.B. 1979. *Dependent Development: The Alliance of Multinational, State and Local Capital in Brazil.* Princeton, NJ: Princeton University Press.

Gallagher, K. 2005. "Globalization and the nation-state: Reasserting policy autonomy for development." In Kevin Gallagher, ed., *Putting Development First: The Importance of Policy Space in the WTO and IFIs.* London: Zed Books, 1–14.

Gereffi, G., and T. Sturgeon. 2005. "The governance of global value chains." *Review of International Political Economy* 12, 1 (Feb.): 78–104.

Gilpin, R. 1975. *U.S. Power and the Multinational Corporation: The Political Economy of Foreign Direct Investment.* New York: Basic Books.

Giuliani, E., C. Pietrobelli, and R. Rabellotti. 2005. "Upgrading in global value chains: Lessons from Latin American clusters." *World Development* 33, 4: 549–73.

Goetz, A.M., and R. Sen Gupta. 1996. "Who takes the credit? Gender, power, and control over loan use in rural credit programs in Bangladesh." *World Development* 24, 1: 45–63.

Greenwood, B.M., A. Bhasin, C.M. Bowler, H. Naylor, and G.A. Targett. 2006. "Capacity strengthening in malaria research: The Gates Malaria Partnership." *Trends in Parasitology* 22, 7: 278–84.

Guillén, M.F., and E. García-Canal. 2009. "The American model of the multinational firm and the 'new' multinationals from emerging economies." *Academy of Management Perspectives* (May): 23–35.

Haslam, P.A. 2007. "The firm rules: Multinationals, policy space and neoliberalism." *Third World Quarterly* 28, 6: 1167–83.

———. and P. Heidrich. 2016. "From neoliberalism to resource nationalism: States, firms and development." In P. Haslam and P. Heidrich, eds, *The Political Economy of Resources and Development: From Neoliberalism to Resource Nationalism.* Milton Park, UK: Routledge.

Hennart, J.-F. 2012. "Emerging market multinationals and the theory of the multinational enterprise." *Global Strategy Journal* 2, 3: 168–87.

Ietto-Gilles, G. 2005. *Transnational Corporations and International Production: Concepts, Theories and Effects.* Cheltenham, UK: Edward Elgar.

Jamali, D., and T. Keshishian. 2009. "Uneasy alliances: Lessons learned from partnerships between businesses and NGOs in the context of CSR." *Journal of Business Ethics* 84: 277–95.

Klein, N. 2015. *This Changes Everything: Capitalism vs. The Climate.* Toronto: Simon & Schuster.

Kobrin, S.J. 1987. "Testing the bargaining hypothesis in the manufacturing sector in developing countries." *International Organization* 41, 4: 609–38.

Kolk, A. 2013. "Partnerships as panacea for addressing global problems? On rationale, context, actors, impact and limitations." In M. Seitanidi and A. Crane, eds, *Social Partnerships and Responsible Business: A Research Handbook.* London: Routledge.

Korten, D.C. *When Corporations Rule the World.* San Francisco: Berrett-Koehler.

Kumar, N. 2007. "Emerging TNCs: Trends, patterns and determinants of outward *FDI* by Indian enterprises." *Transnational Corporations* 16, 1 (Apr.): 1–26.

Milberg, W., and M. Amengual. 2008. *Economic Development and Working Conditions in Export Processing Zones: A Survey of Trends.* Geneva: ILO.

Moran, T.H. 1974. *Multinational Corporations and the Politics of Dependence: Copper in Chile.* Princeton, NJ: Princeton University Press.

———. 1998. "The changing nature of political risk." In T. H. Moran, ed., *Managing International Political Risk.* Malden, Mass.: Blackwell, 7–14.

———. 2005. "How does FDI affect host country development? Using industry case studies to make reliable generalizations." In Theodore H. Moran, Edward M. Graham, and Magnus Bloomström, eds, *Does Foreign Direct Investment Promote Development?* Washington: Institute for International Economics and Center for Global Development, 281–313.

Porter, M.E., and M.R. Kramer. 2011. "Creating shared value: How to reinvent capitalism and unleash a wave of innovation and growth." *Harvard Business Review* (Jan.–Feb.): 62–77.

Ramamurti, R. 2001. "The obsolescing 'bargaining model'? MNC–host developing country relations revisited." *Journal of International Business Studies* 32, 1: 23–39.

Sagafi-Nejad, T., with J.H. Dunning. 2008. *The UN and Transnational Corporations: From Code of Conduct to Global Compact*. Bloomington: Indiana University Press.

Sánchez-Ancochea, D., and K.C. Shadlen. 2008. "Introduction: Globalization, integration, and economic development in the Americas." In D. Sánchez-Ancochea and K.C. Shadlen, eds, *The Political Economy of Hemispheric Integration: Responding to Globalization in the Americas*. New York: Palgrave Macmillan, 1–23.

Stopford, J.H., and S. Strange. 1991. *Rival States, Rival Firms: Competition for World Market Shares*. Cambridge: Cambridge University Press.

Sumner, A. 2005. "Is foreign direct investment good for the poor? A review and stocktake." *Development in Practice* 15, 3 and 4: 269–85.

Thomas, M.D. 1987. "Schumpeterian perspectives on entrepreneurship in economic development: A commentary." *Geoforum* 18, 2: 173–86.

United Nations Conference on Trade and Development (UNCTAD). 1999. *World Investment Report 1999: Foreign Direct Investment and the Challenge of Development*. Geneva: UN.

———. 2004. *International Investment Agreements: Key Issues*, vol. 1. Geneva: UN.

———. 2006. *World Investment Report 2006:* FDI *from Developing and Transition Economies: Implications for Development*. Geneva: UN.

———. 2009. *World Investment Report 2009*, Annex A.1.8, 222–3.

———. 2010. "Latest developments in investor–state dispute settlement." *IIA Issues* Note No. 1. www.-unctad.org/en/docs/webdiaeia20103_en.pdf.

———. 2013. *World Investment Report 2013: Global Value Chains: Investment and Trade for Development*. Annex Table 28, The world's top 100 non-financial TNCs, ranked by foreign assets, 2012. http://unctad.org/en/pages/PublicationWebflyer.aspx?publicationid=588.

———. 2015a. *World Investment Report 2015: Reforming International Investment Governance*. Geneva: UN.

———. 2015b. *World Investment Report 2015: Reforming International Investment Governance*. Geneva: UN. Annex Table 1, FDI inflows by region and economy, 1990–2014. http://unctad.org/en/Pages/DIAE/World%20Investment%20Report/Annex-Tables.aspx.

Utting, P., and A. Zammit. 2006. *Beyond Pragmatism: Appraising UN–Business Partnerships*. Geneva: UNRISD.

van der Wel, P. 2004. "Privatisation by stealth: The global use and abuse of the term 'public–private partnership'." Institute of Social Studies. Working Paper Series No. 394. The Hague: ISS.

Van Harten, G. 2008. "Investment treaty arbitration and its policy implications for capital-importing states." in D. Sánchez-Ancochea and K.C. Shadlen, eds, *The Political Economy of Hemispheric Integration: Responding to Globalization in the Americas*. New York: Palgrave Macmillan, 83–111.

Vernon, R. 1971. *Sovereignty at Bay: The Multinational Spread of US Enterprises*. New York: Basic Books.

Wick, I. 2010. *Women Working in the Shadows: The Informal Economy and Export Processing Zones*. Siegburg, Germany: Südwind Institut für Ökonomie und Ökumene. www.suedwind-institut.de/downloads/2010-03_SW_Women-Working-in-the-Shadows.pdf.

World Bank. 2015. World Development Indicators database. http://databank.worldbank.org/data/reports.aspx?source=2&type=metadata&series=DT.ODA.ALLD.CD#.

Yunus, M. 2003. *Banker to the Poor: The Story of the Grameen Bank*. London: Aurum Press.

12 Civil Society and Development

Henry Veltmeyer

LEARNING OBJECTIVES

- To be able to identify the agents of change in the process of local- or community-based development.
- To understand the role of civil society organizations in the process of alleviating poverty and empowering the poor to act for themselves.

▲ **Activists of the Nepal Federation of Indigenous Nationalities (NFIN) shout anti-government slogans during a general strike rally in Kathmandu. NEFIN is an umbrella organization of 59 Indigenous nationalities that has been fighting for the cultural, economic, and political rights of Indigenous peoples since its establishment in 1991.** | Source: © epa european pressphoto agency b.v./ Alamy Stock Photo

The idea of civil society has achieved prominence over the past two decades in connection with successive waves of democratization that began in Latin America and Eastern Europe and spread across the developing world. A principal feature of this democratization was not so much the restoration of the rule of law as it was the active engagement of people in the public policy formulation process and in the responsibility of governance. This democratization process paralleled a similar process at the economic level (turning over the responsibility for economic development to the private sector and the market, and a reduced role for governments with international co-operation and social participation). In this context of political and economic development, civil society has been widely seen as an agent for limiting authoritarian government, empowering popular movements, reducing the atomizing and unsettling effects of market forces, enforcing political accountability, and improving the quality and inclusiveness of "governance," a term that denotes a particular set of interactions between civil society and governments.

Reconsideration of the limits of government intervention in economic affairs and a related neoliberal attack on the welfare—and developmental—state (see Chapter 7) also have led to an increased awareness of the potential role of civic organizations in the provision of public goods and social services, either separately or in a synergistic relationship with state institutions. Indeed, it is possible to view the turn towards civil society in the provision of hitherto public goods and services as a form of *privatization*: turning over the economy to the "private sector" (profit-oriented or capitalist enterprises) and responsibility for economic and political development to "civil society."[1]

Recourse to the notion of civil society, and the construction of a civil society *discourse*, takes different forms. There are three different traditions in the use of the term, each associated with a particular conception of civil society. One of these, associated with a mainstream form of political science and economics in which politics and economics are treated as analytically distinct systems, can be labelled *liberal*.

The liberal tradition is fundamentally concerned with "political development"—establishing a participatory form of politics and "good," i.e., "democratic," governance. Civil society, from this view, is rooted in the Anglo-American tradition of liberal democratic theory in which civic institutions and political activity are essential components of "political society" based on the principles of citizenship, rights, democratic representation, and the rule of law. On the ideological spectrum (left, centre, right), liberals see civil society as a countervailing force against an unresponsive, corrupt state and exploitative corporations that disregard environmental issues and human rights abuses (Kamat, 2003).

The second tradition, rooted in a more sociological view of the state–society relation and the ideas of Antonio Gramsci, is similarly concerned with the form of politics but sees civil society as a repository of popular resistance to government policies and the basis of a "counter-hegemonic" bloc of social forces engaged in a process of contesting state and other forms of class power. It is based on a radical ideology—a shared belief in the need for radical change. Civil society is thus seen as a repository of the forces of resistance and opposition that can be mobilized into a counter-hegemonic bloc.

The third tradition is associated with international co-operation for development. In this tradition, civil society is viewed as an array of social organizations representing "stakeholders" in a process of economic development, a strategic partner in the war against global poverty waged by the World Bank and other international development associations and agencies. Here, civil society is viewed as an agent for a *participatory* and *empowering* form of *development*. Proponents share a liberal ideology in terms of seeing in civil society the beneficial effects of globalization for democracy and economic progress. On the other hand, conservatives who hold this view of civil society see non-governmental organizations (NGOs) as "false saviours of international development" (Kamat, 2003). The entire project of co-operation for international development (technical and financial assistance to poor developing countries) is seen as misbegotten, more likely to result in a stifling of initiative than to work as a catalyst for improvement in the physical quality of people's lives.

The purpose of this chapter is to deconstruct this civil society discourse. First, we review the origins and contemporary uses of the term. Then we turn towards the development dynamics associated with the contemporary discourse on civil society. This discourse is of two types, one associated with the dynamics of political development and the search for "democratic governance," the other with the search for alternative forms of development initiated from below and within "civil society"—forms that are socially inclusive, equitable, participatory, and empowering. The chapter ends with a brief review of the role of different types of civil society organizations in the development process. The central focus of this review is on non-governmental organizations and **social movements**, elements of civil society conceptualized as agents of anti-globalization—repositories of the forces of resistance against global capitalism in its current neoliberal form.

CIVIL SOCIETY: THE ITINERARY OF A CONCEPT

Definitions of "civil society" are bewilderingly diverse, rooted in alternative social and political philosophies that are hard to reconcile. However, for our purpose it is important to come to some agreement about what it means in the context of current development discourse.

One definition is that of an intermediate realm between the state and the family, populated by organized groups or associations that have some autonomy in relation to the state and are formed voluntarily by members of society to advance their interests, values, or identities. This definition excludes most highly informal associations of the personal network kind as well as families, since they operate in the private sphere. Civil society, by contrast, operates in the public, albeit non-state, sphere. But some kinship organizations above the level of the nuclear or extended family may constitute elements of civil society. Civil society, by this definition, generally excludes profit-oriented or capitalist corporations, although several caveats are in order. Certain types of firms, such as the media and non-profit enterprises, are often important elements of civil society. And when corporations and their CEOs combine to form business associations, these associations can also be regarded as part of civil society.

Civil society includes all manner of social organizations ranging between the family and the state—the state being an apparatus composed of institutions such as governments, the judiciary, the legislature, the armed forces, and any other institution used to determine "who gets what." The United Nations Development Programme (UNDP), the World Bank, and other such agencies of international development adopted the term "civil society" in their discourse precisely because it was so inclusive, containing within its scope the "private sector" (basically, capitalist or multinational corporations governed by the logic of capital accumulation or profit-making). The incorporation of the "private sector" into the development process has been a fundamental aim of these international organizations since 1989 (Mitlin, 1998).

Another consideration is that civil society or non-governmental organizations are generally issue-oriented in their actions rather than class-based, raising questions about whether or not to include social movements. *Social movements* are generally concerned with disputing state power—with bringing about a change in government policies or, like political parties, in governments themselves (albeit in a different way—mobilizing the forces of opposition and resistance rather than participating in elections). In contrast to social movements, civil society in the form of NGOs (or in the voluntary sector) is generally concerned with more specific interest group issues such as the environment, the empowerment of women, human rights, development education, disaster and other forms of relief or emergency aid, or poverty alleviation. Some of these issues also are targeted by some social movements, which is to say that it is possible to mobilize forces for change around these issues. The distinction we make between social movements and non-governmental organizations applies to the development rather than to the political sphere. In this context NGOs are fundamentally concerned with bringing about improvement in socio-economic conditions of the population by means of a change in policy or institutional reform. Social movements, in contrast, tend to have a more confrontational approach in challenging directly the holders and agencies of economic and political power.

The type of organization encompassed by civil society is not the only issue. Social organizations generally take one of three forms: (1) *associations* or *associational* (sharing an organizational objective); (2) *communities* or *community-based* (held together by social bonds and a culture of solidarity, a shared sense of belonging); and (3) *interest groups* or *class-based organizations* (defined by a pursuit of economic interest or political power), such as capitalist enterprises, multinational corporations within the private sector of the economy, and labour unions.

The size and strength of civil society in this organizational context are usually measured in terms of the number of "active" formally constituted social organizations, the density of the resulting social fabric, and the networks that bring people together to act collectively to achieve or to pursue their shared goals and common objectives. A major factor here is the degree to which people rely on governments as opposed to their own social organizations and networks to achieve their goals and objectives. Thus, from the 1940s to the 1970s, with the growth of the welfare and development state (in which governments assumed primary responsibility for both welfare and development), many societies increased their reliance on the government, with a corresponding weakening of civil society. In the 1980s, in a new context involving the insertion of many countries into the system of global capitalism (see discussion below on this "seismic shift"), there was a general retreat of the state, resulting in a corresponding growth and strengthening of civil society.

CIVIL SOCIETY IN CONTEXT

Social change can be analyzed in terms of three dynamic factors: *agency* (the strategies pursued and actions taken by diverse organizations and individuals), *structure* (the institutionalized practices that shape or limit action), and *context* (the specific "situation" or historical conjuncture of objectively given and subjectively experienced "conditions" of social or political action). In regard to the emergence, growth, and strengthening of civil society in the 1980s, six contextual elements, each taking the form of a variable but persistent trend, can be analyzed in terms of three critical dimensions: (1) the actions or policies that provide the driving forces of social change; (2) the social, economic, and political impacts of these actions and policies; and (3) the strategic and political responses to these impacts by different social groups and classes according to their location in the social structure and the broader system of global capitalism.

- *Globalization.* The integration of countries across the world into a new world order in which the forces of economic and political "freedom" are allowed to flourish has had an ambiguous impact on civil society organizations. On the one hand, the invasive pressures of global markets often compromise their autonomy or sovereignty. On the other, globalization—particularly in terms of freer flows of information and communication across national boundaries—has fostered the spread of "transnational communities" (see also Chapter 6) and an incipient global civil society.
- *Democratization.* The spread of democracy, as an idea and value, in recent years has changed the political and institutional environment in which civil society organizations operate (see Chapter 16). In some cases (see Box 12.1), civil society has been the locus of active opposition to authoritarian governments, providing a breeding ground for alternative, participatory, or "democratic" forms of political organization—and governance. In other cases, civil society is marginalized or weakened through state repression or withdrawal from active engagement in politics. Civil society in this context may constitute a locus in which civic values and norms of democratic engagement are nurtured, although greater political freedom can be exploited to advance narrow, self-interested agendas that can exacerbate political conflict and undermine good governance.
- *Privatization.* The rapid economic growth experienced by many developing countries from the 1950s onward was fuelled in large measure by growth of the public sector and a policy of nationalization—taking over from the private sector (the multinational corporations, that is) and buying out firms in the strategic sectors of the economy (oil production, for example). In the 1980s, this policy was reversed with a privatization policy: turning over state firms to private enterprise under the guise of a presumed "efficiency." This new policy allowed capitalist corporations—often multinational in form and foreign-owned—to acquire these enterprises at bargain-basement prices, greatly enriching their new owners (see Chapter 11).

- *Decentralization.* Until 1980 or so, many political scientists (and economists, for that matter) in both liberal and conservative traditions subscribed to the notion that democracy was not necessarily conducive to economic development—that authoritarianism provided a better agent. In the 1980s, however, there was a sea change in this idea, leading to widespread calls for democracy and good governance in the form of a more participatory form of politics and development (see Chapters 9 and 16). To establish an appropriate institutional framework for these developments (also to reduce fiscal pressures on governments), the World Bank argued for the need for a policy of administrative decentralization, with a partnership approach to both local governments and civil society (World Bank, 2004).
- *Economic liberalization.* The improvement in socio-economic conditions in the 1950s and 1960s was based on the active agency of governments in redistributing market-generated wealth and incomes for the common benefit. In the developing countries of the Global South, it was also based on protectionism, a policy designed to protect fledgling industries from the forces of the world market, to give domestic companies a chance to grow by placing restrictions on foreign investment and the operations of multinational corporations in their countries. Under the new economic model of free-market capitalism and **neoliberal globalization**, this policy was reversed.

  Liberalization has had a number of contradictory consequences for civil society. In some contexts, it weakened predatory state structures and limited the scope for "rent-seeking behaviour" by political and bureaucratic elites. Some groups are better placed than others to exploit the opportunities created by liberalization for advancing their own economic agendas, and organizations representing their interests can wield considerable influence over decision-making. The removal of price controls and other restrictions on economic activity are often accompanied by growth of the informal economy and the emergence of a dense network of groups and associations geared towards the advancement of collective economic interests. The removal of safety nets and reduction in government welfare spending gave rise to a proliferation of self-help groups and development associations with a mandate to provide relief and services to people marginalized or impoverished by market reforms.
- *Inclusionary state activism.* The neoliberal economic model based on free-market capitalism in Latin America fell into disrepute almost as soon as it was implemented by governments in the region, and by the end of the 1990s powerful social movements, organized and led by peasants, indigenous communities, and landless rural workers, had brought about the demise of neoliberalism as an economic doctrine. In its place was a more inclusionary form of development based on a new (post-Washington) consensus as to the need to bring the state back into the development process. This, as well as dramatic changes in the world economic system (among them the rise of China and the consequent demand for raw materials and primary commodities composed of natural resources such as minerals and metals), helped bring about in Latin America a new wave of left-leaning or progressive (post-neoliberal) political regimes committed to the use of the revenues derived from the exports of these commodities to reduce the incidence of poverty in their countries. The result has been a significant reduction for many countries in the region in the rate of extreme poverty as well as a reduction of social inequality in the distribution of society's wealth and income (Veltmeyer and Petras, 2013).
- *Deregulation.* State-led development is predicated on government regulation of private economic activity and markets in the public interest. However, from the perspective of firms concerned with maximizing profit-making opportunities, this policy is viewed as an intolerable attack on freedom, resulting in "inefficiency," a distortion of market forces that, if left unhindered, fails to produce an optimal distribution of society's productive resources, wealth, and income. In the 1980s, the perceived "failure" of the state—in the form of a widespread fiscal crisis (an inability to finance costly social and development programs out of government revenues)—created political conditions for a reversal of this regulatory approach.

BOX 12.1 | APPO: Popular Assembly of the People of Oaxaca

CURRENT EVENTS

When a woman advances there is no man who will retreat (on a placard in a political march).

APPO (the Spanish acronym for an organizing body of diverse protest groups) is a coalition of organized social and political groups in southern Mexico. APPO is nothing if not popular, bringing together broad sectors of the community and civil society organizations in a social movement for democratic transformation, as John Gibler (2006) reported:

> On Tuesday, August 1, about 3,000 women marched through downtown Oaxaca City banging metal pots and pans in an oddly melodious cacophony that served as the background for their chants demanding the ousting of Governor Ulises Ruiz. . . .
>
> Once gathered in the central town square—where teachers and other protestors have been camping out since May 22—the women decided to take over the statewide television and radio company. . . . Not a shot was fired. Not a punch was thrown . . . . It took several hours of negotiation before the women were able to fix a live broadcast, during which—still clutching their pots and wooden spoons, dressed in aprons and work clothes—they set out to correct the mistakes in the station's reporting on the violent June 14 attempt by state police to lift the teachers' encampment and demand on the air that the press "tell the truth" about the social movement that is taking over Oaxaca . . . .
>
> On June 16, just two days after the raid, some 500,000 people marched to demand the governor's resignation. . . .

THE ECONOMIC AND POLITICAL DYNAMICS OF DEVELOPMENT AND CIVIL SOCIETY

Development means a combination of improvements in the quality of people's lives—marked by a reduction in or alleviation of poverty, an increased capacity to meet the basic needs of society's members, **sustainable livelihoods**, and empowerment—and the changes in institutionalized practices or structures needed to bring about these improvements. The idea of development can be traced back to the eighteenth-century Enlightenment idea of progress—of the possibility of and necessity for a better form of society characterized by freedom from tyranny, superstition, and poverty, and attaining some degree of social equality. But it was reinvented in 1948 in the context of (1) a post-war world order based on the International Monetary Fund (IMF), the World Bank, and the General Agreement on Tariffs and Trade (GATT); (2) an emerging East–West conflict and Cold War; and (3) a national independence struggle by countries seeking to escape the yoke of colonialism—Pax Britannica in the pre-war period, and Pax Americana in the post-war period (see Chapters 2 and 3).

From the outset of this development process in 1948, signalled by Harry Truman's Point 4 Program of development assistance, to the early 1970s, when the world capitalist system ran out of steam and entered a period of prolonged crisis, state-led development generated an unprecedented period of economic growth and societal transformation (see Chapters 1 and 7). Growth rates, fuelled by rising wages and a rapid growth of domestic markets as well as international trade, exceeded by a factor of two the economic growth rates of previous decades, resulting in an incremental but steady improvement in the physical quality of life and the social conditions of health, education, and welfare. Historians have dubbed these advances the "golden age of capitalism."

In 1973, at the height of an apparent crisis of overproduction, characterized by cutthroat competition, saturated markets and stagflation, sluggish productivity, and falling profits, the capitalist class in the rich countries, the CEOs of its multinational corporations, and governments in their employ or service, abandoned the system that had served them so well. Or, to be more precise, they sought to renovate this system to resolve the crisis of capitalist production by (1) changing the relationship of capital to labour, favouring the former and weakening the latter; (2) incorporating new production technologies and constructing a new regime of accumulation and labour regulation (post-Fordism); (3) relocating labour-intensive industrial production overseas, thereby unwittingly creating a "new international division of labour"; and, above all, (4) bringing about a "new world order" in which the forces of "economic freedom" were liberated from the regulatory apparatus of the welfare-developmental state. The policies that facilitated this process generated epoch-defining changes, a seismic shift in international relations—a new world order in which it was thought that the forces of freedom and democracy could prevail.

By 1990, most countries were aligned to this "new world order" of "globalization" and free-market capitalism. In the 1970s, in the first phase of neoliberal experiments, the implementing agency was a series of military regimes in the Southern Cone of South America—in Chile, Argentina, and Uruguay (Petras and Veltmeyer, 2013). When these neoliberal policy experiments crashed in the early 1980s, a new crop of liberal democratic regimes, forced into line by the realities of a region-wide debt crisis of historic proportions, initiated a second round of "structural reform." They did so with the assistance of an emerging civil society in the so-called "third sector" of non-profit voluntary associations and non-governmental organizations. These organizations, formed in response to the retreat of the state from its erstwhile responsibility for economic development, were enlisted by international financial institutions (IFIs) such as the World Bank and the international community of development associations and aid donors to mediate with the poor—to assist them in their self-development efforts in return for acceptance of their policy advice (market-friendly "reforms" and "good governance").

The literature on these issues is divided. Some see the development NGOs as "false saviours of democracy," enlisted to help rescue capitalism from itself (Hayden, 2002; Kamat, 2003). These authors do not see the role of NGOs as one of delivering economic assistance (through micro-development projects or poverty alleviation funds) but of promoting democracy, a "new activity which the aid agencies and NGOs [originally] embarked [upon] with some trepidation and misgivings," but by the early 1990s this raison d'être "[came] of age" (Ottaway, 2003: vi). Others, however, see them as agents of global capitalism—a "Trojan horse of neoliberal globalization" (Wallace, 2003)—to facilitate the entry of foreign investment and the domestic operations of multinational corporations and, in the process, to help some achieve their imperial dream of world domination.

THE EMERGENCE OF A GLOBAL CIVIL SOCIETY: THE POLITICAL DYNAMICS OF ANTI-GLOBALIZATION

The measures associated with neoliberal policies in the 1990s led to a dramatic increase in social inequalities—disparities in the global and North–South distribution of wealth and poverty, marked by an extension and deepening of existing poverty and a social polarization between the rich and the poor. In the 1990s, this "inequality predicament" (as the United Nations, in a 2005 study, defines it) assumed grotesque proportions. In a world of spreading poverty, neoliberal policies produced a new class of multi-billionaires, the clear "winners" of globalization. In 1996, according to *Forbes* magazine, there were 793 of them, but within a year the number of multi-billionaires had grown to 946. Today *Forbes 2015* lists 1,826 billionaires, up from a then-record 1,125 in 2008. Thirty-four per cent of these super-rich are Americans. In the US, there were just 13 billionaires in 1985 at the dawn of the neoliberal era. Today, after close to three decades of free-market casino capitalism, there are 615, a small group representing the top 0.01 per cent of the US population that has managed to appropriate at least 25 per cent of the wealth produced over the past two decades.[2] But some emerging economies are quickly scaling the rankings: China was in second place with 213 billionaires (12 per cent), adding 71 new billionaires in the last year alone; India had 90 (5 per cent); Russia had 88 (5 per cent); and Brazil had 54 (3 per cent) (Forbes, 2015; Wikipedia, 2015).

Paul Haslam

PHOTO 12.1 | An informal street monument in Buenos Aires commemorating protestors killed during political demonstrations in Argentina, 2001.

The UNDP (2001) has estimated that a roomful of these super-rich, some 358 people, dispose of the equivalent income of 45 per cent of the world's poorest (3.5 billion) who have to subsist on less than $2 a day, a statistic that the UNDP understandably finds "grotesque" and others see as criminal. The total wealth of the world's richest individuals (*Forbes*'s list of billionaires), representing a one-hundred-millionth of the population, increased by 35 per cent to $3.6 trillion in 2010—more than the total wealth of the world's poor. In other words, poverty is the product of the same policies and the same system that generated a very unevenly distributed wealth: wealth for the few, the "winners" of globalization, and poverty for the many, the "losers."

This grotesque situation can be traced out not only at the level of international relations between rich and poor countries but inside wealthy countries such as the US that are dominated by the power of money—and the political power wielded by a ruling class of incredibly wealthy financiers and super-billionaires (Domhoff, 2011). According to Domhoff and the respectable business magazine *The Economist* (21 Jan. 2012: 31), while the richest 1 per cent of Americans accounted for 10 per cent of the national income in 1980 and 15 per cent in 1990, already by 2007 they had managed to appropriate up to 34.6 per cent of the country's wealth. Up to 94 per cent of all the financial wealth created over the past two decades was appropriated by this class of the super-rich, while the purchasing power of average household income over the same period had substantially declined, pushing millions into poverty.

The reign of untrammelled free-market capitalism over the past three decades and the neoliberal policies that the World Bank describes as "pro-growth" and "pro-poor" not only produced mass poverty but have made some individuals incredibly rich. However, the "losers" in the global competition for wealth—or the victims, to be more precise—have not been passive in their response to neoliberal globalization. They have responded by forming social movements in opposition to these policies, in resistance against the dynamics of globalizing capital. These movements have taken different forms in the North and the South. In the Global South, they have been generally led by indigenous communities, peasant farmers, and rural landless workers who have been the major targets and victims of "globalization." The working class, both in its waged/formal and its unwaged/informal forms, is also its victim. But the capacity of the workers to mount either a defensive or an offensive struggle has diminished dramatically over the past two decades, which has meant that the leadership of the popular movement in the Global South now rests with landless rural workers, peasant farmers, and indigenous communities.

As for the North (the rich industrial societies, mostly in Europe and North America), the anti-globalization movement that emerged and took form in the last decade of the twentieth century was based in the major urban centres and was rooted in the middle rather than working class; and it has predominantly taken the form of opposition to the power and agenda of corporate capital, although in 2011 it re-emerged in the US as the Occupy movement. Unlike the South, where anti-globalization is directed against the neoliberal policies of governments, the anti-globalization movement in the North has been most visible in counter-summits to the G8 summits of the most powerful and richest countries, and protests at the periodic gatherings of the World Trade Organization (WTO) and other such organizations that represent the interests of corporate capitalism, and at the World Social Forum, which annually brings together thousands of anti-globalization activists representing hundreds of civil society organizations, to discuss problems and debate strategy.[3] Strictly speaking, neither this broad anti-globalization movement nor the more recent 2011 Occupy movement against the super-rich, the 1 per cent who are estimated to have appropriated up to 90 per cent of the wealth and incomes generated in the US over the past two decades,[4] is against globalization as such but rather against its neoliberal and anti-democratic corporate form (see Chapter 6). In this context, anti-globalization can be seen as a movement formed in the search for "another world," participatory democracy, a more ethical form of globalization, a more equitable and socially inclusive and participatory form of society and development—a democratic alternative to neoliberal globalization and corporate power, free-market capitalism, and imperialism.

In the spring of 2007, the UK Ministry of Defence published a report (*Global Strategic Trends 2007–2036*) warning that the whole system of global capitalism, and with it the new world order, could well be brought down by the mounting forces of resistance. The report argues that excessive inequalities will likely lead to a "resurgence of not only anti-capitalist ideologies . . . but also populism and the revival of Marxism" (2007: 3). It expresses particular concern that the widening global divide in wealth and income has spawned a mass global justice movement that threatens to unite the most diverse forces of resistance and opposition to neoliberal globalization.

The meaning of this anti-globalization movement, and the growth of a transnational or global civil society committed to the search for "another world," is subject to continuing debate. Some see it as a palliative. Others see it as the salvation of humanity on a fast road to self-destruction. But there is no question that it might very well scuttle the best-laid plans of the new world order architects for imperial rule.

CIVIL SOCIETY AND LOCAL DEVELOPMENT

The search for a new development paradigm acquired a particular vigour in the 1980s with the turn towards a "new economic model" prioritizing the free market. Proponents of the new paradigm visualize development as community-based and localized, reaching beyond the state and the market into the localities and communities of the rural poor. The goal in this context is to advance development that is human in form, sustainable in terms of the environment and livelihoods, socially inclusive and equitable, participatory—and initiated "from below," from within civil society as opposed to "from above" or "from outside."

To some extent, this paradigm shift has to do with a long-standing concern with giving development a

Jennifer Rogers

PHOTO 12.2 | A street demonstration in Mexico of citizen groups and workers against the neoliberal policies of the government is met by a police barricade.

social dimension. From the beginning, the study of development was dominated by economics, in which the "social" and the "political" are often abstracted from analysis, treated as "externalities" in a process viewed in strictly economic terms. But in the new paradigm, the social is given more weight, even with regard to capital, the sum total of society's wealth (or income-generating assets). Economists had formulated the theory that economic development was based on capital accumulation and advanced by increasing the rate of savings and productive investment. However, "capital" in this theory was defined purely in economic terms—money invested in the design of new technology, the purchase of labour power, and the transformation of natural resources into commodities or tradable goods. Within the framework of the new paradigm, however, society's productive assets ("capital") are also conceived in social terms—that is, as the norms, institutions, and organizations that promote trust and co-operation among persons in communities and in the wider society. Initially advanced by several sociologists (notably James Coleman and Pierre Bourdieu), this notion of **social capital** was elaborated by leading development scholars such as Robert Chambers and Robert Putnam.

This was the thinking in the 1980s. In the 1990s, the concept of social capital took on a new life, supported and advanced by all manner of scholars, international organizations, and policy-makers in their development discourse. At issue in this discourse was an alternative way of conceiving "development" and fighting the war against world poverty (Durstan, 1999: 104). More specifically, the proponents of this approach claim that the accumulation of social capital based on norms of trust and reciprocal exchange, and a culture of social solidarity, can produce public goods, facilitate the "constitution of sound civil societies," and constitute the poor as "social actors," empowering them to act on their own behalf. As an asset that the poor have in abundance (their only asset, one could add, besides their capacity to labour), social capital promotes self-development of the poor in their localities and communities, alleviating the socio-economic (and psychological) conditions of their poverty.

Robert Putnam's book *Making Democracy Work* (1993) served as the catalyst for this interest in social capital as a research and policy tool. But the rapid spread and ubiquity of the notion in academe, and its wide-ranging applications in research, policy formulation, and practice, have been followed by serious questioning and several concerns. First, what is striking about the concept of social capital is not only the extent of its influence but its enthusiastic acceptance by both scholars and policy-makers. This is evident in the World Bank's notion of social capital as "the glue that holds society together," as the "missing link" in an analysis of the development process (Solow, 2000).

Second, despite the plethora of survey articles that litter the intellectual landscape, the concept is notoriously difficult to define. Most recent contributions to the literature acknowledge this before adding a definition of their own to suit their purpose. The ambiguity of "social capital" is reflected in the suggestion that it is merely a metaphor or a heuristic device and, with regard to the World Bank's formulation, is based on a vicious circle of tautological reasoning without any basis in empirical fact (Portes, 1998).

Third, the concept of social capital is used to describe and explain virtually anything and everything, from the networks formed by the poor, the sick, the criminal, and the corrupt to the social dynamics of the (dys)functional family, schooling, community development, work and organization, democracy and governance, collective action, the intangible assets of the social economy, "the analysis and promotion of peasant-level development," or, indeed, any aspect of social, cultural, and economic activity across time and place—everything, it would seem, except the norms, institutions, and social networks formed by those who constitute what the Australian documentary filmmaker and award-winning journalist John Pilger (2003) terms "the new rulers of the world," the class that runs the global economy and makes its rules.

The final concern about social capital has to do with ideology and politics. What is missing in the analysis informed by the notion of social capital is any concern for the structure of economic and political power. The concept of social capital appears to serve analysts and policy-makers in the same way that postmodern social theory serves analysis: as a means of eluding in thought what for most people is all too real—the dynamic workings of the world capitalist system. The power relations that determine life for most people are inverted: what is essentially a class struggle over the allocation of society's productive resources, a matter of state and economic power, is transmuted into empowerment—a feeling of power gained by individuals through participating in decisions (such as how to spend the poverty alleviation funds that come their way) that affect their livelihoods and supposedly improve the physical quality of their lives. The point is that empowerment means changing oneself (how one feels about one's self) rather than changing the system.

Another criticism is that the concept of social capital is ideologically all too convenient for the powerful and is politically demobilizing. In this connection, Harriss (2001) and others argue that making people responsible for their own development falsely implies that they were responsible for their problems, such as poverty, which draws attention away from the operating structures of the economic and social system. With its focus on "civil society," social capital ignores the dynamics associated with the formal structures and institutions of society's political economy, particularly that of state power.

Critics argue that the way in which the concept of social capital is used has a demobilizing effect on the dynamics of radical change. Local development built on the basis of social capital brings limited improvements, with even more limited or no changes in the existing distribution of "capital" in the form of land and related resources or money in the form of investment capital or credit. Access to these resources—arguably the major factors of economic development—remains in the hands (and institutions) of the rich and powerful, while the poor and powerless are encouraged to exploit their own rather limited resources and to do so without challenging the structures of economic and political power. Some critics regard social capital and empowerment as illusory—not that they are false assumptions but rather a trick used by the rich and powerful to preserve their wealth and keep the have-nots at bay.

NGOs: CATALYSTS FOR DEVELOPMENT OR AGENTS OF OUTSIDE INTERESTS?

The major expression of civil society in the 1980s was the voluntary private association or non-governmental organization, formed in what at the time was defined as the "third sector" (as opposed to the "private sector," composed of profit-making economic enterprises, and the "public sector," organizations and enterprises set up by the government).

At the beginning of the decade, there were relatively few such organizations, most of them voluntary associations to provide poverty relief or to assist communities in their adaptation to the forces of change. By the end of the decade, however, these non-governmental organizations had mushroomed, responding to the vacuum left by the retreating state, assuming responsibilities that it had hitherto fulfilled. While in 1970 there were barely 250 development NGOs working in Latin America, it is estimated that by the end of the 1990s the number had grown to tens of thousands, organized to assist poor communities in the quest for self-development as well as to assist citizens in the struggle to prevent the violation of human rights, advance women's equality, protect the environment, and take on other such concerns of the urban middle class. Political sociologists, armed with a postmodern political imagination, saw this development as the emergence of "new social movements" (Escobar and Alvarez, 1992) concerned with a multitude of issues, not just with state power or transformative social change.

NGOs were enlisted by international organizations such as the World Bank as strategic partners in the war on poverty to act as intermediaries between the providers of financial and technical assistance and the poor communities ravaged by the forces of modernization and abandoned by their governments (at the behest of these same international organizations, it could be added). "Development" here is conceived within the optics of a new paradigm that valorizes "popular participation" and grassroots self-development initiated "from below" with the support of civil society.

To create an appropriate institutional framework for an alternative form of development, the development associations involved in international co-operation promoted a policy of administrative decentralization in developing nations. This policy was incorporated into a new economic model, together with the structural reforms mandated as the cost of admission into the new world order: privatization, financial and trade liberalization, deregulation of markets and private economic activity, democratization, and good governance.

The NGOs were recruited not only to mediate between the aid donors and the poor communities but to promote the virtues of private enterprise and reform. By the 1990s, the marriage between capitalism (the free market) and democracy (free elections) had been consummated, with the NGOs preparing the bridal chamber. In the process, the NGOs helped to dampen the fires of revolutionary fervour among the rural poor, who were encouraged to turn away from the confrontational class politics of the social movements.

There are two fundamental theoretical perspectives on the NGOs in this context. One is to see them as catalysts of an alternative form of development that is participatory, empowering of women and the poor, equitable and socially inclusive, human in form, and sustainable in terms of both the environment and livelihoods. Other scholars, however, take a less sanguine view of these development NGOs, viewing many of them not as change agents but as the stalking horse of neoliberal globalization—a "Trojan horse" for global capitalism—the paid, if at times unwitting, agents of US imperialism (Wallace, 2003). Proponents of this view argue that NGOs do not serve the interests of the rural poor as much as the interests of their masters, the new "rulers of the world," a *transnational capitalist class* composed of corporate CEOs, financiers, and major investors—the guardians of the new world order and its billionaire beneficiaries.

The argument of these scholars is that NGOs are enlisted as front-line soldiers in the war on poverty, in the localities and communities of the poor, to provide

© Cultura RM/Alamy Stock Photo

PHOTO 12.3 | Informal sector employment: A tuk tuk driver waits at Angkor Wat, Cambodia.

what assistance (poverty alleviation funds) might be available and, in the process, to instill respect for the virtues of capitalism and democracy. The war on poverty, it is argued, is simply a charade to mask the real agenda: to create a world safe for capital—to facilitate the entry of foreign investment and the multinational corporations. The implicit mandate of these NGOs, it is further argued, is to help turn the rural poor away from joining social movements and engaging in the confrontational politics of direct action against government policy: to encourage them to seek change and improvements in their lives not by challenging the power structure but by turning inwards—to change not the system but themselves (by "empowering" them to act on their own behalf)—and to seek improvements and change in the local spaces of the power structure rather than challenging the power itself. That is, NGOs are seen as unwitting agents of outside forces and interests, helping to depoliticize the poor in their struggle for change.

CIVIL SOCIETY AND MULTINATIONAL CORPORATIONS

As multinational corporations move into Latin America to take advantage of the extraordinary economic opportunities involved in the extraction and sale on the world market of natural resources and commodities, there is increasing pressure on governments to dampen the voice of civil society organizations working to hold these governments and foreign firms accountable for their actions. In this context the primary role of NGOs and other civil society groups and organizations has been to serve as intermediaries—to intermediate between the communities, on the one hand, and the governments and companies, on the other—to hold the latter accountable for any damage their operations might do to the environment, ensure respect for the culture and human rights of community members, and ensure the engagement of the companies with both the governments and the communities.

However, the actual dynamics of this intermediary role have not been without controversy and debate. On the one hand, some NGOs and other civil society groups and organizations have proven themselves capable of holding governments and companies accountable for their actions. In this context NGOs and other civil society groups and organizations have formed ties with local communities to assist them in their conflicts with the mining companies and have mounted global campaigns against the most symbolic cases to create awareness and hold the mining companies accountable for the negative socio-economic impacts of their operations. In this context, there is increasing pressure on governments to dampen the voice of civil society organizations working to hold the foreign firms accountable for their actions. On the other hand, many NGOs and civil society groups have been more concerned with smoothing the operations of extractive capital and to work with governments in ensuring "community engagement." In this context, civil society organizations tend to be aligned with the foreign companies and the governments in their shared concern with successful project completion. Indeed, in many instances civil society takes the form of NGOs that are set up by the governments or companies, or funded by them. An example of this dual role of NGOs in the development process is given in Box 12.2.

DEVELOPMENT BEYOND NEOLIBERALISM: CIVIL SOCIETY AND THE STATE

The problem with the term "civil society" is that it is so nebulous as to make analysis and prescriptions for action difficult. It includes all manner of social organizations, whose role in the development process must be carefully assessed. For the sake of this assessment, and to facilitate analysis, it is possible to break down "civil society" into three sectors:

1. *A complex of associational-type organizations* (associations formed for a common purpose, such as environmental protection, to advance the status of women, or to promote development or respect for human rights). The anti-globalization movement in the North is an amalgam of such organizations. For the most part, they are located in the cities and are middle-class-based.
2. *Community or grassroots organizations*, making up the "popular sector" of civil society. The Landless Workers' Movement (MST) in Brazil is an example of this type of civil society organization (CSO).
3. *Private-sector interest groups or profit-oriented organizations*. This sector includes the capitalist economic enterprises and multinational corporations that until the 1990s were excluded because they were seen as a large part of the problem.

This chapter has already discussed the role of the first sector, which includes northern development NGOs, the main component of the middle-class sector of civil society activism. (In some contexts, as in India and Latin America, for example, "the new politics" or the politics of the New Left would be included in this grouping.) As for the third, these private-sector organizations are normally excluded from the discourse on development, primarily because as a rule they do not have a development agenda. But in 1989, the UNDP launched a campaign to incorporate the private sector into the development process. For this effort, they used the ideological cover of a more inclusive "civil society" discourse (Mitlin, 1998).

This leaves open for discussion the role of the second sector, namely, grassroots social organizations formed in the localities and communities of the poor. CSOs in this sector arguably have the greatest potential for constituting themselves as "actors." They consist of organizations targeted by international donors and northern NGOs as the object of aid policies and poverty alleviation funding (micro projects). They include social movements, a more politically oriented form of popular organization concerned with bringing about social change through social mobilization and direct action.

The MST (Movimento dos Trabalhadores Rurais Sem Terra or Landless Workers' Movement) in Brazil is a good example of this type of organization. It is dedicated to improving the access of its members to the land, using the politically confrontational tactic of "occupation," as well as organizing for agricultural production on the land, a concern that requires a working

BOX 12.2 | NGOs as Drivers of Community Engagement—To Ensure Successful Project Implementation

CURRENT EVENTS

Case studies show that an investor's willingness and ability to work with governments and local communities from the outset is paramount for successful project completion. The examples of the Toromocho copper mine owned by Chinalco in Peru and Andes Petroleum in Ecuador highlight this lesson particularly well.

In Peru, Chinese state-owned enterprise (SOE) Chinalco's Toromocho mine also borders the Tropical Andes Biodiversity Hotspot. In 2007, Chinalco inherited a commitment to relocate the 5,000 residents of the existing city of Morococha to make way for the mine construction. Morococha is a former mining camp and its water and soil have been badly contaminated from decades of nearby mining operations. Prior to Chinalco's purchase of this project, the Peruvian government was expected to build a new town for the residents, but Chinalco took on the obligation as part of the investment. While the old Morococha had communal latrines and a limited water supply, "Nueva Morococha" promises a modern water and sanitation system. Perhaps most importantly, the move was largely voluntary and the product of dialogue and negotiation among community members, their elected authorities, the central government, and the foreign investor (in this case a Chinese company)—considered the first example of voluntary, participatory community relocation in modern Peruvian history. While it has not been without problems (for example, Chinalco offered each moving family a title to their new homes, but the municipality has delayed issuing them) and there continue to be a number of holdouts, it represents a step forward in Peruvian mining community relations, and a community consultation process that was mediated by a civil society organization (Sanborn and Chonn, 2015).

In Ecuador, however, the community consultation process has not gone so smoothly. Andes Petroleum was given new concessions in early 2014. Ecuador is the only South American country where major Chinese investments exist in an area with extremely high biodiversity in four different species groups as well as traditional indigenous territory, so its respect for social and environmental safeguards are especially important. Until recently, Andes Petroleum (a joint venture between Chinese SOEs Sinopec and CNPC) has had better community relations than most of its competitors (including Ecuadorean SOEs), with fewer protests due to contamination or unfulfilled social obligations. But its real challenge lies ahead, as its current expansion has begun under acrimonious conditions without effective community consultation, as it is alleged by activists that the Secretary of Hydrocarbons (SHE) circumvented state obligations under international law to indigenous communities by obtaining only the approval of the Sápara president instead of seeking the majority approval of the Sápara and Kichwa communities. It is highly probable that the services of some civil society organization will be sought to avoid further conflict and ensure successful project implementation (Ray and Chimienti, 2015).

relationship with the state. Of course, there are less political, more social forms of grassroots organizations as well, such as Via Campesina, a transnational grouping of some 88 peasant and indigenous organizations from at least 25 developing countries (Desmarais, 2007). For such organizations, some closely linked to the anti-globalization movement, their relationship with the state is critical, although it is characterized more by dialogue and co-operation than by the conflict that defines the relationship between most social movements and the state.

The relationship between the state and organizations such as the MST is characterized as much by conflict as by co-operation, because it tends to be marked by dispute and pressure rather than by partnership and dialogue. To push for change and to increase pressure on the state, social movements—and the MST represents an excellent case study of this point—often form alliances with groups and organizations in other sectors of civil society. In the 1990s, for example, the MST expanded its ties to diverse solidarity and advocacy networks, such as the World Social Forum and Via Campesina, that make up what many regard as an emerging "global civil society" (see Box 12.3).

BOX 12.3 | Brazil's Landless Workers' Movement

CURRENT EVENTS

The Movimento dos Trabalhadores Rurais Sem Terra (MST) is a grassroots movement of rural landless workers (peasants) in Brazil formed to bring about land reform through direct collective action—by occupying land that is not in productive or social use and thus subject to expropriation under the 1988 constitution. Over the past two decades the movement has evolved into the largest and most powerful social movement in Latin America, allowing hundreds of thousands of landless small peasant farmers and their households to reclaim their connection to the land and their rural livelihoods.

Conditions for the emergence of the MST could be found in the late 1970s with the rise of liberation theology and pressure from the Catholic Church for the government to address a fundamental issue of land reform—a condition of landlessness for an estimated one million families headed by small peasant farmers. Isolated struggles occurred in rural areas as the impoverished peasantry grew more desperate and began to occupy state land. Officially born in 1984, the MST scored a major victory in 1988 when the constitution was changed to mandate land redistribution.

Over the course of the land struggle the MST evolved to encompass not only a strategy of social mobilization and direct collective action (land occupations) but a social organization of some 60 food co-operatives, a complex of small agricultural industries based on local production, and an organization committed to providing its members a system of alternative education and health services. The MST's literacy program involves 600 educators who work with both adults and adolescents. The movement also monitors 1,000 primary schools in their settlements, in which 2,000 teachers work with about 50,000 children.

The MST opposes previous governments' neoliberal policy regime, gross corruption, and more generally the system that has resulted in an extreme concentration of wealth. Its alternative "Popular Project" includes a program of agrarian reform focused on small, self-sufficient, and environmentally friendly collectives and an end to IMF and World Bank debt repayments in favour of social spending at home. In general, the MST continues to challenge the tenets of neoliberalism: "there is no economic or social reason that impedes every Brazilian having access to land, work, dignified housing, quality public schools, and food. But we need to have the courage to change our government, rethink economic policy and challenge the profits of the powerful" (Manifesto to the Brazilian People, Delegates of the 4th National Congress of the MST, 11 Aug. 2000).

With the support of Via Campesina, an international social movement of peasant farmers (*campesinos*), the MST has evolved into a powerful force of global and local resistance against the dominant model of agricultural production based on large-scale and capital-intensive corporate farming, leading the opposition to the neoliberal model used by governments both in Brazil and in many other countries to guide macroeconomic policy and advance capitalist global production. For its work in leading the global struggle against this model the MST has received a number of international awards, including the Right Livelihood Award and an education award from UNICEF.

As for the relationship between the state and grassroots CSOs, whether non-governmental or social movement in form and action, it is difficult to generalize. One pattern is for social movement-type organizations—such as the MST, Latin America's largest and most dynamic grassroots movement—to take on the central government in the demand for social change. Other grassroots social organizations, in contrast, tend to work with the state at the level of local governments (see Box 12.1). At this level, one can find many cases of "good practice" as well as "local development theory."

GLOBALIZATION, THE STATE, AND CIVIL SOCIETY

A conclusion reached by some analysts of development is that neoliberal globalization is dysfunctional, unethical, and unsustainable (see Chapter 6). The benefits of neoliberal globalization are appropriated by the few, a small group of super-billionaires, while its social costs are borne by the vast majority, many of whom are dispossessed, excluded, or impoverished in the process. In the theory of globalization the benefits of the economic growth generated by the free market will eventually trickle down to the poor. But this is evidently not the case. Apart from the super-rich the only apparent beneficiaries of the globalization process are the "global middle class," who, on the basis of their education, are able to position themselves favourably in the world market and thus improve their life chances. Most of the world's urban and rural poor have neither the opportunities nor the education of this middle class, and thus are socially excluded from any benefits of economic globalization.

Another conclusion, more directly related to the topic of this chapter, is the need for a better balance between the market and the state—to restore the capacity and authority of the state to regulate private economic activity and restrict the power of big capital, as well as the freedom of private interests, and to do so for the public good (Ocampo, Jomo, and Khan, 2007). This does not necessarily mean a return to the welfare and development state. Although the government and regulatory apparatus of the state needs to be reinstituted, it is evident, too, that it needs to be given an entirely new form (see Chapter 7).

People need to assert their "right to development" and to organize—both to empower themselves to act in their collective interest and to advance the local, regional, and national development of society as a whole. This means that the rights of private property need to be restricted, particularly regarding the appropriation of an excessive share of wealth and income. These resources should be shared and distributed more equitably. It also means the abolition of class rule—i.e., reducing the capacity and power of one class, by virtue of its property entitlement (ownership of the means of social production), to set the rules and control who gets what. Above all, it means that civil society should be strengthened and that the relationship between the state and civil society should be democratized.

SUMMARY

This chapter explored the notion of "civil society." In the 1990s the term "civil society" was incorporated into development discourse as it sought to alleviate poverty and to effect social change and "development" in the societies of the Global South on the periphery of the world capitalist system. In this discourse, civil society, a complex of non-governmental organizations, appears as a fundamental agency of social change, replacing the state in this regard. The NGOs, which make up part of civil society and work within it, have become a major object of debate. Some see them as agencies of democracy and participatory development in the struggle for progressive social change. Others, however, see them as agents of the World Bank and other international organizations (as well as of governments in the Global North), engaged in the project of "international co-operation" for the purpose of economic and social development as defined by these major proponents of globalization. At the same time, grassroots social movements in the Global South, such as the MST in Brazil, have entered the discourse to work for a different, and more equitable, world.

QUESTIONS FOR CRITICAL THOUGHT

1. How is civil society constituted—in response to objective changing conditions and trends or as a means of bringing about these conditions?
2. What is the role of civil society in the social change and development process in mediating between donors (and outside forces) and the localities/communities of the poor?
3. Are NGOs a positive factor in the development process? Whose interests do they primarily represent—those of the donors and the guardians of the new world order, or the groups that are socially excluded, marginalized, and poor?
4. What is the best way to advance the interests of the socially excluded, marginalized, and poor—by joining (and encouraging the poor to join) anti-globalization movements for social change or to serve as strategic partners of overseas development associations and their so-called "war on poverty"?
5. Is it possible for development NGOs to support or facilitate self-development of the poor outside the program of international co-operation—without serving as strategic partners of the development associations or multinational corporations and without any funding from them?

SUGGESTED READINGS

Bebbington, Anthony, Samuel Hickey, and Diana C. Mitlin, eds. 2008. *Can NGOs Make a Difference? The Challenge of Development Alternatives*. London: Zed Books.

Craig, D., and D. Porter. 2006. *Development beyond Neoliberalism? Governance, Poverty Reduction and Political Economy*. Abingdon, UK: Routledge.

Keane, John. 2003. *Global Civil Society?* Cambridge: Cambridge University Press.

Munck, Ronaldo. 2007. *Globalization and Contestation: The New Great Counter-Movement*. London: Routledge.

Veltmeyer, Henry. 2007. *Civil Society and the Quest for Social Change*. Halifax: Fernwood.

NOTES

1. The term "civil society" dates back to the eighteenth-century Enlightenment, when moral philosophers such as Adam Ferguson invented the term to distinguish more clearly between "society" and "government" in their writings about "progress." But the term "civil society" disappeared from the map of social scientific discourse until it was resurrected in the 1980s by a generation of social scientists concerned once again with creating a new and better form of society—this time liberated from Soviet authoritarianism as opposed to the class-based and elitist monarchy that was characterized by a ruling, landowning aristocracy, serfdom, monarchy, and an all-powerful church.
2. It is evident that Bill Gates and others who made their fortunes via technical innovations or wealth/job-generating industries or services are in a distinct minority. The vast majority of the world's billionaires used the money of others and speculation to build their fortunes. Many, as in Russia, built their fortunes by looting public assets, pillaging the state's accumulated assets, stealing, and using speculative investment and commodity trading—in construction, telecommunications, chemicals, real estate, agriculture, vodka, foods, land, media, automobiles, and airlines.
3. On this anti-globalization movement see, among others, Engler (2007).
4. On the Occupy movement see, among others, Thompson (2011) as well as the Wikipedia entry "Occupy Movement." Note that Wikipedia most often is an unreliable source of relevant data and studies in this field.

BIBLIOGRAPHY

Desmarais, A.A. 2007. *La Vía Campesina: Globalization and the Power of Peasants.* Halifax and London: Fernwood and Pluto Press.

Domhoff, W. 2011. "Wealth, income, and power. Who rules America?" www2.ucsc.edu/whorulesamerica.

Durston, J. 1999. "Construyendo capital social comunitario." *Revista de* CEPAL no. 69: 103–18.

Engler, M. 2007. *Defining the Anti-Globalization Movement.* Thousand Oaks, Calif.: Sage. http://democracyuprising.com.

Escobar, A., and S.E. Alvarez. 1992. *The Making of Social Movements in Latin America: Identity, Strategy, and Democracy.* Boulder, Colo.: Westview Press.

Forbes. 2015. "Inside the 2015 Forbes billionaires list: Facts and figures." www.forbes.com/sites/kerryadolan/2015/03/02/inside-the-2015-forbes-billionaires-list-facts-and-figures/. Accessed 20 August 2015.

Gibler, J. 2006. "Scenes from the Oaxaca rebellion." *ZNet,* 4 Aug. https://zcomm.org/znetarticle/scenes-from-the-oaxaca-rebellion-by-john-gibler/

Harriss, J. 2001. *Depoliticising Development: The World Bank and Social Capital.* New Delhi: Left Word Books.

Hayden, R. 2002. "Dictatorships of virtue?" *Harvard International Review* 24, 2: 56–61.

Kamat, S. 2003. "NGOs and the new democracy: The false saviours of international development." *Harvard International Review* 25, 1: 48–59.

Mitlin, D. 1998. "The NGO sector and its role in strengthening civil society and securing good governance." In Armanda Bernard, Henry Helmich, and Percy Lehning, eds, *Civil Society and International Development.* Paris: OECD Development Centre.

Ocampo, J.A., K.S. Jomo, and Sarbuland Khan, eds. 2007. *Policy Matters: Economic and Social Policies to Sustain Equitable Development.* London and New York: Orient Longman and Zed Books.

Ottaway, M. 2003. *Democracy Challenged: The Rise of Semi-Authoritarianism.* Washington: Carnegie Endowment for International Peace.

Petras, J., and H. Veltmeyer. 2013. *Social Movements in Latin America: Neoliberalism and Popular Resistance.* Basingstoke, UK: Palgrave Macmillan.

Pilger, J. 2003. *The New Rulers of the World.* London: Verso.

Portes, A. 1998. "Social capital: Its origins and applications in modern sociology." *Annual Review of Sociology* 24: 1–24.

Putnam, R.D., with R. Leonardi and R.Y. Nanetti. 1993. *Making Democracy Work: Civic Traditions in Modern Italy.* Princeton, NJ: Princeton University Press.

Ray, R., and A. Chimienti. 2015. "A line in the equatorial forests: Chinese investment and the environmental and social impacts of extractive industries in Ecuador." Boston: Boston University Global Economic Governance Initiative Working Paper 2015–17.

Sanborn, C., and V. Chonn. 2015. "Chinese investment in Peru's mining industry: Blessing or curse?" Boston: Boston University Global Economic Governance Initiative Working Paper 2015–9.

Solow, R. 2000. "Notes on social capital and economic performance." In Partha Dasgupta and Ismail Serageldin, eds, *Social Capital: A Multi-faceted Perspective.* Washington: World Bank.

UK Ministry of Defence, Development Concepts and Doctrine Centre. 2007. *Global Strategic Trends 2007–2036.* www.dcdc-strategictrends.org.uk.

United Nations Development Programme (UNDP). 2001. *Human Development Report 2001: Making New Technologies Work for Human Development.* New York: UNDP.

———. 2014. *The New Extractivism: A Model for Latin America?* London: Zed Books.

Wallace, T. 2003. "NGO dilemmas: Trojan horses for global neoliberalism?" In *Socialist Register 2004.* London: Merlin Press.

Wikipedia. 2015. "List of countries by the number of US dollar billionaires." https://en.wikipedia.org/wiki/List_of_countries_by_the_number_of_US_dollar_billionaires. Accessed 20 August 2015.

World Bank. 1994. *Governance: The World Bank Experience.* Washington: World Bank.

———. 2004. *Partnerships in Development: Progress in the Fight against Poverty.* Washington: World Bank.

13 China and the Emerging Economies

Jing Gu

LEARNING OBJECTIVES

- To understand changing international development objectives.
- To gain knowledge about China's new development activism.
- To understand factors underpinning co-operation among BRICS countries.
- To acquire critical awareness of new institutions in international development backed by China and the emerging economies.

▲ **Workers fix steel rail track sections to concrete sleepers at the Kathekani T-girder and rail sleeper manufacturing plant, which makes parts for the construction of the new Mombasa-Nairobi Standard Gauge Railway (SGR) line in Tsavo, Kenya. By providing an alternative to roads, the 1,100-kilometre (684-mile) Chinese-financed railway will slash the time and cost of transporting people and goods between East Africa's landlocked nations.** | Source: Riccardo Gangale/Bloomberg via Getty Images

INTRODUCTION

For much of the last century, the world economy and the world of states have been dominated by the economic and political power and influence of the United States and Western economies. For many observers, however, the twenty-first century is already showing signs of a significant shift towards "emerging economies." China has captured the headlines with its dramatic rise to become the world's second largest economy and, in the expectations of many, will soon overtake the United States to claim the top ranking. However, emerging economies are to be found not only in East Asia but also in South Asia, Africa, Latin America, Eurasia, and Eastern Europe. This process of change is perhaps most evident in the coming together of the BRICS countries (Brazil, Russia, India, China, and South Africa), while other economies showing significant growth and economic resilience in recent years are regarded as potentially forming a further wave of emerging economies in Southeast Asia, Eurasia, and Central America.

Emerging economies are widely regarded as driving global growth. Nonetheless, the role and significance of the emerging economies is subject to widespread debate. On the one hand are arguments that these economies offer a break with the past. With their own histories of colonial legacy, impoverishment, conflict, and eventual political stability, recovery, and growth, these countries, proponents claim, have a closer understanding and empathy with the needs and aspirations of the Global South and the billions of people in developing countries. As a consequence, supporters believe they can bring a new approach to critical issues such as international sustainable development. On the other hand, critics argue that little is different, in practice, in the way these economies act in other developing countries, leading some political leaders and commentators in developing countries to label them as new colonialists.

Whichever school of thought one adheres to, these economies, with their growing strength, are having an increasingly significant impact on international development as emerging powers with global reach, importance, and influence. For some, they bring new international development voices and perspectives, perhaps distinct from those of Western powers. Emerging powers are engaged in their own continuing development journey, wrestling with inequities and exclusion. They are also important international development actors. This chapter explores the development trajectories of the emerging powers and the international development implications.

The chapter seeks to develop a sound understanding of the domestic and international development issues central to the emergence of these "economies" or "powers." It explores domestic development implications of their high-speed growth, and assesses their impact on trade, finance, and investment and their growing role as international donors. The discussion begins with an analysis of China's approach to international development before turning to look at the BRICS and other emerging economies.

CHINA'S APPROACH TO INTERNATIONAL DEVELOPMENT

China's role in international development and the implications of that role are subject to intense interest and debate. China's role is immensely controversial, and divides opinion in the global development community. Critics argue that, fundamentally, China is really no different from any other state when it comes to fulfilling its national economic, political, and strategic interests and goals. China's core interest is in accessing raw materials and exporting its labour and goods, while doing little or nothing to counter human rights abuses, corruption, or structural inequalities in its trade and corporate practices. Positive commentaries, however, are more accepting of the so-called "win-win" nature of China's development relations in Africa and elsewhere, pointing to major infrastructural investment improving the sinews of developing-country economies and improving daily lives through social welfare, health, and agricultural technical assistance.

The Chinese government has responded to international criticism that it lacked a clear policy statement on international development and that its approach, therefore, remained opaque. In an attempt to present just such a statement and indicate its evolving thinking on this issue, the government published its first White Paper on Foreign Aid in April 2011 (MOFA, 2011), with a second issued in July 2014 (MOFA, 2014).

The White Papers offer useful insight into China's perspective on international development, one that differs significantly from Western concepts of development in ideational, even ideological, character and set out the principles of foreign aid with "Chinese characteristics" (Box 13.1). These differences mainly derive from China's own experiences of development and as a recipient of foreign aid.

The Chinese government, agencies, and enterprises have been on a steep learning curve as the country's development assistance and technical support to its growing number of development partners in Africa and beyond accelerates, broadens, and deepens (Zhou, 2014). But the formulation of China's approach, a process that had been developing for a few years prior to the issue of the White Papers, is highly complex, involving the legacies of China's own historical experiences, current and anticipated national economic, political, and strategic interests and needs, and the evolving pattern of relationships with other countries and global institutions. This is set within an overarching commitment to ensuring that China's development is peaceful and contributes to building a harmonious world.

To some extent, China's present policy deliberations and international development practices carry the legacy of its turbulent past. As a consequence, China's understanding of "development" has differed markedly from that of many Western countries. While the general Western model is economic as well as ideological (human rights, social welfare, democracy), the Chinese emphasis is on "a wider remit of economic relations" (Gu et al., 2014). In other words, China seeks development partnerships as embedded in the broad spectrum of economic co-operation through trade and investment (particularly in infrastructure capacity-building), as well as in project support and provision of technical know-how.

In addition to this legacy factor is that of institutional policy-making. China's foreign aid policy and implementation responsibilities are spread across four agencies: the State Council, the Ministry of Finance (MOF), the Ministry of Commerce (MOFCOM), and the Ministry of Foreign Affairs (MOFA). The State Council seems to be the body that oversees all aid programs by China, while MOFCOM is the leading agency that co-ordinates China's foreign policy, such as reviewing requests that come from the Ministry of Foreign Affairs that require approval, conducting feasibility studies for aid projects, choosing aid implementers, and conducting project reviews. This raises organizational challenges of co-ordination, capacity, and resources, as well as other difficulties cited by officials including a lack of personnel, limited resources, and the need for a long-term strategy. The institutional infrastructure is further complicated by the myriad of additional agencies engaged in the "development" domain. These include the financial agencies such as the Export-Import Bank of China (Exim Bank); various administrative units at the provincial and municipal

CRITICAL ISSUES

BOX 13.1 | Foreign Aid with Chinese Characteristics

China's first White Paper on Foreign Aid in 2011 emphasized five principles of its foreign aid:

- helping recipient countries build up their self-development capacity;
- imposing no political conditions;
- adhering to equality, mutual benefit, and common development;
- remaining realistic while striving for the best;
- keeping pace with the times and paying attention to reform and innovation.

The 2014 White Paper re-emphasized these five aspects and added one more, "keeping promises," an indication of China's expressed commitment to its overseas development projects.

levels of government; state-owned enterprises and the rapidly growing legion of private firms operating in developing countries; and peak industry associations such as the China–Africa Business Council and bilateral friendship associations exercising their networking influence.

In recent years, China's development approach, both domestically and internationally, has evolved into a broader, deeper, and more complex framework and process (Shambaugh, 2014; Gu et al., 2014). One aspect of this has been greater emphasis placed on promoting and strengthening **people-to-people relationships**. The Chinese government's long-established and preferred approach to its relations with development partners has been that of government-to-government or party-to-party. This is partly a reflection of China's own domestic political culture, which involves a closely regulated civil society, and partly a reluctance to become too deeply involved in the domestic affairs of its partners, potentially compromising its non-interventionist principle. However, there has been criticism in Africa and elsewhere of China's reticence to extend its breadth and depth of engagement. Chinese awareness of this difficulty has led to active encouragement of greater contact between Chinese societal organizations and their counterparts in partner countries. A number of these organizations are semi-civil (i.e., civil society organizations that operate in the civil domain but remain regulated, approved, and monitored by government ministries) bilateral "friendship associations," lodged within the overarching framework of the Chinese People's Association for Friendship with Foreign Countries (CPAFFC), which since 1954 has been responsible for promoting friendly relations with other countries. According to the CPAFFC, it has established "46 China-regional or China-national friendship organisations and established friendly cooperation relationships with nearly 500 nongovernment organisations and institutions in 157 countries" (CPAFFC, n.d.).

China's foreign aid principles are quite distinct from those of many Western states and international institutions (see Box 13.1). Comparing China's current aid policy with the Eight Principles for Economic Aid and Technical Assistance to Other Countries set out by China's former Premier Zhou Enlai in 1964, there has been a clear coherence and consistency in China's aid policy across the intervening decades, as well as a clear divergence with Western aid principles. Recent analyses, however, have examined the evidence that the Chinese government may, after all, be quietly adjusting its stance on non-interference to a gradually more "creative involvement" approach, particularly in Africa, namely respecting sovereignty, consulting on an equal footing, and promoting peace and impartial dialogues (Lu, 2012). The motivation for such a profound change is subject to debate. For some, the rationale is to be found in the heightened exposure and risk to Chinese nationals and enterprises as they increase their presence exponentially across Africa (SIPRI, 2014: vi). Alternative explanations argue that changes actually are a response by Beijing to mounting international criticism.

The Role of the Chinese State and Businesses in Development Co-operation

China's business sector has become increasingly involved in development projects, fuelled in part by its "Going Global" strategy initiated in 2000. This policy used state incentives, including preferential trade access, low interest loans, and Exim Bank support, to promote the outward investment and global expansion of China's leading firms and state-owned enterprises (SOEs).

The engagement of SOEs in development projects is driven both by China's need for raw materials to fuel its domestic growth and by the quest to build up China's own multinational firms in new markets. SOEs have been involved in labour-intensive manufacturing and infrastructure construction in developing countries, often through joint ventures with local private and state-owned enterprises, and have become highly influential in developing countries (see Chapter 11). However, beyond multinational SOEs, a new wave of Chinese private firms and small and medium enterprises (SMEs) also is moving abroad (Gu, 2009). These SMEs are driven by growing domestic competition to seek new market opportunities overseas, but they do so with little co-ordination and direction from the state, and often are underprepared for operating in foreign and new environments.

In recent years, China's economic and political influence in low-income countries has increased dramatically, necessitating enhanced dialogue among disparate development partners. China can offer as advice its recent first-hand experience in achieving economic growth and reducing poverty. For developing countries, these lessons and strategies are more relevant than the experiences of many Development Assistance Committee (DAC) donor countries. Some of China's current challenges are also relevant for developing countries, including those related to income inequality, agriculture, technological innovation, and the environment. China's global reach and influence have become more significant, and nowhere is this more evident than in Africa.

CHINA IN AFRICA

As China's economy has experienced dramatic growth, there has been major growth in both public and private investment in Africa. In the short span of a few years, between 2009 and 2012, the growth rate of Chinese investment reached a remarkable 20.5 per cent. This was matched by the increase in trade. In 2012, the total volume of China–Africa trade reached US$198.49 billion, a year-on-year growth of 19.3 per cent (Government of China, 2013). This expansion in China's engagement with Africa is subject to widespread debate. Opinion is polarized between those, such as He Wenping, who see China's involvement and contribution as adding

CRITICAL ISSUES

BOX 13.2 | Growing Wave of Chinese SMEs in Africa

A new dynamic presence is spreading rapidly and widely across Africa: that of Chinese private enterprises. For these firms, Africa is "the last golden land" of economic opportunity. Why are these enterprises investing in Africa? What are their perspectives on Africa's investment climate?

A growing number of firms are contradicting the stereotype of Chinese firms in Africa. Pushed by intense competition within China's domestic marketplace and pulled by the glint of new opportunities, many small, private manufacturing firms are heading to Africa quite independently of the Chinese government. They take this opportunity in a "three jump" pattern. The first jump is doing business with Africa from China, via exports; the second jump is investing in production in Africa; and the third jump is investing in industrial parks in Africa. This last jump involves Chinese firms clustering in new business parks, collaborating with each other in co-ordinated production.

Yet simultaneously, and contrary to popular perceptions, they are most concerned about their competitive position in China and not by competition from African or other foreign firms in Africa. Estimates of the number of Chinese enterprises in Africa vary considerably. In 2006, the Chinese Export and Import Bank estimated that there were about 800 Chinese companies operating in Africa. Approximately 85 per cent were privately owned. However, evidence from Chinese embassies and the Chinese business communities in Africa indicates that China now has over 3,000 enterprises in Africa. According to one senior Chinese official: "To be honest, we don't know how many firms, especially private firms, invest overseas. There are only a limited number of companies registered with us [in our province]. In fact, I believe that there are more firms. I hope they come to register with us."

The Chinese business sector in Africa, thus, has "enclave" characteristics: enterprises are located together in business parks. They are relatively optimistic about the investment climate in Africa, especially regarding those obstacles created by governments and public policy. However, Africa's prospects for successfully harnessing the Chinese private firms to its development goals depend on how each adapts to the other.

Source: Gu (2011) at http://www.ids.ac.uk/files/dmfile/RsWp365.pdf.

substantial, and much-needed, value-added to Africa's development (He, 2013). Proponents, including South African President Jacob Zuma, see China's engagement as a means by which Africa can begin to reduce its dependency on Western aid and dispense with what are viewed as paternalistic conditionalities forced upon recipients (see Chapter 9). They see China as treating African states "as equals" and point to China's investment, trade, and aid, particularly in building infrastructure, as significant contributors to Africa's development (RT, 2015).

Critics and skeptics, such as Nigerian Central Bank Governor Lamido Sanusi, view the relationship as more "zero-sum" than "win-win" (Sanusi, 2013). Here the primary motivation for China's renewed interest in Africa is its intensifying need for energy and raw materials and for access to Africa's markets for its manufactured products. The critical headlines question China's attitude towards African states accused of human rights violations and corruption. But the criticisms are also much broader and include the use of imported Chinese workers; poor labour and environmental practices; the undercutting of local firms; a weak commitment by many Chinese firms to corporate social responsibility; and a poor record in knowledge and skills transfers. It is argued that China's growing presence puts at risk all the advances in "good governance" made by the international donor community in recent decades (Mwiti, 2015).

The role of the Chinese state as the central driving force and co-ordinating agency behind this increased presence has come under particular scrutiny as China's presence in Africa has grown (Li and Farah, 2013; Piketty and Goldhammer, 2014; Stückelberger, 2015; Strauss and Saavedra, 2009; Brautigam, 2009; Taylor, 2009; He, 2007). Recently, more attention and recognition has been paid to the diverse range of agencies involved and the lack of

AP Photo/Xinhua, Li Xueren

PHOTO 13.1 | **Former Chinese Premier Wen Jiabao embraces a local chief during a visit to Accra, Ghana, in 2006.**

co-ordination between the Chinese state, business, and other organizations operating in Africa. This suggests that the argument that the Chinese state essentially directs Chinese business investment in Africa is overstated (Gu et al. 2016).

As this readjustment of focus was emerging, so was a reassessment of Africa's role. Established wisdom regarded Africa as a passive recipient, reactive rather being than proactive in its engagement with China and other foreign powers. In the revised perspective, the emphasis is on the active role that African governments play in negotiating investments in development (UNECA, 2013; UNCTAD, 2013; Mohan and Lampert, 2013; EU, 2014: article 18), a perspective expressed by the African Union's new vision and strategy, *Agenda 2063*. As the United Nations Economic Commission for Africa (UNECA) argues in relation to the BRICS countries, "The continent also needs to be assertive when negotiating, and to pursue all areas of cooperation to stimulate production and entrepreneurial development" (UNECA, 2013: 3–4).

China's Africa Policy and practice is framed by its foreign policy principles of "Peaceful Development and A Harmonious World" (Government of China, 2005) and the values of political equality, mutual benefit, "win-win" co-operation, cultural exchange, and non-interference. In seeking to understand this, it is necessary to recognize the importance of the close relationship between China's domestic circumstances and its external relations. China's principle of non-interference in the sovereign affairs of its African partners stems from China's own intolerance for foreign interference in its affairs. Moreover, the legitimacy of the Chinese state depends on its ability to deliver economic development to its citizens (Gu et al., 2008). Therefore, while Western states that value civic and political rights talk about "good governance," Chinese officials, who prioritize social and economic rights, talk of "effective governance." Thus, China's approach to governance in Africa is to pay close attention to those who are, in practice, effective partners and to build capacities rather than pressing for the rule of law as a first

PHOTO 13.2 | A Chinese store in Abidjan, Côte d'Ivoire.

priority. China's emphasis on building infrastructure, including transport, hospitals, and education, reflects this prioritization of building capacities. The Chinese slogan "Development first, governance second," underlines China's belief that overcoming state fragility is primarily about improving economic conditions rather than being preoccupied with political governance per se (Gu and Carty, 2014: 57–69).

China has been using diverse means to build relations with developing states, particularly in sub-Saharan Africa, for example, through direct co-operation with the African Union (AU), the African Development Bank (AfDB), and other regional banks (Gu et al., 2014). China's leaders have conducted intensive and extensive diplomacy over the past 25 years, undertaking numerous tours of Africa. It is notable that the first overseas tour of President Xi (elected in 2012 for an initial five-year term and limited to two terms) after his appointment was to Africa. A successful platform has proved to be the Forum on China–Africa Cooperation (FOCAC), established in 2000 to advance partnerships between the African Union and China. As Lan Xue notes, referring to the 2014 FOCAC meeting: "The forum has also become an important platform in extending 'summit diplomacy' to 'people diplomacy' through the involvement of NGOs and business people" (Xue, 2014: 40).

China is not a new donor, but its objectives, mechanisms, and levels of finance have changed significantly. Over the course of its own development experience, its international co-operation has evolved from the ideologically motivated foreign aid of the Mao era to a more pragmatic and flexible strategy involving aid, trade, and Chinese companies "going out" (Shen, 2014). China's leadership has called for the establishment of new multilateral institutions and the deployment of a comprehensive development strategy more reflective of the changing global economic landscape and emerging economies.

Africa and China are central to each other's development co-operation, combining economic, political, strategic, and cultural interests. This is evident not only in the substantial number of diplomatic visits made to Africa by Chinese leaders, government officials, Party representatives, and business and technical co-operation staff and African visits to China, but in the economic statistics. Reciprocal trade flows grew to US$200 billion in 2013, making China Africa's largest trading partner. In his visit to Ethiopia, Nigeria, Angola, and Kenya in May 2014, Premier Le Keqiang announced China's intention to increase this to US$400 billion by 2020 and to increase investment stocks to US$100 billion, compared to US$25 billion in 2013. China would also top up the China Africa Fund, run by the China Development Bank to invest in firms in Africa, by an extra US$2 billion to take its total capitalization to US$5 billion (*China Daily*, 2014). Building on these measures, the May 2014 annual meeting of the African Development Bank approved the creation of an Africa Growing Together Fund (AGTF), a US$2 billion trust fund created by China to enable the Bank to respond to the growing needs of its regional member countries and private-sector clients (AfDB, 2014).

Tony Karumba/AFP/Getty Images

PHOTO 13.3 | Chinese Premier Li Keqiang and Kenyan President Uhuru Kenyatta, 10 May 2014, at State House in the capital, Nairobi.

NEW DEVELOPMENT THINKING AND INSTITUTIONS

Consequently, the most important moves made by China, marking a critical watershed in the direction and focus of its foreign and development policies, are the "Belt and Road" initiative and establishment of the Asian Infrastructure Investment Bank (AIIB). Together, these ambitious initiatives represent the first substantial intervention by China into the institutional architecture of global trade, investment, and financial governance. The importance of these initiatives is not solely economic and financial; it is fundamentally political, representing the first major step by China in acting upon its discontent with the failure to reform the existing global economic and political system. The AIIB, in particular, is a declaration of intent, a challenge and alternative to what it views as Western-centric global financial institutions. For China, the AIIB can bring benefits in terms of demonstrated international leadership and a new avenue through which to extend its influence.

The Belt and the Road Initiative

The **One Belt, One Road initiative** (OBOR) is China's flagship initiative begun under President Xi Jinping. It brings together two separate but interrelated elements: a land-based Silk Road Economic Belt (SREB) and a sea-based twenty-first-century Maritime Silk Road (MSR). The initiative was born in September and October 2013 during President Xi's tours of Central Asia and Southeast Asia. The SREB includes countries situated on the original Silk Road through Central Asia, West Asia, the Middle East, and Europe. The initiative envisages the integration of the region into a cohesive economic area, which will involve investing in infrastructure, widening cultural exchanges, and increasing trade. In addition to this area with its obvious historical roots, the SREB also includes South Asia and Southeast Asia. The MSR is intended to complement the SREB by building partnerships and collaborative relations with countries in Southeast Asia, Oceania, and North Africa as the "Road" traverses the South China Sea, South Pacific, and Indian Ocean.

The initiative is rich in colourful rhetoric, but there is a firm and substantial commitment already evident to help bring the projects to fruition. China has made significant investments totalling approximately US$100 billion. Of this, some US$40 billion has been allocated to the Silk Road Fund (SRF), another US$50 billion to the new Asian Infrastructure Investment Bank (AIIB), and US$10 billion to the BRICS New Development Bank. In President Xi Jinping's view, the SREB and MSR "will promote the trade and investment between China and the countries along the routes, promote the connectivity and new-type industrialisation of countries along the routes, and promote the common development of all countries as well as the peoples' joint enjoyment of the fruits of development. We hope that the annual trade volume between China and the countries along the routes will surpass 2.5 trillion USD in a decade or so" (MOFA, 2015).

IMPORTANT CONCEPTS

BOX 13.3 | One Belt, One Road Priorities

1. *Policy Co-ordination*
   Macroeconomic and development policies, and large-scale projects
2. *Facilities Connectivity*
   Improving land and sea transportation links, ensuring more integrated energy networks and pipelines
3. *Unimpeded Trade*
   Removing investment and trade barriers to facilitate the movement of goods and services, including through creation of free trade zones
4. *Financial Integration*
   Building a "currency stability system, investment and financing system, and credit information system in Asia"; establishing new financing institutions
5. *People-to-People Links*
   Promoting academic links, cultural exchanges, and tourism, sharing information on threats, e.g., epidemics

Asian Infrastructure Investment Bank (AIIB)

The Asian Infrastructure Investment Bank (AIIB) has emerged from an idea first put forward by China in 2013 (Table 13.1). This led to discussions and the formal launch of the proposal in Beijing in October 2014, with the Articles of Agreement signed in late June 2015. As its title indicates, the purpose of the AIIB is to provide much-needed investment in infrastructure capacity in the Asia-Pacific region. The establishment of the AIIB is a direct response to the identified critical need for large-scale investment in many Asia-Pacific countries. According to an assessment by the McKinsey Global Institute, the projected *global* investment for 2015–30 is around US$57.3 trillion (*Wall Street Journal*, 2015). The founding of the AIIB also grew from China's assessment that the heavy dominance of the US and Japan in the ADB and the lack of progress on reform meant that an alternative financial institution was needed.

The AIIB, perhaps unsurprisingly, has proven to be highly controversial. This became evident following press reports that the US opposed the setting up of the AIIB and was conducting quiet, and ultimately unsuccessful, diplomacy to pressure US allies such as Indonesia, Australia, and the UK not to sign up for AIIB membership. US officials were alleged in a *New York Times* report to have lobbied against the development bank to persuade other countries not to join it. The newspaper also stated that "[t]he United States Treasury Department had criticized the bank as a deliberate effort to undercut the World Bank and the Asian Development Bank, international financial institutions established after World War II that are dominated by the United States and Japan . . . . Washington also sees the bank as a political tool for China to pull countries in Southeast Asia closer to its orbit, a soft-power play that promises economic benefits while polishing its image among neighbors anxious about its territorial claims" (*New York Times*, 2014).

TABLE 13.1 | Potential Strengths and Problems for the AIIB

Potential Strengths	Potential Problems
The Bank has a specific focus: specializing in Asia and infrastructure development.	The most challenging aspect of the Bank's work will be to ensure that it balances what is likely to be heavy demand while maintaining its stated principles and standards.
It promises to be more open, transparent, and inclusive than existing multilateral development banks (MDBs).	The Bank will have to address quickly the need to embed openness, transparency, and inclusivity into its organizational culture and governance systems.
The AIIB's founding documents and statements also commit to high professional standards.	As a principal driving force behind the founding of the Bank, China's role in its day-to-day operations will have to be further clarified and justified, especially in relation to other members such as India.
This new institution provides an opportunity for innovation, particularly in terms of the issue of voting rights.	Just how the AIIB is going to work effectively with other MDBs presents a further challenge that requires prioritization in its establishment phase.
The specific regional focus is intended to help promote economic growth, encourage integration, and mobilize financial resources across the region.	The AIIB will have to consider its role and promotion of its members' interests in the wider global institutional architecture.
The Bank also provides for public–private partnerships.	The Bank's structure will need to provide robust project monitoring and problem-solving response mechanisms.
By drawing together regional members into this new multilateral tier of co-operation, it is hoped that existing tensions and differences can be reduced or overcome.	

Scholars, the Chinese government, the World Bank, the African Development Bank, and, more recently, US President Barack Obama, however, have argued that the AIIB should not be seen as competition to other development initiatives but should be viewed as an opportunity for co-operation (Li and He, 2015). Infrastructure needs cannot be filled solely by the AIIB and, thus, co-operation and complementarity with existing institutions are key to the effectiveness of the AIIB. Nonetheless, the AIIB is not just about development finance but is the first real attempt by the Chinese government to institutionalize its financial power globally (Griffith-Jones et al., 2016). The AIIB will not necessarily transform development finance, but it will transform multilateral engagement and global governance.

China and the Post-2015 Sustainable Development Goals (SDGs)

Within the post-2015 debate, China has focused on the question of how to balance economic development, social justice, and environmental protection. Like other middle-income countries, it also has emphasized common but differentiated responsibilities (CBDR), i.e., differential responsibilities within a universal agenda (Leong, 2014), and has stated that at this point in its development, South–South co-operation should serve as a supplement rather than as a replacement for North–South co-operation. In addition to supporting the co-ordinating position of the UN, China sees the AIIB and OBOR assuming crucial roles in post-2015 global development by providing critically needed infrastructural investment and important focal points for common development (Gu, 2015).

In the post-2015 world, sustainable development is a top priority for global development agendas and requires increased commitment and co-operation in development efforts. This era provides opportunity for experts in international relations, trade, climate, and domestic policy to engage in conversation about how each country, as part of a global effort, can contribute to fair and sustainable growth. While the world can count on China to continue to be innovative with new approaches to and partnerships for development, China intends to continue to adhere to its principle of "common but differentiated responsibilities" into the post-2015 era.

THE BRICS AND OTHER EMERGING ECONOMIES

What is an emerging economy or power? As we have already suggested, there are contending answers to this question. Some commentators are even skeptical of the whole idea that there are emerging economies, arguing that while there may well be a strong case for applying the term to China, there is little substance to extend it to other economies as their trajectories of growth and the foundations of political stability are relatively recent and tentative. Such reservations notwithstanding, the BRICS and other emerging economies are a prominent part of the contemporary landscape of international development and a deeper understanding of their role and significance is necessary.

The first point to make is that the range of countries actively engaged in international development co-operation today is much broader and diverse than many might imagine (also see Chapter 6). Beyond the activities of the BRICS, South–South dialogue and co-operation has also involved bilateral and multilateral initiatives with next-wave "emerging economies" such as Indonesia, Mexico, and Turkey. Turkey, for example, has had a development partnership dialogue with Africa reaching back to 1998 and held its Second Turkey–Africa Partnership Summit in November 2014 in Malabo, Equatorial Guinea (RoT, 2014). That being said, it is quite clear that the BRICS countries have particular characteristics that mark them for specific attention in the domain of international development. Beginning from a dialogue process initiated in 2006, the organization and its members have evolved to be important actors. In 2001, Jim O'Neill, at that time the head of Global Economic Research at Goldman Sachs, coined the acronym "BRIC" as a convenient collective term and play on words to describe the four economies he was analyzing in his global economics research paper (O'Neill, 2001). As political impetus for a grouping of these economies, later to be joined by South Africa, the BRIC acronym gained political and institutional currency. BRICS has steadily established itself as an important organization on the international stage.

Commonalities and Differences

The BRICS countries have a number of commonalities and convergences in their approaches to the "development agenda." In terms of commonalities, all the BRICS members have extensive territories and significant populations, and have recorded impressive rates of GDP growth (see Figure 13.2). They accept the idea that the state has a legitimate and important role to play in domestic and international development. Each, with the exception of the Russian Federation, would classify itself as a developing country—although Russia still faces substantial challenges of poverty, inequality, health problems, and deprivation. Other shared characteristics include the recent experience of conflict, poverty, and inequalities; the implementation of successful reforms, resulting in economic recovery and eventual growth and political stability; increasing global influence based in part on their regional dominance; and recent efforts to establish themselves as new sources of international development assistance and co-operation. The BRICS members have also committed to a collective process of institutionalizing their co-operation.

There is a common belief in the importance of **South–South co-operation**. There are two aspects to this co-operation. First, it is seen by the BRICS members to be supplemental to North–South relations, facilitating **triangular development co-operation** strategies and projects between a traditional donor, an emerging donor in the South, and a beneficiary country in the South. Triangular technical co-operation, defined by Brazil as establishing agreements with both developed and developing countries "to acquire and disseminate knowledge applied to social and economic development" (Brazilian Cooperation Agency, n.d.) is a growing component of the emerging architecture of international development promoted by emerging economies, such as Brazil and China. China, for example, works with the UK government on development projects in Africa. This approach nests within a substantial theme of international development co-operation. The Accra Agenda for Action called for further development of triangular co-operation. In response, various organizations and groupings such as ECOSOC, the G8, the UNDP, and the OECD-DAC have held conferences on triangular development co-operation.

Second, although supplementary, South–South co-operation is regarded as vitally important in its own right, providing an important framework and trajectory for developing countries, emerging economies,

IMPORTANT CONCEPTS

BOX 13.4 | What Are the BRICS?

- BRICS is a dialogue and co-operation platform among member states (Brazil, Russia, India, China, and South Africa).
- BRICS started active life in 2009 as BRIC with Brazil, Russia, India, and China and saw South Africa join the group in 2010.
- The grouping accounts for 30 per cent of global land, 43 per cent of global population, 21 per cent of the world's gross domestic product (GDP), 17.3 per cent of global merchandise trade, 12.7 per cent of global commercial services, and 45 per cent of the world's agriculture production.
- The group holds annual BRICS summits, rotating through the membership (eight meetings have been held between 2009 and 2016).
- BRICS countries have increased their share of global GDP threefold in the past 15 years.

Source: BRICS: The Strategy for BRICS Economic Partnership, Official Website of Russia's Presidency in BRICS. http://en.brics2015.ru/documents/.

and BRICS. South–South co-operation emphasizes development partnerships and the BRICS grouping stresses that BRICS are "partners," not "donors." The principles of South–South co-operation have been very important in framing how some of the BRICS (particularly India and Brazil) define themselves as development co-operation providers.

In terms of differences, the BRICS members bring to the grouping very different geographies, histories, cultures, and values as well as different political systems and economic systems. One major difference in political terms, quite evidently, centres on "political democracy" and the way that the term is understood and practised in the respective BRICS member states (see Chapter 16). While India is widely recognized as the world's largest political democracy grounded in a pluralistic, multi-party, representative governmental system, Brazil, Russia, and South Africa have laboured to establish equivalent systems in recent decades, with Brazil and South Africa both stressing the importance of democratization in their development pathways at home and internationally. China, on the other hand, interprets democracy quite distinctly, retaining the paramount and "vanguard" role of the Communist Party as central to the political and social system, both constitutionally and in practice, while promoting a market economy. This diversity gives rise to very different approaches to the role and purpose of civil society and non-governmental organizations, as well as to issues of transparency and accountability, civil and human rights (freedom of expression and the role of the press and other media). Such issues of a domestic nature overflow into international development practices ranging from human rights to corporate social responsibility and the promotion of good governance.

History plays an interesting and important contemporary role. For example, Brazil's initial steps in building development co-operation with states in sub-Saharan Africa reflected a shared experience of Portuguese colonialism and the linguistic and cultural legacies that have remained within the Lusophone countries. This pattern is also evident in China's relations with African development. China's own experience of Portuguese colonialism, on the island of Macao,

Roberto Stuckert Filho/PR

PHOTO 13.4 | BRICS leaders 2014: Russian President Vladimir Putin, Indian Prime Minister Narendra Modi, Brazilian President Dilma Rousseff, Chinese President Xi Jinping, and South African President Jacob Zuma.

provided China with a legitimate basis with which to establish a "Macao Hub," through which to promote, support, and consolidate its relations with Lusophone countries in Africa and Latin America. Brazil's approach has also drawn upon the historical roots with Africa originating in the European colonial slave trade from Africa, offering Brazil an important theme of shared history and familial roots by which to foster and legitimize its development role in Africa within the South–South co-operation and dialogue framework.

The volume of the provision of development assistance also varies, reflecting various factors such as annual rates of growth and changing government, policy, and budget priorities. The recent slowdown in economic growth in Brazil, shifting domestic priorities, and an increasingly commercial character to its development co-operation seem to suggest a drawing-back in its assistance. Other countries, notably India and China, appear to be committed to increasing their assistance provision despite a slowing of their own growth rates (see Figure 13.1).

Institutionalizing BRICS

Is the breadth of issues tackled and the work involved increasing the body of gained infrastructure? BRICS members already have more than 20 institutionalized forms of co-operation, from yearly summits to working groups, addressing international information security, health care, agriculture, science, and technology. Major policy initiatives such as the Contingent Reserve Arrangement (CRA) and the New Development Bank (NDB) are not only key organizational bodies, but are widely regarded as a statement of intent by the BRICS countries to establish substantial alternative financial agencies to those of the IMF and World Bank and to the Western economies.

From its first summit in Yekaterinburg in Russia, the central focus of BRICS has been to tackle what the group's leaders hold to be the exclusivity of a Western club of global financial and political institutions; effectively favouring non-BRICS economies and their enterprises and marginalizing the BRICS countries and other emerging economies and their firms. The Joint Statement of the BRICS Countries' Leaders called for a "greater voice and representation in international financial institutions, and their heads and senior leadership should be appointed through an open, transparent, and merit-based selection process" (BRICS, 2009). Reflecting these concerns, the leaders agreed to create a Business Council and, based on a proposal at the fourth summit held in Delhi in 2012, to work towards establishing joint financial institutions of their own. This dialogue eventually led to the CRA and to the 2014 NDB agreement that came into force in July 2015. The group also operates a BRICS Banking Forum and BRICS Exchanges Alliance (cross-listing shares from over 7,000 BRICS companies with a total capitalization of about US$8 trillion). In the view of some observers, "The establishment of BRICS-led MDBs [multilateral

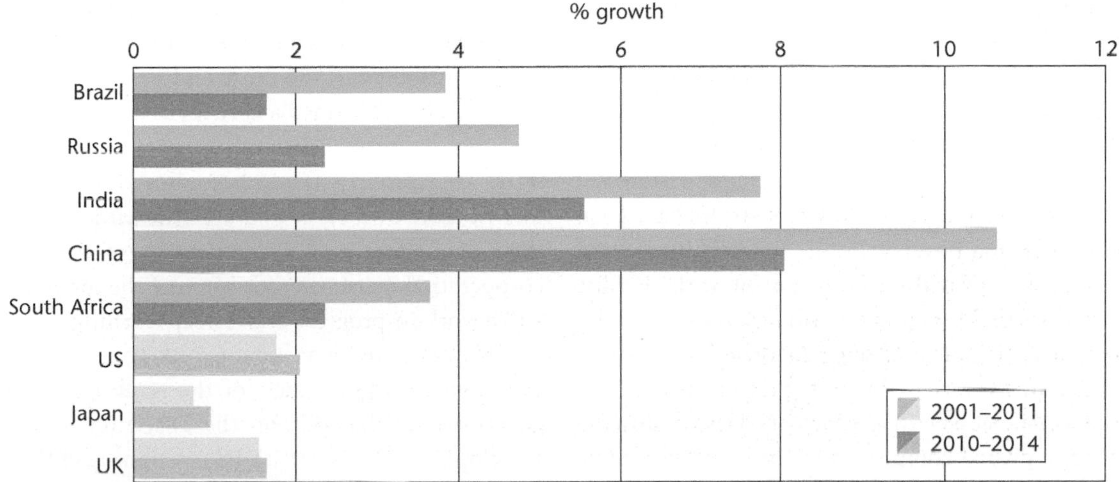

FIGURE 13.1 | Average Annual Growth Rates for the BRICS and Three Major Developed Economies

Source: Walker (2014). Calculated from IMF World Economic Outlook Database, October 2014.

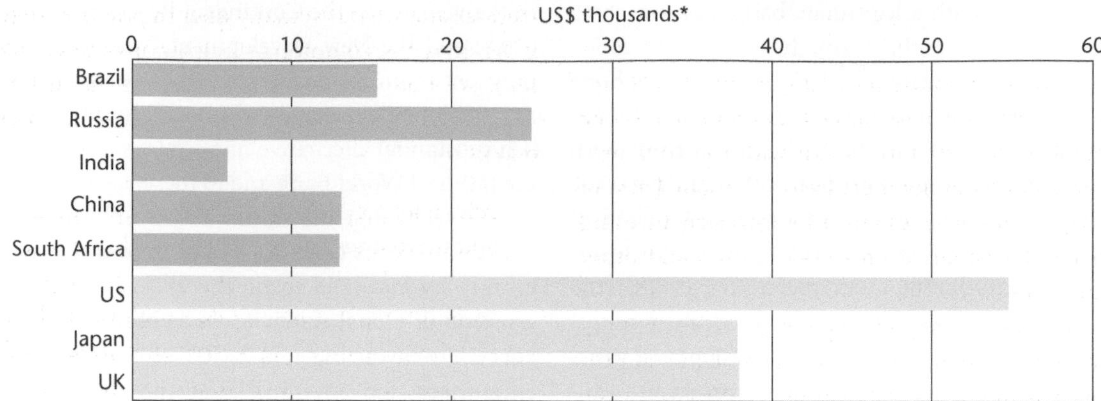

FIGURE 13.2 | GDP Per Capita for the BRICS and Three Major Developed Economies

*Based on purchasing power parity.

Source: Walker (2014). Calculated from IMF World Economic Outlook Database, October 2014.

development banks] will be beneficial for global development to the extent that it helps cover some of the current infrastructure financing gaps. Moreover, the new banks organize a 'voice' for EMDCs [economically more developed countries] and rebalance representation of the non-OECD countries in multilateral development lending. This is likely to speed up reform even in the established multilaterals. Competition is building for the existing Bretton Woods system" (Reisen, 2015: 6).

Unsurprisingly, given the interwoven nature of the international institutional architecture, the agenda of the BRICS is not solely about economic and financial institutional reform but also seeks reform of the United Nations.

The expectations regarding the economic performance and relative weight of the BRICS countries in the global economy have been high, and their average annual growth rates largely met these expectations in the decade through to 2011. Since 2010, however, there has been a slowdown in their growth rates, with Brazil and Russia most affected. Significant strides have been made in reducing poverty, improving health care and education, and providing employment with dignity. Nevertheless, these economies still face substantial development challenges, reflected in their low GDP per capita and by the fact that they are recipients of development assistance as well as providers. Despite this, the BRICS are a pivotal component in the global economic system and much rests on their continued performance.

In terms of international development co-operation, the BRICS have established a declaratory commitment to addressing issues of peace, poverty, and access to health care and education for all, as well as to making sure that global economic growth and sustainable development are an inclusive process. For example, the first BRIC summit called for greater international action to deal with the global food crisis. Nonetheless, up to 2015, the majority of actions were taken directly by BRICS members, rather than collectively through the organization.

The BRICS group has yet to formulate its own institutional development policy and strategy. This is due mainly to two factors. First, as we have already noted, the initial spur to the creation of BRICS was to co-ordinate a response to the global financial crisis and to address the weaknesses in the existing international economic, financial, and political institutions they believe contributed to the crisis and to a weak response to it. This has remained a core focus and goal of BRICS through its several summits. Second, the member states are relatively new to becoming development actors in their own right and are still working through their own ideas and understanding of development co-operation assistance; for some of the members it is still a work-in-progress and a steep learning curve.

However, three factors are likely to change this situation: (1) the creation of the NDB; (2) the intergovernmental dialogue on the Post-2015 Sustainable Development Goals (SDGs); (3) the signing of the Strategy for BRICS Economic Partnership. The NDB has attracted worldwide attention and is worth examining in more detail.

The New Development Bank (NDB)

The process of formulating a distinctive BRICS approach to international sustainable development is one that might be said to have begun with the 2012 proposal for a BRICS development bank. The stated aim of the NDB is to "mobilise resources for infrastructure and sustainable development projects in BRICS and other emerging economies and developing countries." The primary function of the NDB is to provide lending (up to an approved limit of US$34 billion annually) for projects. In focusing on infrastructure, the NDB reflects a widely acknowledged critical need in developing economies for infrastructural investment to support sustainable development and growth.

Are the BRICS Members Really Different?

The central question raised about BRICS is about the extent to which these countries, as a group, represent a new and different approach to international relations and to international sustainable development. The answer involves both the principles upon which BRICS operates and what it actually does in practice. In terms of the shared or common principles or values of BRICS, these are noted in the Ufa Declaration issued at the end of the seventh summit in July 2015 in Russia as follows:

> principles of openness, solidarity, equality and mutual understanding, inclusiveness and mutually beneficial cooperation. We agreed to step up coordinated efforts in responding to emerging challenges, ensuring peace and security, promoting development in a sustainable way, addressing poverty eradication, inequality and unemployment for the benefit of our peoples and the international community. We confirmed our intention to further enhance the collective role of our countries in international affairs." (Ufa Declaration, 2015)

China's President Xi Jinping's speech to the seventh BRICS summit in Ufa, Russia, in July 2015 set out his vision of a BRICS approach emphasizing the need for developing countries to take on more responsibility for their own development while BRICS provides assistance in meeting critical capacity-building needs

IMPORTANT CONCEPTS

BOX 13.5 | BRICS New Development Bank (NDB)

- The NDB is a multilateral development bank operated by the BRICS states (Brazil, Russia, India, China, and South Africa) with an initial capitalization of US$50 billion, rising to an eventual US$100 billion.
- The NDB is headquartered in Shanghai, with an Africa Regional Centre to be established in Johannesburg, South Africa.
- The purpose of the NDB is to "mobilize resources for infrastructure and sustainable development projects in BRICS and other emerging economies and developing countries."
- Each participant country holds an equal number of shares and equal voting rights, and none of the countries will have veto power.
- The BRICS members state that the NDB is not intended to challenge or replace institutions such as the IMF and World Bank, but to support and supplement the work of these organizations, but some observers see the NDB and the same-sized contingent reserve arrangement (CRA) as "institutions that aim to be both competitor and antithesis to the World Bank and International Monetary Fund" (Pizzi, 2015).
- The President of the NDB for the first five years is India's K.V. Kamath.

and promotes further South–South Co-operation. In President Xi's view, "The BRICS nations should also establish a new type of global development partnership, urge the developed countries to shoulder their due responsibilities, and help developing countries improve their self-development capability, so as to narrow the North–South gap, intensify South–South cooperation and seek self-improvement through cooperation on the basis of mutual benefit and win-win." Brazil's approach also stresses the importance of working within the principles and practices of South–South Cooperation "as it enhances general interchange; generates, disseminates and applies technical knowledge; builds human resource capacity; and, mainly, strengthens institutions in all nations involved" (Brazilian Cooperation Agency, n.d.).

What does this mean in practice for international sustainable development? The emphasis is less on the traditional or established idea of "foreign aid," a term and practice believed by the BRICS and other emerging economies to carry connotations of an unequal relationship based on donors and recipients (see Chapter 8). This is particularly salient for these economies as they are, in various ways, recipients of aid as well as contributors. Their approach, therefore, is to move away from the "donor–recipient" aid relationship to form development "partnerships." It also means that, while humanitarian assistance and welfare "aid" are still components of their relationships with developing countries, the substantial weight is on capacity-building for self-help through infrastructural investment and project work, knowledge and skills transfers through partnerships, and self-development.

The Principle of Non-Intervention

A core BRICS principle is non-intervention in the domestic affairs of their partners, retaining the values of mutuality and equality of relations. In other words, the guiding principle is to respect the legal and political sovereignty of partner states by not intervening in their domestic affairs. This principle, of course, is highly controversial and is a focus of pointed criticism from the established, "traditional" Western donors and institutions, which emphasize making assistance contingent on a list of domestic reforms. The principle has a long history, however, including the famous Bandung Conference of newly independent and non-aligned states that met in 1954, with a prime contributor to the declaration from that conference being Chinese Premier Zhou Enlai, who introduced China's own Five Principles of Peaceful Coexistence into the conference debate and final document, principles that remain part of the political position of China and many developing countries today. Yet, while the BRICS countries generally adhere to this principle of non-intervention in their common approach to international development, it is also a source of differentiation between them, most notably with respect to South Africa and Brazil. The South African government and the ruling African National Congress place significant importance on human rights and democracy in international relations and development perspectives. Brazil, for its part, also identifies democracy as a key value and principle in international development, as does India. India, Brazil, and South Africa have established their own grouping, IBSA, that emphasizes democracy as one of its most important principles.

Growing Multilateralism

The development approach of the respective BRICS partners shows they share a number of characteristics, such as regularizing processes of consultation with partners. Much of this is undertaken on a bilateral, state-to-state basis, but there are signs of growing multilateralism, for example, in the Forum on China–Africa Cooperation and in the retreat on the theme of "Unlocking Africa's potential: BRICS and Africa Cooperation on Infrastructure," held between BRICS and African leaders after the fifth BRICS summit held in Durban in 2013, which was focused on the theme of "BRICS and Africa: Partnership for Development, Integration and Industrialization."

In addition, the BRICS members are responding individually to the increased importance of international development by restructuring their international development bureaucracies. In China, as we will see below, international development has taken time to become absorbed into the political agenda. It has taken hold with extensive deliberation over what international assistance means and the form it should take, with the establishment of new research and policy centres and with the publication of the two White

Papers on Foreign Aid. India's growing development co-operation has been consolidated through the creation in 2012 of the Development Partnership Administration (DPA) within the Ministry of External Affairs. The DPA, organized in three divisions that cover project appraisal and lines of credit, capacity-building and disaster relief, and project implementation, reaches out to countries throughout Asia as well as in Africa and Latin America (Government of India, n.d.). South Africa has a new co-ordinating agency, the South African Development Partnership Agency (SADPA), under the Department of International Relations and Cooperation (DIRCO).

Overall, the BRICS and a number of other emerging economies are making an increasing contribution to international development by providing much-needed investment, technical know-how, knowledge, and skills, as well as financial and broader economic and political support. To date, their role remains comparatively small compared to developed economies, but they are catching up rapidly. Many of these economies offer to developing-country partners a common history of colonial or semi-colonial experiences, relatively recent independence, poverty and inequality, and conflict, while also presenting recent histories of successful reform, stability, and growth that are attractive to development partners. Adherence to the principle of non-interference is controversial, particularly with regard to claims of human rights violations in or, as is often alleged, by partner states. However, along with an unwillingness to travel the path of conditionality for assistance—such as structural reforms, principles of non-interference, equality, and mutuality—and a continuing acceptance of the importance of a role of the state in promoting development, all offer a tantalizing alternative to the established sources of development assistance.

CONCLUSION

Global development has reached a critical turning point. In addition to achieving middle-income status, several recipient countries are emerging donors. As the international development community starts down the road of the ambitious post-2015 agenda, China has rapidly expanded its development finance program and has launched new multilateral initiatives. From discourse and pathways of co-operation to new institutions, China has served as an influential driver of shifting development models. With this increasing diversity of actors and development patterns, the international development community now faces difficult questions about how to move forward, and beyond aid, together.

The international community adopted the SDGs at the UN Summit in New York in September 2015. At this significant moment, a fundamental question arose as to the salience of the orthodox, largely Western-derived understanding of and operational approach to international development co-operation. How valid is it in the light of the growing importance of the BRICS and other emerging economies? In classic international relations, emerging powers relate to the existing order in three possible ways: by accepting and being absorbed into the system as a status quo member; by seeking a "revisionist" adjustment within the system to match its own interests; or by a more "revolutionary" rejection of the system in its entirety. How do we classify China and the other emerging economies with respect to the international development co-operation regime? These are hard and complex questions to answer convincingly.

Elements of each stance are to be found in China's approach. China is actively engaged in the international development assistance system and in the regularized system of institutionalized conferences and policy determination procedures; and China is an increasingly assertive and vocal advocate for its position and for developing countries. This position suggests a degree of acceptance of the need to work, at least for the time being, with the existing architecture and underlying principles and values derived mostly from Western origins and precepts.

The BRICS and other emerging countries have been pressing vocally for substantial reforms in the present system, but with limited success. China's approach to aid significantly differs from that of Western donors and is still evolving. Recognition of differences in perspectives behind aid and development remains central to future successful aid co-operation. The institutional context of China's development co-operation is complex. Western donors and external partners must take these differentiated political roles into consideration in order to effectively pursue initiatives such as trilateral development co-operation. It is possible that we are reaching the tipping point where revisionist-reformists move decisively (perhaps reluctantly) to the final "revolutionary" position in rejecting the status quo and replacing it with an alternative system. The first signs are already there.

The increasing presence of the emerging economies has raised the question of what kind of development co-operation we are going to see in the future. This issue is particularly significant in light of the formal agreement on the Sustainable Development Goals in 2015. These goals call for a global partnership to be established to mobilize behind the universal nature of the SDGs and targets. The breadth and scale of the post-2015 development agenda and the complexity of the immense challenge of implementation mean that a multilateral approach is required. The emerging economies and the new perspectives, approaches, and institutions they are bringing with them will need to be recognized as they form an important part of the global partnership.

SUMMARY

This chapter has provided a critical overview of the growing importance and role of China and the emerging economies in international development. It has provided the reader with grounding in the distinctive perspectives and approaches of these new development actors, the innovations they are introducing, and the key issues and debates surrounding their expanding involvement.

For the student reader, the chapter's learning outcomes lie in gaining a greater knowledge and understanding of current development thinking and practice. The inclusion of this chapter in this volume recognizes the increasing importance and influence of these economies in global development. The chapter relates to the wider themes of development addressed in this book, for example, new thinking and practice, the role of the private sector and the emerging post-2015 international institutional development architecture, and the implications of the arrival of these new development actors for development practice.

QUESTIONS FOR CRITICAL THOUGHT

1. Where do the emerging economies fit within the field of development studies?
2. How is "development" understood and practised by the emerging economies?
3. How does China as a growing power, investor, consumer, and donor engage with specific regional and global development regimes?
4. How has China shaped development discourse and the major debates around it?
5. What does the emergence of China and the BRICS mean for traditional donors and other development institutions?

SUGGESTED READINGS

Becker, Uwe, ed. 2014. *The BRICS and Emerging Economies in Comparative Perspective*. Oxford: Routledge.

Economy, Elizabeth C., and Michael Levi. 2014. *By All Means Necessary: How China's Resource Quest is Changing the World*. New York: Oxford University Press.

Gu, Jing, Alex Shankland, and Anuradha Chenoy, eds. 2016. *The BRICS in International Development*. London: Palgrave Macmillan.

O'Neill, Jim. 2011. *The Growth Map: Economic Opportunity in the BRICs and Beyond*, London: Penguin.

Stuenkel, Oliver. 2013. Institutionalizing South–South Cooperation: Towards a New Paradigm? Background Research Paper. High Level Panel on the Post-2015 Development Agenda. www.post2015hlp.org.

BIBLIOGRAPHY

African Development Bank (AFDB). 2014. "AFDB's 2014 annual meetings end in Kigali." www.afdb.org/en/news-and-events/article/afdbs-2014-annual-meetings-end-in-kigali-13208/. Accessed 20 July 2015.

Alden, C., and S. Chichava. 2014. *China and Mozambique: From Comrades to Capitalists*. Auckland Park, South Africa: Jacana.

Brautigam, D. 2009. *The Dragon's Gift: The Real Story of China in Africa*. Oxford: Oxford University Press.

Brazilian Cooperation Agency (ABC). n.d. www.abc.gov.br/training/informacoes/ABC_en.aspx. Accessed 25 July 2015.

BRICS. 2009. "Joint Statement of the BRICS Countries' Leaders." Yekaterinburg, Russia, 16 June. BRICS Information Centre, University of Toronto. www.brics.utoronto.ca/docs/090616-leaders.html. Accessed 15 Aug. 2015.

Chinese–African People's Friendship Association (CAPFA). "About CAPFA." http://en.cpaffc.org.cn/content/details27-656.html. Accessed 10 Aug. 2015.

Chinese People's Association for Friendship with Foreign Countries (CPAFFC). n.d. "About CPAFFC." http://en.cpaffc.org.cn/introduction/agrintr.html. Accessed 18 July 2015.

China Daily. 2014. "Premier Li Visits Africa." 4–11 May. www.chinadaily.com.cn/world/2014livisitafrica/. Accessed 17 July 2015.

European Union (EU). 2014. "The Brussels G7 Summit Declaration." Brussels: European Union. www.consilium.europa.eu/uedocs/cms_Data/docs/pressdata/en/ec/143078.pdf. Politics. Accessed 7 Mar. 2015.

Fues, T., and Y. Jiang. 2014. *The United Nations Post-2015 Agenda for Global Development: Perspectives from China and Europe*. DIE Studies, 84. www.die-gdi.de/uploads/media/Studies_84.pdf. Accessed 5 Mar. 2015.

Government of China. 2005. *China's Peaceful Development Road*. White Paper. State Council Information Office. www.china.org.cn/english/2005/Dec/152669.htm. Accessed 9 Sept. 2015.

———. 2013. *China–Africa Economic and Trade Cooperation (2013)*. Information Office of the State Council, People's Republic of China, Aug.

Government of India, Ministry of External Affairs. n.d. "Development Partnership Administration." Delhi: Ministry of External Affairs. http://mea.gov.in/development-partnership-administration.htm. Accessed 3 June 2016.

Griffith-Jones, S., L. Xiaoyun, J. Gu, and S. Spratt. 2016. "What can the Asian Infrastructure Investment Bank learn from other development banks?" IDS Policy Briefing 113.

Gu, J. 2009. "China's private enterprises in Africa and the implications for African development." *European Journal of Development Research* 21, 4: 570–87.

———. 2011. *The Last Golden Land? Chinese Private Companies Go to Africa*. Brighton: IDS Working Paper 365.

———. 2015. *China's New Silk Road to Development Cooperation: Opportunities and Challenges*. Tokyo: United Nations University Centre for Policy Research.

———. and A. Carty. 2014. "China and African Development: Partnership Not Mentoring." In Gu et al. (2014: 57–69).

———, Y. Chen, and Y. Zhang. 2014. "Understanding China's approaches to international development." IDS Policy Briefing, 75.

———, J. Humphrey, and D. Messner. 2008. "Global governance and developing countries: The implications of the rise of China." *World Development* 36, 2: 274–92.

———, X. Zhang, X. Li, and G. Bloom, eds. 2014. *China and International Development: Challenges and Opportunities. IDS Bulletin*, 45, 4 (July).

———, C. Zhang, A. Vaz, and L. Mukwereza. 2016. "Chinese state capitalism? Rethinking the role of the state and business in Chinese development cooperation in Africa." *World Development* 81: 24–34.

He, W. 2007. "The balancing act of China's Africa policy." *China Security* 3, 3 (Summer): 23–40. World Security Institute.

——— 2013. "China to Africa: Gives it fish and teaches it fishing" [中国对非洲：授其以鱼，更授其以渔]. *Jin Rong Bao Lan*, 6 May 2013. http://finance.sina.com.cn/money/bank/bank_hydt/20130506/200915363934.shtml. Accessed 5 Sept. 2015.

Kitano, N., and Y. Harada. 2014. "Estimating China's foreign aid 2001–2013." JICA-RI Working Paper 78, June. Tokyo: JICA Research Institute. http://jica-ri.jica.go.jp/publication/assets/JICA-RI_WP_No.78_2014.pdf. Accessed 14 July 2015.

Leong, A. 2014. "The principle of common but differentiated responsibilities and the SDGs." post2015.org. 27 May. http://post2015.org/2014/05/27/the-principle-of-common-but-differentiated-responsibilities-and-the-sdgs/. Accessed 9 Sept. 2015.

Li, X., D. Banik, L. Tang, and J. Wu. 2014. "Difference or indifference: China's development assistance unpacked." *IDS Bulletin* 45 (4 July).

——— and W. He. 2015. "China's overseas development assistance." Presentation at Asia Foundation Conference, June.

Li, X., and A.O. Farah. 2013. *China–Africa Relations in an Era of Great Transformations*. London: Ashgate.

Lu, S. 2012. "Some thoughts on the new strategic partnership between China and Africa." Speech given at the Institute of International Strategy at Party School of the Central Committee of the CPC, 19 September. http://ias.zjnu.cn/show.php?id=2627. Cited in Mathieu Duchâtel, Oliver Bräuner, and Zhou Hang. 2014. *Protecting China's Overseas Interests: The Slow Shift away from Non-interference*. Stockholm: SIPRI Policy Paper 41. June. http://books.sipri.org/files/PP/SIPRIPP41.pdf. Accessed 4 Aug. 2015.

Ministry of Foreign Affairs (MOFA). 2011. White Paper on Foreign Aid. Beijing: Government of People's Republic of China.

———. 2015. "Xi Jinping holds talks with representatives of Chinese and foreign entrepreneurs attending BFA annual conference." 29 Mar. www.fmprc.gov.cn/mfa_eng/zxxx_662805/t1250585.shtml. Accessed 15 July 2015.

Mohan, G., and B. Lampert. 2013. "Negotiating China: Reinserting African agency into China–Africa relations." *African Affairs* 112, 446: 92–110.

Mwiti, L. 2015. "China does not support rogue African states, it creates them—new study says." *Mail & Guardian Africa*, 9 Apr. http://mgafrica.com/article/2015-04-07-china-does-not-support-rogue-african-states-it-creates-them-insteadnew-study. Accessed 8 Sept. 2015.

New York Times. 2015. "U.S. Opposing China's Answer to World Bank." 9 Oct.

O'Neill, J. 2001. *Building Better Global Economic BRICs*. Global Economics Paper No: 66, Goldman Sachs, 30 Nov. www.goldmansachs.com/our-thinking/archive/archive-pdfs/build-better-brics.pdf. Accessed 27 July 2015.

Piketty, T., and A. Goldhammer. 2014. *Capital in the Twenty-First Century*. Cambridge, Mass.: Harvard University Press.

Pizzi, M. 2015. "BRICS announce $200B challenge to world financial order." http://america.aljazeera.com/articles/2014/7/15/brics-bank-announced.html. Accessed 20 June 2015.

Reisen, H. 2015. "Will the AIIB and the NDB help reform multilateral development banking?" *Global Policy Journal* 6, 3: 297–304.

Republic of Turkey (RoT). "Turkey–Africa relations." Ministry of Foreign Affairs. www.mfa.gov.tr/turkey-africa-relations.en.mfa. Accessed 17 Aug. 2015.

RT. 2015. "'West still treats Africa as former vassals'—South Africa's Zuma to RT." 10 May. www.rt.com/news/257353-zuma-africa-russia-china-brics/. Accessed 8 Sept. 2015.

Sanusi, L. 2013. "Africa must get real about Chinese ties." *Financial Times*, 11 Mar. www.ft.com/cms/s/0/562692b0-898c-11e2-ad3f-00144feabdc0.html#axzz2PDljcMDF. Accessed 8 Sept. 2015.

Shambaugh. D. 2014. *China Goes Global: The Partial Power*. Oxford: Oxford University Press.

SIPRI. 2014. "Protecting China's overseas interests: The slow shift away from non-interference." *Policy Brief 41*. http://books.sipri.org/files/PP/SIPRIPP41.pdf. Accessed 20 July 2015.

State Council Information Office (SCIO). 2014. "China's foreign aid." July.

Strauss, J.C., and Martha Saavedra, eds. 2009. *China and Africa: Emerging Patterns in Globalization and Development*. Cambridge: Cambridge University Press.

Stückelberger, C. 2015. *Sustainable Business Relations between China and Africa: Report on the Dialogue in South Africa*. Geneva: Globethics.net.

Taylor, I. 2009. "A case of mistaken identity: 'China Inc.' and its 'imperialism' in sub-Saharan Africa." *Asian Politics and Policy* 1, 4: 709–25.

United Nations Economic Commission for Africa (UNECA). 2013. *Africa–BRICS Cooperation: Implications for Growth, Employment and Structural Transformation in Africa*. Addis Ababa: UNECA. www.uneca.org/sites/default/files/PublicationFiles/africa-brics_cooperation_eng.pdf. Accessed 7 Apr. 2014.

Walker, A. 2014. "Whatever happened to the BRICS economies?" 27 Nov. www.bbc.co.uk/news/business-29960335. Accessed 18 July 2015.

Woods, N. 2008."Whose aid? Whose influence? China, emerging donors and the silent revolution in development assistance." *International Affairs* 84, 6: 1205–21.

Wall Street Journal. 2015. "Obama: We're all for the Asian Infrastructure Investment Bank." http://blogs.wsj.com/economics/2015/04/28/obama-were-all-for-the-asian-infrastructure-investment-bank/. Accessed 17 July 2015.

Xinhuanet. http://news.xinhuanet.com/english/china/2014-07/10/c_133474011.htm. Accessed 17 Sept. 2014.

Xue L. 2014. "China's foreign aid." *IDS Bulletin* 45, 4 (July).

Zhou H. 2014. *Foreign Aid in China*. Heidelberg: Springer.

Zhou T. 2013. "Engaging China in international development cooperation." The Asia Foundation. 21 Aug. http://asiafoundation.org/in-asia/2013/08/21/engaging-china-in-international-development-cooperation/. Accessed 15 Oct. 2014.

PART III

Issues in International Development

▲ A woman washes her face at a water pump belonging to the public water distribution service in the center of Goma, Democratic Republic of the Congo, where most of the one million residents of the city do not have clean, uncontaminated tap water in their homes. Goma lies on the edge of one of the largest soft water reservoirs in the world, Lake Kivu, where it rains abundantly, but most people have to go to the lake to fetch water and chlorinate it for drinking, or buy some from sellers.
| Source: JUNIOR D. KANNAH/AFP/Getty Images

14 Debt and Development

Joseph Hanlon and Tim Jones

LEARNING OBJECTIVES

- To learn that lending has a long history and that even lending to developing countries goes back 700 years.
- To understand the roots of the debt crises of the 1980s and 2000s, and the similarities between the most recent financial crisis in the North and earlier debt crises in the Global South.
- To see how lending to developing countries is linked to economic cycles and capital surpluses, and to "loan pushing" and default, and to recognize the role of the South as lender to the North.
- To understand the concepts of illegitimate and odious debt and changes in lending that increase the liability of lenders.

▲ **Two boys stand near a banner in Siby, Mali, where over 200 delegates from seven countries in West Africa met in 2002 to come up with African solutions to African problems, organized by the Malian branch of the anti-globalization Jubilee 2000 committee, which militates in favour of the cancellation of poor countries' debt.** | Source: ISSOUF SANOGO/AFP/Getty Images

Borrowing and lending are often sensible and necessary. Borrowing to cover unexpected expenses or loss of income, such as through sickness or a bad crop, has been common for millennia. Capitalism is based on borrowing for productive investment—a piece of machinery or an irrigation system or simply more stock that will produce increased income to more than repay the initial loan. Most large companies and many countries grow with borrowed money. Many people live in mortgaged houses—rather than save over many years to build a house, they borrow money and repay it over many years, and during that period the borrower can live in a better house.

Banking originated in Babylonia before 2000 BCE, when temples and palaces provided safe places for the storage of valuables—initially deposits of grain and later other goods, including cattle, agricultural implements, and precious metals. By the reign of Hammurabi in Babylon (*c.* 1792–1750 BCE), lending had become common, and his famous code—the first public written code of laws—covers banking and debt.

Initially, people would borrow from relatives, temples, or merchants who might provide goods on credit. Credit-based banking had developed in the Mediterranean world by the fourth century BCE. The Roman Empire developed banking that took deposits and lent money at interest, but this ended with the decline of Rome. Modern banking began to develop in the Mediterranean in the twelfth to fourteenth centuries CE. As banking systems developed, individuals, kings, companies, and even countries borrowed.

But from the beginning, three issues have dominated. First, what happens when the borrower cannot repay? Can the lender take property from the borrower? Can the lender force the borrower to work for him or her? Can the loan become a liability of spouses or children? The Hammurabi code contains two important restrictions. Article 48 says that if a person owes on a loan and the crop fails because of lack of water or a storm, not only does the person not have to make debt payments in that year, but no interest is paid for that year as well. Article 119 says that a man in debt can give himself or his wife, son, or daughter in forced labour to the creditor, but only for three years, after which the debt is considered paid and the person freed.

Second, what can the lender charge the borrower? **Interest** payments are most common, usually a percentage of the outstanding loan each year. The borrower pays back part of the money borrowed—the **principal**—plus interest. The basis of modern commercial banking is to take deposits and pay interest on those deposits and then lend out the money at a higher interest rate, with the difference between the two interest rates covering risk of losses for non-repayment and allowing some profit for the bank. This remains controversial, and **usury**—excessive interest rates—has been an issue down through the ages; most religions allow interest but ban usury. But the Greek philosopher Plato (427–347 BCE) opposed lending at interest. The Qu'ran also opposes lending at interest but permits trading profits and profit from investment, which means that banks should invest in businesses, sharing risk and profit, rather than lending to them.

The third issue has become more important only with the growth of capitalism: what happens if an individual, a company, or a country borrows money for an investment that proves not to be profitable and the loan cannot be repaid? Until the mid-nineteenth century in both the United States and Britain, debtors who failed to repay were thrown into prison. This was replaced by bankruptcy laws that allowed most of the assets of the debtor to be distributed to creditors, thus ending the debt, even if the assets were insufficient to cover full repayment. This proved to be one of the most important provisions of modern capitalism, because it encouraged business people to take risks without the fear of being thrown in debtors' prison. Over the twentieth century, bankruptcy laws became even more liberal, allowing individuals to keep their homes and giving more rights to workers in a company facing bankruptcy—even finding ways to keep a company operating rather than liquidating it to sell its assets. Thus, lenders have come to take an increasing share of the risks of modern capitalism.

LENDING TO DEVELOPING COUNTRIES

Private banks in developed countries have been lending to poorer developing-country governments and businesses for centuries, and the record has often been one of default and political intervention. In his prescient book *The Money Lenders*, Anthony Sampson

(1981: 29–31, 54–6) describes some of the failings of English kings:

> After King Edward I expelled the Jews in 1290 he needed the Italians to finance his wars. . . . To these Italian bankers England was a wild developing country on the edge of the world, a kind of medieval Zaire [now Democratic Republic of the Congo]. Its exports of wool offered prospects of big profits; but with its despotic monarchs, its tribal wars and corrupt courtiers, it had a high country risk. . . . But after King Edward III came to the throne in 1327 he was confident that he could compel his own English merchants to finance his wars; he defaulted on his Italian debts, and the [Florentine] banks of Bardi and Peruzzi collapsed.

A century later, King Edward IV's Wars of the Roses took him deeper into debt. "After trying to reschedule their debts with the King, the Medici Bank had to write off 52,000 florins and close their London office. Rather than refuse deposits," Sampson explains, the Medicis succumbed to the temptation of seeking an outlet for surplus cash in making dangerous loans to princes. "It was a warning relevant to more modern bankers," comments Sampson.

Four centuries later, London was lending to the new United States. "London saw it as a very unreliable developing country, with a black record of embezzlement, fraudulent prospectuses and default," notes Sampson. But the bankers made loans in any case. In 1842, 11 states, including Maryland, Pennsylvania, Mississippi, and Louisiana, defaulted. Setting a precedent that would be used often in later years, Barings Bank simply intervened in local politics. In Maryland, Barings helped to finance candidates in the next election who were willing to repay. "In the elections in 1846 the 'resumptionists' narrowly won, and soon afterwards Maryland raised new taxes which enabled it to repay its debts. The campaign had cost Barings about $15,000; it was worth it," writes Sampson. Mississippi held out. By 1929, the unpaid debt was estimated at $32 million, and as recently as 1980, London banks were still trying to get Mississippi to repay the loans it defaulted on 138 years earlier.

Sometimes there was military action in response. After Mexico defaulted in 1861, Britain, France, and Spain invaded. France installed Ferdinand Maximilian as emperor; he lasted only four years and failed to repay the debts (Eichengreen and Lindert, 1989).

But why do banks lend to foreign governments when it is potentially easy for them to default? In part, they do so because many of these loans are profitable for both parties and are repaid. In his book *Manias, Panics and Crashes*, the eminent economist Charles Kindleberger (2000 [1978]) details his view of economic cycles and international lending. He argues that each cycle starts with a period of real growth involving a rise in profits, often coming from the use of new technologies or new transportation/communication systems such as railways. This growth is linked to a rapid expansion of bank credit. Eventually, money growth outstrips possible productive investments, while investors look for ever higher rates of profit. Increasingly, money goes into speculation, and this is often linked to fraud and swindles. This is the period of "bubbles," or what Kindleberger calls "manias." It usually involves international lending as banks run out of domestic borrowers, become more desperate to lend, and make higher-risk foreign loans—just as the Medicis did with Edward IV in the fifteenth century. Eventually, the bubble bursts, prices fall, and investors try to sell or to collect on their loans. This is the period of "panic" as investors all rush for the exit. The panic feeds on itself, leading to the "crash." Kindleberger points to the tulip mania of 1634, the South Sea Bubble of 1720, the cotton and railway booms of the 1830s, and so on.

The past 250 years have seen four of these cycles:

1. Growth 1780–1820; mania 1820s; crisis 1830s and 1840s.
2. Growth 1850s; mania 1860s; crisis 1870s and 1880s.
3. Growth 1893–1913; mania 1920s; crisis 1930s.
4. Growth 1948–67; mania 1967–79; crises in early 1980s, late 1990s, and 2008, each followed by a new mania.

The 1870s, the 1930s, and the period from 2008 saw crises triggering major global depressions.

After each cycle, there have been retrospective complaints of reckless lending and of **loan pushing**—banks and lending agencies so desperate to lend money that they encourage foreign governments to take loans they do not need and encourage borrowers to live beyond their means. Towards the end of the mania, borrowers are encouraged to take new loans simply to repay old ones. With the panic, lending suddenly stops, borrowers cannot repay, and they default. Francis White, the US assistant secretary of state for Latin American affairs in the early 1930s, commented that "in the carnival days from 1922 to 1929, when money was easy, many American bankers forsook the dignified, aloof attitude traditional of bankers and became, in reality, high pressure salesmen of money, carrying on a cut-throat competition against their fellow bankers, and once they obtained the business, endeavoured to urge larger loans on the borrowing countries" (Drake, 1989: 43). During the 1920s, according to evidence before the Senate Committee on Finance, there were 29 representatives of US financial houses in Colombia alone trying to negotiate loans with the government.

In 1973, the US Federal Reserve governor, Andrew Brimmer, noted that "the main explanation" for the sharp rise in lending to less developed countries was the "failure of demand for loans from borrowers in developed countries to keep pace with the expansion of credit availability" (Darity and Horn, 1988: 8). Brimmer cited a particular form of loan pushing that involves a drastic softening of terms—similar to a drug pusher offering cheap heroin in order to create addiction. In the mid-1970s, international loans had a negative real interest rate—that is, in real terms (taking inflation into account), poor countries had to repay less than they borrowed. Loan pushers in the mania phase stressed that they were literally giving money away. But these loans were on variable interest rates, and in the early 1980s those rates jumped dramatically, setting off the threat of default and fuelling the panic.

International development lending has two phases. In the growth period, lending can be profitable and promote productive investment and growth; indeed, careful borrowing by poorer countries has accelerated industrialization and development by allowing investment in infrastructure and equipment that could not have been afforded otherwise. But in the mania and loan-pushing phases, when bankers are "high pressure salesmen of money," poor countries take unproductive loans they cannot repay.

GOVERNMENTS, POLITICS, THE COLD WAR, AND THE DEBT CRISIS

Initially, most lending was by banks, but increasingly in the late nineteenth and early twentieth centuries, loans were in the form of bonds, which could be sold to individuals and other investors (and which were often highly speculative or fraudulent). During World War I, the United States government became a substantial lender to the countries fighting against Germany. In 1923, it extended the repayment period until 1983 and reduced the interest rate, but in 1934, in the depths of the Depression, Britain and five other European countries defaulted. No further payments were ever made, except by Finland. The debts are still on the books, and the US Treasury reported that as of 30 June 1997, they stood at $33.5 billion. Outstanding World War I debts to the US include $14.6 billion for the UK, $11 billion for France, and $3.2 billion for Italy. But in 2009, the British government confirmed that it had no intention of paying this debt.

World War II was even more expensive, and in 1945 Britain became the world's largest debtor. John Maynard Keynes was sent to Washington, and in December 1945 he negotiated the best deal he could get for Britain—a loan of $3.75 billion at 2 per cent interest. The final repayment was made only in 2006.

(West) Germany was treated differently than it had been after World War I. Rather than enforcing reparations on the defeated country, it received funds through the Marshall Plan and in 1953 half of its debts from both before and after the war were cancelled. Significantly, repayments on the remaining debt were linked to West Germany having a trade surplus, which meant its creditor countries had an incentive to trade with the country (Kaiser, 2013).

The end of World War II brought about four major changes in global politics and economics (some of which had their roots in earlier decades):

- Decolonization began, and many countries became independent.
- The Depression of the 1930s and then the war had made clear that new international institutions were needed, leading to the creation of the United Nations and the two Bretton Woods institutions (BWIs)—the World Bank and the International

Monetary Fund (IMF). The World Bank first lent for European reconstruction and then to newly independent countries (see Chapter 9).

- Major corporations began to arise, increasingly international and often backed by "export credits" (loans given to borrowing governments and companies to import goods from companies in the lending country).
- The advent of nuclear weapons changed the nature of war and of empire. Military power and brute force were no longer the means to conquest, replaced instead by three options. The first option was so-called "low-intensity warfare" in which unacceptable governments were undermined or overthrown by security services backed by limited military force. For example, the United States created or backed opposition movements in Nicaragua, Angola, and Mozambique. The second option involved larger wars but limited (more or less) to single countries, as was the case in Vietnam. The third, and most important for this chapter, was the growing use of non-military means of subjugation—economic power in particular. Thus, loans became an important way of wielding power.

The first example was US lending to Britain in 1945. The United States required Britain to move quickly to free trade and to make the pound convertible to the dollar within 15 months. The outflow of money from Britain was so great that much of the loan was dissipated, and convertibility was abandoned within weeks. But this was an early example of the kind of package of conditions that in the 1970s became known as structural adjustment.

John Perkins, in *Confessions of an Economic Hit Man* (2004), describes working for one of the largest international consulting firms and, indirectly, for the US National Security Agency from 1971 to 1981. He was one of a group of people, he writes, whose job was to produce hugely exaggerated economic growth forecasts to justify vastly oversized electricity, railway, and other infrastructure projects that would be financed by international loans (from both commercial banks and the World Bank). Some money was siphoned off into the foreign bank accounts of these countries' leaders to ensure they would not "notice" that the projects were indeed white elephants. This strategy had two goals. First, contracts would go to US engineering companies (and often the money never left the US). But second, and much more sinister, was a conscious effort to burden the developing country with unpayable debts "so they would present easy targets when we needed favors, including military bases, UN votes, or access to oil and other natural resources" (Perkins, 2004: 15).

The Cold War led to quite extensive lending in order to prop up and tie client dictators to the Western powers, especially to the United States. One study (Hanlon, 2006) estimated that one-quarter of developing-country debt consisted of Cold War loans to Western-backed dictators, such as Joseph Mobutu (see Box 14.1).

THE 1980s DEBT CRISIS AND HIPC INITIATIVE

In 1970, developing-country debt was $69 billion, which may seem like a lot of money, but it proved to be quite small in comparison to what was to come in the following years. The decade of the 1970s was one of Kindleberger's mania periods, with a surplus of capital. There was a sharp increase in loan pushing; in the mid-1970s, global interest rates were 3 per cent lower than global inflation, which meant that real interest rates were negative—countries were being told, in effect, that they could repay *less* than they borrowed. Over the decade, developing-country debt increased sevenfold, to $494 billion in 1980. Figure 14.1 shows both total debt stock and what is called "net transfer on debt"—that is, new loans minus interest payments and principal repayments on old debts—which is thus the actual cash flow into or out of the borrowing country. The top graph shows the sharp increase in debt, while the bottom graph shows that there was a real transfer of money to developing countries in the 1970s.

But by 1984 lenders had raised **real interest rates** to a peak of 12 per cent. In 1982, Mexico could not pay the interest on its $60 billion debt and defaulted, setting off a massive debt crisis. Throughout the remainder of the 1980s, debt was constantly being renegotiated, and new loans and bonds were issued to repay old loans. Most commonly, the new bonds or loans allowed a longer time to pay and sometimes lower interest rates. Money was borrowed to pay even the unpaid interest on old loans, which meant interest was charged on the interest.

Initially, it was hoped that the crisis was temporary and that if debt was rescheduled or refinanced, it could

CRITICAL ISSUES

BOX 14.1 | Congo, Kleptocracy, and the Cold War

General Joseph Mobutu took power in the Congo in 1965, changing the country's name to Zaire. Mobutu may have been on the West's side in the Cold War, but he was also one of the world's most corrupt dictators, and his government was widely described as a "kleptocracy." In 1978, the IMF appointed its own man, Irwin Blumenthal, to a key post in the central bank of Zaire. He resigned in less than a year, writing a memo saying that "the corruptive system in Zaire with all its wicked manifestations is so serious that there is no (repeat no) prospect for Zaire's creditors to get their money back." When Blumenthal wrote his report, Zaire's debt was $4.6 billion. When Mobutu was overthrown and died in 1998, the debt was $12.9 billion, and Mobutu had luxury estates in France and billions of dollars stashed abroad. For once, the private sector saw that they had no chance of getting their money back and stopped lending after 1981. But shortly after the Blumenthal memo, the IMF granted Zaire the largest loan it had ever given an African country. The World Bank was hardly involved in Zaire when Blumenthal wrote his memo, but during the next 15 years it lent $2 billion to Zaire—and was still giving new money to Mobutu as late as 1993. Western governments were the biggest lenders and continued to pour in new money until 1990—even though Zaire had virtually stopped repaying its debts in 1982. In particular, Mobutu provided a home for US covert action against neighbouring Angola, and the US pushed through yet another IMF loan to Zaire, this time over the objections of some IMF officials.

After the overthrow of Mobutu in 1997, Zaire was renamed the Democratic Republic of the Congo (DRC). For 15 years after Mobutu fell, debt payments were made in an ad hoc way as people in the country suffered under various civil wars. The DRC eventually qualified for debt cancellation under the Heavily Indebted Poor Countries initiative in 2010. Its government foreign-owed debt fell from $11 billion to $4 billion, but the remainder of Mobutu's debt has continued to be paid.

be paid off eventually. The IMF and World Bank gave new loans to allow the payment of at least the interest on debts. But it was becoming clear that the crisis was systemic (see, e.g., George, 1988; Payer, 1991; Pineda-Ofreneo, 1991).

Debt is often sold, and this goes back to at least the fifteenth century. Typically a bank or an investor gives cash to the original lender, usually for less than the actual face value of the loan, and takes on the responsibility of collecting the debt. Factoring or invoice selling became a common method of industrial finance in the twentieth century. For example, a company sells goods and sends an invoice requiring a promise of payment in 90 days but then immediately sells the invoice to a finance company; the company is thus paid immediately, which reduces its need for working capital. Bonds are explicitly a form of tradable debt, because the original bondholder, who actually lent the money, can sell the bond to other investors. A market grew up in which developing-country debt was traded, and some countries bought their own debt back at a discount. But as Figure 14.1 shows, that debt was still rising inexorably.

Many of the loans in the 1970s had been made to private companies and banks rather than to governments, and in the 1980s finance ministers in industrialized countries became worried that the debt crisis would lead to the collapse of major banks. So they pushed developing-country governments to take over these private loans—in effect, the North demanded that the South nationalize private debt. BWIs and governments provided bond issues, new loans, and refinancing to take over the private debt, but with conditions linked to free-market and neoliberal economic policies.

By 1996 the World Bank and the IMF accepted that the poorest countries could not sensibly repay their debt, and they launched the **Heavily Indebted Poor Countries Initiative**. It broke new ground by accepting for the first time that some loans made by the two

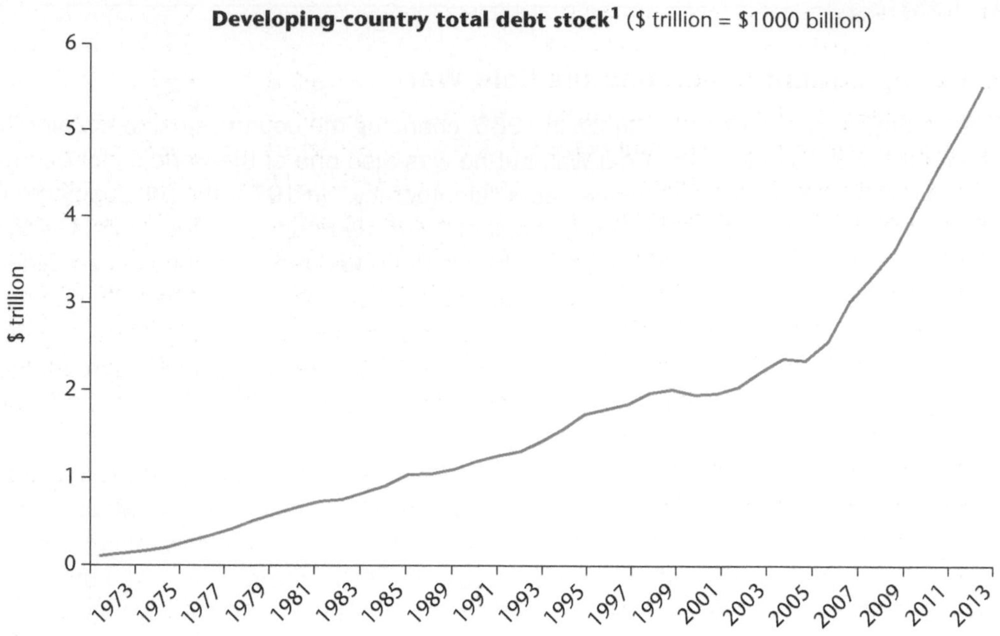

FIGURE 14.1 | Developing-Country Debt and Payments

Notes:

1 "Stock" is the total amount owed.

2 "Developing countries" are those with 2014 GNI (gross national income) per capita of less than $12,746, calculated by the World Bank atlas method.

3 "Net transfer" is the amount of new lending minus interest payments and principal repayments. It is thus the total amount developing countries received from (above the 0 line) or paid to (below the 0 line) all creditors.

Source: World Bank International Debt Statistics, July 2015.

institutions would have to be cancelled. This was to be done in parallel with proportionate debt cancellation by government (bilateral) creditors. The IMF and World Bank handled the negotiations and demanded that developing countries follow strict neoliberal structural adjustment. The process was very complex, and in the first two years there was no debt cancellation.

Meanwhile, Jubilee 2000, an international campaign launched in 1997 (see Box 14.4), called for "cancellation of the unpayable debt of the world's poorest countries by the year 2000 under a fair and transparent process." The campaign was highly successful in three ways. First, it took what had been considered an arcane and technical issue, which supposedly could be understood only by economists, and turned it into an easy-to-understand campaigning issue. Second, it joined together local debt campaigns in numerous countries in the North and South. Third, it gained unexpected support—24 million people from 166 countries signed a petition—and successfully brought pressure on northern governments. At the 1999 meeting of the finance ministers of the Group of Eight (G8) richest countries in Köln, Germany, it was agreed that debt cancellation for heavily indebted poor countries (HIPCs) would be increased from $55 billion to $100 billion. At that time, 41 countries were considered to be HIPCs, and they had $207 billion in debt. But of that, $100 billion was not being serviced anyway—mainly with the agreement of the IMF and World Bank, since most of those countries had Bank and IMF programs. The $100 billion simply would go to writing off debt that the institutions knew would never be repaid—not a particularly generous move. In 2005, the G8 countries finally agreed to cancel more debt, which was actually being paid through a new scheme called the Multilateral Debt Relief Initiative. As of 2015, $130 billion of debt has been cancelled for 36 countries, primarily in sub-Saharan Africa. For many of the countries, debt payments have fallen considerably, though new rounds of lending are threatening to recreate debt crises. This debt cancellation only applied to countries judged to be both heavily indebted and extremely impoverished. Most developing countries were excluded.

The first graph in Figure 14.1 shows that despite a brief drop in 2000 due to debt cancellation, total debt continued to increase. But the huge increase in debt did not bring any benefit to developing countries. The second graph in Figure 14.1 shows that for two decades, despite a massive increase in debt, there was a transfer of money from South to North. For the two decades 1984–2003, total debt tripled from $729 billion to $2,214 billion, yet in the same period poor countries gained nothing and actually gave $350 million to the rich countries as they had to pay more in interest payments and principal repayments than they received in new loans. For 20 years, the developing world gave $48 million to the rich world every day—yet the debt burden increased by $204 million every day. The OECD Development Assistance Committee estimates that total aid (excluding debt relief, technical assistance, and humanitarian aid) in those 20 years was $893 billion, so nearly one-third of aid went right back to the North. Aid and debt cancellation were like using a bucket to try to empty an ever-deeper ocean.

Wikipedia

PHOTO 14.1 | IMF Headquarters, Washington, DC.

The key point is that developing countries in the 1970s did gain money through international borrowing, but in the years since the crisis of the 1980s, they gained nothing. Struggling to repay and sending more and more money to rich countries, they fell deeper and deeper into debt.

THE SOUTH AND THE POOR PAY TO SOLVE THE NORTHERN CRISIS

The previous big crisis was the Great Depression of the 1930s. It largely affected the United States and Europe, while developing countries, notably in Latin America, continued to grow. Within the then industrialized countries, the Depression hit both rich and poor. The rich countries, and mainly the United States, responded to the 1979 crisis by trying to ensure that the Depression of the 1930s was not repeated. They tried to export the crisis to the South and to poorer people within their own countries. Money was to be extracted from the developing countries in order to prevent depression in the industrialized countries, and they used new manias and borrowing to transfer wealth from poor countries and poor people to a small wealthy elite.

The development model that originated in the 1930s Depression and continued through the 1960s and 1970s was state-led growth—not just in the then socialist countries but also in European and Asian capitalist countries and in developing countries following either model. This also led to improving the conditions of poorer people in both North and South and reduced inequality.

But the crisis beginning in the late 1970s was marked by stagnation in the US economy and led to the introduction of an entirely new economic model—neoliberalism. First introduced by Augusto Pinochet after he took power following a US-backed coup in Chile in 1973, it was later adopted by the British government of Margaret Thatcher beginning in 1979 and the US administration of Ronald Reagan from 1981. Linked to right-wing libertarian political philosophies, this policy called for smaller government, privatization, withdrawal of the government from the economy, sharply reduced regulation and reduced power for trade unions, and lower taxes on the rich to encourage them to invest (usually accompanied by lower spending on health and education, on the grounds that the poor should take more responsibility for looking after themselves). An important part of the package was free movement of goods and capital (but not people), so customs barriers and capital controls were removed.

An effect of neoliberalism was increasing inequality, both within countries and between them, as wealth was accumulated by the rich, and notably the wealthiest 1 per cent. By contrast, poor countries and people were forced to borrow to maintain their living standards.

The 1980s saw the developing-country debt crisis, which was followed by new speculative and lending mania. This became so grotesque that there was even a Hollywood film, *Wall Street* (1987), in which the leading character says, "greed, for lack of a better word, is good. Greed is right, greed works." Greed continued until the Asian financial crisis of 1997–9. Then it resumed, and the early 2000s saw an unprecedented mania of borrowing and speculation, leading to the crash of 2008. Whereas the debt crisis of the early 1980s and the Asian financial crisis of the late 1990s largely affected the Global South, the crisis after 2008 affected the industrialized North.

Inequality and Household Debt

Through the 1980s, 1990s, and 2000s inequality rose in many Western countries as the power of trade unions to bargain for higher wages was reduced, taxes on richer people were cut, and financial deregulation made it easier for companies and rich individuals to evade and avoid tax. Relatively more economic output went to the rich through earnings on capital, rather than to ordinary people through wages. The rich spend less of their income than middle- and low-income earners, and instead use it to speculate in financial markets. This led to the boom in financial speculation and increased the supply of loans, and thus debt.

"The gap between rich and poor keeps widening. Growth, if any, has disproportionally benefited higher income groups while lower income households have been left behind" the OECD said in 2015. And it warned that "growing inequality is harmful for economic growth."

The United States Census Bureau (2015) reported that all incomes rose until 1979, but comparing incomes in 2013 with those in 1979, it found that the average real income of the bottom fifth of all families had fallen 11 per cent. The next poorest fifth had incomes the same as in 1979. But for the top 5 per cent, real incomes had increased by 65 per cent.

People were encouraged to borrow in order to maintain their consumption levels. Figure 14.2 shows ballooning US consumer debt. Credit card debt hit $1 trillion in 2007. In the United States, mortgage companies gave home loans to people who were manifestly unable to pay, and like the "loan pushers" of the 1920s and 1970s, they offered low interest initially and encouraged people to borrow more than they needed and to spend the money on consumer goods. The mortgage companies then sold the loans to gullible bankers, who packaged them as allegedly safe investments. By 2006 there were $600 billion in sub-prime mortgages, but they supported $6 trillion of securities and investment vehicles. The crisis came when banks realized that poor people could not repay the outstanding billions of dollars in loans and that the original lenders were taking no responsibility for what was clearly illegitimate lending. The whole house of cards collapsed; not only could the sub-prime mortgages not be repaid, but the loans for the investment vehicles could not be repaid, either. This, in turn, triggered the 2008 economic crisis. But as Figure 14.2 shows, the slowdown in lending was very brief, and the lending mania continued.

Shifting the Crisis to the South

During the Depression of the 1930s, many international borrowers simply defaulted. Europe stopped paying its World War I debt to the US in 1934. Most Latin American borrowers also stopped paying. Why did developing countries not do the same thing and simply not repay after 1979? Why did they, instead, triple their debt simply to repay the initial debt?

The answer is that the US pursued three strategies to shift the ongoing post-1979 crisis onto the Global South:

1. US President Ronald Reagan sharply raised interest rates in the early 1980s, as noted above, which initially created a flow of money from South to North but also triggered the 1980s debt crisis that began in Mexico.
2. The US used "aid" to impose a neoliberal economic model and enforce debt repayment.
3. Borrowing was employed to fuel consumption. Countries were forced to keep dollars as reserves.

The following discussion elaborates these strategies.

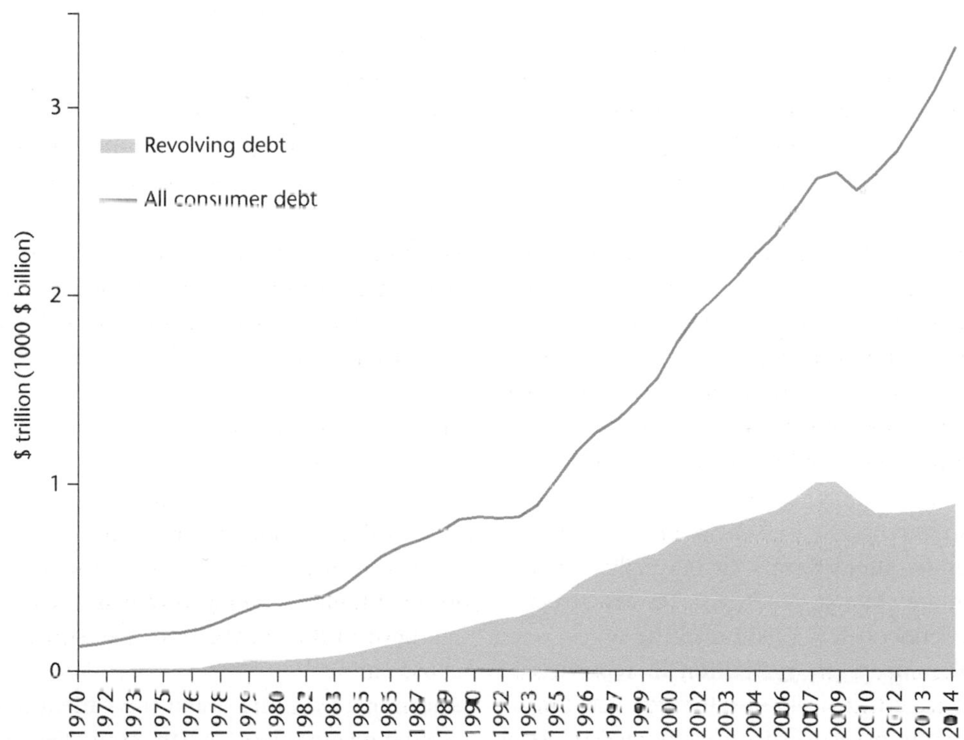

FIGURE 14.2 | United States Consumer Debt

Notes: "Consumer credit" is all outstanding credit extended to individuals for personal expenditures, excluding mortgages. "Revolving credit" mostly comprises credit card loans.

Source: US Federal Reserve System, July 2015.

The major difference between the 1930s and the 1980s was the existence of the Bretton Woods institutions (BWIs). Poor countries became increasingly dependent on "aid," and the "donors" made their aid conditional on recipient countries having World Bank and IMF programs, which in turn imposed two sets of conditions. One was continued debt repayment. Little concession was made for economic problems such as bad crops, and debt bondage lasted indefinitely. Indeed, with respect to the Bretton Woods institutions, developing countries have fewer rights than the citizens of Hammurabi's Babylon did nearly 4,000 years ago.

The second highly controversial condition was that poor countries adopt neoliberal economic policies and what were known as "structural adjustment programs" (also discussed in Chapters 3 and 9). Import-substituting industrialization was the model followed earlier by the now-industrialized countries and was the model being followed by the developing world (Chang, 2002), but the BWIs forced poor countries to open their borders to manufactured goods from the industrialized countries, and instead to adopt a model of export-led growth. This resulted in many countries rapidly expanding the production of agricultural and mineral exports, which in turn meant increased competition and a drop in the prices paid by the rich countries to the poor countries. Cocoa sold for $2,604 a tonne in 1980, less than half that ($1,267) in 1990, and even less in 2000 ($906). Commodity prices began rising again from 2004. But for two decades, the industrialized countries forced the developing world to sell industrial inputs for ever-lower prices while also forcing them to buy imported manufactured goods instead of producing them locally. Debt had become a major weapon of economic power used by the industrialized countries.

Meanwhile, the US was increasingly consuming much more than it produced. The trade deficit (goods and services) was small until the 1990s, when it started to jump, from $31 billion in 1991 to $372 billion in 2000, and $761 billion in 2006 (US Census Bureau, 2015). In other words, the US was importing goods instead of producing them, and it had to borrow money to pay the bills. US public debt in 1940 was $45 billion, and by 1970, it had only risen to $371 billion. But as stagnation set in, the US started to borrow at an unprecedented rate, pushing the debt to $909 billion in 1980, $3 trillion ($3,000 billion) in 1990, $6 trillion in 2000, and $18 trillion by 2015.

The United States had already made another change, the impact of which became clear only later. From 1934, the price of gold had been fixed at $35 per ounce; gold was used as financial reserves by most countries. But the US was having trouble paying for the Vietnam War, and in 1971 President Richard Nixon announced that there would be a free market in gold; the price rose to $140 within two years. As well as helping to pay for the war, this move had a much more subtle effect—instead of gold, US dollars became the world's reserves. Each dollar that a country holds as a reserve is a promise by the US government to eventually provide one dollar in goods. Indeed, reserves are mostly held in US government bonds or as deposits in US banks. US external debt (public and private) jumped from $6 trillion in 2002 to $17 trillion in 2015, with more than $1.3 trillion in US Treasury securities held by China (US Department of the Treasury, 2015). Thus, in effect, countries holding reserves are lending money to the United States.

Figure 14.3 shows that sharp increase in foreign reserves in the twenty-first century. Two very different factors led to the increase in foreign holdings of US bonds and dollars. The East Asian financial crisis of 1997–9 was triggered in part by excessive and speculative international and domestic borrowing, causing the collapse of banks and currencies. With a sudden outflow of speculative capital, Thailand, Malaysia, Indonesia, the Philippines, and South Korea all found themselves unable to pay short-term debt. The IMF and the US offered to "help" but imposed neoliberal conditions requiring that the economies become even more open. This was exactly the wrong response and made the crisis worse. As a result, East Asian countries built up their reserves sharply so that when the next cyclic monetary problem occurred, they would not need to turn to the IMF. That proved to be a wise choice, and they were less affected by the 2008 crash. But in one way, this suited the United States, because middle-income East Asian countries were holding large amounts of dollars—in effect, giving a big loan to the US.

Meanwhile, the IMF insisted that poor countries substantially increase their reserves. They were too poor

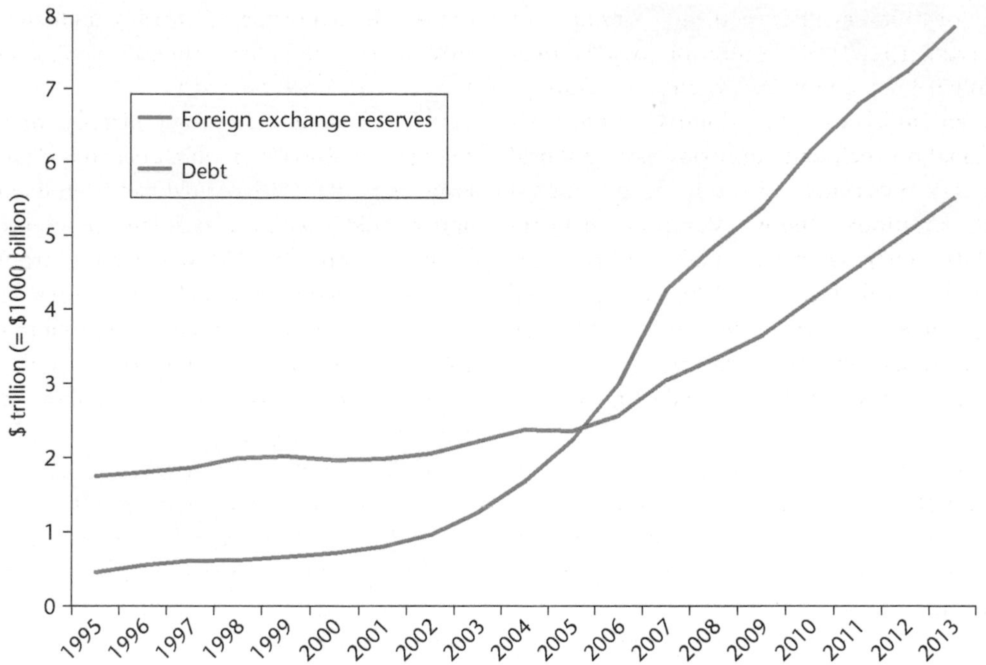

FIGURE 14.3 | Developing-Country Foreign Currency Reserves Compared to External Debt

Note: Debt is external debt stock of "all developing countries," according to the World Bank. Foreign exchange reserves are for "emerging and developing countries," according to the IMF.

to use these reserves to gain independence from the IMF, and many thought the reserves were excessive and that the money would be better spent on development. Figure 14.3 shows foreign reserves held by developing countries and makes clear the dramatic rise from 2003, when the US and its allies needed money to pay for the Iraq war. Reserves of all developing and emerging economies in 1995, before the Asian crisis, were only $456 billion; by 2003 this had risen to $1.3 trillion, and by 2015 to $7.7 trillion, according to the IMF. More than $4 trillion of US public debt is held by foreign governments as reserves. Thus, by forcing poor countries to hold extra reserves, the IMF is, in effect, forcing poor countries to lend to the United States to prop up the US dollar.

Figure 14.3 also shows that since 2005, foreign currency reserves held by developing countries have been larger than their total external debt. In other words, developing countries are net lenders to the US and other industrialized countries—not the other way around. Poor countries are lending more than $2 trillion to the rich countries, preventing a 1930s style depression in the industrialized countries while depressing the economies of the developing countries.

Is Foreign Borrowing Sensible?

The changing nature of international debt in the second half of the twentieth century—and the way that post-1980 debt has mounted astronomically without any apparent benefit to developing countries—raises a question about the whole concept of foreign borrowing.

Poor people well understand the debt trap, constantly borrowing to survive and sinking ever deeper into debt, with debt service payments becoming greater than any benefit gained from the initial borrowing. And yet the other side of borrowing is also obvious. Borrowing to buy a car and having the use of the car while paying off the loan over three years means that because of interest we pay far more than the actual cost of the car or house but we consider it reasonable since

AP Photo/Mahesh Kumar A.

PHOTO 14.2 | Women protest indebtedness resulting from micro-finance loans, Hyderabad, India.

we have the use of the car during that period. And large parts of modern industrial development are based on borrowing money to construct a building or buy a piece of machinery that will make a company more productive and thus sufficiently profitable to pay off the loan. This is exactly the argument used by the World Bank and developing countries alike for foreign borrowing to stimulate more rapid growth.

But economists distinguish between foreign and domestic borrowing. Does a country borrow from its own banks and citizens—say, by issuing bonds—or does it borrow from foreign banks and the World Bank? Economists such as Cheryl Payer (1991) have argued that few countries have successfully developed on the basis of foreign loans, or at least not for very long periods. Foreign borrowing makes very different repayment demands from those of domestic borrowing, and the imposed policies of the Bretton Woods institutions become very important.

Traditionally, countries developed by protecting their infant industries from foreign competition so that these companies could sell their goods locally, become profitable, and repay their loans. The imposed neoliberal model requires that economies be open, which gives no space for local industry to grow and become profitable. Further, foreign borrowing is in currencies of the industrialized world—US dollars or euros. Therefore, the BWIs pushed countries to produce exports they could sell for hard currency, but as everyone produces more of the same exports, the prices fall. At the same time, structural adjustment policies often demanded devaluation of the local currency. All of this made foreign loans much more expensive than domestic ones, and as it turned out, economies simply did not grow rapidly enough to pay the much higher cost of foreign borrowing, because the imposed BWI policies did not promote growth.

WHAT IS THE RESPONSIBILITY OF THE LENDER?

The Philippine dictator Ferdinand Marcos was finally overthrown in 1986 and fled into exile. He had more than $5 billion stashed away in foreign banks, suggesting that up to one-third of the Philippines' foreign borrowing had passed into his very deep pockets. The largest single debt was for the Bataan nuclear power station, built at the foot of a volcano and on an earthquake fault, and financed by the US export credit agency Ex-Im Bank, Union Bank of Switzerland, Bank of Tokyo, and Mitsui and Company, all of which were repaid. In 2007, the Philippines finally paid off the debt for the 30-year-old power station that never should have been built and was never used.

In international law, it is widely accepted that when a government changes, the successor government assumes the laws, contracts, and debts of the previous government. The United States created one of the few exceptions to this convention after it seized Cuba from Spain in 1898. Spain demanded that the US pay Cuba's debts, but the US refused on the grounds that the debt had been "imposed upon the people of Cuba without their consent and by force of arms." Furthermore, the US argued that in such circumstances, "the creditors, from the beginning, took the chances of the investment. The very pledge of the national credit, while it demonstrates on the one hand the national character of the debt, on the other hand proclaims the notorious risk that attended the debt in its origin, and has attended it ever since" (Adams, 1991: 164). The US held a similar view in 2003 after the invasion of Iraq to overthrow the government of Saddam Hussein, when US Treasury Secretary John Snow said, "Certainly the people of Iraq shouldn't be saddled with those debts incurred through the regime of the dictator who is now gone" (Hanlon, 2006: 211).

The name and doctrine of **odious debt** was formalized by Alexander Sack in 1927, who wrote:

> If a despotic power incurs a debt not for the needs or in the interest of the state, but to strengthen its despotic regime, to repress the population that fights against it, etc., this debt is odious to the population of all the state. This debt is not an obligation for the nation; it is a regime's debt, a personal debt of the power that has incurred it, consequently it falls with [the] fall of this power. (Quoted in Adams, 1991: 165)

Surely the same rule regarding odious debt should have been applied to the apartheid regime in South Africa and dictators in Zaire and the Philippines. But lenders, including the World Bank and the IMF, refused to accept that their original lending had been improper.

Although the Jubilee 2000 campaign initially focused simply on "unpayable debt," campaigners increasingly took up the issue of lenders' co-responsibility and of what came to be defined as the broader areas of "illegitimate debt"—loans that were improperly made and that should be the liability of the lender, not the borrower. The Jubilee Debt Campaign in 2015 said that it regarded three-quarters of the developing-country debt still owed to the UK government as "illegitimate," including loans to pay for arms sales to dictators in Indonesia (General Suharto), Iraq (Saddam Hussein), Argentina, Ecuador, Egypt, and Kenya.

Rapidly growing consumer protection in the second half of the twentieth century applies also to lending. Increasingly, lenders take due care to see that a loan is reasonable, that the borrower is competent to borrow, and that the borrower can reasonably be expected to repay. Modern civil and commercial law has broadened contractual obligations in complex business transactions beyond the strict delivery of goods and services to include dissemination of professional advice, discovery of special risks, and so forth, especially if one party is less knowledgeable than the other and therefore must trust the other's superior skills. Neglecting these accessory obligations may be considered a breach of contract. Loans like those to apartheid South Africa, to Mobutu in Zaire, and for the Bataan nuclear plant would simply not be acceptable under domestic law in most industrialized countries. But as Boxes 14.2 and 14.3 show in regard to Argentina and Greece, international lenders still claim the right to make outrageous loans and collect on them.

Three governments have moved on this issue. In 2006 Norway became the first creditor country to acknowledge the concept of **illegitimate debt** and that such debt must be cancelled. That year, Norway

BOX 14.2 | Argentina, Illegitimate Debt, and Vulture Funds

CURRENT EVENTS

During the 1970s lending boom to developing countries, the World Bank, governments (including the US and UK), and Western banks funded the oppressive military junta that, between 1974 and 1983, ran a "Dirty War" against the Argentine people. Over 30,000 people were "disappeared," as the regime tortured and killed trade unionists, students, and anyone believed to be associated with "socialism." The UK government made loans to finance warships, helicopters, and missiles that were later used in the junta's invasion of the British-controlled Malvinas (Falkland Islands) in 1982. Defeat in the Falklands War led to the collapse of the junta. A new government elected in 1983 was saddled with a huge debt, which undermined the economy throughout the 1980s.

In the 1990s, under Carlos Menem, Argentina turned to the IMF and became a poster-child for the neoliberal mix of free-market economic policies, including privatization, trade liberalization, and free movement of capital. Poverty increased but so did foreign funds—until the East Asian financial crisis in 1997, when the foreign capital suddenly flowed out. A four-year recession began in 1998. By the end of 2001, the government debt had become unpayable, costing half of the country's revenues from exports. Argentina defaulted at the start of 2002. After a few months of crisis, poverty began to fall. Prior to the default, in July 2000, after extensive investigations by Alejandro Olmos Gaona and Daniel Marcos, an Argentine federal court found that many Argentine bonds were illegal in origin.

Between 2005 and 2010 Argentina reached deals with 93 per cent of its creditors to pay 30 cents on every dollar that was owed. However, a group of investment funds, called vulture funds, had bought Argentine and Zaire/Congo (see Box 14.1) debt for very low prices during the period when the countries were not paying, and continued to demand full repayment. One fund, FG Hemisphere, bought Zaire debt for $3 million and subsequently claimed over $100 million.

There was then a confusing split in international courts. In 2010 Britain passed a law saying that private companies could only sue HIPCs in British courts for the amount they would have got if they had taken part in the debt relief initiative—effectively enforcing the HIPC settlement on all creditors. This reflects British domestic legal practice, where a debt reduction agreed with most creditors can be enforced on any holdouts. Two Congo vulture funds sued in the British dependency of Jersey and lost their case.

In contrast, in 2013 and 2014, two vulture funds, NML Capital and Aurelius Capital Management, won judgments in the New York courts that Argentina either must pay them in full on its debt or the country would not be allowed to pay any of the creditors who accepted the debt restructuring. This judgment was enforceable because Argentina makes its debt payments through US banks. Argentina initially refused to pay the vulture funds in full, which meant it was unable to pay any of its creditors. But, a newly-elected federal government settled the outstanding debt for US$ 9.3 billion in April 2016 in order to gain access to international credit markets. However, it did so by borrowing more money at high interest rates.

unilaterally cancelled export credit debt for ships that had been used to promote Norwegian shipyards rather than for developmental purposes. And in 2010 it launched the first "creditor audit" of all of its lending to developing countries. On the debtor side, the government of Ecuador established an independent Public Debt Audit Commission in 2007, which found that only 20 per cent of debt was related to development projects and 80 per cent was the result of refinancing old debt with new debt. It found that debt had been

BOX 14.3 | Repeating the 1980s in Greece

CURRENT EVENTS

"Wall Street tactics akin to the ones that fostered subprime mortgages in America have worsened the financial crisis shaking Greece and undermining the euro by enabling European governments to hide their mounting debts," explained the *New York Times* (13 Feb. 2010). From 2001, US investment banks lent money to Greece, but in ways that kept the loans off the books because they would have violated European Union rules. In effect, Greek officials mortgaged the country's airports and highways, pledged future lottery revenues, and bought and sold special bonds. It was loan pushing and sub-prime lending on a global level.

Greece spent double the European average on the military. From 2002 to 2006, Greece was the world's fourth biggest importer of conventional weapons, buying submarines, planes, and tanks from Germany, France, and the United States—on credit. And with loan pushing, two major German companies admitted paying large bribes in Greece (Smith, 2012).

After the 2008 financial crisis, the international lenders responded to Greece exactly as they had to developing countries three decades earlier. First, they pushed up the interest rates being charged to Greece—and by 2010 it was clear the debt was unsustainable and Greece could not pay. A deal was made with a group called the "troika," the IMF, the European Commission, and the European Central Bank, for a bailout. Over the five years 2010–14 the troika provided €252 billion (about $325 billion) in new loans. Of that, €232 billion simply went directly to the previous lenders in principal and interest payments and just €20 billion to the Greek people (Jones, 2015). Much Greek debt was to private banks and companies and the troika's main goal was to protect them, by nationalizing the debt.

Indeed, Greece's debt slightly increased, from €310 billion in 2010 to €317 billion in 2014. Even worse, the lenders imposed the same neoliberal structural adjustment package they had imposed on developing countries in the 1980s, with heavy austerity involving cuts in wages and pensions and sharp increases in taxes. In 2010 the IMF predicted that the austerity would lead to a fall in GDP (gross domestic product) of 1.5 per cent between then and 2014. In fact, the GDP fall was 22 per cent over this period and, with a declining economy, it became harder and harder for Greece to pay. In 2014, real wages were 17 per cent lower than in 2009; two-thirds of young people in Greece were unemployed, and one-in-five people suffered from severe material deprivation.

To be sure, Greece does not need 1,300 tanks and four new submarines. But who is responsible for the loans that paid for them—Greece's poorest pensioners, or the German company that paid bribes to sell its submarines? What responsibility does the IMF have for imposing an austerity package that makes it impossible to repay the IMF loans?

In 2015 the Greek parliament set up a debt audit commission, chaired by the speaker of parliament. It concluded "that Greece should not pay this debt because it is illegal, illegitimate and odious." Many of the initial private loans were given in bad faith by companies and banks that acted "irresponsibly" by not observing their due diligence obligations—to see that the loans were appropriate, followed Greek law, and were repayable. Thus, those banks and companies should carry the risk of their irresponsible actions. The subsequent troika debt "is also illegitimate because it was converted from private to public debt under pressure"; it benefited only private banks and companies and not the Greek people (Hellenic Parliament, 2015).

refinanced in this way in violation of both national and international law, that debt contracts violated Ecuador's sovereignty, and that excessive interest rates amounted to usury. President Rafael Correa declared the debt "illegitimate" and refused further payments. And in Greece, a committee established by parliament raised the issue of illegitimacy in 2015.

Lender–borrower co-responsibilities, as well as odious and illegitimate lending, are now becoming recognized as concepts in international law, and domestic lending concepts such as unfairness and broader obligations of lenders are being taken into account. This has revived calls to establish something similar to the common practice with respect to debt in national laws, and thereby to create an international "bankruptcy" procedure for governments to force all creditors to accept debt reductions. In September 2014, the UN General Assembly voted by 124 to 11 to establish new debt resolution rules. However, those countries voting against included the US, Germany, Japan, and the UK, so it may take several more years before the principle becomes established.

The 2008 Financial Crisis

In 2008 a global financial crisis was triggered not in the South but in the North. The worst financial crisis since the Great Depression of the 1930s was set off first in the United States when the "bubble" burst on lending for "sub-prime mortgages" that could never be repaid. Lehman Brothers, the fourth-largest investment bank in the US, had been dealing heavily in obscure financial instruments based on these unpayable mortgages and went bankrupt. The crisis spread, and five European states (Greece, Portugal, Ireland, Spain, and Cyprus) were unable to repay or refinance their government debt and had to be bailed out by the IMF and European Commission.

CRITICAL ISSUES

BOX 14.4 | The Jubilee Campaign

In the mid-1990s, a global campaign began calling for the debts of 52 countries in the Global South to be cancelled for the millennium. The campaign used the imagery of a "jubilee year"—a year every 7 and/or 49 years recorded in the Jewish scriptures when debts were cancelled and slaves freed. By the year 2000, over 20 million people had signed a petition globally calling for debts to be cancelled, and tens of thousands had marched in protests during G8 summits in Birmingham (UK) and Cologne (Germany).

There were disagreements within the campaign as to how to present the issue. Much campaigning in the Global North focused on the damage debt was causing, without reference to where loans had come from. Campaigners in the Global South—who launched "Jubilee South"—wanted more emphasis on the odious nature of original loans, with their slogan "Don't owe, won't pay."

The global response to the jubilee campaign was the creation and enhancement of the Heavily Indebted Poor Countries Initiative, which by 2015 had led to $130 billion of debt being cancelled for 36 countries. However, the structural changes demanded by the campaign were not implemented. Concepts in the jubilee campaign have continued through global networks such as the African Forum and Network on Debt and Development, Asian Peoples' Movement on Debt and Development, Latin American Network on Debt and Development, and European Network on Debt and Development.

In Spain, Ireland, and Britain, house prices had risen faster than incomes since the early 2000s, and the loan pushers encouraged people to borrow more than the value of the house and use the money for holiday or consumer spending, because they could always sell the house later at a higher price. It was a classic Kindleberger mania. Throughout the boom years of the 2000s, Germany and other "core" European countries lent, through their banks, large amounts to banks and governments in periphery countries such as Greece, Portugal, and Ireland. These loans enabled those countries to buy German exports, maintaining German industrial competitiveness, but building up a debt bomb. With the panic, house prices fell and individuals could not service the loans and banks could not sell the houses to recover the loans, while governments found they could not pay their German loans.

The response was quantitative easing, where central banks in Europe and the US created new money electronically in the hope of stimulating their economies. But more money was created than the banks could use, and as Figure 14.1 shows, this triggered a new lending mania to developing countries. One assessment based on IMF and World Bank predictions shows that two-thirds of low-income countries face large increases in the share of government income spent on debt payments by 2024 (Jones, 2014). It seems much like a return to the 1970s, with loan pushing and excessive lending pointing towards a new debt trap for many developing countries.

SUMMARY

Lending and borrowing, and regulations to control them, go back 4,000 years and international lending goes back 700 years. Loans can be a source of external resources for investment and economic development. However, lenders have their own interests, which have harmed developing countries. Banks with surplus capital have pushed inappropriate loans on countries as part of their speculation. Loans promote exports, especially of weapons. Governments sometimes want to support or to promote political allies, including dictators, regardless of what the money is spent on.

Charles Kindleberger proposed that the global economy runs in cycles of growth, mania, and panic. In the growth period lending can promote development. The mania includes loan pushing that turns to economic bust and panic. This was the case in the 1930s and in the 1980s, which led to two "lost decades of development" across much of the Global South. For two decades, the developing world gave $48 million to the rich world each day—yet every day the debt burden increased by $204 million.

Similarly, the global financial crisis in 2008 was rooted in excessive lending, followed by a sudden bust. And the pattern was repeated. The North printed money through quantitative easing, and some of this surplus money was lent to the South, promoting what would become a new debt crisis.

Meanwhile, within the rich countries, wealth has been transferred from rich to poor while poorer people have been encouraged to borrow to maintain minimal levels of consumption. And the US has built up a huge foreign debt by forcing developing countries to keep US dollars as reserves, making developing countries net lenders to the US and other industrialized countries.

At the heart of lending and borrowing relationships is power. If development is about creating more equal sharing of power in the world, lending has the possibility of doing so, as it is the sharing of resources by those with more. But increasingly, debt has been used as a means of increasing imbalances, increasing wealth and power in industrialized countries, and extracting resources from the Global South and preventing genuine development from taking place.

QUESTIONS FOR CRITICAL THOUGHT

1. Should lenders take more responsibility for improper lending?
2. How would you define "illegitimate lending"?
3. Are developing countries building up excessive reserves in US dollars and thus lending too much to the United States? What are the alternatives?
4. Do developing countries need to borrow internationally?

SUGGESTED READINGS

Chang, Ha-Joon. 2002. *Kicking Away the Ladder.* London: Anthem.

Graeber, David. 2011. *Debt: The First 5,000 Years.* New York: Melville House.

Hanlon, Joseph. 2006. "'Illegitimate' loans: Lenders, not borrowers, are responsible." *Third World Quarterly* 27, 2: 211–26.

Jochnick, Chris., and Fraser A. Preston, eds. 2006. *Sovereign Debt at the Crossroads.* Oxford: Oxford University Press.

Kindleberger, Charles. 1978. *Manias, Panics and Crashes*, 1st edn, London: Basic Books-Macmillan; 4th edn (2000), New York: John Wiley.

Perkins, John. 2004. *Confessions of an Economic Hit Man.* San Francisco: Berrett-Koehler.

BIBLIOGRAPHY

Adams, P. 1991. *Odious Debts.* London: Earthscan.

Chang, H.-J. 2002. *Kicking Away the Ladder.* London: Anthem.

Darity, W., and B. Horn. 1988. *The Loan Pushers: The Role of Commercial Banks in the International Debt Crisis.* Cambridge, Mass.: Ballinger–Harper and Row.

Drake, P. 1989. "Debt and democracy in Latin America, 1920–1980s." In Barbara Stallings and Robert Kaufman, eds, *Debt and Democracy in Latin America.* Boulder, Colo.: Westview.

Eichengreen, B., and P. Lindert. 1989. *The International Debt Crisis in Historical Perspective.* Cambridge, Mass.: MIT Press.

George, S. 1988. *A Fate Worse Than Debt.* London: Penguin.

Hanlon, J. 2006. "'Illegitimate' loans: Lenders, not borrowers, are responsible." *Third World Quarterly* 27, 2: 211–26.

Hellenic Parliament. 2015. *Truth Committee on Public Debt—Preliminary Report.* www.hellenicparliament.gr/UserFiles/f3c70a23-7696-49db-9148-f24dce6a27c8/Report_web.pdf.

International Monetary Fund (IMF). 2009. *Currency Composition of Official Foreign Exchange Reserves (COFER)*, July.

Jones, T. 2014. *Don't Turn the Clock Back: Analysing the Risks of the Lending Boom to Impoverished Countries.* London: Jubilee Debt Campaign. http://jubileedebt.org.uk/reports-briefings/report/dont-turn-clock-back-analysing-risks-lending-boom-impoverished-countries.

———. 2015. *The New Debt Trap: How the Response to the Last Global Financial Crisis Has Laid the Ground for the Next.* London: Jubilee Debt Campaign, July. http://jubileedebt.org.uk/wp-content/uploads/2015/07/The-new-debt-trap_07.15.pdf.

Kaiser, J. 2013. *One Made It Out of the Debt Trap: Lessons from the London Debt Agreement of 1953 for Current Debt Crises.* Friedrich Ebert Stiftung. http://library.fes.de/pdf-files/iez/10137.pdf.

Kindleberger, C. 1978. *Manias, Panics and Crashes*, 1st edn, London: Basic Books-Macmillan; 4th edn (2000), New York: John Wiley.

Organisation for Economic Co-operation and Development (OECD). 2015. *In It Together: Why Less Inequality Benefits All.* Paris: OECD.

Payer, C. 1991. *Lent and Lost: Foreign Credit and Third World Development.* London: Zed Books.

Perkins, J. 2004. *Confessions of an Economic Hit Man.* San Francisco: Berrett-Koehler.

Pineda-Ofreneo, R. 1991. *The Philippines Debt and Poverty.* Oxford: Oxfam.

Sampson, A. 1981. *The Money Lenders*. London: Hodder and Stoughton; e-book 2013, London: Bloomsbury.

Smith, H. 2012. "German 'hypocrisy' over Greek military spending has critics up in arms." *Guardian*, London, 19 Apr.

United States Census Bureau. 2015. www.census.gov/hhes/www/income/data/historical/families/index.html and www.census.gov/foreign-trade/statistics/historical/gands.pdf.

United States Federal Reserve System. 2015. www.federalreserve.gov/releases/g19/HIST/cc_hist_mt_levels.html.

United States Department of the Treasury. 2015. www.treasurydirect.gov/govt/reports/pd/mspd/mspd.htm and www.treasury.gov/resource-center/data-chart-center/tic/Pages/index.aspx.

World Bank. *World Databank: World Development Indicators & Global Development Finance*. http://databank.worldbank.org/ddp/home.do.

15 Free Trade, Fair Trade, and South–South Trade

Gavin Fridell

LEARNING OBJECTIVES

- To discover the differences and debates between "free trade" and "fair trade" theories and practices.
- To situate the dominant trade regime in relation to the past and the current rise of South–South trade.
- To engage in informed discussion on trade policy and its developmental impacts at the local and global levels.
- To understand the politics behind international trade.

▲ **A member of the Lisu hill tribe picks Thai arabica coffee beans at the Thai High coffee farm in Phrao, northern Thailand. The organic fair trade coffee farm was chosen to help produce Black Ivory Coffee. The new brand of coffee is produced by harvesting the beans from the dung of a Thai elephant. It takes 15 to 30 hours for the elephant to digest the beans, then they are plucked from their dung and washed and roasted.** | Source: Paula Bronstein/Getty Images

INTRODUCTION

Over the past decades, world trade has grown at an unprecedented rate. The total value of world exports of merchandise trade increased from $1.2 trillion in 1989 to more than $16.6 trillion in 2013. During this period, several booming Asian economies increased their share of the value of trade exports, whereas the poorest countries in South Asia and sub-Saharan Africa experienced only limited gains—sub-Saharan Africa's share of the value of world merchandise exports increased from an average of around 0.7 per cent per year from 1990 to 1993 to 1.6 per cent from 2009 to 2013 (WITS-UN-COMTRADE, 2015) (see Figure 15.1). While the wealthiest economies have more or less maintained their dominance, several emerging southern giants have increased their weight, while the poorest countries remain well behind. All of these trends have major significance for human development, social change, global politics, and economics.

Because of its significance, international trade seems to find its way into most development debates. The connection between trade and development is made even stronger by the growing number of international "free trade" agreements, which, as many commentators have pointed out, go well beyond trade to include a wide range of rules that intrude on the broader social and economic policies of states (Harvey, 2005; Gill, 2003; Hoogvelt, 2001; McNally, 2006). Consequently, it becomes difficult to discuss perspectives on international trade without getting lost in a conversation around the general theories of development discussed in Part I of this book.

Nonetheless, at the risk of oversimplification, it is possible to speak about two overarching perspectives on trade that generally are apparent in most development works. I will refer to these as a **free trade** perspective and a **fair trade** perspective. Neither of the two perspectives can be precisely defined. Some development thinkers might fit very well into one of the two groups,

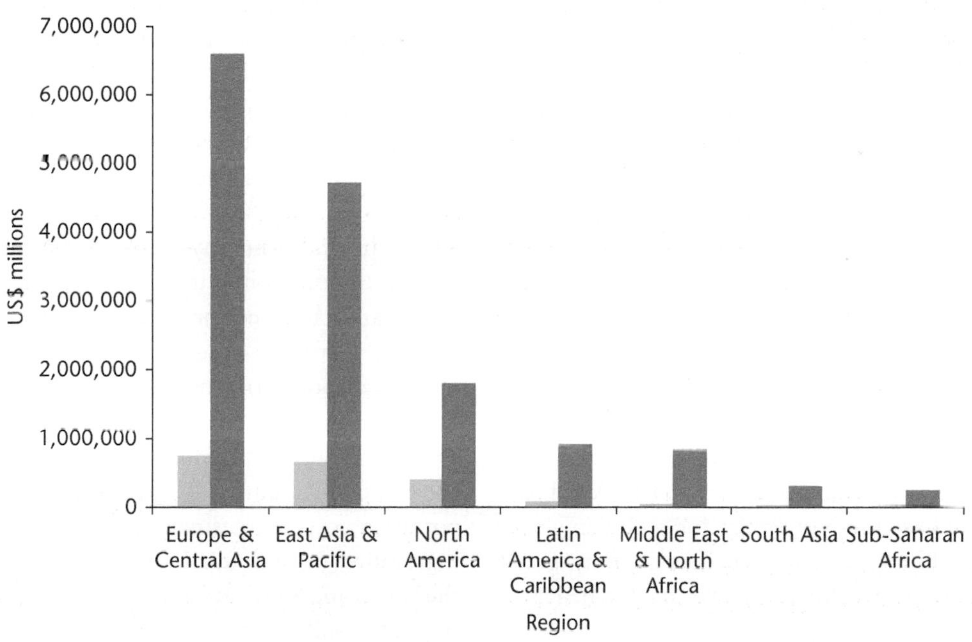

FIGURE 15.1 | World Export Trade

Note: averages exclude data from 1989 for sub-Saharan Africa.

Source: WITS-UN-COMTRADE (2015).

whereas others might fit only partially into a group or present ideas compatible with both. The notion of a free trade perspective and a fair trade perspective is thus a reference not to two cohesive approaches to development but rather to two general overarching assumptions that allow us to talk about general trends—to focus on the forest and not get lost in the trees.

The first of these perspectives, that of *free trade*, is premised on the notion that the removal of barriers to trade and the limitation of state intervention in economic and social interactions will provide the greatest social gains in the North and the South. This is the dominant view today within most official international organizations, such as the World Bank (officially the International Bank for Reconstruction and Development, IBRD), the International Monetary Fund (IMF), and the World Trade Organization (WTO), as well as within many national governments and non-governmental development organizations, although certainly not all.

Free trade moved to the centre of global trade policy in the 1970s, spurred on by the influence of neoliberal thinkers such as economist Milton Friedman (1962) and his University of Chicago disciples, nicknamed "the Chicago Boys." Drawing on neo-classical economic ideals from the nineteenth century, neoliberals are deeply opposed to state intervention in the economy, which they feel is bound to be inefficient and inaccurate because of state officials' limited access to information and their tendency to be biased towards the demands of specific interest groups, such as unions or trade lobbies. The unregulated market, in contrast, offers a "hidden hand" that responds efficiently and accurately to the "rational," self-interested actions of countless individuals through the undistorted market signals of supply and demand. The state is depicted as choking individual liberty and causing economic waste, while the market, as summarized by David Harvey, is viewed as "the best device for mobilizing even the basest of human instincts such as gluttony, greed, and the desire for wealth and power for the benefit of all" (2005: 20–1).

Neoliberal thinkers have been central to advancing a free trade vision based on a particular understanding of the histories of highly industrialized countries, especially the United States and the United Kingdom. They argue that a main driver behind the rapid economic growth experienced by these countries in the eighteenth and nineteenth centuries was a devotion to free trade, which sparked competition, leading to technological innovation and specialization as nations sought to enhance their **comparative advantage**—a concept formulated by David Ricardo in the nineteenth century.

Ricardo's theory held that each nation had an economic advantage relative to other nations for the production of some goods. Thus, Country A might produce both iron and wheat more efficiently than Country B, which also produced the same goods. But Country A might be most efficient at producing iron. Consequently, it would be in the relative interest of both nations if Country A focused on iron and Country B focused on wheat, with the two trading iron and wheat to their mutual benefit. Based on these assumptions, free traders today argue that developing countries need to remove their barriers to trade to gain access to rich countries' technology, products, and investment, while producing and trading those goods for which they have or can develop a comparative economic advantage relative to other nations (Bhagwati, 2002; Sachs, 2005). If each nation specializes in the products for which it has a comparative advantage, all of the nations will benefit in relative terms, making trade not a zero-sum game but rather, in the words of Earth Institute director Jeffrey Sachs, "one that everybody can win" (2005: 31, 54).

Some free trade proponents are less optimistic about its benefits. "New trade theory" advocates Paul Krugman and Anthony Venables argue that transportation and communication advancements have significantly reduced the need for industries to cluster together in regions close to consumer markets to minimize transportation costs. Corporations can now locate themselves wherever labour is cheapest, allowing southern states to promote industrialization through the competitive advantage of cheap labour. As transportation costs increasingly decline, industry increasingly moves to the South. In the end, real wages between the North and South are likely to converge through this process, resulting in a situation "in which the peripheral nations definitely gain and the core nations may well lose" (Krugman and Venables, 1995: 859). While this would not be the rosiest outcome for northern workers, Krugman and Venables argue that protectionist policies in the North would only wreck its competitiveness and unjustly suppress industrialization in the South. In their view, free trade may not bring about a strictly win-win scenario, but it represents the best choice of the available options.

In contrast, the *fair trade* perspective has been even less optimistic about the possibilities of a win-win situation in international trade—unless the terms of North–South trade are readjusted. Fair trade proponents challenge free traders' historical understanding of trade and assert that markets have always been regulated, generally in the interests of the rich and powerful. They argue that the rich nations in the North, as well as the newly industrialized countries (NICs) in East Asia and Latin America, all emerged historically behind a protective wall of import controls, tariffs, levies, quotas, and preferences designed to protect domestic industry and enhance export industry (Chang, 2008; Stiglitz, 2002, 2003). Market regulation, in particular, has been employed by powerful nations to ensure their dominant position in the global division of labour: they demand relatively easy access to raw materials and markets in the South while erecting trade barriers to protect key industries in the North from southern competition. To counter this historical legacy, fair traders argue that market regulation must be used to protect the weak, not the strong, and to create a more equal international trading system (Barratt Brown, 1993).

The strongest proponents of the fair trade perspective tend to be located within a broad school of thought on underdevelopment and dependency theory, which moved to the fore of critical development during the 1960s and 1970s. As discussed in Chapter 3,

PHOTO 15.1 | **Low-priced clothing in a Walmart store. Such clothing is usually manufactured in low-wage developing countries.**

these theorists have argued that the history of colonialism has led to the formation of a world system divided into First World imperialist nations in the North and Third World neo-colonial nations in the South. Rather than southern countries being in a position to enhance their comparative advantage through international trade, their national development is restricted and distorted by the **unequal exchange** of lower-priced primary commodities (such as coffee, tea, cocoa, and bananas) for higher-priced industrial goods, technology, and services from the First World (Frank, 1972; Prebisch, 1950). While some southern NICs have been able to attain rapid industrialization since the 1970s, many of these countries have moved into the low-waged manufacturing stage of production while remaining dependent on the North for advanced technology, services, investment capital, and core markets (Hoogvelt, 2001: 43–6). In this context, international trade does not bring about a win-win scenario for all but, as famously stated by Andre Gunder Frank (1972), the "development of underdevelopment" for the South.

Fair traders criticize free traders for focusing too much on speculative trade models while neglecting the political conditions under which the battle for comparative advantage is carried out and the human impact of this competitive struggle. In many cases, free trade policies present southern producers with a double-edged sword. On the one hand, they result in domestic markets being flooded with high-technology industrial goods produced by northern-based transnational corporations (TNCs) that employ their competitive advantages (including enormous economies of scale) to beat out potential local competitors.

On the other hand, they unleash extensive competition for agricultural and low-waged industrial goods around which poor southern regions hope to eke out their comparative advantage. This is exemplified by the intense competition in the global textile industry. A celebrated blue jeans industry dominated by small producers in Ecuador in the 1980s was devastated by free trade reforms in the 1990s that opened domestic markets to fierce competition from other low-waged jeans producers (see Box 15.1). Similarly, most of

CRITICAL ISSUES

BOX 15.1 | Neoliberalism and "Endogenous" Development: The Jeans Industry in Pelileo, Ecuador

The town of Pelileo in Tungurahua, Ecuador, long had a reputation for its successful blue jeans industry, constructed on the basis of small-scale, family-run textile enterprises. A 1995 World Bank report on Ecuador held up Pelileo's jeans industry as an example of small producers attaining social progress and rural diversification in a neoliberal world. Research conducted by Liisa North (2003), however, revealed that Pelileo was far from a neoliberal success story. The core aspects of Pelileo's development lay in a variety of "endogenous" (internal) factors, including the absence of large estates and servile social relations; the existence of a broad class of efficient, small-scale agriculture producers; Pelileo's long history as a strategic point of commercial exchange; and the early construction of transportation and communication infrastructure in the region. These endogenous factors formed the basis for a boom in the jeans industry in the 1980s, which then declined significantly by the end of the millennium *after* the introduction of neoliberal reforms. Neoliberal structural adjustment programs (SAPs) and the dollarization of Ecuador's currency in the 1990s caused a national economic crisis that reduced domestic demand for jeans, while trade liberalization policies opened the region up to overwhelming competition from other jeans producers. From 1999 to 2000, from 25 to 50 per cent of Pelileo's jeans establishments disappeared. Rather than promoting human development in Pelileo, North (2003: 224) argues that neoliberal reforms were "overwhelmingly destructive" to the town's previously successful endogenous development.

Africa's domestic textile industries have been limited by heavy competition from Asia combined with northern charities dumping second-hand clothes on African markets at unmatchable prices (Bunting, 2005). While industries in Ecuador and Africa have lost out in this competitive environment, low-waged Asian producers have gained, along with giant US retailers like Walmart, which have profited significantly from enhanced access to cheap textiles (Gill, 2003: 210). Outcomes such as these have led fair traders to argue that the poorest countries cannot develop viable industries without active government support at the national and international levels to protect them from overpowering global market forces (Fridell, 2013; Change, 2008; Bello, 2004; Stiglitz, 2003, 2002).

FREE TRADE AND FAIR TRADE SINCE 1945

While free trade is the dominant paradigm today, both fair and free trade perspectives have had significant influences on world trade and development policy, and the tug-of-war between the two overarching approaches is ongoing. In media, academic, and policy circles, the debate frequently focuses on whether the state should or should not intervene in the market. However, regardless of what perspective one adopts, the state remains the essential player in constructing and enforcing the rules around which markets operate (see Chapter 7). While free traders, for example, might find state intervention in the market for social and environmental reasons unacceptable, they do not oppose the need for the state to protect private property rights or to create powerful institutions, like the World Bank, the IMF, and the WTO, to regulate and to enforce free-market policies (Harvey, 2005: 21; McNally, 2006). Consequently, the core issue of debate is less about the *extent* than it is about the *manner* in which the state should regulate the market.

Towards the end of World War II, in July 1944, regulations for an international trade and development regime with various mechanisms for enforcing both free and fair trade policies were adopted at meetings in Bretton Woods, New Hampshire, through a negotiated process dominated by rich countries. In free trade terms, most of the participants at the negotiations viewed protectionist policies prior to the war as having been responsible for the economic chaos of the 1930s, along with the rise of fascism. Consequently, they sought to create a liberal international trading system through the negotiated reduction in trade barriers managed by the General Agreement on Tariffs and Trade (GATT).

Along with this free trade mechanism, however, was a regulated international monetary system, dominated by the US and designed to provide stability for the new trading system. This entailed an exchange rate system pegged to the American dollar, a fixed American dollar–gold convertibility, and international co-operation to control short-term financial flows (Helleiner, 1994; Gowan, 1999). Two key institutions were formed to oversee the system: the IMF, designed to provide short-term loans for countries with balance-of-payment difficulties; and the World Bank, designed to provide long-term financing for development projects (see Chapter 9). The international trade regime that emerged is frequently referred to as one of **embedded liberalism** because it combined a mixture of state intervention to control capital and investment flows with liberal trade objectives (Helleiner, 1994).

Even within the realm of trade, however, the Bretton Woods system allowed for significant regulations to ensure a degree of stability for southern economies. Among the most noteworthy were **commodity control schemes**, which entailed the use of buffer stocks that were built up in times of surplus production and run down in times of shortage. When prices were low, participating countries agreed to withhold a specified amount of their products from the market until prices were forced up. In the 1950s, international agreements under the oversight of the newly formed United Nations (UN) were signed for most major commodities, including coffee, cocoa, cotton, sugar, wheat, tin, rubber, and wool. Over time, most of them subsided for various political-economic reasons; for example, a sugar agreement failed in the 1960s after the United States unilaterally boycotted Cuban sugar amid the Cold War (Barratt Brown, 1993: 89–92; Furtado, 1976: 215–21). Some commodity control schemes, however—in particular, the one for coffee—succeeded in providing important price supports to small producers (see Box 15.2).

CRITICAL ISSUES

BOX 15.2 | Regulating Markets: The International Coffee Agreement

One of the most successful examples of regulating international prices is the International Coffee Agreement (ICA). It was formed in 1963 under pressure from coffee-producing states and was renewed several times until 1989, when major participants, in particular the United States, withdrew their support as part of the movement towards free trade. The ICA was a quota system signed by all major producing and consuming countries designed to stabilize and increase coffee prices by holding a certain amount of coffee beans off the global market to avoid oversupply. John Talbot (2004) has calculated that the ICA resulted in higher coffee bean prices, which translated into a greater retention of coffee income in the South. At the same time, the agreement was plagued by many difficulties, including an inability to deal with the structural causes of oversupply, the failure to do little more than dampen the unpredictable swings of the coffee cycle, and the persistence of conflict among signatory nations over the quota system.

Moreover, the ICA proved to have a minimal effect on how the extra wealth retained in the South was distributed. Countries that pursued social reformist projects that distributed greater resources to small farmers and workers, such as Costa Rica and Colombia, attained better development gains than countries with highly unequal distributions of land and resources, such as El Salvador, Guatemala, and Brazil (Fridell, 2007: 135–72). Yet, as Talbot (2004: 163–95) has noted, overall, ICA-supported prices provided varying degrees of "trickle-down" improvements to the living standards of broad sectors in the South. In contrast, the decades since the end of the ICA have been characterized by extreme market volatility and periodic severe crises for millions of small coffee farmers and workers (Fridell, 2014; Talbot, 2004). In this light, defenders of commodity agreements argue that the ICA was a more successful model for promoting human development than an unregulated, free trade coffee market.

General disillusionment with sluggish economic and trade growth in the South led to the first United Nations Conference on Trade and Development (UNCTAD) in 1964 (see Chapter 10). At the conference, resolutions were passed by a majority of mostly southern nations in favour of a greater transfer of wealth from the North to the South through aid, compensation, and, most importantly, "fairer trade." The strategy for attaining fairer trade focused on two key demands: the replacement of financial aid with efforts to ensure fairer prices for southern commodities through direct subsidies for poor producers (a demand that sparked the slogan "trade not aid"); and a call for northern states to eliminate "unfair" protectionist policies that blocked southern exports and stymied attempts to develop the value-added processing stages of primary production (Barratt Brown, 1993: 92; Furtado, 1976: 221–4). Particularly glaring instances of this system are the escalating tariff rates that continue to be applied to primary products today. For example, the tariff rate for coffee beans entering the EU in 2010 was zero for unprocessed green beans, 7.5 per cent for roasted beans, 9 per cent for decaffeinated roasted beans, and 11.5 per cent for substitutes containing coffee, such as instant coffee (European Commission Database, 2010). This means that coffee countries are, in effect, punished by the EU for processing their beans, stifling coffee manufacturing in the South.

The first UNCTAD failed to address the key demands as northern representatives voted against or abstained from every major resolution. UNCTAD itself, however, was established as an important fair trade forum and research body (Bello, 2004: 34–5). One of its more successful efforts was the promotion of compensatory finance schemes in which producers received compensation when commodity prices dropped below agreed-upon levels. The most notable example of this was the export earnings stabilization system (STABEX) agreement adopted by the European Community in the early 1970s and designed to compensate its ex-colonies—known as the African, Caribbean, and Pacific Group of States (ACP Group). STABEX established target prices for more than 50 products, and the European Community pledged to make up the difference when prices fell below the target. In practice, European nations frequently failed to provide sufficient funds and in some years STABEX failed to meet even 40 per cent of its obligations. Nonetheless, despite its shortcomings, it did provide much-needed price subsidies to poor producers in the South (LeClair, 2002).

UNCTAD, along with other UN bodies, developed into a key advocacy forum wherein southern nations demanded better prices for commodities, preferential access to northern markets, reforms to the international monetary system, new aid flows, and codes of conduct for TNCs. These demands became codified in the UN Programme of Action for the Establishment of a New International Economic Order (NIEO) (1974) and the UN Charter of Economic Rights and Duties of States (1976) (Bello, 2004: 38–41; Hoogvelt, 2001: 41–2). By the end of the decade, however, fair trade was on the decline and the pendulum had swung further in the direction of free trade. Declining economic growth rates in the North compelled more powerful states—in particular the United States, with its burgeoning trade deficit—to seek to pry open southern economies in search of new markets and cheap labour (Helleiner, 1994; Gowan, 1999). The result was a renewed interest in free trade policies.

Among the most powerful mechanisms for the expansion of free trade policies were neoliberal structural adjustment policies (SAPs), which were imposed on highly indebted nations after a series of loan defaults emerging out of the debt crises of the 1980s (see Chapters 9 and 14). In response to the defaults, the IMF offered indebted nations "rescue packages," which included refinancing and rescheduling loan payments on the condition that they agreed to severe cuts to public spending, reducing or eliminating trade barriers and capital controls, and devaluing local currencies to make exports more competitive. By the early 1990s, more than 100 highly indebted southern nations had initiated SAPs. They proved to be ineffective in solving debt crises, and indebted countries had an estimated net outflow of resources to the North of more than $200 billion in the 1980s (Cobridge, 1993: 123–39; Gowan, 1999; Stiglitz, 2003).

What SAPs did accomplish was to usher in a new era of free trade. The political support upon which many fair trade mechanisms had been constructed dissolved, and most declined or disappeared. At the end of 1994, the GATT agreements were ratified at the Uruguay Round, and the WTO was formed, charged with policing and promoting free trade and deregulation among its member states. In 2000, the WTO succeeded in pressuring the European Union and the ACP Group to gradually phase out all preferential trade arrangements, including STABEX. Today, the WTO has 161 members, more than 80 per cent of all countries in the world, all of which have committed, at least officially, to the goals of free trade and market liberalization.

Fair Trade and Social Movements

While the 1980s to the 2000s marked the growth of free trade as the dominant discourse in most official development institutions and government agencies, they also were the decades where considerable challenges emerged to free trade hegemony. Throughout the globe, an array of labour, environmental, indigenous, human rights, and women's groups actively protested against free trade policies and their impacts on local communities (see Chapter 12). These groups put intense pressure on southern governments, some of which grew increasingly resistant to the trade agenda advanced by northern governments and international financial institutions (McNally, 2006; Rosset, 2006). One of the most notable examples of this was the emergence of a coalition of developing countries that refused to settle on a new agreement at the WTO Fifth Ministerial Conference in 2003, an event marked by global protests. The coalition united around a series of demands consistent with both fair trade and free trade ideals, in particular the elimination of northern agricultural export subsidies and protectionist barriers blocking southern commodities (Rosset, 2006). Since 2003, WTO members repeatedly have carried out failed negotiating rounds and have been unable to move ahead with major reforms (although agreement was reached in December 2015 to begin a process of eliminating agricultural export subsidies, the outcome of which remains to be seen). Several of the leaders of the developing coalition have gone on to form the BRICS (Brazil, Russia, India, China, and South Africa) group of states, which has held annual summits since 2010 to promote economic and political co-operation and which has become an influential global association (see Chapter 13).

Outside the state, fair trade ideas have had an influence on a wide variety of social movements. Some of these movements have focused on stemming the tide of global market integration by prioritizing production for local and national markets over international trade. This is exemplified by "food sovereignty" groups like the Landless Workers' Movement (MST) in Brazil, a country with one of the most unequal patterns of landownership in the world. Since 1984, the MST has seized more than 50,000 square kilometres of land, upon which they have settled hundreds of thousands of families and constructed co-operative enterprises, public schools, houses, and health clinics with a view towards farming aimed, first, at local and national markets (Rosset, 2006).

Other movements have sought to attain the integration of poor workers and farmers into global markets under better conditions. Chief among these is the **fair trade network**, which emerged in the post-war era out of a variety of direct-purchase projects that linked northern NGOs to poor and disadvantaged artisans and producers. In the late 1980s, fair trade transitioned into a third-party certification system that verifies private companies through a market-driven model. The network connects small farmers, workers, and craftspeople in the South with organizations and consumers in the North through a system of "fair trade" rules and principles, including democratic organization (of co-operatives or unions), no exploitation of child labour, environmental sustainability, a minimum guaranteed price, and social premiums paid to producer communities to build community infrastructure (Hudson et al., 2014; Fridell, 2007; Jaffee, 2007).

While there are many instances of fair trade bringing meaningful benefits to specific local communities, critics have expressed concern over the limited reach of fair trade because of its dependence on relatively small niche markets in the North. For example, the network's more than 730,000 certified fair trade coffee producers represent less about 3 per cent of the 25 million coffee farmer families worldwide (Fridell, 2007, 2014). Even for those who have been reached by fair trade, its developmental impact is contentious and concerns have been raised around its limited benefits for small farmers (see Box 15.3) and, more recently, rural workers (see Box 15.4).

BOX 15.3 | Fair Trade Coffee in an Unfair World? **CURRENT EVENTS**

Research conducted on fair trade groups in the South suggests that fair trade provides important social and economic benefits to certified producers, although with important qualifications (Hudson et al., 2013; Fridell, 2007; Jaffee, 2007). This can be seen in the case of the Union of Indigenous Communities of the Isthmus Region (UCIRI), one of the most successful fair trade coffee co-operatives in the world, located in Oaxaca, Mexico. Through their participation in fair trade, UCIRI members have attained higher incomes and significantly better access to social services through co-operative projects in health care, education, and training. UCIRI also has constructed its own economic infrastructure, such as coffee-processing and transportation facilities, and has provided its members with enhanced access to credit, technology, and marketing skills. Yet, despite the co-operative's success in combatting extreme misery, UCIRI members still report the persistence of general poverty (Fridell, 2007). Fair trade prices are inadequately low because they must remain somewhat competitive with conventional coffee bean prices. Moreover, UCIRI members remain highly vulnerable to global market and climate conditions beyond their control. A major coffee leaf rust infestation, intensified by the impacts of climate change, destroying coffee harvests throughout Mexico and Central America beginning in 2012, has brought UCIRI to the verge of collapse, with members reporting: "Everything we have fought for over the past 30 years we are losing to climate change and rust" (quoted in Byrne and Sharpe, 2014: 124). How effective can the fair trade network be at the local level against the tide of global forces beyond its control?

BOX 15.4 | Fair Trade and Labour Exploitation CURRENT EVENTS

In 2013 and 2014, several in-depth investigations shook up the fair trade and ethical certification world by suggesting modest, or even less, developmental benefits to certified communities in the South. One report, examining fair trade and UTZ certified coffee in seven regions of Ethiopia, Uganda, and Kenya from 2008 to 2013, concluded that the impact on farmers' total income was "modest and fairly limited"; that "[structural] change of bargaining relations throughout the coffee chain hardly occurred"; and that certification had "not resulted in a widespread perception that coffee farming [was] a profitable business venture" (Hoebink et al., 2014: 8, 12). Another report, examining five cases of sustainably certified cocoa and tea farms in Ecuador, Ghana, and India, was more optimistic, stating that voluntary certification standards revealed "an overall positive impact" on such things as income, while concluding: "We have not found evidence that sustainability standards, especially without significant additional producer support programmes, are able to lift smallholder households out of poverty." Positive impacts on gender inequality were "very limited" and hired labourers were "not reached by sustainability standards" (Nelson and Martin, 2013: 77, 85–6).

Perhaps most surprising of all was a report produced out of the Department of International Development at the School of Oriental and African Studies, University of London, focused specifically on rural wage labourers on fair trade certified coffee, flower, and tea plantations in Ethiopia and Uganda. Based on the extensive gathering of micro-evidence, including over 1,000 "person days of direct field research," the researchers determined that they were unable to find any evidence of positive impacts on wages and working conditions for labourers on fair trade farms. In fact, they conclude that "the data suggests that those employed in areas where there are Fairtrade producer organisations are significantly worse paid, and treated, than those employed for wages in the production of the same commodities in areas without any Fairtrade certified institutions" (Cramer et al., 2014: 16, 18). The authors suggest a key reason for this could be the scale of large, non-fair trade farms, which have the resources to offer better pay and working conditions, and are often highly exposed to public scrutiny. They also point to the specificities of individual farms (which can have good or bad labour conditions for many complex reasons) and to the "blindness" of fair trade standards, which have traditionally focused on small farms while neglecting the rural labourers who work on them (Cramer et al., 2014: 101). Outcomes such as these have sparked considerable debate and point to the need to carefully consider the developmental impacts of fair trade and other voluntary certification schemes as they currently exist.

Concerns also have been raised that the growth of the fair trade network has been driven by the increasing participation of corporations and international institutions that are using token support for fair trade to mask their broader devotion to free trade. Thus, corporations such as Starbucks gain positive publicity for selling 8.1 per cent of its coffee beans as fair trade in 2012, even though over 91 per cent of its beans were not fair trade certified and lacked its rigorous third-party verification. The World Bank has supported fair trade certification, both in its policy documents and by serving fair trade tea and coffee to its employees in Washington, while insisting it must be combined with privatization, liberalization, and deregulation—policies that fair trade groups have traditionally opposed (World Bank, 2013; Fridell, 2007, 2014; Jaffee, 2007). Fair trade author and activist Daniel Jaffee has expressed concern that unless the principles of the fair trade network can be adopted by national and international governing bodies as a matter of state policy, "it might indeed become irrelevant in the face of the larger effects of corporate-led economic globalization" (2007: 266).

Jeff Moore

PHOTO 15.2 | Fair Trade co-founder Francisco VanderHoff examines coffee plants in Buena Vista, Oaxaca, Mexico.

The Scorecard on Free versus Fair Trade

Free trade policies continue to dominate the international trade regime, and their effects continue to spread, with diverse results in different regions in the South. At the same time, the onset of the global economic recession at the start of 2008 reignited debate on the pitfalls of unregulated markets and has given new impetus to advocates for regulated fair trade mechanisms, as discussed below.

While the future of global trade policies remains contentious, some general assessments can be made about their developmental impact on the basis of past performances. In a report by the US-based Center for Economic and Policy Research, *The Scorecard on Globalization*, the authors compare 20 years of embedded liberalism, from 1960 to 1980, during which time fair trade policies were on the rise, to 20 years of neoliberalism, from 1980 to 2000, when free trade policies emerged as the dominant trade paradigm. They determine that despite some of the shortcomings of embedded liberal policies, the 1960s to the 1980s was a period of previously unprecedented overall progress in the South for most major indicators of human development, including life expectancy at birth, GDP per capita, infant and child mortality rates, education, and literacy. In contrast, the decades of neoliberal policies since the 1980s were accompanied by a decline in progress for most of these indicators (Weisbrot et al., 2001). Included among these statistics is economic growth, which slowed significantly after the 1980s for most countries, even while free traders claim it to be a central goal of their policy objectives—GDP per capita in Latin America grew by 75 per cent from 1960 to 1980 compared to only 6 per cent from 1980 to 1998 (Stiglitz,

2003; Weisbrot et al., 2001). If the "scorecard" reads like this, why do free trade policies continue to dominate the international trade agenda?

THE LIMITS OF A TRADE PERSPECTIVE: "IT'S NOT ABOUT FREE TRADE"

Beyond debating the developmental impact of free trade policies, one can also debate the extent to which the many official free trade arrangements genuinely entail freeing trade, which at a minimum involves evenly eliminating trade barriers. The WTO negotiations have failed in this regard, as more powerful countries have used a variety of techniques to warp trade relations in their favour. For example, while rich nations have dramatically reduced their tariff barriers over the past 20 years, they have at the same time increased their use of quotas and non-tariff barriers to trade (Jones, 2010; Rosset, 2006; McNally, 2006; Oxfam International, 2002). Particularly contentious, and a major stumbling block at the WTO, has been the massive use of agricultural subsidies (a non-tariff barrier) by northern states—by one estimate, in 2009 $62 of every $100 that a US farmer earned came from some level of government, amounting to a total annual farm subsidy of $180.8 billion (McKenna, 2010).

Despite the WTO's shortcomings, passionate free trader Jagdish Bhagwati (2008) still prefers its multilateral vision to the burgeoning array of bilateral "free trade" agreements that involve two or a select group of countries. While these agreements may appear to be freeing trade by lowering barriers between specific members, they discriminate against non-members, which in effect erects further barriers to trade for non-members. To Bhagwati, these agreements are not free trade, but rather "preferential trade" agreements, and their widespread growth and adoption since the 1990s is a "pandemic" that threatens the prospects of genuine free trade being negotiated by all WTO members.

If free trade mechanisms are not effective at evenly eliminating trade barriers, political scientist David McNally (2006: 27) provocatively argues that this is because they are "not about free trade." Instead, they have as a key goal that of protecting the property rights of transnational corporations and limiting the rights of states to intervene in their operations for the sake of social, environmental, or developmental concerns. For example, the North American Free Trade Agreement (NAFTA) contains a Chapter 11 that allows foreign investors to sue governments if they believe their company has suffered a loss because of a violation of an array of special investment rights and protections. In the mid-1990s, when the governor of the Mexican state of San Luis Potosi blocked attempts by US-based Metalclad Corporation to build a toxic waste landfill site in the state, the company filed a Chapter 11 complaint. In 2000, the NAFTA tribunal ruled in favour of the company and ordered the Mexican government to pay $16.7 million in damages to the company (McNally, 2006: 43–5).

Since then, dozens of cases have been brought before NAFTA tribunals, awarding millions to corporations and raising concerns of a chilling effect on government policy-makers (Sinclair, 2010). These cases suggest that NAFTA is less about promoting free trade than about formulating a "new constitutionalist framework" that elevates the rights of transnational corporations above the social and environmental concerns of communities and citizens (Gill, 2003). Concerns have been raised recently that the 12-member Trans-Pacific Partnership (TPP), signed in February 2016 and currently awaiting ratification by the member states, contains a similar investor–state dispute mechanism. The manner in which such trade deals as the TPP are crafted in a secretive fashion was highlighted by trade campaigner Stuart Trew, who observed, in regard to the TPP, that "while 600 corporate lobbyists have seen the negotiating texts, they are not made available to the public in any participating country" (2012: 20).

If we accept McNally's premise that the array of agreements and organizations regulating the international trade regime are not concerned primarily with free trade, why do global institutions, national governments, and NGOs persist in discussing and debating trade issues along free trade lines? Some thinkers, drawing on the work of political and cultural theorists like Antonio Gramsci and Michel Foucault, have argued that the concept of "free trade" is most powerfully understood as an ideological tool designed to ensure the "hegemonic" dominance of the world system by the elites in northern countries. Free trade is more than a mere policy proposal; rather, it is a discursive component of a **power/knowledge regime** designed to naturalize and legitimize the current world order (Goldman, 2005; Harvey, 2005) (see Chapter 4).

According to sociologist Michael Goldman, this regime is in part maintained by international organizations such as the World Bank, which produces mountains of reports and policy frameworks that construct "knowledge" about development and what it should or should not entail. The knowledge the Bank produces is not value-neutral but is designed to promote the idea that "there is no connection between increased poverty in the South and increased wealth accumulation in the North, and that such global institutions as the World Bank are composed of mere technocratic experts offering transhistorical truths to those who lack know-how, experience, and skills" (Goldman, 2005: 21). Consequently, while neoliberal policies may not have proved very effective at promoting actual free trade or combatting poverty in the South, the World Bank has spent tens of millions of dollars per year developing reports, working papers, data analyses, seminars, journals, and policy prescriptions to advance the opposite claims. Many of these sources are self-referential, lack the scholarly requirements of independent research, and are produced by officials who tend to share a "scientific esprit de corps that is rare among research institutions" (Goldman, 2005: 101). The result, states Goldman (2005: 103), is that "[k]nowledge is indeed power for the World Bank."

Fair trade concepts are not immune to the above critique, and many have suggested that fair trade ideas remain largely within the discourse of neoliberalism. They assert that despite their differences in approach, both free and fair traders aspire ultimately to competitive markets, open trade, export competitiveness, and a reliance on foreign investment (Bello, 2004; Fridell, 2007; Hart-Landsberg and Burkett, 2005: 13–25; McNally, 2006). Indeed, one of the criticisms

The Image Bank/Simon Rawles/Getty Images

PHOTO 15.3 | A fair trade cotton farmer weighs his crop, Mali.

of neoliberal reforms most frequently made by fair traders is that they do not do enough to promote *true free trade*, which they posit would work in the best interests of the poor and the rich as long as the proper institutional supports are provided (Oxfam International, 2002; Stiglitz, 2002). Critics charge that, when fair traders adopt this position, they inadvertently narrow the development debate down to what is and is not the most effective way to integrate into global markets, while neglecting and obscuring alternative visions of development and trade (Bello, 2004; McNally, 2006).

THE RISE OF SOUTH–SOUTH TRADE

Try as analysts might to predict the future, it is always elusive. Perhaps one of the most unpredictable events to have occurred in the past decade or so has been the much discussed and debated "Rise of the South," which has had major impacts on global trade policy and practice. Several economic giants, led by China, India, and Brazil, have emerged as major players in international trade after decades of rapid economic growth, leading to improved social indicators and enhanced political influence (see Chapters 6 and 13). Flows of South–South foreign direct investment (FDI) grew from $2 billion in 1985 to $60 billion by 2005, and the share of South–South trade composing world merchandise trade grew from 8 per cent in 1980 to 26 per cent by 2011 (UNDP, 2013: 2; Shirotori and Molina, 2009).

Southern giants have emerged as lead players in both importing and exporting goods. China, for example, is the world's second largest economy and second largest exporter, as well as the number-one purchaser of major goods, from cars and pork to timber, gold, and crude oil. Even with products that are relatively "small" in the Chinese market, China is set to become a world leader. Coffee, for example, remains less popular than tea in China, but the country still is predicted to be among the world's top coffee importers by 2020 because of its huge population. The same is true about other southern economic giants. Brazil, long the world's largest coffee producer, became the second largest consumer in 2012 and might yet overtake the United States as the largest coffee-consuming country by the end of the decade (Fridell, 2014; WITS-UN-COMTRADE, 2015).

Southern trading powers have had significant impacts on global trade policy in ways that have both challenged and conformed to the dominant trade agenda. On the one hand, a country like China has accounted for the majority of global poverty reduction since the 1980s—from 1981 to 2005, China's poverty rate declined from 85 to 15 per cent. And yet, while China has been a major trader, its production and trade growth have taken place under massive state involvement in the economy, with regulations on foreign investment and capital and gradual, selective liberalization. This, combined with other examples throughout the South, has given rise to a new emphasis on "pragmatic" trade policies aimed at promoting human development alongside economic growth. In a manner reminiscent of the old fair trade vision, the UNDP (2013: 4) has recently called for these policies to be conducted by "a proactive developmental state" (UNDP, 2013: 4).

On the other hand, the policy impacts driven by southern trading powers have often conformed to the free trade agenda. Brazil, for example, in 2002 famously launched a WTO trade dispute against the United States over subsidies paid to US cotton farmers. In 2005, Brazil won, and the United States agreed to tinker with its subsidy program and offer Brazil US$147 million per year until it reformed its cotton subsidy system. The Brazilian victory was widely celebrated as a sign of the rising South. Critics, however, argued that the winners were not small farmers—who lack the economies of scale to compete with global transnational corporations—but Brazilian agribusiness, dominated by giant, vertically integrated corporations that are now among the world's largest. In policy terms, Kristen Hopewell (2013: 618) has observed that the Brazilian victory signified "an intense focus on liberalizing agriculture markets through the removal of subsidies, rather than advocating policies that would mark a more radical departure from the WTO's traditional neoliberal trade paradigm."

Despite the many unique changes to world trade heralded by the rise of the South, it remains a highly uneven and unequal process, with the greatest gains attained by the most powerful countries and those from the upper and middle classes within countries. The Brazilian cotton dispute was originally depicted as a victory for all southern cotton exporters, in particular the poorest ones in West Africa. In the end, however, most southern countries will not benefit as they lack the ability to compete against Brazilian agribusiness and will not gain access to the millions of dollars paid directly to Brazil as a penalty. Similar inequalities exist within nations (Hopewell, 2013). In China, for example, a key factor in its economic success has been the intensive exploitation of low-paid workers, vulnerable and desperate for work in a world dominated by corporate giants working in partnership with the Chinese state (see Box 15.5).

Some southern projects have sought to directly address uneven development and inequality within and among states, and chart an explicitly alternative or more radical pathway to the dominant trade agenda. Perhaps most notable has been the emergence of ALBA (Bolivarian Alliance for the Peoples of Our America), launched by its lead promoters, Venezuela and Cuba, in 2004, and since expanding to include Antigua and Barbuda, Bolivia, Dominica, Ecuador, Nicaragua, St Lucia, St Vincent and the Grenadines (SVG), and a handful of observer states. ALBA represents a conscious alternative to free trade and proposes a socially oriented regional trade bloc where wealth would be redistributed to poorer members and social issues such as local food sovereignty, access to generic drugs, and environmental rights would take precedence over liberalized trade. Paul Kellogg (2007: 201) states, "where traditional trade deals use language like 'comparative advantage,'" ALBA instead argues that "the political, social, economic and legal asymmetries of both countries have been taken into account." One of ALBA's most successful projects has been a unique agreement wherein Venezuela has sent thousands of barrels of oil a day to Cuba in exchange for Cuba sending thousands of doctors and medical supplies to poor and rural communities in Venezuela, providing medical services and training to 17 million people (Gibbs, 2006: 265–79). This is one of numerous South–South development

CRITICAL ISSUES

BOX 15.5 | Worker Realities and Worker Suicides in China

While China has posted major economic and social gains over the past 30 years, these gains have been distributed highly unequally. While the number of billionaires in China skyrocketed from 3 in 2004 to 354 by 2014, second only to the United States (Baer, 2015), long working days under punishing physical and psychological conditions have confronted millions of low-paid workers—a key ingredient to the country's competitive advantage.

Responding to abysmal working conditions, in 2010, 18 young migrant workers, all between the ages of 17 and 25, attempted suicide at Foxconn Corporation facilities in China. The Taiwanese-owned Foxconn is the world's largest contract manufacturer of electronics, producing half of the world's electronics for major corporations like Apple, HP, Dell, and Nokia, and employing over one million people in China (Ngai and Chan, 2012).

The shocking suicide attempts inspired the creation of the Foxconn Research Group, composed of researchers in China, Hong Kong, and Taiwan, who conducted an extensive investigation into Foxconn labour conditions in nine cities. They determined that workers frequently worked 12 hours a day with only four days off per month; laboured under intense and monotonous conditions with constant surveillance; lived on factory "campuses" under tight control and security; and often experienced "loneliness and fragmented lives." These conditions were facilitated by the state, which provided Foxconn with physical infrastructure, tax breaks, and labour recruitment—including funnelling young "interns" from local schools into Foxconn factories to gain "training." Far from a developmental success story, lead researchers Pun Ngai and Jenny Chan conclude that "Foxconn as a form of monopoly capital generates a global 'race to the bottom' production strategy and repressive mode of management" that deprives migrant workers "of their hopes, their dreams, and their future" (Ngai and Chan, 2012: 402–05).

projects that have emerged in recent years, involving such things as preferential trade arrangements, concessional funding for oil, and various forms of "in-kind" payment and assistance, including a unique project to construct an international airport on the small island state of SVG (see Box 15.6).

ALBA is still in its infancy and faces an uphill battle against many constraints. In particular, some of the most ambitious ALBA projects relied on the oil wealth of Venezuela, which has suffered a great deal with the decline of global oil prices since the 2008 financial crisis. Critics, moreover, have charged that ALBA represents less a coherent alternative to free trade than an attempt by the Venezuelan government to extend its sphere of influence. Yet, while the development of ALBA may in part be driven by the geostrategic interests of Venezuela, a similar critique can also be levelled at international free trade agreements, which often have been adopted by elite-dominated autocratic states under intense pressure from northern powers, the World Bank, the IMF, and the WTO (Ellner, 2007). "Power politics" has always played a central, if unfortunate, role in shaping the nature of modern international trade regimes (Gill, 2003; Gowan, 1999).

THE FUTURE OF INTERNATIONAL TRADE: "DYNAMIC" OR "DEFYING" COMPARATIVE ADVANTAGE?

The rise of southern powers, combined with growing recognition of the failed policies of the 1980s–2000s and the global financial crisis beginning in 2008, has called into question dominant assumptions around the benefits of free trade and sparked a rethinking of global trade policy. Even within the World Bank, long an unwavering promoter of rapid trade liberalization, signs

CRITICAL ISSUES

BOX 15.6 | South–South Co-operation in St Vincent and the Grenadines

The "rise of the South" has brought with it a renewed interest in "a proactive developmental state" not just among the largest southern economies, but also among smaller or more vulnerable ones (UNDP, 2013: 4). One unique example of this has been St Vincent and the Grenadines, where the government of Prime Minister Ralph Gonsalves, in office since 2001, has boosted public spending on social programs (e.g., education and health care) and physical infrastructure (e.g., roads and low-income housing) to combat the negative impacts of the global economic recession and the decline of traditional industries, in particular bananas, which had thrived on the basis of a preferential agreement with the EU until it was quashed by the WTO in the 2000s.

In the wake of declining preferential supports from northern governments, SVG has found increasing assistance from southern partners, including through membership in ALBA. Most notably, since 2008, Venezuela and Cuba have provided SVG with millions of dollars of assistance and soft loans to construct a new international airport designed to promote fresh opportunities for trade, tourism, and services. An estimated $112 million of this assistance—over 40 per cent of the cost of the airport—comes mostly in the form of "in-kind" support, including free engineering services, heavy machinery, wind stations, and an on-site laboratory. Additional support has come from other, non-ALBA countries, including grants and loans from Taiwan, Trinidad and Tobago, Iran, and Libya,and a free Airport Master Plan provided by Mexico (Fridell, 2013; Gonsalves, 2012).

The airport is due for completion by the end of 2016. While projects such as this may not be able to overcome the vulnerability experienced by small island states in a highly uneven global economy, they do point to new and original forms of South–South co-operation that challenge the northern-based consensus around free trade, while supporting governments developing southern-based alternatives to it.

have emerged that a reconsideration of hegemonic trade assumptions is occurring. Justin Lin, Chief Economist and Senior Vice-President of the World Bank, and other prestigious economists have called for a new consensus on "dynamic comparative advantage," based on a recognition that the most successful economies in the world, North and South, relied on government "industrial policy" to encourage manufacturing, research and development, technological advancement, education, employment, training, and entrepreneurialism. While Lin believes, along the lines of conventional free trade thinking, that economic policy ultimately must follow a country's comparative advantage, he departs from this reasoning by arguing that a "facilitating state" should gradually encourage private-sector upgrading and technological advancement (Lin and Chang, 2009).

Departing from this view, economist Ha-Joon Chang argues that *following* comparative advantage is not enough; instead, a developing country must "defy comparative advantage." While comparative advantage is an important consideration, the concept remains limited to a country's current endowments—such as its technological capabilities—and is unable to provide a map for transcending these limitations in the long run. "In the real world," argues Chang, "firms with uncertain prospects need to be created, protected, subsidized, and nurtured, possibly for decades, if industrial upgrading is to be achieved." Reflecting on the historical rise of the Japanese auto industry, he points out, "Japan had to protect its car industry with high tariffs for nearly four decades, provide a lot of direct and indirect subsidies, and virtually ban foreign direct investment in the industry before it could become competitive in the world market" (Lin and Chang, 2009: 491, 501).

The vigorous debate between Lin and Chang offers a welcome revival of long-standing debates over free versus fair trade, centred in particular on what role the state should or should not play in managing markets. Regardless of the debate, however, actual trade policies between states and within international organizations, including the World Bank, have not changed all that much. The particular free trade agenda of the richest and most powerful nations continues to dominate international trade policy, while fair trade alternatives, driven by less powerful supporters, continue to face an uphill political battle. Trade policy is ultimately driven not strictly by the battle of ideas, but by the political and economic interests of competing states in a highly uneven global economy. For development thinkers, however, the ultimate measure of the success of trade projects should be the extent to which they promote and enhance human development. International trade should be merely a means to this end.

SUMMARY

In this chapter, the student learns about two overarching perspectives on trade: *free trade*, premised on the notion that the removal of barriers to trade and the limitation of state intervention in the market will provide the greatest developmental gains for all; and *fair trade*, premised on the belief that the poorest developing countries cannot attain substantial benefits from global trade unless the terms of North–South trade are readjusted and market interventionist mechanisms are employed to support development efforts. These two perspectives, in manifold ways, have dominated post-war policy discourse and debate on trade and development globally, and are of key importance to understanding the dominant development theories and practices. The second half of the chapter discusses the rise of South–South trade and how it has shaken up the old debate on free versus fair trade, giving rise to new and previously unanticipated trade patterns, political and economic impacts, and development agendas. The rise of China and the BRICS, and the return of the "pragmatic" activist state, has injected fresh energy into the old debate, in the form of a new trade policy contest between "dynamic" or "defying" comparative advantage—one that promises to set the stage for trade and development agendas in the years to come.

QUESTIONS FOR CRITICAL THOUGHT

1. What are the major issues of disagreement between "free trade" and "fair trade" perspectives? Are there similarities?
2. Do free traders oppose *any* form of state involvement?
3. In terms of human development, how does the era of neoliberal free trade since the 1980s compare to the previous era of "embedded liberalism"?
4. What are some of the political issues driving free and fair trade policies? Why do the world's most powerful institutions generally support free trade?
5. What has been the impact of the rise of South–South trade on global trade policy? Do you think it has altered things significantly?

SUGGESTED READING

Bhagwati, Jagdish. 2008. *Termites in the Trading System: How Preferential Agreements Undermine Free Trade*. Oxford: Oxford University Press.

Byrne, Stacey, and Errol Sharpe. 2014. *In Pursuit of Justice: Just Us! Coffee Roasters Co-op and the Fair Trade Movement*. Halifax: Fernwood.

Chang, Ha-Joon. 2008. *Bad Samaritans: The Myth of Free Trade and the Secret History of Capitalism*. New York: Bloomsbury Press.

Fridell, Gavin. 2013. *Alternative Trade: Legacies for the Future*. Black Point, NS: Fernwood.

———. 2014. *Coffee*. Cambridge, UK: Polity Press.

McNally, David. 2006. *Another World Is Possible: Globalization and Anti-Capitalism*, rev. edn. Winnipeg: Arbeiter Ring.

BIBLIOGRAPHY

Baer, D. 2015. "This amazing chart shows how fast China is adding billionaires." *Business Insider*, 7 Jan. www.businessinsider.com/chinese-billionaires-increase-over-past-decade-2015-1.

Barratt Brown, M. 1993. *Fair Trade: Reform and Realities in the International Trading System*. London: Zed Books.

Bello, W. 2004. *Deglobalization: Ideas for a New World Economy*. London: Zed Books.

Bhagwati, J. 2002. *Free Trade Today*. Princeton, NJ: Princeton University Press.

———. 2008. *Termites in the Trading System: How Preferential Agreements Undermine Free Trade*. Oxford: Oxford University Press.

Bunting, M. 2005. "The world pays a heavy price for our cheap Christmas miracles." *The Guardian Unlimited*, 19 Dec. www.guardian.co.uk/comment/story/0,,1670279,00.html.

Byrne, S., and E. Sharpe. 2014. *In Pursuit of Justice: Just Us! Coffee Roasters Co-op and the Fair Trade Movement*. Halifax: Fernwood.

Chang, H.-J. 2008. *Bad Samaritans: The Myth of Free Trade and the Secret History of Capitalism*. New York: Bloomsbury Press.

Cobridge, S. 1993. "Ethics in development studies: The example of debt." In F. Schuurman, ed., *Beyond the Impasse: New Directions in Development Theory*. London: Zed Books, 123–39.

Cramer, C., D. Johnston, C. Oya, and J. Sender. 2013. *Fairtrade, Employment and Poverty Reduction in Ethiopia and Uganda: Final Report to DFID*. London: School of Oriental and African Studies, University of London.

Ellner, S. 2007. "Toward a 'multipolar world': Using oil diplomacy to sever Venezuela's dependence." *NACLA Report on the Americas* (Sept./Oct.): 15–22.

European Commission Database. 2010. http://ec.europa.eu/taxation_customs/dds2/taric/taric_consultation.jsp?Lang=en&Taric=0901900000&Expand=true&Area=&Level=2&SimDate=20101023#n0901900000-2. Accessed 22 Oct. 2010.

Frank, A.G. 1972. *Lumpenbourgeoisie: Lumpendevelopment*. New York: Monthly Review Press.

Fridell, G. 2007. *Fair Trade Coffee: The Prospects and Pitfalls of Market-Driven Social Justice*. Toronto: University of Toronto Press.

———. 2013. *Alternative Trade: Legacies for the Future*. Black Point, NS: Fernwood.

———. 2014. *Coffee*. Cambridge, UK: Polity Press.

Furtado, C. 1976. *Economic Development of Latin America*. Cambridge: Cambridge University Press.

Gibbs, T. 2006. "'Business as unusual: What the Chávez era tells us about democracy under globalisation." *Third World Quarterly* 27, 2: 265–79.

Gill, S. 2003. "National in/security on a universal scale." In I. Bakker and S. Gill, eds, *Power, Production and Social Reproduction*. New York: Palgrave Macmillan, 208–23.

Goldman, M. 2005. *Imperial Nature: The World Bank and Struggles for Social Justice in the Age of Globalization*. New Haven: Yale University Press.

Gonsalves, R. 2012. *2012 Budget Speech*. St. Vincent and the Grenadines.

Gowan, P. 1999. *The Global Gamble: Washington's Faustian Bid for World Dominance*. London: Verso.

Hart-Landsberg, M., and P. Burkett. 2005. *China and Socialism: Market Reforms and Class Struggle*. New York: Monthly Review Press.

Harvey, D. 2005. *A Brief History of Neoliberalism*. Oxford: Oxford University Press.

Helleiner, E. 1994. *States and the Reemergence of Global Finance: From Bretton Woods to the 1990s*. Ithaca, NY: Cornell University Press.

Hoebink, P., R. Ruben, W. Elbers, and B. van Rijsbergen. *The Impact of Coffee Certification on Smallholder Farmers in Kenya, Uganda and Ethiopia*. Nijmegen, Netherlands: Centre for International Development Issues Nijmegen (CIDIN), Radboud University.

Hoogvelt, A. 2001. *Globalization and the Postcolonial World: The New Political Economy of Development*. Baltimore: Johns Hopkins University Press.

Hopewell, K. 2013. "New protagonists in global economic governance: Brazilian agribusiness at the WTO." *New Political Economy*. Online First: 9 Jan.

Hudson, M., I. Hudson, and M. Fridell. 2013. *Fair Trade, Sustainability and Social Change*. New York: Palgrave Macmillan.

Jaffee, D. 2007. *Brewing Justice: Fair Trade Coffee, Sustainability, and Survival*. Berkeley: University of California Press.

Jones, K. 2010. *The Doha Blues: Institutional Crisis and Reform in the WTO*. Oxford: Oxford University Press.

Kellogg, P. 2007. "Regional integration in Latin America: Dawn of an alternative to neoliberalism?" *New Political Science* 29, 2: 187–209.

Krugman, P., and A.J. Venables. 1995. "Globalization and the inequality of nations." *Quarterly Journal of Economics* 110, 4: 857–80.

LeClair, M.S. 2002. "Fighting the tide: Alternative trade organizations in the era of global free trade." *World Development* 30, 6: 949–58.

Lin, J., and H.-J. Chang. 2009. "Should industrial policy in developing countries conform to comparative advantage or defy it? A debate between Justin Lin and Ha-Joon Chang." *Development Policy Review* 27, 5: 483–502.

McKenna, B. 2010. "For U.S. farmers, subsidies the best cash crop." *Globe and Mail*, 25 Nov. www.theglobeandmail.com/report-on-business/economy/economy-lab/daily-mix/for-us-farmers-subsidies-the-best-cash-crop/article1813425/.

McNally, D. 2006. *Another World Is Possible: Globalization and Anti-Capitalism*, rev. edn. Winnipeg: Arbeiter Ring.

Nelson, V., and A. Martin. 2013. *Final Technical Report: Assessing the Poverty Impact of Sustainability Standards*. Greenwich, UK: Natural Resources Institute, University of Greenwich.

Ngai, P., and J. Chan. 2012. "Global capital, the state, and Chinese workers: The Foxconn experience." *Modern China* 38, 4: 383–410.

North, L. 2003. "Endogenous rural diversification: Family textile enterprises in Pelileo, Tungurahua." In L. North and J.D. Cameron, eds, *Rural Progress, Rural Decay: Neoliberal Adjustment Policies and Local Initiatives*. Bloomfield, Conn.: Kumarian Press, 207–25.

Oxfam International. 2002. *Rigged Rules and Double Standards: Trade, Globalization, and the Fight against Poverty*. Oxford: Oxfam International. www.oxfam.org.uk/resources/papers/ downloads/trade_report.pdf.

Prebisch, R. 1950. *The Economic Development of Latin America and Its Principal Problems*. New York: UN.

Rosset, P. 2006. *Food Is Different: Why We Must Get the WTO out of Agriculture*. London: Zed Books.

Sachs, J. 2005. *The End of Poverty: Economic Possibilities for Our Time*. New York: Penguin.

Shirotori, M., and A.C. Molina, 2009. *South–South Trade: The Reality Check*. Geneva: UNCTAD.

Sinclair, S. 2010. *NAFTA Chapter 11 Investor–State Disputes*. Ottawa: Canadian Centre for Policy Alternatives, 1 Oct. www.policyalternatives.ca/newsroom/updates/nafta-chapter-11-increasing-threat-public-good.

Stiglitz, J. 2002. *Globalization and Its Discontents*. New York: W.W. Norton.

———. 2003. "Whither reform? Towards a new agenda for Latin America." *CEPAL Review* 80 (Aug.): 7–37.

Talbot, J.M. 2004. *Grounds for Agreement: The Political Economy of the Coffee Commodity Chain*. Oxford: Rowman & Littlefield.

Trew, S. 2012. "An inconvenient trade agreement: Canada begs its way into Trans-Pacific Partnership negotiations, but at what cost?" *Canadian Perspectives* (Autumn). Council of Canadians. www.canadians.org.

United Nations Development Programme (UNDP). 2013. *Human Development Report 2013: The Rise of the South: Human Progress in a Diverse World*. New York: UNDP.

Weisbrot, M., D. Baker, E. Kraev, and J. Chen. 2001. *The Scorecard on Globalization 1980–2000: Twenty Years of Diminished Progress*. Washington: Center for Economic and Policy Research. http://cepr.net/documents/publications/globalization_2001_07_11.htm.

World Bank. 2013. *Project Information Document (Appraisal Stage)—Sustainable Coffee Landscape Project—P127258 (English)*. Washington: World Bank, 8 Feb. http://data.worldbank.org.

World Integrated Trade Solution, United Nations Commodity Trade Statistics Database (WITS-UN-COMTRADE). 2015. http://wits.worldbank.org/trade-visualization.aspx. Accessed 7 July 2015.

16 Democracy

Cédric Jourde

LEARNING OBJECTIVES

- To be able to distinguish between different definitions of democracy.
- To understand the various theories of regime change (democratization; authoritarian backlash) and to be able to apply them concretely to specific countries and situations.
- To understand the dangers that could pull a democratizing country back towards authoritarianism.
- To appreciate the debate surrounding the relationship between democracy and economic and social development.

▲ **Myanmar democracy leader Aung San Suu Kyi waves the flag of the National League for Democracy (NLD) party at the party's fun fair music concert in Yangon, Myanmar. After initiating a nonviolent, pro-democracy movement in 1989, Suu Kyi led her pro-democracy party to victory in the 2015 elections.** | Source: © epa european pressphoto agency b.v./Alamy Stock Photo

The concept of democracy is a source of much debate among researchers studying the politics of developing countries. We will explore four of these debates in this chapter. The first relates to the meaning of democracy: neither scholars nor political actors can agree on a common definition. "Democracy" is a polysemic concept—that is, it is a word with many different meanings. The differences can be very large, not only between countries but also within countries. The second debate concerns the pathways that lead to democracy. Specialists do not agree on the causes or factors that trigger democratic transitions. For example, can we say that the level of economic development is a factor that favours the emergence of democracy? Some believe this is the case, whereas others emphasize entirely different factors. Third, researchers disagree with respect to the factors that hinder (and favour) the consolidation of democratic institutions. Once a country establishes its first democratic institutions, how can we ensure that they will develop fully and not disintegrate a few years after the transition? Finally, the fourth debate revolves around the causal role of democracy: what is the effect of democracy and democratization on social and economic dynamics? Some researchers believe that democracy hinders the economic and social development of the world's poorest countries because it promotes constant competition and political one-upmanship. In contrast, others believe that democracy is the only type of government capable of establishing firm foundations upon which to build a functioning economy and legitimate and just social relations. These are the four main debates explored in this chapter.

CLARIFYING THE CONCEPTS: A DIFFICULT TASK

The first task is to clarify our concepts, since terms in common usage are often ambiguous and admit of multiple definitions. Yet even if we try to be as clear as possible with the terms we use, it is impossible to come to a universally accepted definition.

When scholars consider political institutions in developing countries, their first step is to determine the type of **political regime** in place. "Political regime" refers to the set of principles and rules that govern power relations between society and the state (Przeworski et al., 2000, 18–19). More simply, what political rules connect leaders and citizens? These rules can be formal (such as those written in a constitution) and informal (unwritten and unofficial, yet very effective nonetheless), in which case it is more difficult, but just as important, to know about them (Helmke and Levitsky, 2006). In some cases, those rules and principles can be qualified as democratic, and in other cases, they can instead be qualified as authoritarian.

Usually, democratic regimes are distinguished from **authoritarian regimes**. The latter are regimes in which rules and principles enable state officials to prevent society from participating in the decision-making process; to resort frequently to arbitrary violence against their population; to extract, use, and distribute economic resources in an unaccountable and often violent fashion; and, finally, to avoid any mechanism that would make them accountable for their actions and decisions (Levitsky and Way, 2010: Appendix 1).

Increasingly, researchers also differentiate democracies and authoritarian regimes from a third type of regime. Its name and definition are, once again, the subject of debate: it is usually called a **semi-authoritarian regime** (or a **hybrid regime**). Here we are referring mainly to countries that undertook democratic reforms at the beginning of the 1990s. Although they officially abolished the one-party system and/or removed the military from political office, elites of the old regime still perpetuated (sometimes informally, sometimes in a more formal fashion) a plethora of heavily authoritarian political practices. These practices ranged from the repression of opposition to massive electoral fraud or even to the systematic use of public administration for personal gain (Boogards, 2009; Levitsky and Way, 2010; Wigell, 2008).

In addition, scholars often differentiate between two phases in the process of democratization—**democratic transition** and **democratic consolidation**. "Democratic transition" refers to the phase during which authoritarian institutions and practices are in the process of being reformed and replaced by institutions and practices that are more democratic (or less authoritarian). This transitional phase is characterized by a degree of *uncertainty*; as during all transitions, no one is completely certain about the outcome of the process. It is not clear whether democracy will be achieved, because the actors or forces pushing for democracy are struggling with those attempting to maintain the authoritarian status quo. This phase is distinct from a more stable phase, democratic consolidation, which is characterized by a solidification of the democratic foundations. During this phase, political actors are no longer in debate over *whether* they should conserve the authoritarian regime or adopt a democracy but rather over *how* they should go about reinforcing the democratic regime (Schedler, 2001).

The concepts of democratic transition, democratic consolidation, and even authoritarianism remain, nonetheless, relatively vague unless we clarify the most central concept of this chapter, *democracy*. This concept is a subject of intense debate among researchers, and it is clear that a single and universal definition does not exist. To generalize somewhat, one of the debates reveals a division between two main camps: those who advance a **procedural definition of democracy** and those who propose a **substantive definition of democracy** (Collier and Levitsky, 1997).

Researchers who adopt the procedural approach, which is sometimes labelled "minimalist," argue that a regime is democratic as long as certain basic but fundamental political rules and principles are enforced. First, all citizens can regularly and uninterruptedly choose political representatives who govern in their name. This choice is made through free and fair elections in which any citizen can stand as a candidate as well as being able to participate as a voter, regardless of gender, ethnicity, language, race, religion, social class, or disability. Second, the state must guarantee the fundamental freedoms of all its citizens, in particular rights of participation, assembly, expression, and information. This definition is sometimes characterized

Paul Haslam

PHOTO 16.1 | **A young woman lights a candle for the "disappeared" victims of Argentina's bloody 1976–83 dictatorship, Buenos Aires, Argentina.**

as minimalist because it requires only a minimum number of elements to be present in order to determine whether a regime is democratic or not. This will become increasingly clear when we expand on the substantive approach.

One corollary of the minimalist definition is its universal character: if only a few features are necessary to determine whether a regime is democratic, it entails that democracies can actually be observed, and counted, across time and space. Thus, proponents of the minimalist approach believe that we can count and classify different regimes of the world, either by distinguishing democracies from non-democracies (a binary distinction) or by classifying them according to their degree of democracy and observing the changes that take place from year to year (Munck and Verkuilen, 2002). For example, Larry Diamond (2002: 26) has created a typology that classifies political regimes into six different categories. The most democratic countries are found in the first two categories: "liberal democracies" and "electoral democracies." They are followed by less democratic regimes: "ambiguous regimes," "competitive authoritarian," or "hegemonic electoral authoritarian," and finally, the "politically closed authoritarian" regime. Other researchers, such as those who work for the US-based Freedom House or the Polity V Project, quantify the degree of democracy of each political system in the world by giving them a grade. Freedom House distinguishes between three types of regimes: "free," which is the equivalent of democracy, "partly free," and "not free." Table 16.1 gives us an overview of the evolution of democracy in the world since 1974 (the year that Freedom House started to collect its data). We see, for example, that the number of democratic regimes—grouped together under the "free" category—has significantly increased since 1974. Democracies represented 28 per cent of all the regimes of the world in 1974, increasing to 34 per cent in 1985. Today, at 45 per cent, they represent nearly half of the countries of the world. In contrast, authoritarian regimes—classified under the "not free" category—represented 41 per cent of the regimes in the world in 1974 and represent merely 25 per cent today.

The procedural approach has provoked significant reactions from many scholars who find it too reductionist and minimalist (Zuern, 2009). They propose what is known as the "substantive approach" to emphasize the importance of looking at the "substance" of a democracy, not only its procedures. While they do not challenge the components of the procedural definition, they consider them insufficient. Proponents of this substantive approach usually focus on one of the following three dimensions: cultural, socio-economic, and citizenship.

The cultural-substantive definition is based on the idea that the concept of democracy, while having a certain universal dimension that is understood worldwide, should nevertheless incorporate *local meanings* of the term. According to these researchers, the meaning of the word "democracy" varies from one society to another and even varies strongly within a given society (something often forgotten). Frederic Schaffer (1998) gave a good summary of the problem when he demonstrated that the American understanding of the concept of democracy was not necessarily the same as a Senegalese view; as a matter of fact, even within a country like Senegal, there seems to be a difference between how peasants conceive of democracy

TABLE 16.1 | The Freedom House Classification of Political Regimes

	1974		1985		1991		2015	
Type of Regime	**Total**	**%**	**Total**	**%**	**Total**	**%**	**Total**	**%**
Free	42	28	57	34	76	41	88	45
Partly free	47	31	56	34	66	36	59	30
Not free	63	41	53	32	42	23	48	25

Note: The total number of countries in the survey increased starting from 1991 onward with the independence of the ex-Soviet republics, the disintegration of Yugoslavia and Czechoslovakia, and the independence of countries such as East Timor and Eritrea.

Source: https://freedomhouse.org/sites/default/files/FITW_World_Map_24x16_fa_GF2015.jpg.

BOX 16.1 | Mali and the Freedom House Ranking

CURRENT EVENTS

The case of Mali, one of the poorest countries in the world, provides an illustration of the global tendency that Freedom House has documented. During the 1970s and 1980s, the military regime of Moussa Traoré reigned over Mali, placing this African nation within the category of a "not free" regime. After Traoré's regime was toppled in 1991, however, political actors began to construct a multi-party system and to design a constitution that guaranteed fundamental liberties. As a result, Mali started to receive much higher grades. It moved up into the category of "partly free" countries in 1991–2, then into the category of "free" countries the following year. The regime eventually fell back into the "not free" category in 2012 when a military faction ousted the president through a *coup d'état*, and the country plunged into a war with terrorist organizations and separatist movements in the North. Elections were held in 2013 and the situation slightly improved, with the regime now rated as "partly free."

and how urban, Dakar-based intellectuals understand it. In the United States, according to Schaffer, democracy evokes the notions that were previously highlighted in the procedural definition. In Senegal, *demokaaraasi*, as it is locally called, at least among peasants, evokes notions of solidarity, consensus, and equal treatment among people. He also observed that in Senegal, an election does not have the same meaning that it does in the United States. The act of putting a slip of paper into a ballot box is not seen as "democracy in action"; rather, it is perceived as an economic transaction between a "politician-businessperson" and a "voter-client." Schaffer, like other researchers, defines the concept of democracy as being variable between one national (or sub-national) culture and another.

To say that the basic meaning of democracy varies from one country to another also implies that it can refer to political actors and political dynamics unique to a particular society. For example, when Romain Bertrand (2002) conducted research in Java—the most populous island of Indonesia, an archipelago with around 230 million inhabitants—he realized that if he wanted to understand fully their democratic process, he could not limit himself to analyzing the actors normally studied in Western countries (political parties; governors; civil society activists; military officers; etc.). He had to include actors involved in what can be called "invisible world," the world of "witchcraft," "spirits," and other "invisible forces." Of course, political parties, journalists, non-governmental organizations (NGOs), the central government, and women's movements are democratic actors in Indonesia in exactly the same way they are in a country such as Germany. In Indonesia, however, one must also study the role of "supernatural experts," "forces of the night," and religious leaders who—in the eyes of Indonesians—play a critical role in politics. For Bertrand, as for other researchers, it is not a matter of drawing a caricature of an exotic political system but rather simply of saying that we cannot understand democratization if we focus our analysis only on electoral results and parliamentary reforms.

The second aspect of the substantive approach is socio-economic in nature. The argument put forth here is that the procedural approach is too minimalist because it ignores one of the fundamental characteristics of any political system: the distribution of wealth and economic well-being. Whereas supporters of the procedural approach might classify a country as "democratic" once the electoral cycle is put in place correctly and political freedoms are respected, supporters of the substantive approach might hold that this same country is hardly democratic if it exhibits profound socio-economic inequalities (Zuern, 2009). From the procedural point of view, distribution of wealth has nothing to do with the definition of democracy; in the substantive approach, this issue is at the very heart of democracy. Thus, those who support the substantive approach would paint a very different picture of countries such as South Africa and Brazil. In these countries, there are free elections, and most political liberties are either respected or in the process of being implemented (freedom of expression, right of assembly, and so on). Yet the level of inequality is so high in Brazil, for example—with the richest 10 per cent in 2013 enjoying more than 41.8 per cent of national wealth (compared to 25.7 per cent in Canada), while the poorest 20 per cent of the population have to make do with less than 3.3 per cent (compared to 7.1 per cent in Canada)—that we cannot consider this country as a true democracy. And in South Africa in 2011, the inequality of income distribution was even greater, with the richest 10 per cent having 51.3 per cent of national wealth and the bottom 20 per cent getting only 2.5 per cent (World Bank, 2016). According to this approach, then, democracy is not merely a matter of electoral cycles and individual rights; it also presumes a more equitable distribution of wealth within a country (see Box 16.2).

Finally, the third component of the substantive definition, directly related to the previous one, raises the question of **citizenship**. For supporters of this approach, a democratic regime is one in which all adult citizens are granted a wide range of social and political rights. Moreover, for the regime to be truly democratic, these rights must be applied universally, equally, and systematically. In a number of countries, unfortunately, citizenship is often heterogeneous in that political rights are not respected in a systematic and universal way. For example, in a number of Latin American countries, access to justice, social services, security, or any other public service is unequally distributed and depends on whether a person lives in a city or in the country or even in certain neighbourhoods over others. There are zones of "complete citizenship" but also a number of "brown areas," as Guillermo O'Donnell (2004) calls them. Impunity, arbitrariness, violence, and discrimination based on one's identity (e.g., ethnic, racial, social class, and gender) are the norm in these brown areas. Consequently, while officially everyone is an equal citizen, carrying the same social and political rights, individuals within these countries do not hold equal citizenship in practice. De facto citizenship can vary according to whether one is a native peasant woman, a doctor in a gated community in Rio, or a young Afro-Brazilian living in one of the *favelas* that surround the big cities (Calderia and Holston, 1999). In such cases, the officials who represent the state (i.e., judges, the police, cadastral officers, and, more generally, civil servants) cannot or do not want (the difference is important) to guarantee equal citizenship for all. This infringes on the most fundamental principles

IMPORTANT CONCEPTS

BOX 16.2 | India and Substantive Democracy

During the debates surrounding the drafting of India's first constitution as an independent nation in 1949, Bhim Rao Ambedkar, the leader of the Untouchable (or Dalit) Movement (the most disadvantaged group in the Hindu caste system), argued that India's democratic political institutions were not enough to make India a true democracy. According to Ambedkar, the Indian constitution lacked democratic *substance* because it did not take into account the massive socio-economic gap separating the different social groups of Indian society, notably between the untouchables and the so-called "noble" castes. According to him, limiting the notion of "democracy" to elected assemblies, elections, and political parties was not only insufficient, it was dangerous. Here is what he said in 1949:

> On January 26, 1950 [the date when the new Indian constitution would be enacted], we will enter into a life of contradiction. In politics we will have equality and in social and economic life we will have inequality. . . . We must remove this contradiction as quickly as possible, or else those who suffer from inequality will blow up the structures of political democracy this Assembly has so laboriously built up. (Quoted in Keer, 2005: 415)

of citizenship and constitutes a significant limit to the democratic nature of the regime.

The issue of citizenship also arises in relation to the question "Who is a citizen?" This varies greatly from one country to another. In countries such as the Democratic Republic of the Congo, Côte d'Ivoire, and Malaysia, the formal distinction between citizens and non-citizens who reside on national territory has even been the source of conflict. Some politicians have campaigned for the state to distinguish and discriminate between the "real sons and daughters of the country" (*bumiputri* in Malay, for example) and "foreigners." They argue that foreigners should not be granted the status of citizens. For them, a "foreigner" can be an individual born in the country but whose great-great-grandparents moved into the area 100 years ago. The Chinese in Malaysia and in Indonesia, the Indians in Malaysia, the Malinkes in Côte d'Ivoire, and the Tutsis in the Democratic Republic of the Congo all have seen their citizenship brought into question in recent years because their forefathers and mothers migrated to the country decades ago; occasionally granted citizenship, occasionally having it revoked, their position is always precarious (Bah, 2010). They can no longer buy land, enter the civil service, or even vote. In sum, for this approach, a regime is not worthy of being called democratic if it does not grant full and complete political and social citizenship.

As we can see, although democracy might seem to be a simple concept, it is a source of numerous debates among scholars. Thus, it is not easy to answer the question "What is democracy?" The main point is that it is not necessary to agree on a universally accepted definition—an apparently impossible endeavour—but rather to realize that we must indicate clearly the approach we have chosen and that we must be as clear and precise as possible when we use the concept of democracy.

"WAVES" OF DEMOCRATIZATION

Similarly, explaining why and how countries have democratized is a matter of debate among researchers. This section presents the different approaches researchers use to explain and understand these transitions to democracy.

Before we examine them, we should say a few words about the *historical sequence* of democratic transitions. Samuel Huntington's metaphor of the "wave" (1993) is interesting, despite some limitations, in that it clearly evokes the idea that the process of democratization has often affected a large number of countries simultaneously and within a relatively short period of time, as occurred with varying degrees of success in the Arab world in 2011 (the so-called Arab Spring).

With respect to developing countries, we can divide these transitions into three main historical periods. The first started in the middle of the nineteenth century and lasted until the beginning of the twentieth. During this period, many European, North American, and Latin American countries (such as Chile and Argentina) established representative institutions, with parliaments and heads of state elected by the people and independent judicial systems (Valenzuela, 2000).

The second historical wave began immediately after World War II and ended towards the beginning of the 1960s. As Chapter 2 outlines, this was a period during which a number of colonies obtained their independence. These newly independent countries often inherited democratic institutions that the colonial powers had set up in the final years of colonization. However, a number of them soon were overtaken by some form of authoritarian rule, ranging from single-party systems to military regimes. An important exception was India, which has maintained and developed its democratic institutions ever since independence in 1947, depending, of course, on the definition of democracy we use (see Box 16.2).

Finally, Huntington's "third wave of democratization" started in 1974 with the democratization of Portugal, gained pace at the end of the 1980s, and continues to the present day. Clearly, the way we conceptualize these "waves" depends on how we choose to define democracy and democratization. Also, the fact that numerous authoritarian regimes are going through a democratic transition does not preclude the fact that they may eventually deviate from the democratic model and find themselves transformed into more semi-authoritarian regimes.

EXPLAINING DEMOCRATIZATION: STRUCTURES OR ACTORS? THE NATIONAL OR INTERNATIONAL ARENA?

Various theoretical approaches have been proposed to explain and understand these waves of democratic transition. All studies of the process have to address two central questions, and although these theoretical approaches are presented separately here, in reality they are not mutually exclusive. Indeed, researchers often mix and combine approaches.

First, we can distinguish between the approaches in terms of their *level of analysis*. For some specialists the fundamental causes that explain democratization are to be found at the *international* (or "exogenous") level, while for others these causes are mainly situated at a *national* level (i.e., within the borders of a country, or "endogenous"). Thus, when a scholar states that the end of the Cold War was the principal cause of the third wave of democratization in Africa and Asia in the 1990s, she is suggesting that the most important level of analysis for understanding democratization is the exogenous or international level. Conversely, if a researcher argues that the role played by women's movements and labour unions in a given country explains the democratization of that country's political regime, then she privileges the national or endogenous level of analysis.

Next, researchers have to take a position on a question that has endured since the beginning of the social sciences, that is, the fundamental source of social, economic, and political change. To simplify, we can say that those who identify with Émile Durkheim—a French scholar who was one of the founders of the social sciences—and, to some extent, with Karl Marx propose an approach according to which the fundamental causes of democratic transitions are *structural* or *systemic* in nature. The starting premise is that major social and political phenomena—such as revolutions, ethnic conflicts, or democratization—are the result of changes that take place within large political, economic, institutional, cultural, or social structures. In other words, they are not the product of individual decisions and actions.

Conversely, those who identify with another father of the social sciences, the German Max Weber, assert that the source of social and political change—such as democratic transitions—lies with individuals and their relationships with other people. This approach is an *agency-based explanation*. In this framework, we explain democratization based on the preferences, interests, strategies, and identities of political actors, the information at their disposal and what they *choose* to do with it, their representations of the world, and, of course, the relationships these actors develop with each other (including negotiations, conflicts, tricks, and pacts). In this view, the decisions and actions of political actors, and *not* structural forces over which these actors have no control, explain important political change such as democratization.

Thus, if we combine each of the possible answers to these two questions (international or national; structures or agency), we have four principal approaches: democratic transitions are caused by national structures, international structures, national actors, or international actors. We will now use concrete examples to illustrate each of these four cases.

National Structural Approach

This approach involves explaining the causes of a democratic transition by examining the political, social, and economic structures within the borders of a nation-state. Those who use this approach often argue that changes within a country's social and economic structures are one of the principal causes of democratization (Lipset, 1959; Moore, 1966; Rueschemeyer et al., 1992). Note that the modernization approach described in Chapter 3 has had a direct influence on this theory. Researchers have demonstrated that when the economic structures within a country that is authoritarian begin to develop—especially when the economy is experiencing rapid industrialization and a high rate of urbanization—the social structures of the country are transformed, notably an accelerated growth of the working and middle classes. These classes are concentrated in the major cities and close to the centres of political power. Once they attain a certain size and level of education, they become powerful forces that challenge authoritarian leaders to an unprecedented degree. The authoritarian regime is thus unable to maintain the status quo—namely, a political regime that excludes the majority of the population from the political game. It was easy to deny democratic reform when the majority of the population was scattered in rural areas, without basic education and with barely enough income to pay heed to anything other than daily survival. The situation completely changed, however, with large transformations in economic structures, namely, urbanization and industrialization, which in turn transformed the social structure, increasing levels of education and income for large groups of people who were previously disadvantaged. Supporters of this approach point to a quasi-mechanical effect (a characteristic of structural approaches) in hypothesizing that these economic and social structural transformations will lead to democratic transitions. Taking the recent events in North Africa and the Middle East, some could argue that the main reasons for the ousting of the Ben Ali (Tunisia) and Mubarak (Egypt) regimes are to be found in structural domestic factors. For instance, we could say that a critical cause is the *growing socio-economic gap* between an extremely wealthy but small political elite and a booming class of urban poor and middle classes who are educated but whose conditions of living have declined significantly in recent years (as compared to those of the elite). At a certain point, the social and political exclusion of these large segments of society is no longer viable.

Not all researchers agree on the causal role of structural economic transformations in the process of democratization. Carles Boix (2003), for example, introduced an important nuance, demonstrating that an increase in the level of economic development is not sufficient to generate a transition towards democracy. According to Boix, this transition is statistically more likely to occur if economic development is accompanied by a redistribution of national wealth. To simplify, imagine two countries administered by similar authoritarian regimes. Suppose that both countries experience *similar* economic growth *but* that severe inequalities persist in one country, while growth in the other country is accompanied by a relatively equal distribution of the fruits of development. For Boix, the probability of a democratic transition is much stronger in the second case than in the first.

Other researchers entirely refute the hypothesis of a causal link between the development of socio-economic structures and democratic transition. One of the best-known examples is the work of Adam Przeworski and his colleagues (1997, 2000), who demonstrate that there is practically no statistically significant connection between the level of economic development and the likelihood of democratization. In other words, the fact that an authoritarian regime experiences economic growth has no effect on the probability that this regime will eventually transform itself into a democracy. The thesis of Przeworski and his colleagues is illustrated by the cases of China, Vietnam, and Singapore. While these countries have experienced significant economic and social transformation (economic growth, industrialization, urbanization, and so on), these changes have not led to the democratization of their political regimes. The only significant relationship that these authors found was that the higher the level of economic development, the smaller the chance a democratic regime will collapse and be replaced by an authoritarian regime. On that last point, these researchers would argue that the sudden democratic breakdown in Mali (see Box 16.1) was predictable: one of the poorest countries in the world, Mali's low level of development made it more likely that the democratic regime would succumb to a socio-political crisis and revert to some form of authoritarianism.

International Structural Approach

For some researchers, structural changes are clearly the cause of democratic transitions, but *international* structural change is most important rather than change on a national level. To demonstrate their hypothesis, these researchers point to the two most recent waves of democratization, one that began at the end of the 1940s and the other that started at the end of the 1980s. What was particular about these two periods? The answer, according to these researchers, lies in major transformations of the international system. With respect to the wave that began towards the end of the 1980s, there was a massive change in the international system as the world moved from a bipolar configuration—dominated by the two superpowers of the Cold War—to a unipolar configuration with only one superpower. This change in the international system generated a significant amount of pressure on authoritarian regimes, forcing many of them to undertake democratic reforms. In fact, the dissolution of the Soviet bloc signalled the victory of the model of liberal democracy. Liberal democracy became the norm in the international arena, a norm to which most countries had to adapt. Authoritarian regimes often owed their survival (and very existence) to the structural rivalry between the American and Soviet superpowers. This Cold War rivalry, in effect, had served to subordinate questions about whether a particular country was democratic or not: as long as the authoritarian regime aligned itself with one of the two camps, its survival was guaranteed. Loyalty towards either of the two poles allowed the state to crush any pro-democracy movement within its borders. Once the superpower rivalry disappeared, the authoritarian regime's survival was no longer guaranteed. This international structural transformation exerted more pressure on the authoritarian regimes of the developing world, which in turn increased the likelihood of democratization.

If we apply this hypothesis to the cases of South Africa and Indonesia, for example, the reasoning would be as follows: the only reason these authoritarian regimes were capable of crushing opposition movements was that they held key positions in the international alliance system of the Cold War. The international East–West bipolarity created a system of "international clientelism" in which client states offered their loyalty to one of the two superpowers in return for military, political, economic, and diplomatic support (Clapham, 1996; Afoaku, 2000). Thus, being a geostrategic link between the Atlantic and Indian oceans and surrounded by self-proclaimed Communist regimes, the authoritarian and apartheid regime of South Africa was the recipient of unfailing Western support. As for the Southeast Asian country of Indonesia, it was located in one of the "hottest" regions of the Cold War, right next to the front line of Vietnam and the Indochinese peninsula and fairly close to the two Koreas and the Communist regional superpower, China. Whether in southern Africa or Southeast Asia, the question of authoritarianism was structurally subordinate to or relegated beneath the sole priority of the day: the East–West rivalry. Once the international system was transformed at the end of the 1980s, the South African and Indonesian regimes found themselves vulnerable to the challenge of pro-democracy movements. Democratization was the logical consequence in these two countries. In 1994, the once banned African National Congress won the first free elections and the country elected its first black president, Nelson Mandela. The ANC has won all elections since then. In Indonesia, the de facto military dictatorship of Suharto fell apart in 1998, and the country is today ruled by a civilian president, Joko Widodo, elected in 2014. Even if the Cold War is over, however, the current context of the global fight against terrorism has become a structuring feature of world politics, which once again could provide support for authoritarian regimes—such as in Egypt, Algeria, Pakistan, and Ethiopia—that have positioned themselves for the past decade as allies in the "war on terror" (Pop-Eleches and Robertson, 2015).

On the other hand, specialists of North Africa and the Middle East could argue that the recent uprisings in this region are mostly explained by important global changes. First, the global, worldwide spread of information technologies is a necessary condition, for these have facilitated communication among domestic activists and between these activists and the global public opinion. Furthermore, more than 10 years after the 9/11 attacks in the United States, the international community has been going through a learning curve and is now aware that North African and Middle Eastern autocrats are not necessarily the "solution of last resort against Islamic terrorism" they pretend to be. Hence, without these global structural factors, the regime changes in that region would not have been possible, these scholars would argue.

National Actor Approach

As explained above, agency-based approaches are founded on a very different set of assumptions from those of the two we have just discussed. First, supporters of this approach criticize their counterparts for having an overly mechanistic vision, giving the impression that democratization is an automatic process without the possibility of deviation, contingencies, mistakes, or surprises. Moreover, they argue that the structuralist vision is "teleological" in the sense that it gives an impression—a false and misleading one, according to these critics—that we can know in advance whether a country will democratize (the end point of that process) and how it will go about the transition. According to the supporters of the agency-based approach, transitions are full of uncertainties and contingencies. They really depend on the choices made by a number of actors. For example, the West African countries of Benin and Togo both have similar underdeveloped domestic economic structures and both have evolved within the same international structures, yet Benin democratized in 1991 while Togo remains trapped in authoritarianism. Thus, the factors that really count must be found elsewhere. This "elsewhere"—what makes the difference in democratization—is the role of political *actors*.

Just as with the structural approach, however, the supporters of an agency-based approach are differentiated according to whether they focus on national (endogenous) actors or international (exogenous) actors. Studies that explain democratization by analyzing the struggles between the governing faction of the authoritarian regime and the faction spearheading pro-democracy movements (and the alliances and divisions within each respective faction) are examples of the *national actors* approach. This type of approach has been used to study the case of South Africa, for example. The argument is that South African democratization was made possible because at the end of the 1980s the ruling bloc of the apartheid regime split into two rival factions, each with different interests and strategies. One group was known as the "securocrats" and the other as the "technocrats." The first group was composed of military officers who took a hard line against the democratic and anti-apartheid movements. They were insensitive to the risks entailed by a frontal confrontation with the anti-apartheid movement. The technocrat group, however, was composed of high-level bureaucrats and business people who were more pragmatic (soft-liners) and open to negotiation with their opponents. At the time, this group was led by the newly elected president, Frederik W. de Klerk. This split in the authoritarian regime developed in parallel with a split among opponents of the apartheid regime. On one side was the African National Congress (ANC) led by Nelson Mandela, which was more open to dialogue and envisioned a democratic and multiracial South Africa. On the other side were groups such as the Pan Africanist Congress, which were completely opposed to the presence of a white population on South African territory and the idea of negotiating with the leaders of apartheid. The agency-based approach analyzed the strengths and weaknesses of each of these actors, their ideology, their calculations (and miscalculations), their interests, and the negotiations between the "moderates" of both camps who sought dialogue rather than an absolute confrontation. The argument was that the moderates (of both respective camps) made a political calculation: they estimated that their first preference was unattainable (i.e., to avoid giving in to their adversary), and therefore they agreed to fall back on their second-best option, that being "collusion" or a willingness to play the game of negotiation.

If we look at the recent regime change in North Africa and the Middle East, some could argue that the main reason for the successful ousting of autocrats in Tunisia and Egypt was a split within the ruling elites, in Tunisia between the Ben Ali family and the top officers in the army (the latter becoming increasingly dissatisfied with how the former managed the country's economy and how they appropriated most of the country's resources for themselves), and in Egypt between the Mubarak clan and top army generals (for reasons similar to those of the Tunisians). In both cases, the fall of the regime was possible because key actors in the military and the security apparatus literally stopped supporting the autocrats in power. Had they decided to stick with the leaders, the argument goes, they would still be in power today—or they might have become enmeshed in a civil conflict, as occurred in Libya.

Continuing with the national actor approach, some researchers have conducted in-depth studies of the role of social movements in the process of democratization. They emphasize an often neglected aspect of politics—namely, the capacity to garner support by drawing on symbols, rhetoric (in the true sense of the term), and representations. Often, these social movements spearhead the process of democratization in developing countries, especially since they cannot rely on coercive measures or financial resources. Their main strength is their ability to mobilize a large number of people by way of persuasion and moral arguments, presenting alternative ways of interpreting the political situation and moving people into action. All of this depends on a given movement's strategies, choices, and continuous work.

For example, studies have highlighted the case of a women's movement in Argentina—the Madres (mothers) of the Plaza de Mayo—that emerged in Buenos Aires at the end of the 1970s and the beginning of the 1980s. Argentina had a military dictatorship at the time, and the women were demanding the truth about the disappearance of thousands of youth abducted by the military. These women, without financial or (obviously) military power, managed to create a movement that enjoyed widespread support among the population. They did so because they chose (the notion of choice here is key) the appropriate images and symbols: rather than presenting themselves as "revolutionaries," for instance, they decided to personify the roles of mothers and grandmothers—that is, legitimate and respected actors in Argentinean society. The military dictatorship was trapped by its own rhetoric: it was accustomed to confronting and repressing "revolutionaries," "communists," "terrorists," and even "feminists" (the expressions it used at the time), but in this case it found itself challenged by a segment of Argentinean society representing "traditional" figures—grandmothers, mothers, sisters—and values. Given that the regime had always promoted a traditional conception of Argentinean society, it could not repress the movement. The Madres of the Plaza de Mayo thus dealt a powerful blow to the military junta through the use of symbols and representations that served to delegitimize the regime. The military regime finally stepped down from power in 1983 (Oxhorn, 2001).

In Tunisia and Egypt, diverse social groups, comprising students, young unemployed people, and professionals (teachers, lawyers, etc.) strategically used powerful words and symbols to denounce the autocrats in power. As the state's repression intensified, they made efficient decisions, demonstrating in certain strategic places in Tunis and Cairo, using foreign journalists to show the regime's atrocities, and convincing soldiers and officers not to kill their own compatriots simply to defend a moribund autocrat (Clarke, 2015).

International Actor Approach

Some analysts accept that actors (and their interactions with each other) provoke a number of democratic transitions but hold that the most important actors are those operating in the international arena. Such international actors include foreign states (usually superpowers or regional powers), international organizations, international non-governmental organizations, and other transnational networks (formed around a diaspora or around a particular ideal, such as human rights or women's rights). Authors such as Levitsky and Way (2010), for example, affirm that the "leverage" democratic states have used against authoritarian regimes can play a significant role; the actions of one powerful democratic state over a relatively weak authoritarian state can trigger a democratic transition. Examples of leverage include military pressure and economic sanctions (i.e., "conditionalities"). Levitsky and Way add, however, that these tactics have a relatively modest impact and that many factors undermine their effectiveness, at the level of both the country employing the tactics and the country subject to them. With regard to a powerful democratic country, its willingness to apply leverage is often weakened by competing strategic interests (for instance, a Western government's willingness to impose economic sanctions over a given country may be lessened by influential companies that do business with that country). In a targeted country, authoritarian regimes with considerable military or economic power (or both, as in the case of Iran and China) are more able to resist the democratic pressures exerted by third-party states. Some could argue, for instance, that the toppling of the Ben Ali and Mubarak regimes would have been impossible without the strategic role played by specific international actors. These researchers would say, to illustrate, that had the US government not strongly condemned the two regimes' repressive measures (and used its financial aid as a stick to pressure the Tunisian and—especially—the Egyptian governments), there would have been much less restraint on the part of these regimes, and demonstrators never would have been able to impose the same degree of pressure as they actually did.

Instead of concentrating solely on relations between states, other researchers prefer to analyze the critical role played by non-state actors, such as international institutions, non-governmental organizations, and transnational networks. The latter are conglomerations of people from several countries who come together around common principles such as human rights or democracy. These groups have been able to exert relatively strong pressure on certain authoritarian regimes. Their strength lies in their capacity to bridge the gap between individuals living in democratic countries

AP Photo/Ben Curtis, File

PHOTO 16.2 | The popular uprising for democracy in Egypt: demonstrators in Tahrir Square, Cairo.

and those living in authoritarian regimes. These networks also facilitate the exchange of information and ideas, drawing the attention of the international public to the injustices, atrocities, and repression that exist under an authoritarian regime. They can put pressure on other international actors, including industrialized democracies and international organizations, which in turn exert pressure on the authoritarian regime identified in the activists' campaigns. Keck and Sikkink (1999) have called this technique the boomerang effect, in which activists solicit international actors that are better placed to "hit" the authoritarian regime in question. For these scholars, such actions may not be *sufficient* by themselves, but they are nonetheless *necessary* in explaining many processes of democratization.

It is important to understand that these four distinct approaches are not necessarily mutually exclusive. They are presented separately here both for the sake of clarity and because researchers often do not agree on the virtues and shortcomings of each approach. Certainly, when we wish to analyze a democratic transition in a given country, we are not obliged to choose only one approach. On the contrary, researchers often combine and use several approaches at once.

AFTER DEMOCRATIC TRANSITION: CONSOLIDATION OR A RETURN TO AUTHORITARIAN RULE?

Numerous factors serve to consolidate democratic gains in developing countries, and conversely, other factors might pull a regime back to authoritarianism or semi-authoritarianism.

Here again, researchers offer several explanations. Among the factors that can contribute to democratic consolidation, *popular support* is fundamental.

Research groups connected to the "barometer" institutes (present in every region of the developing world) have carried out opinion polls in many countries to gauge popular support for democratic governments. Although reservations exist with respect to these opinion polls—in particular, that they assume a procedural conception of democracy—they nonetheless provide some interesting indicators. For example, researchers working for the Afrobarometer conducted opinion polls in 19 African countries in 2014–15, asking the same questions of each respondent (Afrobarometer, 2015). The results were revealing: on average, 70 per cent of those polled thought that "democracy is preferable to any other kind of government" and only 9 per cent supported the claim that "in some circumstances, a non-democratic government would be preferable." In Latin America, the Latinobarometro conducted a survey in 2010 that showed a somewhat lower approval rate—averaging 61 per cent approval for the statement "Democracy may have some problems but it is the best system of government." In some countries, such as Uruguay and Venezuela, support was around 75 per cent, but in Guatemala agreement was only at 46 per cent (Latinobarometro, 2010: 25). Clearly, popular support is not a guarantee of democratic consolidation. However, it is certainly a fundamental factor. A country cannot consolidate democracy if the population does not perceive the system as being legitimate in the first place.

A second factor of importance for democratic consolidation is the *institutionalization of defeat*. Indeed, one of the fundamental characteristics of political life in any democracy is that it is normal and legitimate for a government to lose power. Political actors accept defeat in democratic regimes because they know they can run for office again during the next election. Learning to lose and accepting defeat mean that politicians will not seek non-democratic means to regain power, nor will they seek to hold on to power at all costs (Wong and Friedman, 2008).

In many democratizing countries, a defining test is whether those who led authoritarian regimes for years or even decades, and whose willingness to hand over the power they had monopolized for so long was in doubt, will finally accept stepping down. We can think of countries where an institution, the military or a single-party regime, or a dictator monopolized political power. This was the case in Brazil, for instance, where the military and their allies in right-wing parties headed the authoritarian regime for more than 20 years (1965–85). A major test occurred when they eventually conceded defeat to candidates and parties they had repressed during the heyday of the authoritarian era, such as centre-left candidate Fernando Henrique Cardoso (elected president in 1994 and again in 1998), and later Luiz Inácio "Lula" da Silva (2002–10) and Dilma Rousseff (2010–16), both from the popular left. (However, the dismissal from office of President Rousseff in May 2016 could suggest that some political elites who were opposed to the popular left have been gaining some traction.) Likewise, the Institutional Revolutionary Party (PRI) of Mexico, which had held power without interruption since the 1930s, lost the presidential election for the first time in 2000 and again in 2006. The end of this lengthy reign signalled to other political actors that the PRI had finally accepted the idea that voters could shift political power through the ballot box. Similarly, in Africa, many political parties that had governed their respective countries from independence (dating back to the 1960s in most cases) have recently succumbed to defeat. For example, the Socialist Party of Senegal lost the presidential election in 2000 and parliamentary elections in 2001, and in Kenya, the Kenya African National Union party was dislodged from power in 2004 for the first time since independence (1963). In countries that have recently ousted autocrats, as in Tunisia and Egypt, some would argue that the odds of seeing a strong consolidated democracy flourishing depend a lot on whether actors, such as the military and the political elites of the former dominant party, will accept civilians and new political actors and groups attaining power. In Tunisia, the military has not stepped into the transition process, leaving civilians alone in the management of the transition, regardless of whether elections were won by a candidate they favoured or not. But in Egypt, the military eventually deposed and arrested the president who had been elected only a year before, in the aftermath of the Arab Spring. They then decided to organize new elections, which were won by their very own leader, now President of the country, General el-Sissi. Of course, the institutionalization of defeat is not a sufficient condition for speaking of democratic consolidation, but it is nonetheless necessary, just as the other indicators are.

Nevertheless, a number of significant obstacles may surface during the process of democratization, and these can weaken democratic consolidation and can even turn the regime semi-authoritarian. A complete list of obstacles would be too long to elaborate, so we will look at only a few here. First, as supporters of the "substantive" approach to defining democracy often claim, the problem of *socio-economic inequality* is an important factor. This is particularly critical in countries where the process of democratization takes place simultaneously with drastic economic reforms. According to Marcus Kurtz (2004), for instance, the application of neoliberal economic reforms since the 1980s has had disastrous effects on the quality of democracy in Latin America. The economic difficulties these reforms produced seem to have resulted in a lack of political motivation among Latin Americans and reduced the capacity of the most marginalized social classes to undertake sustained collective action.

Another important factor that can derail a country from democratic consolidation is *political violence*, especially when it pertains to identity. In a number of countries, democratization has been concomitant with the development of ethnic, religious, linguistic, or racial violence. In many cases, the authoritarian regime created—or at the very least played up—identity tensions as a means of averting calls for democracy. This has been the case notably in a number of African and Asian countries, where regimes have created and encouraged violence between ethnic or religious communities. For example, some argue that given the level of ethnic and religious tensions in Nigeria, a country of many ethnic groups and languages where terrorist groups have preyed on defenceless villages in northern Nigeria and where armed groups from rival local militias often attack one another in the central regions such as the Plateau State and in the Niger Delta region, democracy will always be difficult to consolidate. Though the Nigerian opposition won the presidential and legislative elections in 2015, for the first time since the transition in 1999, the fact is, they would argue, that the high level of violence continues to be a major threat for democratic consolidation, as it destabilizes the foundations of the country's democratic life (Salehyan and Linebarger, 2015; Houle, 2015).

THE CAUSAL WEIGHT OF DEMOCRATIZATION IN ECONOMIC AND SOCIAL DEVELOPMENT

Instead of looking at the factors that may lead to democratization and democratic consolidation, we now turn to the effects democracy can generate. The causal direction is reversed here. Democracy is not the consequence, but the cause. Debate on the impacts of democracy has continued since a number of developing countries gained independence in the middle of the twentieth century. Many observers believe it was ill-advised for the newly independent states to adopt democracy, claiming that democratic governance could undermine economic and social development. They argue that if a poor country opts for democracy, this type of regime triggers a political cycle that has a devastating effect on the economy.

From this viewpoint, democracies are fundamentally based on short electoral cycles. This encourages politicians to think only of the short term and base their decisions solely on the goal of being re-elected. As a result, these politicians will be inclined to overspend their country's meagre resources on showering the electorate with "gifts," thereby undermining the foundations of an already fragile economy. Politicians also might seek to borrow funds internationally, which can put the country further into debt (see Chapter 14). They also rarely make decisions that are politically difficult but economically necessary (for example, to abolish generous subsidies for an industrial sector that is running a deficit or to sell a failing public enterprise). The logic, then, is that it is preferable, *initially*, for a poor country to set up an authoritarian regime. Then, *after* the authoritarian regime has brought the country to a certain level of economic development, the country should adopt democracy. Samuel Huntington (1968) advanced the argument that military regimes are best placed to resist and repress excessive financial demands from the working class, middle class, peasants, and unions, to name but a few—demands that are impossible for a poor country to meet. The examples that researchers cite most often are those of Chile, Taiwan, and South Korea, countries that would not have achieved such a high level of development without a strong authoritarian regime.

Other researchers contest this argument. Przeworski et al. (2000) found that, statistically, authoritarian regimes do not produce more wealth than democracies. Moreover, according to them, nothing indicates that leaders of authoritarian regimes are necessarily "enlightened despots" who make sound economic or social decisions. A number of authoritarian regimes were governed by dictators or military officers whose sole preoccupation was to satisfy their own personal needs (and the needs of their entourage). Suharto's Indonesia, Marcos's Philippines, the military generals in Nigeria: these and other authoritarian regimes literally pillaged the resources of their country. Even in countries that seemed to grow well for a period of time, such as Tunisia, it has become clear by now that the ruling family had in fact been depleting the country's assets for more than a decade.

Furthermore, some would argue that democracies are much more appropriate in terms of establishing a sound economic base and, more generally, a society that looks after the well-being of its citizens. In democracies, the population holds decision-makers liable for their actions and accountable for their decisions. Democratic decision-makers, so the argument goes, cannot pillage the national resources of their country without paying the price at the next election. Democracy is founded on mechanisms of transparency and checks and balances that reduce the risks and magnitude of corruption, which has disastrous consequences for a country's economic development.

Moreover, to the extent that democracy is a system in which conflicts and tensions between political actors are managed in a peaceful, predictable, and legitimate way—not arbitrarily or through oppression—the risks of political instability and violence are significantly reduced. In the absence of such risks, it is much easier to achieve economic and social development. In addition, given the fact that a democracy is based on holding decision-makers accountable, politicians are institutionally conditioned to adopt inclusive social and economic policies rather than policies that benefit only the favoured few. The ability of the public to replace decision-makers who do not head in this direction is an inevitable constraint that all democratic politicians must face.

SUMMARY

For any country of the world, the potential for socio-economic development is closely related to its political system. One cannot be fully understood without the other. And nowadays, politics in developing countries involves debates about democracy and democratization. Accordingly, this chapter addressed four main issues. (1) Democracy is a central issue globally but its meaning is contested. Some argue for a universal definition that centres on a collection of liberal electoral procedures. For others, democracy is more complex because it is embedded in the specific culture(s) of each society; it also includes other components such as socio-economic rights. (2) Countries can democratize, or fail to do so, for various equally contested reasons. One debate is about the role of domestic factors and international factors: are the prime causes of democratization located *within* the country or are they located at the international level? Second, both actors (politicians, activists, social movements) and large structural forces (i.e., a country's rising level of socio-economic development) are variously seen as the main engines of change. (3) Once democratic institutions and practices are established, various factors can consolidate and strengthen them, or, conversely, can cause their downfall. (4) Democracy and socio-economic development are clearly related one to another, but how exactly? Some believe that only an iron-fisted authoritarian regime is capable of imposing difficult and necessary decisions to foster development. Others point out that many predatory dictators have plundered national resources and that democracy is thus the best form of regime to improve social and economic welfare.

QUESTIONS FOR CRITICAL THOUGHT

1. Compare the different definitions of democracy. Which one seems most convincing to you? Explain why. Beyond the elements presented in this chapter, what additional criteria would you add to arrive at your own personal understanding of democracy?
2. Using developing countries you are familiar with, compare their experiences with democratization. Which of the analytical approaches for explaining democratization seems to be the most convincing in each of these cases? Make a list of the strengths and weaknesses of each approach with respect to the specific cases that interest you.
3. In your view, what factors—in addition to the ones presented in this chapter—are absolutely necessary for democratic consolidation? Using countries that are of interest to you, write a list of obstacles that prevent democratic consolidation. Which of these obstacles pose short-term risk, and which ones might be dangerous over the long term?
4. If you were the head of an international organization such as the United Nations and a country that wanted to establish democracy came to you for advice, what major reforms would you recommend? Are there certain reforms that could be useful for one country but not for another? Why?

SUGGESTED READINGS

Boogards, Matthijs. 2009. "How to classify hybrid regimes? Defective democracy and electoral authoritarianism." *Democratization* 16, 2: 399–423.

Karlstrom, Mikael. 1996. "Imagining democracy: Political culture and democratisation in Buganda." *Africa* 66, 4: 485–505.

Levitsky, Steven, and Lucan Way. 2010. *Competitive Authoritarianism: Hybrid Regimes after the Cold War*. New York: Cambridge University Press.

O'Donnell, Guillermo. 2004. *The Quality of Democracy: Theory and Applications*. Notre Dame, Ind.: University of Notre Dame Press.

Pop-Eleches, G., and G.B. Robertson. 2015. "Structural conditions and democratization." *Journal of Democracy* 26, 3: 144–56.

BIBLIOGRAPHY

Afoaku, O.G. 2000. "US foreign policy and authoritarian regimes: Change and continuity in international clientelism." *Journal of Third World Studies* 17, 2: 13–40.

Afrobarometer. 2009. *Neither Consolidating nor Fully Democratic: The Evolution of African Political Regimes, 1999–2008*. Afrobarometer Briefing Paper No. 67.

Bah, A.B. 2010. "Democracy and civil war: Citizenship and peacemaking in Côte d'Ivoire." *African Affairs* 109, 437: 597–615.

Bertrand, R. 2002. *Indonésie: La démocratie invisible*. Paris: Karthala.

Boix, C. 2003. *Democracy and Distribution*. Cambridge: Cambridge University Press.

Boogards, M. 2009. "How to classify hybrid regimes? Defective democracy and electoral authoritarianism." *Democratization* 16, 2: 399–423.

Clapham, C. 1996. *Africa in the International System: The Politics of State Survival*. Cambridge: Cambridge University Press.

Clarke, K. 2015. "Unexpected brokers of mobilization: Contingency and networks in the 2011 Egyptian uprising." *Comparative Politics* 46, 4: 379–97.

Collier, D., and S. Levitsky. 1997. "Democracy with adjectives: Conceptual innovation in comparative research." *World Politics* 49, 3: 430–51.

Diamond, L. 2002. "Thinking about hybrid regimes." *Journal of Democracy* 13, 2: 21–35.

Helmke, G., and S. Levitsky, eds. 2006. *Informal Institutions and Democracy: Lessons from Latin America*. Baltimore: Johns Hopkins University Press.

Houle, C. 2015. "Ethnic inequality and the dismantling of democracy: A global analysis." *World Politics* 67, 3: 469–505.

Huntington, S. 1968. *Political Order in Changing Societies.* New Haven: Yale University Press.

———. 1993. *The Third Wave: Democratization in the Late Twentieth Century.* Norman: University of Oklahoma Press.

Keck, M.E., and K. Sikkink. 1999. "Transnational advocacy networks in international and regional politics." *International Social Science Journal* 159: 89–101.

Keer, D. 2005. *Dr Ambedkar: Life and Mission.* Mumbai: Popular Prakashan.

Kurtz, M. 2004. "The dilemmas of democracy in the open economy: Lessons from Latin America." *World Politics* 56: 262–302.

Latinobarometro. 2010. *Latinobarometro Report 2010.* Santiago, Chile.

Levitsky, S., and L. Way. 2010. *Competitive Authoritarianism: Hybrid Regimes after the Cold War.* New York: Cambridge University Press.

Lipset, S.M. 1959. "Some social requisites of democracy." *American Political Science Review* 53: 69–105.

Moore, B. 1966. *Social Origins of Dictatorship and Democracy: Lord and Peasant in the Making of the Modern World.* Boston: Beacon Press.

Munck, G., and J. Verkuilen. 2002. "Conceptualizing and measuring democracy: Evaluating alternative indices." *Comparative Political Studies* 35, 5: 5–34.

O'Donnell, G. 2004. *The Quality of Democracy: Theory and Applications.* Notre Dame, Ind.: University of Notre Dame Press.

Oxhorn, P. 2001. "Review: From human rights to citizenship rights: Recent trends in the study of Latin American social movements." *Latin American Research Review* 36, 3: 163–82.

Pop-Eleches, G., and G.B. Robertson. 2015. "Structural conditions and democratization." *Journal of Democracy* 26, 3: 144–56.

Przeworski, A., M.E. Alvarez, J.A. Cheibub, et al. 2000. *Democracy and Development: Political Institutions and Well-Being in the World, 1950–1990.* New York: Cambridge University Press.

Przeworski, A., and L. Fernando. 1997. "Modernization: Theories and facts." *World Politics* 49: 155–83.

Rueschemeyer, D., E. Huber Stephens, and J.D. Stephens. 1992. *Capitalist Development and Democracy.* Chicago: Chicago University Press.

Salehyan, I., and C. Linebarger. 2015. "Elections and social conflict in Africa, 1990–2009." *Studies in Comparative International Development* 50, 1: 23–49.

Schaffer, F. 1998. *Democracy in Translation: Understanding Politics in an Unfamiliar Culture.* Ithaca, NY: Cornell University Press.

Wong, J., and E. Friedman, eds. 2009. *Learning to Lose: Dominant Party Systems and Their Transitions.* New York: Routledge.

World Bank. 2016. "World Bank Indicators: Distribution of income or consumption." http://wdi.worldbank.org/table/2.9.

Zuern, E. 2009. "Democratization as liberation: Competing African perspectives on democracy." *Democratization* 16, 3: 585–603.

17 Climate Change, Environment, and Development

Chukwumerije Okereke and Abu-Bakar S. Massaquoi

LEARNING OBJECTIVES

- To understand the intricate and complex relationship between climate change, environment, and development.
- To learn about the significant historical and more recent developments in the environment, climate change, and development nexus.
- To engage with the key debates, concepts, actors, and institutions in the global governance of environment and sustainable development.

▲ **A Chinese boy runs past a coal-fired power plant near his house on the outskirts of Beijing, China. China's government has set 2030 as a deadline for the country to reach its peak for emissions of carbon dioxide.** | Source: Photo by Kevin Frayer/Getty Images

INTRODUCTION

From its original position as a subject of peripheral concern, the environment has become one of the central topics in international development discourse. Today, climate change, a quintessential environmental problem, is generally recognized as the most important development challenge in the twenty-first century (IPCC, 2014). In addition to acknowledging its many significant direct consequences, development discourse increasingly uses climate change to frame discussions on other important global challenges, such as health, energy, and food security.

For a long period in international development history, the focus of debates and policies was essentially about how to stimulate economic growth, mostly by increasing industrialization and mass consumption in developing countries. A popular philosophy underpinning the emphasis on economic growth was the notion that environmental protection was the preserve of the rich—something that is necessary only after a certain level of economic growth has been attained. This philosophy, which continues to exert powerful influence today, is not without some intuitive appeal. For example, alleviating poverty would seem a natural priority when compared to measuring the size of or closing a hole in the ozone layer. While the former would immediately strike many as a matter of urgent need, the latter, in contrast, might seem to be an exotic and abstract scientific preoccupation. Moreover, common observation shows that developed countries generally tend to have cleaner environments (air, water, etc.) in addition to a higher quality of life. It is difficult to question the many benefits that economic development has brought to poorer countries, for example, an improved mortality rate, better education, improved well-being, and enhanced sanitation.

In recent years, however, the place of the environment in economic development has become a matter of intense academic and public policy debate. The rise of environment as a key issue in international development is rooted in three facts. First is the extensive and increasing impact of humans on all aspects of the environment (IPCC, 2014; Millennium Ecosystem Assessment, 2005). Second, advances in science and technology have afforded not only better understanding of the extent of the environmental damage being caused by humans, but also the tools to communicate and disseminate this information more widely. Consider, for example, the impact of iconic images of environmental degradation in the Nigerian Niger Delta, an entire village in Bangladesh being displaced by flooding induced by climate change, or, more recently, live TV pictures of the BP oil spill in the Gulf of Mexico in 2010. Third, there has been a greater realization of the propensity of environmental degradation to undermine the very basis of economic development and human well-being, for example, air pollution in rapidly developing China.

Since the late 1960s, environmental issues and their links with development have been a subject of increasing international co-operation, with the creation of institutions and multilateral environmental agreements. Currently, the global community has decided to adopt Sustainable Development Goals (SDG) as the overarching framework for a post-2015 development agenda, in a move that perhaps marks the clearest acknowledgement of the environment and development connection. The SDGs build on the eight Millennium Development Goals (MDGs) established through a UN summit in 2000. The Sustainable Development Goals, covering 17 areas including food, water, housing, energy access, and climate change, were officially launched in New York in September 2015 with much pomp and fanfare.

Overall, despite the rise of environment as a central factor in international development and the elaboration of institutions and governance processes at national and global levels, a widespread sense remains that international development efforts are yet to truly incorporate or internalize environmental considerations (Epstein and Buhovac, 2014; Reid, 2013). Over 30 years after the concept of global **sustainable development** was introduced through the Brundtland Report (WCED, 1987) as the guiding principle of economic and international development, there are still no easy answers to the question of how best to effectively combine the goals of environmental protection and economic development at national and global levels (Ehresman and Okereke, 2014).

THE CENTRAL PARADOX AND CONTENDING APPROACHES

The central paradox of the environment–development relationship is that whereas economic development is needed to achieve well-being, the process of economic growth often leads to environmental degradation, which in turn reduces well-being. Differences in understanding the exact nature of this relationship and how to resolve the complex interactions constitute the central challenge of environment–development politics across different scales of governance, from local through national to international levels. In addition, or rather in close relation to this paradox, environmental problems also exhibit two other defining characteristics—the tragedy of commons and the collective action problem (Box 17.1).

Figure 17.1 shows the steady and dramatic increase in the quality of human lives from 1870 to 2007 based on life expectancy at birth, mean years of schooling, expected years of schooling, and gross national income per capita (Escosura, 2013). Measurements based on other development indicators such as infant mortality, the number of people with access to safe drinking water, and the number of undernourished children also show that quality of living has been increasing across all regions of the world (Escosura, 2013).

Advocates of modernization theory (see Chapter 3) are quick to link these improvements to industrialization, urbanization, advances in technology, and increases in global trade. Accordingly, they suggest that economic growth is undeniably a good thing to which all countries should aspire. Moreover, they argue that the best help rich countries can offer poor countries is to export the same development models of state intervention used by the West and to help fast-track poor countries through the various stages of growth (Chambers, 2014).

In addition, some economists have hypothesized that the relationship between economic development and environmental quality takes the form of an inverted U-shape, called the Environmental Kuznets Curve (EKC) (Figure 17.2) (Dietz et al., 2012). The EKC theory suggests that although environmental degradation generally increases as modern economic growth occurs, this increase comes to a halt and then starts to reverse after average income reaches a certain level in the course of development. To date, the modernization theory and the EKC remain highly influential in shaping international environmental and development policies. These approaches suggest that the solution to pollution and environmental degradation resulting from economic growth is, in fact, the pursuit of even more economic development.

IMPORTANT CONCEPTS

BOX 17.1 | Defining "Collective Action Problem" and "Tragedy of the Commons"

Collective action problem describes the situation in which multiple individuals (also communities or countries) would all benefit from a certain action, for example, reducing greenhouse gas emissions that cause climate change, but the associated cost of taking action makes it highly unlikely that any individual can or will undertake and solve the problem alone.

Famously linked to American ecologist Garrett Hardin (1968), the **tragedy of the commons** describes an economic problem in which individual users of a commonly owned resource (say, land for grazing or the atmosphere) each continue to try to reap the greatest benefit from exploiting the resource even when it is apparent that the demand for the resource has overwhelmed the supply. The tragedy is that every individual who consumes an additional unit directly harms others who can no longer enjoy the benefits. Furthermore, the overexploitation, driven by individual gain, Hardin argues will ultimately result in the degradation of the common resource (for an interesting critique of Hardin's thesis, see Ostrom, 1990; Stonich et al., 2002).

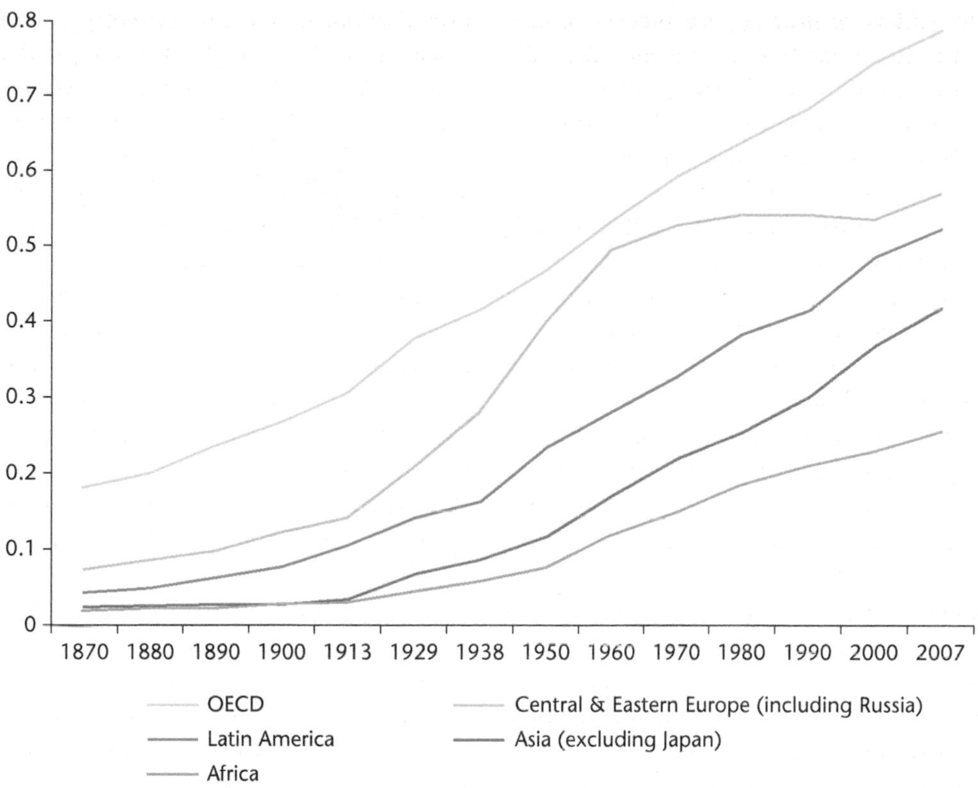

FIGURE 17.1 | World Human Development, 1870–2007

Note: The vertical scale on the left indicates the Human Development Index (HDI), a composite statistic that measures key dimensions of human development.

Source: Adapted from Escosura (2013).

However, it has been noted that the scale of environmental destruction associated with economic development over the decades has become increasingly large. Figure 17.3 is a graph of the global Living Planet Index (LPI), which shows the rapid decline in the number and diversity of vertebrate species living in terrestrial, marine, and freshwater ecosystems. Recent global ecosystem assessment projects have shown that over the past 50 years humans have altered and negatively impacted the natural environment in far more dramatic fashion compared to any other time in human history (Seppelt et al., 2011). Other global assessments also reveal a drastic decrease in world biodiversity, extinction of many species, pollution of various types of ecosystems, and even decrease in levels of happiness (DeFries et al., 2012).

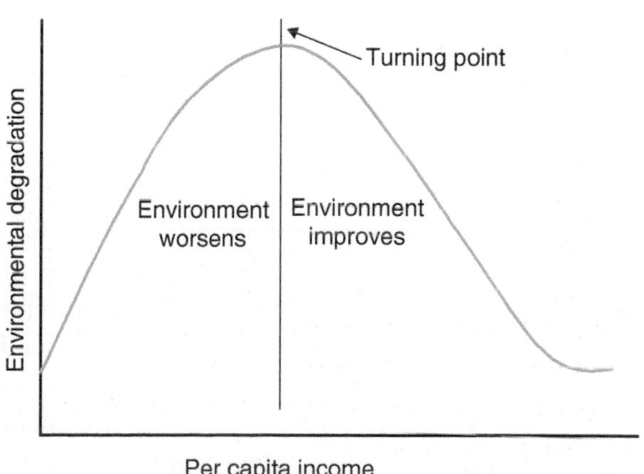

FIGURE 17.2 | Environmental Kuznets Curve

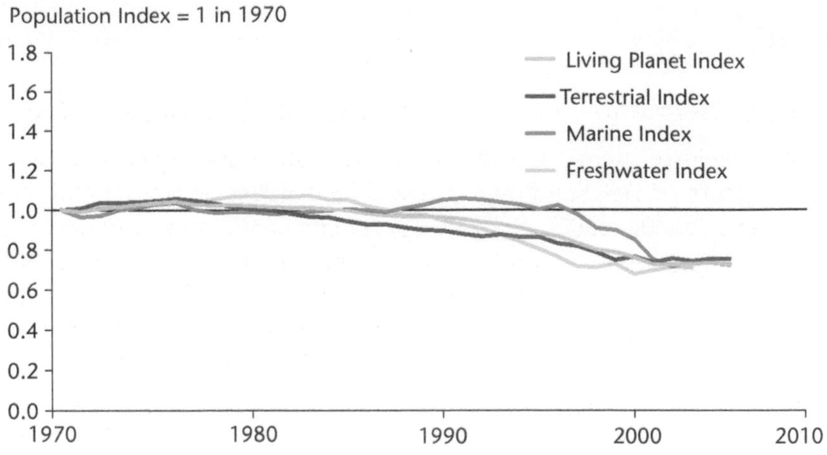

FIGURE 17.3 | Living Planet Index, 1970–2005

Note: The Living Planet Index is an indicator of the state of the world's biodiversity: it measures trends in populations of vertebrate species living in terrestrial, freshwater, and marine ecosysytems.

Source: UNEP-WCMC Living Planet Index available at: www.unep-wcmc.org/system/dataset_file_fields/files/000/000/129/original/Living_Planet_Index._Guidance_for_national_and_regional_use.pdf

Critics have observed that in addition to elevating Western values over indigenous cultures, modernization theory promotes a scale of environmental resource exploitation and consumerism that is ultimately unsustainable (Hannigan, 2014). In addition, the validity of EKC has been challenged. It has been pointed out that the relationship may not hold true for many pollutants, for natural resource use, and for biodiversity conservation, especially when a global perspective is taken. For example, energy and land resource use do not fall as income rises (Dietz et al., 2012). Moreover, it has been argued that many developed countries attained and were able to maintain a certain level of environmental quality only because they were able to get most of their resources from and shifted a high proportion of their pollution to the poor developing countries (Ewing and Rizk, 2008; Wackernagel et al., 1999).

Furthermore, pointing to the degradation of global common pool resources such as the oceans and the atmosphere, and especially the role of Western industrialization in this process, many argue that more modernization can only portend danger for humanity as a whole (Gills, 2015; Takahashi, 2010). That said, many states and citizens in developing countries have not concealed their desire to attain a level of development comparable to the West and a willingness to achieve this goal irrespective of the immediate costs to the environment. The World Bank (2010: 44) sums up the sentiment behind this view rather well by declaring that "it is ethically and politically unacceptable to deny the world's poor the opportunity to ascend the income ladder simply because the rich reached the top first." These observations form the foundation of the argument that only a global approach is sufficient to tackle the problem of environmental degradation and international development (Okereke, 2008). At the same time, it is also argued that the question of how to achieve or maintain economic growth that supports a good quality of living without undermining the natural support base, upon which both growth and lives depend, cannot be met with a simple answer of "just more growth."

A HISTORY OF GLOBAL ENVIRONMENTALISM AND INTERNATIONAL CO-OPERATION FOR SUSTAINABLE DEVELOPMENT

Modern environmentalism can be traced to the early 1960s when various movements, some of which were transnational in nature, campaigned to draw attention to the environmental hazards associated with nuclear weapons testing. Many scholars (e.g., Rootes, 2014;

CRITICAL ISSUES

BOX 17.2 | The Environment–Development Paradox: The Case of China

China has experienced rapid economic growth in the past 30 years, which has resulted in dramatic increases in certain aspects of well-being and a rise of significant environmental challenges. China's manufacturing industries currently produce the highest volume of industrial products in the world, including clothing, electronics, steel, cement, and fertilizer (Zhang, Abbas, and Shishkin, 2012), and recently China ranked fourth for crude oil production globally (National Bureau of Statistics of China, 2012, cited in Zhang et al., 2012). However, this rapid growth fuelled by energy, principally from burning coal, has caused severe environmental problems, especially water and air pollution. China is home to some of the world cities with the worst air pollution (Liu and Diamond, 2005). Respiratory and heart diseases related to air pollution are the leading causes of death in China (Xu et al., 2014), with some studies suggesting that the problem of air pollution costs China up to 10 per cent of GDP every year. China fares equally badly in relation to many other environmental issues. Five of China's cities are in the top 25 of cities most vulnerable to climate change in the world (Maplecroft, 2013). In addition, about 40 per cent of the water in the country's river systems is unfit for human consumption, and the combination of desertification and erosion has swept over almost 30 per cent of China's land over the last two decades (Liu, 2013).

However, a comprehensive understanding of the environmental situation in China requires an acknowledgement of the impact of wider global economic forces and structures (Yang et al., 2013). China may have taken a high polluting route to development at least in part because of politics, national economic interests, and ideological conflicts, which made it difficult for the country to access cleaner technologies from the West. Furthermore, many of the businesses that powered industrial development in China are Western companies interested in maximizing profit and value for their Western shareholders. Today, a vast proportion of the products being made in China are designed for consumption by Western citizens. At the same time, China's real ecological footprint goes far beyond its own borders and reaches far corners of the world, especially Africa, where many Chinese companies are engaged in intensive exploitation of various natural resources including oil, wood, and precious metals (Mol, 2011).

Dryzek, 2013) have linked global environmentalism to the rise of environmental movements in the US. The publication of *Silent Spring* by Rachel Carson in 1962 is often seen as an important landmark. Carson argued that uncontrolled and unexamined pesticide use in the United States, mostly DDT, was harming and killing animal populations (especially birds).

Furthermore, she stressed that through the process of **bioaccumulation**, dangerous amounts of pesticides were finding their way into the human food chain and causing serious harm. Carson was highly critical of capitalism, which she said placed profit above considerations of health and safety. She was also very critical of mainstream science, which she said downplayed or completely ignored the risks and uncertainties associated with widespread pesticide use. Carson's book sparked a vociferous national debate not just about the safety of the use of a number of chemicals, but also about the impact of Western industrialization throughout the world. In the end, the book prompted a reversal in the national pesticide policy and motivated an environmental movement that engendered the establishment of the US Environmental Protection Agency.

Another publication with a far-reaching impact on the rise of global environmentalism was *The Limits to Growth* (Meadows et al., 1972). This book, which originated from research commissioned by the Club of Rome, painted an apocalyptic picture of famine, resource scarcity, hunger, ecosystem collapse, pollution, and reduction in life expectancy, because of what it

ifototrav/iStockphoto

PHOTO 17.1 | Air pollution in Shanghai, China.

described as exponential increase in population and environmental degradation over the last 30 years. Like Carson before them, the authors were critical of materialism and called for environmental regulation and greater emphasis on conservation at the global level.

In response to these currents of opinion for sustainable use of environmental resources the United Nations (UN) organized the United Nations Conference on the Human Environment in 1972 in Stockholm. This was the first-ever environmental conference convened at the United Nations level. Representatives from 113 countries attended, as did others from many international non-governmental organizations, intergovernmental organizations, and other specialized agencies (Egelston, 2013). A key result of the conference was the Stockholm Declaration containing 26 principles aimed at addressing the need to safeguard and improve the human environment. The document reflected on the development–environment nexus, including the idea that environmental protection is fundamental to a good quality of life and the enjoyment of human rights, and that population growth and economic development pose a considerable threat to environmental protection (Dodds, Strauss, and Strong, 2012).

As a follow-up to the conference, the UN General Assembly established the United Nations Environment Programme (UNEP) in 1972. UNEP's core function, as outlined in the original mandate, was to lead the UN's work on environment and its links to international development (see Chapter 10). In 1983, the UN Secretary-General asked Dr Gro Harlem Brundtland, the Norwegian Prime Minister and a public health specialist, to chair a World Commission on Environment and Development (WCED). The launch of the Commission was sparked by a number of high-profile environmental incidents around the world, including a severe drought in Africa that killed about a million people and endangered the livelihoods of 36 million people, and a leak from a pesticide factory in Bhopal, India, which immediately killed more than 2,000 people and injured over 200,000 people. Also notable were an explosion of liquid gas tanks in Mexico City, which killed 1,000 and left thousands more homeless, and the Chernobyl nuclear reactor explosion, which sent nuclear fallout across Europe, increasing the potential risks of human cancers.

Following extensive consultations and meetings across all the continents, the Brundtland Commission published its pioneering report, *Our Common Future*, in April 1987, which brought the term "sustainable development" firmly into public discourse. The report defines sustainable development as "a development that meets the needs of the present generation without compromising the ability of future generations to meet their own needs" (WCED, 1987: 43). It recommended that for sustainable development to be attained, "societies need to meet human needs both by increasing productive potential and by ensuring equitable opportunities for all" (WCED, 1987: 44). In the view of the WCED, sustainable development required the utilization of resources, the arrangement of institutional structures, and the orientation of technology in a manner that fits and improves both current and future potential to meet human needs and aspirations (Ghai and Vivian, 2014; Lafferty and Eckerberg, 2013). Furthermore, the Brundtland Report cited ways of linking environment and development, and stressed the significance of considering the interrelationship and interdependence of economic, environmental, and social issues in framing and implementing development policy decisions to address global environmental challenges (Chatterjee and Finger, 2014).

The 1980s saw some of the most influential advances in climate science and international response to global environmental change (Dryzek, 2013). For example, the Vienna Convention became a framework to protect the ozone layer in 1985, and the Montreal Protocol (a protocol to the Vienna Convention) in 1987 further protected the ozone layer by phasing out the production of substances that cause ozone depletion.

In 1992, the United Nations Conference on Environment and Development (UNCED), commonly known as the Earth Summit, was held in Rio de Janeiro, Brazil. Believed to be the biggest global environment conference ever, the key aim of UNCED was to reinforce the links between environment and development. The meeting produced 21 principles for actualizing sustainable development at the global level, with Principle 4 asserting that "environmental protection shall constitute an integral part of the development process and cannot be considered in isolation from it." In addition, a more detailed blueprint for the protection of the earth and its sustainable development at local levels, known as Agenda 21, was also adopted.

Agenda 21 had a wide-ranging focus, including decreasing deforestation, preventing pollution, alleviating poverty, promoting chemicals management, and avoiding the depletion of natural resources. In full support of the objectives of Agenda 21, the UN General Assembly founded the Commission on Sustainable Development in 1992 as part of the Economic and Social Council. Furthermore, UNCED produced the UN Convention on Biological Diversity (UNCBD), the UN Convention to Combat Desertification (UNCCD), the UN Framework Convention on Climate Change (UNFCCC), and broad Principles on Forest Conservation. A number of global summits of sustainable development have been held since the Rio Earth Summit. These include Rio+10, otherwise known as the World Summit on Sustainable Development, in Johannesburg, South Africa in 2002, and more recently Rio+20 on the theme of the Green Economy, convened once again in Rio de Janeiro.

CLIMATE CHANGE

The earth's climate can be affected by natural elements that are external to the climate system, such as alterations in volcanic activity, solar output, and the earth's orbit around the sun. Of these, the two important issues on time scales of present-day climate change are changes in volcanic activity and changes in solar radiation. Climate change can also be caused by human activities, such as the burning of fossil fuels and the conversion of land for agriculture and forestry. In addition to other environmental impacts, these activities change the land surface and emit various substances to the atmosphere such as carbon dioxide, a greenhouse gas that influences the amount of inward and outward energy and, thus, can have both warming and cooling effects on the climate.

Climate change exemplifies the intricate connections and tensions between global economic development and environmental sustainability perhaps more than any other environmental issue (Okereke and Schroder, 2009). There are at least three points of connection, all of which are of great significance. First, through its severe negative impacts on the natural, human, social, and economic systems of developing countries, climate change could reverse decades of

CURRENT EVENTS

BOX 17.3 | Important Events and Agreements towards an Environmental Regime

1972: United Nations Environment Programme (UNEP) created by UN General Assembly
1973: Convention on International Trade in Endangered Species (CITES)
1979: Bonn Convention on Migratory Species
1985: Vienna Convention for the Protection of the Ozone Layer
1987: Montreal Protocol on Substances that Deplete the Ozone Layer; WCED report, *Our Common Future*, published
1988: Intergovernmental Panel on Climate Change (IPCC) established
1992: United Nations Commission on Environment and Development (UNCED) publishes *Agenda 21*, a blueprint for sustainable development
1992: Convention on Biological Diversity
2000: Cartagena Protocol on Biosafety adopted to address issue of genetically modified organisms
2000: Millennium Declaration: environmental sustainability included as one of eight Millennium Development Goals (MDGs)
2001: Stockholm Convention on Persistent Organic Pollutants (POPs)
2010: Intergovernmental Science-Policy Platform on Biodiversity and Ecosystem Services (IPBES)
2011: UNEP produces the Green Economy Report, *Towards a Green Economy: Pathways to Sustainable Development and Poverty Eradication*, in the context of sustainable development and poverty eradication as the key theme for Rio+20.
2015: Paris Agreement adopted during the 21st Conference of the Parties of the UN Framework Convention on Climate Change (UNFCCC) in Paris
2015: Sustainable Development Goals (SDGs), successor to MDGs

CRITICAL ISSUES

BOX 17.4 | The Post-2015 Sustainable Development Agenda

At the Rio+20 UN Conference on Sustainable Development in 2012, 17 Sustainable Development Goals (SDGs) were identified, and these were adopted by the UN General Assembly in New York in September 2015. The SDGs build on the eight Millennium Development Goals (MDGs) established by the UN in 2000. Before the launch, the SDG process engaged governments, international organizations, and the wider civil society to propose a universal sustainable development agenda, which is likely to extend until 2030. The groundwork also included developing a set of measurable indicators and targets through an intergovernmental Open Working Group (OWG). This 30-member group, established in January 2013, was assigned the responsibility of submitting a report to the UN General Assembly in September 2014. Many member countries see the SDGs as an opportunity to address prevailing and potential sustainable development challenges. Nonetheless, a counter-current has emerged, particularly in respect to ensuring that the SDGs don't end up largely unfunded, like the MDGs. Overall, a lot of hope is being expressed about the SDGs, with many member countries motivated by its promise to offer innovative and transformative approaches to achieving sustainable development, such as new and stronger global partnerships, capacity-building and information-sharing opportunities, and measures to improve accountability through effective monitoring and reporting (https://sustainabledevelopment.un.org/focussdgs.html).

PHOTO 17.2 | A biodiversity display of beans in painted clay pots at the Deccan Development Society (DDS) Biodiversity Festival in Pastapur village, Andhra Pradesh.

international development efforts and further limit the resources available to fight poverty in both rich and poor countries. Some of the potential impacts of climate change in developing countries include increased frequency and severity of extreme climate events, reduced crop yield causing food insecurity, desertification, ecosystem collapse, fresh water shortages, lower incomes and scant economic growth, population displacement, and exposure to new health risks (IPCC, 2007, 2014).

Second, while large-scale economic development is needed to pull billions of citizens in developing countries out of abject poverty, a business-as-usual approach to development will exacerbate the problem of climate change with potentially irreversible long-term consequences (IPCC, 2014, 2007). Furthermore, poverty contributes to environmental degradation and climate change, which in turn increase poverty and underdevelopment—the so-called poverty trap (Okereke and Charlesworth, 2014). A well-known example of this is the relationship between poverty, population growth, and deforestation in developing countries. Third, climate change will considerably shape development choices in developing countries, where governments will need to jump to smarter technologies and more effective and resilient structures (Okereke and Yusuf, 2013). Hence, while climate change poses profound challenges to international development, it also offers unique opportunities to pursue growth and build more resilient economies.

A crucial dimension of climate change is that although its impacts are and will be felt the world over, its current and future impact will fall disproportionately on the world's poor populations who have contributed the least to the problem. The Climate Vulnerability Monitor (2012) indicates that climate change is already contributing to the deaths of nearly 400,000 people a year, 98 per cent of whom reside in poor countries, especially in Africa. Available reports suggest that between 75 million and 250 million people in Africa will be exposed to increased water stress triggered by climate change by 2020, which will significantly affect agricultural production and lead to increasing food insecurity and malnutrition (Kjellstrom, 2015).

These occurrences could increase the costs of adaptation to at least 5 to 10 per cent of Africa's GDP (Tanner and Horn-Phathanothai, 2014). Furthermore, the *Climate Change and Environmental Risk Atlas* (Maplecroft, 2013) noted, for 2015, that the top 10 affected countries were in the Third World (Figure 17.4). These countries, in order of estimated negative impacts, are:

1. Bangladesh
2. Sierra Leone
3. Nigeria
4. South Sudan
5. Chad
6. Haiti
7. Ethiopia
8. Philippines
9. Central African Republic
10. Eritrea

The Climate Regime

Global effort to address climate change has focused on the United Nations Convention on Climate Change (UNFCCC) negotiated in 1992 as part of the UNCED. The Kyoto Protocol is a key component of the UNFCCC because it contains mandatory targets for emissions reduction for states, detailed measures for implementation, and a compliance mechanism, which is the only one of its kind (Hovi, Stokke, and Ulfstein, 2013). In December 2015, during the 21st Conference of the Parties of the UNFCCC in Paris, a new agreement designed to replace Kyoto was adopted (the Paris Agreement). It is intended that the Agreement will come into force in 2020. The Intergovernmental Panel on Climate Change (IPCC) provides crucial scientific evidence for climate policy. The IPCC was established in 1988 by the Executive Council of the World Meteorological Organization (WMO) and United Nations Environment Programme with a mandate to provide the world with a clear scientific view of the current state of knowledge on climate change and its potential environmental and socio-economic impacts. In the same year of its creation, the UN General Assembly endorsed the action by WMO and UNEP in jointly establishing the IPCC and

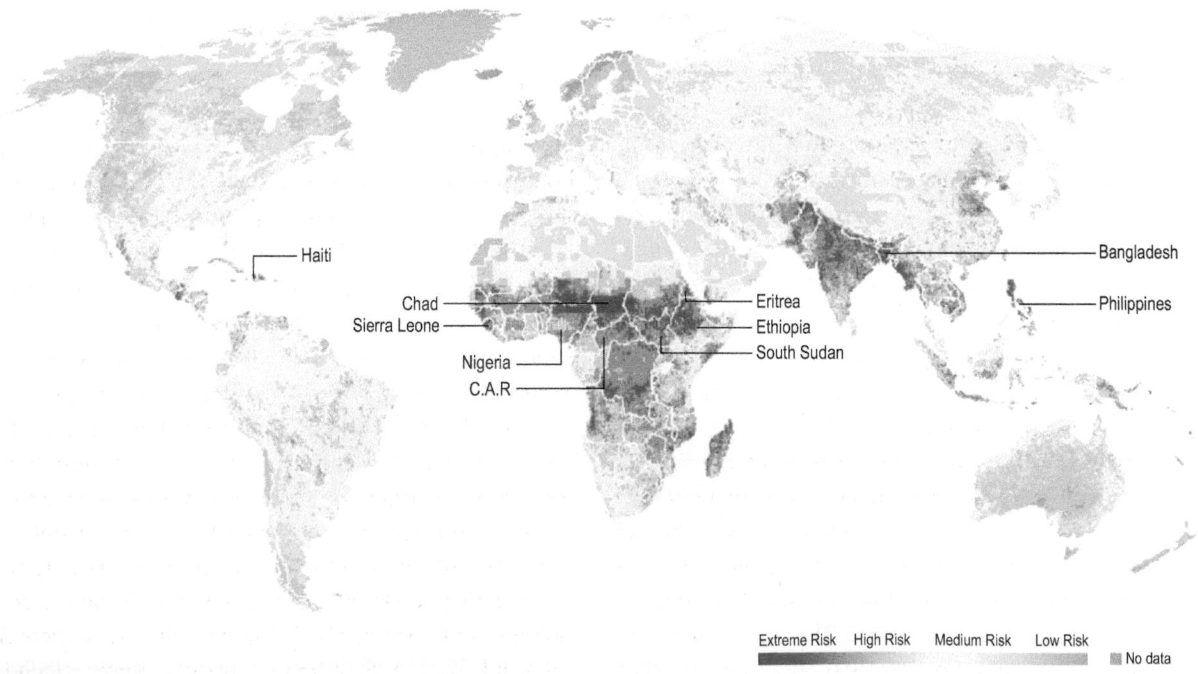

FIGURE 17.4 | Climate Change Vulnerability Index, 2015

Source: Used by permission of Verisk Maplecroft.

BOX 17.5 | Counting the Costs of Climate Change

CURRENT EVENTS

A number of recent reports draw attention to the intricate links between the projected climate risks in developing countries and the future state of the global economy. The *Climate Change and Environmental Risk Atlas*, for example, highlights the extent to which global economic growth is endangered by climate change. The sixth annual edition of the *Atlas* discloses that by 2025, 31 per cent of the global economic yield will be from countries recording "high" or "extreme risks" from the impacts of climate change. This forecast doubles current levels of climate change. A costing using a Climate Change Vulnerability Index (CCVI), which is a core part of the *Atlas,* shows that about 67 countries with a combined yield of $44 trillion will be severely affected by climate change. These estimates confirm that some of the countries upon whose growth the world currently depends, such as China, will be hit extremely hard by climate change if present-day development practices in the public and private sectors go unchanged. In 10 more years beyond 2015, China and India are predicted to record an increase in their GDPs from current levels to $28 trillion and $5 trillion respectively, which will amount to nearly 23 per cent of the world's economic output.

Equally, the situation is grim for most countries in Africa, including Nigeria, the region's largest economy. Recently released climate projections from the Intergovernmental Panel on Climate Change for the period up to 2040 clearly indicate that a significant warming of about 2°C is projected for West Africa, which indicates an increase in rainfall and humidity and severe consequences for communities, governments, and businesses. In the case of Nigeria, which in 2013 was ranked the sixth most climate-vulnerable country in the world according to the CCVI, climate change will mainly affect the oil sector and surrounding communities through erosion and sea level rise. Already the impacts are being felt, with flooding between July and November 2012 resulting in an estimated loss of 500,000 barrels per day in oil production, equal to more than one-fifth of the country's total production capacity (Maplecroft, 2013).

called on the body to submit its first assessment report in time to feed into the United Nations Conference on the Environment and Development in 1992. Today, the IPCC is the world's foremost agency for scientific research on climate change, with five "assessment reports" to its credit, produced in 1990, 1995, 2001, 2007, and 2014.

The UNFCCC and Kyoto Protocol, for their part, may well pass as the most elaborate and complex agreement the world has ever negotiated (Luterbacher and Sprinz, 2001). The regime embraces two main responses in its action against climate change. The first is **mitigation**, which focuses on the reduction of the amounts of greenhouse gas that states and other actors are emitting into the atmosphere. The second is **adaptation**, which focuses on how to cope with the impacts of climate change effects that cannot be mitigated. More recently, the concept of resilience, which considers adaptation as a process of coping with, responding to and recovering from climatic shocks and stresses, has gained prominence (Bahadur, Ibrahim, and Tanner, 2013). Mitigation and adaptation overlap, as the more climate change effects are mitigated, the less the prospect that individuals, communities, and countries will need to adapt. Conversely, some efforts at adaptation, such as planting trees, can also help in mitigation.

Developing countries have consistently demanded an effective global response to climate change with emphasis on urgent and ambitious mitigation efforts by rich countries that are thought to be responsible for the course of climate change at least in historical terms. Second, they call for assistance in terms of finance, technology, and capacity-building to help them increase their adaptation to climate impacts. More recently, low carbon development (LCD) and cognate terms like climate compatible development, low emission

CURRENT EVENTS

BOX 17.6 | Looking Ahead: A Post-2020 Climate Agreement

The overriding purpose of the 1997 Kyoto Protocol was to develop a long-term process for managing climate change, including quantified emission reduction obligations from states. The first commitment period of Kyoto was 2008 to 2012. There are wide differences in opinion about how effective the Kyoto Protocol was. Signatories to the UNFCCC meet every year in what is called the Conference of Parties (COP) to negotiate on various aspects of the international climate agreement. Since 2005, there have been negotiations about how to maintain momentum on climate action after the first commitment period of Kyoto. An agreement was supposed to be reached in Copenhagen (COP-15) in 2009, but this did not happen because of disagreements between states such as China and the US. Since the failure in Copenhagen, much has been done to spark a renewed interest in UNFCCC-led negotiations, with the COPs in Cancun (2010), Durban (2011), and Doha (2012) seen as interventions to rebuild trust between developed and developing countries. Accordingly, in November 2015 an agreement to replace the Kyoto Protocol was signed at the Conference of Parties (COP-21) meeting in Paris, which will come into force in 2020 and provide a framework for long-term global action on climate change. The Paris Agreement, however, is based on voluntary pledges of emission reductions from all countries called Indented Nationally Determined Contributions (INDCs), which will be submitted and reviewed every five years. Despite widespread enthusiasm, some have expressed serious concerns about building a hope for effective global emissions reductions on the voluntary pledges of states. Wide sentiment suggests that the Paris Agreement does not provide enough support for developing countries to enable them to take climate action with regard to mitigation and adaptation.

Source: http://www.rff.org/Publications/Resources/Pages/185-Negotiating-a-Post-2020-Climate-Agreement.aspx.

development strategies (LEDS), and green growth have all become popular in international environmental and sustainable development discourse. Their popularity has stemmed from the notion that they offer a new hope for continued growth in the South while also serving as a soft alternative to hard, quantified GHG emission reduction targets for the developing countries (Nussbaumer, 2009). LCD is also attractive because it appears to hold the promise of reconciling a long and deep conflict between the economic development aspirations of developing countries and the imperative to cut anthropogenic global greenhouse gas emissions that are causing climate change. However, over 20 years since the negotiation of the UNFCCC, there remains a wide sense of frustration from developing countries that the rich countries are not only denying their obligations to reduce emissions and help poor countries adapt to climate change, but that they are surreptitiously conscripting developing countries into undertaking burdensome emission reduction commitments. The Paris Agreement, which will come into effect in 2020, expects all countries (both developed and developing countries) to commit to ambitious emission reduction programs.

Key Actors and Roles

Many actors, including UN agencies, other multilateral organizations such as the European Union and US Agency for International Development (USAID), and transnational public-sector institutions and businesses play crucial roles in global climate governance. For example, the climate change sub-program at UNEP focuses on building the capacity of institutions in developing countries so that they can mainstream climate change decisions into national development strategies. These different strategies are principally linked to the broader UNFCCC framework for global climate governance. Nonetheless, recent developments in the climate regime have led to a renewed interest in multilateral and transnational partnerships outside the UNFCCC structure. These partnerships, such as the G8 and G8+5, largely seek to address climate issues outside the UNFCCC agenda, while others seek to demonstrate the crucial role multilateral institutions play in addressing global environment–development challenges (Green, 2012).

It could be that these responses reflect the failures of the UNFCCC to regulate emissions reductions and stimulate an awareness of their importance, or to provide adequate funds for adaptation in developing countries (Morin and Orsini, 2014). Andonova and colleagues describe the partnerships between the UNFCCC and developing countries in relation to three overlapping roles: information-sharing; capacity-building and implementation; and decision-making (Andonova, Betsill, and Bulkeley, 2009). The main drive, as Bulkeley and Jordan (2012) note, is to outline the priorities of these partnerships for addressing climate change. Conversely, while such partnerships seek to strengthen the UNFCCC process, others, such as the Asia-Pacific Partnership on Clean Development and Climate (APP) created by US President George W. Bush after the withdrawal of the US from the Kyoto Protocol in 2005, enthusiastically wanted to build a parallel framework to the UNFCCC. Nevertheless, the Major Economies Forum on Energy and Climate Change (MEF), which succeeded the APP, has been instrumental in relinking the parties with the UNFCCC (Tanner and Horn-Phathanothai, 2014).

Global climate deliberations have also led to an important set of public- and private-sector multinational responses, including the C40 Climate Leadership Group, an association of 58 of the world's megacities; the Asia Cities Climate Change Resilience Network (ACCCRN) formed by the Rockefeller Foundation; and the World Mayors Council on Climate Change (WMCCC), which seeks to connect industrialized and developing municipalities through an advocacy for city-based climate responses. In the private sector also, a number of consortia have been formed. A notable example is the World Business Council of Sustainable Development (WBCSD), which works with 29 leading world companies from 14 industries to

BOX 17.7 | Governing Climate Change: The UNFCCC **CURRENT EVENTS**

The UN Framework Convention on Climate Change architecture involves 196 country parties, each with a focal point for representation and negotiations, usually located in a ministry dealing with environmental matters. Negotiations are also attended by bilateral and multilateral agencies such as the World Bank and United Nations agencies. The framework categorizes country parties into three groups, the first two of which are interlocking: Annex I parties, numbering 43 and including the European Union (EU), are developed countries and Eastern European "economies in transition"; Annex 2 parties, numbering 24 and including the EU, are members of the Organisation for Economic Co-operation and Development (OECD), and are expected to provide technical and financial assistance to the transitioning economies of the former Soviet bloc and to developing countries to help them in mitigating greenhouse gas emissions and with the impacts of climate change; non-Annex 1 parties consist mostly of developing countries. The UNFCCC is governed through a Conference of Parties (COP) comprising representatives of country parties to the Convention, who meet once a year. During negotiations, countries with common interests tend to form groups to save time and make stronger cases. These groups change, however, depending on the issues being negotiated. Some prominent groupings under the UNFCCC include: the Alliance of Small Island States (AOSIS) comprising 42 countries and observers; the Least Developed Countries (LDCs), consisting of 48 country parties; the African Group, with 53 members from Africa; the EU Delegation comprising the 28 countries of the European Union; and the Umbrella Group, which has no formal members but usually is made up of the United States and some other non-EU developed countries, including Russia, New Zealand, Canada, Japan, and Norway.

develop a "Vision 2050" that describes how a global population of 9 billion will live contentedly within the obtainable natural resource limits (Wilkinson and Mangalagiu, 2012). However, many scholars have pointed out the irony of development agencies like the World Bank and business organizations like WBCSD projecting themselves as leading actors in the efforts to address global environmental problems when, in fact, these actors are actively engaged in activities (e.g., funding the development of dams and coal-fired power station and exploitation of tar sands) that cause environmental degradation (Korten, 2001).

Clearly, a lot of work is required by multiple actors and at multiple scales to stem global environmental degradation and the seeming ineffectiveness of international institutions for environmental and sustainable development governance. Failures of global and country-level institutions to surmount the collective action challenge and offer means through which countries, organizations, and businesses can act together to address pressing challenges of poverty and environmental degradation remain a key global challenge of the twenty-first century.

CONTROVERSIES AND CROSSCUTTING THEMES

Environmental and Climate Justice

One major issue that has dogged international co-operative effort for global governance of climate change and sustainable development is equity and social justice. Contestations for climate justice, mainly in the form of demands for fair treatment by poor countries, have provoked the most vociferous debates and controversies between rich and poor countries in global sustainable development policy circles (Okereke, 2008, 2010). Concern for climate justice has been expressed in many forms. First, poor countries are keen to point out that rich countries are responsible for and have profited disproportionately from the bulk of the pollution that is causing today's global environmental problems. A good example is climate change, where 25 countries account for 75 per cent of historic global emissions (Bulkeley and Newell, 2015).

Second, poor countries point out that they bear a disproportionate burden of global environmental impacts arising from past and current global economic activities as a result of their geographical location, lack of protective infrastructure, and low adaptive and response capacities. This would seem doubly unfair because the rich countries have benefited and still tend to benefit more from these harm-producing activities because of their advantageous position in the global economic structure (Lewis, 2013). Third, poor countries fear that they are not able to participate effectively in the negotiation of global environmental agreements because of poor capacity and structural weaknesses (Okereke and Charlesworth, 2014). They insist that procedural justice is necessary to elaborate rules that are fair to all countries. Fourth, poor countries fear they may be saddled with responsibilities that could undermine their development aspirations. Again, to use climate change as an example, developing countries have pointed out that they have been forced into committing to significant cuts in their own emissions, though they only contributed one-fifth of global emissions between 1850 and 2002 (World Bank, 2005).

Developed countries, for their part, have argued that the fact of a rapidly deteriorating environment demands that all countries must make commitments and sacrifices to help facilitate an effective response (Chasek, Downie, and Brown, 2013). Moreover, they argue that emphasis on historical responsibility for environmental and climate damage is unhelpful and point out that it is hardly justice to seek to punish sons for the sins of their fathers. Rich countries also often suggest that developing countries are the architects of their own poverty and vulnerability through several decades of corruption and poor governance (Rodrik, 2014).

A major equity concept that has been devised to mediate the justice conflict between developed and developing countries is the Common but Differentiated Responsibility and Capability principle (CBDR+C). However, despite its popularity and frequent invocation in environmental agreements and policy circles, the CBDR+C principle has done little to resolve satisfactorily the deep moral impasse that characterizes environmental and climate change bargaining (Okereke, 2008). Developing countries have so often focused on the "differentiated" side of the norm, while developed countries tend to emphasize the "common" side to highlight the need for equal commitment. The result is that while almost all major global environmental agreements negotiated since 1972 contain copious references to equity and justice, many developing countries feel they have made very little progress in securing real justice.

A major argument by developed countries in response to concerns for equity is that a focus on distributive justice—especially in the form of North–South financial or technology transfer—will undermine effective and efficient approaches to deal with climate change. For this reason, developed countries insist that it is much better to use market approaches or instruments in dealing with environmental issues.

In contrast with earlier views that pursuing equality reduces economic efficiency, recent evidence suggests that extensive inequality hinders socio-economic growth and that addressing equity and social justice concerns can deliver fair and lasting development impacts (Acemoglu and Robinson, 2012). In addition, it has been proposed that inequality in access to education and other resources, such as land and credit, can hamper economic growth, since the talents, ideas, views, and experiences of a large proportion of the population are not wholly utilized (Leach et al., 2012).

Nonetheless, market approaches have dominated global environmental and sustainable development rule-making, including policies like the Clean Development Mechanism (CDM), a policy tool formulated in the Kyoto Protocol, that have been crafted as part of solutions for North–South distributive justice (Elah and Okereke, 2014). Through the CDM, developed countries are supposed to get tradable emission credits by investing in emission reduction projects in poor countries. Also, the CDM has been viewed by most developing-country parties as a way of taking the pressure off rich countries that need to make domestic cuts in emissions reductions rather than buy their way out of local liability. In some critical literature, the CDM has been referred to as a form of *carbon colonialism* (Bachram, 2004).

© Dominic Morissette

PHOTO 17.3 | Cleaning up an oil spill, Spain 2003.

What Does Sustainability Mean Anyway?

Another major source of controversy that characterizes global sustainable development policies stems from fundamental differences in the way the very concept of sustainability is understood by different sections of the global community. In its broadest sense, sustainability means the ability of any system to maintain its performance over time. Performance in this context refers to development in relation to the social and individual qualities of life (Tanner and Horn-Phathanothai, 2014). From this understandings, it can be supposed that sustainability is concerned with a "development that lasts," which may require placing an emphasis on safeguarding natural resources (natural capital) that provide a range of services for humans and the environment, or substituting natural capital with other forms of produced capital. In effect, this is a choice between weak sustainability and strong sustainability, respectively (Dietz and Neumayer, 2007).

In respect of a weak sustainability paradigm, the understanding generally is that capital assets are substitutable and the focus ought to be on the total stock of capital. Proponents of weak sustainability commonly assume that natural and produced capital are exchangeable, and that no inequalities exist in the kinds of well-being they produce. Within this perspective, it is thought that it does not matter whether the current generation depletes non-renewable environmental resources or continues to increase carbon emissions, as long as employment, technologies, and basic services are provided in return (Dietz and Neumayer, 2007). Obviously, a weak view of sustainability demands increased monetary compensation for environmental degradation and resulting conditions such as climate change. In contrast, advocates for a strong sustainability paradigm emphasize that some capital assets are more important than others, implying that others cannot be substituted. In their view, policies should be formulated to safeguard environmental resources upon which economic development primarily depends. Within this context, sustainability involves preserving and growing people's capital stock, with a focus on guiding the present generation through taking just as much as they need, so that the next generation will have as much as they will require (Tanner and Horn-Phathanothai, 2014).

Driving Forces behind Environmental Change

The impact of humans on the environment is generally measured using the equation I = PAT. Accordingly, the impact (I) of any population on the environment is expressed as a product of three characteristics: population size (P), its affluence (measured in per-capita consumption) (A), and the prevailing technologies in use (T). In short, impact (I) is calculated as a combined function of *population* (P), *affluence* (A), and *technology* (T).

While this seems simple and straightforward, there is a huge controversy, often reflecting differences in value, about the relative role of the various components and where emphasis should lie in designing global environmental policy. Simply stated, the controversy is often about whether the actual cause of environmental change is *population growth* in developing countries, or *power, affluence*, and *use of technology* in the rich and developed countries. Developed countries often like to focus on the impact of population on the environment. They suggest that a key aspect of global sustainable development policy must include some measure of population control in developing countries. For example, it is projected that the next two decades will see unprecedented growth in urban populations, from three to five billion people, who will mostly live in developing countries. Furthermore, from this perspective, growth in population is believed to be the major cause of the increasing demand for energy, which is expected to rise mainly in developing countries in few a decades (Tanner and Horn-Phathanothai, 2014).

But developing countries often prefer to stress affluence and technology as the main sources of the problem. They point out that most of this stress on the global environment comes from only 25 per cent of the world's population, who consume 75 per cent of global resources (forest, cement, paper, energy, precious metals, etc.). Because of technological growth and affluence, global electricity demand is projected to double by 2030 (from a 2004 baseline) if current consumption trends remain. Tied to this are rapid urbanization and the growth of cities, which account for 60 to 80 per cent of global energy consumption (Kamal-Chaoui and Robert, 2009) (see Chapter 19).

The impact of technology on the environment is far more complex. On the one hand, advances in technology have helped to stem environmental degradation. Common examples are renewable energy and mechanized farming methods used in large-scale food production. On the other hand, advances in technology have made resource depletion much easier and quicker, as evident in large-scale fish trawling in the oceans and deepwater oil exploration. Furthermore, technology has been considered a cause in the widening income inequality gap, as the rich are able to access specialized and expensive equipment to grow their wealth at the expense of poor people, who only benefit from the wages they are paid for working on the rich men's farms and in their industries (Milanović, 2015).

SUMMARY

This chapter has sought to make the case that global environmental challenges are now central in international development discourse. Indeed, environmental issues and international development are so intricately bound that it is inconceivable to ignore environmental issues in any major debate or academic work on development. This chapter provides a foundation for understanding the intricate and complex relationship among climate change, environment, and development. It presents the key historical and more recent developments related to the environment, climate change, and development nexus, and engages with the key debates, concepts, actors, and institutions in the global governance of environment and sustainable development.

While the global community has attempted to respond to these challenges by intensive co-operation marked by the creation of numerous institutions and policies, finding optimum solutions for balancing environmental protection and economic growth, especially in the context of global inequality, remains difficult. It was noted that the main challenge in addressing environment–development problems has to do with the intricate and paradoxical relationship between economic growth and environmental degradation, as well as the fact that global environmental challenges are classic examples of the collective action problem. The chapter also highlights the roles of many other factors, such as ideological differences between the developed and developing countries about the role of the market in solving environmental challenges, the problem of agreeing what "sustainability" means in practice, and fundamental disagreements about how to resolve thorny issues of justice and fairness.

The above difficulties have been further illustrated by exploring the issue of climate change, which has been described as the greatest development challenge of the twenty-first century, with its impacts touching both present and future generations. The chapter shows that, despite wide acknowledgement of the need for urgent and organized response, the likelihood of achieving the level of co-operation required to ensure effective action remains in serious doubt. It is a huge "ask" for international politics, which is marked by power and self-interested calculations of states as well as by societal commitments to luxury and high levels of consumption, to respond to the radical changes in behaviour, structure, and systematic injustice required to address climate change. The chapter underscores the thesis that effective global governance of sustainable development appears to require radical changes in global values, as well as serious attention to questions of justice and fairness.

While there are edited volumes and books on different aspects of the link between environment and development, this chapter provides students with the insights and concepts required to understand and engage with a global debate that is fast evolving as a result of the challenges and choices presented by climate change. As the book at hand is essentially about international development approaches, actors, issues, and practice, this chapter has presented the ways in which development choices conflict with or support arrangements oriented towards environmental protection, climate management, and sustainable development.

QUESTIONS FOR CRITICAL THOUGHT

1. Is environmental degradation an inevitable consequence of economic growth?
2. Why is it so difficult for developed and developing countries to agree on just and equitable policies for the pursuit of global sustainable development?
3. What obligations, if any, do rich countries owe the poorer ones for the damages caused by climate change?
4. Discuss the relative impact of population, affluence, and technology on environmental pollution.

SUGGESTED READINGS

Adams, William M. 2009. *Green Development: Environment and Sustainability in a Developing World.* London and New York: Routledge.

Ehresman, Timothy G., and Chukwumerije Okereke. 2014. "International environmental justice and the quest for a green global economy: Introduction to special issue." *International Environmental Agreements: Politics, Law and Economics* 15, 1: 5–11.

Elliott, Lorraine M. 2004. *The Global Politics of the Environment.* London: Palgrave Macmillan.

Wilson, Gordon, Pamela Furniss, and Richard Kimbowa. 2010. *Environment, Development, and Sustainability: Perspectives and Cases from around the World.* Oxford: Oxford University Press.

World Bank. 2010. *World Development Report 2010.* Washington: World Bank.

BIBLIOGRAPHY

Acemoglu, D., and J. Robinson. 2012. *Why Nations Fail: The Origins of Power, Prosperity and Poverty.* New York: Crown Business.

Andonova, L.B., M.M. Betsill, and H. Bulkeley. 2009. "Transnational climate governance." *Global Environmental Politics* 9, 2: 52–73.

Bahadur, A.V., M. Ibrahim, and T. Tanner. 2013. "Characterising resilience: Unpacking the concept for tackling climate change and development." *Climate and Development* 5, 1: 55–65.

Bachram, H. 2004. "Climate fraud and carbon colonialism: The new trade in greenhouse gases." *Capitalism Nature Socialism* 15, 4: 5–20.

Bulkeley, H., and A. Jordan. 2012. "Transnational environmental governance: New findings and emerging research agendas." *Environment and Planning C: Government and Policy* 30, 4: 556–70.

———, and P. Newell. 2015. *Governing Climate Change.* London: Taylor & Francis.

Chambers, R. 2014. *Rural Development: Putting the Last First.* London: Routledge.

Chasek, P.S., D.L. Downie, and J. Brown. 2013. *Global Environmental Politics.* Boulder, Colo.: Westview Press.

Chatterjee, P., and M. Finger. 2014. *The Earth Brokers: Power, Politics and World Development.* London: Routledge.

Chow, G.C. 2015. *China's Economic Transformation.* New York: John Wiley & Sons.

DeFries, R.S., et al. 2012. "Planetary opportunities: A social contract for global change science to contribute to a sustainable future." *BioScience* 62m 6: 603–6.

Dietz, S., and E. Neumayer. 2007. "Weak and strong sustainability in the SEEA: Concepts and measurement." *Ecological Economics* 61, 4: 617–26.

Dietz, T., E.A. Rosa, and R. York. 2012. "Environmentally efficient well-being: Is there a Kuznets Curve?" *Applied Geography* 32, 1: 21–8.

Dodds, F. 2014. *Earth Summit 2002: A New Deal.* London: Routledge.

Dodds, F., M. Strauss, and M.F. Strong. 2012. *Only One Earth: The Long Road via Rio to Sustainable Development.* London: Routledge.

Dryzek, J.S. 2013. *The Politics of the Earth: Environmental Discourses.* Oxford: Oxford University Press.

Dunn, R. 2012. "In retrospect: Silent Spring." *Nature* 485, 7400: 578–9.

Economy, E.C. 2011. *The River Runs Black: The Environmental Challenge to China's Future*, 2nd edn. Ithaca, NY: Cornell University Press.

Egelston, A.E. 2013. *Sustainable Development.* Dordrecht: Springer Netherlands.

Ehresman, T.G., and C. Okereke. 2014. "International environmental justice and the quest for a green global economy: Introduction to special issue." *International Environmental Agreements: Politics, Law and Economics* 15, 1: 5–11.

Elah, M., and C. Okereke. 2014. "A neo-Gramscian account of carbon markets: The case of the European Union emissions trading scheme and the clean development mechanism." In B. Stephan and R. Lane, eds, *The Politics of Carbon Markets*. Routledge Series in Environmental Policy. London: Routledge, 113–32.

Epstein, M.J., and A. Rejc Buhovac. 2014. *Making Sustainability Work: Best Practices in Managing and Measuring Corporate Social, Environmental, and Economic Impacts*. San Francisco: Berrett-Koehler.

Escosura, L.P. de la. 2013. "World human development: 1870–2007." *Review of Income and Wealth* 61, 2: 240–7.

Ewing, B., and S.M. Rizk. 2008. "The Ecological Footprint Atlas 2008." *Global Footprint Network* (Dec.): 87.

Fuentes-Nieva, R., and I. Pereira. 2010. "The disconnect between indicators of sustainability and human development." Research Paper 2010/34. New York: UNDP.

Ghai, D., and J.M. Vivian. 2014. *Grassroots Environmental Action: People's Participation in Sustainable Development*. London: Routledge.

Gills, B.K. 2015. "Global development in the Anthropocene." *Globalizations* 12, 5.

Green, D. 2012. *From Poverty to Power: How Active Citizens and Effective States Can Change the World*, 2nd edn. London: Oxfam.

Hannigan, J. 2014. *Environmental Sociology*. London: Routledge.

Hardin, G. 1968. "The tragedy of the commons." *Science* 162, 3859: 1243–8.

Hargroves, K., and M.H. Smith. 2013. *The Natural Advantage of Nations: Business Opportunities, Innovation and Governance in the 21st Century*. London: Earthscan.

Hovi, J., O. Stokke, and G. Ulfstein. 2013. *Implementing the Climate Regime: International Compliance*. London: Earthscan.

Intergovernmental Panel on Climate Change. 2007. "An assessment of the Intergovernmental Panel on Climate Change," edited by R.K. Pachauri and A. Reisinger. *Change* 446 (Nov.): 12–17.

———. 2012. *Managing the Risks of Extreme Events and Disasters to Advance Climate Change Adaptation: Special Report of the Intergovernmental Panel on Climate Change*. Cambridge: Cambridge University Press.

———. 2014. *Climate Change 2014: Impacts, Adaptation, and Vulnerability*. Contribution of Working Group II to the *Fifth Assessment Report*. Cambridge: Cambridge University Press.

Kamal-Chaoui, L., and A. Robert. 2009. "Competitive cities and climate change." OECD Regional Working Papers.

Kjellstrom, T. 2015. "Impact of climate conditions on occupational health and related economic losses: A new feature of global and urban health in the context of climate change." *Asia Pacific Journal of Public Health*. 1010539514568711.

Korten, D. 2001. *When Corporations Rule the World*, 2nd edn. Bloomfield, Conn.: Kumarian Press.

Lafferty, W.M., and K. Eckerberg. 2013. *From the Earth Summit to Local Agenda 21: Working Towards Sustainable Development*. London: Routledge.

Leach, M., et al. 2012. "Transforming innovation for sustainability." *Ecology and Society* 17, 2.

Lewis, W.A. 2015. *The Evolution of the International Economic Order*. Princeton, NJ: Princeton University Press.

Liu, J., and J. Diamond. 2005. "China's environment in a globalizing world." *Nature* 435, 7046: 1179–86.

Liu, N. 2013. "Country Report: The People's Republic of China: Criticism levelled at China's revised environmental protection law." *IUCN Academy of Environmental Law eJournal*: 124–31.

Loh, J., et al. 2010. "The Living Planet Index." *The Royal Society* 360, 1454.

Luterbacher, U., and D. F. Sprinz. 2001. *International Relations and Global Climate Change*. Cambridge, Mass.: MIT Press.

Maplecroft (now Verisk Maplecroft). 2013. *Climate Change and Environmental Risk Atlas 2014*. http://maplecroft.com/portfolio/new-analysis/2013/10/30/31-global-economic-output-forecast-face-high-or-extreme-climate-change-risks-2025-maplecroft-risk-atlas/.

Meadows, D.H., D.L. Meadows, J. Randers, and W.W. Behrens. 1972. *The Limits to Growth*. New York.

Milanović, B. 2015. "Global inequality of opportunity: How much of our income is determined by where we live?" *Review of Economics and Statistics* 97, 2: 452–60.

Millennium Ecosystem Assessment. 2005. *Ecosystems and Human Well-Being: Synthesis*. Washington: World Resources Institute.

Mol, A.P.J. 2011. "China's ascent and Africa's environment." *Global Environmental Change* 21, 3: 785–94.

Nussbaumer, P. 2009. "On the contribution of labelled certified emission reductions to sustainable development: A multi-criteria evaluation of CDM projects." *Energy Policy* 37, 1: 91–101.

Okereke, C. 2008. *Global Justice and Neoliberal Environmental Governance: Sustainable Development, Ethics and International Co-operation*. London: Routledge

———. 2008. "Equity norms in global environmental governance." *Global Environmental Politics* 8, 3: 25–50.

———. 2010. "Climate justice and the international regime." *Wiley Interdisciplinary Reviews: Climate Change* 1, 3: 462–74.

———. and M. Charlesworth. 2014. "Environmental and ecological justice." In M. Betsil, K. Hochstetler, and S. Dimitris, eds, *Palgrave Advances in International Environmental Politics*. New York: Palgrave Macmillan, 123–47.

———. and H. Schroeder. 2009. "How can the objectives of justice, development and climate change mitigation be reconciled in the treatment of developing countries in a post-Kyoto settlement?" *Climate and Development* 1: 10–15.

———. and T. Yusuf. 2013. "Low carbon development and energy security in Africa.' In H. Dyer and M. Tombretta, eds, *Global Climate and Energy Security*. Surrey, UK: Edward Elgar, 462–82.

Ostrom, E. 1990. *Governing the Commons: The Evolution of Institutions for Collective Action*. Cambridge: Cambridge University Press.

Pachauri, R. K., et al. 2014. *Climate Change 2014: Synthesis Report. Contribution of Working Groups I, II and III to the Fifth Assessment Report of the Intergovernmental Panel on Climate Change*. Cambridge: Cambridge University Press.

Pearce, D. 2013. *Blueprint 2: Greening the World Economy*. London: Routledge.

Reid, D. 2013. *Sustainable Development: An Introductory Guide*. London: Taylor & Francis.

Robinson, W.C., D.H. Meadows, D.L. Meadows, J. Randers, and W.W. Behrens. 1973. "The Limits to Growth: A Report for the Club of Rome's Project on the Predicament of Mankind." *Demography* 10, 2: 289.

Rodrik, D. 2014. "The past, present, and future of economic growth." *Challenge* 57, 3: 5–39.

Rootes, C., ed. 2014. *Environmental Movements: Local, National and Global*. London: Routledge.

Santoro, M.A. 2015. *China 2020: How Western Business Can—and Should—Influence Social and Political Change in the Coming Decade*. Ithaca, NY: Cornell University Press.

Seppelt, R., C.F. Dormann, F.V. Eppink, S. Lautenbach, and S. Schmidt. 2011. "A quantitative review of ecosystem service studies: Approaches, shortcomings and the road ahead." *Journal of Applied Ecology* 48, 3: 630–6.

Stern, N. 2007. *The Economics of Climate Change: The Stern Review*. Cambridge: Cambridge University Press.

Stonich, S., P.C. Stern, N. Dolsak, T. Dietz, E. Ostrom, and E.U. Weber, eds. 2002. *The Drama of the Commons*. Washington: National Academies Press.

Takahashi, S. 2010. "Surviving modernization: State, community, and the environment in two Japanese fishing towns." Ph.D. dissertation, Rutgers University.

Tanner, T., and L. Horn-Phathanothai. 2014. *Climate Change and Development*. London: Routledge.

Wackernagel, M., et al. 1999. "National natural capital accounting with the ecological footprint concept." *Ecological Economics* 29, 3: 375–90.

Wilkinson, A., and D. Mangalagiu. 2012. "Learning with futures to realise progress towards sustainability: The WBCSD Vision 2050 Initiative." *Futures* 44, 4: 372–84.

World Bank. 2005. *World Resources 2005 : The Wealth of the Poor: Managing Ecosystem to Fight Poverty*. Washington: World Bank.

———. 2010. *Development and Climate Change*. Washington: World Bank.

World Commission on Environment and Development (WCED). 1987. *Our Common Future*. (Brundtland Report). Oxford and New York: Oxford University Press.

Xu, M., et al. 2014. "Spatiotemporal analysis of particulate air pollution and ischemic heart disease mortality in Beijing, China." *Environmental Health* 13, 1: 109.

Yang, S., Y. Bai, S. Wang, and N. Feng. 2013. "Evaluating the transformation of China's industrial development mode during 2000–2009." *Renewable and Sustainable Energy Reviews* 20: 585–94.

Zhang, J., H. Abbas, and P. Shishkin. 2012. "Delivering environmentally sustainable economic growth: The case of China." *Asia Society Policy* (Sept.).

18 Rural Development

Joshua J. Ramisch

LEARNING OBJECTIVES

- To understand and be able to explain the key features of "rurality."
- To use the "sustainable rural livelihoods" concept to understand agriculture in context and to critically assess claims made about smallholder households (e.g., as "rational," "tradition bound," or "multi-locational").
- To learn about and evaluate the paradigm shifts in thinking about rural development.
- To be able to distinguish between the "labour-rich" and "land rich" patterns of rural development and understand the importance of population pressure or other factors on innovation.
- To discover the principal challenges to rural development in the twenty-first century.

▲ **Hmong ethnic hilltribe families harvest rice on a terrace rice field in the northern mountainous province of Yen Bai, Vietnam. The local residents, mostly from the Hmong hill tribe, grow rice in the picturesque terrace fields, which have existed for several centuries. Because of hard farming conditions, locals produce only one rice crop per year.** | Source: HOANG DINH NAM/AFP/Getty Images

> *Agricultural development policies are unduly affected by urban, roadside, dry-season, male-based perceptions of rural life and its problems.*
>
> *Richards (1985: 156)*

INTRODUCTION

While agriculture remains the primary livelihood source for the rural poor (and particularly rural women), for the first time in human history the majority of us (54 per cent according to FAO figures in 2014) live in towns or cities and not in rural areas. Yet the global food crisis that flared in 2008—when food prices spiked and "food riots" challenged governments large and small—reminds us that the problems of rural poverty and agricultural development are far from being resolved (see Box 18.1). Indeed, most (70 per cent) of the world's population earning less than $1 per day is still "rural" (World Bank, 2015). This state of affairs will persist for many decades even with the present rates of urbanization, meaning that "rural development" will remain a crucial element of the developmental agenda long into the twenty-first century.

This chapter introduces the rural face of development in economic, social, and historical terms that reflect the incredible diversity and complexity of rural **livelihoods** and environments. Other recent reviews of rural development (e.g., Scoones, 2015; World Bank, 2007; Ashley and Maxwell, 2001) reaffirm its importance despite a history of failure or only ambiguous successes. Taking a global perspective on development processes that by definition differ according to their local contexts, the chapter begins by exploring the notion of "rurality" and its relevance, and considers the patterns of contemporary rural poverty in relation to past histories of rural transformation and evolving models for rural development. Particular attention is focused on the rise and fall of several important ideas, such as the emphasis on "small farms" or agriculture as the engine of rural development, the benefits and challenges of taking an **integrated approach** to rural problems, and the merits and limitations of **participatory approaches** to rural development.

Perhaps more than most fields of development studies, the history of rural development is tangled with internal contradictions and frustrations at unmet targets. While agriculture has served as the basis for growth and has reduced poverty in many countries, it is also true that livelihoods based largely on subsistence agriculture remain quite vulnerable and are frequently caught in vicious circles or "poverty traps," which are so widespread and enduring that rural poverty can appear inevitable (Ellis, 2000; Barrett et al., 2001). A caustic review almost 40 years ago at the height of interest in rural development noted that "rural development does not usually achieve its objectives" and "[b]y any criteria, successful projects have been the exception rather than the rule" (Williams, 1981: 16–17). Flows of overseas development assistance (ODA) targeting the rural sector stagnated in the early 1980s, then declined until 2007 at an average annual rate of 7 per cent (far steeper than the overall downward trend in ODA) (OECD, 2010: 1). Donor commitments since the 2008 food price crisis have increased agriculture's share of ODA to close to 9 per cent, but this is still much less than the 17 per cent share it held in the early 1980s (OECD, 2015: 1). Neither the Millennium Development Goals (MDGs) nor their Sustainable Development Goal (SDG) successors explicitly acknowledge rural poverty, which therefore fail to recognize where the poor live and how they make their living. The MDGs, for example, only addressed rural poverty indirectly, through targets relating to **food security**, natural resources, and the overall goal of halving poverty by 2015.

PUTTING THE "RURAL" IN CONTEXT

> *The village is the centre; you are peripheral (Indian village leaders' comment to development visitors).*
>
> *Chambers (1983: 46)*

To the development planner (or student), the twenty-first-century world of instant, electronic, global interconnectivity seems at first glance inherently distinct from the world of the peasant. A vast range of places that might be recognizable as "rural" includes farmlands, forests, savannas, pastoral rangelands, mountain villages, and mining or coastal communities. Yet the apparently "obvious" categorical divisions

BOX 18.1 | Global Food Crisis: 2008 and Beyond

CURRENT EVENTS

Through most of the twentieth century, global food production rose and food prices declined, leading many to assume we had entered an unending era of cheap food. However, in early 2008, as the price of oil rose from $70 to peak at $140 a barrel, the prices of most of the world's main agricultural commodities surged to historically unprecedented levels. The rising cost of food and fuel sparked widespread political protest, especially across Asia and Africa, and even led the Haitian prime minister to resign in April after "food riots" killed five people. Global attention to these violent outbursts led to an emergency High-Level Conference on World Food Security in June 2008, and the World Bank dedicated its 2008 World Report to "Agriculture for Development." Rural communities and farmers did not benefit from rising commodity prices—and often suffered greatly—because the costs of purchased inputs were also skyrocketing. The food crisis was overshadowed later in 2008 by the broader banking financial crisis and, for a time, many food prices stabilized or declined as demand fell. However, when prices spiked again in 2011, it was clear that many factors that contributed to the initial crisis remained in place. Critical scholars considered the ongoing crisis a consequence of increasing reliance on capital-intensive, high-input, globalized agriculture that puts pressure on soil, water, non-renewable energy sources, and land itself, with feedback from climate change, dietary changes, and population growth intensifying those pressures (Lang, 2010).

The 2008 food price crisis was clearly linked to suddenly rising oil prices, since globalized industrial agriculture not only uses fossil fuels to run farm machinery and transport crops to market but also transforms them into the fertilizers needed to grow crops intensively (Headey and Fan, 2008). A second factor was reduced global reserves of key commodities (wheat, maize, soybeans, and rice). At the time, many blamed economic growth in China and India for depleting these reserves, but in fact both countries' demand for foodstuffs was stable and self-sufficient over the period (Headey and Fan, 2008). Instead, the accumulated impacts of policy shifts in the Global North were more important, including policies to reduce agricultural overproduction (e.g., reductions in subsidies and environmental conservation programs) and to increase agricultural demand (e.g., initiatives in the US and EU to promote biofuel production from food crops) (Piesse and Thirtle, 2009). Critical outcry about the food security impact of these latter policies has seen biofuel production shift to non-food crops (although see Box 18.4).

A final cause was seasonal or longer-term crop failures in important growing regions (e.g., Australia, Ukraine, and Canada for wheat; Thailand for rice). Global climate change appears to be increasing the variability of production in many of these regions, even as the genetic diversity and water resources that support this production are stretched to their limits.

between "rural" and "urban" (or "local" and "global") may actually be quite ambiguous.

National statistical services distinguish urban populations from rural ones by threshold levels: an urban area must typically contain a certain non-agricultural production base and also a minimum population level or density per square kilometre. Within such frameworks, rural areas therefore become a catch-all defined against the urban: the "not-urban." Conceptualizing "rural" this way is problematic on two counts. First, the thresholds vary considerably between countries and regions: towns as large as 15,000 are considered "rural" in India, while in Honduras the threshold is a settlement of 150 people. This makes aggregated, global comparisons of "rural" data (on poverty or productivity, for example) problematic, although many institutions like the World Bank and Food and Agriculture Organization (FAO) do not hesitate to present aggregated numbers as if "rural" meant the same thing in all places. Second, the diversity of livelihoods found in rural areas (including petty commerce, "cottage" industry or artisanal production, and seasonal or long-term migrations to cities, factories, mines, or ports) blurs the notion that certain activities, or residential patterns, can actually or meaningfully distinguish the "urban" from the "not-urban" (McDowell and de Haan, 1997).

Beyond the logic of national statistical services, we can distinguish at least four enduring, material features of "rurality":

1. A *relative abundance of natural capital* (land, water, soil, trees, wildlife, and other natural resources) and therefore a dependence on (and vulnerability to) the unpredictable elements of the natural environment, including drought or flooding, pests and diseases, and global climate change.
2. A *relative abundance of labour*, which is often structured and negotiated at the household level on the basis of gender and age (e.g., household tasks and the care of crops are often conceptually divided into duties done only by men, by women, or by children). Seasonal or prolonged out-migration of the fittest labourers is often widespread and may adversely affect the quality of the labour actually available in rural areas, particularly at "bottlenecks" of high labour demand in the rural calendar, such as land cultivation, planting, weeding, and harvesting.
3. A *relative isolation* (because of remoteness, internal distances, or the general lack of infrastructure) that translates into a relatively high cost of movement and a relatively limited ability to participate in or influence national politics. As will be discussed, although the lack of infrastructure is a direct result of political indifference or neglect by central authorities, the urbanite's image of rural "isolation" is often much stronger than the reality.
4. A *relative importance of social factors* in stratifying or structuring access to resources that may be equal to or greater than the importance of

Joshua Ramisch

PHOTO 18.1 | A recognizably "rural" landscape of Indonesia, featuring intensively managed rice fields, irrigation networks, family homes, and a reliance on an overwhelmingly female labour force.

market-based mechanisms (if these exist at all). Examples include the likely coexistence of multiple (formal and informal) land tenure regimes (e.g., governing access to farmland, water, fuel wood, pasture rights), the prevalence of reciprocity in social networks (based on kinship, ethnicity, religion, or other groupings), and obligations in hierarchical relationships (such as between elders and younger generations, "native" and "migrant" populations, men and women, "big men" leaders and their "clients," to name just a few).

Each of these features can be challenged and obviously may not be true in all rural places or all time periods. Furthermore, they should not be accepted as politically neutral "facts," unrelated to the urban characteristics against which they are defined. For example, the extractive flow of capital and labour *out* of rural areas to urban areas often sustains the perceived "isolation" or "underdevelopment" of rural areas. Ashley and Maxwell (2001: 407) also point out that rural areas, even ones of great poverty and apparent marginalization, often have much greater income diversity, stronger rural–urban links, and longer-standing interactions with the world economy than is normally assumed. Most of the rural world was transformed, often violently and radically, by the colonial networks of resource exploitation that spanned the globe from the sixteenth to the twentieth centuries (see Chapter 2). Thus, while development planners might imagine that "remote" parts of the world (e.g., much of rural sub-Saharan Africa) would benefit from "linking farmers to markets," these areas have been incorporated into global markets for labour or commodities for centuries, albeit on very unfair and unequal terms (Ferguson, 1994).

Worldwide, rural contexts can be distinguished on the basis of the relative importance of agriculture in GDP growth and the relative levels of rural poverty. In many countries, the rise of national incomes has seen agriculture's share of GDP and labour decline, although these patterns clearly vary according to local contexts and histories. Nonetheless, this apparent process of structural transformation informs much current thinking about the nature of the "rural" economy, such as the categorization of three different "rural worlds" found in the *2008 World Development Report: Agriculture for Development* (World Bank, 2007) (Table 18.1):

- **Agriculture-based countries**, where the contribution of agriculture to overall GDP growth is greater than 20 per cent and where rural poverty accounts for at least 60 per cent of all the people living on less than $1.08 per day. Most countries in this category are found in sub-Saharan Africa.

TABLE 18.1 | Characteristics of the Three "Rural Worlds" in the *2008 World Development Report*

	Agriculture-based countries (*n* = 31)	Transforming countries (*n* = 25)	Urbanized countries (*n* = 18)
Rural population (millions), 2005	417	2,220	255
Rural share of population (%), 2005	68	63	26
GDP per capita (2000 US$)	379	1,068	3,489
Agriculture share of GDP (%)	29	13	6
Annual agricultural GDP growth, 1993–2005 (%)	4.0	2.9	2.2
Annual non-agricultural GDP growth, 1993–2005 (%)	3.5	7.0	2.7
Number of rural poor (millions), 2002*	170	592	32
Rural poverty rate, 2002 (%)*	51	28	13

Note: Averages are weighted and based on 74 countries with at least 5 million people.

*Poverty rate is $1.08/day.

Source: Adapted from World Bank (2008). *World Development Report 2008: Agriculture for Development*. Washington: World Bank. At: go.worldbank.org/ZJIAOSUFUO.

- **Transforming countries,** where agriculture is no longer a major contributor to economic growth (less than 25 per cent of overall GDP growth) but rural poverty remains widespread (at least 60 per cent of total poverty). Most of the world's rural poor—2.2 billion people in 2005—are actually now found in "transforming" countries, including India, China, Indonesia, Morocco, and Thailand. This category includes most of East and South Asia, the Pacific, the Middle East, and North Africa.
- **Urbanized countries,** where rural poverty accounts for less than 60 per cent of overall poverty and agriculture contributes to less than 20 per cent of overall GDP growth. This category includes most countries of Latin America, the Caribbean, Eastern Europe, and Central Asia.

The *2008 World Development Report* presents these categories as part of an evolutionary, modernization-style model, tracking the progress of countries such as China and India from "agriculture-based" to "transforming" or Indonesia from "transforming" to "urbanized" over the 1993–2005 study period. The *Report* assumes that commercial agriculture and off-farm or urban employment will eventually drive growth across all three "rural worlds," and rather optimistically dismisses the many deviations from this model simply as "idiosyncrasies" (World Bank, 2007: 28). However, a dominant theme to be lauded in the *Report* is that heterogeneity does exist between and within countries. For example, even in a strongly "transforming" country like India or an "urbanized" country like Mexico, sub-national regions such as the state of Bihar in India and Chiapas state in Mexico remain strongly agrarian in orientation. This internal heterogeneity has important implications for equity and future rural development and change.

Defining rural areas purely on the basis of spatial or economic features, of course, privileges the knowledge and priorities of urban-based elites. The rural that is "recognizable" to rural inhabitants, in fact, may be based much more on social or cultural attributes: the types of communities and relationships, the crops or animals raised, and the foods consumed. Whereas economic responses to hunger and food insecurity would focus on increasing crop production, the rural solutions might be social, calling on potential reciprocity within social networks to acquire food in times of need (see Box 18.2).

"Peasant" societies, for example, are rural cultures highly reliant on local production, where the distribution of wealth and power at a local level is affected by contact with a nation-state. Such societies are typically highly structured and stratified as a result of that contact, especially on the basis of who owns or controls access to the fundamental resources (land and labour). These hierarchical structures (of landlords, chiefs, or local administrators) are reinforced by cultural, economic, gendered, religious, or cosmological systems and technologies.

Despite such commonalities of structure, peasant societies are complex and varied and have adapted and evolved over centuries around the world as one of the dominant forms of human organization. The resilience of peasant societies (and smallholders more generally) is now well documented, and the contribution of that understanding to rural development theory and practice will be discussed in various forms below. Nonetheless, many of the inherited structural constraints of unjust social orders are overlooked in the *ideal* image of the rural. As a result, the "tradition-bound, conservative peasant" is an image still regularly invoked and looked down upon by leaders and planners or chastised by revolutionaries for not throwing off the yoke of oppressive landlords or village chiefs. To begin to get a sense of the potential that local knowledge and experience can offer rural development, we now consider how rural change has been shaped in various parts of the world.

RURAL TRANSFORMATIONS

Societal Perspectives on Rural Transformation

Contemporary rural development interventions are only the latest forces restructuring rural landscapes and communities. The industrial revolutions that swept the temperate world, from England beginning in the mid-eighteenth century to Japan in the late nineteenth century, were preceded and fuelled by agricultural growth. In previous centuries, the lack of rural opportunities (experienced as rural poverty and misery) had sparked peasant rebellions and uprisings from

CRITICAL ISSUES

BOX 18.2 | Rural Livelihoods and Diversification

A "livelihood" as a whole represents "the capabilities, assets (including both material and social resources) and activities required for a means of living. A livelihood is sustainable when it can cope with and recover from stresses and shocks, maintain or enhance its capabilities and assets, while not undermining the natural resource base" (Scoones, 1998: 5). The concept of sustainable livelihoods is particularly relevant to the rural context, where, for example, the seasonal fluctuations of climate drive the viability of different activities within an agricultural calendar and oblige individuals and households to consider multiple strategies if they are to exploit their environment and flourish.

Livelihood analysis considers how different types of *capital* (financial, natural, social, human, or physical) are combined in a particular *context* (of policy settings, politics, history, agro-ecology, or socio-economic conditions). Different *livelihood strategies* (agricultural intensification or extensification, diversification, or migration), therefore, can be pursued depending on the mediation of *institutional processes* (the matrix of formal or informal institutions or social organizations, such as land tenure or inheritance patterns).

For example, in rural western Kenya a household reported meeting its needs (for food security, school fees, medical services, and funeral expenses) over a six-month period using a range of agricultural and non-agricultural livelihood strategies: cultivating maize and beans (staple crops), cassava (long-term crop), and tea (cash crop) on their own farm; "borrowing" food, fruit, and milk from relatives; growing and selling vegetables; selling firewood; pension money from a retired railway employee; working for day wages and a cooked lunch on neighbours' farms at planting, weeding, and harvest seasons; working as "casual labour" for local woodcutters; selling handicrafts sewn at home; and searching for work as a watchman or bicycle taxi driver in a nearby town (Ramisch and Akech, 2005, unpublished data).

Such strategies represent a combination of *coping* mechanisms to address immediate hardships as well as longer-term *adaptations* (e.g., migration of one or more family members to town in search of work) to adjust to changing conditions or crises and to reduce vulnerability or poverty. Population growth, urbanization, education, global climatic change, and structural adjustment have all called into play a diversity of activities geared towards making a secure livelihood.

the time of the Roman Empire, through medieval Europe and feudal Asia, colonial Latin America and the Caribbean, South and Southeast Asia, and Africa (see Box 18.3). Finally, throughout history colonial powers have exploited the rural sector for resources, stepping up pressure in times of economic hardship to maintain the revenue flow (e.g., the French in West Africa during the 1930s, or the British in India in the 1880s and during Ireland's potato famine in the 1840s).

Although a nation's successful rural development is tied to the opportunities and constraints of its historical context, many scholars have been inspired to use the histories of currently industrialized societies as models. Two countries are often chosen, since their contrasting factor endowments parallel the extremes that still frame much present-day rural poverty: Japan (portrayed as "labour-rich" but with limited land resources) and the United States (portrayed as "land-rich" but with scarce labour until the early twentieth century) (Hayami and Ruttan, 1985; Tomich et al., 1995).

Rural Development in Japan: Intensification

Japan's experience during the Meiji restoration period (1868–1920) was framed by a limited land base and an abundant rural population. New land could not be brought into production because Japan was a fully

IMPORTANT CONCEPTS

BOX 18.3 | Land Tenure and Inequality

Although an agricultural landscape may appear full of "farmers," increasing numbers of the rural poor do not own the land they work on. Land tenure, or the security with which individuals, households, or communities have access to land, is regulated both by customary (traditional norms and practices) and formal legal frameworks. Rights to land range from "usufruct" (use-rights such as cultivation, tree-planting or cutting, grazing, house-building, or drawing water) through to the rights of full "ownership" (e.g., to sell, subdivide, or bequeath land as an inheritance). Many resources crucial to rural livelihoods (such as fisheries, pastures, or seasonal watering points) are managed as "common property" by complex, customary social arrangements that regulate conflicting use-rights.

The complexity of land tenure regimes often also means that the inequality in landownership and use-rights is deeply entrenched. Women in many societies have been excluded from formal land rights, and rely much more than men on informal and customary access to common property resources. In much of Latin America one's position as landlord or tenant farmer is effectively hereditary, while access to land in Africa or Asia is also often structured by long histories of ethnic, caste-based, or racialized power structures. The demand for land reform, to break up large farms or plantations for the benefit of the landless, has fuelled national revolutions (e.g., in Mexico or China) and social movements (e.g., Brazil's contemporary Landless Workers' Movement [MST]). Land reform is hard to achieve if it does not address the underlying power structures. The efforts to redistribute previously white-owned land in post-apartheid South Africa confronted the reality that many landless black households did not have sufficient labour available for farming, and did not have the financial resources either to cope with agricultural risk or even to relocate to the newly freed land (Zimmerman, 2000).

With the emphasis on the rationality of "small farmers" (see below), many rural development projects also have assumed that granting formal legal title to land is essential to securing land rights and creating a land market. Yet, a vast literature shows that simply replacing customary regimes with legal title does not necessarily increase security or willingness to invest in agriculture. For example, in Honduras (Jansen and Roquas, 1998), the land-titling process actually increased conflicts over land, as holders of some customary rights were favoured over others, state intervention in the local community increased to solve conflicts, and conflicts effectively suppressed any potential land market.

settled island nation, and so agricultural production and the rural economy grew over this period through **agricultural intensification**, increasing the overall crop output of the land by increasing inputs of labour, capital, knowledge, and technological resources. Highlights of the Japanese experience include the following:

- Overall production was improved by farmers working relatively small pieces of land (0.5–2.0 hectares), not by industrial agriculture. The smallholder-led strategy focused on improved varieties of the staple crop (rice), increasing reliance on inorganic fertilizers, and increased use of irrigation to manage and regulate water supply.
- As rice production increased, non-farm income opportunities also expanded in the small towns dotting the countryside, maintaining a low degree of inequality in income and lifestyle between rural and urban areas or within rural communities themselves.
- Success depended on the strong collaboration of the leadership and resources of the national government and a national research and extension system to promote the latest scientific knowledge.

- Meiji leaders were under intense external pressure to "modernize" their society by opening up to the outside world as producers and consumers of global goods, a pressure that has been exerted on states gaining independence from colonialism through to the present day forces of globalization.

Seemingly unique aspects of the Japanese experience could be barriers to reproducing this success story in contemporary land-scarce contexts. These include the relative homogeneity of Japanese society (a common language, traditions, and ethnic heritage) and the now-mythologized perception of the enlightened and progressive "vision" of the Meiji leaders. The reality is that more than 200 peasant uprisings, four samurai revolts, and significant internal discord within the government severely constrained the "free hand" that the Meiji rulers supposedly used to reshape their nation (Tomich et al., 1995: 99). Their strongly nationalist desire to industrialize rapidly was matched by an awareness that a growing economy would enrich them, too, and not simply serve the public good. In other words, the policies that effectively stimulated agriculture and the rural non-farm economy appear to represent a happy convergence of factors that might just as easily have led to corruption, rent-seeking, and stagnation.

Rural Development in the US: Extensification

Compared to Japan, the United States had abundant and cheap land but relatively scarce and expensive labour. This meant overall output was increased through agricultural extensification—by expanding the areas cultivated. The following factors were important to the American experience:

- Fertilizers were not a significant input in American agriculture until the 1930s. Before this point, the incentive to intensively manage soil fertility in a given piece of land was outweighed in nearly all locations by the ease with which new, fallow land could be put into cultivation.
- For most of the nineteenth century, agricultural policy was aimed at opening up "virgin" land and creating new family farms, which relied heavily on the household labour (and draft animals) of the settlers themselves.
- Expanding the transportation network was the greatest stimulus to rural development in the interior. Navigable rivers and canals were important in the Northeast and Upper Mississippi, but railroads were the most crucial link between the expanding areas of settler agriculture and the growing urban markets back in the East.

Lessons drawn from the experience of the United States are typically considered most relevant to the African context. For example, Wood (2002) argues that an increasingly prosperous Africa could be "more like America" than land-scarce regions such as Asia and Europe. Since Africa, like the Americas, is land-rich in relation to its population, its primary (rural, agricultural) sector will tend to predominate over its manufacturing sector. With the bulk of its land mass far from the sea and without major navigable waterways, internal transport costs are comparatively higher. This also leads Wood to conclude that a prosperous Africa will have urban, industrial concentrations along its coasts and a less densely settled interior, dominated by agriculture and mining (see Box 18.4).

Cultural and Technological Perspectives on Rural Transformation

To understand the full range of experiences of rural transformation, it is illuminating to consider local patterns of rural technological change. The work of the Danish economist Ester Boserup (1965, 1981) is one of the most comprehensive and useful frameworks for understanding smallholder adaptations cross-culturally. Before Boserup, models of rural transformation assumed that technology was the primary (if not the only) engine of agricultural change. Progress was the ability to command larger sources of energy, and the smallholder in such scenarios was inevitably doomed to obsolescence because human labour would eventually be replaced by draught animals, mechanical power, and fossil fuels (Netting, 1993: 270). Boserup's emphasis on relationships among population density, technological change, agricultural intensification, and markets is of particular value, since these relationships are not presented as part of an evolutionary model of

BOX 18.4 | The Global "Land Rush" CURRENT EVENTS

In the wake of the 2008 food crisis, many countries reconsidered their own food security situation. One response that drew international attention (and criticism) was a rush by foreign companies to acquire large areas of farmland in Africa, Latin America, and Central and Southeast Asia for producing food and biofuel crops for export. When a South Korean company (Daewoo Logistics) tried to lease 1.3 million hectares in Madagascar for growing maize and oil palm for Korean markets, the resulting street protests ultimately overthrew the government in early 2009. The new president, Andry Rajoelina, declared the Daewoo deal dead but the incident drew international attention to similar "land grabs" being proposed across the Global South (Cotula et al., 2009).

Media and activists framed these as "land grabs" since investors from high- and middle-income countries appeared to target low-income countries with abundant land and weak governance. Such leases are typically justified as opportunities for foreign investors to put "underutilized" land to more productive, commercial use through plantation-style agriculture, echoing colonial language and practices. Local and international critics point to disruptive impacts on livelihoods and marginal environments, the high risk of corruption, and the minimal contributions of foreign-owned exports on domestic economies.

While the pace of these types of investments has accelerated since 2004, it is difficult to assess their actual scale, which is cited as anywhere between 15 and 203 million hectares globally since 2000 (Schoneveld, 2014: 34). Many deals are announced quite publicly but never materialize, while potentially more disruptive land-grabbing by domestic elites does not attract the same international attention. Schoneveld's review (2014) of 563 deals in Africa counters the dominant narrative that Chinese or Gulf States' hunger for farmland is driving the "land rush," finding that the majority of investors are from North America and Europe, interested in biofuel rather than food production. Nonetheless, with rural livelihoods and food security already at stake, the added pressure of international capital—whether from new or traditional sources—looking for investment opportunities is a new challenge.

stages or "progressive" change. As such, she breaks with the more rigid formulations suggested by Thomas Malthus and Karl Marx.

Boserup's hypothesis is that an increase in population density is an independent variable sufficient to trigger agricultural intensification and the technical innovations needed to support it. More labour-intensive technologies—such as replacing natural fallows with the spreading of animal manure as a means of improving soil fertility, or replacing digging sticks with hand hoes, ox ploughs, or tractors for cultivation and planting—are only sensibly developed and adopted in the face of the scarcity induced by population pressure. This "pressure" may be due to a population's natural increase, the influx of migrants, or land degradation that reduces the amount of usable land. This relationship between rural population density and agricultural intensification helps to explain why it is not some innate "conservatism" on the part of rural dwellers but rather an entirely rational choice that would keep farmers from adopting the ploughs or purchasing pesticides used by their neighbours in more densely settled landscapes or promoted by an "enlightened" extension agent (Netting, 1993: 263). It also explains why a context of out-migration or other population decreases could rationally lead smallholders to abandon labour-intensive soil conservation methods or to return to "older" methods of land clearance such as burning, even if farmers are aware of more "modern" techniques.

Originally developed from observations of Asian and European smallholder farming systems, Boserup's expected patterns of agricultural intensification have since been validated when applied to population densities in a range of conditions and time periods (see Turner et al., 1993, for Africa). Successful intensification also may be "induced" by forces other than land shortage, such as policy changes or the improvement of infrastructure and better access to markets (Boserup, 1981). These more sophisticated models show how the benefits of intensification may be hindered or missed altogether if not supported by policy, credit and infrastructure development, or access to growing markets.

Malthus, Marx, and Boserup understood the systematic interaction of population, environment (land), and technology (agricultural methods) in different ways. For Malthus in early nineteenth-century Europe, land was the ultimate constraint against population growth. He acknowledged that exogenous technological changes could improve food production (and thus general welfare) but did not see any instances in which such innovations were anything more than random, and certainly not in response to population pressures (Netting, 1993: 278). Marx, on the other hand, concluded that economic growth is powered by exogenous technological change. He saw these changes as guided by the interests of landowners, not rural population density, with greater intensification supporting the extraction of surplus value from the labour of agricultural workers. In contrast, Boserup shows how population growth drives technological innovation and agricultural intensification that can significantly increase the productive potential of a fixed piece of land so that it keeps pace with (or even exceeds) population growth.

MODELS

As the history of rural change suggests, there is no shortage of models or potential ideas about rural development. Since World War II, thinking about rural development has undergone two key paradigm shifts (Ellis and Biggs, 2001). Before the mid-1960s the dominant belief held that smallholder "peasant" agriculture was inherently inefficient and therefore destined to be replaced by more modern forms. The first shift was based on evidence that saw smallholders were "inherently rational" and actually a potential driving force for increased efficiency and productivity. The second shift, in the late 1980s, was from top-down rural development led by national-level policies and the "blueprint" transfer of technologies, towards efforts to make rural development more "participatory," led or at least more controlled by the rural communities themselves at the grassroots.

In the 1950s, the "two-sector" theory of development assumed the small-farm subsistence sector had to be replaced by "modern" activities. This view was exemplified by Sir Arthur Lewis (1954), who postulated that low productivity subsistence agriculture offers a potentially "unlimited supply" of surplus labour that could be attracted to higher-wage activities. The "traditional" sector would therefore eventually vanish as it supplied labour and land resources to "modern" sectors in towns or in industrial agriculture, commercial plantations, or ranches.

The catalyst for the first paradigm shift came with the publication of *Transforming Traditional Agriculture* (Schultz, 1964), which drew lessons from emerging experience in Asia where agriculture took a lead role in economic growth. T.W. Schultz's central proposition was that "traditional" small farmers in fact allocated their limited resources rationally and more efficiently than large-scale farmers, and therefore could lead rural development if given additional resources. This new perspective suggested an emerging industrial sector would be supported by the agricultural contributions of labour, capital, food, foreign exchange (from export crops), and markets for consumer goods. In effect, if it could be shown that the "rural poor" were also "small farmers," growth and equity concerns could be addressed in a single, pro-smallholder, pro-agriculture strategy of rural development—an apparent "win-win" situation.

Such ideas have been incredibly powerful, motivating practitioners of "integrated" rural development and the Green Revolution's pioneers (as well as their successive generations of critics) to see their work as focused on improving the efficiency of smallholders with technologies "appropriate" to their conditions (see Chapter 22). Schultz's ideas continue to hold sway, as in International Fund for Agricultural Development (IFAD) reviews of global data that show the agricultural productivity of "small" farms to be at least twice that of "large" farms in settings as diverse as Colombia, Brazil, India, and Malaysia (IFAD, 2001: 79). The greater productivity of smallholder farmers is attributed to more intensive use of labour and land, particularly in growing higher-value mixes of crops, intercropping, and leaving less land fallow.

The second paradigm shift, towards more "participatory" models of rural development, has also gained broad acceptance since the late 1980s so that it is now used everywhere, from the World Bank to the most radical grassroots NGOs. This shift resulted in part from the perceived failures of large, state-led "integrated rural development" projects in the 1970s and 1980s, when NGOs with alternative models began to enter the spaces created by retreating states. Of course, the disengagement of states from "top-down" rural development projects was further encouraged by international financial and donor actors through structural adjustment (see Chapters 3 and 9).

Figure 18.1 presents a very simplified overview of the evolution of ideas and modes of thinking about rural development over the past half-century. Note that the dominant ideas of a given time period may have taken 10 to 15 years to fully spread from academic circles to policy arenas and practical action, while many minority or dissenting theories and orientations have simmered (or boiled) underneath, even up to the present.

Community Development

The "community development" approach of the 1950s derived from both British experience in "preparing" India for independence in the 1940s and the domestic policy of the United States in the 1930s. Community development then became the guiding logic of American development assistance—primarily in Asia, where rural development was seen as a powerful antidote to communist agrarian movements—and of the United Nations system.

Community development was defined as a process, program, and/or movement involving communities in teaching democratic processes and facilitating transfer of technology to a community for more effective solution of its problems (Holdcroft, 1976: 1–3). The "rural reconstruction" movement in pre-independence India had demonstrated that rural people would take initiative when they realized that they would benefit from community-wide efforts. From these roots, community development programs were assumed to have universal relevance as part of a democratic social movement embracing the idea of a balanced, integrated development of the whole of community life.

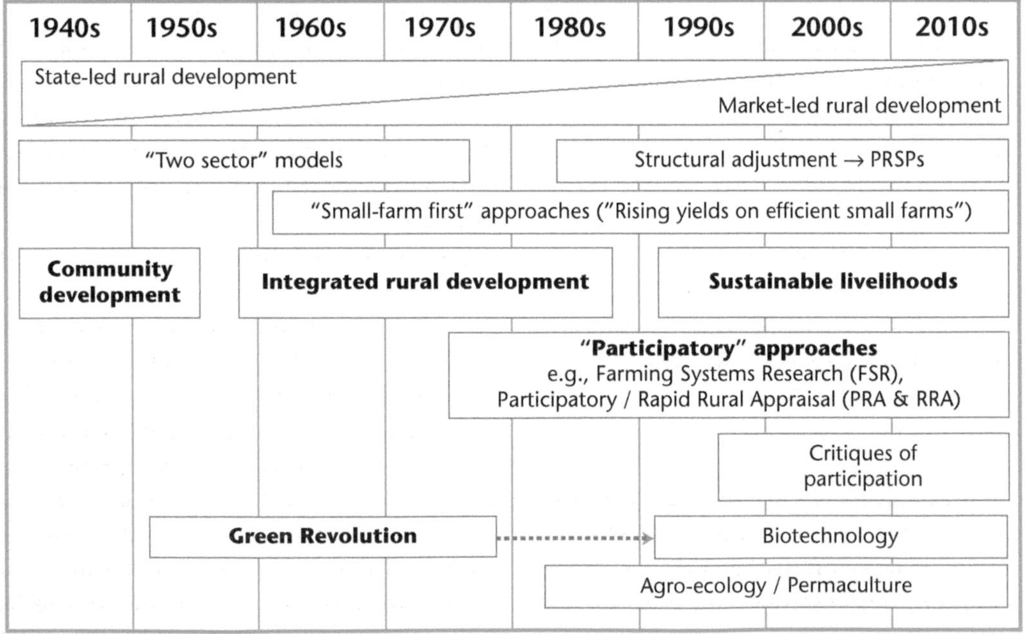

FIGURE 18.1 | Timeline of Dominant Ideas in Rural Development

Source: Adapted and updated from Ellis and Biggs (2001: 439, 442).

The approach flourished through the 1950s, and (as we shall see) has much in common with present-day "sustainable livelihoods" approaches that emphasize a holistic development that is locally "owned" and responds to "felt needs." The approach relied heavily on specially trained civil servants (e.g., "multi-purpose village workers" in India), who would be accountable to and working on behalf of both the local communities and the national governments to facilitate the community development process. This usually spawned a large bureaucracy at the national, regional, and local levels to support and co-ordinate the efforts of technical ministries such as agriculture, education, and health. Given the complexity of co-ordination, community development practitioners increasingly stressed the unique contribution of their own subject matter (e.g., agricultural production, co-operative development, local government, rural education, rural health, social welfare, development economics) while believing that any shortcomings arose from inadequate support from other subject matter areas.

By the mid-1950s, community development programs had become institutionalized standard "models." The price of this oversimplification and standardization was that by the 1960s, most programs were not reaching their stated targets for rural poverty alleviation or food security. As these supposedly universal models contended with local realities, the (usually expatriate) community development specialists' ideals and social scientific perspectives often ran against the interests of the national technical specialists (particularly in agriculture). These tensions were resolved mainly in favour of the more bureaucratically established technical services personnel, to the extent that by 1965 many host-country "development" ministries were absorbed into the more disciplinarily focused ministries of the interior or of agriculture (Holdcroft, 1976: 28).

Integrated Rural Development

The decline of the community development approach fed into two contrasting strains of thought. On the one hand, it led to the emerging emphasis on small-farm growth and agricultural improvement through Green Revolution technologies (see Box 18.5). On the other hand, its lingering influence brought about renewed efforts to promote balanced rural development through even larger-scale "integrated rural development" (IRD) projects, supported by multilateral institutions.

By the late 1960s, the context of rural development had evolved from the community era. Many more countries (particularly in Africa) were newly independent from colonialism and were contending with increasing economic inequality even as the bulk of poverty remained rural. The IRD approach attempted to revive and build on community development while incorporating the new ideas of small-farm efficiency, promoting balanced development strategies that would target all regions of a country instead of relying on urban, industrial growth as the engine of the national economy. The comprehensive nature of IRD strategies also reflected free-market efforts to mirror China's apparent success during the same period in improving production and consumption through rural collectivization.

The appeal of IRD to the World Bank, its greatest proponent, was that the results promised by projects integrated with each other would theoretically outweigh the results of projects implemented on a piecemeal basis. For example, investment in an irrigation system could be combined with improvement of local roads so that surplus agricultural produce could reach other markets. However, the large-scale nature of these projects and the consequently large budgets made them ripe targets for political manipulation as prizes to be shared among governments, donors, and contractors (Ferguson, 1994). Thus, the selection of target locations for IRD projects would become highly political. Leaders with vested interests could divert development funds away from the areas in greatest need, reinforcing existing power structures and inequalities rather than overcoming them.

In general, despite strong donor support, IRD in the 1970s and 1980s had only mixed results. The most common criticisms focused on the projects' top-down nature, supply-driven approach to technical assistance, and heavy, unsustainable, project-specific management structures. While many IRD projects were designed to be replicated elsewhere if successful, most floundered because of numerous obstacles, including fiscal constraints, the shortage of personnel with the appropriate interdisciplinary expertise, and regional differences (e.g., cultural, social, organizational, and administrative) between the pilot and replication sites.

CRITICAL ISSUES

BOX 18.5 | The Green Revolution

> *These and other developments in the field of agriculture contain the makings of a new revolution. It is not a violent Red Revolution like that of the Soviets, nor is it a White Revolution like that of the Shah of Iran. I call it the Green Revolution.*
>
> *(William Gaud,* USAID *director, 1968)*

The so-called Green Revolution of improved crop varieties, fertilizer, and irrigation technologies that transformed South Asia from a famine-prone, food-insecure region into a net exporter of foodstuffs between the mid-1960s and the 1980s is often presented as the greatest success of rural development, if not of agricultural research generally. Many of the plant breeders and agronomists who developed and promoted high-yielding varieties (HYVs) of such staple crops as wheat and rice became household names. Among these leaders in the Green Revolution was Norman Borlaug, who developed disease-resistant, high-yielding varieties of wheat and subsequently won the Nobel Peace Prize in 1970. Innovation continues in plant breeding (and now also in biotechnological methods), broadening the range of crops for which HYVs have been developed and selected for improved drought or pest resistance or tolerance of salinity, soil acidity, or low fertility conditions.

HYVs significantly outperform traditional varieties in the presence of adequate irrigation, pesticides, and fertilizers. In the absence of these inputs (e.g., under the prevailing conditions of most resource-poor farmers), traditional varieties may outperform HYVs. A further criticism of HYVs is that, genetically, they are hybrids, meaning they need to be purchased by a farmer every season rather than saved as seed from the previous season's crop, thus increasing a farmer's production costs. Alternative strategies like agro-ecology or permaculture attempt to intensify production in environmentally and socially sustainable manners by mimicking natural ecosystems (Altieri, 1995), but are faulted by Green Revolution adherents as too labour- and knowledge-intensive to support the demands of current populations and lifestyles (Collier 2008).

Decades later, the Green Revolution remains polarizing: critics argue that increasing production without considering social contexts is both environmentally and socially unsustainable (Patel, 2013). While Green Revolution advocates claim that HYVs have allowed more farmers to grow more food without needing to clear forested lands, such impacts are difficult to measure in practice since increased productivity creates opportunities for landowners to expand their cultivation, forcing less productive farmers to relocate elsewhere. Critics also note negative environmental consequences of increased reliance on commercial fertilizers, the breakdown of soils under continuous cropping, contamination of groundwater, and the loss of biodiversity as HYVs displace local varieties (Shiva, 1991).

Participatory Rural Appraisal

Unlike the grand schemes for rural change promoted by community development or IRD, "participatory rural appraisal" (PRA) is more of a conceptual framework for rural development in the South that stresses putting "farmers first" and "handing over the stick" of control to local communities. An approach popularized by Robert Chambers (1983), it grew out of holistic research traditions such as farming systems research (FSR) and rapid rural appraisal (RRA) to reflect critically on the failure of most rural development programs in the 1970s and 1980s to substantially improve rural livelihoods in large parts of the South.

The assumption is that top-down planning without the adequate involvement of concerned stakeholders

Joshua Ramisch

PHOTO 18.2 | Integrated rural development programs emphasized the export of cash crops as a means for "agriculture-based" or "transforming" countries to derive significant foreign currency earnings. Such dependence on cash crops is still widespread even as commodity prices have declined. Leading cash crops include tea (shown here in Kenya), coffee, cotton, sugar, tobacco, cut flowers, fruits (bananas, oranges), oil palm, spices, and vegetables such as French beans and snow peas.

(especially local people) was one of the core reasons for the failure of previous approaches. The PRA paradigm seeks to incorporate local communities in analyzing, planning, and implementing their own development programs. The key to PRA, which Chambers (1983) repeatedly emphasized and which stands in contrast to the earlier community development approach, is that "experts" must change their paternalistic attitudes towards local people: facilitating change without dominating local processes. While PRA is a family of approaches, methods, and behaviours, rather than a single method, it is now part of standard practice for many development agencies promoting community development.

Development initiatives that emphasize rural people's voices and ways of supporting governments to respond to those voices have had mixed success since their rise in the 1990s. Weaknesses identified include inadequate ownership of the processes by government (e.g., too much has been devolved to isolated NGOs) and consequently weak links with the macro policy environment and the wider processes of governance. These rural development initiatives also have the tendency to see the "rural poor" mainly as "farmers." Such a disciplinarily restricted perspective limits the opportunities to address wider aspects of rural livelihoods, such as the roles of the rural poor as labourers and consumers, or indeed the broader questions of how and why these groups are politically marginalized. As well, many problems are related to sustaining such interventions once their external funding comes to an end.

Finally, "participation" is itself criticized for becoming a "new tyranny" (Cooke and Kothari, 2001) of rhetoric and routines—like community development or IRD before it—that do not actually provide the tools or space for community empowerment. Translating the rhetoric of participation into practice has often proved complicated and resource-demanding. This leads to a cynical view that many projects dress up their top-down, blueprint activities in the current politically correct language of participation, thereby debasing the potential for truly participatory work to develop. Critics would also argue that PRA has strayed from its emancipatory roots and has been co-opted for utilitarian and instrumental purposes: indeed, the World Bank's online "Participatory Sourcebook" is now the largest repository of participatory writing and research.

Sustainable Livelihoods

The sustainable livelihoods approach (see Box 18.2) is the latest attempt to confront the issues of rural poverty in as holistic a manner as possible (Ellis, 2000; Scoones, 2009). Its greatest value, according to its backers, is that it challenges the "farming first" mentality of previous approaches and considers instead the full range of livelihood strategies being pursued in rural areas. Even in agricultural countries, such as most of sub-Saharan Africa, where the persistent image is of subsistence farmers, non-farm (often non-rural) sources may already account for about half (40 to 60 per cent) of average household income and seem to be growing in importance (Barrett et al., 2001: 316). This means it is misleading to assume, just because the rural poor happen to be engaged in farming, that they are therefore farmers or are automatically interested in investing in means to improve those farms with new agricultural technologies.

Clearly, this perspective draws heavily on Chambers's work (1983) on the multiple realities of rural poverty, which is shown to be an outcome not merely of financial or nutritional deprivation but, more importantly, of political and socio-economic exclusion. Sen's definitive work on famines (1981) is also crucial: his argument is that famines occur not because of a lack of food but rather because of inequalities in people's rights (their "entitlements") to access or distribute that food. Finally, we can see roots in the ideas of Boserup and the understanding that decisions about technology are rationally made with reference not only to environmental variables (population density, land quality and availability) but also to socio-economic factors (access to markets, policy or institutional settings).

The livelihoods framework does allow us to better describe and understand the processes occurring in the rural context (see Box 18.6). It is not yet clear, however, whether the sustainable livelihoods approach will be better able to master the interdisciplinary complexity that in the past ultimately limited the implementation of holistic approaches such as community development or IRD. Thus, while the sustainable livelihoods framework is currently *de rigueur* among rural development donors, such support may not be sustained if (as was the case with "integrated" approaches of the 1950s and 1970s) interdisciplinary collaboration means funding potentially critical (or at least skeptical) social research and disciplinary experts who are working towards fundamentally different agendas.

Finally, it is also worth noting that the sustainable livelihoods approach currently vies with a quite different stream of thinking about rural development—namely, the "re-branding" since 1999 of structural adjustment as Poverty Reduction Strategy Papers (PRSPs) (see Chapter 9). These commitments by aid-receiving nations are organized according to economic sectors, meaning that their approach to rural poverty remains heavily centred on agriculture and a persistence of the "two-sector" model. Livelihoods research suggests, of course, that rural poverty reduction depends on inter-sector mobility and adaptability, and diversified, resilient agriculture (Ellis, 2000: 532). However, most PRSPs stick to the neoliberal orthodoxies offered by the *2008 World Development Report* as nearly universal remedies to the heterogeneous poverty of the Global South, such as promoting commercial agriculture and linking farmers to markets.

CHALLENGES

To synthesize across the themes already discussed—the complex nature of "rural" and "local" livelihoods, the diverse histories of rural transformation, and the

CRITICAL ISSUES

BOX 18.6 | Gender Dimensions of Household Livelihoods

While it is convenient to describe "households" as if they were units, they often are fraught with internal dynamics and tensions. Frequently, the most important divisions within households are gendered, although age differences may also intersect powerfully with gender in decision-making and power over household resources such as land and income. The livelihoods framework allows us to look inside the household and its multiple activities to see, for example, who has the power to make (or block) decisions about cropping patterns and labour allocation. In processes of rural development, which involve the introduction of new resources or knowledge alongside the introduction of new labour demands or adaptations, decisions about allocating these benefits and burdens within the household can involve significant internal negotiation.

For example, even if household incomes are rising, the welfare of women and children can worsen. Consider that in many societies, women have the primary responsibility for food preparation, child care, and other domestic tasks such as cleaning and fetching water and fuel. In much of sub-Saharan Africa, women are the main agricultural workers and suppliers of food for the household, to the extent that it is often conceptually useful to refer to "the farmer and her husband" rather than abiding by the patriarchal assumption that the male household head is the "farmer." If the labour demands of new crops or agricultural activities fall mainly on women, as is the case with many input-intensive, Green Revolution technologies (see Box 18.5), they will either have to work much harder than they already do, reduce the time spent caring for children, or both (see Chapter 5).

While some crops may be known culturally as "women's" crops, we do not know in advance whether a new activity also will be considered the responsibility or privilege of women. Very often, cash crops that produce revenue (such as tea, coffee, or sugar cane) are considered to belong to men. However, even staple crops, such as maize, rice, and vegetables, also might become controlled by men if they are commercialized. Household decisions to switch land from staple crops to marketed ones, therefore, may be hotly contested, affecting women's rights over land and its produce, which could have implications for food consumption and allocation within the household. Likewise, intergenerational disputes about labour allocation and whether (or how) to subdivide the household's land can often be pivotal in young people's decisions to migrate out of rural areas.

ever-changing approaches to rural development—we will consider two concluding issues. First, what is the potential for agriculture-led development? And second, is the rural still important in a world of multi-locational households pursuing diverse livelihoods?

Commodities and Agriculture-Led Development

If the current global goal of reducing poverty—as embodied in the PRSPs and Sustainable Development Goals—now depicts rural development as nearly synonymous with agricultural development, there are at least three reasons to be concerned. First, even with recent upward pressures on food prices, the real price of every agricultural commodity has fallen steadily over the long term, making the profitability of agriculture as a business questionable in the absence of subsidies (Ashley and Maxwell, 2001). For example, even accounting for recent price spikes, world cereal prices are nearly 50 per cent lower in real terms than in 1960. This may be advantageous for net food buyers but is not likely to benefit food producers, since the prices of inputs, such as fertilizers, have increased substantially relative to outputs over the same period. Second, agriculture in many parts of the globe confronts environmental limitations, particularly in terms of soil and water (Scoones, 2015). Third, and clearly as a consequence of the first two points, diversification out of agriculture appears to be widespread and increasing, even in dynamic rural economies (Haggblade et al., 2007).

These observations have important implications, especially with the prevailing interest in linking farmers to markets (World Bank, 2007: 118–34). If in many supposedly "agricultural" countries the current agricultural production per capita is insufficient to meet food security needs, then these needs are increasingly being met by food purchased from non-farm and non-rural sources (wage labour, **remittances**, reciprocity) (Barrett et al., 2001; Rigg, 2006). Describing rural Lesotho in the 1980s, where rural communities gained most of their livelihoods from working as migrant labour in South African mines, Ferguson (1994) points out that the conventional wisdom about farmers and markets was actually completely backwards: the rural areas of the country were not the "suppliers" of food but rather the "market" for it. As a result, any further penetration of markets and infrastructure (such as new roads) into Lesotho's rural areas would not raise the farm-gate prices paid to agricultural producers but rather make it even easier for residents of those areas to buy food and give even less incentive to grow food domestically.

Agricultural growth must certainly play a part in pathways out of poverty. Abundant evidence, most recently summarized by the World Bank in its *World Development Report* for 2008 (World Bank, 2007; see also Scoones, 2015; IFAD, 2001; Ellis, 2000), does show that improved or diversified agricultural production will benefit some segments of the rural poor and in some settings will stimulate the rural non-farm economy. But while targeting agriculture is clearly important, it cannot improve the livelihoods of the "rural poor"

PHOTO 18.3 | Sugar cane worker, Philippines. While global sugar prices reached an all-time high in 2011, wages of plantation workers have not risen, meaning that such workers have become steadily impoverished in the world food economy.

as a whole. Not only are non-farm activities becoming central to rural livelihoods, but increasing numbers of households—in "agricultural" countries, not just in "transforming" ones—have no commitment to farming whatsoever (Rigg, 2006: 181).

Blurring the Urban–Rural Divide

A final issue is livelihood diversification and the supposed urban–rural divide. If smallholders are indeed rational, their decisions to leave farming (or at least balance their commitment to farming with other activities) are also clearly rational. The importance of multi-locational households, with members resident in or moving between various communities, economic sectors, and even nation-states, is on the increase (Rigg, 2006). One outcome of this multi-locationality, besides blurring the boundaries between rural and urban identities, has been to boost the importance of remittance income from migrants as a force in rural development, equal to or surpassing that of national investment or international development assistance. In rural Mexico, Mali, and the Philippines, for example, these remittances support infrastructure development and social services to a degree that the government simply cannot, and help to build health clinics, schools, and even roads. This reality could be better supported by migration policy and financial systems to facilitate the direct transfer of funds back to rural areas.

On a deeper level, the increasing irrelevance of the artificial urban–rural divide in terms of livelihoods, markets, and activities also needs to be addressed (see Chapter 19). Assumptions that productivity gains in agriculture will drive increased consumption of non-agricultural goods (e.g., Hayami and Ruttan, 1985) now look flawed and incomplete. The rural non-farm economy today accounts for 35 to 50 per cent of average rural household income across the Global South (Haggblade et al., 2007). Given the range of livelihood strategies now pursued in rural areas, "rural" and "urban" may not be so easily distinguished on the basis of economic activities. But since non-farm opportunities in rural areas are often barely more productive than agriculture, they deserve to be developed in their own right.

SUMMARY

This chapter has demonstrated two key ways in which thinking about rural development has evolved. The first is how attitudes that smallholder "peasant" agriculture is inefficient and outmoded must confront evidence that smallholders are "inherently rational" and therefore the potential driving force of increased efficiency and productivity. The second is the rising challenge to top-down rural development made by more participatory approaches led by, or at least more controlled by, rural communities, which acknowledge that rural "sustainable livelihoods" do not always rely solely on farming. Targeting agriculture is therefore necessary, but not sufficient, for rural development. The ongoing food crisis illustrates that agricultural development, rural development, and food security are not synonymous, and we cannot emphasize increased production without attention to social and environmental impacts. Rural development in the twenty-first century will need to learn from the diversity of rural people's present and past experiences if it is to contend with climate change, land pressures, and volatile commodity prices.

QUESTIONS FOR CRITICAL THOUGHT

1. Do rural and urban areas differ in meaningful ways in regard to livelihoods and alleviating poverty? How do episodes like the 2008 global food crisis change or reinforce any distinctions or differences?
2. Considering the long history of failed rural development projects, does Boserup's model of agricultural intensification and technological change provide any better explanation of this failure than the perspectives of Malthus or Marx?

3. Considering the various rural development models of the past 50 years, how can the development challenges move beyond arguments of specialist versus generalist knowledge or of top-down versus bottom-up approaches?
4. In a world where over a billion people are food insecure, to what extent can or should agriculture lead rural development?

SUGGESTED READINGS

Chambers, Robert. 1983. *Rural Development: Putting the Last First*. London: Longman.

Patel, Raj. 2008. *Stuffed and Starved: The Hidden Battle for the World Food System*. Brooklyn, NY: Melville House.

Scoones, Ian. 2015. *Sustainable Livelihoods and Rural Development*. Halifax: Fernwood.

Sen, Amartya. 1981. *Poverty and Famines: An Essay on Entitlements and Deprivation*. Baltimore: Johns Hopkins University Press.

World Bank. 2007. *World Development Report 2008: Agriculture for Development*. Washington: World Bank.

BIBLIOGRAPHY

Altieri, M. 1995. *Agroecology: The Science of Sustainable Agriculture*, 2nd edn. London: IT Publications.

Ashley, C., and S. Maxwell. 2001. "Rethinking rural development." *Development Policy Review* 19, 4: 395–425.

Barrett, C.B., T. Reardon, and P. Webb. 2001. "Nonfarm income diversification and household livelihood strategies in rural Africa: Concepts, dynamics, and policy implications." *Food Policy* 26: 315–31.

Boserup, E. 1965. *The Conditions of Agricultural Growth*. New York: Aldine.

———. 1981. *Population and Technological Change: A Study of Long Term Trends*. Chicago: University of Chicago Press.

Chambers, R. 1983. *Rural Development: Putting the Last First*. London: Longman.

Collier, P. 2008. "The politics of hunger: How illusion and greed fan the food crisis." *Foreign Affairs* 87, 6: 67–79.

Cooke, B., and U. Kothari. 2001. *Participation: The New Tyranny?* London: Zed Books.

Cotula, L., S. Vermeulen, R. Leonard, and J. Keeley. 2009. *Land Grab or Development Opportunity? Agricultural Investment and International Land Deals in Africa*. London and Rome: IIED/FAO/IFAD. www.ifad.org/pub/land/land_grab.pdf.

Ellis, F. 2000. *Rural Livelihoods and Diversity in Developing Countries*. Oxford: Oxford University Press.

——— and S. Biggs. 2001. "Evolving themes in rural development: 1950s–2000s." *Development Policy Review* 19, 4: 437–48.

Ferguson, J. 1994. *The Anti-Politics Machine: "Development," Depoliticization, and Bureaucratic Power in Lesotho*. Cambridge: Cambridge University Press.

Haggblade, S., P.B.R Hazell, and T. Reardon, eds. 2007. *Transforming the Rural Nonfarm Economy: Opportunities and Threats in the Developing World*. Washington: IFPRI.

Hayami, Y., and V.W. Ruttan. 1985. *Agricultural Development: An International Perspective*, 2nd edn. Baltimore: Johns Hopkins University Press.

Headey, D., and S. Fan. 2008. "Anatomy of a crisis: The causes and consequences of surging food prices." *Agricultural Economics* 39 (Supplement 1): 375–91.

Holdcroft, L.E. 1976. "The rise and fall of community development in developing countries, 1950–65: A critical analysis and an annotated bibliography." MSU Rural Development Papers no. 2. East Lansing: Department of Agricultural Economics, Michigan State University.

International Fund for Agricultural Development (IFAD). 2011. *Rural Poverty Report 2011: New Realities, New Challenges: New Opportunities for Tomorrow's Generation*. Oxford: Oxford University Press.

Jansen, K., and E. Roquas. 1998. "Modernizing insecurity: The land titling project in Honduras." *Development and Change* 29: 81–106.

Lang, T. 2010. "Crisis? What crisis? The normality of the current food crisis." *Journal of Agrarian Change* 10, 1: 87–97.

Lewis, W.A. 1954. "Economic development with unlimited supplies of labor." *The Manchester School* 22: 139–91.

McDowell, C., and A. de Haan. 1997. "Migration and sustainable livelihoods." IDS Working Paper 65. Brighton, UK: University of Sussex.

Netting, R. 1993. *Smallholders, Householders: Farm Families and the Ecology of Intensive, Sustainable Agriculture.* Stanford, Calif.: Stanford University Press.

OECD. 2010. *Measuring Aid to Agriculture (data to 2007–8).* OECD-DAC (Apr.). www.oecd.org/dac/stats/44116307.pdf.

———. 2015. *Aid to Agriculture and Rural Development—Data to 2012–13.* OECD-DAC (Mar.). http://bit.ly/1UkRIhh.

Patel, R. 2013. "The long Green Revolution." *Journal of Peasant Studies* 40, 1: 1–63.

Piesse, J., and C. Thirtle. 2009. "Three bubbles and a panic: An explanatory review of recent food commodity price events." *Food Policy* 34: 119–29.

Richards, P. 1985. *Indigenous Agricultural Revolution: Ecology and Food Production in West Africa.* London: Hutchinson.

Rigg, J. 2006. "Land, farming, livelihoods, and poverty: Rethinking the links in the rural South." *World Development* 34, 1: 180–202.

Schoneveld, G.C. 2014. "The geographic and sectoral patterns of large-scale farmland investments in sub-Saharan Africa." *Food Policy* 48: 34-50.

Schultz, T.W. 1964. *Transforming Traditional Agriculture.* New Haven: Yale University Press.

Scoones, I. 1998. "Sustainable rural livelihoods: A framework for analysis." IDS Working Paper 72. Brighton, UK: University of Sussex.

———. 2009. "Livelihoods perspectives and rural development." *Journal of Peasant Studies* 36, 1: 171–96.

———. 2015. *Sustainable Livelihoods and Rural Development.* Halifax: Fernwood.

Sen, A. 1981. *Poverty and Famines: An Essay on Entitlements and Deprivation.* Baltimore: Johns Hopkins University Press.

Shiva, V. 1991. *The Violence of the Green Revolution: Third World Agriculture, Ecology and Politics.* London: Zed Books.

Tomich, T., P. Kilby, and B. F. Johnston. 1995. *Transforming Agrarian Economies: Opportunities Seized, Opportunities Missed.* Ithaca, NY: Cornell University Press.

Turner, B.L., G. Hyden, and R. W. Kates. 1993. *Population Growth and Agricultural Change in Africa.* Gainesville: University of Florida Press.

Williams, G. 1981. "The World Bank and the peasant problem." In J. Heyer et al., eds, *Rural Development in Tropical Africa.* London: Macmillan.

Wood, A. 2002. *Could Africa Be More Like America?* http://ssrn.com/abstract=315240.

World Bank. 2007. *World Development Report 2008: Agriculture for Development.* Washington: World Bank.

Zimmerman, F.J. 2000. "Barriers to participation of the poor in South Africa's land redistribution." *World Development* 28, 8: 1439–60.

19 Urban Development: Cities in the Global South

Anne Latendresse, Lisa Bornstein, and Jane Reid

LEARNING OBJECTIVES

- To understand global trends in urbanization and factors contributing to the urbanization of developing countries.
- To become familiar with key concepts and theoretical approaches to understanding and interpreting the transformation of urban areas in developing countries.
- To appreciate the central development issues for cities in the Global South, with specific reference to shelter and sustainability.
- To learn about the major players in urban development—private developers, international agencies, governments, NGOs, and urban movements—and be able to provide examples of their role in contemporary urban restructuring.

▲ **Residents in the "pacified" Pavao-Pavaozinho *favela* community in Rio de Janeiro, Brazil. The *favela* stands above famed Copacabana and Ipanema beaches, two of Rio's wealthiest neighborhoods. The government recently created a commission with the objective to increase social projects in *favela* communities that have a Pacifying Police Unit (UPP). The new aim acknowledges that the communities, many of which remain plagued by violence and other issues, cannot be "pacified" solely by police operations.** | Source: Photo by Mario Tama/Getty Images

INTRODUCTION

In 2014, an estimated 54 per cent of the planet's population—3.9 billion people—resided in urban areas (UN, 2014a). According to the United Nations (UN), the world's **urban** population is growing at a faster rate than the total population of the planet, and most of this growth will occur in the Global South. By 2050, two-thirds of humanity will live in cities (UN, 2014a). This shift is justly seen as a significant revolution in human history, marked as it had been with a scattering of cities—some great, some small—in a landscape dominated by rural settlement patterns and associated livelihoods. In the words of Anna Tibaijuko (2007), former executive director of the United Nations Human Settlements Programme (UN-Habitat), the human species has now become "Homo Urbanus."

Cities have come to play an increasingly important role in shaping possibilities for human development and economic well-being. Urban dwellers need livelihoods, shelter, services (from water to education), and ways to meaningfully engage with the society in which they live. Equally important, "living gently on the land" has become a pressing reality, as the environmental consequences of resource-intensive and waste-generating human activities have wreaked havoc at the local, regional, and global scales (see Chapter 17). Yet, despite these imperatives, the relationship between urbanization and human well-being is one of mixed results. Cities are places of growth and opportunity. Cities also reflect inequalities and unevenness in wider development; they may grow because of an increase in trade flows, or because of immigration provoked by crises elsewhere. Urban processes—the design and construction of the built environment, and the act of living in cities—generate development challenges. Socio-spatial inequality and segregation, for example, have become dominant features of urban areas throughout the world, starkly depicted by some observers as a planned city for the richest and upper-middle-class inhabitants, and unplanned settlements or homelessness for the poorest. Such contrasts are apparent in cities throughout the world, whether in the wealthiest areas, those in the midst of economic crises (e.g., Greece), conflict (e.g., Syria and South Sudan), or disaster (e.g., Nepal), or those simply undergoing ordinary (uneven) development. At the same time, cities are places of innovation—social, political, economic, and technological—and of struggles for citizenship, democracy, and individual and collective freedoms (Isin, 2000; Harvey, 2013).

Urban agglomerations of the Global South, the focus of this chapter, are often depicted as large, polluted cities surrounded by a belt of slums. This image is not so far from the reality: Delhi has 25 million inhabitants (the second largest city in the world after Tokyo), Shanghai has 24 million, and São Paulo, Mumbai, and Mexico City have 21 million each (UN, 2014a). Many cities of the Global South are characterized by high levels of inequality and burgeoning demand for state and humanitarian services.

The vast majority of cities have a troubled relationship with their surroundings, and cities of the Global South are no exception. Cities are large consumers of water and energy resources, and producers of greenhouse gas emissions and industrial and residential waste. Cities depend on rural areas for food and other resources, yet often expand onto and consume agricultural and open land. Such expansion can bring needed infrastructure and economic opportunities to the urban periphery; it also can generate processes of speculative "land-grabbing" and displacement of rural and small-town residents, while reducing nearby sources of food, water, and energy. Immigrants—both economic migrants seeking a better quality of life than that available in their places of origin and **refugees** displaced by conflict, disaster, environmental, economic, or other crises—swell the numbers of urban residents. Moreover, it is already known that climate change and its manifestations seriously affect populations of developing countries, particularly inhabitants of slums and informal neighbourhoods (World Bank, 2015). Given the severity of the challenges, an important issue for the future will be how urban actors—governments, the private sector, community groups, and international partners—confront these challenges in innovative ways.

This chapter examines urbanization in relation to development. We tackle the phenomenon as a historical process of spatial transformation that has demographic, economic, political, social, and cultural dimensions. In the first part, we present major trends and patterns of urbanization occurring in developing countries and review the main factors contributing to it. The second part focuses on the urban crisis faced by cities and governments of developing countries since the 1980s and explores implications for the living conditions of city inhabitants. We introduce the elements of the crisis, cover the main debates about its causes as posited in the fields of geography and sociology, and identify key challenges. The third part of the chapter examines these challenges in greater depth, discussing spatial expressions of deepening environmental challenges and socio-economic inequalities; our focus is on shelter. Finally, we consider central actors in urban development and provide indications of collective actions by local actors, movements, and municipal governments that seek to promote more just and sustainable forms of urban development.

UNDERSTANDING URBANIZATION

Urbanization is the transition over time of a rural society to a more urban one (known also as "urban transformation"). It is a process that has modified and continues to modify the spatial distribution of the population in every region of the globe. We can therefore refer to the "rate of urbanization" or "urbanization level" in a country or region by comparing the population living in cities to the total population.

The evolution of cities and towns has been influenced by the physical characteristics of the environment, their role within larger political and economic territories, their internal economic structure and activities, the dominant model of development, daily life, culture, and customs. In addition to historical legacies, in the contemporary era the state, private sector, civil society, social movements, and citizens all contribute in distinct ways to city-making. For these reasons, cities and towns vary greatly over time and space.

Yet researchers, planners, and geographers seek a definition of a city that is relevant regardless of country, region, or historical period of study. Today, most researchers agree on the following elements: a politically and administratively defined territory; a relatively high population size and density; the presence of a division of labour and functional diversity; and social organization based on complex and varied interrelations.

Once the city is defined qualitatively, what is the threshold at which it is possible to say that it is indeed an urban entity? And on what basis can researchers and observers monitor the urbanization of a country and compare it to that of other countries and other regions?

One of the main problems is that the threshold defining an urban entity differs from one country to another. For example, an urban centre in Canada is an area with at least 1,000 people and a population density of at least 400 people per square kilometre; and in Botswana, in southern Africa, a city is an agglomeration of 5,000 or more people where at least 75 per cent of the economic activity is non-agricultural. Population growth on the periphery of a city may or may not be counted as urban; in India, for example, city boundaries are slow to adjust, since reclassification of land as urban carries with it requirements for costly municipal provision of services.

Data on urbanization typically are supplied by a country's census or national statistical agency, which uses its own definitional criteria. In addition to the absence of a universal definition, the uneven quality of data collection produced in various countries reduces the reliability of information and, therefore, leads to difficulties when comparative analyses are necessary. For example, slum dwellers, squatters, and homeless people are difficult to count accurately since they lack a formal place of residence. The World Bank and United Nations compile nationally collected data for comparative and country-specific purposes: the data allow tracking of human welfare and progress towards development goals (such as the Millennium Development Goals or MDGs) over time; assessment of development policies and urban programs; and consideration of local conditions in policy formulation and funding decisions. International agencies may conduct independent household surveys to supplement national data, but most information comes from local sources based on local criteria and definitions.

URBANIZATION ACROSS TIME AND SPACE

Available data allow comparison of global levels of **urban population** by region and time period (see Figure 19.1). Latin America and the Caribbean began their **urban transition**—shifting to a majority urban population—about six decades ago. Today, just over 80 per cent of the total populations of these regions live

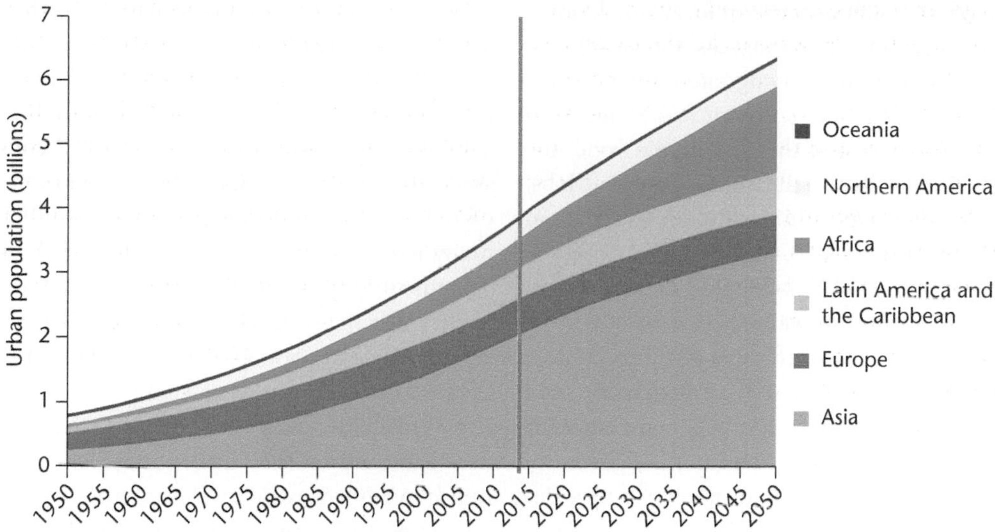

FIGURE 19.1 | Urban Population by Region, 1950–2050
Source: UN (2014b: 12).

in cities. Asia and Africa, where the urban population currently is estimated at 39 per cent, began this process later. However, Asia already contains half of the world's urban population, half of the world's cities of at least one million people, and half of the mega-cities of 10 million or more inhabitants (UN, 2014a). Africa has the world's highest **urban growth rate**, of between 3 and 4 per cent per year, but China and India alone account for 37 per cent of the world's population, and in both cases the urban population continues to grow dramatically: the cities of just three countries, China, India, and Nigeria, are projected to account for one-third of the increase in the world's urban population (some 900 million residents) by 2050. Growth of large agglomerations is expected to continue: in 2014, there were 28 mega-cities of 10 million or more, housing one-eighth of the world's population; by 2030, there will be 41 such mega-cities. Most of these mega-cities are located in the Global South. In parallel, smaller cities remain important; nearly half the world's city dwellers reside in settlement areas of less than 500,000 people (UN, 2014a).

Rural–urban migration and **natural increase** fuel the growth of cities now, as in the past. Migration is the major cause of city growth in China, where over 260 million rural Chinese have migrated to urban areas in the past 10 years. Elsewhere, natural increase—the excess of births over deaths—accounts for approximately 60 per cent of urban population growth (UNFPA, 2007). Reclassifying previously rural areas as urban, such as when fringe areas and neighbouring villages are incorporated into a metropolitan area, also contributes to the swelling of urban populations.

In other respects, contemporary urbanization dynamics are distinct from those of past eras. Urbanization of Europe and North America occurred in a period marked by industrialization and economic growth. Throughout the nineteenth and early twentieth centuries, the state played a crucial role, creating the economic and physical infrastructure to support urban growth: rail and road systems supported the growth of new cities, towns, and suburbs; landownership and banking systems facilitated real estate booms and home ownership; and social welfare systems helped assure subsidized housing, job creation, and a safety net for many of those in need of assistance.

Urbanization in the Global South has differed because of both historical and contemporary factors. For example, colonization accelerated urbanization and the structuring of cities around colonial relations (King, 1990). In some instances, colonialism disrupted existing settlement patterns, for example, by creating separate quarters in the city for settlers and their institutions, often at the expense of local inhabitants. Post-independence did not, in most cases, reverse colonial patterns of city location along international trade routes, or the internal dualistic structure of cities, with their "modern" quarter and the "traditional" one, the latter housing the majority of the migrants seeking jobs, education, and other opportunities in the post-colonial city (Drakakis-Smith, 2000). Countries urbanizing today do so in the context of globalization, neoliberalism, and, in many cases, in the wake of structural adjustment programs, as discussed in other chapters. Unlike in past eras, where industrialization, urbanization, and economic growth occurred together, contemporary restructuring of economic activities and the advent of information and communication technologies have decoupled such relations. Indeed, with the exception of certain parts of Asia such as China, urbanization happening in the South entails neither industrialization nor economic growth (Glaeser, 2014; Gollin et al., 2013). This situation explains why certain experts refer to the "urbanization of poverty" (UNFPA, 2007), a trend most visible in the housing sector: 863 million people today live in informal settlements and slums (UN-Habitat, 2014). Indeed, as Sylvia Chant (2013: 9) contends, "prosperity is not an inevitable outcome of urbanization," and instead, in much of the Global South, cities are places where "poor living standards . . . socioeconomic disparities, and lack of decent work opportunities" predominate, "often associated with violence, crime, insecurity, and mental and physical ill-health."

International, regional, and local forces and actors influence the rate and distribution of urban growth in direct and indirect ways. Public, private, and internationally funded projects may prompt particular forms of urbanization; for example, the construction of roads opens up areas of the country to settlement, labour-saving agricultural technologies usually prompt rural–urban migration, and the construction of dams usually displaces people. Disasters and conflict may force rural people to move to the cities. However, these forces are entwined with wider economic and political relations as well as the policies of international bodies such as the UN and the World Bank (see Chapter 9). Indeed, globalization—understood as a contemporary process of restructuring economic, political, and cultural dimensions of the world order—engenders socio-spatial restructuring at different scales (global, regional, national, and sub-national) that directly affects urban areas (see Chapter 6).

All of these shifts are accompanied by an environmental crisis that many see as linked to, if not largely caused by, the forms of production and consumption associated with the city. The consequences include climate change, and increasing risks and hazards for many (see Chapter 17). These factors make urban development in the contemporary period more complex, particularly in poorer countries of the world, where basic challenges of development become intertwined with those of urbanization.

While cities have long been associated with disorder, chaos, and violence, throughout history they also are linked to human creativity (Mumford, 1961). Technological innovations—from the first agricultural revolution of the neolithic age to the Industrial Revolution and, most recently, the information revolution, have been prompted by the needs of urban development and have profoundly restructured urban form and urban life. The polis in Greece gave birth to democratic practices, and these city-states evoked the birth of citizenship (Hall, 1998). The history of cities is a reminder that spatial concentration has prompted humans to create new technologies, and new political institutions and practices, at times leading to innovative solutions to urban problems.

The developmental and sustainability challenges associated with urbanism are reflected in the following observations:

1. The location, pace, and scale of urbanization underway are unprecedented in human history.
2. Urbanization and urbanism are associated with a new geography of economic activity, political alliances, and socio-economic outcomes. More specifically, cities are part of a global urban network in which distinctive forms of urban development, polarization, instability, and environmental stress are emerging both within cities and among them.
3. Cities are major resource users and producers of wealth, but not all cities consume nature in the same way or at the same levels. Moreover, environmental risks and poor-quality environments are unequally distributed, with low-income people disproportionately vulnerable.
4. The capacity, resources, and political will to address urban, developmental, and environmental

problems are often most lacking in the places where they are most needed. Nonetheless, efforts to address problems and create better cities are apparent, with some highly innovative initiatives emerging from even the poorest and least well-resourced countries.

URBAN CRISIS AND THE CHALLENGE OF SUSTAINABLE URBAN DEVELOPMENT

Some experts at the UN and other research agencies have used the term "urban crisis" to denote the contradictory effects of urban population growth; in this view, urban growth, fuelled by individual hopes for a better life, has social, economic, and ecological effects that weaken cities' potential as places to live. To support such an argument, experts point to the example of peasants who arrive in the city in search of a better life but end up residing in a cardboard shack, unemployed. Students and scholars of development recognize, in contrast to such arguments, that blaming migrants for their own urban misfortunes misses the forces that shape opportunities, in both rural and urban areas, for migrants and long-term residents alike. It is true that many urban dwellers live in informal settlements. Or they may work informally in an employment relationship "not subject to labour legislation, income taxation, social protection or other employment benefits" (ILO, 2013a), constituting the so-called informal sector that includes street vendors and shoeshine boys (see Chapter 11). However, informality in shelter and employment, rather than an outcome of overpopulation per se or of individual aspirations for a better life, must be seen as consequences of wider structures, policies, and practices. These structures, policies, and practices create the various dimensions of an urban crisis, as well as the bases for sustainable urban development.

The cases of shelter and disasters are illustrative. Housing shortages are often linked to highly unequal land tenure patterns and to the difficulties newly independent states face in establishing communal infrastructure such as housing, sanitation, and public transit. These forces combine to create a crisis, one that is only aggravated by the structural adjustment programs imposed by international institutions such as the World Bank and the International Monetary Fund (IMF) (Davis, 2006). Lack of sufficient adequate housing at prices and locations accessible to low-income households, coupled with lack of decent work, prompt many people—from schoolteachers and government bureaucrats to unemployed youth—to rely on informal housing for shelter and informal work for primary or supplementary income.

Alongside these now-recognized phenomena, new problems are coming to light, particularly in terms of natural catastrophes, environmental crises, and global climate change. The earthquakes that hit Kathmandu in April 2015 killed over 8,000 people, landslides washed away nearly 300 people in Rio de Janeiro in March 2010, and the 1984 gas leak from a Union Carbide chemical plant in Bhopal, India, killed several thousand people immediately and caused long-term health impacts for many more over a longer period. In each case, these events reveal a link between socio-economic inequalities and environmental risk. Indeed, underlying social, economic, and political vulnerabilities increase the risk of disasters. Low-income populations are the most vulnerable to the impacts of climate change (IPCC, 2014; World Bank, 2015). Post-disaster reconstruction specialist Gonzalo Lizarralde (2015: 130) identifies poor building techniques, construction in areas prone to disaster, and "less tangible characteristics that put people in fragile situations, such as . . . lack of property titles or insurance and limited education" as among the many "unsafe circumstances that societies develop and institutions tolerate." In this sense, he observes, disasters are never strictly "natural." Vulnerability is socially constructed.

It is important to ask whether there are links between these various crises. In other words, are they different crises with independent causes, or are we dealing with a global crisis that affects the food and agriculture system, the environment, and cities, or even a crisis that is both systemic and sectoral? While some experts adopt a **Malthusian approach** and continue to see population growth as a main cause of the urban crisis, others look to the links between the global economy and the forms of urban development occurring in both industrialized and developing countries. For theorists such as David Harvey and Immanuel Wallerstein, the current chaos is not caused by *crises*; rather, one systemic crisis, based on capitalism as a mode of production, is the root cause

Johan Douma

PHOTO 19.1 | Slum dwellers on Boeng Kak Lake in Cambodia are vulnerable to the increased frequency and severity of storms.

of various ills facing humanity. This crisis is exacerbated by international policies and institutions.

Today, even the World Bank recognizes the failure of the policies previously put forward for human and economic development, including in urban areas. Urban theorists, civil society organizations, and social movements question how the economic system is shaping cities in different parts of the world. A growing number of researchers now call for better urban planning regulations, economic development stimuli, and infrastructure and services provision, as well as the need for participation of communities.

CITIES, GLOBALIZATION, AND SOCIO-SPATIAL FRAGMENTATION

Urban theorists argue that globalization has its own spatial expressions and relations; and they have documented the resulting spatial and socio-economic characteristics of cities. Saskia Sassen's *The Global City* (1991) examines in depth the very large cities that are international financial centres, such as New York, Tokyo, and London. **Global cities**, she contends, fulfill their global functions through the spatial concentration of high-level international command functions and linked business services (for example, advertising, insurance, and business advisory companies). As Sassen (1998) observes, "The new growth sectors, the new organizational capacities of firms, and the new technologies—all three interrelated—are contributing to produce not only a new geography of centrality but also a new geography of marginality."

Castells (1996) agrees, seeing in these cities the nodes of a form of globalization that maintains financial control over modes of production in some global cities, while the sites of production of goods are transferred from developed to developing countries. Some metropolises in the Global South are now part of this network of major metropolitan areas that concentrate power and economic and financial flows. Shanghai, São Paulo, and Singapore are finance centres for the global economy, while Dubai acts as a transport hub and Bangalore is a centre for information technology. They are part of the circle of major urban areas at the heart of the world economy.

Even Dhaka in Bangladesh and Lagos in Nigeria, both large cities that are economically and politically marginalized, are shaped by global systems. The design, urban fabric, and infrastructure of their downtowns resemble those of many large cities in developed countries. They are marked by the presence of an affluent class that is part of the international elite and whose lifestyles and consumption patterns resemble those of other major urban cities (Jenks et al., 2008). Local officials may turn their backs on "traditional," "informal," and "unregulated" ways of using urban space (planting crops in the city, street vending, etc.) in favour of speculative and spectacular urban projects, a form of development also associated with a loss of community and civic space, a lack of public amenities, and the severe environmental degradation of urban areas. Indeed, the most ecologically unsustainable aspects of cities in wealthy regions—high consumption, massive waste, automobile dependency, low-density sprawl, and continued reliance on high levels of resource extraction (from agricultural land to groundwater to oil and other minerals)—are increasingly characteristic of other parts of the world. Economic and spatial polarization is a core element.

In all these cases, the city fabric reflects exposure to the global economy and has generated new forms of entrepreneurial city-building. The built environment has become an object of speculation, while simultaneously being reshaped to serve the needs of a growing cadre—in some cities—of people in new economic activities (from data processing and call-centres to software development and high-level management). Gated communities, elite downtown condos, and slums are recurrent elements of these cities (Marcuse, 2008; Caldeira, 2000). Property-led development, with an emphasis on revitalizing older parts of the city for new international functions, is apparent in diverse cities of the world (e.g., Mexico City, Bangkok, Singapore, and Cape Town). Global events, such as summits of world leaders and the Olympics, and megaprojects are actively pursued as a means to better brand major

luoman/iStockohoto

PHOTO 19.2 | *Favela* (slum) in Rio de Janeiro, Brazil.

cities and make them ever more visible on the world stage (Bornstein, 2010) (see Box 19.1). While such investment dynamics result in revitalization of older urban areas and provision, in some cases, of major urban infrastructure, the consequences for ordinary city residents are less certain; evictions, displacement, and security crackdowns rather than improved quality of life are common (Davis and Monk, 2008).

BOX 19.1 | Competing for the Olympics

CURRENT EVENTS

Competition for the Olympics starts well before the lighting of the Olympic flame. While much of our attention focuses on the years of preparation undergone by athletes, cities also prepare, hone their offerings, and compete: hosting the Olympics, and other international sporting events, is seen as a prize in itself, one that places the host city and country on the podium of the world stage. Historically, few countries in the Global South acted as hosts. In recent years, various rising economies have sought such status, often submitting repeat bids in their efforts to "win the gold." Almaty, Baku, Beijing, Doha, Istanbul, and Rio de Janeiro have submitted bids to host the Summer or Winter Olympics in the last decade and are likely to do so again. Cities compete actively, perhaps ruthlessly, and at considerable cost in the bidding game.

City governments and local chambers of commerce generally see international sporting events as a good investment. Major upgrades in local facilities and infrastructure are needed to satisfy international requirements; Beijing used the 2010 Summer Olympics to introduce a subway system, reconfigure the city around a modern core, construct arenas of striking architectural design, and attract international investment and tourism. Local promoters hope this visibility and the physical upgrades will be long-term assets for profit-making: that the city will become a destination for other sporting events, conferences, independent tourism, investment, and trade. The construction jobs, lucrative media contracts, thousands of tourists, and global visibility are argued to benefit government, private-sector promoters, and local residents.

The reality is often quite different. A strong bid means demonstrating that the "conditions for a successful event" are in place: economic and political stability, high-level security, land availability, and easy, comfortable access for the many visitors—athletes and non-athletes alike—to the various venues. These imperatives have led to a slew of negative policies and practices associated with international games that include displacement of low-income people who occupy desired lands; relocation of homeless and other "undesirables" in the days and weeks leading up to the event; rushed, low-quality construction that both reduces the life of infrastructure and endangers the lives of the construction workers on the projects; and branding of the city and event for a "mass audience" at the expense of local culture. And few long-term benefits may materialize. Tourism and investment may not outlast the event itself. Facilities, whose construction costs may take decades to pay off, may end up underused.

There are alternatives. In some cases, local civil society groups have mobilized to oppose the bid, construction plans, or associated human rights abuses. For instance, in South Africa, StreetNet International joined with refugee, sex worker, and slum dweller organizations to protest evictions in advance of the World Cup (Robbins, 2012). In other cases, such as Cape Town's unsuccessful 2004 Olympic bid, promoters partnered with civil society to ensure benefits—such as job training, environmental clean-up, and investment in needed social infrastructure—would flow to local people. Meanwhile, international campaigns, such as that spearheaded by Transparency International (2014: 5–6), have called for major reforms, including independent oversight of international sport associations and bidding criteria that "make internationally accepted and binding standards on fundamental rights (e.g. human rights) and anti-corruption a prerequisite for any event."

PHOTO 19.3 | UNHCR refugee camp.

In sum, numerous global forces affect the urban form of metropolitan areas. Four trends are apparent: a rise in new types of cities that play important co-ordinating roles in the global economy; new spatial tendencies of fragmentation, fracturing, and polarization within globalized cities; a parallel rise in inequality, poverty, and vulnerability; and an increase in new forms of governance that emphasize local strategies for economic growth in the spatial order—and thus a more entrepreneurial-state stance towards promotion of the city—over other development needs.

In the next section, two contemporary challenges that illustrate these dynamics are discussed, namely population displacement and shelter.

THE EXPANSION OF SLUMS

As noted above, slums are a feature of contemporary urbanization (see Box 19.3). Whether they are called *bidonvilles*, shantytowns, *poblaciones*, *favelas*, or slums, these informal housing areas are present on all continents. There were 792 million people living in slums in 2000, and 863 million in 2014 (UN-Habitat, 2014). China has the highest number of slum dwellers (180 million) and India is second (104 million). However, in some countries, nearly all housing is inadequate or produced via informal means. Sub-Saharan Africa overall has 70 per cent of its population (199.5 million) living in slums and, the Central African Republic has a striking 96 per cent of the population classified as slum dwellers (UN-Habitat, 2014).

In some parts of the world, informal settlements are located within the formal city, as in Rio de Janeiro in Brazil. Elsewhere, slums create one or more belts surrounding the city. Davis (2006) observes that the rise of mega-cities has been paralleled by the rise of mega-slums, linked together into continuous swaths of informal housing that lack sanitation, water, roads, and other services. At a human level, this means that a vast proportion of people in the world live in places where water is polluted and there are no adequate basic services; overcrowding means that privacy is non-existent, housing is makeshift, and there is little possibility of securely holding land.

BOX 19.2 | Refugees, the Displaced, and Host Cities

CURRENT EVENTS

Images of "boat people" in overloaded vessels leaving Africa for Europe and of thousands of Haitians crowded into tents following the 2010 earthquake have drawn attention to a major phenomenon of the twenty-first century: human displacement and forced migration. In 2014 alone, 33.3 million people had no option but to leave their houses and lands to seek refuge elsewhere. The reasons are threefold: "natural" catastrophes including those linked to climate change; war and conflict; and economic factors. Most of those displaced from their homes, "some 60 per cent of the total 14.4 million refugees and 80 per cent of the 38 million internally displaced people (IDPs)," end up in cities (UN-Habitat, 2015a). The massive and unplanned arrival of refugees or displaced people in urban areas is generating new, and highly visible, tensions: observers point to the massive scale of displacement, the difficulty in untangling so-called opportunistic reasons for movement (i.e., economic migrants who opt to move in search of a better economic future) from crisis-related reasons (such as war or an earthquake), and the perceived competition newcomers could pose for scarce urban jobs, services, and shelter. Such considerations may, in some countries, outweigh or parallel a humanitarian, compassionate response of welcome and assistance.

In other instances, ongoing conflict, lack of resources, political will, and/or institutional capacity have meant "temporary" shelter for displaced populations persists for years or decades. The cases of Somali and Palestinian refugee camps are illustrative (see Brynen and El-Rifai, 2007; Roberts, 2010; IDMC, 2015). Refugee settlements, often located on the fringe of existing cities, have become part of the wider urban conglomeration, albeit under UN authority and with distinct characteristics. Typically, the tents that predominate at first are replaced by small houses of permanent construction, and basic services such as water, sanitation, and electricity are provided. Physical conditions come to resemble those of surrounding areas, that is, with significant variation across the region, quite poor, for example, in Palestinian camps in Jordan and Lebanon (Roberts, 2010) and better in Gaza and the West Bank (Brynen and El-Rifai, 2007: 36). Overcrowding is common, with self-built extensions to homes frequent. Camp residents remain vulnerable; for instance, although the Somali residents of Kenya's Dadaab refugee camp have access to education and basic services lacking in their conflict-torn areas of origin, they do not have the right to work, vote, or remain long-term in Kenya (Warner, 2015). Indeed, as is true of other displaced people, these refugees and their descendants have not been able to take part fully in the political, economic, and civic life of nearby cities.

In the most basic sense, slums form for two reasons: (1) the growth of the population outpaces the production of housing for low- and moderate-income households; and (2) governments—and other urban actors—cannot find means to provide shelter for those households, whether by stimulating private developers to build more housing, undertaking state production of housing, or planning settlements in which informal construction could be accompanied by service provision and better settlement planning. Historic legacies play a part as well and include concentrated ownership of land; lack of investment in sanitation and water services; settlement in areas prone to hazards or far from the city's economic hubs; and limited land made available for formal production of low-income housing (Davis, 2006). Regulations can make it difficult for poor households to gain title to land or its use, and government neglect or active destruction of informal housing also contributes to the ongoing growth of slums. Davis (2006: 62) further blames "the current neoliberal economic orthodoxy" for exacerbating the housing shortage by shrinking government programs and privatizing

IMPORTANT CONCEPTS

BOX 19.3 | What Is a Slum?

A slum household lacks *one or more* of the following five conditions:

1. Durable housing that is built on a non-hazardous location and can adequately protect inhabitants from climatic conditions.
2. Sufficient living area, where not more than three people share the same room.
3. Access to improved water in sufficient amounts and at an affordable price, without requiring extreme effort.
4. Access to sanitation in the form of a private toilet or a public toilet shared with a reasonable number of people.
5. Secure tenure, through documentation or de facto protection against forced evictions.

Source: Adapted from UN-Habitat (2008).

housing markets. Finally, in recent years, globalization and the competition between cities to attract investments have favoured speculation and high prices for better-located real estate, worsening the living conditions of lower-income households, who are pushed to the outskirts of the formal city.

Whether slum dwellers reside in central areas or the periphery of the city, they are exposed to a variety of risks. Environmental health hazards of poorly serviced and planned settlements, such as exposure to industrial toxins or lack of clean water, are compounded by the more recent impacts of a changing climate (Anderson et al., 2008; Aguilar, 2009). While these settlements are poorly regulated and serviced by government, they are places where people establish homes, form friendships, start small businesses, and survive as best they can; rather than clearance of slums or their residents, most researchers and many advocacy organizations call for policy reforms that would improve conditions and grant expanded political voice for slum dwellers. A focus on regularization of ownership and titles to property, a dominant approach to slum upgrading in the 2000s, has now been replaced by approaches that improve conditions, ideally in situ; the risk remains of relocation of slum residents to more peripheral parts of the city, as centrally located lands are redeveloped for spectacle or speculation (see Box 19.1).

Slum dwellers lack decent employment in addition to decent housing, and the numbers of unemployed and underemployed have swelled with the recent economic crisis. Youth unemployment is at record highs, with the International Labour Organization (ILO) reporting an increase from 11.9 per cent unemployment in 2007 to 12.6 per cent in 2013—that represents 73.4 million economically active youth aged 15–24 who could not find work. In developing countries, economic crises also mean reduced hours and wages for those who are employed, a rise in working poverty, greater difficulty for women to find work, and a turn to informal economic activities (ILO, 2013). One promising direction is urban agriculture (see Box 19.4). A second is municipal infrastructure; as cities grow and age, there is a pressing need to invest in the expansion, maintenance, and repair of water, sewage, transport, and power systems, and employment-generating approaches could provide job growth (ILO, 2006). The ILO has coined the phrase "decent work" in its platform for action, and has pushed—in partnership with local governments, unions, and rights-based groups—to incorporate clauses protecting the health, safety, and dignity of workers into trade agreements and the MDG replacement, the UN 2030 Agenda for Sustainable Development (UN, 2015b).

IMPORTANT CONCEPTS

BOX 19.4 | Urban Agriculture: A Survival Strategy for Poor Urban Dwellers?

Growing food in urban areas is a long-standing practice, from the hanging gardens of Babylon to the present. For many years, however, urban agriculture virtually disappeared from cities throughout the world; restrictions on food production by city managers who feared associated nuisances, the industrialization of food production, and the availability of refrigeration conspired to shift food systems away from local production. Yet, beginning in the 1970s, urban agriculture began to reappear. Small home gardens and urban farms emerged in major cities of Africa, Asia, and Latin America. Community farming also blossomed in some cities of the developed world.

To explain the re-emergence of urban agriculture, researchers point to the "economic worsening of the situation of the poor as a consequence of structural adjustment programs" (Ratta and Nasr, 1996, in Bryld, 2003), rapid urbanization, and a lack of inexpensive transport for agricultural products coming from rural areas. For urban households, urban agriculture is a strategy to enhance food security. Indeed, it is "one of the most important factors in improving childhood nutrition, by increasing both access to food and nutritional quality" (Halweil and Nierenberg, 2007: 50). Moreover, it can contribute to local economies in terms of jobs and incomes, better management of waste, and improved quality of life.

Some 800 million people were engaged in urban agriculture by the mid-1990s, the majority in Asia (UNDP, 1996). Among them, 200 million engaged in production for the market. The Food and Agriculture Organization (FAO) estimates that 130 million African and 230 million Latin American urban dwellers plant fruit and vegetables to supplement their diets or incomes (FAO, 2015). For some it is their only source of income, as in Yaoundé, Cameroon, where 70 per cent of urban farmers have no other work, and in Cairo, Egypt, where rooftop gardening provides income-earning possibilities for teenage women who—for cultural reasons—cannot leave the home. Income and output from urban farms can be significant. As Bryld (2003) mentions, "In Africa, urban cultivation has become a permanent part of the landscape. Today, 70 per cent of the poultry food consumed in Kampala is produced within the city boundaries. In Kathmandu and Zambia, more than a third of the subsistence food production is produced within the city." Urban farming can make efficient use of resources (such as wastewater and organic waste), uses less water and land for equivalent outputs than conventional farming, and can help prevent erosion, cleanse water in sensitive areas, and provide nutrients for urban wildlife (Halweil and Nierenberg, 2007). Yet barriers to expanded urban agriculture remain, including conflicts over land tenure and pressures to build. Additional areas for municipal support include repeal of regulations prohibiting urban agriculture, designation of uncontaminated lands for cultivation, and establishment of local markets and distribution networks.

FORCES OF CHANGE: INTERNATIONAL INSTITUTIONS, LOCAL GOVERNMENTS, AND GRASSROOTS INITIATIVES

The World Bank has emerged as a major player in the field of urban development. Its urban focus emerged in the 1970s out of the recognition that "because they serve as reserves for capital and for research, as sites of concentrated production, and of modern consumption, cities are becoming major economic players" (Osmont, 1995: 7). The policies of the World Bank and other institutions and agencies have deepened many of the pernicious trends described above. World Bank urban policy has entailed limited public intervention, privatization of land and real estate, promotion of free

BOX 19.5 | The New Urban Agenda and Habitat III CURRENT EVENTS

The United Nations' third Conference on Housing and Sustainable Urban Development, Habitat III, was held in Quito, Ecuador, in October 2016. The Habitat Conference brought together stakeholders from across the world to review progress, highlight urban challenges, and lay out global goals and commitments for the next 20 years. The aim of Habitat III was to identify "drivers of change" that will help governments and other stakeholders manage urban areas in a socially, environmentally, and economically sustainable way. One potential driver is a New Urban Agenda, a policy document prepared for adoption during the conference. Diverse stakeholders provided input to the New Urban Agenda with policy papers (www.unhabitat.org/issue-papers-and-policy-units), committee meetings in New York, Nairobi and Jakarta, and dialogues (www.habitat3.org/sitemap). Discussions focused on identifying ways to support:

- patterns of urban growth that support other forms of sustainable development, such as the growth of "green economy" practices;
- urban plans and policies that reach beyond the traditional boundaries of the city and connect urban, peri-urban, and rural areas;
- institutional arrangements at the national and sub-national levels that enable governments to effectively deliver the New Urban Agenda.

The UN sees an important role for young people in the formulation of the New Urban Agenda. It is estimated that by 2030, as many as 60 per cent of all urban dwellers will be under the age of 18. Currently, cities, especially those in the Global South, provide youth with insufficient access to education and employment. By engaging with Habitat III, youth, it is hoped, can have the opportunity to raise awareness of the needs of young urban dwellers, their participation in urban life, and their potential contributions to the planning and management of our cities.

markets for housing, and decreases in assistance to residents (Renard, 2003: 242). In short, the city becomes a laissez-faire playing field.

During the 1990s the Bank recognized the failure of its interventions. According to Renard (2003), it is now shifting towards an emphasis on local governance and urban planning. In addition, the rhetoric of the Bank and other actors such as UN-Habitat now emphasizes citizen participation, such as in the Habitat III consultations (see Box 19.5) or participatory budgeting (see Box 19.6). This change in terminology, support for the active involvement of NGOs and civil society as major players in sustainable urban development, and the promotion of participatory democracy indicate a turning point in World Bank thinking. However, some question the value of this new discourse within the Bank, and caution that the Bank may take lessons learned from urban movements or innovative cities and strip them of their potential for social transformation. In such cases, citizen and civil society participation could be incorporated into technocratic and managerial approaches to the city instead of into popular mobilization processes that aim for the transformation of social and political relations.

THE RIGHT TO THE CITY

This shift in rhetoric has coincided with the failure of structural adjustment programs imposed on many countries by the World Bank and with the outbreak of urban riots in Casablanca, Tunis, Cairo, and other cities in the late 1980s. It also coincided with the

IMPORTANT CONCEPTS

BOX 19.6 | Participatory Budgets and Local Democracy

In 1989, Porto Alegre, Brazil, initiated participatory budgeting. This is a process of involving city residents and key local stakeholders, such as unions and neighbourhood committees, in the preparation of the city's investment budget. The process, named a Best Practice in Good Governance by UN-Habitat in 1996, relies on direct participation and on representation: residents in each neighbourhood identify priorities for investment for their district and region through direct participation, and then elect representatives to the city-wide budgeting process. Participatory budgeting is an important breakthrough in governance and urban planning: it provides a mechanism for redistributing resources in the city, improves transparency and increases accountability of elected officials, and contributes to the renewal of local democracy (Abers, 2001; Latendresse, 2006). Following the example of Porto Alegre, about 1,500 other cities in the world have experimented with various forms of participatory budgets. Both large urban centres—Johannesburg, Cologne, and Chicago—and less well-known municipalities—Rosario, Argentina; Entebbe, Uganda; Dondo, Mozambique; and Zwolen, Poland—have introduced some level of participatory budgeting.

emergence, since the early 1990s, of various initiatives around the world to promote appropriation of the city and its neighbourhoods by residents. Practices associated with participatory democracy, such as the experience of participatory budgeting in Brazil and in several other cities in the world, are a small-scale answer to the urban crisis.

The World Urban Social Forum and other networks seeking to create just, ecologically sustainable, inclusive, and democratic cities have begun to draw on the theoretical concept of the *right to the city* developed by the sociologist Henri Lefebvre. Lefebvre affirmed the right of those living in cities (regardless of their citizenship status, class, gender, ethnic, linguistic, religious, or other identity) to take part in the definition of the city. Thousands of local actors, including municipalities, as well as worldwide urban movements, aspire to see this right recognized along with other social and economic human rights. A network of institutions and NGOs has developed a World Charter for the Right to the City. The preamble of the Charter (2005) outlines this right:

> The Right to the City broadens the traditional focus on improvement of peoples' quality of life based on housing and the neighbourhood, to encompass quality of life at the scale of the city and its rural surroundings, as a mechanism of protection of the population that lives in cities or regions with rapid urbanization processes. This implies initiating a new way of promotion, respect, defense and fulfillment of the civil, political, economic, social, cultural and environmental rights guaranteed in regional and international human rights instruments.

Alongside this collective project of the global justice movement, actors in the public and private sectors are experimenting with new practices that converge in the same direction: the need to integrate the poorest populations, as well as women, indigenous people, ethnic minorities, and other marginalized social groups (see Box 19.7). Without idealizing the scope of these initiatives, which face many obstacles and constraints, it is important to note that they are exploring new avenues for participatory governance and sustainable urban planning and will contribute some elements, however modest, to the response to the urban crisis.

Paul Haslam

PHOTO 19.4 | Sao Paulo, one of the largest cities in the world.
Paul Haslam

IMPORTANT CONCEPTS

BOX 19.7 Gender and Housing Rights

The Right to Housing is the "right to live somewhere in security, peace and dignity" (UN-CESCR, 1991). Access to secure and decent housing provides psychological and physical security; it is also a means to struggle against poverty and inequality. Once a family has access to decent housing conditions, adults are able to concentrate their efforts on income-generation or improvements to their living conditions while children are more likely to have access to education. The right to adequate housing has emerged as a key policy agenda for housing movements, NGOs, and international agencies, one that increasingly is recognized as tied to gender equality. As Miraftab (2001: 154, 156) observes:

> Housing is a key resource for women; it is an asset important to their economic condition and central to their physical and social well-being. It is the site of child rearing and income generation and a nexus for social networks of support and community-based reliance. . . . Housing is a significant economic asset to women that contributes to their independence, economic security and bargaining power with men in their households and in society at large. Most importantly, it helps women determine their own futures and make the decisions that affect their lives.

Despite progress against gender discrimination, women disproportionately lack adequate housing (Chant, 2013; UN-IANWGE, 2009). Women head about 20 per cent of urban households worldwide but, in many countries, they do not have full rights to inheritance or property tenure. Where basic services are not supplied to the home or immediate neighbourhood, it is women and girls who typically fetch water or gather fuelwood, often at great distances, impinging on time for income-generation, schooling, and child care. And it is women and girls whose safety and comfort is most compromised by lack of sanitation, toilets, street lighting, and

(continued)

secure public transport: for instance, since they work at home in greater numbers, they are exposed to the environmental and health risks of poor infrastructure (such as diseases linked to poor drainage, open defecation, and decomposing rubbish) while lack of separate-sex toilets in schools may lead adolescent girls to drop out or be targeted for sexual violence. The vulnerability and insecurity faced by women and girls, in both the public and private realms, limit their ability to access services and pursue economic opportunities; gender-based violence is especially high under conditions of conflict, disaster, and their aftermath.

In urban areas, priorities to reverse and reduce gender inequalities include combatting overt forms of discrimination—such as biases in ownership, inheritance, and land titling regulations, in hiring and remuneration, or in political representation—and overcoming "gender blindness" in the planning and provision of urban services. Researchers from the World Bank and independent university studies "consistently show that when mothers have greater control over resources, more resources are allocated to food and to children's health (including nutrition) and education" (UN-IANWGE, 2009). The 1996 Habitat Agenda advocates for community mortgage programs that can help provide women with the access to capital, credit, land, technology, information, and other resources they need to improve their situation. Gender blindness—that is, the ignorance of and indifference to the distinct needs and priorities of women and of groups of women, such as the elderly, professionals, the informally employed, and students—is another barrier to change, and one that becomes of increasing importance as overt discrimination is eliminated. Bolivia, Colombia, Honduras, Peru, and Venezuela have changed how the head of a household is defined, allowing women to be recognized as responsible for and to sign legal documents (including ownership and loan contracts) on behalf of the family (Rolnik, 2011). Other important initiatives include the UN-Habitat Land Security and Urban Governance's campaign for property regulation reform, and, sharing similar goals, the Global Land Tool Network (GLTN) promotion of tools to facilitate women's access to property (land and housing).

FUTURE NEEDS

Cities—and the lifestyles of those who live, produce, and recreate in them—will need to radically shift towards more sustainable forms. It is in the cities that the decisive action to mitigate climate change and adapt to new environmental patterns must occur. Certainly, many coastal cities will need to adapt to rising sea levels, and changing weather and climate patterns will impact inland cities as well. "It is particularly ironic that the battle to save the world's remaining healthy ecosystems will be won or lost, not in tropical forests or coral reefs that are threatened, but on the streets of the most unnatural landscapes on the planet" (Worldwatch Institute, 2007: xxiv). Challenges of livelihoods, employment, and shelter are pressing. There is insufficient "productive and decent" employment for urban residents, with numerous implications for human welfare and service provision. The lack of adequate shelter experienced by one in seven urban residents in developing countries must be addressed immediately. While urbanization does not guarantee development, efforts to promote social justice, rights to the city, and sustainable settlements attest to the potential of cities as sites of innovative solutions to human problems.

SUMMARY

In this chapter, we have treated urbanization as a process that develops differently, depending on the region of the world, and we have examined demographic, economic, political, social, and environmental dimensions. This perspective allows the student to distinguish the current context in developing countries from the experience of industrialization in the industrialized countries. We underline that the globalization of the economy, which directly affects cities as places of production and consumption, and neoliberalism, which transformed the role and nature of the state, are structural factors that impacted cities and their ability to absorb growing numbers of inhabitants. Urbanization in most developing countries has occurred without industrialization or growth, contributing to the urbanization of poverty. Urban crisis is manifested, most notably, in the inequalities visible in slums side-by-side with rich areas. The arrival of migrants displaced by natural disasters, conflict, or economic reasons affects the ability of cities to cope. Students should note that cities occupy a paradoxical position. On the one hand, they contribute to environmental crises, on the other, they offer new opportunities for people to engage their municipalities to solve these problems: for example, through participatory governance, civil society movements, and urban agriculture.

QUESTIONS FOR CRITICAL THOUGHT

1. What distinguishes the urbanization of developing countries from that of developed countries?
2. What is meant by the term "urbanization of poverty"? What are the links between urbanization and development?
3. What are the main components of the urban crisis that has hit developing countries?
4. Why do slums emerge? What could be done to better provide poor households, women, and refugees with adequate shelter?
5. Explain some of the dilemmas raised by community participation and grassroots initiatives in the management of urban development.

SUGGESTED READINGS

Aguilar, Lorena. 2009. "Women and climate change." In Linda Starke, ed., *State of the World 2009: Into a Warming World*. New York: Worldwatch and W.W. Norton, 59–62.

Lizarralde, Gonzalo. 2015. *The Invisible Houses: Rethinking and Redesigning Low-Cost Housing in Developing Countries*. Hoboken, NJ: Taylor and Francis.

Miraftab, Faranak, and Neema Kudhu. 2014. *Cities of the Global South Reader*. New York: Routledge.

Moulaert, Frank, Erik Swyngedouw, Flavia Martinelli, and Sara Gonzalez, eds. 2010. *Can Neighbourhoods Save the City? Community Development and Social Innovation*. Abingdon, UK: Routledge.

BIBLIOGRAPHY

Aguilar, L. 2009. "Women and climate change." In Linda Starke, ed., *State of the World 2009: Into a Warming World*. New York: Worldwatch and W.W. Norton, 59–62.

Anderson, E.R., E.A. Cherrington, L. Tremblay-Boyer, A.I. Flores, and E. Sempris. 2008. "Identifying critical areas for conservation: Biodiversity and climate change in Central America, Mexico and the Dominican Republic." *Biodiversity* 9: 89–99.

Beall, J. 2002. "Globalisation and social exclusion in cities." *Environment and Urbanization* 14, 1: 41–51.

Bornstein, L. 2010. "Mega-projects, city-building and community benefits." *City, Culture and Society* 1, 4: 199–206.

Brookings-LSE Project on Internal Displacement. 2014. *Climate Change and Internal Displacement*. Washington: Brookings Institution.

Brynen, R., and R. El-Rifai. 2007. *Palestinian Refugees: Challenges of Repatriation and Development*. Ottawa: IDRC.

Caldeira, T. 2000. *City of Walls*. Berkeley: University of California Press.

Castells, M. 1996. *The Rise of the Network Society*. Oxford: Blackwell.

Chant, S. 2013. "Cities through a 'gender lens': A golden 'urban age' for women in the global South?" *Environment and Urbanization* 25, 1: 9–29.

Davis, M. 2006. *Planet of Slums*. London: Verso.

——— and R. Monk. 2008. *Evil Paradises: Dreamworlds of Neoliberalism*. New York: New Press.

Drakakis-Smith, D., 2000. *Third World Cities*, 2nd edn. London: Routledge.

ECHO. 2015. "ECHO Factsheet, Syria Crisis." http://ec.europa.eu/echo/files/aid/countries/factsheets/syria_en.pdf.

Food and Agriculture Organization of the United Nations (FAO). 2015. "Cities of despair—or opportunity?" www.fao.org/ag/agp/greenercities/en/whyuph/index.html.

Friedmann, J., and G. Wolff. 1982. "World city formation." *International Journal of Urban and Regional Research* 6, 3: 309–44.

Glaeser, E.L. 2014. "A world of cities: The causes and consequences of urbanization in poorer countries." *Journal of the European Economic Association* 12: 1154–99.

Gollin, D., R. Jedwab, and D. Vollrath. 2013. "Urbanization with and without Industrialization." www.uh.edu/econpapers/RePEc/hou/wpaper/2013-290-26.pdf.

Hall, P. 1998. *Cities in Civilization.* New York: Fromm International.

Harvey, D. 1982. *The Limits to Capital.* Chicago: University of Chicago Press.

———. 2013. *Rebel Cities: From the Right to the City to the Urban Revolution.* London: Verso.

Haysom, S. 2013. *Sanctuary in the City? Urban Displacement and Vulnerability. Final Report.* London: Humanitarian Policy Group, Overseas Development Institute.

Intergovernmental Panel on Climate Change (IPCC). 2014. *Climate Change 2014: Impacts, Adaptation, and Vulnerability.* New York: Cambridge University Press.

International Labour Organization (ILO). 2006. *The Future of Urban Employment.* Second United Nations Conference on Human Settlements (Habitat II). Geneva: ILO.

———. 2013. "Jobs and livelihoods in the post-2015 development agenda." *ILO Concept Note* No. 2.

Isin, E. 2000. *Democracy, Citizenship and the Global City.* London: Routledge.

Jenks, M., D. Kozak, and P. Takkanon. 2008. *World Cities and Urban Form: Fragmented, Polycentric, Sustainable?* London: Routledge.

King, A. 1990. *Urbanism, Colonialism and the World-Economy: Cultural and Spatial Foundations of the World Urban System.* London: Routledge.

Lizarralde, G. 2015. *The Invisible Houses: Rethinking and Redesigning Low-Cost Housing in Developing Countries.* Hoboken, NJ: Taylor and Francis.

Lorinc, J. 2008. *Cities.* Toronto: Groundwood Press.

Marcuse, P. 2008. "Globalization and the forms of cities." In Jenks et al. (2008).

Massey, D. 1984. *Spatial Divisions of Labor: Social Structures and the Geography of Production.*New York: Methuen.

Miraftab, F. 2001. "Risks and opportunities in gender gaps to access shelter: A platform for intervention." *International Journal of Politics, Culture, and Society* 15, 1: 143–60.

Mumford, L. 1961. *The City in History.* New York: Harcourt, Brace & World.

Osmont, A. 1995. *La banque mondiale et les villes: Du développement à l'ajustement.* Paris: Karthala.

Pielke, R., Jr. 2015. "Obstacles to accountability in international sports governance." In Transparency International, *Global Corruption Report: Sport.* www.transparency.org/files/content/feature/1.4_ObstaclesToAccountability_Pielke_GCRSport.pdf. Accessed 7 Sept. 2015.

Piketty, T. 2014. *Capital in the 21st Century.* Translated by A. Goldhammer. Cambridge, Mass.: Harvard University Press.

Renard, V. 2003. "Recherche urbaine et coopération avec les pays en développement: A la recherche d'un nouveau paradigme?" In A. Osmont and C. Goldblum, eds, *Villes et citadins dans la mondialisation.* Paris: Karthala.

Robbins, G. 2012. "Major international events and the working poor." *WEIGO Technical Brief* 5.

Roberts, R. 2010. *Palestinians in Lebanon: Refugees Living with Long-term Displacement.* Ottawa: I.B.Tauris.

Rolnik, R., 2011. *Report of the Special Rapporteur on adequate housing as a component of the right to an adequate standard of living, and on the right to non-discrimination in this context.* Human Rights Council, 19th session Agenda item 3, General Assembly of United Nations.

Sassen, S. 1991, 2001. *The Global City: New York, London, Tokyo.* Princeton, NJ: Princeton University Press.

———. 1998. "Urban economy and fading distance." Second Megacities Lecture, The Hague, Nov. www.brooklynsoc.org/courses/5/sassen.html. Accessed 7 Sept. 2015.

Smith, D.A. 1996. *Third World Cities in Global Perspective: The Political Economy of Uneven Urbanization.* Boulder, Colo.: Westview Press.

Tibaijuko, A. 2007. "Keynote address on water for thirsty cities." Opening Plenary Session, Stockholm World Water Week.

Transparency International. 2014. *Working Paper 2/2014: Corruption and Sport: Building Integrity to Prevent Abuses.* www.transparency.org/whatwedo/publication/working_paper_2_2014_corruption_and_sport_building_integrity_to_prevent_abu. Accessed 7 Sept. 2015.

United Nations. 2014a. *World Urbanization Prospects: The 2014 Revision.* Highlights. New York: UN Population Division, Department of Economic and Social Affairs.

United Nations. 2014b. *World Urbanization Prospects: The 2014 Revision.* New York: UN Population Division, Department of Economic and Social Affairs.

———. 2015a. *Cities and Climate Change and Disaster Risk Reduction.* UN Conference on Housing and Sustainable Development (Habitat III) Issue Paper. New York: UN Task Team for Habitat III.

———. 2015b. *Transforming Our World: The 2030 Agenda for Sustainable Development.* Finalized text for adoption, 1 Aug.

United Nations Committee on Economic, Social and Cultural Rights (UN-CESCR). 2001. "General Comment No.4, The right to adequate housing." Sixth session, 1991, U.N. Doc. E/1992/23, annex III at 114 (1991). www.refworld.org/docid/47a7079a1.html.

UN-Habitat. 2008. *State of the World's Cities 2010/2011.* London: Earthscan.

———. 2014. *State of the World's Cities 2012/2013.* New York: UN.

United Nations High Commissioner for Refugees (UNHCR). 2001. *Guiding Principles on Internal Displacement.* www.unhcr.org/43ce1cff2.html. Accessed 6 Aug. 2015.

———, IDMC Observatoire des situations de déplacement interne, and Norwegian Refugee Group. 2014. "33,3 millions de personnes déplacées par les conflits à travers le monde : le Nigéria figure parmi les cinq pays les plus touchés." Communiqué de presse.

United Nations-IANWGE. 2009. "Gender equality and sustainable urbanisation fact sheet." Inter-Agency Network on Women and Gender Equality (IANWGE), WomenWatch. www.un.org/womenwatch/feature/urban/factsheet.html.

United Nations Population Fund (UNFPA). 2007. *State of the World Population 2007: Unleashing the Potential of Urban Growth.* New York: UNFPA.

United Nations Radio. 2015. "Interview with Frank Santana, Coordinator, Resettlement Project, International Organization for Migration." Program broadcast by MINUSTAH-FM, Jan. 2015, on behalf of United Nations Radio.

Warner, Gregory. 2015. "How the world's largest refugee camp remade a generation of Somalis." *Morning Edition*, National Public Radio, 28 May. www.npr.org/sections/goatsandsoda/2015/05/28/410003537/their-life-in-a-refugee-camp-might-be-better-than-life-back-at-home.

World Bank. 2015. "Climate change complicates efforts to end poverty." *World Bank News*, 6 Feb. www.worldbank.org/en/news/feature/2015/02/06/climate-change-complicates-efforts-end-poverty.

World Charter for the Right to the City. 2005. Trans. Jodi Grahl. www.urbanreinventors.net/3/wsf.pdf. Accessed 25 Oct. 2010.

Worldwatch Institute. 2007. *State of the World: Our Urban Future.* New York: W.W. Norton.

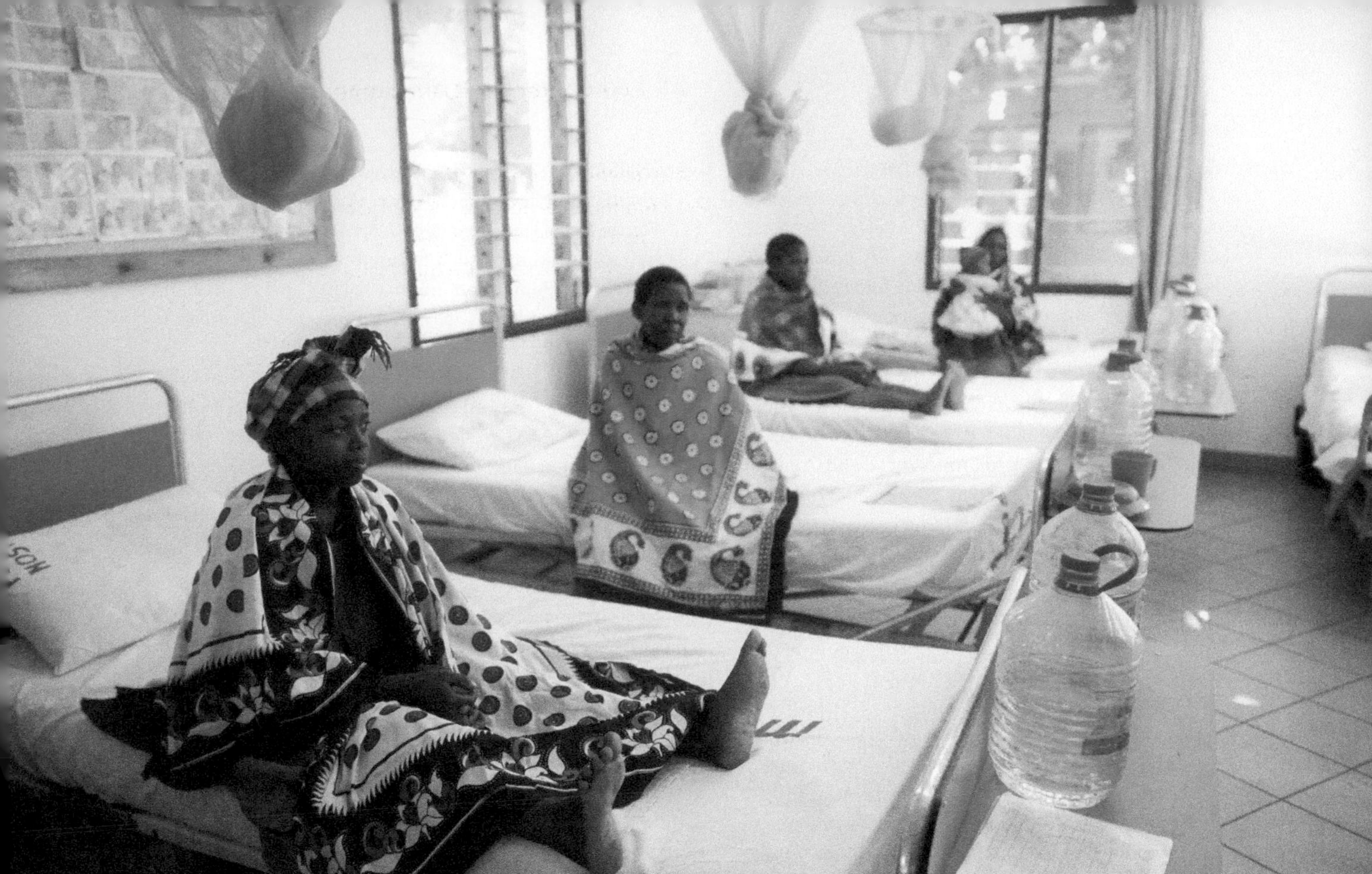

20 Development and Health

Ted Schrecker

LEARNING OBJECTIVES

- To achieve familiarity with key concepts such as social determinants of health and socio-economic gradients in health.
- To be able to assess arguments about the relative contribution of health care or health systems and social determinants of health to socio-economic gradients in health and population health status.
- To be able to identify and assess the potential effects on health of domestic social and economic policy and international development policy in areas that are superficially unrelated to health.
- To become familiar with major elements of the changing landscape of global health governance.
- To be able to assess the prospects for future improvements in population health outside the high-income countries in light of key developments in the international political economy.

▲ **Female patients waiting on hospital beds in the Comprehensive Community Based Rehabilitation in Tanzania (CCBRT) hospital.** | Source: Photo by Thomas Trutschel/Photothek via Getty Images

INTRODUCTION: WEALTH, HEALTH, AND THE REST OF THE STORY

Imagine for a moment a series of disasters that killed almost 800 people every day for a year: the equivalent of three or four daily crashes of crowded airliners. Such a situation would quickly be regarded as a humanitarian emergency: the stuff of headlines, especially if ways of preventing the events were well known and widely practised in some parts of the world. This is the casualty count from complications of pregnancy and childbirth, which kill an estimated 289,000 women per year—poor women, in poor countries. In Canada, a woman's lifetime risk of dying from complications of pregnancy or childbirth is one in 5,200; across the whole of sub-Saharan Africa, the world's poorest region, it is estimated at one in 38 (MMEIG, 2014).

The most basic explanation for this disparity has to do with wealth and poverty. One recent estimate is that providing a bare minimum of essential health services for all the residents of a low-income country would cost an average of US$86 per person, per year (in 2012 dollars; Centre on Global Health Security, 2014). This sum would not buy anything like the care most readers of this chapter take for granted, yet is several times what many low-income countries spend on health care. For example, in 2012 the public budget for health care, adjusted for purchasing power, was US$27 per person in Bangladesh, US$37 in Ethiopia, and US$23 in Madagascar (WHO, 2015b). Meanwhile, high-income countries spend thousands of dollars per person per year on their health-care systems, which operate in facilities like the US cancer centre shown in Photo 20.1. In many poor countries, resources for cancer care are almost non-existent despite rapid increases in the number of cases (Knaul, Anderson, Bradley, et al., 2010; Livingston, 2013).

Low-income countries, in particular, cannot realistically provide even a bare minimum standard of care without external resources, which is why development assistance for health (DAH)—discussed later in the chapter—is so important. Domestic priorities also come into play, and the health of the poor and marginalized may simply not be high on the agenda. For example, in 2001 the member states of the African Union (AU) committed (without a deadline) to increasing public spending on health to 15 per cent of general government expenditure. A decade later, only six of 53 AU member states had met this target (Committee of Experts, 2011); AU finance ministers had unsuccessfully attempted to force its abandonment. And in 2015 a newly elected Indian government announced a 16 per cent cut in its health budget (Mudur, 2015), even though India's performance on basic indicators like literacy, immunization, and child nutrition lags well behind some even poorer countries (Drèze and Sen, 2013: 40, 45–80). Protection of health, especially the health of the poor, is merely one competitor among many for policy attention and state resources, just as it is in wealthier countries. Further complicating the story, a number of low-income countries (such as Cuba, Sri Lanka, and Costa Rica) and regions within countries (India's Kerala state is the example most often cited) have achieved *Good Health at Low Cost*—the title of a 1985 study of such jurisdictions (Halstead, Walsh, and Warren, 1985). More recent research identifies Bangladesh, Ethiopia, Kyrgyzstan, Thailand, and the Indian state of Tamil Nadu as jurisdictions that have achieved substantial improvements in health despite low public expenditure levels, although health systems are in no respect comparable to those in the high-income world (Balabanova, Mills, Conteh, et al., 2013).

Health care is only one of the influences on health, and in many contexts is less important than **social determinants of health**: conditions under which people live and work that affect their opportunities to lead healthy lives. These were the focus of a commission established by the World Health Organization (WHO), whose 2008 report was organized around eliminating health inequities: unjust and avoidable inequalities in health (Commission on Social Determinants of Health, 2008). Some of the more extreme illustrations: despite progress over the past decades, and with some uncertainties about data quality (as is often the case), an estimated 795 million people in the world suffer from chronically insufficient caloric intake, the most extreme form of malnutrition (FAO, 2015). Paradoxically, according to WHO there are now roughly twice as many people in the world who are overweight (WHO, 2015a)—another form of malnutrition and one that may actually have more serious consequences for health because of links with cardiovascular disease, diabetes, and

Ted Schrecker

PHOTO 20.1 | One building on the campus of the M.D. Anderson Cancer Center, Houston, Texas.

other non-communicable diseases (Dixon, 2010). This is an important aspect of, and contributor to, the **double burden of disease** (Box 20.1). Again, despite recent progress, more than 600 million people lack access to clean drinking water and 2.4 billion lack access to basic sanitation (UNICEF and WHO, 2015). This is one of several ways economic deprivation creates situations in which daily routines of living are themselves hazardous. Charcoal or dung smoke from heating and indoor cooking is a major contributor to respiratory disease among the world's poor (Kurmi, Lam, and Ayres, 2012). It is estimated that more than 800 million people now live in slums, including 62 per cent of the urban population of sub-Saharan Africa (UN-Habitat, 2013: 112); there is room for disagreement about definitions, but on almost any definition slums do not provide a healthy environment (see Chapter 19).

"GREAT DIVIDES" AND SOCIO-ECONOMIC GRADIENTS

Against the background of casualty figures like those that began the chapter, one of the "great divides" in health and development is whether the glass should be considered half empty or half full. Those in the latter camp emphasize progress in such areas as measles control, where deaths dropped from 548,000 in 2004 to 158,000 in 2012 as a result of large-scale immunization campaigns (Perry, Gacic-Dobo, Dabbagh, et al., 2014), or the twelvefold increase between 2003 and 2013 in the number of people living with HIV whose lives are being prolonged by access to antiretrovirals (UNAIDS, 2012, 2014). Even the optimists concede the importance of intensive efforts to ensure that progress continues. Another such divide involves the relative priority that

CRITICAL ISSUES

BOX 20.1 | The Double Burden of Disease

For a long time, population health researchers believed that countries would undergo a relatively standardized **epidemiological transition** as they grew richer. Infectious or communicable diseases, many of which disproportionately affect children, would decline in importance as causes of death while deaths from non-communicable diseases such as cardiovascular disease and cancer, which normally affect people later in life, would increase. Although reductions in infant and under-5 mortality make an important contribution to the improvement in health status that often accompanies increases in income in low- and middle-income countries (LMICs), the full picture is more complicated.

Communicable diseases continue to take a toll in the low-income world. Roughly 95 per cent of new HIV infections now occur in LMICs, especially in sub-Saharan Africa, where AIDS kills 1.1 million people per year despite increases in access to antiretroviral therapy (UNAIDS, 2014). Malaria and tuberculosis continue to kill an estimated 600,000 and 1.3 million people per year, respectively, despite considerable progress in recent years (United Nations, 2014) and despite the demonstrated effectiveness of relatively low-cost solutions. At the same time, people in LMICs are increasingly exposed to industrial pollution; to risk factors for non-communicable diseases such as cardiovascular disease and diabetes, exemplified by rapid increases in overweight and obesity; and to road traffic accidents, which kill an estimated 1.1 million people per year in LMICs. The number of non-fatal injuries, often resulting in permanent disability, is vastly larger and even less well documented (WHO, 2013). The double burden of disease refers to the persistence of communicable diseases in parallel with the rapidly growing prevalence of non-communicable diseases and injuries—often thought, stereotypically but inaccurately, to be diseases of wealth.

As with most other causes of disability and death, a pronounced **socio-economic gradient** exists in road traffic injuries: pedestrians and users of unsafe or unregulated forms of public transportation, many of whom have little hope of ever affording a vehicle, are disproportionately likely to be injured or killed on the roads. The toll is expected to increase as members of the expanding middle class buy more cars, while health systems are unable to afford anything approaching high-income countries' standards of expensive trauma care.

should be accorded to promoting advances in medical care (biomedical approaches) and to social determinants of health.

The Lancet, one of the world's leading medical journals, often commissions long, multi-authored review articles on topics of special interest. In 2013 and 2014, two of these *Lancet* articles articulated dramatically different visions for global health. The lead authors of one article (Jamison, Summers, Alleyne, et al., 2013a) were two former World Bank economists, one (Lawrence Summers) also a former US Secretary of the Treasury. The second team (Ottersen, Dasgupta, Blouin, et al., 2014) was led by a neuroscientist, the president of the University of Oslo, and included Sir Michael Marmot, the distinguished epidemiologist who chaired WHO's Commission on Social Determinants of Health. This second team focused on "power asymmetries" and the "political determinants of health" in a globalized world; its treatment of biomedical interventions was limited to considering the role of trade agreements in restricting access to essential medicines. The first team dismissed policies to address the social determinants of health in a paragraph and concentrated on how best to develop and diffuse biomedical interventions, although it did concede the importance of such health promotion measures as high alcohol and tobacco taxes, along with taxes or regulations addressing highly processed foods. They also argued that improved health could accelerate economic growth (Jamison et al., 2013a: 1912–18), although their own assessment of evidence for this point falls back in part on "the inherent plausibility of the finding" (Jamison, Summers, Alleyne, et al., 2013b).

The tension between these approaches is partly illusory. No amount of poverty reduction will produce an effective measles vaccine or treatment for HIV infection. Conversely, vaccines and therapeutics cannot address the problems of deprivation-related indoor air pollution, or the rapid dietary transitions that lead to increases in overweight and obesity. A critical point for development policy is that neither perspective provides support for policy nostrums that prioritize economic growth in the expectation that health improvements will follow, sooner or later. This is not a caricature. A 2001 article in the *British Medical Journal* (Feachem, 2001) claimed that "globalization is good for your health, mostly" because countries that integrate into the global economy more rapidly, specifically through trade liberalization, experience more rapid growth and are therefore better able to reduce poverty. For several reasons, some explored in the next section of the chapter, few responsible researchers would now support this claim without numerous qualifications.

The historical record is clear that health improvements do not follow automatically or rapidly from economic growth. Historian Simon Szreter (1999) has shown that during a period of rapid economic growth associated with industrialization in nineteenth-century England and Wales, national average life expectancy remained constant (at 41 years) through most of the century, but in the crucibles of industrialization, cities like Manchester and Birmingham, it plunged to 29 years by the 1830s and did not recover for several decades. (To put the chronology into perspective, Friedrich Engels's *The Condition of the Working Class in England*, graphically describing conditions that endangered life and health, was published in 1845.) Szreter explains the eventual improvement with reference to the provision of water and sanitation services by local governments, responding to demands from an alliance of the newly enfranchised working class and an industrial and mercantile bourgeoisie concerned about the health of its workforce. As he puts it: "The relationship between market-led, rapid economic growth and human health and welfare . . . is critically mediated by politics" (Szreter, 1999: 146). Underscoring this point, many jurisdictions that have achieved rapid improvements in population health have done so not only by committing resources to health care but also through education, rural development, and prioritizing the empowerment of women (Balabanova et al., 2013)—what has been referred to as investing in "social growth" (Riley, 2008) as well as economic growth. Further social science research is needed on the political conditions under which health and the reduction of health inequalities are more or less likely to become policy priorities in LMICs.

So far, this chapter has discussed health outcome data in terms of national averages. Such averages can be misleading; they conceal substantial socio-economically patterned differences in health: **social gradients** or **socio-economic gradients** (Commission on Social Determinants of Health, 2008: 30–2). Figure 20.1 shows the gradient in mortality among children five years old and younger (under-5 mortality rate or U5MR, a common health indicator) in six LMICs; note that not only the absolute values but also the steepness of the gradient vary substantially. Such differences are not confined to LMICs and are observed within much smaller areas than those defined by national borders. Within the borders of the small English local authority where I live and work, the difference in male life expectancy at birth between the most and least deprived districts is 17 years (Public Health England, 2015), comparable to the difference in national average male life expectancy between the United Kingdom and Senegal. Infant mortality (death before the age of one year) is 10 times as common in the poorest area of Washington, DC, the capital of the United States, as in the richest area (Save the Children, 2015: 42).

Socio-economic gradients are important to understandings of development and health for at least two reasons. First, they exist even in high-income jurisdictions that (in theory) offer universal access to health care independently of ability to pay, like the United Kingdom, which suggests the importance of social determinants of health in explaining health inequalities. Second, especially in middle- and high-income countries, socio-economic gradients in health are only partly attributable to the effects of material deprivation. Marmot's studies of British public servants (the Whitehall studies, referring to the street in London where the main offices of the British public service historically

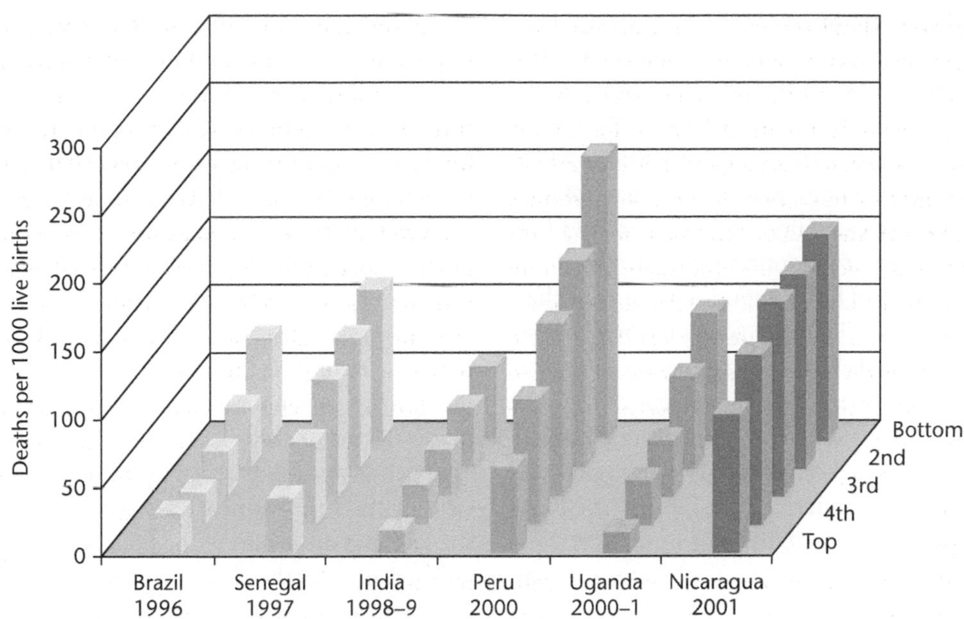

FIGURE 20.1 | Gradient in Under-5 Mortality Rate by Household Income Quintile, Selected Countries

Source: Data from Gwatkin, Rutstein, Johnson et al. (2007).

were located) are central to the research literature on socio-economic gradients. They showed a gradient in various health outcomes across a population none of whom were living in poverty or affected by inadequate nutrition or insalubrious housing; in most cases they also enjoyed considerable job security. Marmot has argued powerfully, with reference to well-established physiological effects of psychosocial stress, for an explanation based on the quite different ways in which stress is experienced depending on one's access to economic resources and position within a social hierarchy (Marmot, 2004).

GLOBALIZATION AND HEALTH: TRADE AND INVESTMENT AGREEMENTS AS A CASE STUDY

An extensive literature now exists on the relation between globalization and health (see, e.g., Labonté, Schrecker, Packer, and Runnels, 2009; Blouin, Chopra, and van der Hoeven, 2009; Ruckert and Labonté, 2012; Schrecker, 2014a, 2014b), which is clearly an area of concern for development policy. This chapter concentrates on one specific area: the implications for health of the changing nature of the international trade law and policy regime, which provides essential legal infrastructure for the global reorganization of production, commerce, and finance. The first rounds of multilateral trade negotiations and agreements after World War II focused on reducing tariffs (customs duties). Tariffs, along with quotas on imports and some forms of product standards, operate "at the border," figuratively if not literally. By contrast, many elements of contemporary trade and investment agreements take effect "behind the border," by limiting the range of government actions that might have the consequence of restricting trade or limiting the profitability of foreign investment. The effect, and often the intent, is to limit governments' **policy space**: "the freedom, scope, and mechanisms that governments have to choose, design, and implement public policies to fulfill their aims" (Koivusalo, Schrecker, and Labonté, 2009: 105). This is true of several agreements that came into force in 1995 as part of the WTO regime, but also of some agreements like the North American Free Trade Agreement (NAFTA) that predate the WTO.

One example is the harmonization of intellectual property (IP) protection under the WTO Agreement on

Trade-Related Aspects of Intellectual Property Rights (TRIPS). TRIPS was driven in the first instance by transnational, mainly US, corporations: "in effect, twelve corporations made public law for the world" (Sell, 2003: 96); they included pharmaceutical giants Bristol-Myers (now Bristol-Myers Squibb), Merck, and Pfizer. A subsequent civil society campaign organized around lowering the prices of patented antiretroviral drugs to treat HIV/AIDS, in the face of bitter opposition from the pharmaceutical industry (Gellman, 2000; 't Hoen, Berger, Calmy, et al., 2011), also led to the adoption in 2001 of the Declaration on the TRIPS Agreement and Public Health (Doha Declaration), which established the principle that health concerns could outweigh intellectual property protections under certain conditions. However, initial use of this flexibility was slow (Kerry and Lee, 2007), and even a decade later the issuance of compulsory licences—which override patent protection—had been limited, with "few instances" of compulsory licences for diseases other than AIDS, and no compulsory licences "for high-impact diseases with patented treatments such as malaria, multi-drug resistant tuberculosis, or sepsis." The authors of the cited study concluded "that the barriers" to using TRIPs flexibilities "go well beyond the lack of production capacity, and likely extend to health system incapacity, political pressure against CLs [compulsory licences], and the legislative difficulties of issuing a CL" (Beall and Kuhn, 2012).

Meanwhile, the United States in particular actively pursued IP protection that goes beyond TRIPS ("TRIPS-plus" provisions) in bilateral and regional trade and investment agreements, such as an agreement with several Central American countries and the Dominican Republic (CAFTA-DR) that has kept off the Guatemalan market even some generic drugs that are available in the US (Roffe, Von Braun, and Vivas-Eugui, 2008; Shaffer and Brenner, 2009; Correa, 2013: 903–4). Such agreements often reflect fundamental inequalities of bargaining power, in that governments must make substantial concessions in order to secure modest gains in access to the markets of a much larger and richer trading partner (Shadlen, 2005). As in the case of (non-)investment in national health systems, the fact that the health of the poor is most immediately affected may further limit the political salience of access to medicines. This said, IP protection is probably less important in terms of the overall pattern of access to medical advances than a more fundamental problem: diseases that affect mainly or exclusively the poor are not commercially attractive in terms of research investment (Box 20.2).

A trade policy impact of quite a different kind involves the relation between trade liberalization and the **nutrition transition** to diets high in sugar and fat, now occurring in many LMICs more rapidly than it did in high-income countries (Popkin, 2007). An important

CRITICAL ISSUES

BOX 20.2 | The 10/90 Gap and Health Research

Private for-profit firms, mainly pharmaceutical firms, now substantially outspend governments worldwide on health research (Burke and Matlin, 2008: 28), but the objectives and accountabilities involved are quite different. The result is a continuing mismatch between health research priorities and the illnesses of primary concern outside the industrialized world: the so-called **10/90 gap**, referring to the fact that 10 per cent or less of the world's health research spending is directed to the conditions that account for 90 per cent of the global burden of disease. The poor do not constitute a market of sufficient size to attract research funding based on anticipation of commercially viable products. Between 1975 and 2010, only a handful of the thousands of new pharmaceutical entities developed were for treatment of tuberculosis, tropical diseases, and other neglected conditions of the poor (Balasegaram, Childs, and Arkinstall, 2014: 251). The need, therefore, is not only for reform of IP protection regimes, but also and more fundamentally for multilateral initiatives to change how medical research and innovation are financed and to mobilize new sources of funds (Moon, Bermudez, and 't Hoen, 2012).

driver of the transition is rapid transformation of food systems by imports of ultra-processed foods (Monteiro, Moubarac, Cannon, et al., 2013) and by foreign investment in supermarkets, food processing, and fast-food chains (Popkin, 2014)—facilitated by a liberalized trade and investment regime (Hawkes, Chopra, and Friel, 2009; Thow, Snowdon, Labonté, et al., 2015). A strong correlation has been found between the level of foreign investment as a percentage of GDP and "greater exposure to unhealthy food commodities, especially for soft drinks, processed foods and alcohol" across 50 LMICs, and LMICs that have trade agreements with the US have per capita levels of soft-drink consumption more than 50 per cent higher than those that do not (Stuckler, McKee, Ebrahim, et al., 2012). According to a trade publication "McDonald's arrived in Chile targeting the segment of children, but over time, the customer base has expanded from not just children to also their parents, as well as young people. This strategy has allowed this brand to claim an important part of the category, and it has established itself amongst consumers of fast food" (Euromonitor, 2011).

The combination of farm subsidies in the US and the removal of trade and investment barriers between the US and Mexico under NAFTA led to rapid transformation of the Mexican food system: "exporting obesity" (Clark, Hawkes, Murphy, et al., 2012). Specifically, US exports of subsidized corn to Mexico, partly as high-fructose corn syrup (HFCS), rose sharply after a 2006 WTO dispute settlement ruling invalidated a Mexican tax on soft drinks sweetened with anything other than cane sugar; HFCS is thought by some researchers to play a significant role in the rising incidence of diabetes (Goran, Ulijaszek, and Ventura, 2013). Perhaps predictably, Mexican prevalence of overweight and obesity is now comparable to US levels. The agricultural subsidy programs that enable US exporters to underprice Mexican producers remain

Sunitha Pilli/iStockphoto

PHOTO 20.2 | Clean water is essential to public health.

permissible under the current trade law regime, and the US has doggedly resisted efforts to end them. At the very least, such conflicts between trade and health policy objectives suggest the need for greater "policy coherence" (Blouin, Drager, and Heymann, 2008). Are the international institutions established to protect and promote health up to the task? More fundamentally, is the issue one of coherence, or one of a project of neoliberal globalization that systematically subordinates health protection to commercial objectives?

THE CHANGING LANDSCAPE OF GLOBAL HEALTH AND DEVELOPMENT POLICY

The increasingly complex twenty-first-century global health policy landscape is often discussed in terms of global health governance. The term reflects the lack of a supranational authority and the expanding role of organizations that are neither agencies of national governments nor multilateral agencies in the conventional mould. Only a few of the most important actors and institutions are discussed here (for more detail see, e.g., Youde, 2012; Hein, 2013).

WHO is the UN system agency with primary responsibility for health protection, with its constitution designating it "as the directing and co-ordinating authority on international health work" (see also Chapter 10). Its 193 member states meet annually as the World Health Assembly (WHA) to set policy, which is overseen by a 34-member executive board. It operates 147 country offices and six regional offices as well as its Geneva secretariat. Since 2006–7, WHO has operated on an annual budget of approximately US$4 billion, which represents a substantial decline once inflation is taken into account. In recent years only about 25 per cent of that amount represented "assessed contributions" paid as part of members' UN obligations (WHO, 2014). For the balance, WHO must rely on discretionary contributions from member states, meaning that WHO programming and priorities are donor-driven to a degree that is often difficult to discover (People's Health Movement, Medact, and Global Equity Gauge Alliance, 2008: 224–39). WHO is further constrained by the fact that, in the words of the editor of *The Lancet*, it is "intergovernmental, not supra-governmental," and thus lacks any source of authority apart from the co-operation and commitment of member states (Horton, 2009: 28). In recent years, while pressures for WHO reform intensify, the organization is increasingly seen as irrelevant. "One of the fiercest conflicts in global health, concerning the TRIPS agreement and access to medicines, unfolded with WHO playing only a marginal role" (Hein, 2013: 56), and WHO came in for criticism over the slowness of its response to the Ebola outbreak of 2014 (Box 20.4).

WHO once sought leadership in promoting comprehensive primary health care (CPHC), a strategy for integrating prevention and treatment at the core of the goal of achieving "Health for All in the Year 2000," which was endorsed by member states in 1978 at the Alma-Ata Conference. The vision articulated at Alma-Ata (since renamed Almaty), Kazakhstan, included not only comprehensive access to health care, but also many elements that would now be described in terms of social determinants of health (Box 20.3). For various reasons, WHO failed to defend effectively this admittedly ambitious vision against critics, both within the medical and health communities (including within WHO itself) and outside them (Brown, Cueto, and Fee, 2006; Lawn et al., 2008). Meanwhile, the much larger and richer World Bank and International Monetary Fund (IMF) emerged as decisive players in development policy, with both direct and indirect influence on health and health systems. The Bank's importance derives both from its role as a channel of development finance and from its formidable research budget for gathering and analyzing data. As a result of this capability, the policy advice it provides is often incorrectly perceived as beyond politics and ideology (see Chapter 9).

Historically, the Bank aggressively promoted a market-dominated concept of health-sector reform that favoured private provision and financing, including reliance on user fees, with the public sector as a residual provider of a limited, "cost-effective" set of interventions (Rowden, 2013), an approach that may have contributed to the eventual demise of WHO's commitment to CPHC (Hall and Taylor, 2003). "The Bank's argument, presented as one tenet of a broader neoliberal economic agenda, that health care was largely a private not a public good, and thus deliverable through

CRITICAL ISSUES

BOX 20.3 | The Alma-Ata Vision

Primary health care . . . (2) addresses the main health problems in the community, providing promotive, preventive, curative, and rehabilitative services accordingly; (3) includes at least: education concerning prevailing health problems and the methods of preventing and controlling them; promotion of food supply and proper nutrition; an adequate supply of safe water and basic sanitation; maternal and child health care, including family planning; immunisation against the major infectious diseases; prevention and control of locally endemic diseases; appropriate treatment of common diseases and injuries; and provision of essential drugs; (4) involves, in addition to the health sector, all related sectors and aspects of national and community development, in particular agriculture, animal husbandry, food, industry, education, housing, public works, communications, and other sectors . . . . and demands the coordinated efforts of all those sectors . . . . (6) should be sustained by integrated, functional, and mutually supportive referral systems, leading to the progressive improvement of comprehensive health care for all, and giving priority to those most in need . . . .

All governments should launch and sustain primary health care as part of a comprehensive national health system in coordination with other sectors.

Source: Alma-Ata Declaration, 1978, as reproduced in Lawn, Rohde, Rifkin, et al. (2008).

the market, proved influential throughout the latter decades of the twentieth century, spilling over into the 21st" (Harmer and Buse, 2014: 3). The Bank is now less dogmatic in its enthusiasm for private financing, in the context of growing global support for universal health coverage (Rowden, 2013), discussed in the concluding section of the chapter.

In addition to promoting private health financing, the Bank often acted in concert with the IMF during the era of structural adjustment lending (discussed in Chapters 3, 9, and 14), demanding a relatively standard package of macroeconomic policies designed primarily to ensure that debt service payments to external creditors could be maintained. Destructive effects on social determinants of health were documented in an authoritative UNICEF study as early as 1987 (Cornia, Jolly, and Stewart, 1987), yet throughout the first decade of the century the IMF continued to demand strict limits to the growth of public expenditures on health and education, even when funds had been committed by donors, because of concerns about potential domestic inflation and about currency appreciation that would reduce the competitiveness of exports (Ooms and Schrecker, 2005; Independent Evaluation Office, 2007; Working Group, 2007). Among other consequences, the weakening of African national health systems may have compromised responses to the Ebola outbreak of 2014 (Box 20.4).

Perhaps the strongest indication that health is now firmly established as an element of the foreign policy agenda of the high income countries is the increasing value of development assistance for health (DAH). On recent estimates, this figure increased from US$6.9 billion in 1990 to US$35.9 billion in 2014 (Dieleman, Graves, and Johnson, 2015; figures in 2014 dollars), including funds from private sources like the Bill & Melinda Gates Foundation but not assistance for programs in such areas as water, sanitation, and nutrition that may have important health benefits. DAH cannot offset the far larger outflows of funds from most developing regions associated with debt servicing (see Chapter 14) and capital flight (see Ndikumana, Boyce, and Ndiaye, 2014), but it nevertheless serves as a rough indicator of the extent of policy concern.

It is useful to distinguish between sources of DAH (the originators or "donors") and channels (the institutions by way of which it reaches its eventual users in destination countries). National governments, the United States in particular, are the dominant sources of DAH, much of which is disbursed through the channels of their own bilateral aid agencies (such as Canada's Ministry of International Development within Global Affairs Canada and the United Kingdom's Department for International Development). Middle-income countries like the BRICS (Brazil, Russia, India, China, and South Africa) are becoming increasingly important as sources of development assistance and direct investment (Harmer, Xiao, Missoni, et al., 2013); so far their policy influence through development assistance—as distinct from direct investment, at least in the case of China—has been modest, but this may well change in the future (see Chapter 13).

National governments also disburse funds through channels like the World Bank and an expanding range of hybrid, multi-sectoral, and multilateral organizations. The Global Fund to Fight HIV/AIDS, Tuberculosis and Malaria (the Global Fund), the most important of these, was established by the G8 countries in 2001, at least partly to avoid the bureaucracy that was seen by the United States in particular as compromising WHO and the UN system more generally. The Global Fund operates like an international granting council, mainly funded by high-income country governments; its board includes representatives of donor and recipient governments, non-governmental organizations, and the private sector. As of 2014, it had disbursed US$30.9 billion (in 2014 dollars) (Dieleman et al., 2015) to projects that must first be proposed by recipient country applicants and then approved by a scientific review panel. Like other ventures of its kind, the Global Fund has been criticized for emphasizing "vertical," disease-specific programs at the expense of efforts to support overall health system strengthening. The limits of vertical programming, which has achieved demonstrated successes, may be less of a concern than the Global Fund's lack of stable long-term funding: it relies on periodic "voluntary replenishment conferences" where it in effect passes around a hat. After the financial crisis of 2008, the Fund was temporarily forced to suspend support for all new projects (Moszynski, 2011).

The increased importance of the Bill & Melinda Gates Foundation (BMGF) signals what may be a longer-term shift to supporting development and health through private wealth rather than public resources (People's Health Movement et al., 2008: 240–59). BMGF's resources enable it to spend more annually than the value of assessed contributions to WHO. Health promotion pioneer Ilona Kickbusch and a colleague have described this as "a scandal of global health governance" in which WHO member states "are giving up their major instrument to drive health policy and ensure health security" (Kickbusch and Payne, 2004). By 2014, BMGF had spent US$21.6 billion (2014 dollars) on health programming, or 5.7 per cent of total DAH from all sources since 1999 (Dieleman et al., 2015). Critics have commented on the large number of Foundation grants awarded to US-based recipients (McCoy, Kembhavi, Patel, et al., 2009: 1650), and have drawn a parallel between the rise of the BMGF and the influence of the Rockefeller Foundation on international public health policy in the twentieth century: "Each was started by the richest, most ruthless and innovative capitalist of his day" (Birn, 2014: 1/27).

New kinds of co-ordinating institutions have emerged in response to the multiplication of actors in global health. One of these is the H8 or Health 8, established in 2007, which comprises senior officials of four UN agencies (the Joint United Nations Programme on HIV/AIDS or UNAIDS, which is itself a multi-organizational partnership, UNICEF, the UN Population Fund, and WHO); the World Bank; the Global Fund; the Global Alliance for Vaccines and Immunization (GAVI, another hybrid institution); and BMGF. It is indicative of the changing global health architecture that the World Bank, BMGF, and two hybrid institutions participate on an equal footing with UN system agencies that are at least formally accountable through the UN General Assembly. Like WHO, such co-ordinating institutions depend entirely on the good faith and commitment of their members; so far, also like WHO, they reflect little or no recognition of the health consequences of choices about such matters as trade, macroeconomic policy, and public finance. This limitation assumes special importance in view of a number of challenges for development policy and health that lie ahead.

DEVELOPMENT AND HEALTH: THE UNCERTAIN FUTURE

One of the most immediate concerns in global health remains the mobilization of additional financing for health systems. Based on the earlier cited estimate of US$86 per person per year as the minimum

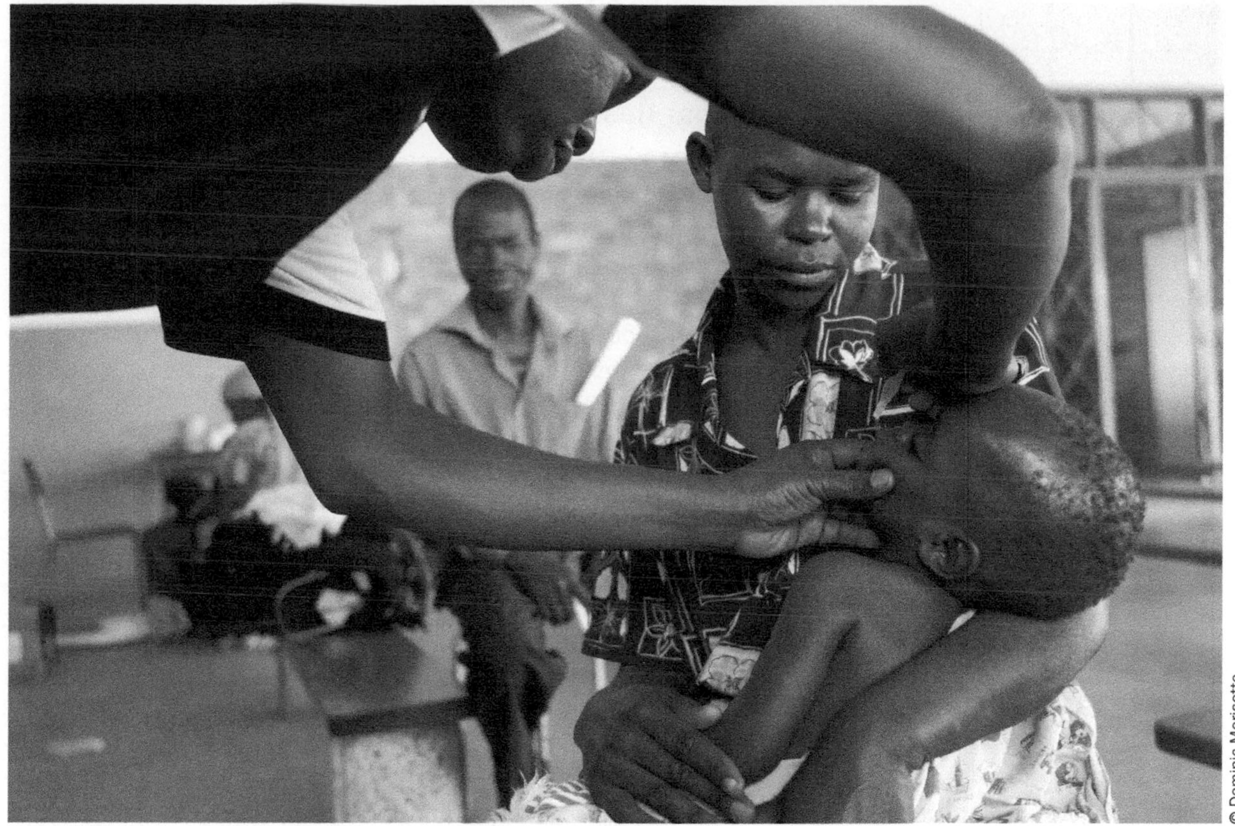
© Dominic Morisette

PHOTO 20.3 | Health clinic in Gulu, Uganda.

cost of basic health care, the annual "financing gap" amounts to US$196 billion (2012 dollars) (Centre on Global Health Security, 2014), or several times the current value of DAH. This is a very large amount in terms of its potential impact; it is also trivial in comparison with annual military spending worldwide, including in some DAH recipient countries, or the US$14 trillion in cash and credit guarantees that were mobilized to bail out financial institutions during the 2008 crisis (Bank of England, 2009). Such comparisons leave aside important questions of implementation, effectiveness, and accountability (Sridhar, 2010), but nevertheless raise issues of global justice, which could indeed be the subject of a separate chapter.

What motivates donors to allocate resources to improving health outside their borders? The simplest answer involves concern about the spread of communicable diseases like influenza and SARS. Document-based research on health and foreign policy has found that security-oriented rationales, specifically the fear of international epidemics, predominate (Labonté and Gagnon, 2010)—as shown, for example, by the characterization of HIV/AIDS "as a threat to both human and national security" at the time of the UN General Assembly special session on HIV in 2001 (McInnes, 2009). The political power of security concerns was underscored by responses to the Ebola outbreak of 2014 (Box 20.4). "This justification may explain why non-communicable diseases rank low in aid and development discourse" (Labonté and Gagnon, 2010: 5): Australians, Britons, Canadians, or Germans have little to fear from (for example) maternal and child mortality or rising traffic fatality counts in low-income countries. At the same time, security is not the only motivation for DAH, and in at least some contexts it is probably driven by genuinely

CRITICAL ISSUES

BOX 20.4 | Ebola: Lessons for Global Health Policy and Politics

Responses in the high-income world to the 2014 outbreak of Ebola virus disease in West Africa represented an extreme example of the fear factor at work. The *New York Times* reported on 10 March that "[t]he world [had] spent more than $4 billion fighting Ebola," and in December 2014 President Obama had called on Congress to support US$6.2 billion in emergency funding. In March, there were still only four confirmed cases in the US. The effects of the disease are fearsome, but it cannot be transmitted by asymptomatic individuals, and it was pointed out at the time that: "The numbers of children dying every day from preventable causes are far greater than from this Ebola outbreak. One key difference, of course, is that these health problems do not board planes to Europe or North America" (Wright, Hanna, and Mailfert, 2015). In the aftermath of the outbreak, WHO was criticized by its own internal review panel for its limited emergency response capability (Stocking, Muyembe-Tamfun, Shuaib, et al., 2015); the panel attributed this failure both to budget constraints and to management shortcomings, and drew attention more generally to problems of financing research and development related to neglected diseases. Less widely recognized was the fact that "the conspicuous unpreparedness of countries like Guinea, Liberia, and Sierra Leone [was] a direct consequence of years of insufficient public investment in the underlying public health infrastructure," attributable at least in part to the IMF's obsession with fiscal restraint (Rowden, 2014; see also Kentikelenis, King, McKee, et al., 2015).

altruistic concerns. Here is one of several areas where detailed research that gets inside the "black box" of the policy process will be useful.

This is true in particular of the shift towards universal health coverage (UHC) as a priority for development and health policy. Milestones include the 2008 G8 Summit, which focused on health system strengthening (Reich and Takemi, 2009); WHO's 2010 *World Health Report*, organized around the move towards universal coverage; and a 2012 resolution of the UN General Assembly urging governments "to urgently and significantly scale up efforts to accelerate the transition towards universal access to affordable and quality health-care services" (United Nations, 2012). The imperative here involves not only protecting health, but protecting people against the economic effects of the lack of coverage: it is estimated that 100 million people a year are driven into poverty by the need for out-of-pocket health spending (Xu, Evans, Carrin, et al., 2007). It remains to be seen how effectively the substantial resources needed to provide UHC, especially in low-income countries, will be mobilized, and the extent to which (especially in middle-income countries) domestic revenues can be drawn upon. The meaning of UHC is also contested terrain. Support for UHC would appear a decisive repudiation of the market-oriented World Bank view that was hegemonic at the end of the last century, but Sengupta (2013) warns that UHC as a policy objective is fully compatible with a model in which coverage is universal but confined to a limited range of interventions, while governments function as managers of a health system and purchasers of care from private, for-profit providers. He argues that this is in fact the model envisioned by many promoters of UHC and the one that characterizes current efforts to move toward UHC in Brazil and India. Thus, UHC can actually "end up decreasing equity and efficiency in health systems" (Sengupta, 2013: 20). This could happen, for instance, if UHC were implemented in a way that concentrated resources in clinical services at the expense of prevention, within or outside the health sector (Schmidt, Gostin, and Emanuel, 2015).

A further important element of context is the changing nature of global capitalism itself. The financial crisis of 2008 could have transformed the global health and development policy landscape in a number of ways, potentially foregrounding issues of justice within and across borders. However, it is remarkable how quickly the relevant policy discourses returned to incrementalism and business as usual. Meanwhile, evidence accumulates that capitalism is assuming new and distinctly predatory forms on a global scale. Sassen (2010) writes of a "savage sorting of winners and losers" on multiple scales associated with neoliberal globalization, and a former chief economist of the World Bank (Bourguignon, 2015) is one of many academic authors who argue that globalization is magnifying economic inequalities, especially within national borders. The implications for health and health inequalities are far from clear, but the possibility must be considered that even well-intentioned strategies organized around new therapies and expanded access to care will be undermined by the effects of rising levels of inequality and economic insecurity, and by domestic political resistance from those who see little gain from solidaristic health and social policies.

SUMMARY

From this chapter you will have gained a basic understanding of the causes of health inequalities between and within rich and poor countries. The chapter described some notable successes in improving health outside the high-income world, but also identified several challenges, including the double burden of disease and the inadequacy of resources for health despite substantial increases in development assistance. The chapter emphasized the importance of macro-scale processes such as the negotiation of trade and investment agreements that may create collateral damage to health, and a mechanism for financing health research that leads to neglect of diseases of the poor. It also described a set of institutions for making decisions about global health and development that are increasingly complex and fragmented. Whether these institutions will be able to mobilize the resources needed to reduce health inequalities remains uncertain, as does the impact on health and health inequalities of the changing nature of the world's economic systems.

QUESTIONS FOR CRITICAL THOUGHT

1. Do the moral obligations with respect to health inequalities within your country differ from those that involve health inequalities between your own country and other, poorer ones? If so, how and why?
2. You are a senior official in the health ministry of a low- or middle-income country, trying to help the health minister make the case for an increase in your ministry's budget to her cabinet or parliamentary colleagues. What arguments would you be most likely to use, and why? What sources of opposition would you expect to encounter?
3. You are a senior official in a national government department or agency with responsibilities for international development and health in a high-income country, trying to help your minister or cabinet secretary make the case to her cabinet and legislative colleagues *either:*
   (a) that your country should make an additional multi-year commitment to development assistance for health, *or:*
   (b) that your country should assess its future trade policy commitments in terms of their effects on health in LMICs.
   What arguments would you be most likely to use, and why? What sources of opposition would you anticipate?
4. Imagine that you are a journalist in the year 2025, looking back on developments in global health since 2015. Write an imaginary history of no more than 1,000 words in which you identify the three most significant developments and explain how and why they occurred.

SUGGESTED READINGS

Birn, Anne-Emanuelle, Yogan Pillay, and Timothy H. Holtz. 2009. *Textbook of International Health: Global Health in a Dynamic World*, 4th edn. New York: Oxford University Press, 2016.

Farmer, Paul. 2003. *Pathologies of Power: Health, Human Rights and the New War on the Poor.* Berkeley: University of California Press.

Krieger, Nancy. 2011. *Epidemiology and the People's Health: Theory and Context.* Oxford: Oxford University Press.

Schrecker, Ted, and Clare Bambra. 2015. *How Politics Makes Us Sick: Neoliberal Epidemics.* Houndmills, UK: Palgrave Macmillan.

BIBLIOGRAPHY

Balabanova, D., A. Mills, L. Conteh, B. Akkazieva, H. Banteyerga, U. Dash, et al. 2013. "Good health at low cost 25 years on: Lessons for the future of health systems strengthening." *The Lancet* 381: 2118–33.

Balasegaram, M., M. Childs, and J. Arkinstall. 2014. "The fight for global access to essential health commodities." In G. Yamey, G. Brown and S. Wamala, eds., *The Handbook of Global Health Policy.* New York: John Wiley & Sons, 245–66.

Bank of England. 2009. *Financial Stability Report*, No. 25. London: Bank of England. www.bankofengland.co.uk/publications/fsr/2009/fsrfull0906.pdf.

Beall, R., and R. Kuhn. 2012. "Trends in compulsory licensing of pharmaceuticals since the Doha Declaration: A database analysis." *PLoS Med* 9, e1001154.

Birn, A.-E. 2014. "Philanthrocapitalism, past and present: The Rockefeller Foundation, the Gates Foundation, and the setting(s) of the international/global health agenda." *Hypothesis* 12, E6.

Blouin, C., M. Chopra, and R. van der Hoeven. 2009. "Trade and social determinants of health." *The Lancet* 373: 502–7.

———, N. Drager, and J. Heymann, eds. 2008. *Trade and Health: Seeking Common Ground.* Montreal and Kingston: McGill-Queen's University Press.

Bourguignon, F. 2015. *The Globalization of Inequality.* Princeton, NJ: Princeton University Press.

Brown, T.M., M. Cueto, and E. Fee. 2006. "The World Health Organization and the transition from "international" to "global" public health." *American Journal of Public Health* 96: 62–72.

Burke, M.A., and S.A. Matlin. 2008. *Monitoring Financial Flows for Health Research 2008: Prioritizing Research for Health Equity.* Geneva: Global Forum for Health Research. www.globalforumhealth.org/layout/set/print/content/download/480/3028/file/s14888e.pdf.

Centre on Global Health Security Working Group on Health Financing. 2014. *Shared Responsibilities for Health: A Coherent Global Framework for Health Financing.* Chatham House Report. London: Chatham House. www.chathamhouse.org/sites/files/chathamhouse/field/field_document/20140521HealthFinancing.pdf.

Clark, S.E., C. Hawkes, S.M.E. Murphy, K.A. Hansen-Kuhn, and D. Wallinga. 2012. "Exporting obesity: US farm and trade policy and the transformation of the Mexican consumer food environment." *International Journal of Occupational and Environmental Health* 18: 53–64.

Commission on Social Determinants of Health. 2008. *Closing the Gap in a Generation: Health Equity through Action on the Social Determinants of Health (Final Report).* Geneva: WHO. http://whqlibdoc.who.int/publications/2008/9789241563703_eng.pdf.

Committee of Experts of the 4th Joint Annual Meetings of the AU Conference of Ministers of Economy and Finance and ECA Conference of African Ministers of Finance Planning and Economic Development. 2011. *Investment in Health Is an Investment in Economic Development.* E/ECA/COE/30/5/Rev.1. Addis Ababa: United Nations Economic Commission for Africa. www.uneca.org/cfm/2011/documents/English/Investment-inHealth.pdf.

Cornia, G.A., R. Jolly, and F. Stewart, eds. 1987. *Adjustment with a Human Face, vol.1: Protecting the Vulnerable and Promoting Growth.* Oxford: Clarendon Press.

Correa, C.M. 2013. "High costs, negligible benefits from intellectual property provisions in FTAs." *IIC—International Review of Intellectual Property and Competition Law* 44: 902–5.

Dieleman, J.L., C. Graves, and E. Johnson. 2015. "Sources and focus of health development assistance, 1990–2014." *Journal of the American Medical Association* 313: 2359–68.

Dixon, J.B. 2010. "The effect of obesity on health outcomes." *Molecular and Cellular Endocrinology* 316 104–8.

Drèze, J., and A. Sen. 2013. *An Uncertain Glory: India and Its Contradictions*. London: Allen Lane.

Euromonitor. 2011. "Fast food in Chile." www.euromonitor.com/fast-food-in-chile/report.

Feachem, R.G.A. 2001. "Globalisation is good for your health, mostly." *British Medical Journal* 323: 504–6.

Food and Agriculture Organization of the United Nations (FAO). 2015. *The State of Food Insecurity in the World (SOFI) 2015—Meeting the 2015 International Hunger Targets: Taking Stock of Uneven Progress*. Rome: FAO. www.fao.org/3/a-i4646e.pdf.

Gellman, B. 2000. "An unequal calculus of life and death: As millions perished in pandemic, firms debated access to drugs." *Washington Post*, 27 Dec. www.washingtonpost.com/wp-dyn/content/article/2006/06/09/AR2006060901287_pf.html.

Goran, M.I., S.J. Ulijaszek, and E.E. Ventura. 2013. "High fructose corn syrup and diabetes prevalence: A global perspective." *Global Public Health* 8: 55–64.

Gwatkin, D.R., S. Rutstein, K. Johnson, E. Suliman, E., A. Wagstaff, and A. Amouzou. 2007. *Socio-Economic Differences in Health, Nutrition and Population within Developing Countries: An Overview*. Washington: World Bank. http://go.worldbank.org/XJK7WKSE40.

Hall, J.J., and R. Taylor. 2003. "Health for all beyond 2000: The demise of the Alma-Ata Declaration and primary health care in developing countries." *Medical Journal of Australia* 178: 17–20.

Halstead, S.B., J.A. Walsh, and K.S. Warren, eds. 1985. *Good Health at Low Cost*. New York: Rockefeller Foundation.

Harmer, A., and K. Buse. 2014. "The BRICS—a paradigm shift in global health?" *Contemporary Politics* 20: 127–45.

Harmer, A., Y. Xiao, E. Missoni, and F. Tediosi. 2013. "'BRICS without straw'? A systematic literature review of newly emerging economies' influence in global health." *Globalization and Health* 9: 15.

Hawkes, C., M. Chopra, and S. Friel. 2009. "Globalization, trade, and the nutrition transition. In Labonté et al. (2009: 235–62).

Hein, W. 2013. "The new dynamics of global health governance." In I. Kickbusch, G. Lister, M. Told, and N. Drager, eds, *Global Health Diplomacy*. New York: Springer, 55–72.

Horton, R. 2009. "Global science and social movements: Towards a rational politics of global health." *International Health* 1: 26–30.

Independent Evaluation Office, International Monetary Fund. 2007. *The IMF and Aid to Sub-Saharan Africa*. Washington: IMF. www.imf.org/external/np/ieo/2007/ssa/eng/pdf/report.pdf.

Jamison, D.T., L.H. Summers, G. Alleyne, K.J. Arrow, S. Berkley, A. Binagwaho, et al. 2013a. "Global health 2035: A world converging within a generation." *The Lancet* 382: 1898–1955.

——— et al. 2013b. "Global health 2035: A world converging within a generation—Supplementary web appendix 2: Summary of the evidence on the association between health and income." *The Lancet*. doi: 10.1016/S0140-6736(13)62105-4.

Kentikelenis, A., L. King, M. McKee, and D. Stuckler. 2015. "The International Monetary Fund and the Ebola outbreak." *The Lancet Global Health* 3: e69–e70.

Kerry, V.B., and K. Lee. 2007. "TRIPS, the Doha Declaration and paragraph 6 decision: What are the remaining steps for protecting access to medicines?" *Globalization and Health* 3.

Kickbusch, I., and L. Payne. 2004. "Constructing global public health in the 21st century." In *Meeting on Global Health Governance and Accountability*, Cambridge, Mass.: Harvard University. Geneva: Kickbusch Health Consult. www.ilonakickbusch.com/global-health-governance/GlobalHealth.pdf.

Knaul, F.M., B. Anderson, C. Bradley, and D. Kerr. 2010. "Access to cancer treatment in low- and middle-income countries: An essential part of global cancer control." CanTreat Position Paper. http://papers.ssrn.com/sol3/papers.cfm?abstract_id=2055441.

Koivusalo, M., T. Schrecker, and R. Labonté. 2009. "Globalization and policy space for health and social determinants of health." In Labonté et al. (2009: 105–30).

Kurmi, O.P., K.B.H. Lam, and J.G. Ayres. 2012. "Indoor air pollution and the lung in low- and medium-income countries." *European Respiratory Journal* 40: 239–54.

Labonté, R., T. Schrecker, C. Packer, and V. Runnels, eds. 2009. *Globalization and Health: Pathways, Evidence and Policy*. New York: Routledge.

——— and M. Gagnon. 2010. "Framing health and foreign policy: Lessons for global health diplomacy." *Globalization and Health* 6: 14.

Lawn, J.E., J. Rohde, S. Rifkin, M. Were, V.K. Paul, and M. Chopra. 2008. "Alma-Ata 30 years on: Revolutionary, relevant, and time to revitalise." *The Lancet* 372: 917–27.

Livingston, J. 2013. "Cancer in the shadow of the AIDS epidemic in southern Africa." *The Oncologist* 18: 783–6.

McCoy, D., G. Kembhavi, J. Patel, and A. Luintel. 2009. "The Bill & Melinda Gates Foundation's grant-making programme for global health." *The Lancet* 373: 1645–53.

McInnes, C. 2009. "National security and global health governance." In O.D. Williams and A. Kay, eds, *Global Health Governance: Crisis, Institutions and Political Economy*. Houndmills, UK: Palgrave Macmillan, 42–59.

Marmot, M. 2004. *Status Syndrome: How Your Social Standing Directly Affects Your Health and Life Expectancy*. London: Bloomsbury.

Maternal Mortality Estimation Inter-Agency Group (MMEIG). 2014. *Trends in Maternal Mortality: 1990 to 2013—Estimates by WHO, UNICEF, UNFPA, the World Bank and the United Nations Population Division*. Geneva: WHO. http://apps.who.int/iris/bitstream/10665/112682/2/9789241507226_eng.pdf.

Monteiro, C.A., J.C. Moubarac, G. Cannon, S.W. Ng, and B. Popkin. 2013. "Ultra-processed products are becoming dominant in the global food system." *Obesity Reviews* 14: 21–8.

Moon, S., J. Bermudez, and E. 't Hoen. 2012. "Innovation and access to medicines for neglected populations: Could a treaty address a broken pharmaceutical R&D system?" *PLoS Medicine* 9: e1001218.

Moszynski, P. 2011. "Global Fund suspends new projects until 2014 because of lack of funding." *British Medical Journal* 343: d7755.

Mudur, G. 2015. "Experts question how India will meet promises on public health after cut in budget for 2015–16." *British Medical Journal* 350: h1244.

Ndikumana, L., J.K. Boyce, and A.S. Ndiaye. 2014. *Capital Flight: Measurement and Drivers*, Working Paper No. 363. Amherst, Mass.: Political Economy Research Institute, University of Massachusetts. www.peri.umass.edu/fileadmin/pdf/working_papers/working_papers_351-400/WP363.pdf.

Ooms, G., and T. Schrecker. 2005. "Viewpoint: Expenditure ceilings, multilateral financial institutions, and the health of poor populations." *The Lancet* 365: 1821–3.

Ottersen, O.P., J. Dasgupta, C. Blouin, P. Buss, V. Chongsuvivatwong, J. Frenk, et al. 2014. "The political origins of health inequity: Prospects for change." *The Lancet* 383: 630–67.

People's Health Movement, Medact, and Global Equity Gauge Alliance. 2008. *Global Health Watch 2: An Alternative World Health Report*. London: Zed Books.

Perry, R.T., M. Gacic-Dobo, A. Dabbagh, M.N. Mulders, P.M. Strebel, J.M. Okwo-Bele, et al. 2014. "Global control and regional elimination of measles, 2000–2012." *MMWR: Morbidity and Mortality Weekly Report* 63: 103–7.

Popkin, B.M. 2007. "Global context of obesity." In S. Kumanyika and R.C. Brownson, eds, *Handbook of Obesity Prevention*. New York: Springer, 227–38.

———. 2014. "Nutrition, agriculture and the global food system in low and middle income countries." *Food Policy* 47: 91–6.

Public Health England. 2015. "Health Profile 2015: Stockton-on-Tees Unitary Authority." London: Public Health England. www.apho.org.uk/resource/view.aspx?RID=171624.

Reich, M.R., and K. Takemi. 2009. "G8 and strengthening of health systems: Follow-up to the Toyako summit." *The Lancet* 373: 508–15.

Riley, J.C. 2008. *Low Income, Social Growth and Good Health: A History of Twelve Countries*. Berkeley: University of California Press.

Roffe, P., J. Von Braun, and D. Vivas-Eugui. 2008. "A new generation of regional and bilateral trade agreements: Lessons from the US-CAFTA-DR agreement." In Blouin et al. (2008: 41–89).

Rowden, R. 2013. "The ghosts of user fees past: Exploring accountability for victims of a 30-year economic policy mistake." *Health and Human Rights* 15: 175–85.

———. 2014. "West Africa's financial immune deficiency." *Foreign Policy*, 30 Oct. http://foreignpolicy.com/2014/10/30'west-africa-financial-immune-deficiency/.

Ruckert, A., and R. Labonté. 2012. "The global financial crisis and health equity: Toward a conceptual framework." *Critical Public Health* 22: 267–79.

Sassen, S. 2010. "A savage sorting of winners and losers: Contemporary versions of primitive accumulation." *Globalizations* 7: 23–50.

Save the Children. 2015. *State of the World's Mothers: The Urban Disadvantage*. Fairfield, Conn.: Save the Children Federation. www.savethechildren.org/atf/cf/%7B9def2ebe-10ae-432c-9bd0-df91d2eba74a%7D/SOWM_2015.PDF.

Schmidt, H., L.O. Gostin, and E.J. Emanuel. 2015. "Public health, universal health coverage, and Sustainable Development Goals: can they coexist?" *The Lancet*. doi: org/10.1016/S0140-6736(15)60244-6.

Schrecker, T. 2014a. "Changing cartographies of health in a globalizing world." *Medicine Anthropology Theory* 1.

———. 2014b. "Globalization and health." In B. Jennings, L. Eckenwiler, G. Kaebnick, B. Koenig, S. Krimsky, S. Latham, and M. Mercurio, eds, *Bioethics*, 4th edn. Farmington Hills, Mich.: Macmillan Reference, 1363–70.

Sell, S.K. 2003. *Private Power, Public Law: The Globalization of Intellectual Property Rights*. Cambridge: Cambridge University Press.

Sengupta, A. 2013. *Universal Health Coverage: Beyond Rhetoric*. Occasional Paper No. 20. Kingston, Ont.: Municipal Services Project. www.municipalservicesproject.org/sites/municipalservicesproject.org/files/publications/OccasionalPaper20_Sengupta_Universal_Health_Coverage_Beyond_Rhetoric_Nov2013_0.pdf.

Shadlen, K.C. 2005. "Exchanging development for market access? Deep integration and industrial policy under multilateral and regional-bilateral trade agreements." *Review of International Political Economy* 12: 750–75.

Shaffer, E.R., and J.E. Brenner. 2009. "A trade agreement's impact on access to generic drugs." *Health Affairs* 28: w957–w968.

Sridhar, D. 2010. "Seven challenges in international development assistance for health." *Journal of Law, Medicine & Ethics* 38: 459–69.

Stocking, B., J.-J. Muyembe-Tamfun, F. Shuaib, C. Alberto-Banatin, J. Frenk, and I. Kickbusch. 2015. *Report of the Ebola Interim Assessment Panel*. Geneva: WHO.

Stuckler, D., M. McKee, S. Ebrahim, and S. Basu. 2012. "Manufacturing epidemics: The role of global producers in increased consumption of unhealthy commodities including processed foods, alcohol, and tobacco." *PLoS Med* 9: e1001235.

Szreter, S. 1999. "Rapid economic growth and 'the four Ds' of disruption, deprivation, disease and death: Public health lessons from nineteenth-century Britain for twenty-first-century China?" *Tropical Medicine and International Health* 4: 146–52.

't Hoen, E., J. Berger, A. Calmy, asnd S. Moon. 2011. "Driving a decade of change: HIV/AIDS, patents and access to medicines for all." *Journal of the International AIDS Society* 14: 15.

Thow, A.M., W. Snowdon, R. Labonté, D. Gleeson, D. Stuckler, L. Hattersley, et al. 2015. "Will the next generation of preferential trade and investment agreements undermine prevention of noncommunicable diseases? A prospective policy analysis of the Trans-Pacific Partnership Agreement." *Health Policy* 119: 88–96.

UNAIDS. 2012. *Report on the Global AIDS Epidemic 2012*. Geneva: UNAIDS. www.unaids.org/en/media/unaids/contentassets/documents/epidemiology/2012/gr2012/20121120_UNAIDS_Global_Report_2012_en.pdf.

———. 2014. *The Gap Report 2014*. www.unaids.org/en/resources/campaigns/2014/2014gapreport/slides/.

UN-Habitat. 2013. *State of the World's Cities 2012/2013: Prosperity of Cities*. New York: Routledge. http://unhabitat.org/?wpdmact=process&did=MTQ3My5ob3RsaW5r.

UNICEF and WHO. 2015. *Progress on Sanitation and Drinking Water: 2015 Update and MDG Assessment*. Geneva: WHO.

United Nations. 2012. "Global health and foreign policy." General Assembly resolution No. A/67/L.36. New York: UN. www.un.org/ga/search/view_doc.asp?symbol=A/67/L.36.

———. 2014. *The Millennium Development Goals Report 2014*. New York: UN. www.un.org/millenniumgoals/2014%20MDG%20report/MDG%202014%20English%20web.pdf.

Working Group on IMF Programs and Health Spending. 2007. *Does the IMF Constrain Health Spending in Poor Countries? Evidence and an Agenda for Action*. Washington: Center for Global Development. www.cgdev.org/doc/IMF/IMF_Report.pdf.

World Health Organization (WHO). 2010. *World Health Report 2010: Health Systems Financing—The Path to Universal Coverage*. Geneva: WHO. www.who.int/whr/2010/en/index.html.

———. 2013. *Global Status Report on Road Safety 2013*. Geneva: WHO. www.who.int/iris/bitstream/10665/78256/1/9789241564564_eng.pdf.

———. 2014. *Programme Budget 2014–15*. Geneva: WHO. www.who.int/about/resources_planning/PB14-15_en.pdf?ua=1.

———. 2015a. "Obesity and overweight." www.who.int/mediacentre/factsheets/fs311/en/.

———. 2015b. *World Health Statistics 2015*. Geneva: WHO. http://apps.who.int/iris/bitstream/10665/170250/1/9789240694439_eng.pdf?ua=1&ua=1.

Wright, S., L. Hanna, and M. Mailfert. 2015. *A Wake-Up Call: Lessons from Ebola for the World's Health Systems*. London: Save the Children. www.savethechildren.org/atf/cf/%7B9def2ebe-10ae-432c-9bd0-df91d2eba74a%7D/WAKE%20UP%20CALL%20REPORT%20PDF.PDF.

Xu, K., D.B. Evans, G. Carrin, A.M. Aguilar-Rivera, P. Musgrove, and T. Evans. 2007. "Protecting households from catastrophic health spending." *Health Affairs* 26: 972–83.

Youde, J. 2012. *Global Health Governance*. Cambridge: Polity.

21 Conflict and Development

Torunn Wimpelmann and Astri Suhrke

LEARNING OBJECTIVES

- To understand the liberal view of the relationship between conflict and development.
- To discover why and how the liberal theory of violence has been challenged and alternative perspectives developed.
- To learn how policy measures to contain violent conflict have been conceived and implemented and how these measures are related to different understandings of the conflict–development nexus.

▲ **A mother from the village of Malual Kon, in South Sudan, reunites with two of her children who had fought for, but are now demobilized by, the rebel army in Sudan. Child soldiers have been used on both sides of the conflict, being either forcibly recruited or joining forces to protect themselves and their communities. The United Nations Children's Fund (UNICEF) estimates that 15,000 to 16,000 children may have been used by armed forces and groups in the conflict.** | Source: Photo by Cyril LE TOURNEUR/Gamma-Rapho via Getty Images

This chapter introduces the ways in which social scientists have understood the relationship between conflict and development. Within this wide and controversial field of inquiry, the chapter identifies two main perspectives:

1. The liberal view, which sees underdevelopment as a cause of conflict and development as a way out of strife and towards peace.
2. A competing perspective, which sees conflict as integral to development. Development is therefore likely to produce conflict, although violent conflict may be contained by proper policy measures.

The first part of the chapter lays out these two perspectives and different methods of assessing whether conflict is part of development or outside it. The second part takes the reader to recent issues of development and peace, particularly the field of **peace-building** and Western interventionism to illustrate how these different theories play out in practice.

POSING THE QUESTION

Conflict is the opposite of development—war is development in reverse. This was the message of a major 2003 report on civil wars from World Bank researchers that was influential at a time when the Western peace-building regime was at its height. The study concluded that "[w]hen development succeeds, countries become safer; when development fails, countries experience greater risk of being caught in a **conflict trap**" (Collier et al., 2003). At first glance, this seemed persuasive. Wars destroy lives, property, and the environment. As such, it is "development in reverse." Most recent wars, moreover, had taken place in poor countries in Africa, Asia, and Latin America. Western Europe and North America—by most accounts the richest and most developed countries in the world—have experienced very little war since World War II. The Balkan wars in the 1990s appeared to many as a shock, a ghost from a past it was assumed Europe had left behind.

On closer examination, however, the picture is not so simple. Violence may set back "development," but it also may sweep away older structures and make way for change. Nor is national development necessarily a ticket to safety, either for self or for others. Countries considered as being "developed" have been subject to violent civil strife, such as race riots in the United States, separatist violence in Spain, sectarian fighting in Northern Ireland, and terrorist attacks in London. If we add international violence, we find that NATO members in recent years have repeatedly attacked other states (Iraq in 1991 and 2003, Kosovo and Serbia in 1999, Afghanistan in 2001, and Libya in 2011). At the other end of the development spectrum there is also some variation. Among the 10 least developed countries according to the Human Development Index of the United Nations Development Programme (UNDP), some have escaped what seemed to be a conflict trap (e.g., Mozambique and Niger), while others have experienced recurrent conflict (e.g., the Democratic Republic of Congo and Burundi) (UNDP, 2014). Perhaps some are poor and underdeveloped because of recurrent violence caused primarily by other factors.

Social scientists, philosophers, and historians have long tried to understand the relationship between violence and development. Among the many perspectives and interpretations, two main streams are notable. A **liberal theory of violence**, which approximates the World Bank report cited above, considers violence an aberration and as the opposite of development. The implication—sometimes spelled out—is that development is a way out of violence. From a very different perspective, violence is "at the heart of societal transformations," as Christopher Cramer writes, and also a frequent companion in the "expansionary modernism" of Western states (Cramer, 2006). If violence is at least potentially inherent in the very process of social change, there is little prospect for an exit from strife—unless we declare "the end of history" (as some Western writers indeed did when the Soviet Union collapsed) (Fukuyama, 1992).

These perspectives will be explored below. We start with the proposition that underdevelopment leads to conflict and that development, therefore, is a way to reduce conflict. We then examine the competing view that development is a conflictual process and must be understood and studied as such, although the violent manifestations may vary and arguably can be modified. Finally, we discuss how ideas about the relationship between conflict and development have shaped—and to a degree also justified—Western-led interventions in conflict areas.

But first, a brief note on definitions, approaches, and methods.

Photo by Thomas Trutschel/Photothek via Getty Images

PHOTO 21.1 | Training for carpenters at the vocational school Young Africa, Mozambique. Learning new skills is often used to encourage demobilized soldiers to return to civilian life in post-conflict societies, such as Mozambique.

DEFINITIONS, APPROACHES, AND METHODS

A discussion of the relationship between development and conflict obviously depends on how development is defined. Empirical studies in the positivist tradition typically disaggregate development along one or several dimensions—economic, social, and political—in order to assess the relationship to conflict. For instance, if development is understood primarily in terms of macroeconomic indicators (e.g., gross domestic product or GDP), one can investigate the relationship between growth rates and the incidence of conflict. If the focus is on social development, indicators of education, health, and distribution of material goods would be relevant. Ethnic diversity and divisions are classic indicators in studies of national integration. Elections, levels of corruption, or freedom of speech are used to indicate political development. Many recent studies have analyzed the relationship between such dimensions statistically, using indicators from generally accessible data banks.[1]

A very different approach is "the grand narrative," which seeks to uncover the essence of the development process as it has unfolded historically. The classical scholars here are Karl Marx (1818–83) and Max Weber (1864–1920). Writing at a time of rapid change and much violence in Europe as well as beyond, they tried to understand "development" and the processes and patterns of social change. For Marx, development cannot be separated from conflict or understood as independent of it. Conflict is intrinsic to the development process, the motor that drives it forward as power and resources are redistributed to different classes and peoples. In a continuation of this grand narrative, Lenin argued that imperialism was the highest stage of capitalism; the imperialist nations, the "most developed" in conventional terms, would then succumb to war against each other (see Chapter 2).

In Weber's grand narrative, by contrast, capitalism is peaceful, emerging through rationalization and the efficiency of social and economic relations. Industrial capitalism overcomes its own internal tensions through rational planning and orderly competition for power within an arena of secular politics. The rules of competition are guarded by a state that has a legitimate monopoly of force. "Modernity," then, is associated with societies ruled primarily by reason as enshrined in predictable, efficient, and secular institutions. This all suggests an exit from violence. In this tradition, a recent major effort to understand how societies develop mechanisms to ensure social order finds democratic institutions are of critical importance (North et al., 2009).

Conflict, Violence, and War

So far, we have used the terms "conflict," "violence," and "war" interchangeably, but the meaning of these words is a debate in itself. "Conflict" is generally understood to mean tension between opposing views, interests, or wills. Conflicts may or may not involve violence, even if we allow for the many meanings of "violence." The most obvious and common-sense meaning is physical violence. But there is also "structural violence," a concept launched by peace researcher Johan Galtung in the 1950s to denote extreme and systematic inequality, and "symbolic violence," understood in the tradition of French sociologist Pierre Bourdieu as internalized humiliation among the weak and legitimation of inequality and hierarchy. In the following exploration, we will focus on physical violence, particularly war.

War has long been considered a unique category of conflict. "War" suggests that special attention is warranted: it signals extraordinary violence, a situation when normal rules do not apply but special rules have been developed (as in international law governing warfare). In the social sciences, war has usually been studied separately from other forms of violence. Typically, students of international relations and political science study "war," while anthropologists and sociologists study "violence."

Within political science, one approach to the study of war in relation to development is to treat war as a discrete event, the appearance of which can be examined statistically in relation to other factors believed to be its causes or (more rarely) consequences. Large databases have been established for this purpose since the 1960s, with data on events classified as internal and international wars, as well as some hybrid forms. Classification systems are controversial, particularly with regard to the definition of "civil war." The most widely used data sets have both quantitative measures (1,000 battle-related deaths per year or per duration of the conflict) and qualitative data such as organization of the belligerent parties (usually states or rebels with some organization) and the incompatibility of their aims.[2]

Use of these databases to determine the links between war and development, such as the World Bank study cited above, is subject to some limitations. One problem is the unreliability of raw data from war zones, particularly in conflicts where the belligerent parties are armed factions with no centralized organization and where human rights monitors have poor access. Estimates of casualties during the 1989–97 war in Liberia, for instance, vary from 60,000 to 200,000. Use of different thresholds of casualties will produce different frequencies of war. No current data sets have indicators for intensity, although this clearly affects the impact of wars on society and hence on development in all its dimensions. For example, a thousand deaths in civil strife is much less significant for national development in a country of more than one billion people (India) than it is for a state with just under one million (Timor-Leste). Moreover, what should be counted as battle-related deaths? In the classic image of warfare, war is fought on the battlefield between opposing armies. In many contemporary conflicts, violence is diverse, carried out by militias as well as state or rebel armies, and civilians are often the victims. It is unclear how massacres of unarmed people should be counted (most civil war data sets do not include the massacre of an estimated half a million to one million people in Rwanda in 1994, since it was mostly a one-sided genocide). Likewise, current civil war data sets rarely include deaths from war-related famine and disease, even though these typically outnumber battlefield deaths and often continue into peacetime at abnormally high rates. Difficulties also arise as to how we should treat complex and continuing wars, such as the recurring violence in Afghanistan during the past four decades.

Another way to consider war is to place it in its historical and sociological setting. We can then examine organized violence as part of a social process of transformation, with causes and functions that cannot be understood if abstracted from their context and entered into a data set. This approach permits a deeper inquiry about not only the causes of violence, but also how violence can open the way for the formation of social capital and new institutions. In this way, the developmental as well as destructive functions of war are brought out. This approach is favoured by anthropologists and economists and political scientists working in the tradition of **political economy** (Cramer, 2006; Richards, 2005; Keen, 2001).

CONFLICT AND DEVELOPMENT: PERSPECTIVES AND FINDINGS

When development theory became an academic field of study after World War II, it was largely based on the premise that development and conflict are separate phenomena and appear sequentially: development stops when conflict starts and can continue when conflict subsides. In line with this, aid provided during

CRITICAL ISSUES

BOX 21.1 | War as a Complex "Event"

If we were to plot "the war in Afghanistan" as one event in a database, that clearly would be misleading. The first phase started in April 1978, when the Afghan Communists seized power and the militant resistance formed. A year and a half later, the Soviets invaded, and the resistance started receiving international arms support and training. It was now an internationalized civil war. In 1989, the last Soviet soldiers withdrew, and after a brief peace, Afghan factions turned on each other in a full-scale civil war. That lasted roughly until 1996, when the Taliban seized Kabul, thereby wielding power over some 90 percent of the entire country. In October 2001, US-led forces invaded the country and, with the help of local factions, defeated the Taliban. After a brief peace, violence resumed and soon grew into a serious insurgency that challenged the government and the international forces in almost all parts of the country.

How would we approach these Afghan conflicts using a qualitative approach? Starting from the notion that war and development are not necessarily mutually exclusive, a first task is to explore what kinds of governing structures, social relations, and economic activity developed during this long period of upheaval. In some areas, warlords emerged; in other areas, traditional leaders or new political movements held sway. Many of them conducted "foreign relations" with outside governments or agencies. Social and economic capital accumulated during periods of warfare was invested in times of (relative) peace for personal or community benefits. Thus, after the Taliban lost power, one of the first public acts of the "warlord of Herat" in western Afghanistan, Ismail Khan, was to beautify public parks and restore the magnificent mosaic arches that grace the entrance to the city. The Taliban regime itself represented an early stage of state formation by introducing a uniform system of social regulation and justice.

Nevertheless, the most obvious impact of the long wars was destruction. Successive waves of fighting left a trail of death and disintegration. Families and communities were displaced. The legal economy stagnated. Infrastructure was destroyed. Violence was pervasive—not only organized warfare among fighting units but also alleged war crimes, crimes against humanity, and massive human rights violations. For those close to the event, it was difficult to see that this kind of destruction could be the foundation for new development.

conflict was humanitarian relief designed to save lives, not aid to support long-term development processes. As a result, there was little effort to explore the relationship between development and conflict. Only in the past decade or so has this separation been challenged within mainstream development studies and practice.

Underdevelopment as a Cause of Conflict—Development as the Foundation for Peace

A powerful theme within Western liberal thinking is that modernization and economic progress will bring stability. Drawing on Weber's concept of modernity as secularism and rationalism, Western political scientists produced a huge "modernization" literature in the 1960s (see Chapter 3). Societies would develop and modernize by establishing effectively functioning bureaucracies, streamlining individual affinities away from primordial or ethnic identities towards larger national loyalties, incorporating modern technology, and putting foreign aid to good use. The political development component was usually understood as the establishment of representative institutions that could aggregate interests and provide checks and balances on executive power.

In fact, progress along this path was uneven, sometimes abandoned, and often strewn with violence. The deviations became increasingly clear as the Cold War between the superpowers was played out in what was then called the Third World. The United States and the Soviet Union exploited local divisions in order to enhance their own interests, a process that in several cases turned into "proxy wars" in Africa and Latin America. More generally, the Cold War meant that Western states reshaped the modernization agenda to fit the anti-Communist struggle. This often meant supporting military strongmen rather than democratic forces (as in Southeast Asia and South America) and promoting groups that in Weberian terms were distinctly "unmodern." The latter included patrimonial bureaucracies that served individual rulers, such as Joseph-Désiré Mobutu, President of Zaire from 1965 to 1997, as well as movements seeking unity between state and religion, such as the Afghan mujahedeen who fought the Soviets in the 1980s.

The Democratic Peace

The old idea that democracies and peace belong together was reborn in new research in the 1980s. This work was inspired by Immanuel Kant's *Perpetual Peace*, a small pamphlet written in 1795 in the shadow of the French Revolution and Napoleon's rising power. *Perpetual Peace* outlined the conditions for peace *among* states. Prominent among these conditions was a republican constitution (which did not mean democracy in the form of majority rule) and free trade encouraging economic interdependence. Prosperous burghers, Kant believed, would not want to send their sons into battle or pay for the national debt incurred by war. Economic interdependence would make it difficult in practice for states to fight each other. The 1980s version of this thesis launched by American political scientists held that "democratic" states very seldom went to war against each other, with "democratic" defined as periodic competitive elections and universal adult suffrage. Here, it seemed, was a clear link between one dimension of development (political democracy) and the absence of at least some kinds of violence (Rummel, 1975–81; Doyle, 1983). A flurry of further studies confirmed the link. These studies relied on statistical analysis and provided little explanation for *why* countries with regular elections and adult suffrage did not fight each other. Yet—as critics pointed out—these countries did not shy away from going to war against weaker states or entities, as demonstrated, for instance, by the history of US military interventions in Central America, France's war against the Algerian independence movement, and, just the decade before this literature developed, the long US war in Vietnam. In an earlier period, European states with at least some democratic features had readily gone to war to establish and maintain empires. In other words, the democratic constitution of a state clearly produced only a selective peace.

The promises of political democracy held out by liberal theory seemed less ambiguous with respect to internal wars. Using statistical analysis of data to compare types and frequency of internal disturbances with indicators of democracy, one leading American scholar found a clear pattern (Rummel, 1997). Non-democratic countries were much more likely than democratic ones to experience internal violence of almost all kinds, ranging from civil wars to political assassinations and terrorist bombings. Subsequent studies using statistical methods affirmed the point but added a significant elaboration. Countries defined as autocratic are as stable as democracies when it comes to internal conflict. It is the countries in between—the "anocracies" with both autocratic and democratic features—that are statistically most likely to experience internal violence (Hegre et al., 2001; Fearon and Laitin, 2003).

Other studies using qualitative methods confirmed a pattern more in accord with the competing prism of development as a conflictual process. The European experience suggested that democratization has been associated with war. In the 150 years between the French Revolution and World War II, European states underwent what today we would call a period of rapid economic and political development. The process fuelled nationalism and wars. "States being dragged by social change into a transition to democracy," Edward Mansfield and Jack Snyder conclude, "have been more likely to participate in wars and more likely to start them than have states whose [political] regimes did not change" in the direction of greater democracy (Mansfield and Snyder, cited in Snyder, 2000: 20).

More recently, the "Arab Spring" demonstrates that attempted transitions to more democratic politics can be extremely destabilizing. After decades of stable but autocratic rule in Tunisia, Egypt, Syria, and Libya, popular movements for democracy rapidly were replaced by civil war (Syria and Libya) or heightened repression (Egypt). Only one country (Tunisia) emerged relatively peacefully. Yet it must be noted that different paths of the transitions had quite complex causes, including external interventions and violent countermoves by the old regimes.

Ethnicity

Modernization theory assumed that as societies made the transition to modernity, identities related to clan, tribe, village, or ethnic group would become less important and gradually be submerged by a higher national identity. The point was supported by scholars of nationalism, such as Ernest Gellner (1983), who argued that growth of national identities paralleled the growth of a modern market economy. By extension, **ethnic conflict** would become less pronounced. World events in the 1990s, however, suggested otherwise. Did the rise of apparent ethnic conflict in the disintegration of the Soviet Union and Yugoslavia represent a slip back to an earlier stage, or was it a challenge to the idea that modernity would reduce ethnicity? Perhaps "ethnic conflict" itself was a problematic concept.

To many analysts, the conflicts in the Balkans and the former Soviet Union were triggered by the collapse of Cold War constraints that previously had kept ethnic animosities in check. Some suggested that the Balkans were trapped in ancient hatreds that modernization had not quite neutralized. The view was popularized by widely read authors such as Robert Kaplan and the military historian John Keegan,[3] who viewed the wars in Yugoslavia and the Caucasus as a breakdown of civilized order, or as primitive tribal conflicts that "only anthropologists can understand" (Keegan cited in Cramer, 2006). Conflicts in sub-Saharan Africa, including the genocide in Rwanda, were viewed through a similar lens in much of the international media and by popular writers. In a widely read article in 1994, Kaplan discussed developments in Africa under the title: "The coming anarchy: How scarcity, crime, overpopulation, tribalism, and disease are rapidly destroying the social fabric of our planet" (Kaplan, 1994).

Yet historians and political scientists have documented how ethnic identities have been profoundly shaped by processes of modernization, including the colonial experience. British colonial rulers, in particular, institutionalized and reified ethnic identities in subtle and not-so-subtle divide-and-rule strategies (see Chapter 2). As constantly created and recreated, ethnic identity cannot be understood simply as a feature of tradition. If ethnic identity is constructed and malleable, as numerous studies suggest, that makes the idea of ethnic conflict more complex than the "ancient hatreds" thesis claims (Horowitz, 1985). Moreover, even conflicts that follow and are fuelled by ethnic divisions are frequently intertwined with economic and political interests in a very complex manner. The Rwandan genocide and the Balkan War in the early 1990s illustrate the point (see Box 21.2).

Inequality

Efforts to reduce systemic and overlapping social, economic, and political inequalities have been at the heart of the development process in many countries. In a few historically rare cases this has taken the form of social revolutions (as in France, Russia, and China). At times, such struggles have been intertwined with the fight for independence from colonial rule (e.g., Algeria and Vietnam). Conflicts born of structural inequalities also have led to more recent civil wars. During the 1970s and 1980s, landless or poor peasants and workers fought the landed oligarchy that controlled the state and its armed forces in Central America. In Nepal, caste and class coincided to create highly unequal access to education, economic opportunity, and political power. In both cases, radical movements mobilized the disenfranchised to challenge the structure of power. The wars ended in compromise peace settlements in Central America and, eventually, in Nepal as well in 2006.

Well-known cases such as these have raised questions as to whether sharp inequality leads to violent upheaval. Statistical analysis shows no clear link between inequality and level of conflict, yet stubborn evidence from historical cases of wars and revolutions suggests that inequality does matter.

The most obvious explanation is that systematic inequality is a necessary but not sufficient condition for violent social transformation. "The mere existence of privations is not enough to cause an insurrection; if it were, the masses would always be in revolt,"

Chr. Michelsen Institute/Jan Isaksen

PHOTO 21.2 | A weapons cache, southern Africa.

Leon Trotsky observed in his *History of the Russian Revolution*. Dissatisfaction and despair are the raw material of violent change but not sufficient for a rebellion to materialize, let alone succeed. Organized revolt against the status quo requires mobilizing people (or solving what is often called "the collective action" problem) and finding resources and support (consistent international support seems critical to success), and progress requires an accelerated weakening of the state that typically started as more powerful than the rebels. All these conditions help explain the three major revolutions in modern history—in France, Russia, and China (Skocpol, 1979). Importantly, when unequal access to political, economic, and social resources coincide with cultural differences among groups, the divisions will deepen. Coincidental boundaries among groups, what Frances Stewart (2002) calls horizontal inequalities, are more likely to produce political instability and conflict than cross-cutting divisions.

State Failure

During the last two decades, "state failure" has been an influential concept in the literature on underdevelopment and conflict. Western-based analysts and aid organizations identified a number of "failed states" in the post-colonial world, defined by the inability of governments to perform core functions associated with the modern state, such as upholding a monopoly of violence or providing basic services (Suhrke, 2015). Somalia, which has been without a functioning central government for most of the time since 1991, is often featured as the prototypical failed state, but other

CRITICAL ISSUES

BOX 21.2 | Primitive Ethnic Violence?

Some 800,000 persons were killed in Rwanda in 1994. The victims were mainly ethnic Tutsi, while the perpetrators were mainly Hutu. Many outside observers initially attributed the violence to long-standing tribal animosities between the Hutu and the Tutsi. Yet these ethnic identities were in part a product of Belgian colonial policy, which deliberately treated the two as separate peoples and issued ethnic identity cards to institutionalize the division. The 1994 massacres were triggered by conflicts over concrete issues (power-sharing in the government, distribution of economic aid) and an uneasy military standoff between the (Hutu-led) government and (Tutsi) rebel forces. A radical Hutu faction that controlled the state had meticulously planned and organized the massacres. The machete was the weapon of choice—which seemed to symbolize the primitive nature of the society and the violence it produced—but modern guns bought on the international market or received through aid agreements with France were also used with decisive effect.

The violent breakup of the Socialist Federal Republic of Yugoslavia, it is commonly said, was caused by ancient ethnic hatreds among Serbs, Croats, and Muslims, released after Tito's socialist regime came to an end. These hatreds further defined the war, characterized by ethnic cleansing and massacres of members of "the other" ethnic group. A more careful consideration of the dynamic of the breakup suggests a different picture. Socialist Yugoslavia had consisted of six republics, each with mixed populations. The system was finely balanced by interlocking rights on the individual, republican, and federal levels. After Tito's death in 1980, and with the encouragement of Western governments and the international financial institutions, Yugoslavia moved towards a market economy and political reform. With both economic and political reform on the table, the political contest intensified. Leaders in the various republics started to make appeals in terms of "national" (i.e., "ethnic") interests. Then, as Susan Woodward writes, a cycle of mutual insecurity and exclusion developed:

> [U]nder the budgetary austerities of macroeconomic stabilization, debt repayment, and economic reform in the 1980s . . . political nationalism began to take an exclusionary form. Individuals and politicians first claimed social and economic rights for their national group against others, as they faced worsening unemployment, frozen wages, and declining welfare funds, and then escalated those claims to political rights over capital assets and territory in moves towards exclusive states' rights for the republics, in the name of their majority nation . . . and, eventually independence. (Woodward, 1999: 81)

countries such as Afghanistan and the Central African Republic also made the list.

At the same time, economists pointed to the importance of a well-functioning state for economic growth. The terms "state failure" and "state fragility" were used by the Organisation for Economic Co-operation and Development (OECD) to develop guidelines for aid to states that failed to pursue policies that donor agencies considered necessary for development. As a result, "state failure" became a rather elastic concept, which could mean anything from governments adopting the "wrong" economic policies, to a situation without a government in any meaningful sense. Gradually, a policy consensus emerged to the effect that all these aspects of state failure were interlinked, so that failure in one field would reinforce failure in another (Wimpelmann, 2006). The related notion of vicious cycles and virtuous cycles rested on the premise that the elements of what is commonly associated with Western modernity are mutually reinforcing. As such, the "failed state" fitted neatly within the framework of a liberal theory of development as a way out of, or separate from, conflict.

© Dominic Morissette

PHOTO 21.3 | Peace process: weapon destruction by demobilized guerrillas under UN supervision, El Salvador, 1992.

DEVELOPMENT AS A CONFLICTUAL PROCESS: NO DEVELOPMENT WITHOUT CONFLICT?

Social Change as a Source of Instability

As noted above, the competing paradigm is that periods of change—whether economic growth or decline, political transitions, or social innovation—are associated with conflict. Existing institutions come under pressure and may be unable to control or integrate new forces, demands, and collective actors. Change is likely to be uneven and create a sense of relative deprivation, injustice, and threat among the losers. Men rebel, the political scientist Ted Gurr wrote in 1970, when they feel they are worse off than their relevant reference groups, and change is likely to produce precisely such differences. Rapid cultural change likewise tends to create individual anxiety, the sociologist Émile Durkheim noted more than 100 years ago. When accompanied by rapid and uneven economic change, it may stimulate radical reactions. Contemporary versions of this argument often appear in relation to "globalization," which has increased communication among societies but also accentuated the often unequal distribution of benefits (see Chapter 6).

Conservative writers who accepted the weaknesses of the liberal theory of violence and development warned that social change was a source of instability and conflict and looked for ways to contain the effects, particularly bottom-up violence by mobs, rebels, and revolutionaries. A notable example of this genre among contemporary social scientists is Samuel Huntington, whose influential 1968 book pointed to the dangers of rapid modernization and development (Huntington, 1968). The critical issue of development,

Huntington concluded, was the question of order. To secure order, social mobilization must not proceed ahead of the building of institutions. His conclusion was a faint echo of the classic conservative lament of Edmund Burke, who believed the common people were an ignorant rabble and considered the revolutionaries at the time of the French Revolution to be stupid, cruel barbarians.

Violence in Development

In a radical perspective, the more interesting link between conflict and social change is the role of violence in social transformations. The premise here is that development is necessarily a conflictual process because it involves redistribution of power and resources; this typically involves violence in some form or other. An obvious example is the colonization of Asia, Africa, and the Americas. Often established and maintained through violence, European domination facilitated the flow of resources that underpinned the Industrial Revolution in the West. To what extent the colonial experience also paved the way for later development in the post-colonial states is more controversial.

The great trailblazer for this line of thinking is Karl Marx. For Marx, violence played an important role in social change. He held that history could be understood through modes of production, characterized by the technical and material inputs into production as well as the social relations that men enter into when producing. As the transition from one mode of production to another entailed a complete change of the relations of production, it meant that property rights and hence the distribution of resources radically changed. Such processes were accentuated by the use of force; as he put it, "revolutions are not made through laws."

In *Capital*, Marx described how he saw the transition to the capitalist mode of production as having emerged through a process he called primitive accumulation. His account of primitive accumulation was closely linked to his understanding of capitalism, which he saw as historically distinct: capitalists owned the means of production, whereas workers had to sell their labour to survive because they had no other means (e.g., land) of subsistence. This state of affairs—in which capitalists owned all the means of production and workers none—had not come about naturally. Rather, it was a result of a process of primitive accumulation that entailed "conquest, enslavement, robbery, murder, briefly force" (Marx, 1867: ch. 26). A prominent example of primitive accumulation is the enclosure process in fifteenth- and sixteenth-century England, when peasants were evicted, often forcibly, from land that had previously been treated as commons. Similar processes, Marx noted, took place in Scotland and Ireland as English soldiers were sent to enforce the claims of landlords. Often, whole villages were burned and destroyed.

Primitive accumulation did not occur only within Europe. The colonial system facilitated the accumulation of riches from Asia, Africa, and America to capitalists in Europe, Marx wrote. Here, the methods of primitive accumulation were especially brutal. "The treasures captured outside Europe by undisguised looting, enslavement, and murder floated back to the mother country and were there turned into capital" (Marx, 1867: ch. 31).

While rebuking classical political economists for painting a rosy picture of the origins of capitalism, Marx nevertheless concluded that capitalism represented technological and economic improvement that would pave the way for socialism. The transition to socialism would likewise necessitate violence, he predicted, although less so than in the transition to capitalism.[4] After socialism, however, social harmony would prevail. In this regard, Marx appears as a modernist thinker: he envisaged human history as a matter of continual progress towards an emancipatory end point.

Influential contemporary social scientists have likewise examined the role of violence in development. Drawing on Marx's historical analysis, Barrington Moore produced a now-classic study of the origins of the industrial democracies in the United States, France, and England, which showed that they grew out of civil wars, slavery, physical violence, and structural violence in the form of systematic oppression. The critical transformations in the development of these democracies were violent. For instance, by destroying the conditions for a plantation economy based on slave labour, the civil war in the United States laid the foundation for the modern industrial development of the nation and the growth of the middle class (Moore, 1966).

The development of the modern state in the European experience also has been a violent process.

Charles Tilly famously described early European state-building as "our largest example of organised crime" (Tilly, 1985: 167). Tilly depicted heads of states-in-the-making as self-interested entrepreneurs in the business of producing organized violence. As they set about to eliminate internal and external rivals who threatened their monopoly of violence, these rulers entered into alliances with moneyed clients, merchants, landowners, and so on. These alliances functioned as a bargain. Rulers, needing funding for their war efforts, sold military protection to their clients. Their protection, however, was of a double nature. While the rulers sold their clients protection against enemies, both within and outside the rulers' territory, they also sold their clients protection against the rulers. Clients who did not pay risked facing the rulers' coercive powers. In effect, it was a protection racket. Thus, Tilly argued, organized crime was at the heart of early state formation.

Much recent literature on "war economies," sometimes referred to as the **political economy of war**, also belongs to a tradition that sees violence as intertwined with development. These scholars call for analysis of the *dynamics* of violent conflict in developing countries, including the economic transactions taking place through and during violence. Until recently, researchers have tended to put violence in a "black box," as David Keen (2001) argues. Whereas the causes of conflict are investigated, conflict itself has been seen as a breakdown of "normal" life: more or less a nothingness or wholly negative condition not worth exploring in its own right. It follows that during violent conflict, there is no development; rather, violent conflict constitutes

BOX 21.3 | Sierra Leone's "Blood Diamonds"

CURRENT EVENTS

In 2000, a Canadian NGO published a report on the ongoing war in Sierra Leone called *The Heart of the Matter: Sierra Leone, Diamonds and Human Security*. It began: "This study is about how diamonds—small pieces of carbon with no great intrinsic value—have been the cause of widespread death, destruction and misery for almost a decade in the small West African country of Sierra Leone." The authors argued that diamonds played a central and hitherto unacknowledged part in the brutal war. The levels of violence in Sierra Leone, the authors argued, could only have been sustained through diamond trafficking. Indeed, they said, "the point of the war may not actually have been to win it, but to engage in profitable crime under the cover of warfare." The report urged the International community to address the issue. It received worldwide attention and contributed to an international momentum to stop the trade in "conflict diamonds." One result was the establishment of the Kimberley Process, a global certification system to trace the origin of diamonds, designed to stop international trade in diamonds by rebel groups who use the profits to finance violent conflict against UN-recognized governments.

Some argued, however, that the focus on diamonds risked reducing the war, and particularly the rebel movement Revolutionary United Front (RUF), to a simple greed for diamonds, thus obscuring the political dimension of the conflict. For instance, when the RUF leader Foday Sankoh was appointed head of the commission for mineral resources as part of a 1999 peace deal, this was seen by many merely as a confirmation that the movement, all along, only had been after control of the diamond fields. The case supported a more general argument that African wars were driven by individual "greed, not grievances" (Collier and Hoeffler, 2004). Yet, this conflict—as many others—was deeply rooted in political exclusion and deteriorating living conditions. This had been a mobilizing factor for many rebel soldiers. The wartime diamond economy, moreover, did not represent a radical departure from peacetime practices in trade and production. A regional network of illicit production and trade in diamonds had existed for decades before the war. The RUF and other factions had been able to tap into and sometimes alter these structures, but they did not replace them completely and often entered into alliances with established traders, miners, and exporters. Thus, many of the actors in the Sierra Leone diamond industry remained the same through war and peace.

J. Andrew Grant

PHOTO 21.4 | The Kimberley Process, by establishing the certification of diamonds on the world market as conflict-free, has sought to end the international trade in diamonds used by rebel groups to finance conflict, notably in sub-Saharan Africa.

a pause or even a setback in the development process. Keen and others (e.g., Cramer, 2006) assert, in contrast, that war is no such "nothingness." War also entails intense economic activity and often involves a significant transformation of power relations and the control of resources. Hence, violence and development do not always occupy separate social spaces.

DEALING WITH THE DEVELOPMENT–CONFLICT NEXUS: INTERVENTION AND PEACE-BUILDING

The end of the Cold War opened up space for new and unprecedented forms of Western intervention in conflict areas. A reinvigorated UN engaged actively to end wars that had been fuelled by superpower rivalry. Peace settlements and post-war reconstruction followed in short order in Central America (Nicaragua, El Salvador, Guatemala), Asia (Cambodia), and southern Africa (Mozambique). At the same time, the collapse of the bipolar international order created new forms of upheavals. Turbulent transitions occurred at the rim of the ex-Soviet Union (in the Caucasus and the Balkans). In the Horn of Africa, regimes that had been propped up by the superpowers collapsed (Somalia). Elsewhere in Africa, new violence developed as well—in Rwanda and Zaire, Sierra Leone and Liberia. To deal with these conflicts, the UN system honed its "peace-building" skills.

UN Secretary-General Boutros Boutros-Ghali defined the UN agenda in a 1992 document, *The Agenda for Peace*. Just after the turn of the century, more than 20 major operations had been undertaken. Most had

CRITICAL ISSUES

BOX 21.4 | Accounting for the Non-Violent Actors in Conflict Settings

Much of the literature on war and conflict tends to emphasize the agency of perpetrators and beneficiaries of violence. The focus is on warlords, faction leaders, and conflict entrepreneurs. Such perspectives sometimes extend into peace-building processes as well. For instance, power-sharing deals, amnesty, or concessions to natural resources often are offered to military leaders as incentives to give up violence.

In this landscape, "ordinary people" frequently appear simply as victims, innocent civilians who are caught up in the mayhem. Some scholars, however, have stressed that people living in conflict zones must be recognized as active participants in the conflict setting. They are not merely victims but agents, adopting strategies of surviving and resisting conflict (Goodhand, 2006). Gilgan (2001) calls for more research on why and how people choose *not* to fight. She suggests that people actively oppose violent domination through non-compliance, political dissidence, and flight and that outside intervention must recognize such acts of resistance to violence.

This also means that peace processes must be careful not to further marginalize local communities vis-à-vis armed factions. Often, only those who have picked up guns are included in the peace negotiations. The numerous peace talks in southern Somalia were sometimes criticized for focusing too much on "warlords" at the cost of traditional authorities and civil society, thereby conferring political legitimacy on anyone who had gained military power:

> Outsiders' insistence on holding high profile, centralized peace conferences for Somalia gives warlords incentives to continue fighting. If they are disruptive enough to defeat peace proposals, they get included in talks, which subsequently increases their reputation and consolidates their position. If they "only" represent legitimate interests of a local community, they have a tendency to be forced to concede powers. Thus, the international community empowers the violent warlords. (Hanson, 2003: 72)

a military component of peacekeepers as well as an administrative structure to co-ordinate myriad social, economic, and political reconstruction activities. "Peace-building" by this time had come to mean an increasingly standardized package of post-war aid, designed to provide security (by UN soldiers and police), promote demilitarization of the belligerent armies or factions, encourage refugees to return, restart or kick-start the economy, restore or democratize political institutions, ensure the rule of law and respect for human rights, and—sometimes—establish accountability mechanisms for war crimes and massive human rights violations perpetrated during the conflict.

The premise of the standard peace-building package was an expanded version of what we referred to earlier as "the democratic peace." In the peace-building context, it involved both economic and political reforms and became known as "the liberal peace." The essence was a set of reforms believed to constitute the foundation for peaceful reconstruction and development. Political reforms typically meant elections, with participation of political parties and the establishment of plural institutions. Civil society organizations and a free media were encouraged. On the economic side, reforms focused on market mechanisms, a minimalist but effective state, and macroeconomic stability. In addition, human rights monitoring was strengthened and legal reforms patterned on Western legal traditions were initiated. The package was firmly anchored in the tradition of Western liberalism.

That these traditions would serve as reference points for post-war reconstruction and development in Asia, Africa, and Latin America was hardly surprising at a time when the Soviet Union had collapsed and socialism seemed a defunct concept. In ideological terms, political and economic liberalism was the dominant paradigm in the post-Cold War world. Recent Western scholarship, as we have seen, also seemed to affirm that this was a solid foundation for domestic and international peace. World Bank research recommended rapid post-war growth to sustain the peace. The case for political democracy and peace was often celebrated in triumphalist terms, as exemplified by an American scholar and co-founder, in 2000, of the new *Journal of Democracy*:

> The experience of this century offers important lessons. Countries that govern themselves in a truly democratic fashion do not go to war with one another . . . [they] do not "ethnically" cleanse their own populations . . . [they] do not sponsor terrorism . . . [they] do not build weapons of mass destruction to use on or to threaten one another. . . . [They] form more reliable, open and enduring trading partnerships . . . [they] are more environmentally responsible because they must answer to their own citizens. (Larry Diamond, cited in Paris, 2004: 35)

The limitations of the liberal theory of violence as a guide to understanding the relationship between development and conflict have been noted above. In addition, some scholars now asked whether liberal institutions were particularly *ill*-suited as a framework for post-war reconstruction. A trenchant critical analysis in this regard was developed by Roland Paris in *At War's End* (2004). Liberalism, he noted, invites open competition, whether in the market or in the political arena. Countries emerging from civil war, however, are more in need of integrative mechanisms to overcome the divisive events of the past and reconstitute themselves as functioning societies. Above all, this requires structures of guidance, stability, and predictability—in short, institutions that can regulate access to economic and political power. Hence, in an echo of the Huntingtonian prescription of the 1960s, Paris recommended the development of institutions before introducing liberal reforms in order to strengthen peace.

The combination of large aid flows and high policy relevance turned peace-building studies into a growth industry. Much was applied research that assessed the impact of particular projects, but there was also a considerable body of more academic work. For example, Doyle and Sambanis (2006) examined factors associated with the degree and kind of peace established in the post-war period within countries that had recently undergone violent conflict. Using comparative and quantitative studies, they found that the post-conflict package helped to stabilize peace at least in the sense that it prevented relapse into full-scale war. Other analysts worked in the tradition of critical analysis to understand the functions of peace-building in relation to the political, strategic, or organizational interests of the "peace-builders" (Duffield, 2001; Chandler, 2006; Cunliffe, 2012).

If the post–Cold War peace-building agenda was always entangled in Western foreign policy interests, the attacks in the US on 11 September 2001 and the ensuing "war on terror" sharpened the geopolitical aspects of subsequent interventions. In Afghanistan and Iraq, military combat operations that had little to do with conventional UN peacekeeping coexisted with the more familiar and multilateral "peace-building" efforts, such as UN-led political transitions and economic development programs overseen by the World Bank. Even when the UN deployed its own soldiers, under the umbrella of a UN operation, they were increasingly expected not to keep peace, but to produce it, through robust use of force. By 2015, it was estimated that two-thirds of UN peacekeepers were deployed in the midst of ongoing conflict, as opposed to implementation of peace agreements already in place (de Coning, 2015). The techniques and mandates of the wars in Iraq and Afghanistan were increasingly reproduced in UN operations. In Mali, for instance, UN peacekeepers were mandated to undertake the extension of "state authority" and stabilization, tasks far removed from the conventional peacekeeping role of a neutral arbitrator and monitor operating in relation to recognized and consenting parties to a conflict. In the Democratic Republic of Congo, the UN in 2012 set up an "intervention brigade" tasked to carry out targeted offensive operations to neutralize armed groups that threatened state authority and civilian security. The result of these developments was to make international interventions in conflict settings more controversial, and the work of field staff, both military and civilian, much more dangerous.

Elsewhere, the UN became closely associated with what in much of the Muslim world was viewed as Western imperialism (by authorizing the bombing

BOX 21.5 | COIN: Winning Wars through Development?

CURRENT EVENTS

The first decade of the 2000s saw the codification of a US military doctrine for counter-insurgency (COIN for short). Promoted by high-profile US commanders operating in Iraq, such as Stanley McChrystal and David Petraeus, COIN drew explicitly on the experience of the colonial wars of France and Britain. Its proponents argued that in order to defeat insurgencies such as those facing Western militaries in Afghanistan and Iraq, it was not enough to defeat the enemy on the battlefield. The population had to be won over to support the government and its military forces and to deny the insurgents the space to operate. The "Coinistas" held that the key to winning the population was avoiding large civilian casualties, establishing "good governance" in the form of representative government, basic social services, and development. Tactically, the COIN approach was expressed in the phrase "clear, hold, build," where the military would clear an area of insurgents, hold it through the establishment of military checkpoints and patrols, and thereby allow military and civilian actors to build peace and development to generate popular support for the new order.

In practice, COIN proved less straightforward to implement, as the Afghanistan experience demonstrated. Civilian casualties were large. Aid agencies central to the "building" phase of COIN proved reluctant or ineffective partners. Some refused the close collaboration that COIN presumed, fearing it would compromise the neutrality on which they depended, or that it negated key criteria for development assistance based on needs and sustainability. The alternative was to bring in private contractors, but they, too, had difficulty working in areas that the military struggled to "clear" of insurgents and where their freedom to move outside of military bases was restricted. The result during the "surge" in Afghanistan was an enormous waste of resources, as COIN dictated rapid disbursement of aid, but implementing capacity was weak and the conflict permitted very little access for oversight.

A more fundamental problem was the idea that the population could be "won over" simply by a checklist of good governance and service delivery. The international military often struggled to deal with the subtleties of local politics, where loyalties did not follow neat ideas of corrupt "bad guys" and non-corrupt "good guys." An alternative approach would have been to support political settlements at the local and national level.

of Libya in 2011), or a front line in the US-led war on terror (by working closely with the US in Afghanistan). These developments further eroded the traditional UN role as an impartial builder and keeper of the peace.

Two decades after the UN's agenda for peace in 1992 set the stage for international peace-building, there were clear signs that the enthusiasm for state-building and modernization as part of a larger peace-building package had dwindled. The difficulties experienced in Iraq and Afghanistan—two enormously costly and inconclusive interventions—encouraged the search for new approaches to deal with post-war situations. State-building and modernization "from scratch" now seemed too ambitious and unrealistic. Instead, peace-building programs had to be more pragmatic, building on existing institutions and elites, whatever their nature. Some scholars called for "hybrid" approaches that mobilized "traditional" and local practices (Boege et al., 2009), worked with local elites and within the logic of local politics (De Waal, 2009), or privileged traditional or informal justice as an alternative to reforming the formal system of justice. More generally, the emphasis was less on transformation and development, or "progress," and more on short-term stabilization through the strengthening of existing power structures (see Box 21.5).

At the same time, the international order that had enabled unprecedented peace-building interventions for two decades after the Cold War was shifting. Following unsuccessful campaigns in Iraq and Afghanistan, the debacle in Libya, which imploded after NATO's bombing removed its leader, Mu'ammer Gaddafi, and financial difficulties in Europe and the US, the "West" was no longer the evident global hegemon it had been. The first firm sign of change came with Syria, where a devastating conflict by 2015 had displaced a fourth of the population but prompted no UN-authorized military intervention to establish peace. Instead, as during the Cold War, the world community was politically divided and collectively reduced to only provide some humanitarian relief. Even access to distribute that aid was sharply limited by the violence itself.

LEARNING FROM HISTORY

Prepositions and conjunctions can be tricky. The title of this chapter, "Conflict *and* Development," suggests that violence is a separate thing that can be extracted from a country's historical development. This is certainly the starting point of many studies, particularly recent research that relies on statistical analysis. But the chapter could also be titled "Conflict *in* Development" to convey a different perspective—namely, that conflict is embedded in development understood as social change. Such change often becomes violent, especially during major social transformations. To study conflict *in* development therefore requires placing events in their broader historical and deeper sociological contexts. The careful student can learn from both approaches.

A related implication is the geographic location of conflict. If we understand conflict as part of development, we can more readily recognize conflict—and its potential for violence—as part of the history of nations that today are "developed." The prosperous, industrialized political democracies of the North are both directly and indirectly founded on conflict, violence, and suffering.

Violent conflict is not something that primarily afflicts the latecomers to development or involves gruesome war tactics (such as amputating limbs, as RUF rebels in Sierra Leone did, or beheadings as the Islamic State militants carry out) that are uniquely barbarian. Exercising "memory" in relation to our own past, as Christopher Cramer calls it, is a precondition for understanding and addressing the conflict potential in all forms of development.

SUMMARY

This chapter provided an overview of how the relationship between conflict and development has been understood and analyzed in social science. It identifies two main strands. One strand views the lack of development as a cause of conflict and therefore sees development as a cure; the other conceives of development as generating conflict or as a conflictual process in itself. The chapter examined various attempts to make a causal link between underdevelopment and conflict, whether underdevelopment has been understood as the absence of economic opportunities or democracy, as inequality, or as ethnic loyalties. The chapter then discussed conservative and radical claims that development might be associated with conflict. The conservative version warns against the destabilizing effects of rapid development, while the radical view understands development as an often violent redistribution of resources and power, calling to attention the violent past of Western capitalism.

Finally, the chapter considered international efforts—often called "peace-building"—to help reconstruct societies emerging from violence. Today, peace-building operations premised on the assumption that development and "state-building" are necessary tools to recover from violent conflict might be ceding ground to a more realist position, which sees large-scale transformation of war-torn societies as difficult or costly. It was argued that this shift must be seen in connection with the changing position of Western countries, whose foreign policy interests and ideologies had underpinned much of the peace-building enterprise.

QUESTIONS FOR CRITICAL THOUGHT

1. Taking a developed country you are familiar with, what do you think the role of conflict, especially violent conflict, has been in its development?
2. Taking a developing country today that you are familiar with, do you see any parallels with the role of conflict in its development? What accounts for similarities and differences?
3. What are the implications of using the term "conflict and development" versus "conflict in development"?
4. Why, and in what ways, does choice of methodology matter in analyzing the relationship between conflict and development?
5. What are the strengths and weaknesses of contemporary peace operations?
6. Take one or several components of peace-building (e.g., UN peacekeepers, refugee return, elections, economic reconstruction), and consider how they can promote peace or have unintended effects.

SUGGESTED READINGS

Chandler, David. 2006. *Empire in Denial*. London: Pluto.

Collier, Paul, et al. 2003. *Breaking the Conflict Trap: Civil War and Development Policy*. Washington: World Bank and Oxford University Press.

Cramer, Christopher. 2006. *Civil War Is Not a Stupid Thing: Accounting for Violence in Developing Countries*. London: Hurst.

Huntington, Samuel P. 1968. *Political Order in Changing Societies*. New Haven: Yale University Press.

North, Douglass C., John J. Wallis, and Barry R. Weingast. 2009. *Violence and Social Orders: A Conceptual Framework for Interpreting Recorded Human History*. Cambridge: Cambridge University Press.

Tilly, Charles. 1985. "War making and state making as organised crime." In Peter B. Evans, Dietrich Rueschemeyer, and Theda Skocpol, eds, *Bringing the State Back In*. Cambridge: Cambridge University Press, 169–91.

Wood, Elizabeth J. 2003. *Insurgent Collective Action and Civil War in El Salvador*. New York: Cambridge University Press.

NOTES

1. For instance, Polity on democracy (www.cidcm.umd.edu/polity), the World Bank on economic statistics (http://econ.worldbank.org), and the UNDP on socio-economic indicators (http://hdr.undp.org).
2. Among the best known are the Correlates of War project (www.correlatesofwar.org) and UCDP/PRIO Armed Conflict Data Set (http://new.prio.no/CSCW-Datasets/Data-on-Armed-Conflict/UppsalaPRIOArmed-Conflicts-Dataset).
3. Robert Kaplan's "The coming anarchy" was hugely influential in the US.
4. "[I]n the former case [transition from feudalism to capitalism], we had the expropriation of the mass of the people by a few usurpers; in the latter [transition from capitalism to socialism], we have the expropriation of a few usurpers by the mass of the people" (Marx, 1867: ch. 32).

BIBLIOGRAPHY

Boege, V., A. Brown, K. Clements, and A. Nolan. 2009. "Building peace and political community in hybrid political orders." *International Peacekeeping* 16: 599–615.

Chandler, D. 2006. *Empire in Denial*. London: Pluto.

Collier, P., et al. 2003. *Breaking the Conflict Trap: Civil War and Development Policy*. Washington: World Bank and Oxford University Press.

———, and A. Hoeffler. 2004. "Greed and grievance in civil wars." *Oxford Economic Papers* 56, 4: 563–95.

Cramer, C. 2002. "Homo economicus goes to war: Methodological individualism, rational choice and the political economy of war." *World Development* 30, 11: 1845–64.

———. 2006. *Civil War Is Not a Stupid Thing: Accounting for Violence in Developing Countries*. London: Hurst.

———. 2009. "Trajectories of accumulation through war and peace." In R. Paris and T. Sisk, eds, *The Dilemmas of Statebuilding*. London, Routledge, 129–48.

Cunliffe, P. 2012. "Still the spectre at the feast: Comparisons between peacekeeping and imperialism in peacekeeping studies today." *International Peacekeeping* 19, 4: 426–42.

de Coning, C. 2015. "Offensive and stabilization mandates." In M. Peter, ed., *United Nations Peace Operations: Aligning Principles and Practice*. Oslo: Norwegian Institute of International Affairs, 17–19.

De Waal, A. 2009. "Mission without end? Peacekeeping in the African political marketplace." *International Affairs* 85: 99–113.

Doyle, W. 1983. "Kant, liberal legacies, and foreign affairs, parts 1 and 2." *Philosophy and Public Affairs* 12: 205–35, 324–53.

——— and N. Sambanis. 2006. *Making War and Building Peace: United Nations Peace Operations*. Princeton, NJ: Princeton University Press.

Duffield, M. 2001. *Global Governance and the New Wars*. London: Zed Books.

Fearon, J.D., and D.D. Laitin. 2003. "Ethnicity, insurgency, and civil war." *American Political Science Review* 97, 1: 75–90.

Fukuyama, F. 1992. *The End of History and the Last Man*. London: Hamish Hamilton.

Gellner, E. 1983. *Nations and Nationalism*. Oxford: Blackwell.

Gilgan, M. 2001. "The rationality of resistance: Alternative for engagement in complex emergencies." *Disasters* 25, 1: 1–18.

Goodhand, J. 2006. *Aiding Peace? The Role of NGOs in Armed Conflict*. Bourton on Dunsmore, Rugby, UK: ITDG.

Gurr, T. 1970. *Why Men Rebel*. Princeton, NJ: Princeton University Press.

Hansen, S. J. 2003. "Warlords and peace strategies: The case of Somalia." *Journal of Conflict Studies* 22, 2: 57–78.

Hegre, H., T. Ellingsen, S. Gates, et al. 2001. "Toward a democratic civil peace? Democracy, political change and civil war 1816–1992." *American Political Science Review* 95, 1: 33–48.

Horowitz, D.L. 1985. *Ethnic Groups in Conflict*. Berkeley: University of California Press.

Huntington, S.P. 1968. *Political Order in Changing Societies*. New Haven: Yale University Press.

Jones, S. 2000. *Of Centaurs and Doves: Guatemala's Peace Process*. Boulder, Colo.: Westview.

Kaplan, R.D. 1994. "The coming anarchy." *Atlantic Monthly* (Feb.).

Keen, D. 2001. "The political economy of war." In F. Stewart, V. Fitzgerald, et al., eds, *War and Under-Development*, vol. 1: *The Economic and Social Consequences of Conflict*. Oxford: Oxford University Press.

Marx, K. 1867. *Capital*, vol. 1.

Moore, B. 1966. *Social Origins of Dictatorship and Democracy: Lord and Peasant in the Making of the Modern World*. Boston: Beacon Press.

Paris, R. 2004. *At War's End*. New York: Cambridge University Press.

Richards, P. 2005. *No War, No Peace: An Anthropology of Contemporary Armed Conflicts*. Oxford: James Currey.

Rummel, R.J. 1975–81. *Understanding Conflict and War*, 5 vols. New York: Sage.

———. 1997. *Power Kills: Democracy as a Method of Nonviolence*. Piscataway, NJ: Transaction.

Skocpol, T. 1979. *States and Social Revolutions*. New York: Cambridge University Press.

Smilie, I., L. Gberie, and R. Hazleton. 2000. *The Heart of the Matter: Sierra Leone, Diamonds and Human Security*. Ottawa: Partnership Africa Canada. www.pacweb.org/Documents/diamonds_KP/heart_ of_the_matter_summary-Eng-Jan2000.pdf.

Snyder, J. 2000. *From Voting to Violence*. New York: W.W. Norton.

Stewart, F. 2002. "Horizontal inequalities as a source of conflict." In F.O. Hampson and D.M. Malone, eds, *Reaction to Conflict Prevention: Opportunities for the UN System*. Boulder, Colo.: Lynne Rienner.

Suhrke, A. 2015. "The long decade of statebuilding." In C.A. Crocker, F.O. Hampson, and P. Aall, eds, *Managing Conflict in a World Adrift*. Washington: US Institute of Peace.

Tilly, C. 1985. "War making and state making as organised crime." In P.B. Evans, D. Rueschemeyer, and T. Skocpol, eds, *Bringing the State Back In*. Cambridge: Cambridge University Press, 169–91.

United Nations Development Programme (UNDP). 2006. *Human Development Report 2006: Beyond Scarcity: Power, Poverty and the Global Water Crisis*. Geneva: UNDP. hdr.undp. org/hdr2006/statistics.

Wimpelmann, T. 2006. *The Aid Agencies and the Fragile States Agenda*. CMI Working Paper WP 2006: 21. Bergen, Norway: Chr. Michelsen Institute

Wood, E.J. 2003. *Insurgent Collective Action and Civil War in El Salvador*. New York: Cambridge University Press.

Woodward, S.L. 1999. "Bosnia and Herzegovina: How not to end civil war." In B.F. Walter and J. Snyder, eds, *Civil Wars, Insecurity, and Intervention*. New York: Columbia University Press.

22 Information Technologies and Development

Erwin A. Alampay

LEARNING OBJECTIVES

- To understand the challenges in transplanting appropriate technologies for development.
- To develop a critical understanding of the effects of technologies on societies, institutions, work, and individuals.
- To appreciate the growing role played by information and communication technologies (ICTs) in development.
- To consider if Internet access is a human right.

▲ **Female youth volunteers at a computer literacy training center, run by the Afghan Red Crescent Society (ARCS) in Herat, Afghanistan. There are 10 computers and 160 youths attend the classes in shifts.** | Source: Photo by Shehzad Noorani/Majority World/UIG via Getty Images

In 1998, the World Bank's annual *World Development Report* focused on the theme "Knowledge for Development." In 2016, the *World Development Report* looked at how the Internet affects the lives of people all over the world. In a way, these reports are interlinked, given that information is central to the things people do and access to it is important to their development. As such, some even call for Internet access to be considered a basic human right. This is partly explained by the fact that in a rapidly developing digitized society, more and more people need information communication technologies to access basic services (e.g., water and health care), look for opportunities, and exercise their freedoms (of expression, opinion).

This chapter explains how information and systems for sending and receiving it can be used for development and governance. We begin with a brief discussion of the relationship between technology and development, then focus on information and communication technologies (ICTs). ICTs discussed here are not limited to computers and the Internet. We also consider such ICTs as radio, television, telephone, and indigenous information systems that may be available and more appropriate for some contexts. ICTs can impact economies, how society organizes itself, and how people work. This chapter examines these effects and investigates important policy issues connected to them.

TECHNOLOGY AND SOCIETY

> *Every technology is both a burden and a blessing; not either-or, but this-and-that.*
>
> *Postman (1992: 4–5)*

Defining Technology

Technology is considered "the science and art of getting things done through the application of skills and knowledge" (Smillie, 2000: 69). It may require the organization and use of physical infrastructure, machinery and equipment, knowledge, and skills. Using technology is not simply a matter of obtaining machines and needed infrastructure but also of putting people's knowledge and skills to use and applying them. In other words, technology refers to the practical application of science to solve real-world problems.

Technology Creation and Diffusion

Technology can be developed and transferred in a number of ways. Resource abundance and shortages play an important role in the development and diffusion of technologies. A good example of this is the need for grain and the resulting Green Revolution (see Chapter 18). The Green Revolution was a campaign to develop higher-yielding strains of rice and wheat in the 1960s and 1970s. A cross-bred variety of rice was developed that doubled traditional yields, and from 1982 to 1992 production of cereals grew in Asia by 25 per cent and in Africa by 41 per cent (Smillie, 2000).

While technologies can be created, they can also be bought, copied, and stolen. Commerce and warfare have also been contributors to technological development and diffusion. Early trading between China and other Asian countries, for instance, brought with it the diffusion of technologies for papermaking, textiles, gunpowder, and porcelain. Aztec, Maya, and Inca technology for intercropping *ipil-ipil* with maize was transferred to Asia by the galleon trade (Smillie, 2000). Arabian traders helped to spread Chinese steel technology and Arabian medical knowledge. In more recent times, Japan, Korea, and Taiwan developed their automobile, electronics, and computer industries based on Western technologies.

The contribution of warfare to technological innovation has included the use of crossbows, guns and gunpowder, and mathematics to optimize distribution systems and decode messages. Space travel, for instance, is linked to the development of land-based missile technologies. Similarly, the Internet developed from the need to secure communications in the event of a nuclear attack. Moreover, technological disparities between civilizations have led to the conquest of nations. A good example of this is how the greatly outnumbered Spaniards were able to defeat the Incas in the 1500s because of their guns, steel weapons, armour, and horses (Diamond, 1999).

Appropriate Technology

Technology transfer, however, is not easy to accomplish. In developing countries and marginalized communities, it is necessary to consider the socio-economic and environmental context into which a technology will be transplanted. The term **appropriate technology** has its origin in the work of Fritz Schumacher on the kinds of technology that fit small-scale, grassroots, and community-centred organizations. These technologies are appropriate to the environmental, cultural, and economic context in which they are used. An appropriate technology is not a "poorer" technology. What is important is that it works, is suitable for the context, and is sustainable. Some examples of appropriate technologies include a polio vaccine that only requires a drop on the tongue, heat-stable vaccines that do not require refrigeration, vaccine cocktails in a single shot (UNDP, 2001: 28), inexpensive hand water pumps, fuel-efficient stoves, cheap electricity provided by windmills (Smillie, 2000), earthbags for building houses, bottled solar lights (see https://www.youtube.com/watch?v=cQCHvO2Ho_o), water rollers that ease the transport of clean water (see www.hipporoller.org), and simple latrines that help reduce the incidence of blindness by reducing the population of flies that transmit the bacteria that causes trachoma (see www.cartercenter.org). Appropriate technologies typically require fewer resources, cost less, and have minimal negative impacts on the environment. They also tap the existing knowledge of local people and use local natural resources (see Box 22.1).

Technological Determinism versus Social Determinism

The interaction between technology and society can be viewed in two ways: through technological determinism or through social determinism.

Technological determinism suggests that technology drives the evolution of society. The idea is that technology begets technology and that society is continually reformed in the wake of this process (Ling, 2007). For example, the printing press contributed to the Protestant Reformation by giving more people access to the Bible and permitting individual interpretations of God's word.

Social determinism, on the other hand, considers social interaction as having primacy in terms of the development and use of technologies. Thus, a technology, while originally intended to function in a particular way, can be reinterpreted and used in other ways. From this viewpoint, technology is not inherently good or bad, since the outcome depends largely on how it is used. For example, nuclear technology can be used to provide society with energy but has also been used for war. A hand tractor originally intended for plowing farms has been reinvented as a means of public transportation in some rural villages in the Philippines, and gill nets are being used to catch crab rather than fish. In the context of development, this interpretation highlights the

IMPORTANT CONCEPTS

BOX 22.1 | Appropriate Housing Technology: Earthbags

An example of a feasible, low-cost housing technology that has been adopted in some developing countries is the earthbag (see www.earthbagbuilding.com). This natural building alternative, evolved from military bunker construction techniques, uses bags filled with local, natural materials, hence the term "earthbags." It reduces construction costs by lowering the production and transportation costs of building materials. After being filled, the bags are stacked like bricks. Houses are often domed, much like igloos. The method is durable and non-toxic, and can provide good insulation.

However, the transfer of technologies is not always perfect. In one site, the final layer of plaster was not placed correctly and did not adhere to the mud fill that was applied over the earthbag structure. Hence, plants ended up growing naturally in the earthen medium because seeds or roots were present in the bags at the time they were used (see www.earthbagbuilding.com/projects/clinic.htm).

Reuters/Alamy Stock Photo

PHOTO 22.1 | Farmers plough a rice field with a water buffalo, locally called "carabao", and a hand tractor in a village in Dinalupihan town, northwest Philippines.

importance of focusing on people, on what they can do with technology, and on building their capacities.

Some technologies, however, are particularly closed. They are difficult to reinterpret and use in ways other than originally intended, while others are relatively open. Information and communication technologies are particularly open. Hence, while the telephone was originally intended for use by business, people soon found other, more social and personal applications for it. The same goes for the Internet, which is used not only by scientists, researchers, and the military (as originally intended) but also by ordinary people looking for recipes, life partners, and entertainment.

A very specific example of "openness" in this field is the open data movement. Open data can be freely used, reused, and redistributed by anyone—subject only, at most, to the requirement to attribute and share. The logic with this is that, often, the best use of data is not necessarily known to the originator of the data, but rather by other stakeholders in society since people could look at the same data differently.

In the "Hole in the Wall" project in India, engineers conducted an experiment to test whether people in slum areas can independently learn to use an Internet-connected computer without instruction (see www.hole-in-the-wall.com). Among the findings was how quickly children embraced the technology and were able to develop their own vocabulary for teaching each other about it.[1]

In the field of development studies, however, the issue of whether technology shapes organizations or whether society defines how technologies are used may not be as important as the effects that result from the interaction between society and technology.

Technology and Development

According to the United Nations Development Programme (UNDP, 2001: 27), many technologies can be used for human development to increase incomes, improve people's health, allow them to live longer and enjoy better lives, and permit them to participate fully in their communities. However, as Postman (1992) suggests, technology is both a burden and a blessing.

Fire, gunpowder, steam engines, electricity and nuclear energy, trains, airplanes, the telegraph, telephones—history is full of examples of technologies that have changed the course of human development, but not necessarily for the better. Thus, while technologies are often seen as indicators of modernization and material progress, they also have created new social conflicts. During the Industrial Revolution, for instance, technology created tensions not only between man and nature but also among men with different relationships to technology. Owners of capital were pitted against owners of land, progress against tradition, and capital against labour (Briggs, 1963). As Jared Diamond aptly puts it, "technology, in the form of weapons and transport, has provided the direct means by which some peoples have expanded their realms and conquered other people" (1999: 241).

Technologies also are identifiable with historical eras. For instance, some would consider that what mechanization did for the Industrial Revolution, computer technology is doing for the Information Age (Naisbitt, 1984, cited in Webster, 2000: 8). The discovery of the steam engine and later electrical production spurred the Industrial Revolution and resulted in the transformation of major social institutions such as the family, the church, cities, and working life. In Western societies, the family moved from being a multi-generational unit of production and reproduction to become more nuclear, with a mother, a father, and children, and with economic production shifted to other work sites than the household. The church lost much of its power, cities grew larger, and organizations became bureaucratized (Ling, 2007). Similarly, an important question today is how information and communication technologies are changing society and these same institutions (see Table 22.1).

THE INFORMATION SOCIETY

Information and communication technologies are arguably the defining technologies of contemporary life. ICTs encompass both the equipment and the services that facilitate the electronic capture, processing, and display of information (Torrero and Braun, 2006: 3). They include computer technologies (computers, the Internet), telecommunications (mobile phones), audiovisual technologies (DVDs, cameras, MP4s), broadcasting (radio, television), and newer technologies that combine these functions (e.g., smartphones, tablets).

Convergence and Interactivity

New ICTs are the product of technological convergence between old and new networks of technologies. Older technologies, such as radio and television, were characterized by one-way provision of communication. People were passive recipients of information. New ICTs are characterized by "interactivity" whereby communication is two-way and people have a choice in selecting the information they want while also creating new content for others.

In the near future, the issue of old versus new ICT may no longer be salient, since *convergence* has resulted in the "old" media of TV, radio, and telephones becoming digital. Furthermore, developed countries can also learn from the innovation occurring in less developed countries. For example, text messaging, which has been popular in less developed countries, has been adopted in some development projects. Projects like Frontline SMS, which allows anyone to text-message with a large group of people, now are used even among communities in developed countries in the West (see www.frontlinesms.com).

Approaches to Understanding the Information Society

Five arguments can be made for considering the world today as an "information society": technological, economic, occupational, spatial, and cultural (Webster, 2000).

TABLE 22.1 | Comparison between the Industrial Age and the Information Age

	Industrial Age	Information Age
Productive Input	Energy (steam, electricity); machines	Information; ICTs
Output	Products	Services
Organizations	Large factories	Networked organizations
Workers	Organized labour	Individualization

Sources: Adapted from Castells (2000); Rubery and Grimshaw (2001); Ling (2007); Winter and Taylor (2001).

The *technological* argument emphasizes the impressive technological innovations in information processing, storage, and transmission. It is driven by the "convergence" of telecommunications, broadcasting, and computing technologies and the creation of networks of terminals among people and organizations that have provided people with new ways of working.

The *economic* perspective on the information society derives from the work of Fritz Machlup (Machlup, 1984, cited in Webster, 2000), and measures the information society in economic terms by classifying technologies according to five broad primary industry groups: education (e.g., libraries, universities), media (radio, television, advertising), information machines (computer equipment, musical instruments), information services (law, insurance, medicine), and other information activities (research and development, non-profit work). By quantifying the economic contributions of these industries, one can calculate the growing economic significance of information and knowledge in today's society.

The *occupational* argument focuses on occupational change and the apparent predominance of occupations based on informational work (more teachers, lawyers, and entertainers than builders and coal miners, for example). This perspective is often used in combination with the economic perspective. In this view, the distribution of occupations has shifted towards a "white-collar society" and away from industrial labour. A simplification of this dichotomy argues that in the industrial sector, workers create, process, and handle physical goods, while in the information sector, workers create, process, and handle information.

The *spatial* perspective is based on the informational networks that now connect locations and affect how society organizes around time and space, thereby leading to a "flat world" (Friedman, 2005). This allows organizations to operate 24 hours a day, with offices, factories, suppliers, and employees located all over the world, as a result of the global ICT infrastructure that links them together, thereby making ICTs crucial drivers of globalization.

The *cultural* argument recognizes the extraordinary increase in information in social circulation because of television, the Internet, cell phones, and other devices. As a result, the behaviour and values of people in the highly urbanized cities of the world may be more similar than among people within the same country who are less connected to the global information network.

These five approaches to examining the idea of a global information society remain problematic, however. Identifying the types of economic activity that constitute the information society is somewhat subjective. Also, just about every profession deals with information and many of these professions have existed for a long time. Furthermore, at what point (in terms of percentage of GNP or readiness for e-commerce) can we say that a nation already constitutes an information society?

Credit card use, for instance, is important for participating in online commerce. However, except for high-income countries, the rest of the world hardly has access to credit cards (see Table 22.2). Does this mean only high-income countries participate in information societies? Or are there different types of information societies whose economies function differently, as exemplified by the unique take-up of mobile money use in the sub-Saharan region? The differences among these regions clearly suggest that nuances in development need to be understood in relation to the "information society."

Finally, networks among people in the same occupation or profession have been around since long before the creation of the Internet. Examples include machine technicians, salespersons, lawyers, teachers, and doctors. Taking such phenomena into account, how does one identify the point at which the information society came to be?

From a pragmatic viewpoint, it may not matter whether we are in an information society or not. What matters is recognizing that ICTs are affecting society economically, socially, and culturally. Societies are confronted with the growing importance of information products, an increase in information itself, the essential role of ICTs in many services and activities, and the need for information processing in trading and finance. Hence, it is important to understand what is happening in the interaction between society and ICTS, and what the implications of this interaction are for development.

TABLE 22.2 | Types of Accounts and Payment Methods, by Region, 2011, Share of Population (%)

Regions/Groups	Debit Card	Account at a Formal Financial Institution	Cheques Used for Payments	Electronic Payments Used for Payments	Mobile Phones Used to Pay Bills	Mobile Phones Used to Receive Money	Mobile Phones Used to Send Money	Credit Card
High-income countries	61.4	89.5	33.4	55.2	–	–	–	49.8
Other economies								
East Asia and Oceania	34.5	54.9	1.7	6.1	1.3	1.2	1	6.6
Europe and Central Asia	36.4	44.9	3.7	7.8	3	2.7	2.5	16.2
Latin America and Caribbean	28.8	39.3	3.9	10.3	1.8	1.9	0.8	18.4
Middle East and North Africa	9.1	17.7	4.1	2.2	1	2.4	1.3	2.4
South Asia	7.2	33	6.6	1.6	2	1.9	0.8	1.6
Sub-Saharan Africa	15.5	24	3.3	4	3	14.6	11.2	2.9
World	30.4	50.5	9.4	14.5	2	3	2.2	14.8

Source: Global Financial Inclusion Database, from UNCTAD Information Economy Report 2015, p. 37. Reprinted with the permission of the United Nations.

Linking ICTs to Development

There are generally two sides to the ICT and development debate. Optimists, consistent with the discourse on *modernization* and *globalization,* tend to embrace ICTs. Modernization theory explains how societal development must go through a series of stages, with each phase having a different technological base of production (see Chapter 3). In an information society, that base would be information technology, following the same modernization logic of radio to Internet, analog to digital. Furthermore, economies of the world have become more integrated, aided by information technology, as a result of globalization (see Chapter 6). Only over the past few decades has a technological infrastructure developed to permit the global economy to function as a unit on a planetary scale. This technological infrastructure includes telecommunications, information systems, micro-electronic processing, air transportation, cargo systems, and international business services all over the world (Castells, 1999).

In both the modernization and the globalization perspectives, information technologies play a part in development. According to modernization theory, ICTs can be seen as a potential means of closing the gap between nations. ICTs even allow countries to leapfrog stages of economic growth by modernizing a country's production system and increasing competitiveness at a faster rate than in the past (Castells, 1999). ICTs are viewed as an important aspect of a nation's ability to participate in global markets. Others argue that ICTs have helped level the playing field, as evidenced by the shift of knowledge and information-based work to less developed countries through outsourcing (Friedman, 2005). On the other side are the skeptics, influenced by the dependency and post-colonial discourse, who highlight the growing disparities in access and the inequalities that also permeate the online world.

The *dependency* paradigm, in particular, views development in one country as inevitably implying

Luis Barnola/IRDC

PHOTO 22.2 | The Asháninka, an indigenous tribe in the village of Marankiari Bajo, Peru, view the Internet as a means to share their traditions, while strengthening their culture and language.

underdevelopment in another—a sort of global zero-sum game—and sees this as implicit in the nature of capitalism (see Chapter 3). This perspective is consistent with world systems theory, which views development as a dynamic link between core regions of development and peripheral areas. Core regions are characterized by high income, advanced technologies, and diversified products, while peripheral areas have lower wages, rudimentary technology, and simple production mixes (Taylor, 1989, cited in Malecki, 1997). For instance, call-centres, which have been a growth industry in English-speaking developing countries such as India and the Philippines, are viewed by some as just another modern-day sweatshop. The system is automated to queue calls in ways to minimize idle time among workers. This contributes to negative effects of call-centre work such as lack of sleep, lack of exercise, increase in drinking and smoking, and less time for the family (Hechanova, 2007). Odd work schedules, coupled with the mentally and physically stressful nature of the work, are leading to high turnover rates in these types of jobs.

Hence, the core–periphery dichotomy that was evident during colonial times and the industrial era continues in the information age, with the idea of *divides* continuing to persist. As Castells explains, a network society has the "simultaneous capacity to include and exclude people, territories and activities," and this is characteristic of "the new global economy as constituted in the information age" (1999: 5).

Just as nations have to clarify their position with respect to these development perspectives, they also have to clarify the role of ICTs in their development policies, since ICT use is also value-laden, cultural, and contextual. For instance, as a tool for governance, ICTs can be used to increase control, just as they can be used to empower. They can be used to develop national identity, just as they can be used to better understand other cultures. In the end, ICT is a tool, and it is up to the owners or users of the technology to decide how it will be used for development—whether in commerce, education, health, or governance.

ICTS AND SOCIETY

Access to ICTs can help communities. Most important are the efficiency gains they provide. Access to phones, for example, helps to reduce travel time and transportation costs because physical commutes are no longer necessary to communicate. It also provides more security, especially for those isolated in remote areas or in dangerous locations, since access to ICTs enables people to communicate more quickly with police, hospitals, and emergency response services. Examples include the 911 emergency phone line and tsunami warning systems. Furthermore, with an increasingly mobile but dispersed population, ICTs are useful in maintaining family ties and in some cases have stemmed migration because businesses have outsourced various processes to developing countries.

There are various views on how ICTs affect society and development. Some are optimistic and focus on the benefits that ICTs can bring, including access to economic opportunities, more efficient work, and instantaneous access to better and more relevant information. In a "networked economy," those included in the network have the opportunity to share and increase their life chances, while those who are excluded have fewer opportunities and roles (Castells, 1999). Hence, to keep pace with other countries, every nation must be able to participate in the information economy. This creates skepticism among some observers, who caution that ICTs simply support existing social divides. For them, the information society widens the gap between the rich and the poor because of differences in their access to ICTs, their capabilities for using them, and the ways that they can apply them. Some also view ICTs as irrelevant to the majority of the poor and a possible negative influence on people's culture and lives (see Box 22.2).

More pragmatic observers, however, see ICTs as having varied effects on different groups and regions across the world. Consequently, they see the challenge is in making ICTs more relevant to different groups (see Box 22.3).

Optimistic View

The optimists see the use of ICTs as a necessity that helps to encourage the sustainable development of individuals, communities, and nations. At the World Summit on the Information Society (WSIS) in 2003, ICTs were considered crucial to development because they can be used in public administration, business, education, health, and environmental protection. They are seen as useful in alleviating poverty by expanding people's opportunities for economic development. They also are seen as tools that provide people with access to information that can be used to undertake production, participate in the labour markets, and conduct reciprocal exchanges with other people.

The growing share of ICTs in world economic output is cited as evidence of their importance. The most optimistic see ICTs as providing developing countries with an opportunity to "leapfrog" stages of development and achieve the level of development of the West. In fact, studies have found some beneficial relationships in terms of economic growth when a critical mass of access to ICTs such as mobile phones (Waverman et al., 2005) and broadband (Katz, 2012) is reached, with the impact being more significant in developing than in developed countries. Mobile phones, in particular, have been found to have an impact on agricultural markets (fish and grains) by reducing the dispersion of prices across markets, leading to improved welfare of fishermen and consumers (Aker and Mbiti, 2010).

CRITICAL ISSUES

BOX 22.2 | Three Separate Worlds

No country is purely based on services or information. Verzola (1998) argues that one of three sectors will dominate: agricultural, industrial, or informational (that is, the service sector). This creates three disparate worlds and could lead to a widening gap between rich and poor societies.

The agricultural sector produces living matter for consumption; the industrial sector produces non-living finished goods from natural resources; and the information sector produces non-material goods based on high information content. In trade terms, this equates producing 160 pounds of coffee (if coffee costs $1 per pound) with producing one television set at $160 or selling one copy of the latest Microsoft Office Professional for the same price.

The unique characteristic of information—never wearing out, never being used up, and easily copied with minimal input of labour and materials—gives a significant advantage to societies with economies based more on information over those based more on agriculture or industry.

CRITICAL ISSUES

BOX 22.3 | Global Care Chains

An interesting example of the balance between positive and negative views of ICTs is the concept of "global care chains," which are a "series of personal links between people across the globe based on paid or unpaid work of caring" (Hochschild, 2001: 131, cited in Munk, 2005). These chains emerged as a result of greater numbers of women obtaining employment in "post-industrial" occupations created by the growing economic reliance on information as a commodity. The need for non-manual skills has particularly benefited women, in terms of new jobs it has created for them. However, the increase in the proportion of women in the labour force has had an impact on the nuclear family in developed countries. It has fuelled a desire for migrant domestic workers from the South to serve families in the North (Thomas and Ling, 2011). Similarly, those who stay in their countries of origin but serve the needs of the North through outsourced services do so at odd hours. Thus, traditional family arrangements in developing countries are affected.

Pessimistic View

An opposing view about ICTs is that they only will increase existing inequalities and social divides. Evidence for this perspective is taken from cases demonstrating that areas that have long benefited from excellent physical access and have been dominant politically and economically are the ones benefiting from greater access to information technologies (Niles and Hanson, 2003). Historically, the introduction of new telecommunications has generally increased inequality, benefited mostly the wealthy, and had little impact on quality of life for the poor (Forestier et al., 2003). The idea that development results from linking poor nations to ICTs—the Internet in particular—was considered a myth (*The Economist*, 2005a). However, evidence is already emerging to nuance its impact on different countries' development (Waverman et al., 2005, ITU, 2012). Nonetheless, while ICTs have been instrumental in the development of India's information technology industry, this has not helped to reduce inequality between the rich and poor in Indian society (UNDP, 2001; Warschauer, 2004). To understand why the gap continues to increase, one simply needs to visualize the price and cost differential between commodities (see Box 22.2). Original software may cost $100 and can be duplicated at zero cost in minimal time. Contrast that to a farmer, who would need vast inputs in resources and time to produce the same value in agricultural produce. Finally, for some countries, the utopian ideal of an information society requiring investment in ICTs is overshadowed by the more pressing basic needs of shelter, food, and health care.

Pragmatic View

The pragmatic view sees ICTs as playing a role in a country's development if applied appropriately. Anecdotal evidence shows that access to a telephone, for instance, can have a dramatic effect on the quality of life of the rural poor. For example, Bangladesh's Grameen Village phone ladies were celebrated as a good model for areas where there is no widespread access to telephones. Grameen provided micro-loans for women to start mobile phone businesses, in which they would buy a phone and then charge other villagers per call. At one point, village phone ladies were earning three times the average national income. However, as access to mobile phones in Bangladesh has increased, the income from this "shared-access model" has declined. Nonetheless, the model can still be viable in places where telephone access remains limited.

Hence, whether ICTs are useful for development or not still depends on overcoming the same socio-economic barriers that contribute to underdevelopment in the first place. Strategies for using ICTs should consider their fit in the local context. In

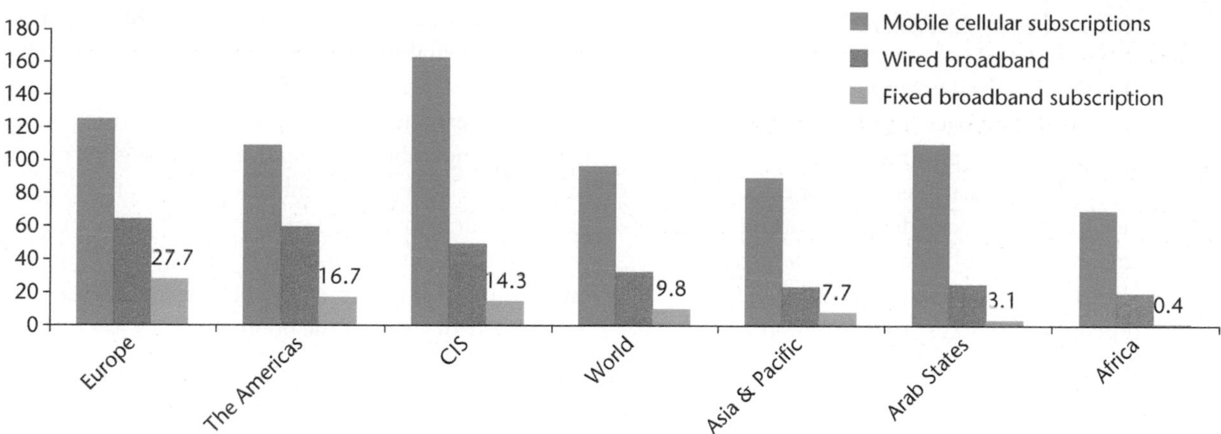

FIGURE 22.1 | ICT Subscribers per 100 Inhabitants, by World Region, 2014

Note: CIS is the Commonwealth of Independent States (formerly the USSR)

Source: ITU (2014).

addition, innovative public policies are required to make sure that technologies are not only tools for progress but also socially inclusive.

THE DIGITAL DIVIDE

At the World Summit on the Information Society, representatives of governments and civil society organizations from 175 countries declared their common desire and commitment to building a fairer society:

> a people-centred, inclusive and development-oriented Information Society, where everyone can create, access, utilize, and share information and knowledge, enabling individuals, communities and peoples to achieve their full potential in promoting their sustainable development and improving their quality of life. (WSIS, 2003: 1)

The challenge of making a more inclusive information society means overcoming the **digital divide**. The digital divide refers to the difference between groups in their access to and use of ICTs. Manifestations of this divide are commonly seen between countries, rich and poor, genders, urban and rural areas, young and old, and the educated and uneducated. The divide is usually measured in terms of the number of ICT users (e.g., fixed broadband subscribers) per inhabitant in a population.

The digital divide, however, is a relative concept. The International Telecommunications Union (ITU) reported that by the end of 2014, almost 44 per cent of households in the world had Internet access at home. However, there is a huge difference across regions, with 78 per cent in European homes having access, compared to only 11 per cent in Africa. Furthermore, in Africa, fixed broadband subscription in 2014 stood at only 0.4 per cent compared to 27.7 per cent in Europe (see Figure 22.1).

Optimists would argue that access is always on the upswing, given that the technology is rapidly developing (see Box 22.4) and its capacity exponentially increases at the same time that the cost decreases. Pragmatists, however, would point out that any progress towards access among the marginalized should be examined against the progress made by developed countries. For others, the idea of a digital divide may be passé or irrelevant, because those who need ICTs in the more developed countries already have them and those who do not have access do not really need them. Anecdotal evidence, however, suggests that access to ICTs can make a difference to people who have been deprived of it, even as there is clear evidence that such a divide exists between and within countries (see Box 22.5).

In the end, the issue of whether the divide is increasing or not is less important than the question of how to bridge it. Bridging the digital divide is important for a number of reasons. The primary reasons are to provide access to basic services and to promote social equality.

Access to Basic Services

Access to ICTs is a basic component of civic life that some developed countries aim to guarantee for their citizens. The primary argument for universal access to ICTs, in fact, is security-related, not economic. Telephone service is often considered important for the security and reduced isolation of remote areas. Health, crime, disaster, and other emergencies can be handled better if people have access to telecommunication systems. Also important is how more information for education, career, civic life, and safety purposes is made available on the Internet, especially on websites. Even social welfare services can be administered and offered electronically, an example of which is the delivery of m-money for conditional cash transfers and salaries (see Box 22.4).

Social Equality

For people in developing countries without Internet access, bridging the digital divide is a means of sharing the wide range of opportunities already available to those who are connected (i.e., the rich, people in urban areas, the educated). It gives them a means for participating and making better decisions (see Sen, 1999: chs 1 and 24). This is especially important in the exercise of good governance (see Chapters 7, 9, and 16). It varies from the simple ability to search and access government information to more ambitious visions of increased public participation in elections and decision-making processes. Direct participation through ICTs would only be possible if access to these technologies were available to all strata of the population.

From an economic standpoint, the development and use of ICTs is widely believed to be a source of competitive advantage. Hence, the ability to harness their potential is important so that no one is left behind.

If ICTs play an increasingly important role in continued learning and career advancement, then meaningful education in their use is necessary. Unless such education is widely available, the existing digital divide discriminates against children of lower socio-economic status. However, offering long-distance education through ICTs can potentially reduce the cost of education, especially at the post-secondary level, since the cost of relocation and travel can be a disincentive to continuing in school. In fact, this was the prime

CRITICAL ISSUES

BOX 22.4 | Mobile Money

Over half of the people in the world are unbanked, that is, they do not use formal financial services to save and borrow. This lack of access to financial services can exclude people with important need for capital. Hence, improving access to financial services is important for development because it can facilitate economic growth and help reduce income inequality.

With the growth in access to mobile phones in developing countries, there has been considerable optimism regarding their use as a conduit for reaching the unbanked, particularly through the development of mobile phone-based financial services. New electronic payment systems based on the mobile phone are referred to as "mobile money," that is, "services that connect consumers financially through mobile phones. Mobile money allows for any mobile phone subscriber—whether banked or unbanked—to deposit value into their mobile account, send value via a simple handset to another mobile subscriber, and allow the recipient to turn that value back into cash easily and cheaply." M-money can be used for both transfers (m-money transfer) and payments (mobile payments). Systems like MPESA (in Kenya), WIZZIT (in South Africa), and GCASH (in the Philippines) were pioneered in the less developed countries, which also shows how technology transfer can be adopted from "less developed" places. In addition, m-money has been used in the delivery of conditional cash transfers, loans, salaries, and remittances.

BOX 22.5 | Leapfrogging Stages of ICT Development CURRENT EVENTS

Given how rapidly ICTs are developing today, many are optimistic that developing societies and communities are likely to catch up. Part of this optimism has to do with ICTs not only becoming more powerful, but also becoming more affordable. This is attributable to Moore's law, which states that the number of transistors on a chip doubles about every two years and leads to a rapid and continuing advance in computing power per unit cost. On this basis, the power of computers per unit cost doubles every 24 months. A similar law has held for hard disk storage cost per unit of information and random access memory. Hence, the technology is getting better while also becoming more affordable. Hopefully, this helps make it more accessible to the poor. For instance, in 2010, the Indian Institute of Technology and the Indian Institute of Science came up with a $35 touchscreen laptop. The "tablet," which can be run on solar power, is an example of how Moore's law, along with the declining cost of ICTs, is levelling access to ICTs, with technology appropriately developed for its context.

These advancements in ICT contribute to the concept of **leapfrogging**, which is a theory of development in which developing countries skip inferior, less efficient, more expensive, or more polluting technologies and industries and move directly to more advanced ones. A frequent example is countries that move directly from having no telephones to having cellular phones, skipping the stage of land-line telephones altogether. The same is happening with Internet access being made available through mobile broadband. The benefit of leapfrogging in information technologies is that it promotes greater access to information and ICTs that is at par with the developed world.

motivation behind Mahabir Pun's quest to provide Internet service to his high school in Nepal (Box 22.6). Students in the villages can now not only access more information but also listen to guest teachers from distant places through the Internet.

Factors Contributing to the Digital Divide

Several factors work against equal Internet access and use. These factors include distribution, affordability, skills, and motivation.

Unequal diffusion/distribution of technologies. The disparity among nations often begins with a lack of access to technological infrastructure. Access is often prioritized for urban centres and business areas. This explains the divide between urban and rural communities. The availability of technologies in a community, however, does not guarantee usage. Social barriers also need to be overcome for technologies to become useful. Foremost among these barriers are gender differences, lack of education, and insufficient motivation.

Affordability. Even within urban enclaves where ICTs are commonplace, one barrier to usage is sometimes the cost of obtaining and using them. This contributes to disparities in the use of ICTs among the rich and the poor. The popularity of cell phones over land-line telephones in developing countries, for instance, was driven by the availability of prepaid cards that allowed customers to overcome barriers to ownership when credit histories were often a prerequisite.

Skills. Differences in the use of ICTs are also related to educational attainment. The more educated tend to use ICTs more. A gender dimension is also apparent, especially in places where women have less access to education and are therefore less likely to have access to or use for ICTs.

Motivation. The motivation difference is especially true with regard to the young and the old. Older people tend to have a harder time adapting to new technologies, partly because they are quite used to life without them. Motivation also is related to the relevance of the technologies to a person's occupation. White-collar professionals, for instance, may find more uses for ICTs than farmers and fishermen do.

CRITICAL ISSUES

BOX 22.6 | Bridging the Digital Divide: The Case of Nepal Wireless

This is Mahabir Pun's story of how he brought the Internet to his village.

In 1997, I wished to get Internet in my village for the first time after Himanchal High School got four used computers as presents from the students of a school in Australia. Internet and e-mail were quite new terms then. Students from Billanook College in Melbourne collected the computers and raised money to ship them to Nepal. Our dream then was to have the students of the two schools communicate with each other through e-mail. That dream did not come true instantly because there was no phone line in the village to connect to the Internet.

I tried everything to get a telephone line. Initially we got a radio phone for the village, but it did not work well. I tried to find ways to get a satellite phone; however, the cost was beyond our means. I asked political leaders and officers of the Nepal telephone company for help, but nothing happened. I kept asking people for ideas. I wrote a short e-mail to the BBC in 2001, asking if they knew anyone who could suggest ideas for getting cheaper Internet connection to my village. They wrote articles about my school and the computers we had built in wooden boxes. That article changed everything: I got responses with ideas from people all over the world.

As a result of the BBC article, we received two volunteers in early 2002 who knew about wireless networking. We experimented with wireless cards to test the connection between two villages which were 1.5 kilometres apart across a river valley. We used ordinary TV dish antennas and home-built antennas for the testing. The test was successful. Later on, many people from around the world helped provide more ideas about the wireless technology. Others donated equipment for access points for the project. Additional tests were done to connect my village to Pokhara (the nearest city with an Internet Service Provider [ISP]) using an ordinary TV satellite antenna. We pointed the antenna towards the mountain range that was stretching between Pokhara and my village. These mountains were the main obstacle for us. To overcome it, we used a tall tree on the top of the mountain as a relay station.

We had partial success. We found that we could connect to Pokhara because we could connect to Pokhara from a relay station hill. However, we could not connect to Pokhara directly from the village that time even though we tried everything we could. I played with the access points for a few more weeks. I figured out that I could connect to Pokhara if I set the transfer rate of the radio at 2 Mbps, put the access points further apart, and put a screen made of aluminum foil in between them. It worked well but there was shortage of power to run the radios all day. We had connection only for a couple of hours every day.

It took seven years for my wish to be fulfilled. Eventually, we got a grant from a foundation, which was used to buy additional equipment. We have come a long way in the past three years, but we still have to go further to bring the full benefit of the Wi-fi technology to the villagers.

Source: Abridged from nepalwireless.net/story01.php; see http://www.nepalconnection.org.np/about-mahabir-pun/.

USING ICTs FOR DEVELOPMENT

The use of ICTs for development requires an integrated approach that accounts for access to the ICT infrastructure, the content and applications that can be used intensively, and building the necessary capabilities to use them, before it can impact on development (see Figure 22.2). Universal service/universal access policies deal with bridging the divide in access to ICTs.

Universal service in telecommunications is defined as "making affordable a defined minimum service of specified quality to all users at an affordable price'"

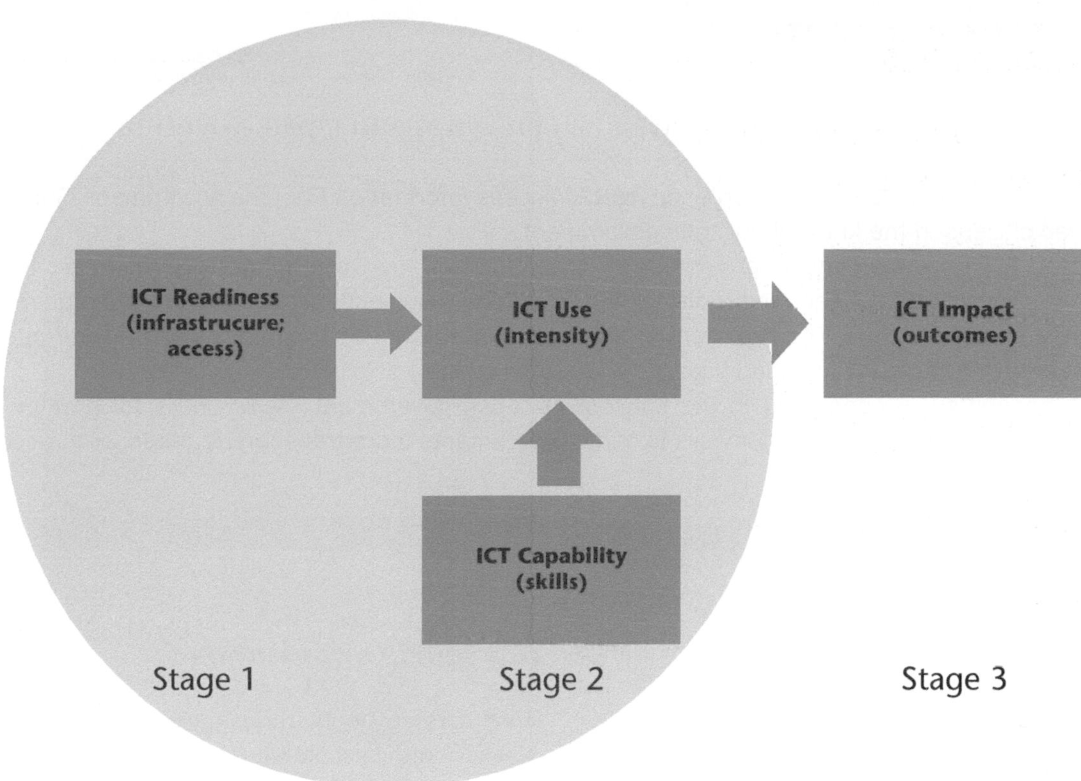

FIGURE 22.2 | ICT Development Index Framework towards an Information Society
Source: Adapted from ITU (2014).

(Prosser, 1997: 80). The focus of universal service policies is to promote "'universal' availability of connections by individual households to public telecommunications networks" (Intven, 2000: 1). This means that universal service is based on the availability of ICTs in homes.

Universal access, on the other hand, refers to "a situation where every person has a reasonable means of access to a publicly available telephone . . . [which] may be provided through pay telephones, community telephone centers, teleboutiques, community Internet access terminals and similar means" (Intven, 2000: 1). It is often measured in terms of the proportion of people in the population with access (i.e., percentage of people with cell phones). Countries have varied definitions of access. Some define it in terms of distance (e.g., a pay phone within 20 kilometres of most people), while others define it with respect to time (e.g., a telephone within a 10-minute walk) (Panos Institute, 2004).

Both universal service and universal access are based on the *affordability*, *accessibility*, and *quality* of basic telecommunication services. The primary difference is that universal service is focused on the availability of services in all homes, whereas universal access aims to have basic telecommunication services available in all communities. Policies are crucial in making this possible (see Box 22.6).

With the convergence of technologies and the development of wireless technologies such as the cell phone, 4G, and TV White Space, "universal access" and "universal service" have evolved to refer to access to the types of services or functions a technology can deliver. Developing countries are now moving towards access to the Internet, in particular broadband Internet, as their primary universal access objective.

Creating Value: Developing Relevant Content

Using ICTs for development, first and foremost, requires understanding the information needs and rights

IMPORTANT CONCEPTS

BOX 22.7 | Freedom of Information, Open Data, and Open Government

Freedom of information laws give people the right to access information from the government. Such laws often keep citizens in the know about their government.

Related to this is the concept of **open data**. According to Open Data Handbook, this refers to data that can be freely used, reused, and redistributed by anyone—subject only, at most, to the requirement to attribute and share alike. The argument for open data is that the best use of data is left for people/stakeholders, not necessarily the original generator of that data.

Both concepts are connected to the concept of "open government," which calls for greater civic participation in public affairs, and for ways to make governments more transparent, responsive, accountable, and effective.

of people (see Box 22.8). This understanding should come from the intended users in the community. But because people have different uses and needs, there are calls for more "open data," with the idea that it is people, in their respective contexts, who are in the best position to know how to use data. It is from this that innovation in content use will follow (see Box 22.7).

Providing Qualitative Transformation: Making ICT Use Relevant to People

It cannot be assumed that ICTs alone can make a significant impact on an individual, an organization, or a government. Their impact also depends on the capacities and values of the people using the technology. Thus, investing in ICTs requires shaping people and developing the necessary skills to permit them to succeed.

In fact, even though newer ICTs are more "user-friendly" than those of the past, they still require some degree of skill to operate. Being able to navigate the Internet to find useful information requires the ability to discriminate between what is useful and relevant and what is not. This is why more educated people have been better able to take advantage of the benefits offered by the Internet, such as surfing the World Wide Web, e-mailing, using social networks, and creating content.

ICTs and Organizations

Since ICTs are tools, their impact on organizations depends on the people who design what the system is supposed to do and on how people, in the end, use it. Thus, the impact also depends on what the user wants the technology to be rather than just on the technology itself. While the available technology defines to some extent the limits of what can and cannot be done in an organization, in the final analysis, how ICTs are used tends to be socially determined by their managers.

Internal versus External Focus

ICTs can be used to make internal processes within companies more efficient (e.g., automation). They can also be used to network different systems within organizations. Systems also can be designed to increase interaction between an organization and its clients. This can be done by offering feedback mechanisms through telephone hotlines, websites, or e-mail. Automated systems and business process outsourcing to other parts of the world also can enable an organization to offer services around the clock, seven days a week.

Flexibility versus Control

ICTs can be used to make work easier and empowering. This can be done by giving people greater access to

IMPORTANT CONCEPTS

BOX 22.8 | Implementing Universality: Regulatory Measures to Fund It

Several policy and regulatory measures can be pursued to make universal access to ICTs possible.

1. *Market-based reforms.* In cases where the government had owned the telecommunication operations, evidence has shown that a marked improvement in access to services occurred following privatization. Other reform measures include opening the market to more competition and cost-based pricing.
2. *Mandatory service obligations.* Service obligations are imposed through licence conditions or other regulatory measures. This may be through a policy requiring providers to serve all customers who are willing to pay the prescribed rates, or policies prescribing geographic limits to areas where service is mandatory.
3. *Cross-subsidies.* Surplus revenue earned from profitable services could be used to cover losses from unprofitable areas or services (e.g., long-distance rates subsidizing local rates, business rates subsidizing residential rates).
4. *Universality funds.* This refers to independently administered funds that collect revenue from various sources and provide targeted subsidies to implement universality programs. These sources may include government-appropriated budgets, charges for interconnection services, levies on subscribers, or providers (Intven, 2000).

different kinds of information within an organization (e.g., through local networks with access to internal databases) and outside the organization (e.g., providing Internet access during working hours). However, ICTs can also expand control over what employees are doing by increasing the managers' span of control—thanks to cell phones, for example, employees can be reached anytime and anywhere.

ICTs and Work

The impact of ICTs on employment is mixed, just as it is in other facets of development. On the plus side, new kinds of jobs have been created. Some examples are call-centre operators, computer programmers, knowledge managers, systems administrators, web designers, online tutors, and medical transcribers. In addition, ICTs can provide flexibility in careers and work opportunities, since people are no longer limited by their location and the opportunities available there. They expand work opportunities available to people, giving them easier access to information about work in different parts of the world. Such information can enable people in developing countries to earn higher pay than what the local market would normally provide. It also can help workers balance their work and family life.

On the negative side, however, jobs can be made obsolete. Automated teller machines, for instance, take the place of bank tellers. Lawyers no longer rely on secretaries to type their briefs. There's less need for messengers and telegraph operators. Services outsourced to developing countries take jobs away from other parts of the world. While people may have more employment opportunities, they also face more competition for those jobs.

There are other drawbacks to always being "connected." For some people, being accessible at all times opens the way to intrusion into their private space instead of helping balance work and family life. Moreover, ICTs can create a distraction that could lead to lower productivity—even abuse and addiction. Because the Internet is content-rich, employees sometimes venture to websites or activities that are not work-related.

PHOTO 22.3 | Technology helped protestors bring down the Mubarak regime in 2011: Tahrir Square, Egypt.

CRITICAL ISSUES

BOX 22.9 | Communication Rights Issues Pertaining to Content

There are a number of issues with respect to developing content for the information society. Among these are free access to useful and relevant information, freedom of expression, and the preservation of local cultures.

Open access versus intellectual property rights. Open access is important, especially when considering the social and economic necessity of sharing the benefits of technological developments and access to data (see Box 22.8). It becomes controversial, however, when pitted against commercial interests in terms of ownership and intellectual property rights. An example is the battle between proprietary software like Microsoft Explorer and open-source software, such as Firefox, that does the same thing. Interestingly, in the World Wide Web, voluntarism and sense of community remain very much alive. This is evident in the numerous journals and websites that provide open access—i.e., free, immediate, permanent, full-text, online access—for any user, web-wide, to digital scientific and scholarly materials, and the growth of open-source software online.

Censorship versus freedom of expression. On the negative side, there is concern about the potentially harmful and dangerous content carried in ICTs, especially pornography and gambling, as well as sites that encourage terrorism, foster hatred of identifiable groups, and teach how to improvise explosive weapons. Hence, states are concerned about regulating content. On the other hand, some people worry that increased regulation, especially in the form of censorship, might curtail people's freedoms to express, communicate, and access useful information. For instance, in 2007 in Burma, thousands of Buddhist monks marched for freedom in the streets of Yangon. The state attempted to prevent the story from coming out by cutting off access to the Internet. Nonetheless, activists and journalists were able to smuggle images and video captured on mobile phones and broadcast these on YouTube. This generated worldwide condemnation of and concern over the events occurring in Burma. Similar attempts to control the Internet occurred during what is now referred to as the Arab Spring, the wave of demonstrations in the Arab world from late 2010 to early 2012 that forced a number of governments out of power. Some refer to it as the "Twitter revolution" in part to recognize the use of social media to organize and raise awareness among the population.

However, even governments in developed countries like the United States are not immune from wanting some regulation of online content because of "national security." This was the case, for instance, with WikiLeaks, a whistleblower website that posted classified and sensitive documents about the wars in Iraq and Afghanistan.

Security versus privacy. Along with censorship, another form of regulation is increasing surveillance and monitoring of online communications. This is because of the growing view among states that cyberspace is now a national security concern. Hence, some governments try to exert some control over companies who own and operate in cyberspace. This has become an issue among companies such as Google and Yahoo! that operate in closed societies and non-democratic countries, including China and the United Arab Emirates, as it raises ethical issues regarding the privacy of users and possible harassment of activists, regime opponents, and free-speech advocates.

The issue of security versus privacy gained further prominence through the case of Edward Snowden, who in 2013 revealed several global surveillance programs run by the US National Security Agency. Some sectors now consider him a hero, while others see him as a traitor. Another instance was the dispute between the FBI and Apple where the FBI demanded help to mine data from an iPhone used by a terrorist in the San Bernardino, California, shootings in 2015. Apple's position was that people around the world deserve data protection, security, and privacy, and sacrificing one over the other actually puts people at greater risk.

Diversity of content. One important issue with ICTs is the dominance of content created in the West. For example, the predominant language on the Internet is English, which may not be the first language of choice in many countries of the world. Hence, some groups fear that ICTs can endanger local cultures and heritage. Furthermore, news conglomerates, often owned by a few powerful people, may present biased perspectives on world events. Thus, an important challenge is to diversify the content, provide information that celebrates different cultures, acknowledge differences in viewpoints, and provide more information in local languages.

These include answering personal e-mail, using instant messaging, playing games, viewing movies and pornography, and gambling.

Thus, balancing the benefits and hazards of providing Internet access in the workplace has become a policy concern in organizations and in countries around the globe. Determining who should have access and restrictions in terms of time and content are pertinent issues in the workplace today, just as they are issues for states.

In the end, ICTs are not a panacea for making corrupt governments less corrupt, bad organizations good, or incompetent individuals competent. However, as with other technologies, ICTs in the hands of good people can make the people themselves and their society better. That is what ICT for development strives for.

SUMMARY

In this chapter, the student has learned about the growing role of information and communication technologies in everyday life and development in general. However, these "digital dividends" are not guaranteed, and there are uneven outcomes among regions, genders, and income classes. For it to lead to positive outcomes for all requires addressing non-digital complements, such as differences in access to infrastructure, addressing inequalities in levels of education, and putting in place regulations that expand opportunities for people to obtain more affordable and good quality services.

Finally, with the increased pervasiveness of ICTs, emerging issues also affect the basic human rights that governments must consider. Among these are rights of privacy, security, free expression, intellectual property, and open access to knowledge.

QUESTIONS FOR CRITICAL THOUGHT

1. What factors initially contributed to the digital divide in the Nepalese case discussed in the chapter? How did the community overcome these problems? Could this solution to the digital divide be replicated in other developing communities? Can such technology transfer be sustained?
2. Consider the case of earthbags (see Box 22.1). Is this technology appropriate for any place? How can problems identified in the case be fixed or avoided in the future? What lessons does it offer about the transplanting of technologies from one context to another?
3. What do you think are the benefits and problems that social media like Twitter and Facebook bring to society? What can people or organizations do to ensure that these media bring more good than harm?
4. There is a statistically significant relationship between the ICT Development Index and 20 (out of 48) Millennium Development Goal indicators for which sufficient data are available (e.g., infant mortality, maternal health, combatting hunger) (ITU, 2014). Do you think this would be sufficient evidence to say access to ICTs should be considered as a basic human right?

SUGGESTED READINGS

Deibert, Ronald J., John G. Palfrey, Rafal Rohozinski, and Jonathan Zittrain, eds. 2010. *Access Controlled: The Shaping of Power, Rights, and Rule in Cyberspace.* Cambridge, Mass.: MIT Press.

Katz, James, ed. 2011. *Mobile Communications: Dimensions of Social Policy.* Piscataway, NJ: Transaction.

Smillie, Ian. 2000. *Mastering the Machine Revisited: Poverty, Aid and Technology.* Bourton on Dunsmore, Rugby, UK: ITDG.

United Nations Development Programme (UNDP). 2001. *Human Development Report 2001: Making New Technologies Work for Human Development.* New York: UN. http://hdr.undp.org/reports/global/2001/en.

Webster, Frank. 2000. *Theories of the Information Society.* London and New York: Routledge.

World Bank. 2016. *World Development Report 2016: Digital Dividends: 2016.* Washington: World Bank.

NOTE

1. See the Hole in the Wall Project, at www.ncl.ac.uk/egwest/holeinthewall.html.

BIBLIOGRAPHY

Aker, J.C., and I.M. Mbiti. 2010. "Mobile phones and economic development in Africa." Center for Global Development, Working Paper 211.

Alampay, E.A. 2006. "Analysing socio-demographic differences in the access and use of ICTs in the Philippines using the capability approach." *Electronic Journal of Information Systems in Developing Countries* 27. www.ejisdc.org/ojs2/index.php/ejisdc.

Briggs, A. 1963. "Technology and economic development." In Scientific American, *Technology and Development*. New York: Alfred A. Knopf, 3–18.

Castells, M. 1999. "Information technology, globalization and social development." UNRISD Discussion Paper no. 114, Sept.

———. 2000. *The Information Age: Economy, Society and Culture*, vol. 1: *The Rise of the Network Society*, 2nd edn. Cambridge, Mass.: Blackwell.

Diamond, J. 1999. *Guns, Germs and Steel: The Fates of Human Societies*. New York: W.W. Norton.

Economist, The. 2005a. "The real digital divide." 12 Mar., 9.

Forestier, E., J. Grace, and C. Kenny. 2003. "Can information and communication technologies be pro-poor?" *Telecommunications Policy* 26: 623–46.

Friedman, T.L. 2005. *The World Is Flat: A Brief History of the Twenty-First Century*. New York: Farrar, Strauss and Giroux.

Hechanova, R. 2007. "The view from the other side: The impact of business process outsourcing on the wellbeing and identity of Filipino call center workers." Paper presented at the Living the Information Society Conference, 23–4 Apr., Makati City, Philippines.

International Telecommunication Union (ITU). 2014. *Measuring the Information Society Report*. Geneva: ITU.

Katz, R. 2012. *The Impact of Broadband on the Economy: Research to Date and Policy Issues*. Geneva: ITU, Apr.

Ling, R. 2007. "What would Durkheim have thought?" Plenary paper presented at the Living the Information Society Conference, Makati City, Philippines, 23 Apr.

Malecki, E. 1997. *Technology and Economic Development: The Dynamics of Local, Regional and National Competitiveness*, 2nd edn. Harlow, UK: Longman.

Munk, R. 2005. *Globalization and Social Exclusion: A Transformationalist Perspective*. Bloomfield, Conn.: Kumarian Press.

Niles, S., and S. Hanson. 2003. "A new era of accessibility." *URISA Journal* 15: 35–41.

Rubery, J., and D. Grimshaw. 2001. "ICTs and employment: The problem of job quality." *International Labour Review* 140, 2: 165–92.

Panos Institute. 2004. *Completing the Revolution: The Challenge of Rural Telephony in Africa*. London: Panos Institute.

Postman, N. 1992. "Technopoly." In N. Postman, *The Surrender of Culture to Technology*. New York: Vintage Books.

Prosser, T. 1997. *The Law and Regulators*. Oxford: Clarendon.

Schech, S. 2002. "Wired for change: The links between ICTs and development discourses." *Journal of International Development* 14: 13–23.

Sen, A. 1999. *Development as Freedom*. New York: Anchor Books.

Smillie, I. 2000. *Mastering the Machine Revisited: Poverty, Aid and Technology*. Bourton on Dunsmore, Rugby, UK: ITDG.

Thomas, M., and S.S. Lim. 2011. "On maids and mobile phones: ICT use by female migrant workers in Singapore and its policy implications." In J. Katz, ed., *Mobile Communication and Social Policy*. Piscataway, NJ: Transaction.

United Nations Development Programme (UNDP). 2001. *Human Development Report 2001: Making New Technologies Work for Human Development*. New York: UNDP.

Verzola, R. 1998. "Towards a political economy of information." In F. Rosario-Braid and R. Tuazon, eds, *A Reader on Information and Communication Technology*

Planning for Development. Manila: Asian Institute of Journalism and Communication, 94–104.

Warschauer, M. 2004. *Technology and Social Inclusion: Rethinking the Digital Divide*. Cambridge, Mass.: MIT Press.

Waverman, L., M. Meschi, and M. Fuss. 2005. *The Impact of Telecoms on Economic Growth in Developing Countries*. Vodafone Policy Paper Series, 2. London.

Webster, F. 2000. *Theories of the Information Society*. London and New York: Routledge.

Winters, S.J., and S.L. Taylor. 2001. "The role of information technology in the transformation of work: A comparison of post-industrial, industrial, and proto-industrial organization." In J. Yates and J. Van Maanen, eds, *Information Technology and Organizational Transformation: History, Rhetoric, and Practice*. Thousand Oaks, Calif.: Sage.

World Summit on the Information Society (WSIS). 2003. *Declaration of Principles*. Document WSIS-03/GENEVA/DOC/4-E. 12 Dec.

23 Culture and Development

Nissim Mannathukkaren

LEARNING OBJECTIVES

- To understand the concept of culture and to dispel the many myths surrounding it.
- To learn about the relationship between culture and development.
- To develop an intercultural understanding.

▲ **Hindu nationalist Bharatiya Janata Party convention goers are serenaded by ekkalam players during BJP festivities in Jaipur, Rajasthan state, India.** | Source: Photo by Robert Nickelsberg/The LIFE Images Collection/Getty Images

INTRODUCTION

Culture is one of the most misunderstood concepts in the lexicon. It is often used rather loosely, denoting entirely contradictory meanings. Misunderstandings about culture have serious implications. In fact, in recent history, there are hardly any conflicts, major or minor, that have not entailed invoking the concept of culture in some way. It seems that in an age when humankind has achieved the highest level of economic prosperity and scientific and technological advancement, culture and its varied manifestations have acquired an all-pervasive influence as a concept that can explain almost anything. In academia, one of the most important examples of this is the theorist Samuel Huntington's revival of his "clash of civilizations" argument to explain the reality of the post-9/11 world. Such arguments, as we will discuss in this chapter, have only solidified misunderstandings about the concept of culture in popular discourse, thus further exacerbating the conflicts ostensibly rooted in culture. This possibility for aggravating or even causing conflict places a greater responsibility on academics to develop a better understanding of the term.

In the sphere of development, culture has also assumed an unprecedented significance in explaining phenomena such as poverty, economic growth, violence, and so on. From the policy formulations of international financial institutions, such as the World Bank and the International Monetary Fund (IMF), to the theoretical and practical programs of non-governmental organizations (NGOs), culture has become the centre of attention. Hence, we see the ubiquity of words such as "community," "ethnicity," and "gender" in the development discourse and the differences associated with these concepts. This is in marked contrast to the dominant tendency of twentieth-century development theory and practice, which excluded questions of culture.

Since the Enlightenment in eighteenth-century Europe, Western thought has been dominated by an outlook that placed its faith in human reason instead of in an extraneous supernatural authority, such as the God of Judeo-Christian religions. Reason was a universal human trait and hence was not the property of any one cultural group or formation. Reason was supposed to liberate human beings from superstitions, serfdom, and poverty and take them on the path of progress. Development, until quite recently, was based on this philosophical assumption. The means of realizing this assumption was through a project of modernization, which would destroy archaic institutions and relations. Industrialization and urbanization were the ideal and the necessary outcomes of this process of modernization (Escobar, 1997: 86). All this was made possible by "rationality, the highest expression of which was science" (Shanin, 1997: 65).

Irrespective of cultural differences, all societies could follow this path of modernization. But this universal project of development based on reason, and above culture, did not materialize. Moreover, the glorious tenets of the Enlightenment—liberty, equality, and fraternity—have still not been accepted by all societies. Even in societies that have accepted these values as core constitutional principles, it is liberty (mainly economic liberty) that has gained precedence. Since the emergence of capitalism and, more specifically, the Industrial Revolution, "the ceaseless production of endlessly proliferating material goods" (Sainath, 2006: 66) has increasingly connoted progress. Therefore, it was not surprising that the entire development enterprise, as implemented in the Third World, mainly meant revolutionizing the economic forces of production, a cause for which all other questions, including cultural, were sacrificed (see Box 23.1).

Recent criticisms that have emerged from a *post-modern* and *post-colonial* perspective have looked at the Enlightenment values, including the crowning of reason and science, as European constructions that have been imposed on the rest of the world (see Chapter 4). Thus, the experience of colonialism, imperialism, and development, and the monstrosities caused by them, put a serious question mark on the efficacy of reason itself. We stand at a juncture, therefore, in which the ideas and values that ruled our consciousness for two to three centuries have been deeply questioned—chief among them being the conception that all societies have a similar path to pursue and a similar goal to achieve. Instead, we see the emphasis on diversity and "difference" and the multiple paths and endeavours characterizing different cultural formations. Therefore, the current explosion of the use of the concept of culture can be seen as a justifiable backlash against ignoring culture for so long.

CRITICAL ISSUES

BOX 23.1 | Development sans Culture

The adoption of modernization and scientific rationality has led to an inevitable conflict between the world views of the modernizing elites and the masses who still continue traditional ways of living. Therefore, development in many southern societies has seen rural peasants being subjected to policies constructed by the educated bureaucrats from the cities. One example is the relief package announced by the government of India in 2006 for the debt-ridden farmers of western India, which included the distribution of cattle to people who had never used them before and in a region that is deficient in water and fodder. Ultimately, the result of the government's promoting dairying in a region not suited for it was that the farmers spent a lot of labour time in tending to the cattle, as well as the equivalent of three people's daily wages on the sustenance of one cow, with hardly any return from it (Sainath, 2006). Such examples abound in the history of the development era, not only in the South but also in the North–South relationship, seen especially in the devastating policies designed by institutions like the World Bank without due consideration to the local, material, and cultural contexts of a region.

In the course of this chapter, we will look at culture in its varied manifestations and its relationship to development. One of the main goals will be to dispel the many myths that surround the concept of culture. After setting out a plausible definition of culture, we will deal with one of the important debates that characterizes the field: the cultural versus the material. Understanding the relationship between these two spheres is crucial to clearing up some of the misconceptions about the concept of culture. In the final section, we focus on the **turn towards culture** as an explanatory variable to understand development and the reasons and implications of such a turn.

WHAT IS CULTURE?

If we are to clear up misunderstandings about the term "culture," the first step is to develop a precise definition of the concept. "Culture" derives from the Latin word *cultura* and in its initial usage referred to the cultivation or the nurturing of animals or crops. From the sixteenth century onward, this original usage was extended to include human beings and the cultivation of the mind. Gradually, it took on the connotation of a "progressive process of human development, a movement towards refinement and order and away from barbarism and savagery" (Thompson, 1990: 124, 126). Affinities with the Enlightenment idea of progress are visible here. Similarly, culture can be seen as "a state or process of human perfection, in terms of certain absolute or universal values" (Williams, 1961: 41). One of the problems in defining culture in this fashion is that it can acquire an elitist and evolutionary connotation, suggesting that culture is the property of a few people while the majority lack culture, and that culture can be attained only at a certain stage of development. This elitist belief is common in many societies, but it took its most pronounced form in the European encounter with non-Europeans, especially colonized people. This is the reason why the colonizing enterprise was also a civilizing mission—to bring culture to the "primitives" (see Chapter 2).

This notion of the inferiority of non-European cultures began to be corrected only with the emergence of the discipline of anthropology towards the end of the nineteenth century. Rather than seeing culture as an evolutionary movement to a predestined state of perfection defined by Europeans, anthropology began to look at cultures, especially non-Western ones, without any preconceived notions of inferiority (Benhabib, 2001: 3). E.B. Tylor, one of the famous first-generation anthropologists, described culture as "that complex whole which includes knowledge, belief, art, morals, law, custom, and any other capabilities and habits acquired by man as a member of society" (quoted in Thompson,

1990: 128). Similarly, culture can be seen as "a description of a particular way of life, which expresses certain meanings and values not only in art and learning but also in institutions and ordinary behaviour." This definition will "include analysis of elements in the way of life that to followers of the other definitions are not 'culture' at all: the organization of production, the structure of the family, the structure of institutions which express or govern social relationships, the characteristic forms through which members of the society communicate" (Williams, 1961: 41, 42). These definitions are devoid of the Eurocentric assumptions of the evolutionary and elitist concept of culture that we saw above. They do not seek to pass an evaluative judgment about what is good or bad. However, these definitions can become very broad, encompassing almost everything that human beings do. This renders them somewhat vague and imprecise (Thompson, 1990: 130). It is therefore imperative that we move beyond both the elitist and the anthropological understandings of culture, while retaining what is useful in them.

It has been argued that the distinctive feature of humans is that we have fully developed language (Thompson, 1990). Therefore, a good starting point is to focus the study of culture on the symbolic. According to the distinguished anthropologist Clifford Geertz, "man is an animal suspended in webs of significance he himself has spun" (1973: 5). Culture becomes important because human beings do not just inhabit a world that is objective and natural. It is also simultaneously a world that is constructed and subjective. This means that human beings develop and attribute their own meanings to the objective world they inhabit. And these meanings may vary from one society to another. Here, it would be productive to follow Thompson: "culture is the pattern of meanings embodied in symbolic forms, including actions, utterances and meaningful objects of various kinds, by virtue of which individuals communicate with one another and share their experiences, conceptions and beliefs" (Thompson, 1990: 132). But this is only the first step towards a proper understanding, especially when we are seeking to understand culture's relationship with development.

The variety of understandings about culture is mainly a result of the genuine complexity of cultural formations that exist in the world. At the same time, it would be fruitful to develop a definition that eliminates some of the myths that surround culture. Thus, the evolutionary definition, which holds that culture is a constant movement towards perfection, would not make sense unless we understood the elements that constitute this idea of perfection and the actual social and historical contexts that produce different ideas of perfection. At the same time, we have to account for values that do not meet the criterion of perfection. There is also the need to avoid definitions that narrowly treat culture as a mere by-product of other, "real" interests in society (Williams, 1961: 43–4, 46). That does not help us to understand what is intrinsic to the sphere of culture. However, the study of culture cannot remain at the level of culture alone either; it should move on from a mere study of symbolic forms to a study of them in "relation to the historically specific and socially structured contexts and processes within which, and by means of which, these symbolic forms are produced, transmitted and received" (Thompson, 1990: 136). For example, while we can easily identify with many of the themes in William Shakespeare's plays, it would be wrong to assume that we can learn all about the culture of the period from the plays alone; instead, they have to be placed within and understood in relation to the context of sixteenth-century England.

THE CULTURAL VERSUS THE MATERIAL

It would be a fascinating enterprise to study transformations throughout history in the cultural sphere along with transformations in the material sphere. Of course, we must acknowledge that, in reality, these spheres are inextricably intertwined and that only for heuristic purposes do we try to make such distinctions. It would be going along with a wrong, though commonsensical, understanding that the symbolic is somehow beyond all determinations and influences. The economic aspect, for example, is a very important facet of the interrelationship between culture and other elements in society. In fact, many misunderstandings about culture stem from the belief that culture can be analyzed without understanding its interlinkages with the economic dimension, which would include the forces of production (land, labour, machinery) and the relations of production (the relationship between classes in the process of economic production). How can we understand the cultural forms of the present without an in-depth look into how capitalism—the dominant mode of production of our time—functions? It has to be kept in mind that the practice and interpretation of cultural forms cannot be entirely random. The capitalist mode of production (as any other mode of production) structures in various ways the cultural forms that are produced. How is it possible, as Garnham asks, to study multiculturalism without studying the movement of labour and people that created it in the first place? How is it possible to study mass-mediated cultural forms without understanding the broadcasting institutions that produced them? Similarly, how can we understand shopping and advertising without understanding the processes of manufacturing and retailing (Garnham, 1998: 611)? These questions especially highlight the inextricable linkages between culture and development. In the present these linkages have acquired an extra-local character and culture has been "caught up in processes of commodification and transmission that are now global in character" (Thompson, 1990: 124).

Technology plays a crucial role in present-day culture. The ways in which modern means of communication and commodification have shaped culture show that culture does not exist in a vacuum but is constantly shaped by material forces. For example, communication technologies like the Internet and mobile phones have had a significant impact on the cultural meanings of human relationships and interaction, especially in the Global South, where the paradoxes produced by the coexistence of modern and traditional ways of life are very pronounced (see Chapter 22). Technologies such as photography and printing also have completely altered our relationship to the past. This new way of recording culture has a significant impact (both negative and positive), especially on indigenous cultures with strong oral traditions, societies that transmit their culture across generations without a writing system. Similarly, science exerts an influence on cultural forms. The detective story genre, for example, would not have been possible in any age other than the scientific age. Detective stories "could only appeal to—in fact, only be *comprehensible* to—an audience accustomed to think in scientific terms: to survey the data, set up a hypothesis, test it by seeing whether it caught the murderer" (Macdonald, 1964: 37).

Even as the economic mode of production, along with the level of science and technology, sets a limit to the kinds of cultural forms that are produced, we have to avoid conceiving of this relationship as mechanical. The most difficult task is to understand this relationship in a non-reductive manner—that is, to study culture without reducing it to changes in the economic sphere (or vice versa) (see Box 23.2). Development, for a long time, was undertaken with the

IMPORTANT CONCEPTS

BOX 23.2 | Are Hunter-Gatherers Poor?

The ideology of modernization and development characterized pre-modern subsistence economies as societies existing in precarious and extremely difficult conditions. The anthropologist Marshall Sahlins, in a famous study on the hunting and gathering tribes, has questioned characterizing a lack of material possessions as poverty. Sahlins instead argues that the lack of material possessions does not make these tribes poor but rather free. In their own evaluation, this lack is a positive cultural fact, for they privilege the freedom of movement over material accumulation (see Sahlins, 1997). It is important to ask here why our modern criteria would label people with such few wants as poor rather than as affluent, as Sahlins does.

belief that culture did not matter and that culture would mechanically adjust itself to changes in the economic sphere, the consequences of which could be deleterious. One example is the introduction of smallpox vaccination by the British in colonies while outlawing existing indigenous techniques that were intrinsically linked with religious practice and worship (see Marglin, 1990: 8). Cultural forms produced under capitalism are not necessarily homogeneous, since "the capitalist mode of production does not demand, require, or determine, any one form of politics" (Garnham, 1998: 605). While the United States, Japan, and the United Kingdom are all capitalist societies, their cultures are not identical. These cultural variations show that culture cannot be explained merely by the distinction between the owners of the means of production and wage labour, as is the case in capitalism (Grossberg, 1998: 614). While economic practices "determine the distribution of practices and commodities," they do not totally determine the meanings circulated by these practices (Grossberg, 1998: 618).

One of the most important debates within the social science tradition since its origin has been the materialism versus idealism debate. The former asserts the primacy of material factors in social change, while the latter focuses on cultural factors, mental phenomena, and ideas. As we suggested above, this kind of binary distinction is problematic because of the interlinked nature of social phenomena. Privileging one over the other does not aid us in arriving at a proper understanding of culture or development. For instance, it has been a common practice among modernization theorists and also within popular discourse to blame the slowness of economic growth on the "backward" mentality and superstitious beliefs of "traditional" societies. These views, in the absence of an understanding of material factors, portray development as primarily governed by thought processes.

Paul Haslam

PHOTO 23.1 | Religion is important in Latin America: the statue of Christ the Redeemer, Rio de Janeiro, Brazil.

Here, social phenomena such as poverty can be blamed on the poor themselves for their lack of "correct" thinking (Allen, 2002: 454). On the other hand, material factors such as forces of production do not develop on their own. Labour is not a physical activity alone but also involves a mental component. Modern science and technology could not have originated unless the belief in the sacredness of nature had been substantially altered. Similarly, capitalism could not have originated or flourished without continuous savings and investments, which required a radical change in the meanings attributed to money and its use.

Nonetheless, it should be understood that conscious acts and agency themselves can turn into a structure: "structures created and perpetuated by a multitude of conscious, individual acts [can] develop some sort of internal logic, or institutional imperative, over and above these acts" (Femia, 1981: 119). Very often, the economic realm, because of its centrality to the sustenance and reproduction of human life, develops such structures with their own logic and dynamism, which are not easily circumvented except by the combined agency of a very large number of people. In this sense the economic sphere, along with other material factors such as natural and physical resources, is seen to limit the "the range of possible outcomes" of cultural imagination without mechanically determining them. Ultimately, what outcome becomes a reality is still decided by "free political and ideological activity" (Femia, 1981: 119). Here, it is also important to recognize what is intrinsic and unique to each sphere beyond its interlinkages with and determinations by other spheres.

Culture and development thus are intrinsically interlinked. With recent revisions to our understanding of development, following theorists such as the Nobel laureate Amartya Sen, from mere economic development to the enhancement of human freedom in the broadest sense, development has begun to include the enhancement of cultural freedom as well. Economic development also can lead to enhanced resources that can enable the exploration of a society's cultural history through historical excavations and research. Sen argues that culture can thus become one of the basic ends of development. Culture plays another role for Sen: as a means of development. As we observed above, symbolic understandings can govern behaviour, including people's economic behaviour (see Box 23.3). Thus, cultural traditions and norms can play an important role in influencing economic success and achievement. In addition, they can constitute an important source of economic investment and returns through activities such as tourism promotion, which has other positive benefits, including cultural contact and interaction (Sen, 2001: 1–4).

IMPORTANT CONCEPTS

BOX 23.3 | The Protestant Ethic

The most famous theory regarding cultural influence on economic behaviour is Max Weber's theory of the **Protestant ethic**, in which certain characteristics of Protestantism (especially Calvinism), such as valuing austerity, discipline, and hard work to attain material wealth and success as a route to personal salvation, were considered by Weber as having played a major role in the origin of capitalism. The theory has been criticized heavily for its inability to explain the economic success of Catholic countries such as France and Italy and non-Christian Asian countries in the twentieth century. However, the Japanese economic miracle has been attributed to a different set of cultural values, "which emphasized group responsibility, company loyalty, interpersonal trust and implicit contracts that bind individual conduct." These values originate from a variety of cultural traditions, including Japan's history of feudalism, Confucian ethics, and the "Samurai code of honour" (Sen, 2001: 6–7, 11). In "transitional" and "developing" countries, it is claimed that one of the important cultural barriers to efficient economic growth is the problem of corruption. Former socialist economies such as those of Russia and Eastern European countries are examples of this phenomenon (Sen, 2001: 14).

CULTURE AS DOMINATION AND CULTURE AS RESISTANCE

One of the biggest myths about culture is that it is an ahistorical entity—something that persists without change. Thus, for example, whenever there is a discussion about religion or religious texts, especially from the point of view of the faithful, the general tendency has been to see them in abstract, universal, and essentialist terms. The fact that they originated in a particular period, respond to particular needs, are subject to many kinds of contestation, and change accordingly throughout history is rarely recognized. Culture is as much determined by relations of power as any other sphere is. No work of art or ritual is above a particular point of view or interest. Cultural forms "are always produced or enacted in particular social historical circumstances, by specific individuals drawing on certain resources and endowed with varying degrees of power and authority" (Thompson, 1990: 135). Cultural phenomena are distributed, received, and interpreted by individuals and groups placed in different power locations and with different material interests. The interpretation of cultural phenomena varies according to these differences. In short, cultural phenomena are not benign; rather, they are immersed in relations of power. And these relations of power cannot be reduced to economic relations or class power. They exist in other spheres, such as gender relations, relations between ethnic and religious communities, and nation-states.

Thus, the practice of cultural forms and the enjoyment of symbolic objects are not activities devoid of ideology. Very often, symbolic objects provide the cultural underpinnings of a dominant mode of development. Not all classes and groups in society influence the formation of culture equally. In this sense, the ideological and material interests of the ruling class and the dominant groups tend to dominate the art and culture of any period. The social scientific tradition inaugurated by Karl Marx and Friedrich Engels was the first to theorize about this phenomenon.

Once we understand that culture is characterized by power relations and the obvious resistances they produce, it becomes easier to dispel the myth that cultures are homogeneous wholes. This myth essentializes "the idea of culture as the property of an ethnic group or race"; it reifies "cultures as separate entities by overemphasizing their boundedness and distinctness" (Terence Turner, quoted in Benhabib, 2001: 4). Such claims of cultural homogeneity and distinctness, for instance, are routinely made in relation to nationalism, one of the most potent cultural forces in the present world. The culture–development linkage is very clearly demonstrated in the nation-state: the concept of the "nation" provides the cultural underpinning for the state's pursuit of development. But what is crucial from our perspective is the two-faced nature of nationalism: even when the nation seeks to be a community of people, it is in reality characterized by hierarchy and domination and the perpetration of exploitation and exclusions. Nationalism, in the present, becomes a cultural ideology that seeks to paper over the inequities generated by the development process (see Box 23.4).

Culture, then, is not a static entity. Since all the elements of the bygone cultural past cannot be known or practised as a part of a tradition, the question of selection invariably crops up. Here, the selection of particular aspects of a period's culture will be governed by many kinds of dominant interests, including class interests. The student of development should relate the particular selection and interpretations of tradition and culture to each period's development context to see how the interplay between material and cultural factors is influenced by various classes and groups in society. Development studies should endeavour to examine how certain symbolic forms and ideas gain dominance rather than seeing them as natural phenomena. It then may be obvious that many of the ideas and symbolic forms that appear as universal and abstract actually originate in particular dominant groups—either class-based or otherwise (see Box 23.5).

The ways in which cultural understandings are a necessary basis of bringing about new forms of development are seen clearly in this phase of capitalist globalization. Capitalism and the promise of material affluence that comes with it become the new common sense across the developing world, dismantling older ways of living focused less on material goals. Leslie Sklair (1991) has argued that the value system central to capitalist modernization is the "culture–ideology of consumerism." Capitalism is a system built on the relentless pursuit of profits, which can happen only with production of more and more goods, the

CRITICAL ISSUES

BOX 23.4 | The Myth of Nationalism

Many homogeneous nationalisms that exist or are pursued today actually mirror the dominant ethnic group's culture at the cost of the minority nationalities and ethnic groups. A good example would be the recent efforts by Hindu fundamentalists to define Indian nationalism as Hindu, an approach that seeks to erase the diversity of one of the most multicultural societies in history. Indian society is home to all the major religions of the world and, besides Hinduism, India is the birthplace of Buddhism, Jainism, and Sikhism, of which there are millions of adherents. Despite Hindus being the majority in India, the country has the third largest Muslim population in the world as well as a substantial number of Christians and followers of the Baha'i faith and of other "minor" religious traditions. The right-wing Hindu nationalists' attempt to build a majoritarian nationalism, often through violent means, has led to the loss of many lives. Nationalists have also used religion in an instrumental fashion to garner the support of the majority Hindus. In placing religious and cultural issues such as the building of temples and protection of Hinduism at the top of the agenda and in positing religious minorities such as Muslims (or other nations such as Pakistan) as the main enemy, Hindu nationalists glossed over the fundamental divisions in society between the owners of capital and land and the labouring masses, high and low castes, and men and women that mark all religious communities, including the Hindu majority. As a result, during their tenure in government from 1998 to 2004 no attempt was made to level these hierarchies. For example, despite the fact that the Indian economy was growing at one of the fastest rates in the world, the country actually went down on the Human Development Index (HDI) from 124th to 127th, suggesting that the boom in the economy benefited only the rich and the middle classes. In such an instance, nationalism becomes a rhetoric for political gain and entrenchment, but it is not capable of meeting the material needs of even the majority community it claims to speak for. It merely becomes a symbolic tool in the hands of the powerful to mobilize the support of the powerless, while also constituting a source of cultural pride for the classes that are included in the economic growth.

IMPORTANT CONCEPTS

BOX 23.5 | The "American Dream"

An example of how certain ideas gain universal acceptance and acquire an ideological form is the idea of the "American dream," according to which if a person has talent and works hard, she or he can lead a successful and prosperous life. This dream drives millions of people from all over the world to move to the US. While the concept contains an element of truth, it hides the fact that the United States, despite its wealth, is the least egalitarian society in the Global North, and structural inequalities based on class and race (among other factors) prevent a majority of immigrants from attaining their dream.

commodification of new objects, and the creation of new wants (some of which, over a short or longer period, are elevated to become needs). The mass media and the entertainment industry have been the main vehicles for promoting new practices of the culture–ideology of consumerism in the Third World. "[T]he promise of the 1970s that satellite television would revolutionize education, public health and nutrition, and eliminate illiteracy throughout the urban and rural Third World, has been largely unrealized" (Sklair, 1991: 165).

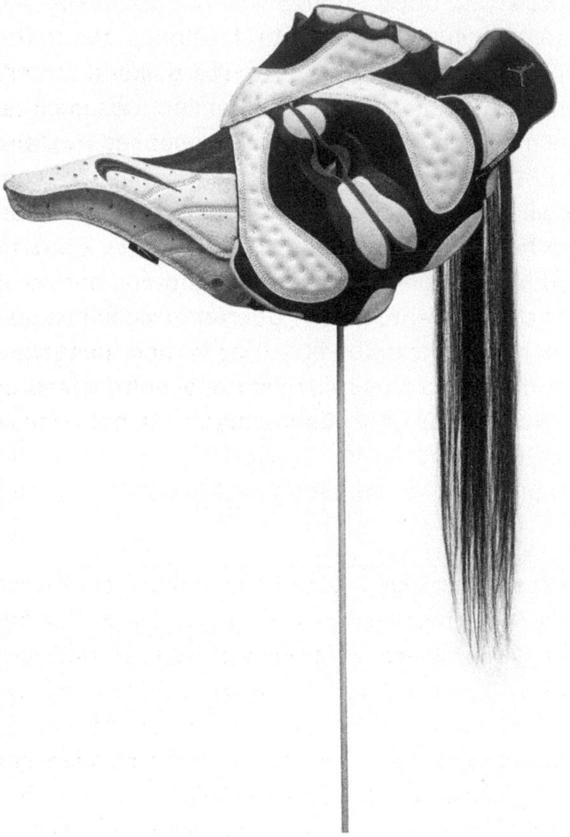

Courtesy of Catriona Jeffries, Vancouver. Photo: Trevor Mills, Vancouver Art Gallery.

PHOTO 23.2 | Brian Jungen, a Canadian artist, uses modern consumerist artifacts (such as the Nike footwear here) and reworks them to resemble specified references to First Nations cultures, thus creating new meanings to represent the complex relationship of the indigenous people to the modern capitalist world.

This is especially true for the Third World, where consumption practices modelled on Western lifestyles engineered by the mass media have brought about serious contradictions and a skewed relationship between production and consumption (see Box 23.6). The masses have been exposed to the glitzy and glamorous world of new global market culture without the material means to afford this culture. And culture-based economic activities such as tourism can have harmful consequences because of excessive commercialization—selling exoticized versions of "traditional" cultures primarily to rich Western tourists.

Despite this, there is a **double movement** in the domain of culture. While the dominant elements seek to control and rein in the subordinate elements, the latter are not passive actors; they are constantly seeking to resist these attempts despite the fact that the contest is unequal because of the power possessed by the dominant elements (Hall, 1998: 443, 447). This follows the Marxist theoretician Antonio Gramsci, who argued that cultural struggle is not a one-sided process in which the ruling or dominant culture simply overruns or decimates the subordinate culture—as is a common misconception—but is a complex process of struggle in which the former can become dominant only by accommodating the latter in some measure (Bennett, 1986: xv). Therefore, against the common belief that cultural practices and objects come with inherent meanings, it has to be emphasized that meanings are created in the process of struggle and contestation. Thus, all cultures are contradictory, containing different elements that intersect and overlap in the course of struggle (Hall, 1998: 452). Culture, therefore, is a process rather than a finished form (see Box 23.7).

Nevertheless, one of the main reasons for the appropriation of subordinate and critical culture by the dominant culture is the fact that the power and the means of cultural production are concentrated in the hands of dominant classes and cultural industries. For example, in the early 1990s, the international music recording industry was an oligopoly consisting of six companies (During, 1993: 16). This is an instance of the economic mode of production in a particular

CRITICAL ISSUES

BOX 23.6 | The Culture–Ideology of Consumption

The "culture–ideology" of consumption has deleterious consequences for the developing world. The focus on attaining a lifestyle associated with the developed West has led to an ignorance of the fulfilling of the basic necessities of the vast majority of impoverished people in developing societies. Capitalism is built on the philosophy of "planned obsolescence" in which goods are built such that they last only for short periods of time. The Apple campaign asking consumers to "think different" and the frenzy with which they flock to buy the latest versions of Apple products every few months is an example of this planned obsolescence and its success. Other than the cultural implications of this relentless production and consumption of goods, what is of graver concern is the material consequence of the exploding rates of garbage production. The "Golden Age of Capitalism" in the West was also the "Golden Age of Garbage"—between 1960 and 1980 solid waste increased fourfold in the United States (Mannathukkaren, 2012). But the problem of waste is hidden in the developed world through egregious practices like waste imperialism—waste being dumped and treated in regions/countries where the marginalized populations live. Now this perilous feature of garbage and waste of capitalist development is affecting the developing world, which has non-existent waste disposal systems. Scholars estimate that South Asia will be the "fastest growing region for waste in the world by 2025" (Mannathukkaren, 2014). Even the hopes of avoiding industrialization's catastrophic production of waste and pollutants by transitioning to a digital world are a chimera. The fastest-growing component of waste in the world is electronic waste. It is estimated that e-waste from computers and mobile phones will go up by between 5 and 18 times, respectively, in India alone by 2020. What is most dangerous is the fact that 90 per cent of this waste is recycled in the informal sector in absolutely hazardous conditions and involving 4.5 million children (Mannathukkaren, 2014). This situation is not alien to other countries in the Global South.

period acting as the limiting force and it shows the inevitable intertwining of cultural and material domination (see Box 23.8).

THE CULTURAL TURN

We have seen briefly how the values of the Enlightenment have been subject to scrutiny in the recent past. In fact, the biggest theme animating the field of development is the cultural question. Recourse to explanations based on culture has also been the result of a general consensus about an impasse in development studies: the inability or the failure of much of development theory to explain reality, especially in the South (Booth, 1994). From the 1980s, the endeavour has been to envision an alternative path to development—of which the building block is culture. It can be summarized as "the challenge . . . to find ways of increasing well-being without indiscriminately destroying valued ways of living and 'knowing' and without placing unbearable strains on the environment" (Jayawardena, 1990: vi). This search for an alternative was premised on the supposed failure of the Western model of development, which had been dominant especially over the past 60-odd years (see Chapter 4). The blind imitation of this model by the non-West, especially poor countries, has led to their ruin, according to critics:

> It is taken as axiomatic that intellectual frameworks borrowed from other historical, cultural and political environments can no longer be effective in understanding the complex realities

CRITICAL ISSUES

BOX 23.7 | Symbolic Struggles

Even as the culture of dominant groups and ruling classes tries to control the culture of subordinate people, the latter mounts resistance. This has been a constant feature in all societies across the ages. Thus, no dominant ideology can ever be completely dominant. Unless we factor in resistance waged at the symbolic and material levels, we will not be able to explain social change. Such resistance has been brilliantly theorized by James Scott, especially through his study of the peasantry in Malaysia. According to Scott, despite the lack of material means and avenues to challenge the dominance of powerful groups, the powerless resort to symbolic struggles in innovative and anonymous ways. Beyond the surface appearance of a placid acceptance of dominant culture, the cultural sphere is actually simmering with "gossip, folktales, songs, gestures, jokes, and theater of the powerless" through which they mount a critique of power (Scott, 1990: xii).

We would not generally associate these things (along with others, such as rumour, linguistic tricks, metaphors, and euphemisms) as anything to do with politics or the struggle for power, but they do constitute an important part of the symbolic armoury of the powerless. Gossip, for instance, especially gossip that seeks to destroy the reputation of superiors, is a tool used by the dominated to ensure that the former do not exceed acceptable levels of oppression (Scott, 1990: 137, 142–3). Similarly, symbolic resistance to new economic modes of production, such as capitalism, that cause a tremendous disruption to traditional ways of agrarian life (which, despite the lack of many modern freedoms, was secure in many other aspects) can be seen in many parts of the South. One example is the belief by displaced peasantry in Colombia and Bolivia that capitalist proletarianization and commoditization are intimately associated with the spirit of evil, and thus unnatural (see Taussig, 1980).

> of the other, fundamentally different cultures and contexts, or in giving direction to social changes underway in them. The additional question is how to use the total knowledge systems that are available in the South to facilitate this understanding. (Wignaraja, 1993: 6)

It was as much a case of the West dominating the non-West as the latter's actively looking towards the former in awe. After all, throughout the years of colonialism, the colonized were inculcated in systems of education that glorified Western ways of living. Colonialism drew its justification by portraying the colonized as "children" who needed to be looked after (Nandy, 1983). What this did was largely erase indigenous ways of life and knowledge. This erasure altered the course of the histories of colonized societies and has had real effects in the post-colonial period. Almost all of these societies are victims not only of economic underdevelopment but also of cultural underdevelopment. Hence, we see the adoption of the languages of the erstwhile European rulers as official languages in these societies: 38 African countries have adopted a European language as their official language (Dhaouadi, 1988: 220). This has serious implications, for it systematically undermines native languages and, therefore, cultures, since much of what we call culture is expressed through language and the unique thought processes imbued within specific languages. The acceptance of a non-native language within a country also creates a divide between elites, who have fluency in European languages, and subordinate groups, who do not. Equally significant are the substantial changes brought about in the sphere of family and personal law. The diversity in the types of families that characterized "traditional" societies was replaced by the ideal of the European nuclear family. The collapse of joint and extended families, for example, has had deep psychosocial consequences that have not been overcome in the rapidly modernizing societies of the South.

IMPORTANT CONCEPTS

BOX 23.8 | Che as a Capitalist Icon

One of the best examples of the appropriation of a subordinate and critical culture by dominant culture is the symbolic figure of Che Guevara, a leading Marxist revolutionary of the twentieth century who fought alongside Fidel Castro during the Cuban revolution in the late 1950s and became a minister in Castro's government, and who was captured and executed in 1967 while working to organize an uprising in Bolivia. If he was the inspiration of many a socialist insurrection in the 1960s and 1970s, his ruggedly handsome visage now mainly adorns billboards and designer wear created by the capitalist market and his name is used to sell numerous products, such as cigarettes (see photo below). Here, the symbol of Che, as a result of its appropriation by the forces of capital, acquires a totally different meaning from what he stood for as a revolutionary who sought to overthrow the influences of Western capitalism in Latin America.

According to those who have questioned this domination, "[w]hat passes today for the truth of the history of humankind (that is, progressive access of every nation to the benefits of development) is actually based upon the way in which Western society—to the exclusion of all others—has conceptualized its relationship to the past and the future" (Rist, 1997: 44). Or, as more emphatically put by Jonathan Crush (1995: 11), "development discourse is rooted in the rise of the West, in the history of capitalism, in modernity and globalization of Western state institutions, disciplines, cultures and mechanisms of exploitation."

PHOTO 23.3 | Che Guevara—the appropriation of a radical symbol by the capitalist mass culture.

Academic theories also were implicated in ethnocentrism. This was clearly obvious with theories such as modernization that posited one goal for all of the so-called Third World countries—to become like the West (see Chapter 3). Modernization theory operated with dichotomies such as tradition/modernity or backward/advanced, with a clear privileging of the second category. It was as if the entire history of Third World countries did not matter and what mattered was the future alone, in which they would become "modernized." Even dependency and other Marxist inspired theories that arose as a critique of modernization were deemed ethnocentric because they operated "within the same discursive space of development" (Arturo Escobar, cited in Crush, 1995: 20) by not questioning the basic assumptions of development, such as industrialization and growth. Moreover, they unwittingly replicated the structure of modernization through categories such as developed/underdeveloped and centre/periphery. Again, what happened inside the periphery (the "Third World" countries) was less important than what the core (the "First World" countries) did to it. It was disenchantment with these theories that led to the emergence of the "post" discourse: for example, postmodern, post-colonial, post-development (see Rahnema and Bawtree, 1997). This discourse seeks to go beyond the assumptions of many of the interrelated projects that governed humankind in the recent past: modernity, colonialism, development, and so on. It has sought to lay the blame for the current state of the world on modernity, that is, the period since the Enlightenment that has elevated reason to a privileged position (see Chapter 4).

In their search for an alternative, the critics of modernity looked towards traditional and indigenous cultural systems and to a recovery of the practices associated with them, which had been dismissed as "backward, irrational, superstitious, obscurantist" by the Western paradigm of development. If the West is characterized by *episteme*—the impersonal, a negative moral connotation attached to labour, control over nature, and a negative view of illness—non-Western traditional societies are characterized by *techne*—the personal, a divine conception of manual labour, control over the self, and illness as a necessary imbalance (Marglin, 1990: 8–26). Moreover, non-Western societies embraced the "participation of the people in decisions that affected their lives; sharing and caring for the community beyond individual self-interest; trust, innocence, simplicity, thrift; a work ethic with a fine-tuned balance between work and leisure; harmony with nature and a rational use of resources; communal ownership of the commons; and complementarity between men and women" (Wignaraja, 1993: 20). These values would constitute the fulcrum of an alternative path.

The theories that have arisen under the "post" rubric have taught us to look at non-Western societies without the coloured lens constructed elsewhere. Classic texts such as Edward Said's *Orientalism* deconstructed many commonplace assumptions about the Orient. Said's work showed that the Orient the Occident knew was more a construction than reality. It exposed the deep linkages between knowledge and power (in this case, colonial power). According to Said, "the essence of Orientalism is the ineradicable distinction between Western superiority and Oriental inferiority" (Said, 1978: 42). What the critique of modernity, colonialism, and development did was reclaim the history, the culture, and the agency of the colonized, thus giving them a sense of identity. More important, it put a question mark over the assumption that the Western way constituted the only path to civilization and development. The concept of development, which until recently connoted mere economic development, was redefined and expanded as a result.

Despite these achievements, the theories inspired by postmodernism are ridden with problems. Most have adopted an extreme stance vis-à-vis modernity and development, ultimately proving counterproductive for the marginalized and oppressed for whom the theories claim to speak. The fundamental problem is that culture becomes an all-encompassing explanatory variable. At the same time, culture appears to be detached from all other elements in society. Culture is seen as a homogeneous and essentialist whole, without fissures and conflicts. Hence, the large generalized categories such as West/East or North/South, colonizer/colonized, and modernity/tradition replicate the dichotomies created by mainstream theories such as modernization. Fear of the universalizing tendencies of modernity and the Western development model makes the postmodern-inspired theories essentialize tradition and adopt an uncritical attitude towards it. Consider, for example, Marglin's comment: "it may be readily agreed that the sacrifice of a young woman on an altar in traditional society is barbarous, but in and of itself it is no more barbaric than the sacrifice of a young man on a battle field in modern society" (Marglin, 1990: 12). Such a view ignores (despite the presence of ideological inculcation in both) the fact that in the second case, physical coercion is absent (except in conscription).

Similar exercises of seeing culture in benign terms can lead to defending practices such as female circumcision rather than analyzing them in terms of power relations—in this case, patriarchy. Therefore, these theories ultimately end up as a nativist and "Third Worldist" discourse, uncritically upholding tradition, religion, community, and so on while ignoring issues such as internal hierarchies and oppression within these categories. A critique of practices such as the

PHOTO 23.4 | The impact of colonialism on the culture of a society: the Cahhatrapati Shivaji Terminus (previously known as Victoria Terminus), built in the Victorian Gothic style by the British, Mumbai, India.

sacrifice of women on their husbands' funeral pyres and female circumcision does not have to come from a perspective that glorifies Western standards of justice. Criticism and opposition are already present in these "traditional" societies, as demonstrated by the fact that coercion, especially physical coercion, is often required to enforce norms.

Societies in the non-Western world are supposed to have a divine conception of manual labour. But if that were the case, how did a caste system based on an occupational division of labour with a clear privileging of mental over manual labour emerge in India? Why were the "lower" castes performing the menial tasks subjected to deep oppression for centuries? Similarly, the non-Western world is supposed to be characterized by a harmonious relationship with nature. But, as David Harvey (1993: 29) points out regarding "pre-modern" China, "[t]he Chinese may have ecologically sensitive traditions of Tao, Buddhism and Confucianism . . . but the historical geography of de-forestation, land degradation, river erosion and flooding . . . contains not a few environmental events which would be regarded as catastrophes by modern-day standards." These contradictions cannot be explained by the simple categorization of East/West and tradition/modernity. Ultimately, although postmodern theories start out "with the intention of preaching tolerance and the recognition of difference, . . . [they come] dangerously close to a celebration of repression" (Kiely, 1995: 159).

These theories cannot avoid the slide into **cultural relativism**, because they refuse to acknowledge any kind of universalism. Once they argue that cultural practices are not necessarily right or wrong because "there is no way of assessing their truth or falsity apart from people's beliefs" (Marglin, 1990: 13), their justification of repressive practices becomes inevitable. Despite

IMPORTANT CONCEPTS

BOX 23.9 | Universal Values

The traditional and modern ways of living do not have to be absolutely disparate, as postmodern criticisms imply. For example, among the Boran tribal people, traditionally pastoral nomads living mainly in Ethiopia, the concept that comes closest to development is *fidnaa*. It basically denotes a variety of things including growth and reproduction of vital resources, "lack of fear and hunger, freedom from worries about one's nearest and dearest . . . [and an] egalitarian and expanding social order that extends to neighbouring peoples" (Dahl and Megerssa, 1997: 55). The commonalities between this concept and the modern development enterprise are striking.

Thus, we come back to the problem that we started out with: culture is as marked by relations of power as any other sphere in society and is continuously changing according to the nature of contestation and struggle. The other major flaw in the postmodern theoretical framework is the nearly total absence in it of an analysis of material relationships. This is very obvious in the post-colonial analysis of colonialism, in which colonial exploitation without material relations becomes mere Western cultural domination. Economic exploitation itself takes a back seat. Therefore, European domination appears unrelated to capitalism. As Dirlik argues, "Without capitalism as the foundation for European power and the motive force of its globalization, Eurocentrism would have been just another ethnocentrism . . . [post-colonialism] fails to explain why this particular ethnocentrism was able to define modern global history, and itself as the universal aspiration and the end of that history, in contrast to the regionalism or localism of other ethnocentrisms" (Dirlik, 1997: 68).

In post-colonial theory, there is an obsessive focus on the colonial past and Eurocentrism that takes away an engagement with the present. Thus, the current internationalization and globalization initiated by late capitalism, of a scale unimaginable before, and the exploitation inherent in these processes cannot be countered by culturalism, especially when capitalism is increasingly becoming Asian-dominated. When almost the entire globe has come under the sway of capital and commodification, it is not feasible to simply reject modernity or development. This is all the more true when the poor and marginalized, who constitute the vast majority of the world's population, also embrace values such as equality and democracy and seek goods such as health, education, shelter, and security that modernity has to offer yet so far have been available to only a minority. Without an internally differentiated view that takes into account the different classes, castes, and groups within broad categories such as the East, the South, or traditional societies and their different (as well as common) experiences under modernity and capitalism, any alternative proposal based on culture alone that aims to go beyond development can only be incoherent. More important, it can only help the ruling classes and elites in these deeply non-egalitarian societies to maintain their power, using the legitimacy of cultural difference. Rather than indulge in a romantic celebration of Eastern cultures, an alternative development project should include not only cultural decolonization but also a material transformation that would eliminate all kinds of exploitation, including economic exploitation that is perpetrated both by the West and by indigenous classes and groups within the "Third World." To this end, the critical resources of the West and the East, as well as modernity and tradition, would have to be mobilized (see Box 23.10).

the fact that colonialism and the Western development model have used universalism instrumentally to their own benefit and subverted some of its core principles, there are problems in abandoning the concept itself. Postmodern accounts have one-sidedly reduced modernity and the Enlightenment to being indissolubly associated with domination, alienation, deprivation, and so on. This ignores the fact that the Enlightenment was also founded on values such as liberty, equality, and fraternity, which have inspired countless struggles against oppression all over the world, not just in Europe. More important, these values are attractive because of their deep affinity to at least some of the values in non-Western societies (see Box 23.9). Although modernity is a distinct period in human history and constitutes a break with earlier periods in significant ways, as we saw above, criticism of oppression or the struggle for equality cannot be said to be merely European or modern; intimations of Enlightenment ideas can be found in different parts of the world and in previous periods of history. They are embedded in various ritual practices, such as the "carnival in Catholic countries, the Feast of Krishna in India, the Saturnalia in classical Rome, the war festival in Buddhist Southeast Asia . . . [and] have provided the ideological basis of many revolts" (Scott, 1990: 80).

The abuse of Enlightenment values does not mean that we should therefore dismantle the entire European critical tradition. An abandonment of universalism would make any talk of social justice impossible, and any oppression, including slavery, could be justified on cultural grounds. As Martha Nussbaum argues, "to give up on all evaluation and, in particular, on a normative account of the human being and human functioning [is] to turn things over to the free play of forces in a world situation in which the social forces affecting the lives of women, minorities, and the poor are rarely benign" (Nussbaum, 1992: 212). To overcome cultural

CRITICAL ISSUES

BOX 23.10 | "Asian Values"

The resort to culture for legitimacy (of rule) by the elites is seen in the propagation of the "Asian values" thesis by the first Prime Minister of Singapore, Lee Kuan Yew, who argued that Asian culture is more conducive to discipline and order rather than to freedom and liberty (which suited the West). Such vast generalizations justifying authoritarianism are grievously erroneous, for they completely ignore the enormous diversity that exists within these large blocks called Asia and the West. Once we examine this diversity, we might find a different reality from the one outlined by Lee Kuan Yew. It would be even more obvious if we looked into the accounts of the marginalized and the oppressed, who would have a totally different understanding of discipline and order from that of the ruling classes.

The "Asian values" thesis also has been used as a cultural explanation for the economic success of Japan, China, and Southeast Asian countries. But again, as Amartya Sen argues, the problem is that the thesis is too broad, and ultimately inadequate for explaining the specificities of the different countries. For example, how do the different traditions of Confucianism, Buddhism, and Shintoism prevalent in the region explain the same phenomenon of capitalist success? Moreover, the application of the thesis is further complicated by the success of Islamic Indonesia and Malaysia and the emerging economic power of Hindu-dominated India. Thus, the thesis boils down to a cultural "grand theory" that seeks to explain major economic, political, and social outcomes across the world in terms of cultural differences—the kind of theory that, as in this case, does so rather unsuccessfully (Sen, 2001: 11–13).

relativism, Charles Taylor proposes that we talk in a "language of perspicuous contrast" that would allow us to "formulate both their way of life and ours as alternative possibilities in relation to some human constants at work in both" (Taylor, 1985: 126). Such constants obviously rise above the particularities of different cultures and constitute the basis of a universalist understanding. This is a dialogic process in which the West has as much to learn from the non-West as the latter from the former (see Box 23.9). Only such an understanding will act as a check on the use of culture by the ruling classes to justify authoritarianism.

SUMMARY

One of the main goals of this chapter has been to dispel the many myths that surround the concept of culture and to demonstrate that development is not merely a material process. Students would have also learned that while a focus on culture in relation to development is vital, societal processes cannot be reduced to a single explanatory variable such as culture. In reality, these processes cannot as easily be broken down into various elements, such as culture, politics, and economics, as they are in academic analysis. All elements are interlinked and cannot be abstracted and studied in isolation. Therefore, development does not make sense at all without an understanding of the meanings and the cultural value attributed to it by the people who are subjected to it. At the same time, these meanings cannot be entirely disparate because of certain universal features of the human condition—and also because the same material processes of commodification and marketization are taking place across the world. The task for the development studies student is to negotiate the lines between acknowledging the importance of human agency, the process of creating meanings, and understanding the structural limitations imposed by material factors on cultural imaginations.

QUESTIONS FOR CRITICAL THOUGHT

1. Distinguish between the cultural and the material.
2. What is the role of culture in development?
3. Given cultural differences, can/should development have the same goals across societies?
4. Make a case for and against cultural relativism.
5. Identify instances where struggles for development have assumed cultural forms.

SUGGESTED READINGS

Dacosta, Dia, ed. 2010. Special Issue on "Relocating culture in development and development in culture." *Third World Quarterly* 31, 4: 501–674.

Kothari, Uma. 2006. "An agenda for thinking about 'race' in development." *Progress in Development Studies* 6, 1: 9–23.

Schech, Susanne, and Jane Haggis. 2000. *Culture and Development: A Critical Introduction.* Malden, Mass.: Blackwell.

——, eds. 2002. *Development: A Cultural Studies Reader.* Oxford: Blackwell.

Venkatesan, Soumhya, and Thomas Yarrow, eds. 2012. *Differentiating Development: Beyond an Anthropology of Critique.* Oxford: Berghahn.

BIBLIOGRAPHY

Allen, T. 2002. "Taking culture seriously." In T. Allen and A. Thomas, eds, *Poverty and Development into the 21st Century*, rev. edn. Oxford and New York: Open University in association with Oxford University Press, 443–66.

Anderson, P. 1998. *The Origins of Modernity*. London: Verso.

Benhabib, S. 2001. *The Claims of Culture: Equality and Diversity in the Global Era*. Princeton, NJ: Princeton University Press.

Bennett, T. 1986. "Introduction: Popular culture and the 'turn to Gramsci'." In T. Bennett, C. Mercer, and J. Woollacott, eds, *Popular Culture and Social Relations*. Milton Keynes, UK, and Philadelphia: Open University Press, xi–xix.

Booth, D. 1994. *"Rethinking social development: An overview." In D. Booth, ed., Rethinking Social Development: Theory, Practice and Research*. London: Longman, 277–97.

Crush, J. 1995. "Introduction: Imagining development." In J. Crush, ed., *Power of Development*. London and New York: Routledge, 1–23.

Dahl, G., and G. Megerssa. 1997. "The spiral of the ram's horn: Boran concepts of development." In Rahnema and Bawtree (1997: 51–64).

Dhaouadi, M. 1988. "An operational analysis of the phenomenon of the other underdevelopment in the Arab world and in the Third World." *International Sociology* 3, 3: 219–34.

Dirlik, A. 1997. *The Postcolonial Aura: Third World Criticism in the Age of Global Capitalism*. Boulder, Colo.: Westview.

During, S. 1993. "Introduction." In S. During, ed., *The Cultural Studies Reader*. London and New York: Routledge, 1–25.

Escobar, A. 1995. "Imagining a post-development era." In J. Crush, *Power of Development*. London: Routledge, 211–27.

———. 1997. "The making and the unmaking of the Third World through development." In Rahnema and Bawtree (1997: 85–93).

Femia, J.V. 1981. *Gramsci's Political Thought: Hegemony, Consciousness, and the Revolutionary Process*. Oxford: Clarendon.

Freund, C.P. 2002. "In praise of vulgarity: How commercial culture liberates Islam—and the West." Mar. www.reason .com/news/show/28344.html. Accessed 21 Sept. 2007.

Garnham, N. 1998. "Political economy and cultural studies: Reconciliation or divorce?" In Storey (1998: 604–12).

Geertz, C. 1973. *The Interpretation of Cultures*. New York: Basic Books.

Gellner, E. 1983. *Nations and Nationalism*. Ithaca, NY: Cornell University Press.

Grossberg, L. 1998. "Cultural studies vs. political economy: Is anybody else bored with this debate?" In Storey (1998: 613–24).

Hall, S. 1998. "Notes on deconstructing 'the popular'." In Storey (1998: 442–53).

Harvey, D. 1993. "The nature of environment: Dialectics of social and environmental change." *Socialist Register* 1–51.

Jayawardena, L. 1990. "Foreword." In F. Apffel Marglin and S. Marglin, eds, *Dominating Knowledge: Development, Culture and Resistance*. London: Clarendon.

Kiely, R. 1995. *Sociology and Development: The Impasse and Beyond*. London: UCL Press.

Macdonald, D. 1964. "A theory of mass culture." In B. Rosenberg and D.W. White, eds, *Mass Culture: The Popular Arts in America*. Glencoe, Ill.: Free Press, 59–73.

Mannathukkaren, N. 2012. "Garbage as our alter ego." *The Hindu*, 3 Nov.

———. 2014. "Watch your waste." *The Hindu*, 6 Sept.

Marglin, S. 1990. "Towards the decolonization of the mind." In F. Apffel Marglin and S. Marglin, eds, *Dominating Knowledge: Development, Culture and Resistance*. London: Clarendon, 1–27.

Nandy, A. 1995. *The Savage Freud and Other Essays on Possible and Retrievable Selves*. Princeton, NJ: Princeton University Press.

Nussbaum, M. 1992. "Human functioning and social justice." *Political Theory* 20, 2: 202–46.

Rahnema, M., and V. Bawtree, eds. 1997. *The Post-Development Reader*. London: Zed Books.

Rist, G. 1997. *The History of Development: From Western Origins to Global Faith*. London: Zed Books.

Sahlins, M. 1997. "The original affluent society." In Rahnema and Bawtree (1997: 3–21).

Said, E.W. 1978. *Orientalism*. New York: Vintage Books.

Sainath, P. 2006. "Till the cows come home." *The Hindu*, 23 Nov.

Scott, J.C. 1990. *Dominations and the Arts of Resistance*. New Haven: Yale University Press.

Sen, A. 2001. "Culture and development." Paper presented at the World Bank meeting, 13 Dec., Tokyo. www .worldbank.org/prem/poverty/culture/book/sen.htm. Accessed 26 Sept. 2007.

Shanin, T. 1997. "The idea of progress." In Rahnema and Bawtree (1997: 65–72).

Sklair, L. 1991. *Sociology of the Global System*. Baltimore: Johns Hopkins University Press.

Storey, J., ed. 1998. *Cultural Theory and Popular Culture: A Reader*, 2nd edn. Hemel Hempstead, UK: Prentice-Hall.

Taussig, M. 1980. *The Devil and Commodity Fetishism in South America*. Chapel Hill: University of North Carolina Press.

Taylor, C. 1985. *Philosophy and the Human Sciences: Philosophical Papers*, vol. 2. Cambridge: Cambridge University Press.

Thompson, J.B. 1990. *Ideology and Modern Culture: Critical Social Theory in the Era of Mass Communication*. Cambridge: Polity Press.

Wignaraja, P. 1993. "Rethinking democracy and development." In P. Wignaraja, ed., *New Social Movements in the South: Empowering the People*. New Delhi: Vistaar, 4–35.

Williams, R. 1961. *The Long Revolution*. New York: Columbia University Press.

PART IV

Practice in International Development

▲ **Woman planting rice in Bali.** | Source: Photo by Jorge Fernández/LightRocket via Getty Images

24 Understanding Global Poverty Reduction: Ideas, Actors, and Institutions

David Hulme and Sophie King

LEARNING OBJECTIVES

- To understand how different conceptualizations of poverty have shaped the kinds of approaches and targets applied to the challenge of poverty reduction since the 1950s.
- To understand the ideological underpinnings of these different conceptualizations and how they are linked to international political and economic struggles between powerful actors.
- To evaluate progress in achieving poverty reduction around the world, including in terms of changing attitudes towards poverty and inequality.

▲ **The Micro-Gardens Project in Dakar was initiated in 1999 within the framework of a Technical Cooperation Programme between the Food and Agriculture Organization (FAO) and the Senegalese Government, with the primary objective of poverty reduction by providing fresh vegetables to poor families, thereby improving their food supply and nutrition.** | Source: Erick-Christian Ahounou/AFP/Getty Images

Placing global poverty eradication on the international agenda in the 1990s was not the result of some natural moral progression. Nor was it accidental. It arose out of the interaction of social forces within the historic structure of that era, as individuals, groups, organizations, networks, nations, and associations of nations pursued their goals and collaborated with and/or contested each other. Most of these actors promoted what they believed to be in their self-interest: that the spread of capitalism, and therefore economic globalization, would benefit all of the world's people; that policies and programs could be introduced to reduce flows of illegal immigrants from poorer countries into richer countries; that programs could be devised to discourage the recruitment of young men into "terrorist" organizations; that images of altruism could improve a country's or organization's standing in international circles. Many other self-interested reasons related to power, profit, and security also were motivating factors. But these were also tempered by compassion and informed by various moral visions of the world that many actors sought to live in and to bequeath to future generations. Such visions have been grounded in a genuine desire to improve the lives of very poor people; a belief that social and economic inequality had to be reduced; a commitment to reducing the impact of climate change on poorer people and preventing environmental destruction; and religious beliefs and other moral sentiments. Part of this moral vision focused on extreme poverty and was favoured by a historic moment, the turn of the millennium, which created an opportunity to push the issue of poverty up the international agenda.

This chapter seeks to explain how the idea of global poverty eradication emerged and was institutionalized in initiatives like the Millennium Development Goals (MDGs) and $1.25-a-day poverty measures, and also will evaluate progress in achieving international agendas. It begins by tracing the historical and ideological underpinnings of poverty in social and development thought, and how concepts like poverty and ideas about how it can be reduced have come to shape development approaches and practices in the contemporary era. The chapter then examines how the complex interplay between such ideas and a diversity of actors and institutions (of differing degrees of power and influence) has led to significant but insufficient achievements towards global poverty reduction.

POVERTY IN SOCIAL AND DEVELOPMENT THEORY

Contemporary ideas and concerns about poverty—especially the recently constructed idea of global poverty (Hulme, 2015)—are closely interwoven with development thought, but many of poverty's conceptual roots lie in the historical analysis of social problems in Western Europe. In the late eighteenth and nineteenth centuries, as the Enlightenment unfolded, European social thought began to address poverty as a core issue. This included the search by de Condorcet and Paine for an end to poverty; the warnings from Burke and Malthus of the dangers of such radical thinking; Marx and Engels's examinations of the evolution of capitalism and class relations; and the identification by Booth and Rowntree of who exactly was poor. Many ideas from these times—including the separation of the "deserving" and "undeserving" poor, the role of charity, poverty as a structural or individual phenomenon, poverty lines, targeting, and welfare dependency—continue to influence contemporary development thinking. Such debates have tremendous practical significance. If poverty is understood as a lack of individual or household income, policies to increase income are likely to be prioritized. By contrast, if poverty is conceptualized along other dimensions, such as limited access to basic education and health services, policies to expand and improve access to basic services are more likely to be prescribed.

Across different schools of development theory there are considerable tensions between those who pursue concepts of poverty that facilitate measurement (narrow, means-based, absolute, and objective) and those who believe that such simplifications are flawed as they avoid the more structural aspects of poverty essential to understanding how poverty is produced and reproduced. The "measurement camp" is usually occupied by economists, econometricians, quantitative sociologists, and social statisticians. Governments, international agencies, and policy-makers gravitate towards this camp. In the "structuralist camp" are critical sociologists, anthropologists, political economists, and heterodox economists. Their analyses are most often picked up and supported by activist non-governmental

IMPORTANT CONCEPTS

BOX 24.1 | What Is Poverty?

Understandings of poverty can broadly be grouped into four oppositional conceptualizations: narrow versus broad; absolute and relative; objective and subjective; and whether poverty can be understood in terms of individual agency or social structures.

Narrow versus broad conceptualizations. A narrow approach is easily comprehensible and measurable, while a broader approach explores the multi-faceted nature of poverty and the processes that create, maintain, or reduce poverty. At the narrow end of this continuum are national poverty lines focused on income-based measures. Broader conceptualizations view poverty as a set of multi-dimensional material and non-material deprivations. An example is Amartya Sen's work on capabilities (Sen, 2001; see Box 24.3), which was instrumental in establishing the UN's Human Development Index (HDI). From Sen's perspective, people experience poverty when they are deprived of basic capabilities: the ability to avoid hunger, become literate, and appear in public without shame, or take part in social activities, for example.

Absolute and relative poverty. Absolute perspectives interpret poverty as occurring when people cannot meet their minimum physical needs because of lack of income. This leads to an unambiguous poverty line. This method is simple and measurable and focuses on **basic human needs**. Major technical concerns arise, however, in dealing with differences in the minimum amount of nutrition that people need, for example, according to age, health status, employment, and household size. Those advocating a relative conceptualization recognize that human beings are social actors, and argue that poverty must be defined relative to others in a society. For some, relative poverty is only a small step in the right direction. It is **relational poverty** that needs to be analyzed—not merely income inequality but the unequal power relations between different groups in a society (see, for example, du Toit, 2009).

Objective and subjective measurements. "Objective" measurements such as the $1.25-a-day poverty line are specified by researchers who decide who is poor and non-poor according to rigorously conceptualized definitions and survey analyses, permitting comparisons to be made over time and space. Critics question the objectivity of such measures, which inevitably involve explicit or implicit value judgments by the researchers. "Subjective" measures of poverty are made by people about their own status and others in their community or society. This has the advantage of letting those most knowledgeable about the experience of poverty determine how poverty is defined and measured, but the disadvantage is that people living in different areas may set different criteria that may change over time, making comparison difficult.

Human agency versus social structure. These contrasting conceptualizations of the underlying causes and solutions to poverty are particularly important for understanding debates about relationships between poverty and inequality. Agency-based approaches benefit from the simplicity and precision of thinking in terms of individual behaviour and experiences of poverty. Structuralists argue that the units of analysis are multiple (class, gender, race, and others) and overlapping, and that behaviours are complex and, at best, only partly predictable. Both approaches have their strengths and weaknesses, and Giddens (1984) has proposed a conceptual means—structuration—of integrating both approaches.

CRITICAL ISSUES

BOX 24.2 | How Many Poor People Are There and Where Do They Live?

Counting the global poor is a highly contested issue. There are heated philosophical debates about whether poverty is absolute or relative, setting poverty lines, and whether poverty should be measured in terms of income/consumption or in multi-dimensional terms. In addition, the data are often of low quality and are difficult to compare across different country contexts. Despite these problems, there is broad agreement among analysts about some key parameters:

- Extreme poverty has decreased in all regions of the world since 1980, and especially in East Asia.
- The greatest numbers of extremely poor people live in South Asia and sub-Saharan Africa.
- Somewhere between 1.2 billion and 1.6 billion people were extremely poor around 2010.
- Poverty is deepest in sub-Saharan Africa, i.e., on average poor Africans experience higher levels of deprivation than poor people in other regions.
- Around 2.5 billion to 2.9 billion people could be viewed as being poor if one adopts a $2-a-day or relative poverty line.

Source: Hulme (2015, drawing on Ravaillon and Chen, 2014, and OPHI, 2014)

organizations (NGOs) and civil society groups, trade unionists, environmentalists, and left-of-centre political parties. The diehard measurers argue that qualitative approaches lack rigour and permit the analysts to select non-representative empirical materials to advance their argument. The diehard qualitative analysts argue that by focusing on what is readily measurable at the individual and household level, these dominant measurement approaches neglect the analysis of culture, identity, agency, and social structure that are central to the processes that create wealth and poverty (see Chambers, 1983).

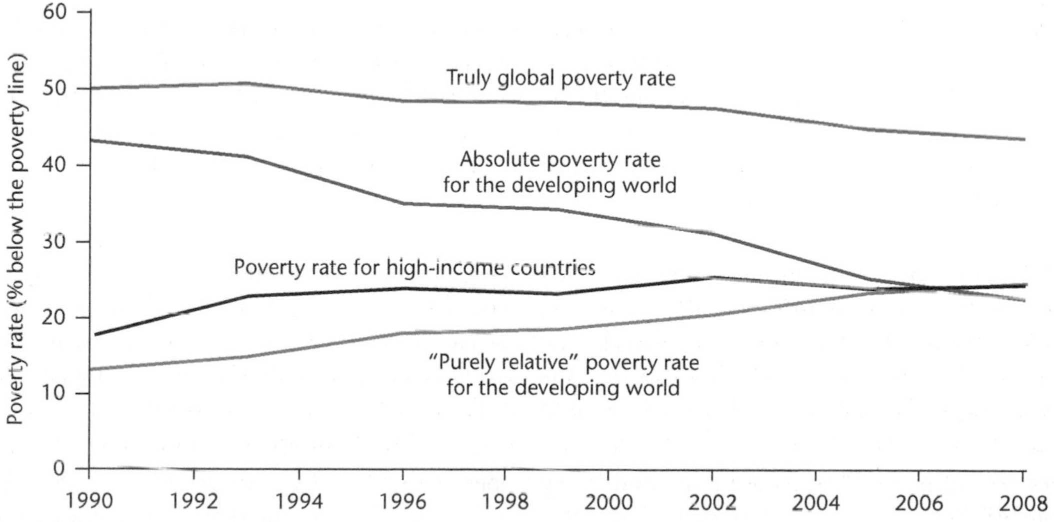

FIGURE 24.1 | Truly Global Poverty Rates

Source: Ravallion and Chen (2013: 261) © 2013 University of Durham and John Wiley & Sons, Ltd

DEVELOPMENT AS POVERTY REDUCTION: A BRIEF HISTORY

While mass poverty was the norm across Asia and Africa (and much of Latin America, the Caribbean, and the Pacific) during the era of independence from colonial rule, reducing poverty was rarely an explicit analytical or policy focus in the 1950s and 1960s in the way it became so in the early 1970s and in the mid-1990s (Hulme, 2015). Rather, it was thought that the pursuit of modernization and economic growth, through the transfer of finance, technology, and institutions from the US/Europe or the Soviet Union, would transform economic and social conditions, including poverty.

For all except a few East Asian countries, post-World War II promises of modernization were not delivered. This led to two different responses. First, from the developing world came the structuralist analysis that "underdevelopment" (Fanon, 1961) was blocking economic and social progress. Africa, Asia, and Latin America (the periphery) were underdeveloped because of their relationships with the US and Europe (the core), which meant that development required the reform of the core's exploitative relations with the periphery rather than "foreign aid" from advanced nations. These radical ideas were prepared to shift to revolutionary if required, identifying their priority for action as tackling the root causes of poverty and underdevelopment, namely, the structures and relationships of post-colonial capitalism (see Chapter 2).

In the early 1970s, development thought in the major international agencies began to focus directly on poverty. The International Labour Organization (ILO) and other UN agencies proposed a **basic needs approach** to development that encouraged national governments and aid donors to prioritize policies, budgets, and actions that would ensure disadvantaged people were able to access a minimum level of well-being, including food, water, shelter, and primary education. In 1974, the World Bank began promoting a greater focus on rural development rather than urban industrialization (see Chapters 18 and 19). While "basic needs" and "rural development" both sought to reduce poverty directly, the former focused more on state-provided social protection, while the latter focused on income generation and enterprise promotion. This emphasis on poverty analysis and direct poverty reduction within development thinking and practice was to prove only a brief interlude, however. By the late 1970s, neoliberal ideas were ascendant around the globe, and over the 1980s and 1990s the Washington Consensus (Williamson, 1990) and its structural adjustment policies dominated the intellectual and policy agenda, arguing that economic growth was the key to development. This could be achieved if countries deregulated, privatized, and liberalized; as a side effect, poverty would automatically be reduced (see Chapters 3 and 9).

The year 1990 marked a tipping point in the evolution of ideas about development and how poverty was positioned within development thought. Against the backdrop of the end of the Cold War and growing doubts about structural adjustment, the World Bank's *World Development Report 1990* chose poverty as its theme, acknowledging the need for economic reform to be accompanied by social policies. The report presented the first serious attempt to count the world's poor using a common measure. It introduced the dollar-a-day head count measure of global poverty and estimated that around 1.1 billion people lived in extreme poverty. More significantly, the United Nations Development Programme (UNDP) published the first *Human Development Report* in 1990, promoting the idea of human development as an alternative to economic growth as a concept and goal. This facilitated the promotion of a broader understanding of poverty reduction compared to previous measurements of income and consumption poverty, and made this alternative more accessible to a wider group of professionals and the media. It gave left-of-centre scholars and social activists a relatively coherent framework from which to argue for policy change.

The processes leading to the creation of the poverty-obsessed Millennium Development Goals (MDGs) (Hulme, 2010) can also be traced back to 1990, when the World Summit for Children in New York achieved political commitment for setting concrete targets to improve the prospects of the world's children. Then, in 1995, the World Summit on Social Development (WSSD) in Copenhagen pushed global poverty reduction onto the international agenda, stimulating an unprecedented conceptual, empirical, and policy focus on poverty. It was here that a global consensus (with 117 heads of state and government present) was

Paul Haslam

PHOTO 24.1 | An elderly musician earns his keep by performing on the street, Rosario, Argentina.

first reached for placing poverty reduction as the priority goal for development (UNDP, 1997: 108). The WSSD approved the target of eradicating dollar-a-day poverty. Implicitly, it drew on the idea of human development, viewing poverty as multi-dimensional. After Copenhagen, explaining how poverty would be tackled became a significant focus of international relations and development thought.

The debates and declarations of the global conferences and summits of the 1990s were impressive. They led to increased media coverage of the issues and raised public awareness about development and poverty. However, action after these events, with the exception of the Child Summit, was often relatively limited and levels of official development assistance (ODA) continued to decline. This created unease among the OECD's Development Assistance Committee (DAC)—leading it to produce a report in 1996 that listed seven International Development Goals (IDGs) in an attempt to generate public support for foreign aid. These goals brought together components from the declarations of recent summits and conferences, although the Copenhagen commitment to eradicating poverty was converted into halving extreme poverty by 2015. The IDGs achieved political traction in some OECD countries, such as the UK, but had little impact over other powerful actors, including the United States, the World Bank, and the IMF (Hulme, 2010). In developing countries, the poverty-focused IDGs had little or no resonance, coming as they did from a document produced entirely by rich countries in which promises of "partnership" sounded like well-worn rhetoric. However, this list would make a comeback.

In 1998, the global poverty agenda continued to be reshaped in preparation for the UN's Millennium Assembly, held in New York in September 2000. The UN's new Secretary-General, Kofi Annan, was keen to make global poverty reduction central to the UN agenda. He identified four main themes for the Millennium Assembly. The second of these was "development, including poverty eradication," signifying the institutionalization of the shift in development thought that had emerged at Copenhagen. Development was no longer about economic growth and generalized improvements in welfare; rather, it was synonymous with targeted poverty eradication (or at least poverty reduction). Between 1998 and 2000, a complex set of formal and informal negotiations and releases of competing reports sought to specify exactly what poverty eradication/reduction was. The aid donors of the OECD pushed their conceptual and strategic preferences based on the original IDGs and supported by the World Bank and IMF. In parallel, the UN was producing a declaration for the Millennium Summit, a document that had to satisfy a larger constituency with very different interests: the 189 members of the UN General Assembly.

Over the summer of 2000 there were frantic negotiations about what should finally go into the *Millennium Declaration* regarding goals of development and poverty eradication. With around 150 heads of government or state due to attend, the Millennium Summit had to be a success. As the big day approached, a compromise was reached that included goals for rich countries (for aid, debt, trade, and policy reforms) and strengthened the goals related to gender equality and child and maternal mortality. These additions, deletions, and compromises worked. The *Millennium Declaration* was unanimously approved at the UN General Assembly on 18 September 2000, and what had once been "development" officially became "development and poverty eradication" (UN, 2000). Negotiations over 2001 eventually led to the creation of a task force comprising officials from the DAC (representing OECD), World Bank, IMF, and UNDP. This was the task force that finalized the Millennium Development Goals (MDGs).

While the MDGs, and recently the post-2015 development agenda, have remained important in official public discussions (which remain excessively influenced by the aid industry's interests), keeping global poverty genuinely on the international agenda has been difficult. Other priorities—terrorism, trade policy, economic growth, national security, energy security, the financial crisis—have proved more pressing, and national self-interest remains the dominant force in international negotiations, as evidenced by the lack of progress over climate change and discussed in more detail below (and in Chapter 17). Contemporary development thought could be seen as having moved to a synthesis position combining elements of structuralism with liberalism—so that growth, inequality, and poverty all have a major analytical role—or to an uneasy compromise in which liberals promote the analysis of market-based growth by demonstrating growth's (absolute) poverty-reducing effects, and structuralists seek to promote the analysis of inequality through more relativist and relational poverty analysis.

REDUCING POVERTY: IDEAS, ACTORS, AND INSTITUTIONS

Following this brief history of the rise of the poverty reduction agenda within international development, this section of the chapter analyzes the interplay of ideas, institutions, material capabilities, and national interests that have underpinned the chain of events and the ways in which initiatives like the MDGs have played out over time and up to the present in deliberations over the post-2015 development agenda.

Ideas and Actors

The idea of reframing international development as global poverty eradication, rather than neoliberal growth, gradually emerged over the 1990s. The moral case for focusing on the poor and poorest had long been known. The negative effects of structural adjustment programs had meant that the World Bank had been forced to pursue "social dimensions" and social fund initiatives since the late 1980s. In essence these were direct poverty reduction programs, so the Bank had some recent experience of poverty reduction. The pressure for policy change from critics of structural adjustment, allied to the need that the Bank's new President, James Wolfensohn, perceived to transform the institution's image (Mallaby, 2004), made poverty reduction a politically attractive goal. But, how would poverty reduction be conceptualized?

This was where the idea of human development came in. The idea had provided general support for UN conferences and associated declarations throughout the 1990s. While it has several variants, it promoted two specific theoretical strands that became underpinnings for efforts to tackle global poverty. These particularly shaped the MDGs. First, it advanced the case that development strategies needed to directly pursue the goals of development, and not just the means (economic growth). Human development provided an overarching conceptual framework for arguing that education and health improvements, gender equality, and other goals were not only good in their own right but were essential components of the pursuit of a dynamic vision of the good life. Social goals should not play second fiddle to economic goals; they had to be pursued on an equal footing.

Second, when the conveners of the UN Social Summit in Copenhagen, the OECD's DAC and the UN Secretariat, drew up lists of goals they could explicitly or implicitly argue that a list was needed as development and poverty reduction were multi-dimensional. Lists of goals were not mere "shopping lists" reflecting a failure to analyze problems and select priorities (a criticism that had partly undermined UN promoted "basic needs" strategies in the 1980s). Rather, multiple goals were essential for any rigorously thought out poverty reduction effort. While the processes behind the placing of items on such lists involved complex interactions of ideas, empirical evidence, political interests, and personal values, human development provided a well-reasoned case for multi-dimensional lists. In the background were the works of Nobel Laureate Amartya Sen. His name, along with others, could be cited in an iconic fashion to show that a deep theoretical coherence lay behind such lists.

But human development needed to reach an accommodation with ideas about economic growth if it was going to be acceptable to those interests that dominated decision-making in the most powerful institutions and nation-states. The idea that economic growth was essential for global poverty reduction, alongside the self-interest of the countries, corporations, and people doing well out of capitalist development, meant that the MDGs had not merely to include but had to be headed by the goal of reducing income poverty (i.e., raising incomes through growth).

IMPORTANT CONCEPTS

BOX 24.3 | Sen's Framework for Conceptualizing Human Development

The conceptual foundations of the capability approach can be found in Amartya Sen's critiques of traditional welfare economics, which focuses on resource- (income, commodity command, asset) and utility- (happiness, desire-fulfillment) based concepts of well-being. Sen rejects these frameworks in favour of a more direct approach for measuring human well-being and development, which concerns itself with the full range of human function(ing)s and capabilities people have reason to value. Sen's framework makes the following distinctions:

- *Functionings.* "The concept of 'functionings' . . . reflects the various things a person may value doing or being. The valued functionings may vary from elementary ones, such as being adequately nourished and being free from avoidable disease, to very complex activities or personal states, such as being able to take part in the life of the community and having self-respect" (Sen, 2001: 75).
- *Capability or freedom.* "A person's 'capability' refers to the alternative combinations of functionings that are feasible for her to achieve. Capability is thus a kind of freedom: the substantive freedom to achieve alternative functioning combinations (or, less formally put, the freedom to achieve various life-styles)" (Sen, 2001: 75).
- *Development.* The expansion of freedom is the primary end and principal means of development. Development involves the expansion of human capabilities and the enrichment of human lives.

Source: Adapted from Clark (2006); Sen (2001).

Chr. Michelsen Institute/John Barnes

PHOTO 24.2 | Local women collect water at the borehole, Mozambique.

Importantly, the MDGs identified goals but did not specify the strategy that would be followed to pursue such goals. Should poverty reduction strategies be led by growth or human development? This would have required an agreement between the different sets of institutions and interests championing these choices. Such an agreement was infeasible and so the goals were as far as the specification went. The concrete policy choices would be battled over, ideationally and politically, through processes like Poverty Reduction Strategy Papers (PRSPs) and Mid-Term Expenditure Frameworks (MTEFs).

The idea of human development was not just challenged by those with material interests in maintaining the status quo. Other institutions also contested the emerging super-norm of the MDGs. The very strong human development case for reproductive health was challenged by the Vatican and a handful of conservative Islamic states. As a result, the International Conference on Population and Development's reproductive health goal disappeared during the hidden negotiations to finalize the *Millennium Declaration* in 2000.

The ideational adjunct to human development, in terms of the MDGs and plans to achieve the MDGs, was **results-based management (RBM)**. (For more information on RBM, see Chapters 8, 25, and 27.) This did not directly contribute to the content of global goals and strategies but it determined the form they took. This reflected the interests of the wealthy aid donor countries and especially their politicians and senior public servants, who wanted to be able to explain to their publics that aid would not be wasted because "best practice" management tools would ensure effectiveness. The common-sense nature and linearity of RBM made it attractive—set targets, monitor achievement, and reward staff on the basis of performance. For the aid-financed programs of the DAC membership, World Bank, and UN it was particularly attractive. The widely reported under-performance of aid in earlier decades would not occur in the future as RBM methods would ensure high levels of performance.

RBM influenced the idea of global poverty eradication in three main ways. First, it determined the structure of the MDGs (and has continued to shape the UN Sustainable Development Goals of 2015), and explains why they are a nested hierarchy of goals, targets, and indicators focused on time-bound "outcomes." RBM theory argues that goals must be SMART—stretching, measurable, achievable, realistic, and time-bound—and this thinking was applied to the goals emerging from UN conferences.

Second, it shaped the specification of goals. While determining what is "achievable" is not an exact science, one sees this tenet in operation with the $1.25-a-day poverty target. At the 1995 World Summit for Social Development in Copenhagen this was set as "eradicating" extreme poverty. RBM thinking about this target reduced it to the elastic but feasible goal of "halving" extreme poverty by 2015. Previously, the IDGs had targeted halving the *proportion*, rather than the absolute number, of people living in extreme poverty. When expected population growth is taken into account, achieving a 50 per cent reduction in the proportion of people in extreme poverty equates to only an approximate 19 per cent reduction in the number of people in extreme poverty. The target is therefore considerably less ambitious than it might at first appear (see Pogge, 2004).

Third, the idea of RBM meant that the pursuit of global poverty eradication was focused on measurables: this meant that politically contentious goals, such as human rights and participation, could be avoided on the technical grounds that they were difficult to measure. China had particular concerns about human rights, which it viewed as the imposition of Western models on its development strategy, and countries in Southeast Asia argued that "Asian values," such as a focus on the collective good, were neglected in ideas of participation that focused on the individual. These issues could be placed in the introductions and conclusions of key documents as "principles," but not in the lists that were to guide resource allocation and plans of action. As a result, the variety of human development that lay behind the Millennium vision of ending poverty was more about "meeting basic needs" than "promoting human rights."

Institutions

A vast number and range of institutions have shaped, and continue to shape, thinking and action (or lack of action) on global poverty. These include the UN General Assembly and UN specialized agencies, the G8 and G20, the OECD's DAC, the World Bank and IMF, bilateral development agencies, the finance ministries of developing countries, social movements, the Holy See, NGOs, think-tanks, and epistemic communities. Often these institutions form formal and/or informal networks and coalitions, such as Jubilee 2000, in pursuit of their aims.

The UN has been central to the reframing of international development as global poverty eradication through the conferences and summits of the early and mid-1990s, the formulation of the *Millennium Declaration* and MDGs (1998–2001), and subsequent plans for MDG implementation. This has involved the UN General Assembly, the UN Secretariat, the UNDP, and other specialized agencies. Early on the UN's main contribution was as a convener, pulling together international conferences and world summits and persuading member states to negotiate and agree to socially progressive declarations. Some parts of the UN apparatus made major efforts and contributions. The UNDP played a central ideational role by promoting the concept of human development, as an alternative to neoliberal economic growth, throughout the 1990s. UNICEF operated highly effectively: it relaunched UN summitry, steered child development to the heart of poverty eradication (and the MDGs), and, pursuing a human rights approach, achieved the Convention on the Rights of the Child (see Chapter 10).

However, the UN Secretariat was often walking a tight rope, tasked with brokering agreements between its members, and other groups that had very different interests and ideas about what improving the human condition meant and how global poverty reduction might be achieved. As pointed out above, the Secretariat had to focus on "what should be achieved" but not on "how it should be achieved." The Secretariat brokered the "final" MDG deal in 2001 with the incorporation of Goal 8 into the MDGs—what rich countries should do. This made MDG implementation plans feasible but also created an Achilles heel—the lack of specification of Goal 8 targets did not strengthen accountability mechanisms and meant that the world's most powerful countries could continue with business as usual.

Within the broader UN system, but at the opposite end in terms of its contribution to focusing on global poverty eradication, was the IMF. While it participated in key activities, such as being one of the four members of the technical committee that finalized the MDG goals, and it renamed its key products (e.g., the Poverty Reduction and Growth Facility), there is little evidence that its actions or culture were impacted by the shift of focus to poverty eradication. The IMF has been reluctant to embrace goals that go beyond neoliberal priorities of economic stability and economic growth (Hulme, 2010). It has been able to give an impression of being part of global agreements on poverty eradication but has only changed its thinking and practice at a snail's pace.

The World Bank has played a major role in thinking and action about global poverty eradication. The work of its Research Department in developing the idea of dollar-a-day poverty helped persuade many rich world politicians that global poverty counted (because apparently precise figures could be produced about it). The design of PRSPs was closely associated with the Bank. While it is not possible to classify the Bank's practice of poverty eradication as easily as it is that of the IMF, it is clear that Bank rhetoric—about participatory assessments of poverty and shifting to country ownership of PRSPs—moved well ahead of its actions. In particular, during the early 2000s, parts of the Bank's Research Department mounted a powerful campaign to prove that economic liberalization always led to poverty reduction. This supported a continuation of the neoliberal policies of the 1980s and 1990s and, although this was eventually discredited, it weakened attempts to broaden the focus of PRSPs beyond market-based economic policies (see Chapter 9).

Civil society groups (social movements, NGOs, faith groups, and others) were an influential force in the promotion of the idea of global poverty eradication and in its specification. Their profile and capacity had risen greatly since the end of the Cold War and they gained access to UN events and became powerful advocates for a range of international norms aimed at reducing human deprivation and inequality and promoting human rights. Particularly effective was the Jubilee 2000 coalition (see Chapter 14). Some groups aspired to promote an agreement around an alternative development that did not merely reject neoliberalism but was actively anti-capitalist (see Chapter 12). However, they were bitterly disappointed about the configuration of the final MDGs, which accepted that globalization would be the means for economic growth. They were also dismayed that the major responsibilities for implementing poverty eradication were left to the IMF and World Bank.

The types of institution that might have been able to advance ideas that would have forced change on the IMF and World Bank—a powerful social movement for poverty eradication or a coherent epistemic community promoting human development or human rights—did not emerge at the Millennium moment. The progress made with the idea of human development was the result of shifting networks and coalitions of actors and did not produce a robust institutional support for the idea. The idea of human development made progress, but still it fell between stools. It did not lead to the emergence of a self-fuelling social movement that could consistently place human development on the political agenda when decisions were being made.

Nor did an epistemic community emerge (in academia, the professions, and the media) that could agree on a tightly defined analytical and causal framework that could capture and dominate decision-making in key institutions, as had the neoliberal epistemic community at the IMF, World Bank, US Treasury, and ministries of finance around the world. Human development, however, might be a concept that does not lend itself easily to form the base for an epistemic community. It is broad, it recognizes the need for deliberation and debate (and thus eschews the type of elite domination that made the neoliberal epistemic community so powerful), and it is multi-disciplinary.

MATERIAL CAPABILITIES AND NATIONAL INTERESTS

Humanity now has the material capabilities (the technological and organizational capabilities with productive and destructive potentials), following Robert Cox's critical political economy, to dramatically reduce or eradicate extreme poverty across the world. A redistribution of a small part of these capabilities would permit the poor to meet their needs for basic goods and services. In practice, reforming access to these capabilities has proved very difficult. The national governments and associations of governments that might rewrite "the rules of the game" for access to and use of such resources have been prepared to reach general agreement on the need for change, but key members and groups of members oppose specific changes (such as increasing their aid budgets or reforming the governance of the World Bank and IMF). This is partly because of active opposition to changes driven by national self-interest and partly due to a more passive lack of interest in global poverty reduction. For most high-income and upper middle-income countries (and their governments, citizens, and corporations), poverty in other countries is neither a high priority nor a pressing public issue.

So, while material capabilities in the aggregate create the opportunity for global poverty eradication, the contemporary distribution of those capabilities sets the limits on achieving this goal. The concentration of capabilities in the United States, until recently the world's only superpower (economically and technologically), means that it has been in a unique position to shape the evolution of goals and plans for tackling global poverty. It has appeared to be deeply ambivalent about how to respond to the challenge of global poverty. At times it has supported the processes, as in 2002, when President George W. Bush spoke enthusiastically at the Monterrey Finance for Development Summit and announced massive increases in US foreign aid (Lancaster, 2008). At other times it has appeared to oppose international efforts, as in 2005, when John Bolton (then US Ambassador to the UN) sought to have the terms "Millennium Development Goals" and "poverty" removed from the "Millennium plus Five" General Assembly declaration (McArthur, 2013). Despite this ambivalence, the United States is central to most efforts and activities to end poverty: directly, through its vast resources and influence over institutions such as the IMF, World Bank, and G7/8; and indirectly, as every other actor (governments, multilateral and bilateral agencies, social movements, NGOs, activists, celebrities) in the process asks, "what is the US position on this?"

The power of the United States, deriving from its material capabilities, has had many impacts on the evolution of efforts to tackle extreme poverty. Most significantly, in 2000, the framing of global goals and plans of action had to be done in a way that ensured the United States would be a part of global efforts—this set limits on how radical they could be. While the ideas behind the UN conferences and summits (and later the IDGs and MDGs) dismissed the thinking and prescriptions of the Washington Consensus, those who proposed new ways of thinking could not imagine challenging the idea or practice of free-market global capitalism as the basis for the improvement of the human condition. Hence, MDG Goal 1/Target 1 is personal income growth, which highlighted the need for economic growth. How this goal was to be achieved—by rapidly opening up an economy and encouraging foreign direct investment or through state-led industrial policy to guide the establishment of infant industries—was not specified, as that would have led to argument and the blocking of an agreement. Similarly, the MDGs' focus on reducing extreme absolute poverty was acceptable to the United States (and many of its allies and business interests more generally).

But move on to 2015 and things have changed dramatically. Economic growth in the BRICS (especially Brazil, India, and China) has redistributed material capabilities to the "emerging powers" and a group of "emerging middle powers" (Turkey, Indonesia, Mexico, South Africa) (see Chapter 13). The forms of negotiation about global goals have also changed dramatically in terms of leading actors and ideas. Brazil, in particular, has played a leading role promoting a Rio+20 agenda (the follow-up to the 1992 Earth Summit) and in mobilizing the G77 (today, the 130 UN member states who see themselves as "developing countries"). It has converted the Post-2015 Development Agenda into the Sustainable Development Goals (SDGs). The SDGs incorporate most of the poverty agenda of the MDGs but move well beyond it. They (i) target the eradication of poverty; (ii) set goals for achieving sustainable production processes and consumption patterns; and (iii) seek to promote inclusive economic growth. Inequality is no longer "off" the agenda and a goal has

IMPORTANT CONCEPTS

BOX 24.4 | The United Nations Open Working Group Recommendations for the Sustainable Development Goals (SDGs)

Goal 1 End poverty in all its forms everywhere.
Goal 2 End hunger, achieve food security and improved nutrition, and promote sustainable agriculture.
Goal 3 Ensure healthy lives and promote well-being for all at all ages.
Goal 4 Ensure inclusive and equitable quality education and promote lifelong learning opportunities for all.
Goal 5 Achieve gender equality and empower all women and girls.
Goal 6 Ensure availability and sustainable management of water and sanitation for all.
Goal 7 Ensure access to affordable, reliable, sustainable, and modern energy for all.
Goal 8 Promote inclusive and sustainable economic growth, and full and productive employment and decent work for all.
Goal 9 Build resilient infrastructure, promote inclusive and sustainable industrialization, and foster innovation.
Goal 10 Reduce inequality within and among countries.
Goal 11 Make cities and human settlements inclusive, safe, resilient, and sustainable.
Goal 12 Ensure sustainable consumption and production patterns.
Goal 13 Take urgent action to combat climate change and its impacts.
Goal 14 Conserve and sustainably use the oceans, seas, and marine resources for sustainable development.
Goal 15 Protect, restore, and promote sustainable use of terrestrial ecosystems, sustainably manage forests, combat desertification, and halt and reverse land degradation and halt biodiversity loss.
Goal 16 Promote peaceful and inclusive societies for sustainable development, provide access to justice for all, and build effective, accountable, and inclusive institutions at all levels.
Goal 17 Strengthen the means of implementation and revitalize the global partnership for sustainable development.

Source: Adapted from Open Working Group proposal for Sustainable Development Goals at http://sustainabledevelopment.un.org/focussdgs.html.

been set for "reducing inequality within and across countries." As in 2000, these goals are to be achieved through a "global partnership," with a recognition that the millennium goal partnership was not achieved.

At one level it might be argued that the shift from the poverty-reducing MDGs to the broader SDGs means that global poverty has slipped down the international agenda. But if one takes a close look at the SDGs, one can argue that they have moved from targeted poverty-reduction to prosperity and well-being for all (including future generations). They promise to tackle the root causes of poverty—increasing inequality, conflict, and violence; weak institutions; an unfair global trade system; access to technology—rather than just the proximate symptoms.

WHAT HAS BEEN ACHIEVED?

Assessing what has been achieved by recent efforts for global poverty reduction is a complex task that has generated hundreds of reports and many data sets. A summary of MDG performance to 2014 is provided in Table 24.1 (and updates can be found at www.un.org).

TABLE 24.1 | Progress with the MDGs to 2014

MDG	1990–2015
1. Halve extreme poverty	Target already achieved because of 80 per cent reduction in China. South Asia close to target but sub-Saharan Africa significantly off track.
2. Universal primary education	Close to target but will not be achieved in sub-Saharan Africa and South Asia and progress has slackened.
3. Gender equality	Close to achievement at primary and secondary school level but other targets are lagging.
4. Reduce child mortality by two-thirds	Substantial progress but target will not be achieved. Sub-Saharan Africa significantly off track.
5. Reduce maternal mortality by three-quarters	Least progress of all the MDGs with 300,000 pregnancy-related deaths per annum. Very problematic in sub-Saharan Africa and South Asia.
6. Combat HIV/AIDS, malaria, and other diseases	Most countries face difficulties in meeting targets. HIV/AIDS is a particular problem and worst in sub-Saharan Africa. Malaria target on track but big challenges remain.
7. Environmental sustainability	Global greenhouse emissions have massively increased and deforestation remains a threat. Unsafe water and lack of sanitation remain widespread.
8. Develop a global partnership	No evidence of a step change in relationships. • Decline in aid reversed but levels well below 0.7 per cent target. • Debt burden of developing countries much lower than 2000. • Trade talks stalled. • Climate change—limited progress.

Sources: United Nations (2014) and author.

The accuracy of this information varies from indicator to indicator because of the poor quality of much of the underlying data and problems of estimation. Assessing how twenty-first-century efforts to end poverty (MDGs, Financing for Development, PRSPs, etc.) have contributed to these changes in levels of human development is even more difficult, as this would require isolating the contribution of each mechanism from that of many other factors (such as economic growth in China, global warming, the war in the Democratic Republic of Congo, patterns of rainfall in Asia and Africa, food prices, or the global financial collapse of 2008). Such assessments also vary with the perspective taken: should we assume that anything less than 100 per cent achievement for all eight MDG goals is failure or does partial achievement represent significant progress? Does China's overachievement in reducing extreme income poverty and other targets partially compensate for underperformance in other parts of the world? Or, given doubts about the data and time lags between policy change and outcome change, should the focus be on process changes and trying to identify whether or not a step change occurred in international and national efforts to reduce poverty around 2000?

MDG Performance

The most recent data (UN, 2014) provide grounds for being both deeply impressed with poverty reduction achievements since 1990 and deeply alarmed by the remaining scale of human deprivation, continued environmental degradation, and lack of progress towards "global partnerships." On the positive side, the period since 1990 has witnessed the reduction of income/consumption poverty at historically unprecedented rates. Using the global poverty line of US$1.25-a-day and the 2005 purchasing power parities (PPPs), then, by 2010, the MDG Goal #1/Target #1 was achieved five years earlier than targeted. Projections indicate that by 2015, US$1.25-a-day poverty will have dropped from around 42 per cent of humanity in 1990 to 15 per cent.

As a headline figure this is almost a two-thirds reduction in extreme poverty in 25 years: not the "eradication" target declared at the World Summit on Social

Chr. Michelsen Institute/Arne Strand

PHOTO 24.3 | Reconstruction in Mymane, Afghanistan.

Development at Copenhagen in 1995, but better than the "halving the proportion" target of the MDGs. Two qualifications to this good news need to be borne in mind, however. First, much of this achievement has been concentrated in China (but at what costs to workers and the environment?). Progress in sub-Saharan Africa, and to a lesser degree in South Asia, has been much weaker. Second, there are big questions about how much of this extraordinary achievement can be attributed to international action to tackle global poverty. Autonomous policy change in China in the late 1970s and 1980s—land and agrarian reform and the opening up of the economy to international trade—may be responsible for much income poverty reduction.

On the negative side, the maternal mortality goal has proved very difficult to make progress on; global emissions of carbon dioxide are 50 per cent higher than in 1990; and there has been little progress towards a genuine global partnership for development (for example, the governance of the World Bank and IMF is virtually unchanged). Moving beyond the headlines, there are complex patterns of MDG achievement in different regions and countries and for different goals. Some of these are outlined below.

In 2000, the *Millennium Declaration* recognized Africa's "special needs." Despite increased economic growth and improvements in human development indicators (especially a recent decline in infant mortality), this special status is still justified. This is the region of the world where MDG progress has been most challenging and, even bearing in mind that the MDG specification makes Africa's achievements appear worse than they are (Easterly, 2009), progress has been unsatisfactory. Between 1990 and 2010, extreme poverty has been well below the trend needed to "halve" poverty (the decline has only been from 56 per cent in 1990 to 48 per cent in 2010) and only a 36 per cent reduction is estimated by 2015 (UN, 2014). This is clearly disappointing: but it must be noted that this is a decline—poverty has reduced greatly in sub-Saharan Africa despite the impression from parts of the media that "things are getting worse."

Human development achievements are also disappointing: there has been only limited progress on universal primary education; gender equality in primary education has moved relatively slowly (from 52 per cent in 1990 to 78 per cent in 2012); child mortality has declined but is at much higher levels than other regions (98 deaths per 1,000 births in 2012, compared to South Asia's 58 deaths per 1,000 births); maternal mortality is more than twice South Asia's rate; and the region has encountered great difficulty in achieving HIV/AIDS reduction targets. The picture is not uniform across the continent, and there are outstanding examples of progress. For example, several sub-Saharan countries have made significant strides in tackling the incidence of malaria, and it is estimated that between 2000 and 2012 more than 3 million child deaths were averted by anti-malaria interventions. Rwanda increased the proportion of children under five sleeping under insecticide-treated bed nets from 4 per cent in 2000 to 56 per cent in 2008. Countries that have achieved high coverage of malaria interventions, notably Benin, Madagascar, Rwanda, and Tanzania, have seen declines of more than 50 per cent in severe malaria cases and deaths in health facilities (UN, 2009: 36). Significant progress is being made in certain areas, but Africa still clearly merits special attention.

In terms of specific goals, then, the picture again is mixed. The goal of achieving universal primary education is likely to come close to achievement in 2015 but sub-Saharan Africa and South Asia will lag. A key concern about this goal is whether the progress on the numbers of children enrolled in schools has impacted negatively on educational quality (schooling without learning) and led to high dropout rates, especially by the poorest children. There is substantial achievement in terms of gender equality at the primary school level but less at the secondary school level as substantial male:female gaps remain in sub-Saharan Africa and South Asia. Work-related indicators (labour force participation, occupational levels, and wages) continue to reveal significant gender gaps. The relative position of women in most countries is progressing but the pace is often very slow.

Both good news and bad news can be identified on the health targets. Child mortality has fallen in all regions and is on target to reduce by three-quarters (1990–2015) in East Asia, Latin America, and the Middle East and North Africa (although it must be noted that instability in the latter region, especially in Iraq, Syria, and Libya, means that in some countries infant and maternal mortality has increased and life expectancy has lowered dramatically). At the same time, progress in sub-Saharan Africa has been limited and easily preventable deaths remain high. Maternal mortality is the goal for which progress has been most limited. Each year more than 300,000 women die from pregnancy-related health problems. In 2013, sub-Saharan Africa (510 deaths per 100,000 live births) and South Asia (190 deaths per 100,000 live births) remained especially problematic. Most countries and regions face difficulties achieving HIV/AIDS targets, and this is an exceptionally severe problem in sub-Saharan Africa. Halting the incidence of malaria and tuberculosis also remains a challenge as drug resistance has been building up.

In terms of environmental sustainability, the target on access to water is likely to be met globally and in many countries, though there are questions about how "safe" much of this water is. However, the sanitation target has made more limited progress especially in sub-Saharan Africa and South Asia. More than one billion people routinely practice open defecation, and this is a particular problem in India. Global CO_2 emissions have increased significantly since 1990, renewable water resources in many parts of the world are becoming scarcer, and deforestation rates remain high.

The lack of quantitative targets for the goal of developing a global partnership means this cannot be judged against specific measures. However, with aid at less than half of the 0.7 per cent target, the stalled Doha trade round, and slow progress on the mitigation of global warming, it seems reasonable to state that the rich world has broken its promises.

CONCLUSIONS

If one rates the significance of an idea by how widely cited it is, then the last 15 to 20 years have been a bumper time for poverty (Ravallion, 2011). Since the

CP Images/Shehzad Noorani

PHOTO 24.4 | A woman carries her belongings in earthquake-devastated Port-au-Prince, Haiti.

demise of structural adjustment and the end of the Cold War, the concept of poverty reduction has risen in prominence and has been very closely associated with international development—indeed, leading agencies have at times seen these two as synonymous. Whether this has been advantageous or disadvantageous to poor people is unclear.

At the current juncture it would seem that a synthesis of two traditionally oppositional ideological camps may be occurring (Brett, 2009) around theories of poverty, which recognizes that both states and markets have to work to improve human well-being. Analysts of both structuralist and liberal tendencies have coalesced around a "promote growth, reduce poverty, and strengthen institutions" framework. The international financial institutions (IFIs) have shifted away from one-size-fits-all policy prescriptions to a greater focus on customized national poverty reduction strategies (PRSs) and institutional development.

However, whether this is a genuine synthesis or merely a temporary lull in the structuralism versus liberalism contestations remains to be seen. Both sides may agree that poverty reduction is a good thing, but a yawning chasm remains between those who theorize that the cause of poverty is inequality (and to whom reducing national and international inequality is the paramount issue) and those who theorize it is lack of growth (and to whom releasing the power of the market to increase growth is the top priority). The burgeoning consultations, debates, and meetings about the post-2015 development agenda have been shaping the future of poverty in development thinking. Analysts of a structuralist tendency were concerned that with British Prime Minister David Cameron as the OECD's representative on the three-person UN steering committee, the next set of goals will shift towards market-based growth. Scholar-activists such as Richard Jolly and colleagues (2012) argued for a set of goals that placed reducing inequality at their heart. These liberal versus structuralist debates will rumble on, and with 17 goals and 167 targets the SDGs appear to be a new compromise on the goals of development—not a synthesis—between these two intellectual camps. Poverty heads the SDGs but they are a much longer and more complex set of goals than the MDGs.

SUMMARY

This chapter has sought to introduce the concept of "poverty" and explain why ending poverty, or at least poverty reduction, across the world gained entry to the international agenda in the 1990s and crystallized into the MDGs (approved by the entire UN membership) and now heads the post-2015 SDGs. Ideas were of great importance, especially the reformist idea of pursuing human development in all countries and the existence of a measuring stick (the dollar-a-day poverty line) that would make it possible to count how many people were escaping extreme income poverty. A vast number of formal and informal institutions shaped and used these ideas in contests to achieve their goals of either social mission or self-interest. At one level this can be seen as a contest between the ideas of the Bretton Woods institutions (the Washington Consensus built around economic development) and the other UN agencies (human development). However, the processes of interaction—G7/8 meetings; UN summits; regional conferences; civil society protests; the annual World Economic Forum in Davos, Switzerland; and a million more—meant there were no clear sides and no one fully understood what the products of debates would be. The material capabilities of particular nation-states, and particularly the collapse of the Soviet Union's economic power, underpinned these processes. The growing wealth of the world made it reasonable to argue that, at the very least, the basic needs of all of humanity could be met. And . . . it was a time for some stardust. A new millennium demanded that world leaders come up with something grand: they could not come up with a real vision, but they could agree (eventually) to a negotiated set of anti-poverty goals.

QUESTIONS FOR CRITICAL THOUGHT

1. What are the links between how poverty has been conceptualized and approaches to poverty measurement and poverty reduction?
2. Have international commitments to poverty reduction been driven more by national interests or by altruism?
3. What has shaped the character of global social movements for poverty eradication?
4. How is the emergence of new powers like Brazil, India, and China shaping the international poverty reduction agenda?

SUGGESTED READING

Deaton, Angus. 2013. *The Great Escape: Health, Wealth and the Origins of Inequality.* Princeton, NJ: Princeton University Press.

Hulme, David. 2015. *Global Poverty: Global Governance and Poor People in the Post-2015 Era.* London: Routledge.

Pogge, Thomas. 2008. *World Poverty and Human Rights: Cosmopolitan Responsibilities and Reforms.* Cambridge: Polity.

BIBLIOGRAPHY

Chambers, R. 1983. *Rural Development: Putting the Last First.* Abingdon, UK: Routledge.

Clark, D. 2006. "Capability approach." In D. Clark, ed., *The Elgar Companion to Development Studies.* Cheltenham: Edward Elgar, 32–44.

Du Toit, A. 2009. "Poverty measurement blues." In T. Addison, D. Hulme, and R. Kanbur, eds, *Poverty Dynamics: Interdisciplinary Perspectives.* Oxford: Oxford University Press, 225–46.

Easterly, W. 2009. "How the MDGs are unfair to Africa." *World Development* 37, 1: 26–35.

Fanon, F. 1961. *The Wretched of the Earth.* New York: Penguin Modern Classics.

Giddens, A. 1984. *The Constitution of Society: Outline of the Theory of Structuration.* Berkeley: University of California Press.

Hulme, D. 2010. "The making of the Millennium Development Goals: Human development meets results-based management in an imperfect world." In J. Clapp and R. Wilkinson, eds, *Global Governance, Poverty and Inequality.* London: Routledge, 135–61.

Jolly, R., G.A. Cornia, D. Elson, C. Fortin, S. Griffith-Jones, G. Helleiner, R.E. van der Hoeven, R. Kaplinsky, R. Morgan, I. Ortiz, R. Pearson, and F. Stewart. 2012. *Be Outraged: There Are Alternatives.* EUR-ISS-EDEM. Rotterdam: International Institute of Social Studies, Erasmus University. http://hdl.handle.net/1765/38332. Accessed 16 Sept. 2015.

Lancaster, C. 2008. *George Bush's Foreign Aid: Transformation or Chaos?* Washington: Brookings Institution Press, 2008.

McArthur, J. 2013. "Own the goals: What the Millennium Development Goals have accomplished." www.brookings.edu/research/articles/2013/02/21-millennium-dev-goals-mcarthur. Accessed 16 Sept. 2015.

Mallaby, S. 2004. *The World's Banker: Story of Failed States, Financial Crises, and the Wealth and Poverty of Nations.* New York: Penguin.

OPHI. 2014. "Global Multidimensional Poverty Index, Oxford Poverty and Human Development Initiative." www.ophi.org.uk/. Accessed 16 Sept. 2015.

Pogge, T. 2004. "The first United Nations Millennium Development Goal: A cause for celebration?" *Journal of Human Development and Capabilities* 5, 3: 377–97.

Ravallion, M., and S. Chen. 2013. "A proposal for truly global poverty measures." *Global Policy* 4, 3: 258–65.

Sen, A. 2001. *Development as Freedom.* Oxford: Oxford University Press.

United Nations. 2009. *The Millennium Development Goals Report 2009.* New York: UN.

———. 2014. *The Millennium Development Goals Report 2014.* New York: UN.

Williamson, J. 1990. "What Washington means by policy reform." In J. Williamson, ed., *Latin American Adjustment: How Much Has Happened?* Washington: Institute for International Economics, 5–38.

25 Measuring and Evaluating Poverty

Keetie Roelen

LEARNING OBJECTIVES

- To learn about the evolution of thinking about poverty across time and place.
- To understand different approaches for measuring and interpreting poverty.
- To appreciate the importance of using complementary measurement.
- To understand the use of poverty measurement for policy.

▲ **A woodcutter rides in a train in Manikpur railway station, India, with his wood for sale. Collection and sale of firewood in nearby markets is a regular source of income for families with little or no productive land.** | Source: Photo by Akshay Gupta/Pacific Press/LightRocket via Getty Images

INTRODUCTION

Poverty must be one of the most frequently used words in international development and development studies. But what do we actually mean when we use the term "poverty"? And do we all mean the same thing? This is highly unlikely. Ask someone living in Sierra Leone about what it means to be poor and she or he will probably give you a very different answer compared to someone living in Switzerland. Ask a child what poverty means to him or her and you are likely to get a very different response than from an adult. And if you were able to ask someone a century ago about what "living in poverty" meant, you would have received a very different answer than if you were to ask someone the same question today.

To help gain an understanding of the different concepts and measures of poverty, this chapter examines how thinking about poverty has evolved over time and discusses main schools of thought that have shaped poverty debates up to the present. We then consider key questions around measuring poverty by discussing the two main approaches to poverty measurement in more detail, namely, monetary poverty and multi-dimensional poverty. Finally, the chapter examines the extent to which these approaches provide similar or different pictures of poverty and reflects on implications for policy and practice.

Keetie Roelen

PHOTO 25.1 | Woman and child in front of grass house, Burundi.

EVOLUTION OF THINKING ON POVERTY

I saw an old cottage of clay,
And only of mud was the floor;
It was all falling into decay,
And the snow drifted in at the door.

Yet there a poor family dwelt,
In a hovel so dismal and rude;
And though gnawing hunger they felt,
They had not a morsel of food.

The children were crying for bread,
And to their poor mother they'd run;
"Oh, give us some breakfast," they said,
Alas! their poor mother had none.

Excerpt from "Poverty" by Jane Taylor (1783–1824)

The excerpt from the poem "Poverty" poignantly reflects how poverty was conceived in the nineteenth century in England, referring to hunger and harsh living conditions. The first comprehensive poverty studies were undertaken in England around the turn of the twentieth century. Charles Booth mapped living conditions in London (see photo of Booth's map of London) by investigating various areas of people's lives, including work and working conditions, housing conditions, urban environment, and religious life. Benjamin Rowntree conducted a similar study in York a few years later to highlight that urban poverty was not a phenomenon exclusive to the metropolis of London. He focused on whether city dwellers were able to acquire basic necessities such as food, fuel, and clothing and calculated a minimum weekly sum of money

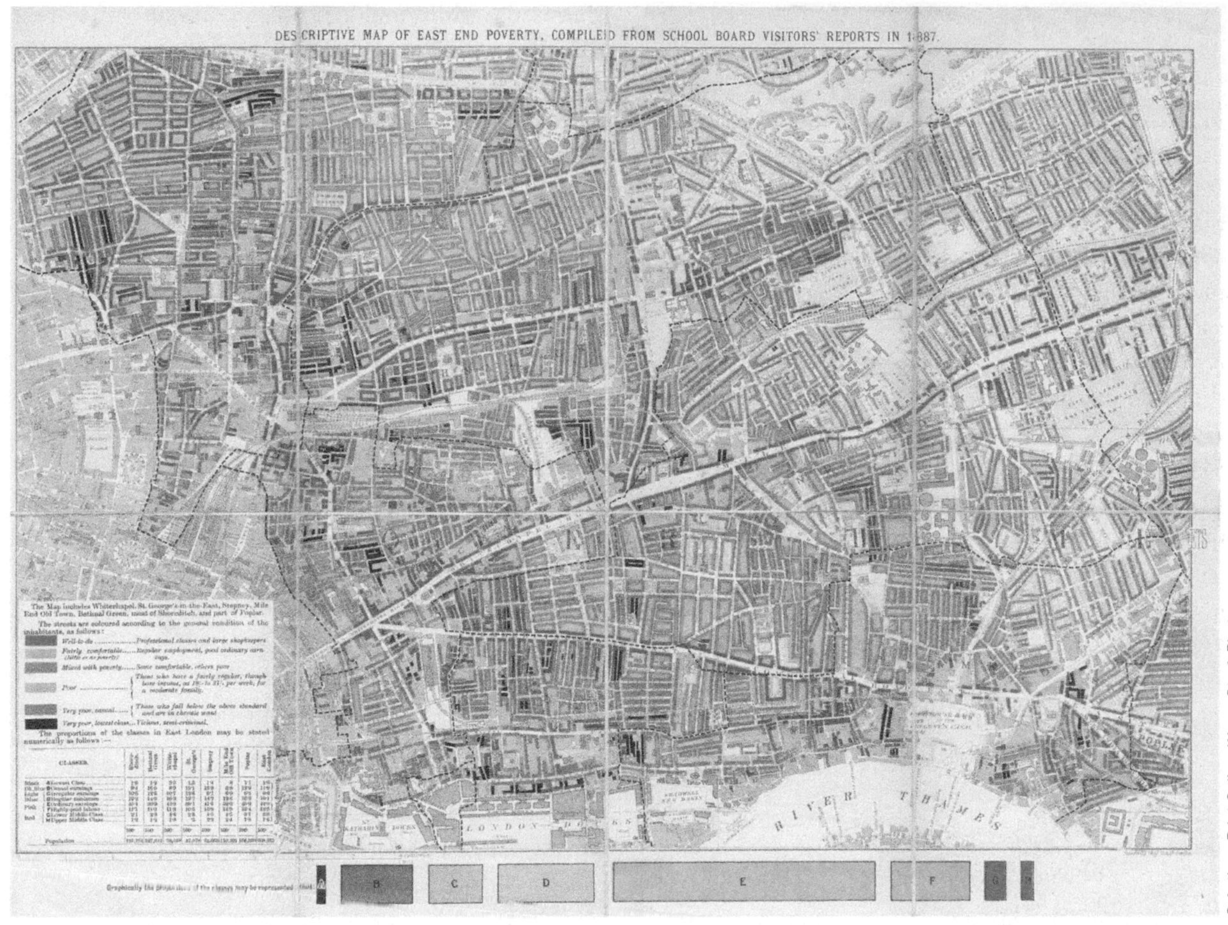

PHOTO 25.2 | Charles Booth's map of London poverty in 1889.

necessary to enable families to secure the necessities of a healthy life, thereby becoming one of the founding fathers of what remains the dominant approach in poverty measurement.

Studies focusing on people's living conditions and comparing those to a threshold of basic necessities were replicated in many different areas and countries in the first half of the twentieth century. As living conditions in Europe and other Western countries improved, notions of the meaning of poverty shifted towards thinking about poverty as the inability to live lives that are considered the norm or appropriate in that time and place rather than the inability to secure a minimum level of basic needs. This led to a shift in thinking from **absolute poverty** to **relative poverty**. One of the first scholars to consider this concept was Peter Townsend, who said that poverty was about: "The absence or inadequacy of those diets, amenities, standards, services and activities which are common or customary in society" (Townsend, 1979). In other words, poverty was no longer about being able to meet a basic minimum level of living standards but about being able to live and do as others in society.

Around the same time that thinking moved from absolute to relative poverty, an Indian economist and philosopher, Amartya Sen, argued that poverty is not all about income or living standards but rather about having the capabilities to achieve and live the lives that people value. His "capability approach" and its influence on thinking about development and poverty reduction were so groundbreaking that he was awarded the Nobel Prize in Economics in 1998.

Anders Wiklund/SCANPIX/CP

PHOTO 25.3 | Amartya Sen (*left*) receiving Nobel Prize in 1998.

In terms of poverty measurement, it inspired wider thinking around multi-dimensional poverty and the notion that poverty is a broader concept and should include more indicators for it to capture all the different elements.

The issue of poverty measurement and the "right" approach has remained and remains the subject of extensive academic research and policy debate. Although somewhat crude, the division between monetary and multi-dimensional approaches to poverty measurement is widely maintained, largely informed by normative, conceptual, and empirical underpinnings. Monetary approaches focus on the availability of monetary resources as the main indicator of living standards, while multi-dimensional approaches take into account a broader spectrum of living conditions. Monetary poverty measurement is therefore also referred to as an indirect approach to poverty measurement as it considers the means to an end rather than the end itself (Hulme, 2015).

MONETARY POVERTY

Monetary poverty remains the most prominent approach in measuring poverty (Sumner, 2007) and is based on a number of assumptions about how monetary resources can be translated into fulfillment of basic needs. What makes the monetary approach so appealing is its intuitive nature and that the use of money as the main indicator makes for a very versatile measure that can provide information about the number of people living in poverty but also about how poor they are and where they are.

Despite its basic intuitive nature, how to measure monetary poverty has been widely debated. This includes questions around how to determine someone's welfare, how to decide on a minimum threshold (the poverty line), and how to measure poverty.

The Welfare Measure

The first step in establishing whether someone is poor or not in the monetary approach requires measuring someone's welfare or looking at how much money someone has at his or her disposal. This might appear a straightforward exercise, particularly when living in high-income countries: you simply consider how much income someone earns. This is not the case, however, in either high-income countries or low-income countries. For example, people might earn income from multiple sources and pay different types of taxes over those income sources. People might also earn income with different frequencies: a permanent job may provide the same income every month; seasonal or temporary jobs may provide income at variable and unpredictable intervals; and the sale of a house or land will constitute a large one-off flow of income. In low-income countries these issues are often compounded as most people do not have formal or permanent jobs, income flows are highly variable, and income earnings can be in cash or in-kind.

Given the complexities involved, a degree of common practice has emerged to determine the amount of monetary resources available. An important element of that practice in low- and middle-income countries is to consider how much someone consumes or spends, rather than earns, as income. This might be more appropriate for a number of reasons. First, income fluctuates much more than consumption does; while the income one earns might be dependent on the season, for example, a basic level of consumption is maintained throughout the year. Second, income is usually under-reported as people are either reluctant to share full information about their earnings or may not know the full extent of their income, particularly if there are multiple income sources. Consumption and spending are less contentious to report and might be easier to track in a diary, for example. Finally, income may not take the form of money, particularly in developing countries. People could be paid in food items, for example, or could not be paid at all but survive on their own food production. Taking consumption as the welfare measure would account for all food that is eaten, regardless of whether it is purchased with money or homegrown (see Deaton and Grosh, 2000, for further discussion).

It should be noted that welfare is usually established at the household level. Individual consumption, spending, or earning patterns are aggregated to household level, culminating into an indication of the level of monetary resources available in the household as a whole. The rationale for doing so is that resources are generally shared across household members but individual members may not equally contribute to such resources. Children are a case in point: they do not earn an income by themselves but share in their household's overall income. When referring to welfare at the individual level, household-level measures of welfare will have been translated back to the individual level by dividing the total resources across all household members.

The Poverty Line

After having established how to measure welfare, the next step is to establish what level of welfare constitutes poverty or not. In order to make this decision, one needs to set a threshold that divides the population into poor and non-poor on the basis of their welfare level—a poverty line. If someone's welfare is lower than the **poverty line**, that person is considered poor. As is the case for establishing the welfare measure, setting the poverty line is a complex and contentious process.

An important consideration is whether the poverty line should be absolute or relative. Should the poverty line represent a minimum standard of living—the method employed by Benjamin Rowntree—or should it be related to the society's wider living conditions—as proposed by Peter Townsend? Although most high-income countries employ both types of poverty lines, the relative poverty line has gained prominence in the last two decades and is now most widely used in European countries. This is in recognition of the fact that even if everyone in society might be able to secure minimum needs for survival, some may not be able to participate in society according to conventional living standards. Absolute poverty lines remain the most widely used method in low-income countries.

An absolute poverty line is usually based on the costs of a minimum consumption basket. Many countries apply a method calculating the cost of a basket of food typically consumed to provide a daily caloric intake of 2,300 calories (Hulme, 2015). This amount is complemented with a non-food share to account for costs of important non-food items such as shelter, clothing, and cooking fuel. The first poverty line is often referred to as the "extreme poverty line" or "food poverty line," while the second poverty line is often simply called the "poverty line" (Hulme, 2015). Box 25.1 describes how absolute poverty lines are calculated in Myanmar.

The absolute poverty lines described above are national poverty lines that will be different depending on the country under consideration, making them very useful for in-country analysis but less helpful for cross-country comparisons. International poverty lines serve the purpose of measuring absolute poverty at a global scale; the World Bank's International Extreme Poverty Line (IEPL) is the most widely used measure. It is also known as the "dollar a day" line, as this was its value when the line was first established in 1990. The line has been adjusted a few times since and currently stands at US$1.25 in 2005 purchasing power parity (PPP). PPP refers to the process of taking account of the differences in the costs of living across countries: even after the application of

IMPORTANT CONCEPTS

BOX 25.1 | Setting the Food Poverty Line and Poverty Line in Myanmar

Two poverty lines are presented in [Myanmar's] *Poverty Profile* based on the Integrated Household Living Conditions Assessment, the "food poverty" and "poverty" lines. The food poverty line measures how much consumption expenditure is required to meet basic caloric needs only. The poverty line simply adds an allowance for non-food expenditure. . . .

The Food Poverty Line

There are five basic steps which are required to set the food poverty line:

- First, a "poor" reference group is selected, which, in the present case, is the second quartile (25 per cent) of the consumption distribution, i.e. the bottom 25–50 per cent.
- Second, the number of calories consumed by this reference group is calculated. This step requires information on the quantities of food items consumed and the caloric content of these food items.
- Third, the minimum required caloric intake is calculated for different population groups based on nutritional norms. In Myanmar, different calorie requirements have been set for males, females, children and urban/rural dwellers.
- Fourth, the food actually consumed by the reference group is "scaled up or down" until it reaches the minimum required level of caloric intake. In practice, this means that the "basket" of foods consumed stays the same but the level is increased or decreased.
- Finally, the cost of this new scaled food basket is calculated, and represents the food poverty line.

It should be noted that the "food poverty" line is very meagre indeed. It represents the amount required to meet caloric requirements assuming that *all* household income is spent on food. As such, it represents a level of extreme hardship.

The Poverty Line

The poverty line retains all of the above steps and simply adds an allowance of non-food expenditure. Three additional steps are required:

- First, the non-food share in consumption expenditure of the reference group is calculated.
- Second, a monetary value is assigned to this share (by multiplying it by the food poverty line).
- Third, the monetary value is added to the food poverty line to arrive at the poverty line.

Calculated in this way, the poverty line represents a minimum of food and non-food expenditures based on the consumption pattern of the second quartile of the consumption distribution.

Source: IHLCA (2011: 5–6).

exchange rates, the amount of food (or any other goods) that you would be able to purchase with US$1.25 in Norway would be very different from what you would be able to purchase in Niger, for example. To ensure that the IEPL reflects the ability to purchase the same basket of goods anywhere in the world—the same purchasing power—adjustments have to be made using purchasing power parity (PPP) exchange rates. As such, the IEPL of US$1.25

IMPORTANT CONCEPTS

BOX 25.2 | The "Big Mac Index"

A simplified and more intuitive version of PPP exchange rates is the "Big Mac Index." The Big Mac Index was invented by *The Economist* in 1986 as a light-hearted and simplified version of the PPP principle, calculating the price of a highly standardized product—the Big Mac—in US dollars using market exchange rates. The Big Mac PPP exchange rate between two countries is obtained by dividing the price of a Big Mac in one country (in its currency) by the price of a Big Mac in another country (in its currency). This value is then compared with the actual exchange rate; if it is lower, then the first currency is under-valued (according to PPP theory) compared with the second, and conversely, if it is higher, then the first currency is over-valued.

Source: *The Economist*: http://www.economist.com/content/big-mac-index.

in 2005 PPP reflects the purchasing power of US$1.25 in the United States in 2005 (Sillers, 2015).

Critics of absolute poverty lines have argued that they objectify people as "cattle or livestock—being reared, not part of society" (Hulme, 2015: 61) and that poverty needs to be defined in relation to whether people are integrated and able to participate in society. Relative poverty measures aim to do so by using countries' average living conditions as a benchmark rather than minimum needs for survival. The most commonly used relative poverty line is 60 per cent of median income, which is referred to as the "at-risk-of-poverty" line and applied to all 28 countries in the European Union. As the poverty line is tied to median income in a given country, the value of such poverty lines differs considerably across countries (Eurostat, 2015). Also, while an absolute poverty line allows for the eradication of poverty—it is possible for all people to gain an income that is higher than the absolute poverty line—there will always be a degree of poverty when employing a

IMPORTANT CONCEPTS

BOX 25.3 | Relative Poverty in Middle-Income Countries

Tying the poverty line to the income distribution of a given country ensures that poverty measures account for the cost of social inclusion rather than merely the cost of basic needs. The attributes of social inclusion will differ from one country to the next. They could include owning a car that allows for the daily commute to work, having the ability to go on a school trip with other classmates, or making contributions to important family celebrations such as weddings and funerals. Adam Smith—one of the founding fathers of economic theory—referred to linen shirts as an attribute of social inclusion in the context of Europe in the eighteenth century: "A linen shirt, for example, is, strictly speaking, not a necessary of life. The Greeks and Romans lived, I suppose, very comfortably though they had no linen. But in the present times, through the greater part of Europe, a creditable day-labourer would be ashamed to appear in public without a linen shirt, the want of which would be supposed to denote that disgraceful degree of poverty" (Smith, 1776: part 2 article 4).

relative poverty line because the line is pegged against the proportion of a country's income distribution.

The Poverty Measure

After having decided on the welfare measure and poverty line, the next step entails establishing poverty measures that allow for aggregating information at the household or individual level into meaningful information about poverty. The so-called Foster-Greer-Thorbecke (FGT) poverty measures distinguish three types of measures that each provide different information about poverty: (1) the headcount index, (2) the poverty gap index, and (3) the poverty severity index (see Box 25.4).

The first measure—the **poverty headcount index**—is the most intuitive and widely used measure and simply indicates what proportion of the population lives in poverty. It is calculated by counting the number of people below the poverty line and dividing that by the total population. This is illustrated in Figure 25.1 by the dashed lines for Countries I and II; in both countries, 50 per cent of the population have a level of monetary resources below the poverty line.

The second measure—the **poverty gap index**—provides insight into how deep poverty is. It does so by taking into account the level of monetary resources and its distance to the poverty line for every poor household or individual, representing individual shortfalls from the poverty line. These individual shortfalls are aggregated and represent the poverty gap in a country, as is represented by the dashed arrows in Figure 25.1. The overall poverty gap is then divided by the poverty line and averaged across the total population. Thereby the measure represents "[t]he sum of these poverty gaps [and] gives the minimum cost of eliminating poverty, if transfers were perfectly targeted" (World Bank, 2005: 69). The poverty gap index is an important measure for providing information on the depth of poverty. It should also be noted that two countries can have identical poverty headcount ratios but very different outcomes in terms of the poverty gap ratio, as reflected for Countries I and II in Figure 25.1. While half of the population is poor in both countries, poverty is "deeper" in Country II since the combined gap between monetary resources and the poverty line of those people living in poverty is larger.

The third measure—the **poverty severity index**—is the least intuitive of the FGT measures but gives an indication of how severe poverty is. It is calculated by giving greater weight to larger poverty gaps by "squaring" individual poverty gaps before dividing them by the poverty line and averaging this across the total population. It can also be seen as a measure that takes inequality among the poor into account by giving greater weight to those who are further away from the poverty line.

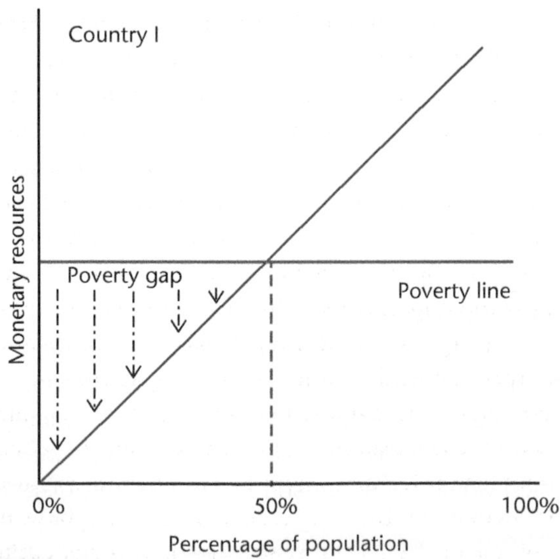

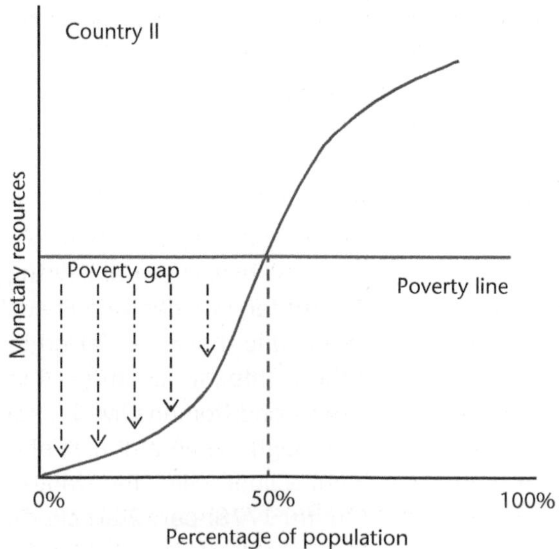

FIGURE 25.1 | Poverty Gap

IMPORTANT CONCEPTS

BOX 25.4 | Foster-Greer-Thorbecke (FGT) Class of Poverty Measures

The equation below represents the formal mathematical notation of the FGT class of poverty measures, where N is the size of the population, z is the poverty line, and G_i is the shortfall from the poverty line. It includes all three measures in one equation by varying the value for α. If $\alpha = 0$, the equation represents the proportion of people living below the poverty line or the poverty headcount index (also noted as P_0). If $\alpha = 1$, the equation represents the average shortfall as a proportion of the poverty line or the poverty gap ratio (also noted as P_1). If $\alpha = 2$, the equation gives greater weight to larger shortfalls and represents the squared poverty gap index or the poverty severity index (also noted as P_2).

$$P_\alpha = \frac{1}{N}\sum_{i=1}^{N}\left(\frac{G_i}{z}\right)^\alpha$$

For a more detailed discussion, see World Bank (2005: ch. 4).

MULTI-DIMENSIONAL POVERTY

The measurement of multi-dimensional poverty can be said to follow from heated debates around whether poverty should be understood as the lack of means to achieve a minimum standard of living or as the actual shortfall from such a standard of living (Hulme, 2015). As indicated earlier, monetary poverty approaches essentially focus on the "means to an end," based on the assumption that monetary resources can be translated into non-monetary outcomes. Multi-dimensional measures challenge that assumption and aim to capture elements of standard of living more directly.

There are many shortcomings of the monetary approach, mostly related to the underlying assumptions discussed previously (Bourguignon and Chakravarty, 2003). A first drawback relates to the assumption that everything necessary for a minimum standard of living can be expressed in monetary terms. A second shortcoming relates to the assumption that everything can be bought on markets and that such markets function perfectly. This is not necessarily the case, particularly in developing countries. Third, monetary approaches assume that a given level of income is also spent on the minimum required set of basic needs, which may not necessarily be the case. Finally, monetary approaches assume that income at the household level is distributed to individual members in equal measure or in such a way that it meets individuals' requirements.

In addition to these conceptual challenges of the monetary approach, empirical findings in the 1970s also fuelled doubts about whether a purely economic view fairly reflected reality on the ground in terms of wider living conditions. In 1978, for example, Streeten and Burki found that: "In spite of unprecedently [*sic*] and unexpectedly high growth rates during the last twenty-five years, and in spite of improvements in such social indicators as literacy and infant mortality, pessimism is widespread. The pessimism prevails because aggregate economic growth appears to have done very little for the poorer half of the Third World's rapidly growing populations" (Streeten and Burki, 1978: 411).

In light of these conceptual and empirical challenges, multi-dimensional poverty approaches were developed. As indicated earlier, the work by Amartya Sen on the capability approach (see Box 25.5) laid the foundation for many approaches that were developed subsequently. These approaches include the basic needs approaches (Streeten, 1984, 1981) and social exclusion methods (Marlier et al., 2009). Basic needs approaches

IMPORTANT CONCEPTS

BOX 25.5 | Sen's Capability Approach

While the capability approach originates from the 1970s, Amartya Sen's *Development as Freedom* (1999) provides helpful insight into the meaning of the approach. He specifically sets the capability approach apart from the monetary approach by stating that the "capability approach" addresses poverty as "the deprivation of basic capabilities rather than merely as lowness of incomes." The space it operates in is "that of the substantive freedoms—the capabilities—to choose a life that one has reason to value" (Sen, 1999: 74). Capabilities thus refer to being able to do or be according to someone's values, thereby taking into account a complex combination of an individual's set of valued choices and degree of freedom and agency to act upon such choices. Sen writes that "[c]apability is thus a kind of freedom: the substantive freedom to achieve . . . various lifestyles. For example, an affluent person who fasts may have the same functioning achievement in terms of eating . . . as a destitute person who is forced to starve, but the first person does have a different 'capability set' than the second (the first can choose to eat well and be well nourished in a way the second cannot" (Sen, 1999: 75). Given the focus on individual values and freedom to live up to such values, Sen has always been opposed to formulating a universal set of capabilities. Other scholars operationalizing the capability approach, most notably Martha Nussbaum, advocate a more prescriptive approach that includes the establishment of context-specific lists of basic capabilities.

build on the notion that a set of universal basic needs holds across time and place and thereby mirrors absolute poverty as described as part of monetary poverty measurement. Social exclusion methods emerged in Europe in the 1970s and are grounded in concepts of inclusivity and participation, postulating that poverty measures should reflect whether people are able to participate in the society as measured against standards that are relevant in that place and at that time. They therefore resemble relative poverty measures as discussed above. Although multi-dimensional poverty approaches take different perspectives on what various dimensions are to be included (which can sometimes include income), they share the common ground that poverty cannot be assessed on the basis of income alone (also see Chapters 1 and 24).

The measurement of multi-dimensional poverty is not without debate or caveats, however. Choices inherent to the incorporation of multiple dimensions of poverty in poverty measures are normative and subject to value judgments. Often such choices are made implicitly, making multi-dimensional poverty estimates susceptible to misinterpretation (Roelen, Gassmann, and Neubourg, 2009) and controversy (Klasen, 2000). One of the most contentious issues in measuring multiple dimensions of poverty appears to be that of aggregation and the extent to which information on single indicators or dimensions should be combined into composite numbers or, rather, should be used at face value. Ferreira and Lugo (2013) distinguish between those favouring "scalar indices" versus a "dashboard" approach. Proponents of scalar indices value the capability to rank countries, households, or other units of analysis and subsequently to be able to use such rankings in policy, communication, and advocacy (Birdsall, 2011). Aggregate indices can be strong in providing quick overviews of main trends and inequalities, for example. Opponents of such indices denounce the ambiguity in the choice of dimensions, thresholds, and weighting schemes that is inherent in the aggregation of individual indicators into a composite index (Ravallion, 2011).

As such, the construction of multi-dimensional measures is scrutinized to the same (if not greater) degree as monetary measures are. The questions to ask and steps to take when measuring multi-dimensional poverty are also much the same as they are for monetary poverty and include the establishment of a welfare measure, poverty line, and poverty measure. Practice around multi-dimensional poverty measurement is much less harmonized, however, and these three different questions are more intertwined, making it difficult to discuss these steps one by one. We will therefore discuss two prominent approaches—the Human Development Index (HDI) and the Multidimensional Poverty Index (MPI)—detailing the steps for each of these approaches.

Human Development Index (HDI)

The Human Development Index (HDI) was first published in the UNDP's annual *Human Development Report* (*HDR*) in 1990 to provide an alternative to economic criteria for assessing the development of a country, most notably the gross domestic product (GDP) or gross national income (GNI). As highlighted on the UNDP website: "The HDI was created to emphasize that people and their capabilities should be the ultimate criteria for assessing the development of a country, not economic growth alone" (UNDP, 2015).

The HDI is a summary measure of average achievement in three dimensions of human development: experiencing a long and healthy life; being knowledgeable; and having a decent standard of living. Information about these three different dimensions is collected at the country level and assessed against minimum and maximum values. For example, the aspect of living a long and healthy life is measured by considering average life expectancy at birth in a given country and normalizing this indicator using a minimum value of 20 years and maximum value of 85 years. A total of four indicators are included in the HDI—one for health, two for education, and one for living standards—with minimum and maximum values serving as benchmarks for each of these. The overall HDI score is calculated by taking the average score across all three domains (UNDP, 2015). This means that there is no threshold or cut-off below which a country is deemed to be deprived or to perform poorly; the HDI aims to allow for comparisons over time and across countries.

The HDI is grounded in Sen's capability approach, and although it only includes three dimensions and arguably only covers a limited range of issues beyond economic development, it presented an important shift from focusing solely on economic indicators for assessing global and regional progress towards development. The fairly intuitive inclusion of dimensions has also added to its popularity, making it one of the most popular tools for comparing a country's progress towards development across time or to other countries.

Multidimensional Poverty Index (MPI)

In 2010, UNDP extended its set of indicators by including the Multidimensional Poverty Index (MPI) in its annual *Human Development Report* (*HDR*). The MPI has been developed by the Oxford Poverty and Human Development Initiative (OPHI) and is distinct from the HDI as it captures information at the household level rather than national level. This means that one can analyze the extent to which households suffer multiple deprivations at the same time.

The MPI includes information on the same three domains as included in the HDI—education, health, and standard of living. The range of indicators within domains is more extensive, however, with two indicators in the education domain, two indicators in the health domain, and six indicators in the living standards domain. There is a threshold for each indicator determining whether a household is deprived with respect to that indicator or not. If a household is deprived in more than 33.3 per cent of the weighted dimensions, it is considered poor. The MPI poverty rate simply reflects the proportion of people living in households that do not meet this threshold.

The measure has been found to be rigorous, easy to disaggregate by domain and demographic group and to be useful for policy, and adaptable to different contexts. Since its development in 2010, the MPI has been calculated for the majority of low- and middle-income countries, thereby representing the first official effort to calculate the number of poor individuals globally through a multidimensional index and offering a complement to the international monetary poverty measures. Using this measure, more than a third of the combined population in the 91 countries covered by the MPI lived in poverty in 2014 (for further information, see Alkire and Foster, 2015; OPHI/BMZ, 2015; UNDP, 2015).

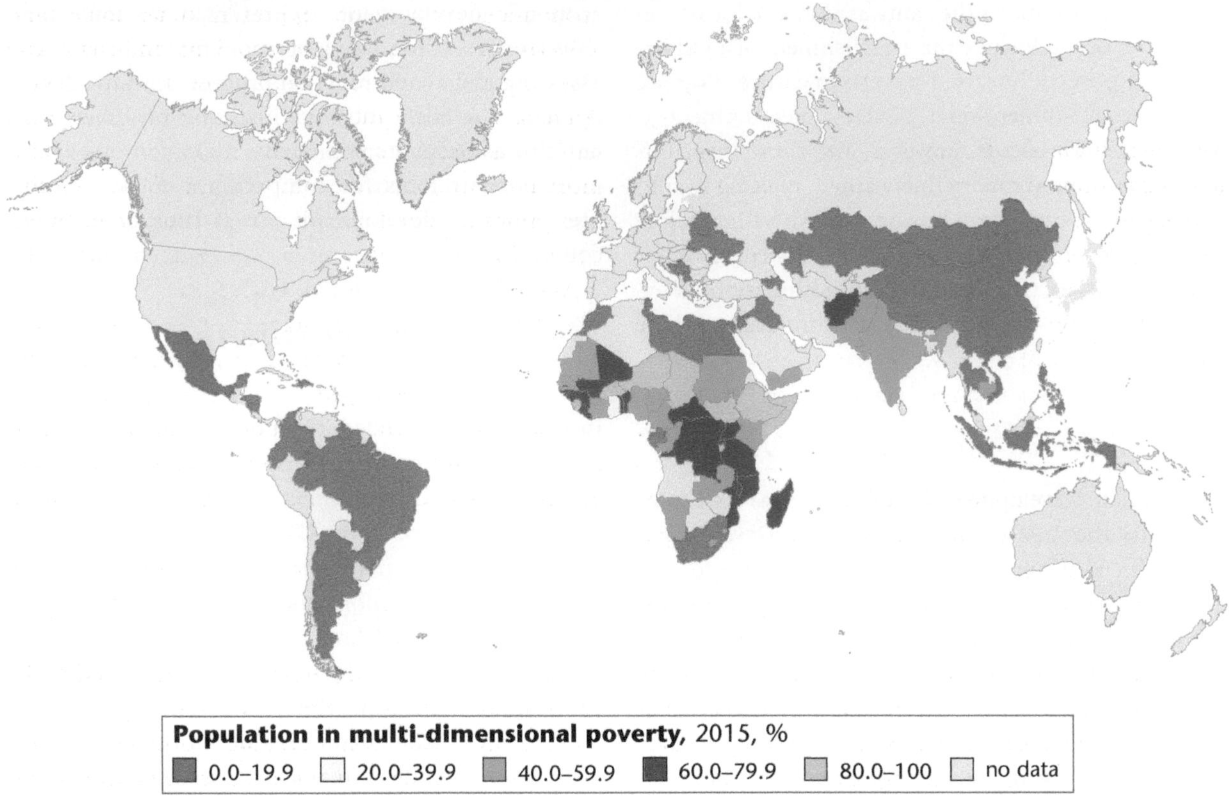

FIGURE 25.2 | The Unlucky 1.6 Billion: Multi-Dimensional Poverty across the Globe

Source: *The Economist* (2015).

CRITICAL ISSUES

BOX 25.6 | Individual Poverty Measure

One of the criticisms of the monetary approach is that income is measured at the household level and that assumptions are made about the extent to which this is shared within the household and poverty is distributed across household members. This is of particular concern when considering the situation of vulnerable groups such as children and women (Vijaya, Lahoti, and Swaminathan, 2014). Although widely expressed with respect to monetary approaches, this critique also holds for many multi-dimensional approaches to poverty measurement, including the MPI, as indicators refer to issues at the household rather than individual level. The Individual Deprivation Measure (IDM) was developed to address this shortcoming and particularly to give insight into differences in multi-dimensional poverty across gender. It does so by including mostly indicators that are measured at the individual level, such as those related to health care, clothing, personal care and hygiene, and freedom from violence. Such a measure presents an improvement in terms of capturing poverty status at the individual level but poses challenges in terms of data availability because many of the indicators are not available in current data sets.

Source: Wisor et al. (2014)

DIFFERENT MEASURES, DIFFERENT OUTCOMES

The discussion above makes it clear that monetary and multi-dimensional poverty approaches differ with respect to their conceptual and normative underpinnings about the extent to which monetary resources may be translated into non-monetary outcomes. As highlighted by Amartya Sen, capability-based or multi-dimensional approaches focus on what is intrinsically important while income-based approaches focus on what is instrumentally important (Sen, 1999). But one might ask whether such theoretical differences make a difference in practice: does the use of different approaches to measurement also lead to different pictures of poverty?

Conceptual and normative dissonance between monetary and multi-dimensional poverty approaches is increasingly corroborated by empirical findings. The evidence base regarding incongruent outcomes when using different measures is rapidly expanding. Studies investigating the mismatch of poverty outcomes often explore two elements, namely, the extent to which measures report different headcount rates and to what extent they identify different groups as being poor or deprived. Findings from existing studies largely suggest that the use of monetary and multi-dimensional measures results in different pictures of poverty, pointing towards a modest, even limited, overlap of results. Evidence originates from high-income countries (Klasen, 2000; Tran, Alkire, and Klasen, 2015; Laderchi, Saith, and Stewart, 2003) and low- and middle income country settings (Bradshaw and Finch, 2003; Perry, 2002; Wagle, 2009), and indicates that monetary and multi-dimensional poverty measures do in fact lead to different headcount rates and that these different approaches identify different groups as being poor. Such differences are exemplified even further when asking people about their own experiences of living in poverty.

Different Poverty Rates

Studies that compare monetary and multi-dimensional poverty rates highlight that the use of different measures gives rise to differential levels of poverty. Figure 25.3 maps monetary poverty and multi-dimensional child poverty in 28 countries in sub-Saharan Africa and shows that the two measures are not strongly related. Monetary poverty rates are considerably lower than multi-dimensional child poverty rates for most countries included, such as Ethiopia and Chad. Notable exceptions include Burundi and Rwanda, where monetary poverty is higher than multi-dimensional child poverty (Plavgo and De Milliano, 2014).

These differences in magnitude have been found not only in sub-Saharan Africa or with respect to child poverty but are observed more generally. In Mexico, Pakistan, and Egypt, for instance, there are twice as many multi-dimensionally poor as there are poor using the $1.25-a-day poverty measures (*The Economist*, 2015).

Different Poverty Groups

While a comparison of poverty rates indicates that the proportions of poor people are different depending on the measure under consideration, it does not give insight into the extent to which the same people are affected by both types of poverty. In other words, when monetary poverty rates are lower, it does not necessarily mean that those who are monetary poor are also multi-dimensionally poor. Venn diagrams represent a useful method for analyzing the extent to which poverty measures identify the same groups as being poor or not. They include circles that represent groups identified as being monetary or multi-dimensionally poor with the degree of overlap between those circles indicating to what extent the group experiencing monetary poverty also experiences multi-dimensional poverty and vice versa.

Figure 25.4 presents Venn diagrams showing the overlap between monetary and multi-dimensional child poverty in Ethiopia for 1999, 2004, and 2009 and Vietnam for 2004, 2006, and 2008. Children are either categorized as non-poor (group C), both monetary and multi-dimensionally poor (group AB), exclusively multi-dimensionally poor (group A), or exclusively monetary poor (group B). Analysis points towards size differences with substantial groups of children being either multi-dimensionally poor (A) or only monetary poor (B). The diagrams show that groups of children being either monetary or multi-dimensionally poor

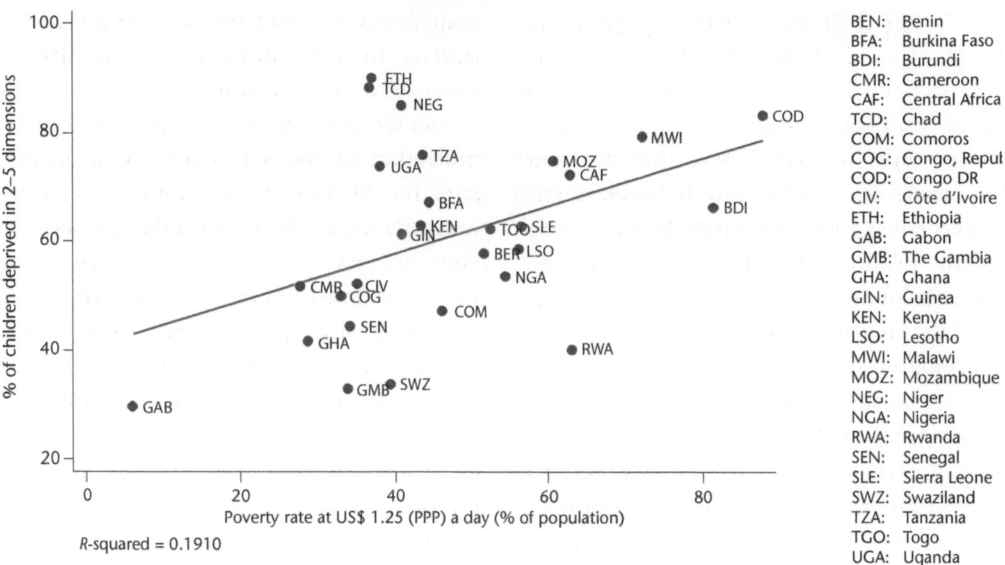

FIGURE 25.3 | Correlation between Monetary Poverty and Multi-Dimensional Child Poverty in 28 Sub-Saharan Countries

Source: Plavgo and De Milliano (2014). Analysing Child Poverty and Depravation in sub-Saharan Africa: CC-MODA - Cross Country Multiple Overlapping Deprivation Analysis, Innocenti Working Paper No. 2014-19, UNICEF Office of Research, Florence.

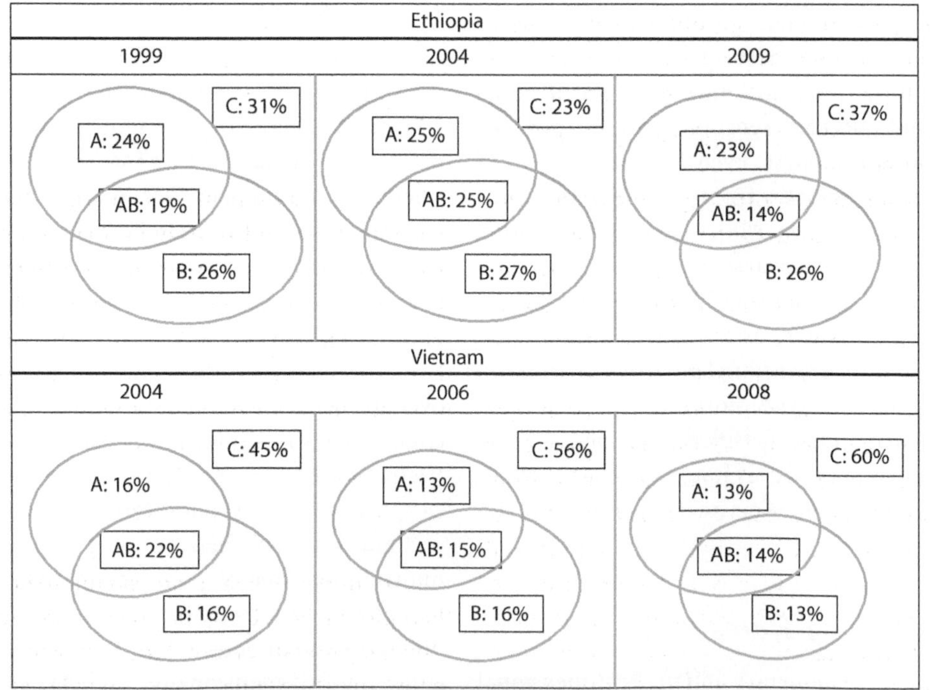

FIGURE 25.4 | Venn Diagrams: Monetary and Multi-Dimensional Child Poverty in Ethiopia and Vietnam

Source: Adapted from Roelen (2015).

are largest in Ethiopia. This can partly be explained by the indicators that are included in the measure of multi-dimensional child poverty, which include school attendance, the number of hours worked on farming, and the number of hours worked on domestic chores. While there is a positive link between monetary resources available in the household and school attendance, the relationship between the numbers of hours that children work on farming or doing domestic chores and household wealth is less clear and sometimes negative, as children's work contributes to household wealth. Indicators included in the Vietnamese measure of multi-dimensional child poverty are more related to basic needs such as water, sanitation, and shelter and therefore more strongly linked to household wealth. But despite a stronger link between monetary and non-monetary outcomes, children in Vietnam living in multi-dimensional poverty are not necessarily monetary poor and vice versa (Roelen, 2015).

Different Experiences

The discussion above highlights how different measures of poverty paint different pictures in terms of the numbers of people who are poor but also about what types of deprivation they suffer. Such differences are further exemplified when asking people about their living conditions and their own assessment of whether they are poor or not.

Arguments for the importance of including people's voices in development processes were pioneered by Robert Chambers in the 1980s when he advocated for "putting the last first" and putting experiences of the poor, marginalized, and destitute at the centre of development (Chambers, 1983). One of the first large-scale efforts that involved asking poor people about their living conditions was the report *Voices of the Poor* (Narayan, 1999). It included information from 47 countries, highlighting that poverty is a painful experience, consists of many interlinked and interlocked dimensions, and places undue weight on households and families (Narayan, 1999). The study was groundbreaking as it presented the first comprehensive effort to understand what people understood poverty to mean and how they were faring with respect to those conditions. Not only did this provide an important expansion of the evidence base on poverty, it also emphasized the limitations of conventional measures in capturing the complexities of living in poverty.

An example from Rwanda provides a pertinent illustration of the dissonance between outcomes as measured by poverty measures and as experienced by people themselves. Rwanda has seen widespread economic growth and great advances in both monetary and multi-dimensional poverty reduction, but an assessment of lived experiences, derived by asking Rwandans about their own views of the development process, suggests "that life is not actually improving for many Rwandans, that their wellbeing is poorly represented by some of the simple development indicators" (Dawson, 2015: 65). The dissonance between people's own experiences and those reflected in monetary and multi-dimensional indicators of poverty was linked to lack of political freedom and participation in developmental processes. While programs such as "villagization" and housing modernization have contributed to improved living conditions, as measured by indicators related to shelter and access to services, the oppressive process of implementation (with people being forced to move) has led to negative impacts for many Rwandans (Dawson, 2015).

POVERTY MEASUREMENT AND POLICY

Poverty measurement is crucial for informing policy-making and improving the lives of people living in poverty and vulnerability. Information about the number of people living in poverty, who and where they are, and how poor they are is crucial for ensuring that programs reach the right people and address the most pertinent issues, and for monitoring progress towards reaching goals and objectives.

Identifying Groups for Intervention

Poverty measurement is crucial for identifying groups that should benefit from policies and interventions. Monetary measures have long been used for establishing a poverty profile, which provides an overview of who and where poor people are. Such a poverty profile often considers variations by household characteristics (gender of the household head, educational attainment of the household head), community characteristics (communities with or without a paved road or hospital), and geography (urban versus rural areas; region) (Haughton and Khandker, 2009). An assessment of poverty patterns across such groups can help to direct limited resources to groups of people who are most in need.

Figure 25.5 provides an example of the identification of the most deprived regions in Nepal. An analysis of monetary poverty rates across regions highlights large disparities in terms of the proportions of people living in poverty (or poverty headcount indices). The regions around the capital of Kathmandu, in the Central Region, have poverty rates lower than the national poverty rate, while proportions of people living in poverty are much higher in the western part of the country. Many development programs therefore focus their efforts on this relatively disadvantaged area of the country.

Targeting of policies and programs can also occur at the household level, such as social assistance programs that provide regular cash transfers to those living in poverty. The amount of income earned in a household often determines eligibility for such programs. In South Africa, for example, the Child Support Grant (CSG) supports children living in poor families with a monthly cash transfer, with income thresholds of R3,300 per month for single caregivers and R6,300 per month for married couples (Black Sash, 2015).

The use of poverty measures for targeting policies and programs is not limited to monetary approaches. Multi-dimensional poverty approaches, and the MPI in particular, are increasingly being adopted as official poverty measures for informing

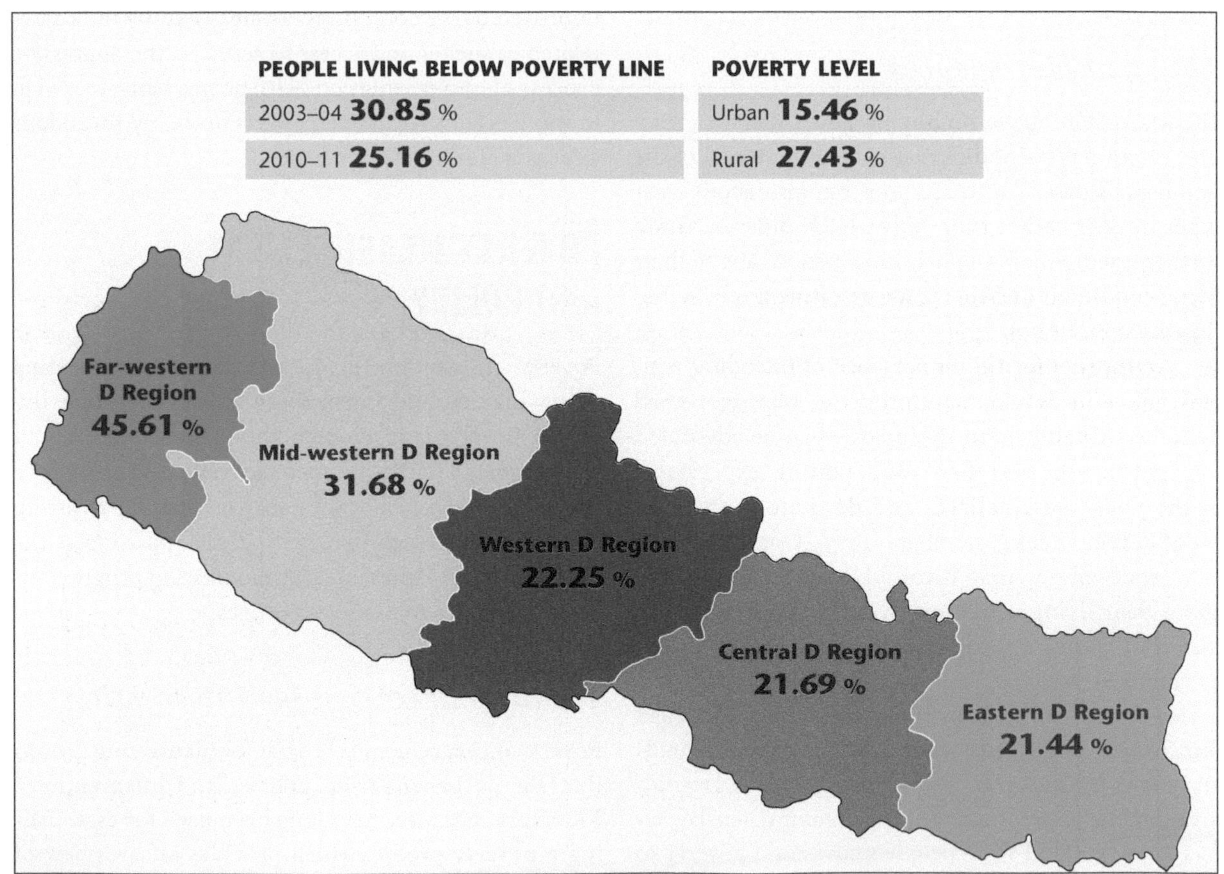

FIGURE 25.5 | Monetary Poverty in Nepal

Source: Nepal Living Standards Survey (NLSS) at www.unicef.org/evaldatabase/files/Conducting_an_Institutional_Assessment_and_Providing_Capacity_Development_and_Training_on_Social_Protection_in_Nepal.pdf

and guiding policy formulation. In Colombia, for example, a country-specific MPI was developed to inform national policy-making processes, including the identification of particularly deprived areas and groups of people that receive policy priority. The National Development Plan 2014–2018 targets two regions with the highest incidences of multi-dimensional poverty—the Pacific and the Atlantic—while the MPI and income poverty measures are used in conjunction for targeting social programs such as Families in Action Plus and UNIDOS (OPHI/BMZ, 2015).

Identifying Policy Areas for Intervention

Poverty measurement is also important for identifying policy areas of particular concern or that should receive priority. Multi-dimensional poverty measures are particularly helpful in this respect because their inclusion of different dimensions of poverty allows for drawing direct linkages to policy areas. As noted by Neubourg, Roelen, and Gassmann (2009: 52), "the profile of people being deprived on several dimensions also reveals where to direct attention when designing social policy."

The use of the MPI in Colombia illustrates how a multi-dimensional poverty measure can also inform decision-making in policy from this perspective. The national MPI was further developed to construct a measure that can be applied at the municipal level using census data, thereby allowing for the creation of local poverty maps to target social intervention programs within municipalities (OPHI/BMZ 2015). A study focusing on Villapinzon municipality in Cundinamarca illustrated that the application of such a local measure, in combination with discussions with local residents, can help to identify and prioritize areas for intervention and convince local authorities to adapt policies accordingly. Housing conditions (overcrowding), education (low levels of education and illiteracy), and labour market conditions (high rates of informal employment) were found to be areas of most urgent concern in the municipality (Torres and Bautista Hernandez, 2015).

IMPORTANT CONCEPTS

BOX 25.7 | Gross National Happiness (GNH) Index in Bhutan

For decades Bhutan has rejected conventional economic measures of development and poverty but instead focused on non-economic aspects of life. "Gross National Happiness" was first proposed in the 1970s by the King of Bhutan, Jigme SingyeWangchuck, and has led to national development being measured using the "Gross National Happiness (GNH) Index." The dedicated website describes the initiative as follows:

> The concept implies that sustainable development should take a holistic approach towards notions of progress and give equal importance to non-economic aspects of wellbeing. The concept of GNH has often been explained by its four pillars: good governance, sustainable socio-economic development, cultural preservation, and environmental conservation. Lately the four pillars have been further classified into nine domains in order to create widespread understanding of GNH and to reflect the holistic range of GNH values. The nine domains are: psychological wellbeing, health, education, time use, cultural diversity and resilience, good governance, community vitality, ecological diversity and resilience, and living standards. The domains represent each of the components of wellbeing of the Bhutanese people, and the term "wellbeing" here refers to fulfilling conditions of a "good life" as per the values and principles laid down by the concept of Gross National Happiness.

Source: GNH Index/Bhutan GNH Index at http://www.grossnationalhappiness.com/articles/.

Monitoring Progress

A third important reason for measuring poverty is to monitor progress towards goals and targets in terms of development policy and poverty reduction. From a global perspective, Sustainable Development Goal (SDG) #1, on the eradication of all forms of extreme poverty, includes a target to eradicate extreme poverty everywhere using the $1.25-a-day measure as well as a target to reduce poverty according to national definitions by at least half (OWG SDG, 2014). While monetary measures remain dominant, multi-dimensional poverty approaches, and the MPI in particular, are increasingly being adopted as official poverty measures for informing and guiding policy formulation at the national level.

Colombia's adoption of a country-specific MPI again provides a pertinent illustration. In 2011, President Juan Manuel Santos announced a new National Development Plan with a strong focus on poverty reduction. A Colombian Multidimensional Poverty Index (MPI-Colombia) was included in the Plan as a tool for setting poverty reduction targets and measuring progress towards reaching those targets. The most recent National Development Plan of 2015 expands the role of this country-specific multi-dimensional poverty measure even further by including specific targets for each of the dimensions and indicators included in the MPI. The reporting system employs a "traffic light" tool that triggers alerts when progress towards any indicator falls off track. A special ministerial cabinet commission was established to ensure that progress towards achieving such targets is on track (OPHI/BMZ, 2015), thereby ensuring that progress is not merely tracked but also that policy-makers are held to account.

Other countries have followed suit, including Chile, where the government announced its new national Multidimensional Poverty Index (MPI) along with its new income poverty measure in January 2015, and the Philippines, where the government included a multi-dimensional poverty measure in the Philippine Development Plan (2011–16) (OPHI/BMZ, 2015). Bhutan is one of the few countries that has long denounced the singular use of economic indicators and focused on wider measures of development instead (see Box 25.7).

SUMMARY

This chapter examined the evaluation of thinking around poverty, the main approaches to poverty measurement, and the importance of poverty measurement for policy. It is evident that poverty is a fluid concept and that its meaning differs depending on time, place, and group under consideration. Monetary poverty and multi-dimensional poverty represent two broad but main categories of poverty measurement. While monetary poverty measurement has dominated development discourse until recently (and some may argue it still does), multi-dimensional poverty measurement has gained prominence and is now considered a viable or preferred alternative by some. Ultimately, poverty is in the "eye of the beholder": different approaches to poverty measurement suggest different magnitudes of the problem and identify different groups as being poor. Complementary and comprehensive poverty measurement is therefore essential for gaining insight into the reality on the ground and allowing for the formulation of adequate and appropriate policies.

QUESTIONS FOR CRITICAL THOUGHT

1. Is there an optimal way for measuring poverty and if so, what would it look like? Would this differ for low- and high-income countries and why? Would this differ for different groups in society? Explain.
2. Do monetary and multi-dimensional approaches to poverty measurement allow for the voices of people living in poverty to be included? How can poverty measures be inclusive?
3. How does the use of different poverty measures influence policies for eradicating or reducing poverty? Do different measures play a different role?

SUGGESTED READINGS

Alkire, Sabina, James Foster, Suman Seth, Maria Emma Santos, Jose Manuel Roche, and Paola Ballon. 2015. *Multidimensional Poverty Measurement and Analysis.* Oxford: Oxford University Press.

Haughton, Jonathan, and Shahidur Khandker. 2009. *Handbook on Poverty and Inequality.* Washington: World Bank.

Kakwani, Nanak, and Jacques Silber. 2007. *The Many Dimensions of Poverty.* Basingstoke: Palgrave Macmillan.

Sen, Amartya. 1999. *Development as Freedom.* Oxford: Oxford University Press.

BIBLIOGRAPHY

Birdsall, N. 2011. "Comment on multi-dimensional indices." *Journal of Economic Inequality* 9, 3: 489–91. doi: 10.1007/s10888-011-9195-y.

Black Sash. 2015. *You and Your Rights.* Social Grants 2015/2016. www.blacksash.org.za/images/yourrights/allgrants_eng_june05.pdf. Accessed 4 Aug. 2015.

Bourguignon, F., and S. Chakravarty. 2003. "The measurement of multidimensional poverty." *Journal of Economic Inequality* 1, 1: 25–49.

Bradshaw, J., and N. Finch. 2003. "Overlaps in dimensions of poverty." *Journal of Social Policy* 32: 513–25.

Chambers, R. 1983. *Rural Development: Putting the Last First.* Essex, UK: Longmans Scientific and Technical Publishers; New York: John Wiley.

Dawson, N. 2015. "Bringing context to poverty in rural Rwanda: Added value and challenges of mixed methods approaches." In K. Roelen and L. Camfield, eds, *Mixed Methods Research in Poverty and Vulnerability. Sharing Ideas and Learning Lessons.* Basingstoke, UK: Palgrave Macmillan, 61–86.

Deaton, A., and M. Grosh, 2000, "Consumption." In M. Grosh and P. Glewwe, eds, *Designing Household Survey Questionnaires for Developing Countries: Lessons from 15 Years of the Living Standards Measurement Study,* vol. 1. Washington: World Bank, ch. 5.

Economist, The. 2015. www.economist.com/blogs/freeexchange/2015/06/multidimensional-poverty?fsrc=scn/tw_ec/the_poorest_quarter.

Eurostat. 2015. "Statistics explained. Income distribution statistics." http://ec.europa.eu/eurostat/statistics-explained/index.php/Income_distribution_statistics. Accessed 8 Sept. 2015.

Ferreira, F.H.G., and M.A. Lugo. 2013. "Multidimensional poverty analysis: Looking for a middle ground." *World Bank Research Observer* 28, 2: 220–35. doi: 10.1093/wbro/lks013.

Haughton, J., and S. Khandker. 2009. *Handbook on Poverty and Inequality.* Washington: World Bank.

Hulme, D. 2015. *Global Poverty. Global Governance and Poor People in the Post-2015 Era.* Abingdon, UK: Routledge.

IHLCA Project Technical Unit. 2011. *Integrated Household Living Conditions Survey in Myanmar (2009–2010) Poverty Profile.* Yangon: Ministry of National Planning and Development, UNDP, UNICEF, SIDA.

Klasen, S. 2000. "Measuring poverty and deprivation in South Africa." *Review of Income and Wealth* 46, 1: 33–58.

Laderchi, C.R., R. Saith, and F. Stewart. 2003. "Does it matter that we do not agree on the definition of poverty? A comparison of four approaches." *Oxford Development Studies* 31, 3: 243–73.

Marlier, E., B. Cantillon, B. Nolan, and K. Van den Bosch. 2009. "Developing and learning from measures of social inclusion in the European Union." Paper presented at Measuring Poverty, Income Inequality, and Social Exclusion—Lessons from Europe conference, Paris, 16–17 Mar.

Narayan, D. 1999. *Can Anyone Hear Us? Voices from 47 Countries. Voices of the Poor,* vol. 1. Washington: World Bank.

Neubourg, C. de, K. Roelen, and F. Gassmann. 2009. "Making poverty analyses richer–Multidimensional poverty research for policy design." In K. De Boyser, C. Dewilde, D. Dierckx, and J. Friedrichs, eds, *Between the Social and the Spatial: Exploring Multiple Dimensions of Poverty and Social Exclusion.* Abingdon, UK: Ashgate, 35–56.

Oxford Poverty and Human Development Initiative and German Federal Ministry for Economic Cooperation and Development (OPHI/BMZ). 2015 *Measuring Multidimensional Poverty: Insights from around the World.* Oxford: OPHI and BMZ.

Perry, B. 2002. "The mismatch between income measures and direct outcome measures of poverty." *Social Policy Journal of New Zealand* 19: 101–27.

Plavgo, I., and M. de Milliano. 2014. *Multidimensional Child Deprivation and Monetary Poverty in Sub-Saharan Africa.* MODA In Brief 7. Innocenti Working Paper No. 2014–19. Florence: Office of Research, Innocenti.

Ravallion, M. 2011. "On multidimensional indices of poverty." *World Bank Policy Research Working Paper* no. 5580.

Roelen, K. 2015. "Reducing all forms of child poverty: The importance of comprehensive measurement." IDS Policy Briefing 98. Brighton, UK: IDS.

———, F. Gassmann, and C. de Neubourg. 2009. "The importance of choice and definition for the measurement of child poverty: The Case of Vietnam." *Child Indicators Research* 2, 3: 245–63.

Sillers, D. 2015. "Is $1.82 the new $1.25? Choosing the next international extreme poverty line." USAID Economics Brief. Washington: US Agency for International Development.

Smith, A. 1776. *An Enquiry into the Nature and Causes of the Wealth of Nations*, Book 5, Chapter 2.

Streeten, P. 1981. *First Things First: Meeting Basic Human Needs in Developing Countries.* New York: Oxford University Press.

———. 1984. "Basic needs: Some unsettled questions." *World Development* 12, 9: 973–8.

———and S.J. Burki. 1978. "Basic needs: Some issues." *World Development* 6, 3: 411–21.

Torres, M.F., and E. Bautista Hernandez. 2015. "An inclusive proposal for the use of mixed methods in studying poverty: An application to a Colombian municipality." In K. Roelen and L. Camfield, eds, *Mixed Methods Research in Poverty and Vulnerability: Sharing Ideas and Learning Lessons.* Basingstoke, UK: Palgrave Macmillan, 173–96.

Townsend, P. 1979. *Poverty in the United Kingdom.* London: Allen Lane and Penguin Books

Tran, V.Q., S. Alkire, and S. Klasen. 2015. "Static and dynamic disparities between monetary and multidimensional poverty measurement: Evidence from Vietnam." *OPHI Working Paper No. 97.*

Vijaya, R.M., R. Lahoti, and H. Swaminathan. 2014. "Moving from the household to the individual: Multidimensional poverty analysis." *World Development 59: 70–81.* doi: http://dx.doi.org/10.1016/j.worlddev.2014.01.029.

UNDP. 2015. "Multidimensional Poverty Index." http://hdr.undp.org/en/content/multidimensional-poverty-index-mpi. Accessed 7 Sept. 2015.

Wagle, U. 2009. "Capability deprivation and income poverty in the United States, 1994 and 2004: Measurement outcomes and demographic profiles." *Social Indicators Research* 94, 3: 509–33.

World Bank. 2005. *Poverty Manual.* Washington: World Bank.

26 Inequality and Social Policy

Arjan de Haan

LEARNING OBJECTIVES

- To understand the importance of inequality and how it is different from poverty.
- To become familiar with the concept of and approaches to social policy.
- To understand why approaches differ for technical and political reasons.
- To learn how social policy success can be measured.

▲ **Brazilian Maria Nilza shows her Bolsa Familia social plan card in Serra Azul, Brazil. Bolsa Familia attempts to both reduce short-term poverty and fight long-term poverty by increasing human capital through conditional cash transfers. It is currently the largest conditional cash transfer program in the world and has been responsible for a significant reduction in child labour and a 20 per cent drop in inequality in Brazil since its implementation in 2001.** | Source: VANDERLEI ALMEIDA/AFP/Getty Images

INTRODUCTION

Global poverty has been reduced significantly over the last few decades, supported by economic growth and by policies that have benefited poor populations directly. But inequality has increased in many countries, particularly in countries such as China where economic growth has been rapid. In other countries, notably in Latin America, income inequalities are very high, and in South Africa and India, for example, social or group inequalities are a central challenge of development policy. Even in the poorest countries, inequalities matter, including those between men and women. This chapter will examine why inequality is important for development, and under what conditions social policy can be useful in addressing it.

We discuss the differences and similarities between inequality and poverty. Addressing inequalities requires a broader set of policies than addressing poverty. This chapter introduces the concept of social policy for that purpose: the broad set of public policies that impact the well-being of entire populations. It shows that the history of social policies is complex, context-dependent, and ideologically driven. A wide range of instruments exists, in terms of financing and organization, which can be targeted on individuals as well as groups. Social policy is subject to political pressure, and its benefits are not always distributed towards the poorest. Examining and comparing different kinds of social policy is important to understand and measure their impact on vulnerable populations.

WHAT IS INEQUALITY?

The Millennium Development Goals (MDGs) principally emphasized poverty reduction. MDG #1 called for the reduction of people living on $1 per day poverty. (The aspirational Sustainable Development Goals [SDGs] adopted by the United Nations in 2015 revised this figure upward to $1.25 per day in SDG #1.) This is an example of an "absolute poverty" approach, which counts the number of people living below a certain, minimum standard of living. In the MDG/SDG approach, this is a poverty line that is internationally established and comparable; countries also have poverty lines tailored to their specific circumstances.

How is inequality different from poverty? Is not a country that has, say, a larger number of people below a poverty line more unequal? The answer is: it depends. The extent of equality or inequality does not only depend on how many people are poor, but also on how many people are not poor, or rich. It also depends on *how poor* poor people are, and *how rich* the rest of the population is. This chapter discusses how important these differences are for policy-making, but first we explain the key nuances in how we can understand inequality.

Inequality of Outcome

Inequality can be defined and measured in two main ways: inequality of *outcome*, and inequality of *opportunity*. Inequality of outcome, put simply, refers to how wealth or well-being is distributed across a population. This can be measured in income, assets, land, health, education levels, etc. If in a population of 100 people, each person has 1 per cent of the income, this country has perfect equality; if one person has all the available income or land, this country has maximum inequality. In practice, of course, all countries fall somewhere in between these extremes.

A number of indicators describe inequality. Let's take the stylized example above to demonstrate these. The **Gini coefficient** is possibly the most commonly used measure. Its value varies between 0 for perfect equality and 1 for complete inequality. The Gini coefficient for selected countries is shown in Table 26.1. Technically, the Gini reflects the area between the line of actual income distribution, also known as the Lorenz curve, and the line representing perfect equality (the 45-degree line): the larger the space between the two lines, the higher the Gini. Global income inequality is estimated to be about 0.65. High-inequality countries like Brazil and South Africa have Gini coefficients of 0.60, while in many European countries it is 0.30 or lower; importantly, in the latter case, this refers to net income, after taxation.

A second main measure is **income shares**, based on a description of populations in, usually, 5 or 10 income groups (called quintiles and deciles, respectively). If a country is perfectly equal, of course, all income

IMPORTANT CONCEPTS

BOX 26.1 | How Is Income Measured?

This rather simple question, of key importance for both poverty and inequality measures, does not have as simple an answer as may be expected. In richer countries, a person's or household's income or what they spend can be measured fairly accurately. For most agricultural families in poorer countries, however, only a part of what they produce and consume is monetized (bought or sold on the market). To reflect such households' poverty or well-being, measurement focuses on consumption, with long lists of the goods such households consume, which are then converted into monetary value. This is how it is possible, also, to identify people living under or above the extreme poverty cut-off of $1.25 per day: this is not actually $1.25 of income, but instead reflects a bundle of goods that represent a minimum level of living.

Such measurements take households as their basis. This, too, is not uncomplicated. A household unit can mean different things in different contexts. Extended households, or households with migrants, for example, complicate measurement. Deciding what a household's minimum needs are requires assumptions about the diverse needs of adults and children. Finally, measuring the welfare and poverty of households does not tell us anything about inequalities within those households. In particular, it does not give insight into gender inequalities (see Chapter 5).

Moreover, such measures of poverty are static. A household's current income in itself does not predict the risks of falling into poverty or the possibility of improving well-being. There is research that examines mobility in and out of poverty or across incomes, thus taking a more dynamic perspective. For social policy this distinction is important because many social policy instruments focus on risk and (social) insurance—in other words helping people protect themselves against temporary shortfalls in income—which tend to be least available for the poor.

groups have equal income shares: each decile has 10 per cent of the total income. In the completely unequal country, the top 1 per cent has 100 per cent of the income. Mexico and Colombia are among the most unequal countries, with the richest 1 per cent of the population holding over 20 per cent of the total income;

TABLE 26.1 | Measures of Inequality in a Sample of Countries

	GDP/Capita (PPP $)	Gini Coefficient	Income Share Top 10%	Income Share Lowest 20%	Extreme Poverty Headcount $1.25/day (PPP) (%)
Brazil	15,413	53	42	3	4
China	12,609	37	30	5	6
Colombia	12,447	54	42	3	6
Denmark	42,777	27	22	9	0
Mexico	16,496	48	39	5	1
United Kingdom	37,614	38	29	6	0
United States	52,118	41	30	5	0

Source: World Development Indicators, online, most recent year available. PPP means purchasing power parity, an instrument to allow comparison of the prices of goods across countries.

in Denmark this is 9 per cent.[1] These examples—summarized in Table 26.1—refer to inequality across a country's population; as with poverty measures, this can also be used at an international level, as well as at sub-national and group levels.

How do these inequality measures compare to the poverty measures? While the two are not unrelated, it is not necessarily the case that more unequal countries have more poor people. This depends on two issues. First, how high or low the poverty line is set relative to the average income: in the imaginary perfectly equal country it is possible that all people live below the poverty line, if that line was above the average income. In reality, some low-income countries—like China in 1978—have low inequality and high poverty rates. Second, income inequality can change without a change in poverty rates: if income shifts from the top decile to the somewhat-less-rich, income inequality improves without a change in poverty rates. Or income inequality can worsen while poverty goes down, as has been the case in China, which harbours the big success story of poverty reduction since the early 1980s. China's poverty rate declined from 84 per cent of the population in 1980 to 16 per cent in 2005. Poverty reduction was directly related to the very high rates of economic growth, on average 8 per cent per year during that period. But inequality rose, too: from a Gini coefficient of 0.29 to 0.42 over the same period.[2]

Inequality of Opportunity

The three measures discussed so far—the Gini coefficient, income deciles, poverty rates—all refer to "outcome" measures. There are important political and ideological differences regarding the question of how much these matter. While many people would concur that Gini coefficients at Latin American or South African levels are too high, this does not necessarily mean there is agreement on the causes of inequality or on the appropriate policy responses. Economists have argued that inequality is an inevitable fact of economic life, as it is associated with the incentives necessary for a well-functioning economy. China, as mentioned above, which experienced rapidly rising inequality since the late 1970s, is a case in point: the reforms started in 1978 were meant to restore producer incentives and succeeded in doing so, at the cost of the previous egalitarian structure. It is important to stress also that there is no agreement on how much inequality is good for an economy. Chinese leaders, for example, thought the rising inequality throughout the 1980s was inevitable, but showed great concern when income inequalities started to reach Latin American levels.

For many people, what matters is whether "opportunities" are reasonably equally distributed and fair, even if outcomes are less equal. In fact, complete equality of outcome is practically impossible: people have different talents, or—even if they have the same chances—may apply different efforts to increase their income. However, most people agree that everybody should have the same opportunity to earn and improve their income, live a healthy life, become educated, etc. Similarly, there is usually a great degree of agreement that policies should help to create a "level playing field": not to make sure that outcomes are the same for everybody, but that everybody has the same opportunity to improve their situation.

Inequality in opportunity—deemed unfair—can relate to two things: differences in social treatment or discrimination, often related to gender, race, or ethnic group; and differences in conditions in family background and resources (social class). In a "meritocratic" view, inequality of outcome due to different efforts is deemed fair (or at least not necessarily unfair), and inequality due to different opportunities is not. For example, different performances in education (outcome) are not necessarily unfair, but certain groups being unable to go to school (opportunity) is. Measurement of inequality of opportunity is more complex than measuring inequality of outcomes. Most of the existing research has focused on assessing whether inequality in outcomes is due to discrimination against certain individuals or groups.

Individuals and Groups

Most of the above discussion on measuring inequality refers to individuals. An equally important question—often politically sensitive—is about inequality between groups, based on race, ethnicity, caste, and gender. These inequalities often have deep historical roots.

Boaz Rottem / Alamy Stock Photo

PHOTO 26.1 | While poverty in China has decreased in recent decades, inequality has also risen.

South Africa is one of the world's most unequal countries measured by individuals' income. Apartheid created enormous group differences between blacks and whites. At the heart of the economic differences was the allocation of land along racial lines, but discrimination existed in all spheres of social and economic life. Since the end of Apartheid in 1994, the group differences have diminished somewhat, partly

CRITICAL ISSUES

BOX 26.2 | Views on the Need for More Equality

The World Values Survey, administered in about 50 countries across the world, asks people if they think "incomes should be made more equal" or whether "we need larger income differences as incentives for individual effort." Respondents are asked to score these views on a 1–10 scale. This shows that in very unequal countries such as Brazil a high percentage of people do think inequalities should be reduced (26 per cent in Brazil scored a 1). In Chile and China as well, support for more equality is relatively high. In South Africa, on the other hand, support for reducing inequality is much lower. In relatively equal Sweden, there is still support for reducing inequality, more so than in the relatively unequal US. During the 2000s, in most countries public support for redistribution increased.

Sources: http://www.worldvaluessurvey.org/WVSOnline.jsp; IMF (2014).

because of specific empowerment policies, which we discuss below. But this has been accompanied by growing inequalities *within* the black population.

South Africa's group inequalities, rooted in colonial history, are to some extent unique, but Latin American countries' social group differences also are significant and have similar colonial origins. India's social group differences have longer and indigenous roots, even though colonialism documented them in detail and probably reinforced them. There are at least three marked types of socio-economic differences in India. First, "Adivasi" groups (first nations or indigenous—"scheduled tribes" in administrative language) suffer from deeper poverty, isolation, and lack of access to productive land. Second, India's caste system is the world's most complicated system of group differentiation, with "dalits" (untouchables, or scheduled castes) being most deprived both economically and socially. Third, inequalities exist between religious groups, with Muslims deprived compared to the Hindu population, and equally large inequalities are found within these groups.

Gender inequality is the most common form of inequality across societies. As previously mentioned, the standard poverty and inequality measures provide us with little insight, as these take households as the unit of analysis. But there are many other measures that show how women are disadvantaged in various contexts. Women tend to earn lower wages than men, including when they have the same jobs and levels of education (ILO, 2014). Earning lower wages often also means women are disadvantaged with respect to pensions, if these are proportional to income earned. In what is called the informal sector, or jobs marked by low productivity and lack of social protection, women tend to have lower incomes too. In rural economies, women tend to have less access and fewer rights with respect to land, agricultural inputs, and extension services (see Chapter 5).

A key aspect of gender inequality is women's role in the "care economy" and time spent on those activities (Razavi and Shireen, 2006). Social norms determine that women have greater responsibility within the household, in duties of cooking, care for children and elderly, etc. They often spend very long hours in these activities, and in poorer places this is often compounded by the absence of basic facilities. In certain regions, women are expected not to work outside the household. Where they do such work outside the household, they usually carry a double burden of continuing to have the main responsibility for care work, and their care responsibility often reduces any career opportunities that may exist.

Why Does Inequality Matter?

Why is inequality important? Two types of arguments, based on "intrinsic" and "instrumental" reasons, are usually considered.

Many people consider inequality as *intrinsically* unfair. In particular, as mentioned, there is a great deal of agreement that all people should have equal opportunities, and civil rights and the anti-Apartheid movements have focused on this aspect. There is generally less consensus about the moral case for equality of outcomes. National governments differ substantially in the extent to which they redistribute incomes: European countries do this much more than the United States, for example, and in developing countries redistribution of income is even more limited.

Second, inequality is important because it can have negative economic or political effects, so-called *instrumental* reasons. While economists argue that a degree of inequality is important for economic incentives, certain forms of inequality may also reduce individuals' or groups' chances to fully contribute to the economy. For example, research has shown that women's lack of access to productive opportunities reduces overall economic growth. This form of inequality is thus of great potential importance in low-income and rural economies. But, as a report by the World Economic Forum (2014) argues, countries marked by more gender equality also are more competitive. The reason for this is not difficult to imagine: when there are economic barriers for half the population, the economy as a whole is likely to suffer. Also, inequalities can have an impact on saving and spending patterns: rich people tend to save more of their total income and spend less of their total, thus potentially reducing stimulus to the economy.

Moreover, there can be political consequences to high or rising inequalities. Inequality can influence voting behaviour. According to the so-called median voter hypothesis, higher inequality—or the perception

imageBROKER / Alamy Stock Photo

PHOTO 26.2 | When women do work outside the household, they usually carry a double burden of continuing to have the main responsibility for care work, and their care responsibility often reduces any career opportunities that may exist.

thereof—is likely to lead to increased pressure to redistribute income. Higher inequality can also lead to direct protests: the worldwide 99 per cent movement is a recent example (see Chapter 6). While it seems intuitive that people might protest excessive income inequality, it is important to stress that these are usually complex phenomena. For example, the growth in protests in China since the early 1990s is often associated with growing inequalities. But research shows that they tend to be caused by feelings of injustice—often a consequence of corruption and land appropriation—not by rising income inequalities per se (Whyte, 2010).

Thus, the reasons why inequality matters are much more complex than we may have thought initially. The types and levels of inequality matter. Norms of fairness differ across countries and can change over time. In addition, diverse policies aim to address inequalities, as described next.

Social Policy for Development

In developing countries, policies have mostly focused on addressing poverty, particularly through a targeted approach, and with success. But these targeted approaches are also part of a broader set of policies and approaches that impact the entire population. We use the notion of social policy for this purpose.

Social policy is a broader concept than poverty alleviation. According to the Nigerian sociologist Tade Akin Aina, social policy analysis needs to focus on the:

> systematic and deliberate interventions in the social life of a country to ensure the satisfaction of the basic needs and the well-being of the majority of its citizens. This is seen as an expression of socially desirable goals through legislation, institutions, and administrative

> programs and practices. . . . [and] is thus a broader concept than . . . social work and social welfare. (Aina, 1999: 73)

There are no generally agreed definitions of social policy. In fact, the term "social policy" is not widely recognized in the field of development studies, where a number of overlapping terms exist: "anti-poverty programs and policies"; "human development policies," particularly related to health and education; "social protection"; and "social security."[3] Aina's definition clearly distinguishes social policy from social work and social welfare, which are generally regarded as more "residual" or reactive programs designed for disadvantaged groups, whereas his broad definition focuses on the role of the state in public provision of services to the entire population.

As with the different definitions of inequality, defining "social policy" is not merely a technical or academic question. For some, social policy is merely about measures to mitigate the negative consequences of markets and economic processes, such as temporary crises—often labelled a "safety net" or "welfarist" approach. For others, including Aina, social policies need to be broader, and they create the preconditions for market processes and even for nation-building. The first argue for a minimalist state, the second for a more interventionist state (see Chapter 7).

In this chapter, we include mainly health, education, social security or protection, and affirmative action within the discussion of social policy. For reasons of space, we do not focus on housing policies, or policies related to unemployment, labour markets, and minimum wages. It is also important to emphasize that poverty reduction is not only the result of social or anti-poverty policies: it is also affected directly by economic growth and economic policies, but for reasons of space these are not discussed here either.

How Much Do Countries Spend on Social Policy?

In broad definitional terms, social policy consists of—and data exist for—three sectors: education, health, and social protection. Developing countries on average spend about 4.5 per cent of their gross domestic product (GDP) on health, 3 per cent on education, and 2 per cent on social protection (also see Chapter 20). However, there is a large variation in how much countries spend, as Figure 26.1 shows for health and education (the graph includes "outliers" such as the Persian Gulf states, which spend relatively little). There are important regional differences: Latin American countries tend to have relatively high spending, and East Asian countries traditionally keep spending low.

As countries become richer, they start spending more on each of those sectors, in both absolute and relative terms. For example, many rich countries spend more than 20 per cent of their GDP on social protection alone. Peter Lindert (2004) calls this process "growing public": his in-depth study of the history of the welfare state shows that governments take increasing

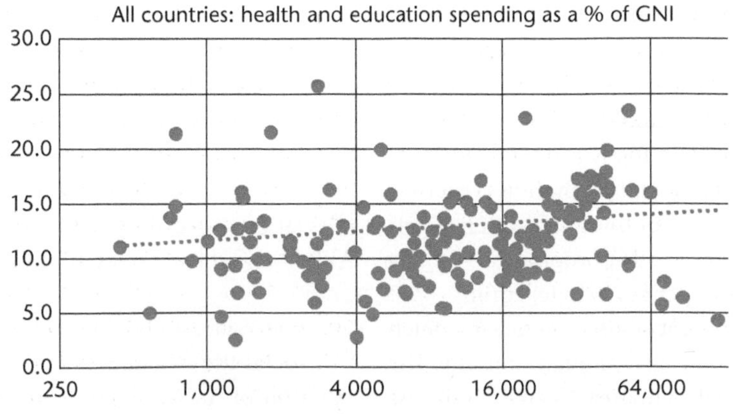

FIGURE 26.1 | Patterns in Public Social Policy Spending

Note: GNI logged.
Source: Compiled by the author, based on data from the *Human Development Report, 2014*.

responsibility for public welfare as their countries grow richer.

The data in Figure 26.1 show *government* spending. Although the topic of this chapter is public spending, it is important to put these figures in the context of private spending by individuals on their social needs. In India, for example, despite a public commitment to **universal health care**, the government spends 1.2 per cent of GDP, while private spending constitutes 1.8 per cent. High shares of private spending suggest access to services is unequally distributed, as the better-off can pay for additional services. While these inequalities exist in countries like the US, in poorer countries inequality in access is even more acute: poor people lack access to essential care, and if they have to pay for access, spending often leads to personal indebtedness.

Governments raise resources to pay for social policy in different ways, and this can have a big impact on inequalities. In high-income countries, a large share of government revenue comes from personal income taxes, which are often *progressive*, meaning that people earning higher incomes pay a higher *share* of their income as tax. In low-income countries, governments rely relatively more on indirect taxes (such as the value-added tax, VAT) and the taxation of natural resources. The low levels of direct taxation can be explained by the fact that fewer people in low-income countries are salaried workers and by weak tax administrations, generous exemptions, and low compliance.

To understand the impact of social policy on inequality (or poverty), it is important to look at both government spending programs (also known as transfers) and taxation. This can be done through benefit incidence analysis, which uses household survey data to analyze how much households receive and have to pay in taxes. In OECD countries, transfers and taxes jointly reduce inequality on average by 12 percentage points, from a Gini of 0.41 to 0.29 in 11 countries studied. In developing countries, this impact is much smaller: in 12 countries studied the net impact was a decline of about 3 percentage points (Bastagli, 2015; Caminada and Goudswaard, 2012).

The smaller impact of government transfers and taxes is in part due to the lower overall levels of taxation and spending. Also, developing countries raise revenues through indirect taxation, such as on consumption. This is often less progressive than direct taxation, as poorer people spend a larger share of their income on consumption goods than richer people. Finally, not all spending on social services leads to reduction of inequalities. For example, pensions provided to people working in the formal and government sectors, if supported through general taxation, benefit the middle classes rather than the poorest. Government spending on expensive hospitals in urban areas also benefits the better-off more than the people who live far away and are poorer.

How Does Social Policy Emerge?

Social policies develop under the influence of a range of factors (Gough, 2008). Politics is always a key factor, as we describe below. Social policies also evolve alongside major societal and economic change, often in reaction to major crises.

Urbanization and industrialization have played a key role in the emergence of social policies. Historically, for rural areas, public policies have often remained restricted to poor relief and mere temporary measures during droughts and floods. More permanent policies were thought to be unnecessary, as rural populations were thought to have traditional safety nets, particularly the support of families and sometimes of local community and religious organizations. Even for migrant workers, who moved from rural to urban areas for work, rural safety nets were seen by policy-makers as making social policy unnecessary.

Urbanization creates a new demand for social policies—even though living standards may be higher than in rural areas. This demand is not simply about (migrant) workers and growing trade unions claiming new rights. Equally important have been concerns of urban elites, including about safety. Urbanization can lead to new (infectious) diseases, making health and hygiene services a necessity (see Chapters 19 and 20).

Economic crises often prompt or create political opportunities for new social policies. The New Deal in the US was a policy response to the extended economic crisis of the Great Depression and the visible deprivation of large groups of people. In a series of both successful and failed steps, this radically changed the role of the US federal state. The UK welfare state, including its national health system, was designed during World War II. In East Asia, the 1997 financial crisis led to an expansion of what had been very limited social policies. Similarly, social policies often emerge from emergency relief, with temporary institutions becoming permanent, such as some of the major NGOs in Bangladesh (see below).

International connections can play an important role as well. European welfare states learned from each other's experiences. Germany and the Nordic countries industrialized later than other countries and started to introduce social policies relatively early in their development. In newly independent countries, while new social policies were often a central plank in leaders' plans for nation-building, practices and traditions of colonial powers continued to play an important role. In aid-dependent countries, international agencies play an important role in setting the agenda: while some have been criticized for introducing neoliberal approaches to the developing world, they have also been a main supporter of primary health care and education, and of increasingly new forms of social protection in developing countries.

Who Implements Social Policy?

In both developing and richer countries, diverse actors are involved in social policy implementation: private, public, and not-for-profit or non-governmental organizations.

In many countries private spending on health care, for example, is larger than public spending. This means that most health care is provided by medical professionals operating privately. Private spending, provision, and insurance are not usually considered "social" policy, but in practice these are part of the overall provisioning of services and hence should be part of an overall analysis of social policy.

In systems of universal care, services are provided by public institutions. Service providers are usually employees in government service, and government authorities decide what services will be available. In federally organized countries, states or provinces often have a key role in setting these social policies. This can lead to complex and overlapping responsibilities, as is the case in India where Centrally Sponsored Schemes implement health and education policies, sometimes bypassing the states that should have primary responsibility for those functions.

A third type of actor in provision of social services is neither public nor private, but includes various types of non-state, not-for-profit organizations. Historically, charitable and often religious-oriented organizations provided poor relief. Co-operative organizations provided forms of support to members, such as farmers and artisanal workers. A relatively new type of provider of social services is the social enterprise. These are distinct from charitable organizations as they aim to generate a financial return as well as a social or environmental good. They make their money from selling goods and services, but reinvest their profits back into the business or the local community (see Chapter 11). Such activities for the "bottom of the pyramid" (Prahalad and Hart, 2002) are often set up by large companies with the objective of reaching poor consumers: for example, Unilever (India) created cheap water filters for the poor. Aravind Eye Care hospitals in India were set up by an individual doctor, using cross-subsidization to provide health care to all.

In international development, non-governmental organizations play an important role, in a variety of ways. Some organizations play a role in implementing government policies or donor projects (involving international NGOs like Oxfam or World Vision), often operating in geographical areas where government services are limited. Other organizations have played a more independent role. In Bangladesh, the Grameen Bank and BRAC (the Bangladesh Rural Advancement Committee) have reached millions of poor people through micro-finance and other empowerment programs.

Governments also have a key role in *regulation* of social policy (to ensure that services are actually available even if not provided by government itself). Usually, this role as regulator is supported by independent or semi-independent institutions, such as elected school boards, health care councils or pension fund boards.

Developing countries often continue to have universal aspirations, but in principle the implementation is in fragmented fashion. In most cases, the implementation of social policies involves all three types of actors (public, private, and non-profit). As previously mentioned, India committed itself to universal health provisions, but private provision and, increasingly, insurance have come to play an important role, as government spending remains very low and quality of services is considered poor. Many NGOs are important in this respect, often serving the poorest communities.

The type of actor implementing social policies changes over time. European welfare states grew as states incrementally provided more services publicly, taking over functions that had been provided privately but also taking over or unifying services provided by charitable organizations. Governments keen to reduce the public sector's role in social provision often try to enhance the role of non-governmental organizations.

Social Policy: Fiscal Drain or Economic Investment?

A common concern about government spending on social policies is that they absorb large amounts of governments', and hence taxpayers', money. This is a concern not only because of the need to balance government budgets, but also because such spending may crowd out other forms of investment. Also, many fear that providing people with benefits—for example, against unemployment—will reduce their incentive to work.

However, spending on social policies is also an investment. While pensions are often a substantial contributor to government deficits, pension funds can play an important role for the saving capacity of countries. Investing in broad-based education is good for entire economies, as it leads to a better-educated workforce, and hence the potential for increasing productivity. The East Asian economic miracle was helped by a well-functioning education system. Similarly, public health is an essential condition for a healthy labour force and, therefore, for a vibrant economy. Public child care and maternity leave can encourage more mothers into the workforce, and thus is good for the economy as a whole.

Social protection, too, can play an important economic function. A well-designed safety net ensures that people—and human capital—are protected during crises. England's Poor Law during the period from 1601 to 1834 may have helped the country's competitiveness. The system provided basic benefits, improving health status. The benefits were portable, not tied to a permanent residence, thus enhancing possibilities of migration to find work elsewhere (Smith, 2008). Similarly, small cash transfers that are often feared to reduce work incentives have also been found to do the opposite, providing people with the means to search for jobs or diversify rural livelihoods (Mathers and Slater, 2014). Economies that are more internationally oriented tend to spend more on social protection: the reason is that social protection is essential to absorb the economic shocks that tend to afflict open economies (Rodrik, 1998).

Of course, this does not mean that all social policy spending is productive. Not all spending is "good" spending: there can be wastage and corruption. In many cases, spending does not benefit the poor: health spending can be focused on tertiary care such as expensive hospitals in cities. Many relatively poor countries have well-developed public pensions for civil servants, taking up a large share of public social spending; its benefits to the poor, and hence to economies as a whole, are limited.

The Politics of Social Policy

The relationship between democracy and social policy is complex. Amartya Sen (1999) emphasized the importance of democracy and freedom of expression in preventing famine. Non-democratic governments have expanded social provisions, too, and at times have done so effectively. Social policy also can contribute to democratization, notably through education and the norms expressed in the curriculum. This section discusses how political processes and development of social policy interacts.

Peter Lindert's study (2004) argues that economic growth and public spending are compatible. The welfare state can look like a "free lunch," and investments in health care and maternity benefits are economically productive. But, Lindert asks, how do governments make the right choices? Democratic process and political coalitions play a crucial role in ensuring that public finances are well managed and that they do not excessively benefit one group over another or distort unduly. Well-functioning political systems facilitate both the growth and the reform of social policies when these start to expand in directions thought to be unfair or ineffective. In this regard, democracy, in which the poor have a voice, is an essential condition for good social policy.

To understand how social policies evolve, it is critical to understand the politics behind them. This has been analyzed in detail for OECD countries (see Box 26.3). In democracies, leftist or social democratic

IMPORTANT CONCEPTS

BOX 26.3 | Social Policy Regimes

The way national histories and politics have impacted the shape of social policies in OECD countries is analyzed in the classic work of Danish sociologist, Gøsta Esping-Andersen (1990):

> A *liberal* regime, with its roots in the nineteenth-century English political economy, has a strong bias towards targeting of social assistance and a narrow definition of both risk and state responsibility.
>
> A *corporatist* approach is more common in continental Europe, where, historically, both liberalism and socialism have played small roles. In this approach, risk is pooled through membership, usually compulsory, based on professional status or sectoral occupation.
>
> A third approach is *universalistic*, based on an ideology of national solidarity and the idea of pooling all risks under one umbrella. Nordic social democratic welfare regimes—which emerged after periods of violent civil strife—have emphasized universalism. Trade unions have regarded it as means to strengthen solidarity across classes.

While such approaches are less distinct in developing countries, this characterization can be valuable in understanding the different approaches to social policy. In Latin America corporatism has played an important role, following industrialization in the 1930s, with social security limited to those in government services and large firms; recent new social protection programs aim to extend this corporatist approach. East Asian policies also have displayed such characteristics, while maintaining low government spending. South Asian policies show the history of English colonialism. In Africa such historical traditions seem least distinct, partly because aid dependence has a distinct impact on social policies.

parties tend to be strong supporters of progressive social policies. But non-democratic governments create social policies too. The German "social state" (*Sozialstaat*) was developed in the 1870s under the conservative government of Otto von Bismarck, with the aim of gaining support from the working classes and undermining the growing socialist movement.

In China, social policies are implemented as part of a strategy to maintain political power and to strengthen the idea of China as a nation (de Haan, 2010). Under Mao Zedong, after 1949, China built up broad-based social policies with guaranteed access to basic social services, although these policies privileged urban over rural populations. With economic reforms, inequalities in income and access to basic services—particularly health services, which were effectively privatized—rose. Over time, pressure increased on China's leaders—who since 1978 have focused on high economic growth and ensuring full employment—to address growing inequalities. From the early 2000s on, this pressure led to renewed social policy initiatives, which became encapsulated under the "harmonious society" efforts of Hu Jintao and Wen Jiabao. This happened as part of the Communist Party's explicit aim to continue to remain in power. It was a response to growing pressure and numbers of protests across the country. Finally, growing threats of epidemics—HIV/AIDS, SARS—helped to convince China's leaders of the need for public policies to ensure a well-functioning health system.

Processes of political democratization and extension of citizens' rights often are accompanied by expansion of social policies. Under Apartheid, South Africa's social policies discriminated heavily against non-white populations. Since the transition, a range of new social policies have been put in place or existing ones have been expanded. The South Africa Child Support Grant was introduced in 1998, replacing a discriminatory provision, and now benefits about 10 million children of poor families. In South Korea, economic transformation was followed by political democratization, which in turn contributed to expansion of previously very frugal social policies during the 1990s. In Latin America, the expansion of social protection policies accompanied the return of democracy, which followed a period of dictatorship; it was part of the "social contract" between the new democratic leaders and poorer groups, in the context of very high inequalities.

In democracies, social policies can play a key role in electoral strategies and debates. In India, "Abolish Poverty" was the slogan of Indira Gandhi's successful election bid in 1971. This was followed by the creation of numerous targeted poverty programs. The national employment scheme of the 2000s was associated with the Congress Party, while Prime Minister Narender Modi, who was elected in 2014, has focused on sanitation. Such political drivers can play an important role in expanding social provisions, but they can also lead to inefficiencies and various overlapping schemes. At local levels, there are often similar electoral promises, and co-ordination can be problematic.

The development of social policy is usually not only the result of contestation at the political level, but also of that among service providers and government departments. The establishment of universal health systems is typically (including in the China example mentioned above) based on a compromise between public authorities and doctors who had previously operated privately.

Social-political histories are thus critical in understanding how countries' specific social policies evolve. Within these, technical approaches can be distinguished, which we discuss next.

APPROACHES TO SOCIAL POLICY

The social policy notion used above focuses on provision of social services to a country's entire population, and thus has a strong normative character. In practice, provision can be achieved in different ways, and social provisions can be biased towards specific groups, for example, urban populations. Here we consider the main technical approaches within the field of social policy, keeping in mind that the definitions of terms can differ.

Social Security

Social security is traditionally defined, particularly by the International Labour Organization (ILO), as contributory health, pension, and unemployment protection. It protects workers and usually their families against the risk of falling ill. Employers and workers usually both contribute to funds, and this can be supplemented by governments from general taxes.

The ILO estimates that about 20 per cent of the world's population has adequate social security coverage of this kind. In Africa and South Asia this is less than 10 per cent. Social security tends to be restricted to occupational groups; historically, these groups have tried to protect themselves collectively against specific risks. Social security coverage tends to be low because only people in wage employment in larger firms or government employment have access to it. People working within agriculture and in the informal sector have no access, and in many developing countries the proportion of people in the informal sector has not been declining.

Efforts have been made to extend social security to workers in the informal sector, such as by the Self-Employed Women's Association (SEWA) in India. SEWA is based in Ahmedabad, a city that used to have a flourishing textile industry. It organizes women working in the informal sector, with 1.8 million members across India. It advocates for recognition and extension of provisions that are available to the formal sector, and sees contributory social insurance schemes as empowering. It also provides an "integrated insurance program" to cover the "life-cycle needs" of women, "such as illness, widowhood, accident, fire, communal riots, floods," etc.[4] However, such initiatives have remained limited, and they are not effective substitutes for well-functioning health systems.

Countries have continued to develop health services based on social insurance principles. South Korea increased the coverage of health insurance from 20 per cent in 1977 to full coverage in 1989, and in rural China a medical system based on insurance principles has been in place since the mid-2000s. In Ghana, a national health insurance system has been developed since 2000. Like other newly independent countries, Ghana at independence set up tax-financed health provisions, and it then introduced user fees (with exemptions) during the 1970s and 1980s. Since the late 1990s, and particularly with the elections in 2000, policy has tried to abolish this "cash-and-carry" system through the establishment of a health insurance system.[5]

Contribution-based approaches are often combined with free access to services or tax-based provisions. Costa Rica combines health insurance with free access to health care. Pension systems in many countries are multi-tiered, with a tax-financed pension for the entire population (which is a very important redistributive mechanism), company-based pension funds that allow employees to build up additional savings, and/or private individual funds.

Universalism

At the time of developing countries' independence, only small proportions of their populations had such social security benefits, and provisions to the rest of the largely rural populations were very limited indeed. Faced with such disparities, many governments set out to create universal provisions in health and education. This had considerable success, for example, in Zimbabwe and Zambia, where the numbers of health centres and schools expanded rapidly during the 1960s and 1970s.

The expansion of social services came to a halt with the onset of economic crisis and structural adjustment. Alongside insistence by international financial institutions on reducing fiscal deficits and enhancing efficiency, one of the most controversial changes, supported by international donors, was the introduction of user fees for health care. According to critique from organizations like UNICEF (Cornia et al., 1987), this led to a reversal of the progress made during the first decades after independence.

In transition economies, structural adjustment stressed the need to reform extensive social security systems, but in many cases political opposition halted such reforms. Chile has been regarded as one of the success cases in the social security reform arena, moving towards an individual contribution-based system. These reforms have been heavily criticized because of concerns that they would reduce access to services by the poorest, but they are also credited with increasing the country's savings capacity.

Partly responding to the international criticism of structural adjustment, donors have continued to emphasize universal provision of health care and education, particularly at primary levels. Many of the donor initiatives came in the form of "vertical" programs, including by now very significant private organizations such as the Gates Foundation, focusing on specific diseases (HIV/AIDS, malaria, worms) and groups (mothers, children). These vertical programs have had success, though, according to some, with limited attention to strengthening the capacity of health systems (see Chapter 20).

Targeting

Since the 1980s, the principle of **targeting** has become firmly rooted in policy practice, notably of international agencies that showed increasing concern to ensure benefits reached those people who most needed them (also see Chapters 24 and 25). Examples include India's public food distribution scheme. In the 1960s it established a food distribution system intended for the entire population. To reduce costs and to ensure benefits went to those with more urgent needs, during the 1990s this was converted into a targeted system. Now only people living below the poverty line can obtain subsidized food rations. In the late 1980s the World Bank introduced "social funds," as described in Box 26.4, to mitigate the negative impact of structural adjustment.

The focus on targeted poverty actions has been particularly marked in Latin America. A new generation of programs has focused on cash transfers to the poor. Programs such as Bolsa Familia in Brazil provide cash, allowing beneficiary households—with a key role for women—to decide what to use it for. Often, this is combined with an obligation to enter children into school and health services. The benefits are targeted towards households with an income below a defined threshold. Bolsa Familia in 2006 provided an average of US$24 per month for 10 million families with a per capita monthly income below US$34.

CRITICAL ISSUES

BOX 26.4 | Social Funds

During the 1980s period of stabilization and adjustment the World Bank started to look for ways in which the impact of economic crises could be ameliorated, focusing on people directly impacted by crises. The main approach to this was named a "social fund." The first of these was the Bolivia Emergency Social Fund (ESF), which aimed to address the social costs of adjustment for miners laid off with the closing of state-run mines. Social funds in Ghana and Uganda were set up in a similar vein. In 2000, social funds existed in over 50 countries, with total expenditure amounting to US$9 billion. They remained a small part of social security activities in most countries, but the approach has greatly influenced international development in social policy.

Social funds are provided as loans to countries, usually co-financed with recipient contributions to ensure activities have ownership and sustainability. The social funds serve as an intermediary that channels resources to small-scale projects for poor and vulnerable groups. They are institutionally distinct from government sectoral policies and services. The funds support local groups, local NGOs, small firms, and entrepreneurial projects within a set menu of eligible projects, thus trying to ensure quick and targeted interventions. Over time, the emphasis of the social fund approach has shifted from short-term emergency relief towards more general developmental programs, and also has become closely connected to community-driven development.

While the move towards targeting has been criticized by those who see it as a move away from rights-based universalism, targeted programs have been successful in reducing poverty, particularly in Latin America. They have also helped to reduce inequality: research has shown that about one-fifth of the reduction in Latin America's inequality during the 2000s was due to cash transfers (Lustig et al., 2013).

To make targeting work is not always easy. There are two main methods: one is *self-targeting*, applied through public works, for example. The general idea is that wages on public works schemes are low and/or work requirements so severe that only people who really need it will enter the scheme. In India, the Maharashtra Employment Guarantee Scheme operated successfully from the late 1960s, with the work requirement seen as key to targeting and avoiding dependency. This experience was used, and adapted, in the creation in 2004 of India's Mahatma Gandhi National Rural Employment Guarantee Act (MGNREGA; http://nrega.nic.in/netnrega/home.aspx).

The other method is *administrative targeting*: benefits are provided to households that meet certain eligibility criteria, typically having an income below a set threshold. For example, in Brazil's Bolsa Familia, in 2010, families with a monthly income of less than R$140 (about US$85) received R$22 for young and R$33 for older children. Families with a per capita income below R$70 received an additional R$68.

While targeting of benefits may seem desirable, it has a number of disadvantages. There are administrative costs to targeting, and it may be difficult in developing countries with limited administrative capacity. Inevitably, there is "leakage": some of the benefits are likely to go to non-eligible households. Targeting also can have a stigmatizing effect, as it singles out a group of people as "poor" and as "beneficiaries," dividing them according to specific programs and group characteristics. Finally, there is the question of political support, whether middle classes are likely to support programs from which they themselves derive no benefits (there is actually little evidence of such lack of support in Latin American countries).

Within the social policy literature, there are large differences of opinion about the desirability of targeting. On the one hand, targeting was promoted strongly, as mentioned, in the 1980s by the World Bank, and more recently, following the success of the new social protection programs in Latin America. Others emphasize the need for universalism. Thandika Mkandawire (2005) in particular has argued that universal social policy approaches have tended to go hand in hand with successful development and that the costs of targeting outweigh the benefits. In practice, most social policy systems combine universalism—or at least aspirations for universalism—with some forms of targeting.

Affirmative Action

Inequalities between groups are important in many countries and of a very different nature from inequalities between individuals. In many countries, policies vis-à-vis social groups have played a critical role in the development of the broader social policy framework.[6] For example, South African social policies since 1994 have focused on addressing the disparities created under Apartheid. Old age pensions and child grants have been flagship cash transfer schemes, broadening the previous discriminatory policies to include the entire population—while not affirmative action as such, the main beneficiaries have been the black population. The program Black Economic Empowerment (BEE, later Broad-based Economic Empowerment) was introduced to make economic activity representative of the country's racial structure, for example, through skills development and preferential procurement.

In India, support for deprived groups is enshrined in the Constitution and is delivered through elaborate administrative and financial mechanisms. Affirmative action exists in three areas: legal safeguards against discrimination; education and empowerment of deprived groups; and quotas, called "reservation," in government services, admission in public educational institutions, and seats in central, state, and local legislative and administrative bodies. Nepal has introduced policies to address inequalities for deprived castes similar to India's.

The politics of affirmative action is distinct. Malaysia introduced elaborate affirmative action as part of the New Economic Policy after racial riots in 1969, aiming to provide equal opportunities to the indigenous population. In India, affirmative action has become a central feature of many policies, even though they were introduced with the expectation that they were only temporary measures. Also, these policies have been extended to an increasing number of social groups ("other backwards castes") that claimed they were also deprived, and have been the subject of much debate and political mobilization (including at universities) (Shah, 2002).

Affirmative action is among the most disputed forms of social policy. While racial differences were made central in Malaysia and South Africa, they were not in Rwanda after the genocide, and China's poverty policies focus on minority-area regions rather than social groups per se. In some cases, it is argued that the focus should be on economic rather than social/racial differences. There is also a concern that affirmative action creates a "creamy layer," that the benefits—for example, quotas in universities—go to only a small group within the larger deprived groups. India's extensive system of affirmative action has come to lead its own life in the administrative structure and as part of electoral politics, arguably without equal attention to addressing discrimination in legal, economic, and social spheres, as has been the case in the US with its strong civil rights movement.

Social Policy and Citizens' Rights

The welfare states in OECD countries are distinct not only because of the extensive government involvement in providing social services, but also because these were introduced as a right for all citizens, defining a new relationship between the state and its citizens. Many newly independent countries also introduced social provisions as a right for their populations. India's MGNREGA has a rights-based orientation, with a guarantee of a number of days of work for everybody who wants to access the program.

While rights emerged from protracted processes of social contestation in OECD countries, in developing countries the achievement of those rights has been much more limited. This, however, is no reason to dismiss the notion of rights. Social policies are part of the way in which the relationship between the state and citizens is defined. In South Africa, social policies contributed to Apartheid, and after the end of apartheid, social policies have had a key role in addressing inequalities and discrimination.

New social protection policies in countries such as Brazil have been discussed in the literature as the formation of a new "social contract," part of the new democratic regime's attempts to enhance legitimacy through addressing inequalities. The political drivers behind such programs always imply a risk that a change in government could result in the end of the schemes, but thus far this has not happened. The maintenance of the program has been facilitated by its popularity among the large number of beneficiaries, which creates expectations and a sense of entitlement (even if not formally a "right"), as well as evidence that these schemes have achieved their intended objectives.

In Africa, many social policies are supported by the international community and development aid. In fact, under the Millennium Development Goals and supported by international summits, a large share of aid did go to social sectors, perhaps at the cost of supporting economic policies. Project funding in social sectors, altruistic and voluntary in nature, has led to improved outcomes. Often, however, these improvements have been achieved through setting up "project implementation" units, which have tended to function parallel to mainstream policy institutions and, therefore, have not necessarily strengthened the accountability of service provisions and state-citizen relationships. Developing countries often finance temporary programs with international support, thus avoiding difficult political and economic choices that are necessary for long-term programs. Sustainable social policy provisions and citizens' rights—or the progressive realization of rights—are closely interwoven. They are part of political processes and broader social contestation that generates support for social policy implementation and the taxation necessary to fund it.

CONCLUSION: MEASURING SOCIAL POLICY SUCCESS

Compared to policies for reducing poverty, addressing inequality is harder to measure and evaluate. It involves assessing changes in well-being of the entire population. Targeted approaches to reducing poverty can be assessed through measuring the impact on specific groups. This is not easy: for example, one needs to understand the counter-factual, that is, what would have happened in the absence of a policy or intervention. But the question of impact on inequality—and the broader sets of policies that this chapter has discussed—of course requires a broader set of tools to assess success.

In the first place, the financing of social policies is important. The way social policies are funded and implemented can be more or less progressive. Contribution-based approaches have large advantages related to political sustainability, but are less suitable for the most marginalized and those working in the informal sector. General taxation is crucial for building up redistributive social policies, but methods of taxation matter a great deal, and it is critical to assess the net redistributive impact of governments' policies.

Second, social policies are multi-sectoral. Good instruments exist to assess the impact of health and education policies and cash transfers. However, the well-being of populations and inequalities within these populations depend on the composite of these measures. Governments need to choose in which sector to invest their resources: as described, health care has tended to be relatively neglected. There are no hard and fast rules on what the composition of an overall public policy should be, but good policy analysis needs to take into account the impact of all sectors—of health, education, social protection, etc.—on the well-being of the population.

Third, good social policy analysis is also political analysis. It is important to recognize the political nature of social policy formulation, their constituencies, and, therefore, how these vary across countries. Ideological differences are critical, and are here to stay. For example, in some contexts inequality of opportunity is regarded as the critical criterion of a public policy, whereas in other contexts it is inequality of outcome. Similarly, social or group differences drive public policy and measurement in some areas, whereas individual inequalities are the main concern elsewhere.

Finally, there are no simple measures of universalism. Social policies necessarily imply a mix of universal policies (such as primary education or health care, in many countries) and targeted policies (such as unemployment benefits). They usually imply a mix of tax-financed policies and contribution-based policies, such as in multi-tier pension systems. Complete universalism, like complete equality, does not exist and may not be desirable, but it is important to develop a comprehensive assessment in support of the aspiration towards universalism.

SUMMARY

This chapter has sought to explain the importance of inequality in international development and how this differs from poverty. There has been growing recognition that inequality is important in low-income countries as well as in high-income countries, and it is of increasing significance in countries that have experienced rapid economic growth.

Inequality, as we have seen, can be measured. The reasons why inequality matters are complex, and may be more so than one might initially think. The types and levels of inequality matter, and norms of fairness and equality differ across countries or regions, as well as change over time.

In addition, diverse policies aim to address inequalities. The chapter introduced a broad notion of social policy, emphasizing that there is no right or wrong definition, and there are political reasons for adopting one or another. The way governments tax is equally important, particularly to assess the net redistributive impact of government policy. History has shown that governments over time are able to and have developed better instruments to address inequalities. But these paths and ideologies that drive social policy are diverse. Social policy analysis needs to understand the political motivations and constituencies, and the different social policy approaches that emerge from this.

QUESTIONS FOR CRITICAL THOUGHT

1. To what extent should development policy for low-income countries focus on poverty or inequality?
2. What are the advantages and disadvantages of using a broad notion of social policy, compared to sectoral approaches or those that focus on the negative consequences of economic growth?
3. What are the advantages and disadvantages of policies that focus on individual inequalities as compared to those that focus on group inequalities? Are there differences in this respect for low-income versus higher-income countries?
4. Do you agree that the development of social policy is a political exercise? If so, what does this mean for the role that international development policy can play?

SUGGESTED READINGS

Barrientos, Armando, Jasmine Gideon, and Maxine Molyneux. 2008. "New developments in Latin America's social policy." *Development and Change* 39, 5: 759–74.

Esping-Andersen, Gøsta. 1990. *The Three Worlds of Welfare Capitalism*. Princeton, NJ: Princeton University Press.

Gough, Ian. 2008. "European welfare states: Explanations and lessons for developing countries." In Anis A. Dani and Arjan de Haan, eds, *Inclusive States: Social Policy and Structural Inequalities*. Washington: World Bank, 39–72.

Mkandawire, Thandika, ed. 2004. *Social Policy in a Development Context*. UNRISD. Basingstoke, UK: Palgrave Macmillan.

Razavi, Shahra, and Shireen Hassim, eds. 2006. *Gender and Social Policy in a Global Context: Uncovering the Gendered Structure of "the Social."* Basingstoke, UK: Palgrave.

NOTES

1. http://oxfamblogs.org/fp2p/who-is-the-richest-man-in-history/.
2. See de Haan (2013) for a more detailed description and sources. This also illustrates the different patterns compared to India, where inequality rose less but poverty declined less.
3. Currently, the term "social protection" is used mainly with reference to the new generation of conditional

cash transfers, implemented with much success in Latin America. The term "social security" usually refers to contribution-based social provisions.

4. In 2012 VimoSEWA had about 100,000 members (www.sewainsurance.org/).

5. www.who.int/healthsystems/topics/financing/health report/GhanaNo2Final.pdf.

6. De Haan and Thorat (2011) describe these for the emerging economies of Brazil, China, India, and South Africa.

BIBLIOGRAPHY

Aina, T.A. 1999. "West and Central Africa: Social policy for reconstruction and development." In D. Morales-Gómez, ed., *Transnational Social Policies: The New Challenges of Globalization*. London: Earthscan, 69–87.

Bastagli, F. 2015. "Bringing taxation into social policy analysis and planning." Working Paper 421. London: ODI. www.odi.org/publications/9671-bringing-taxation-into-social-protection-analysis-planning.

Caminada, K., and K. Goudswaard. 2012. "The redistributive effect of social transfer programmes and taxes: A decomposition across countries." *International Social Security Review* 65, 3: 27–48.

Cornia, G.A., R. Jolly, and F. Stewart. 1987. *Adjustment with a Human Face*. Oxford: Clarendon Press.

De Haan, A. 2010. "The financial crisis and China's 'Harmonious Society'." *Journal of Current Chinese Affairs* 2.

———. 2013. *The Social Policies of Emerging Economies: Growth and Welfare in China and India*. Working Paper No. 110. Brasilia: UNDP, International Policy Centre for Inclusive Growth. www.ipc-undp.org/pub/IPCWorkingPaper110.pdf.

——— and S.K. Thorat. 2011. "Addressing group inequalities: Social inclusion policies in emerging economies' great transformation." *European Journal of Development Research* 24, 1: 105–24.

Esping-Andersen, G. 1990. *The Three Worlds of Welfare Capitalism*. Princeton, NJ: Princeton University Press.

International Labour Organization (ILO). 2014. *Global Wage Report 2014/15*. Geneva: ILO. www.ilo.org/global/about-the-ilo/newsroom/news/WCMS_324651/lang--en/index.htm.

International Monetary Fund (IMF). 2014. "Fiscal policy and income inequality." www.imf.org/external/np/fad/inequality/.

Lindert, P.H. 2004. *Growing Public: Social Spending and Economic Growth since the Eighteenth Century*, 2 vols. Cambridge: Cambridge University Press.

Lustig, N., C. Pessino, and J. Scott. 2013. "The impact of taxes and social spending on inequality and poverty in Argentina, Bolivia, Brazil, Mexico, Peru and Uruguay: An overview." *Commitment to Equity*, Working Paper No. 13. www.commitmentoequity.org. Accessed 9 Apr. 2013.

Mathers, N., and R. Slater. 2014. "Social protection and growth: Research synthesis." London: ODI. www.odi.org/publications/8663-social-protection-economic-growth.

Mkandawire, T. 2005. *Targeting and Universalism in Poverty Reduction*. Working Paper No. 23. Geneva: UNRISD.

Prahalad, C.K., and S.L. Hart. 2002. "The fortune at the bottom of the pyramid." *Strategy and Business* 26: 1–14.

Razavi, S., and H. Shireen, eds. 2006. Gender and Social Policy in a Global Context: Uncovering the Gendered Structure of "the Social." Basingstoke, UK: Palgrave.

Rodrik, D. 1998. "Why do open economies have bigger governments?" *Journal of Political Economy* 106, 5.

Sen, A. 1999. *Development as Freedom*. Oxford: Oxford University Press.

Shah, G. 2002. "Introduction: Caste and democratic politics." In G. Shah, ed., *Caste and Democratic Politics in India*. Delhi: Permanent Black.

Smith, R.M. 2008. "Social security as developmental institution? Extending the solar case for the relative efficacy of poor relief provisions under the old English Poor Law." Working Paper No. 56. Manchester: Brooks World Poverty Institute, University of Manchester.

Whyte, M.K. 2010. *Myth of the Social Volcano: Perceptions of Inequality and Distributive Injustice in Contemporary China*. Stanford, Calif.: Stanford University Press.

World Economic Forum. 2104. *The Global Gender Gap Report 2014*. www.weforum.org/reports/global-gender-gap-report-2014.

27 Planning and Appraising Development Projects

David Potts

LEARNING OBJECTIVES

- To understand the nature of development projects and their role in development.
- To learn about the sources of project identification.
- To discover the processes involved in project planning.
- To understand the criteria used for project appraisal and how they are determined.
- To be able to distinguish between financial and economic analysis and their meaning and purpose.

▲ **Fixing a road like this one in Papua New Guinea would help users but has no sales benefits so how do we decide whether the benefits justify the costs?** | Source: ARIS MESSINIS/AFP/Getty Images

WHAT IS A PROJECT?

The word "project" is used in many different ways, but in the context of development planning a project can be thought of as an investment of scarce resources in the expectation of future benefit. If resources are scarce they have to be used effectively, so development projects have to be planned with a clear objective in mind. A project has to have geographical and/or organizational boundaries so that we know what is included in the project and what isn't. A project is also time bound in that it has both a start and an end. Often, the end of a project as a project does not mean that the activities finish. It just means that they become part of the routine operation of the organization responsible for the project.

The association of projects with investment is important because we expect the early stages of the project to incur net costs to society but that these costs will eventually lead to net benefits. The methods used for appraising projects are designed specifically to take account of the comparison of early net costs with later net benefits. These methods include cost-benefit analysis, where project benefits can be measured fairly easily, and cost-effectiveness analysis, where valuation of benefits is more difficult, particularly in the health and education sectors.

Project Planning for Development

Projects can be undertaken by all sorts of organizations with different motivation. However, when we attach the word "development" to the word "project" it implies that the project is intended to contribute to development. The use and meaning of the term "development" is contentious and is discussed extensively in Chapter 1 of this book. For the purposes of this chapter I will use the following definition: "Development . . . implies the improvement over time and on a sustainable basis of the level and distribution of income and the physical and human resource basis" (Potts, 2002: 11).

A development project, therefore, has to contribute to development in the sense indicated above and its value should be judged on that contribution. We have to go beyond the simple measures of profitability used in private-sector projects to assess the overall welfare impact in a way that is appropriate to the type and scale of the project under consideration. This does not mean that private-sector projects cannot be development projects. It just means that development impact is not the same as private profitability. For this reason, when development banks fund private-sector projects, financial profitability would be regarded as a necessary constraint rather than the development objective. A development project must be financially sustainable or it will not work, but it must also contribute to development objectives. Project planning for development therefore implies the use of resources in ways that prioritize enhancement of the welfare of those groups in most need. In short, development projects should contribute to poverty reduction. This has implications for both the *design* of development projects (determining objectives and the means to achieve them) and the *appraisal* of their value (ensuring that benefits are greater than costs for the economy as a whole and that an adequate proportion of those benefits will go to the poor). This chapter will therefore pay particular attention to project design approaches and to the techniques of cost-benefit analysis.

The Role of Projects in Development

The role of projects in development has been the subject of considerable debate over the last 50 years. In the late 1960s and the 1970s there was growing disillusion with the results of macroeconomic planning in developing countries and regarding the impact of trade protection policies on market prices and related incentives. A number of major publications focused on the need to ensure the economic viability of productive-sector projects, particularly those involving substitution for imports (Marglin, 1967; Little and Mirrlees, 1969, 1974; UNIDO, 1972; Squire and van der Tak, 1975). Development funding from aid donors and development banks placed greater emphasis on ensuring the viability of specific projects rather than the contribution of those projects to wider programs. It was implicitly assumed that, as long as an individual project could be shown to be economically viable, it would contribute to development. The issues surrounding the economic policies of recipient governments were debated, but donor influence was exerted mainly through the choice of projects rather than the overall orientation of government policy. A great deal of donor funding was directed into investment projects and training planners in developing countries in the planning and appraisal of such projects.

In the late 1970s and early 1980s policy changes in the major donor countries, particularly the UK and the US, coincided with the declining influence of the Soviet Union. This led to greater pressure on aid-recipient governments to change their policies, particularly by reducing the role of the state in the directly productive sectors of industry and agriculture. Increasing donor influence on policy issues through structural adjustment programs changed the kind of projects that donors would fund, with an emphasis on the infrastructure and social sectors. The prevailing donor view was that most industrial and agricultural projects should be funded by the private sector and that investment in the social sectors, in particular, would be done on the basis of sector programs rather than projects. In the period 1975–9, 43 per cent of World Bank projects were in the agriculture, rural development, and energy and mining sectors, while only 10 per cent were in education, health, public-sector governance, social protection, and the environment. In the period 2003–7 the proportions were 23 per cent and 41 per cent, respectively (IEG, 2010: 7). Valuation of benefits in the social sectors is more difficult and contentious than for directly productive and infrastructure projects, and they are more likely to be planned as part of a wider program. Consequently, external funding of training in project analysis received less priority, and project planning capacity in many developing countries tended to decline.

By the late 1980s the legitimacy of donor influence on recipient country policies was more widely if reluctantly accepted by those countries, partly because they had little alternative. As a result, by the late 1990s,

SAM PANTHAKY/AFP/Getty Images

PHOTO 27.1 | Indian farmers pluck ripe tomatoes in a field in the village of Alindra. How do we know if a project, like a tomato canning operation is commercially viable? See how to calculate it, using the full schedule of tables available in the online content for this chapter.

donor funding packages contained a mixture of policy interventions and support to capital and recurrent spending in key sectors such as health and education. This program approach led to a decline in the relative importance placed on projects by donors and an emphasis on sector-based development support, partly because of a perceived weak impact of project-based aid on growth and poverty reduction "in the presence of poor policies" (Burnside and Dollar, 2000: 847). This change in emphasis was reflected in the Paris Declaration (OECD, 2005), which recommended harmonization of aid donor assistance in "co-ordinated programmes aligned with national development strategies" rather than individual donor-planned projects. A contrast was drawn between the so-called "project approach" and "sector wide approaches" (SWAPs). The "project approach" was perceived to be narrow in focus and failing in terms of overall coherence. The emphasis placed by donors on the planning and appraisal of projects was therefore reduced. However, the idea that a systematic approach to planning could involve *both* coherent sector strategies *and* well-planned projects seemed to be overlooked (see Chapter 8).

By 2010 a review of the use of cost-benefit analysis (CBA) at the World Bank (IEG, 2010) found that the proportion of World Bank projects for which CBA was undertaken had fallen from 70 per cent in the 1970s to 25 per cent in the early 2000s. Partly this was due to a shift in lending towards sectors for which CBA is not usually undertaken. However, although performance improvements were observed in those sectors that do use CBA, there was a general decline in its use. There also seemed to be a failure on the part of donors to recognize that, even if they were no longer using a "project approach" to define their programs, this did not mean that the investments did not have to be planned. A review by two IMF economists (Cordella and Dell'Ariccia, 2003) suggested that budget support was more effective when the aid program was relatively small compared to the resources of the recipients, while project aid was more effective when the aid program was relatively large. Less aid-dependent countries presumably have greater capacity to plan their projects effectively. While some projects fail even when they appear to have been well planned, the quality of planning can normally be expected to have a positive impact on project performance, so good project planning does matter.

THE PROJECT PROCESS

The most widely known model of the development of a project is the "Project Cycle," originally developed by Baum (1970, 1978). This model was developed for the World Bank and reflected the processes of that organization (Figure 27.1). Essentially, a project goes through the processes of identification, preparation, appraisal, implementation, and evaluation. The cycle is completed when the evaluation process leads to a new project idea and the cycle starts over again.

There have been many criticisms of the model for its simplicity and rigidity and the fact that it does not recognize the possibility of abandonment or termination. A number of alternative and more detailed models have been put forward (e.g., Rondinelli, 1977; Goodman and Love, 1979; MacArthur, 1994). Picciotto and Weaving (1994) developed a new version for the World Bank that emphasized participation, flexibility, and accounting for the interests of stakeholders. An alternative approach that relates project development to the various processes and stages but allows for modification of design as well as termination is the "Project Spiral" (Potts, 2002: 16). In this model the process of project development is conceived as a series of concentric circles that may eventually lead to project implementation but may also involve changes in project design or simply abandoning the idea. An emphasis is placed on the various aspects of the **project environment** in the

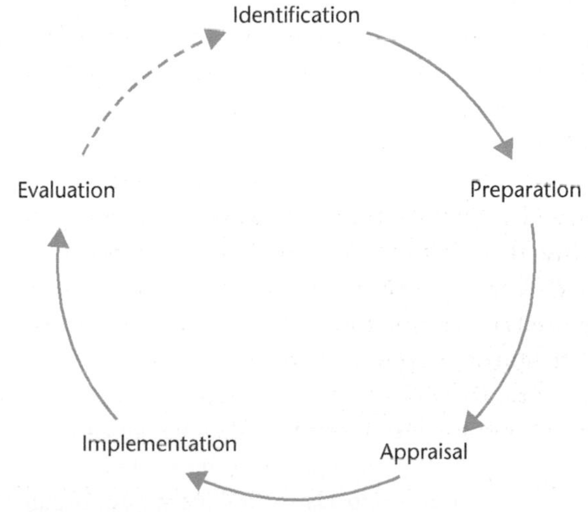

FIGURE 27.1 | The Project Cycle

Source: Baum (1978).

identification of projects and the process of project development. It is important to recognize that it is better to abandon or redesign a bad project than to continue to sink more and more resources into something that is likely to fail.

Despite criticisms of the simplicity of the original Baum model, very similar models are still used (see, e.g., EC, 2004: 16) and they may be well suited to the programming procedures of aid agencies. This association of project planning procedures in general with procedures that are specific to aid agencies has contributed to the rather misleading impression that procedures designed for aid programming are equally valid for the far larger number of projects funded internally by developing-country governments and other organizations in both the public and private sectors. In reality, such models are useful to describe some processes but may need to be adapted to reflect priorities and practices of the organizations concerned. More generally, projects can be identified and planned in a more or less systematic process that *may* eventually lead to project implementation but does not necessarily do so in all cases if at any stage of the process it is determined that the project is unlikely to succeed.

Identifying Projects

The project planning process starts with project identification. Essentially, project ideas are derived from the project environment. It is at this stage that the need for sector strategies becomes important. The idea that sector planning should be combined with more detailed project planning is not new. As early as 1965 Singer argued that development projects could not logically be divorced from their planning context. A project is more likely to succeed if it is part of a coherent program that identifies constraints to be overcome and opportunities that can be taken, as well as alternative solutions. Such a program often may include a number of related projects that are important if both the program and the constituent projects are to be successful.

Programs can be sector-based (e.g., a sector plan or program), but they can also be geographically based (e.g., a regional plan) or organizationally based (e.g., plans and proposals from government organizations, private-sector companies, NGOs, or community groups). Often projects involve partners so the project idea may be derived from the interaction of different partners.

A project idea has to be based on the existence of either a problem to solve or an opportunity to exploit (e.g., the existence of an underutilized resource). The process of identifying projects is therefore often based on problem-solving techniques or reviews of resource availability. A useful approach to developing project ideas was first introduced by the German development agency GTZ in 1983 and has been used systematically since 1987 (GTZ, 1997: 29). The approach was given the German acronym ZOPP, which can be translated as "objective (or goal) oriented project planning (OOPP)." The approach has been combined with a tool originally developed by USAID in 1969 called the logical framework (LF). The combination of OOPP with the LF is often described as the **logical framework approach** (LFA). A more recent explanation of these processes and their variants is provided in the European Commission's *Project Cycle Management Guidelines* (2004).

Assuming that a problem (or an opportunity) has been identified, the first stage in OOPP is to identify the relevant stakeholders, that is, the people who are likely to be involved in a potential project or those who might be affected either positively or negatively. The purposes of the exercise are:

1. to ensure that resources are targeted to meet the needs of priority groups;
2. to make appropriate arrangements for co-ordination and participation;
3. to understand and address potential areas of conflict in project design.

The next stage is sometimes described as "problem analysis" and is designed to allow a systematic analysis of causes and effects. One of the tools that can be used for problem analysis is the problem tree (Figure 27.2).[1] This approach is designed to identify the core problem that a project is supposed to solve by building a chain of causes and effects. The starting point is for the relevant stakeholders to brainstorm what they believe to be problems and then, collectively, to select a "starter problem." The problems are then arranged in a tree to determine cause and effect. Those problems that are caused by the starter problem are placed above the starter problem and those that cause the starter problem are placed below. The various problems are then connected by arrows to determine the hierarchy of problems and their causes. In the process of analysis the core problem at the centre of the tree might no longer be seen as the original starter problem, as those doing the analysis get a better understanding of cause and effect.

Once the problem tree has been constructed the next stage is to determine how the problems can be solved. This is described as "objectives analysis." In this process the negative situations indicated in the problem tree are replaced by positive outcomes that are supposed to be "realistic" and "achievable." The idea is then to determine the measures required to achieve those outcomes. The problem tree is replaced by an objectives tree in which the negative statements are replaced by solutions. In a pure project case this would simply consist of the activities needed in the project. However, in many cases other actions (e.g., policy decisions) may be necessary for the project activities to work. These may become conditions that have to be satisfied before the project planning process can start; otherwise, assumptions that are made, if wrong, might affect project outcomes.

The process of objectives analysis might result in multiple strategies to satisfy the intended objectives. It is at this stage that detailed planning of the activities takes place with the purpose of determining the most appropriate set of actions to resolve the identified set of problems. This is described as "alternatives analysis" or "analysis of strategies." In this stage the possible strategies that could potentially resolve the problem are compared and the most promising approaches are identified for further analysis. In the case illustrated in Figure 27.2, part of the solution might be a project to improve wastewater treatment facilities. This could be combined with a public education program, but successful implementation might depend on tougher legislation and enforcement (Figure 27.3). Whether the education program and the wastewater treatment facilities should be a single project or two related projects under different organizations is open to question.

In some cases it may be that a project is not the most sensible way to solve the problem, particularly if the problem is caused by policy failure or a shortage of recurrent resources, such as funding for the operating costs of a wastewater facility. In such cases the process would lead to recommendations for policy changes or an increased recurrent budget in specific areas. Only if the problem analysis identifies a need for specific investments as a critical issue is a project approach appropriate for solving the problem identified.

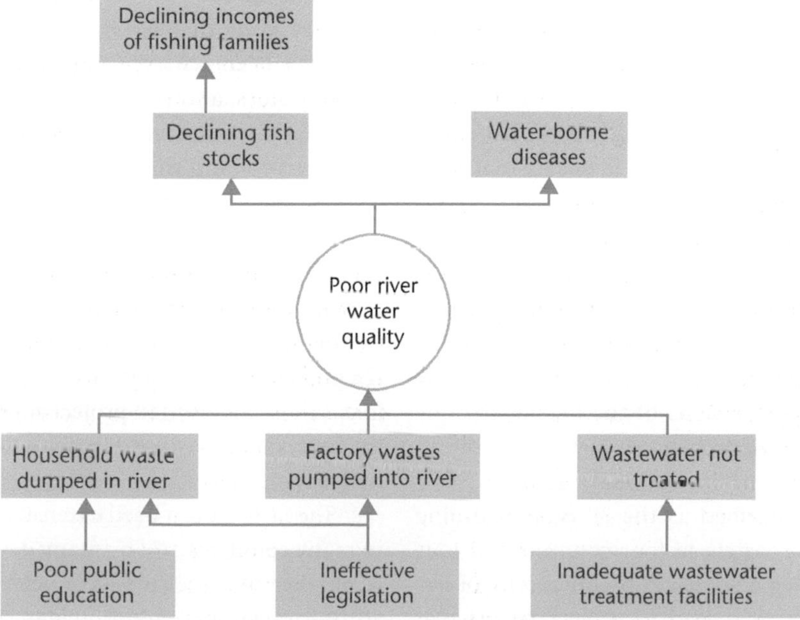

FIGURE 27.2 | A Problem Tree

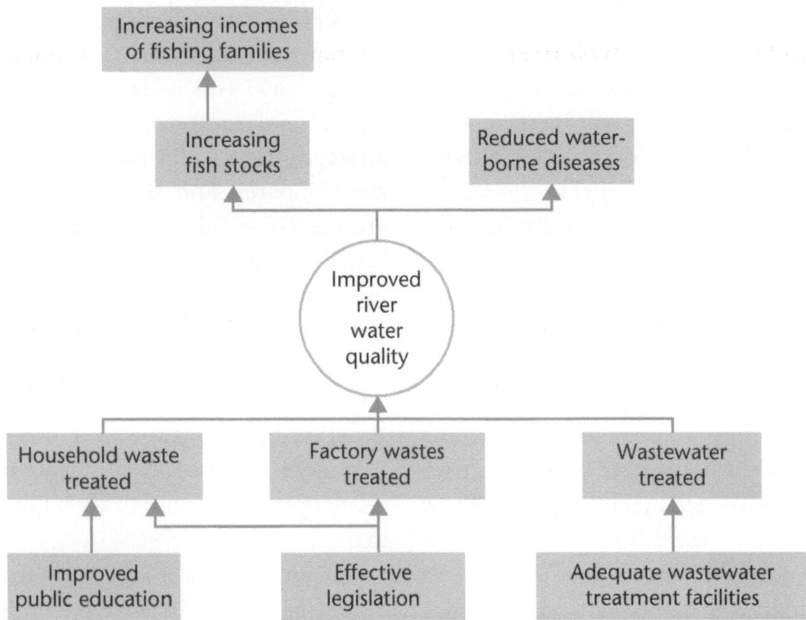

FIGURE 27.3 | Objectives Analysis: A Solution Tree

PLANNING PROJECTS AND THE LOGICAL FRAMEWORK

When there is a clear idea of the problem to be solved or the opportunity to be exploited, and when it is also clear that some form of investment is required, it is possible to start to plan the project. In doing this, the problem tree helps to define the measures to be taken by the project and may also help to identify particular issues that might affect the project but lie outside its jurisdiction. At this point an approach is needed to ensure that what is proposed is logically consistent with the defined objectives and to define what the project might be. The LF provides a tool that helps in clarifying project design. It is also the final stage in what has come to be known as the LFA, although it was developed earlier and can be used as a stand-alone tool.

There are various versions of the LF, but the one illustrated here is the approach used by the European Commission, based on the original German ZOPP model, originally described as the "Project Planning Matrix." The LF is a matrix of four columns and four rows. The vertical logic relates to the hierarchy of objectives. Project *activities* lead to project *results* that contribute to a development outcome or *purpose* that contributes to a wider *overall objective* or development impact. This vertical logic can be examined to ensure that the investment proposed in the project actually contributes to the intended outcome. If a project component does not contribute to the outcome, why is it there?

The columns provide a *description* of the various objective levels, the *indicators* that show whether objectives have been achieved, the *means of verification* for the indicators, and the important underlying *assumptions* that must hold if each level is to be achieved. The indicators column shows the most important things to be monitored during the implementation of the project and the means of verification column shows where the necessary information can be found. It provides guidance for the development of reporting systems for project management. The assumptions column highlights the potential causes of project failure and therefore informs those involved in project appraisal of some of the indicators that may need to be tested through sensitivity analysis.

The LF has been used extensively in many variants in many countries and by many development agencies. A number of criticisms have been raised in the literature (e.g., Gasper, 2000; Reidar, 2003; Bakewell and Garbutt, 2005). Some critics have described the LF as a

Project Description	Indicators	Means of Verification	Assumptions
Overall objective Improve family health Increase incomes of fishing families	 Incidence of water-borne diseases reduced by 50% Value of fish sales increase by 20% (date)	 Hospital and clinic records Fishing catch records	 Sustainable fishing practices adopted
Purpose Improved river water quality	National water pollution standard reached by (date)	Water quality surveys	Waste treatment process effective Public awareness campaign effective
Results Reduced volume of wastes and wastewater discharged into river	Volume of waste in water reduced by 80% by (date)	Survey of households and factories	Upstream river flows and water quality maintained at specified level
Activities Rehabilitate waste treatment plant Public health awareness program	New plant completed and in operation (date) program delivered (date)	Project monitoring reports	

FIGURE 27.4 | An Example of a Logical Framework: The Project Planning Matrix

"lockframe" (Gasper, 2000) that restricts creative thinking because of the rigidity of a 4 × 4 matrix. There are also questions about the terminology used for different levels and the number of levels in the vertical hierarchy. It is not always easy to determine what to put into each level. The version of the LF from the Norwegian Agency for Development Co-operation (NORAD, 1999) has five levels with "inputs" at the lowest level, and the indicators and means of verification are combined so that there are only three columns. There are also different opinions as to whether the assumptions column should only include factors outside the control of the project management.

The LF shown in Figure 27.4 is a simplified illustration of what is involved that also illustrates some of the issues that have been raised. In Figure 27.4 there are two "overall objectives." Some would argue, as in the original version of ZOPP, that there should only be one overall goal. This can be achieved easily by adding the word "and" but it doesn't address the point that multiple goals can lead to confusion about what is most important. Strictly speaking, the effectiveness of the water treatment facility is in the control of the project management, but this is a critical assumption. In some cases of complex projects with multiple stakeholders it may be difficult to fit the project into only four levels. Should we accept the general idea but adapt the tool to the particular needs of the project in question?

One of the most important points to be made about the LF is that it only ensures that the project is logical. It does not ensure that the design proposed is the best design, nor does it ensure that the benefits of the project exceed the costs. This is the subject of project appraisal.

PROJECT APPRAISAL

Project planning is essentially about project feasibility. Will the project work? Tools like the LF and other project identification and design tools help to make sure that the proposed activities of the project will contribute to the proposed output. However, if we want to judge whether a project is a good thing we need to consider four major issues:

1. Do the overall benefits of the project exceed the costs?
2. Do the net benefits to key stakeholders exceed their costs, i.e., do they have the incentive to participate as assumed?
3. Is the distribution of the costs and benefits of the project such that it can be said to contribute to the development objective?
4. Is the risk of failure sufficiently low for all relevant stakeholders?

To answer these questions for projects with benefits that can be valued without too much difficulty we need some of the tools of **cost-benefit analysis (CBA)**. CBA can be done from the point of view of an individual organization, group, or enterprise. This is described as *financial analysis*. It can also be done from the national economic point of view. This is described as *economic analysis*. Economic analysis can also be adapted to determine who gets the benefits and who pays the costs. This can be described as *distribution analysis*.

In cases where benefits may be difficult to value, particularly in some social-sector projects, we may decide to use the tools of **cost-effectiveness analysis (CEA)**. CEA can also be done from financial, economic, and distributional viewpoints.

Basic Principles of Cost-Benefit Analysis

The first basic principle of CBA is that overall benefits should exceed costs. This is a weaker criterion than the traditional economists' concept of Pareto optimality where a welfare improvement is only certain if everybody is better off. CBA has traditionally adopted the Hicks-Kaldor criterion that welfare improvement occurs if gainers can potentially compensate losers even if the compensation does not take place. CBA therefore allows for the possibility that there may be losers as well as winners, although it is recognized that in some circumstances it may be necessary to compensate the losers. The issue of the distribution of costs and benefits has some significance in such cases.

An important issue for CBA is the timing of costs and benefits. When investment takes place, net benefits in the early part of the project will probably be negative, and later on in the project life the benefits will exceed the costs. Where net benefits are initially negative and later positive, we have to have a means to compare benefits and costs at different points of time. The decision criteria used for CBA are based on the principle of time preference. It is assumed that people prefer to have benefits earlier rather than later, so the weight given to costs and benefits in the future is lower than the weight given to present costs and benefits. The standard measures used for comparing costs and benefits over time therefore assume that a *discount rate (r)* is applied to costs and benefits over time with the weight applied to each year falling by a given percentage. By definition the weight given to the present is 1.0 and the *present values* (*PVs*) of costs and benefits are calculated by applying discount factors (*DFs*) to costs and benefits in future years.

The higher the value of *r*, the more weight we put on the present in relation to the future. The issue of choosing the discount rate is therefore related to intergenerational issues such as conservation of the environment.

IMPORTANT CONCEPTS

BOX 27.1 | Discount Factors

If r is the discount rate and t is the year in the project life, the discount factor (DF_t) is given by:

$$DF_t = 1/(1+r)^t$$

If the discount rate is 8%, the discount factor for Year 1 of a project is 1/1.08 = 0.926 and a benefit or cost of \$100 in Year 1 of the project would have a *PV* of \$100 × 0.926 = \$92.60. The same benefit or cost in Year 2 would have a value of \$100 × $(1/(1.08)^2)$ = \$85.70.

In estimating the costs and benefits of any project it is useful to distinguish between three categories of costs, namely, investment costs, operating costs, and working capital. Clearly all projects also have some source of revenue, which comes from sales in the case of a commercial project. These categories of costs and benefits will be illustrated with a simplified example of a tomato concentrate project. All values are expressed in thousands of domestic dollars (D$).[2]

Investment costs are the initial costs required to establish the project and often include replacement costs for items that have an operational life less than the life of the project. Vehicles are replaced in Year 6 and the remaining assets are sold at the end of the project life in Year 10. This *residual value* is recorded as a negative cost.

For projects with outputs that are sold the benefits can be described as revenue. However, although all projects should have some benefits, they do not necessarily all have sales revenue. For example, road projects with no toll deliver benefits to road users but they do not have any sales. The distinction between the internal costs and benefits of a project and the wider impact on society marks the distinction between financial and economic analysis. In our example revenue comes from sales. Note that the value of sales is not always the same as that of production because projects will normally keep some stocks of output to ensure a regular supply to customers. In our example the stocks are sold off in the final operating year.

Operating costs are the costs incurred in running the project and can be *variable*, i.e., they relate to the level of activity of the project, or *fixed*, i.e., unchanged by the level of activity. Sometimes particular categories of cost may include a mixture of fixed and variable costs, e.g., maintenance and operational workers.

Working capital includes stocks of materials required for the normal operation of a project as well as stocks of finished goods (for projects with a physical output) and also financial working capital, mainly credit given by the project to customers (accounts receivable) and credit received from suppliers (accounts payable). Note that what is recorded as a cost is the increase in working capital because the stocks from one period are used or sold in the following period and are therefore recorded in the operating costs. Likewise, credit received or given in one period is paid for or received in the following period. At the end of the project life all the stocks of materials are used up, stocks of output are sold, outstanding credit is recovered, and debts are paid off.

Once the costs and benefits are determined they can be set out on a year-by-year basis in an **annual statement of costs and benefits**. This is sometimes described, for financial analysis, as a *cash flow* or, in economic analysis, as a *resource statement*. In this chapter the term "annual statement of costs and benefits" will be used and qualified by factors such as whether it relates to economic or financial costs and benefits and whether it is set out in constant or current prices. Normally, CBA is conducted in constant prices of the year in which the project is planned to avoid any distortion induced by assumptions about inflation. An example of such a statement for our project is given in Table 27.1.

It can be seen that net revenue is negative in Years 1 and 2 and positive in all subsequent years. What is now required is a method to determine whether this is a

TABLE 27.1 | Annual Statement of Costs and Benefits (D$ '000 constant market prices)

Year	1	2	3	4	5	6	7	8	9	10
Investment costs	4,050.0	100.0				100.0				–1,150.0
Operating costs		2,407.0	4,712.0	4,950.0	4,950.0	4,950.0	4,950.0	4,950.0	4,950.0	
Incremental working capital		430.2	458.0	24.5	0.0	0.0	0.0	0.0	–912.7	
Total costs	4,050.0	2,937.2	5,170.0	4,974.5	4,950.0	5,050.0	4,950.0	4,950.0	4,037.3	–1,150.0
Revenue		2,700.0	5,700.0	6,000.0	6,000.0	6,000.0	6,000.0	6,000.0	6,000.0	
Net revenue	–4,050.0	–237.2	530.0	1,025.5	1,050.0	950.0	1,050.0	1,050.0	1,962.7	1,150.0

IMPORTANT CONCEPTS

BOX 27.2 | The Net Present Value (NPV)

This is simply the sum of the net benefits in each year multiplied by the discount factor for that year:

$$\text{NPV} = \sum_{t=1}^{n} \frac{(B_t - C_t)}{(1+r)^t}$$

The NPV can be calculated using standard spreadsheet functions (e.g., =NPV in Excel).

good project. If we simply add up all the net benefits we do not take any account of the timing of the costs and benefits. As indicated earlier, one way of dealing with time is to apply the method of discounting. The most obvious indicator to use if the discount rate is known is the *net present value* (NPV).

If the NPV is positive at the given discount rate, the project is accepted. If the discount rate is known and there is no problem to secure investment resources (no capital rationing) and no problem of uncertainty about the values of the costs and benefits, the NPV gives a clear and unequivocal decision rule. For this reason it is regarded as the most reliable indicator of the value of a project both for yes/no decisions and for ranking projects (Belli et al., 2002: 217–19; Curry and Weiss, 2000: 55; Potts, 2002: 73). The NPV indicated in Table 27.1 is positive at an 8 per cent discount rate and so the project is acceptable at that rate.

If the discount rate is not known or is uncertain an alternative indicator can be used. This is the *internal rate of return* (IRR). The IRR indicated in Table 27.1 is 13.5 per cent so the project is acceptable at all discount rates up to 13.5 per cent.

The IRR is a measure of the efficiency of investment. It is common practice to estimate both the NPV at specified discount rates and the IRR in order to get a clear indication of the value of a project, but the NPV is regarded as more reliable because the IRR can be misleading when ranking projects (Belli et al., 2002: 222). An example of such a situation is the case of a road improvement project where the benefits are measured by vehicle operating cost savings. Assuming a situation of increasing traffic and a deteriorating road, the potential vehicle operating cost savings will increase every year and the value of the IRR will always increase if the project is delayed (Potts, 2002: 76–7). However, because the process of discounting reduces the value of future benefits, the *size* of the NPV is reduced if the project is delayed so the NPV can be used to determine the best time to start the road project.

IMPORTANT CONCEPTS

BOX 27.3 | The Internal Rate of Return (IRR)

The IRR can be defined as the discount rate at which the NPV is zero or the *switching value* for the NPV at which the NPV changes from a positive to a negative value.

$$\text{IRR} = r \text{ where NPV} = 0$$

The IRR can be estimated by estimating the NPV at different discount rates and interpolating, but it is easier and more accurate to use a spreadsheet function (e.g., =IRR in Excel).

Another measure that was widely used when CBA was first adopted is the *benefit-cost ratio* (BCR). This measures the ratio of the discounted value of benefits to the discounted value of costs. A project is acceptable if the BCR is greater than one. This indicator is generally not recommended, partly because different variants can lead to inconsistency and partly because, like the IRR, it is a measure of the efficiency of conversion of costs into benefits and does not indicate the absolute size of the net benefits (Potts, 2002: 69–71). The simple BCR for our project (discounted benefits divided by discounted costs) at 8 per cent discount rate is 1.04, which is greater than one so the project is acceptable.

FINANCIAL ANALYSIS

So far the analysis has simply measured the costs and benefits to the project as a whole. There is no indication of how it is to be financed. Net benefits in Years 1 and 2 are negative but we do not know how these costs will be financed. We assume that the project will be financed partly by the shareholders and partly by a loan from a development bank with an interest rate of 8 per cent. A loan of D$2.5 million is taken out in Year 1, interest due in Year 2 is accumulated into the principal sum of the loan, and the loan is repaid in equal total instalments of interest and principal over a period of eight years from Year 2 to Year 9.

To construct a financial analysis for the project it is necessary to draw up a *depreciation schedule*. In CBA depreciation is *not* included because the costs and benefits are set out in full in the years when they occur. However, we do need a measure of depreciation for financial analysis because governments allow enterprises to write off part of the value of their investment costs as a cost in each year of the asset life. It is assumed that buildings and machinery have potential lives of 20 and 10 years, respectively, and vehicles have a life of four years. It is further assumed that depreciation is calculated on a straight-line basis.

The values in the depreciation schedule are not needed for the CBA, but they are needed to work out how much tax the enterprise will have to pay. This is estimated from the *profit and loss account* or *income statement*. Net pre-tax profit is estimated by deducting operating costs, depreciation and loan interest from the project revenue. Interest includes unpaid interest on the basis of the accruals principle in accounting.

The most important schedule for the financial analysis is the *cash flow* shown in Table 27.2. This shows the flows of cash into and out of the project. Although the annual net cash flow can be negative in some years (in Year 3 in this case), the cumulative cash flow must always be positive; otherwise, the project runs out of money and will not work. Financial analysis is not just about profitability—it is also about whether the financial plan will work.

The return to shareholders can be estimated by deducting the value of their share capital contribution from the annual net cash flow. This can then be discounted to estimate the NPV and IRR to the shareholders. This is an important indicator because the return to the shareholders should exceed the return on their next best alternative investment—either the next best project or the return they could get from lending their money to a bank. In this case the IRR to equity (13.3 per cent) is very similar to the overall IRR to the project (13.5 per cent).

The example used is a commercial project because it illustrates a full set of schedules that might be required. Clearly, a profit and loss account is not relevant to a non-commercial project so the financial analysis of a non-commercial project would not include such a statement. However, a cash flow statement is needed for any project because we need to know that the sources of project funds will be enough to pay for the project activities. Running out of money is a very common cause of project delay or even project failure. Sometimes this is related to inflation and, in principle, financial analysis should be conducted in current prices. This introduces complications that are outside the scope of this chapter.[3]

Measures like the NPV and IRR relate the value of initial net costs to later net benefits and are relevant to activities that involve initial investment costs followed by later net benefits. Not all project activities involve investment so sometimes it is necessary to use different indicators. This is particularly the case for projects that involve changes in cropping patterns of smallholder farmers. In the project example used here it is assumed that the factory will get its supply of tomatoes from farmers who would otherwise grow rice. There is no investment of money for the farmers but there are changes in costs and revenue. It is assumed that tomato yields for farmers in the first year are lower than in

TABLE 27.2 | Cash Flow (D$ '000)

Year	1	2	3	4	5	6	7	8	9	10
Cash Inflow										
Equity capital	1,600.0	400.0								
Loan	2,500.0									
Sales		2,700.0	5,700.0	6,000.0	6,000.0	6,000.0	6,000.0	6,000.0	6,000.0	
Total annual cash inflow	4,100.0	3,100.0	5,700.0	6,000.0	6,000.0	6,000.0	6,000.0	6,000.0	6,000.0	
Cash outflow										
Investment	4,050.0	100.0				100.0				–1,150.0
Incremental working capital		430.2	458.0	24.5					–912.7	
Operating costs		2,407.0	4,712.0	4,950.0	4,950.0	4,950.0	4,950.0	4,950.0	4,950.0	
Loan interest			216.0	191.8	165.6	137.4	106.9	74.0	38.4	
Loan repayment			302.6	326.8	352.9	381.2	411.7	444.6	480.2	
Tax			34.5	145.0	152.8	161.3	170.4	180.3	191.0	
Total annual cash outflow	4,050.0	2,937.2	5,723.1	5,638.1	5,621.4	5,729.9	5,639.0	5,648.9	4,746.9	–1,150.0
Annual net cash flow	50.0	162.8	–23.1	361.9	378.6	270.1	361.0	351.1	1,253.1	1,150.0
Cumulative balance C/F	50.0	212.8	189.7	551.7	930.3	1,200.4	1,561.4	1,912.5	3,165.6	4,315.6
Return to equity	–1,550.0	–237.2	–23.1	361.9	378.6	270.1	361.0	351.1	1,253.1	1,150.0
NPV to equity at 8%	596.9									
IRR to equity	13.3%									

Tim Gainey / Alamy Stock Photo

PHOTO 27.2 | A farmer transporting tomatoes to market on a bullock cart in Puttaparthi, India. The return to labour from tomatoes is significantly better than for rice, but the amount of labour involved is greater.

subsequent years because they are a new crop. Farmers use their own family labour so there is no financial cost of labour, but there is an *opportunity cost* represented partly by the alternative of growing rice and partly by the alternative of other work or leisure time.

An important indicator for small farmers is the return per labour day. The return to labour from tomatoes is significantly better than for rice from the second operating year but the amount of labour involved is greater. This could imply either forgone leisure time or forgone income opportunities such as casual labour for other farmers.

The aggregate incremental benefits and costs to farmers can be determined by multiplying the individual costs and benefits by the number of farmers. In order to derive a measure of overall benefit to the farmers, an opportunity cost of D$10 per day has been assumed. Opportunity cost is an important concept for economic analysis. It is defined as the next best alternative use of a resource. In this case it is assumed that the next best alternative for a farmer to working on his/her own farm is to work as an unskilled labourer on another farm for D$10 per day. This is slightly below the return to labour for the rice crop.[4]

Having undertaken the financial analysis of the project, it becomes clear that a number of different stakeholders are involved in any project and financial analysis can be done for each of those stakeholders. This raises the obvious question as to whose benefits we are concerned about. The individual enterprise is primarily concerned about private profitability, but in our example we also know that if the project was not profitable to the tomato farmers, they would not have the incentive to supply tomatoes to the factory. Likewise, if the bank believed that it would be unable to get its money back, it would be unwilling to give the loan. The overall benefits of the project are shared between the project owners, the bank, the farmers, and the government, as well as the organizations supplying and receiving credit. If a project is to work, all of those parties would have to be satisfied with the outcome. In addition, if the government has to grant planning permission for the project and if the bank is a development bank, they may be concerned about the wider economic and distributional impact of the project. To analyze this we need to undertake an economic analysis.

ECONOMIC ANALYSIS

Economic analysis of projects is concerned with the overall impact of the project on the national economy. A first estimate can be obtained by adding together the costs and benefits to different stakeholders identified in the financial analysis. Most of these are covered by the annual statement provided in Table 27.1. However, we have now also estimated the benefits to the farmers. If we add the farmers to the analysis, the value of the tomatoes disappears because they are costs to the factory and equal and opposite benefits to the farmers, as shown in Table 27.3. It can be seen that the project now has a very high internal rate of return (22.5 per cent) and the NPV has more than doubled. Over 60 per cent of the benefits go to the farmers. From an economic point of view the project appears to be very good. It is profitable to the owners, and it provides a significant income increase to the farmers who might be regarded as relatively poor. The economic case for the project appears to be very strong.

If we believe that the prices of the goods and services used or created by the project provided good indicators of economic value we might be satisfied that the project should go ahead. However, before such a conclusion can be reached there are four questions we need to ask:

1. Are there any **externalities** arising from the project? One important potential question relates to the impact on the environment. Does the project enhance or damage the environment and how do we measure environmental costs and benefits?
2. Are the prices used in the analysis good indicators of economic cost or value? The most important issues here are the impact of the project on foreign exchange, taxes, and workers' incomes. These issues are generally taken into account through the uses of *shadow prices*.
3. Can the benefits of the project be measured in money terms? This question is particularly important for health projects since the benefits are derived from reductions in sickness and premature death. What value do we put on a human life or relief from sickness or pain? Similar questions arise in relation to education projects but are slightly less controversial.
4. How certain are we about the values we have estimated for costs and benefits? What is the likelihood that our estimates will be so inaccurate that they change the conclusion about project viability? The techniques of sensitivity and risk analysis can be used to answer these questions.

Externalities and the Environment

Measurement of external costs and benefits is one of the most important aspects of economic analysis.

TABLE 27.3 | Distribution of Costs and Benefits (Market Prices)

Year	1	2	3	4	5	6	7	8	9	10
Shareholders	–1,550.0	–237.2	–23.1	361.9	378.6	270.1	361.0	351.1	1,253.1	1,150.0
Bank	–2,500.0		518.6	518.6	518.6	518.6	518.6	518.6	518.6	
Net creditors		163.2	185.0	18.5					–366.7	
Government			34.5	145.0	152.8	161.3	170.4	180.3	191.0	
Farmers		21.5	428.0	428.0	428.0	428.0	428.0	428.0	385.2	
Total benefits	–4,050.0	–52.5	1,143.0	1,472.0	1,478.0	1,378.0	1,478.0	1,478.0	1,981.2	1,150.0
NPV at 8%	3,253.4									
IRR	22.5%									

Externalities can be defined as benefits or costs that are imposed by a project on another group without an equivalent charge for benefits or compensation for costs. For some sectors, such as roads, benefits may be entirely in the form of externalities. These include the benefits of vehicle operating cost savings, time savings, and reduced accidents, as well as any effects on overall economic activity. Measurement of the benefits of transport projects is not particularly problematic in principle, although forecasts of traffic can be subject to considerable uncertainty[5] and tracing the effects of traffic changes on air pollution can be difficult when traffic may be diverted from one route to another. Most large-scale transport projects are subject to some form of economic CBA in which the measurement of external benefits is often the most important exercise.

Environmental externalities are more important for some sectors than others. Energy projects are particularly likely to require some form of environmental assessment, as are most water projects. Industrial projects often have implications for air and water quality. Agricultural projects can involve water pollution from agro-chemicals and damage to watersheds from forest clearance. Environmental assessment in CBA is concerned with measuring the effects and allocating a value to them.

The basic principles underlying environmental valuation relate to the reasons why an environmental resource might be considered to have some value and the effect of the project on that value. Environmental values can be divided into use value (e.g., alternative uses of land) and non-use value, where a resource is valued for reasons not related to its use that may include moral issues such as the right of rare species of animal to exist (World Bank, 1998: 3). Clearly, measurement of environmental values in economic terms is much less problematic when it is based on measurable use values. The general rule for economic analysis is to measure and value what is possible and to give a qualitative assessment of those issues that are important but not easily measured. Approaches to the measurement of environmental externalities are often related to issues of compensation for environmental damage. If a project is likely to damage the environment, what form of compensation measures should be undertaken and who should pay? In principle the polluter should pay, but it is not always easy to enforce this rule and it is not always easy to measure the cost. If the polluter does pay, some of the costs may be passed on to consumers through higher prices. Anand (2012) provides a summary of some of the issues and approaches to environmental valuation.

Shadow Prices

Much of the early literature relating to CBA in a developing-country context related to the use of shadow prices. In particular, it was believed that a typical developing country was characterized by foreign exchange shortages, high levels of unemployment or underemployment of unskilled labour, and high levels of taxes on trade, including import duties to protect import substitution industries and taxes on primary commodity exports. It was argued that the official exchange rate undervalued foreign exchange costs and benefits, taxes distorted the economic values of traded goods, and minimum wage levels overstated the opportunity cost of unskilled labour in the formal sector. It was therefore necessary to make the following adjustments to the analysis of projects at market prices:

1. Adjust all foreign exchange costs and benefits upward to take account of the relative scarcity of foreign exchange using a *shadow exchange rate* (SER). This is usually expressed as a ratio of the SER to the official exchange rate.
2. Remove all elements of tax from the prices since taxes are transfers from the taxpayer to the government, not real resource costs. The shadow price for taxes is therefore zero by definition.
3. Adjust formal-sector unskilled labour costs downward to take account of unemployment and underemployment using a *shadow wage rate* (SWR); this is usually expressed as a ratio of the SWR to the average market price of unskilled labour in the formal sector.

Essentially this process was intended to ensure that the shadow prices used would represent the opportunity costs of the resource concerned. This kind of analysis can be very informative in identifying the economic value of a project to the nation, as well as indirect distributive impacts, but it can also be quite demanding in terms of data requirements.

COST-EFFECTIVENESS ANALYSIS AND THE SOCIAL SECTORS

CBA is not necessarily feasible for all projects. This applies particularly to the health sector, where CBA would require the estimation of values for human life and relief of suffering, but it also relates to other areas such as primary education where universal public provision is regarded as a policy goal. The question is not whether to provide the service but how to use the available resources as efficiently as possible. There are two main approaches to cost-effectiveness analysis (CEA). The first can be described as the "efficiency approach," where the objective is to achieve the maximum output for a given budget. The second is the "economy approach," where the objective is to achieve a given target for the minimum cost.

SENSITIVITY AND RISK ANALYSIS

All forms of project analysis make assumptions about the future, which is inherently uncertain. It is therefore clear that any of the estimates that go into CBA or CEA have a margin of error. No analysis of a project is complete without testing some of the main assumptions. What percentage change in the value of the benefits reduces the NPV to zero? How sensitive is the project result to changes in the most important cost items? How sensitive is the project to delay? In principle, sensitivity analysis should be conducted for all the most important variables. Decisions can then be made on the basis of information on the potential benefits of a project balanced by knowledge of the potential risks if some outcomes differ from what was assumed in the plan.

SUMMARY

This chapter introduced the definition of a development project and some of the debates about the relative importance of projects in development planning. It was argued that, while such projects need to be planned in a wider sector context, it remains important that project investments are identified and planned in a systematic way and appraised to ensure that they make a positive contribution. Some of the useful tools for planning and designing projects are included in the logical framework approach, which has been used by many development agencies. Projects in different sectors can be appraised using the techniques of CBA and CEA. The first stage in CBA is to set out the costs and benefits at market prices to determine potential overall viability. This can then be further refined into a financial analysis to determine the financial profitability of commercial projects and to ensure that the financial plan of any project will work. To determine whether a project is a good thing from the national point of view, it is necessary to consider potential external costs and benefits, including those associated with environmental impact. It is also necessary to undertake an economic analysis using shadow prices if market prices are not perceived to reflect economic costs or values. In the process it is possible to undertake a distribution analysis to determine whether the benefits go to target groups, particularly those that are relatively poor. For some sectors, particularly in the social sectors where benefits may be difficult to value, it may not be possible to do CBA. In such cases it may be possible to undertake CEA to ensure that expenditure is relevant and efficient. Finally, it is important to account for the margin of error in the estimates made to determine whether the risk of failure is excessively high.

QUESTIONS FOR CRITICAL THOUGHT

1. What defines a project as a development project?
2. Is detailed project planning useful or is it a waste of time and money?
3. Does the LFA provide a helpful way to design a project? What are its weaknesses?
4. Is it practically possible to take account of environmental costs and benefits in CBA?
5. Is the use of shadow prices necessary in a world of liberalized markets?
6. Can CEA provide an effective way to prioritize spending in the social sectors?

SUGGESTED READINGS

Curry, Steve, and John Weiss. 2000. *Project Analysis in Developing Countries*. London: Macmillan.

Belli, Pedro, Jock Anderson, Howard Barnum, John Dixon, and Jee-Peng Tan. 2002. *Economic Analysis of Investment Operations*. Washington: World Bank. (1998 version available at www.d-ria.ru/blog/wp-content /uploads/2010/11/WBHandbookEA.pdf.)

European Commission. 2004. *Aid Delivery Methods: Volume 1, Project Cycle Management Guidelines*. Brussels: EC. http://ec.europa.eu/europeaid/sites/devco/ files/methodology-aid-delivery-methods-project-cycle-management-200403_en_2.pdf.

Potts, David. 2002. *Project Planning and Analysis for Development*. Boulder, Colo.: Lynne Rienner

Weiss, John, and David Potts, eds. 2012. *Current Issues in Project Analysis for Development*. Cheltenham, UK: Edward Elgar.

NOTES

1. The example used in Figures 27.2, 27.3, and 27.4 is a simplified derivation of a more comprehensive example used in EC (2004).
2. Only the summary tables are included here. Spreadsheet tables for the example project described below can be accessed from the Oxford University Press Canada website for this volume. A spreadsheet example also is provided in Campbell and Brown (2003).
3. For a more detailed discussion of some of these issues, see Potts (1996, 2002: ch. 16).
4. For more detailed discussions of issues related to assessment of costs and benefits to farmers, the classic source is Gittinger (1982). Another useful source is FAO (1995). See also Potts (2002: ch. 6).
5. A useful source of information on appraisal of road projects is a series of notes that can be found at http://web.worldbank.org/WBSITE/EXTERNAL/TOPICS/EXTTRANSPORT/0,,contentMDK:20457194~menuPK:1323557~pagePK:210058~piPK:210062~theSitePK:337116,00.html. TRRL (1988) is also useful for general principles.

BIBLIOGRAPHY

Anand, P.B. 2012. "Environmental valuation." In John Weiss and David Potts, eds, *Current Issues in Project Analysis for Development*. Cheltenham, UK: Edward Elgar.

Bakewell, O., and A. Garbutt. 2005. *The Use and Abuse of the Logical Framework Approach*. Stockholm: Swedish International Development Cooperation Agency. www.intrac.org/data/files/resources/518/The-Use-and-Abuse-of-the-Logical-Framework-Approach.pdf.

Baum, W. 1978. "The World Bank Project Cycle." *Finance and Development* 15, 4, 10–17.

Burnside, C., and D. Dollar. 2000. "Aid, policies, and growth." *American Economic Review* 90, 4: 847–68

Campbell, H., and R. Brown. 2003. *Benefit-Cost Analysis*. Cambridge: Cambridge University Press

Cordella, T., and G. Dell'Ariccia. 2003. "Budget support versus project aid." IMF Working Paper WP/03/88. www.imf.org/external/pubs/ft/wp/2003/wp0388.pdf.

Dale, R. 2003. "The Logical Framework: An easy escape, a straightjacket, or a useful planning tool?" *Development in Practice* 13, 1: 57–70

European Commission (EC). 2004. *Project Cycle Management Guidelines*. Brussels: Europe Aid Cooperation Office. https://ec.europa.eu/europeaid/sites/devco/files /methodology-aid-delivery-methods-project-cycle-management-200403_en_2.pdf.

Food and Agriculture Organization (FAO). 1995. *Guideline for the Design of Agricultural Investment Projects*. FAO Investment Centre Technical Paper No. 7. Rome: FAO. ftp://ftp.fao.org/docrep/fao/008/v4810e/v4810e00.pdf

GTZ. 1997. *ZOPP—Objectives-oriented Project Planning: A Planning Guide for New and Ongoing projects and Programmes*. Eschborn: GTZ. http://gametlibrary .worldbank.org/FILES/194_Guidelines%20for%20 Project%20Planning%20using%20ZOPP%20-%20GTZ.pdf.

Gasper, D. 2000. "Evaluating the 'Logical Framework Approach': Towards learning-oriented development evaluation." *Public Administration and Development* 20, 1: 17–28.

Gittinger, J.P. 1982. *Economic Analysis of Agricultural Projects*. Baltimore: Johns Hopkins University Press.

Goodman, L., and R. Love. 1979. *Management of Development Projects: An International Case Study Approach*. Oxford: Pergamon.

Independent Evaluation Group (IEG). 2010. *Cost Benefit Analysis in World Bank Projects*. Washington: World Bank. http://ieg.worldbank.org/Data/reports/chapters/cba_full_report1.pdf.

Little, I., and J. Mirrlees. 1969. *Manual of Industrial Project Analysis in Developing Countries*, vol. 2. Paris: OECD.

——— and ———. 1974. *Project Appraisal and Planning for Developing Countries*. London: Heinemann.

MacArthur, J. 1994. "The project sequence: A composite view of the project cycle." In J. MacArthur and J. Weiss, eds, *Agriculture, Projects and Development*. Aldershot, UK: Avebury

Murray-Webster, R., and P. Simon. 2007. *Starting Out in Project Management*. High Wycombe, UK: APM Publishing.

Norwegian Agency for Development Co-operation (NORAD). 1999. *The Logical Framework Approach (LFA): Handbook for Objectives Oriented Project Planning*. Oslo: NORAD. www.ccop.or.th/ppm/document/home/LFA%20by%20NORAD%20Handbook.pdf.

Organisation for Economic Co-operation and Development (OECD). 2005. *The Paris Declaration on Aid Effectiveness and the Accra Agenda for Action*. www.oecd.org/dac/effectiveness/45827300.pdf.

Picciotto, R., and R. Weaving. 1994. "A new project cycle for the World Bank." *Finance and Development* 31, 4.

Potts, D. 1996. "When prices change: Consistency in the financial analysis of projects." *Project Appraisal* 11, 1: 27–40.

Rondinelli, D., ed. 1977. *Planning Development Projects*. Stroudsburg, Penn.: Dowden, Hutchinson and Ross

Squire, L., and H. van der Tak. 1975. *Economic Analysis of Projects*. Washington: World Bank.

Transport and Road Research Laboratory (TRRL). 1988. *Overseas Road Note No. 5: A Guide to Road Project Appraisal*. Crowthorne, UK: Transport and Road Research Laboratory. www.transport-links.org/transport_links/filearea/publications/1_701_Overseas%20Road%20Note%2005.PDF.

United Nations Industrial Development Organization (UNIDO). 1972. *Guidelines for Project Evaluation*. New York: United Nations.

World Bank Environment Department. 1998. "Economic analysis and environmental assessment." Environmental Assessment Sourcebook Update Number 23, Apr. http://siteresources.worldbank.org/INTSAFEPOL/1142947-1118039018606/20526257/Update23EconomicAnalysisAndEAApril1998.pdf.

28 Humanitarian Assistance and Intervention

Laura Hammond

LEARNING OBJECTIVES

- To learn about the history of humanitarianism and its emergence as a field of practice and study.
- To understand the ways that humanitarianism—in both theory and practice—borrows from development yet is also in many ways distinctive.
- To discover the assumptions that underlie humanitarianism and the challenges it faces.
- To appreciate the ethical dilemmas inherent in humanitarian action.
- To understand how humanitarianism relates to wider questions about political economy, globalization, and international relations.

▲ **A young boy receives a box of food from an employee of the United Arab Emirates (UAE) Red Crescent at a distribution centre in Afgoye, Somalia. Over 5,000 internally displaced persons were given food by this humanitarian organization during the mission.** | Source: AFP/Stringer/Getty Images

INTRODUCTION

Humanitarian assistance and the associated subject of humanitarian intervention are often seen as being related to, though still distinct from, development practice. This chapter will consider the points of continuity and disjuncture between humanitarian assistance and intervention, on the one hand, and development, on the other, suggesting that there is much that we can borrow from the study of development that may inform our understanding of humanitarian action. We will consider the historical and political processes that have shaped contemporary humanitarian enterprises and debates, the specific norms that guide them, and the ways in which the field both affects and is affected by development processes.

Humanitarian assistance is sometimes referred to as "development on steroids," referring to the fact that it focuses on short-term, rapidly provided assistance to relieve immediate suffering. Humanitarian assistance is also sometimes hailed as being "apolitical" in that it tries to relieve human suffering but for the most part does not try to address the underlying structural causes of that suffering or to provide more systemic support to prevent recurrence of suffering. That, of course, is an oversimplification, since the dividing lines between humanitarian and development assistance are blurred.

For the purposes of this chapter, humanitarian assistance is defined as assistance that is primarily aimed at providing emergency life-saving support to people affected by crisis. Humanitarian assistance is typically short-term, although it can be prolonged if the crisis does not subside or if people are unable to regain their self-sufficiency relatively quickly. Those who provide humanitarian assistance, as we shall see, usually attempt to do so according to the principles of impartiality and neutrality, although these principles can be more aspirational than actual.

Humanitarian assistance can be provided in response to human-made or natural disasters. Natural disasters are often categorized as either of slow onset (drought, leading to famine, for instance) in that they develop over several years, progressively eroding people's asset bases, or sudden onset (storms, earthquakes, tsunami, floods, volcanic eruptions), whereby people experience a shock to their livelihoods with little or no warning. Even where these hazards are unavoidable, their impact on human populations is in part a function of the governance system in place, particularly the extent to which preparedness and response are effectively managed.

Conflict, of course, is a human-made disaster that can be either sudden or slowly escalating. Very often conflict and natural disasters occur simultaneously, creating what are called complex political emergencies (CPEs) that can take an enormous toll on the ability of local communities to survive. As we shall see in this chapter, however, whether caused by nature or people, all disasters and their responses are also affected by political factors—by political choices, funding priorities, state-society relations, and other dynamics involving power.

A HISTORY OF HUMANITARIAN ACTION

The history of humanitarian action is a long one and is linked to faith-based traditions of charity, compassion, and care that can be seen in all of the world's religions. Yet the emergence of a distinct field of humanitarian thought and action is the product of specific historical, ideological, and political interactions. Understanding these processes helps to inform our understanding of humanitarianism today.

Michael Barnett, in his *Empire of Humanity: A History of Humanitarianism* (2011), identifies three major periods in the history of the field: the *age of imperial humanitarianism, the age of neo-humanitarianism*, and the *age of liberal humanitarianism*. We will consider each of these periods in turn, setting the ground for a consideration of issues facing contemporary humanitarianism.

The Age of Imperial Humanitarianism, 1800–1945

Barnett describes the age of imperial humanitarianism as beginning in 1800 and lasting until the end of World War II in 1945. He notes that in the early nineteenth century, notions of charity and compassion rode on the back of the colonial political projects (see Chapter 2). The idea that the Christian West stood as a force for spreading a particular kind of compassionate international community took root. Many of the first humanitarians were missionaries and private citizens who seized upon the spread of colonialism to import their brand of assistance into areas seen to be in need of both spiritual and material salvation.

Out of this general widening of the sense of community, and in the face of political upheaval in Europe, came a series of events that have been credited with giving birth to modern humanitarianism. Swiss businessman Henri Dunant, on his way to meet with the French emperor, Napoleon III, happened upon the battlefield at Solferino, Italy, on 24 June 1859 immediately after a day of heavy fighting between French and Austro-Hungarian troops. Injured soldiers were still lying on the battlefield and more than 9,000 casualties were sheltering in the local village with virtually no medical care available. Moved by the suffering that he saw on both sides, he helped organize relief for the troops, mobilizing villagers to help care for the wounded and even successfully appealing for the release of several Austrian doctors who had been captured to assist in the effort (Bugnion, 2012: 1303–4).

Dunant returned to Geneva and organized a group of prominent members of the elite Genevois society to establish the Permanent International Committee for the Relief of Wounded Soldiers, which later became the International Committee of the Red Cross (ICRC). Central to the work of the Red Cross were the principles of impartiality—providing assistance to whoever needed it—and neutrality—not taking sides in the conflict. (We will consider these principles later on in the chapter.) Over the past 150 years, the ICRC has led the way in responding to the needs of those affected by war and disaster. While today it responds to the needs of both combatants and civilians, at first the focus of this work was on responding to the needs of wounded soldiers and prisoners of war. In 1921, the League of Red Cross and Red Crescent Societies was founded to provide support to those affected by natural disasters, effectively creating what has come to be known as the Red Cross/Red Crescent Movement.

The evolution of the Red Cross/Red Crescent movement and other humanitarian organizations (which were overwhelmingly private voluntary organizations rather than government-funded bodies) during these years followed the principles that Barnett identifies as being characteristic of the age of imperial humanitarianism: an extension of European, and largely Christian, principles of compassion and charity to others who needed it. During this time some of what were to become the world's largest privately funded organizations were founded: Save the Children was founded in 1919 by Eglantyne Jebb to provide assistance to all children affected by World War I regardless of their nationality. Oxfam (formerly the Oxford Committee for Famine Relief) was founded in 1942 to provide assistance to people affected by famine in Greece.

The years between the world wars saw a rapid transformation of the humanitarian landscape. The founding of the League of Nations in 1919 and its eventual expansion into what became the United Nations in 1945 was both an expression and a driver of an internationalist focus that changed the shape not only of international relations but of humanitarian thought and action as well. In 1921 the League of Nations created the High Commission for Refugees to address the problem of mass displacement of people across Europe. Although the HCR would go on to expand significantly in size and mandate after World War II, during its first years it was largely focused on a particular group. Barnett (2011: 88) observes:

> Overwhelmed by the sheer number of displaced persons and their demands, many private charity groups lobbied states to create a new international agency to aid the relief effort. Also, and perhaps most important, states believed that mass population movement was destabilizing Europe. Yet there were real limits on the number of people they were prepared to help. Although refugees were strewn across Europe, Western states were unwilling to recognize their presence and restricted the HCR's mandate to the Russian refugees. Also, the category of refugee was defined in part as someone forced to flee because of persecution—a politically loaded charge that they were prepared to level only at the Soviet Union. States also limited the HCR to coordination and refused to give it any operational capacity. And because the HCR was not expected to do all that much, states gave it a meagre budget to match.

The outbreak of World War II would force an expansion of the ideas of humanitarianism, a shift from episodic and situational alliances and actions to more durable and universal commitment to a movement supporting humanity.

The Age of Neo-Humanitarianism, 1945–89

The political commitment to a global community of nations during the 1940s grew in part out of a resolve to prevent the kinds of wars that the world had just endured. At the same time, there was a resolve to address the legacies of these wars—population displacement, physical and social destruction, and economic stagnation. The immediate post-war years saw the passing of the Universal Declaration of Human Rights (1948), the Geneva Conventions (1949) relating to the conduct of war, and the Geneva Convention Relating to the Status of Refugees (1951), all of which have become important instruments of international law that have guided the development of humanitarian action.

Perhaps the most important instrument to pave the way for the expansion of humanitarian action to address the needs of civilians affected by conflict came with the adoption of the Geneva Conventions in 1949. These four conventions set out a blueprint for the "rules of war" and include provisions for the humane treatment of those affected by war, both combatants and civilians. The Fourth Convention Relating to the Protection of Civilian Persons in Time of War explicitly provides that "an impartial humanitarian body, such as the International Committee of the Red Cross, may offer its services to the Parties to the conflict." This simple sentence, arguably more than any other, has paved the way for non-governmental organizations (NGOs) seeking to provide humanitarian assistance to victims of war to claim a right to accessing these populations. Indeed, this right, reflecting another right of civilians to be assisted when they are affected by conflict, has become the guiding mission for many humanitarian organizations.

In the immediate aftermath of World War II the focus of international humanitarian efforts was on post-war reconstruction and reacting to the problem of population displacement in Europe. New humanitarian organizations were founded; for example, CARE (formerly the Committee for American Remittances to Europe) was established in 1945 to help with the post-war reconstruction effort, and it remains one of the largest relief organizations in the world in the beginning of the twenty-first century.

However, the liberation wars associated with the end of colonialism and the increasing entrenchment of the Cold War, resulting in proxy wars in Africa, Asia, and Latin America, drove the humanitarian project to take on a progressively more global focus. Relief organizations that had never operated outside of Europe now launched relief efforts in places as far from their European and North American bases as Indochina (during the late 1960s and early 1970s), Biafra (Nigeria) in the late 1960s, and Nicaragua during the 1980s. Still, despite the expansion into the Global South, power over directing the humanitarian enterprise still remained vested with head offices in North America and Europe.

The proxy wars by which the United States and Soviet Union fought their Cold War led to bitter conflicts in such diverse places as Angola, Ethiopia, Somalia, Afghanistan, and throughout Central America. These conflicts brought both non-governmental actors and intergovernmental humanitarian response to new areas. Although most NGOs attempted to stake a claim to being non-political, their assistance had great geopolitical significance, and both superpowers sought to use humanitarian assistance as a tool to promote their interests, and conversely to cast humanitarian suffering as a by-product of their opponent's influence.

This period also saw the beginning of what has come to be known as the **CNN effect**, the broadcasting of humanitarian emergencies onto television screens around the world. Such coverage was first seen on a global scale in 1984, when the BBC's coverage of the famine in Ethiopia shocked the world and prompted an outpouring of donations from private citizens throughout Europe and North America. This crisis received even more attention when the world's biggest rock bands staged the Live Aid concerts in the US and UK simultaneously in July 1985 and recorded singles to benefit the relief. This "celebritization" of disaster response has continued to the present day in ways that have been helpful as well as problematic (see Franks, 2013; Müller, 2013).

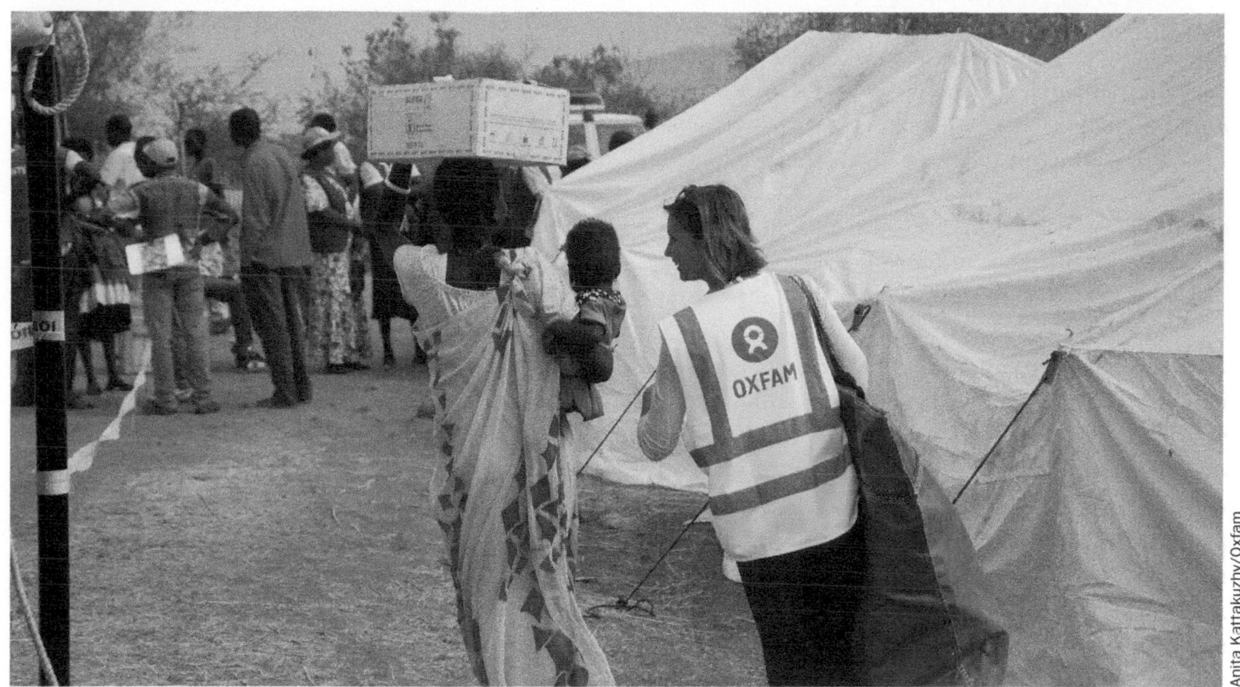

PHOTO 28.1 | Oxfam is an example of a Dunantist organization, believing humanitarian work should be neutral and independent.

The Age of Liberal Humanitarianism, 1989–Present

The end of the Cold War, brought about by the disintegration of the Soviet Union, and the dramatic reshifting of global political power resulted in what Barnett calls the age of liberal humanitarianism. This period was at first characterized by the collapse of states that had been previously propped up by superpower patronage. National budgets whose militaries had been bloated with bilateral aid money from one superpower or the other found themselves bankrupt, and their lack of investment in health, education, and economic development resulted in crushing poverty for large swaths of their populations.

Humanitarian actors stepped in to fill some of these gaps—in some cases providing life-saving support to victims of conflict, but also often becoming involved in providing the most basic forms of social support. Here the lines between relief and development work became more blurred (one could argue that they had never been fully distinct) and NGOs in some cases became like "mini-states" providing assistance that ideally (had they been strong enough) states should have provided themselves.

At the same time, the post-Cold War era has seen a rise in what has come to be seen as **humanitarian intervention**—military intervention motivated or justified at least in part with reference to humanitarian objectives of saving lives or relieving suffering. The military interventions in Iraq in 1990 and again in 2003, Somalia in 1993, Afghanistan in 2001, and the Balkans in the mid-1990s are all examples of interventions for which humanitarian motives were claimed. In each of these cases civilian and military humanitarian actors have been brought into close and sometimes uncomfortable proximity with one another. In 2001 the principle of the "responsibility to protect" (R2P) was introduced. This principle asserts that a state's authority and legitimacy come not from its control over a geographic area but rather from its commitment to ensure that its citizens' basic rights are safeguarded (ICISS, 2001). The Responsibility to Protect movement has gained significant traction in the years since (see www.responsibilitytoprotect.org), and the R2P principle is gradually gaining acceptance as a basic requirement for both states and—crucially—for non-state actors who aspire to one day take the reins of formal state power. The deliberate instrumentalization of aid by donors active on the battlefield to support strategic military objectives, which themselves are conceived of and justified with reference to humanitarian objectives, has met with resistance from most civilian humanitarians. Humanitarian assistance, for many donors, has come to be seen as a key asset to be used in the process of liberal peacebuilding. Humanitarian actors have found it difficult (in some cases impossible) to work in areas where military campaigns are being waged. Conflict actors do not always make distinctions between civilian humanitarian groups and rival military actors, and the risks for the former can be very high (see Hammond, 2008).

The age of liberal humanitarianism has seen a dramatic expansion in the number of humanitarian organizations working in the sector and in the number of individuals employed in it. The number of people employed in the humanitarian sector is difficult to estimate, although the Aid Workers Security Database estimates that in 2013 there were 450,000 humanitarian aid workers. The sector has undergone a rapid process of professionalization, whereby humanitarian workers are expected to bring more sophisticated technical skills, managerial capabilities, and cultural and political sensitivity and analytic abilities to their work (Slim, 1995).

DUNANTIST AND WILSONIAN HUMANITARIAN ORGANIZATIONS

Amid the proliferating world of humanitarian organizations, a few types have emerged. These can be roughly divided into two groups: Dunantist and Wilsonian organizations (see Stoddard, 2003). Dunantist organizations align themselves closely with humanitarian principles of neutrality and impartiality (see below) as well as independence, in the tradition of Red Cross movement founder Henri Dunant. Although not all are as purist as the Red Cross/Red Crescent movement members, they see these principles as important to adhere to in order to maintain access to populations in need. They actively shirk association with political actors, seeking to carve out a "humanitarian space" where they can operate without the interference of political interests. Examples of Dunantist organizations include Oxfam, Concern Worldwide, and in some cases Médecins Sans Frontières (see Stoddard, 2003).

Wilsonian organizations (named with reference to US President Woodrow Wilson) recognize that humanitarian assistance is inherently political and has the potential to be used to promote positive political outcomes. These organizations are often, though not always, closely tied to governments with an interest in the politics of the particular humanitarian setting; they may also be receiving financial support from these governments. Often frustrated with the non-interventionist stance of Dunantist organizations, Wilsonian actors reason that humanitarian aid can be used to help influence political relations in positive ways to help bring about a political solution. This, they argue, can help to alleviate suffering in a more comprehensive and possibly more long-lasting way. Dunantists counter this position by arguing that such an interventionist position also can have the potential to do real harm to populations in need and to worsen an already dire humanitarian situation. Examples of Wilsonian organizations include CARE, World Vision, and the International Rescue Committee (see Stoddard, 2003).

As we shall see, in recent years other trends in humanitarianism have been gaining recognition and strength, particularly those faith-based organizations that operate out of solidarity with a particular group or political movement. While motivated by a similar understanding of the potential power of humanitarianism to alter political dynamics, they may be rooted in political objectives that differ markedly from those associated with the Western ideal of Wilsonian humanitarianism.

CONTEMPORARY CHALLENGES TO HUMANITARIANISM

Concentration of Funds

Today the field of humanitarianism is a multi-billion dollar industry—in 2014, \$18.7 billion were contributed by governments, and \$5.8 billion came from

IMPORTANT CONCEPTS

BOX 28.1 | Two Sides of the Same Coin: Dunantist and Wilsonian NGOs

International Committee of the Red Cross (ICRC)

The ICRC—the classic Dunantist organization—is a unique kind of NGO in that it is the only non-governmental body with an explicit mandate to provide relief to victims of war. In addition to providing medical support, food aid, and other life-saving assistance, the ICRC also carries out activities not generally included in the suite of services of a relief NGO, such as visitation of prison inmates and prisoners of war, family reunification, and monitoring of adherence to international humanitarian law. Much of the ICRC's funding does come from governments (83 per cent in 2014 from individual governments and another 9 per cent from the European Community's Humanitarian Office) (ICRC, 2015), but it insists on setting its own spending priorities and does not take "tightly earmarked" funds from donors (ICRC, 2015). It avoids becoming overly dependent on a single donor by drawing on a wide pool of donors for its work. Its budget in 2014 was $1.85 billion.

Catholic Relief Services (CRS)

Since its founding in 1943 to respond to the needs of World War II survivors in Europe, Catholic Relief Services (CRS) has been one of the primary recipients of US government funding. Long guided by a passionate faith-based and anti-Communist agenda, CRS used US and other funding to gradually expand in the post–World War II era to become one of the largest global relief organizations. Today, the organization works in 101 countries. Its 2014 Annual Report indicates that 62 per cent of its total income was derived from US public sources. In the first half of 2016, CRS received over $216 million from the US for humanitarian emergency work, the third largest recipient of US government funds (after the UN High Commissioner for Refugees and the World Food Programme) (http://fts.unocha.org).

CRS represents a category of faith-based NGOs that "see their humanitarian programmes as straddling the church and the secular world, combining social and religious goals" (Stoddard, 2003). While CRS is overtly a faith-based organization, even some of the more professedly secular organizations have roots in religious precepts and traditions. Thus, despite the CRS profile as religious it also falls into the category that Stoddard describes as being "Wilsonian" in that it has consistently worked closely with US funding on relief and development work that aligns with the foreign policy objectives of the US government. This can be seen, for instance, in the fact that CRS has continued to work in Afghanistan with USAID funding long after most other major NGOs departed over concerns about their inability to operate safely as independent aid actors.

private sources for humanitarian assistance (GHA, 2015). Figure 28.1 shows the generally steady increase in funding for humanitarian operations since 2009, employing hundreds of thousands of people all over the world. Despite this proliferation of humanitarian actors, there is a heavy concentration of wealth and power within a very few non-governmental organizations. The five largest NGOs—Médecins Sans Frontières (MSF), Save the Children Fund, Oxfam, World Vision, and the International Rescue Committee—accounted for 31 per cent of all humanitarian expenditure in 2013. The remaining 69 per cent was divided among hundreds of other smaller organizations (Humanitarian Outcomes, 2015).

Figure 28.1 shows the breakdown of humanitarian funding between government or EU funding and private sources. Private funding for humanitarian response—including philanthropic donations from large foundations but also including smaller contributions from members of the public, often in response to

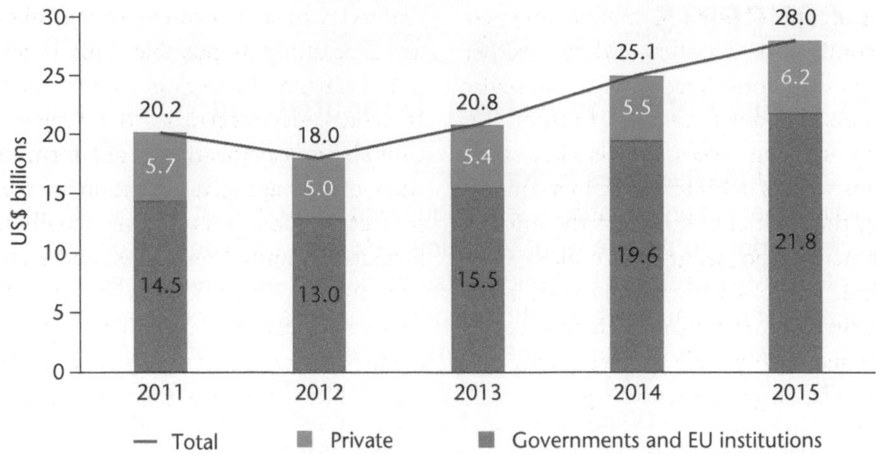

FIGURE 28.1 | Global Government and Private Humanitarian Assistance, 2011–15

Source: Figure developed for the Global Humanitarian Assistance Report 2016, published by Development Initiatives: http://devinit.org/#!/GHA2016

specific disaster appeals—has been increasing in recent years. While some NGOs rely heavily on private donations—some national chapters of MSF, for instance, do not take government money of any kind—others are heavily reliant on funding from government humanitarian budgets. Some try to maintain their independence by seeking funding from multiple donors at once or by refusing to use a certain government's funds if they believe that to do so would pose a challenge to their neutrality.

Principled Action: Preserving Neutrality, Impartiality, and Independence

In 1965, the International Red Cross and Red Crescent Movement adopted a set of fundamental principles concerning humanitarian action. These include the principles of humanity, neutrality, impartiality, independence, voluntary service, unity, and universality. Since then, other humanitarian organizations have adopted positions aligned with one or more of these principles, most commonly those of neutrality, impartiality, humanity, and independence. We will examine these four principles here.

Today, most humanitarian organizations not aligned with conflict actors declare an allegiance to the principle of impartiality, or the imperative to provide assistance to all who need it, regardless of their position in relation to the conflict or their ethnicity, race, religion, gender, age, or other distinction. Many also declare positions of neutrality, of not taking sides in a conflict and of not engaging in activities of a "political, racial, religious or ideological nature" (www.icrc.org). Although in other contexts they are often used interchangeably, impartiality and neutrality are not the same things in the humanitarian world. Being neutral does not necessarily mean that one is committed to impartiality. Being impartial in a very uneven conflict, where the numbers of casualties are disproportionate, may mean that one responds to suffering more on one side than the other, which may give the impression of having taken sides. Upholding both of these principles, as the members of the Red Cross movement attempt to do, can be extremely difficult. When one has limited resources and the needs are very high, for instance, decisions about who should receive assistance and who should not can begin to look very much like the kind of triage decisions made in a hospital emergency room. Different organizations may interpret these principles in different ways. (For a longer examination of the neutrality and impartiality principles, and the way that they have shifted over time, see Hammond, 2015).

Another often staunchly defended humanitarian principle is independence—the insistence on working without being influenced by donors, governments, or other political actors. In part, independence may be seen to stem from positions of impartiality and neutrality. Overarching the entire humanitarian enterprise is the principle of humanity, of helping people affected by conflicts or disasters. Taken together, these four principles are considered essential to maintaining access to populations in need and responding to life-threatening suffering. Access here is a key objective. Organizations seen as not interfering in a conflict, or not criticizing the political aspects of the affected country's government response, are more likely to be allowed to continue to work in sensitive areas. Those that do not abide by these principles, their proponents argue, risk losing access to people in need. Some also argue that they may face a greater risk of being targeted by combatants, although there is evidence that sometimes adhering to principled humanitarian action may expose workers to greater levels of risk (see Hammond, 2008). They are therefore not able to provide protection and assistance, nor are they able—through their functions as witnesses to suffering—to prevent abuses and violations of humanitarian law. Of course, having access to populations in crisis does not always stop abuses or provide protection, but it has been shown very often to be effective at minimizing them.

Principled humanitarian action has attracted strong criticism at key moments in history. One of the most extreme examples of this concerned the Red Cross during World War II. In the interests of maintaining access to people in need, the Red Cross was quiet about what it knew about the killings going on in European Nazi concentration camps. Its defenders have argued that if it had spoken out, the Red Cross would have been expelled from the camps and would not have been able to do the good work it was able to do in spite of the situation. However, the organization has been widely criticized for turning its back on victims of the Holocaust; the controversy continues to plague the organization more than 70 years later (Moorehead, 1998; Favez, 1999).

Ethical Dilemmas

The examples above highlight the difficult ethical terrain within which humanitarian organizations must work. It is virtually impossible to escape these dilemmas. At its most basic, the goal of humanitarian action is to save lives, but this imperative is muddied by several subsidiary goals—to do no harm (not to let aid contribute, even indirectly, to the suffering of people) and to try to steer a course of ethical decision-making as successfully as possible. This is no easy task; one might say that the work of a humanitarian practitioner is 90 per cent concerned with trying to make judgment calls about prioritization of aid, forms of response, and ways of managing information in which there is no perfect solution. This is done usually with limited information, limited resources, and restricted authority or mandate. Humanitarian workers often feel that no solution is cost-free, and that they are therefore condemned to try to find the "least-worst" option among a range of less than ideal possible actions.

WHOSE RESPONSIBILITY TO RESPOND?

Government Responses

When disaster strikes, the first responsibility to respond rests with the government of the affected country. In countries where disaster is a frequent occurrence, governments often have well-developed early warning, preparedness, and response capabilities and institutions. Ethiopia has one of the oldest and most comprehensive famine early warning systems; developed in the aftermath of the 1984–5 famine, it has been effective at facilitating response to recurrent droughts and floods. Several potential famines have been averted over the past 25 years. In Bangladesh, also highly vulnerable to disaster—in this case floods and cyclones—the government has worked closely with civil society to build a reasonably responsive early warning, preparedness, and response system.

Often the need for humanitarian and emergency assistance is greater than even a well-organized government can respond to. In such cases it seeks supplementary support from its own civil society as well as from international actors. This most often takes the form of a request to the United Nations and international NGOs to provide assistance on an emergency basis. If the UN and NGOs are already working in the country, response even to sudden-onset disasters can be provided often within a matter of only 24 hours. Where the affected area is very remote or the relationships with international actors are not already in place, the response may be slower.

CRITICAL ISSUES

BOX 28.2 | To Stay or Go? Weighing the Costs and Benefits of Working in Ethically Challenging Environments: Goma, 1994

A prime example of the difficult, some say impossible, choices that humanitarian actors sometimes have to make involved the positioning of humanitarian NGOs in what was then eastern Zaire (now the Democratic Republic of Congo) following the 1994 genocide in Rwanda. **Refugees** living in the camps around Goma included not only those who had escaped the violence, but also some who had played a role—directly or indirectly—in perpetrating it. The camps were being used as recruitment bases, recuperation bases, and mobilization sites by the Rwandan Hutu-dominated Interahamwe. Humanitarian organizations were faced with a choice between two problematic positions: either continue to stay in the camps and provide assistance to all refugees regardless of whether they had played a role in the genocide (a choice that the United Nations High Commissioner for Refugees and several large international NGOs took) or withdraw from the camps on the grounds that the assistance being provided was being used against civilians and was prolonging the violence (a position taken ultimately by Médecins Sans Frontières France and Belgium). Fiona Terry, who was working in the camps at the time, writes in her book *Condemned to Repeat: The Paradox of Humanitarian Action* (2004) about the impossibility of there being a "right" and principled path to take. She defends, however, the ultimate decision taken by MSF to leave the camp on the grounds that continuing to provide assistance to the refugees would only further the violence and prolong the suffering of those who were innocent. Similar dilemmas have faced humanitarian workers in Darfur, Sudan, in the early 2000s, in Afghanistan since the early 2000s, in Ethiopia during the civil war and famine of the 1980s, and in Somalia in the buildup to the 2011 famine.

UN-Led Models of Assistance

Once a request for assistance has been given, humanitarian actors must work quickly to respond. This requires not only procuring the necessary food, health supplies, sanitation kits, or other items, but also working out how best to provide the assistance to the affected population. The United Nations and its specialized agencies (the UN High Commissioner for Refugees [UNHCR], UNICEF, the World Food Programme, the World Health Organization, the Food and Agricultural Organization, and others) serve important functions not only as service providers but also in co-ordinating information and response during times of crisis (see Chapter 10).

The United Nations Consolidated Appeal Process (CAP) can mobilize funds for disaster and emergency response—all of the concerned UN agencies will issue a joint appeal to respond to all of the emergency needs, and will then present the appeal to donors for a co-ordinated response. Importantly, however, funds provided in response to the CAP—usually by foreign governments—are given to the United Nations and do not include funding for NGOs: those must be raised by individual organizations or consortia (such as the Disasters Emergency Committee, which raises funds on behalf of 13 different organizations). The task of co-ordinating all of these different organizations, their different work, and the potentially vast sums of money that they mobilize is enormous.

In many cases, the UN works through what it calls clusters. Each cluster (sanitation, water and hygiene, food security, camp settlement and co-ordination, etc.) has a lead UN agency that directs the sectoral response. This helps to minimize duplication of services and ensure that gaps are filled. Co-ordination with non-UN agencies, however, can be difficult, since some NGOs may choose to co-operate with the UN clusters while some prefer to be more independent and to work on their own.

Humanitarian early warning and response mechanisms are only effective when they are paid attention to by donors and implementers. Often donors respond too late, when humanitarian conditions have deteriorated to emergency levels. In such cases even the fastest, most efficient response cannot prevent all suffering. Getting donors to provide adequate resources in good time to prevent an escalation of suffering is crucial. This requires acting on available early information about rainfall, food prices, livestock conditions, nutrition levels, and migration patterns, among other indicators. It also requires donors prioritizing one crisis among others. Donors' responses to humanitarian appeals not only reflect the severity of the problem but are also influenced by the political and security interests, the historical relations, and the public perceptions within particular donor countries. Some kinds of crisis—in countries seen as strategically insignificant or where vulnerability and suffering are harder to see (such as chronic diseases like HIV/AIDS or tuberculosis)—are particularly difficult to raise funds for.

Non-Governmental Actors—Traditional and "Emergent"

Much of the history of humanitarian action has been told through the prism of the experience of the United Nations agencies and/or Western international humanitarian organizations, yet other actors are also often involved. Sometimes referred to as "new," "non-traditional," or "emergent" actors, in fact they are often none of these. Rather, what is often "new" is that well-established bodies—for instance, Islamic Relief, which was established in 1985—or types of activity—such as diaspora groups—are being *recognized* for the first time as playing an important and influential role in humanitarian affairs. That said, it is true that humanitarian action is changing due to the increased involvement of donors outside the Development Assistance Committee (DAC) of the OECD—donors such as Brazil, Saudi Arabia, Turkey, China, India, and the United Arab Emirates (see Chapter 13). It is also changing as a result of the involvement of large private foundations such as the Bill & Melinda Gates Foundation (which now has a budget larger than that of the World Health Organization), the Google Foundation, and the Ikea Foundation (which partners with UNHCR to provide shelter support to refugees), to name a few. In other cases there are, indeed, new NGOs, some but not all formed by people with experience working for humanitarian organizations. Exactly what kinds of influence these different players will have on humanitarian action is difficult to predict precisely.

In particular crises, these changing dynamics can have a profound impact on the overall response. In Somalia in 2011, $350 million was reportedly provided in famine relief to organizations working outside the UN's Consolidated Appeal structure. Much of this money was distributed through the Organization for Islamic Cooperation, which had much better access to the worst-affected areas than the UN did.

It is clear that the shape of humanitarianism is changing. The absolute control over humanitarian affairs by Western actors and interests, which has been the hallmark of most modern humanitarian action, is beginning to change. The effects of these changing dynamics are seen most dramatically in areas where donors and the larger and better-funded NGOs have the most interest. Donors from the Persian Gulf countries, for instance, tend to respond most to crises in countries with large Muslim populations. Thus, the overall effects of these changes are unevenly distributed.

THE CHALLENGES OF LONG-TERM RECOVERY

Despite the increase in funding for humanitarian assistance in recent years, there are still not enough funds available to meet the needs of all crisis-affected populations everywhere. One implication of this is that even in situations where humanitarian response is robust, it tends to be short-lived. Once emergency conditions subside and the worst of a crisis is over, donors tend to shift their resources to other crises seen as more pressing. This leaves affected populations without adequate resources to recover fully from the disaster; they remain in a state of enhanced vulnerability to suffering should conditions deteriorate once more.

A family affected by drought, for instance, may have lost all of its livestock and been forced to move into the nearest urban centre to receive food aid handouts during the drought. Once the rains return, however, if they do not have enough money to be able to rebuild their herds, then they cannot return to their pastoral way of life and they remain dependent on welfare. Or if they have only a few animals, they may start to farm again, but if drought strikes again it will only take the loss of a few animals to push them over the threshold and into destitution again.

HUMANITARIAN ACCOUNTABILITY

An important set of questions with regard to humanitarian action revolves around the issue of accountability. While donors set a high standard for ensuring that the funds they provide are used for the purposes for which they are intended, there is a relative lack of **downward accountability**. Very rarely are the views of the intended recipients of aid taken into account in determining whether assistance has been effective. Where there is a lack of effectiveness on the ground, aid recipients usually do not have recourse to a complaints system. As in the development sector, there is usually no penalty for humanitarian work that does not go well.

Some actors are attempting to redress this problem by developing codes of conduct or accountability frameworks. NGOs agree to abide by these rules voluntarily, but there is usually no enforcement mechanism to ensure that they remain compliant. The Core Humanitarian Standard Alliance (CHS Alliance), with a membership of approximately 250 local and international NGOs, has been working on strengthening both bottom-up accountability and top-down accountability, and has developed a nine-point set of Core Humanitarian Standards for use by communities affected by disasters, conflict, or poverty, aid workers, and humanitarian organizations. The principles of the CHS are shown in Figure 28.2.

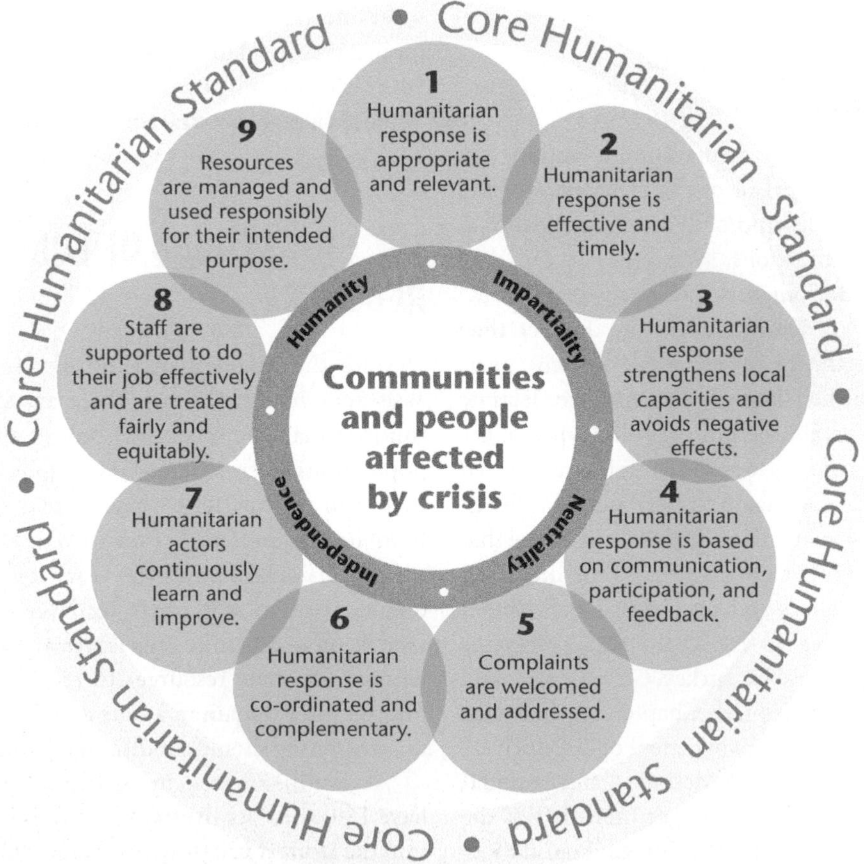

FIGURE 28.2 | Core Humanitarian Standards

Source: This diagram shows the Nine Commitments in the Core Humanitarian Standard on Quality and Accountability (CHS). The CHS was published by the CHS Alliance, Groupe URD and Sphere Project in 2014.

Resilience

Increasingly, humanitarian practitioners are recognizing that those who are best able to respond to crisis are those affected by it. As soon as disaster strikes, survivors will focus their energies and resources on two things: mitigating the impact of the crisis and managing their own recovery. Humanitarian assistance is most effective when it supports the efforts that people are already engaged in, or would be if they had the resources.

Clearly, an individual's, family's, or community's ability to withstand the impact of a hazard or to recover from a disaster depends on how vulnerable they are when the shock occurs. If they are already extremely poor, have no savings or other assets to call upon, and are not in a position to get assistance from their relatives and neighbours, they will be more severely affected than if they do have such resources.

The ability to adapt to and recover from hazards and crisis is referred to as **resilience**. Resilience is something that individuals, families, communities, organizations, and governments may have, although in the humanitarian context the focus is on building, drawing upon, and protecting the resilience of those who are most affected by crisis. A resilient household will be able to meet its essential needs now and in the future, will have at least a small cushion of assets (financial savings, livestock, other property, etc.), and will be able to respond to shocks without jeopardizing the well-being of the household. This also requires a level of preparedness and knowledge about the kinds of hazards that are likely to occur and how people have responded to them in the past. Resilience has become something of a buzzword in humanitarian circles in recent years, but at its core is a recognition of the centrality of the agency of those

ZUMA Press, Inc. / Alamy Stock Photo

PHOTO 28.2 | WHO and Catholic Relief Services work together to show health workers how to wear personal protective gear for an Ebola outbreak

who are most affected by crisis and the need to build on that resource at all times.

POLITICAL ECONOMY OF HUMANITARIAN ASSISTANCE

Taking a somewhat wider perspective on the humanitarian sphere, there are important considerations about how humanitarian assistance and interventions are shaped by, and in some cases can themselves help to shape, political dynamics at national and international levels.

Even though they are generally claimed to be separate from political interests, the high value of humanitarian aid flows can make them a powerful political tool. The ways that humanitarian funds are disbursed are often driven by political considerations—donors are more likely to provide more funds to their allies or to countries where they have significant economic, political, or strategic interest—or cultural ties—than to countries where they do not. For recipients, humanitarian aid, like development resources, may represent a major source of foreign exchange, a significant opportunity for generating local employment, and a chance to generate other funds for economic development.

In situations of protracted crisis, humanitarian aid may take the place of economic activity that has been disrupted. Obtaining access to aid can then become an end in itself for political actors, warlords, and others. An aid economy is often generated, which powerful actors have an interest in perpetuating and manipulating so that they can continue to benefit. Recovery from crisis in such situations involves figuring out how to disentangle the aid economy from the rest of the economy, or removing the incentives that the aid economy provides. This can be enormously difficult, and even dangerous, if those who hold control over aid resources are not willing to peacefully relinquish their stranglehold. Ideally, it may be possible to generate economic and political opportunity elsewhere, thereby removing the incentives of such rent-seeking behaviour (see Keen, 1991).

RESEARCH AND THE HUMANITARIAN FUTURE

For social scientists, research concerning humanitarian action can be difficult. Access to the work of humanitarian actors and to crisis-affected individuals and communities can require a well-established network of contacts. Even then, there may be practical considerations concerning security. Focusing research on the experiences of suffering, or on the work involved in saving lives, can be ethically problematic as well.

Even where direct fieldwork is not involved, there can be a lack of availability of reliable data. Data on nutrition levels, migration flows, morbidity and mortality rates, and other indicators may be unavailable or of varying quality. Wherever possible, triangulation of data is needed to support conclusions drawn. Data quality is improving in some areas. Financial information is now more available than it has been in the past thanks to sources such as the UN's Financial Tracking System (http://fts.unocha.org) and the Global Humanitarian Assistance initiative (www.globalhumanitarianassistance.org). Information about aid worker security is available now as well (see http://aidworkersecurity.org). Much of this data is provided on a self-reporting basis, which tends to mean that the figures are an under-representation. Large gaps in data continue to exist in other areas.

While it is not possible to prevent all crises in the future, it is possible to sketch a few characteristics of the humanitarian future. First, the expansion in the numbers of people who are targeted for assistance, the number of people employed in the sector, and the amounts of money raised for humanitarian response are certain to continue to increase. Second, it is likely that the proliferation of different kinds of actors will continue. This may result in additional funding being made available for response, but it will also present certain challenges with regard to co-ordination and professionalization.

A third dynamic is that as militarized humanitarianism continues to be exercised, including UN peacekeeping and peace enforcement activities but also multilateral interventions staged independently of the UN, the objectives of working independently and from positions of neutrality and impartiality will become ever more contested and hazardous.

Finally, as understanding about the connection between vulnerability and resilience is developed, there may—with any luck—be a possibility for forging stronger ties between efforts to promote development and those to promote preparedness and recovery from disasters.

SUMMARY

This chapter has provided a snapshot of many of the most important issues facing humanitarian actors, researchers of humanitarianism, and affected populations. It has provided an overview of the history of modern humanitarian action, showing the major organizing principles and forces that have shaped the contemporary sector. It has also highlighted some of the difficulties encountered by those engaged in providing humanitarian assistance, from navigating difficult ethical terrain to negotiating the core humanitarian principles of independence, neutrality, impartiality, and even humanity itself. It has considered the various types of actors, the funding they rely on to carry out their work, and the wider political economy implications that humanitarian assistance poses in terms of foreign relations, foreign policy, and aid economies.

While linked in many ways to the wider field of development studies, humanitarian studies has a dynamic of its own. Its importance in the coming years looks set to increase. It is therefore a fertile area of study both in its own right and in relation to wider development questions.

QUESTIONS FOR CRITICAL THOUGHT

1. Consider a current or recent humanitarian emergency in a developing country and explain how the response has affected wider development processes and conditions.
2. How might an aid economy perpetuate a humanitarian crisis? Which actors may have an interest in continued crisis and what might their individual motivations be?
3. Why is protecting and abiding by humanitarian principles (humanity, independence, neutrality, and impartiality) difficult? What are the ethical dilemmas that such principled approaches may entail?
4. What ethical and practical considerations are involved in conducting research on humanitarian issues? Do these considerations differ significantly from the kinds of considerations one might face in researching development more broadly?

SUGGESTED READINGS

Barnett, Michael. 2013. *Empire of Humanity: A History of Humanitarianism*. Ithaca, NY: Cornell University Press.

Mac Ginty, Roger, and Jenny H. Peterson. 2015. *The Routledge Companion to Humanitarian Action*. Abingdon, UK: Routledge.

Sezgin, Zeynep, and Dennis Dijkzeul. 2015. *The New Humanitarians in International Practice: Emerging Actors and Contested Principles*. London: Routledge.

Stoddard, Abby. 2003. "Humanitarian NGOs: Challenges and trends." *HPG Briefing* Number 12, July. London: Humanitarian Policy Group, Overseas Development Institute, 2003. www.odi.org/sites/odi.org.uk/files/odi-assets/publications-opinion-files/349.pdf.

BIBLIOGRAPHY

Aid Worker Security Database. 2015. "Aid Worker Security Report 2015: Figures at a Glance." https://aidworkersecurity.org/sites/default/files/HO_AidWorkerSecPreview_1015_G.PDF.V1.pdf.

Barnett, M. 2013. *Empire of Humanity: A History of Humanitarianism*. Ithaca, NY: Cornell University Press.

Bugnion, F. 2012. "Birth of an idea: The founding of the International Committee of the Red Cross and of the International Red Cross and Red Crescent Movement: From Solferino to the original Geneva Convention (1859–1864)." *International Review of the Red Cross* 94, 888: 1299–1338.

Favez, J.-C. 1999. *The Red Cross and the Holocaust*. Translated by J. Fletcher and B. Fletcher. Cambridge: Cambridge University Press.

Financial Tracking Service. http://fts.unocha.org.

Franks, S. 2013. *Reporting Disasters: Famine, Aid, Politics and the Media*. London: Hurst & Company.

Global Humanitarian Assistance (GHA). 2015. *Global Humanitarian Assistance Report 2015*. www.globalhumanitarianassistance.org.

Hammond, L. 2008. "The power of holding humanitarianism hostage and the myth of protective principles." In Michael N. Barnett and Thomas G. Weiss, eds, *Humanitarianism in Question: Politics, Power, Ethics*. Ithaca, NY: Cornell University Press, 172–95.

———. 2015. "Neutrality and impartiality." In Mac Ginty and Peterson (2015: 87–97).

Humanitarian Outcomes. 2015. *The State of the Humanitarian System: 2015 Edition*, London: ALNAP. www.humanitarianoutcomes.org/sites/default/files/alnap-sohs-2015-web.pdf.

Integrated Regional Information Network (IRIN). www.irinnews.org.

International Commission on Intervention and State Sovereignty (ICISS), Gareth J. Evans, Mohamed Sahnoun, and International Development Research Centre (Canada), eds. 2001. *The Responsibility to Protect: Report of the International Commission on Intervention and State Sovereignty*. Ottawa: International Development Research Centre.

International Committee of the Red Cross. "Geneva Conventions and commentaries." www.icrc.org/en/war-and-law/treaties-customary-law/geneva-conventions.

International Committee of the Red Cross (ICRC). 2015. *International Committee of the Red Cross Annual Report*. Geneva: ICRC.

Keen, D. 1994. *The Benefits of Famine: A Political Economy of Famine and Relief in Southwestern Sudan, 1983–1989*. Princeton, NJ: Princeton University Press.

Mac Ginty, R., and J.H. Peterson, eds. 2015. *Routledge Companion to Humanitarian Action*. Abingdon, UK: Routledge.

Moorehead, C. 1999. *Dunant's Dream: War, Switzerland and the History of the Red Cross*. New York: Carroll & Graf.

Müller, T.R. 2013. "The long shadow of band aid humanitarianism: Revisiting the dynamics between famine and celebrity." *Third World Quarterly* 34, 3 (Apr.): 470–84. doi: 10.1080/01436597.2013.785342.

Redfield, P. 2013. *Life in Crisis: The Ethical Journey of Doctors without Borders*. Berkeley: University of California Press.

ReliefWeb. www.reliefeweb.int.

Slim, H. 1995. "The continuing metamorphosis of the humanitarian practitioner: Some new colours for an endangered chameleon." *Disasters* 19, 2: 110–26. doi: 10.1111/j.1467-7717.1995.tb00362.x.

Stoddard, A. 2003. "Humanitarian NGOs: Challenges and trends." *HPG Briefing* Number 12, July. London: Humanitarian Policy Group, Overseas Development Institute, 2003. www.odi.org/sites/odi.org.uk/files/odi-assets/publications-opinion-files/349.pdf.

Terry, F. 2002. *Condemned to Repeat? The Paradox of Humanitarian Action*. Ithaca, NY: Cornell University Press.

United Nations. 1948. Universal Declaration of Human Rights. www.un.org/en/universal-declaration-human-rights/.

United Nations High Commissioner for Refugees (UNHCR). "The 1951 Refugee Convention." www.unhcr.org/pages/49da0e466.html.

Walker, P., and C. Russ. 2010. "Professionalizing the humanitarian sector: A scoping study." Enhancing Learning and Research for Humanitarian Assistance (ELRHA), Apr. www.elrha.org/wp-content/uploads/2015/01/Professionalising_the_humanitarian_sector.pdf.

29 Ethics of Development

Des Gasper

LEARNING OBJECTIVES

- To understand development ethics as an essential dimension of international development studies, for explanatory work and self-awareness as well as for evaluation and policy design.
- To recognize issues for values-sensitive thinking about development: in conceptualizing costs and benefits, considering who bears them, and asking which types of change process are legitimate.
- To become alert to which issues, identities, and interests get considered and which get downgraded or ignored.
- To identify relevant tools in development ethics for description, analysis/evaluation, and action.

▲ **Villagers protest under the banner of the Narmada Bachao Andolan (NBA) by standing in chin-deep water to demand replacement for land lost by flooding that occurred when water levels were raised at the Omkareshwar and Indira Sagar dams. Dam projects propose obvious ethical questions because they involve *known, intended* damage.** | Source: epa european pressphoto agency b.v. Alamy Stock Photo

INTRODUCTION

Avatar, the 2009 film by Canadian director James Cameron that is sometimes listed as the highest-grossing movie of all time, is set in the twenty-second century. Humans have found in a remote star system the moon Pandora, which contains sites rich in the technically vital mineral *unobtanium*. The Resources Development Administration (RDA) commences displacement of the indigenous humanoid people and destruction of their forest environment and sacred sites in order to extract the mineral by open-pit mining. When the humanoids refuse to move, the RDA embarks on their removal by force and—when it is considered necessary—their extermination. RDA ethnographers have been living with the indigenes, through periodic transference to bodies that can live in the alien environment. They are under instructions to learn about the indigenes and persuade them to move but become sympathetic to their situation and decide to defend and ultimately to side with them.

Development in human societies involves value-laden choices. Different choices and ways of thinking about development bring greatly different outcomes for different people. We should try to think openly, carefully, and fairly about the priorities and principles that guide these choices, about which groups are favoured, neglected, or even sacrificed, and about the choices involved also in the related ways of thinking. Besides its importance for guiding action, attention to values is important for trying to understand people. Humans hold and use and are partly driven by values, including ethical ideas; and the types of ethical ideas they hold affect their motivation for thinking empathetically about other people and for engaging in action. Powerful groups often keep values concealed and deny choices, to hide who is favoured, neglected, or sacrificed. The key role of development ethics is to reveal, reflect on, and assess these choices, and to add a voice for those who otherwise are unreasonably neglected or sacrificed.

International development studies arose in the post–World War II era because of the inadequacy of simply adopting and applying the forms of economics, sociology, political science, etc. that had emerged during the previous two centuries in Europe and North America and had become consolidated as separate disciplines to describe industrialized commodity-oriented nation-states. To try to understand and promote prospective transitions in the rest of the world from low-income agriculture-based rural societies to affluent, industrialized, predominantly urban societies, more integrative and dynamic perspectives were needed. Attention was required to the constraints and opportunities for low-income countries and people, who now lived in a world dominated and transformed by the power of rich groups and countries. Existing disciplines reflected in various ways the perspectives and interests of established richer groups and richer countries. Consequently, they neglected some issues, including the explication and debate of values used in thinking about and promoting "development."

From the 1950s, a field of thought called "development ethics" emerged as a strand within, or partner of, international development studies. It was a response to many issues concerning how a society (and our global society) is moving into the future. First, there are perceptions that much poverty is both undeserved and removable, including much sickness and insecurity and unhappiness; that many processes of further impoverishment are also undeserved and avoidable; and that distribution of the costs and benefits of development is often unbalanced and unfair, including through infliction of undeserved, unconsulted, and uncompensated harm. Second, what should be assessed as the true costs and benefits of development? What is the significance of culture? And to what justifiable extent are values culturally relative? Third, what is appropriate distribution over time in regard to laying burdens on people in the present or on future generations? Fourth, who bears which responsibilities, including to refrain from harming, to compensate for harm, to prevent harm occurring, and/or to help more extensively if one can do so? Fifth, who should be involved in consultation and decision-making on all this and how?

It is no coincidence that, reflecting the modern world's combination of economic interconnection and potential for technology-based improvements, attention to development ethics has grown since the mid-twentieth century as images of children and babies from around the world—often suffering children or babies—have become more widely distributed. Small children and babies bear no responsibility for their own situation and have little unaided ability to

IMPORTANT CONCEPTS

BOX 29.1 | Questions in Development Ethics

- What meaning is given to "development" in the sense of progress, well-being, or improvement?
- Which values underlie this meaning of "development," and which values in practice determine the allocation of attention and the prioritizations made in development processes? Are values of human well-being, justice and human dignity adequately reflected in practice? How can attention to those values be supported?
- Who is gaining and who is losing in social change? Who bears the costs of "development"? Is it fair?
- Why do unfair arrangements arise? How can they be prevented or mitigated?
- How should we respond to the painful—sometimes "cruel"—choices between different values and groups that can arise in development policy/programs/projects?
- How can one construct well-reasoned alternatives to prevailing practices that violate values of justice, well-being, and dignity—alternatives in ways of thinking and in strategy, policy, and practice?
- Who has responsibilities (and "response-abilities")—to act, to desist, to compensate—in regard to violations of values of justice, human well-being, and dignity?

respond. The following question arose, as articulated, for example, by Martha Nussbaum (2004: 3): to what extent, if any, should "the chance of being born in one nation rather than another pervasively [determine] the life chances of every child who is born"?

HISTORICAL CONTEXT

In principle, the gains from more productive use of a location's resources and opportunities should bring benefits for all parties and not be at the expense of existing occupants or of the workforce used to bring these resources into more productive use. In practice, this has very often not happened, in the past and presently. Although development studies and development ethics under those names arose in the post-1945 era, the broad ideas of development, underdevelopment, and development ethics do not date from 1945 or 1949, the year of President Truman's oft-cited inaugural speech. "Development" language in regard to issues of socio-economic change and improvement had already been long-established around the world since at least the early nineteenth century (see Cowen and Shenton, 1996). Further, behind the particular words used, "the issues with which 'development studies' deals are some of the great issues (of justice, of equality and inequality, of the nature of the 'good' life) with which human beings have been preoccupied since the days of Plato and Aristotle" (Kitching, 1982: viii). Indeed, these concerns go back in time even earlier, and in all parts of the world.

In particular, international development studies returns to the issues and formats in the social studies and humanities of the seventeenth to nineteenth centuries that were aiming to make sense of a world in transformation, before these areas of thought became artificially separated, formalized, and abstracted in imitation of the natural sciences. The "great issues" that Kitching refers to were prominent in the writings of John Locke (1632–1704), Immanuel Kant (1724–1804), John Stuart Mill (1806–73), and Karl Marx (1818–83), among others. The contemporary Indian-British philosopher Bhikhu Parekh (1935–) warns, though, that all four of those great thinkers were in fundamental ways Eurocentric (Parekh, 1997). They wrote emphatically of the necessity of European rule over other countries, but had never visited, let alone lived, outside

Europe. In this respect, present-day development ethics should and mostly does adopt a more informed and inclusive perspective. Many of its themes concern relations between actors who have great relative power and others who are marked by extreme relative weakness, and the responses to these disparities. The responses, historically, have frequently included processes of Othering, exploitation, and extermination, but sometimes, in contrast, responses have involved growth of mutual respect, sympathy, and co-operation.

Avatar's themes match many contemporary "resource-grab" situations on Earth. They echo, too, the seizure of the Americas in the sixteenth to nineteenth centuries and the subjugation and decimation of Native Americans by European invaders driven by desire for precious resources while confident in their technological advantage over the indigenous peoples and believing in their own radical biological and cultural superiority. Many colonizers held that the Native Americans were subhuman or damned creatures of the devil; not only were they non-Christian but they reportedly engaged in human sacrifice and cannibalism. The Catholic priest Bartolomé de las Casas (1484–1566), who wrote a chilling account of their subjugation (*A Brief Account of the Destruction of the Indies* [1552]), was the most famous defender of Native Americans' human status and corresponding rights. Las Casas was a forerunner of universal human rights thinking and of the liberation theology movement.

Development ethics considers comparable present-day situations where there are opportunities for enormous gain through application of modern technology to resources worldwide and yet many of the people affected are harshly excluded or exploited. This no longer occurs through formal systems of slavery but often in successor arrangements in which, for example, workers may have no contracts, may never get paid, or are otherwise deceived and trafficked and/or work at high risk of injury (as reportedly do many of the over 100 million internal migrants in China; see Pai, 2013). In many instances, local people have been brusquely displaced to make room for new projects from which they do not benefit.

Various systems of thought in the sixteenth through nineteenth centuries put forward justifications not only for European expansion but for the subjugation and **dispossession** of non-European populations. Hugo Grotius (1583–1645), known as the father of international law, crafted arguments for why the expansionist Dutch Republic had the right to sail and trade in whichever seas it could reach—for the sea is not enclosable and is open to all—and at the same time to occupy and enclose lands around the world and continue to own them even when its personnel were not present. He invoked the analogy that a theatre seat, once taken, can be temporarily left vacant and rightfully not be available for others (Arneil, 1992). What supposed right had the colonizing European power to take such lands in the first place? First, "for the reason that uncultivated land ought not to be considered occupied" (Grotius, *The Law of War and Peace*; cited in Arneil, 1992: 592); and second, because "men who are like beasts" and especially "those who feed on human flesh" can rightfully be punished by dispossession (cited in Arneil, 1992: 594). Other authors declared that many of the non-European populations lived in a savage and disorderly "state of nature," a war of all against all, and that their absence of private landholding implied that the resources concerned had no owner and so could be rightfully taken by the Europeans.

Most famous among these authors was John Locke, philosophical father of the English Revolution of 1688 and long-term secretary to the Lord Proprietors of Carolina, the English colony that later became the American states of North Carolina and South Carolina. Like Grotius, he held that lands not cultivated could be deemed unoccupied; hunter-gatherers could be rightfully displaced or subordinated by new, more intensive users, without compensation.

> Land that is left wholly to Nature, that hath no improvement of Pasturage, Tillage or Planting, is called, as indeed it is, *wast[e] . . . As much Land* as a Man Tills, Plants, Improves, Cultivates, and can use the Product of, so much is his *Property.* (Locke, *Two Treatises on Government*, II, para. 26, cited in Arneil, 1992: 601)

Locke and similar thinkers, and the European governments they advised, declared that communally held Native American lands were "wastelands" with no owner, and were open for rightful acquisition and enclosure by Europeans who would, at least in theory, fell trees and/or establish crops or livestock. Other arguments became added, though, supposedly to justify why the felling and cultivation could be done for the Europeans by slaves brought from Africa. The history of the subsequent centuries-long struggles against legally established slavery and various forms of quasi-slavery is both depressing and uplifting. The slow rise of ethically based resistance (Crawford, 2002; Gasper, 2006) provides many lessons for practically oriented development ethics.

Current development ethics work similarly assesses present-day systems of thought and practice, to see whose interests they give attention to and respect and whose they downplay or ignore. Development ethics brings to the fore who has gained and who has lost, and explores principles and practical procedures and alternatives for ethically better outcomes.

JUSTICE AND HARM; RIGHTS AND RESPONSIBILITIES

We saw that Nussbaum asked how far should "the chance of being born in one nation rather than another pervasively [determine] the life chances of every child who is born"? A sister question applies to the chance of being born in one family rather than another within a country, and here most countries take some steps to ensure access by all resident children to certain basic goods. How have people reasoned about these questions? Nussbaum (2004) comments on some major traditions, elements of which may become combined. Such ideas have been applied both to the intra-country cases and, nowadays, increasingly to international relations.

Three Relevant Philosophical Traditions

One tradition is natural law ethics, in which ethical implications are proposed based on the nature of human beings and their environment. There are various such ethics, according to how human nature and "the human condition" are interpreted, as we saw above. Las Casas, Grotius, and Locke all reasoned partly in this way, but making different interpretations. Human rights thinking too comes from this tradition, in the line of Las Casas: humans are seen as a single species, with a common worth and common necessities, and they are both deserving and capable of mutual respect and sympathy.

A second great tradition is utilitarianism, which grew out of the type of rational calculation fostered by business and markets: costs and benefits should be calculated, summed, and compared. Predominant now in business-dominated societies is an economic variant of utilitarianism that we can call "money-tarianism" (Gasper, 2004): costs and benefits are assessed in terms of monetized market values. This tends to lead to the following: only monetized effects are included; a rich person's well-being becomes considered more important, because greater purchasing power brings greater monetary impact; interpersonal distribution is sometimes treated as unimportant so that gains for the rich can outweigh costs for the poor, even the deaths of the poor because those have little or no monetary weight. Saving some minutes of business people's time can be used to justify ever more air travel that, through its impact on greenhouse gases and climate change, may cost lives of some of the poorest and most vulnerable people around the world, especially infants (Noll, 2011; WHO, 2014).

A third tradition is social contract theory, which asks: what do or would participants freely agree? It treats the participants, in important respects, as free, equal, and intelligent; everyone seeks his/her own advantage and together they negotiate a contract that supposedly gives advantage to all. This bargaining may be specified as being between all households within a nation-state, as outlined in John Rawls's *A Theory of Justice*; or only between full citizens (in John Locke's context, white male property holders); or between states, as in Rawls's *The Law of Peoples*; or, instead, between all human beings seen as members of a global society. Social contract theory sometimes ignores the record of history, by assuming that countries are self-enclosed and have engaged in free and equal inter-country negotiation; and even when formulated in the context of such an immigrant nation as the United States, it can ignore migration (as Rawls did in *A Theory of Justice*) or rule it out as irregular (as he did in *The Law of Peoples*).

To return to the case of human babies, why, considers Nussbaum, should their life chances be determined by their good or bad luck of nation of birth? No baby is responsible for its parents, and arguably the idea of a fair "social contract" should be at the level of the whole world. In addition, she asks how far any contract model, about relations between basically equal bargainers, is relevant as the primary construct for talking about justice (Nussbaum, 2004, 2006). Why not adopt a start-point that more adequately reflects our humanity, including our unequal strength plus our social nature? Humans are "people who want to live with others. A central part of our own good . . . is to produce, and live in, a world that is morally decent, a world in which all human beings have what they need to live a life with human dignity," she argues (Nussbaum, 2004: 12; see also Etzioni, 1988). Hence, she presents instead a particular type of human rights ethic (Nussbaum, 2006, 2011).

Minimizing Harm and Neglect in Displacement and in Business Operations

Much work in development ethics has involved application of and debate between different broad theories about appropriate distribution, such as those just mentioned. Some work debates different possible degrees of ethical responsibility: to ensure equal treatment or equal outcomes or fulfillment of minimum basic rights. Other work has concentrated on a restricted set of issues concerning the infliction, avoidance of, and remedies for harm. These issues are especially pressing and important in development studies, and it may be easier to make progress by applying the principles of avoiding doing harm to others (Pogge, 2008) and of taking responsibility for the effects of one's actions and therefore compensating others for harm done to them, wherever they might live (O'Neill, 1996). These issues may offer more scope for reaching agreements, such as that it is unacceptable to inflict basic harm on babies, as through climate change, and that it is unacceptable to externalize costs onto other people rather than to pay the full costs of what one initiated and benefited from. An important example of proceeding in this way is provided by Penz, Drydyk, and Bose (2011), who discuss the rights of persons potentially or actually displaced by development projects (Box 29.2). Rather than follow one specific theory of appropriate distribution, they use a more general principle of "minimizing harm and neglect" (2011: 118).

The Ruggie Framework and Principles for business corporations' public responsibilities, discussed next, provide a second important and instructive example. They have achieved broad endorsement and contributed to significant progress after decades, indeed centuries, of near-deadlock in this area.

Beginning in the 1940s the world's governments have endorsed a series of major conventions on human rights. Over those same decades the activities and power of global business corporations grew enormously, but their human rights responsibilities remained disputed and ambiguous. Corporations have often transgressed human rights and continue too often to do so: in land acquisition and displacement of local populations; in inflicting environmental damage; and by participating in extreme exploitation of workers at the bottom of global supply chains. Major conflicts and campaigns have resulted. Human rights advocates demanded that corporations adopt all the human rights obligations in international human rights law. Businesses replied that they are not governments and that they "do good by doing well," i.e., by making profits; in other words, they have argued that "the only business of business is business" and that they should be left alone, except perhaps to self-regulate and voluntarily follow self-defined codes. Organized business has had the power and government backing to block anything more extensive. In the late 1990s United Nations Secretary-General Kofi Annan took a first step beyond this deadlock by bringing forward a more ambitious voluntary code, the Global Compact. In 2005 he mandated his chief adviser in that exercise, Harvard professor John Ruggie, to lead a second stage. Ruggie's book, *Just Business* (2013), describes his approach and the results achieved.

Ruggie decided not to put forward a perfectionist proposal that would lead to no agreement and hence no progress. Instead, he proposed, first, to draw out the implications of existing human rights agreements, not try for a special new convention for businesses. Second, rather than treating corporations as if they have the same responsibilities as states—to promote, advance, and protect all the human rights specified in all the conventions—his approach focuses on the obligation of businesses to not violate the rights indicated in the four foremost existing agreements (the 1948

Mike Goldwater/Alamy Stock Photo

PHOTO 29.1 | A family trapped on a roof during the Bangladesh floods of 1998 receives a delivery. Floods are one of the unintended consequences of development and climate change.

Universal Declaration of Human Rights; the two 1966 human rights covenants—on civil and political rights and on economic, social, and cultural rights; and the 1998 ILO Declaration of Fundamental Principles and Rights at Work). The principle of non-violation is hard for businesses and their backers to object to. Third, he indicated practical implications of that principle and procedures for getting case-by-case negotiated compromises between conflicting objectives, rather than falsely assuming that covenants and laws can foresee all details and resolve all cases in advance.

In 2008 Ruggie presented the Protect, Respect, and Remedy Framework, followed in 2011 by Guiding Principles that provide suggestions about operationalization. The duties to protect and promote human rights lie primarily on states; the duty to not infringe human rights, in contrast, rests on all agents, including corporations; and citizens have a right to have access to systems for remedy of human rights violations. Corporations' duty to not violate human rights must be complemented by showing respect for the people they interact with and affect. Ruggie underlined that if corporations and their agents do not show this respect, then small conflicts are likely to escalate into bigger ones.

Ruggie's Guiding Principles provide advice on how to institutionalize human rights responsibilities. States' duties to protect imply that they must, for example, establish suitable corporate laws and regulation systems, as well as well-designed agreements with investors. Citizens' rights for remedy require the provision of adequate court systems, plus relevant national administrative mechanisms and company-level grievance mechanisms since those are often more economical and more readily attainable. Corporations' duties include respect for international law and human rights conventions even when those are not ratified or adopted

CRITICAL ISSUES

BOX 29.2 | Adjudicating Development-Forced Displacement: "Talk Softly and Carry a Big Boomerang"

Core development processes—expansion of cities, construction of irrigation and transport systems, generation and distribution of energy, mining projects, and so on—often physically displace many people. An estimated 10–15 million people each year are directly displaced. For centuries, displacement frequently has occurred with little or no consultation with, compensation to, or benefit for the displaced people, and in many contemporary cases this continues. Such displacement often mainly involves people who are relatively or absolutely poor, for the sake of bringing benefits mainly to people who are already better off. It removes livelihoods and can bring massive cultural and psychological disruption. In their book *Displacement by Development*, Canadian scholars Peter Penz, Jay Drydyk, and Pablo Bose propose a detailed ethical approach for appropriately taking into consideration both the potential benefits from development investments and the rights and interests of people liable to suffer through displacement. It deepens ideas in the report of the World Commission on Dams (2000).

Penz et al. elaborate a rights-based approach, but without absolute rights: no one, they argue, has an absolute right not to be displaced. More fundamental are the rights to participate in open and fair processes of decision-making, to be moved only for good reasons, to have equitable sharing of costs (not disproportionate costs for victimized persons), and to share equitably in benefits. "Good reasons" means that the physical development that would cause the displacement satisfies values of "responsible development" (Penz et al., 2011: 13): the promotion of human well-being and security, and respect for equity, participation and empowerment, cultural freedom, environmental sustainability, and (other) human rights and fair procedures. These are the values governments worldwide have repeatedly endorsed in international declarations and conventions.

A justified project should produce enough benefits that any people to be displaced can be treated decently, gaining rather than being broken through the project. What is a responsible project plan and what is adequate compensation must be determined through a fair procedure for adjudication of claims and resolution of disputes, with participation of those affected. *Displacement by Development* applies these principles in detail to propose rights and responsibilities of governments, investors, local residents, and international agencies.

The work of Penz et al. grew out of experience with large dam projects. Similar lessons emerged from study of conflicts over mines: lack of respect for human rights leads to conflict (and, thus, less profitability), whereas respect for human rights helps resolve conflict. Centrally important are *human rights principles* of accountability, transparency, and participation. They are more important than any *human rights norms* about what people should rightly receive, for norms can become ignored when the principles are absent. People care most about being treated with respect and wish to feel involved in the processes of balancing between competing values. They may agree to some sacrifices if they feel fairly and respectfully treated overall; such feelings depend on transparency and participation.

To initiate and sustain these processes of negotiation and adjudication and to hold governments and corporations accountable typically relies on the energies of networks of NGOs and social movements at local, national, and global levels. Only in this way can local struggles be connected to actors—national and international media, consumers, rating agencies, etc.—who are able to make large corporations and governments think again. This is the **boomerang model** of how human rights ideas exercise influence

(Risse, Ropp, and Sikkink, 1999); the boomerang of global pressure substitutes for the military "big stick" that an interventionist US President in the early twentieth century, Teddy Roosevelt, combined with "speaking softly." Human rights have served as a forceful, universally understandable language that can link and energize these networks worldwide, to gain a place at the negotiation table and to increase the mutual respect and acceptance essential for co-operation to create superior ways forward.

Source: Adapted from Gasper (2016).

or respected in a particular country (for example, in a "failed state"); and, of vital importance, they imply that businesses must show **due diligence** in respect to these duties. The businesses must have and use adequate systems that check on how far they respect human rights and repair failings, in the same way that they must have and follow systems to show due diligence in regard to, for example, financial risks.

Human Rights, Human Development, and Human Security

Human rights thinking and practice compose perhaps the biggest stream of development ethics. The human rights movement that was consolidated under the new United Nations in the 1940s chose to focus not on underlying doctrine but on consensual commitments. Such commitments can be supported on the basis of different ethical traditions, religious or secular. We will not go further into human rights approaches, for which there is a huge literature (see, e.g., Uvin, 2004; Gasper, 2007). Note, though, that broader development ethics work exists partly because human rights approaches, while essential, are not sufficient.

Human rights thinking tends to represent values in a rigid format: definite rights to which correspond definite duties of definite duty-holders. This rigidity is its strength, helping to make the claims enforceable, but is also its limitation. It leads, for example, to difficulties when values clash, as they inevitably do. Even the Christian theological language of "indivisibility" that is used in human rights conventions cannot resolve such clashes. Additional discourses for thinking about values and threats to values are necessary.

A **human development discourse**, often based on the capability approaches of Amartya Sen (1999) and Martha Nussbaum (2011), is a popular partner (see Chapter 1). Such approaches talk about facilitating access by people to values that they have reason to value. **Human security discourse** focuses on threats to the fulfillment of people's priority needs (see, e.g., United Nations General Assembly Resolution 66/290 of 2012). It is more flexible than rights language because it does not consider threats only to values that are treated as ethically inviolable; and further, it focuses on the systems of interconnecting and intersecting factors that generate threats for particular people (Gasper, 2012). Extended rights-based approaches sometimes work in a similar fashion even if under a different name. Such a rights-based approach should "look at underlying causes of poverty (and not symptoms) and therefore necessarily [build] partnerships between a large range of stakeholders; including the linkage between citizen and state, thus creating systems and mechanisms that ensure that all actors are accountable for the development process" (A. Burden of CARE USA, cited in United Nations Development Group [UNDG] report; summary at UNDG, n.d.).

REFLECTION ON MEANINGS OF WELL-BEING AND ILL-BEING

Conceptions of Development: How Much Room for Alternatives?

While development paths involve value-laden choices about which values to prioritize and pursue, development discourse typically includes strong elements of asserted necessity: claims that progress inevitably and indisputably requires some particular actions or path. The notion of "development" was strongly influenced by thinking in biology about the life path of an organism. Each organism has inherent potentials to achieve some pre-set ends; an infant animal, for example, can learn to walk but in most cases not to fly, and human beings in very favourable circumstances can live 100 years but never 1,000 years like some trees. The conception of development as the unfolding of a necessary path of progress is strong in some thinking in engineering, business, and economics. It can lead to lack of attention to alternatives and to value principles for designing and assessing alternatives.

The unilinear model contains these components:

- Progress—fundamental improvement—has a universal meaning, content, and destination, though there can be local variation in details.
- In broad terms, there is a universally necessary path to this progress—involving science, investment, economic growth, urbanization, etc.—though again there can be local variation in details.
- Given the belief in a universal path to a universal destination, there is a lack of sensitivity to alternative paths and alternative destinations and to how development paths differently affect different groups and values.

The more that the path and meaning of progress are seen as universally necessary, the less patience and attention go to securing the interests of marginal groups; instead, the entrepreneurial "developers" must stride forward and others must bear what they must bear as the necessary price of long-term progress. "We must break eggs in order to make omelettes" was a famous slogan that reportedly originated with British Colonial Secretary Joseph Chamberlain (1836–1914).

A second major idea—that national economic product is the central measure of progress—has contributed to hiding the choices of priorities and the choices between alternative paths. National economic product measures volume of monetized activity. So, first, it is a measure of activity rather than of valuable achievement; it includes, for example, the costs of medical bills, not the length and healthiness of people's lives. Second, besides inappropriately including costs, it excludes many types of major value, such as friendship, justice, peace, dignity, identity, and so on. Third, national economic product ignores how costs and benefits are distributed across different people and across generations; for example, much monetized activity can occur at the expense of exhausting resources and bequeathing problems to future generations. Unfortunately, business leaders and political leaders have frequently acted as if all important values are subsumed within gross national product (GNP), and as if any other values should be sacrificed for the sake of GNP growth. Development became equated to GNP. What other important values should be considered? Indeed, to what extent is GNP truly important, or at best just one possible means towards well-being—and not always a good one?

Ethics of Ill-Being

It makes sense to start with ill-being. As we saw, to identify harm or what is wrong may be easier than agreeing on what is good. The one thing that every theory of well-being agrees on is that suffering is undesirable (Phillips, 2006). Various dimensions of ill-being require separate attention, however; one cannot simply compare and sum different types. Narayan highlights **voicelessness** and powerlessness, for example, in her summary of the *Voices of the Poor* study, which reviewed over 60,000 interviews with poor people:

> The study establishes, first, that poverty is multidimensional and has important noneconomic dimensions; second, that poverty is always specific to a location and a social group, and awareness of these specifics is essential . . . ; and third, that despite [these] differences in the way poverty is experienced by different groups and in different places, there are striking commonalities. . . . Poor people's lives are characterized by powerlessness and voicelessness . . . . (Narayan, 2000: 18)

Worse than suffering is undeserved suffering. Historically, and still currently, ruling groups nationally and internationally often have argued that most of the suffering poor deserve their situation, because of misdeeds in a previous life or alleged indolence or incompetence. "The deserving poor" were a minority. We saw that European invaders of the New World mostly considered the indigenous peoples incompetent wasters of resources who did not even deserve their own lands. We noted how especially inapplicable these sorts of argument are in relation to babies and children.

Of critical ethical significance is undeserved avoidable suffering. Modern technology and riches make it relatively easily possible to fulfill basic needs around the world, notably children's health and education needs. Yet, health research funding has been and remains overwhelmingly focused not on the diseases of the people who live short, vulnerable lives, but on further extension of the lives and comfort of the rich. Transferring just eight days of global military budgets would cover the additional annual costs required for achieving good-quality universal pre-primary, primary, and lower secondary education, according to UNESCO (2015: 8).

These are cases of non-inclusion in the benefits of economic development. We saw earlier cases of deliberate exclusion by forcible displacement. Other cases concern "collateral damage" through negative externalities of economic expansion, like climate deterioration. Others still, such as frequent farmer suicides in India, involve "disadvantageous inclusion"; farmers are seduced into taking large loans for high-input agriculture, and these loans can bankrupt them in climatically adverse years.

Ethics of Well-Being

A strong liberal strand in development ethics, as in the work of Amartya Sen, proposes leaving the choice of priorities to personal and societal reflection, with that reflection and choice as themselves central features in "the good life." Nonetheless, Sen recognizes the priority for a good life of fulfillment of some universal basic needs, such as in nutrition, education, and health. This needs-fulfillment can be seen as the removal of fundamental elements of ill-being, including most notably not living a full, healthy lifespan.

Beyond those elements, well-being research (summarized in Phillips, 2006) does suggest some shared fundamentals of well-being. Etzioni (2012) highlights three elements: (1) personal relationships and friendship; (2) intellectual/spiritual life; (3) social participation and contribution. Much other well-being research underlines the prime importance of physical and mental health; balanced time budgets, not only monetary budgets, including having enough time for recreation, reflection, and participation; quality of work-time; and feeling treated with respect and dignity, including eventually in the process of dying. Chilean development theorist Manfred Max-Neef's model of human needs reflects much of this: for all areas of need it considers not only a dimension of Having but also dimensions of Being, Doing, and Interacting.

The Universal Declaration of Human Rights and similar documents do not leave elements of the good life purely to be discussed afresh in each situation, without any constitutional prioritization, for that would leave too much power to the powerful. Market capitalism, for example, has built-in biases towards supplying "information" that says that having more commodities will bring all good things for everyone (who is deserving) and urges us that economic growth should never end and is essential for social order. At the same time, market capitalism undersupplies information that is hard to make a profit from, including information about some non-commodity aspects of life and about negative side effects of commodity-centred society.

Much work in development ethics considers the human quest for meaning and identity, a quest that unfortunately also can take undesirable forms such as nationalist aggression, environmental destruction, or religious zealotry. Denis Goulet (1971) analyzed "The Cruel Choice" felt in many cultures regarding a perceived need to abandon types of behaviour and tradition that constituted their felt identity as the price of "catching up" with foreign powers and hence maintaining independence and respect; Peter Berger (1974) explored the associated "calculus of meaning." Such issues remain of central importance. The 2015 encyclical of Pope Francis, "On Care for Our Common Home," is one recent exploration, as are the Latin American schools of thought and practice on *buen vivir* or living well (Gudynas, 2011).

Box 29.3 looks at the thought-provoking case of Japan, which illustrates choices faced and made in national development and the ethical significance of those choices. These included its intense orientation towards nationalist values, which led it to become a colonial

CRITICAL ISSUES

BOX 29.3 | Japan: The "Calculus of Meaning"

Between the 1850s and 1890s Japan moved from deliberate isolation from the rest of the world during the previous 200 years to become the first non-Western industrialized country. It radically transformed itself in order to "catch up" with the West. Paradoxically, it did so in order to remain distinctive, unique, and independent from the West, the same reasons for which it had closed itself off in the seventeenth century. In 1853–4, the militarily and economically vastly stronger United States dictated to Japan that it must reopen to foreign trade or the country would be forced open. The ruling Japanese elites acquiesced, in order not to become a subject country like India. In 1871–3, more than half the leadership of the "Meiji Revolution" then spent almost two years travelling across the United States and Europe to learn about "the great principles which are to be our guide in the future." This Iwakura Mission's report noted that "the wealth and prosperity one sees now in Europe dates to an appreciable degree from the period after 1800. It has taken scarcely 40 years to produce" (cited in Pyle, 2007: 85). The Mission saw that different paths of transformation were possible and explicitly rejected the crude exploitation and squalor of Britain's *laissez-faire* Industrial Revolution.

Already by 1895 Japan was strong enough to graduate to be a so-called "civilized" country and to impose itself on its weaker neighbours, China and Korea. While reinforcing Japanese pride in a supposed unique "Japanese spirit," the extraordinary success in imitating selected Western patterns and models left cultural self-doubt: we have copied the West, but what are we now? Japan continued for decades to seek strength and status through imitating the West and at the same time trying to compensate for feelings of lost identity. By the 1930s Japan sought to impose itself further across East Asia, in pursuit of natural resources and Great Power status. Faced with American demands that it withdraw, backed by trade embargos, Japanese leaders this time refused. Proud in their felt strength and supposed uniqueness, angry at Western domination, and unwilling to "lose face," Japan's nationalist elites chose in 1941 to attack their far stronger antagonist, leading to years of war, destruction and death, and eventual crushing defeat. Post-war Japan has rebuilt on the basis not only of national solidarity and ambition, but also now of a strong strand of declared universalist ethics.

Source: Based on Pyle (2007).

power that dictated to other countries, and its search for sources of status and self-respect that could apparently not be fully satisfied only by economic advance.

ACTIVITIES AND TOOLS IN DEVELOPMENT ETHICS

Development ethics thinking and action can be seen as having three aspects: first, observation, experience, and exposure; second, conceptualizing, analyzing, and theorizing; third, attempted application, adaptation, and new learning. The three aspects are to some extent a sequence of stages, but they occur also in parallel and in continuing interaction. Each involves particular skills and potential pitfalls.

Observation, Exposure, Sensitization

This first stage includes a "look-and-feel" phase. Writers and speakers and those we encounter invite us (or we ask ourselves) to "Look at this experience—think and feel about it." They ask for our attention, widen our awareness, perhaps open our eyes and broaden our categories. Exposure also brings a risk of desensitization: we can stop noticing things that become familiar. Some exposure is direct, through fieldwork, visits, "gap years," and so on. This direct exposure can have a special force, if it is not merely "development tourism." Box 29.4 explains the method of "immersion visits," nowadays used sometimes for senior development bureaucrats.

Most of our exposure to other people's lives must be second-hand, through research literature, novels, newspapers, television, films, and other people's accounts. These

IMPORTANT CONCEPTS

BOX 29.4 | Immersion Visits: Putting Yourself in Other People's Shoes

During the past 20 years, "immersion visits" have been talked about and sometimes practised in development bureaucracies. Some senior and mid-level staff may spend a few days, including at least two nights, sharing the lives of poor people. Often they report dramatic changes in their perspective. This box draws on a survey of such experiences by Irvine et al. (2004).

- "I have asked myself what would have happened if I had spent one week per year in a village somewhere over the last decade. I am quite sure it would have made a difference to me. Ten different contexts, and a number of faces and names to have in mind when reading, thinking, writing, taking decisions and arguing in our bureaucracy." (Respondent, cited by Irvine et al., 2004: 4)

The reports of dramatic learning come not only from foreign staff. The following quotations are from Tanzanian staff members of an international NGO, after an immersion visit within their own country (Irvine et al., 2004: 12).

- "I thought I knew about village life as my roots are in the village and I still visit family in my village from time to time. But I know nothing about what it is like to be poor and how hidden this kind of poverty can be."
- "I've worked in rural villages for more than 20 years but I never had an experience like this."
- "Even village leaders could not tell you what we experienced for ourselves."
- "I could not believe that the family only had one broken hoe to cultivate with. It was like trying to dig with a teaspoon. I will never forget that."

Even a two-week, not merely two-day, visit would not be enough to understand adequately other people's life-worlds. But brief exposures under the right circumstances can help visitors to realize that they do not understand what they thought they did, and to motivate them to try to better understand. The functions of immersion visits for development professionals, ranging from short stays to "gap years," include:

- To learn, about a very complex world; to see interconnections and go beyond stereotypes.
- To update, in a fast-changing world.
- To get beneath the artificial surfaces on display during brief official visits.
- To have time to listen and watch, not only to talk, and to learn also from children and the old.
- To counteract the centralizing, generalizing tendencies of managerial thought in big organizations.
- To stimulate "double-loop learning," i.e., rethinking of models and assumptions, not just feeding new data into existing mental programs.
- To gain credibility as a professional, commentator, and contributor.
- To become more empathetic, sympathetic, and motivated.

sources give us access to far wider ranges of experience than we could have directly, and they come in forms that are selected and organized to make a point. In particular, imaginative literature and films form a treasure store of influential and often insightful interpretations of human living. Sometimes "the trained sensibilities of a novelist or a poet may provide a richer source of social insight than, say, the impression of untrained informants on which so much of sociological research currently rests" (Coser, 1963: 3; see also Lewis, Rodgers, and Woolcock, 2014). However, we need to be cautious in regard to authors' interpretations and our own interpretations of the authors. As discussed later, tools of discourse analysis can help us to better identify and assess these interpretations.

Why can imaginative literature and films be such influential sources (whether for good or ill)? Several of the reasons apply also to real stories, historical accounts, and biographies, but Nussbaum argues that imaginative literature has an extra power because it takes us richly and vividly into the lives, thoughts, and emotions of a wide range of protagonists. Her book *Poetic Justice* shows how effectively Charles Dickens's novel *Hard Times* refuted the narrow "money-tarian" perspectives that underlay the inhumane industrialization in nineteenth-century Britain, perspectives that Japan's Meiji Revolution leaders also rejected. Compared to the abstracted and often generalized talk in social science, political ideologies, and official documents, stories show case-specifics and thus deepen our understanding of local dynamics; they show people's emotions and calculations; they show important interactions of types that we are unable to model in social science; they present the multi-faceted combinations and coincidences that arise in real situations and that can have major consequences; and they involve and educate (for good or ill) our emotions, because they help us to think about—indeed, almost experience—what someone else's life is like and what our own life would be like if we were equally exposed. The ethnographers in *Avatar* come to know literally what it is like to live as the indigenes do, through the transference of their minds into bodies like those of the indigenes. Films, novels, and the best journalism and travel accounts can take us in that same direction.

Even much less detailed forms of case illustration, real or imaginary, can be important in ethical thinking when they help us to put ourselves in other people's shoes (Rifkin, 2010) and/or to grasp the implications of particular circumstances and combinations (Gasper, 2000, 2004). So cases of various degrees of detail are used in philosophical theorizing and in policy analysis training for the second and third stages in development ethics.

Analysis and Theorization

The stage of systematizing ideas can begin with an "identify and describe" phase. One seeks to clarify value choices encountered in situations and to describe the systems of values present, for example, in important documents, policies, theories, and institutions. That phase blends into the next, of trying to further analyze and assess these ideas. Activities here include clarifying concepts and checking logic, including the degree of mutual consistency of different values, partly through examining implications and asking: What do you think your stated values will bring if fulfilled? And how can your higher-level values in fact be furthered? If felt necessary, one can attempt some synthesis and innovation of ideas, even system-building. This theorizing should grow out of close interfacing with a real-world context of experience and practice; otherwise, disasters arise, such as a theory of justice that ignores an essential real-world feature like migration. These phases of thinking match those in "value-critical policy analysis" (e.g., Schmidt, 2006; Schön and Rein, 1994), which involves identifying existing intellectual frames and what they include and exclude, by using tools such as indicated in the first half of Box 29.5 (see, e.g., Gasper, 2004), then comparing and assessing the frames and trying, where necessary, to craft more adequate alternatives by using tools indicated in the second half of Box 29.5 (see, e.g., Gasper, 2006).

Consider two examples of using such methods. First, a review of development literatures in India during its decades of independence shows continuous strong reference to visions of economic and technological transformation, at the same time as disputed and changing pictures of the public sector versus private business. This is not surprising, but the methods also reveal some less obvious continuous relative blind spots, such as the lack of attention to sanitation facilities for ordinary and poor people and to the enormous numbers of informal-sector migrant workers and their families.

Second, comparison of two global reports on the challenge of climate change for low-income

IMPORTANT CONCEPTS

BOX 29.5 | Basic Questions and Tools in Value-Sensitive Discourse Analysis and Philosophical Ethics

Discourse Analysis/Frame Analysis

Preliminary. Ask who wrote the text, for what audience and purpose, and how this should affect your interpretation of it.

Categories. Identify the categories and labels used in the text; and those that were *not* used. Reflect on the *system* of categories. Look especially at the "cast of characters" and at who is ignored (e.g., perhaps migrants, non-nationals, women, children).

Figurative language. Identify the key metaphors used; they provide clues about the assumptions and way of thinking, the way of making sense of complexity. Study also the other attention-grabbers and attention-organizers: the choice of examples, the use of images and proverbs.

Values. Identify the praise and criticism language; this provides clues about the unstated values, conclusions, and proposals, in addition to the stated ones.

Frameworks of inclusion/exclusion. From the above steps and other indicators such as the recurrent vocabulary used, identify which issues, identities, and interests receive consideration (e.g., economic growth?) and which do not (e.g., external effects; unintended effects; adequate access of poor people to water and sanitation; morbidity and mortality among the poor; the language of human rights?).

Ethics

Preliminary. Do not assume that nouns in language are necessarily definite things in reality. (For example, do not assume "development" is an entity/phenomenon like biological evolution or electricity.)

History. Who did what? Who caused the problem? Who contributed well and deserves reward?

Role reversal tests and empathetic reflection:

1. Ask what would be my feelings if X happened to me/my family/friends/familiars.
2. Ask how other people feel when X happens to them/their families/friends/familiars.

Consequences and other implications. Ask what would be the requirements and the results of acting on the basis of a given idea/principle.

Consistency. For each view/principle/action ask: is it consistent with the proponent's (e.g., my) other beliefs and commitments? (For example, the Jubilee 2000 debt-relief campaign found that all the countries that had insisted on full repayment of least-developed-country debts had themselves had major instances of receiving debt relief or forgiveness or of repudiating debts.)

countries—the United Nations *Human Development Report 2007/8* and the World Bank's *World Development Report 2010*—reveals two different mental worlds, reflecting different priority values (Gasper et al., 2013). Table 29.1 compares word counts in their almost identical-length executive summaries. The United Nations report refers intensively to issues of justice, human rights, and the interests of "our children and grandchildren"; the World Bank report never mentions human rights and emphasizes, instead, efficiency, consumption, and management towards "climate-smart" solutions. The different patterns of vocabulary help us to identify more vividly and confidently the different guiding values of the two reports.

TABLE 29.1 | Vocabularies of the Overview Chapters in the *Human Development Report 2007/8* and *World Development Report 2010*

	HDR	WDR
we	56	11
children	11	3
future generations	19	0
the world's poor	17	0
human	102	8
human rights	11	0
efficiency/efficient/ inefficient/inefficiency	21	48
effective	2	12
climate-smart	0	9
consumption	7	19
threshold/s	7	1
manage/(mis)management/ mismanaging	6	26

Source: Adapted from Gasper et al. (2013)

Application, Adaptation, Action

Applying ethical awareness and ethical analysis in practical ways calls for further types of skill. It does not happen automatically and effortlessly. Pure philosophy does not and cannot solve all problems. Practical ethics is therefore more than just "applied" ethics, more than just applying general theories. We have to use imperfect general ideas together with typically imperfect data about a range of relevant factors to look at distinctive real cases, in which the need for action often seems urgent. We need to identify good enough estimations, not play with philosophy for philosophy's sake; and we have to deal with the limitations of any system of ideas when applied and, usually, the need to negotiate and compromise with other idea systems. (Hence the fulfillment of basic needs has a special importance, because these are necessary conditions for people to follow any more elaborate ethic, such as of satisfaction or freedom or virtue or spiritual growth.) Case studies and stories are useful here too,

UN Photo/Jean-Marc Ferré

PHOTO 29.2 | The UN Human Rights Council unanimously adopted the UN Guiding Principles on Business and Human Rights. Here, we see a collective response to ethical challenges and development.

for learning how to better grapple with choices in real situations. The cases deepen our thinking beyond the theories. The questions at the end of this chapter include two such discussion cases.

One fundamental challenge is how to deal with uncertainty, not ignore that it exists, and deal with how the associated risks are distributed across different groups and persons. For example, much discussion of risks arising from the climate change generated by economic development based on fossil fuels is actually about the risk, given our uncertainty about exact future impacts, of unnecessarily reducing economic growth due to excessive precautionary responses. That sort of discussion reflects the concerns of people who feel they benefit from existing and future production and are little exposed to its costs. Also requiring attention, though, are the risks of damage to the health, lives, and livelihoods of marginal people, usually in poor countries. Those risks may rank higher in importance than the first set when we bring almost any ethical theory into the discussion (Gasper, 2012).

Another fundamental challenge concerns how to get ethical concerns onto organizational and public agendas, and gain attention in a sustained way for weaker groups and uncomfortable issues such as displaced people and basic sanitation. Ideas of human rights, human development, human security, and so on should feed not only into critical evaluations of existing outcomes, but into the problem identification and problem definition done by powerful organizations and into the design of action alternatives. Indicators are one key to capturing attention. It is often argued that many social issues—such as the quality of childhood, local culture, and social networks—should not be assessed in monetary terms. However, they may still require strong non-monetary indicators if they are to influence public decision-making and be converted into enforceable responsibilities. (For one currently debated example, regarding children's rights, see www.kidsrightsindex.org/.)

Transferring ethical criteria and critiques into influence and action requires creative thinking. Box 29.6

IMPORTANT CONCEPTS

BOX 29.6 | Policy Instruments for Promoting Human Rights

"Carrots and sticks"

- Laws, rules, litigation
- Monitoring—using vivid attention-grabbing indicators
- "Naming and shaming" of violators
- Intra-national and international sanctions and intervention
- Reparations
- Affirmative action policies
- Victim empowerment
- Capacity and skills investment in agencies for these activities

"Sermons and dialogue"

- Education: in primary and secondary schools, and via public information
- Education: especially in university schools of law, business, engineering, and policy and governance—to influence systems of planning, design, and evaluation
- Voluntary codes, guidelines
- Museums, monuments, and other instruments of memory
- Public debate; mass media
- Truth and reconciliation commissions; transformative public dialogues
- Capacity and skills investment for these activities, including for listening, mediation, innovative problem-solving

Hispalois/Wikipedia

PHOTO 29.3 | Statue portraying Bartolomé de las Casas who defended indigenous peoples in Mexico against Spanish colonial exploitation. Las Casas' work is an example of the importance of reflection, empathy, and taking a stand on human rights.

presents the example of the very broad range of policy instruments that are relevant for promoting human rights.

CONCLUSION

Development ethics themes and tools apply and connect to many topics besides those concentrated on in this chapter: for example, religions, migration to urban areas and other countries, transnational connections, tourism, and the global impacts of consumption patterns. You are encouraged to apply the themes and tools to areas covered by the other chapters. Further, the root concerns of development ethics—an insistence on not automatically equating societal improvement to economic growth, not ignoring costs of many types and their distribution, and looking for and comparing value and strategy alternatives—apply also for rich countries. By thinking qualitatively about what are costs and benefits, harm, and personal and societal priorities, what is deserved and what not, and relations between generations, development ethics as a field of thought helps development studies and development policy to treat human lives more seriously.

SUMMARY

This chapter introduced some of the major areas in ethics of national and global development: asking what is the nature of well-being and ill-being and what should be meant by desirable "development"; considering ideas about equitable distribution of the costs and benefits from change; assessing debates around what are ethically legitimate rights and the responsibilities in relation to infringement of those rights; and underlying all these, examining how concepts of development typically contain and depend on values and on conceptions of the elements of living as a human being. It discussed examples that reflect central development themes, including appropriation of valuable natural resources, as in the colonization of the Americas; displacement of resident populations, as in major infrastructure investments and mining projects; and the global operations of huge businesses and their associated human rights obligations. It presented also some tools for value-sensitive observation and critical analysis and for connecting such concerns to practical action.

QUESTIONS FOR CRITICAL THOUGHT

1. Watch this five-minute film on farmer suicides: www.youtube.com/watch?v=Av6dx9yNiCA. Which ethical principles do different speakers appeal to? Are there other ethical principles you consider relevant here? What more would you like to know about the case in order to answer these questions better?
2. Watch the following 12-minute film on deforestation and displacement of people in Latin America to make way for soya farms: www.youtube.com/watch?v=fzdnCmLHvNQ&feature=related. Soya is exported to Europe and used for factory farming of animals. Try to identify all the groups involved. Which ethical principles do different speakers appeal to? Are other ethical principles relevant in this case? Do the principles conflict with each other? How can one try to analyze and resolve such conflicts? Why does this type of harm, conflict, and exclusion arise? What would you like to know more about the case?
3. *Life in a Day* is a crowd-sourced documentary of extracts from the lives of hundreds of people around the world on 24 July 2010 (available on YouTube). Consider commonalities and differences in the values that you see among them.
4. The Norwegian anthropologist Fredrik Barth proposed that subjectively chosen definitions of development are more effective for furthering action and improvement. So, is part of development to make one's own definition of development? What is your definition?
5. Examine a recent development policy report. Identify the concepts, categories, "cast of characters," and value criteria used in the report, how different groups are characterized, and which issues and groups are downgraded or omitted.

SUGGESTED READINGS

Gasper, Des. 2004. *The Ethics of Development*. Edinburgh: Edinburgh University Press.

———. 2007. "Human rights, human needs, human development, human security." *Forum for Development Studies* 34, 1: 9–43.

Nussbaum, Martha C. 1995. *Poetic Justice: The Literary Imagination and Public Life*. Boston: Beacon Press.

———. 2011. *Creating Capabilities: The Human Development Approach*. Cambridge, Mass.: Harvard University Press.

Ruggie, John G. 2013. *Just Business: Multinational Corporations and Human Rights*. New York: W.W. Norton.

BIBLIOGRAPHY

Arneil, B. 1992. "John Locke, natural law and colonialism." *History of Political Thought* 13, 4: 587–603.

Berger, P. 1974. *Pyramids of Sacrifice: Political Ethics and Social Change*. New York: Basic Books.

Coser, L.A. 1963. *Sociology through Literature: An Introductory Reader*. Englewood Cliffs,NJ: Prentice-Hall.

Cowen, M.P., and R.W. Shenton. 1996. *Doctrines of Development*, London: Routledge.

Crawford, N. 2002. *Argument and Change in World Politics*. Cambridge: Cambridge University Press.

Etzioni, A. 1988: *The Moral Dimension: Toward a New Economics*. New York: Free Press.

———. 2012. "You Don't Need to Buy This." www.youtube.com/watch?v=FN3z8gtDUFE.

Gasper, D. 2000. "Anecdotes, situations, histories—Reflections on the use of cases in thinking about ethics and development practice." *Development and Change* 31, 5: 1055–83.

———. 2004. "Studying aid: Some methods." In J. Gould and H.S. Marcussen, eds, *Ethnographies of Aid*. Roskilde, Denmark: Roskilde University, International Development Studies, 45–92.

———. 2006. "What is the point of development ethics?" *Ethics and Economics* 4, 2.

———. 2012. "Climate change—The need for a human rights agenda within a framework of shared human security." *Social Research: An International Quarterly of the Social Sciences* 79, 4: 983–1014.

———. 2016. "The ethics of economic development and human displacement." In G. DeMartino and D. McCloskey, eds, *Oxford Handbook on Professional Economic Ethics*. New York: Oxford University Press, 534–57.

———, A.V. Portocarrero, and A.L. St Clair. 2013. "The framing of climate change and development: A comparative analysis of the *Human Development Report 2007/8* and the *World Development Report 2010*." *Global Environmental Change* 23, 1: 28–39.

Goulet, D. 1971. *The Cruel Choice: A New Concept in the Theory of Development*. New York: Atheneum.

Gudynas, E. 2011. "Buen vivir: Today's tomorrow." *Development* 54, 4: 441–7.

Irvine, R., R. Chambers, and R. Eyben. 2004. *Learning from Poor People's Experience: Immersions*. Brighton, UK: Institute of Development Studies.

Kitching, G. 1982. *Development and Underdevelopment in Historical Perspective*. London: Methuen.

Las Casas, B. de. 1552. *A Brief Account of the Destruction of the Indies*. www.gutenberg.org/cache/epub/20321/pg20321-images.html.

Lewis, D., D. Rodgers, and M. Woolcock. 2014. "The fiction of development: Literary representation as a source of authoritative knowledge." In Lewis, Rodgers, and Woolcock, eds, *Popular Representations of Development: Insights from Novels, Films, Television, and Social Media*. New York: Routledge.

Max-Neef, M. 1991. *Human Scale Development*. New York: Apex.

Narayan, D. 2000. "Poverty is powerlessness and voicelessness." *Finance and Development* 37: 18–21.

Nolt, J. 2011. "How harmful are the average American's greenhouse gas emissions?" *Ethics, Policy & Environment* 14, 1: 3–10.

Nussbaum, M. 2004. "Beyond the social contract: Capabilities and global justice." *Oxford Development Studies* 32, 1: 3–18.

———. 2006. *Frontiers of Justice*. Cambridge, Mass.: Harvard University Press.

O'Neill, O. 1996. *Towards Justice and Virtue*. Cambridge: Cambridge University Press.

Pai, H.-H. 2013. *Scattered Sand: The Story of China's Rural Migrants*. London: Verso.

Parekh, B. 1997. "The West and its others." In K. Ansell-Pearson, B. Parry, and J. Squires, eds, *Cultural Readings of Imperialism*. London: Lawrence & Wishart, 173–93.

Penz, P., J. Drydyk, and P. Bose, 2011: *Displacement by Development*. Cambridge: Cambridge Univ. Press.

Phillips, D. 2006. *Quality of Life*. Abingdon, UK: Routledge.

Pogge, T. 2008. *World Poverty and Human Rights*. Cambridge: Polity Press.

Pyle, K. 2007. *Japan Rising*. New York: Public Affairs.

Rawls, J. 1971. *A Theory of Justice*. Cambridge, Mass.: Harvard University Press.

———. 1999. *The Law of Peoples*. Cambridge, Mass.: Harvard University Press.

Rifkin, J. 2010. "The empathic civilisation." RSA Animate. www.youtube.com/watch?v=l7AWnfFRc7g&feature=related.

Risse, T., S. Ropp, and K. Sikkink, eds. 1999. *The Power of Human Rights: International Norms and Domestic Change*. Cambridge: Cambridge University Press.

Sen, A. 1999. *Development as Freedom*. New York: Oxford University Press.

Schmidt, R. 2006. "Value-critical policy analysis." In D. Yanow and P. Schwartz-Shea, eds, *Interpretation and Method*. Armonk, NY: M.E. Sharpe, 300–15.

Schön, D., and M. Rein. 1994. *Frame Reflection: Towards the Resolution of Intractable Policy Controversies*. New York: Basic Books.

UNESCO. 2015. *Pricing the Right to Education: The Cost of Reaching New Targets by 2030*. Paris: UNESCO. http://unesdoc.unesco.org/images/0023/002321/232197E.pdf.

United Nations Development Group. n.d. "Final summary of e-discussion: What do human rights principles mean for daily development work?" http://hrbaportal.org/wp-content/files/1238763225summary.doc.

Uvin, P. 2004. *Human Rights and Development*. Bloomfield, Conn.: Kumarian Press.

World Bank. 2010. *World Development Report 2010: Development and Climate Change*. Washington: World Bank.

World Commission on Dams. 2000. *Dams and Development*. London: Earthscan.

World Health Organization (WHO). 2014. *Quantitative Risk Assessment of the Effects of Climate Change on Selected Causes of Death, 2030s and 2050s*. Geneva: WHO.

GLOSSARY

absolute poverty The inability to meet a basic minimum level of living standards due to lack of income or resources, i.e., the minimum level of income required for physical survival. The World Bank defines this level as US$1.25 per day measured at international *purchasing power parity*.

adaptation Action to assist in coping with the effects of climate change, such as construction of barriers to protect against rising sea levels.

agricultural extensification A means of increasing food production only through an expansion of the total area cultivated and not by increasing the rate of labour or capital inputs.

agricultural intensification A means of increasing the amount of food produced by a given area of land through the use of additional labour or capital, such as the increased use of manure or fertilizer, planting more crops per year, or using higher-yielding crop varieties, irrigation, or more labour or chemicals for weed and pest control.

agriculture-based countries Countries where agriculture is a dominant component of overall GDP and of GDP growth and where most of the poor are in rural areas.

alternative development People-centred, participatory approaches to development that seek to de-objectify the recipients of aid and involve them in the process of their own material improvement, in contrast to Western development models that are seen to impose "solutions" to "problems" on aid recipients.

alternatives New ways of thinking and doing. Promoted by global ethics as a way of improving human well-being and dignity.

annual statement of costs and benefits Accounting tool sometimes described as a cash flow (for financial analysis) or as a resource statement (in economic analysis).

appropriate technology Technologies that suit the environmental, cultural, and economic contexts to which they are transferred.

authoritarian regimes Regimes in which state officials prevent society from participating in the decision-making process; frequently resort to arbitrary violence against society; extract, use, and distribute economic resources in an arbitrary and often violent fashion; and are rarely held accountable (Médard, 1991).

basic human needs Minimum acceptable levels for food, nutrition, drinking water, health, education, and shelter.

basic needs approach An approach to development popularized in the 1970s that encouraged national governments and aid donors to prioritize policies, budgets, and actions that would ensure disadvantaged people were able to access a minimum level of well-being, including food, water, shelter, and primary education.

bilateral Agreements or relations involving only two governments; often distinguished from broader multilateral agreements, institutions, or relationships.

bilateral aid or bilateral assistance Foreign aid provided by the government of one country (usually industrialized) directly to the government of another country (usually developing).

bilateral investment treaties Agreements that enunciate the principles of treatment that foreign investors are entitled to receive from host governments and that permit multinational corporations to sue host governments in international arbitration tribunals for breach of obligations.

bioaccumulation The accumulation of substances such as pesticides or other chemicals in an organism, occurring when an organism absorbs a toxic substance at a rate greater than that at which the substance is lost.

bluewash A play on the word "whitewash," which suggests that UN agencies (known for their blue logos) can cover up the flaws of the private sector by associating with them.

boomerang pattern, model, effect, or strategy A concept developed by Margaret Keck and Kathryn Sikkink to explain how local non-governmental organizations can influence their own governments by pressuring actors external to the country, such as international organizations or the home government of a multinational corporation, which in turn directly pressure the government in question.

Bretton Woods institutions The World Bank and the International Monetary Fund, so called because they were founded in Bretton Woods, New Hampshire, in 1944.

Bretton Woods system A system of fixed exchange rates between countries to promote financial stability and international trade, implemented following World War II, in which all national currencies were pegged to the US dollar, which in turn was backed by gold until 1971, when the US went off the gold standard. This system laid the basis for the original roles of the International Monetary Fund and the World Bank.

buen vivir To live a full (good) life, a post-development concept derived from the cosmology of numerous indigenous societies that emphasizes the oneness of all animate (and inanimate) beings in nature, and thus is contrary to the notion that nature must be conquered and governed.

capability approach A method of understanding poverty and development developed by Nobel Prize–winning economist Amartya Sen, who argues that development should not be seen simply as rising income levels but rather as an increase in individuals' substantive freedoms and ability to make choices they value.

capitalism The economic organization of society based on private ownership and control of the means of production whereby people are free to sell their labour in the marketplace. Owners of the means of production are able to make profit, and accumulate more capital, by paying wage workers less than what the owners earn through the sale of the products.

chartered company A company that received monopoly commercial rights from a state ruler for the purpose of promoting trade and exploration in a specific geographic area. Chartered companies, such as the East India Company and the Hudson's Bay Company, served as vehicles for European overseas expansion, becoming vitally important in the seventeenth century.

citizenship A status conferred on the inhabitants of a state, which provides them with a wide range of social and political rights, including the right to vote, to access state services (such as education and legal counselling), and to have a fair trial. For a regime to be truly democratic, these rights must be applied equally, fairly, and systematically (everywhere and at any time) (O'Donnell, 2004).

civil and political rights Rights based on the Universal Declaration of Human Rights that establish an individual's right to be free from state oppression and to participate in the political process. Civil and political rights are the principal rights recognized in the West.

civil society The collectivity of social organizations that are not controlled by the state or business, such as church groups, environmental lobbies, and so on. The presence and active participation of civil society organizations is thought to be a necessary if not sufficient guarantee of democracy, good governance, and participatory development.

clientelism A situation where political actors support the economic interests of particular groups in society in exchange for their loyalty. Typically, resources are exchanged for political support. When states need to cut such private deals to stay in power, the national interest and the possibility for enacting policies and applying resources that lead to collective development are often lost.

climate change A pattern of change affecting global or regional climate, as measured by yardsticks such as average temperature and rainfall, or an alteration in frequency of extreme weather conditions. Both natural processes and human activity may cause this variation.

CNN effect The broadcasting of humanitarian emergencies onto television screens around the world—first seen globally in 1984 with BBC coverage of a famine in Ethiopia—which can stimulate public interest.

collective action problem A situation in which multiple individuals (also communities or countries) would all benefit from a certain action (e.g., reducing greenhouse gas emissions), but the associated cost of taking action makes it highly unlikely that any individual can or will undertake and solve the problem alone.

colonialism The territorial conquest, occupation, and direct control of one country by another. In some instances, it also involved large-scale settlement and nearly always brought systems of great political inequality and economic exploitation.

colonization The processes of occupation and administration of a territory, country, or region by another and the consequences of these processes.

commodity control schemes Internationally managed commodity agreements that entailed participating nation-states agreeing to adhere to country-specific quotas for the amount of their product they could sell on the market in order to force prices up and keep them relatively stable. Agreements were signed for most major tropical commodities in the 1950s; by the end of the 1980s, most of them had become defunct.

common pool resources Goods consisting of natural or human-made resource systems (e.g., a community forest or fishing ground), the size or characteristics of which make it difficult, but not impossible, to define recognized users and exclude other users altogether; also called common property resources.

communitarianism The ethical standpoint that individuals belong to a political and social community, that this is a factor of key moral relevance, and that a social order that fosters communal bonds is morally preferable to an individualistic social order. Often contrasted with liberalism.

comparative advantage A theory of international trade formulated by David Ricardo in the nineteenth century according to which each nation has an economic advantage relative to other nations for the production of some goods. Consequently, the theory assumes that it would be to the relative benefit of all nations to focus on producing those goods for which they have the strongest comparative advantage and then trade with each other for the goods for which they do not.

compradorial Term coined by radical theorists to describe the ties of the developing state to external interests, whether foreign governments, investors, or military, and to the local resource-owning and internationally oriented capitalist class. Thus a formally independent state can be considered under the influence of foreign interests.

comprehensive primary health care A model of health system design that emphasizes strengthening of universally accessible basic health services and integrating health care with social and economic development. It is often contrasted with selective primary health care, a model that emphasizes biomedical interventions directed at specific diseases or risk factors and assessed for their "cost-effectiveness."

conflict trap Grounded in the liberal theory of violence, an argument claiming that countries that have experienced civil war are likely to plunge into renewed violence unless the conditions that gave rise to war in the first place—underdevelopment—are addressed. The concept was promoted in a 2003 World Bank report, *Breaking the Conflict Trap.*

corporate social responsibility The idea that corporations have a moral responsibility beyond their shareholders to a broader set of individuals and groups, known as stakeholders, affected by the activities of the firm, including employees and local communities. Corporate social responsibility is a voluntary commitment of firms to improve the quality of their relationship with stakeholders.

cosmopolitanism An ethical position that holds national boundaries to be irrelevant to questions of justice and argues that our common humanity entails a set of shared values and responsibilities to people around the world regardless of where we were born or currently live.

cost-benefit analysis Detailed measurement and comparison of the dollar value in costs and benefits of a proposed project.

cost-effectiveness analysis Analysis of a proposed project in terms of its relevancy or efficiency, as in health or education, where it is difficult to place a specific dollar value on such things as a human life, relief from suffering, or the education of a primary school cohort.

cultural relativism The theoretical position that holds that the values and beliefs of a cultural formation have to be evaluated on the basis of standards internal to that culture. While cultural relativism is helpful in countering notions of ethnocentrism—the belief in the superiority of one's own culture—if taken to the extreme, it can ignore the many universal features of human physical and social life across different cultures.

cultural turn The theoretical trajectory that many disciplines in the social sciences have taken in the past couple of decades. It basically uses culture as an explanatory variable to understand society and social transformation.

culture A complex concept referring to the web of meanings and understandings generated by identifiable groups of people about themselves and the natural world and the ability to convey these meanings and understandings through symbols, actions, and utterances.

degrowth Economic, social, and political movement based on ecological principles and anti-consumerist, anti-capitalist ideas.

democracy (procedural definition) Democracy as defined by rules for free and fair elections, with broad citizen participation and the guarantee of fundamental freedoms.

democracy (substantive definition) Combination of universal attributes of "democracy" with local meanings of the term, often including substantive socio-economic outcomes such as greater income equality and lower poverty rates.

democratic consolidation A phase of democratization characterized by a solidification of the democratic foundations in which there is no uncertainty as to whether political actors want to conserve the authoritarian regime or adopt a democracy, but rather about how they should go about reinforcing the democratic system (Schedler, 2001).

democratic transition The period when authoritarian institutions and practices are in the process of being reformed and replaced by institutions and practices that are more democratic (or less authoritarian). It is an uncertain phase in which actors or forces pushing for democracy are struggling with those attempting to maintain the authoritarian status quo.

deterritorialization The delocalization of economic activities, as well as the adoption by states of common policies on major issues governing the economy and society.

development economics A new branch of economics that emerged after World War II that is specifically concerned with the challenges of developing countries; associated with Sir Arthur Lewis, among others.

"development tourists" A derogatory term to describe well-paid development consultants who jet in and out of countries, stay in five-star hotels, and dispense advice with little knowledge of local conditions.

digital divide The difference between groups in their access to and use of information and communication technologies.

discourse A system of representation (words, language) linked to power that shapes and limits the way we see the world. Used by postmodern and post-colonial scholars.

discrimination The unfair treatment of a person or group as a result of prejudice. It includes sexism and sexual discrimination.

dispossession The alienation of people from their land, resources, livelihoods, and/or other human rights.

distribution of income How the average wealth of a country is divided among the population. Distribution of income may be measured by comparing the average wealth of different deciles (tenths) or quintiles (fifths) of the population or by a measure such as the Gini coefficient; also known as income inequality.

donors Governments of countries or international agencies that provide foreign aid.

double burden of disease A pattern in which continued substantial prevalence of communicable diseases, which have historically been regarded as "diseases of poverty," coexists with rising incidence of non-communicable "diseases of affluence" like cardiovascular disease, diabetes, and cancer.

double movement A concept from Karl Polanyi who argued that as capitalism extends its influence over society, a popular backlash, or resistance, is produced to roll back this influence and insulate human relations from the market.

downward accountability The idea that aid recipients should have a voice in assessments of the effectiveness of that aid, for example, through access to a "complaints system."

due diligence With regard to development ethics, the idea that corporations must make a reasonable effort to ensure that they respect human rights and repair failings.

economic, social, and cultural rights Based on the International Covenant on Economic, Social and Cultural Rights (ICESCR) of 1966, rights that are mostly substantive guarantees of a minimum standard of living. Not generally accepted by Western countries, these rights are mostly promoted, but not implemented, by developing countries as a way to justify more aid transfers from rich countries.

emancipatory An adjective used to describe civil, social, and political freedoms-enhancing activities and practices, as in emancipatory social movements, ideas, and outcomes.

embedded autonomy A term popularized by Peter B. Evans that suggests that an effective developmental state should have embedded information-sharing networks with foreign and domestic elites yet also retain some degree of autonomy from them that allows the state to regulate and discipline the private sector.

embedded liberalism A concept referring to the international trade and development regime that emerged out of the Bretton Woods negotiations in 1944 and lasted until the 1970s. It entailed a mixture of international state intervention to control capital and investment flows with liberal trade objectives.

emerging multinational corporations (EMNCs) Multinational corporations based in developing countries, particularly dynamic emerging economies such as Brazil, China, India, and South Africa.

empowerment The capacity of individuals for self-development—to act and participate in decisions that affect their livelihoods and living standards. In practice, it refers to an enhanced sense of participation, to change oneself rather than the operating structures of the "system." In reference to gender, it indicates change in gender relations that challenges assumptions about power, helping, achieving, and succeeding.

enclave Operations by a company that have few beneficial links to the rest of the economy, often thought to be associated with extractive industry and multinational corporations.

entrepreneur/entrepreneurship People with a special ability to combine the factors of production in new and innovative ways to cause economic growth.

epidemiological transition Like demographic transition, a concept describing population-scale changes. It is based on the observation that, as per capita income increases, mortality rates from infectious and pest-borne diseases decrease, in part as a result of better sanitation and nutrition. Since many of these diseases disproportionately affect infants and children, the effect is to increase life expectancy. Because of the double burden of disease, the concept must be used with caution as it applies to the contemporary situation of low- and middle-income countries.

essentialize To reduce a group of people to simplistic defining characteristics. For example, women in developing countries are often portrayed as mothers or victims with little agency, or they are stripped to essentialist stereotypes of femininity.

ethnic conflict A form of conflict that some analysts see as generated by ethnic difference and animosities per se, requiring little additional explanation. Others regard ethnicity as one among several factors, and some reject the term's analytical value altogether.

Eurocentric, Eurocentrism A bias towards glorifying the values, practices, and historical developmental experience of Europe and North America. It is important to remember that the rise of Europe and North America had multiple causes, which may or may not support the idea that development elsewhere should follow the same steps.

European External Action Service (EEAS) European Commission "super ministry" for foreign affairs, established in 2010.

externalities Benefits or costs that are imposed by a project on another group without an equivalent charge for benefits or compensation for costs, such as the impact a project can have on the environment.

fair trade A political-economic concept that has gained popularity since World War II, premised on a belief in the need for international market regulation in the interests of poorer southern nations to combat the historical legacy of colonialism, dependency, and underdevelopment. Proponents of fair trade tend to focus on two issues: the development and expansion of interventionist mechanisms to ensure fair prices and living standards for farmers and workers in the Global South, and the elimination of "unfair" protectionist policies in the North.

fair trade network A network that connects small farmers, workers, and craftspeople in the South with organizations and consumers in the North through a system of "fair trade" rules and principles, including democratic organization (of co-operatives or unions), no exploitation of child labour, environmental sustainability, a minimum guaranteed price, and social premiums paid to producer communities to build community infrastructure.

food security The ability (derived from land, labour, capital, and/or political power) to meet food consumption needs either directly (from farming, livestock keeping, fishing, or hunting) or indirectly (through purchase or trade).

foreign direct investment (FDI) Investment made across national borders that has a physical presence or corporate form (such as a branch plant) and, therefore, a degree of control over how the investment is put to use, as differentiated from indirect investment, also known as portfolio capital or foreign portfolio investment.

foreign portfolio investment (FPI) Investments not made in an enterprise form that include the purchase of foreign debt, loans, and stock market investments on foreign stock exchanges. Portfolio capital may flow into or out of a developing country more rapidly than foreign direct investment, leading to financial instability and balance-of-payments crises.

Foster-Greer-Thorbecke (FGT) Class of poverty measures of three types, each of which provides different information about poverty: (1) the headcount index, (2) the poverty gap index, and (3) the poverty severity index.

"Fourth World" The most underprivileged and oppressed peoples within the so-called developed countries and Third World countries. It is used to speak about a population that suffers from economic, and social exclusion and, more generally, about stateless nations. The term was first used by the Canadian Aboriginal leader George Manuel and Michael Posluns in their book, *The Fourth World: An Indian Reality* (1974), to designate those indigenous peoples who continue to experience internal colonialism by settler societies.

free trade A political-economic concept popularized in the nineteenth century, premised on the belief that the removal of barriers to trade and the limitation of state intervention in economic and social interactions within and between nation-states would provide the greatest social gains for all countries involved. Significantly revived since the 1970s, free trade is supported on the grounds that state regulation of the market is inherently inefficient and wasteful while an unregulated market operates as an efficient "hidden hand" that responds accurately to undistorted market signals of supply and demand.

GDP per capita The most widely used indicator of economic development, which measures the total market value of the goods and services produced in an economy (gross domestic product) divided by the number of people in that economy. GDP per capita is a measure of the average wealth in a country and does not account for how that wealth is distributed.

gender mainstreaming The integration of gender into all facets of policies and programs in all political, economic, and societal spheres.

Gini coefficient Commonly used measure for determining income inequality within a country. Its value varies between 0 for perfect equality and 1 for complete inequality.

global cities Major urban centres such as London, Tokyo, New York, and Paris that fulfill global functions through the spatial concentration of high-level international command functions and linked business services, including finance, trade, transportation, advertising, insurance, and business advisory capacities.

global civil society Non-state actors acting at the global level and engaging with global institutions and processes.

global ethics The field of study examining questions of morality at the level of the world, such as international justice, distribution of wealth among nations or among peoples of different nations, global trade, and humanitarian activity.

global health governance The array of international organizations, ranging from the World Health Organization and the World Bank to large health-oriented foundations such as the Bill & Melinda Gates Foundation, that oversee and shape global health, but without any supranational authority.

globalization The economic, sociological, and cultural process by which nation-states, organizations, and individuals become increasingly interlinked and interdependent.

Global South A concept introduced by Filipino political economist Walden Bello to underline the unequal global distribution of resources between the developed countries and the less developed countries, mostly (though not exclusively) located in the South.

global value chains Concept developed in the 1990s to describe how multinational corporations organize their production across borders in "chains" of related activities, many of which may be performed by distinct firms. Typically, the higher-value-added activities are found in the developed countries where the head offices of MNCs are located, while low-value-added and labour-intensive parts of the production process are contributed by local firms in developing countries.

good governance The idea that in order for market-oriented development strategies to be effective, the political systems that surround them must be accountable, transparent, responsive, efficient, and inclusive.

governance Rules of procedure and regulation designed to maintain order—or political order—without direct government involvement or with as little government action as possible, by engaging non-state institutions or civil society stakeholders in the process of maintaining order. The definition of who constitutes a stakeholder and how their input should be taken into account is the subject of much debate.

Green Economy Theme of the Rio+20 Summit; an economy that results in reducing environmental risks and ecological scarcities, and that aims for sustainable development.

greenhouse gases (GHGs) Natural and industrial gases that trap heat from the earth and thus warm the Earth's temperature. The Kyoto Protocol restricts emissions of six greenhouse gases: natural (carbon dioxide, nitrous oxide, and methane) and industrial (perfluorocarbons, hydrofluorocarbons, and sulphur hexafluoride).

Heavily Indebted Poor Countries Initiative (HIPC) A 1996 arrangement between the Bretton Woods institutions and some large government donors to cancel some of the debts of the poorest countries if they implemented structural adjustment programs.

hegemonic power A great power or group of powers that can bring pressures or inducements to bear on other states such that they lose some or most of their freedom of action in practical terms (though not their formal sovereignty). A hegemonic power can affect other states' behaviour by way of economic, military, and other material incentives but also by way of ideology, policy formulas, and other non-material influences.

human development discourse An approach to development ethics that avoids being loaded down by ideological and religious assumptions by focusing on facilitating access to values that people have reason to value, following the capability approaches of Amartya Sen and Martha Nussbaum.

Human Development Index (HDI) A composite measure established by the UNDP of three equally weighted factors: a long and healthy life, knowledge, and standard of living. A long and healthy life is measured by life expectancy at birth; knowledge is a composite of the adult literacy rate and the combined gross enrolment ratio for primary, secondary, and post-secondary schools; and standard of living is measured by GDP per capita. In this respect, the index recognizes that income levels are important but that other factors are also important in human development.

humanitarian assistance Emergency life saving support to people affected by a crisis focused on short-term, rapidly provided assistance to relieve immediate suffering but that for the most part does not try to address the underlying structural causes or prevent recurrence of that suffering.

humanitarian intervention Military intervention motivated or justified at least in part with reference to humanitarian objectives of saving lives or relieving suffering.

human security discourse An approach to conceptualizing development ethics that focuses on threats to the fulfillment of people's priority needs.

illegitimate debt A loan that should not have been made and thus reflects misconduct by the lender. Such a debt is the responsibility of the lender, not the borrower.

imperialism A political and economic system by which wealthy and powerful states control the political and economic life of other societies. Most forms of imperialism involve long-distance commercial ties, with or without direct political ties.

income shares Measure of income equality/inequality based on a description of populations in 5 or 10 income groups (called quintiles and deciles, respectively) and the percentage of total income earned by each group. If a country were perfectly equal, each decile or quintile would have an equal share of total income.

indirect rule A system of governance by which colonial powers recognized and supported the legitimacy of indigenous authorities and legal systems insofar as they were subordinate and useful to the colonial state and used those authorities as intermediaries to govern the local population.

industrial capitalism Form of capitalism in which production shifts from small-scale individual production to large-scale centralized production in factories, with an increasingly complex division of labour. Work tasks are normally split into small, routinized activities, as on an assembly line.

Industrial Revolution The transition from rural, agrarian economies to urban-based factory production, associated with the harnessing of steam power as an energy source. First identified in eighteenth-century England, the Industrial Revolution eventually brought enormous political, social, and cultural change throughout nineteenth-century Europe.

informal economy Part of the economy where individuals and enterprises do business without being officially registered or regulated. Usually associated with small or micro-enterprises.

informality The condition of existing in the informal economy, including having weak property rights, poor access to financing, and limited potential for growth.

information and communication technologies (ICTs) The equipment and services that facilitate the electronic capture, processing, and display of information. These include computer technologies (computers, the Internet), telecommunications (cellular and land-line phones), audiovisual technologies (DVDs, cameras, MP3s), and broadcasting (radio, television).

integrated approach An interdisciplinary ideal that acknowledges the complexity and interconnected nature of rural development problems. Such approaches and projects attempt to co-ordinate teams of disciplinary specialists, including those with agricultural, environmental, nutritional health, social, economic, and political expertise.

interest The amount that must be paid by the borrower in addition to the principal and that provides the lender's profit and security against risk.

intergovernmental Relations or agreements between governments.

Keynesian policies Policies to stimulate economic growth through state intervention in market processes, based on the idea that capitalist markets require state regulation to correct problems that emerge from the operation of free markets, after twentieth-century British economist John Maynard Keynes.

knowledge-based institutes and activities Institutions and activities that owe their influence to the scientific generation of new ideas, techniques, and processes. Many organizations of the UN system exhibit influence based on knowledge.

laissez-faire Literally, "leave to do," the idea being to allow individuals to pursue their own interests through market transactions without state interference. "Perfect competition" is believed to result in optimal and more rational outcomes than state regulation.

leapfrogging Theory of development in which developing countries skip inferior, less efficient, more expensive, or more polluting technologies and industries and move directly to more advanced ones.

legitimacy The idea that governments require the consent of their populations to rule. A government that lacks general support from its population is said to be illegitimate.

liberal theory of violence A view that progress or development reduces the likelihood of violent conflict. In this view, conflict is regarded as a setback for development.

libertarian The ethical standpoint that holds individual freedom to be the highest moral principle and that it should not be infringed upon by the collectivity, society, or the state. Key individual rights, according to libertarianism, include the rights to acquire and retain property. Individual rights should never be breached in favour of the collective good.

Listian industrialization Also known as infant industry protection, the idea, derived from nineteenth-century German-American economist Friedrich List, that national industries may need to be protected from external competition, at least in the early phase of development, by tariffs that raise the cost of products exported by other countries' industries.

livelihood The capabilities, assets (material and social), and activities required for a means of living (Scoones, 1998: 5).

loan pushing Banks or lending agencies encouraging borrowers to take loans they do not need or cannot afford to repay.

logical framework approach A method for identifying potentially viable projects originally developed by USAID and involving the identification of stakeholders affected by the project, problems to be solved, possible solutions, and realistic objectives and activities. The logical framework is supposed to ensure that planning of a development project is logically consistent with project objectives.

Malthusian approach The view that population growth is a main cause of economic crisis, including poverty, malnutrition, and unemployment, after Thomas Malthus, an English cleric and political/economic theorist of the late eighteenth and early nineteenth centuries.

masculinities A concept that recognizes that masculine identities, both individually and collectively, are socially constructed and historically shifting. Since the making of men's role is not the manifestation of an inner essence, this opens a space for alternative masculinities to challenge hegemonic definitions of manhood by strengthening men's resistance to violence and sexual domination, and by engaging young men in gender equality.

micro-finance Small loans targeted at small family businesses, often run by women.

Millennium Development Goals Eight objectives established by the United Nations in 2000 related to global development and aimed at eradicating extreme poverty and improving gender equality, under-5 mortality rates, educational opportunity, environmental sustainability, and health outcomes (especially in regard to HIV/AIDS and malaria) by the year 2015.

mitigation Action that will reduce man-made climate change, including action to reduce greenhouse gas emissions or absorb greenhouse gases in the atmosphere.

moderate poverty An income level that indicates income deprivation and insecurity but at which actual physical survival is not threatened. Moderate poverty is typically considered to be an income of US$2 per day at international purchasing power parity.

monetary poverty Poverty expressed as a shortfall in monetary resources, which can be measured in terms of consumption, expenditures, or income.

multi-dimensional poverty Poverty expressed as an accumulation of deprivation in a range of dimensions of life, which often include access to education, access to health care, housing conditions, access to safe drinking water, and use of hygienic sanitation facilities.

multilateral, multilateralism Arrangements among three or more states, commonly for peaceful purposes over extended periods. Such arrangements can help governments improve their standing, influence, security, or economic advantage.

multinational corporations Corporations that invest across national borders and/or establish branch plants, subsidiaries, or other operations in more than one country. Usually used as a synonym of "transnational corporations" and "multinational enterprises" but favoured by social scientists and the media.

multinational enterprise A corporation that invests across national borders and/or establishes branch plants, subsidiaries, or other operations in more than one country. Usually used as a synonym of "transnational corporation" and "multinational corporation" but favoured by international business studies.

nation Refers both to a well-defined territorial and political entity and to a population that identifies itself as a common group in juxtaposition to others. The distinction is important; for example, we frequently discuss Basque nationalism even though a Basque government does not exist.

natural increase The positive difference between the number of births and number of deaths in a given population.

natural law ethics An ethical view whereby ethical implications are proposed based on the nature of human beings and their environment, from which human rights thinking is derived.

neo-colonialism The perpetuation of exploitative economic relationships between a developed and a developing country, despite the formal political independence of the latter.

neoliberal globalization An economic doctrine that repudiates the role of the state in the economy, preferring to leave the economy in the hands of the market, and that promotes the integration of economies and societies across the world into the "new world order"—a global economy based on the principles of liberalism and capitalism.

neoliberalism A mainstream international economic theory positing that markets are almost always the best decision-makers in terms of efficient resource allocation and that trade and investment flows across borders are optimized when there are as few restrictions as possible. The term "neo" distinguishes the creed from classical liberalism and indicates that some mainstream economists do recognize that there are certain market failures that must be addressed.

new international division of labour (NIDL) The new role of certain countries in the semi-periphery in providing cheap labour for manufacturing processes to multinational corporations, in contrast to the earlier international division of labour, which saw developed countries specializing in manufactures and developing countries specializing in commodities. The majority of this cheap labour is female.

non-governmental organizations (NGOs) First established in the 1960s in the form of "private voluntary organizations." They serve a range of contradictory purposes, some charitable, some political. Such organizations are often supported by governments and sometimes serve not to promote change but to sustain the existing order. The World Bank favours them as a strategic partner in the war on poverty and as instruments of good governance.

nutrition transition A shift to diets high in sugar and fat, now occurring in many low- and middle-income countries as an unintended consequence of trade liberalization and the increased consumption of processed foods.

obsolescing bargaining model A model of state–firm relations developed by Raymond Vernon that argues that each actor—state and firm—wants to capture a greater share of the benefits of foreign investment and that over time the relative strength of each actor changes. At the time of the investment, the multinational corporation is in the stronger position, but over time, the initial contract over the terms of investment erodes as the state becomes more powerful.

odious debt A loan to a dictatorship or despotic regime that does not benefit the people and may be used to repress the population that fights against the regime. Such a debt is not an obligation for the nation; it is a personal debt of the regime and need not be repaid by the successor regime.

official development assistance (ODA) As defined by Western donors in 1969, flows to developing countries and multilateral institutions provided by official agencies that meet the tests of (a) promoting the economic development and welfare of developing countries as the main objective and (b) containing a grant element of at least 25 per cent. Often referred to as "foreign aid."

OLI paradigm Developed by John H. Dunning and also known as the "eclectic" approach, a theory arguing that the internationalization of multinational corporations can be explained through the interaction of three factors related to its ownership (O), location-specific (L), and internalization (I) advantages, relative to non-internationalized firms.

One Belt, One Road Initiative China's flagship initiative under President Xi Jinping to bring together two separate but interrelated elements: a land-based Silk Road Economic Belt (SREB) and a sea-based twenty-first-century Maritime Silk Road (MSR).

open data Data that can be freely used, reused, and redistributed (shared) by anyone.

oppression The unjust or cruel exercise of authority or power, such as the systematic, institutionalized, and elite-sanctioned mistreatment of and/or discrimination against a group in society by another group or by people acting as agents of the society as a whole.

othering Viewing those unlike oneself and one's own cultural/social/ethnic/racial group or gender as worth less (in intelligence, skills, knowledge, wisdom) than oneself and one's own group.

participatory approach An ideological and philosophical commitment to an ideal that rural development is controlled by the full range of rural actors with a stake in it.

peace-building Generally, activities directed towards the establishment or consolidation of peace. A more narrow meaning refers to activities by international actors in countries emerging from civil wars, designed to prevent the recurrence of conflict.

people-to-people relationships Chinese concept of diplomacy through promoting academic links, cultural exchanges, and tourism, and sharing information on threats such as epidemics.

peripheral capitalism A concept developed by dependency theorists, who argued that the capitalist world economy could be divided into core and peripheral (and in some cases semi-peripheral) regions. In the periphery, capitalism develops differently from the way it developed in core countries and is characterized as externally directed, less dynamic, and more exclusionary and unjust than in currently developed countries.

policy space The real room that governments have to enact policy, given the constraints imposed on them by international agreements and multinational corporations.

political economy Interdisciplinary study of interactions or relationships between production and trade and power and politics.

political economy of war A term normally referring to the relationship between economic activities, power structures, and violence during wartime.

political regime The set of principles and rules that govern power relations between society and the state (Przeworski et al., 2000, 18–19).

positionality An awareness by researchers or development practitioners of the social situation and power relationships in which they are embedded. This awareness, particularly their position relative to the local people with whom they interact, helps development researchers and practitioners make better decisions and reduce their negative impact.

poverty gap index A measure that helps to show the depth of poverty. It does so by taking into account the level of monetary resources and its distance to the poverty line of every poor household or individual. These individual shortfalls are aggregated and represent the poverty gap in a country.

poverty headcount index The most intuitive and widely used measure of poverty, which simply indicates what proportion of the population lives in poverty. It is calculated by counting the number of people below the poverty line and dividing that by the total population.

poverty line The threshold below which an individual or household is considered to be poor.

Poverty Reduction Strategy Papers (PRSPs) A refashioning of the IMF and World Bank's structural adjustment programs in the later 1990s. PRSPs are intended to cover a wide range of social, economic, and political reforms, including a firm commitment to good governance, and to increase country ownership of reforms.

poverty severity index A measure that reflects the severity of poverty by giving greater weight to greater shortfalls from the poverty line.

power/knowledge regime A conception of political power that explores not just an international regime's direct political-economic power but also its knowledge-producing power. With this concept, sociologist Michael Goldman argues that an international organization like the World Bank does not produce value-neutral knowledge but rather constructs a power/knowledge regime designed to naturalize and legitimize a world order skewed in the interest of rich northern countries.

principal The amount of money initially borrowed.

project environment The various factors and actors that affect the planning and implementation of a development project.

Protestant ethic The most famous theory regarding cultural influence on economic behaviour, posited by Max Weber, which holds that certain characteristics of Protestantism (especially Calvinism), such as valuing austerity, discipline, and hard work to attain material wealth and success as a route to personal salvation, played a major role in the origin of capitalism.

public–private partnerships Related to privatization, usually involving the provision of public services by private companies working together with state agencies, often through government subcontracting to private companies, which are thought to be able to provide the service more cheaply, have more incentives to cut costs and respond to customers, and have the expertise to apply the latest techniques and management to the problem. For example, new roads in Mexico have been built by private companies that retain the ability to charge tolls over a period of several decades to recover their costs.

purchasing power parity A comparative indicator based on an exchange rate that equates the price of a basket of identical traded goods and services in two countries.

quantitative easing Gradual increase in the money supply based on a central bank's purchase of financial assets from private banks. Used to stimulate the US and European economies after the Great Recession of the 2010s.

radical feminist Perspective that calls for a reordering of society and the economy to rid it of all forms of patriarchy and male supremacy, if necessary through means beyond the political process.

real interest rate The rate of interest charged, less the rate of inflation.

recipients Governments that receive foreign aid.

refugee As defined in the United Nations Convention Relating to the Status of Refugees (1951), someone who is "outside his own country, owing to a well-founded fear of persecution, for reasons of race, religion, nationality, membership of a particular social group, or political opinion." This limited definition now includes those who have fled their country because of conflict or environmental or natural disaster, as well as those who are internal refugees, having fled an area within a country to another region in the same country.

regulatory chill The possibility that good public policy could be withdrawn or never proposed because of the government's fear of being sued by affected foreign investors.

relational poverty The unequal power relations between different groups in a society.

relative poverty, Poverty that does not threaten a person's daily survival but in which that person may not have the income necessary to fully participate in his or her society. Relative poverty is often the principal kind of poverty in developed countries.

resilience Ability to adapt to and recover from hazards and crisis.

results-based management (RBM) Management based on the measurement and specification of problems, goals, and expected results intended to improve the effectiveness of development projects.

rights-based ethic Fundamental entitlement to act or be treated in specific ways based on moral claims. Justifications for rights-based morality are complex, but they include the idea that we have rights because we have interests or because of our status.

rural–urban migration The movement of people from rural to urban areas within a country, caused by such factors as changes in agricultural production, the effects of climate change (e.g., floods, desertification), and the hope for employment.

"scramble for Africa" The rapid and disorderly colonization of Africa by European powers following the 1884 Berlin Conference.

self-determination A principle in customary international law and diplomacy according to which all peoples have the right to "freely determine their political status and freely pursue their economic, social and cultural development" (International Covenants on Civil and Political Rights and on Economic, Social and Cultural Rights). The right of all peoples to self-determination is embodied in several treaties and can be implemented in diverse ways.

semi-authoritarian regimes (hybrid regimes) Regimes that have democratized their formal institutions (removed a one-party system and/or the military from political office) but in which elites of the old authoritarian regime still perpetuate (sometimes informally, sometimes in a more formal fashion) a plethora of heavily authoritarian political practices.

shared value The idea that businesses can enhance their competitiveness by focusing on social problems in co-operation with government and non-governmental organizations.

social capital The networks of relationships between individuals and communities that provide, to a greater or lesser extent, support in times of financial, health, and emotional need and connections in terms of securing employment; broad and diffuse social trust.

social contract theory View of ethical reasoning that asks what participants would freely agree as being just to all. Commonly associated with Thomas Hobbes, John Locke, and John Rawls.

social determinants of health Social, economic, and environmental conditions under which people live and work that affect their opportunity to lead healthy lives. Access to health care is only one of many social determinants of health, which lie largely outside the domain of the health-care professions and the mandate of government ministries or other agencies concerned with health.

social determinism (of technology) The view that social interaction is most important in terms of the development and use of tools and technologies.

socialist feminist Perspective focused on gender inequality in the workplace, and with holding socialist objectives for gender and income equality. Argues for greater state involvement to abolish all forms of discrimination against women and all manifestations of patriarchy in society and politics.

social movements Groups of individuals in civil society who join together to seek social change through collective action, such as workers' movements, civil rights movements, and environmental movements.

social or socio-economic gradient A pattern, found in rich and poor societies alike, in which health status varies with income, wealth, education, or some other indicator of socio-economic status. In other words, health improves with wealth, income, education, and other assets.

social policy "[S]ystematic and deliberate interventions in the social life of a country to ensure the satisfaction of the basic needs and the well-being of the majority of its citizens" (Aina, 1999: 73).

South–South co-operation Co-operative state-initiated social, cultural, and economic activities between and among countries of the Global South.

sphere of influence Geographical and political areas over which major powers can expect their wishes to be respected because of their ability to threaten, intimidate, or persuade governments and non-state actors. Frequently used in reference to the Cold War partition of much of the world between American and Soviet spheres of influence.

state A government and its various agencies of administration, control, and service that make decisions on behalf of a political and territorially defined entity. It is important to point out that the state itself can be rife with internal conflicts, reflecting wider divisions within society.

state autonomy The degree of "insulation" that a state enjoys from social and external forces in making decisions. Originated in neo-Marxist literature that asked if the capitalist state could be relatively independent from the bourgeoisie (dominant capitalist class).

state capacity The bureaucratic and technical ability of a state to design and implement policy decisions. Commonly used to suggest that developing states may not be as capable as their counterparts in the North. Based on Max Weber's theory of the state.

structural adjustment A controversial series of economic and social reforms promoted by the IMF and World Bank following the 1982 debt crisis that aimed to promote economic development through minimizing the role of the state in societies and liberalizing markets.

sustainable development Defined by the World Commission on Environment and Development (Brundtland Commission) in 1987 as development that meets the needs of the present without compromising the ability of future generations to meet their own needs.

sustainable livelihoods "A livelihood is sustainable when it can cope with and recover from stresses and shocks and maintain or enhance its capabilities and assets both now and in the future, while not undermining the natural resources base" (Chambers and Conway, 1992, cited in Shaffer, 2002: 30).

targeting Directing social programs and assistance to those groups within a total population who are in the greatest need so that, for example, only those below the poverty line can received subsidized food rations.

technical functionalism The original design principle for the United Nations system, which separated the developmental functions of the organization by professional and technical category.

technological determinism The notion that technology drives the evolution of society.

technology "The science and art of getting things done through the application of skills and knowledge" (Smilie, 2000: 69), or the capacity to organize and use physical infrastructure, machinery and equipment, knowledge, and skills; the practical application of science to solve real-world problems.

10/90 gap The fact that worldwide, less than 10 per cent of health research spending addresses conditions that account for 90 per cent of the global burden of illness and death, almost entirely in low- and middle-income countries.

tied aid Foreign aid that must be used to purchase goods and services from the donor country.

time and space, contraction of An effect of modern communication and transportation techniques that have changed the way in which economic and social relations are constructed and perceived, giving the appearance that time runs more quickly and the distance between places has been reduced.

tragedy of the commons As introduced by Garrett Hardin, the overexploitation and resulting degradation of environmental resources as a result of individuals rationally pursuing personal gain with resources that are held in common by a group of people or by all people, such as common pasture (the commons), the oceans and their resources, or the air we breathe.

transfer price The internal price that a multinational corporation attributes to a product it trades across borders between different branches of its organization. That price is fixed by administrative decision, not the operation of supply and demand. There is some concern that multinationals may use strategic transfer pricing to reduce their overall tax burden by spreading it across more than one country.

transforming countries Countries where agriculture is no longer a major contributor to economic growth but where rural poverty remains widespread.

transnational corporations Corporations that invest across national borders and/or establish branch plants, subsidiaries, or other operations in more than one country. Usually used as a synonym of "multinational corporations" and "multinational enterprises" but favoured by the United Nations system in its reports and publications.

transnational feminism A type of post-colonial theorizing of women's differences that emphasizes the importance of incorporating political economy into analyses of gender and development; challenged by some for primarily being a product of feminist academics from the Global South situated at institutions in the Global North.

triad The most powerful capitalist areas, which dominate the world economy: North America, Western Europe, and Japan.

triangular development co-operation Strategies and projects between a traditional donor, an emerging donor in the South, and a beneficiary country in the South.

turn towards culture An alternative path to developmentwith the aim of finding "ways of increasing well-being without indiscriminately destroying valued ways of living and 'knowing'" (Jayawardena, 1990: vi). Contrasts with a supposed failed Western and Eurocentric model, of which culture is the building block.

unequal exchange A theory of international trade popularized by underdevelopment and dependency theorists in the 1960s and 1970s. It states that Third World countries, rather than being in a position to enhance their comparative advantage through international trade, have their national development restricted and distorted by the "'unequal exchange" of lower-priced primary commodities (such as coffee, tea, cocoa, and bananas) for higher-priced industrial goods, technology, and services from the First World.

United Nations (UN) Founded in 1945 to replace the League of Nations and aimed at facilitating co-operation in international law, international peace and security, and economic and social development, as well as in human rights issues and humanitarian affairs. The UN is currently composed of 193 recognized independent states, with its headquarters located in New York City on international territory.

universal access (to ICTs) A situation in which every person has a reasonable means of access to a publicly available telecommunication service, which may be provided through pay telephones, community telephone centres, teleboutiques, community Internet access terminals, or similar means.

universal health care Government-funded medical services provided to all members of a society.

universal service (to ICTs) Making available a defined minimum telecommunication service of specified quality to all users at an affordable price.

upgrading The idea that firms can learn and improve the quality of the products they produce, eventually moving into higher-skill and higher-value-added activities, even within a global value chain.

urban Settlements or localities defined as "urban," as opposed to "rural" or "non-urban," by national statistical agencies, based on population size, population density, and/or government structure.

urban growth rate The increase in the number of people who live in towns and cities, measured in either relative or absolute terms.

Urbanized countries Where rural poverty accounts for less than 60 per cent of overall poverty and agriculture contributes to less than 20 per cent of overall GDP growth.

urbanization The process of transition from a rural to a more urban society. Statistically, urbanization reflects an increasing proportion of the population living in settlements defined as urban, primarily through net rural-to-urban migration and, in some countries, as a result of immigration. The level of urbanization is the percentage of the total population living in towns and cities, while the rate of urbanization is the rate at which it grows.

urban population Proportion of the total population living in urban areas.

urban transition The passage from a predominantly rural to a predominantly urban society.

usury Excessive interest rates.

utilitarianism A view of development that grew out of the type of rational calculation fostered by business and markets: costs and benefits should be calculated, summed, and compared. Such a view tends to give short shrift to ethical considerations in development.

voicelessness A problem for many poor people who are unable to make themselves or their problems heard by authorities. Underlined in Narayan's *Voices of the Poor* study for the World Bank.

Washington Consensus A tacit agreement between the International Monetary Fund, the World Bank, and the US executive branch over the development policies that developing countries should follow. This neoliberal orthodoxy formed around the key issues of macroeconomic prudence, export-oriented growth, and economic liberalization.

Weberian View associated with sociologist Max Weber that accepts the rational-purposeful institutionality of a modern state, regardless of its origin. Contrasts with a neo-patrimonial state.

white man's burden The idea that (white) Europeans and Americans have a duty to colonize and rule over peoples in other parts of the world because of the alleged superiority of European culture. Both the subject peoples and the act of colonization are seen as the "burden." This idea was used as a justification for colonial empires in the nineteenth century.

White Papers on Foreign Aid (China) Chinese government documents of 2011 and 2014 outlining that country's perspective on international development, which differs ideologically and ideationally from Western concepts of development and assistance, especially in regard to a view of "partnership" rather than "donor" and "recipient," and in relation to alleged non-interference in the governance practices of the receiving country.

INDEX

Note: Page numbers in **bold** type indicate figures and illustrations.